COMMEMORATIVE EDITION

THE WORLD ALMANAC®

THE COMPLETE 1868 ORIGINAL AND SELECTIONS FROM 25, 50, AND 100 YEARS AGO

Edited by
June Foley, Mark Hoffman,
and Tom McGuire,
editors of *The World Almanac*®
and Book of Facts

PHAROS BOOKS
A SCRIPPS HOWARD COMPANY
NEW YORK

First published in 1992.

Library of Congress Cataloging-in-Publication Data
The World Almanac commemorative edition / by the editors of The
   World Almanac.
   p.   cm.
   ISBN 0-88687-729-6.—ISBN 0-88687-728-8 (pbk.)
   1. Almanacs, American. 2. History, Modern.
AM71.W67   1992
031—dc20
                                                    92-24501
                                                    CIP

Printed in the United States of America

World Almanac
An Imprint of Pharos Books
A Scripps Howard Company
New York, NY 10166

10 9 8 7 6 5 4 3 2 1

CONTENTS

PREFACE

It would be inspiring to believe that the first editors of *The World Almanac* in 1868 knew that their creation would still be renewing itself 125 years later in a world they would hardly recognize. However, today's editors are, of course, firmly grounded in fact and can only look back and appreciate their predecessors' efforts and results. As the 20th century draws to a close and we look back to the world of 1868, there are many areas of interest which naturally lead to comparison and contrast. In an attempt to draw parallels or to highlight uniqueness in order to bring some thematic unity to this commemorative edition, we have included advertisements, tables, charts, summaries of the year's events, and selected special features from editions 25 (1968), 50 (1943), and 100 (1893) years ago, as well as the entire original 1868 edition. Upon examination, these features will readily lead you, loyal readers, to reach your own conclusions concerning the past 125 years and the current state of affairs. As today's *World Almanac* editors celebrate the 125th anniversary of the first printing, we follow tradition and leave social, political, and moral conjecture to the reading public. It is with this tradition in mind that this special edition is presented. For 125 years, *The World Almanac* has provided up-to-date, accurate, comprehensible information on an encyclopedic range of historical and current topics to readers of all ages, from all segments of society. The editorial purpose of *The World Almanac* has never strayed: past and present, it is a single-volume, general reference book encompassing a wide variety of useful (a most "relative" term as all past and present editors learn) information and a contemporary record of well-known and influential people and important issues, and this commemorative edition is intended to serve much the same purpose.

This volume is organized by year and by general categories to emphasize the distinct qualities of each year's selections in addition to drawing attention to the similarities in coverage through the years. The individual items were chosen not only to reflect world events over the past 125 years, but to create an aura of authenticity for each era represented.

The World Almanac was first published in 1868 by *The New York World* newspaper. It was intended to be a handbook for journalists of that paper, and was used to provide background information or profiles concerning current events. (The name of the publication comes directly from the newspaper, which was known as "The World," thus The *World* Almanac.) The 1868 edition had 120 pages and was sold for about 20 cents.

The first editor of *The World Almanac* was a newspaperman whose name was never recorded. In fact, until 1923, no editor or staff member was named in the publication. The first known editor was Robert Hunt Lyman, also a newspaperman.

Publication was suspended in 1876, but in 1886, famed and powerful publisher Joseph Pulitzer, who had purchased *The World* and was quickly making it one of the most influential papers in the nation, revived *The World Almanac*, determined to make it a "compendium of universal knowledge." The same year, the Statue of Liberty was dedicated, with Pulitzer leading the fund drive. A picture of Lady Liberty was imprinted on the cover of the 1886 edition, and we have tried to recapture this spirit by reproducing the Statue on this commemorative edition. By 1894, the book claimed 500,000 "habitual users," and had changed its name to *The World Almanac and Encyclopedia*, which remained the title until 1923 when it was changed to its present title: *The World Almanac and Book of Facts*.

We are often asked how the book has changed over the years. Actually, it hasn't changed in any dramatic way; it has grown along with the nation and the world. The early emphasis on New York City not only reflected a regional slant, it represented the relative "smallness" of the rest of the U.S. As New York, Boston, Philadelphia, and Washington, D.C. became less dominant in U.S. affairs, and as the rest of the world became more accessible through the dynamic development of transportation and communication, *The World Almanac*'s contents grew to cover the expanding base of information made available and of interest to the ever-growing general population. As is the case in history itself, events, individuals, natural environmental changes, and humankind's technological, medical, and social discoveries and innovations have had the most notable influence on the contents of our publication.

For example, World War I not only brought the U.S. out of its isolationist policy, it led the editors to create a "Nations of the World" section, although the European/American bias continued until the 1950s, as can be seen in the 1943 edition where the profiles of the U.S. and the British Empire are prominent while the rest of the world is listed under the heading "Other Nations." The stock market crash of 1929 is another example of an event leading to changes in coverage, as the editors began to place a new emphasis on economic matters. During World War II, *The World Almanac* boasted that GIs around the globe carried the book and were proud to keep it near their pinups of Betty Grable. In fact, in 1944 and 1946, at the request of the government, *The World Almanac* had special print runs of over 100,000 copies for distribution to the armed forces. Additionally, the war had an obvious effect on the book's contents, as every battle was described (as shown in our selections from the 1943 edition). Another effect of the war was a paper shortage, and the publishers and editors pitched in by cutting more than 100 pages of the book. They did this by eliminating the advertising, which had been part of the book since its inception. The ads, some of which have been included in our selections, vividly evoke the past and show, among other things, Americans' interest in re-inventing themselves through education, especially "self-help" guides; they also document our preoccupation with digestive problems, weight loss or gain, and, of course, getting rich quickly.

In the 1960s, the civil rights movement was manifested in the book as population, economic, and employment data began to show minorities' positions in the U.S. The women's movement also had a major impact, with coverage of the role of "influential" women as well as all women in society portrayed in data and in feature articles. The Vietnam War, the energy crisis, the concern for the environment, Watergate, and consumerism all have had an impact on the makeup of *The World Almanac* in recent years. Most recently, Reaganomics, tax reform, and the changing world of the former Soviet Union and Eastern Europe have had an obvious and dramatic influence on our coverage and editorial focus, as have the social issues of AIDS, homelessness, poverty, racism, drug abuse, crime, and education.

In offering his congratulations on our 125th anniversary, Mayor David N. Dinkins of New York City said: "When I speak to schoolchildren, I remind them to stay in school and study. By studying hard, I tell them, they will learn to reason. Knowledge and the ability to reason are things that can never be taken away or suppressed. The unjust may be able to imprison a person's body, but they cannot imprison his or her mind. That is why sources of information like *The World Almanac* are so important. They provide the vital facts that permit knowledge to grow."

We hope that you will enjoy this commemorative edition, and that we will be able to "grow" together for many years to come.

The Editors

June Foley   Mark Hoffman   Thomas McGuire

Almanac

1868.

ESTABLISHED 1861.

The Great American
TEA COMPANY
Nos. 81 & 88 VESEY STREET,

HAVE JUST RECEIVED

TWO FULL CARGOES OF THE FINEST NEW CROP TEAS.

22,000 HALF CHESTS by Ship "Golden State."
12,000 HALF CHESTS by Ship "George Shotton."

In addition to these large cargoes of Black and Japan Teas, the Company are constantly receiving large invoices of the finest quality of Green Teas from the Moyune district of China, which are unrivaled for fineness and delicacy of flavor.

To give our readers an idea of the profits which have been made in the Tea trade, we will start with the American houses, leaving out of the account entirely the profits of the Chinese factors.

1st. The American house in China or Japan makes large profits on their sales or shipments, and some of the richest retired merchants in the country have made their immense fortunes through their houses in China.

2d. The Banker makes large profits upon the foreign exchange used in the purchase of Teas.

3d. The Importer makes a profit of 30 to 50 per cent. in many cases.

4th. On its arrival here it is sold by the cargo, and the Purchaser sells it to the Speculator in invoices of 1000 to 2000 packages, at an average profit of about 10 per cent.

5th. The Speculator sells it to the Wholesale Tea Dealer in lines at a profit of 10 to 15 per cent.

6th. The Wholesale Tea Dealer sells it to the Wholesale Grocer in lots to suit his trade, at a profit of about 10 per cent.

7th. The Wholesale Grocer sells it to the Retail Dealer at a profit of 15 to 25 per cent.

8th. The Retailer sells it to the consumer for ALL THE PROFIT HE CAN GET.

When you have added to these EIGHT profits as many brokerages, cartages, storages, cooperages and wastes, and add the original cost of the Tea, it will be perceived what the consumer has to pay. And now we propose to show why we can sell so very much lower than other dealers.

We propose to do away with all these various profits and brokerages, cartages, storages, cooperages and wastes, with the exception of a small commission paid for purchasing to our correspondents in China and Japan, one cartage, and a small profit to ourselves—which, on our large sales, will amply pay us.

By our system of supplying Clubs throughout the country, consumers in all parts of the United States can receive their Teas at the same price (with the small additional expense of transportation) as though they bought them at our warehouses in this city.

Some parties inquire of us how they shall proceed to get up a Club. The answer is simply this: Let each person wishing to join in a Club say how much tea or coffee he wants, and select the kind and price from our Price List, as published in the paper or in our circulars. Write the names, kinds and amounts plainly on the list as seen in the Club Order published below, and when the Club is complete send it to us by mail, and we will put up each party's goods in separate packages, and mark the name upon them, with the cost, so there need be no confusion in their distribution—each party getting exactly what he orders, and no more. The cost of transportation the members can divide equitably among themselves.

Parties sending Club or other orders for less than thirty dollars had better send Post-office Drafts or money with their orders, to save the expense of collections by express; but larger orders we will forward by express, to collect on delivery.

Hereafter we will send a complimentary package to the party getting up the Club. Our profits are small, but we will be as liberal as we can afford. We send no complimentary package for Clubs less than $30.

Parties getting their Teas of us may confidently rely upon getting them pure and fresh, as they come direct from the Custom House stores to our Warehouses.

We warrant all the goods we sell to give entire satisfaction. If they are not satisfactory they can be returned at our expense within 30 days, and have the money refunded.

The Company have selected the following kinds from their stock, which they recommend to meet the wants of clubs. They are sold at cargo prices, the same as the Company sell them in New York, as the list of prices will show.

PRICE LIST OF TEAS.

OOLONG (Black), 70c., 80c., 90c., best $1 per pound.
MIXED (Green and Black), 70c., 80c., 90c., best $1 per pound.
ENGLISH BREAKFAST (Black), 80c., 90c., $1, $1.10, best $1.20 per pound.
IMPERIAL (Green), 80c., 90c., $1, $1.10, best $1.25 per pound.
YOUNG HYSON (Green), 80c., 90c., $1, $1.10, best $1.25 per pound.
UNCOLORED JAPAN, 90c., $1, $1.10, best $1.25 per pound.
GUNPOWDER (Green), $1.25, best $1.50 per pound.

COFFEES ROASTED AND GROUND DAILY.

GROUND COFFEE, 20c., 25c., 30c., 35c., best 40c. per pound. Hotels, Saloons, Boarding-house keepers, and Families who use large quantities of Coffee, can economize in that article by using our FRENCH BREAKFAST AND DINNER COFFEE, which we sell at the low price of 30c. per pound, and warrant to give perfect satisfaction.

Consumers can save from 50c. to $1 per pound by purchasing their Teas of "*The Great American Tea Company*," Nos. 31 and 33 Vesey Street.

N. B.—All villages and towns where a large number reside, by Clubbing together, can reduce the cost of their Teas and Coffees about one-third, (besides Express charges,) by sending directly to " The Great American Tea Company."

BEWARE of all concerns that advertise themselves as branches of our Establishment, or copy our name either wholly or in part, as they are *bogus* or *imitations*. We have no branches, and do not, in any case, authorize the use of our name.

Post-Office Orders and Drafts, make payable to the order of " Great American Tea Company." Direct letters and orders to

The Great American Tea Company,

Nos. 31 & 33 VESEY STREET, N. Y.

POST OFFICE BOX, 5,643, NEW YORK CITY.

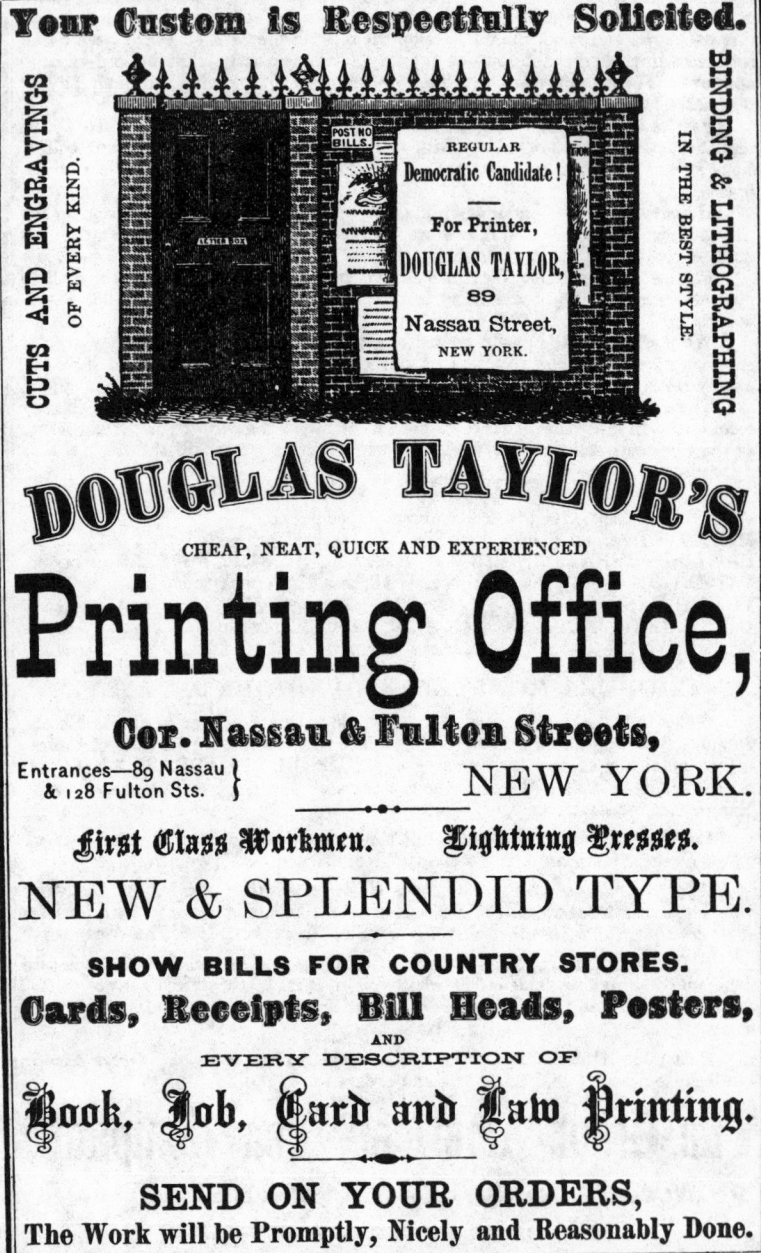

THE WORLD ALMANAC FOR 1868.

Eclipses in 1868.

In the year 1868 there will be two eclipses, both of the Sun, and a transit of Mercury over the Sun's disc.

I. An annular eclipse of the Sun, February 22, invisible in the United States, but visible in South America, Africa, and a small portion of Europe.

II. A total eclipse of the Sun, August 17th, invisible in the United States. This eclipse will be visible in portions of Asia and Africa and in Australia.

III. A transit of Mercury over the Sun's disc, November 4th, invisible in the United States, but partly visible in Europe.

NOTE.—It will be observed that none of the eclipses for 1868 are visible in the United States.

Table of Sixty-one Bright Stars.

To ascertain when any star or constellation found in the following Table will be on the meridian, *add* the numbers opposite in the left hand column of figures to the time of "*Sidereal Noon*," found in the calendar pages. For the RISING of a star, *subtract* the number opposite in the right-hand column of figures from its meridian passage. For the setting of a star, *add* the same number to its meridian passage. Those marked (....) revolve in a circle of perpetual apparition, and do not rise nor set north of the latitude of New York (40° 42' 40''), for which latitude the semi-diurnal arcs are calculated. The civil day begins at the preceding midnight, and consequently 24 hours after midnight, or 12 hours from noon is *morning* of the succeeding day; and 24 hours to 36 hours from noon is *evening* of the next day. The table is arranged in the order of culmination.

NAME OF STAR.	On Meridian. H. M.	Rises & Sets. H. M.	NAME OF STAR.	On Meridian. H. M.	Rises & Sets. H. M.
α Andromedæ (Alpheratz)...	0 2	7 49	γ Leonis (Al Gieba).........	10 11	7 14
γ Pegasi (Algenib).........	0 7	6 50	β' Ursæ Majoris } Pointers...	10 52	....
α Cassiopeæ (Schedir).......	0 33	....	α Ursæ Majoris } Pointers...	10 54	....
β Ceti.....................	0 37	4 52	β Leonis (Denebola).........	11 40	6 53
β Andromedæ (Merach)....	1 2	8 26	γ Ursæ Majoris (Phad).....	11 45	....
α Ursa Minoris (Polaris)....	1 11	....	β Corvi....................	12 26	4 36
β Arietis.................	1 47	7 14	ε Ursæ Majoris (Alioth).....	12 46	....
γ Andromedæ (Almaach)...	1 56	9 18	α Virginis (Spica).........	13 16	5 22
α Piscium.................	1 55	6 6	η Ursæ Majoris............	13 40	....
α Arietis.................	1 59	7 23	α Bootis (Arcturus).......	14 7	7 11
α Ceti (Menkar)...........	2 55	6 11	β Ursæ Minoris...........	14 49	....
α Persei (Algenib).........	3 14	....	β Libræ..................	15 7	5 28
η Tauri (Seven Stars).......	3 39	7 27	α Coronæ Borealis.........	15 27	7 43
α Tauri (Aldebaran)........	4 28	6 57	α Serpentis...............	15 35	6 23
α Aurigæ (Capella)........	5 6	10 11	β' Scorpii................	15 55	4 49
β Orionis (Rigel)...........	5 7	5 30	α Scorpii (Antares)........	16 19	4 19
β Tauri (El Nath).........	5 17	7 50	α Herculis...............	17 6	6 51
γ Orionis (Bellatrix).......	5 17	6 20	α Ophiuchi...............	17 26	6 44
δ Orionis (Mintaka).......	5 24	5 58	β Draconis...............	17 25	....
ε Orionis (Anilam)........	5 29	5 54	γ Draconis...............	17 51	....
ς Orionis (Alnitak)........	5 33	5 52	α Lyræ (Vega).............	18 30	8 52
α Columbæ (Phaet)........	5 34	3 37	β Lyræ..................	18 42	8 16
α Orionis (Betelguese)......	5 47	6 25	α Aquilæ (Altair).........	19 41	6 29
α Canis Majoris (Sirius).....	6 38	5 0	α Cygni (Denebola).......	20 34	9 59
ε Canis Majoris (Adhara)...	6 52	4 7	α Cephei.................	21 12	....
α²Geminor (Castor).........	7 25	8 10	β Aquarii................	21 21	5 38
α Canis Minoris (Procyon)..	7 31	6 18	α Aquarii................	21 56	5 56
β Geminor (Pollux)........	7 36	7 49	α Piscium Aus. (Formalhaut)	22 47	4 0
ς Argus (Naos).............	7 58	2 58	β Pegasi (Scheat).........	22 54	7 44
α Hydra (Alphard)........	9 20	5 31	α Pegasi (Markab)........	22 54	6 50
α Leonis (Regulus)..........	10 0	6 43	Vernal Equinox............		5 59

The Planets.

MERCURY will be brightest and at the most favorable situation for visibility about Feb. 17th, June 13th and Oct. 9th, being then in the west and evening star soon after sun-set; also, April 7th, Aug. 6th and Nov. 24th, in the east as morning star, just before sun-rise.

VENUS will be the evening star until July 16th, then morning star until the end of the year. It will be at its greatest brilliancy about June 9th, and may often some days before and after that date be seen during the afternoon with the naked eye, crossing the meridian about 3 o'clock, P. M.; again, after passing the inferior conjunction, and becoming morning star. It attains its greatest brilliancy about August 21st, and may be seen in the forenoon about 2 h. ¾ in advance of the Sun.

MARS will be morning star throughout the entire year, but will not be at all conspicuous before May or June, but will continue to grow brighter throughout the year.

JUPITER will be evening star until March 10th, and morning star until Oct. 1st, and evening star the rest of the year. It will be, however, too near the Sun to be conspicuous before the end of May, and will increase in brightness until Oct. 1st, when it will be brightest, being then in opposition.

SATURN will be morning star until May 23, then evening star till Nov. 29, and morning star the rest of the year. It will be brightest about May 23d.

Conjunctions of the Planets, and other Phenomena.

Month.	Aspect.	Time.	Distance Apart.
		D. H. M.	° ′
Jan'y..	♂ ☌ ☉	2 0 55 m	
	☉ in Perigee.	2 11 13 e.	
	☿ ☌ ♂	17 4 22 e.	☿ 0 56 S.
	♄ ☌ ●	19 10 17 m	♄ 3 19 S.
	☿ Sup. ☌ ☉	23 8 43 e.	
	♂ ☌ ●	24 3 59 m	♂ 4 9 S.
	☿ ☌ ●	24 6 5 e.	☿ 4 48 S.
	♀ ☌ ●	27 9 3 m	♀ 1 21 S.
	♀ ☌ ♃	30 3 56 e.	♀ 0 23 S.
Febr'y	♄ ☌ ●	15 8 30 e.	♄ 3 22 S.
	☿ ☌ ♃	17 0 29 e.	☿ 1 32 N.
	☿ gr. elon. E.	20 3 3 e.	☿ 18 9 E.
	♃ ☌ ●	24 9 48 m	♃ 0 3 N.
	♄ □ ☉	24 11 30 m	
	☿ ☌ ●	25 4 48 m	☿ 3 58 N.
	♀ ☌ ●	26 11 7 m	♀ 3 11 N.
	☿ stationary.	27 9 41 m	
March.	☿ ☌ ♃	5 0 13 m	☿ 5 6 N.
	☿ inf. ☌ ☉	8 5 2 m	
	♃ ☌ ☉	10 11 1 m	
	♄ ☌ ●	14 5 57 m	♄ 3 16 S.
	☿ ☌ ♂	16 11 5 e.	☿ 3 20 N.
	☿ ☌ ●	22 2 33 m	☿ 1 16 N.
	♂ ☌ ●	22 11 50 m	♂ 0 16 S.
	♃ ☌ ●	23 5 21 m	♃ 0 39 N.
	♀ ☌ ●	27 8 47 m	♀ 6 46 N.
April..	☿ gr. elon. W.	4 1 9 e.	☿ 27 47 W.
	♂ ☌ ♃	8 10 10 m	♂ 0 1 N.
	♄ ☌ ●	10 1 39 e.	♄ 3 5 S.
	☿ ☌ ♃	13 8 36 m	☿ 1 41 S.
	☿ ☌ ♂	17 4 23 e.	☿ 1 51 S.
	♃ ☌ ●	20 1 28 m	♃ 1 51 N.
	♂ ☌ ●	20 1 17 e.	♂ 1 55 N.
	☿ ☌ ●	20 6 8 e.	☿ 0 15 N.
	♀ ☌ ●	25 2 20 m	♀ 7 52 N.
May...	♀ gr. elon. E.	7 5 31 m	♀ 45 31 E.
	♄ ☌ ●	7 7 50 e.	♄ 2 58 S.
	☿ Sup. ☌ ☉	15 0 23 m	
	♃ ☌ ●	17 8 58 e.	♃ 1 50 N.
	♂ ☌ ●	19 2 31 e.	♂ 3 40 N.
	☿ ☌ ●	22 4 29 e.	☿ 6 27 N.
	♄ ☍ ☉	23 1 45 m	
	♀ ☌ ●	25 9 15 m	♀ 6 20 N.
June..	♄ ☌ ●	3 11 29 e.	♄ 2 59 S.
	♃ ☌ ●	14 2 12 e.	♃ 2 19 N.
	☿ gr. elon. E.	16 7 14 e.	☿ 24 51 E.
	♂ ☌ ●	17 2 0 e.	♂ 4 42 N.
	☿ ☌ ●	22 3 46 m	☿ 2 31 N.
	♀ ☌ ●	22 3 32 e.	♀ 2 3 N.
	♀ stationary.	23 8 33 e.	
	☿ stationary.	30 3 26 e.	
July..	♄ ☌ ●	1 2 12 m	♄ 3 10 S.
	☉ in Apogee.	1 9 0 m	
July..	♃ □ ☉	4 10 4 m	
	♃ ☌ ●	12 3 25 m	♃ 2 36 N.
	☿ Inf. ☌ ☉	14 6 16 m	
	♂ ☌ ●	16 11 45 m	♂ 4 57 N.
	♀ Inf. ☌ ☉	16 0 22 e.	
	☿ ☌ ●	19 3 35 m	☿ 1 39 S.
	♀ ☌ ●	19 8 28 m	♀ 2 57 S.
	☿ stationary.	24 6 42 e.	
	☿ ☌ ♀	27 5 30 m	☿ 3 19 N.
	♄ ☌ ●	28 6 10 m	♄ 3 24 S.
Aug...	♄ stationary.	2 8 4 e.	
	☿ gr. elon. W.	3 2 40 m	☿ 19 15 W.
	♃ stationary.	3 3 57 e.	
	♀ "	7 1 16 m	
	♃ ☌ ●	8 11 16 m	♃ 2 36 N.
	♂ ☌ ●	14 6 56 m	♂ 4 36 N.
	♀ ☌ ●	15 10 46 m	♀ 2 49 S.
	☿ ☌ ●	17 6 20 m	☿ 2 31 N.
	♄ □ ☉	22 0 49 m	
	♄ ☌ ●	24 1 23 e.	♄ 3 33 S.
	♀ sup. ☌ ☉	28 7 42 m	
Sept...	♃ ☌ ●	4 1 57 e.	♃ 2 22 N.
	♂ ☌ ●	11 10 38 e.	♂ 3 53 N.
	♀ ☌ ●	13 1 30 m	♀ 1 11 S.
	☿ ☌ ●	17 8 45 m	☿ 3 57 S.
	♄ ☌ ●	21 0 29 m	♄ 3 32 S.
	♀ gr. elon. W.	25 2 0 e.	♀ 46 9 W.
Oct....	♃ ☌ ●	1 1 56 e.	♃ 2 3 N.
	♃ ☍ ☉	1 9 55 e.	
	♂ ☌ ●	10 9 59 m	♂ 2 57 N.
	♀ ☌ ●	12 9 14 m	♀ 0 56 S.
	☿ gr. elon. W.	13 0 18 m	☿ 24 54 E.
	☿ ☌ ●	17 9 47 m	☿ 8 24 S.
	♄ ☌ ●	18. 2 35 e.	♄ 3 25 S.
	☿ stationary.	25 3 12 m	
	♃ ☌ ●	28 3 5 e.	♃ 1 56 N.
Nov...	☿ inf. ☌ ☉	5 1 38 m	
	♂ ☌ ●	7 3 58 e.	♂ 2 5 N.
	♀ ☌ ●	10 11 59 e.	♀ 2 2 S.
	☿ ☌ ●	12 11 44 e.	☿ 2 59 S.
	☿ stationary.	13 10 55 e.	
	♄ ☌ ●	15 5 49 m	♄ 3 17 N.
	☿ gr. elon. W.	21 4 15 e.	☿ 19 51 W.
	♃ ☌ ●	23 8 21 e.	♃ 2 9 N.
	♃ stationary.	29 0 34 e.	
	♄ ☌ ☉	29 6 51 e.	
Dec...	♂ ☌ ●	5 3 33 e.	♂ 1 38 N.
	♀ ☌ ●	10 8 31 e.	♀ 3 13 S.
	☿ ☌ ●	12 7 30 e.	☿ 4 41 S.
	♄ ☌ ●	12 8 10 e.	♄ 3 12 S.
	☿ ☌ ♄	13 1 10 m	☿ 1 28 S.
	♃ ☌ ●	22 6 21 m	♃ 2 37 N.
	♃ □ ☉	26 7 30 e.	

CHARACTERS EXPLAINED.—☿ Mercury, ♀ Venus, ♂ Mars, ♃ Jupiter, ♄ Saturn, ● Moon, ☉ Sun, ☍ Opposition or half a circle apart, □ Quadrature or quarter of a circle apart, ☌ Conjunction or together, having the same *right ascension* or longitude; gr. elon., greatest elongation or farthest distance from the Sun; stationary, when the planet is without apparent motion, and is about to move in a direction contrary to that it last had. The above table enables us to find the planets throughout the year.

Occultations.

The Moon will occult or eclipse the star Aldebaran (*α Tauri*), Jan. 7th, visible; the star disappears 1h. 17m. morning, and reappears 2h. 20m. at Washington. Again, March 28th, invisible at Washington, as the star is below the horizon. On Nov. 27th Aldebaran will again be occulted; disappears 5h. 54m., evening, reappears 6h. 51m. at Washington.

The Seasons.

Spring begins March 20th, 2h. 27m. morning.	Autumn begins September 22d, 1h. 25m. evening.
Summer begins June 20th, 10h. 54m. evening.	Winter begins December 21st, 7h. 20 m. morning.

Notable Days and Periods.

Dominical Letters, E D; Epact, 6; Golden Number, 7; Solar Cycle, 1; Roman Indiction, 11; Julian Period, 6,581.

The 93d year of American Independence begins July 4; the year 1285 of the Mohammedan Era begins April 24th, 1868.

EXPLANATION.—The Epact expresses the Moon's age on the first day of the year, and is used to determine Easter, which depends on the Moon, being always the first Sunday after the first full Moon after the vernal equinox, (March 21st.) The Golden Number is the number of years that have elapsed since a new Moon full on January 1st. It is obtained by adding one to the date, and dividing by 19, the number of years in a cycle. From eleven times the golden number subtract 10 and divide by 30, subtract one, and the remainder is the epact. The epact subtracted from 24 gives the number of days from March 21st to the next ecclesiastical full Moon, and the following Sunday, shown by the Dominical letter, is Easter Sunday.

The Sun, Moon, Earth and Bright Stars of the Year.

There are many facts connected with astronomy which are as common as household words, but which most persons are prone not to remember readily. Some figures, showing the dimensions and positions of the leading planets, may not, therefore, be amiss. We condense them from the observations of Dr. Chambers, a celebrated English Astronomer: The Sun's distance from the Earth is 91,430,000 British statute miles. Its diameter is not less than 882,000 miles, or rather more than one hundred and eleven times the diameter of the Earth. It has a circumference of 2,646,000 miles, while the Earth's circumference is only 25,000 miles. The Sun's light is transmitted 2,700 millions of miles, and its light exceeds that of the Moon 801,072 times. The solar volume, or bulk, is 1,400,000 times greater than that of the Earth, and exceeds five hundred times the aggregate bulk of all the bodies of the planetary system. The Moon, as the Earth's satellite, is to us the most important of the secondary planets. It revolves round the Earth at a mean distance of 238,833 miles, but by the eccentricity of its orbit, it may reach from the Earth to a distance of 251,947 miles, or approach it to within 228,719 miles. Its real diameter is 2,162 English miles. The Earth is a planet, in all essential respects similar to Mars and Venus, its nearest neighbors. It revolves round the Sun at a mean distance of 91,430,000 miles; but by the eccentricity of its orbit, this distance may either extend to 92,965,000 miles, or contract to 89,894,000 miles.

The bright stars of the year 1868 are to be Mercury, Venus, Mars, Saturn, and Jupiter. The planets are called morning or evening stars when they are to the west of the Sun, and arise before it, and when to the east, and set after it. In the case of Venus it is alternately about 290 days a morning and evening star. Mercury is of the old planets the one nearest the Sun, round which it revolves at a mean distance of 39,392,000 miles; but owing to the eccentricity of its orbit, this distance may either extend to 42,665,000 miles, or fall as low as 28,119,000 miles. Its real diameter is set down at 2,962 miles. Next in order of distance from the Sun, after Mercury, is Venus, which revolves round the Sun at a mean distance of 66,131,000 miles. The eccentricity of its orbit being less, the extremes of distances are only 66,585,000 miles and 65,777,000 miles. The real diameter of Venus is supposed to be 7,510 miles, or about the same as the Earth's. Mars is the first planet exterior to the Earth, in the order of distance, from the Sun. It revolves round the Sun at a mean distance of 139,312,000 miles, which, on orbital eccentricity, may augment to 152,284,000 miles, or diminish to 126,340,000 miles. Its real diameter is somewhat less than 5,000 miles. Mars and the Earth come nearly to the same relative position every twenty-three years, but several centuries must elapse before precise coincidence occurs. Jupiter, the largest planet of our system, revolves round the Sun at a mean distance of 475,693,000 miles, but the eccentricity of its orbit is such, that the planet may recede from the Sun 488,603,000 miles, or approach it to within 452,782,000 miles. Its equatorial diameter is 68,400 miles or thereabout. Inferior in size alone, Saturn may fairly be pronounced the most interesting member of the Solar system. It revolves round the Sun at a mean distance of 872,134,000 miles, which an orbital eccentricity may increase to 921,105,000 miles, or diminish to 823,164,000 miles. Its equatorial diameter may be taken at 71,904 miles. Saturn's ring is double, and the nearest is three times as broad as the other, the one being 20,000 miles and the second 7,200 miles; the space between them is 2,839 miles.

Influence of the Moon upon the Weather.

It is important not only to seamen and navigators, but to everybody, to know the character of the Moon's influence upon the Earth. The world-renowned Navigator, Captain Horsburg, in one of his numerous works, presents the following chances of change of weather:

1st. The chances of change (of weather and wind), particularly so if any one phase of the Moon happens at or nigh apogee or perigee, the greatest being at the time of perigee from any one single point.

2d. The New Moon next to the perigee is likely to be accompanied with the greatest changes of weather.

3d. At New Moon, coinciding with the perigee, the greatest change may be expected, and the chances are as great as thirty-three to one that a change of weather takes place.

4th. New Moon coinciding with apogee, seven to one that a change takes place.

5th. Full Moon coinciding with perigee, ten to one a change occurs.

6th. Full Moon coinciding with apogee, eight to one a change happens.

7th. If a New Moon coinciding with perigee when the Sun is on the equator, the chance of change of weather is very great.

8th. If at the autumnal equinox any of the lunar points coincide, there will be a great probability of a change so as to cause a typhoon on the south coast of the Chinese Sea—probably a storm or gale situated nigh the Tropic of Cancer.

9th. The changes of weather do not happen always precisely at the lunar points, but, like the tides, sometimes vary a little in time from those points, for a change of weather often precedes one or two days the change of the Moon.

10th. Let it be remembered that the changes of the Moon are more likely to be accompanied by stormy weather than at the full, and also that the blowing or stormy weather prevails more in dark nights than when much of the Moon's disc is illuminated.

By reference to the almanac these points are always known. If when the Sun's semi-diameter and horizontal parallax of the Moon are the greatest, she is then in that part of her orbit nearest the Earth, and is in what is termed *perigee;* and when the Sun's semi-diameter and horizontal parallax are the least, she then is at her greatest distance from the Earth, and is in *apogee.*

In support of the influence of the Moon on the Earth, a few extracts from the published works of the late Dr. Adam Clarke may be of service to the farmer and useful to the sailor. He says:

1st. If the New Moon happens between the hours of 10 P. M. and midnight in summer, it being in the northern hemisphere, the probability is the weather will be fine for the space of the next seven days. This calculation is from and between the hours of 10 o'clock at night and 2 o'clock the following morning; and it further adds that the nearer the New Moon is to midnight, the fairer will be the weather for the next seven days.

2d. The nearer to mid-day or noon the phases of the Moon happen, the more foul or wet the weather may be expected to be during the next seven days, and the calculation for this is in the space from 10 in the morning till 2 o'clock in the afternoon. This observation refers principally to summer, although it affects spring and autumn nearly in the same ratio.

3d. If the last quarter of the Moon takes place between 10 and 12 o'clock in the forenoon, if in the summer, there will be frequent showers of rain, and if in the winter, the weather will be cold and rainy, if the wind is westerly, and snow if in the east.

4th. The nigher to midnight the full change, first or last quarter, happens, the fairer will be the weather for the next seven days.

5th. If the Moon falls at or nigh mid-day or noon, there will be snow or rain in winter, and if in the summer months, very rainy. The space of this calculation is from noon to 2 P. M.

6th. If the New Moon is between the hours of 11 P. M. and one hour after midnight, the fairer the weather will be the next seven days, but if in winter, and the wind in the south, it is most likely to rain.

8th. If the Full Moon happens to take place between 10 o'clock at night and midnight, expect it to be fair in summer and fair and frost in winter.

9th. To know the effect the Moon's phases have upon the weather or wind, and to predict with certainty, reference should be had to her situation as regards her orbit, whether east. west, north or south of the observer, and if at or nigh the meridian.

Discovery of Two New Planets.

Professor J. C. Watson, of the Michigan University, alleges that he has discovered two new planets during the year 1867, one in August and one in September. The first is said to be in the constellation of Cetus, which lies about 6½ degrees west of Mera Ceti, the wonderful variable star; it is also 38 degrees SW. of the Pleiades, and rises about 11 P. M., being invisible through any but telescopes of superior power. It is situated, according to astronomical phraseology, in the right ascension, 1 degree and 40 minutes, and in declination, 3 degrees and 10 minutes south, and is at present moving west and south. The second one is said to be situated in the right ascension, 14 degrees and 15 minutes, and declension 6 degrees and 10 minutes north, and is thought to be equal in brilliancy to a star of the eleventh magnitude. The heavenly bodies discovered by Prof. Watson are probably asteroids, which consist of a group of small planets, revolving between the orbits of Jupiter and Mars. The first was discovered in January, 1801; the fifth in December, 1845; the forty-third, April 16, 1851; the forty-seventh, October 3, 1857, by Mr. James Ferguson, at the National Observatory, Washington, D. C.: and the fifty-first at Rheims, in France, December 24, 1857, by Mr. Laurent, of the Assay Office. If, therefore, Professor J. C. Watson has discovered a new planet, the three discovered in modern times have been by an Englishman, a Frenchman, and an American.

The Mohammedan Calendar.

The Mohammedan year is Lunar. The months consist alternately of 29 and 30 days; to the last month an intercalary day is added eleven times in a period of 30 years. These are called *abounding-years*, corresponding to our leap-years, and consist of 355 days; the common year being 354. These abounding-years are the 2d, 5th, 7th, 10th, 13th, 15th, 18th, 21st, 24th, 26th and the 29th, making 32 of our years nearly equal to 33 Mohammedan years.

ANNO HEGIRAH, 1285. A. D., 1868.

Their year commences with		Length.	Corresponding to April 22d.
1st month	Moharrem	30	
2d	„ Sepher	29	
3d	„ Rebb-ul-evvel	30	
4th	„ Rebb-ul-Akhur	29	
5th	„ Jem ad-ul-Evvel	30	
6th	„ ad-ul-Akhur	29	
7th	„ ejeb	30	
8th	„ Shaban	29	
9th	„ Ramadan or Ramazan	30	
10th	„ Sheval	29	
11th	„ Zee-'l-Kaddeh	30	
12th	„ Zee-'l-Hijjeh	29	

Jewish Calendar.

The year 5628, of 12 months, began Sept. 30, 1867, and ends Sept. 16, 1868.

MONTH.	BEGINS.	MONTH.	BEGINS.
4 nebet	December 27, 1867	10 Tammuz	June 21
5 Sebat	January 25, 1868	11 Ab	July 20
6 Adar	February 24, „	12 Elul	August 19
7 Nisan	March 24, „	1 Tisri	September 17
8 Ijar	April 23, „	2 Chesvan	October 17
9 Swan	May 22, „	3 Kisler	November 15

The Purim festival will be celebrated on March 8, 1969; the Jewish Passover on April 7, and Pentecost on May 27.

The new Jewish Year, 5629, begins September 17, and the Day of Atonement occurs on the 27th of the same month.

The Positivist's Calendar.

The year 1868 is the 80th year of the Great Crisis.

	MONTH.	BEGINS.	LENGTH.
1	Moses	January 1	28
2	Homer	January 29	28
3	Aristotle	February 26	28
4	Archimedes	March 26	28
5	Cæsar	April 23	28
6	St. Paul	May 21	28
7	Charlemagne	June 18	28
8	Dante	July 16	28
9	Guttemburg	August 13	28
10	Shakspeare	September 10	28
11	Descartes	October 8	28
12	Frederick	November 5	28
13	Bichat	December 8	28

Universal Festival of the Dead.   General Festival of Holy Women.

Extension of the Elective Franchise at the North.

February 6th, 1867, the Tennessee House of Representatives passed a law striking the word "white" from the franchise law, by a vote of 38 to 25. February 18th, the Senate concurred, by a vote of 14 to 7. Subsequently the Supreme Court of the State sustained the constitutionality of the law. In Ohio, October, 1867, an amendment extending the elective franchise to negroes was rejected by a majority of 38,353, and counting the votes cast for Governor and not cast on this question, by 50,618. Negro suffrage was defeated, in November, in Minnesota by 1,298, and in Kansas by 8,523 majority; in Kansas female suffrage was also defeated. In New Jersey negro suffrage was indirectly presented to the people, it being understood that the Republican candidates for members of the legislature would favor an amendment to the State constitution embodying this feature; the result was a Democratic majority of 16,354. By act of Congress (passed by House, Jan. 18, 1866, by Senate, Dec. 13, 1866) negro suffrage was established in the District of Columbia.

New and Valuable Tide Table of 110 Places.

To find the time of high-water at any of the places named in the following table, add the time indicated in the first column of figures to the time of "Moon South," found in the calendar pages. EXAMPLE: Required the time of high-water at New Haven for May 4th and 7th. For the 3d, Moon South, at 9h. 55m. in the afternoon, which added to 11h. 16m. gives 21h. or 9h. 11m. of the morning of the 4th for time of high-water. On the 7th, Moon South at 0h. 24m. morning, which added as before, gives 11h. 40m. in the morning for high-water. There are two tides during the passage of the Moon from the meridian, around to the meridian again, and they are about 12h. 26m. apart.

PLACES.	Establish't of Port.	Height of Spring Tide.	Neap Tide.
NOR'EAST CO'ST	H. M.	FT.	FT
Hanniwell's Pt.	11 15	9 3	7 0
Portland	11 25	9 9	7 6
Portsmouth	11 23	9 9	7 6
Newburyport	11 22	9 1	6 6
Rockport	10 57	10 2	7 1
Salem	11 13	10 6	7 6
Boston Light	11 12	10 9	8 1
Boston	11 27	11 3	8 5
Plymouth	11 19	11 4	9 0
Wellfleet	11 5	13 2	9 2
Provincetown	11 22	10 8	7 7
Monomoy	11 58	5 3	2 6
Nantucket	12 24	3 6	2 6
Hyannis	12 22	3 9	1 8
Edgartown	12 16	2 5	1 6
Holmes' Hole	11 43	1 8	1 3
Tarpaulin Cove	8 4	2 8	1 8
Wood'sHole(N)	7 59	4 7	3 1
Wood'sHole(S)	8 34	2 0	1 2
Menemsha Lgt.	7 45	3 9	1 8
Quick's Hle.(N)	7 31	4 3	2 9
Quick's Hole(S)	7 36	3 8	2 3
Cuttyhunk	7 40	4 2	2 9
Kettle Cove	7 48	5 0	3 7
Bird Is'ld Lgt.	7 59	5 3	3 5
New Bedford	7 57	4 6	2 8
Newport	7 45	4 6	3 1
Point Judith	7 32	3 7	2 6
Rock Island	7 36	3 5	2 0
Montauk Point.	8 20	2 4	1 8
Sandy Hook	7 29	5 6	4 0
New York	8 13	5 4	3 4
HUDSON RIVER.			
Dobb's Ferry	9 19	4 4	2 7
Tarrytown	9 57	4 0	2 7
Verplanck's Pt.	10 8	8 8	2 5
West Point	11 2	3 2	2 0
Poughkeepsie	12 34	3 9	2 4
Tivoli	1 24	4 6	3 2
Stuyvesant	3 23	4 4	3 0

PLACES.	Establish't of Port.	Height of Spring Tide.	Neap Tide.
	H. M.	FT.	FT
Castleton	4 29	3 0	2 3
Greenbush	4 22	5 5	1 9
L. IS'LD. SOUND			
Watch Hill	9 0	3 1	2 4
Stonington	9 7	3 2	2 2
Little Gull Is'ld	9 38	2 9	2 3
New London	9 28	3 1	2 1
New Haven	11 16	6 2	5 2
Bridgeport	11 11	8 0	4 7
Oyster Bay	11 7	9 2	5 4
Sand's Point	11 13	8 9	6 4
New Rochelle	11 22	8 6	6 6
Throg's Neck	11 20	9 2	6 1
JERSEY COAST.			
Cold Sprg. Inlet	7 32	5 4	3 6
Cape Ma y Lan.	8 19	6 0	4 3
DEL'RE BAY,&c			
Delaw'e Brkw'r	8 0	4 5	3 0
Higbie's C May	8 33	6 2	3 9
Egg Island Lgt.	9 4	7 0	5 1
Mahon's River.	9 52	6 9	5 0
Newcastle	11 53	6 9	6 6
Philadelphia	1 18	6 8	5 1
CHESA'PKE, &c.			
Old Pt. Comfort	8 17	3 0	2 0
Point Lookout.	0 32	1 9	0 7
Annapolis	4 38	1 0	0 8
Bodkin Light.	5 42	1 3	0 8
Baltimore	6 33	1 5	0 9
Washington	7 44	3 4	2 0
City Point.	2 11	3 0	2 5
Richmond	4 32	3 4	2 3
Tappahannock	0 42	1 9	1 3
SOU'N COAST.			
Hatteras Inlet.	7 4	2 2	1 8
Beaufort (N.C).	7 26	3 3	2 2
Bald Head	7 26	5 0	3 4
Smithville	7 19	5 5	3 8

PLACES.	Establish't of Port.	Height of Spring Tide.	Neap Tide.
	H- M.	FT.	FT
Wilmington	9 6	3 1	2 2
GeorgetownEnt	7 56	4 7	2 7
Bull's Isl'd Bay.	7 16	5 7	8 7
Charleston	7 26	6 0	4 1
St. Helena Sd.	7 8	7 4	4 4
Ft. Pulaski	7 20	8 0	5 9
Savannah	8 13	7 6	5 5
Doboy Light	7 33	7 8	5 4
St. Simon's.	7 43	8 2	5 4
Ft. Clinch	7 53	6 7	5 3
St. John's Riv.	7 28	5 5	3 7
St. Augustine	8 21	4 9	3 6
Cape Florida	8 34	1 8	1 2
Indian Key.	8 23	2 2	1 3
Sand Key	8 40	2 0	0 6
Key West.	9 30	1 5	0 9
Tortugas	9 56	1 5	0 6
Charlotte Har.	13 9	1 3	0 8
Tampa Bay.	11 21	3 2	1 6
Cedar Keys.	13 15	3 2	1 6
St. Marks.	13 38	2 9	1 4
WEST'ENCOAST.			
San Diego	9 38	5 0	2 3
San Pedro	9 39	4 7	2 2
Cuyler's Harbor	9 25	5 1	2 8
San Luis Obispo	10 8	4 8	2 4
Monterey	10 22	4 3	2 5
Soth. Farrallone	10 37	4 4	2 8
San Francisco.	12 6	4 3	2 8
Mare Island	18 40	5 2	4 1
Benicia	14 10	5 1	3 7
Ravenswood	12 36	7 3	4 9
Bodego	11 17	4 7	2 7
Humboldt Bay.	12 2	5 5	3 5
Port Orford	11 26	6 8	3 7
Astoria	12 42	7 4	4 6
Nee-ah-Harbor	12 33	7 4	4 8
Pt. Townshend	8 49	5 5	4 0
Stellacoom	4 46	11 1	7 2
Semi-ah-moBay	4 50	6 6	4 8

Morning Stars.

Venus (♀) after July 16.
Mars (♂) from January 2 to November 13.
Jupiter (♃) from March 10 to July 4.
Saturn (♄) until Feb. 24, and after Nov. 29.

Evening Stars.

Venus until July 16.
Mars until after Jan. 2, and after Nov. 13.
Jupiter until March 10, and after July 4.
Saturn from February 24, to November 29.

To Ascertain the Length of the Day and Night.

At any time of the year add twelve hours to the time of the Sun's setting, and from the sum subtract the time of rising, for the length of the day. Subtract the time of setting from twelve hours, and to the remainder add the time of rising next morning, for the length of the night. These rules are equally true for apparent time.

COTTON.

We subjoin statistics of the crop of American Cotton for the year ending 1st Sept., with comparative statements:

Receipts and Exports of Cotton (Bales) from September 1, 1866, to September 1, 1867, and Stocks at latter date.

PORTS.	Rec'pts year end'g Sept. 1, 1867.	Rec'pts year end'g Sept. 1, 1866.	Exported year ending Sept. 1, 1867, to Great Britain	France.	Other F'reign.	Total.	Stocks, Sept. 1, 1867.
New Orleans	702,131	711,629	403,521	160,852	54,567	618,940	15,256
Alabama	239,516	429,102	145,566	4,352	3,506	153,424	3,714
South Carolina	162,247	112,462	75,547	3,524	1,825	80,896	1,228
Georgia	248,601	258,798	111,592	959	1,550	114,101	633
Texas	186,495	175,065	60,751	....	16,173	76,913	3,233
Florida	57,451	149,432	3,019	....	....	3,109	5
North Carolina	38,623	64,653	534	....	....	534	......
Virginia	127,867	39,093	13,011	....	....	13,011	2,589
New York	119,601	141,659	375,206	28,460	66,002	469,668	41,497
Boston	33,462	21,066	16,624	....	390	17,014	10,000
Philadelphia	58,556	52,728	3,155	....	....	3,155	3,000
Baltimore	2,721	3,300	7,820	....	155	7,975	2,000
Shipped to manuf's from Tenn., &c...	42,000	35,000	....	....	....	....	......
Total	2,019,271	2,193,987	1,216,336	198,147	144,168	1,558,661	83,155
Last year	2,193,987	....	1,258,277	222,593	71,817	1,552,457	281,179
Increase this year	....	....	....	....	64,325	6,204	......
Decrease this year	174,716	....	41,931	24,446	....	....	198,024

Total Crop for Twenty Years (Bales).

1865–6.....2,193,987	1858–9.....3,851,481	1854–5.....2,847,339	1850–1.....2,355,257
1861–5..(no record)	1857–8.....3,113,962	1853–4.....2,930,027	1849–50...2,096,706
1860–1.....3,656,086	1856–7.....2,939,519	1852–3.....3,262,883	1848–9.....2,728,596
1859–60....4,669,770	1855–6.....3,527,845	1851–2.....3,015,029	1847–8.....2,347,634

The crop of Sea Island the past year has been as follows: Florida, 12,632 bales; Georgia, 7,646 bales; South Carolina, 12,060 bales—total, 32,328 bales. The crop of Sea Islands during the former years has been as follows:

1853–4 ....bales, 39,686	1856–7 ....bales, 45,314
1854–5................... 40,841	1857–8................... 40,566
1855–6................... 44,512	1858–9................... 47,592

Consumption of Cotton at the North.

Total crop of the United States, as above stated		2,019,271
Stock on hand commencement of year, September 1, 1866—		
In Southern ports	162,836	
In Northern ports	120,856—	283,692
Total supply during the year ending September 1, 1867		2,302,963
Of this supply there has been		
Exported to foreign ports during the year	1,558,737	
Burnt at New York	5,068	
Burnt in the South	6,122	
Now on hand (September 1, 1867)—		
In Northern ports	56,497	
In Southern Ports	26,658—1,653,132	
Total consumed in the United States during the year ending September 1, 1867		649,831
Estimated consumption in the Southern States		70,000
Consumption in the Northern States for the year		579,831

This, as will be seen, is equal to a consumption in the Northern States of about 11,000 bales per week. The total consumption in the United States each year since 1853, has been as follows:

Year.	Total, U. S.	Year.	Total, U. S.	Year.	Total, U. S.
1853–4 ....bales, 737,236	1857–8 ....bales, 595,562	1861–5........bales, no record
1854–5............... 766,412	1858–9............... 927,651	1865–6............... 667,292
1855–6............... 770,739	1859–60............. 972,043	1866–7............... 656,307
1856–7............... 819,936	1860–1............. 843,740	

Prices of Cotton at New York and Liverpool on the First Tuesday of each Month for two years.

DATE.	1866–7. New York.	1866–7. Liverpool.	1865–6 New York.	1865–6 Liverpool.	DATE.	1866–7. New York.	1866–7. Liverpool.	1865–6. New York.	1865–6. Liverpool.
	CTS.	D.	CTS.	D.		CTS.	D.	CTS.	D.
September 7...	32	13	44	18½	March 1........	32	13⅜	44	18⅞
October 5......	39½	14⅝	49	24	April 5.........	27½	12⅝	38	18
November 2...	39	15	56	20½	May 3..........	27	11½	33	13¾
December 7...	33½	14	49	....	June 7.........	27	11⅜	37	13
January 4.....	35½	15¼	51	20¼	July 5..........	26	10½	35	14
February 1....	33½	14¾	48	18½	August 2......	28	10¼	36	14

Imports of Cotton at Liverpool for years ending August 31, 1867 and 1866, and Stock at Dates.

	Imports. Year end. Aug. 31, 1867.	Imports. Year end. Aug. 31, 1866.	Stocks. Aug. 31, 1867.	Stocks. Aug. 31, 1866.	Stocks. Aug. 31, 1865.
American ....bales,	1,239,614	1,260,709	313,550	334,010	29,980
Brazilian.....................	397,983	449,670	128,190	109,330	34,480
Egyptian, Smyrna, &c.......	203,293	262,409	48,500	38,540	56,150
West Indian..................	101,226	107,701	27,900	23,120	13,820
East Indian..................	1,159,426	1,558,838	273,850	423,310	245,870
China and Japan............	4,616	14,852	1,570	7,830	31,460
Total....................	3,106,158	3,654,179	793,560	936,140	411,760
Stock at London..............................			96,680	93,259	61,460
" at Havre..............................			102,000	180,000	36,000
" at other ports (estimated)....................			30,000	25,000	20,000
Total Stocks in Europe........................			1,022,240	1,231,153	529,220

The current estimate at this writing of the crop of 1867–8, is 2,500,000 bales.

Condition of the National Banks.

The following is an abstract of the quarterly reports of all the National Banking Associations in the United States, on the first Mondays of July and October, 1867:

RESOURCES.	July, 1867.	Oct., 1867.*
Loans and Discounts, including overdrafts........................	$588,100,703 62	$609,608,095 35
U. S. Bonds deposited to secure circulation........................	367,735,250 00	388,540,150 00
U. S. Bonds and Securities deposited to secure deposits............	38,302,750 00	38,211,450 00
U. S. Bonds and Securities on hand	45,629,300 00	42,173,150 00
Other Stocks, Bonds and Mortgages	21,452,040 43	21,375,403 92
Due from National Banks...	92,287,906 39	95,212,308 45
Due from other Banks and Bankers..............................	9,603,442 12	8,386,600 60
Real Estate, Furniture, &c..	19,755,023 70	20,637,011 95
Current Expenses	3,217,747 70	5,295,738 33
Premiums..	3,361,247 11	2,758,753 78
Checks and other Cash Items......................................	128,255,674 49	134,550,948 96
Bills of National Banks..	16,128,898 00	11,838,056 00
Bills of other Banks..	531,264 00	333,209 00
Specie..	9,602,072 97	10,253,114 80
Legal Tender Notes and Fractional Currency.....................	102,431,346 96	100,511,924 83
Compound Interest Notes...	75,456,915 00	56,866,440 00
Total..	$1,491,433,582 49	$1,496,552,355 97
LIABILITIES.		
Capital Stock paid in..	$418,123,148 50	$419,973,415 00
Surplus Fund...	63,229,585 62	66,695,587 01
Undivided Profits	30,586,670 80	33,592,032 41
National Bank Notes Outstanding.................................	291,491,038 00	293,804,831 00
State Bank Notes Outstanding	4,422,505 00	4,092,153 00
Individual Deposits..	537,882,949 91	537,922,575 83
United States Deposits..	29,764,089 09	23,078,315 71
Deposits of U. S. Disbursing Officers.............................	3,407,608 19	4,637,264 92
Due to National Banks..	89,817,032 74	93,111,240 89
Due to other Banks and Bankers	22,608,954 58	19,644,940 20
Total..	$1,491,433,532 49	$1,496,552,355 97

JOHN JAY KNOX, *Deputy and Acting Comptroller.*

*Including all statements except 1st N. B. Portland, Oregon, capital $100,000.

PHASES OF THE MOON.

MOON.		Boston.	N. York.	Wash'ton.	D.	Venus South.	Mars South.	Jupiter South.	Saturn South.	SUN AT NOON MARK
	D.	H. M.	H. M.	H. M.		P. M.	P. M.	P. M.	MORN.	H. M. S.
					1	1 47	0 4	3 46	9 17	12 3 37
1st Quar	2	11 18 ev.	11 6 ev.	10 54 ev.	7	1 54	0 1	3 26	8 56	12 6 2½
Full....	9	6 7 ev.	5 57 ev.	5 45 ev.	13	2 0 A. M.	3 7	8 35	12 8 47	
3d Quar.	16	0 20 ev.	0 8 ev.	11 56 m.	19	2 6	11 54	2 48	8 13	12 10 5½
New....	24	2 34 ev.	2 22 ev.	2 10 ev.	25	2 11	11 50	2 30	7 52	12 12 30

The lower portion of the page consists of rotated (vertical) calendar columns for four regions: "CALENDAR FOR Charleston; North Carolina, Tennessee, Georgia, Alabama, Mississippi and Louisiana.", "CALENDAR FOR Washington; Maryland, Virginia, Kentucky, Missouri and California.", "CALENDAR FOR New York City, Philadelphia, Connecticut, New Jersey, Pennsylvania, Ohio, Indiana and Illinois.", and "CALENDAR FOR Boston; New England, New York State, Michigan, Wisconsin, Iowa and Oregon." Each with columns for H.W., Moon Sets, Sun Sets, Sun Rises. Below are rows for MOON SOUTH. (Even.), SIDEREAL NOON. (Even.), DAY OF WEEK, and DAY OF MONTH.

PHASES OF THE MOON.

MOON.		Boston.	New York.	Wash'ton.
	D.	H. M.	H. M.	H. M.
1st Quar	1	1 32 ev.	1 20 ev.	1 8 ev.
Full....	8	4 51 m.	4 39 m.	4 27 m.
3d Quar.	15	4 32 m.	4 20 m.	4 8 m.
New....	23	9 36 m.	9 24 m.	9 12 m.

D.	Venus South. P. M.	Mars South. MORN.	Jupiter South. P. M.	Saturn South. MORN.	Sun at noon mark H. M. S.
1	2 15	11 45	2 8	7 26	12 13 48
7	2 18	11 40	1 49	7 4	12 14 22
13	2 21	11 36	1 31	6 42	12 14 28
19	2 24	11 31	1 13	6 20	12 14 7
25	2 26	11 26	0 54	5 57	12 13 22

CALENDAR FOR Charleston; North Carolina, Tennessee, Georgia, Alabama, Mississippi and Louisiana.

H.W. CH'TON. H. M.	MOON SETS. H. M.	SUN SETS. H. M.	SUN RISES. H. M.
0 30	morn.	5 33	6 55
1 25	0 55	5 34	6 55
2 28	1 58	5 34	6 54
3 37	2 59	5 35	6 53
4 45	rises.	5 36	6 52
5 48	6 17	5 37	6 51
6 40	7 24	5 38	6 50
8 28	8 29	5 39	6 49
9 16	9 33	5 40	6 48
10 48	10 33	5 41	6 47
11 35	11 32	5 43	6 46
ev. 18	morn.	5 44	6 45
2 18	0 28	5 45	6 45
3 14	1 23	5 46	6 44
4 11	2 15	5 47	6 43
3 51	3 6	5 48	6 42
5 36	3 52	5 49	6 41
6 17	4 36	5 50	6 40
7 55	5 19	5 51	6 39
8 32	5 57	5 52	6 37
9 45	sets.	5 53	6 36
10 30	7 4	5 54	6 35
11 14	7 59	5 55	6 34
morn.	8 55	5 56	6 33
9 52	5 57	6 32
10 30	5 57	6 31
10 49	5 58	6 30
11 49	5 58	6 29

CALENDAR FOR Washington; Maryland, Virginia, Kentucky, Missouri and California.

MOON SETS. H. M.	SUN SETS. H. M.	SUN RISES. H. M.
0 3	5 20	7 7
2 10	5 22	7 6
3 15	5 23	7 5
4 18	5 24	7 4
5 18	5 25	7 3
6 14	5 26	7 1
rises.	5 27	7 0
7 18	5 29	6 59
8 27	5 30	6 58
9 34	5 31	6 57
10 37	5 32	6 56
11 40	5 33	6 55
0 40	5 34	6 53
1 36	5 35	6 52
2 31	5 37	6 51
3 21	5 38	6 50
4 51	5 39	6 48
5 32	5 40	6 47
6 7	5 41	6 46
sets.	5 42	6 45
6 59	5 44	6 43
7 57	5 45	6 42
8 53	5 46	6 40
9 56	5 47	6 39
10 58	5 48	6 38
morn.	5 49	6 36
	5 50	6 35
	5 51	6 33
	5 52	

CALENDAR FOR New York City; Philadelphia, Connecticut, New Jersey, Pennsylvania, Ohio, Indiana and Illinois.

H.W. N.Y. H. M.	MOON SETS. H. M.	SUN SETS. H. M.	SUN RISES. H. M.
1 16	0 5	5 16	7 11
2 11	2 8	5 18	7 10
3 15	3 13	5 19	7 9
4 22	4 19	5 20	7 8
5 30	5 22	5 21	7 7
6 34	6 18	5 22	7 6
7 32	rises.	5 24	7 5
8 22	7 15	5 25	7 3
9 15	8 27	5 26	7 2
10 46	9 34	5 28	7 0
11 32	10 38	5 30	6 59
ev. 21	11 43	5 31	6 57
1 12	morn.	5 32	6 56
2	0 43	5 33	6 54
3 59	1 40	5 35	6 52
4 55	2 33	5 37	6 51
5 48	3 25	5 39	6 50
6 37	4 12	5 40	6 48
7 21	4 55	5 41	6 47
7 58	5 35	5 43	6 45
8 38	sets.	5 44	6 44
9 18	6 58	5 45	6 42
9 56	7 57	5 47	6 41
10 32	8 53	5 48	6 39
11 12	9 57	5 49	6 38
11 59	10 11	5 50	6 36
morn.	morn.		6 35

CALENDAR FOR Boston; New England, New York State, Michigan, Wisconsin, Iowa and Oregon.

H.W. BOSTON. H. M.	MOON SETS. H. M.	SUN SETS. H. M.	SUN RISES. H. M.
4 29	0 7	5 13	7 15
5 29	2 11	5 14	7 14
6 37	2 17	5 15	7 13
7 37	3 23	5 17	7 12
8 45	4 27	5 18	7 10
9 48	5 22	5 20	7 9
10 48	rises.	5 21	7 8
11 40	7 8	5 22	7 6
ev. 28	8 26	5 24	7 5
1 16	9 35	5 25	7 3
2 2	10 40	5 27	7 1
2 49	11 45	5 28	7 0
3 35	morn.	5 30	6 58
4 24	0 46	5 31	6 56
5 19	1 44	5 33	6 55
6 17	2 30	5 34	6 53
7 11	3 17	5 35	6 52
8 11	4 59	5 36	6 50
9 3	5 39	5 38	6 49
9 51	6 13	5 39	6 48
10 36	sets.	5 40	6 44
11 16	6 57	5 43	6 42
11 55	7 57	5 44	6 41
morn.	8 54	5 45	6 40
0 32	9 59	5 46	6 38
1 10	11 11	5 48	6 36
1 48	morn.	5 49	6 35
2 30			
3 13			

	MOON SOUTH.		SIDEREAL NOON.
H. M.	Even.	Even.	H. M.
6 10	15	3	35
6 3	11	3	31
7 59	7	3	27
8 58	3	3	23
9 59	59	3	19

DAY OF WEEK.	Sa	M	Tu	W	Th	Fr	Sa	Su	M	Tu	W	Th	Fr	Sa	Su	M	Tu	W	Th	Fr	Sa	Su	M	Tu	W	Th	Fr	Sa
DAY OF MONTH.	1	2	3	4	5	6	7	8	9	10	11	12	13	14	15	16	17	18	19	20	21	22	23	24	25	26	27	28	29

3d Month.] MARCH, 1868. [31 Days.

PHASES OF THE MOON.

MOON.		Boston.	N. York.	Wash'ton.
	D.	H. M.	H. M.	H. M.
1st Quar.	1	12 5 ev.	11 53 ev.	11 41 ev.
Full....	8	3 38 ev.	3 26 ev.	3 14 ev.
3d Quar.	15	10 44 ev.	10 32 ev.	10 20 ev.
New....	24	2 15 m.	2 3 m.	1 50 m.
1st Quar.	31	7 41 m.	7 29 m.	7 17 m.

D.	Venus South. P. M.	Mars South. MORN.	Jupiter South.	Saturn South. MORN.	Sun at noon mark H. M. S.
1	2 29	11 22	0 39	5 38	12 12 25
7	2 31	11 16	0 21	5 15	12 11 3
13	2 34	11 10	0 3	4 51	12 9 27
19	2 37	11 4	morn.	4 28	12 7 42
25	2 41	10 5	11 26	4 4	12 5 53

CALENDAR FOR Charleston; N. Carolina, Tennessee, Georgia, Alabama, Mississippi and Louisiana.

CALENDAR FOR Washington; Maryland, Virginia, Kentucky, Missouri and California.

CALENDAR FOR New York City, Philadelphia, Connecticut, New Jersey, Pennsylvania, Ohio, Indiana and Illinois.

CALENDAR FOR Boston; New England, New York State, Michigan, Wisconsin, Iowa and Oregon.

Day of Month	Day of Week
1	Su
2	M
3	Tu
4	W
5	Th
6	Fr
7	Sa
8	Su
9	M
10	Tu
11	W
12	Th
13	Fr
14	Sa
15	Su
16	M
17	Tu
18	W
19	Th
20	Fr
21	Sa
22	Su
23	M
24	Tu
25	W
26	Th
27	Fr
28	Sa
29	Su
30	M
31	Tu

PHASES OF THE MOON.

MOON.	D.	Boston. H. M.	N. York. H. M.	Wash'ton. H. M.
Full....	7	2 33 m.	2 21 m.	2 9 m.
3d Quar	14	5 50 ev.	5 38 ev.	5 26 ev.
New ...	22	3 36 ev.	3 24 ev.	3 12 ev.
1st Quar	29	1 34 ev.	1 22 ev.	1 10 ev.

D.	Venus South. P.M.	Mars South. MORN.	Jupiter South. MORN.	Saturn South. MORN.	Sun at Noon Mark H. M. S.
1	2 46	10 51	11 5	3 36	12 3 45
7	2 50	10 44	10 46	3 11	12 1 59
13	2 54	10 38	10 28	2 47	12 0 21
19	2 58	10 31	10 9	2 22	11 58 56
25	3 2	10 24	9 50	1 57	11 57 47

CALENDAR FOR Charleston; North Carolina, Tennessee, Georgia, Alabama, Mississippi and Louisiana. — columns: Sun Rises, Sun Sets, Moon Sets, H. W. Ch'ton.

CALENDAR FOR Washington; Maryland, Virginia, Kentucky, Missouri and California. — columns: Sun Rises, Sun Sets, Moon Sets.

CALENDAR FOR New York City; Philadelphia, Connecticut, New Jersey, Pennsylvania, Ohio, Indiana and Illinois. — columns: Sun Rises, Sun Sets, Moon Sets, H. W. N. Y.

CALENDAR FOR Boston; New England, New York State, Michigan, Wisconsin, Iowa and Oregon. — columns: Sun Rises, Sun Sets, Moon Sets, H. W. Boston.

Moon South Even.	Sidereal Noon Morn.	Day of Week	Day of Month
7 34	11 19	W	1
8 31	11 15	Th	2
9 26	11 11	Fr	3
10 20	11 7	Sa	4
11 12	11 3	S	5
morn.	10 59	M	6
0 3	10 55	Tu	7
0 54	10 51	W	8
1 44	10 47	Th	9
2 34	10 43	Fr	10
3 24	10 39	Sa	11
4 14	10 35	S	12
5 1	10 32	M	13
5 51	10 28	Tu	14
6 38	10 24	W	15
7 24	10 20	Th	16
8 9	10 16	Fr	17
8 54	10 12	Sa	18
9 38	10 8	S	19
10 24	10 4	M	20
11 10	10 0	Tu	21
11 58	9 56	W	22
ev.48	9 52	Th	23
1 41	9 48	Fr	24
2 36	9 44	Sa	25
3 34	9 40	S	26
4 32	9 36	M	27
5 30	9 33	Tu	28
6 26	9 29	W	29
7 21	9 25	Th	30

5th Month.]   **MAY, 1868.**   **[31 Days.**

PHASES OF THE MOON.

MOON.		Boston.	N. York.	Wash'ton.
	D.	H. M.	H. M.	H. M.
Full....	6	1 53 ev.	1 41 ev.	1 29 ev.
3d Quar.	14	0 31 ev.	0 19 ev.	0 7 ev.
New ...	22	1 52 m.	1 40 m.	1 28 m.
1st Quar	28	6 58 ev.	6 46 ev.	6 34 ev.

D.	Venus South.	Mars South.	Jupiter South.	Saturn South.	SUN AT NOON MARK
	P. M.	MORN.	MORN.	MORN.	H. M. S.
1	3 6	10 13	9 32	1 32	11 56 54
7	3 9	10 11	9 13	1 6	11 56 21
13	3 11	10 4	8 54	0 41	11 56 8
19	3 11	9 58	8 34	0 16	11 56 16
25	3 8	9 51	8 15	EVEN.	11 56 44

[The remainder of the page consists of dense multi-region calendar tables (Calendar for Charleston, North Carolina, etc.; Washington, Maryland, etc.; New York City, Philadelphia, etc.; Boston, New England, etc.) with columns for H.W., Moon Sets, Sun Sets, Sun Rises, and rows for Moon South, Sidereal Noon, Day of Week, Day of Month.]

6th Month.] JUNE, 1868. [30 Days.

PHASES OF THE MOON.

MOON.	Boston.	N. York.	Wash'ton.
	D. H. M.	H. M.	H. M.
Full....	5 2 9 m.	1 59 m.	1 47 m.
3d Quar.	13 5 29 m.	5 17 m.	5 5 m.
New....	20 10 1 m.	9 49 m.	9 37 m.
1stQuar.	27 1 6 m.	0 54 m.	0 42 m.

D.	Venus South. P. M.	Mars South. MORN.	Jupiter South. MORN.	Saturn South. P. M.	SUN AT NOON MARK H. M. S.
1	3 2	9 43	7 52	11 16	11 57 38
7	2 54	9 37	7 32	10 51	11 58 39
13	2 41	9 31	7 12	10 26	11 59 38
19	2 24	9 24	6 51	10 0	12 1 8
25	2 2	9 18	6 30	9 36	12 2 26

CALENDAR FOR Charleston; North Carolina, Tennessee, Georgia, Alabama, Mississippi and Louisiana. — H. W. Ch'ton, Moon sets, Sun sets, Sun rises.

CALENDAR FOR Washington; Maryland, Virginia, Kentucky, Missouri and California. — Moon sets, Sun sets, Sun rises.

CALENDAR FOR New York City; Philadelphia, Connecticut, New Jersey, Pennsylvania, Ohio, Indiana and Illinois. — H. W. N. Y., Moon sets, Sun sets, Sun rises.

CALENDAR FOR Boston; New England, New York State, Michigan, Wisconsin, Iowa and Oregon. — H. W. Boston, Moon sets, Sun sets, Sun rises.

MOON SOUTH. Even.
SIDEREAL NOON. Morn.
DAY OF WEEK
DAY OF MONTH

7th Month.]   JULY, 1868.   [31 Days.

PHASES OF THE MOON.

MOON.	D.	Boston. H. M.	N. York. H. M.	Wash'ton. H. M.
Full....	4	3 55 ev.	3 43 ev.	3 31 ev.
3d Quar.	12	7 56 ev.	7 44 ev.	7 32 ev.
New ...	19	5 12 ev.	5 0 ev.	4 48 ev.
1st Quar	26	9 7 m.	8 55 m.	8 43 m.

D.	Venus South. P. M.	Mars South. MORN.	Jupiter South. MORN.	Saturn South. P. N.	Sun at Noon Mark H. M. S.
1	1 34	9 12	6 9	9 11	12 3 38
7	1 0	9 6	5 38	8 46	12 4 40
13	0 22	9 0	5 26	8 22	12 5 29
19	MORN.	8 54	5 3	7 57	12 6 1
25	11 5	8 48	4 41	7 33	12 6 14

CALENDAR FOR Charleston; North Carolina, Tennessee, Georgia, Alabama, Mississippi and Louisiana.

Sun rises. H. M.	Sun sets. H. M.	Moon sets. H. M.	H. W. Ch'ton. H. M.
4 55	7 12	2 38	4 51
4 55	7 12	3 20	5 42
4 56	7 12	rises.	6 29
4 56	7 11	6 59	7 14
4 57	7 11	7 44	7 55
4 57	7 11	8 25	8 36
4 58	7 11	9 3	9 14
4 58	7 11	9 39	9 54
4 59	7 10	10 13	10 33
4 59	7 10	10 45	11 14
5 0	7 10	11 52	11 56
5 1	7 9	morn.	ev.43
5 1	7 9	0 30	1 34
5 2	7 9	1 55	2 31
5 2	7 8	2 47	3 34
5 3	7 8	3 43	4 38
5 4	7 7	sets.	5 38
5 4	7 7	7 48	6 36
5 5	7 6	8 37	7 30
5 6	7 6	9 23	8 21
5 6	7 5	10 3	9 13
5 7	7 5	10 43	10 1
5 8	7 4	11 59	10 51
5 9	7 3	sets.	11 41
5 10	7 2	7 48	morn.
5 10	7 1	8 37	0 33
5 11	7 0	9 23	1 27
5 12	6 59	1 19	2 27
5 12	6 59	2 49	3 24

CALENDAR FOR Washington; Maryland, Virginia, Kentucky, Missouri and California.

Sun rises. H. M.	Sun sets. H. M.	Moon sets. H. M.
4 39	7 28	2 24
4 39	7 28	3 3
4 40	7 28	3 47
4 40	7 27	rises.
4 41	7 27	8 39
4 42	7 27	9 15
4 43	7 27	9 48
4 44	7 26	10 18
4 45	7 26	10 49
4 46	7 25	11 24
4 47	7 25	11 48
4 47	7 24	morn.
4 48	7 24	0 22
4 49	7 23	0 59
4 50	7 23	1 41
4 51	7 22	2 30
4 52	7 21	3 26
4 53	7 20	sets.
4 54	7 19	8 0
4 55	7 18	8 48
4 56	7 17	9 28
4 57	7 16	10 5
4 58	7 15	10 39
4 59	7 14	11 48
5 0	7 13	morn.
5 0	7 12	0 5
5 1	7 10	1 46
5 2	6 59	2 32

CALENDAR FOR New York City; Philadelphia, Connecticut, New Jersey, Pennsylvania, Ohio, Indiana and Illinois.

Sun rises. H. M.	Sun sets. H. M.	Moon sets. H. M.	H. W. N. Y. H. M.
4 33	7 34	2 21	5 36
4 34	7 34	2 58	6 28
4 34	7 34	3 43	7 15
4 35	7 34	rises.	7 56
4 35	7 33	8 43	8 39
4 36	7 33	9 18	9 22
4 37	7 33	9 50	10 8
4 38	7 32	10 19	10 38
4 38	7 32	10 49	11 16
4 39	7 31	11 24	11 39
4 40	7 31	11 47	ev.43
4 41	7 30	morn.	1 29
4 42	7 29	0 56	2 20
4 43	7 28	1 37	3 18
4 44	7 27	2 26	4 17
4 45	7 27	3 22	6 23
4 46	7 26	sets.	5 21
4 47	7 25	8 3	8 14
4 49	7 24	8 50	9 9
4 50	7 23	9 29	10 0
4 50	7 21	10 5	10 47
4 51	7 21	10 38	11 35
4 52	7 19	11 46	morn.
4 53	7 18	morn.	1 14
4 54	7 17	0 59	1 19
4 55	7 16	1 42	3 5
4 56	7 24	2 27	6 2

CALENDAR FOR Boston; New England, New York State, Michigan, Wisconsin, Iowa and Oregon.

Sun rises. H. M.	Sun sets. H. M.	Moon sets. H. M.	H. W. Boston. H. M.
4 28	7 40	2 17	8 51
4 28	7 39	2 54	9 42
4 29	7 39	3 38	10 30
4 29	7 39	rises.	11 14
4 30	7 39	8 47	11 57
4 30	7 38	9 21	ev.35
4 31	7 38	9 53	1 15
4 31	7 38	10 21	1 53
4 32	7 37	10 50	2 34
4 33	7 37	11 24	3 7
4 34	7 36	11 46	3 14
4 35	7 35	morn.	3 58
4 36	7 35	0 18	4 43
4 37	7 34	0 53	5 35
4 38	7 33	1 33	6 32
4 39	7 32	2 21	7 37
4 40	7 31	3 17	8 37
4 41	7 31	sets.	11 31
4 42	7 30	8 7	morn.
4 43	7 29	8 53	0 22
4 44	7 28	9 31	1 14
4 45	7 27	10 6	2 4
4 46	7 27	10 38	2 52
4 47	7 26	11 10	3 41
4 48	7 25	11 43	5 29
4 49	7 24	morn.	6 27
4 50	7 22	0 55	8 5
4 51	7 20	1 37	8 23
4 52	7 2	2 23	9 16

MOON SOUTH. Even. H. M.	SIDEREAL NOON. Morn. H. M.	DAY OF WEEK.	DAY OF MONTH.
9 53	5 21	W	1
10 42	5 17	Th	2
11 31	5 13	Fr	3
morn.	5 9	Sa	4
0 20	5 5	M	5
1 8	5 1	Tu	6
1 54	4 57	W	7
2 39	4 53	Th	8
3 23	4 49	Fr	9
4 7	4 46	Sa	10
4 50	4 42	M	11
5 33	4 38	Tu	12
6 18	4 34	W	13
7 6	4 30	Th	14
7 56	4 26	Fr	15
8 51	4 22	Sa	16
9 48	4 18	M	17
11 52	4 14	Tu	18
ev.53	4 10	W	19
1 53	4 6	M	20
2 50	4 2	Tu	21
3 43	3 58	W	22
3 35	3 54	Th	23
5 24	3 51	Fr	24
6 13	3 47	Sa	25
2	3 43	M	26
7 50	3 39	Tu	27
8 39	3 35	W	28
9 28	3 31	Th	29
8 28	3 27	Fr	30
10 17	3 23		31

PHASES OF THE MOON.

MOON.	Boston.	N. York.	Wash'ton.	D.	Venus South. MORN.	Mars South. MORN.	Jupiter South. MORN.	Saturn South. P.M.	SUN AT NOON MARK H. M. S.
	H. M.	H. M.	H. M.						
Full.... 3	7 8 m.	6 56 m.	6 44 m.	1	10 27	8 41	4 14	7 6	12 6 1
3d Quar. 11	7 44 m.	7 32 m.	7 20 m.	7	10 1	8 35	3 50	6 42	12 5 26
New.... 17	0 27 m.	0 15 m.	0 3 m.	13	9 40	8 29	3 26	6 19	12 4 31
1st Quar. 24	8 3 ev.	7 51 ev.	7 39 ev.	19	9 25	8 22	3 1	5 56	12 3 16
				25	9 14	8 15	2 36	5 33	12 1 45

CALENDAR FOR Charleston; North Carolina, Tennessee, Georgia, Alabama, Mississippi and Louisiana.

SUN RISES.	SUN SETS.	MOON SETS.	H. W. CH'TON.
5 13	6 58	3 39	6 5
5 13	6 58	rises.	6 52
5 14	6 57	7 40	7 30
5 15	6 56	8 14	8 10
5 15	6 55	8 48	8 47
5 16	6 54	9 20	9 25
5 17	6 53	9 54	10 3
5 18	6 52	10 25	10 41
5 19	6 51	11 6	11 22
5 19	6 50	11 47	ev. 6
5 20	6 49	morn.	0 59
5 21	6 48	0 34	1 59
5 21	6 47	1 27	3 5
5 22	6 46	2 26	4 11
5 23	6 45	3 31	5 19
5 23	6 44	sets.	6 21
5 24	6 43	7 11	7 17
5 25	6 42	7 55	8 6
5 25	6 41	8 36	8 53
5 26	6 40	9 16	9 40
5 27	6 38	9 57	10 27
5 28	6 37	10 35	11 14
5 28	6 36	11 17	morn.
5 29	6 35	12 0	0 3
5 30	6 34	morn.	0 51
5 31	6 31	0 47	1 56
5 31	6 30	1 35	2 57
5 32	6 30	2 25	4 49
5 32	6 28	3 17	5 38
5 33	6 27	4 10	6 23

CALENDAR FOR Washington; Maryland, Virginia, Kentucky, Missouri and California.

SUN RISES. H. M.	SUN SETS. H. M.	MOON SETS.
5 7	7 11	3 21
5 8	7 10	4 13
5 9	7 9	rises.
5 9	7 8	7 50
5 10	7 7	8 22
5 11	7 5	8 52
5 11	7 4	9 22
5 12	7 3	9 51
5 13	7 2	10 22
5 13	7 0	10 56
5 14	6 58	11 35
5 15	6 57	morn.
5 16	6 56	0 18
5 16	6 54	1 10
5 17	6 53	2 8
5 18	6 52	3 15
5 19	6 50	4 25
5 20	6 49	sets.
5 21	6 48	7 59
5 22	6 46	8 36
5 23	6 45	9 13
5 23	6 43	9 48
5 24	6 42	10 24
5 25	6 41	11 4
5 26	6 39	11 44
5 27	6 38	morn.
5 27	6 37	0 29
5 28	6 35	1 17
5 28	6 34	2 8
5 29	6 32	3 58

CALENDAR FOR New York City; Philadelphia, Connecticut, New Jersey, Pennsylvania, Ohio, Indiana and Illinois.

SUN RISES. H. M.	SUN SETS.	MOON SETS.	H. W. N. Y.
4 57	7 15	3 11	6 52
4 58	7 14	4 13	7 35
4 59	7 13	rises.	8 13
5 0	7 12	7 52	8 54
5 1	7 10	8 24	9 33
5 2	7 9	8 53	10 10
5 3	7 8	9 22	10 45
5 4	7 7	9 50	11 23
5 4	7 6	10 21	ev.
5 5	7 4	10 54	0 53
5 6	7 2	11 32	1 46
5 7	7 1	morn.	2 46
5 9	6 59	0 14	3 50
5 10	6 58	1 6	4 58
5 11	6 57	2 4	6 7
5 12	6 55	3 10	7 7
5 13	6 54	4 22	7 59
5 14	6 53	sets.	8 51
5 15	6 51	8 36	9 39
5 16	6 50	9 12	10 24
5 17	6 48	9 46	11 9
5 18	6 47	10 21	11 59
5 19	6 45	10 59	morn.
5 20	6 44	11 39	0 50
5 22	6 41	morn.	1 44
5 23	6 40	0 25	2 42
5 24	6 37	1 13	3 41
5 25	6 36	2 5	4 39
5 26	6 34	2 58	5 24
		3 54	6 7

CALENDAR FOR Boston; New England, New York State, Michigan, Wisconsin, Iowa and Oregon.

SUN RISES. H. M.	SUN SETS.	MOON SETS.	H. W. BOSTON.
4 53	7 19	3 12	10 5
4 54	7 18	4	10 51
4 55	7 17	rises.	ev. 9
4 56	7 16	7 55	0 38
4 57	7 15	8 26	1 24
4 58	7 14	8 54	2 2
4 59	7 12	9 22	2 41
5 0	7 11	9 49	3 22
5 1	7 10	10 19	4 6
5 2	7 8	10 51	4 50
5 3	7 6	11 28	6 0
5 4	7 5	morn.	7 5
5 5	7 3	0 10	8 14
5 6	7 1	1 1	9 20
5 7	6 59	1 59	10 6
5 9	6 58	3 6	11 16
5 10	6 57	4 18	morn.
5 11	6 55	sets.	0 53
5 12	6 54	8 31	1 40
5 13	6 52	9 11	2 27
5 14	6 50	9 44	3 14
5 15	6 49	10 18	4 3
5 16	6 47	10 55	4 57
5 17	6 46	11 35	5 56
5 18	6 44	morn.	6 56
5 20	6 43	0 20	7 49
5 21	6 41	1 1	8 49
5 22	6 39	1 59	9 38
5 23	6 38	2 54	10 23
5 24	6 36	3 51	

MOON SOUTH.

Morn. Even. H. M.
2 5
11 52
morn.
0 37
1 22
2 8
2 48
3 31
4 8
4 48
5 39
6 39
7 33
8 31
9 32
10 33
11 34
ev. 33
1 29
2 23
3 16
4 7
4 57
5 46
6 36
7 25
8 14
9 1
9 49
10 35
11 20

SIDEREAL NOON.

Morn. H. M.
3 19
3 15
3 11
3 7
3 3
2 59
2 55
2 52
2 48
2 44
2 40
2 36
2 32
2 28
2 24
2 20
2 16
2 12
2 8
2 4
2 0
1 57
1 53
1 49
1 45
1 41
1 37
1 33
1 29
1 25
1 21

DAY OF WEEK.

Sa 31 | M | Tu | W | Th | Fr | Sa 32 | M | Tu | W | Th | Fr | Sa 33 | M | Tu | W | Th | Fr | Sa 34 | M | Tu | W | Th | Fr | Sa 35 | M

DAY OF MONTH.

1 2 3 4 5 6 7 8 9 10 11 12 13 14 15 16 17 18 19 20 21 22 23 24 25 26 27 28 29 30 31

9th Month.] SEPTEMBER, 1868. [30 Days.

PHASES OF THE MOON.

MOON.		Boston.		N. York.		Wash'ton.	
	D.	H. M.		H. M.		H. M.	
Full....	1	11 13 ev.		11 1 ev.		10 49 ev.	
3d Quar.	9	5 20 ev.		5 8 ev.		4 56 ev.	
New ...	16	8 35 m.		8 23 m.		8 11 m.	
1st Quar	23	10 38 m.		10 26 m.		10 14 m.	

D.	Venus Sonth. MORN.	Mars South. MORN.	Jupiter South. MORN.	Saturn South. P. M.	SUN AT NOON MARK H. M. S.
1	9 5	8 7	2 7	5 7	11 59 39
7	9 0	7 59	1 41	4 44	11 57 41
13	8 57	7 52	1 15	4 22	11 55 36
19	8 56	7 43	0 49	4 0	11 53 30
25	8 56	7 35	0 23	3 38	11 51 25

CALENDAR FOR Charleston; North Carolina, Tennessee, Georgia, Alabama, Mississippi and Louisiana.

H. W. Ch'ton.	Moon rises.	Sun sets.	Sun rises.
7 42	rises.	6 25	5 34
8 17	6 49	6 24	5 35
8 54	7 22	6 22	5 35
9 32	7 55	6 21	5 36
10 11	8 29	6 20	5 37
10 53	9 5	6 19	5 37
11 40	9 45	6 17	5 38
ev.35	10 29	6 16	5 39
1 37	11 17	6 15	5 39
2 45	morn.	6 13	5 40
3 36	0 12	6 12	5 41
4 2	1 14	6 11	5 42
5 8	2 18	6 9	5 43
6 57	3 24	6 8	5 43
7 45	4 34	6 7	5 44
8 29	sets.	6 5	5 45
9 15	7 8	6 4	5 45
10 1	7 48	6 2	5 46
10 46	8 30	6 1	5 46
morn.	9 11	5 58	5 47
0 27	9 55	5 57	5 48
1 23	10 42	5 56	5 48
2 22	11 29	5 54	5 50
3 20	morn.	5 53	5 50
4 14	0 19	5 52	5 51
5 0	1 12	5 51	5 52
5 50	2 57	5 49	5 52
6 31	3 50	5 48	5 53
	4 43	5 46	5 53

CALENDAR FOR Washington; Maryland, Virginia, Kentucky, Missouri and California.

H. W.	Moon rises.	Sun sets.	Sun rises.
7 47	rises.	6 30	5 29
6 55	6 57	6 29	5 30
7 25	7 26	6 27	5 31
7 54	7 54	6 26	5 32
8 58	8 55	6 24	5 33
9 33	9 30	6 23	5 33
10 14	10 10	6 21	5 34
11 1	10 57	6 20	5 35
11 55	11 51	6 18	5 35
morn.	morn.	6 17	5 36
0 56	0 52	6 15	5 37
1 52	1 58	6 13	5 38
3 12	3 0	6 12	5 39
4 23	4 21	6 10	5 40
sets.	sets.	6 8	5 41
5 7	5 7	6 7	5 42
7 4	7 4	6 5	5 43
8 19	8 11	6 3	5 44
8 58	8 58	6 1	5 45
9 39	9 39	5 59	5 46
10 24	10 24	5 57	5 47
11 11	11 11	5 56	5 48
morn.	morn.	5 54	5 49
0 2	0 2	5 53	5 50
0 55	0 55	5 51	5 51
1 50	1 50	5 49	5 52
2 45	2 42	5 48	5 53
3 41	3 37	5 46	5 54
4 37	4 36	5 46	5 55

CALENDAR FOR New York City; Philadelphia, Connecticut, New Jersey, Pennsylvania, Ohio, Indiana and Illinois.

H. W. N. Y.	Moon rises.	Sun sets.	Sun rises.
7 47	rises.	6 32	5 27
8 24	6 57	6 31	5 28
9 3	7 26	6 29	5 29
9 40	7 54	6 28	5 30
10 17	8 23	6 26	5 31
10 53	8 55	6 25	5 32
11 37	9 30	6 23	5 33
ev.26	10 10	6 21	5 34
1 22	10 57	6 19	5 35
2 23	11 51	6 18	5 36
3 31	morn.	6 16	5 37
4 41	0 52	6 15	5 38
5 49	1 58	6 13	5 39
6 41	3 0	6 11	5 40
8 26	4 21	6 9	5 41
9 16	sets.	6 8	5 42
10 1	6 48	6 6	5 43
10 43	7 41	6 4	5 44
11 29	8 17	6 3	5 45
morn.	8 35	6 1	5 46
0 20	9 20	5 59	5 47
1 14	10 7	5 58	5 48
2 8	10 54	5 56	5 49
3 8	11 58	5 54	5 50
4 4	morn.	5 53	5 51
4 58	0 51	5 51	5 52
5 50	1 47	5 49	5 53
6 36	2 42	5 47	5 55
7 16	3 37	5 46	5 56
	4 36	5 44	5 58

CALENDAR FOR Boston; New England, New York State, Michigan, Wisconsin, Iowa and Oregon.

H. W. Boston.	Moon rises.	Sun sets.	Sun rises.
11 4	rises.	6 34	5 25
11 41	6 58	6 33	5 26
ev.17	7 26	6 31	5 27
0 54	7 53	6 29	5 28
1 32	8 22	6 27	5 29
2 11	8 53	6 26	5 31
2 54	9 27	6 24	5 32
3 40	10 0	6 23	5 33
4 35	10 52	6 21	5 34
5 46	morn.	6 19	5 35
6 56	0 47	6 17	5 36
9 3	1 54	6 15	5 38
10 3	4 19	6 13	5 39
10 58	sets.	6 12	5 40
11 44	6 33	6 10	5 41
morn.	7 39	6 8	5 42
0 29	8 14	6 6	5 44
1 15	8 51	6 5	5 45
2 0	9 31	6 3	5 47
2 46	10 15	5 59	5 48
3 34	morn.	5 57	5 50
4 27	0 47	5 56	5 51
5 23	1 43	5 52	5 53
6 22	2 39	5 49	5 54
7 20	3 35	5 47	5 55
8 14	4 35	5 45	5 56
9 7		5 43	
9 50			
10 32			

		MOON SOUTH. Morn. H. M.
		morn.
		0 4
		0 47
		1 30
		2 14
		2 58
		3 45
		4 34
		5 26
		6 20
		7 17
		8 16
		9 16
		10 14
		11 7
		ev. 1
		1 54
		2 46
		3 37
		4 28
		5 19
		6 8
		6 57
		7 45
		8 31
		9 17
		10 1
		10 44
		11 28

	SIDEREAL NOON. Morn. H. M.
	1 17
	1 13
	1 9
	1 5
	1 1
	0 58
	0 54
	0 50
	0 46
	0 42
	0 38
	0 34
	0 30
	0 26
	0 22
	0 18
	0 14
	0 10
	0 6
	even.
	11 51
	11 47
	11 43
	11 39
	11 35
	11 31
	11 27
	11 23
	11 19

DAY OF WEEK.	DAY OF MONTH.
Tu	1
W	2
Th	3
Fr	4
Sa	5
S	6
M	7
Tu	8
W	9
Th	10
Fr	11
Sa	12
S	13
M	14
Tu	15
W	16
Th	17
Fr	18
Sa	19
S	20
M	21
Tu	22
W	23
Th	24
Fr	25
Sa	26
S	27
M	28
Tu	29
W	30

10th Month.]   OCTOBER, 1868.   [31 Days.

PHASES OF THE MOON.

MOON.	Boston.	N. York.	Wash'ton.	D.	Venus South. MORN.	Mars South. MORN.	Jupiter South. P.M.	Saturn South. P.M.	SUN AT NOON MARK
	H. M.	H. M.	H. M.		H. M.	H. M.	H. M.	H. M.	H. M. S.
Full.... 1	3 14 ev.	3 2 ev.	2 50 ev.	1	8 56	7 26	11 52	3 17	11 49 27
3d Quar. 9	1 29 m.	1 17 m.	1 5 m.	7	8 57	7 17	11 25	2 56	11 47 39
New... 15	6 17 ev.	6 5 ev.	5 53 ev.	13	8 59	7 6	10 59	2 34	11 46 8
1st Quar 23	4 58 m.	4 46 m.	4 34 m.	19	9 1	6 56	10 32	2 13	11 44 56
Full.... 31	6 21 m.	6 9 m.	5 57 m.	25	9 2	6 45	10 6	1 52	11 44 6

CALENDAR FOR Charleston; N. Carolina, Tennessee, Georgia, Alabama, Mississippi and Louisiana. — columns: Sun Rises, Sun Sets, Moon Rises, H.W. Ch't'n.

CALENDAR FOR Washington; Maryland, Virginia, Kentucky, Missouri and California. — columns: Sun Rises, Sun Sets, Moon Rises.

CALENDAR FOR New York City; Philadelphia, Connecticut, New Jersey, Pennsylvania, Ohio, Indiana and Illinois. — columns: Sun Rises, Sun Sets, Moon Rises, H.W. N.Y.

CALENDAR FOR Boston; New England, New York State, Michigan, Wisconsin, Iowa and Oregon. — columns: Sun Rises, Sun Sets, Moon Rises, H.W. Boston.

MOON SOUTH.	SIDEREAL NOON.	DAY OF WEEK.	DAY OF MONTH.
Morn. / Even.	H. M.		

11th Month.]   **NOVEMBER, 1868.**   **[30 Days.**

PHASES OF THE MOON.

MOON.	D.	Boston. H. M.	N. York. H. M.	Wash'ton. H. M.
3d Quar.	7	9 3 m.	8 51 m.	8 39 m.
New ...	14	6 11 m.	5 59 m.	5 47 m.
1st Quar	22	2 2 m.	1 50 m.	1 38 m.
Full....	29	8 16 ev.	8 4 ev.	7 52 ev.

P.	Venus South. MORN.	Mars South. MORN.	Jupiter South. P. M.	Saturn South. P. M.	Sun at noon mark H. M. S.
1	9 5	6 32	9 36	1 28	11 43 41
7	9 7	6 20	9 11	1 7	11 43 51
13	9 10	6 7	8 46	0 46	11 44 32
19	9 13	5 53	8 21	0 26	11 45 44
25	9 16	5 39	7 57	0 5	11 47 23

(Calendar tables for the several regions — Charleston, North Carolina, Tennessee, Georgia, Alabama, Mississippi and Louisiana; Washington, Maryland, Virginia, Kentucky, Missouri and California; New York City, Philadelphia, Connecticut, New Jersey, Pennsylvania, Ohio, Indiana and Illinois; Boston, New England, New York State, Michigan, Wisconsin, Iowa and Oregon — with columns for H.W., Moon Rises, Sun Sets, Sun Rises; followed by Moon South, Sidereal Noon, Day of Week, Day of Month.)

PHASES OF THE MOON.

MOON.		Boston.	N. York.	Wash'ton.
	D.	H. M.	H. M.	H. M.
3d Quar.	6	4 50 ev.	4 38 ev.	4 26 ev.
New ...	13	8 49 ev.	8 37 ev.	8 25 ev.
1st Quar	21	11 44 ev.	11 32 ev.	11 20 ev.
Full....	29	9 3 m.	8 51 m.	8 39 m.

D.	Venus South. MORN.	Mars South. MORN.	Jupiter South. P. M.	Saturn South. MORN.	SUN AT NOON MARK. H. M. S.
1	9 20	5 24	7 34	11 44	11 49 29
7	9 24	5 8	7 10	11 24	11 51 58
13	9 30	4 51	6 48	11 3	11 54 45
19	9 35	4 32	6 25	10 42	11 57 41
25	9 42	4 12	6 3	10 22	12 0 41

CALENDAR FOR Charleston; North Carolina, Tennessee, Georgia, Alabama, Mississippi and Louisiana.

SUN RISES.	SUN SETS.	MOON RISES.	H. W. CH'TON.
6 45	4 54	6 50	8 20
6 45	4 54	7 50	9 17
6 46	4 54	8 53	10 0
6 47	4 54	9 58	11 55
6 48	4 54	morn.	ev.53
6 49	4 54	0 4	1 53
6 49	4 54	1 9	2 57
6 50	4 54	2 9	3 54
6 51	4 54	3 12	4 51
6 52	4 54	4 13	5 44
6 53	4 55	5 15	6 33
6 54	4 55	sets.	7 20
6 54	4 55	5 39	7 55
6 55	4 55	6 41	8 46
6 56	4 56	7 33	9 29
6 56	4 56	8 27	10 12
6 57	4 57	9 21	10 53
6 58	4 57	10 14	11 35
6 58	4 57	11 7	morn.
6 59	4 58	morn.	0 20
6 59	4 59	0 1	1 8
7 0	4 59	0 54	1 57
7 1	5 0	1 48	2 52
7 1	5 1	2 44	3 44
7 2	5 1	3 44	4 35
7 2	5 2	sets.	5 29
7 3	5 3	5 34	6 29
7 3	5 4	6 37	7 20
7 3	5 4	7 46	8 11
7 3	5 5	rises.	9 3

CALENDAR FOR Washington; Maryland, Virginia, Kentucky, Missouri and California.

SUN RISES.	SUN SETS.	MOON RISES.
7 0	4 38	6 31
7 1	4 38	7 31
7 2	4 37	8 36
7 3	4 37	9 45
7 4	4 37	10 52
7 5	4 37	morn.
7 6	4 38	2 13
7 7	4 38	3 16
7 9	4 38	4 22
7 10	4 38	5 26
7 11	4 38	6 27
7 12	4 39	sets.
7 13	4 39	6 34
7 14	4 39	7 18
7 15	4 40	8 13
7 16	4 41	9 8
7 17	4 42	11 0
7 18	4 42	11 54
7 19	4 43	morn.
7 19	4 44	0 53
7 19	4 45	1 49
7 19	4 47	2 52
7 19	4 48	rises.
		6 20
		7 30

CALENDAR FOR New York City; Philadelphia, Connecticut, New Jersey, Pennsylvania, Ohio, Indiana and Illinois.

SUN RISES.	SUN SETS.	MOON RISES.	H. W. N.Y.
7 6	4 33	6 26	9 13
7 7	4 33	7 27	10 3
7 8	4 32	8 33	10 51
7 9	4 32	9 42	11 45
7 10	4 32	10 50	ev.42
7 11	4 32	11 57	1 40
7 12	4 32	morn.	2 39
7 13	4 32	2 13	3 41
7 14	4 32	3 18	4 39
7 15	4 32	4 24	5 36
7 16	4 32	5 29	6 30
7 17	4 33	6 32	7 18
7 18	4 33	sets.	8 2
7 19	4 33	6 29	8 47
7 19	4 34	7 14	9 33
7 20	4 34	8 7	10 15
7 21	4 34	9 5	10 54
7 22	4 35	10 10	11 37
7 22	4 36	11 54	morn.
7 23	4 36	morn.	0 21
7 23	4 37	0 54	1 6
7 24	4 38	1 51	2 43
7 24	4 39	2 54	3 36
7 25	4 40	3 55	4 30
7 25	4 40	rises.	5 21
	4 41	6 6	6 14
	4 42	6 16	8 4
		7 26	9 49

CALENDAR FOR Boston; New England, New York State, Michigan, Wisconsin, Iowa and Oregon.

SUN RISES.	SUN SETS.	MOON RISES.	H. W. BOSTON.
7 11	4 28	6 21	ev.36
7 12	4 28	7 22	1 24
7 13	4 28	8 28	2 15
7 14	4 27	9 38	3 0
7 15	4 27	10 47	3 55
7 16	4 27	11 56	4 53
7 17	4 27	morn.	5 54
7 18	4 27	1 6	6 56
7 19	4 27	2 14	7 54
7 20	4 27	3 20	8 51
7 21	4 27	4 26	9 44
7 22	4 27	5 33	10 33
7 23	4 28	6 36	11 20
7 23	4 28	sets.	morn.
7 24	4 28	6 24	0 46
7 25	4 28	8 5	1 30
7 26	4 29	8 5	2 12
7 27	4 29	9 2	2 53
7 27	4 30	9 59	3 35
7 28	4 30	10 57	4 19
7 28	4 31	11 53	5 8
7 30	4 32	morn.	5 57
7 30	4 33	0 54	6 51
7 32	4 33	1 52	7 45
7 33	4 34	2 56	8 42
7 34	4 35	3 58	9 35
7 35	4 36	6 11	10 30
7 36	4 37	rises.	11 21
7 36		6 11	ev.12
7 37		7 22	1 3

MOON SOUTH. Morn. H. M.	0 58 1 56 2 53 3 53 4 49 5 42 6 34 7 25 8 14 9 4 9 55 10 46 11 38 ev.29 1 21 2 11 2 58 3 45 4 29 5 12 5 55 6 37 7 21 8 6 8 55 9 46 10 42 morn. 0 41 1 41		
SIDEREAL NOON. Even. H. M.	7 15 7 12 7 8 7 0 6 56 6 52 6 48 6 40 6 36 6 32 6 28 6 24 6 20 6 16 6 13 6 9 6 5 6 1 5 57 5 53 5 49 5 45 5 41 5 37 5 33 5 29 5 25 5 21 5 17		
DAY OF WEEK.	Tu W Th Fr Sa **49** M Tu W Th Fr Sa **50** M Tu W Th Fr Sa **51** M Tu W Th Fr Sa **52** M Tu W Th		
DAY OF MONTH.	1 2 3 4 5 6 7 8 9 10 11 12 13 14 15 16 17 18 19 20 21 22 23 24 25 26 27 28 29 30 31		

RECONSTRUCTION.

There are three acts on the subject of Reconstruction: The first was passed March 2, 1867, at the Second Session of the Thirty-ninth Congress; the second, or Supplemental act, was passed March 23, 1867, at the First Session of the Fortieth Congress; and the third, or Explanatory act, was passed July 19, 1867, at the Extra Session of the Fortieth Congress. The acts are as follows:

Reconstruction Act of Thirty-ninth Congress.

AN ACT to provide for the more efficient government of the rebel States.

Whereas no legal State governments or adequate protection for life or property now exist in the rebel States of Virginia, North Carolina, South Carolina, Georgia, Mississippi, Alabama, Louisiana, Florida, Texas, and Arkansas; and whereas it is necessary that peace and good order should be enforced in said States until loyal and republican State governments can be legally established; Therefore—

Be it enacted, &c., That said rebel States shall be divided into military districts and made subject to the military authority of the United States, as hereinafter prescribed, and for that purpose Virginia shall constitute the first district; North Carolina and South Carolina the second district: Georgia, Alabama, and Florida the third district; Mississippi, and Arkansas the fourth district; and Louisiana and Texas the fifth district.

SEC. 2. That it shall be the duty of the President to assign to the command of each of said districts an officer of the army, not below the rank of brigadier general, and to detail a sufficient military force to enable such officer to perform his duties and enforce his authority within the district to which he is assigned.

SEC. 3. That it shall be the duty of each officer assigned as aforesaid to protect all persons in their rights of person and property, to suppress insurrection, disorder, and violence, and to punish, or cause to be punished, all disturbers of the public peace and criminals, and to this end he may allow local civil tribunals to take jurisdiction of and to try offenders. or, when in his judgment it may be necessary for the trial of offenders, he shall have power to organize military commissions or tribunals for that purpose; and all interference under color of State authority with the exercise of military authority under this act shall be null and void.

SEC. 4. That all persons put under military arrest by virtue of this act shall be tried without unnecessary delay, and no cruel or unusual punishment shall be inflicted; and no sentence of any military commission or tribunal hereby authorized, affecting the life or liberty of any person, shall be executed until it is approved by the officer in command of the district; and the laws and regulations for the government of the army shall not be affected by this act, except in so far as they conflict with its provisions: *Provided*, That no sentence of death under the provisions of this act shall be carried into effect without the approval of the President.

SEC. 5. That when the people of any one of said rebel States shall have formed a constitution of government in conformity with the Constitution of the United States in all respects, framed by a convention of delegates elected by the male citizens of said State twenty-one years old and upward, of whatever race, color, or previous condition, who have been resident in said State for one year previous to the day of such election, except such as may be disfranchised for participation in the rebellion or for felony at common law, and when such constitution shall provide that the elective franchise shall be enjoyed by all such persons as have the qualifications herein stated for electors of delegates, and when such constitution shall be ratified by a majority of the persons voting on the question of ratification who are qualified as electors for delegates, and when such constitution shall have been submitted to Congress for examination and approval, and Congress shall have approved the same, and when said State, by a vote of its legislature elected under said constitution shall have adopted the amendment to the Constitution of the United States, proposed by the thirty-ninth Congress, and known as article fourteen, and when said article shall have become a part of the Constitution of the United States, said State shall be declared entitled to representation in Congress, and senators and representatives shall be admitted therefrom on their taking the oaths prescribed by law, and then and thereafter the preceding sections of this act shall be inoperative in said State: *Provided*, That no person excluded from the privilege of holding office by said proposed amendment to the Constitution of the United States shall be eligible to election as a member of the convention to frame a constitution for any of said rebel States, nor shall any such person vote for members of such convention.

SEC. 6. That until the people of said rebel States shall be by law admitted to representation in the Congress of the United States, any civil governments which may exist therein shall be deemed provisional only, and in all respects subject to the paramount authority of the United States at any time to abolish, modify, control, or supersede the same; and in all elections to any office under such provisional governments all persons shall be entitled to vote, and none

others, who are entitled to vote under the provisions of the fifth section of this act; and no person shall be eligible to any office under any such provisional governments who would be disqualified from holding office under the provisions of the third article of said constitutional amendment.

Passed March 2, 1867.

Proposed 14th Constitutional Amendment.

The following is the proposed constitutional amendment referred to in section five:

ARTICLE XIV.

SECTION 1. All persons born or naturalized in the United States, and subject to the jurisdiction thereof, are citizens of the United States, and of the State wherein they reside. No State shall make or enforce any law which shall abridge the privileges or immunities of citizens of the United States; nor shall any State deprive any person of life, liberty, or property without due process of law, nor deny to any person within its jurisdiction the equal protection of the laws.

SEC. 2. Representatives shall be apportioned among the several States according to their respective numbers, counting the whole number of persons in each State, excluding Indians not taxed. But when the right to vote at any election for the choice of electors for President and Vice-President of the United States, representatives in Congress, the executive and judicial officers of a State, or the members of the Legislature thereof, is denied to any of the male inhabitants of such State, being twenty-one years of age and citizens of the United States, or in any way abridged, except for participation in rebellion or other crime, the basis of representation therein shall be reduced in the proportion which the number of such male citizens shall bear to the whole number of male citizens twenty-one years of age in such State.

SEC. 3. No person shall be a senator or representative in Congress, or elector of President and Vice-President, or hold any office, civil or military, under the United States or under any State, who, having previously taken an oath as a member of Congress, or as an officer of the United States, or as a member of any State Legislature, or as an executive or judicial officer of any State, to support the Constitution of the United States, shall have engaged in insurrection or rebellion against the same, or giving aid or comfort to the enemies thereof. But Congress may, by a vote of two-thirds of each house, remove such disability.

SEC. 4. The validity of the public debt of the United States authorized by law, including debts incurred for payment of pensions and bounties for services in suppressing insurrection or rebellion shall not be questioned. But neither the United States nor any State shall assume to pay any debt or obligation incurred in aid of insurrection or rebellion against the United States, or any claim for the loss or emancipation of any slave; but all such debts, obligations, and claims shall be held illegal and void.

SEC. 5. The Congress shall have power to enforce, by appropriate legislation, the provisions of this article.

➡ Passed June 13, 1866.

Supplemental Reconstruction Act of Fortieth Congress.

AN ACT supplementary to an act entitled "An act to provide for the more efficient government of the rebel States," passed March 2d, eighteen hundred and sixty-seven, and to facilitate restoration.

Be it enacted, &c., That before the first day of September, eighteen hundred and sixty-seven, the commanding general in each district defined by an act entitled "An act to provide for the more efficient government of the rebel States," passed March second, eighteen hundred and sixty-seven, shall cause a registration to be made of the male citizens of the United States, twenty-one years of age and upwards, resident in each county or parish in the State or States included in his district, which registration shall include only those persons who are qualified to vote for delegates by the act aforesaid, and who shall have taken and subscribed the following oath or affirmation: "I, ———, do solemnly swear (or affirm), in the presence of Almighty God, that I am a citizen of the State of ———; that I have

resided in said State for ——— months next preceding this day, and now reside in the county of ———, or the parish of ———, in said State (as the case may be); that I am twenty-one years old; that I have not been disfranchised for participation in any rebellion or civil war against the United States, nor for felony committed against the laws of any State or of the United States; that I have never been a member of any State legislature, nor held any executive or judicial office in any State, and afterwards engaged in insurrection or rebellion against the United States or given aid or comfort to the enemies thereof; that I have never taken an oath as a member of Congress of the United States, or as an officer of the United States, or as a member of any State legislature, or as an executive or judicial officer of any State, to support the Constitution of the United States, and afterwards engaged in insurrection or rebellion against the United States or given aid or comfort to the enemies thereof; that I will faithfully support the Constitution and obey the laws of the United States, and will, to the best of my ability, encourage others so to do, so help me God;" which oath or affirmation may be administered by any registering officer.

SEC. 2. That after the completion of the registration hereby provided for in any State, at such time and places therein as the commanding general shall appoint and direct, of which at least thirty days' public notice shall be given, an election shall be held of delegates to a convention for the purpose of establishing a constitution and civil government for such State loyal to the Union, said convention in each State, except Virginia, to consist of the same number of members as the most numerous branch of the State legislature of such State in the year eighteen hundred and sixty, to be apportioned among the several districts, counties, or parishes of such State by the commanding general, giving each representation in the ratio of voters registered as aforesaid as nearly as may be. The convention in Virginia shall consist of the same number of members as represented the territory now constituting Virginia in the most numerous branch of the legislature of said State in the year eighteen hundred and sixty, to be apportioned as aforesaid.

SEC. 3. That at said election the registered voters of each State shall vote for or against a convention to form a constitution therefor under this act. Those voting in favor of such a convention shall have written or printed on the ballots by which they vote for delegates, as aforesaid, the words "For a convention," and those voting against such a convention shall have written or printed on such ballots the words "Against a convention." The persons appointed to superintend said election, and to make return of the votes given thereat, as herein provided, shall count and make return of the votes given for and against a convention; and the commanding general to whom the same shall have been returned shall ascertain and declare the total vote in each State for and against a convention. If a majority of the votes given on that question shall be for a convention, then such convention shall be held as hereinafter provided; but if a majority of said votes shall be against a convention, then no such convention shall be held under this act: *Provided*, That such convention shall not be held unless a majority of all such registered voters shall have voted on the question of holding such convention.

SEC. 4. That the commanding general of each district shall appoint as many boards of registration as may be necessary, consisting of three loyal officers or persons, to make and complete the registration, superintend the election, and make return to him of the votes, lists of voters, and of the persons elected as delegates by a plurality of the votes cast at said election; and upon receiving said returns he shall open the same, ascertain the persons elected as dele-

gates according to the returns of the officers who conducted said election, and make proclamation thereof; and if a majority of the votes given on that question shall be for a convention, the commanding general, within sixty days from the date of election, shall notify the delegates to assemble in convention, at a time and place to be mentioned in the notification, and said convention, when organized, shall proceed to frame a constitution and civil government according to the provisions of this act and the act to which it is supplementary; and when the same shall have been so framed, said constitution shall be submitted by the convention for ratification to the persons registered under the provisions of this act at an election to be conducted by the officers or persons appointed or to be appointed by the commanding general, as hereinbefore provided, and to be held after the expiration of thirty days from the date of notice thereof, to be given by said convention; and the returns thereof shall be made to the commanding general of the district.

SEC. 5. That if, according to said returns, the constitution shall be ratified by a majority of the votes of the registered electors qualified as herein specified, cast at said election (at least one-half of all the registered voters voting upon the question of such ratification), the president of the convention shall transmit a copy of the same, duly certified, to the President of the United States, who shall forthwith transmit the same to Congress, if then in session, and if not in session, then immediately upon its next assembling; and if it shall, moreover, appear to Congress that the election was one at which all the registered and qualified electors in the State had an opportunity to vote freely and without restraint, fear, or the influence of fraud, and if the Congress shall be satisfied that such constitution meets the approval of a majority of all the qualified electors in the State, and if the said constitution shall be declared by Congress to be in conformity with the provisions of the act to which this is supplementary, and the other provisions of said act shall have been complied with, and the said constitution shall be approved by Congress, the State shall be declared entitled to representation, and senators and representatives shall be admitted therefrom as therein provided.

SEC. 6. That all elections in the States mentioned in the said "Act to provide for the more efficient government of the rebel States," shall, during the operation of said act, be by ballot; and all officers making the said registration of voters and conducting said elections shall, before entering upon the discharge of their duties, take and subscribe the oath prescribed by the act approved July second, eighteen hundred and sixty-two, entitled "An act to prescribe an oath of office:" *Provided*, That if any person shall knowingly and falsely take and subscribe any oath in this act prescribed, such person so offending and being thereof duly convicted, shall be subject to the pains, penalties, and disabilities which by law are provided for the punishment of the crime of wilful and corrupt perjury.

SEC. 7. That all expenses incurred by the several commanding generals, or by virtue of any orders issued, or appointments made, by them, under or by virtue of this act, shall be paid out of any moneys in the treasury not otherwise appropriated.

SEC. 8. That the convention for each State shall prescribe the fees, salary, and compensation to be paid to all delegates and other officers and agents herein authorized or necessary to carry into effect the purposes of this act not herein otherwise provided for, and shall provide for the levy and collection of such taxes on the property in such State as may be necessary to pay the same.

SEC. 9. That the word article, in the sixth section of the act to which this is supplementary, shall be construed to mean section.

Passed March 23, 1867.

Additional Explanatory Act.

AN ACT supplementary to an act entitled "An act to provide for the more efficient government of the rebel States," passed on the second day of March, eighteen hundred and sixty-seven, and the act supplementary thereto, passed on the twenty-third day of March, eighteen hundred and sixty-seven.

Be it enacted, &c., That it is hereby declared to have been the true intent and meaning of the act of second day of March, one thousand eight hundred and sixty-seven, entitled, "An act to provide for the more efficient government of the rebel States," and of the act supplementary thereto, passed on the twenty-third day of March, in the year one thousand eight hundred and sixty-seven, that the governments then existing in the rebel States of Virginia, North Carolina, South Carolina, Georgia, Mississippi, Alabama, Louisiana, Florida, Texas, and Arkansas, were not legal State governments; and that thereafter said governments, if continued, were to be continued subject in all respects to the military commanders of the respective districts, and to the paramount authority of Congress.

SEC. 2. That the commander of any district named in said act shall have power, subject to the disapproval of the General of the Army of the United States, and to have effect till disapproved, whenever in the opinion of such commander the proper administration of said act shall require it, to suspend or remove from office, or from the performance of official duties and the exercise of official powers, any officer or person holding or exercising or professing to hold or exercise, any civil or military office or duty in such district under any power, election, appointment, or authority derived from, or granted by, or claimed under, any so-called State or the government thereof, or any municipal or other division thereof; and upon such suspension or removal such commander, subject to the disapproval of the General as aforesaid, shall have power to provide from time to time for the performance of the said duties of such officer or person so suspended or removed, by the detail of some competent officer or soldier of the army, or by the appointment of some other person, to perform the same, and to fill vacancies occasioned by death, resignation, or otherwise.

SEC. 3. That the General of the Army of the United States shall be invested with all the powers of suspension, removal, appointment, and detail granted in the preceding section to district commanders.

SEC. 4. That the acts of the officers of the army already done in removing in said districts persons exercising the functions of civil officers, and appointing others in their stead, are hereby confirmed: Provided, That any person heretofore or hereafter appointed by any district commander to exercise the functions of any civil office may be removed either by the military officer in command of the district, or by the General of the Army. And it shall be the duty of such commander to remove from office, as aforesaid, all persons who are disloyal to the government of the United States, or who use their official influence in any manner to hinder, delay, prevent, or obstruct the due and proper administration of this act and the acts to which it is supplementary.

SEC. 5. That the boards of registration provided for in the act entitled "An act supplementary to an act entitled 'An act to provide for the more efficient government of the rebel States,' passed March two, eighteen hundred and sixty-seven, and to facilitate restoration," passed March twenty-three, eighteen hundred and sixty-seven, shall have power, and it shall be their duty before allowing the registration of any person, to ascertain, upon such facts or information as they can obtain, whether such person is entitled to be registered under said act, and the oath required by said act shall not be conclusive on such question, and no person shall be registered unless such board shall decide that he is entitled thereto; and such board shall also have power to examine, under oath, (to be administered by any member of such board) any one touching the qualification of any person claiming registration; but in every case of refusal by the board to register an applicant, and in every case of striking his name from the list as hereinafter provided, the board shall make a note or memorandum, which shall be returned with the registration list to the commanding general of the district, setting forth the grounds of such refusal or such striking from the list: Provided, That no person shall be disqualified as member of any board of registration by reason of race or color.

SEC. 6. That the true intent and meaning

of the oath prescribed in said supplementary act is, (among other things,) that no person who has been a member of the legislature of any State, or who has held any executive or judicial office in any State, whether he has taken an oath to support the Constitution of the United States or not, and whether he was holding such office at the commencement of the rebellion, or had held it before, and who has afterwards engaged in insurrection or rebellion against the United States, or given aid or comfort to the enemies thereof, is entitled to be registered or to vote; and the words "executive or judicial office in any State" in said oath mentioned shall be construed to include all civil offices created by law for the administration of any general law of a State, or for the administration of justice.

SEC. 7. That the time for completing the original registration provided for in said act may, in the discretion of the commander of any district, be extended to the first day of October, eighteen hundred and sixty-seven; and the boards of registration shall have power, and it shall be their duty, commencing fourteen days prior to any election under said act, and upon reasonable public notice of the time and place thereof, to revise, for a period of five days, the registration lists, and upon being satisfied that any person not entitled thereto has been registered, to strike the name of such person from the list, and such person shall not be allowed to vote. And such board shall also, during the same period, add to such registry the names of all persons who at that time possess the qualifications required by said act who have not been already registered; and no person shall, at any time, be entitled to be registered or to vote by reason of any executive pardon or amnesty for any act or thing which, without such pardon or amnesty, would disqualify him from registration or voting.

SEC. 8. That section four of said last-named act shall be construed to authorize the commanding general named therein, whenever he shall deem it needful, to remove any member of a board of registration and to appoint another in his stead, and to fill any vacancy in such board.

SEC. 9. That all members of said boards of registration, and all persons hereafter elected or appointed to office in said military districts, under any so-called State or municipal authority, or by detail or appointment of the district commanders, shall be required to take and to subscribe the oath of office prescribed by law for officers of the United States.

SEC. 10. That no district commander or member of the board of registration, or any of the officers or appointees acting under them, shall be bound in his action by any opinion of any civil officer of the United States.

SEC. 11. That all the provisions of this act and of the acts to which this is supplementary shall be construed liberally, to the end that all the intents thereof may be fully and perfectly carried out.

Passed July 19, 1867.

Steps Towards Restoration—Presiden Lincoln's Plan.

Before referring to the action of the Thirty-ninth and Fortieth Congresses, we propose to give a brief resume of what Presidents Lincoln and Johnson attempted, and what the Southern States themselves did to restore their relations to the Union.

President Lincoln, and with him a majority of his party, almost up to the time of the surrender of the Confederate armies, believed that the war was for the sole purpose of "restoring the Union." This belief was based upon the declaration of Congress, which, as early as July 23, 1861, passed a resolution, that the war was only "to defend and maintain the supremacy of the Union, with all the dignity, equality, and rights of the several States unimpared." Mr. Lincoln's own often-expressed fear was, that, after a conquered peace, the Southern States might refuse the proffer of restoration. President Johnson, in his speech of February 22, 1866, says, that when he came to Washington to be inaugurated as Vice President, in his first interview with Mr. Lincoln, in a conversation relative to the Southern States, Mr. Lincoln said: "My great and sole desire has been to preserve these States intact under the Constitution, as they were before; and there should be an amendment to the Constitution which would *compel* the States to send their Sen-

ators and Representatives to the Congress of the United States." Mr. Lincoln's early acts, indorsed by Congress and approved by the Republican party, looked to this sort of restoration. His first efforts were in Louisiana. New Orleans was captured in April, 1862, and shortly after, as General Butler testified before the Committee on the Conduct of the War, it was intimated to him from Washington that the election of two members of Congress from Louisiana would be desirable; and he further testified that he sent General Weitzel to make an expedition into the Lafourche district for the express purpose of including territory enough within the Federal lines to warrant the election of a second Congressman. Eight months (Nov. 14, 1862,) after the occupation of New Orleans, by command of General Butler, Military Governor, Brigadier General G. F. Shepley issued an order in which he said: "Whereas the State of Louisiana is now, and has been, without any Representatives in the Thirty-seventh Congress of the United States of America; and whereas, a very large majority of the citizens of the First and Second Congressional Districts in this State, by taking the oath of allegiance, have given evidence of their loyalty and obedience to the Constitution and laws of the United States," *et cetera*, the election of two members of Congress was ordered. Accordingly, in December, Messrs. Hahn and Flanders were elected from those districts, and went to Washington, but were refused seats. Still further, under the direction of the President, a reorganization of the State government was ordered; the State constitution was revised by a convention, submitted to the people, and ratified; a legislature was chosen; in March, 1864, Michael Hahn was elected Governor by the people; subsequently, the legislature chose United States Senators, one of whom was Hahn, then Governor; and in the following popular election J. Madison Wells was chosen Governor of the State. Although the United States Senators and Representatives elect were refused admission, the State Government, as re-organized under the Lincoln-Banks plan, was never interfered with by Congress till the final Reconstruction acts were passed.

Incidentally, it is a matter of history that the unhappy Olustee expedition, in 1863, was undertaken mainly for the purpose of "opening up" a Congressional District in Florida; indeed, President Lincoln may be said to have been represented on the ground in the person of his Private Secretary, Mr. John Hay, who accompanied this unfortunate expedition.

President Lincoln's efforts at restoration in Tennessee date from his appointment of Andrew Johnson as Military Governor of that State. Governor Johnson began the work of reorganization by calling a convention, which forever abolished slavery in the State, declared the ordinance of secession null and void, and repudiated the rebel debt. Under the reorganization effected by Andrew Johnson, William G. Brownlow, March 4, 1865, was elected Governor by a popular vote. Congress never interfered with this reorganization or reconstruction of the State; and Tennessee, Louisiana and Florida were the only States in which Mr. Lincoln was able to accomplish anything in the way of "restoration."

The Policy of President Johnson.

By the death of Mr. Lincoln, Andrew Johnson succeeded to the Presidency, April 15, 1865. No extra session of Congress was called, and until the opening of the Thirty-ninth Congress, in December, Mr. Johnson faithfully carried out the policy of his predecessor, by holding out inducements to the Southern States to reorganize their governments, and to restore as rapidly as possible their rightful relations to the Union. He issued an order, April 29, 1865, removing unnecessary commercial restrictions in certain parts of the States of Tennessee, Virginia, North Carolina, South Carolina, Georgia, Florida, Alabama, Mississippi, and in Louisiana, east of the Mississippi River; an order May 9, 1865, re-establishing the authority of the United States and the execution of the laws in Virginia, and recognizing Governor Pierpoint's administration; declaring Southern ports, except those in Texas, open, May 22, 1865; a Proclamation of Amnesty, May 29, 1865, based on President Lincoln's proclamations of December 8, 1863, and March 26, 1864. On the same day, in conformity with the action of his predecessor, he appointed William W. Holden Provisional Governor of North Carolina; and, subsequently, in June and July, he appointed other Provisional Governors, as follows: William L. Sharkey, for Mississippi; James Johnson, for Georgia; Andrew J. Hamilton, for Texas; Lewis F. Parsons, for Alabama; Benjamin F. Perry, for South Carolina; and William Marvin, for Florida. Previous to the assembling of Congress, in December, other orders and proclamations of the President, relating to the Southern States, were the following: A Proclamation June 13, 1865, respecting commercial intercourse, and the suppression of the rebellion in Tennessee; June 23, rescinding the blockade; August 29, further removal of commercial restrictions; October 12, withdrawal of martial law from Kentucky; and December 1, annulling the suspension of the *habeas corpus*.

Action of the Southern States.

President Johnson lost no opportunity to convey to the South the "conditions" upon which the early restoration of the States might reasonably be expected. The States themselves must abolish slavery forever within their own borders; they must declare the secession ordinances null and void; they must repudiate the rebel debt; and their senators and representatives elect must be able to take the test oath. The Provisional Governors were authorized, and, in some instances, ordered, to proceed with the reorganization of the State governments, by calling conventions to revise the State constitutions; and the inducement was held out that a reorganization on the foregoing plan would result in a speedy resumption of their electoral privileges by the people, for the choice of State and local officers, and for the election of representatives to Congress from all the States. The main qualification for an elector for delegates to the convention was the exhibition of his duly-certified signature to the Amnesty Oath contained in the President's proclamation of May 29, 1865.

Delegates to the conventions were accordingly elected in the several States. In North Carolina the convention met in October, 1865, declared the secession ordinance null and void, and passed ordinances prohibiting slavery forever in the State, repudiating the rebel debt, and dividing the State into seven Congressional Districts. November 9, these ordinances were submitted to the people and approved; and on the same day State officers and members of Congress were elected. December 1, the legislature ratified the anti-slavery amendment; and December 15, Jonathan Worth, elected in November, was qualified as Governor of the State. In Mississippi the convention met August 14, and passed the required ordinances respecting slavery in the State and the secession ordinance. On the first Monday in October, State officers and members of Congress were elected. The legislature met October 16, and the next day Benjamin G. Humphreys was inaugurated Governor. November 27, the legislatnre declined to ratify the anti-slavery amendment. The Georgia convention submitted the anti-slavery, anti-secession and rebel debt repudiation ordinances to the people; November 15, State officers and members of Congress were elected; and December 5, the legislature ratified the anti-slavery amendment. The Alabama convention passed the required ordinances. In November State officers, (R. M. Patton, Governor,) and members of Congress were elected; December 2, the legislature ratified the anti-slavery amendment, and December 5, Provisional Governor Parsons received a telegram from Secretary Seward, conveying the congratulations of the President, that, by its vote ratifying the anti-slavery amendment, the State of Alabama "being the twenty-seventh, fills up the complement of two-thirds, and *gives the amendment finishing effect as a part of the organic law of the land.*" South Carolina, by order of Provisional Governor Perry, called a convention, which

ordered a State election October 18, when James L. Orr, was elected Governor. November 13, the legislature ratified the anti-slavery amendment, and November 22, members of Congress were elected. Florida annulled the secession ordinance, abolished slavery, and repudiated the rebel debt. November 29, State officers and a representative to Congress were elected: and December 28, the legislature ratified the anti-slavery amendment. In Virginia the administration of Governor Francis H. Pierpoint, having been recognizedby the President's order of May 9, 1865, the State government continued without interruption; and October 12, 1865, representatives in Congress were elected. From the date of Brownlow's election, March 4, 1865, as Governor of Tennessee, the government in that State has been unmolested by Congress. Texas annulled the secession ordinance, abolished slavery, and repudiated the rebel debt. The provisional government of Hamilton was followed by an elected State government, headed by Governor Throckmorton. In October, 1865, when Isaac Murphy was elected Governor of Arkansas, President Johnson telegraphed to him that there would be no interference with the "present organization of State government," and added, "I have learned * * * that all is working well, and you will proceed and resume the former relations with the Federal Government, and all the aid in the power of the government will be given in restoring the State to its former relations."

The Policy of Congress—Reconstruction vs. Restoration.

The foregoing sums up the principal points in the action and efforts of President Lincoln, President Johnson, and the Southern States, to reorganize and restore those States to their normal condition in respect of the other States. During the Summer and Autumn of 1865, Mr. Johnson made brief addresses to different delegations, and held interviews with men of note from all parts of the country, in which he clearly enunciated the plan then in progress, its complete success so far, and his implicit belief that it would result in an easy, speedy, and complete restoration of the Union. These views, widely disseminated, led to a general confidence throughout the country that the settlement of the questions at issue was near at hand; and the effect upon the business and industrial interests of the country was everywhere manifest. As the President telegraphed to Governor Murphy, of Arkansas, "all was working well."

The Thirty-ninth Congress met, and, December 4, the President sent in his first annual message, in which he recited the steps already taken in the Southern States, their then condition and situation, and made the first official announcement of his policy, by declaring what he believed to be the duty of Congress towards those States. But the Republican majority had yet to announce its plan of "reconstruction;" and

meanwhile, the representatives elect from the Southern States—rejected at roll call when the House organized—were waiting, with their credentials, for admission at the doors. Caucus and Congress declared that, as each House had the constitutional right to decide with regard to the qualifications of its own members, the Southern members elect, for the present at least, should be excluded. The first step was the appointment, December 13, 1865, of what soon became the "Joint Committee on Reconstruction," but which, under the concurrent resolution authorizing the appointment, was simply and only a committee to "inquire into the condition" of the Southern States, "and to report whether they, or any of them, are entitled to be represented in either House of Congress." December 18, the President, in response to a resolution of the Senate, sent in a message "on the late insurrectionary States," in which he stated that, "as the result of the measures instituted by the Executive, with the view of inducing a resumption of the functions of the States comprehended in the inquiry of the Senate, the people in North Carolina, South Carolina, Georgia, Alabama, Mississippi, Louisiana, Arkansas, and Tennessee, have reorganized their respective State governments, and are yielding obedience to the laws and government of the United States with more willingness and greater prompti- tude than, under the circumstances could reasonably have been anticipated;" and he further reported what these States had done. This message was accompanied by the report of General Grant, in which he said, that, after a tour of inspection through the South, he was "satisfied that the mass of thinking men of the South accept the present situation of affairs in good faith," and that his observations led him "to the conclusion that the citizens of the Southern States are anxious to return to self-govern- ment within the Union as soon as possible." Senator Sumner characterized this report as a "whitewashing" one.

Congress was now almost wholly devoted to what was called "Reconstruction," and Congress confided the sole management and conduct of the matter to the Joint Commit- tee, to whom all papers, resolutions, or any- thing relating to the readmission or restor- ation of the Southern States, or referring in any sense to Southern affairs, were, by a vote of both Houses, to be referred without debate. The action, or rather, inaction, of this Committee, is too widely known to need extended comment. But there was a show of work—now and then a report of "progress," or something equally vague and intangible; and whenever the country, and even Congress, became impatient and clamored for a "report," the invariable sop to Cerberus was another impracticable "Constitutional amendment," sure to be slaughtered in the Senate if it ever passed the House. More than six months elapsed before the Committee favored Congress and the country with its first formal report; but this interval (with months more) is pre- sumed to have been employed in taking "testimony" with regard to the "loyalty" of the Southern States—which testimony was subsequently embodied in an octavo volume of 800 pages. The impatience of the country was manifest almost as soon as the Committee began to hold its secret sessions. February 20, 1866, Mr. Stevens reported from the Committee to the House of Representatives a resolution "that, in order to *close agitation* upon a question which seems *likely to disturb the action of the Government*, as well as to quiet the un- certainty which is *agitating the minds* of the people of the eleven States, * * no Sena- tor or Representative shall be admitted into either branch of Congress from any of said States until Congress shall have declared such State entitled to such representation." The House passed the resolution; the next day, on motion of Mr. Stevens, the House

tabled a motion (by Mr. Stevens) to recon- sider the vote on the resolution; and, March 2, the Senate passed it! The passage, veto, and repassage of the Civil Rights bill follow- ed. As the weeks wore on, the question of Reconstruction—in the form of various reso- lutions proposed and tabled, or passed to-day and reconsidered to-morrow, or amendments amended in the Senate and re-amended in the House—was ever flying, like a shuttle- cock, between the two ends of the Capitol. At last, June 18, 1866, Mr. Fessenden, in the Senate, and Mr. Stevens, in the House, submitted the long-looked-for report of the Joint Committee on Reconstruction. This very voluminous paper recited at length the points of opposition, in the Congressional plan, to the policy of the President; but it proposed no definite means, immediate or prospective, for the readmission to repre- sentation of the Southern States; and con- sidering that the committee was one of "inquiry," it afforded an infinitesimally small amount of information. It admitted that "the people of *most* of the States lately in rebellion had, under the advice of the President, *organized local governments*, and some of them had *acceded to the terms* proposed by him;" but it declared that the Southern States have "forfeited all civil and political rights and privileges under the Constitution," and that "they can only be restored thereto by the permission and authority of that constitutional power against which they rebelled and by which they were subdued;" and the conclusion of the Committee, therefore, was "that the so- called Confederate States are not at present entitled to representation in the Congress of the United States." Mr. Reverdy Johnson, in the Senate, and Mr. Rogers, in the House, in a minority report, June 22, presented an elaborate and able argument in favor of the speedy readmission of the Southern States, and said that the minority had "not thought it necessary to examine into the legality of the measures adopted, either by the late or present President, for the resto- ration of the Southern States." It was "sufficient for their purpose to say that, if those of President Johnson were not justi- fied by the Constitution, the same may at least be said of those of his predecessor. * * The motives of neither President, however, whether the measures were legal or not, are liable to censure. The sole object of each was to effect *a complete and early union of all the States ;* to make the general govern- ment, as it did at first, embrace all, and to extend its authority and secure its privi- leges and blessings to all alike."

The Proposed Fourteenth Constitutional Amendment.

The attention of the Joint Committee on Reconstruction was early directed to the supposed necessity of an amendment to the Constitution with regard to representation in Congress. Mr. Stevens, Jan. 22, 1866, re- ported from the Reconstruction Committee an article, proposing to exclude from the basis of representation all who were denied

the elective franchise "on account of race or color." Sundry substitutes or amend- ments to the proposed amendment were offered, and, January 30, it was recommitted to the Committee without instructions. The next day, Mr. Stevens offered sub- stantially the same amendment, omit- ting only the apportionment of "direct taxes," as well as "representatives" upon the proposed basis. Mr. Schenck, of Ohio, offered a substitute, which was disagreed to. February 13, Mr. Bingham reported from the Reconstruction Committee, in the House, another Constitutional amendment, proposing to give Congress the power to make certain laws for the government of all the States; and Mr. Fessenden, the same day, reported this wholesale reconstruction measure in the Senate. The House at once recommitted it; fifteen days afterwards, Mr. Bingham reported the same amendment again; the House then, instead of returning it to the Committee, "postponed its consideration" to April 10, and never called it up; in the Senate it was instantly "laid over," and not again considered! March 9, the Senate rejected the Constitutional amendment reported by Mr. Stevens, January 31, in the House. April 30, Mr. Stevens, from the same Committee, reported a paradoxical bill "to provide for restoring the States lately in insurrection to their *full political rights*," by fettering those States with the political restrictions embodied in the proposed 14th Constitutional amendment, the first draft of which was presented in this bill. At the same time, Mr. Stevens reported from the Reconstruction Committee another joint resolution proposing a Constitutional amendment, mainly the same as the now proposed 14th in respect of the clause relating to the apportionment of representatives, but containing a section excluding "until the 4th day of July, 1870, all persons who voluntarily adhered to the late insurrection, giving it aid and comfort, from the right to vote for representatives in Congress, and for electors for President and Vice President of the United States." May 10, this resolution, with Mr. Stevens' proposed Constitutional amendment containing the "until 1870" disfranchising section, passed the House—yeas 128, nays, 37,—and was sent to the Senate, where it was amended according to the present text, and was passed by a vote of 33 to 11—5 Senators absent. The House accepted and passed the amendment June 13, as it came from the Senate, by a vote 138 to 36. The professed importance of the proposed amendment makes the following seem at least singular: Five days after the passage of the amendment, a concurrent resolution of the two Houses was referred to Secretary Seward, "That the President of the United States be requested to transmit forthwith to the executives of the several States, copies of the article of amendment proposed by Congress to the State legislatures to amend the Constitution of the United States, passed June 13, 1866," *et cetera ;* two days later, June 20, the Secretary of State communicated this request to the President, with the information that the amendment was brought to the State Department June

16, and *on that day* transmitted to the Governors of the several States. Thus, Congress, on the 18th, was oblivious of the fact that "somebody" had attended to the transmission of the amendment on the 16th, and until the 20th, the President was presumed to be (officially) ignorant that the proposed amendment was in existence. That he *was* aware of the fact, however, he took pains to inform Congress in a special message, in which he said: "Even in ordinary times any questions of amending the Constitution must be justly regarded as of paramount importance. This importance is at the present time enhanced by the fact that the joint resolution was not submitted by the two Houses for the approval of the President, and that of the thirty-six States which constitute the Union eleven are excluded from representation in either House of Congress, although, with the single exception of Texas, they have been entirely restored to all their functions as States, in conformity with the organic law of the land, and have appeared at the national capitol by Senators and Representatives, who have applied for and have been refused admission to the vacant seats." He further observed "that the steps taken by the Secretary of State are to be considered as purely ministerial, and in no sense whatever committing the executive to an approval or a recommendation of the amendment to the State legislatures or to the people."

So the proposed amendment went to the States. Tennessee, July 12, 1866, was the first to ratify it; and, July 23, Congress passed a joint resolution, approved by the President July 24, "restoring Tennessee to her relations to the Union." The two Senators and five Representatives elect from that State at once qualified and took their seats—the three remaining Representatives qualifying in December following. During October, November, and December, 1866, and in January and February, 1867, Alabama, Arkansas, Florida, Georgia, Louisiana, Mississippi, North Carolina, South Carolina, Texas and Virginia rejected it; Iowa, California and Nebraska have not acted upon it; and in 1866 and 1867, twenty remaining States ratified it. After the admission of Tennessee, for a long while the proposed amendment seemed to excite little attention. Indeed, in February, 1867, an effort was made to prepare a substitute, and such an amendment, said to be satisfactory to the President, and including a section which would remove from the basis of representation all persons denied the elective franchise "on account of race or color," was submitted, as a test, to the legislature of North Carolina, but was rejected. The proposed 14th amendment, however, derives a new interest and importance from its incorporation in, and connection with, the Reconstruction acts.

Further Efforts of the President.

President Johnson, April 2, 1866, issued a Proclamation that the rebellion had ended. In answer to the inquiry of James H. Bell, Secretary of State of Texas, he sent a tele-

gram, July 28, 1866, directing that the legislature could assemble August 6, "without hinderance"; that the Governor elect (Throckmorton) could be inaugurated "without hinderance"; and, that thereafter "the Provisional Governor would be relieved, and the government transferred to the elected authorities of Texas." August 20, 1866, he issued a Proclamation declaring the insurrection at an end, and civil authority existing throughout the United States. September 7, 1867, he issued an Amnesty Proclamation, modifying the Proclamation of May 29, 1865, wherein "fourteen extensive classes of persons were altogether excepted and excluded from the benefits thereof," so that "the full and beneficent pardon conceded" in that Proclamation "should be opened and further extended to a large number of the persons who, by its aforesaid exceptions, have been hitherto excluded from Executive clemency."

Reconstruction by Congress.

The Second Session of the Thirty-ninth Congress began December 3, 1866, and, the same day, the President sent in his second annual message which was mainly devoted to restoration; to an exposition and defence of his own position; and to a recital of what had been done already towards "the gradual restoration of the States, in which the insurrection occurred, to their relations with the Federal Government." Since "the coercion of arms" had been superseded by civil authority, he said, in all of those States, "the people, by their voluntary action, are maintaining their governments in full activity and complete operation." What remained to be done was "the admission to Congress of loyal Senators and Representatives," and this, he thought, was "imperatively demanded by every consideration of national interest, sound policy, and equal justice."

The vague and unsatisfactory majority report (June 18, 1866), of the Joint Committee on Reconstruction, had only suggested something, and had decided upon nothing; so when Congress reassembled in December, the dominant party was still "at sea" in search of a definite plan for reconstruction. A step in obstruction, however, was at once taken in the House, by passing a bill, December 3, repealing the 13th section of the act of July 17, 1862, authorizing the President by proclamation "to extend to persons who may have participated in the existing rebellion * * pardon and amnesty." [The Senate passed this bill, January 7, 1867, and it became a law by the failure of the President to return it within ten days after its presentation to him.] On the second day of the Session, the House instructed the Committee on Territories to inquire into the expediency of providing Territorial Governments for "the several districts of country" formerly occupied by "the once existing States"—the resolution naming all the Southern States excepting Tennessee. December 6, Senator Sumner introduced six resolutions "declaring the true principles of reconstruction," to wit, "the jurisdiction of Congress over the whole subject," and "illegality of the existing governments in the rebel States," and their exclusion "from representation in Congress and from voting on Constitutional amendments." December 13, Mr. Stevens, in the House, introduced a bill for the civil government of North Carolina. In the Senate, Mr. Trumbull presented memorials for the abrogation of the State governments of Virginia and Louisiana, and the substitution of territorial governments, declaring that "Congress has complete jurisdiction over the whole subject." The District of Columbia was reconstructed by a bill, December 13-14, giving the negroes resident therein the right of suffrage; and Congress adjourned for the holidays, reassembling January 3, 1867. The President, January 7, vetoed the District negro-suffrage bill, and it was at once repassed over the veto.

Several days in January were devoted to debate upon a bill presented by Mr. Stevens, in the House, as a substitute for the Reconstruction Committee Bill; and for the Stevens substitute, Mr. James M. Ashley, of Ohio, offered another substitute, in the form of an amendment, declaring the existing governments in the Southern States invalid, and all their action null and void, except so far as they shall be ratified by State governments hereafter legally organized; all male citizens, without regard to race or former condition of servitude are to take part in the formation of the new State governments; meanwhile, a "Provisional Committee of Safety" of five "loyal" citizens would take charge of the State and of the election of delegates to a Convention to appoint a Provisional Governor and other officers, and to frame a State Constitution; if this Constitution—which *must* embody certain "points" stated in the Ashley amendment—was satisfactory to Congress, and if certain other conditions are complied with, the reconstructed State might be declared entitled to all the rights, privileges, *et cetera*, of "a State in the American Union." This elaborate scheme, together with the Stevens plan, protracted the debate to January 26, when Mr. Ashley withdrew his substitute; and on the 28th the whole matter was referred back to the Reconstruction Committee. February 9, Mr. Banks, of Massachusetts, offered a proposition to send "a commission of three persons," to be appointed, one by the Senate, one by the House, and one by the War Department, "to re-establish civil government" in Louisiana.

Meanwhile, February 6, Mr. Stevens, from the Committee on Reconstruction, reported a bill "to provide for the more efficient government of the insurrectionary States." This bill, as originally introduced, did not differ greatly from the text of the bill finally passed by Congress. It declared that the governments in the Southern States were set up without the authority of Congress, and *without the sanction of the people;*" and that these "so-pretended governments *countenance and encourage lawlessness and crime!*" These sentences were omitted, and other expressions were modified, in the final bill. On the 13th, the House considered Mr. Stevens' bill, and Mr. Blaine, of Maine, moved its reference to the Judiciary Committee, with instructions to report it back, with an amendment that any State ratifying the proposed 14th Constitutional amendment, conforming its constitution and laws thereto, the people of the State ratifying, and Congress approving the same, such State should be entitled to representation in Congress, and the bill should become inoperative in that State. Mr. Blaine's amendment was lost, 69 ayes to 95 nays, and the bill, as reported by Mr. Stevens, was passed by a vote of 109 to 55. It came up in the Senate, February 15, and Reverdy Johnson offered the Blaine (House) amendment. Senator Wilson offered a bill declaring that "the Constitutional amendment, having been ratified by the requisite number of States, had now become a part of the Constitution of the United States;" but the bill, in substance, called for a further ratification by "the States lately in insurrection;" and proposed when any State should so ratify, secure impartial suffrage, and comply with other conditions, such State shall "be declared entitled to representation in Congress." The Johnson-Blaine amendment and Wilson's bill were disagreed to; and, February 16, Senator Sherman presented a substitute for the Stevens bill as it came from the House, which was adopted by a vote of 29 to 10—13 Senators not voting. The House, February 19, refused to concur in this bill, and asked for a committee of conference; the Senate refused; the House then added an amendment, and passed the bill, 98 to 70; and the Senate, February 20, accepting the House amendment by a vote of 35 to 7, passed the bill in its present form.

The bill was returned to the House, March 2, by the President with his veto. The declaration that there was "no adequate protection for life and property" in the Southern States, was not supported by any evidence which had come to the President's knowledge; all his information convinced him that "the masses of the Southern people * * are completely united in the effort to reorganize their society on the basis of peace, and to restore their mutual prosperity as rapidly and as completely as their circumstances will permit;" the bill seems "to show on its face that the establishment of peace and good order is not its real object;" he then recites the *political* portions of the bill, and says, "the excuse given for the bill in the preamble is admitted by the bill itself not to be real;" he submits to Congress "whether this measure is not in its whole character, scope, and object, without precedent and without authority, and in palpable conflict with the plainest provisions of the Constitution;" "the power given to the commanding officer over all the people of each district is that of an absolute monarch; his mere will is to take the place of all law;" and "the purpose and object of the bill, the general intent which prevades it from beginning to end, is to change the entire structure and character of the State governments, and to compel them, by force, to the adoption of organic laws and regulations which they are unwilling to accept if left to themselves." These were among the main objections urged by the President to the bill—its despotism, its political purpose, and its unconstitutionality. Notwithstanding the objections, the House, by a vote of 135 to 48, and the Senate, by a vote of 38 to 10, immediately passed the bill over the veto, and it became a law March 2, 1867.

The bill having thus become a law, the President immediately proceeded to put it into execution by the appointment of the following Military Commanders of the five districts:

First District—Virginia: General J. M. Schofield; headquarters, Richmond, Va.

Second District—North Carolina and South Carolina: General D. E. Sickles; headquarters, Columbia, S. C.

Third District—Georgia, Florida, and Alabama: Headquarters, Montgomery, Ala., General G. H. Thomas—at whose request General John Pope was subsequently assigned to this command, General Thomas retaining command of the Department of the Cumberland.

Fourth District—Mississippi and Arkansas: General E. O. C. Ord; headquarters, Vicksburg, Miss.

Fifth District—Louisiana and Texas: General P. H. Sheridan; headquarters, New Orleans.

These Generals at once proceeded to their respective departments, and assumed their commands.

Supplemental Reconstruction.

The Thirty-ninth Congress expired, and the Fortieth Congress immediately entered upon its First Session, March 4, 1867. The Reconstruction Committee's bill, supplementary to the act of March 2, and making provisions for carrying out the details of that act, was passed March 18. In this bill (we give the complete text elsewhere) there is nothing about the insecurity of life and property in the Southern States, and the consequent necessity for military protection and intervention, but it simply provides for the political reconstruction foreshadowed in the original act. The President, March 23, returned this bill with his veto, in which he reiterated the objections to the original bill, as applicable to this, and presented new objections, prominent among others—that the people themselves are to have no voice in conducting the registration or election; that the Conventions would not represent the citizens of the States; and that, if, as the bill pre-supposes, negro suffrage is essential to a republican form of government, "the work of reconstruction may as well begin in Ohio as in Virginia, in Pennsylvania as in North Carolina." Notwithstanding the veto, the Senate repassed the bill by a vote of 40 to 7, and the House by a vote of 114 to 25, and it became a law, March 23, 1867. The President approved, March 30, a joint resolution providing for the expenses of "carrying into effect" the Reconstruction act, on the ground that the seventh section of the supplementary act provided that the expenses incurred under that act "should be paid out of any moneys in the Treasury not otherwise appropriated;" whereas the joint resolution limits the appropriation to $500,000; and as the President considered this limitation "as a very necessary check against unlimited expenditures and liabilities," he "felt bound to approve the resolution, without modifying in any manner his objections, heretofore stated, against the original and supplementary acts."

Congress adjourned March 31, and reassembled July 4. In April, the States of Georgia and Mississippi presented petitions to the Supreme Court of the United States to issue injunctions prohibiting the President and district commanders from taking any measures to carry out the provisions of the Reconstruction acts. Chief Justice Chase, April 15, delivered the opinion of the Court on the Mississippi application for an injunction to restrain the President and General Ord from executing certain acts in Mississippi and Arkansas, showing "the impropriety of such interference," which, said the Court, "will clearly be seen upon consideration of its probable consequences"—in substance as follows: If the President should refuse obedience, the Court is without power to enforce its process; and if the President complied, the House might impeach him for refusing to execute the act of Congress; a bill praying an injunction against the execution of an act of Congress by the incumbent of the Presidential office cannot be received, whether it describes him as President, or simply as a citizen of a State. Motion for leave to file the bill was therefore denied. In the case of the State of Georgia against certain officers, the Attorney-General made no objection to the policy of the bill, and leave was granted to file that bill. The State of Georgia is complainant against Edwin M. Stanton, Ulysses S. Grant, and John Pope; and, April 16, a subpœna was issued in the case, these men to appear before the Supreme Court, December 2, 1867, to answer to the bill of complaint of the State of Georgia. Notwithstanding the full details of the Supplemental act, the district commanders generally put their own construction upon the Reconstruction acts, and in registration and other matters were mainly a law unto themselves. Accordingly, at the request of the President, Attorney-General Stansbery furnished an opinion upon the interpretation of the Military Government bills, so far as they related to registration and the right of voting, and this opinion made the number of disfranchised persons less than had been generally supposed; and the President issued an order to the district commanders to

govern themselves by the opinion of the Attorney-General. Meanwhile, registration offices were opened in every section of the South, and, during the summer, sundry members of Congress, among others Senator Wilson, of Massachusetts, and Representative William D. Kelly, of Pennsylvania, traversed the country, addressing large gatherings of negroes, and urging them to vote the Republican ticket.

According to adjournment, Congress reassembled July 4. In answer to the inquiry, President Johnson stated that he had no communications to make to either House. At the outset, resolutions were introduced declaring that further legislation, at this session, upon reconstruction would be inexpedient, and that the business should be confined to removing obstructions placed, or likely to be placed, in the way of the execution of the acts heretofore adopted. But several bills were at once introduced into both Houses, with a view of defining and explaining the original and supplementary acts. These were referred to the Reconstruction Committee, and resulted in a bill, the text of which is given under the head of the Explanatory Reconstruction Act, which was passed, July 13, in the House by a vote of 111 to 23, and, in the Senate, by a vote of 31 to 6—sixteen Senators absent or not voting. Congress having thus declared what was "the true intent and meaning" of the act of March 2, 1867, the bill went to the President, who returned it, July 19, with his veto, in which he declared that all his previous objections to the former bills applied to this, with others specially pertinent, since it appears by this declaratory act that the military government over ten States is to have "unlimited authority over the Courts and over all the officers of the State, legislative, executive, and judicial;" it gives military commanders the power to suspend or remove from office any officer or person holding any civil or military office or duty in their districts; they are authorized to fill vacancies thus created by the detail of any officer, or soldier of the army, thus transferring such officer or soldier into a civil officer, so that he may be a Governor, a Legislator, or a Judge, however unfit for the duty. He then urges that the legal existence of the States now made military districts, has been recognized in various ways by Congress and the Courts; by the appointment of District-Attorneys and Marshals; the Internal Revenue laws describe them as States; the Chief-Justice has recently held a Circuit Court in North Carolina, and if North Carolina is not a State, every proceeding of that Court was null and void. In concluding this veto, the President referred to the attempts made by Congress to strip the Executive Department of some of its constitutional powers, and declared his intention, while the obligation rested on him as Chief Executive, to see that the laws are faithfully executed, never willingly to surrender the trust or the powers given for their execution. The bill was repassed over the veto, in the House by a vote of 100 to 22, and in the Senate by a vote of 30 to 6—seventeen Senators not voting or absent. Congress then passed a bill appropriating $1,675,000, "for the purpose of carrying out the Reconstruction acts," which the President vetoed; but it was repassed over the veto, in the House by 100 to 24, and in the Senate by 32 to 4. The House passed a vote of thanks to Generals Sheridan, Sickles, Pope, and Schofield, for services as Department Commanders; and received, July 12, from Secretary Stanton, copies of all the correspondence between the War Department and the District Commanders. The passage of the Explanatory act was the main business of the short session of sixteen days; and Congress, July 20, adjourned, to reassemble November 21, 1867.

This summary includes what President Lincoln, President Johnson, and the Southern States have attempted in the way of restoration, and what the Thirty-ninth and Fortieth Congresses have done towards reconstruction.

The Military Districts.

The assignment of commanders to the military districts was by orders issued from the headquarters of the army, March 11, 12, and 15, 1867. From the moment of their arrival at their respective commands, the several generals proceeded to carry out the "act to provide for the more efficient government of the rebel States," by making arrangements to regulate and control all local elections in accordance with what they presumed to be the views and desires of the dominant party in Congress. Order No. 1, March 13, of General J. M. Schofield, commanding the First District (Virginia), declared that "all officers under the existing provisional government of the State" might "continue to perform the duties of their respective offices * * until their successors shall be duly elected and qualified according to the act of Congress." April 2, he issued an order respecting boards of registration, detailing for the board five captains of the regular army. The same day he issued another order suspending all elections, State, county, or municipal, till the registration should be completed; and April 5, another order, stating that all officers hereafter elected or appointed, in addition to the oath of office prescribed by the State, must take the Test Oath prescribed by Congress. In the Second District, in an order dated March 21, General D. E. Sickles declared that "the civil government now existing in North Carolina and South Carolina is provisional only, and in all respects subject to the paramount authority of the United States, at any time to abolish, modify, control, or supersede the same." April 1, he refused to permit the election of a Sheriff in Richland District, telegraphing to the general in command that when the term of the present incumbent expired, a successor would be "appointed." In the Third District (Georgia, Florida, and Alabama), General Wager Swayne ordered, March 28, that "by direction of General Grant, all State and local elections * * are disallowed pending the arrival of the District Commander (John Pope) and his order in the premises." General Pope's first order, April 1, announced that "no elections would be held in any of the States comprised in this military district, except such as are provided for in the act of Congress, and in the manner therein established;" and that vacancies occurring "before the prescribed registration of voters is completed will be filled by appointment of the general commanding the district." April 8, he ordered that the district commanders should appoint "supervisors of registration." In the Fourth District (Mississippi and Arkansas), General E. O. C. Ord announced his appointment and assumption of his command March 28, and stated that such orders as were necessary to carry out the acts of March 2 and 23 would be duly published. In the Fifth District (Louisiana and Texas), March 9, General Sheridan prohibited an election for certain city officers in New Orleans, ordered by the Legislature for March 11, "that body, at a special session, having refused to postpone said election." March 27, he removed from office Andrew S Herron, Attorney-General of the State of Louisiana; James T. Monroe, Mayor of New Orleans; and Edmund Abell, Judge of the First District Court of New Orleans, and appointed other officers in their places. April 10, he appointed a Board of Registers for the Parish of Orleans, and Brevet Brigadier-General J. W. Forsyth was directed "to supervise the Board of Registration." April 13, he appointed a Military Commission, to try such persons as might be brought before it. In all the districts orders were issued declaring that the military administrations would be conducted according to the acts of Congress of March 2 and 23.

It will be seen that, from the outset, the district commanders administered the acts of March solely with reference to the military manipulation of elections. They, however, used their own discretion in regard to other matters. In Mobile, General Swayne, by command of General Pope, forbade the police from wearing gray uniform, as the City Council had directed. Subsequently, several policemen were removed, and, in every instance, negroes were substituted. In South Carolina, May 20, General Sickles issued an order prohibiting the distillation of grain. May 24, General Pope issued an order districting Georgia and Alabama for purposes of registration, placing a negro on every Board of Registration. In Virginia, May 28, General Schofield ordered the appointment of military commissioners, to be selected from officers of the army and the Freedmen's Bureau, and to command (with "sufficient military force") "all local police or other forces." These Commissioners were "clothed with all the power of magistrates," and when they tried a man, the commanding general was to give a decision on report of the case; but till such decision was announced, "the orders of the Military Commission will be paramount." While each commander was thus placing his own construction upon the acts of Congress, in June the President issued an order that the military commanders should guide themselves, in their interpretation of the Reconstruction acts, by the opinion of the Att'y-General—whereupon Gen. Sickles resigned the command of the Second District. June 4, Gen. Sheridan removed Gov. Wells, of Louisiana. Subsequently, the Attorney-General furnished a second opinion, that the district commanders had no right to remove civil officers. Nevertheless, July 30, Gen. Sheridan issued a special order removing Gov. Throckmorton, of Texas, and appointing Mr. E. P. Pease in his place.

The correspondence between the War Department and the district commanders, called for by the House, and furnished by Secretary Stanton, July 12, affords the information that Gens. Pope and Sheridan had inquired whether the opinion of the Attorney-General as to registration, &c., was to be considered binding upon them, and that Gen. Grant had replied that it had not be. n put in the form of an order, and he presumed it was not so intended by the President; the commanders were directed to put their own construction upon the military bills, till ordered to do otherwise. In expressing his dissent from Gen. Ord's views respecting registration in the 4th District, Gen. Grant says: "The law, however, makes the district commanders *their own interpreters* of their power or duty under it; and, in my opinion, the Attorney-General or myself can no more than give our opinion of the meaning of the law; neither can enforce his views against the judgment of those made responsible for the faithful execution of the law, the district commanders."

President Johnson, August 17, prepared an order removing Gen. Sheridan from the 5th District, and appointing Gen. Thomas to that command. This order was submitted, for suggestion, to Gen. Grant, and a correspondence followed, Gen. Grant urging the retention of Sheridan in his command. The President replied at length, stating that Sheridan's rule had been of "absolute tyranny," that his course had even "seriously interfered with a harmonious, satisfactory, and speedy execution of the acts of Congress," and that alone was "sufficient to justify a change." Gen. Grant yielded, and, August 26, issued the President's order removing Gen. Sheridan, and Gen. Hancock was assigned to the command. At the same time the order was issued removing Gen. Sickles from command of the Second District, and assigning Gen. Canby in his place. The President, September 3, issued a proclamation declaring that military officers are sworn to obey the orders of the President, and enjoining all military and civil officers "to render due submission to the laws and

decrees of the Courts of the United States," and to "sustain the authority of the law," and "to maintain the supremacy of the Federal Constitution." General Sickles, considering this proclamation a censure of his course as Commander of the Second District, addressed to General Grant a vindication of his conduct. He had ordered one of his officers to disregard a certain process issued by the United States District Court; General Grant ordered Sickles to obey the process; but subsequently, upon receipt of Sickles' statement of the case in question, General Grant rescinded his order. Afterwards General Sickles complied with the process of the Court. Immediately before Sickles' removal, the President received, August 24, an opinion from Acting Attorney-General Binckley, that the course cf General Sickles was wholly unwarranted, a manifest usurpation of power; that it was the duty of the Executive to maintain the authority of the Judiciary; and that the President should promptly repress the contumacy thus disclosed to him. Whereupon, General Sickles was removed.

Meanwhile, in all the districts registration was conducted under military supervision—every opportunity being afforded to the negroes, and every restriction being thrown in the way of the great body of whites by the boards of registration. On another page will be found the results of this remarkable registration. Subsequent elections in several of the districts were still more under military control, in many instances negroes coming in armed battalions to the polls; and formal charges have been made that in several cases arms and equipments for these negro political organizations were issued from the military commands and from agencies of the Freedmen's Bureau. These elections were to decide for or against calling conventions to frame new State constitutions, and to provide for the appointment of provisional civil officers. Whether or not the conventions were under military control, is sufficiently indicated in the case of the convention convened at Montgomery, Alabama, November 5. Agents and employes of the Freedmen's Bureau are declared to have been "members" of the convention. General Pope went from Atlanta, Georgia, and was in Montgomery when the convention opened. After the organization, November 8, the following resolution was introduced:

Resolved, That a committee of five be appointed to *wait upon Major-General Pope, and confer with him in regard to organizing a provisional government for this State*, and vacating all offices of the pretended government within the next twenty days.

This resolution was tabled by the close vote of 45 to 42, and led to the adoption of yet more summary measures. The convention was declared by one member to be "not a popular assembly, but a *Congressional* Convention;" and the proceedings at Montgomery represent the method of "military" reconstruction in the other districts.

ACTS OF CONGRESS.

Synopsis of the principal Acts and Resolutions passed at the Second Session of the Thirty-ninth Congress, and at the First Session and July Session of the Fortieth Congress.

III. *Negro Suffrage*—Regulates the elective franchise in the District of Columbia, so as to permit negroes to vote. [Vetoed, and Repassed January 8, 1867.]

V. *Penitentiaries*—Appropriates $20,000 for the Territory of Washington, and $40,000 in each of the Territories of Nebraska, Colorado, Idaho, Montana, Arizona, and Dakota, for the erection of penitentiaries. [Approved January 14, 1867.]

VI. *Congress*—Enacts that, in addition to the present regular times of meeting of Congress, hereafter Congress shall meet at noon, March 4. [January 22, 1867.]

X. *Suffrage in the Territories*—Forbids denial of the elective franchise in any of the Territories on account of race or color. [Not returned by the President, and became a law without his approval.]

XIII. *Counterfeiting*—Provides for the punishment of the crimes of forgery and counterfeiting of the public securities and currency. [February 5, 1867.]

XIV. *Habeas Corpus*—Amends the act of May 11, 1866, relating to *habeas corpus*, and regulating judicial proceedings in certain cases. [February 5, 1867.]

XV. *United States Courts*—Amends the act of September, 24, 1789, to establish the judicial courts of the United States. [February 5, 1867.]

XIX. *Pensions*—Authorizes the appointment of agents, not more than three in any State or Territory, to hold office for four years. [February 5, 1867.]

XXI. *Nebraska*—Accepts and ratifies the Constitution and State government formed by the people, and admits Nebraska to the Union upon the condition that " there shall be no denial of the elective franchise, or of any other rights, to any person, by reason of race or color, excepting Indians not taxed." [Passed over the President's veto, February 8, 1867.]

XXVI. *Congressional Library*—Provides that every proprietor who copyrights a book, pamphlet, map, chart, musical composition, engraving, or photograph, and does not deposit a copy within one month of publication in the Library of Congress, is subject to a penalty of $25. [February 18, 1867.]

XXVII. *Prize Money* — Authorizes payment of prize money to certain officers and men of the signal corps with Admiral Farragut in the action of Mobile Bay, August 5, 1864. [February 18, 1867.]

XXIX. *League Island*—Authorizes the acceptance of League Island, in the Delaware River, for naval purposes, provided the navy yard at Philadelphia shall be dispensed with and disposed of. [February 18, 1867.]

XXXII. *Organization of the House of Representatives*—Instructs the Clerk of the next preceding Congress to prepare for the first meeting of the subsequent Congress a roll of representatives elect, but putting on the roll only the names of claimants for seats from States represented in the preceding Congress. If the Clerk is prevented from making such a roll for his successor, the Sergeant-at-Arms and, in his disability, the Doorkeeper of the House, must do it. [Not returned in time, and became a law without the approval of the President.]

XXXIV. *Pensions*—Appropriates $33,280,000 to pay invalid and other pensions for the year ending June 30, 1868. [February 22, 1867.]

XXXVII. *National Cemeteries*—Provides for the establishment and protection of national cemeteries for the burial of deceased sailors and soldiers. [February 22, 1867.]

XLIV. *Mississippi River* — Authorizes the construction of a submerged tubular bridge across the Mississippi, at St. Louis. [February 25, 1867.]

XLV. *Oregon*—Grants land to the State of Oregon to aid in the construction of a military wagon road from Dallas City, on the Columbia River, to Fort Bois, on the Snake River. [February 25, 1867.]

LI. *Steam Navigation*—Amends the act of July 25, 1866, to provide for the safety of the lives of passengers on board vessels propelled by steam, and to regulate the salaries of steamboat inspectors. [February 25, 1867.]

LXV. *Montana*—Amends the act providing for the temporary government of Montana Territory, and forbids the legislatures of all the territories from granting private charters or special privileges, but they may, by general incorporation acts, permit persons to associate themselves as bodies corporate for mining, &c. [March 2, 1867.]

LXVI. *Idaho*—Amends the act for the government of Idaho, making legislative assemblies biennial, and members of the council to be elected for a term of four years. [March 2, 1867.]

XLVIII. *Reconstruction* — Provides for " the more efficient government of the rebel States." [The full text of this bill is given elsewhere. Passed over the President's veto, March 2, 1867.]

LXIX. *Tenure of Office Bill*—[The full text is given elsewhere. Passed over the President's veto, March 2, 1867.]

LXX. *President's Acts and Proclamations*—Declares valid and conclusive all acts, proclamations, and orders of the President, or acts done by his authority or approval after March 4, 1861, and before July 1, 1866, respecting martial law, military trials by courts-martial, or military commissions, or the arrest, imprisonment, and trial or persons charged with participation in the late rebellion as aiders or abettors thereof, or as guilty of any disloyal practice; and the proceedings of all courts-martial and military commissions are made valid, as if these acts and proceedings had been done under the direction of Congress, and in pursuance of laws previously enacted and expressly authorizing and directing the same to be done. [March 2, 1867.]

LXXIII. *Education*—Establishes a Department of Education to collect statistics showing the condition and progress of education in the several States and Territories; to diffuse information with regard to school systems, and generally to promote the cause of education throughout the country. [March 2, 1867.]

LXXXIV. *Volunteers* — Declares the rights, rank, pay, privileges, &c., of volunteer officers as regards the regular army. [March 2, 1867.]

LXXXIV. *Revenue* — Amends existing laws relating to internal revenue. [March 2, 1867.]

LXXXIX. *Navy*—Amends certain acts in relation to the navy; gives the commandant of the main corps the rank and pay of a brigadier-general of the army; regulates the number, and manner of appointment, of midshipmen at the Naval Academy; and entitles officers on the retired and reserved lists promotion as their several dates on the active list are promoted; but without additional pay. [March 2, 1867.]

XC. *Brevets*—Authorizes the conference of brevets upon army officers for gallant conduct in the volunteer service. [March 2, 1867.]

XCI. *Bankrupt Law*—Establishes an uniform system of bankruptcy throughout the United States; and various sections are devoted to the administration of the law in courts of bankruptcy; appeals and practice; assignments and assignees; debts and proof of claims; property perishable and in dispute; examination of bankrupts; distribution of the bankrupt's estate; the bankrupt's discharge and its effect; preferences and fraudulent conveyances declared void; bankruptcy of partnerships and corporations; dates and depositions; involuntary bankruptcy; superseding the bankrupt proceedings by arrangement; penalties against bankrupts; penalties against officers; fees and costs; and the meaning of terms and computation of time. [March 2, 1867.]

XCV. *Imprisonment for Debt*—Is supplementary to the several acts of Congress abolishing imprisonment for debt. [March 2, 1867.]

XCVII. *Ocean Mails* — Authorizes the establishment of ocean mail steamship service between the United States and the Hawaiian Islands, at a cost of not more than $75,000 for twelve round trips a year, and the contractors must be citizens of the United States. [March 2, 1867.]

XCIX. *Land Claims*—Extends the provisions of the act "for the final adjustment of private land claims in the States of Florida, Louisiana, and Missouri." [March 2, 1867.]

CII. *Peonage*—Abolishes the system of peonage in New Mexico and in the other parts of the United States. [March 2, 1867.]

CIV. *California*—Grants lands to aid in constructing a railroad from Stockton to the town of Copperopolis, in California. [March 2, 1867.]

CXII. *Revenue* — Provides for an increased revenue from imported clothing, combing, carpet and other similar wools. [March 2, 1867.]

Public Resolutions.

No. 2. *Paris Exposition*—Instructs Commissioner of Agriculture to prepare specimens of the cereal productions of the United States, for exhibition at Paris. [Approved January 11, 1867.]

No. 3. *Soldiers' Medals*—Authorizes distribution through the mails, free of postage, of certain medals to honorably discharged soldiers, or to relatives of the killed or of those who died in service, in West Virginia. [January 14, 1867.]

No. 4. *New York City Post-Office*—Authorizes the Mayor, Postmaster, and others, to purchase site for Post-office building on lower portion of City Hall Park, for $500-000; and authorizes same Commission to procure plans and estimates for suitable building. [January 22, 1867.]

No. 6. *Disabled Volunteers' Asylum*—Authorizes the Secretary of War to transfer certain land at Point Lookout, Maryland, to the National Asylum for Disabled Volunteers. [January 29, 1867.]

No. 8. *Internal Revenue*—Amends existing laws relating to alcohol and burning fluid. [February 5, 1867.]

No. 9. *Militia*—Provides for payment of certain Kentucky Militia forces. [February 8, 1867.]

No. 10. *Alcohol*—Provides, in certain cases, for the removal of alcohol from bonded warehouses free from internal tax. [February 18, 1867.]

No. 11. *Ocean Mails*—Authorizes the employment of ocean mail service between San Francisco and Portland, Oregon, at a cost not to exceed $25,000 a year. [February 18, 1867.]

No. 12. *Pensions*—Gives pensions to widows of revolutionary soldiers at increased rate the soldiers would be entitled to under existing laws, if now living. [Feb. 18, 1867.]

No. 13. *New York Harbor*—Appropriates $38,500 to purchase David's Island. [February 18, 1867.]

No. 14. *Customs*—Extends the time for codifying laws relating to customs to January 1, 1868. [February 22, 1867.]

No. 15. *Lieutenant-Commander S. L. Breese, U. S. N.*—Restores him, with same rank, to active list from retired list. [February 22, 1867.]

No. 16. *For Sufferers at the South*—Assigns a public vessel to carry food to Charleston, Savannah, and Mobile. [February 22, 1867.]

No. 17. *Isthmus Canal*—Authorizes Secretary of Navy to furnish facilities in aid of survey for a ship canal to connect the Atlantic and Pacific at the Isthmus of Darien. [February 25, 1867.]

No. 19. *West Virginia*—To provide for ascertaining and apportioning the proper quota of direct tax of 1861 in West Virginia. [February 25, 1867.]

No. 20. *More Pay*—Gives additional compensation to certain employes in the civil service at Washington. [February 28, 1867.]

No. 21. *Tennessee*—Extends the provisions of the act in regard to agricultural colleges to Tennessee. [February 28, 1867.]

No. 22. *Quarantine*—Extends the time for the use of certain vessels for quarantine purposes at the Port of New York. [February 28, 1867.]

No. 26. *Statue of General Scott*—Appropriates $20,000 for a bronze equestrian statue (contract with Henry K. Brown, Newburg, N. Y.,) of Lieutenant-General Winfield Scott, for Franklin square, Washington. [March 2, 1867.]

No. 27. *Secession Sympathizers* — Prohibits payments of all accounts, claims, or demands accruing previous to April 13, 1861, to persons not known to have been opposed to the rebellion and in favor of its suppression. [March 2, 1867.]

No. 28. *Repeal of Duties*—Exempts from duty machinery imported for the manufacture of beet sugar, and repeals, in section 5 of the act of June 30, 1864, the paragraph "On castings, mohair cloth," &c. [March 2, 1867.]

No. 30. *National Banks*—Authorizes refunding any excess of duty paid to the Treasury by national banks. [March 2, 1867.]

No. 31. *Quartermasters' Stores*—Provides payment for stores furnished forces under General Lew. Wallace in 1863. [March 2, 1867.]

No. 32. *Isthmus Canal*—The Secretary of State directed to obtain authority from the United States of Columbia to make surveys at the Isthmus of Darien. [March 2, 1867.]

No. 33. *Lincoln*—Congress thanks Brazil for resolutions of sorrow and sympathy on the death of President Lincoln. [March 2, 1867.]

No. 34. *Boston Post-Office*—Authorizes a commission to select a site for a post-office and sub-treasury building in Boston. [March 2, 1867.]

No. 36. *Public Documents*—Provides for exchange of public documents with foreign countries for benefit of Congressional Library. [March 2, 1867.]

No. 37. *Kansas*—Grants land for bridge purposes to State of Kansas. [Mar. 2, 1867.]

No. 38. *Atlantic Cable* — Thanks Cyrus W. Field, and awards a gold medal, for his Atlantic Cable services. [March 2, 1867.]

No. 40. *Shipwreck Services* — Awards a gold chronometer to Captain James G. Smith, for rescuing persons from brig E. H. Fitler. [March 2, 1867.]

Appropriations.

In the foregoing synopsis of acts and resolutions by the Thirty-ninth Congress (Second Session) the appropriation bills are omitted. The following sums were appropriated, and are added to the amount appropriated at the First Session of the same Congress:

Deficiencies for the year ending June 30, 1868	$1,185,953
Post Office Department	19,138,000
Pensions	33,280,000
Consular and diplomatic	1,425,454
Military Academy	368,913
Legislative, Executive, and Judicial	23,387,971
Sundry civil expenses	5,307,191
Army	23,874,454
Repair of public works	1,290,006
Naval service	16,297,241
Indian Department	3,022,003
Repair and completion of certain public works	4,702,781
Deficiencies ending June 30, 1867	10,493,439
Miscellaneous	1,421,163
Total	$145,139,560
Appropriations of the first session	155,890,018
Total for the entire Congress	$301,029,588

Fortieth Congress—First Session.

IV. *Destitute Soldiers*—Furnishes every invalid soldier, who is an inmate of any regularly constituted " Soldiers' Home," with a complete suit of clothing. [Approved March 22, 1867.]

VI. *Reconstruction*—Act of March 23, 1867, supplementary to the act of March 2. [The full text is given elsewhere.]

VII. *Nebraska*—Provides for a District and Circuit Court of the United States for the District of Nebraska. [March 25, 1867.]

VIII. *Internal Revenue*—Exempts wrapping paper, made from wood or corn-stalks, from internal tax. [March 26, 1867.]

XI. *Boston Harbor*—Appropriates $5,000 to purchase a site for a fort on Long Island, in Boston harbor. [March 28, 1867.]

XII. *Atlantic Dock*—Authorizes sale of government warehouse on Atlantic Dock, Brooklyn. [March 28, 1867.]

XIV. *Indiana and Ohio*—Reimburses Indiana and Ohio for money expended in enrolling, equipping, and provisioning milia for the service of the United States. March 30, 1867.]

XV. *Ocean Telegraph*—Gives the American Atlantic Cable Telegraph Company of New York the right to lay, land, and operate cables on the Atlantic coast, except on the coast of Florida. [March 30, 1867.]

XVI. *Pennsylvania* — Makes Chester, Pennsylvania, a port of delivery. [March 30, 1867.]

XVII. *Patent Office*—Increases the force in the Patent Office. [March 30, 1867.]

XVIII. *Lincoln*—Incorporates the Lincoln Monument Association. [March 30, 1867.]

XX. *Colorado*—Amends the organic act of Colorado Territory, making legislative sessions biennial; and members of the council to be elected for the term of four years.

XXI. *Soldiers and Sailors' Orphan Home*—Provides for the support, in part, of the National Soldiers and Sailors' Orphan Home, in the District of Columbia, by an appropriation of $5,000.

XXII. *Nebraska*—Extends to the State of Nebraska, the provisions of the act relating to agricultural colleges.

[July Session, 1867.]

Reconstruction—The Explanatory Reconstruction Act, passed July 19, 1867. [The full text is given elsewhere.]

Indians—Appoints a commission to establish peace with certain hostile tribes; to establish security for person and property along the lines of railroad now building to the Pacific; to select districts with tillable and grazing ground for permanent homes for Indians; $150,000 are appropriated for these objects; and $300,000 to subsist friendly Indians separating themselves from hostile tribes and seeking protection; if the commissioners fail to secure the consent of the Indians to remove to the reservations, and fail to secure peace, the Secretary of War is authorized to accept four thousand mounted volunteers to suppress Indian hostilities. [Approved July 20, 1867.]

Venezuela—Authorizes the appointment of a commissioner at $3,000, and $10 per diem traveling expenses, to carry into effect the convention of April 25, 1866, with the republic of Venezuela for the adjustment of claims of citizens of the U. S. on the government of that republic. [July 20, 1867.]

Public Resolutions.

No. 1. *Paris Exposition*—Provides additional facilities to enable the people of the United States to participate in the advantages of the Universal Exposition at Paris in 1867. [Approved March 12, 1867.]

No. 3. *George Peabody*—Presents the thanks of Congress to George Peabody for giving two million dollars for the promotion of education in the South, and awards a gold medal. [March 16, 1867.]

No. 4. *Destitute Negroes*—Appropriates $15,000 for the relief of destitute negroes in the District of Columbia. [March 16, 1867.]

No. 7. *Soldiers' Asylum* — Authorizes Secretary of War to turn over certain property at Camp Chase, Ohio, for the use of the National Asylum for Disabled Volunteer Soldiers. [March 22, 1867.]

No. 9. *Ship Canal*—Authorizes provision to be made for survey of a ship canal to connect Lakes Erie and Ontario for military, naval, and commercial purposes. [March 22, 1867.]

No. 13. *Works of Art*—Authorizes the importation of certain works of art free of duty; also, steam ploughs imported during the fiscal year as models, or for experimental purposes. [March 26, 1867.]

No. 14. *New Mexico*—Makes valid the laws passed by the Legislature at Santa Fe from December 3, 1866, to January 31, 1867. [March 26, 1867.]

No. 15. *Diplomatic Uniforms*—Prohibits all persons in the diplomatic service of the United States from wearing any uniform or official costume not previously authorized. [March 27, 1867.]

No. 18. *Congressional Salaries*—Authorizes Members of Congress to draw their pay, at the rate established by law, at the end of each month. [March 30, 1867.]

No. 19. *Duties*—Amends the "act to provide for increased revenue from imported wool," &c. [March 30, 1867.]

No. 20. *Ship Canal*—Authorizes surveys and estimates for a ship canal around the Falls of the Ohio River on the Indiana side; also an estimate of the expense of completing the Louisville and Portland Canal on the Kentucky side of said falls; the expense to be defrayed from appropriations already made. [March 30, 1867.]

No. 23. *Agricultural College Scrip*—Forbids the further issue or delivery of Agricultural College scrip to any of the Southern States excepting Tennessee. [Mar. 30, 1867.]

No. 27. *Survey of Rivers*—Authorizes the employment of five civil engineers to execute the surveys of Western and Northwestern rivers. [March 30, 1867.]

No. 28. *The Suffering South*—Authorizes distribution, through Freedmen's Bureau, of supplies of food to prevent starvation and want to "all classes" of destitute people in the South where the crops have failed. [March 30, 1867.]

No. 29. *Seeds for the South*—Transfers $50,000 from Freedmen's Bureau to Agricultural Department to purchase cereal seeds for distribution in the Southern States. [March 30, 1867.]

No. 30. *Arms for Tennessee*—Furnishes arms and equipments for ten thousand militia in Tennessee. [March 30, 1867.]

No. 31. *Drafted Slaves*—Suspends all proceedings in relation to payment for slaves drafted or received as volunteers in the military service of the United States. [March 30, 1867.)

No. 32. *Reconstruction* — Appropriates $500,000 to carry into effect the Reconstruction acts. [March 30, 1867.]

No. 34. *Brooklyn Navy-Yard* — Authorizes the purchase of the Ruggles property, without the previous assent of the State of New York. [March 30, 1867.]

[July Session, 1867.]

Reconstruction — Appropriates one million dollars to carry into effect the Reconstruction acts. [Passed over veto, July 19,'67]

Crete—Expressing sympathy with the suffering people of Crete.

Proclamations.

March 1, 1867—Proclamation declaring Nebraska a State in the Union.

September 3, 1867—Warns all persons against obstructing or hindering the execution of the Constitution or the laws ; and enjoining all military and civil officers " to render due submission to these laws and the decrees of the courts of the United States ; and to give all the aid in their power necessary to the prompt execution of all said laws, decrees, judgments, and processes.

September 7, 1867—Extending Full Pardon to Certain Persons Who Were Engaged in the Late Rebellion.

Whereas, in the month of July, anno Domini 1861, the two Houses of Congress, with extraordinary unanimity, solemnly declared that the war then existing was not waged on the part of the government in any spirit of oppression, nor for any purpose of conquest or subjugation, nor purpose of overthrowing or interfering with the rights or established institutions of the States, but to defend and maintain the supremacy of the Constitution, and to preserve the Union with all the dignity, equality, and rights of the several States unimpaired, and that as soon as these objects should be accomplished the war ought to cease;

And whereas, the President of the United States, on the eighth day of December, anno Domini 1863, and on the twenty-sixth day of March, anno Domini 1864, did, with the objects of suppressing the then existing rebellion, of inducing all persons to return to their loyalty, and of restoring the authority of the United States, issue proclamations offering amnesty and pardon to all persons who had directly or indirectly participated in the then existing rebellion, except as in those proclamations was specified and reserved;

And whereas, the President of the United States did, on the twenty-ninth day of May, anno Domini 1865, issue a further proclamation with the same objects before mentioned, and to the end that the authority of the government of the United States might be restored, and that peace, order, and freedom might be established, and the President did, by the said last-mentioned proclamation, proclaim and declare that he thereby granted to all persons who had directly or indirectly participated in the then existing rebellion, except as therein excepted, amnesty and pardon, with restoration of all rights and property, except as to slaves, and except in certain cases where legal proceedings had been instituted, but upon condition that such persons should take and subscribe an oath therein prescribed, which oath should be registered for permanent preservation;

And whereas, in and by the said last-mentioned proclamation of the twenty-ninth day of May, anno Domini 1865, fourteen extensive classes of persons, therein specially described, were altogether excepted and excluded from the benefits thereof;

And whereas, the President of the United States did, on the second day of April, anno Domini 1866. issue a proclamation declaring that the insurrection was at an end, and was thenceforth to be so regarded;

And whereas, there now exists no organized armed resistance of misguided citizens or others to the authority of the United States in the States of Georgia, South Carolina, Virginia, North Carolina, Tennessee, Alabama, Louisiana, Arkansas, Mississippi, Florida, and Texas, and the laws can be sustained and enforced therein by the proper civil authority, State or Federal, and the people of said States are well and loyally disposed, and have conformed, or, if permitted to do so, will conform in their legislation to the condition of affairs growing out of the amendment to the Constitution of the United States prohibiting slavery within the limits and jurisdiction of the United States ;

And whereas, there no longer exists any reasonable ground to apprehend, within the States which were involved in the late rebellion, any renewal thereof, or any unlawful resistance by the people of said States to the Constitution and laws of the United States ;

And whereas, large standing armies, military occupation, martial law, military tribunals, and the suspension of the privilege of the writ of *habeas corpus* and the right of trial by jury, are, in time of peace, dangerous to public liberty, incompatible with the individual rights of the citizen, contrary to the genius and spirit of our free institutions, and exhaustive of the national resources, and ought not, therefore, to be sanctioned or allowed, except in cases of actual necessity for repelling invasion or suppressing insurrection or rebellion;

And whereas, a retaliatory or vindictive policy, attended by unnecessary disqualifications, pains, penalties, confiscations, and disfranchisements, now, as always, could only tend to hinder reconciliation among the people and national restoration, while it must seriously embarrass, obstruct, and repress popular energies and national industry and enterprise;

And whereas, for these reasons, it is now deemed essential to the public welfare, and to the more perfect restoration of constitutional law and order, that the said last-mentioned proclamation, so as aforesaid issued on the twenty-ninth day of May, anno Domini 1865, should be modified, and that the full and beneficent pardon conceded thereby should be opened and further extended to a large number of the persons who, by its aforesaid exceptions, have been hitherto excluded from executive clemency;

Now, therefore, be it known that I, Andrew Johnson, President of the United States, do hereby proclaim and declare that the full pardon described in the said proclamation of the twenty-ninth day of May, anno Domini, 1865, shall henceforth be opened and extended to all persons who, directly or indirectly, participated in the late rebellion, with the restoration of all privileges, immunities, and rights of property, except as to property with regard to slaves, and except in cases of legal proceedings under the laws of the United States; but upon this condition, nevertheless: that every such person who shall seek to avail himself of this proclamation shall take and subscribe the following oath, and shall cause the same to be registered for permanent preservation, in the same manner and with the same effect as with the oath prescribed in the said proclamation of the twenty-ninth day of May, 1865, namely:

" I, ———— ————, do solemnly swear (or affirm), in presence of Almighty God, that I will henceforth faithfully support, protect, and defend the Constitution of the United States, and the Union of the States thereunder; and that I will, in like manner, abide by and faithfully support all laws and proclamations which have been made during the late rebellion with reference to the emancipation of slaves. So help me God."

The following persons, and no others, are excluded from the benefits of this proclamation, and of the said proclamation of the twenty-ninth day of May, 1865, namely:

First. The chief or pretended chief executive officers, including the President, the Vice-President, and all heads of departments of the pretended confederate or rebel government, and all who were agents thereof in foreign states and countries, and all who held, or pretended to hold, in the service of the said pretended confederate government, a military rank or title above the grade of brigadier-general, or naval rank or title above that of captain, and all who were or pretended to be Governors of States, while maintaining, aiding, abetting, or submitting to and acquiescing in the rebellion.

Second. All persons who in any way treated otherwise than as lawful prisoners of war persons who in any capacity were employed or engaged in the military or naval service of the United States.

Third. All persons who, at the time they may seek to obtain the benefits of this proclamation, are actually in civil, military, or naval confinement or custody, or legally held to bail, either before or after conviction, and all persons who were engaged directly or indirectly in the assassination of the late President of the United States, or in any plot or conspiracy in any manner therewith connected.

In testimony whereof, I have signed these presents with my hand, and have caused the seal of the United States to be hereunto affixed.

Done at the City of Washington, the seventh day of September, in the year of our Lord one thousand [SEAL.] eight hundred and sixty-seven, and of the independence of the United States of America the ninety-second.

ANDREW JOHNSON.

By the President;

WILLIAM H. SEWARD, Sec. of State.

Tenure of Office Bill.

AN ACT regulating the tenure of certain civil offices.

Be it enacted &c., That every person holding any civil office to which he has been appointed by and with the advice and consent of the Senate, and every person who shall hereafter be appointed to any such office, and shall become duly qualified to act therein, is, and shall be, entitled to hold such office until a successor shall have been in like manner appointed and duly qualified, except as herein otherwise provided: *Provided*, That the Secretaries of State, of the Treasury, of War, of the Navy, and of the Interior, the Postmaster General, and the Attorney General, shall hold their offices respectively for and during the term of the President by whom they may have been appointed and for one month thereafter, subject to removal by and with the advice and consent of the Senate.

SEC. 2. That when any officer appointed as aforesaid, excepting judges of the United States courts, shall, during a recess of the Senate, be shown, by evidence satisfactory to the President, to be guilty of misconduct in office, or crime, or for any reason shall become incapable or legally disqualified to perform its duties, in such case, and in no other, the President may suspend such officer and designate some suitable person to perform temporarily the duties of such office until the next meeting of the Senate, and until the case shall be acted upon by the

Senate; and such person so designated shall take the oaths and give the bonds required by law to be taken and given by the person duly appointed to fill such office; and in such case it shall be the duty of the President, within twenty days after the first day of such next meeting of the Senate, to report to the Senate such suspension, with the evidence and reasons for his action in the case and the name of the person so designated to perform the duties of such office. And if the Senate shall concur in such suspension and advise and consent to the removal of such officer, they shall so certify to the President, who may thereupon remove such officer, and, by and with the advice and consent of the Senate, appoint another person to such office. But if the Senate shall refuse to concur in such suspension, such officer so suspended shall forthwith resume the functions of his office, and the powers of the person so performing its duties in his stead shall cease, and the official salary and emoluments of such officer shall, during such suspension, belong to the person so performing the duties thereof, and not to the officer so suspended: *Provided, however,* That the President, in case he shall become satisfied that such suspension was made on insufficient grounds, shall be authorized, at any time before reporting such suspension to the Senate as above provided, to revoke such suspension and reinstate such officer in the performance of the duties of his office.

SEC. 3. That the President shall have power to fill all vacancies which may happen during the recess of the Senate, by reason of death or resignation, by granting commissions which shall expire at the end of their next session thereafter. And if no appointment, by and with the advice and consent of the Senate, shall be made to such office so vacant or temporarily filled as aforesaid during such next session of the Senate, such office shall remain in abeyance, without any salary, fees or emoluments attached thereto, until the same shall be filled by appointment thereto, by and with the advice and consent of the Senate; and during such time all the powers and duties belonging to such office shall be exercised by such other officer as may by law exercise such powers and duties in case of a vacancy in such office.

SEC. 4. That nothing in this act contained shall be construed to extend the term of any office the duration of which is limited by law.

SEC. 5. That if any person shall, contrary to the provisions of this act, accept any appointment to or employment in any office, or shall hold or exercise, or attempt to hold or exercise, any such office or employment, he shall be deemed, and is hereby declared to be, guilty of a high misdemeanor, and, upon trial and conviction thereof, he shall be punished therefor by a fine not exceeding ten thousand dollars, or by imprisonment not exceeding five years, or both said punishments, in the discretion of the court.

SEC. 6. That every removal, appointment, or employment, made, had, or exercised, contrary to the provisions of this act, and the making, signing, sealing, countersigning, or issuing of any commission or letter of authority for or in respect to any such appointment or employment, shall be deemed, and are hereby declared to be high misdemeanors, and, upon trial and conviction thereof, every person guilty thereof shall be punished by a fine not exceeding ten thousand dollars, or by imprisonment not exceeding five years, or both said punishments, in the discretion of the court: *Provided,* That the President shall have power to make out and deliver, after the adjournment of the Senate, commissions for all officers whose appointment shall have been advised and consented to by the Senate.

SEC. 7. That it shall be the duty of the Secretary of the Senate, at the close of each session thereof, to deliver to the Secretary of the Treasury, and to each of his Assistants, and to each of the Auditors, and to each of the Comptrollers in the Treasury, and to the Treasurer, and to the Register of the Treasury, a full and complete list, duly certified, of all persons who shall have been nominated to and rejected by the Senate during such session, and a like list of all the offices to which nominations shall have been made and not confirmed and filled at such session.

SEC. 8. That whenever the President shall, without the advice and consent of the Senate, designate, authorize, or employ any person to perform the duties of any office, he shall forthwith notify the Secretary of the Treasury thereof; and it shall be the duty of the Secretary of the Treasury thereupon to communicate such notice to all the proper accounting and disbursing officers of his department.

SEC. 9. That no money shall be paid or received from the treasury, or paid or received from or retained out of any public moneys or funds of the United States, whether in the treasury or not, to or by or for the benefit of any person appointed to or authorized to act in or holding or exercising the duties or functions of any office contrary to the provisions of this act; nor shall any claim, account, voucher, order, certificate, warrant, or other instrument providing for or relating to such payment, receipt, or retention, be presented, passed, allowed, approved, certified, or paid by any officer of the United States, or by any person exercising the functions or performing the duties of any office or place of trust under the United States, for or in respect to such office, or the exercising or performing the functions or duties thereof; and every person who shall violate any of the provisions of this section shall be deemed guilty of a high misdemeanor, and, upon trial and conviction thereof, shall be punished therefor by a fine not exceeding ten thousand dollars, or by imprisonment not exceeding ten years, or both said punishments, in the discretion of the court.

Passed March 2, 1867.

The President's Veto.

To the Senate of the United States :

I have carefully examined the bill "to regulate the tenure of certain civil offices." The material portion of the bill is contained in the first section, and is of the effect following, namely : * * * These provisions are qualified by a reservation in the fourth section, "that nothing contained in the bill shall be construed to extend the term of any office, the duration of which is limited by law." In effect the bill provides that the President shall not remove from their places any of the civil officers whose terms of service are not limited by law, without the advice and consent of the Senate of the United States. The bill in this respect conflicts, in my judgment, with the Constitution of the United States. The question, as Congress is well aware, is by no means a new one. That the power of removal is constitutionally vested in the President of the United States is a principle which has been not more distinctly declared by judicial authority and judicial commentators than it has been uniformly practiced upon by the legislative and executive departments of the government. The question arose in the House of Representatives so early as the 16th of June, 1789, on the bill for establishing an executive department denominated "The Department of Foreign Affairs." The first clause of the bill, after recapitulating the functions of that officer and defining his duties, had these words: "to be removable from office by the President of the United States." It was moved to strike out these words, and the motion was sustained with great ability and vigor. It was insisted that the President could not constitutionally exercise the power of removal exclusively of the Senate; that the Federalist so interpreted the Constitution when arguing for its adoption by the several States; that the Constitution had nowhere given the President power of removal, either expressly or by strong implication, but, on the contrary, had distinctly provided for removals from office by impeachment only. A construction which denied the power of removal by the President was further maintained by arguments drawn from the danger of the abuse of the power; from the supposed tendency of an exposure of public officers to capricious removal to impair the efficiency of the civil service; from the alleged injustice and hardship of displacing incumbents dependent upon their official stations without sufficient consideration; from a supposed want of responsibility on the part of the President, and from an imagined defect of guarantees against a vicious President who might incline to abuse the power. On the other hand, an exclusive power of removal by the President was defended as a true exposition of the text of the Constitution. It was maintained that there are certain causes for which persons ought to be removed from office without being guilty of treason, bribery, or malfea-

sance, and that the nature of things demands that it should be so. "Suppose," it was said, " a man becomes insane by the visitation of God, and is likely to ruin our affairs, are the hands of the government to be confined from warding off the evil ? Suppose a person in office, not possessing the talents he was judged to have at the time of the appointment, is the error not to be corrected ? Suppose he acquires vicious habits and incurable indolence, or total neglect of the duties of his office, which shall work mischief to the public welfare, is there no way to arrest the threatened danger ? Suppose he becomes odious and unpopular by reason of the measures he pursues—and this he may do without committing any positive offence against the law—must he preserve his office in despite of the popular will ? Suppose him grasping for his own aggrandizement and the elevation of his connections by every means short of the treason defined by the Constitution, hurrying your affairs to the precipice of destruction, endangering your domestic tranquility, plundering you of the means of defence, alienating the affections of your allies and promoting the spirit of discord must the tardy, tedious, desultory road by way of impeachment be traveled to overtake the man who, barely confining himself within the letter of the law, is employed in drawing off the vital principle of the government. The nature of things, the great object of society, the express objects of the Constitution itself, require that this thing should be otherwise. To unite the Senate with the President in the exercise of the power," it was said, " would involve us in the most serious difficulty. Suppose a discovery of any of those events should take place when the Senate is not in session, how is the remedy to be applied ? The evil could be avoided in no other way than by the Senate sitting always." In regard to the danger of the power being abused if exercised by one man, it was said "that the danger is as great with respect to the Senate, who are assembled from various parts of the continent with different impressions and opinions;" "that such a body is more likely to misuse the power of removal than the man whom the united voice of America calls to the Presidential chair. As the nature of government requires the power of removal," it was maintained " that it should be exercised in this way by the hand capable of exerting itself with effect; and the power must be conferred on the President by the Constitution as the executive officer of the government." Mr. Madison, whose adverse opinion in the Federalist had been relied upon by those who denied the exclusive power, now participated in the debate. He declared that he had reviewed his former opinions, and he summed up the whole case as follows : " The Constitution affirms that the executive power is vested in the President. Are there exceptions to this proposition ? Yes, there are. The Constitution says that in appointing to office, the Senate shall be associated with the President, unless in the case of inferior officers, when the law shall otherwise direct. Have we (that is, Congress) a right to extend this exception? I believe not. If the Constitution has invested all executive power in the President, I venture to assert that the legislature has no right to diminish or modify his executive authority. The question now resolves itself into this: Is the power of displacing an executive power? I conceive that if any power whatsoever is in the Executive, it is the power of appointing, overseeing, and controlling those who execute the laws. If the Constitution had not qualified the power of the President in appointing to office by associating the Senate with him in that business, would it not be clear that he would have the right, by virtue of his executive power, to make such appointment? Should we be authorized, in defiance of that clause in the Constitution—'The executive power shall be vested in the President'—to unite the Senate with the President in the appointment to office? I conceive not. If it is admitted that we should not be authorized to do this, I think it may be disputed whether we have a right to associate them in removing persons from office, the one power being as much of an executive nature as the other; and the first one is authorized by being excepted out of the general rule established by the Constitution in these words: 'The executive power shall be vested in the President.'" The question thus ably and exhaustively argued, was decided by the House of Representatives, by a vote of thirty-four to twenty, in favor of the principle that the executive power of removal is vested by the Constitution in the Executive, and in the Senate by the casting vote of the Vice-President. The question has often been raised in subsequent times of high excitement, and the practice of the government has nevertheless conformed in all cases to the decision thus early made. The question was revived during the administration of President Jackson, who made, as is well recollected, a very large number of removals, which were made an occasion of close and rigorous scrutiny and remonstrance. The subject was long and earnestly debated in the Senate, and the early construction of the Constitution was nevertheless freely accepted as binding and conclusive upon Congress.

Chancellor Kent's remarks on the subject are as follows: "On the first organization of the government it was made a question whether the power of removal in case of officers appointed to hold at pleasure resided nowhere but in the body which appointed, and, of course, whether the consent of the Senate was not requisite to remove. This was the construction given to the Constitution while it was pending for ratification before the State conventions, by the author of the Federalist. But the construction which was given to the Constitution by Congress, after great consideration and discussion, was different. The words of the act (establishing the Treasury Department) are: 'And whenever the same shall be removed from office by the President of the United States, or in any other case of vacancy in the office, the assistant shall act.' This amounted to a legislative construction of the Constitution, and it has ever since been acquiesced in and acted upon as a decisive authority in the case. It applies equally to every other officer of the government appointed by the President, whose term of duration is not specially declared. It is supported by the weighty reason that the subordinate officers in the executive department ought to hold at the pleasure of the head of the department, because he is invested generally with the executive authority, and the participation in that authority by the Senate was an exception to a general principle and ought to be taken strictly. The President is the great responsible officer for the faithful execution of the law, and the power of removal was incidental to that duty, and might often be requisite to fulfil it." Thus has the important question presented by this bill been settled, in the language of the late Daniel Webster, (who, while dissenting from it, admitted that it was settled,) by construction, settled by precedent, settled by the practice of the government, and settled by statute. The events of the last war furnished a practical confirmation of the wisdom of the Constitution as it has hitherto been maintained, in many of its parts, including that which is now the subject of consideration. When the war broke out rebel enemies, traitors, abettors, and sympathizers were found in every department of the government, as well in the civil service as in the land and naval military service. They were found in Congress and among the keepers of the Capitol; in foreign missions; in each and all of the executive departments; in the judicial service; in the Post office, and among the agents for conducting Indian affairs. Upon probable suspicion they were promptly displaced by my predecessor, so far as they held their offices under executive authority, and their duties were confided to new and loyal successors. No complaints against that power or doubts of its wisdom were entertained in any quarter. I sincerely trust and believe that no such civil war is likely to occur again. I cannot doubt, however, that in whatever form, and on whatever occasion sedition can raise an effort to hinder, or embarrass, or defeat, the legitimate action of this government, whether by preventing the collection of revenue, or disturbing the public peace, or separating the States, or betraying the country to a foreign enemy, the power of removal from office by the Executive, as it has heretofore existed and been practiced, will be found indispensable. Under these circumstances, as a depository of the executive authority of the nation, I do not feel at liberty to unite with Congress in reversing it by giving my approval to the bill. At the early day when this question was settled, and, indeed, at the several periods when it has subsequently been agitated, the success of the Constitution of the United States, as a new and peculiar system of free representative government, was held doubtful in other countries, and was even a subject of patriotic apprehension among the American people themselves. A trial of nearly eighty years, through the vicissitudes of foreign conflicts and of civil war, is confidently regarded as having extinguished all such doubts and apprehensions for the future. During that eighty years the people of the United States have enjoyed a measure of security, peace, prosperity, and happiness, never surpassed by any nation. It cannot be doubted that the triumphant success of the Constitution is due to the wonderful wisdom with which the functions of government were distributed between the three principal departments—the legislative, the executive, and the judicial—and to the fidelity with which each has confined itself or been confined by the general voice of the nation within its peculiar and proper sphere. While a just, proper, and watchful jealousy of executive power constantly prevails, as it ought ever to prevail, yet it is equally true that an efficient Executive, capable, in the language of the oath prescribed to the President, of executing the laws and, within the sphere of executive action, of preserving, protecting, and defending the Constitution of the United States, is an indispensable security for tranquility at home, and peace, honor,

and safety abroad. Governments have been erected in many countries upon our model. If one or many of them have thus far failed in fully securing to their people the benefits which we have derived from our system, it may be confidently asserted that their misfortune has resulted from their unfortunate failure to maintain the integrity of each of the three great departments while preserving harmony among them all. Having at an early period accepted the Constitution in regard to the executive office in the sense in which it was interpreted with the concurrence of its founders, I have found no sufficient grounds in the arguments now opposed to that construction, or in any assumed necessity of the times, for changing those opinions. For these reasons I return the bill to the Senate, in which House it originated, for the further consideration of Congress which the Constitution prescribes. Insomuch as the several parts of the bill which I have not considered are matters chiefly of detail, and are based altogether upon the theory of the Constitution from which I am obliged to dissent, I have not thought it necessary to examine them with a view to make them an occasion of distinct and special objections. Whenever administration fails, or seems to fail, in securing any of the great ends for which republican government is established, the proper course seems to be to renew the original spirit and forms of the Constitution itself.

WASHINGTON, March 2, 1867.

National Debts.

The following official statement of the present indebtedness of nations is given in gold dollars, reckoning for foreign nations, where the statements were made in pounds, for convenience, five dollars to the pound sterling:

UNITED STATES.
Debt Bearing Coin Interest.

	October 1.	November 1.
Five per cent. Bonds	$198,431,350	$198,845,350
Six per cent. Bonds of 1867 and 1868	14,707,941	14,690,941
Six per cent. Bonds, '81	283,676,600	283,676,600
Six per cent. Five-Twenty Bonds	1,235,380,750	1,267,898,100
Navy Pension Fund	13,000,000	13,000,000
Total	$1,745,196,741	$1,778,110,991

Debt Bearing Currency Interest.

Six per cent. Bonds	$16,746,000	$18,042,000
Three Year Compound Interest Notes	78,839,580	62,558,940
Three Year Seven-Thirty Notes	365,489,100	334,607,700
Three per cent. Certificates		11,560,000
Total	$461,074,680	$426,768,640

Matured Debt not Presented for Payment.

Three Year Seven-Thirty Notes, due August 15, 1867	$4,250,000	$3,371,100
Compound Interest Notes, matured June 10, July 15, August 15, 1867	7,483,100	9,316,100
Bonds, Texas Indemnity	262,000	262,000
Treasury Notes, Act July 17, 1861, and prior thereto	164,511	163,661
Bonds, April 15, 1842	54,061	54,061
Treasury Notes, March 3, 1863	959,380	868,240
Temporary Loan	5,012,203	4,168,375
Certificates of Indebtedness	36,000	34,000
Total	$18,221,236	$18,237,538

Debt Bearing no Interest.

United States notes	$361,164,844	$357,154,844
Fractional currency	29,864,713	30,706,433
Gold certificates of deposit	14,867,820	14,514,206
Total	$405,897,377	$402,385,677
Total debt	$2,630,389,456	$2,625,502,848
Coin in Treasury	103,296,659	111,540,317
Currency in Treasury	31,813,349	22,458,080
Total	$135,112,009	$133,998,399
Amount of debt, less cash in Treasury	$2,495,277,446	$2,491,504,450
Reduction since last statement		$3,772,996

The foregoing is a correct statement of the public debt, as appears from the books and Treasurers' returns in the Department, on the 1st of November, 1867.
(Signed) HUGH McCULLOCH,
Secretary of the Treasury.

The aggregate debt of the States is estimated at $250,000,000.

BRITISH AND COLONIAL DEBTS.

Great Britain, funded and un-funded	$3,750,000,000		New South Wales	30,000,000
Bank of England	55,000,000		New Zealand	13,000,000
Antigua	125,000		Nova Scotia	4,850,000
British Columbia	625,000		Queensland	4,250,000
British Guiana	2,950,000		South Australia	4,350,000
British India	575,000,000		Pasmania	1,400,000
Canada	62,500,000		Trinidad	1,250,000
Cape of Good Hope	3,600,000		Victoria	42,500,000
Ceylon	2,250,000		Total	$4,570,695,000
Jamaica	3,930,000		Supposing the annual rate of	
Mauritius	5,000,000		interest, on the average, to	
Natal	1,250,000		be 4 per cent., the total	
New Brunswick	6,000,000		would be, premium	$182,827,800
Newfoundland	865,000			

OTHER FOREIGN DEBTS.

Argentine Confederation	$13,250,000		Italy	850,000,000
Austria	1,275,000,000		Mexico	317,500,000
Belgium	130,000,000		Morocco	2,200,000
Bolivia	5,000,000		Netherlands	420,000,000
Brazil	73,500,000		Peru	50,000,000
Chili	13,250,000		Portugal	100,000,000
Cuba	2,800,000		Prussia	200,000,000
Danubian Principalities	10,900,000		Russia	1,215,000,000
Denmark	25,000,000		Salvador	2,000,000
Equador	9,125,000		Spain	820,000,000
Egypt	75,000,000		Sweden and Norway	25,000,000
France	2,460,000,000		Turkey	355,000,000
New Grenada	37,500,000		Uruguay	5,000,000
Greece	75,000,000		Venezuela	33,471,750
Guatemala	500,000			
Hanover	36,013,705		Total	$8,960,260,455
Hanse Towns	23,250,000			

The National Domain.

What are called the "Land States and Territories" contain one billion and nearly five hundred million acres. The last report of the Commissioner of the General Land Office gives the number of acres of public lands surveyed up to June 30th, 1866, as 474,160,551, and the number of acres not yet surveyed as 991,308,249. Only the merest fraction of our public lands is settled upon, and the whole vast area is open for free homesteads. The following table gives the area of the Land States and Territories:

	Acres.	Sq. miles.
Wisconsin	34,511,360	53,924
Iowa	35,228,800	55,045
Minnesota	53,459,840	83,531
Kansas	52,043,520	81,318
Nebraska	48,636,800	75,995
California	120,947,840	188,981
Nevada	52,184,960	81,539
Oregon	60,975,360	95,274
Washington Territory	44,796,160	69,994
Colorado Territory	66,880,000	104,500
Utah Territory	68,084,480	106,382

Arizona Territory.....	80,730,240	126,140
New Mexico Territory.	77,538,640	121,201
Dacotah Territory.....	153,982,080	240,597
Idaho Territory.......	58,196,480	90,932
Montana Territory....	92,016,640	148,776
Missouri	41,824,000	65,350
Alabama	32,462,080	50,722
Mississippi...........	30,179,840	47,156
Louisiana	26,461,440	41,346
Arkansas	33,406,720	52,198
Florida	37,931,520	59,268
Ohio	25,576,960	39,964
Indiana	21,637,760	33,809
Michigan	36,128,640	58,451
Illinois...............	35,462,400	55,410
Indian Territory......	41,154,240	68,991
Alaska................	238,000,000	371,875
Total 1,703,468,800	2,661,670	

New York has 46,000 square miles. Nevada has twice as many square miles as New York, and Kansas and Nebraska have each nearly twice as many. Colorado and Utah are more than twice as large as New York; Montana more than three times, California more than four times, and Dacotah more than five times. 7,000,000 acres of public lands have been disposed of during the past year. There are now 37,000 miles of completed railroad in this country, which, since their commencement is at the rate of 1,000 miles a year. In course of construction 17,860 miles of railroad. For these roads completed, and for those in contemplation, the government has granted over 184,800,000 acres of land, and to the Pacific Roads over 24,000 acres of land.

Growth of Cereals in 1867.

From the reports to the Agricultural Bureau at Washington, the following statements respecting the growth of cereals in the United States in 1867, are compiled:

Wheat.—While few localities have exhibited large yields per acre, and some have caused comparative disappointment by an average product less than was confidently expected at harvesting, the sum total in bushels will exceed that of any harvest hitherto gathered in this country. It will surmount the figures of last year by forty to fifty millions; but will not reach the amount which should have been attained, upon the ratio of increase made between 1850 and 1860, by twenty millions. As an approximate estimate, upon present data, 220,000,000 to 225,000,000 bushels may be received as the crop of the entire country for 1867. In some of the Eastern States, in Texas, and Kansas, the figures scarcely equal those of last year; in Texas the reduction is fully half. In the Northwestern States the increase is variable and moderate, as follows: Illinois, 7 per cent.; Minnesota, 8 per cent.; Michigan, 13; Iowa, 15; Wisconsin, 16. The belt of States in the Ohio valley, which suffered so unusually last year, and made but four, five, six, or eight-tenths of a crop respectively, and averaged together but half a crop, have made a heavy increase upon those figures. The largest is made by Ohio, 130 per cent., as might be expected, the deficiency having been greatest there; Indiana is placed at 85 per cent. increase; West Virginia, 51; Kentucky, 38. In the Atlantic States the greatest deficiency last year was in Pennsylvania, and the increase there this year is 57 per cent. The Southern States show a material enlargement in the area of wheat, from an evident intention to become more nearly self-supporting and independent than formerly. This is particularly noticeable in Virginia, Georgia, Alabama, Tennessee, and Arkansas. The quality of wheat is greatly superior to that of last year; it is almost universally sound and dry, but in many localities there may be found from a third to a half deficient in weight, lacking in plumpness, or slightly shriveled, and passing as No. 2, being less than 58 pounds to the bushel. There is also a greater tendency to cleanliness and care in preparing the grain for the market. High prices and the marked discrimination of buyers are doing good service in this direction. Old wheat will show a reduction as compared with last year, when the old stock was also small. The stock of old wheat has not been reduced so low for many years, if ever.

Oats.—The yield of oats has proved less than was expected in Maine, Vermont, New York, Virginia, Mississippi, Texas, Tennessee, and Kentucky; in Michigan, no increase over last year is reported, but most of the Western States have made a comparative gain. As in the case of corn and wheat, the majority of the Southern States added to their area in oats, and have a larger product. The quality and yield are a fair average in Ohio, Indiana, and Illinois; in Wisconsin, Minnesota, and Iowa, they are generally of superior quality, and have threshed out very satisfactorily. The aggregate estimate will exceed 280,000,000 bushels—about three per cent. above that of 1866.

Rye.—This grain has made a very uniform growth and yielded an average product, with few exceptions. The report indicates a larger total product than last year, and the quality is uniform in most of the States. Those which show a slight depreciation are Maine, New Hampshire, Vermont, Rhode Island, Delaware, Virginia, Tennessee, and Nebraska. In the Southern States the crop is generally good. The estimate for all the States excepting those on the Pacific is 21,900,000 bushels. This is an increase of four per cent. over the product of last year.

Barley.—The barley crop is slightly deficient—about a half million bushels, or four per cent. as compared with the crop of last year. Illinois, Kansas, Pennsylvania, New York, and all the Eastern States, except Massachusetts and Connecticut, share in the deficiency. New York being the principal grower, producing nearly forty per cent. of the crop, a deficiency there of thirteen per cent. is equivalent to half a million bushels. The comparative losses and gains of all the other States together will balance each other.

Corn.—West Virginia, Kentucky, Ohio, Indiana, and Illinois, a belt of which suffered last year by the winter-killing of wheat, were affected by a drought of considerable severity, which will cause a heavy reduction of the general aggregate. The tenor of the reports for this district differ little from those of September. To offset this deficiency in part, an increase, ranging from 7 to 17 per cent., is reported for the States of Michigan, Wisconsin, Minnesota, Iowa, and Kansas. Delaware, Virginia, and North Carolina have small crops, and Pennsylvania is slightly deficient. The States further north and east have generally shown a slight increase, and the Southern States have made a comparatively heavy increase. The quality is uniformly good, leaving no doubt that the value of the entire crop, after deducting the deficiency in the Ohio valley, and allowing for an increase in almost all the other States, will be greater, not only in cash, but in the intrinsic life-sustaining and pork-producing power, than that of last year. As the deficiency occurs in the centre of the commercial pork-packing district, it will affect unduly the market, both for corn and pork, making the scarcity more prominent, while the comparative abundance of the South will greatly reduce the demand upon the West.

Religious Denominations in the United States.

The following statistics of churches and religious denominations in the United States, are from the report of Rev. Henry B. Smith, D.D., of the Union Theological Seminary, New York, to the Evangelical Alliance in session at Amsterdam, in 1867:

NUMBER OF CHURCHES, ETC., IN THE UNITED STATES.

	Churches.	Communicants.
Roman Catholics..	3,800	4,000,000
Methodists........	10,460	2,000,000
Baptists...........	17,220	1,690,000
Presbyterians	5,000	700,000
Lutherans.........	2,900	323,800
Congregationalists.	2,780	267,400
Protestant Episcopalians..........	2,300	161,200
German Reformed	1,100	210,000
Dutch Reformed..	440	60,000

United Brethren, about 3,000 societies. Moravians about 12,000 communicants. Unitarians about 300 churches. Universalists include about 600,000 of the population. Friends or Quakers, orthodox, about 54,000 members. Friends or Quakers, Hicksites, about 40,000 members.

Freemasonry in the World.

It is estimated that at present, in round numbers, there are 1,250,000 Free and Accepted Masons scattered upon the face of the globe. Of this number some 150,000 are in England; 100,000 in Scotland, and 50,000 in Ireland. There are 60,000 on the Continent of Europe; 800,000 in the United States, and 50,000 in other parts of the world.

Odd Fellowship in the United States.

The Grand Secretary of the Order in the United States, reports the membership at the present time to be 217,886, there having been an accession the past year of 33,764 members. The receipts for the past year have been $1,965,718.1, of which $1,760,123.56 were from bodies under the jurisdiction of the Grand Lodge, and $505,593.45 from bodies under the jurisdiction of the Grand Encampment. The total relief dispensed in the same time was $690,675.97, of which $625,820.25 were by the bodies under the jurisdiction of the Grand Lodge. The relief dispensed by the bodies under the jurisdiction of the Grand Encampment was $64,855 12.

Gold Yield of the Country.

The Gold yield of this country for the year 1867, is estimated as follows: Montana, $10,000,000; Idaho, $6,000,000; Oregon, $2,000,000; Colorado, 5,000,000; Nevada, $10,000,000; California, $25,000,000, and miscellaneous, $5,000,000. Total, $63,000,000.

St. Thomas.

This island in the West Indies will become the property of the United States so soon as Congress ratifies the treaty for its purchase, and makes the requisite appropriation. It is situate Lat. 18° 20′ 24″ N., Long. 64° 55′ 45″ W. Greatest length from E. to W., 17 miles; greatest breadth about 4½ miles. It contains 45 square miles, and 28,800 acres. Only about 2,500 acres are under cultivation, the soil being sandy and not fertile. Population, 12,800.

The number of births registered in London and twelve other large towns during the week ending October 19, 1867, was 4,397. Those in London alone were 2,171. The excess of births over deaths in the United Kingdom is now more than a thousand a day. In England it is 250,000 a year: in Ireland, 70,000; in Scotland, 40,000; and Wales makes up the balance. Allowing for emigration, the rate of increase is now estimated at 200,000 a year. The emigration from the United Kingdom in 52 years has exceeded six millions, and the decrease in Ireland during the last twenty-two years from this cause is 2,738,099. In 1845 the population of that country was estimated to be 8,295,061, in 1857 the estimate is 5,556,962.

Ohio is now the chief wool growing State, having 6,608,052 sheep, out of 32,650,797 in the whole United States. In 1866 the live stock of Ohio was valued at $151,000,000, which is greater than any other State except New York.

Tobacco Crop of the United States.

Statistics of the Tobacco Crop of the United States are very imperfectly kept; those for Kentucky and the Ohio River especially so. It is difficult to arrive at accurate figures, but the following will be found approximately correct:

STATEMENT OF RECEIPTS OF HOGSHEADS AT SEABOARD MARKETS IN FIVE YEARS.

	N. York.	N. Orlns.	Virginia.	Baltimore.	Total.
1863,	68,983	....	....	52,043	121,026
1864,	132,701	...	....	53,255	185,956
1865,	87,112	....	35,000	45,362	167,474
1866,	61,169	14,064	26,822	47,789	149,824
1867,*	82,322	13,164	41,640	66,132	203,268

* Two months partly estimated.

STATEMENT OF INSPECTIONS.

Virginia, for year ending
Oct. 1st, at Richmond.. 26,374
Petersburgh, etc.......... 17,404—43,778
Maryland and Ohio, for year
ending Nov. 1st, at Balt.. 42,504
Ohio...................... 21,606—64,110
Kentucky, etc., for year ending Nov. 1st, at Louisville 41,420
At Cincinnati, St. Louis, etc., estimated,......... 30,000
Total,.................... 179,318

ESTIMATES FOR 1867.
The estimates of the crop of 1867 are as follows:
Virginia, hogsheads................ 45,000
Maryland,.......................... 27,000
Ohio,.............................. 9,000
Kentucky,.......................... 68,000

Total for 1867, hhds............. 149,000
Estimates of the crop of Seed Leaf Tobacco for three years:

	1865.	1866.	1867.
Massachusetts and Connecticut, (cases)......	25,000	30,000	20,000
New York "	8,000	6,000	1,500
Pennsylvania "	8,000	5,000	2,000
Ohio, "	12,000	20,000	10,000
Western States, (cases).	5,000	5,000	2,000
Total cases........	58,000	66,000	35,500

It will be observed, that both in "Leaf and "Seed Leaf," a much smaller crop was raised in 1867, than in 1866; upon which prices have advanced from 2 to 5 cents per pound. The following is a statement of the

EXPORTS OF TOBACCO FROM THE UNITED STATES, FOR THE YEAR ENDING NOV. 1, 1867.

To	Hhds.	Cases.	Bales.	Cer's & tcs.	Stems hhds.	Bales.	Pkgs. & bxs.	Manf'd lbs.
Great Britain..........	24,000	2,722	232	614	86	....	1,368	1,368,776
Sweden.................	342	....	....	....	20	....	....	....
Germany...............	50,735	38,570	19,642	8	4,748	924	735	293,450
Belgium...............	6,553	891	13	....	....	....	....	70,171
Holland...............	27,310	279	....	2	1,774	....	18	17,276
Italy.................	20,026	21	....	....	....	....	29	49,876
France................	16,841	25	99	....	154	....	....	18,215
Spain, Gibraltar, &c...	11,870	1,935	20	....	....	....	1,029	663,028
Mediterranean.........	1,096	61	....	....	....	....	51	72,605
Austria...............	14	....	....	....	....	....	....	....
Africa, &c............	2,052	371	1,213	....	....	....	691	178,940
China, India, &c......	....	2,662	97	15	....	....	320	3,142
Australia, &c........	100	902	20	50	....	....	2,714	3,995,437
B. N. Am. Provinces..	712	318	194	....	....	....	6,438	342,733
South America........	249	1,823	3,375	24	....	....	973	702,145
West Indies...........	929	1,411	7,695	8	....	....	790	822,762
East Indies...........	7	372	....	....	....	....	....	....
Mexico................	8	76	231	....	....	....	....	4,571
Honolulu, &c..........	....	234	....	....	....	....	58	....
All others............	25	....	....	....	....	....	50	10,513
Total since...........	165,560	52,675	32,831	716	6,801	924	15,276	8,646,142

The following table indicates the ports from which the above exports have been shipped:

From	Hhds.	Cases.	Bales.	Tcs. & crns.	Stems hhds.	bls.	Bxs. & Pkgs.	Lbs.
New York.............	85,040	47,248	28,797	425	2,668	924	5,575	8,211,548
Baltimore.............	68,145	132	....	4	4,133	....	142	290,981
Boston................	1,618	4,783	3,659	65	....	....	8,152	4,516
Portland..............	34	14	....	....	....	....	563	....
New Orleans...........	9,769	....	263	....	....	....	8	....
Philadelphia..........	28	31	47	....	....	....	....	139,097
San Francisco.........	....	498	65	....	....	....	369	....
Virginia..............	926	29	....	222	....	....	467	....
Total since Nov. 1..	165,560	52,675	32,831	716	6,801	924	15,276	8,646,142

Prices during the year 1867, show a general advance of 20 per cent., in consequence of diminished growth, an active export, and considerable speculation. The diminished growth is attributable to disorganized labor, high rates of wages, and unfavorable climatic influences.

IMPORTANT EVENTS IN 1867.

JANUARY.

1. Napoleon makes a very pacific speech to the Diplomatic Corps.

2. Heavy battle between Cretans and Turks, and defeat of the latter.—Earthquake in Algeria; shocks also felt at Spa, Belgium.

3. Congress reassembles after holidays.

4. Ohio ratifies proposed 14th Constitutional Amendment.

5. Financial panic at Havana abates.

7. President vetoes District Suffrage bill. —Alabama rejects the proposed 14th Constitutional Amendment.

8. Ashley's House resolution of Impeachment referred to Judiciary Committee—109 to 66.—Great Jackson banquet in Washington; President makes a speech.—Kentucky rejects proposed 14th Constitutional Amendment. — Missouri ratifies proposed 14th Constitutional Amendment.

9. Virginia rejects proposed 14th Constitutional Amendment.—Large list of pardoned confederates sent in to Senate.

10. Congress passes bill for universal suffrage in the Territories.—New York ratifies Constitutional Amendment.—The Porte issues an important belligerent note to all the powers about trouble between Turkey and Greece.

11. Kansas ratifies Constitutional Amendment.

12. The Porte calls 150,000 men into service.

13. Great fire in Yokohama, Japan—loss, $5,000,000; and in Janesville, Wisconsin—loss, $1,200,000.—Capital of the Canadian Confederation removed from Ottawa to Quebec.

14. Violent tempest in Bay of Naples.

15. Ice breaks on lake in Regent Park, London, and forty-one skaters drowned.— First detachment of French troops from Mexico arrive in France.—Illinois ratifies the Constitutional Amendment.—West Virginia ratifies Constitutional Amendment.

16. West Washington Market, New York, almost wholly consumed by fire, with immense destruction of provisions and produce. — Commencement of terribly cold term. Ferry-boats in North and East River, detained for hours in ice drift.—Minnesota, West Virginia, and Maine ratify Constitutional Amendment. — Minister King, at Rome, is "invited" to remove the American chapel outside the city walls.

17. Greatest snow storm in New York since 1856. Pennsylvania ratifies proposed Constitutional Amendment.

19. The Porte agrees to evacuate forts held by Turks in principality of Servia.

20. Napoleon issues an important decree relating to the Chamber, press, and people. All the members of his Cabinet tender resignations; but six are not accepted.—Another great snow storm, general through the North.—Indians troublesome; and 8,000 United States troops ordered to the plains.

22. Destructive fires in Vicksburg, Mobile, and New Orleans.—Prince Alfred declines to accept the yacht Henrietta as a gift. —Settlement of difficulties, growing out of firing upon Italian vessels, between Turkey and Italy, Turkey paying indemnity.—Rappahannock case settled, by Board of Admiralty in London, in favor of United States. —Nevada ratifies proposed Constitutional Amendment.

23. President approves bill authorizing future meetings of Congress March 4.—East River bridged by ice; thousands of people cross on foot.—Wholesale seizure of steamers at Mobile for revenue infractions.—Indiana ratifies proposed Constutional Amendment.

25. The Danish formally annexed to the German Confederation.—President vetoes the Colorado admission bill.

29. President vetoes the Nebraska admission bill.

FEBRUARY.

3. Serious labor riots in France and Belgium.

4. Capital punishment abolished in Italy.

6. Evacuation of the City of Mexico by French forces.—Delaware rejects proposed Constitutional Amendment.—Louisiana rejects proposed Constitutional Amendment.

7. Mr. George Peabody announces his gift of $1,200,000 for educational purposes in the South and Southwest. Wisconsin ratifies proposed Constitutional Amendment. — Rhode Island ratifies proposed Constitutional Amendment.

8. Nebraska admitted to the Union.—Outbreak of Fenian disturbances in South of Ireland.

9. Balize, at Southwest Pass, Mississippi River, totally destroyed by fire—Destructive fires in Mobile; loss $900,000.

11. Reform procession of 20,000 men in London.

14. Napoleon makes an important speech to the Corps Legislatif.

15. Official announcement in Parliament that the rebellion in Ireland is ended.

18. The Swatara brings John H. Surratt to Washington.

20. Birth of third daughter of Princess of Wales.

24. Communication between Vera Cruz and City of Mexico suspended.

28. Juarez declares amnesty in Mexico for political offences previous to date. Defeat of Miramon by Escobedo in two engagements near Zacatecas confirmed.

MARCH.

1. Opening of the new Academy of Music in New York.

2. President vetoes Reconstruction bill, No. 1.—Five magistrates in Norfolk, Va.,

arrested for refusing to receive negro testimony.

3. Steamship Andalusia, of New York, burned at sea; cargo and five lives lost.

4. Thirty-ninth Congress adjourned, and Fortieth Congress assembled.—Important changes, growing out of reform movement, in British Cabinet.

5. Attempt of 1,000 negroes to vote, under Reconstruction act, at Alexandria Va., and votes not received.

6. Terrible earthquake at Aletekene, Levant; 1,000 lives lost.—Fenian agitations in Ireland renewed.

7. Ashley, of Ohio, again introduces impeachment resolutions in the House.

9. Reorganization of Derby (British) ministry.

10. Attempt to assassinate Victor Emanuel, of Italy, near Milan.—Marshal Bazaine and the last of the French troops leave Mexico.

11. Ireland quiet again, and Fenian bands dispersed.

13. General Grant issues order assigning commanders to the Southern military districts.—Steamer Mercury sinks in Arkansas River; 25 lives lost.

14. Great cable banquet in Liverpool.

20. Labor riots renewed in France.—Massachusetts ratifies proposed Constitutional Amendment.

21. Gathering of Fenians at St. Albans, Vt.—Hostilities between Russia and Bokara suspended.

22. Maximilian at Queretaro tries to force his way through the Liberal lines, and is repulsed with great loss; sends commissioners to Juarez offering to surrender on conditions, which are declined; Miramon mortally wounded.

23. President vetoes Supplementary Reconstruction bill.—Winter Garden Theatre, New York, destroyed by fire.

25. Opening of Chicago lake tunnel.

27. The North German Parliament adopts the new constitution.

28. Insurrection at Port au Prince, Hayti, resulting in abdication of President Geffrard and accession of Salnave.

30.—Announcement in Washington of the Russian cession of Alaska to the United States.—Congress adjourns to July 4.

APRIL.

1. Democratic victory in Connecticut State Election.—Inauguration of Paris Exposition.

2. Puebla, Mexico, surrender to Diaz; 63 Imperialists shot.

4. Lindell House, St. Louis, burnt; loss $1,000,000.—Coalpit explosion, Chesterfield County, Va., 69 lives lost.

5. Secretary Seward sends a messenger to Juarez, to ask that Maximilian may be spared.

8. Abolition of slavery in Brazil; to take full effect in 20 years.

9. Senate confirms the Alaska treaty.—Deed conveys site in City Hall Park for N. Y. Post Office.—Commencement of Fenian trials in Dublin.

12. Liberal victory of San Cristobal in Mexico.—Garibaldi issues a revolutionary proclamation.

13. Mexican Liberals capture Puebla.

16. Gov. Fenton vetoes Broadway, N. Y., Surface Railroad bill.

19. Cretan victory over Turks at Heraclion.

22. Arrival of Japanese embassy at New York.—30,000 tailors strike in Paris.—Tailors' strike in London.

27. Agreement between France and Prussia that the Fortress of Luxemburg shall be dismantled.

29. *Coup d' etat* in Bogota; Mosquera proclaimed Dictator.

MAY.

3. President receives Japanese Commissioners. Argument in United States Supreme Court in the Georgia and Mississippi injunction (Reconstruction) cases.—Eight hour riots in Chicago.—20,000 Liberals besiege and bombard the city of Mexico.-Prussia accepts the proposition for the neutralization of Luxemburg.

6. Great Reform meeting in Hyde Park, London.—Maximilian attempts to cut his way through the Liberal lines at Queretaro, and is repulsed.

8. Meeting of the Peace Conference in London.

9. General strike movement in the United States and abroad.-Negro riot at Richmond, Virginia.

11. Completion of the Russian telegraph to the mouth of the Amoor River, Siberia.

13. Jefferson Davis admitted to bail. $100,000, in U. S. District Court, at Richmond.

14. Kelly-Radical riot at Memphis, Tenn.

15. Russia ratifies the Alaska cession treaty.—A large number of insurgents arrested at Madrid.—Queretaro captured and Maximilian taken prisoner.

17. Attorney-General Stanberry's opinion on the disfranchising clauses of Reconstruction Act sent to the District commanders.—George Bancroft appointed U. S. Minister to Berlin.

18. Napoleon and King William of Prussia, sign the Luxemburg treaty.—City of London votes £500 for a statue to George Peabody.

20. The Sultan grants the title of king to the Viceroy of Egypt.

21. Steamer Wisconsin burned near Cape Vincent, Lake Ontario, 30 lives lost.-Steamship Santiago de Cuba, from Nicaragua to New York, ashore at Atlantic City, N. J., 7 lives lost.

22. Derby race in England: "Hermit" comes in winner in the midst of a snow storm.

23. Queen's proclamation declaring the Dominion of Canada.

24. Gen Pope orders the districting of Georgia and Alabama for registration.

JUNE.

2. President starts on Southern journey.

3. General Sheridan removes Gov. Welles, of La.—Austria begins to fortify Vienna.

4. New York State Constitutional Convention sits at Albany.-Departure from New York of raft "Nonpariel," to cross the Atlantic.

5. Lord Monck appointed Viceroy of the Dominion of Canada.

6. Alexander of Russia, narrowly escapes assassination in Paris—Sheridan appoints B. F. Flanders, Governor of Louisiana. —Frightful boiler explosion in Philadelphia, 20 lives lost.

7. Forcible ejection of Gov. Welles, of Louisiana.

8. Francis Joseph, of Austria, crowned king of Hungary.—Alex. R. Rangabe, first Greek Minister to the United States, arrives at New York.

9. Mosquera, dictator of Colombia, taken prisoner at Bogota.

10. Hartford Carpet Co's buildings burned at Tariffville, Conn.; loss $1,190,000.

11. Egypt becomes a separate sovereignty.

12. Mexican Liberals capture Santa Anna at Sisal.

13. Attack of U. S. Gunboats Hartford and Wyoming on the Island of Formosa, to avenge the murder of the crew of the bark Rover, wrecked March 12.—Steamboat George Sharkey sinks in Mississippi river, several lives lost.

18. Formidable "anti-Popery" riots in Birmingham, England.—Important Cabinet meeting on Reconstruction, and proceedings officially published.

19. Execution of Maximilian at Queretaro.—Burning of American Varieties Theatre, in Philadelphia; 12 men killed and several injured by a falling wall.

20. President's proclamation making public the Russian-American Alaska treaty.—General Longstreet pardoned.—City of Mexico surrenders to the Liberals.

21. President's reception in New York, on his way to Boston, to lay corner stone of Masonic Hall.—Attempted insurrection in Rome.—The Porte refuses to accede to request of the great powers on the Candian Question.-Alexander suspends confiscations in Poland.

23. Yellow Fever appears in New Orleans.

27. Vera Cruz surrenders to the Liberals.

29. Grand celebration of the 18th centenary of St Peter's martyrdom at Rome.

30. Earthquake at Salvador.

JULY.

1. Distribution of prizes at Paris Exposition.—Address of 490 Bishops to the Pope.

3. Congress assembles in extraordinary session.

4. Corner-stone of New Tammany Hall. laid in New York.—Dunderberg departs from New York for France.

5. Diplomatic relations between France and Mexico suspended.

6. Ismael Pacha, King of Egypt, arrives in London,

11. Reciprocity treaty between United States and the Hawaiian Islands.—Discovery of conspiracy against the life of Queen Isabella, and 2,000 arrests in Madrid.

12. Sultan arrives in London.—Twelve

more of Maximilian's generals shot at Queretaro.

15. House of Commons passes Reform bill.—Napoleon warns Victor Emanuel of the threatening movements of Garibaldi. Juarez's proclamation to Mexico.

18. Great banquet to the Sultan in London.

19. President vetoes Supplementary Reconstruction Bill.—Garibaldi announces that the time has come to liberate Rome.

20. Congress adjourns to Nov. 21.

22. France abolishes imprisonment for debt. Re-establishment of the Provincial Assembly in Russia.

23. Radical riot at Rodgersville, Tenn.; 2 men killed, and 37 wounded.—Poland absorbed as a province of the Russian Empire.

24. Woman suffrage proposition rejected by the New York State Constitutional Convention, 125 to 19.—Radical riot at Knoxville, Tenn.

25. Candian war ends.—Radical Convention at Charleston, S. C.

26. Raft "Nonpareil," from New York, June 14, arrives at Southampton.—Napoleon asks King William of Prussia to surrender the Danish districts of North Schleswig to Denmark.

27. State dinner by Napoleon to Admiral Farragut.

30. General Sheridan removes Governor Throckmorton, of Texas.—More than 100 men killed in a mine explosion in Moravia.

AUGUST

1. Election for State officers and members of Congress in Tennessee; Brownlow re-elected.—Radical (Botts) State Convention at Richmond, Va.—Sheridan "readjusts" the New Orleans Board of Aldermen.

2. Sharp fight with and defeat of Indians near Fort Phil. Kearney, Nebraska.—King William of Prussia by proclamation assumes the duties of sovereign of the North German States.—Bott's Convention at Richmond adjourns.

3. The Dunderberg arrives at Cherbourg in 13 days 17 hours from New York.—Cholera report in Italy shows 32,074 deaths from January to July.

5. Kentucky State election; Democratic victory.—President Johnson asks Secretary Stanton to resign; he refuses.—Napoleon addresses the foreign Commissioners to the Exposition.

6. House of Lords passes the Reform bill,

9. Treaty of Peace between Russia and Bokara.

11. Surrat's trial begins in Washington.

12. Stanton suspended, and Gen. Grant appointed Secretary of War, ad interim.

14. "Dexter," at Buffalo races, makes the shortest time on record, in 2.17¼.

15. Turkey refuses intervention in the Candian affair.—Great rain storm along the whole Atlantic coast.

16. Internationa. co-operative Congress forbidden to assemble in Paris.

17. Gen. Sheridan relieved at New Orleans; Gen. Mower left in command.

19. National Labor Congress meets at Chicago.

20. Close of the U. S. Legation at Rome. —Salzberg, conference between Emperors of France and Austria.

21. Spanish authority restored in Catalonia and other insurrectionary districts.

23. St. Petersburg ovation to Farragut.—End of three days' fight near Fort Hayes, Kansas, and U. S. troops defeated.

24. U. S. Attorney-General's opinion on Reconstruction Acts.—The Mexican Liberal forces enter Monteray.

26. Gen. Sickles replaced by General Canby at Charleston.

28. First train over the Mount Cenis (Alps) railway.

29. Gen. Grant instructs District commanders not to reinstate deposed civil officers.

SEPTEMBER.

2. Hawaian Legislature passes the U. S. Reciprocity Treaty.—The Porte announces the close of the Candian War.

3. President's Proclamation concerning the maintenance of Civil Law in the South. —National Congress of Fenians at Cleveland, O.—Vermont State Election, (Repub.) —N. Y. Steamship George Cromwell ashore on the Florida coast.

4. North Carolina Radical State Convention at Raleigh.—California State Election; Democratic victory.

6. Railway train thrown into Naugatuck River, near Thomaston, Conn.; 10 persons drowned.—Breakage of dam of West Hartford, Conn., Reservoir; great damage. Accident on Fair Grounds near Burlington, Vt.; Amphitheatre seats break down, injuring more than 50 people, some fatally.

8. President issues Amnesty Proclamation.

9. Maine State Election; Republican; Governor Chamberlain re-elected by a majority reduced 16,000 since 1866.—Boiler explosion in 28th street, N. Y.; 4 killed, six injured.—Radical Peace Congress at Geneva, Garibaldi present.

10. Telegraph communication by Cable with Cuba.

11. American-Canadian 6 mile boat-race at Springfield, Mass.; America wins in 29 m., 38 sec.—St. Leger English race won by "Achievement;" stakes £5,235.

13. Revolutionists fight Salnave's troops at Fort Biasson, Hayti.

14. Turkish general amnesty to Greek insurgents.

16. Great fire at St. Pierre, Miquelon; 200 houses destroyed.

17. Dedication of Antietam National cemetery.

18. New Constitution adopted by popular vote in Maryland.

19. Sinking of steamer Dean Richmond by the Vanderbilt in Hudson River—serious Fenian disturbance in Manchester, England.

20. Peace declared with the Brules, Ogallallas and Sioux, at North Platte, Nebraska.

22. Garibaldi proclaims revolution; counter proclamation by Victor Emanuel—

Brownlow summons troops to Nashville, Tenn., "to enforce the franchise law."

23. Stephen R. Mallory, ex-Secretary Confederate Navy, pardoned.

24. Arrest of Garibaldi while crossing the Roman frontier—France sends troops to Rome—Conflict in Limerick, Ireland, between troops and people—Assembling of the Pan-Anglican Synod in Lambeth Palace—New York Constitutional Convention adjourns to November 12.

26. Garibaldian uprising in various parts of Italy.

27. Election on question of Convention in Louisiana—Burning of New Orleans—Philadelphia steamship Tioga at sea; passengers and crew saved.

30. Negro riots in Savannah, Ga.—Garibaldi refuses to give parole not to engage in hostilities against the Papal States.

OCTOBER.

1. Reconstruction election on question of Convention in Alabama—Cyclone at Hong Kong; several ships wrecked and damage on shore $10,000,000—Garibaldi sent to Caprera; escapes and is re-captured at Leghorn and sent back.

2. Alexandria demands the cession of Candia to Greece.

3. Democratic State Convention at Albany —R. M. T. Hunter, ex-Confederate Secretary War, pardoned—Destructive gale and flood at Galveston, Texas—Paraguayans defeated by Brazilians near Humiata, with loss of 500 men—Garibaldians fight with Papal troops in the province of Viterbo—City of Hamburgh refuses to join the Zollverein—Whiskey riots in Philadelphia.

6. Engagement near Abrazzi frontier and Papal troops driven back by the Garibaldians to Rome—Sanguinary fight between Turks and Montenegrins on Turkish frontier.

7. Tornado at Matamoras, Mexico; loss $3,000,000—Presidential electors meet at Sinola, Mexico, and cast entire vote for Benito Juarez.

8. State Elections in Iowa, (Rep.) Pennsylvania, (Dem.) and Ohio (Rep.)—Ohio gives a majority of 38,353 against negro suffrage.

9. Maryland Democratic State Convention—The Italian "Party of Action" defeated near Montali Vieta—Gale on coast of Labrador, 30 vessels and 40 lives lost.

10. Discovery of forged U. S. Bonds in large quantities.

11. General Mendoza's revolt against President Acosta, Colombia.

14. Papal-Garibaldian battle near Verola; Papal troops defeated.

16. Fenian alarm in England; troops and gunboats dispatched to Ireland.

18. Garibaldi escapes from Caprera.

19. Nerola and Orte, towns occupied by Garibaldians, carried by Papal troops—Explosion at Hoosac Tunnel, Mass.; 13 lives lost.

22. Virginia election on Convention question.

24. Election in West Virginia—Rebellion quelled in Venezuela—Fight within half a

mile of Rome; attack on Viterbo; Garibaldians repul·ed.

25. Fight near Monte Rotondo; Garibaldians victorious.

27. French fleet at Cherbourg starts for Italy—Victor Emanuel issues proclamation denouncing Garibaldi—Marriage of George I. of Greece to daughter of Duke Constantine at St. Petersburg.

28. French troops from Toulon land at Civita Vecchia—British Abyssinian expedition, 12 ships, leaves Aden for Zolla.

29. Elections in Florida and Georgia on Convention question—Hurricane at St. Thomas; 83 vessels sunk or ashore; 1014 lives lost; and $8,000,000 damage to property on land.

30. Hurricane at St. Domingo; 200 lives lost—Italian army crosses Papal frontiers; Garibaldi ordered to disarm and disband his forces—Santa Anna sentenced to eight years banishment from Mexico, and goes to Havana.

31. Bavaria and Wurtemburg join the Zollverein.

NOVEMBER.

1. Arrival of French troops at Rome.

2. Dickens' farewell dinner in London—Successful debut of Miss Kellogg in Her Majesty's Theatre—Gen. Sherman's order announcing Indian war at an end.

3. Garibaldi near Tivoli; is beaten by Papal troops; he retreats to Monte Rotondo, where battle is renewed, and he is again beaten with a loss of 1200 killed and wounded and 2000 prisoners—Hurricane at St. Thomas. W. I.; 5 steamers and 60 vessels wrecked; 1014 lives lost; and town nearly destroyed by tornado.

4. Garibaldi and his son captured on the way to Florence.

5. Elections in New York, (Dem.) New Jersey, (Dem.) Massachusetts, (Rep.) Maryland, (Dem.) Michigan, (Rep.) Minnesota, (Rep.) 1298 against negro suffrage, Kansas, (Rep.) 8523 against negro suffrage and 9692 against female suffrage, Wisconsin, (Rep.)—Serious bread riots at Exeter, England—Alabama reconstruction Constitutional Convention meet at Montgomery.

6. Garibaldi imprisoned in Piedmont—Italian troops recalled from Papal territory—Conservative State Convention at Columbia, S. C.—James A. Seddon, ex-Confederate Secretary of War, pardoned.

7. Hurricane at Porto Rico; 200 lives lost—Tornado at Tortola.

8. Boiler explosion at Pittsburgh, Pa.; 12 killed and 30 injured—Colliery explosion in Glamorgan, Wales, more than 300 lives lost—Formal transfer of Alaska at New Archangel to Gen. Rosseau on behalf of United States.

12. Severe earthquake in Jamaica.

14. Meteoric showers—Mount Vesuvius in volcanic action—Denmark concludes treaty ceding and selling to U. S. for $11,500,000, the W. I. islands St. Thomas, San Juan and Santa Cruz.

15. Reconstruction Convention election in Florida and Arkansas.

18. Maximilian's remains delivered to Austrian admiral Tegethoff—Earthquake at Porto Rica—Emperor Napoleon's speech to Corps Legislatif, "accepting frankly" the change of situation across the Rhine.

19. Election on question of Convention in North Carolina, South Carolina and Mississippi—Queen's speech to Parliament.

20. Great Western Railway workshops burnt at Hamilton, C. W.

21. Congress re-assembles in extraordinary session—Gen. Mower makes sweeping removals of civil officers in New Orleans—Collision on Cincinnati and Dayton (O.) railway at Lockland; entire train consumed and 5 passengers burned to death.

22. Jeff. Davis returns to Richmond.

23. 299 arrivals at New York of sailing and steam vessels, the largest number ever reported in one day—Execution of Fenians Allen, Larkin and Gould at Manchester, Eng.—The Pope orders release of all captive Garibaldians.

25. House Judiciary Committee reports in favor of impeachment; 2 minority reports—Glycerine explosion at South Bergen, N. J., 9 killed and several injured.

DISTINGUISHED DEAD.

JANUARY.

6. Marquis de Larochejaquelin, senior member of the Chamber of Deputies, at Pecq, France.

11. Alexander Smith, poet, at Edinburg.

20. Nathaniel Parker Willis, poet, author and editor, at Idlewild, Hudson River, aged 66.

21. M. Victor Cousin, philosopher, at Paris, aged 75.

29. C. A. Davis, "Jack Downing," at New York, aged 72.

30. Ezekiel F. Chambers, Judge Supreme Court of Maryland, in Kent County.

31. Philip Johnson, M. C., Easton, Pennsylvania, died at Washington.

FEBRUARY.

2. Washington Hunt, ex-Governor, M. C., &c., at New York, aged 56.

13. Alexander Dallas Bache, Superintendent U. S. Coast Survey, at Newport, R. I., aged 61.

18. Earl of Camperdown, England.

22. Daniel Devlin, City Chamberlain, at New York, aged 55.

27. James D. B. DeBow, editor, author, statistician, at Elizabeth, New Jersey, aged 47.

27. Gen. Aaron Ward, ex M. C., at Sing Sing, N. Y. Also, in February, Earl Brownlow, of England; and the Austrian Archduke Stephen.

MARCH.

6. Bishop Soule, senior bishop of the Methodist Church, at Nashville, Tenn., aged 84.

6. Charles F. Browne, "Artemus Ward," at Southampton, England, aged 37.

15. Hiram Woodruff, a celebrated turfman, at New York.

18. Jesse Hoyt, politician, at New York.
17. Rev. Jacob Panborn, Presiding Elder, Methodist Church, at Concord, N. H., aged 79. Also in March, President Thomas Hunt, of the University of Louisiana, at New Orleans; and Admiral Sir Phipps Hornby, of the British navy.

APRIL.

4. George W. Randolph, ex-Secretary of War, Virginia.
16. Henry Bowen, ex-Secretary of State of Rhode Island—Rev. Dr. D. Field, at Stockbridge, Mass., aged 86—Also in April, Earl Rivers, England, Rt. Rev. John Timon, Bishop of Buffalo; and Sir Robert Smlke, architect of the British Museum, 87 years.

MAY.

11. Joseph A. Wright, U. S. Minister at Berlin, aged 57.
17. Gen, Mendez, shot in Mexico.
24. Sir Archibald Alison, historian, aged 75.
30. Gen. Castilla, chief of revolt against Prado's government, at Arica, Peru—Also in May, Hon. Joseph Lumpkin, of Georgia, Sup. Court at Athens; John Povey, actor, at London, aged 67; Mdme. Persiani, singer, at Paris.

JUNE.

4. Gen. W. A. Blount, in Beanfort Co., N. C.—Rev. Joel Hawes, D. D., Hartford.
13. Lt. Com. Alex. S. McKenzie, U. S. N., killed at Formosa.
19. Maximilian of Hapsburg, 35 years old; Gen. Thomas Mejia, and Gen. Miguel Miramon, shot at Queretaro—Isaac Newton, Commissioner of Agriculture, at Washington—Also in June, Judge William Lyons, Richmond, Va.

JULY.

1. Rear Admiral Geo. F. Pearson, U. S. N., at the Portsmouth Navy Yard, age 68.—Gen. Thomas Francis Meagher, Secretary Montana, drowned near Fort Benton, age 44.
3. Lazarus W. Powell, ex-Governor and ex-United States Senator, at Henderson, Ky., age 55.
5. Associate Justice U. S. Supreme Court, James M. Wayne, at Washington.
6. John A. King, ex-Governor, &c., at Jamaica, L. I.
12. Dr. Higgin, Bishop of Derry, Ireland. —Gen. Vidaurri shot at City of Mexico.
30. Catherine M. Sedgwick, author, at Stockbridge, Mass., age 69.—R. C. Purgear, ex-M. C., in Yadkin Co., N. C.—Also in July, A. N. O. Totten, ex-Judge, Sup. Court, Tenn; James A. Banks, Speaker of Assembly, Nevada, killed by Indians; and ex-King Otho, of Greece.

AUGUST.

1. Manuel Cavallo, Chilean Minister to Brussels.
2. William T. Coggeshall, U. S. Minister at Eucador.
6. David R. Porter, ex-Governor, at Harrisburg, Penn.
9. Wm. W. Scrugham, Judge Sup. Court at Yonkers, N. Y.
18. Gen. O'Horan, shot at City of Mexico.
19. Wm. B. Campbell, ex-Governor and M. C., at Lebanon, Tenn.

21. Gen. Juan Alvarez, in Mexico.
22. Jeremiah Day, LL. D., D. D., ex-President of Yale College, at New Haven, age 94—Hon. E. D. Beach, lawyer, Springfield, Mass., age 58.
25. Pierre Flavian Turgeon, R. C. Archbishop of Quebec.
27. Michael Faraday, chemist, London, 73 years old.
28. A. A. L. M. Velpeau, physician, at Paris, age 72—Also in August, Marie Sophie Amelie, ex-Queen of Naples; Cardinal Louis Alteri; Dr. John C. Warren and Dr. James Jackson, of Boston; Wm. A. Bradley, Washington; Ira Aldridge, colored tragedian, in Poland; Soulouque, ex-Emperor of Hayti; Pierce Butler, in Georgia; and Captain Cresswell, R. N. who claimed discovery of Arctic N. W. passage in 1853.

SEPTEMBER.

3. James A. McDougall, ex-U. S. Senator Cal., at Albany, age 50.
8. John L. Helm, governor, at Elizabeth, Ky.
9. Dr. Louis Desire Veron, journalist, at Paris, age 69—Dr. Thomas Howe Taylor, rector of Grace Church, New York—Wm. Hagadorn, editor, at Harlem, N. Y.—Eustace W. Barron, Banker, City of Mexico.
19. Sir Frederick W. A. Bruce, Brit. Min. to U. S. at Boston, age 53.
24. Joachim Manzano, Captain-General of Cuba, at Havana.
28. Charles A. King, LL. D., ex-President Columbia College, at Rome, age 78—Gen. Sterling Price, at St. Louis—Also in September, Gen. Yell, of Arkansas; and ex-Chancellor Blackburn, England, age 86.

OCTOBER.

3. Thomas E. Noell, M. C., 3d Dist. Missouri, at St. Louis, age 29.
4. Elias Howe, jr., inventor, Brooklyn, 48 years old—Avonia Jones (Mrs. G.V. Brooke) actress, New York, age 28.
6. Peter Lorillard, New York merchant, at Saratoga, age 72—Achille Fould, ex-Minister of Finance, Paris, age 67.
13. L. Silliman Ives, ex-Episcopal Bishop of North Carolina, at Manhattanville, N. Y.
21. George Wilkins Kendall, Editor *N. O. Picayune*, in Texas, age 60.
30. John A. Andrew, ex-Governor Massachusetts, at Boston, age 49.

NOVEMBER.

1. Lord Wm. Rosse, astronomer, London, age 67.
5. Alexander W. Bradford, late Surrogate, at New York, age 53.
13. Nathaniel Bullock, oldest grad. Brown University and oldest member of the bar in Rhode Island, at Bristol, age 89.
14. Gen. Stevens, ex-Conf. and Supt. of the Vera Cruz and Mexican railway, at Vera Cruz.
19. Fitz Greene Halleck, poet, at Guildford, Conn., age 72—Also in November, Marshall Leopold O'Donnell, ex-Captain General of Cuba, at Baritz, France. 58.

RATES OF FOREIGN POSTAGE.

The standard single rate to Great Britain is half oz. avoirdupois ; to France and the Continent (by French Mails) it is 15 grammes, or quarter oz. avoirdupois.

The asterisk (*) indicates that prepayment of the rate to which it is affixed is optional, in all other cases prepayment is required.

	Letters not exceed'g quarter oz.	Letters not exceeding half oz.	Newspapers.
	cts.	cts.	cts.
England, Ireland, Scotland and Wales		12	2

[By the new postal convention, *Printed Matter* may now be transmitted in the mails between the United States and Great Britain at the following charges:—

Newspapers and circulars, under 2 oz. in weight, each 2 cents.

Books, per single rate of 4 oz. 6 cents.

Pamphlets, and other printed matter over 2 oz., per single rate of 4 oz., 4 cents.

Samples of merchandise, seeds, &c., per single rate of 4 oz., 8 cents. No packet is allowed to exceed 24 inches in length by 12 inches in breadth and 12 inches in thickness.

These rates must be *fully prepaid in stamps,* or the package will not be forwarded. Letters and packets may be *registered* at an extra fee of 8 cents—to be prepaid.]

German States and Free Cities, including Austria, Bavaria, Baden, Bremen, Brunswick, Frankfort, Hamburg, Hanover, Lubec, Luxemburg, Mecklenburg, Oldenburg, Prussia, Saxe-Altenburg, Coburg-Gotha, Meiningen, Weimar, Saxony and Wurtemburg.

	cts.	cts.	cts.
By Prussian closed mail.......		*30	6
" " " " except Baden, if prepaid		28	
By French mail.............	*21	*42	
" Bremen mail.............		*15	
Exceptions:			
Bremen by Bremen steamer..		*10	
Hamburg by Hamburg " ..		*10	2
Luxemburg by Bremen " ..		*15	3
Australia, British mail, *via* Southampton		33	6
Australia, British mail, *via* Marseilles	39	45	8
Australia, ship mail, from New York or Boston.............		5	2
Australia, French mail, (South Australia compulsory).......	*30	60	
Australia, Bremen or Hamburg mail, *via* Marseilles and Suez.		37	
Australia, Bremen or Hamburg mail, *via* Trieste		55	
Azores, British mail, *via* Portugal	29	*37	8
Belgium, French mail.........	*21	*42	
" closed mail, *via* England		*27	5
Belgium, open mail, *via* London, American packet......		21	2
Belgium, open mail, *via* London, British packet.........		5	2
China, British mail, *via* Southampton		45	6
China, British mail, *via* Marseilles		53	8
China, British mail, by Bremen or Hamburg mail, *via* Trieste		55	
China, Bremen or Hamburg mail, *via* Marseilles and Suez		37	
China, French mail.........	30	60	2
China, San Francisco mail, thence by ship.........		3	
Constantinople, Prussian closed mail		*35	6
Constantinople, French mail..	*30	*60	2
" Bremen or Hamburg mail.................		*32	
Constantinople, open mail, *via* London, American packet...		21	2
Constantinople, open mail, *via* British packet..............		5	2
Cuba		10	2
East Indies, open mail, *via* London, American packet........		21	6
East Indies, open mail, *via* London, British packet..........		5	6
East Indies, Prussian closed mail, *via* Trieste.............		70	13
East Indies, Prussian closed mail, *via* English Possessions		38	10
East Indies, Bremen or Hamburg mail, *via* Marseilles and Suez		37	
East Indies, Bremen or Hamburg mail, *via* Trieste........		55	
East Indies, French mail......	30	60	
Egypt, (except Alexandria), British mail, *via* Southamp'n		33	6
Egypt (except Alexandria) British mail, *via* Marseilles	33	45	8
Egypt (except Alexandria) Prussian closed mail.........		38	6
Egypt (except Alexandria) Bremen or Hamburg Mail.......		30	
Egypt (except Alexandria) French mail.................	30	60	2
Egypt to Alexandria, Prussian closed mail................		*35	10
Egypt to Alexandria, Prussian closed mail, prepaid.........		30	
Egypt to Alexandria, Bremen or Hamburg mail.............		30	
Egypt to Alexandria, French mail...................	*30	*60	2
Egypt to Alexandria, open mail, *via* England, American packet		21	4
Egypt to Alexandria, open mail, *via* England, British packet..		5	4
France......................	*15	*30	2
Greece, open mail, *via* London, American packet............		21	4
Greece, open mail, *via* London, British packet............		5	4
Greece, French mail...........	*30	*60	
Greece, Bremen or Hamburg mail...................		*35	

	cts.	cts.	cts.		cts.	cts.	cts.
Hong Kong, British mail, *via* Marseilles..................		53	8	Russia, French mail........	*30	*60	2
Hong Kong, British mail, *via* Southampton		45	6	Sandwich Islands, *via* San Francisco....................		3	2
Hong Kong, French mail	30	60	2	Sardinian States, Prussian closed mail..................		*42	6
Hong Kong, Bremen or Hamburg mail...................		30		Sardinian States, Prussian closed mail, prepaid..........		40	
Hong Kong, Prussian closed mail................		38	10	Sardinian States, Bremen or Hamburg mail		*23	
Japan, British mail, *via* Southampton		45	6	Sardinian States, French mail..	*21	*42	
Japan, British mail, *via* Marseilles........................		53	8	South American States, *Atlantic Coast. Via* England.....		45	4
Japan, French mail	30	60		South American States, for Brazil alone, from New York.		*10	2
Jerusalem, British mail		33	4	South American States, for Argentine Republic and Uruguay, *via* Bordeaux.......	30	60	
" French mail........	*30	*60		South American States, *Pacific Coast.* Peru..................		22	6
Mexico.......................		10	2	South American States, Ecuador, Bolivia and Chili........		34	6
Naples (Kingdom of), Prussian closed mail..................		30	6	Spain, French mail............	21	42	
Naples (Kingdom of), French mail......................	*21	*42	2	Spain, Bremen or Hamburg mail..........................		25	
Naples (Kingdom of), Bremen or Hamburg mail.............		22		Spain, British mail, American packet		21	2
Portugal, British mail, *via* England.......................	33	45	8	Spain, British mail, British packet		5	2
Portugal, Bremen or Hamburg mail		25		Sweden, Prussian closed mail..		*33	6
Portugal, French mail, *via* Behobia	21	42		Sweden, Prussian closed mail, prepaid		34	
Portugal, French mail, *via* Bordeaux and Lisbon............	30	60		Sweden, Bremen or Hamburg mail		*21	
Roman or Papal States, Prussian closed mail..............		46	6	Sweden, French mail...........	*33	*66	2
Roman or Papal States, French mail....................	*27	*54	2	Switzerland, Prussian closed ml.		*35	6
Roman or Papal States, Bremen or Hamburg mail.............		*28		Switzerland, Prussian closed mail, prepaid..............		33	
Russia, Prussian closed mail ...		*37	6	Switzerland, French mail......	*21	*42	2
Russia, Prussian closed mail, prepaid.......................		35		Switzerland, Bremen or Hamburg mail...................		*19	
Russia, Bremen or Hamburg mail......................		*20		West Indies, British		10	2

RATES OF DOMESTIC POSTAGE.

LETTERS.
The standard single-rate weight is ½ oz. avoirdupois.
Single-rate letter, throughout the United States....................3 cents
For each additional ½ oz. or fraction............................3 "
Drop-letters, for local delivery, ...2 "

NEWSPAPERS.
The standard single-rate is 4 oz. avoirdupois. Prepaid quarterly or yearly.
Daily (7 times a week)....35 cts. per quarter
Daily (6 times a week)....30 cts. per quarter
Tri-weekly................15 cts. per quarter
Semi-weekly.............10 cts. per quarter
Weekly................... 5 cts. per quarter
Rates must be prepaid quarterly or yearly, *The standard single rate is 4 oz.*

PERIODICALS.
Semi-weekly............. 6 cts. per quarter
Monthly.................. 3 cts. per quarter
Quarterly................ 1 ct. per quarter
Newsdealers may receive their packages of periodicals and newspapers at the same rates as subscribers.

TRANSIENT PRINTED MATTER.
Books, for each single rate of 4 oz. 4 cents

Circulars, not exceeding three in one envelope constituting a single rate 2 cents
Miscellaneous mailable matter, for single rate of 4 oz. avoirdupois .. 2 cents
Prepayment by stamps is required for all postage on transient printed matter.
The maximum weight of any package of printed or miscellaneous matter is 4 lbs. avoirdupois.

Registration.—Letters may be registered on payment of a fee of 20 cents, but the government takes no responsibility for safe carriage, or compensation in case of loss.

Money Orders.—All principal post-offices now receive small sums of money and issue drafts for the same upon other post-offices, subject to the following charges and regulations:
On orders not exceeding $20........10 cts.
Over $20 and not exceeding $50....25 "
No fractions of cents to be introduced.
The Order is only payable at the office upon which it is drawn. The Order should be collected within one year from its date. After once paying an Order, by *whomsoever presented*, the Department will be liable to no further claim.

UNITED STATES GOVERNMENT.

JANUARY 1, 1868.

THE EXECUTIVE.

ANDREW JOHNSON, of Tennessee, *President of the United States*.....Salary $25,000
BENJAMIN F. WADE, of Ohio, *President pro tempore of the Senate*...,   "   8,000

THE CABINET.

WILLIAM H. SEWARD, of New York, *Secretary of State*........Salary $8,000
HUGH M'CULLOCH, of Indiana, *Secretary of the Treasury*.......   "   8,000
ULYSSES S. GRANT, of Illinois, *Secretary of War, ad interim*..
GIDEON WELLES, of Connecticut, *Secretary of the Navy*........   "   8,000
ORVILLE H. BROWNING, of Illinois, *Secretary of the Interior*..   "   8,000
HENRY STANBERY, of Ohio, *Attorney General*.................   "   8,000
ALEXANDER W. RANDALL, of Wisconsin, *Postmaster-General*,   "   8,000

THE JUDICIARY.

SUPREME COURT OF THE UNITED STATES.

SALMON P. CHASE, of Ohio, *Chief Justice*, Salary $6,500.

ASSOCIATE JUSTICES, Salary, $6,000.

NATHAN CLIFFORD, of Maine, VACANCY.   SAMUEL F. MILLER, of Iowa,
SAMUEL NELSON, of N. Y.,   DAVID DAVIS, of Ill.,   STEPHEN J. FIELD, of Cal.,
ROBERT C. GRIER, of Penna., NOAH H. SWAYNE, of Ohio, VACANCY.

Court meets at Washington, D. C, first Monday in December.

MINISTERS TO FOREIGN COUNTRIES.

ENVOYS EXTRAORDINARY AND MINISTERS PLENIPOTENTIARY.

Country.	Capital.	Ministers.	Salary.	Appointed
Austria	Vienna	(Vacant)	$12,000	
Brazil	Rio Janeiro	James Watson Webb, N. Y.	12,000	1861
Chili	Santiago	Judson Kilpatrick, N. J	10,000	1865
China	Pekin	Anson Burlingame, Mass	12,000	1861
France	Paris	John A. Dix, N. Y	17,500	1866
Great Britain	London	Charles Francis Adams, Mass.	17,500	1861
Italy	Florence	George P. Marsh, Vt	12,000	1861
Mexico	City of Mexico	(Vacant)	12,000	
Prussia	Berlin	George Bancroft, N. Y.	12,000	1867
Russia	St. Petersburg	Cassius M. Clay, Ky	12,000	1863
Spain	Madrid	John P. Hale, N. H	12,000	1865

MINISTERS RESIDENT.

Country.	Capital.	Ministers.	Salary.	Appointed
Argentine Republic	Buenos Ayres	Alexander Asboth, Mo	$7,500	1860
Belgium	Brussels	Henry S. Sanford, Conn	7,500	1861
Bolivia	La Paz	Allen A. Hall, Tenn	7,500	1863
Costa Rica	San Jose	Albert G. Lawrence, R. I.	7,500	1866
Denmark	Copenhagen	George H. Yeaman, Ky	7,500	1865
Ecuador	Quito	(Vacant)	7,500	
Guatemala	Guatemala City	Fitz Henry Warren, Iowa	7,500	1865
Hawaiian Islands	Honolulu	Edward M. McCook, Ohio	7,500	1866
Honduras	Comayagua	Richard H. Rousseau, Ky	7,500	1866
Japan	Yedo	R. B. Van Valkenburgh, N. Y.	7,500	1866
Netherlands	Hague	Hugh Ewing, Kansas	7,500	1866
Nicaragua	Nicaragua	Andrew B. Dickinson, N. Y	7,500	1863
Paraguay	Asuncion	Charles A. Washburn, Cal	7,500	1861
Peru	Lima	Alvin P. Hovey, Ind	7,500	
Portugal	Lisbon	James E. Harvey, Pa	7,500	1861
Salvador	San Salvador	Alpheus S. Williams	7,500	
Sweden & Norway	Stockholm	(Vacant)	7,500	
Switzerland	Berne	George Harrington, D.C.	7,500	1865
Turkey	Constantinople	Edward Joy Morris, Pa	7,500	1861
U. S. of Colombia	Bogota	Allen A. Burton, Ky	7,500	1861
Venezuela	Caracas	James Wilson, Ind	7,500	1866

MINISTERS RESIDENT AND CONSULS GENERAL.

Country.	Capital.	Ministers.	Salary.	Appointed
Hayti	Port au Prince	Henry E. Peck, Ohio	7,500	1865
Liberia	Monrovia	John Seys, Tenn	4,000	1866

FOREIGN LEGATIONS IN THE UNITED STATES.

ENVOYS EXTRAORDINARY AND MINISTERS PLENIPOTENTIARY.

Argentine Republic..Don Colonel Domingo
            F. Sarmiento.
Austria...........Baron Von Frankenstein.
Brazil...................... ....La de P. Flurry.
Denmark .....˙...........Col. H. Dollener.
France........ ....M. J. Berthemy.
Great Britain..........*Francis Close Ford.
Italy...........................M. Cerutti.

Mexico..........Senor Don Matias Romero.
Netherlands......................A. Mazel.
Peru............Senor Don Antonia Garcia.
Prussia.................Baron Von Gerolt.
Russia..............M. Edward de Stoeckl.
Spain....................Don Fecundi Goni.
U. S. of Colombia...Gen. Eustorjio Salgar.
Venezuela.......Senor Don Blas Bruzual.

MINISTERS RESIDENT.

Belgium.................Maurice Delfosse.
Hayti...........................Col. Raester.

Sweden & Norway...Baron de Wetterstedt.

CHARGES D'AFFAIRS.

Bremen.................A. Schumacker.
Chili..........Senor Alberto Blest Gana.
Costa Rica, Senor Don Ezequiel Gutierrez.

Hanseatic Republic.......Johannes Rosing.
Hawaiian Islands...........Chas. A. Harris.
Liberia..............Henry M. Schieffelin.
Portugal......M. Manuol Garcia da Roza.

*In charge ; Edwd. Thornton, min. ap. ——

FORTIETH CONGRESS.

The first session of the Fortieth Congress commenced on Monday, March 4, 1867 ; on March 20th an adjournment was had to Wednesday, July 3: on July 20th a further adjournment was had to Thursday, Nov 21. Second regular session commenced Dec. 2.

SENATE.

BENJAMIN F. WADE, of Ohio, President.   JOHN W. FORNEY, of Pennsylvania, *Clerk.*
[Democrats in *Italics.*   Republicans in Roman.]

CALIFORNIA.	Term Ex.	NEVADA.	Term Ex.
John Conness...........................1869		William M. Stewart...................:...1869	
Cornelius Cole...........................1873		James W. Nye.........................1873	
CONNECTICUT.		**NEW HAMPSHIRE.**	
James Dixon...........................1869		Aaron H. Cragin.......................1871	
Orris S. Ferry.........................1873		James W. Patterson....... 1873	
DELAWARE.		**NEW JERSEY.**	
Jas. A. Bayard......................1869		Frederick T. Frelinghuysen............1869	
Willard Saulsbury...................1871		Alexander G. Cattell..................1871	
ILLINOIS.		**NEW YORK.**	
Richard Yates...........................1871		Edwin D. Morgan.....................1869	
Lyman Trumbull.......................1873		Roscoe Conkling.....................1873	
INDIANA.		**OHIO.**	
Thomas A. Hendricks.................1869		Benjamin F. Wade...................1869	
Oliver P. Morton.......................1873		John Sherman.......................1873	
IOWA.		**OREGON.**	
James W. Grimes......................1871		George H. Williams...................1871	
James Harlan...........................1873		Henry C. Corbett....................1873	
KANSAS.		**PENNSYLVANIA.**	
Edmund G. Ross.......................1871		*Charles R. Buckalew*.................1869	
Samuel C. Pomeroy...................1873		Simon Cameron......................1873	
KENTUCKY.		**RHODE ISLAND.**	
James Guthrie.........................1871		William Sprague.....................1869	
Garret Davis..........................1873		Henry B. Anthony...................1871	
MAINE.		**TENNESSEE.**	
Lot M. Morrill...........................1869		*David T. Patterson*..................1869	
Wm. P. Fessenden.....................1871		Joseph S. Fowler.....................1871	
MARYLAND.		**VERMONT.**	
Reverdy Johnson......................1869		George F. Edmunds...................1869	
Philip F. Thomas....................1873		Justin S. Morrill......................1873	
MASSACHUSETTS.		**WEST VIRGINIA.**	
Charles Sumner........................1869		Peter G. Van Winkle........ 1869	
Henry Wilson...........................1871		Waitman T. Willey....................1871	
MICHIGAN.		**WISCONSIN.**	
Zachariah Chandler....................1869		James R. Doolittle....................1869	
Jacob M. Howard.......................1871		Timothy O. Howe.....................1873	
MINNESOTA.		**RECAPITULATION.**	
Alexander Ramsey......................1869		Republicans.............................. 45	
Daniel S. Norton........................1871		Democrats................................. 9	
MISSOURI.			
John B. Henderson......................1869		Republican majority..................... 36	
Charles D. Drake..........: 1873		John Evans and James B. Chaffee, have	
NEBRASKA.		been elected Senators from Colorado, to	
Thomas W. Tipton.......:..............1869		take their seats when that State is admitted	
John M. Thayer....... ....:871		to the Union. * Not yet admitted.	

HOUSE OF REPRESENTATIVES,

SCHUYLER COLFAX, of Indiana, *Speaker.* EDWARD MCPHERSON, of Pennsylvania, *Clerk.*

Democrats in *Italic ;* Republicans, in Roman. Those marked with a star (*) were members of the XXXIXth Congress.

CALIFORNIA.

1* *Samuel B. Axtell.*
2* William Higby.
3 *Jas. A. Johnson.*

CONNECTICUT.

1 *R. D. Hubbard.*
2 *Julius Hotchkiss.*
3 H. H. Starkweather.
4 *William H. Barnum.*

DELAWARE.

1* *John A. Nicholson.*

ILLINOIS.

At Large—John A. Logan.
1. Norman B. Judd.
2* John F. Farnsworth.
3* Elihu B. Washburne.
4* Abner C. Harding.
5* Ebon C. Ingersoll.
6* Burton C. Cook.
7* Henry P. H. Bromwell.
8* Shelby M. Cullom.
9* *Lewis W. Ross.*
10 *Albert G. Burr.*
11* *Samuel S. Marshall.*
12* *Jehu Baker.*
13 Green B. Raum.

INDIANA.

1* *William E. Niblack.*
2* *Michael C. Kerr.*
3 Morton C. Hunter.
4 *William S. Holman.*
5* George W. Julian.
6 John Coburn
7* Henry D. Washburn.
8* Godlove S. Orth.
9* Schuyler Colfax.
10 William Williams.
11 John P. C. Shanks.

IOWA.

1* James F. Wilson.
2* Hiram Price.
3* William B. Allison.
4 William Loughridge.
5 Granville M. Dodge.
6* Asahel W. Hubbard.

KANSAS.

1* Sidney Clarke.

KENTUCKY.

1* *Lawrence S. Trimble.*
2 *John Young Brown.*
3 *John S Gollady.*
4 *J. Proctor Knott.*
5 *Asa P. Grover.*
6 *Thomas L. Jones.*
7 *James B. Beck.*
8 *George M. Adams*
9 *John D. Young.*

MAINE.

1* John Lynch.
2* Sidney Perham.
3* James G. Blaine.
4 John A. Peters.
5* Frederick A. Pike.

MARYLAND.

1* *Hiram McCullough.*
2 *Stevenson Archer.*
3* *Charles E. Phelps.*
4* Francis Thomas.
5 *Frederick Stone.*

MASSACHUSETTS.

1* Thomas D. Eliot.
2* Oakes Ames.
3 Ginery Twitchell.
4* Samuel Hooper.
5 Benj. F. Butler.
6* Nathaniel P. Banks.
7* George S. Boutwell.
8* John D. Baldwin.
9* Wm. B. Washburn.
10* Henry L. Dawes.

MICHIGAN.

1* Fernando C. Beaman.
2* Charles Upson.
3 Austin Blair.
4* Thomas W. Ferry.
5* Row. E. Trowbridge.
6* John F. Driggs.

MINNESOTA.

1* William Windom.
2* Ignatius Donnelly.

MISSOURI.

1 William A. Pile.
2 Carman A. Newcomb.
3 *James R. McCormick.*
4 John J. Gravelly.
5* Joseph W. McClurg.
6* Robert T. Van Horn.
7* Benjamin F. Loan.
8* John F. Benjamin.
9* George W. Anderson.

NEBRASKA.

1 John Taffe.

NEVADA.

1* Delos R. Ashley.

NEW HAMPSHIRE.

1 Jacob H. Ela.
2 Aaron F. Stevens.
3 Jacob Benton.

NEW JERSEY.

1 William Moore.
2 *Charles Haight.*
3* *Charles Sitgreaves.*
4 John Hill.
5 George A. Halsey.

NEW YORK.

1* *Stephen Taber.*
2 *Demas Barnes.*
3 *Wm. E. Robinson.*
4 *John Fox.*
5 *John Morrissey.*
6 *Thomas E. Stewart.*
7* *John W. Chanler.*
8 *James Brooks.*
9 *Fernando Wood.*
10 William H. Robertson.
14 Charles H. Van Wyck.
12* John H. Ketcham.
13 Thomas Cornell.
14 *John V. L. Pruyn.*
15* John A. Griswold.
16 Orange Ferris.
17* Calvin T. Hulburd.
18* James M. Marvin.
19 William C. Fields.
20* Addison H. Laflin.
21 Alexander H. Bailey.
22 John C. Churchill.
23 Dennis McCarthy.
24* Theodore M. Pomeroy.
25 William H. Kelsey.
26 William S. Lincoln.
27* Hamilton Ward.
28 Lewis Selye.
29* Burt Van Horn.
30* *James M. Humphrey.*
31* Henry Van Aernam.

OHIO.

1* Benjamin Eggleston.
2 *Samuel F. Cary.*
3* Robert C. Schenck.
4* William Lawrence.
5 *William Mungen.*
6* Reader W. Clarke.
7* Samuel S. Shellabarger.
8 Cornelius S. Hamilton.
9* Ralph P. Buckland.
10* James M. Ashley.
11 John T. Wilson.
12 *Philadel. Van Trump.*
13 *George W. Morgan.*
14* Martin Welker.
15* Tobias A. Plants.
16* John A. Bingham.
17* Ephraim R. Eckley.
18* Rufus P. Spaulding.
19* James A. Garfield.

OREGON.

1 Rufus Mallory.

PENNSYLVANIA.

1* *Samuel J. Randall.*
2* Charles O'Neill.
3* Leonard Myers.
4* William D. Kelley.
5 Caleb N. Taylor.
6* *Benj. M. Boyer.*
7* John M. Broomall.
8 *J. Lawrence Getz.*
9* Thaddeus Stevens.
10 Henry L. Cake.
11 *Daniel M. Van Auken.*
12 *George W. Woodward.*
13* Ulysses Mercur.

14* George F. Miller.
15* *Adam J. Glossbrenner.*
16* Wm. H Koontz.
17 Daniel J. Morrell.
18* Stephen F. Wilson.
19* Glenni W. Scofield.
20 Darwin A. Finney.
21 John Covode.
22* James K. Moorhead.
23* Thomas Williams.
24* George V. Lawrence.

RHODE ISLAND.

1* Thomas A. Jenckes.
2* Nathan F. Dixon.

TENNESSEE.

1 Roderick R. Butler.
2* Horace Maynard.
3* William B. Stokes.
4 James Mullins.
5 John Trimble.
6 Samuel M. Arnell.
7* Isaac R. Hawkins.
8 David A. Nunn.

VERMONT.

1* Fred. E. Woodbridge.
2 Luke P. Poland.
3 Worthington C. Smith.

WEST VIRGINIA.

1* Chester D. Hubbard.
2 Benjamin M. Kitchen.
3 Daniel Polsley.

WISCONSIN.

1* Halbert E. Paine.
2 Benj. F. Hopkins.
3* Amasa Cobb.
4* *Charles A. Eldridge.*
2* Philetus Sawyer.
3 Cad. C. Washburne.

DELEGATES.

ARIZONA.
Coles Bashford.

COLORADO.
Geo. M. Chilcott.

DACOTAH.
Walter A. Burleigh.

IDAHO.
E. D. Holbrook.

MONTANA.
James M. Kavanaugh.

NEW MEXICO.
†*Charles P. Clever.*

UTAH.
William H. Hooper.

WASHINGTON.
Alvin Flanders.

RECAPITULATION,
Republicans,...................... 144
Democrats,........................ 50
<hr>
Republican majority,............ 94
† Contested.

ELECTION RETURNS,

BY STATES, COUNTIES AND CONGRESSIONAL DISTRICTS.

MAINE.

COUNTIES	Governor, 1867.		Governor, 1866.		President, 1864.	
	Pills-bury. Dem.	Cham-b'lain. Rep.	Pills-bury. Dem.	Cham-b'lain. Rep.	Mc-Clel'n Dem.	Lin-coln. Rep.
Androscg'n.	1829	3424	1914	4352	2165	3646
Aroostook..	1038	1607	1508	1931	818	1162
Cumberl'nd	5724	7009	5774	8680	6487	8071
Franklin...	1647	2270	1453	2626	1803	2251
Hancock...	1989	2649	1855	3334	2574	3441
Kennebec ..	4032	5820	2723	7098	3347	6803
Knox......	2843	2464	2189	2723	2379	2532
Lincoln....	2156	2100	2010	2675	2504	2536
Oxford.....	3032	3800	3114	4535	3163	4206
Penobscot..	4350	6641	4212	8655	4343	7124
Piscataquis.	1694	1490	949	1812	1012	1628
Sagadahoc..	1181	1877	814	2523	1120	2671
Somerset...	3015	3815	2674	4362	2850	3854
Waldo.....	3018	3427	2367	4069	2817	3938
Washingt'n	2735	2930	2451	3433	3000	3174
York.......	6051	6139	5880	6809	5368	6594
Soldiers' V.	....	....	....	....	738	4174
Total ...	45644	57462	41947	69637	46988	67805

The official vote of the election for Governor in 1867, is not declared until January, 1868, and did not reach us, therefore, in time for publication in the WORLD ALMANAC. The above returns of the vote of 1867, include 453 cities, towns and plantations. The 31 small towns and plantations yet to be heard from, voted in 1866 as follows: Pillsbury, (Dem.) 628; Chamberlain, (Rep.) 576.

STATE OFFICERS.—Joshua L. Chamberlain, Governor; Ephraim Flint, Secretary of State; Nathan G. Hichborn, Treasurer.

CONGRESS, 1866.

Dists.	Dem.		Rep.		Rep. Maj.
1	Sweat..	11653	Lynch..	15611	3958
2	Morrill..	7363	Perham..	13784	6421
3	Heath..	8313	Blaine..	14909	6591
4	Weston.	6564	Peters..	12059	5195
5	Crosby..	7973	Pike....	12351	4378

STATE LEGISLATURE, 1867–8.

	Senate.	House.	Joint Bal.
Republicans	23	106	134
Democrats	3	45	48
Republican Majority ...	25	61	86

RHODE ISLAND.

COUNTIES.	Governor, 1867.		Governor, 1866.		President, 1864.	
	Pierce Dem.	Burn-side, Rep.	Pierce Dem.	Burn-side, Rep.	Mc Clel'n Dem.	Lin-coln, Rep.
Bristol....	210	403	175	389	449	780
Kent......	333	751	209	628	815	1365
Newport ...	291	955	232	1332	844	1773
Providence.	2091	4181	1878	4535	5369	8152
Washingt'n	415	1264	322	1260	993	1622
Total.....	3340	7554	2816	8197	8470	13692

STATE OFFICERS. — Governor, Ambrose E. Burnside; Lieut.-Governor, William Greene.

Secretary of State, John R. Bartlett; Attorney-General, Willard Sayles; Treasurer, George W. Tew.
STATE DEBT.—War Debt, $3,626,500. No Civil Debt.

CONGRESS, 1867.

Dists.	Dem.		Rep.
Eastern......		Jenckes........	4560

Thomas A. Jenckes elected without opposition.

| Western....Carder.....1497 | Dixon ....2754 |

Nathan F. Dixon over Carder, 1257.

STATE LEGISLATURE, 1867–8.

	Senate.	House.	Joint Bal.
Republicans	28	64	92
Democrats	6	8	14
Republican Majority....	22	56	78

MASSACHUSETTS.

COUNTIES.	Governor, 1867.		Governor, 1866.		President, 1864.	
	Ad-ams. Dem.	Bul-lock. Rep.	Sweet-ser. Dem.	Bul-lock. Rep.	Mc-Clel'n Dem.	Lin-coln. Rep.
Barnstable..	997	2230	325	2036	701	3994
Berkshire..	3773	4137	2369	4004	3363	5314
Bristol.....	3137	8407	901	5884	2173	9736
Dukes......	99	270	74	373	138	475
Essex......	10893	13472	3953	13142	5691	17237
Franklin...	1392	3429	670	3222	1289	4376
Hampden ..	3906	4551	1798	4302	2994	6356
Hampshire..	1345	4353	314	3790	866	5036
Middlesex..	14345	17974	5249	17520	9597	22318
Nantucket ..	40	521	39	331	36	486
Norfolk	7862	8074	2945	8308	5502	11040
Plymouth ..	3943	6442	1260	5507	2512	7610
Suffolk.....	9908	8555	4276	10454	8367	14692
Worcester..	8810	16091	2948	13107	5615	18072
Total.....	70360	98306	26671	91980	48744	126742

STATE OFFICERS.—Governor, A. H. Bullock; Lieut.-Governor, Wm. Claflin; Secretary of State, Oliver Warner; Treasurer, J. H. Loud; Auditor, H. S. Briggs; Attorney-General, Chas. Allen.

STATE DEBT.—Civil Debt, $11,065,744.69; War Debt, $16,573,173.60; Total, $27,638,918.29, of which amount, $16,926,587.92 is provided for, leaving a balance of $10,712,330.37.

STATE LEGISLATURE, 1868.

	Council.	Senate.	House.
Republicans	7	28	178
Democrats	1	12	62
Republican Majority.......	6	16	116

CONGRESS, 1866.

Dist.	Dem.		Rep.		Rep. Maj.
1	Ellis.......	1539	Eliot ..	8184	6645
2	Ide	2456	Ames ..	9581	7125
3	Aspinwall ..	2601	Twichell..	6084	3483
4	Wightman ..	3183	Hooper..	7902	4719
5	Northend ..	2838	Butler..	9021	6183
6	Prince	3366	Banks..	10075	6709
7	Saltonstall.	2885	Boutwell..	9847	6962
8	Williams ..	1901	Baldwin..	9039	7138
9	Haywood.	1768	Washburne	11895	10127
10	Chapin..	4185	Dawes..	8125	3940

NEW HAMPSHIRE.

COUNTIES.	Governor, 1867.		Governor, 1866.		President, 1864.	
	Sinclair. Dem.	Harriman. Rep.	Sinclair. Dem.	Smyth Rep.	McClel'n Dem.	Lincoln. Rep.
Belknap....	2172	1966	2066	1922	2216	1855
Carroll.....	2397	1967	2305	1883	2509	1782
Cheshire....	2242	3371	2190	3421	2444	3492
Coos........	1462	1291	1376	1230	1459	1116
Grafton....	4594	4471	4229	4533	4574	4337
Hillsboro'..	5566	6549	5229	6335	5325	6378
Merrimac...	4707	4541	4480	4544	4768	4374
Rockingh'm	5062	5967	4477	5857	4477	5822
Strafford...	2551	3484	2392	3218	2550	3094
Sullivan....	1910	2202	1813	2194	2022	2279
Soldiers' V..					690	2066
Total......	32663	35809	30481	35137	33034	36595

STATE OFFICERS. — Walter Harriman, Governor; John D. Lyman, Secretary of State; Peter Sanborn, Treasurer.

STATE DEBT.—$3,747,776.95.

CONGRESS, 1867.

1st District.	D. Marcy. Dem.	J. H. Ella. Rep.
Belknap......................	2182	1966
Carroll......................	2395	1955
Rockingham..................	5103	5931
Strafford....................	2565	3385
Total......................	12247	13243

J. H. Ella over D. Marcy, 996.

2d District.	E. W. Harrington.	A. F. Stevens.
Hillsborough..................	5611	6611
Merrimac.....................	4694	4649
Total......................	10305	11260

A. F. Stevens over E. W. Harrington, 955.

3d District.	H. Bingham.	J. Benton.
Cheshire.....................	2241	3346
Coos.........................	1433	1121
Grafton......................	4663	4598
Sullivan.....................	1909	2229
Total......................	10246	11294

J. Benton over H. Bingham, 1048.

STATE LEGISLATURE, 1867—8.

	Senate.	House.	Joint Bal.
Republicans.............	9	202	211
Democrats..............	3	128	131
Republican Majority.....	6	74	80

CONNECTICUT.

COUNTIES.	Governor, 1867.		Governor, 1866.		President, 1864.	
	English. Dem.	Hawley. Rep.	English. Dem.	Hawley. Rep.	McClel'n Dem.	Lincoln. Rep.
Fairfield....	7805	7698	7339	7094	7193	7368
Hartford....	9678	9072	8937	8618	8680	8692
Litchfield...	5058	5019	4653	4771	4423	4997
Middlesex..	3174	3340	2939	3206	3107	3113
New Haven	11696	9379	10784	8630	9638	8761
New Lond'n	5437	5833	4607	5610	4919	5662
Tolland....	2281	2455	2032	2479	2152	2430
Windham..	2436	3782	2144	3566	2173	3668
Total.....	47575	46585	43433	43974	42285	44691

STATE OFFICERS.—James E. English, Governor; Ephraim H. Hyde, Lieut.-Governor; Leverett E. Pease, Secretary of State; Edward S. Moseley, Treasurer; Jesse Olney, Comptroller.

STATE DEBT.—Funded Debt, $9,828,400; Sinking Fund, $1,211,767.35; Bank Stock and Cash, $955,-155.09.

CONGRESS, 1867.

Districts.	Dem.	Rep.
I.	Hubbard.	Deming.
Hartford....9699	9049	
Tolland......2925	2428	
Total......11994	11477	

R. D. Hubbard over H. C. Deming, 517.

II.	Hotchkiss.	Northrup.
New Haven 11550	9599	
Middlesex.. 3180	3338	
Total......14730	12937	

Julius Hotchkiss over Cyrus Northrup, 1793.

III.	Martin.	Starkw'r
N. London ..5399	5841	
Windham...2428	3882	
Total........7827	9723	

H. H. Starkweather over Earl Martin, 1896.

IV.	W H. Bar.	P. T. Bar.
Fairfield....7848	7360	
Litchfield...5235	4743	
Total......13083	12103	

W. H. Barnum over P. T. Barnum, 980.

STATE LEGISLATURE, 1867—8.

	Senate.	House.	Joint Bal.
Republicans.............11	124	135
Democrats.............10	113	123
Republican Majority..... 1	11	12

TOWN ELECTIONS.—At the town elections in Oct. and Nov., 1867, the Democrats carried 86 and the Republicans 75; first time in 14 years that the Democrats have carried a majority of the towns.

VOTE BY TOWNS.
FAIRFIELD COUNTY.

TOWNS.	Governor, 1867.		Governor, 1866.	
	English. Dem.	Hawley. Rep.	English. Dem.	Hawley. Rep.
Bridgeport...	1395	1452	1325	1324
Brookfield....	164	108	152	111
Bethel.......	139	228	135	207
Darien.......	121	168	124	163
Danbury.....	734	784	724	714
Easton.......	182	151	167	133
Fairfield.....	402	455	359	431
Greenwich...	645	415	612	375
Huntington..	193	144	166	138
Monroe......	201	119	184	109
New Canaan.	232	282	202	258
New Fairfield.	116	90	106	91
Newtown....	424	275	396	273
Norwalk.....	713	940	651	838
Redding.....	155	177	131	162
Ridgefield...	212	255	186	298
Stamford....	577	665	557	631
Sherman.....	115	75	111	73
Stratford....	217	274	221	267
Trumbull....	181	136	190	124
Weston......	174	66	159	64
Wilton......	162	230	163	192
Westport....	351	213	315	189
Total.......	7805	7698	7337	7094

HARTFORD COUNTY.

TOWNS.	Governor, 1867.		Governor, 1866.	
	English. Dem.	Hawley. Rep.	English. Dem.	Hawley. Rep.
Avon........	85	126	84	128
Berlin.......	235	257	199	256
Bloomfield...	223	117	208	123
Bristol......	428	389	388	338
Burlington...	190	73	173	70
Canton......	232	280	194	278
East Hartford.	314	329	289	323
East Windsor.	238	263	228	284
East Granby.	134	75	120	65
Enfield......	299	394	238	399
Farmington..	291	396	268	357
Glastenbury.	373	324	322	357
Granby......	189	207	178	198
Hartland....	109	67	112	78
Hartford....	3216	2746	2991	2512
Manchester..	268	393	216	339
Marlborough.	95	40	84	60
New Britain.	635	603	618	535
Rocky Hill..	126	85	140	86
Simsbury....	210	209	180	222
Southington.	428	341	397	309
South Windsor	212	170	203	172

HARTFORD CO.—*continued.*

TOWNS.	Governor, 1867. English. Dem.	Governor, 1867. Hawley. Rep.	Governor, 1866. English. Dem.	Governor, 1866. Hawley. Rep.
Suffield	356	359	322	370
West Hartford	130	178	129	167
Wethersfield	202	278	211	253
Windsor	266	244	255	229
Windsor Locks	194	129	191	120
Total	9678	9072	8937	8619

LITCHFIELD COUNTY.

TOWNS.	1867 Dem.	1867 Rep.	1866 Dem.	1866 Rep.
Barkhamsted	158	176	137	176
Bethlehem	93	81	100	73
Bridgewater	191	45	175	46
Canaan	200	103	166	97
Colebrook	134	135	124	144
Cornwall	165	202	162	197
Goshen	97	154	79	145
Harwinton	83	136	73	127
Kent	168	192	183	162
Litchfield	353	302	367	303
Morris	128	67	95	64
New Hartford	224	268	193	269
New Milford	395	379	357	376
Norfolk	119	162	111	168
North Canaan	178	126	180	121
Plymouth	292	461	300	426
Roxbury	153	91	155	94
Salisbury	426	250	355	228
Sharon	329	209	270	238
Torrington	229	327	188	252
Warren	85	76	85	71
Washington	193	167	192	146
Watertown	123	226	108	222
Winchester	328	419	277	381
Woodbury	214	265	222	243
Total	5058	5019	4654	4771

MIDDLESEX COUNTY.

TOWNS.	1867 Dem.	1867 Rep.	1866 Dem.	1866 Rep.
Chatham	180	216	194	199
Chester	92	131	79	139
Clinton	141	194	132	190
Cromwell	172	135	158	126
Durham	118	140	114	150
East Haddam	251	368	223	319
Essex	170	244	144	223
Haddam	316	192	302	172
Killingworth	171	80	157	83
Middletown	905	824	935	910
Old Saybrook	106	114	89	116
Portland	292	248	242	259
Saybrook	97	183	82	183
Westbrook	96	141	88	139
*Middlefield	67	130	....	....
Total	3174	3340	2933	3206

*New town in 1867.

NEW HAVEN COUNTY.

TOWNS.	1867 Dem.	1867 Rep.	1866 Dem.	1866 Rep.
Bethany	141	69	135	66
Branford	355	180	340	177
Cheshire	263	198	251	185
Derby	566	603	487	531
East Haven	257	307	238	300
Guilford	265	317	251	329
Hampden	319	214	289	194
Madison	226	235	221	244
Meriden	731	1030	702	805
Middlebury	66	91	54	89
Milford	382	318	378	301
Naugatuck	314	202	298	186
New Haven	5035	3235	4553	2998
North Branford	93	122	110	128
North Haven	156	193	151	181

NEW HAVEN CO.—*continued.*

TOWNS.	Governor, 1867. English. Dem.	Governor, 1867. Hawley. Rep.	Governor, 1866. English. Dem.	Governor, 1866. Hawley. Rep.
Orange	160	245	169	224
Oxford	172	133	176	124
Prospect	61	76	60	84
Seymour	254	203	224	157
Southbury	181	134	167	118
Wallingford	390	255	365	243
Waterbury	1175	860	1031	816
Wolcott	68	36	69	36
Woodbridge	66	123	65	114
Total	11696	9379	10784	8630

NEW LONDON COUNTY.

TOWNS.	1867 Dem.	1867 Rep.	1866 Dem.	1866 Rep.
Bozrah	74	105	92	114
Colchester	267	361	216	232
East Lyme	160	156	153	145
Franklin	68	81	79	98
Griswold	166	245	113	224
Groton	416	483	318	459
Lebanon	144	279	140	265
Ledyard	161	141	137	129
Lisbon	72	55	80	58
Lyme	129	141	110	160
Montville	179	227	163	222
New London	823	783	689	773
North Stonington	188	254	165	275
Norwich	1135	1444	953	1354
Old Lyme	154	115	131	111
Preston	293	146	273	150
Salem	82	77	84	68
Sprague	175	118	116	101
Stonington	477	545	360	481
Waterford	254	177	236	191
Total	5437	5833	4608	5610

TOLLAND COUNTY.

TOWNS.	1867 Dem.	1867 Rep.	1866 Dem.	1866 Rep.
Andover	70	62	68	77
Bolton	90	47	94	52
Columbia	112	91	116	75
Coventry	157	261	142	236
Ellington	154	164	161	179
Hebron	143	144	125	154
Mansfield	203	257	190	246
Somers	184	153	150	166
Stafford	429	377	396	395
Tolland	188	122	169	128
Union	106	86	99	75
Vernon	344	351	227	555
Willington	101	140	95	151
Total	2281	2455	2032	2479

WINDHAM COUNTY.

TOWNS.	1867 Dem.	1867 Rep.	1866 Dem.	1866 Rep.
Ashford	165	146	157	150
Brooklyn	114	210	114	198
Canterbury	186	169	155	158
Chaplin	72	88	75	97
Eastford	85	124	82	117
Hampton	73	126	59	133
Killingly	376	511	287	479
Plainfield	275	230	251	274
Pomfret	107	187	89	180
Putnam	113	284	85	256
Scotland	71	87	84	97
Sterling	117	93	100	88
Thompson	157	395	135	345
Voluntown	117	133	90	139
Windham	249	470	220	436
Woodstock	159	439	161	419
Total	2436	3782	2144	3566

NEW YORK.

COUNTIES.	Sec. of State, 1867.		Governor, 1866.		Cons. Conv'n. 1866.		Sec. of State, 1865.		Governor, 1864.		President, 1864.	
	Nelson. Dem.	McKean. Rep.	Hoffman. Dem.	Fenton. Rep.	Agst.	For.	Slocum. Dem.	Barlow. Rep.	Seymour. Dem.	Fenton. Rep.	McClel'n Dem.	Lincoln. Rep.
Albany	12292	10486	11320	11534	6413	12149	9919	9762	12929	10250	12934	10204
Allegany	2736	5640	2621	6330	2612	6173	1911	4626	2555	6262	2561	6238
Broome	3589	4731	3375	5173	2607	5227	2367	3965	3144	4995	3139	5001
Cattaraugus	3563	4826	3418	5728	2959	5537	2495	3975	3518	5576	3575	5505
Cayuga	4393	6776	4075	7723	2124	7457	3498	6120	4403	7560	4408	7534
Chautauqua	4053	7614	3814	8750	3552	8445	2797	6015	3952	8762	3992	8700
Chemung	3511	3168	3382	3467	3265	3420	2928	2787	3110	3307	3109	3292
Chenango	4057	5125	3980	5571	3844	5495	3162	4581	4021	5509	4033	5362
Clinton	3188	3445	3589	3699	2700	3166	2551	2741	3540	3486	3546	3471
Columbia	5016	4846	4883	5155	4794	5060	4582	4427	5236	4906	5240	4876
Cortland	2095	3477	2030	3872	1814	3787	1592	3115	2082	4005	2063	3983
Delaware	4226	4887	3968	5348	3856	5210	2979	4338	4206	5338	4249	5297
Dutchess	6700	6827	6081	7281	5839	6971	5340	6068	6593	7300	6643	7202
Erie	13530	11774	13122	12538	2564	7958	19951	11547	13398	13055	13370	13062
Essex	1971	2892	1903	3089	920	2949	1537	2466	2163	3229	2164	3224
Franklin	2060	2756	1953	2858	930	2625	1219	2154	1859	2863	1837	2838
Fulton	2553	2796	2669	3283	2559	3098	2519	2785	2884	2984	2887	2792
Genesee	2543	3531	2495	3918	2353	3830	2210	3291	2760	4050	2772	4030
Greene	3706	2820	3532	3210	3280	3082	3036	2568	3891	3121	3897	3087
Hamilton	450	222	with Fulton		with Fulton		with Fulton		with Fulton		with Fulton	
Herkimer	3949	4698	3831	5182	2217	4998	3183	4241	4173	5114	4207	5087
Jefferson	5506	7296	5314	8147	5156	7929	4428	6815	5313	8603	5842	8590
Kings	22391	17787	29166	19634	26175	19419	20342	18933	25663	20745	25726	20836
Lewis	2781	2882	2670	3182	2001	3143	1870	2399	2896	3111	2911	3078
Livingston	3149	4076	3118	4555	2290	4903	2813	3706	3535	4600	3553	4581
Madison	3743	5362	3519	5923	3299	5804	2872	4586	3744	6221	3748	6183
Monroe	8234	9023	8227	10006	4169	8646	6738	8154	9078	10247	9107	10203
Montgomery	3812	3306	3615	3619	3163	3550	3270	3219	3900	3536	3908	3517
New York	85764	26098	80667	33492	46193	35055	53128	28740	73537	36310	73709	36686
Niagara	4339	4147	3989	4716	3711	4569	3732	3986	4277	4845	4287	4839
Oneida	10555	11158	11121	12431	1958	11630	8036	9857	10923	12075	10916	12049
Onondaga	8456	10268	8028	11566	7982	11279	7310	9815	8697	11022	8713	10996
Ontario	3845	4780	3672	5371	3475	5208	3057	4291	3957	5457	3989	5409
Orange	6891	6592	6497	7167	6399	7090	5120	5803	6605	6820	6633	6783
Orleans	2216	3219	2106	3585	1543	3330	1961	2981	2442	3769	2458	3754
Oswego	5442	7726	5480	8368	5349	8111	4395	6745	6220	8798	6238	8793
Otsego	5763	5740	5797	6335	4683	5952	4802	5093	6050	6167	6047	6151
Putnam	1599	1182	1430	1329	1094	1188	1114	1046	1616	1446	1618	1443
Queens	5098	2841	4574	3611	4206	3494	3721	2928	5405	4307	5400	4284
Rensselaer	9375	8892	7504	9580	6712	9409	7368	7823	9375	9174	9377	9158
Richmond	2415	1912	2479	1508	1857	1639	1732	1371	2886	1584	2874	1564
Rockland	2081	1232	1973	1559	1787	1574	1609	1099	2293	1428	2287	1445
St. Lawrence	3593	9657	3146	10648	829	10155	2229	7369	4053	10904	4048	10863
Saratoga	4956	5475	4191	6078	4173	5950	3842	5135	4713	5923	4715	5908
Schenectady	2182	2223	1998	2469	1138	2594	1951	2424	2308	2284	2309	2263
Schoharie	4311	2634	4642	3092	4341	3130	3765	2846	4793	2886	4801	2870
Schuyler	1883	2292	1884	2576	1650	2242	1547	2161	1890	2570	1893	2576
Seneca	3128	2419	3114	2767	2607	2548	2744	2434	3249	2703	3267	2680
Steuben	5989	6830	5507	8021	5355	7772	4262	6030	5804	8123	5813	8099
Suffolk	3813	3316	3573	4083	3511	3979	2489	3273	4038	4327	4027	4305
Sullivan	3355	2761	3521	2987	2627	2489	2759	2459	3548	2973	3548	2960
Tioga	2979	3652	2779	3959	2744	3889	2006	3131	3014	3789	3018	3780
Tompkins	2926	3935	2952	4456	2879	4338	2437	3621	3006	4509	2996	4518
Ulster	7396	6131	7150	6769	5756	6327	5536	5346	7719	6958	7766	6900
Warren	2361	2473	1944	2522	912	2029	1821	2023	2153	2447	2169	2399
Washington	3507	5498	3035	5972	2041	5824	2552	4867	3659	6236	3642	6221
Wayne	3913	5152	4026	6021	2434	5711	3436	4873	4413	6117	4392	6122
Westchester	9253	6328	8293	7519	6337	7187	6076	5515	9310	7616	9355	7607
Wyoming	2314	3546	2298	4105	1497	3977	1724	3403	2563	4146	2568	4123
Yates	1632	2631	1476	2878	929	2784	1313	2322	1704	3049	1693	3036
Soldiers' Vote							435	801				
Total	373029	325099	352526	366315	256364	352854	273198	301055	361264	369657	361986	368735

STATE OFFICERS.—Governor, Reuben E. Fenton; Lieut.-Governor, Stewart L. Woodford; Secretary of State, Homer A. Nelson; Comptroller, William F. Allen; Treasurer, William H. Bristol; Attorney-General, M. B. Champlain; State Engineer, Van Rensselaer Richmond.

STATE DEBT, Sept. 30, 1867.—General Fund, $5,642,622.22; Contingent, $130,000.00; Canal, $15,733,-060.00; Bounty, $26,862,000.00; Total, $48,367,682.22.

VOTE FOR OTHER STATE OFFICERS.—1867.

Democratic.

Comptroller	Wm. F. Allen	Vote	372517
Treasurer	Wm. H. Bristol	"	372769
Attorney-General	M. B. Champlain	"	372648
State Engineer	V. R. Richmond	"	372967
Canal Commissioner	John D. Fay	"	372786
State Prison Inspector	Solomon Scheu	"	372928
Judge of Court of Appeals	Martin Grover	"	364849

Republican.

Thos. Hillhouse	Vote	325658
Theo. B. Gates	"	325201
Joshua M. Van Cott	"	325328
A. C. Powell	"	324775
J. M. Hammond	"	325509
G. De La Matyr	"	325018
Charles Mason	"	324477

Vote for Justices of the Supreme Court.—1867.
Democrats in *Italics*; Republicans in Roman.

	Elected.	Vote.	Opponents.	Vote.
1st District	*Albert Cardozo*	84381	Freeman J. Fithian	25968
2d District	*Abraham B. Tappan*	66250	Stephen W. Fullerton	40946
3d District	*Rufus W. Peckham*	65871	No opponent	
4th District	Augustus Bockes	41430	*Wm. C. Cooke*	3563
5th District	*Le Roy Morgan*	50102	No opponent	
6th District	*John M. Parker*	42254	Jesse Palmer	25411
7th District	James C. Smith	41519	*Josiah T. Miller*	34106
8th District	George Barker	43911	*Harlow L. Comstock*	35273

NEW YORK STATE BY ELECTION DISTRICTS.

ALBANY COUNTY.

	Sec. State, 1867.		Governor, 1836.	
	Nelson. Dem.	McKean. Rep.	Hoffman. Dem.	Fenton. Rep.
Albany City				
Ward 1, E.D.	315	93	280	82
M.D.	404	151	353	156
W.D.	633	187	544	252
2, E.D.	483	257	416	298
W.D.	221	146	174	174
3, E.D.	245	150	271	136
W.D.	300	324	318	299
4, E.D.	156	158	156	179
W.D.	198	281	184	272
5	198	185	160	210
6	320	373	304	406
7, E.D.	407	102	412	121
W.D.	434	209	413	226
8, E.D.	393	501	346	527
S.D.	571	232	540	241
9, E.D.	176	293	162	291
M.D.	251	302	234	342
W.D.	427	343	341	379
10, E.D.	308	358	305	382
M.D.	267	375	276	373
W.D.	410	528	317	627
Total City	7117	5548	6506	5973
Dist.				
Bethlh'm 1	215	183	202	196
2	116	237	109	251
3	196	131	194	142
Berne 1	112	103	105	132
2	141	171	100	204
3	82	71	45	102
Coeymans 1	151	111	139	108
2	170	89	172	103
3	145	38	122	54
Guilderl'd 1	89	203	82	202
2	104	173	104	185
3	81	110	82	109
Knox 1	59	189	36	236
2	63	87	56	103
N. Scotla'd 1	120	121	112	118
2	112	154	99	170
3	101	160	95	184
Rensel'lle 1	148	141	133	160
2	179	70	180	73
3	116	48	111	54
Watervliet 1	242	204	222	217
2	342	313	331	400
3	458	188	450	211
4	299	250	290	299
5	243	205	226	239
6	120	196	116	220
7	194	222	175	242
8	158	239	160	253
9	69	68	66	88
10	262	144	208	178
Westerlo 1	131	104	112	119
2	177	210	180	211
Total	12292	10486	11320	11533

ALLEGANY COUNTY.

	Nelson. Dem.	McKean. Rep.	Hoffman. Dem.	Fenton. Rep.
Alfred	32	272	38	296
Allen	10	165	7	196
Alma	81	43	78	51

ALLEGANY CO.—continued.

	Sec. State, 1867.		Governor, 1866.	
	Nel. Dem.	Mc Kean Rep.	Hoff- man. Dem.	Fen- ton. Rep.
Almond	191	206	218	232
Amity	157	278	163	305
Andover	131	233	114	274
Angelica	104	261	108	279
Belfast	125	204	109	225
Birdsall	85	63	75	83
Bolivar	75	142	69	157
Burns	94	148	86	113
Caneadea	174	200	114	214
Centreville	34	165	34	200
Clarksville	25	135	37	168
Cuba	214	291	221	314
Friendship	157	257	146	292
Genesee	28	183	25	207
Granger	20	182	23	207
Grove	94	88	70	108
Hume	94	322	86	342
Independ'e	71	215	58	223
New Huds'n	55	184	55	228
Rushford	57	280	46	335
Scio	174	268	178	223
Ward	47	81	58	101
Wellesville	217	314	241	340
West Alm'd	54	108	49	152
Willing	65	163	52	170
Wirt	71	249	63	264
Total	2736	5640	2621	6330

BROOME COUNTY.

	Nel. Dem.	Mc Kean Rep.	Hoff- man. Dem.	Fen- ton. Rep.
Dist.				
Bing. City 1	276	297	301	396
2	140	199	254	369
3	169	198	237	263
4	257	307	124	151
5	72	61		
Town 1	76	65		
2	60	106		
Barker	166	189	136	213
Chenango	103	222	93	259
Conklin	122	124	117	131
Dist.				
Colesville 1	135	240	153	238
2	85	88	85	89
3	86	127	102	140
Fenton	116	170		
Kirkwood 1	86	74	75	86
2	66	61	79	74
Lisle 1	86	207	77	232
2	57	181	40	189
Maine 1	63	259	56	279
2	66	56	70	61
Nanticoke	74	130	63	162
Port Crane			97	241
Sandford 1	257	165	245	192
2	48	49	45	57
3	28	65	34	75
Triangle	169	280	152	279
Union	84	85	75	85
Vestal 1	174	231	187	251
2	236	205	234	255
Windsor 1	192	300	182	346
2	40	60	40	70
Total	3589	4731	3375	5173

CATTARAUGUS COUNTY.

	Sec. State, 1867.		Governor, 1866.	
	Nelson. Dem.	Mc-Kean Rep.	Nelson. Dem.	Mc-Kean Rep.
Allegany	236	184	205	197
Dist.				
Ashford 1	78	95	69	118
2	62	91	54	122
Carrolton	86	63	85	93
Coldspring	101	96	124	89
Dist.				
Connew'go 1	65	89	55	100
2	38	89	44	92
Dayton	77	142	77	176
East Otto	79	153	93	173
Ellicotville	175	144	165	152
Farmers'lle	57	152	49	205
Franklin'lle	182	154	175	175
Freedom	61	196	63	241
Gr't Valley	138	162	117	190
Hinsdale	188	127	150	181
Humphrey	94	92	85	91
Ischua	98	83	82	112
Leon	72	189	88	320
Lit'le Valley	64	138	52	151
Lyndon	53	123	47	161
Machias	73	155	64	202
Mansfield	41	155	68	177
Napoli	64	166	69	193
New Albion	130	187	152	209
Olean	261	252	236	297
Otto	74	159	78	193
Perrysbur'h	116	195	110	198
Persea	171	119	173	141
Portville	118	215	104	256
Randolph	50	241	146	288
Salamanc'a	197	180	189	188
S'th Valley	41	49	28	87
Yorkshire	123	192	122	240
Total	3563	4826	3418	5728

CAYUGA COUNTY.

	Nelson. Dem.	Mc-Kean Rep.	Nelson. Dem.	Mc-Kean Rep.
Ward				
Auburn 1	323	471	258	434
2	162	304	130	353
3	186	321	182	298
4	336	318	283	328
Dist.				
Aurelius 1	149	120	121	130
2	137	114	142	126
Brutus	189	327	172	371
Cato	147	308	109	362
Conquest	196	191	199	233
Fleming	85	176	66	189
Genoa 1	74	193	62	242
2	64	176	63	205
Ira	170	264	191	275
Ledyard	105	273	107	333
Locke	60	173	61	216
Mentz	255	248	251	262
Montezuma	158	99	128	137
Moravia	161	272	158	313
Niles 1	123	121	112	164
2	99	63		126
Owasco	96	139	80	161
Scipio	119	238	116	286
Sempronius	86	177	81	199

CAYUGA CO.—continued.

TOWNS.	Sec. State, 1867.		Governor, 1866.	
	Nelson. Dem.	McKean. Rep.	Hoffman. Dem.	Fenton. Rep.
Bennett.....	124	212	117	252
Springport..	211	240	210	251
Sterling.....	189	321	189	408
Summerhill	58	182	61	213
Throop.....	114	143	113	156
Venice.....	97	294	90	352
Victory.....	139	262	150	300
Total.....	4393	6776	4075	7723

CHAUTAUQUA COUNTY.

TOWNS.	Nelson. Dem.	McKean. Rep.	Hoffman. Dem.	Fenton. Rep.
Arkwright...	71	112	79	162
Busti......	109	280	116	326
Carroll.....	43	250	42	310
Charlotte...	230	159	217	209
Dist.				
Chautau'a 1	182	240	157	258
" 2	58	141	52	158
Che'y Creek	87	176	80	218
Clymer.....	33	258	29	265
Dist.				
Dunkirk...1	186	102	194	138
" 2	97	139	95	163
" 3	289	156	263	191
Ellery......	82	303	95	349
Dist.				
Ellicott...1	122	414	107	473
" 2	204	459	174	505
Ellington...	55	293	58	340
French Cr'k	55	130	49	139
Gerry......	36	195	33	269
Dist.				
Hanover..1	122	117	98	152
" 2	145	109	148	185
" 3	64	97	55	120
" 4	69	82	61	105
Harmony .1	47	223	53	246
" 2	30	364	31	385
" 3	37	92	32	108
Kiantone...	36	72	28	96
Mina.......	80	148	71	166
Poland.....	48	269	33	296
Dist.				
Pomfret...1	128	197	139	215
" 2	155	196	136	211
" 3	81	94	95	109
Portland....	163	225	165	255
Ripley......	165	207	127	216
Sheridan...	136	154	127	195
Sherman...	62	247	57	253
Stockton...	171	236	160	283
Villenova...	120	189	116	217
Dist.				
Westfield..1	229	360	205	282
" 2	16	69	17	87
Total.....	4053	7614	3814	8750

CHEMUNG COUNTY.

TOWNS.	Nelson. Dem.	McKean. Rep.	Hoffman. Dem.	Fenton. Rep.
Ashland....	102	124		
Baldwin....	129	105	123	110
Big Flats...	219	164	230	195
Catlin......	149	145	158	179
Chemung...	190	242	171	258
Elmira.....	106	108	101	140
Ward.				
Elmira Cit.1	137	202	129	188
" 2	277	165	403	371
" 3	307	278	275	299
" 4	309	228	319	266
" 5	194	203	181	204
" 6	140	186		
Erin.......	195	100	168	122
Dist.				
Horsch'ds 1	202	256	205	272
" 2	109	50	107	46

CHEMUNG CO.—continued.

TOWNS.	Sec. State, 1867.		Governor, 1866.	
	Nelson. Dem.	McKean. Rep.	Hoffman. Dem.	Fenton. Rep.
S'port, dis. 1	139	63	209	186
" 2	179	115	153	149
Van Etten..	197	117	218	114
Dist.				
Veteran...1	69	108	74	124
" 2	162	209	158	244
	0	0		
Total.....	3511	3168	3382	3467

CHENANGO COUNTY.

TOWNS.	Nelson. Dem.	McKean. Rep.	Hoffman. Dem.	Fenton. Rep.
Afton......	187	259	157	272
Bainbridge.	177	262	170	277
Columbus..	50	240	54	280
Coventry...	160	198	151	229
German....	67	94	66	107
Dist.				
Greene...1	176	166	192	174
" 2	266	253	264	264
Guilford...1	169	95	167	102
" 2	89	228	89	278
Lincklaen..	45	169	44	198
McDonough	167	157	170	149
Dist.				
N. Berlin..1	140	186	136	199
" 2	135	131	140	133
Norwich ..1	258	229	268	223
N. Norw'h 1	62	100	65	114
" 2	24	38	17	44
Otselic.....	120	236	134	237
Dist.				
Oxford....1	172	176	187	190
" 2	189	209	178	220
Pharsalia..1	179	96	170	111
Pitcher....	131	173	130	182
Plymouth..	143	193	139	220
Preston....	123	93	127	109
Dist.				
Sherburne..	221	411	186	463
Dist.				
Smithville 1	118	57	116	92
" 2	133	72	129	92
Smyrna....	87	263	76	331
Total.....	4057	5125	3980	5571

CLINTON COUNTY.

TOWNS.	Nelson. Dem.	McKean. Rep.	Hoffman. Dem.	Fenton. Rep.
Dist.				
Ausable...1	99	109	116	115
" 2	141	107	122	125
Altona.....	101	148	141	152
Beekma'ton	170	274	256	266
Blackbro'k1	196	112	188	109
" 2	71	39	48	67
Champlain.	338	295	320	309
Dist.				
Chazy....1	118	119	111	147
" 2	40	234	51	293
Clinton...1	88	30	111	26
" 2	114	9	139	10
Dannemora	37	141	50	131
Dist.				
Ellenburg'1	97	92	111	91
" 2	196	128	179	123
Mooers....1	103	179	113	183
" 2	113	208	130	227
Peru......1	123	175	132	178
" 2	82	122	123	140
Plattsbur'1	286	210	356	215
" 2	103	96	107	113
" 3	171	168	201	157
Saranac...1	152	192	207	254
" 2	83	87	93	88
Sch'lerFalls	166	171	184	188
Total.....	3188	3445	3589	3699

COLUMBIA COUNTY.

TOWNS.	Sec. State, 1867.		Governor, 1866.	
	Nelson. Dem.	McKean. Rep.	Hoffman. Dem.	Fenton. Rep.
Ancram....	223	163	197	180
Austrelitz..	125	162	118	196
Canaan....	133	274	152	280
Dist.				
Chatham..1	246	305	234	312
" 2	202	195	203	197
Claverack.1	122	135	121	148
" 2	153	114	158	112
" 3	127	132	123	152
Clermont..	154	45	172	52
Dist.				
Copake...1	51	61	169	255
" 2	150	155		
Gallatin...1	74	121	85	121
" 2	29	102	39	96
Germanto'n	133	140	105	177
Ghent.....	249	310	224	334
Greenport.	143	164	153	146
Dist.				
Hillsdale..1	209	182	195	199
" 2	55	27	57	28
" 3	40	93	44	21
Ward.				
Hudson...1	197	152	177	172
" 2	273	171	247	183
" 3	197	217	171	237
" 4	255	236	248	251
Dist.				
Kinderh'k 1	229	156	225	167
" 2	210	254	231	223
Livingston..	196	229	204	235
N. Lebanon	217	170	215	193
Stockport ..	171	135	138	177
Dist.				
Stuyvesant1	78	68	85	56
" 2	176	119	162	125
Taghkanic..	208	129	231	128
Total.....	5016	4846	4883	5155

CORTLAND COUNTY.

TOWNS.	Nelson. Dem.	McKean. Rep.	Hoffman. Dem.	Fenton. Rep.
Cincinnatus	140	150	134	175
Dist.				
Cortl'ville 1	180	405	161	411
" 2	165	203	147	223
" 3	85	219	75	247
Cuyler.....	58	209	49	255
Freetown ..	63	126	67	144
Harford....	50	162	46	164
Dist.				
Homer....1	56	128	60	150
" 2	105	229	96	269
" 3	79	268	72	283
Lapeer.....	73	92	71	102
Marathon..	154	210	133	224
Preble.....	153	134	148	138
Scott......	54	212	62	222
Solon......	126	67	140	83
Taylor.....	88	160	82	177
Truxton....	179	158	195	192
Dist.				
Virgil.....1	121	177	124	221
" 2	45	59	46	67
Willett.....	121	109	122	125
Total.....	2095	3477	2030	3872

DELAWARE COUNTY.

TOWNS.	Nelson. Dem.	McKean. Rep.	Hoffman. Dem.	Fenton. Rep.
Dist.				
Andes.....1	92	265	70	296
" 2	126	79	94	93
Bovina.....	63	172	60	192
Dist.				
Colchester 1	123	205	101	181
" 2	51	63	34	51
" 3	77	71	65	65
Davenport 1	150	103	149	128

DELAWARE CO.—continued.

TOWNS.	Sec. State, 1867. Nelson, Dem.	McKean, Rep.	Governor, 1866. Hoffman, Dem.	Fenton, Rep.
Dist.				
Davenport 2	147	88	157	83
Delhi......1	147	206	130	222
"......2	113	198	113	219
Franklin..1	154	288	123	300
"......2	73	147	64	162
"......3	41	61	47	66
Hamden...	73	316	64	358
Dist.				
Hancock..1	87	84	72	79
"......2	207	191	226	158
Harperfield	138	155	146	176
Dist.				
Kortright.1	126	86	133	101
"......2	109	81	108	90
Masonville.	189	194	175	219
Meredith...	113	210	114	241
Middlet'n.1	130	88	116	93
"......2	267	121	239	142
"......3	55	50	48	70
Roxbury..1	73	53	71	59
"......2	35	45	39	61
"......3	218	85	206	104
Sidney.....	282	190	265	177
Stamford...	187	185	194	201
Dist.				
Tompkins 1	126	164	119	211
"......2	227	231	201	294
Walton....	237	412	225	456
Total.....	4226	4887	3968	5348

DUTCHESS COUNTY.

TOWNS.	Nelson, Dem.	McKean, Rep.	Hoffman, Dem.	Fenton, Rep.
Dist.				
Amenia...1	156	177	120	157
"......2	69	115	61	124
Beekman...	95	188	55	208
Dist.				
Clinton....1	105	137	88	148
"......2	101	117	101	114
Dover.....1	143	161	114	195
"......2	116	104	100	102
E. Fishkill.1	96	97	97	64
"......2	71	59	58	67
"......3	169	58	161	59
Fishkill...1	235	192	207	227
"......2	220	212	232	236
"......3	166	177	158	209
"......4	165	143	163	159
"......5	90	67	98	60
Hyde Park1	146	133	133	137
"......2	154	96	154	103
Lagrange..	216	235	206	227
Dist.				
Milan.....1	46	72	45	75
"......2	113	131	114	127
Northeast..	194	217	180	242
Pawling...	140	273	118	293
Pine Plains	133	166	118	212
Pleas't Val.	224	204	192	225
Dist.				
P'keepsie..1	205	129	187	146
"......2	119	168	112	168
Ward.				
P'kep. Cit. 1	404	233	350	247
"......2	363	275	326	283
"......3	196	284	152	339
"......4	227	289	206	263
"......5	191	259	155	264
"......6	146	221	124	227
Dist.				
Red Hook 1	249	152	276	186
"......2	344	94	249	117
Rhinebeck 1	200	186	179	213
"......2	170	205	145	229
Stanford...1	148	154	144	145
"......2	65	125	57	134

DUTCHESS CO.—continued.

TOWNS.	Nelson, Dem.	McKean, Rep.	Hoffman, Dem.	Fenton, Rep.
Union Vale Dist.	104	228	96	230
Wash'ton..1	118	157	111	165
"......2	188	157	139	165
Total.....	6700	6827	6081	7281

ERIE COUNTY.

TOWNS.	Nelson, Dem.	McKean, Rep.	Hoffman, Dem.	Fenton, Rep.
Dist.				
Alden......1	122	121	123	136
"......2	147	50	188	59
Amherst..1	248	213	301	209
"......2	154	29	166	47
Aurora....1	153	201	166	230
"......2	41	90	53	103
Boston.....1	212	114	216	134
"......2	128	106	129	125
Chicktaw'a	166	159	165	180
Dist.				
Clarence..1	82	118	83	124
"......2	114	216	145	251
Colden....	187	119	199	155
Dist.				
Collins....1	55	171	53	193
"......2	76	146	87	156
Concord...1	130	229	136	254
"......2	58	69	76	94
"......3	63	58	61	70
E. Hamb'gh	198	212	206	247
Dist.				
Eden......1	93	37	98	48
"......2	152	150	140	168
Elma......1	156	104	149	126
"......2	120	54	120	75
Evans.....1	58	102	66	101
"......2	138	92	133	197
Grand Isl'd	99	79	96	91
Hamburgh.	311	170	351	181
Dist.				
Holland....1	177	107	182	132
Lancaster.1	331	179	305	194
"......2	80	95	89	161
Marilla....	214	185	198	205
Dist.				
Newstead..1	93	132	100	155
"......2	119	195	130	267
Dist.				
N. Collins.1	30	129	34	148
"......2	76	64	87	85
Sardinia...	150	213	179	239
Tonawanda	307	135	324	131
Wales.....	132	163	134	186
W. Seneca.	223	108	238	137
Total towns	5493	5015	5708	5734

BUFFALO.

Ward. Dist.	Nelson, Dem.	McKean, Rep.	Hoffman, Dem.	Fenton, Rep.
1	324	111	283	109
...... 2	332	98	312	93
...... 3	395	163	352	160
2 1	210	160	191	73
...... 2	185	301	148	298
...... 3	143	271	127	263
3 1	312	288	262	306
...... 2	213	229	279	240
4 1	161	173	156	173
...... 2	257	224	242	228
...... 3	262	223	229	217
5 1	321	303	298	309
...... 2	477	207	440	245
...... 3	213	259	195	226
6 1	326	149	293	189
...... 2	276	281	241	314
...... 3	333	136	355	148
7 1	307	279	243	309

ERIE CO.—continued.

Ward. Dist.	Nelson, Dem.	McKean, Rep.	Hoffman, Dem.	Fenton, Rep.
7 2	159	158	125	179
...... 3	381	229	440	129
8 1	245	153	202	154
...... 2	371	216	308	218
9 1	214	322	217	318
...... 2	216	333	200	334
10 1	267	341	212	309
...... 2	216	370	231	337
11 1	214	210	196	236
...... 2	109	163	82	161
12 1	295	226	239	248
...... 2	117	47	100	44
13 1	186	136	168	146
Total City..	8037	6759	7414	6804
Total Coun.	13530	11774	13122	12538

ESSEX COUNTY.

TOWNS.	Nelson, Dem.	McKean, Rep.	Hoffman, Dem.	Fenton, Rep.
Dist.				
Chest'field 1	155	175	159	171
"......2	34	44	40	46
Crownpoint	100	374	69	451
Elizabeth'n	62	201	63	224
Essex.....	146	126	150	124
Dist.				
Jay......1	109	115	70	144
"......2	123	74	118	78
Keene.....	15	109	28	107
Lewis.....	142	154	152	174
Minerva...	81	53	91	56
Dist.				
Moriah...1	157	247	173	260
"......2	198	97	212	98
Newcomb..	4	24	..	31
North Elba.	41	32	43	33
N. Hudson..	29	59	28	71
Dist.				
St.Armn'd 1	13	33	10	33
"......2	2	12	1	22
Schroon....	119	188	121	188
Ticonder'ga	148	294	153	301
Westport...	150	182	107	198
Willsboro'h	111	160	96	168
Wilming't'n	32	127	19	121
Total.....	1971	2892	1903	3089

FRANKLIN COUNTY.

TOWNS.	Nelson, Dem.	McKean, Rep.	Hoffman, Dem.	Fenton, Rep.
Bangor....	105	350	102	334
Bellmont...	96	106	82	114
Dist.				
Bombay...1	91	83	87	98
"......2	57	15	61	14
Brandon...	48	95	38	92
Brighton...	11	25	11	21
Burke.....	190	166	169	174
Chateau'y 1	114	90	108	117
"......2	191	92	196	119
Constable...	97	131	95	134
Dickinson..	43	312	38	298
Duane.....	31	20	33	29
Ft. Covin'tn	145	243	129	253
Dist.				
Franklin...1	51	21	42	20
"......2	65	84	52	81
Harrietst'n.	32	19	42	25
Dist.				
Malone....1	160	326	151	313
"......2	247	290	234	312
Moira.....	167	164	179	160
Westville...	119	124	110	150
Total.....	2060	2756	1958	2858

FULTON COUNTY.

TOWNS.	Sec. State, 1867.		Governor, 1866.	
	Nelson, Dem.	Mc Kean Rep.	Hoffman, Dem.	Fenton, Rep.
Bleecker ...	158	30	115	61
Broadalbin.	249	280	191	327
Caroga	104	36	75	42
Ephratah ..	254	194	224	235
Dist.				
Johnstown 1	300	287	289	292
" 2	322	774	255	797
" 3	199	288	179	309
Mayfield ..1	164	186	136	193
" ..2	59	115	56	128
Northamp'n.	272	179	243	186
Dist.				
Oppenh'im 1	254	197	160	88
" 2			82	132
Perth	91	130	88	130
Stratford...	127	100	109	129
Total....	2553	2796	2202	3039

GENESEE COUNTY.

Alabama...	79	238	88	275
Alexander.	124	228	113	260
Bergen	174	223	190	233
Byron	103	228	102	265
Bethany....	125	216	128	238
Dist.				
Batavia...1	171	197	234	289
" ..2	218	162	296	304
" ..3	224	174		
Darien....	165	203	197	253
Elba ...	185	256	187	230
Dist.				
Le Roy...1	234	292	252	297
" ..2	137	188	149	210
Oakfield ..	97	181	91	205
Pavilion ..	137	201	139	241
Dist.				
Pembroke.1	94	168	85	208
" 2	137	174	127	178
Stafford....	119	202	117	232
Total....	2543	3531	2495	3918

GREENE COUNTY.

Dist.				
Athens....1	243	167	253	225
" ..2	56	79	55	94
Ashland...	78	148	76	51
Dist.				
Cairo......1	248	178	246	177
" ..2	54	51	46	66
Catskill ...1	282	244	259	246
" ..2	162	85	110	99
" ..3	112	152	94	165
" ..4	123	126	124	145
Coxsackie 1	287	283	264	309
" 2	124	59	95	71
Durham...1	203	150	200	161
" ..2	103	126	108	139
Greenville.	256	245	263	262
Halcott....	64	28	62	37
Dist.				
Hunter...1	94	29	108	42
" ..2	64	72	59	95
Jewett	149	109	132	128
Dist.				
Lexington 1	115	23	123	37
" 2	119	38	121	41
N. Balti're 1	223	109	200	138
" 2	131	89	126	93
Prattsville..	214	70	217	83
Windham..	213	150	191	206
Total....	3706	2820	3532	3210

HAMILTON COUNTY.

TOWNS.	Sec. State, 1867.		Governor, 1866.	
	Nelson, Dem.	Mc Kean Rep.	Hoffman, Dem.	Fenton, Rep.
Arietta....	14	11	17	4
Benson.....	82	13	105	8
Hope.......	98	43	104	43
Ind. Lake..	21	22	25	21
Lake Pleas't	50	20	38	41
Long Lake..	50	48	5	49
Morehouse..	34	7	43	12
Wells	146	58	130	66
Total....	450	222	467	244

HERKIMER COUNTY.

Columbia ..	160	259	154	309
Danube	136	194	139	207
Fairfield ...	110	211	111	237
Dist.				
Frankfort.1	223	229	233	259
" 2	54	114	55	153
Ger. Flats.1	359	265	356	291
" 2	196	356	191	327
Herkimer..	389	253	395	265
Litchfield ..	134	163	130	195
Dist.				
Little Falls 1	502	397	473	425
" 2	218	104	234	100
Manheim...	246	181	223	196
Newport ...	117	296	115	347
Norway	111	104	110	127
Ohio.......	116	99	78	115
Dist.				
Russia....1	59	249	46	270
" ..2	82	81	81	93
Salisbury..	161	290	140	306
Schuyler...	125	200	134	236
Stark......	152	195	157	215
Warren	195	197	185	210
Dist.				
Wilmurt...1	5	29	3	23
" ..2	4	2	5	1
Winfield....	97	231	81	275
Total....	3349	4698	3831	5182

JEFFERSON COUNTY.

Dist.				
Adams....1	114	226	125	252
" 2	68	250	75	295
Alexand'a 1	135	70	124	91
" 2	63	142	59	157
" 3	106	99	115	118
Antwerp..1	150	313	167	354
" ..2	77	72	69	85
Brownville 1	87	89	83	104
" 2	59	81	58	89
" 3	38	92	31	139
" 4	62	170	55	170
C. Vincent 1	221	179	193	196
" 2	111	65	102	86
Champion..	140	279	140	313
Dist.				
Clayton...1	132	124	127	152
" ..2	230	180	231	198
Ellisburgh.1	195	242	191	245
" 2	119	233	127	242
" 3	85	254	90	289
Henderson..	152	247	139	273
Dist.				
Hounsfield 1	147	131	155	149
" 2	28	80	31	92
" 3	50	85	61	99
Le Ray...1	177	195	176	203
" ..2	93	205	106	213
Lorraine ...	146	146	128	169
Dist.				
Lyme.....1	81	96	75	122
" 2	101	106	88	130
" 3	49	56	51	62

JEFFERSON CO.—*continued.*

TOWNS.	Sec. State, 1867.		Governor, 1866.	
	Nelson, Dem.	Mc Kean Rep.	Hoffman, Dem.	Fenton, Rep.
Dist.				
Orleans....1	46	54	40	58
" 2	79	113	71	128
" 3	59	55	54	60
" 4	63	55	61	73
Pamelia...1	162	170	160	177
" ..2	66	110	54	119
Philadelp'a	187	157	178	189
Rodman ...	93	261	87	309
Dist.				
Rutland...1	49	149	56	156
" ..2	86	122	95	133
Theresa ...	219	253	215	296
Dist.				
Waterto'n 1	253	248	234	268
" 2	171	245	173	255
" 3	186	193	154	209
" 4	134	105	128	113
Wilna....1	202	222	180	225
" ..2	99	73	86	78
" ..3	47	136	46	144
Worth.....	83	68	70	70
Total....	5506	7296	5314	8147

KINGS COUNTY.

BROOKLYN.				
Ward. Dist.				
1 1	260	290	230	339
2	371	124	357	163
Total....	631	414	587	502
2 1	458	66	494	82
2	217	64	217	79
3	525	132	536	155
Total....	1200	262	1247	316
3 1	248	246	232	292
2	281	304	276	345
3	223	347	165	400
Total....	752	897	673	1037
4 1	310	270	294	324
2	344	172	421	350
3	311	250	357	306
4	145	144		
Total....	1110	836	1072	980
5 1	681	40	614	40
2	372	40	329	64
3	476	113	445	90
4	215	116	207	118
5	243	112	221	131
6	473	100	428	123
Total....	2490	521	2244	566
6 1	510	87	525	108
2	453	137	470	164
3	593	267	577	352
4	548	208	514	216
5	410	217	373	242
Total....	2514	916	2459	1082
7 1	413	230	357	223
2	414	162	361	176
3	222	261	232	294
4	264	261	221	287
5	219	190	211	206
Total....	1532	1104	1382	1186

KINGS CO.—continued.

TOWNS.	Sec. State, 1867. Nelson Dem.	McKean Rep.	Governor, 1867. Hoffman Dem.	Fenton Rep.
Ward. Dist.				
8 1	249	179	194	168
2	158	144	343	210
3	230	88	378	136
4	443	142	289	127
5	324	108		
Total....	1404	661	1204	641
9 1	532	142	471	161
2	532	46	453	113
3	253	178	207	183
4	319	114	245	120
5	306	292	229	312
6	533	150	507	196
7	245	184	145	173
Total....	2720	1106	2257	1258
10 1	271	240	243	283
2	456	114	422	141
3	317	206	251	225
4	460	158	431	203
5	638	76	544	89
6	258	222	198	276
7	271	166	222	206
8	352	237	293	270
Total....	3023	1419	2604	1693
11 1	296	219	280	246
2	340	103	292	121
3	224	229	215	274
4	336	247	321	312
5	189	323	168	369
6	428	88	351	137
Total....	1815	1209	1627	1459
12 1	679	41	670	55
2	190	12	137	18
3	437	13	407	11
4	445	88	394	130
Total....	1751	154	1608	214
13 1	279	200	224	234
2	302	333	267	389
3	264	225	267	265
4	296	356	230	411
5	146	177	123	233
6	111	157	111	171
Total....	1398	1448	1222	1703
14 1	573	82	538	73
2	477	65	469	170
3	326	90	317	121
4	207	145	233	187
5	313	74	285	86
Total....	1896	456	1842	637
15 1	319	109	191	125
2	238	261	330	308
3	186	215	356	410
4	173	167		
5	279	176		
Total....	1095	928	867	843
16 1	272	207	249	240
2	282	169	257	222
3	374	167	351	173
4	273	209	262	201
5	380	192	400	161
6	405	131	403	144
Total....	1986	1075	1922	1141

KINGS CO.—continued.

TOWNS.	Sec. State, 1867. Nelson Dem.	McKean Rep.	Governor, 1866. Hoffman Dem.	Fenton Rep.
Ward. Dist.				
17 1	474	381	469	447
2	345	316	296	430
3	220	302		
Total....	1039	999	765	877
18 1	338	183	290	176
2	302	252	270	232
Total....	640	435	560	408
19 1	213	191	162	178
2	218	274	187	284
3	311	245	283	270
Total....	742	710	632	732
20 1	316	316	280	292
2	391	333	381	378
3	137	140	118	157
4	119	137	107	142
5	235	409	264	402
6	105	213	80	201
Total....	1303	1548	1230	1572
Total City..	31030	17252	27974	18996
New Lots..	532	162	478	252
Flatbush...	269	136	218	168
Flatlands..	193	95	124	143
N. Utrecht..	277	79	249	12
Gravesend.	160	63	123	93
Total....	32391	17787	29166	19634

LEWIS COUNTY.

TOWNS.	Nelson Dem.	McKean Rep.	Hoffman Dem.	Fenton Rep.
Dist.				
Croghan..1	103	45	90	60
" ..2	137	35	157	46
Denmark .1	70	151	68	188
" 2	64	200	62	222
Diana......1	34	22	44	30
" ..2	47	15	52	20
" ..3	74	76	70	89
Greig......1	106	84	75	93
" ..2	123	121	95	125
Harrisburg.	110	152	110	164
H. Market.	143	33	192	42
Lewis......	159	56	154	58
Leyden....1	82	161	80	178
" ..2	124	70	112	75
Lowville...	212	378	188	390
Martinsb'g1	58	122	60	134
" 2	100	207	82	218
Montague..	64	76	75	91
N. Bremen.1	173	89	172	89
" 2	76	6	61	6
Osceola...	78	63	66	69
Pinckney..	154	130	139	155
Turin......1	86	168	66	185
" ..2	38	83	37	92
Watson....	136	121	121	124
Dist.				
W. Turin .1	103	156	115	175
" ..2	57	56	53	53
" ..3	70	6	74	11
Total....	2781	2882	2670	3182

LIVINGSTON COUNTY.

TOWNS.	Nelson Dem.	McKean Rep.	Hoffman Dem.	Fenton Rep.
Dist.				
Avon......1	46	142	49	161
" ..2	157	113	150	125
" ..3	31	38	35	42
Caledonia..1	111	169	109	204
Conesus....1	94	185	94	196

LIVINGSTON CO.—continued.

TOWNS.	Sec. State, 1867. Nelson Dem.	McKean Rep.	Governor, 1866. Hoffman Dem.	Fenton Rep.
Dist.				
Geneseo...1	122	190	124	193
" ..2	93	151	90	166
Groveland .1	113	111	117	131
Leicester ..2	170	202	143	215
Lima.......	223	326	219	352
Dist.				
Livonia ...1	86	140	85	157
" ..2	78	249	83	256
Mt. Morris 1	319	183	300	212
" 2	64	64	56	73
" 3	85	83	80	108
N. Dans'lle1	195	164	189	160
" ..2	239	149	236	161
Nunda 1	130	119	137	153
" ..2	93	178	100	192
Ossian....	108	119	115	125
Portage....	110	146	106	180
Sparta.....	151	130	146	145
Dist.				
Spr'gwater1	47	104	51	118
" 2	60	195	65	251
West Sparta	124	132	134	127
Dist.				
York......1	54	205	58	250
" ..2	46	96	47	102
Total....	3149	4076	3118	4555

MADISON COUNTY.

TOWNS.	Nelson Dem.	McKean Rep.	Hoffman Dem.	Fenton Rep.
Dist.				
Brookfield 1	33	142	39	150
" 2	112	182	109	210
" 3	105	102	98	123
" 4	57	52	58	63
Cazenovia 1	86	149	73	175
" 2	143	220	143	241
" 3	153	178	132	192
De Ruyter..	89	285	89	284
Dist.				
Eaton......1	152	257	137	263
" ..2	159	259	129	272
Fenner.....	128	169	111	197
Georgeto'n 2	92	255	70	279
Dist.				
Hamilton 1	126	313	106	304
" 2	161	251	138	305
Lebanon ..1	44	150	26	181
" ..2	70	100	57	113
Lenox.....1	113	115	128	137
" ..2	385	402	375	410
" ..3	190	153	179	191
" ..4	186	265	163	281
Madison...1	184	322	178	355
Nelson....1	117	96	105	108
" ..2	66	117	55	133
Smithfield..	58	190	68	227
Stockbridge	160	238	167	244
Dist.				
Sullivan ...1	278	124	267	157
" ..2	158	60	167	69
" ..3	68	82	79	95
" ..4	43	66	47	78
" ..5	27	67	28	86
Total....	3743	5363	3519	5923

MONROE COUNTY.

TOWNS.	Nelson Dem.	McKean Rep.	Hoffman Dem.	Fenton Rep.
Dist.				
Brighton..1	184	110	156	126
" ..2	82	125	68	148
Chili......	176	154	182	160
Clarkson ..1	166	238	158	261
Gates......	299	146	229	294
Dist.				
Greece 1	223	121	264	140
" ..2	143	123	157	137

MONROE CO.—continued.

TOWNS.	Sec. State, 1867. Nelson. Dem.	Mc-Kean Rep.	Governor, 1866. Hoffman. Dem.	Fenton. Rep.
Hamlin.....	100	314	94	343
Dist.				
Henrietta..1	71	131	63	153
"" 2	122	99	130	96
Irondequ't 1	166	68	161	78
"" 2	134	88	157	110
Mendon...1	174	135	162	146
"" 2	116	128	134	143
Ogden	238	270	238	304
Dist.				
Parma 1	99	157	90	171
"" 2	60	216	43	241
Penfield...1	120	191	135	224
"" 2	38	116	36	155
Perrinton .1	191	255	197	274
"" 2	70	98	69	152
Pittsford ...	201	186	208	203
Riga.......	146	214	149	227
Rush	120	169	143	193
Dist.				
Sweden ...1	73	170	73	193
"" 2	235	318	204	316
Webster ..1	108	212	115	225
"" 2	69	119	71	146
Wheatl'nd 1	88	187	93	195
"" 2	96	85	98	96
Total towns	4037	4943	4097	5580
Ward.				
Rochester..1	267	207	272	236
"" 2	345	282	339	289
"" 3	319	464	350	481
"" 4	266	287	247	302
"" 5	440	303	429	339
"" 6	300	274	312	276
"" 7	200	301	171	343
"" 8	447	314	433	365
"" 9	363	363	374	371
"" 10	216	237	212	269
"" 11	372	211	359	367
"" 12	254	288	236	319
"" 13	234	274	208	253
"" 14	184	275	186	314
Total.......	4197	4080	4128	4424
Tot. county.	8234	9023	8225	10004

MONTGOMERY COUNTY.

TOWNS.	Sec. State, 1867. Nelson. Dem.	Mc-Kean Rep.	Governor, 1866. Hoffman. Dem.	Fenton. Rep.
Dist.				
Amsterd'm1	287	340	240	370
"" 2	371	101	281	313
Canajoharie				
1	347	262	336	288
"" 2	117	161	105	184
Charleston 1	53	116	54	114
"" 2	89	143	114	150
Florida....1	120	141	119	162
"" 2	174	93	155	107
"" 3	92	26	102	32
Glen....1	170	119	201	110
"" 2	66	48	53	64
"" 3	79	96	89	104
Minden...1	336	359	280	430
"" 2	59	97	56	102
"" 3	99	65	86	96
Mohawk..1	101	104	85	107
"" 2	254	211	248	206
Palatine ..1	233	90	248	96
"" 2	139	149	125	182
Root.......1	141	108	121	52
"" 2	191	95	117	91
"" 3			106	78
St. John'lle1	294	179	294	181
Total.....	3812	3306	3615	3619

NEW YORK COUNTY.

Ward.	Dist.	Sec. State, 1867. Nelson. Dem.	Mc-Kean Rep.	Governor, 1866. Hoffman. Dem.	Fenton. Rep.
1	1	631	19	672	35
	2	580	20	607	40
	3	607	25	647	38
	4	127	32	107	40
	5	136	25	157	26
Total.....		2081	121	2190	179
2	1	123	46	126	93
	2	132	32	141	41
Total.....		255	78	267	134
3	1	292	67	289	85
	2	131	39	124	66
	3	131	28	124	33
	4	46	9	56	12
Total.....		600	143	593	196
4	1	371	77	341	132
	2	615	59	557	107
	3	438	36	474	59
	4	328	21	297	26
	5	331	34	296	35
	6	272	82	290	43
	7	401	66	395	41
Total.....		2756	375	2650	443
5	1	97	33	114	45
	2	112	21	121	44
	3	315	94	312	117
	4	240	181	207	236
	5	315	51	324	62
	6	372	86	336	125
	7	371	80	341	91
	8	395	40	397	63
Total.....		2187	586	2152	803
6	1	30	19	35	25
	2	114	8	119	14
	3	327	29	323	50
	4	260	32	294	57
	5	497	29	459	30
	6	678	5	634	24
	7	265	15	230	28
	8	198	18	176	33
	9	728	21	768	22
	10	203	10	216	14
Total.....		3300	186	3254	297
7	1	415	60	338	94
	2	664	30	662	47
	3	367	90	357	99
	4	221	37	218	64
	5	544	74	523	125
	6	543	105	443	246
	7	307	58	242	122
	8	379	70	345	104
	9	517	75	489	114
	10	591	41	555	69
	11	491	60	483	58
Total.....		5049	700	4656	1142
8	1	285	34	264	70
	2	559	88	546	140
	3	279	96	260	121
	4	197	78	217	98
	5	351	26	352	54
	6	335	69	277	89
	7	507	87	478	174

NEW YORK CO.—continued.

Ward.	Dist.	Sec. State, 1867. Nelson. Dem.	Mc-Kean Rep.	Governor, 1866. Hoffman. Dem.	Fenton. Rep.
8	8	343	192	372	211
	9	344	121	319	162
	10	300	73	294	110
	11	321	72	281	98
	12	292	29	260	54
Total.....		4113	964	3920	1381
9	1	355	88	341	95
	2	328	157	316	193
	3	299	132	313	154
	4	206	261	228	295
	5	287	229	276	286
	6	273	212	262	255
	7	309	272	317	319
	8	141	91	102	124
	9	161	110	173	156
	10	153	126	128	141
	11	202	214	203	251
	12	187	197	182	193
	13	233	77	227	95
	14	381	163	354	179
	15	265	193	262	204
	16	289	187	313	206
	17	168	48	160	61
Total.....		4237	2748	4187	3207
10	1	410	104	373	151
	2	425	113	413	193
	3	394	109	345	188
	4	466	111	436	163
	5	396	86	364	145
	6	438	85	358	138
	7	425	75	373	144
	8	509	122	495	162
Total.....		3453	805	3157	1284
11	1	349	23	350	57
	2	504	49	508	80
	3	418	44	411	62
	4	351	112	355	178
	5	392	115	311	105
	6	194	40	208	70
	7	441	30	446	52
	8	392	44	384	77
	9	193	91	211	121
	10	199	81	217	95
	11	251	75	246	108
	12	306	28	304	80
	13	418	57	393	83
	14	308	100	297	116
	15	239	37	216	33
	16	352	73	335	60
	17	266	41	250	57
	18	450	42	404	72
	19	276	43	282	65
Total.....		6229	1125	6128	1601
12	1	280	119	293	115
	2	517	179	464	231
	3	399	152	331	150
	4	403	243	387	227
	5	511	394	512	422
	6	306	220	261	254
	7	337	72	359	53
	8	393	208	336	205
Total.....		3076	1586	2943	1657
13	1	460	134	414	170
	2	234	67	482	191
	3	288	91	565	103

NEW YORK CO.—continued.

TOWNS.	Sec. State 1867. Nelson, Dem.	McKean Rep.	Governor 1866. Hoffman, Dem.	Fenton, Rep.
Ward. Dist.				
13				
4	304	67	467	97
5	454	58	832	156
6	242	75	263	126
7	412	68	193	68
8	260	77	337	114
9	311	144	..	..
10	297	93	..	..
Total	3212	874	3053	1025
14				
1	250	22	209	47
2	395	9	137	16
3	288	25	274	40
4	478	23	467	51
5	276	58	278	89
6	443	48	420	95
7	278	63	275	77
8	315	24	266	52
9	596	30	551	75
10	230	25	219	59
Total	3549	327	3396	601
15				
1	260	184	234	228
2	292	111	274	123
3	278	99	299	78
4	260	217	234	285
5	106	100	89	124
6	140	136	151	169
7	114	147	80	175
8	416	154	396	112
9	156	138	165	182
10	173	104	171	133
11	140	100	146	119
Total	2335	1490	2229	1728
16				
1	293	160	251	198
2	352	173	329	184
3	553	200	507	219
4	199	187	203	236
5	221	171	217	176
6	309	152	275	184
7	309	123	303	142
8	389	189	406	220
9	225	226	250	257
10	195	156	171	227
11	153	165	133	212
12	421	190	403	233
13	87	31	89	39
14	127	54	110	67
Total	3834	2177	3647	2594
17				
1	335	101	295	157
2	421	101	397	163
3	407	99	386	144
4	328	103	300	139
5	341	120	336	166
6	195	101	208	130
7	225	123	235	151
8	329	101	319	140
9	115	61	99	93
10	252	52	243	78
11	189	171	179	193
12	251	175	220	214
13	403	99	404	98
14	453	31	464	47
15	416	54	369	91
16	306	69	283	109
17	357	69	349	114
18	459	70	478	105
19	343	64	319	120
20	455	58	449	77
21	447	25	430	68
22	421	82	412	147

NEW YORK CO.—continued.

TOWNS.	Nelson, Dem.	McKean Rep.	Hoffman, Dem.	Fenton, Rep.
Ward. Dist.				
23	442	66	465	78
24	577	28	489	47
Total	8487	2020	8128	2869
18				
1	198	146	191	226
2	223	235	184	331
3	281	234	241	329
4	261	227	186	223
5	217	223	232	231
6	249	91	373	244
7	283	82	353	233
8	274	103	200	93
9	77	83	258	128
10	196	82	386	82
11	268	94	401	148
12	399	90	325	58
13	289	84	568	37
14	310	38	315	53
15	388	15	560	58
16	386	27	..	..
17	263	25	..	..
18	138	5	..	..
19	457	19	..	..
20	169	29	..	..
Total	5320	1923	4783	2484
19				
1	275	81	265	119
2	287	72	252	105
3	98	53	78	56
4	613	109	429	118
5	132	59	124	103
6	452	166	375	240
7	294	52	236	106
8	376	139	293	204
9	124	77	103	68
10	481	125	353	157
11	294	213	252	242
12	402	88	341	116
13	144	25	148	33
14	153	45	113	45
15	142	61	142	60
16	366	189	341	229
17	431	200	386	262
Total	5064	1753	4210	2263
20				
1	384	31	355	48
2	336	169	299	182
3	451	112	413	182
4	370	138	258	66
5	247	105	214	103
6	431	64	372	97
7	447	26	356	55
8	159	100	142	127
9	84	107	82	115
10	116	103	104	135
11	120	95	150	140
12	321	140	243	177
13	459	50	410	88
14	327	86	333	119
15	329	86	282	118
16	351	104	370	123
17	417	102	418	137
18	342	92	351	135
19	248	97	262	104
20	224	42	320	148
21	192	111	190	184
22	237	66	215	86
Total	6592	2026	6109	2669
21				
1	313	131	285	159
2	471	94	407	110
3	521	117	457	153

NEW YORK CO.—continued.

TOWNS.	Nelson, Dem.	McKean Rep.	Hoffman, Dem.	Fenton, Rep.
Ward. Dist.				
4	585	89	473	133
5	552	88	494	111
6	316	63	264	66
7	377	82	264	128
8	171	143	164	180
9	265	144	206	193
10	353	224	281	256
11	272	208	232	236
12	207	160	176	205
13	191	253	182	303
14	193	241	178	298
Total	4795	2037	4063	2530
22				
1	460	182	443	237
2	454	83	479	102
3	290	225	282	275
4	439	180	428	201
5	198	115	186	133
6	280	147	257	186
7	280	167	284	226
8	237	107	241	117
9	354	132	322	194
10	158	63	161	72
11	253	118	201	108
12	204	53	185	60
13	397	157	386	179
14	347	65	290	83
15	410	45	359	72
16	308	112	286	92
17	171	94	172	78
Total	5240	2045	4962	2415
Total city	85764	26098	80677	33492

NIAGARA COUNTY.

TOWNS.	Nelson, Dem.	McKean Rep.	Hoffman, Dem.	Fenton, Rep.
Cambria...	151	234	148	262
Hartland..1	153	205	148	251
Lewiston..1	190	121	154	138
Lockport..1	55	109	45	124
Lockport..2	232	281	202	336
Lockp't cit.1	334	295	279	344
" 2	269	155	275	155
" 3	299	395	264	393
" 4	183	166	152	185
Newfane..1	133	124	143	42
" 2	182	183	204	213
Niagara..1	322	157	231	213
" 2	232	101	216	121
Pendleton...	159	137	143	150
Porter...	163	211	151	236
Royalton..1	225	180	213	223
" 2	257	232	255	243
Somerset...1	101	161	113	296
Wheatfi'd.1	79	70	88	69
Wilson...1	272	41	247	66
" 2	154	201	154	220
" 3	83	141	64	161
Total	4339	4147	3969	4716

ONEIDA COUNTY.

TOWNS.	Nelson, Dem.	McKean Rep.	Hoffman, Dem.	Fenton, Rep.
Annsville...	327	248	322	312
Augusta...	204	231	204	311
Ava...	123	127	120	144
Boonville...	387	542	467	584
Bridgwater...	87	156	105	198
Camden...	258	481	286	559
Deerfield...	236	244	369	235
Florence...	362	121	434	137

ONEIDA CO.—continued.

TOWNS.	Sec. State, 1867.		Governor, 1866.	
	Nelson, Dem.	McKean, Rep.	Hoffman, Dem.	Fenton, Rep.
Floyd	176	130	168	143
Kirkland	422	516	436	528
Lee	319	230	357	333
Marcy	177	157	202	182
Marshall	178	273	193	294
N. Hartford	235	597	272	590
Paris	218	475	236	557
Remsen	228	310	247	402
Rome	1318	785	1195	804
Sangerfield	317	239	317	253
Steuben	86	210	112	236
Trenton	202	518	201	612
Utica Wd. 1	209	109	227	123
" ...2	388	229	372	271
" ...3	339	435	374	404
" ...4	236	462	321	488
" ...5	500	178	511	230
" ...6	545	334	562	389
" ...7	365	381	361	418
Total Utica	2632	2131	2731	2313
Vernon	276	203	260	432
Verona	491	519	608	639
Vienna	352	291	368	356
Western	301	214	302	253
Westmor'd	265	417	263	580
Whiteston.	368	513	336	544
Total	10555	11158	11121	12431

ONONDAGA COUNTY.

TOWNS.	Sec. State, 1867.		Governor, 1866.	
	Nelson, Dem.	McKean, Rep.	Hoffman, Dem.	Fenton, Rep.
Dist.				
Camillus..1	142	140	127	178
" ...2	137	123	133	132
Cicero....1	68	241	63	297
" ...2	46	107	54	125
" ...3	36	91	31	99
Clay....1	172	269	177	224
" ...2	43	145	34	180
De Witt..1	168	150	157	180
" ...2	116	161	135	165
Elbridge ..1	175	129	179	144
" ...2	219	232	246	267
Fabius ...1	102	221	88	252
" ...2	39	113	27	125
Goddes...	283	353	235	332
Lafayette..1	60	92	69	88
" ...2	145	178	151	223
Lysander..1	187	205	185	239
" ...2	194	412	189	462
Manlius...1	144	188	141	218
" ...2	152	285	123	312
" ...3	74	55	85	67
" ...4	135	97	138	104
" ...5	57	45	59	60
Marcellus.1	117	186	105	208
" ...2	55	110	53	124
Onondaga.1	107	250	97	279
" ...2	237	177	220	223
" ...3	135	184	127	213
Otisco.....	138	156	135	204
Pompey...1	122	128	115	162
" ...2	93	239	97	290
" ...3	87	85	87	85
Salina....1	154	158	188	157
" ...2	69	76	67	93
Skancatc's1	149	196	140	207
" ...2	237	233	215	232
Spafford..1	74	84	61	106
" ...2	51	123	42	145
Tully......	130	233	136	260
Dist.				
Van Buren1	126	121	135	128
" ...2	188	275	135	234
Total towns	5189	7070	5023	8023

ONONDAGA CO.—continued.

TOWNS.	Sec. State, 1867.		Governor, 1866.	
	Nelson, Dem.	McKean, Rep.	Hoffman, Dem.	Fenton, Rep.
SYRACUSE.				
Ward. Dist.				
1 1	216	219	213	234
" 2	217	113	175	135
2 1	225	105	241	102
" 2	277	258	258	307
3	308	193	297	228
4 1	163	313	136	321
" 2	232	236	269	261
5	444	407	381	423
6 1	331	392	233	418
" 2	89	115	86	126
7 1	294	379	253	453
" 2	211	129	186	171
8	240	349	183	374
Total city ..	3367	3198	3000	3543
" county	8456	10268	8023	11566

ONTARIO COUNTY.

TOWNS.				
Bristol....	104	222	111	250
Canadice...	45	122	36	141
Dist.				
Canada'a l	231	280	267	302
" 2	291	274	266	275
" 3	42	155	41	184
E. Bloomsf'd	181	257	163	230
Farmington	81	234	68	274
Dist.				
Gorham...1	125	107	127	100
" ...2	52	83	48	92
" ...3	59	104	53	114
Hopewell..	163	180	160	223
Dist.				
Manches'r 1	151	140	147	164
" 2	154	105	140	118
" 3	66	74	60	95
Naples	165	305	137	336
Dist.				
Phelps...1	250	277	275	305
" ...2	90	147	85	172
" ...3	188	77	198	101
Richmond..	85	230	71	248
Dist.				
Seneca....1	330	229	366	268
" ...2	261	275	258	308
" ...3	98	156	100	180
" ...4	67	126	66	139
So. Bristol..	191	128	104	128
Victor....	262	265	248	290
W. B'mfield	92	229	75	275
Total....	3345	4780	3673	5371

ORANGE COUNTY

TOWNS.				
Dist.				
Bl'g Grove1	90	160	91	180
" 2	69	83	80	105
Chester....	195	181	209	202
Dist.				
Cornwall..1	271	207	246	223
" ...2	193	168	169	130
Crawford ..	273	151	282	181
Dist.				
Deerpark..1	79	59	78	58
" 2	77	41	73	50
" 3	455	462	392	508
" 4	96	72	83	88
Goshen...1	318	237	297	231
" ...2	105	61	88	63
Greenvill..	188	58	193	72
Ham'burgh	153	68	133	80
Minisink...	138	87	157	78
Dist.				
Monroe...1	197	123	83	67
" ...2	63	239	60	237
" ...3	145	158	142	141

ORANGE CO.—continued.

TOWNS.	Sec. State, 1867.		Governor, 1866.	
	Nelson, Dem.	McKean, Rep.	Hoffman, Dem.	Fenton, Rep.
Dist.				
M'tgomery1	211	193	209	215
" 2	139	232	134	255
Mount Hope	201	181	214	196
Dist.				
Newburgh 1	126	126	116	126
" 2	119	83	113	82
" 3	75	101	76	98
" 4	..	..	..	..
Ward.				
N'bu'h city1	357	277	334	308
" 2	377	397	382	442
" 3	214	374	176	383
" 4	218	331	237	338
Dist.				
N. Windsor1	124	62	108	79
" 2	98	71	89	84
" 3	64	39	64	50
Wallkill...1	435	644	376	621
" 2	131	129	131	129
" 3	145	158	145	158
Warwick..1	155	86	153	84
" 2	100	119	87	131
" 3	238	219	235	249
" 4	42	42	37	63
Wawaya'a.	242	173	216	213
Total.....	6891	6592	6497	7167

ORLEANS COUNTY.

TOWNS.				
Dist.				
Barre....1	338	440	388	461
" 2	94	208	92	232
" 3	77	178	73	197
Carlton..1	80	151	82	155
" 2	69	196	61	227
Clarendon.	198	181	203	201
Gaines....	158	248	161	288
Kendall...	163	231	161	250
Dist.				
Murray...1	154	131	153	139
" 2	130	91	124	117
Ridgeway.1	78	146	67	167
" 2	201	300	140	367
" 3	107	119	94	137
Shelby	244	337	216	344
Yates	107	263	91	303
Total.....	2316	3219	2106	2585

OSWEGO COUNTY.

TOWNS.				
Albion......	192	228	184	279
Amboy....	139	146	127	164
Boylston...	56	123	61	143
Dist.				
Constantia.	184	136	231	138
" 2	135	142	130	202
Granby...1	192	220	201	257
" 2	126	137	131	164
Hannibal ..1	94	253	92	281
" 2	95	137	101	158
Hastings..1	98	117	96	123
" 2	123	260	137	297
Mexico....1	97	293	71	329
" 2	110	293	103	310
New Haven	63	314	52	347
Orwell....	94	133	109	169
Oswego...1	103	183	130	185
" 2	97	137	80	139
Ward.				
Oswego cit.1	309	263	303	249
" 2	311	263	315	255
" 3	378	483	398	444
" 4	323	454	341	410
Parish....	138	246	137	263
Palermo....	99	315	116	346

OSWEGO CO.—continued.

TOWNS.	Sec. State 1867. Nelson. Dem.	McKean. Rep.	Governor. 1866. Hoffman. Dem.	Fenton. Rep.
Redfield....	86	93	97	94
Dist.				
Richland ..1	154	247	149	256
" ..2	143	219	142	268
Schræppel ..1	243	198	223	218
" 2	75	151	85	154
Sandy Cr'k	188	336	200	378
Scriba.....	220	299	187	352
Dist.				
Volncy....1	209	325	211	351
" ...2	245	204	217	236
" ...3	45	147	53	162
W. Monroe.	95	103	112	117
W'mstown.	184	103	168	130
Total.....	5442	7726	5480	8358

OTSEGO COUNTY.

TOWNS.	Nelson. Dem.	McKean. Rep.	Hoffman. Dem.	Fenton. Rep.
Burlington.	172	191	173	223
Butternuts..	170	334	156	393
Cherry V'lly	286	204	288	224
Decatur...	110	102	116	114
Dist.				
Edmeston.1	161	134	165	152
" 2	22	94	25	120
Exeter.....	109	247	113	256
Hartwick..1	154	151	160	177
" 2	129	105	130	125
Laurens...1	156	189	149	199
" ..2	71	87	65	97
Maryland..	283	264	283	285
Middlefield1	83	76	88	81
" 3	152	89	166	98
" 3	130	77	141	76
Milford...	311	237	330	276
Morris....1	227	258	331	276
" 2	12	33	16	37
New Lisbon	221	173	234	184
Dist.				
Onconta...1	197	187	175	178
" 2	87	155	91	152
Otego 2	271	252	251	285
Dist.				
Otsego 1	303	233	287	292
" 2	184	233	189	251
Pittsfield..	134	175	149	190
Plainfield .	83	211	76	236
Dist.				
Richfield ..1	108	129	156	276
" 2	50	132		
Roseboom..	167	206	166	215
Dist.				
Springfield1	142	59	201	122
" 2	138	65	198	140
Westford ..1	181	149	190	165
Dist.				
Worcester 1	203	139	196	215
" 2	97	34	97	40
Unadilla...1	161	88	176	93
" 2	238	133	233	150
Total.....	5763	5740	5797	6335

PUTNAM COUNTY

TOWNS.	Nelson. Dem.	McKean. Rep.	Hoffman. Dem.	Fenton. Rep.
Dist.				
Carmel....1	173	125	159	140
" ...2	104	121	89	121
Kent	200	150	154	157
Patterson .	102	136	108	197
Dist.				
Phillipst'n 1	73	73	73	74
" 2	87	62	76	70
" 3	353	156	319	200
Putn'm Val.	236	83	192	124
Southeast..	265	216	260	246
Total.....	1639	1182	1430	1329

QUEENS COUNTY.

TOWNS.	Sec. State 1867. Nelson. Dem.	McKean. Rep.	Governor. 1866. Hoffman. Dem.	Fenton. Rep.
Dist.				
Flushing ..1	156	83	121	126
" ..2	175	174	142	190
" ..3	299	73	255	103
" ..4	250	108	200	122
" ..5	166	44	181	73
Hempste'd 1	198	169	91	220
" 2	249	169	221	232
" 3	204	150	229	193
" 4	138	219	123	251
" 5	106	88	96	134
Jamaica..1	347	113	294	130
" ..2	362	168	317	225
Newtown..1	232	96	178	130
" 2	366	146	310	190
" 3	329	111	323	166
" 4	462	75	347	96
N. Hemp'd1	150	188	212	192
" 2	160	180	146	217
Oyster Bay1	244	187	265	183
" 2	290	215	278	258
" 3	101	56	94	85
" 4	139	69	151	95
Total.....	5098	2841	4574	3611

RENSSELAER COUNTY.

TOWNS.	Nelson. Dem.	McKean. Rep.	Hoffman. Dem.	Fenton. Rep.
Berlin......	195	268	202	257
Dist.				
Brunswick 1	274	156	215	202
" 2	78	183	65	176
E. Gr'bush 1	128	114	99	121
" 2	77	51	71	48
Grafton....	119	265	199	283
Dist.				
Greenbush 1	342	139	310	159
" 2	221	121	223	108
Hoosick ..1	204	337	232	341
" 2	96	127	107	133
" 3	54	61	51	64
L'inburgh..1	235	350	185	409
" 2	285	320	209	339
Nassau....1	141	230	107	249
" 2	127	155	100	201
N. Gr'bush 1	203	158	169	177
" 2	117	69	104	61
Petersbur'h	185	216	119	235
Dist.				
Pittstown..1	166	267	132	276
" 2	128	217	84	214
Pocstenkill1	150	113	150	114
" 2	106	68	75	89
Sandlake ..1	130	186	91	216
" 2	150	112	124	139
Schaght'kel	164	127	140	136
" 2	139	201	103	258
Schodack .1	288	225	252	229
" 2	279	144	246	161
Stephento'n	172	286	126	321
Total towns	5043	5276	4230	5715
Ward.				
TROY.....1	476	338	404	350
" ..2	334	581	254	597
" ..3	152	320	114	327
" ..4	218	470	215	496
" ..5	219	394	157	391
" ..6	391	215	284	270
" ..7	511	373	435	395
" ..8	778	225	580	307
" ..9	609	183	506	225
" ..10	464	457	325	507
Total city..	4332	3616	3274	3365
" county	9375	8893	7504	9580

RICHMOND COUNTY.

TOWNS.	Sec. State 1867. Nelson. Dem.	McKean. Rep.	Governor. 1866. Hoffman. Dem.	Fenton. Rep.
Dist.				
Castleton..1	284	139	321	144
" ..2	240	128	230	171
" ..3	164	144	151	174
Middleto'n1	181	68	191	79
" 2	432	148	382	151
" 3	48	29	74	40
Northfield.1	218	117	216	144
" 2	68	50	91	79
" 3	130	34	128	50
Southfield.1	89	45	85	60
" 2	280	85	339	88
Westfield .1	143	125	119	181
" 2	138	99	152	147
Total.....	2415	1212	2479	1508

ROCKLAND COUNTY.

TOWNS.	Nelson. Dem.	McKean. Rep.	Hoffman. Dem.	Fenton. Rep.
Dist.				
Clarksto'n 1	178	37	182	39
" 2	118	46	118	67
" 3	191	105	203	130
Haverst'w 1	69	101	89	164
" 2	263	123	215	152
Orangeto'n1	241	158	208	178
" 2	266	198	257	229
" 3	64	72	72	81
Ramapo...1	114	63	119	84
" 2	131	106	104	171
" 3	165	105	164	134
Stony Point	281	118	242	137
Total.....	2081	1232	1973	1559

ST. LAWRENCE COUNTY.

TOWNS.	Nelson. Dem.	McKean. Rep.	Hoffman. Dem.	Fenton. Rep.
Dist.				
Brasher....1	70	80	66	96
" ...2	87	151	74	164
Canton....1	197	207	178	214
" ...2	38	121	27	128
" ...3	66	79	69	87
" ...4	49	103	50	101
" ...5	77	220	78	213
Colton.....2	56	181	42	207
Dist.				
De Kalb...1	60	279	38	318
" ...2	25	122	18	143
Depeyster.	42	186	42	199
Edwards...	58	132	55	158
Fine.......	9	83	14	85
Fowler....	115	192	106	238
Dist.				
Governeur 1	114	334	89	380
" 2	25	48	24	57
Hammond..	48	261	53	290
Hermon....	111	190	123	236
Hopkinton.	57	267	36	266
Lawrence..	84	391	80	418
Dist.				
Lisbon....1	37	208	37	230
" ...2	33	218	26	229
" ...3	15	141	8	148
" ...4	22	115	20	133
Louisville .	134	183	133	199
Macomb ..1	38	92	28	109
" ..2	54	53	47	66
Madrid....1	84	313	72	347
Massena...1	121	249	130	276
Morristown	65	310	48	343
Norfolk ...1	159	209	157	237
Dist.				
Osw'gatc'e1	211	202	167	212
" ...2	76	83	54	113
" ...3	40	191	28	230
" ...4	164	246	132	267
" ...5	130	143	89	159

ST. LAWRENCE CO.—continued.

TOWNS.	Sec. State, 1867 Nelson, Dem.	Sec. State, 1867 McKean, Rep.	Governor, 1866 Hoffman, Dem.	Governor, 1866 Fenton, Rep.
Dist.				
Parishville 1	31	273	14	318
" 2	3	74	6	76
Pierpont ..1	50	265	48	289
" ..2	5	102	4	96
Pitcairn....	24	82	24	89
Dist.				
Potsdam ..1	56	297	49	310
" ..2	39	185	30	205
" ..3	27	132	20	150
" ..4	48	220	42	237
" ..5	51	147	39	141
Rossie....1	70	79	93	103
" 2	37	75	32	103
Russell....	137	279	133	317
Dist.				
Stockholm 1	68	247	49	278
" 2	34	329	24	317
Waddingt'n	142	288	121	335
Total....	**3593**	**9657**	**3146**	**10648**

SARATOGA COUNTY.

TOWNS.	Nelson, Dem.	McKean, Rep.	Hoffman, Dem.	Fenton, Rep.
Ballston...	266	194	262	196
Dist.				
Charlton ..1	108	132	101	151
" ..2	57	58	54	60
Clifton P'k1	144	128	139	147
" 2	126	173	94	211
Corinth	70	243	48	265
Day	149	78	121	83
Edinburgh..	204	160	169	190
Galway	227	237	207	272
Dist.				
Greenfield 1	83	271	57	292
" 2	95	130	77	144
Hadley....	58	133	38	146
Halfmoon.1	147	195	133	225
" 2	135	157	132	158
Malta......	132	158	106	185
Dist.				
Milton 1	291	274	262	307
" 2	182	224	165	228
Moreau....	195	238	153	250
N'umberl'd.	168	184	132	212
Providence.	134	156	108	159
Dist.				
Saratoga ..1	94	168	85	164
" ..2	323	202	182	315
S'a Springs1	205	258	152	302
" 2	240	340	177	365
" 3	251	186	238	205
Stillwater 1	170	107	164	111
" 2	173	190	160	210
Waterford..	425	315	386	330
Wilton	106	186	89	195
Total....	**4956**	**5475**	**4191**	**6078**

SCHENECTADY COUNTY.

TOWNS.	Nelson, Dem.	McKean, Rep.	Hoffman, Dem.	Fenton, Rep.
Dist.				
Duanesb'h 1	71	136	63	150
" 2	117	94	98	103
" 3	96	158	91	93
Glenville..1	89	80	88	103
" 2	169	132	162	145
" 3	102	106	94	107
Niskayuna.	115	101	95	122
Dist.				
Princet'n .1	27	78	21	92
" 2	50	53	50	46
Rotterdam 1	68	107	59	110
" 2	123	107	115	110
" 3	43	108	60	101
Ward.				
Schenect'y1	176	116	156	134

SCHENECTADY CO.—continued.

TOWNS.	Nelson, Dem.	McKean, Rep.	Hoffman, Dem.	Fenton, Rep.
Schenect'y2	185	171	166	205
" 3	256	180	233	229
" 4	309	285	259	320
" 5	136	211	188	199
Total....	**2182**	**2223**	**1998**	**2460**

SCHOHARIE COUNTY.

TOWNS.	Nelson, Dem.	McKean, Rep.	Hoffman, Dem.	Fenton, Rep.
Blenheim ..	158	107	166	124
Dist.				
Broome....1	82	82	81	102
" ..2	94	72	97	74
" ..3	20	68	25	69
Carlisle....	218	168	239	175
Cobleskill..	401	195	422	192
Conesville..	165	83	206	111
Esperance..	111	183	109	198
Dist.				
Fulton.....1	160	28	186	38
" 2	152	67	153	78
" 3	116	41	121	47
Gilboa 1	44	69	47	75
" 2	119	75	106	93
" 3	51	103	63	123
Jefferson ..	143	196	150	244
Dist.				
Middleb'h.1	340	111	366	155
" 2	78	56	85	73
Richmo'lle 1	160	37	172	49
" 2	158	135	176	147
Schoharie .1	346	117	366	140
" 2	123	48	127	140
Seward	268	131	311	140
Sharon	342	189	356	277
Dist.				
Summitt ..1	163	91	183	105
" ..2	75	42	90	48
Wright.....	234	150	239	165
Total....	**4311**	**2634**	**4642**	**3092**

SCHUYLER COUNTY.

TOWNS.	Nelson, Dem.	McKean, Rep.	Hoffman, Dem.	Fenton, Rep.
Catharine..	126	218	125	237
Cayuta....	118	50	127	58
Dist.				
Dix.......1	345	247	297	270
" 2	92	114	83	153
Hector....1	85	209	82	255
" 2	74	149	69	178
" 3	217	165	187	186
" 4	100	216	105	229
Montour...	148	224	172	261
Orange	252	212	267	215
Reading....	119	214	138	232
Tyrone	207	264	232	302
Total....	**1883**	**2282**	**1884**	**2576**

SENECA COUNTY.

TOWNS.	Nelson, Dem.	McKean, Rep.	Hoffman, Dem.	Fenton, Rep.
Dist.				
Covert....1	152	109	156	128
" 2	136	113	132	129
Fayette ...1	191	97	188	109
" ...2	153	93	135	103
" ...3	119	87	109	88
Junius	146	139	145	165
Lodi.......	234	235	228	247
Dist.				
Ovid.......1	177	167	167	196
" 2	68	96	67	112
Romulus...1	211	152	215	196
Dist.				
Sen'a Falls1	108	129	110	129
" 2	196	188	185	215
" 3	243	80	245	118
" 4	164	123	167	175
Tyre........	147	147	157	166

SENECA CO.—continued.

TOWNS.	Nelson, Dem.	McKean, Rep.	Hoffman, Dem.	Fenton, Rep.
Dist.				
Varick....1	112	67	120	76
" 2	93	92	89	104
Waterloo..1	163	100	165	114
" 2	315	207	333	218
Total....	**3128**	**2419**	**3114**	**2767**

STEUBEN COUNTY.

TOWNS.	Nelson, Dem.	McKean, Rep.	Hoffman, Dem.	Fenton, Rep.
Addison...	205	170	215	200
Avoca.....	174	215	171	272
Dist.				
Bath......1	117	55	118	83
" 2	200	202	190	222
" 3	172	264	168	299
" 4	81	156	87	182
Bradford...	131	108	130	127
Cameron...	93	171	88	191
Dist.				
Campbell..1	47	121	32	178
" ..2	62	74	61	86
Canisteo...	174	245	140	283
Caton.....	60	208	62	276
Dist.				
Cohocton .1	149	173	131	197
" 2	86	120	86	132
Corning...1	379	379	333	438
" 2	239	123	188	194
Dansville..	228	132	242	162
Erwin.....	201	186	171	221
Fremont...	121	123	121	145
Greenwood	112	140	93	146
Hartsville..	69	100	63	113
Hornby....	107	165	109	181
Dist.				
Horn'ville 1	208	202	193	229
" 2	321	250	311	287
Howard...1	118	145	119	174
" 2	54	108	43	132
Jasper.....	106	250	82	262
Lindley....	67	122	56	141
Dist.				
Prattsbu'h 1	181	205	172	230
" 2	121	33	131	53
Pulteney...	147	179	144	200
Rathbone..	121	128	94	154
Thurston..	91	151	79	189
Troupsbu'h	159	243	127	284
Tuscarora..	80	202	63	203
Urbana	214	223	184	272
Wayland..	281	157	267	207
Wayne	85	103	67	121
West Union	121	107	106	111
Wheeler...	171	114	156	137
Woodhull..	127	278	114	307
Total....	**5989**	**6830**	**5507**	**8021**

SUFFOLK COUNTY.

TOWNS.	Nelson, Dem.	McKean, Rep.	Hoffman, Dem.	Fenton, Rep.
Brookha'n 1	279	160	234	202
" 2	71	38	85	51
" 3	162	67	181	115
" 4	83	53	82	66
" 5	214	215	217	218
" 6	124	134	105	156
E. Hamp'n1	63	80	78	103
" 2	40	33	41	33
" 3	41	26	32	41
" 4	36	19	29	37
Hunting'n 1	317	217	302	290
" 2	191	133	202	171
" 3	176	77	162	111
" 4	213	170	182	199
Islip......1	98	100	94	115
" 2	81	39	64	81
" 3	90	92	96	135

SUFFOLK CO.—continued.

TOWNS.	Sec. State, 1867. Nelson. Dem.	McKean Rep.	Governor, 1866. Hoffman Dem.	Fenton Rep.
Dist.				
Riverhead 1	57	82	55	32
" 2	190	237	157	257
" 3	83	77	78	82
Shelter Isl'd	29	39	32	48
Smithtown	175	84	151	130
Dist.				
S'hampton 1	150	161	134	202
" 2	70	157	60	188
" 3	87	84	81	94
" 4	83	110	90	156
" 5	45	78	53	90
Southold 1	58	94	53	101
" 2	285	136	231	149
" 3	125	194	110	235
" 4	106	180	102	195
Total	3813	3316	3572	4083

SULLIVAN COUNTY.

TOWNS.	Nelson Dem.	McKean Rep.	Hoffman Dem.	Fenton Rep.
Dist.				
Bethel 1	137	94	133	92
" 2	135	152	156	157
Callicoon 1	295	126	355	141
Dist.				
Cochecton 1	220	89	231	98
" 2	237	45	239	53
Fallaburgh 1	58	56	56	82
" 2	234	277	201	312
Forestb'gh 1	78	41	74	49
" 2	35	20	39	22
Fremont 1	231	115	218	152
Highland 2	83	72	88	75
Dist.				
Liberty 1	121	113	139	128
" 2	166	168	180	179
Lumberla'd	125	33	143	48
Dist.				
Mamaka'g 1	103	166	119	196
" 2	123	148	151	158
" 3	66	131	72	129
Neversink 1	75	59	69	70
" 2	187	180	191	202
Rockland 1	167	211	152	177
Dist.				
Thompson 1	118	102	116	111
" 2	219	228	236	224
" 3	42	78	60	74
Tusten	110	52	103	58
Total	3355	2761	3521	2987

TIOGA COUNTY.

TOWNS.	Nelson Dem.	McKean Rep.	Hoffman Dem.	Fenton Rep.
Dist.				
Barton 1	112	129	199	369
" 2	133	52	77	89
" 3	78	76	134	48
" 4	119	236	—	—
Berkshire	94	157	95	174
Candor 1	307	324	260	361
" 2	116	91	132	94
" 3	56	68	50	76
Newa'k Val	138	384	135	408
Nichols	152	263	119	283
Dist.				
Owego 1	231	329	217	338
" 2	183	175	163	201
" 3	138	92	114	112
" 4	67	86	61	105
" 5	337	483	301	514
Richford	118	181	118	193
Spencer	194	244	196	265
Tioga 1	175	107	167	124
" 2	103	64	106	82
" 3	94	73	94	86
" 4	34	38	39	37
Total	2979	3652	2779	3959

TOMPKINS COUNTY.

TOWNS.	Sec. State, 1867. Nelson. Dem.	McKean Rep.	Governor, 1866. Hoffman Dem.	Fenton Rep.
Dist.				
Caroline 1	90	146	94	165
" 2	100	190	108	199
Danby	158	279	142	335
Dist.				
Dryden 1	127	116	141	144
" 2	93	100	92	136
" 3	95	369	95	404
" 4	20	120	19	143
Enfield	205	229	220	241
Dist.				
Groton 1	48	74	59	93
" 2	91	282	99	312
" 3	79	151	89	174
Ithaca 1	260	240	253	275
" 2	327	261	308	287
" 3	247	837	250	358
Lansing 1	86	157	90	173
" 2	103	74	109	93
" 3	142	106	138	131
Newfield 1	274	266	280	275
" 2	78	47	74	61
Ulysses 1	195	465	191	308
" 2	108	121	101	146
Total	2926	3935	2952	4456

ULSTER COUNTY.

TOWNS.	Nelson Dem.	McKean Rep.	Hoffman Dem.	Fenton Rep.
Dist.				
Denning 1	77	56	72	40
" 2	37	25	38	29
Esopus 1	167	133	179	158
" 2	50	139	42	145
" 3	123	104	115	222
Gardiner	253	145	222	163
Dist.				
Hardenb'h 1	29	24	21	30
" 2	38	21	41	20
Hurley 1	131	220	118	199
" 2	46	83	46	85
Kingston 1	262	288	260	305
" 2	293	311	295	353
" 3	272	178	382	322
" 4	161	89	177	109
" 5	313	179	271	173
" 6	336	134	339	147
Lloyd 1	124	80	98	111
" 2	180	163	167	189
Marbleto'n 1	202	172	183	167
" 2	123	180	118	198
Marlboro'h 1	112	162	104	187
" 2	114	114	90	142
New Paltz	212	232	197	232
Dist.				
Olive 1	312	184	326	218
" 2	67	33	67	45
Plattekill 1	77	119	62	157
" 2	86	78	75	96
Rochester 1	261	140	257	124
" 2	127	73	122	98
" 3	67	50	61	34
Rosendale	309	228	295	237
Saugerties 1	355	264	202	374
" 2	199	272	381	340
" 3	157	116	203	194
" 4	181	151	—	—
Shandaken 1	187	100	206	119
" 2	131	77	101	101
Shawan'k 1	161	82	168	105
" 2	236	101	253	114
Wawarsi'g 1	258	320	284	328
" 2	225	177	243	146
" 3	87	99	110	133
" 4	121	50	122	46
Woodstock	139	198	137	219
Total	7398	6131	7150	6769

WARREN COUNTY.

TOWNS.	Sec. State, 1867. Nelson. Dem.	McKean Rep.	Governor, 1866. Hoffman Dem.	Fenton Rep.
Bolton	105	173	94	161
Caldwell	155	95	130	100
Dist.				
Chester 1	159	165	129	171
" 2	119	113	90	117
Hague	79	64	81	72
Horicon	139	175	97	193
Dist.				
Johnsbu'h 1	268	152	240	153
" 2	27	78	23	89
Luzerne	69	193	54	183
Dist.				
Queensb'g 1	132	104	100	119
" 2	134	195	104	192
" 3	267	271	233	269
" 4	121	306	99	295
Stoney Cr'k	121	124	111	127
Thurman	122	134	123	115
Warrensb'h	254	131	236	156
Total	2261	2473	1944	2522

WASHINGTON COUNTY.

TOWNS.	Nelson Dem.	McKean Rep.	Hoffman Dem.	Fenton Rep.
Argyle 1	92	215	88	227
" 2	80	218	62	243
Cambridge 1	89	153	89	170
" 2	73	162	69	161
Dresden	54	75	52	88
Dist.				
Easton 1	38	221	41	275
" 2	69	164	44	194
" 3	56	65	48	74
Fort Ann 1	135	129	132	136
" 2	68	84	49	95
" 3	44	45	45	45
Fo't Edw'd 1	387	334	339	319
" 2	74	79	59	75
Granville 1	122	186	100	209
" 2	111	258	118	269
Greenwich 1	96	300	65	306
" 2	74	151	44	191
" 3	126	86	96	105
Hampton	58	99	38	112
Hartford	111	306	114	336
Dist.				
Hebron 1	105	209	83	240
" 2	48	100	51	112
Jackson	111	198	72	210
Dist.				
Kingsbury 1	66	147	60	174
" 2	264	287	257	303
Putnam	12	113	12	117
Dist.				
Salem 1	191	303	167	304
" 2	56	147	49	154
White Cr'k 1	91	221	80	247
" 2	135	106	99	126
Whitehall 1	234	143	215	150
" 2	237	194	199	200
Total	3507	5498	3035	5972

WAYNE COUNTY.

TOWNS.	Nelson Dem.	McKean Rep.	Hoffman Dem.	Fenton Rep.
Dist.				
Arcadia 1	173	111	178	131
" 2	105	171	90	214
" 3	277	249	266	266
Butler	131	282	114	331
Galen 1	57	95	74	105
" 2	31	70	38	84
" 3	288	375	336	423
Huron	159	220	150	258
Dist.				
Lyons 1	83	43	99	48
" 2	209	164	215	187
" 3	257	219	259	235

WAYNE CO.—continued.

TOWNS.	Sec. State, 1867.		Governor, 1866.	
	Nelson. Dem.	Mc-Kean. Rep.	Hoffman. Dem.	Fenton. Rep.
Dist.				
Macedon..1	153	140	136	164
" 2	61	145	59	163
Marion	66	308	70	377
Ontario	114	308	146	383
Dist.				
Palmyra ...1	327	322	312	363
" 2	62	96	58	109
Rose........	151	253	194	304
Savannah..	156	230	177	266
Dist.				
Sodus 1	115	237	137	289
" 2	205	186	217	208
" 3	87	72	74	95
Walworth.	120	255	140	319
Dist.				
Williams'n1	87	183	95	208
" 2	80	118	81	144
Walcott ...1	162	147	162	178
" 2	158	151	149	169
Total	8913	5152	4026	6021

WESTCHESTER COUNTY.

Bedford.....	320	414	309	479
Cortlandt..	781	898	712	812
E. Chester..	509	329	505	416
Greenbu'gh	831	439	702	595
Harrison ...	109	59	71	96
Lewisbor'h.	96	237	86	238
Mamaron'k	119	58	103	76

WESTCHESTER CO.—continued.

TOWNS.	Sec. State, 1867.		Governor, 1866.	
	Nelson. Dem.	Mc-Kean. Rep.	Hoffman. Dem.	Fenton. Rep.
Morrisania.	1268	496	1074	523
Mt. Pleas'nt	515	234	458	353
New Castle.	169	238	149	253
N. Rochelle.	318	166	351	242
Nth Castle.	224	168	198	195
N'th Salem.	80	213	72	247
Ossining....	577	512	592	495
Pelham.....	110	37	93	29
Poundridge	138	134	134	145
Rye.........	406	234	345	308
Scarsdale...	39	32	37	34
Somers......	133	169	134	187
Westchest'r	349	131	338	160
West Farms	583	255	513	356
White Pl'n.	225	140	210	157
Yonkers....	972	665	849	840
Yorktown..	266	187	258	223
Total	9253	6328	8293	7519

WYOMING COUNTY.

Arcade.....	153	179	155	189
Attica......	246	294	228	303
Benningt'n.	242	160	256	210
Castile.....	122	334	111	369
Covington..	44	171	42	223
Eagle.......	151	175	148	206
Gainesville.	104	243	110	287
Gene'e Fa's	65	117	61	130
Java........	255	129	261	166
Middlebury	95	273	85	284

WYOMING CO.—continued.

TOWNS.	Sec. State, 1867.		Governor, 1866.	
	Nelson. Dem.	Mc-Kean. Rep.	Hoffman. Dem.	Fenton. Rep.
Orangeville	72	155	79	178
Perry.......	104	396	109	452
Pike........	84	300	62	355
Sheldon....	159	117	167	177
Warsaw.....	269	385	252	442
Weath'sfi'd	149	118	169	134
Total	2314	3546	2298	4105

YATES COUNTY.

Barrington.	159	187	160	207
Dist.				
Benton....1	100	246	89	266
" 2	50	120	48	238
Italy.......	76	211	53	224
Dist.				
Jerusalem.1	71	135	71	145
" 2	170	185	132	237
Middlesex..	66	224	44	228
Dist.				
Milo.......1	133	249	121	246
" 2	107	103	91	123
" 3	205	192	183	193
Potter.....1	33	132	32	141
" 2	114	179	32	137
" 3	—	—	75	64
Starkey....1	98	164	94	185
" 2	86	171	82	207
Torry	164	133	169	137
Total	1632	2631	1476	2878

CONGRESS, 1867.

Special Election, to fill vacancy, occasioned by resignation of Roscoe Conkling.

Dist.	Dem. Bailey.	Rep. Stryker.
Oneida..10,515		11,182

Alex. H. Bailey over John Stryker, 667.

CONGRESS 1866.

Dists.	Dem. Taber	Rep. Gleason
I. Queens...4,508....3,679		
Richmond.2,454....1,527		
Suffolk ...3,496....4,156		
Total...10,458....9,362		

Stephen Taber over Wm. H. Gleason, 1,096

II.
Brooklyn (part) and towns of

	Dem. Rep. I.D. Barnes V.Brunt Hughes
K'gs co.15,614 8,965 384	

Demas Barnes over J. A. VanBrunt, 6,629; over all 6,245.

III.
Brooklyn (part)

	Robinson Chittenden
	12,634 10,803

Wm. E. Robinson over S. B. Chittenden, 1,831

IV.
N. Y. City,
1, 2, 3, 4, 5, 6, 8 Wards.

	Fox. Greeley.
	14,003. 3,743

John Fox, over Horace Greeley, 10,260.

V.
N. Y. City,
7, 10, 13, 14 Wards.

	Morrissay. Elliott. Taylor.
	9,162 2,293 6,503

John Morrissay (Dem.) over Nelson Taylor (Ind.), 2,659; over Eneas Elliott (Rep.), 6,869.

VI.
N. Y. City,
9, 15, 16 Wards.

	Stewart. Spencer. Stevenson.
	9,452 6,955 711

Thos. E. Stewart (Con.) Over Chas. S. Spencer (Rep.), 2,497; over Geo. Stevenson (Ind.), 8,741.

VII.
N. Y. City,
11, 17 Wards.

	Chanler. Steinbrenner.
	11,503 6,743

John W. Chanler over Geo. F. Steinbrenner, 4,760.

VIII.
N. Y. City.
18, 20, 21 Wards.

	Brooks. Cannon.
	13,816 8,210

James Brooks over Le Grand B. Cannon, 5,606; over Cannon and Elizabeth Cady Stanton(Ind.), 5,582.

IX.
N. Y. City.
12, 19, 21 Wards.

	Wood. Darling.
	9,605 7,995

Fernando Wood over Wm. A. Darling, 1,610.

X.

	Radford. Robertson.
Putnam ...1,409	1,351
Rockland..1,868	1,620
Westchst'r.6,680	9,041
Total....9,957	12,012

Wm. H. Robertson over Wm. Radford, 2,055.

XI.

	Anderson. Van Wyck.
Orange....6,471	7,150
Sullivan ..3,462	3,044
Total....9,933	10,194

Chas. H. Van Wyck over Isaac Anderson, 261.

XII.

	Collier. Ketcham.
Columbia.4,881	5,128
Dutchess.3,959	7,407
Total...10,840	12,535

John H. Ketcham over Casper P. Collier, 1,695.

XIII.

	Tuthill. Cornell.
Greene...3,481	3,258
Ulster ...6,698	7,263
Total...10,179	10,521

Thos. Cornell over Jos. Tuthill, 342.

XIV.

	Pruyn. Ramsey.
Albany ..11,088	11,757
Schoharie 4,532	3,215
Total...15,620	14,972

John V. L. Pruyn over Joa. H. Ramsey, 648.

XV.

	Milliman. Griswold.
Rensselaer7,313	9,756
Wash'g'n.3,060	5,933
Total...10,373	15,689

John A. Griswold over Nat. B. Milliman, 5,316.

XVI.

	Hoyle. Ferris.
Clinton ..3,592	3,687
Essex....1,897	3,124
Warren...1,923	2,530
Total...7,412	9,341

Orange Ferris over Geo. V. Hoyle, 1,929.

XVII.

	Lawrence. Hulburd.
Franklin..1,960	2,840
St.Lawr'e.3,156	10,609
Total...5,116	13,449

Calvin T. Hulburd over D. W. Lawrence, 8,333.

XVIII.

	Horton. Marvin.
Fulton & Ham'tn 2,648	3,283
Montgm'y 3,618	3,579
Saratoga. 4,107	6,143
Schen'tdy 1,969	2,491
Total...12,342	15,496

James M. Marvin over Thos. R. Horton, 3,154.

XIX.

	Johnson. Fields.
Chenango 3,963	5,589
Delaware 3,892	5,351
Otsego... 5,766	6,337
Total...13,621	17,277

Wm. C. Fields over S. C. Johnson, 3,656.

XX.

	Lansing. Laflin.
Herkimer..3,807	5,192
Jefferson..5,254	8,127
Lewis.......2,673	3,179
Total...11,734	16,498

Addison H. Laflin over Ed. S. Lansing, 4,764.

XXI. Kellogg. Conkling.
Oneida..11,053   12,470
Roscoe Conkling over
Palmer V. Kellogg, 1,417.

XXII. Perry. Churchill.
Madison ..3,500   5,938
Oswego ...5,327   8,523

Total..8,827   14,461
John C. Churchill over
Albertus Perry, 5,634.

XXIII. Ruger. McCarthy.
Cortland.2,053   3,731
Onond'a..7,913   11,529

Total..9,966   15,260
Dennis McCarthy over
Wm. C. Ruger, 5,294.

XXIV. Humphreys. Pomeroy.
Cayuga..4,172   7,550
Seneca ..3,147   2,710
Wayne...4,085   5,929

Total..11,404   16,189
Theo. M. Pomeroy over
Geo. Humphreys, 4,785.

XXV. Chesebro. Kelsey.
Livingston 3,141   4,445
Ontario...3,715   5,317
Yates......1,478   2,875

Total...8,334   12,637
Wm. H. Kelsey over
H. O. Chesebro, 4,303.

XXVI. McCormick. Lincoln.
Broome..3,341   5,207
Schuyler.1,880   2,580

Tioga....2,682   4,017
Tompkin.2,946   4,460

Total..10,849   16,264
Wm. S. Lincoln over
H. McCormick, 5,415.

XXVII. Collins. Ward.
Allegany...2,596   6,324
Chemung..3,407   3,434
Steuben....5,432   7,992

Total...11,435   17,750
Hamilton Ward over
Jno. G. Collins, 6,315.

XXVIII. Selye. Hart.
Monroe....10,293   7,634
Orleans....2,498   3,123

Total......12,791   10,757
Lewis Seyle (Ind. Rep.)
over Roswell Hart, 2,034.

XXIX. Comstock. Van Horn.
Genesec.2,623   3,717
Niagara. 4,076   4,554
Wyom'g 2,432   8,933

Total...9,131   12,204
Burt Van Horn over H.
S. Comstock, 3,073.

XXX. Humphrey. Clapp.
Erie 13,402   12,085
James M. Humphrey
over A. M. Clapp, 1,317.

XXXI. Risley. Van Aernam.
Cattar's 3,443   5,692
Chaut'a 3,856   8,713

Total .7,299   14,405
Henry Van Aernam
over H. A. Risley, 7,106.

NEW YORK STATE LEGISLATURE, 1868.

SENATE.

[Democrats in *Italics*; Republicans in Roman.]

Dist.	Members.	Vote.	Maj.	Opponents.	Vote
1	*Lewis A. Edwards*	11226	3336	Jeremiah Simonson	7390
2	*James F. Pierce*	13690	2978	Wm. W. Goodrich	9712
3	*Henry C. Murphy	17914	9947	Geo. P. Willey	7967
4	*William M. Tweed*	16144	6537	James E. Kerrigan	5966
				And. W. Leggatt	2175
				Thos. Montgomery	1466
5	*Michael Norton*	11218	733	William B. White	6206
				Chas. Blauvelt	2160
				John Keyser	2119
6	*Thomas J. Creamer*	16122	10235	Wm. T. Ashman	3578
				Jno. H. McKinley	2309
7	*John J. Bradley*	11389	5839	Christopher Pullman	5950
			5891	John Hardy	5448
8	*Henry W. Genet*	8180	2786	Wilson Berryman	5394
			3207	Michael Tuomey	4973
9	*William Caldwell*	12352	3104	James W. Husted	9248
10	*William M. Graham*	10087	633	Henry R. Low	9454
11	Abiah W. Palmer	12032	685	Jacob B. Jewett	11376
12	Francis S. Thayer	14386	1601	Alfred H. Griswold	12785
13	*A. Bleeker Banks*	11974	1166	Chas. H. Adams	10808
14	*George Beach*	10955	2016	Joshua Fiero, Jr	8939
15	*Charles Stanford, (Ind.)	14467	1202	Adam W. Kline	13225
16	Matthew Hale	8829	1436	Melville A. Sheldon	7393
17	Abraham X. Parker	12333	6674	Wm. H. Wallace	5659
18	*John O'Donnell	10017	1647	Levi H. Brown	8370
19	*Samuel Campbell	10975	259	Geo. H. Sanford	10716
20	J. B. Van Patten	10303	530	De Witt C. Bates	9773
21	Abner C. Mattoon	12855	3562	Robt. C. Kenyon	9293
22	Geo. N. Kennedy	13346	2453	Henry S. Randall	10883
23	*John F. Hubbard, Jr	12740	247	Dan'l. Waterbury	12493
24	Orlow W. Chapman	12299	2810	Oliver C. Crocker	9489
25	*Stephen K. Williams	11505	3075	E. J. T. Martin	8430
26	*Charles J. Folger	9815	1244	D. A. Ogden	8571
27	*John J. Nicks	12223	4354	J. L. McDowell	7869
28	Lewis H. Morgan	8627	76	Wm. H. Bowman	8551
29	*Richard Crowley	10878	1812	Sherman B. Piper	9066
30	*Wolcott J. Humphrey	13048	4798	Samuel D. Faulkner	8250
31	Asher P. Nichols	13378	1521	James Sheldon	11857
32	*Lorenzo Morris*	7022	912	Walter L. Sessions	6110
			203	A. F. Allen	6819

* Re-elected.

Democrats, 15; Republicans, 16; Independent, 1,

ASSEMBLY.

[Democrats in *Italics* ; Republicans in Roman.]

County.	Dist.	Members.	Vote.	Maj.	Opponents.	Vote.
Albany	1	*John C. Chism*	2852	23	John Flagler	2829
do	2	*Francis H. Woods*	3082	373	Henry Smith	2709
do	3	*Jackson A. Sumner*	3948	1110	Lemon Thomson	2838
do	4	*Theo. Van Valkenburg*	2372	328	Oscar F. Potter	2044
Allegany		Silas Richardson	5597	2852	*Samuel Swayne*	2745
Broome		Chauncey C. Bennett	4689	1070	*Fred. H. Perry*	3619
Cattaraugus	1	*Jonas K. Button*	2204	772	Gideon Searl	1432
do	2	E. C. Topliff	2140	142	*L. J. Jenks*	1998
Cayuga	1	Charles H. Weed	3107	796	*Oliver Wood*	2311
do	2	Sanford Gifford	3602	1553	*Jno. Cuyendall*	2049
Chautauqua	1	Matthew P. Bemus	2021	725	*T. S. Moggs*	1296
				376	Horace H. Glidden	1645
do	2	Winfield S. Cameron	4041	1527	*John S. Beggs*	2514
Chemung		*Edmund Miller*	3551	503	George W. Buck	3048
Chenango		*Frederick Juliand	5080	992	Harris H. Beecher	4098
Clinton		William F. Cook	3362	95	*Royal Corbin*	3267
Columbia	1	*Harper W. Rogers*	2773	419	Robt. F. Groat	2354
do	2	*Stephen H. Wendover*	2391	88	*Abm. Vosburgh*	2303
Cortland		Raymond T. Babcock	3394	1255	*A. L. Chamberlain*	2139
Delaware	1	Albert E. Sullard	2598	643	*Wm. H. Bradford*	1955
do	2	*Edward L. Burhans*	2297	40	George C. Gibbs	2257
Dutchess	1	*Augustus A. Brush*	3362	212	*John W. Storms*	3150
do	2	*Alfred T. Ackert*	3567	183	Mark D. Wilbur	3384
Erie	1	*George J. Balmer*	2701	656	John Hoy	2045
do	2	*Richard Flach*	2821	496	George W. Bull	2325
do	3	*L. P. Dayton*	2581	42	Benj. H. Austin, Jr	2539
do	4	*Alpheus Prince*	2546	508	Henry Eastabrook	2038
do	5	James Rider	2791	126	*Philip D. Riley*	2665
Essex		Samuel E. Root	2868	892	*Henry D. Graves*	1976
Franklin		Edmund F. Sargent	2770	733	*B. S. W. Clark*	2037
Ful. & Ham'n		*Samuel W. Buell*	3188	369	Cyrus H. Kellogg	2819
Genesee		*Henry F. Tarbox	3446	839	Sanford Wilber	2607
Greene		*James Loughran*	3707	922	Samuel Stimpson	2785
Herkimer		E. W. Stannard	4597	583	*N. W. Taylor*	4014
Jefferson	1	*Lafayette J. Bigelow*	3505	1196	*Samuel T. Tifft*	2309
do	2	*Andrew Cornwall*	3576	402	Albert D. Shaw	3174
Kings	1	*Patrick Burns*	3837	2573	Wm. H. Parker	1264
do	2	*William S. Andrews*	3563	709	E. L. Sanderson	2854
do	3	*Patrick Keady*	2493	852	— O'Keefe	1641
do	4	*F. A. Mallison*	4336	2683	H. B. Bradshaw	1653
do	5	*William C. Jones*	2852	349	F. T. Parsons	2503
do	6	Jacob Worth	2229	30	*John Raber*	2190
do	7	*Caleb L. Smith*	3302	1407	Geo. W. Buckridge	1855
do	8	*Dewitt C. Tower*	2587	92	David E. Austin	2495
do	9	*John C. Jacobs*	4081	2480	Jno. L. Guischard	1601
Lewis		John F. Mann	2830	28	*Charles G. Riggs*	2802
Livingston		Lewis E. Smith	4007	805	*Robt. Vallance*	3202
Madison	1	G. Wellington	2916	1420	*S. P. Smith*	1496
do	2	Robert Stewart	2438	242	*John Wilson*	2196
Monroe	1	John M. Davis	2141	99	*D. B. De Land*	2042
do	2	Nehemiah C. Bradstreet	4149	57	Henry Cribben	4092
do	3	*Abner J. Wood*	2430	135	Jas. H. Warren	2295
Montgomery		*Angell Matthewson*	3923	734	D. W. Ten Brook	3189
New-York	1	*Michael C. Murphy*	3751	2250	Charles Moore	1501
				3002	Joseph C. Scully	749
do	2	*Denis Burns*	2639	1101	*James Donovan*	1538
				1542	*Constantine Donoho*	1097
do	3	*Daniel O'Reilly*	4268	4134	John McGibney	134
do	4	*John Galvin*	3545	1825	*John Glass*	1720
				3166	Isaac Wolf	379
do	5	*Christopher Johnson*	2778	1296	Christopher Monahan	1482
				1692	Chas. T. Polhamus	1126
				2009	*Thos. J. Bogan*	679
do	6	*Timothy J. Campbell*	1484	52	*Fred'k Zimmer*	1432
				695	James O. Ellery	789
				1255	Eden L. Rosemon	229
				1293	*Frank Duffy*	191

County.	Dist.	Members.	Vote.	Maj.	Opponents.	Vote.
New York....	7	James Riley	1733	380	Jas. A. Richmond..	1353
				655	Wm. P. Richardson......	1078
				1957	Michael Cassidy	1773
do	...8	*James Reed	3730	2370	Nich. F. Eberhardt.......	1360
				3417	Michael Clark...........	313
do	9	William G. Bergen......	3319	1440	Geo. F. Coddington......	1879
				2799	Ed. F. Brown..........	520
do	...10	Anthony Hartman......	3197	2199	Herman F. Bauer........	998
				2213	Samuel Mullen..........	984
do	...11	Peter Trainer..........	2644	514	John V. Gridley..........	2130
do	...12	William B. Quinn......	2620	1002	John A. Dinkell........	1618
				1790	James McCarthy........	830
				687	Chas. P. Shaw...........	1904
do	...13	James C. Moran........	2591	2333	Ed. J. Montague	258
				2400	Thos. Crawford........	191
				1258	Alex. H. Mulligan.......	721
do	...14	James McKiever........	1979	1283	Chas. H. Whalen........	696
				1576	John Nugent.............	403
				1775	Lewis W. Maires.........	204
				434	Austin V. Pettit.........	1623
				785	Wm. J. Stewart..	1272
do	...15	*Alexander Frear......	2057	1447	John Murray.............	610
				1648	Sol. B. Noble............	409
				279	Wm. Baird.	1473
do	...16	*James Irving...........	1752	449	Henry Rowley...........	1303
				587	Michael S. Lambert......	1165
do	...17	Frederick H. Flagge....	2313	436	Joel W. Mason..........	1877
				469	James Kelly............	1844
				1066	Samuel S. Urmy.........	1432
do	...18	Lawrence D. Kiernan...	2498	1373	Michael Fay.............	1125
				2067	P. H. McDonough........	431
				130	Joshua D. Minor........	936
do	...19	William L. Wiley......	1066	579	John Quinn............	487
				106	Henry Clausen, Jr.....	2090
do	...20	George B. Van Brunt.....	2196	1456	John Keegan............	743
				336	Robert Brown...........	1201
do	...21	William Hitchman......	1537	434	Wm. H. McCarthy......	1103
				511	Michael Hallaran........	1026
Niagara	1	Ransom M. Skeels.......	2432	246	Henry F. Cady.........	2186
do	2	Benjamin Farley.....	1914	25	Wm. Samways........	1889
Oneida......	1	William H. Chapman...	2770	94	John French..........	2676
do	2	Alanson B. Cady.........	2949	410	Oscar B. Gridley.......	2539
do	3	James Stevens.........	2631	378	John J. Parry.........	2253
do	4	Ambrose Nicholson.....	3014	434	George J. Flint.......	2580
Onondaga...	1	Augustus G. S. Allis...	3429	558	John C. Munro........	2871
do	2	Luke Ranney...........	3447	586	Axella F. Tracy......	2861
do	3	Hiram Eaton...........	3138	316	Henry J. Mowry......	2822
Ontario	1	Henry Ray............	2331	183	Delos W. Colvin......	2148
do	2	*Samuel H. Torrey.....	2037	311	Walter S. Hubbell......	1726
Orange	1	W. C. H. Sherman.....	2963	21	Geo. K. Smith........	2942
do	2	John H. Reeves.........	3854	702	Geo. Wiggins........	3152
Orleans......		*Edmund L. Pitts.......	3264	1110	Geo. Mather..........	2154
Oswego......	1	John A. Place.........	2287	205	Leverett A. Card.....	2082
do	2	James D. Lasher.......	2262	214	Edmund Merry.......	2048
do	3	Alvin Richardson.......	2373	350	Frank S. Low.........	2023
Otsego......	1	Myron J. Hubbard......	2840	62	Davis W. Bates.......	2778
do	2	William C. Bentley.....	2939	61	Henry R. Washbon....	2878
Putnam......		Samuel D. Humpary...	1478	223	S. Mable..............	1255
Queens......	1	*Francis Skillman......	2156	799	Daniel D. Robbins......	1337
do	2	John B. Madden.......	2670	1196	B. Hendrickson........	1474
Rensselaer....	1	John L. Flagg.........	4684	1342	Jno. L. Blanchard......	3442
do ...	2	Jared A. Wells........	2717	673	Albert S. Pease.......	2044
do ...	3	Harris B. Howard.....	3082	680	B. J. Van Hoesen.....	2402
Richmond.....		John Decker..........	2336	1096	Samuel R. Brick......	1240
Rockland		Thomas Lawrence.....	1940	606	John J. Cole.........	1334
St. Lawrence.	1	*George M. Gleason	3017	1937	T. J. Hazleton.......	1080
do	2	Julius W. Palmer......	3357	2031	W. H. Sawyer........	1326
do	3	R. H. Andrews..........	3215	2338	M. H. Knapp.........	877
Saratoga	1	*T. G. Younglove	2722	44	C. M. Noxon.........	2678
do	2	Alembert Pond........	2735	459	C. A. Russell........	2276
Schenectady..		Robert Furman.........	1921	149	Charles G. Ellis........	1772

County.	Dist.	Members.	Vote.	Maj.	Opponents.	Vots.
Schoharie....		*William S. Clark.....	4352	1777	Moses S. Wilcox.........	2575
Schuyler.....		George Clark.........	2240	336	Anson N. Ackley........	1904
Seneca.......		David D. Lefler.........	3034	575	James Flood...........	2459
Steuben	1	John F. Little.........	3022	460	A. Hadden.............	2562
do	2	Lyman Balcom..........	3945	712	B. F. Balcom...........	3133
Suffolk....		James W. Halsey........	3808	491	Wm. R. Post..........	3317
Sullivan.....		*David G. Starr......	3272	473	Thomas Crary.......	2799
Tioga.......		Oliver H. P. Kinney.....	3569	510	Chauncey L. Rich..	3059
Tompkins....		*John H. Selkreg.....	3875	2927	S. C. Reynolds.........	2927
Ulster.......	1	Wm. Lounsbury.......	2517	529	Wm. T. Swart.........	1988
do	2	Abm. E. Hasbrouck....	2602	472	Louis Bevier..........	2130
do	3	Theodore Guigon.....	2375	533	D. C. Griffin..........	1842
Warren......		Nicholas B. La Bau.....	2384	54	G. R. Martine...........	2330
Washington..	1	David Underwood.....	3100	1406	Henry C. Gray.........	1694
do	2	Nathaniel Dailey......	2152	152	Geo. Northrup........	2000
Wayne......	1	Dewitt Parshall.......	2857	701	R. F. Norris..........	2156
do	2	Elijah M. K. Glen.....	2216	458	H. P. Underhill.......	1758
Westchester.	1	*Samuel M. Purdy.....	3913	3913	No opposition........	
do ..	2	*Geo. J. Penfield.....	3202	1134	David Downs..........	2068
do ..	3	Henry C. Nelson.....	2802	91	David W. Travis.......	2711
Wyoming....		*William Bristol........	3485	1189	R. T. Shearman.......	2296
Yates......		Oliver S. Williams......	2169	151	Charles S. Hoyt.........	2018

*Re-elected.
Democrats, 73; Republicans, 55;

RECAPITULATION.

	Senate.	Assembly.	Joint. Bal.
Democrats,......................................	15	73	88
Republicans,...................................	16	55	71
Independent,...................................	1		
		—	—
Democratic majority,...........................		18	17

NEW YORK STATE CONSTITUTIONAL CONVENTION, 1867.

The following are the names of the members of the New York State Constitutional Convention, elected April 23d. 1867 Convention met June 4th, 1867.

DELEGATES AT LARGE.

Democrats.

Augustus Schell,
George Law,
Henry C. Murphy,
Homer A. Nelson,
*David L. Seymour,
Jacob Hardinburgh,
Smith M. Weed,
Alonzo C. Paige,
Francis Kernan,
George F. Comstock,
John Magee,
Henry D. Barto,
Sanford E. Church,
Henry D. Cheesbro,
Joseph G. Masten,
Marshall B. Champlain.
* Since Deceased.

Republicans.

Waldo Hutchins,
William M. Evarts,
George Opdyke,
A. J. H. Duganne,
George Wm. Curtis,
Horace Greeley,
Joshua M. Van Cott,
Ira Harris,
Erastus Cook,
Martin J. Townsend,
†William A. Wheeler,
Charles Andrews,
Tracey Beadle,
Charles J. Folger,
Erastus Prosser,
Augustus Frank.
† President of the Convention.

DELEGATES FROM SENATORIAL DISTRICTS.

[Democrats in *Italics* ; Republicans in Roman.]

Dist.
1. *Solomon Townsend,*
   Selah B. Strong,
   Wm. Wickham,
   Erastus Brooks.
2. *Wm. D. Vedder,*
   S. J. Colahan,
   John J. Schumaker,
   Tunis G. Bergen.

Dist.
3. *John P. Rolfe,*
   W. L. Livingston,
   Charles Lowery,
   Daniel P. Barnard.
4. *Samuel A. Garvin,*
   Abraham D. Lawrence,
   John S. Burrill,
   Charles P. Daly.

Dist.
5. *James Moncrief,*
   Norman Stratton,
   Elbridge T. Gerry,
   Henry Rogers.
6. A. D. Russell,
   F. W. Leow,
   Gideon J. Tucker,
   Magnus Gross.

Dist.
7. *Edwards Pierrepont,* *A. L. Robertson,* *James Brooks,* *Samuel J. Tilden.*
8. *R. L. Larramore,* *John E. Devlin,* *C. W. Monell,* *Wm. Hitchman.*
9. *A. B. Tappan,* *Robert Cochran,* *A. B. Conger,* *Wm. H. Morris.*
10. Gideon Wales, E. V. R. Luddington, Stephen W. Fullerton, William H. Houston.
11. John S. Gould, Francis Sylvester, B. Platt Carpenter, Wilson C. Sheldon.
12. John M. Francis, J. P. Armstrong, Cornelius L. Allen, Adolphus Hitchcock.
13. *Erastus Corning,* *William Cassidy,* *Amasa J. Parker,* *James Roy.*
14. *Manly B. Mattice,* *E. P. Moore,* *M. Schoonmaker,* *Solomon G. Young.*
15. Horace E. Smith, Hezekiah Baker, Judson S. Landon,

Dist.
15. Alembert Pond.
16. George M. Beckwith, N. G. Axtell, Matthew Hale, A. J. Cherretree.
17. William P. Brown, Leslie W. Russell, Edwin A. Merritt, Joel J. Seaver.
18. Wilton H. Merwin, James A. Bell, Marcus Buckford, Edward A. Brown.
19. Richard W. Sherman, Theodore W. Dwight, Benj. H. Huntington, George Williams.
20. E. C. Terry, John Eddy, Edgar Graves, O. B. Beales.
21. Linsley M. Lee, Elias Root, Loring Fowler, Lester M. Case.
22. Thomas G. Alvord, *L. Harris Hiscock, Patrick Corbett, Horatio Ballard.
23. E. H Prindle, John Grant, Samuel F. Miller, Hobart Krum.
24. Milo G. Goodrich, Stanton D. Hand,

Dist.
24. C. E. Parker, O. D. H Kinney.
25. George Rathbun, Charles C. Dwight, Orrin Archer, L. S. Ketchum.
26. M. H. Lawrence, E. G. Lapham, Angus McDonald, Sterling G. Hadley.
27. David Ramsey, George T. Spencer, Elijah P. Brooks, Abraham Lawrence.
28. Jerome Fuller, L. B. Ely, Wm. A. Reynolds, Freeman Clarke.
29. Levi T. Brown, George T. Flager, Seth Wakeman, Benjamin Field.
30. Wm. H. Merrill, Isaac L. Endress, John M. Hammond, Edward J. Farnham.
31. *Israel T. Hatch,* *George W. Clinton,* *Allen Potter,* *J. A. Verplanck.*
32. George Barker, Augustus F. Allen, Norman M. Allen, Henry Van Campen.

* Died June 4, 1867, and succeeded by his brother, Frank Hiscock.

RECAPITULATION.

	At Large.	Dist.	Total.
Republicans	16	81	97
Democrats	16	47	63
Rep. majority		34	34

NEW YORK COUNTY AND CHARTER ELECTIONS, 1867.

WARDS.	SHERIFF O'Brien. Tam.	SHERIFF Connolly. Moz.	SHERIFF Abbe. Rep.	CLERK Loew. Tam.	CLERK Conner. Moz.	CLERK Walsh. D.Un.	CLERK Haggerty. Rep.	D.A. Hall. T.&M.	D.A. Waterbury. D.U.	D.A. Hawkins. Rep.	MAYOR Hoffman. Tam.	MAYOR Wood. Moz.	MAYOR Darling. Rep.
1	1251	790	176	1195	534	357	122	1838	202	121	1668	281	58
2	141	107	94	110	146	34	45	204	31	74	219	52	53
3	266	330	156	280	216	104	136	493	101	147	431	135	86
4	1725	1221	223	1375	395	1257	150	1980	939	174	2186	688	131
5	626	1542	618	889	732	646	597	1340	882	532	1483	740	348
6	1685	1644	222	1658	580	1152	132	2541	797	160	2754	787	119
7	3138	1840	848	1816	1197	1959	524	4347	561	726	3579	1329	517
8	1803	2222	1012	1688	1575	835	1057	3443	622	1007	3153	887	628
9	2007	2090	2925	1746	1940	846	2219	3418	795	2770	3353	1079	1881
10	1589	1778	874	2462	798	330	651	2387	412	800	2997	467	502
11	3457	2551	1210	4207	2260	279	801	5681	324	1128	5019	1359	798
12	1194	1816	1633	1335	1301	514	1486	2482	563	1584	2261	914	1090
13	1338	1800	935	1580	1143	378	671	2785	409	933	2307	830	543
14	1668	1831	388	1362	1102	1058	309	2522	1019	345	2346	1152	223
15	1258	1003	1527	1117	917	212	1155	1949	294	1431	1931	390	979
16	1872	1849	2280	1741	1982	398	1938	3149	439	2158	2670	1318	1522
17	4429	4607	2047	5526	2276	552	1771	7363	1032	1383	6348	1752	1424
18	3216	2069	1945	2670	1818	914	1795	4549	852	1652	3663	1748	1487
19	2235	2586	1861	2170	2598	497	1528	4194	750	1732	3075	1692	1655
20	2882	3691	2142	3264	1690	1695	2009	4260	2308	2081	4070	2293	1426
21	3692	1094	2079	3112	1350	463	1939	4409	459	2014	3806	830	1511
22	1299	4105	1962	1822	2186	1273	1942	3996	1346	1974	3057	2104	1502
Total	42771	41955	27277	43125	29136	15833	23217	70030	15127	25623	63081	22827	18483

VERMONT.

COUNTIES.	Governor, 1867. Ed-wards Dem.	Page Rep.	Governor, 1866. Dav-enp't. Dem.	Dill-ing'm Rep.	President, 1864. Mc Clel'n Dem.	Lin-coln. Rep.
Addison....	252	2553	246	2537	344	3567
Bennington	1244	2773	830	1820	1021	2333
Caledonia..	1135	2266	1129	2389	1115	2731
Chittenden.	986	2777	958	3402	923	3227
Essex.	340	640	309	638	385	613
Franklin..	1058	2308	1067	2601	1156	2689
Grand Isle.	168	367	173	386	168	370
Lamoille,..	435	1124	441	1597	531	1760
Orange.....	1406	2728	1455	2859	1701	3365
Orleans....	659	1917	635	2490	626	2703
Rutland....	993	3265	1067	3437	1247	4789
Washt'n...	1241	2551	1245	2901	1552	3633
Windham..	761	2428	874	2953	1232	4183
Windsor....	832	3997	863	4107	1320	6440
Total.....	11510	31694	11292	34117	13321	42419

STATE OFFICERS — John B. Page, Governor; Stephen Thomas, Lieut. Governor; George Nichols, Secretary of State; John A. Page, Treasurer

LEGISLATURE, 1867—8

	Senat.	House.	Joint Bal.
Republicans............	29	213....	242
Democrats........	1	25....	26
Rep. Majority.	28	188....	216

CONGRESS, 1866.

Districts	Dem. Wells.	Rep. Woodbridge.
I		
Addison..............	201	2594
Bennington.........	797	1887
Rutland.............	873	3317
Washington.......	1165	2770
Total............	3,036	10,568

F. E. Woodbridge over Wells, 7,582.

	Chase.	Poland.
II		
Caledonia...........	1042	2207
Orange..	1329	2374
Windham.........	823	2777
Windsor..........	741	3486
Total...........	3,935	10,844

Luke P. Poland over Chase, 6,909.

	Brigham.	Addis.	Smith.
III			
Chittenden..........	641	926	1597
Essex..........	162	19	402
Franklin..........	808	949	1215
Grand Isle..........	120	258	123
Lamoille..........	397	332	877
Orleans..........	552	310	1516
Total..........	2,680	2,794	5,730

W. C. Smith over Brigham, 3,050; over Addis 2,936; over all 210.

OHIO.

COUNTIES.	Governor, 1867. Thurman Dem.	Hayes Rep.	Const'l Amd't 1867. No.	Yes.	Governor, 1865. Morgan Dem.	Cox. Rep.	President, 1864. Mc Clel'n Dem.	Lin-coln. Rep.
Adams.....	2300	1982	2427	1745	1770	1962	1932	2088
Allen.....	2624	1737	2717	1364	2152	1623	2241	1865
Ashland...	2464	2161	2577	1979	2319	2030	2281	3156
Ashtabula.	1377	5061	1295	4787	961	4069	1039	6054
Athens....	1701	2598	1904	2278	1160	2541	1318	3024
Anglaize..	2713	925	2839	760	2049	918	2374	1164
Belmont...	3971	3412	4212	3018	3289	3363	3496	3422
Brown.....	3266	2407	3386	2171	2879	2610	2933	2699
Butler....	4896	2800	5060	2505	4245	2981	4310	3219
Carroll...	1289	1634	1380	1485	1177	1632	1223	1794
Champaign	2159	2623	2375	2238	1625	2440	1755	2753
Clarke....	2113	3290	2392	2869	1719	2946	1641	3709
Clermont..	3737	3246	4001	2789	3307	3336	3318	3303
Clinton...	1638	2634	1764	2417	1353	2328	1397	2758
Columbiana	2919	4237	3029	3943	2371	3705	2501	4547
Coshocton.	2619	2102	2734	1761	2374	1979	2447	2125
Crawford..	3497	1864	3578	1703	2911	1759	3112	1954
Cuyahoga..	7436	9673	7858	8989	5809	7472	5856	9957
Darke.....	3246	2661	3529	2389	2605	2637	2704	2595
Defiance ..	1855	1009	1893	944	1509	849	1594	1163
Delaware ..	2311	2727	2514	2444	1669	2491	1892	2827
Erie......	1989	2480	2169	2219	1651	2143	1829	3483
Fairfield..	3940	2056	4058	1809	3394	2351	3510	2484
Fayette...	1543	1733	1717	1435	1087	1547	1243	1860
Franklin..	7255	4600	7707	4032	6236	4296	5756	4920
Fulton....	1146	1902	1329	1789	879	1511	970	1965
Gallia....	1902	2001	2207	1521	1051	2095	1174	2826
Geauga....	630	2654	708	2512	526	2201	491	2986
Greene....	1857	3615	1957	3403	1523	2873	1556	3886
Guernsey..	2052	2549	2126	2420	1853	2053	1980	2684
Hamilton..	18437	19961	20796	16119	13605	17943	16548	22700
Hancock...	2509	2172	2625	1994	2228	2120	2300	2177
Hardin....	1770	1770	1838	1629	1302	1644	1457	1613
Harrison..	1660	2112	1820	1870	1467	1969	1563	2178
Henry.....	1545	955	1587	896	1268	811	1271	924
Highland..	2885	2881	3074	2607	2063	2695	2582	3105
Hocking...	2129	1179	2193	1057	1691	1265	1887	1384
Holmes....	2988	957	3011	868	2558	948	2683	1068
Huron.....	2273	3682	2228	3431	1944	3202	2090	4441
Jackson...	1621	1857	1916	1615	1102	1558	1317	1955
Jefferson..	2202	2969	2371	2706	1589	2843	732	3375
Knox......	2811	2814	2995	2530	2438	2629	2523	2856
Lake......	830	2392	910	2216	625	2103	582	2781

LEGISLATURE, 1868—

	Senate.	House.	Joint Bal.
Democrats....18		56..........	74
Republicans....17		49..........	66
Dem. Majority, 1		7............	8

CONGRESS, 1867.

Special Election in 2d District, to fill vacancy occasioned by the resignation of R. B. Hayes.

	Cary. Dem.	Smith. Rer.
Hamilton Co.............	2699 9390	9431

Sam'l F. Cary over R'd Smith, 959.

CONGRESS, 1866.

Districts.	Dem.	Rep.
I.	Pendleton.	Eggleston.
Hamilton..............	9496	10422

Benjamin Eggleston over Geo. H. Pendleton, 926.

II.	Cook.	Hayes.
	8981	11549

Rutherford B. Hayes over Theodore Cook, 2558.

III.	Ward.	Schenck.
Butler..............	4747	2887
Montgomery.........	5962	5534
Preble..............	1764	2709
Warren..............	1787	3897
Total..............	13960	15027

Robert C. Schenck over J. Durbin Ward, 1,067.

IV	McKinney.	Lawrence.
Champaign.................	1867	2706
Darke.............	2911	2879
Logan.............	1653	2568
Miami.............	2549	3688
Shelby.............	2079	1472
Total.............	11059	13313

Wm. Lawrence over J. F. McKin-ney, 2,254.

	Mungen.	Walker.
Allen.............	2255	1858
Anglaize.............	2239	1037
Hancock.............	2361	2256
Hardin.............	1439	1746

COUNTIES.	Thur-man.	Hayes	No.	Yes.	Mor-gan.	Cox.	Mc Clel'n	Lin-coln.
Lawrence..	2258	2009	2771	1098	1261	1847	1113	2962
Licking...	4441	3133	4838	2767	3804	3152	3860	3322
Logan.....	1837	2516	1943	2318	1487	2302	1617	2577
Lorain	1807	4095	1944	3857	1674	3474	1650	4568
Lucas	2655	3844	3074	3220	1713	2942	2095	3794
Madison...	1533	1515	1710	1240	1157	1391	1165	1671
Mahoning.	2602	2898	2642	2733	2134	2504	2422	3042
Marion....	1953	1377	2046	1160	1657	1460	1690	1441
Medina....	1686	2626	1745	2486	1636	2521	1629	2925
Meigs.....	2185	2773	2425	2368	1493	2450	1464	3493
Mercer....	2323	696	2355	588	1798	730	1926	826
Miami	2810	3352	2964	3004	2289	3175	2348	3791
Monroe....	3477	1111	3535	936	2783	1177	3200	1411
Montgom'y.	6282	5602	6648	4956	5034	5063	5284	5526
Morgan....	1953	2403	2033	2266	1628	2220	1727	2606
Morrow ...	1801	2240	1893	2087	1560	2105	1672	2405
Muskingum	4671	4315	4949	3851	3903	3972	3897	4421
Noble	1873	2009	1937	1865	1588	1949	1722	2122
Ottawa....	1260	808	1303	731	920	697	842	822
Paulding ..	666	761	727	614	352	502	363	805
Perry......	2090	1599	2178	1457	1774	1713	1864	1823
Pickaway..	2870	1882	3060	1572	2423	2111	2527	2201
Pike.......	1770	973	1890	766	1333	905	1941	1049
Portage....	2317	3342	2386	3188	1932	2853	1918	3478
Preble.....	1867	2422	1938	2285	1524	2333	1706	2719
Putnam....	2020	972	2077	866	1493	875	1710	1117
Richland..	3691	3067	3815	2859	3278	2874	3401	3187
Ross.......	3837	2889	4056	2556	3125	3022	3200	3381
Sandusky..	2834	2261	2948	2067	2355	2161	2375	2297
Scioto	2535	2327	2636	1831	1936	2205	2051	2799
Seneca.....	3584	2739	3709	2453	3030	2807	3311	3085
Shelby.....	2393	1350	2482	1162	1886	1412	2028	1603
Stark......	4821	4669	4976	4316	4026	4447	4290	4797
Summit ...	2274	3942	2403	3675	1879	3220	1823	4192
Trumbull..	2189	4525	2222	4243	1851	3989	1907	5089
Tuscarawas	3483	2746	3600	2715	3048	2715	3129	3030
Union	1537	2123	1562	1905	1173	1930	1255	2128
Van Wert..	1408	1408	1451	1242	1153	1247	1201	1294
Vinton.....	1634	1302	1706	1137	1168	1137	1323	1119
Warren....	1905	3638	2079	3321	1499	3229	1595	3851
Washingt'n	3718	3722	3868	3416	3042	3439	3056	4028
Wayne.....	3703	3313	3783	3123	3257	3053	3413	3181
Williams..	1801	2199	1885	2052	1388	1662	1425	2197
Wood	1800	2420	1974	2200	1408	2036	1492	2586
Wyandotte.	2183	1609	2258	1487	1869	1673	1874	1740
Total.....	240622	243605	255340	216987	193697	223632	205568	265154

V.
Mercer......2012 763
Van Wert....1296 1483
Wyandotte...1922 1734

Total.........13524 10872
Wm. Mungen over Moses B. Walker, 2652.

VI.   Howard. Clarke.
Brown.............3107 2806
Clermont..........3644 3395
Clinton...........1510 2831
Fayette...........1328 1795
Highland..........2678 3019

Total.........12267 13846
R. W. Clarke over Wm. Howard, 1579.

VII.   Miller. Shellabarger.
Clarke............1960 3522
Franklin..........6505 4614
Greene............1598 3945
Madison...........1453 1606

Total.........11516 13687
Samuel Shellabarger over Thomas Miller, 2171.

VIII.   Reid. Hamilton.
Delaware..........1983 2793
Marion............1676 1523
Morrow............1613 2237
Richland..........3316 2955
Union.............1270 2902

Total............9858 11710
C. S. Hamilton over Wm. P. Reid, 1852.

IX.   Finefrock. Buckland.
Crawford..........3173 1996
Erie..............1787 2990
Huron.............2050 4005
Ottawa............1044 885
Sandusky..........2554 2392
Seneca............3336 2963

Total.........13944 15231
R. P. Buckland over T. P. Finefrock, 1287.

X.   Commager. Ashley.
Defiance..........1671 1054
Fulton............1066 2041
Henry.............1393 1008
Lucas.............2851 3937
Paulding..........494 735
Putnam............1959 1133
Williams..........1633 2261
Wood..............1889 2705

Total.........12956 14873
J. M. Ashley over H. S. Commager, 1,917.

The Constitutional Amendment included negro suffrage and the disfranchisement of deserters.

STATE OFFICERS.—Rutherford B. Hayes, Governor; John C. Lee, Lieut.-Governor; William H. Smith, Secretary of State; John Welch, Auditor; Sidney S. Warner, Treasurer; William H. West, Attorney General; Moses R. Brailey, Comptroller.

STATE DEBT.—Civil Debt in 1861, $13,954,233.89; War Debt, $1,612,039.45; Total, $15,566,273.34. Redeemed since 1861, $4,386,570.78; Present Debt, $11,179,702.56.

XI.   Moore. Wilson.
Adams......2016 2060
Gallia......1369 2475
Jackson.....1678 1619
Lawrence....1397 2334
Scioto......2120 2621
Vinton......1365 1374

Total......9945 12783
John T. Wilson over Oscar F. Moore, 2,838.

XII.   VanTrump. Jones.
Fairfield....3417 2137
Hocking......1811 1113
Perry........1908 1720
Pickaway.....2531 2065
Pike.........1513 1040
Ross.........3366 3261

Total......14546 11336
P. Van Trump over Wells S. Jones, 3,210.

XIII.   Morgan. Delano.
Coshocton...2468 2100
Knox........2537 2913
Licking.....4020 3397
Muskingum...4203 4547

Total......13228 12957
Geo. W. Morgan over Columbus Delano, 271.

XIV.   Young. Welker.
Ashland.....2210 2167
Holmes......2808 868
Lorain......1720 4361
Medina......1645 2761
Wayne.......3404 3337

Total......11787 13494
Martin Welker over J. B. Young, 1,707.

XV.   Follett. Plants.
Athens......1212 2640
Meigs.......1676 2884
Monroe......2866 1067
Morgan......1827 2436
Washington..3171 3789

Total......10752 12816
T. A. Plants over M. D. Follett, 2,064.

XVI.   Mitchner. Bingham.
Belmont.....3569 3505
Guernsey....1913 2705
Harrison....1538 2086
Noble.......1701 2147
Tuscarawas..3226 2926

Total......11947 13369
John A. Bingham over C. H. Mitchner, 1,422.

XVII.   Schaefer. Eckley.
Carroll.....1164 1713
Columbiana..2378 4248
Jefferson...1761 3174
Stark........3979 4782

Total......9275 13917
Eph. R. Eckley over Louis Schaefer, 4,642.

XVIII.   Payne. Spalding.
Cuyahoga....5714 8447
Lake........578 2362
Summit......1687 3670

Total.......7974 14479
R. P. Spalding over Oliver H. Payne, 6,505.

XIX.   Coolman. Garfield.
Ashtabula... 931 5001
Geauga......401 2488
Mahoning....2275 2933
Portage.....1982 3342
Trumbull....1787 4598

Total.......7376 18362
Jas. A. Garfield over D. C. Coolman, 10,986.

PENNSYLVANIA.

COUNTIES.	Justice Sup. Court, 1867. Shars-wood. Dem.	Justice Sup. Court, 1867. Will-iams. Rep.	Governor, 1866. Cly-mer. Dem.	Governor, 1866. Geary Rep.	President, 1864. Mc Ciel'n Dem.	President, 1864. Lin-coln. Rep.
Adams	2829	2437	3126	2910	3016	2612
Allegheny	9994	16333	12795	20511	13414	21519
Armstrong	2934	3235	3078	3758	3211	3526
Beaver	2278	2818	2385	3310	2304	3237
Bedford	2644	2305	2835	2591	2752	2336
Berks	11912	6117	13288	7121	13266	6710
Blair	2590	3113	2768	3520	2686	3292
Bradford	2638	5846	3091	7134	3007	6865
Bucks	6910	6224	7399	6805	7335	6436
Butler	2662	2939	3061	3544	2947	3475
Cambria	3020	2068	3295	2643	3036	2244
Cameron	300	358	303	374	232	325
Carbon	2124	1687	2339	1906	2251	1721
Centre	3473	2790	3565	3094	3399	2817
Chester	5853	7751	6221	8500	5987	8446
Clarion	2603	1410	2813	1776	2833	1780
Clearfield	2740	1477	2786	1650	2801	1516
Clinton	2228	1602	2337	1754	2135	1666
Columbia	3453	1696	3583	1965	3467	1914
Crawford	4018	5400	4969	6714	4526	6441
Cumberl'd	4231	3451	4567	4030	4354	3604
Dauphin	3847	5247	4301	5691	4220	5444
Delaware	2148	3207	2262	3647	2145	3664
Elk	756	286	916	376	835	348
Erie	3428	5504	3957	7237	3722	6911
Fayette	3859	3184	4359	3569	4126	3221
Franklin	3962	3773	4106	4229	3821	3862
Fulton	1019	709	1055	775	906	694
Forest	319	289	76	100	62	85
Greene	2753	1343	3230	1699	3074	583
Hunting'n	2258	3009	2239	3248	2477	3321
Indiana	1867	3608	2109	4458	2197	4329
Jefferson	1851	1806	1912	2015	1877	1820
Juniata	1665	1368	1814	1516	1753	1437
Lancaster	7475	12799	8592	14592	8448	14469
Lawrence	1281	2833	1410	3560	1389	3408
Lebanon	2501	3625	2696	4194	2779	3780
Lehigh	5141	3514	5731	4159	5920	3908
Luzerne	10404	7985	12387	8733	10045	7645
Lycoming	4357	3604	4448	3871	4207	3401
McKean	545	705	714	877	652	767
Mercer	3414	3935	3757	4416	3569	4220
Mifflin	1769	1565	1835	1725	1718	1643
Monroe	2359	543	2699	705	2698	685
Montgom'y	7683	6586	8342	7286	7943	6872
Montour	1383	1006	1523	1130	1496	1130
Northam'n	5979	3027	6870	3559	6944	3726
Northum'ld	3469	3023	3829	3361	3608	2915
Perry	2292	2427	2495	2581	2446	2406
Philadelph.	52075	49587	48817	54205	44032	55797
Pike	901	235	1084	360	1180	260
Potter	481	1134	620	1346	680	1380
Schuylkill	8380	7256	10514	8793	9540	7851
Somerset	1541	2756	1759	3062	1719	2788
Snyder	1199	1630	1326	1792	1368	1679
Sullivan	683	421	761	436	660	369
Susqueh'na	2690	3947	2981	4429	2959	4203
Tioga	1425	4090	1628	4791	1584	4673
Union	1200	1675	1287	1991	1352	1945
Venango	2610	3040	3492	4409	3341	3849
Warren	1459	2131	1572	2687	1505	2541
Washingt'n	4513	4618	4712	4977	4579	4951
Wayne	2586	2330	2883	2357	3989	2274
Westmor'ld	5645	4212	6113	5406	5977	4650
Wyoming	1474	1357	1499	1408	1402	1337
York	7671	4848	8780	5896	8500	5668
Total	267751	266824	290096	307274	276316	296391

STATE OFFICERS.—John W. Geary, Governor; John F. Hartranft, Auditor-General; Francis Jordon, Secretary of State; Jacob M. Campbell, Surveyor-General.

STATE DEBT.—Civil Debt, $32,801,302.16; War Debt, $2,820,750.00.

STATE LEGISLATURE, 1868.

	Senate.	House.	Joint Bal.
Republicans	20	54	74
Democrats	13	46	59
Rep. Majority	7	8	15

CONGRESS, 1867.

Special Election in 12th Congressional District, to fill vacancy occasioned by the death of Chas. Denison.

	G. W. Woodward. W. W. Ketcham.
Counties.	Dem.	Rep.
Luzerne	10155	8274
Susquehanna	2468	3804
Total	12623	12078

G. W. Woodward over W. W. Ketcham, 545.

VOTE OF PHILA.,1867.
Judge of Supreme Court.

Wards.	Sharswood. Dem.	Williams. Rep.
1	1778	2002
2	3095	2093
3	2081	1148
4	2401	872
5	1966	946
6	1490	951
7	1827	2185
8	1483	1475
9	1543	1699
10	1514	2456
11	1671	903
12	1646	1189
13	1744	1905
14	1722	2249
15	2942	3963
16	1915	1682
17	2278	1141
18	1896	2570
19	2606	2586
20	3782	3766
21	1049	1322
22	1472	2036
23	4556	1958
24	1681	1608
25	1491	919
26	1826	2417
27	868	969
28	747	729
Total	52069	49469
Co.K, 4th Art. 2		60
Co.L, 4th Art. 2		58
Total	52074	49587

Total number of votes cast, exclusive of the 123 by the soldiers, 101,538; total number registered, 144,272.

CONGRESS, 1866.

Districts	Dem.	Rep.
I.	Randall.	Gibbons.
Phil. W'd 2	3095	2319
3	1951	1251
4	2194	925
5	1885	1056
6	1435	1112
11	1632	1065
Total	12192	7728

S. J. Randall over Chas. Gibbons, 4,464.

II.	Hulme.	O'Neill.
Phil. W'd 1	1599	2011
7	1790	2304
8	1419	1542
9	1518	1788
10	1456	2546
26	1693	2415
Total	9475	13612

Chas. O'Neill over John Hulme, 3,137.

III.	Buckwalter.	Myers.
Phil. W'd 12	1476	1535
13	1599	2160
16	1870	1793
17	2291	1368
18	1835	2323
19	2445	2841
Total	11516	12520

Leonard Myers over C. Buckwalter, 1,004.

IV.	Welsh.	Kelley.
Phil. W'd 14	1699	2484
15	2809	3699
20	3948	3782
21	1697	2013
24	1574	1566
27	856	1027
Total	12126	14551

Wm. D. Kelley over John Welsh, 2,425.

V.	Ross.	Taylor.
Phil. W'd 22	1848	2383
23	1551	2061
25	1472	997
Bucks Co.	7429	6818
Total	11800	12259

C. M. Taylor over H. P. Ross, 459.

VI.	Boyer.	Thomas.
Lehigh	5674	4180
Montgomery	8335	7267
Total	14009	11447

B. M. Boyer over David Thomas, 2,562.

VII.	Pratt.	Broomall.
Chester	6247	8450
Delaware	2284	3561
Total	8531	12011

J. N. Broomall over N. Pratt, 3,480.

VIII.	Getz.	Lincoln.
Berks	13188	6999
Lincoln	6,189.
J. L. Getz over D. J.

J. L. Getz over D. J. Lincoln, 6,189.

IX.	Reynolds	Stevens.
Lancaster	8675	14298

Thad. Stevens over S. H. Reynolds, 5,623.

X.	Gloninger.	Cake.
Lebanon	2729	4157
Schuylkill	10242	9029
Total	12971	13186

H. L. Cake over C. D. Gloninger, 215.

XI.	Van Anken.	Lilly.
Carbons	2339	1906
Monroe	2699	705
Northam'n	6870	3896

Pike......	1096	360
Wayne....	2903	2328
Total....	15907	9121
D. M. Van Auten over		
Wm. Lilly, 6,786.		

XII. Denison. Archibald.

Luzerne ...	12311	8831
Susq'hann.	2969	4443
Total.....	15280	13274
Chas. Denison over		
Jas. Archibald, 2,006.		

XIII. Elwell. Mercur.

Bradford ..	3185	7078
Columbia..	3644	1907
Montour ..	1550	1114
Sullivan..	762	435
Wyoming ..	1512	1406
Total	10653	11940
Ulysses Mercur over		
Wm. Elwell, 1,287.		

XIV. Bower. Miller.

Dauphin ..	4320	5675
Juniata....	1834	1499
Northuml'd	3830	3347
Snyder.....	1392	1715
Union......	1299	1951
Total.....	12675	14190
George F. Miller over		
Bower, 1515.		

XV Glossbren'r. Henders'n.

Cumberl'd ..	4565	4005
Perry......	2506	2581
York......	8759	5903
Total.....	15830	12489
A. J. Glossbrenner		
over R. M. Henderson,		
3341.		

XVI. Sharpe. Koontz.

Adams.....	3134	2901
Bedford....	2850	2575
Franklin..	4162	4278
Fulton.....	1073	756
Somerset ..	1745	3079
Total.....	12964	13589
Wm. H. Koontz over		
Sharpe, 625.		

XVII. Johnston. Morrell.

Blair......	2736	3554
Cambria...	3415	2791
Huntingd'n	2259	3226
Mifflin....	1838	1727
Total.....	9979	11298
D. J. Morrell over R. L.		
Johnston, 1319.		

XVIII. Wright. Wilson.

Centre.....	3592	3070
Clinton....	2352	1736
Lycoming..	4462	3845
Potter......	628	1330
Tioga.......	1654	4753
Total.....	12688	14734
S. F. Wilson over T.		
F. Wright, 2046.		

XIX. Scott. Scofield.

Cameron ...	305	372
Clearfield..	2791	1646
Elk.......	936	359
Erie.......	4094	7128
Forest.....	77	99
Jefferson...	1944	1986
McKean....	739	851
Warren....	1595	2663
Total.....	12481	15107
G. W. Scofield over W.		
L. Scott, 2626.		

XX. McCalmont. Finney.

Clarion....		
Crawford..		
Mercer....		
Venango...		
Total.....	15222	17106
D. A. Finney over A.		
B. McCalmont, 1884.		

XXI. Wier. Covode.

Fayette....	4370	3594
Indiana....	2142	4409
W'tmorel'd	6157	5020
Total.....	12669	13023
Jno. Covode over Wier		
354.		

XXII. Switzer. Moorhead.

All'h'y,(P't)	9655	12720
J. K. Moorhead over J.		
B. Switzer, 3065.		

XXIII. Childs. Williams.

All h'y,(P't)		
Armstrong.		
Butler.....		
Total.....	10012	14197
Thos. Williams over B.		
G. Childs, 4185.		

XXIV. Montg'y. Lawrence.

Beaver....	2424	3283
Green.....	3270	1649
Lawrence..	1426	3550
Washg'tn..	4783	4903
Total.....	11853	13391
G. V. Lawrence over		
W. Montgomery, 1538.		

COUNTIES.	Dem.	Rep.	Run- yon. Dem.	Ward. Rep.	Mc- Clel'n Dem.	Lin- coln. Rep.
Morris...	3566	3104	3506	3702	3587	3222
Ocean ...	860	1048	811	1421	791	1292
Passaic ...	3157	2933	2666	3365	2773	2934
Salem	1884	2275	2017	2379	2164	2221
Somerset...	2243	1598	2225	2022	2334	1923
Sussex	3148	2393	3215	1815	3164	1621
Union.....	3288	2229	2408	2776	2866	2381
Warren ...	2479	833	3584	2249	3706	2006
Total....	67468	51114	61736	67525	63021	60723

There was no General State Election in 1867; the figures given under that year, in the above table, are those of the average vote for Members of the Legislature and County Officers.

STATE OFFICERS.—Governor, Marcus L. Ward; Secretary of State, Horace V. Congar; Treasurer, Howard Ivins; Comptroller, Wm. K. McDonald; Attorney-General, George M. Robeson.

STATE DEBT.—Bonded war debt, $3,295,600, of which $593,400 is taxable. Towards liquidation of this, $89,500 was received January 1, 1868. There is also a sinking fund of $350,000. No civil debt.

STATE LEGISLATURE, 1868.—

	Senate.	House.	Joint Bal.
Democrats.......	11	46	57
Republicans......	10	14	24
Dem. majority....	1	32	33

VOTE OF NEWARK.

WARDS.	Mayor, 1867.		Governor, 1865.		President, 1864.	
	Big- elow. Dem.	Ped- die. Rep.	Run- yon. Dem.	Ward. Rep.	Mc- Clel'n Dem.	Lin- coln. Rep.
1......	493	649	517	938	556	777
2.......	585	729	616	920	639	743
3.......	379	729	384	972	411	785
4.......	533	624	587	832	707	710
5.......	451	437	811	681	720	522
6.......	514	544	527	578	529	476
7.......	867	576	959	701	942	513
8.......	440	331	433	360	394	259
9.......	331	659	263	873	285	738
10......	605	525	556	599	527	428
11......	258	124	239	157	233	111
12......	674	185	373	122	350	75
13......	592	675	689	767	685	541
Total....	6722	6787	6954	8500	6981	6678

CONGRESS, 1866.

Dist.	Dem. Slape.	Rep. Moore.
I.		
Atlantic	759	1292
Camden	2572	3370
Cape May ..	368	673
Gloucester .	1354	2029
Cumberland	1701	2736
Salem.......	2204	2368
Total....	9108	12468

Wm. Moore over Slape, 3360.

II.	Haight.	Newell.
Burlington..	4414	5122
Ocean......	982	1339
Monmouth..	4717	3131
Mercer......	3712	3884
Total.....	13825	13476

Chas Haight over New- ell, 349.

III.	Sitgreaves.	Davidson.
Hunterdon..	4091	2944
Middlesex...	3504	3273
Somerset....	2192	1950
Union.......	2759	2814
Warren.....	3222	1974
Total.....	15768	12955

Chas. Sitgreaves over Davidson, 2813.

IV.	Rogers.	Hill.
Bergen......	2178	1645
Essex (part)	2123	3054
Morris.....	3129	3781
Passaic	2862	3419
Sussex.....	3107	1962
Total.....	13399	13861

John Hill over Rogers, 462.

V.	Gilchrist.	Halsey.
Newark.....	6289	7920
Hudson....	5558	4862
Total.....	11847	12782

G. A. Halsey over Gil- christ, 933.

NEW JERSEY.

COUNTIES.	Legislature, 1857.		Governor, 1865.		President, 1864.	
	Dem.	Rep.	Run- yon. Dem.	Ward. Rep.	Mc- Clel'n Dem.	Lin- coln. Rep.
Atlantic	982	1078	1024	1262	1062	117
Bergen.....	2206	786	2281	1811	2431	1554
Burlington .	5080	4463	3919	5387	4176	5280
Camden....	3356	2741	2767	3365	2758	3332
Cape May..	652	632	440	735	557	761
Cumberla'd	2540	2589	856	2743	2034	2669
Essex	9498	9702	9114	11617	9239	9402
Gloucester..	1727	1758	1393	2083	1404	1998
Hudson	6439	3545	5279	5157	6397	4616
Hunterdon .	3979	2072	4369	3094	4355	2631
Mercer.....	4032	3627	3767	4118	3792	3726
Middlesex..	3935	2855	3470	3379	3740	3037
Monmouth..	2558 no op		4197	3145	4410	3001

MARYLAND.

COUNTIES.	Governor, 1867.		New Const'n. 1867.		President. 1864.	
	Bowie Dem.	Bond. Rep.	Yes.	No.	Mc-Clel'n Dem.	Lin-coln. Rep.
Alleghany..	2884	2175	2059	1779	1990	2455
Anne Aru'l.	1695	150	1282	199	1574	416
Bal. City...	19912	4846	16126	5627	2953	14978
Bal. Co....	4131	1324	3285	1532	2391	2402
Calvert....	881	9	337	168	669	62
Caroline...	1005	231	766	262	270	728
Carroll.....	2815	2291	2187	1920	1885	2056
Cecil......	2513	1588	1773	1214	1520	1757
Charles....	1279	7	791	17	961	27
Dorchester.	1571	341	1384	362	1361	626
Frederick..	4185	3705	3307	2929	2302	3553
Harford ...	2297	896	1879	749	1650	1259
Howard....	1210	335	728	368	778	579
Kent.......	1420	136	1010	346	1269	413
Montgom'y.	1675	320	913	654	1542	496
Pr'ce Geo's.	2055	78	995	149	1550	197
Q'n Ann's.	1757	95	1214	176	1482	384
St. Mary's.	1519	40	746	119	986	99
Somerset..	1315	137	1257	1042	2111	644
Talbot.....	1273	138	1080	255	267	578
Washingt'n	3332	2913	2658	2527	1402	2980
Wicomico..	1615	310				
Worcester..	1401	135	1236	680	1506	664
Soldiers V't					331	2800
Total.....	63739	22110	47152	23036	32739	40153

STATE OFFICERS—Governor, Ogden Bowie; Attorney General, I. D. Jones; Controller, Wm. J. Leonard; Commissioner of Agriculture, W. S. McPherson.

STATE LEGISLATURE, 1868.   *Senate.   House.*
Democrats.................... 25   85
No Republicans in either house.

CONGRESS, 1866.

Dist.	Dem.	Vote.	Rep.	Vote.	Maj.
1. H. McCulloch,	11729	S. A. Graham..	4052	7677	
2. S. Archer....	7091	J. L. Thomas,Jr	5014	2077	
3. C. E. Phelps..	5548	Jos. J. Stewart.	4568	980	
4. W.P. Maulsby	9230	Francis Thomas	11252	2022	
5. Fred'k Stone.	8708	Wm. J. Albert..	2032	6676	

DELAWARE.

COUNTIES.	Governor, 1866.		President, 1864.	
	Sauls-bury. Dem.	Riddle Rep.	Mc-Clel'n Dem.	Lin-coln. Rep.
Kent..................	2725	1796	2402	1652
New Castle	4248	4428	3813	4274
Sussex	2837	2374	2552	2229
Total	9810	8598	8767	8155

STATE OFFICERS—Gove Saulsbury, Governor; Curtis W. Wright, Secretary of State; William I. Clark, Treasurer; Robert Lambden, Auditor; Jacob Moore, Attorney General.

STATE DEBT—$1,242,000,00, all contracted during the war, previous to which time Delaware had no debt.

STATE LEGISLATURE, 1868—
	Senate.	House.	Joint Bal.
Democrats............	6	15........	21
Republicans...........	3	5........	8
Dem. majority........	3	10........	13

CONGRESS, 1866.
Dem.   *Rep.*
J. A. Nicholson ....9983.... J. L. McKim...8553
John A. Nicholson over J. L. McKim, 1,380

OREGON.

COUNTIES.	Governor, 1866.	
	Kelly Dem.	Woods Rep.
Baker	299	283
Benton	494	537
Clackhamas	560	682
Clatsop	48	117
Columbia	104	89
Coos	85	135
Curry	42	58
Douglas	545	631
Grant	254	317
Jackson	691	562
Josephine	179	153
Lane	700	579
Linn	1233	1015
Marion	833	1390
Multnomah	1025	1205
Polk	565	560
Tillamook	39	47
Umatilla	517	270
Umpqua		
Union	416	285
Wasco	413	355
Washington	359	465
Yamhill	555	568
Total	9956	10283

STATE OFFICERS.—Governor, Geo. L. Woods; Secretary of State, Samuel E. May; Treasurer, E. N. Cook.

STATE LEGISLATURE—
	Senate.	House.	Joint Bal.
Republicans.........14		24	38
Democrats......... 8		23	31
Rep. Majority,..... 6		1	7

CONGRESS, 1866.
Fay, *Dem.*   Mallory, *Rep*
9809   10362
Rufus Mallory over Fay, 553.

KENTUCKY.

COUNTIES.	Governor, 1867.			Clerk Court Ap., 1866.		President. 1864.	
	Helm. Dem.	Bar-nes. Rep.	Kin-kead In. D.	Du-vall. Dem.	Hob-son. Rep.	...-c Cl'n Dem.	Lin-coln. Rep.
Adair	550	324	420	535	675	627	59
Allen	526	93	400	725	472	547	29
Anderson ...	736	109	36	882	266	272	34
Ballard	1130	69	8	1268	145	541	351
Barren	1354	284	78	1535	708	737	55
Bath	1026	464	77	950	760	451	132
Boone	1411	147	28	1505	329	1063	200
Bourbon	1081	97	59	1317	320	850	274
Boyd	575	406	16	554	501	493	202
Boyle	707	133	63	845	316	532	129
Bracken	901	220	55	1202	733	922	268
Breathitt ..	419	218	8				
Breckinri'e	1079	429	130	1165	811	995	42
Bullitt	524	4	113	730	307	624	14
Butler	439	634	47	392	752	414	99
Caldwell ...	776	249	38	807	472	351	294
Calloway ...	1094	106	27	1169	183		
Campbell ..	1631	1129		1889	1619	1286	1504
Carroll	696	16	12	755	168	324	82
Carter	583	776	7	475	861	345	367
Casey	429	439	123	331	575	507	127
Christian ..	1060	383	154	1287	884	636	376
Clarke	850	179	145	936	413	690	130
Clay	288	418	223	223	661	186	312
Clinton	104	175	198	58	571	215	3
Crittenden.	587	665	82	212	471	252	424
Cumberla'd	443	173	120	394	394	302	33
Davies	1618	147	150	1951	495	1134	37
Edmondson	295	178	80	249	385	215	48
Estill......	461	648	47	506	811	303	470

	Dem.	Rep.	In.D.	Dem.	Rep.	Dem.	Rep.
Fayette....	1607	541	190	1769	824	496	882
Fleming....	1184	837	80	1153	989	701	357
Franklin...	1370	224	216	1273	534	689	253
Floyd......	781	209		626	196		
Fulton.....	650	6		692	38	61	86
Gallatin...	512	46	14	587	155	391	109
Garrard....	643	299	57	753	632	460	467
Grant......	798	389	10	970	682	372	220
Graves.....	1434	444	47	1586	553	769	642
Grayson....	767	312	252	769	681	716	114
Green......	592	26	421	622	510	591	
Greenup....	642	703	12	464	641	431	596
Hancock....	760	44	57	674	229	366	18
Harden....	1352	205	99	1552	930	1010	833
Harlan.....	75	428	1	87	642	51	287
Harrison...	1331	179	26	1586	473	820	256
Hart......	860	90	756	850	780	1051	40
Henderson..	1098	50	10	1309	156	949	30
Henry......	1044	26	383	1167	591	1168	111
Hickman....	885	45	2	872	73	223	289
Hopkins....	946	253	9	1117	517	492	47
Jackson....	19	511	14	30	523	29	345
Jefferson..	5422	570	887	6002	3720	6404	2066
Jessomine..	626	127	59	780	198	612	195
Johnson....	284	560	6	264	617		
Josh Bell..	52	432	15				
Kenton....	2011	876	9	2410	1508	1374	1716
Knox.......	124	759	188	90	987	197	629
Larue......	461	64	404	549	538	700	17
Laurel.....	199	670	145	159	706	188	444
Lawrence...	874	528	7	664	633	380	191
Letcher....	227	274					
Lewis......	744	962	15	735	912	391	645
Lincoln....	745	169	150	831	569	801	109
Livingston.	619	68	3	755	161	217	246
Logan......	1574	148	116	1706	568	508	290
Lyon.......	448	104	26	509	158	105	60
Madison....	1258	614	112	1388	1067	700	800
Magoflin...	322	325	3	297	280	79	23
Marion.....	1034	73	669	1074	410	1119	28
Marshall...	904	117	6	999	179	147	149
Mason......	1711	411	127	1734	1047	1197	368
McCracken..	817	139	34	1098	307	323	515
McLean.....	529	23	329	586	435	504	62
Meade......	929	18	48	902	159	630	3
Mercer.....	840	196	133	1090	725	627	271
Metcalfe...	461	119	320	420	568	505	24
Monroe.....	359	619	13			326	84
Montg'ry...	746	158	109	753	313	813	401
Morgan.....	745	223	6	648	197	52	
Muklenb'g..	757	451	20	889	696	597	225
Nelson.....	1151	12	133	1314	171	968	17
Nichols....	895	345	26	1116	483	528	244
Ohio.......	853	554	100	1007	865	765	367
Oldham.....	620	6	197	683	286	588	31
Owen.......	1870	72	25	2274	211		
Owsley.....	82	698	116	84	690	96	348
Pendleton..	1038	544		1225	877	688	629
Perry......	153	366	2				
Pike.......	650	381	12	497	475		
Powell.....	156	133	28	212	188	227	27
Pulaski....	490	1740	339	508	1377	615	1059
Robertson..	621	90	12				
Rockcastle.	346	568	105	257	553	259	428
Rowan......	158	274	2			23	49
Russell....	360	367	97	207	530	459	15
Scott......	1291	94	85	1535	207	567	87
Shelby.....	1207	32	366	1421	427	990	18
Simpson....	539	36	25	749	181	430	6
Spencer....	475	3	96	596	107	351	1
Taylor.....	388	3	442	451	314	489	30
Todd.......	697	160	84	846	438	388	105
Trigg......	1021	34	123	1097	317	452	42
Trimble....	710	3	20	826	64	385	12
Union......	1341	147	5	1287	175	428	98
Warren.....	1211	117	310	1602	686	1444	163
Washingt'n.	666	223	598	797	822	810	73
Wayne......	553	354	125	582	613	546	89
Webster....	832	337	2	913	325	311	77
Whitley....	60	945	59	10	1207	71	731
Woodford...	787	37	73	679	141	564	28
Wolfe......	457	291	1	304	210		
Soldiers V'e						2823	1194
Total.....	90225	33939	13167	95979	58035	64301	27786

STATE OFFICERS.—Governor, John W. Stevenson; Secretary of State, Samuel B. Churchill; Assistant Secretary, William T. Samuels; Attorney-General, John Rodman; Auditor, W. T. Samuels; Treasurer, Alfred Allen; Register of Land Office, James A. Dawson; Supt. Public Intruction, Z. F. Smith.

STATE DEBT.—$4,611,199.45, of which $544,000 is war debt.

STATE LEGISLATURE.

	Senate.	House.	Joint Bal.
Democrats............	31	90	121
Republicans..........	7	10	17
Dem. majority.....	24	80	104

Special election in 3rd Congressional District to fill vacancy occasioned by death of Elijah Hise.

Counties.	Dem. Golladay.	Ind. Jackman.	Rep. Curd.
Allen.................	451	101	59
Barren................	1094	60	102
Clinton..............	86	81	15
Cumberland...........	425	84	5
Hart.................	848	40	49
Logan................	1011	5	347
Monroe...............	344		
Metcalfe.............	440	21	8
Russell..............	341	368	
Simpson..............	265		220
Todd.................	576	13	43
Warren...............	738	77	327
Total............	6619	850	1175

J. S. Golladay over J. R. Curd, 5444; over W. T. Jackman, 5769: over both, 4594.

CONGRESS, 1867.

Dist.	Dem.	Rep.
1.	Trimble.	Symmes
Fulton.....	443	3
Hickman....	638	10
Ballard....	944	98
McCracken..	695	204
Graves.....	1345	341
Marshall...	656	109
Calloway...	872	81
Trigg......	886	95
Lyon.......	339	38
Caldwell...	621	203
Livingston.	502	66
Crittenden.	436	381
Union......	713	70
Webster....	697	81
Total....	9787	1780

L. S. Trimble over G. G. Symmes, 8007.

II.	Brown.	Smith.
Christian..	890	439
Hopkins....	959	216
Muhlenb'g..	653	548
Henderson..	1083	61
Davies.....	1663	184
McLean.....	512	44
Ohio.......	769	392
Hancock....	543	53
Breakinri'e	843	264
Grayson....	569	153
Butler.....	233	442
Edmonson...	205	20
Total....	8922	2816

B. C. Ritter (Ind.) received 1,155 votes. J. Y. Brown over S. E. Smith, 6,106; over both, 4,951.

III.	Hise.	Blakey.
Russell....	249	95
Cumberla'd.	272	27
Clinton....	128	46
Monroe.....	359	378
Metcalfe...	316	
Barren.....	1041	56
Allen......	511	82
Simpson...	566	23
Warren....	1302	69
Todd......	683	113
Logan.....	1634	118
Hart......	679	117
Total....	7740	1201

Elijah Hise over G. D.

IV.	Knott.	Taylor.
Meade.....	580	17
Adair.....	435	338
Hardin....	1162	263
Bullitt...	442	56
Larue.....	359	176
Marion....	925	92
Washingt'n	619	538
Nelson....	767	45
Spencer...	307	33
Taylor....	349	46
Green.....	450	140
Shelby....	976	99
Anderson..	598	140
Casey.....	230	294
Total....	8199	2277

W. J. Heady (Ind.) received 508 votes. J. P. Knott over M. C. Taylor 5,922; over both 5,414.

V.	Grover.	Jacob.
Jefferson.	3754	1520
Oldham....	536	240
Henry.....	876	534
Owen......	1962	123
Total....	7118	2417

W. A. Bullitt (Rep.) received 742 votes. A. P. Grover over R. T. Jacob, 4,701; over both, 3,959.

VI.	Jones.	Rankin.
Gallatin..	362	59
Harrison..	1361	362
Boone.....	1118	183
Trimble...	648	10
Grant.....	735	358

Kenton	1700	974
Campbell ..	1100	799
Pendleton..	920	478
Bracken ..	984	330
Carroll	560	34
Total....	**9488**	**3587**

T. L. Jones over W. S. Rankin, 5,901.

VII. — Beck. Brown.

Franklin..	848	130
Nicholas ..	1024	298
Bourbon..	1046	91
Clarke.....	763	162
Fayette ...	1257	302
Scott......	1218	68
Jessamine..	614	142
Woodford..	651	24
Mercer	934	210
Boyle......	667	104
Lincoln ..	694	133
Total ...	**9716**	**1664**

C. Hanson (Ind.) received 1,388 votes. J. B. Beck over W. Brown, 8,052; over both, 6,664.

VIII. — Adams. Rice.

Pulaski....	1000	1040
Rockcastle.	419	275
Madison ..	1319	707
Estill	367	507
Jackson ...	73	426
Laurel	399	496
Whitley ...	399	608
Owsley.....	195	461

Clay......	482	348
Knox......	549	659
Harlan....	173	537
Breathitt...	347	127
Perry	181	262
Wayne....	593	275
Garrard ...	710	309
Wolfe.....	403	195
Total.....	**7609**	**7244**

G. M. Adams over M. J. Rice, 365.

IX. — Young. McKee.

Mason	1509	627
Lewis.....	593	931
Greenup ..	456	551
Boyd......	421	425
Powell	157	152
Fleming ...	1033	818
Rowan	135	278
Carter	390	831
Lawrence..	548	472
Morgan....	598	265
Johnson ...	251	465
Floyd.....	557	248
Pike	458	455
Magoffin ..	221	308
M'gomery..	731	167
Bath	984	567
Total.....	**9042**	**7563**

T. M. Green (Ind.) received 862 votes. J. D. Young over S. McKee, 1,479; over both, 617.

STATE OFFICERS—Governor, Wm. G. Brownlow; Secretary of State, A. J. Fletcher; Comptroller, G. W. Blackburn; Treasurer, J. R. Henry.

STATE DEBT—$37,062,323.

STATE LEGISLATURE, 1868—

	Senate.	House.	Joint Bal.
Republicans...........	25	80	105
Democrats.............		4	4
Rep. majority.	25	76	101

CONGRESS, 1867

Dist.	Dem. White.	Rep. Butler.
I.		
Johnson ...	35	598
Carter	66	918
Sullivan ...	22	709
Washing'n .	93	1314
Hawkins ..	183	1093
Hancock ..	21	578
Greene....	807	1537
Cocke.....	56	924
Jefferson ..	166	2106
Granger ...	240	852
Sevier	88	1343
Total	**1777**	**11972**

R. R. Butler over J. White, 10,195.

II.	Williams.	Maynard.
Claiborne..	156	824
Union	207	660
Knox......	1031	2875
Campbell ..	219	653
Scott......	4	288
Morgan....	103	194
Anderson ..		
Blount	344	1393
Monroe ...	151	980
Polk......	45	213
McMinn ...	380	1296
Bradley ...	291	1098
Roane	108	1520
Total	**3039**	**11994**

Horace Maynard over John Williams, 8,955.

III.	Fleming.	Stokes.
Meigs	126	359
Rhea......	30	259
Hamilton ..	173	1503
Marion	24	486
Grundy	49	46
Bledsoe....	51	408
Van Buren.	9	71
Sequatchie.	7	125
Warren ...	154	418
White	25	360
Smith	269	1000
Cumberl'd .	7	250
Putnam....		
Jackson....	307	643
Macon.....	47	596
Overton ...	9	414
De Kalb....	158	862
Hentress...	171	233
Total.....	**1616**	**8033**

Wm. B. Stokes over Eli G. Fleming, 6,417.

IV.	Cooper.	Mullins.
Rutherford.	380	2932
Cannon....	164	430
Coffee.....	431	223
Franklin...	329	692
Lincoln...	277	774
Bedford...	987	1719
Marshall..	474	816
Giles......	179	1862
Total.....	**3221**	**9448**

James Mullins over Edmund Cooper, 6227.

V.	Peyton.	Trimble.
Williamson	600	1687
Davidson ..	980	5367
Wilson	783	1212
Sumner....	233	545
Robertson..	510	338
Cheatham..	58	208
Total.....	**3163**	**9357**

John Trimble over Bailey Peyton, 6,194.

VI.	Thomas.	Arnell.
Lawrence..	48	204
Wayne....	25	608
Hardin ..	114	879
Decatur...	76	193
Perry.....	67	209
Lewis.....	1	74
Maury....	239	2823
Hickman ..	129	259
Humphreys	142	260
Dickson...	123	314
Mt'gomery.	582	1525
Stewart ...	631	248
Total.....	**2170**	**7596**

S. M. Arnell over D. B. Thomas, 5,426.

VII.	Coldwell.	Hawkins.
Benton ...	13	271
Henry.....	19	
Weakley...	303	791
Obion.....	55	284
Dyer......	35	390
Gibson	233	704
Lauderdale	154	287
Henderson.	104	786
Carroll....	65	1557
Total	**981**	**5000**

J. R. Hawkins over W. P. Coldwell, 4,019.

VIII.	Leftwitch.	Nunn.
McNairy ...	126	589
Hardeman..	625	378
Fayette ...	529	1428
Shelby....	2745	4414
Tipton....	1275	178
Madison ...	498	352
Haywood...	391	1718
Total.....	**6189**	**9057**

David Nunn over J. W. Leftwitch, 2,868.

TENNESSEE.

COUNTIES.	Governor, 1867. Etheridge Dem.	Brownlow Rep.
Anderson .	335	643
Blount	344	1381
Bledsoe....	60	395
Bedford....	918	1786
Benton	21	261
Bradley....	288	1094
Campbell ..	188	639
Carter	66	921
Claiborne..	159	795
Cocke.....	59	938
Cannon....	157	430
Cumberl'd.	4	250
Cheatham..	58	207
Coffee.....	413	235
Carroll....	69	1592
Davidson ..	939	5456
De Kalb...	142	864
Dyer......	46	316
Decatur....	63	207
Dickson...	117	321
Franklin...	313	702
Fentress...		220
Fayette....	513	1143
Granger ...	237	857
Greene....	802	1530
Grundy....	59	45
Gibson	277	687
Giles.....	153	1879
Hancock...	20	579
Hawkins...	136	1107
Hamilton..	502	1480
Hardin....	117	875
Hickman ..	117	262
Humphreys	131	267
Hardeman..	693	446
Henderson.	112	785
Henry.....	19	
Haywood..	442	1655
Jefferson..	161	2112
Johnson....	42	623
Jackson....	342	636
Knox......	1021	2681
Lawrence..	48	203
Lincoln ..	267	780
Lewis.....	1	74
Lauderdale	162	296
McMinn...	387	1295
Meigs.....	135	353
Marion....	30	472
Monroe....	161	977
Maury....	238	2817
Morgan....	100	179
Montg'ry..	588	1527
Marshall...	449	831
Macon.....	47	600
McNairy...	127	608
Madison...	503	343
Overton ...	17	411
Obion.....	67	272
Polk......	48	211
Putnam....		
Perry.....	62	216
Rhea......	55	252
Roane.....	109	1503
Robertson.	493	348
Rutherford.	361	2937
Stewart...	631	252
Sumner....	224	891
Sevier.....	86	1353
Scott......	9	250
Sullivan...	22	776
Sequatchie.	14	122
Smith.....	278	993
Shelby....	2735	4419
Tipton....	1273	178
Union.....	208	648
Van Buren.	11	67
Wilson....	789	1248
Warren....	158	415
Wayne....	24	622
White.....	29	356
Williamson	574	1704
Washingt'n	102	1296
Weakley...	232	769
Soldiers V't		818
Total.....	**22548**	**74484**

CALIFORNIA.

COUNTIES.	Governor, 1867. Haight. Dem.	Gorham. Rep.	Justice Sup. Court, 1865. Hartley. Dem.	Sanderson. Rep.	President, 1864. McClel'n Dem.	Lincoln. Rep.
Alameda.....	1092	1266	453	850	811	1467
Alpine......	106	149	121	288	228	384
Amador.....	1358	1076	945	919	1199	1392
Butte......	1148	882	773	1207	1117	1739
Calaveras...	1380	1250	1035	1423	1564	2071
Colusa.....	554	197	344	163	425	274
C'tra Costa.	599	719	518	669	522	958
Del Norte..	178	150	100	122	139	167
El Dorado..	1835	1579	1299	1753	2122	2949
Fresno.....	325	47	199	44	359	92
Humboldt..	393	657	192	392	262	423
Inyo.......	106	95				
Kern.......	385	164				
Klamath...	215	136	103	86	122	139
Lake......	508	221	238	97	405	213
Lassen.....	103	162	101	207	236	318
Los Angeles	989	927	642	359	744	555
Marin.....	344	515			410	685
Mariposa...	835	599	512	499	842	767
Mendocino.	898	512	517	276	778	576
Merced.....	255	52	147	41	218	76
Mono......	101	117	22	52	138	167
Monterey ..	544	414	186	191	364	415
Napa......	750	655	276	375	592	575
Nevada.....	2283	2176	1195	2088	1793	2784
Placer.....	1590	1672	859	1449	1474	2314
Plumas.....	708	781	553	616	669	828
Sacramento	2141	1677	1400	2099	1763	4192
San B'dino	426	234	244	155	493	243
San Diego..	179	82	54	15	197	97
San F'cisco.	10571	6363	5307	5673	8352	12665
San Joaq'in	1592	1668	721	1076	1427	1849
S. L. Obispo	177	242	67	110	149	259
San Mateo.	355	427	39	309	377	600
S. Barbara.	301	309	171	182	80	343
S'ta Clara..	2031	1839	681	1303	1202	1930
Santa Cruz.	703	868	194	551	452	974
Shasta.....	512	541	280	566	562	909
Sierra.....	698	955	600	1147	1037	2151
Siskiyou....	985	744	634	718	957	925
Solano.....	1228	1155	688	853	908	1255
Sonoma....	2565	1625			2336	2026
Stanislaus..	451	219	282	156	346	277
Sutter.....	660	555	371	389	586	677
Tehama....	373	326	141	227	363	482
Trinity.....	444	509	318	506	461	653
Tulare.....	618	255	528	410	639	528
Tuolumne.	1350	1068	973	888	1566	1589
Yolo......	796	573	488	506	475	653
Yuba......	1178	1155	934	1206	1333	1870
Soldiers V't					237	2600
Total.....	49905	40359	26245	33221	43841	62134

C. T. Fay was nominated as an independent candidate by the republicans, who were disaffected with the nomination of Geo. C. Gorham; he received but 2,088 votes in the whole State, his largest vote in any county being only 470.

On the 16th of October there was an election for Justice of the Supreme Court and Superintendent of Public Instruction, the candidates being:

Justice of Sup. Ct.	Supt. Pub. Ins.
Royal T. Sprague, (D,)	O. P. Fitzgerald, (D.)
John Currey, (R.)	John Swett, (R.)

The vote was light, and both the Democratic candidates were elected by small majorities, Sprague by 2,539 and Fitzgerald by 696.

STATE OFFICERS—Governor, Henry H. Haight; Lieut. Governor, William Holden; Secretary of State, H. L. Nichols; Comptroller, Robert Watt; Attorney-General, Joseph Hamilton; Surveyor-General, John W. Bost.

STATE DEBT—Civil Debt, $3,491,000; war debt, $1,635,000; total (all funded), $5,126,000.

STATE LEGISLATURE—

	Senate.	House.	Joint Bal.
Democrats...............	17	52	69
Republicans.............	23	28	51
Dem. majority..........	*6	24	18

*Rep. majority.

CONGRESS. 1867.

Dist.	Dem.	Rep.
I.	Axtell.	Phelps.
Fresno.....	321	54
Inyo......	104	102
Kern......	381	172
L. Angeles.	984	742
Mariposa..	799	661
Merced....	253	56
Monterey..	529	433
S. B'nard'o	418	248
San Diego..	173	89
S. F'cisco..	10249	7150
S.L.Obispo.	180	252
San Mateo.	360	435
S. Barbara.	305	311
S'ta Clara..	2000	1896
Santa Cruz	672	921
Stanislaus..	447	225
Tulare.....	618	252
Total.....	18793	13989

S. B. Axtell over T. G. Phelps, 4,804.

II.	Coffroth.	Higby.
Alpine.....	103	179
Amador....	1347	1151
Alemada..	1038	1346
Calaveras..	1324	1322
C'tra Costa	565	765
Eldorado ..	1818	1735
Mono......	91	141
Nevada....	2193	2428
Placer.....	1424	1907
Sacramento	2025	2232
San Joaquin	1550	1731
Tuolumne...	1308	1116
Total.....	14786	16053

William Higby over Jas. W. Coffroth, 1,267.

III.	Johnson.	Hartson.
Butte......	1102	1080
Colusa.....	527	258
Del Norte..	175	155
Humboldt..	371	693
Klamath...	213	145
Lake......	503	234
Lassen....	102	181
Marin.....	315	544
Mendocino.	874	555
Napa......	707	736
Plumas....	698	834
Shasta....	498	612
Sierra....	667	1115
Siskiyou...	959	829
Solano....	1178	1256
Sonoma...	2159	1699
Sutter....	644	609
Tehama...	367	345
Trinity...	413	599
Yolo.....	782	711
Yuba.....	1153	1244
Total.....	14767	14394

Jas. A. Johnson over C. Hartson, 373.

INDIANA.

COUNTIES.	Sec'y of State, 1866. Manson. Dem.	Trusler. Rep.	President, 1864. McClel'n Dem.	Lincoln. Rep.
Adams.................	1273	635	1156	485
Allen................	4929	2841	4932	2244
Bartholomew......	2374	2144	2051	1545
Benton..	376	513	272	380
Blackford............	607	527	475	355
Boone................	2169	2408	1651	2134
Brown................	1025	423	821	288
Carroll..............	1804	1820	1583	1431
Cass.................	2797	2221	2086	1836
Clark................	2644	1870	1986	1683
Clay.................	1643	1432	1407	1088
Clinton..............	1706	1706	1501	1413
Crawford............	976	974	709	706
Davies...............	1555	1529	1399	1227
Dearborn............	2909	2251	2420	2117
Decatur.............	1914	2339	1559	2172
DeKalb..............	1721	1830	1472	1484
Delaware............	508	2307	588	2405
Dubois..............	1679	441	1454	396
Elkhart.............	2337	2690	2000	2253
Fayette.............	983	1335	860	1318
Floyd...............	2386	1865	2055	1457
Fountain............	2007	1899	1818	1562
Franklin	2517	1538	2316	1399
Fulton..............	1336	1270	1099	987
Gibson..............	1737	1716	1516	1297
Grant...............	1366	1837	1238	1547
Greene..............	1675	1758	1515	1212
Hamilton............	1822	3157	1093	3225
Hancock.............	1471	1315	1337	1369
Harrison............	2021	1746	1780	1329
Hendricks...........	1256	2907	832	2622
Henry...............	1203	2774	1057	3027
Howard..............	1166	1963	932	1728

COUNTIES.	Man-son. Dem.	Trus-ler. Rep.	Mc-Clel'n Dem.	Lin-coln. Rep.
Huntington..	2003	1890	1685	1597
Jackson	2321	1490	1795	1187
Jasper	361	756	286	585
Jay	1350	1430	1143	1103
Jefferson	2276	2926	1777	2758
Jennings	1286	1936	1079	1817
Johnson	1999	1618	1715	1532
Knox	2051	1743	1817	1348
Kosciusko	2052	2658	1808	2188
Lagrange	921	1793	796	1583
Lake	674	1452	461	1275
Laporte	2661	2974	2145	2766
Lawrence	1427	1811	1085	1421
Madison	2271	1787	2057	1535
Marion	5610	6779	3486	10952
Marshall	2209	1848	1589	1206
Martin	1140	825	817	576
Miami	2084	2099	1717	1831
Monroe	1381	1585	1210	1203
Montgomery	2565	2573	2260	2228
Morgan	1457	2053	1283	1793
Newton	342	474	274	350
Noble	1896	2494	1550	1992
Ohio	481	628	381	592
Orange	1260	1233	1020	940
Owen	1629	1441	1522	1063
Parke	1903	2274	1236	2121
Perry	1392	1444	1042	1112
Pike	1184	1239	972	920
Porter	1257	1762	936	1469
Posey	1794	1896	1585	1357
Pulaski	823	632	718	488
Putnam	2388	2384	2155	1968
Randolph	1183	2593	1168	2371
Ripley	2087	2187	1750	1826
Rush	1935	2130	1680	1881
Scott	837	749	742	586
Shelby	2466	2138	2223	1837
Spencer	1796	1990	1427	1558
Starke	315	294	247	217
Steuben	762	1819	610	1642
St. Joseph	1928	2739	1558	2188
Sullivan	2214	1243	2059	795
Switzerland	1125	1495	855	1440
Tippecanoe	3210	3460	2775	3489
Tipton	1181	935	1019	731
Union	640	883	592	832
Vanderburg	2717	2919	2114	2735
Vermillion	740	1197	752	1044
Vigo	2867	3186	2167	2887
Wabash	1376	2957	1229	2461
Warren	916	1450	761	1373
Warrick	1662	1575	1441	1247
Washington	2020	1757	1799	1242
Wayne	2105	4360	1529	4238
Wells	1423	1091	1235	846
White	1163	1191	899	940
Whitely	1534	1327	1327	1062
Total	**155102**	**169618**	**130233**	**150422**

There was no general election in 1867, but the vote for county officers showed democratic gains.

State Officers. — Governor, Conrad Baker; Secretary of State, Nelson Trusler; Auditor, T. B. McCarty; Treasurer, Nathan Kimball; Attorney General, D. E. Williamson.

State Debt. — Civil debt, $4,592,304.33; war debt, $395,000. Total, $4,987,304.33, of which amount $1,026,117 is provided for, leaving a balance of $3,961,187.33.

State Legislature, 1868—

	Senate.	House.	Joint Bal.
Republicans	31	64	95
Democrats	19	36	55
Rep. majority	12	28	40

CONGRESS, 1866.

I.

	Dem. Niblack.	Rep. DeBruler.
Davies	1556	1529
Dubois	1670	442
Gibson	1740	1716
Knox	2054	1731
Martin	1145	830
Pike	1168	1245
Posey	1784	1903
Spencer	1779	2001
Vanderb'h	2698	2930
Warick	1661	1578
Total	17255	15905

Wm. E. Niblack over De Bruler, 1,350.

II.

	Kerr.	Gresham.
Clarke	2616	1888
Crawford	968	953
Floyd	2357	1890
Harrison	2009	1756
Orange	1256	1239
Perry	1380	1456
Scott	829	753
Washingt'n	2006	1743
Total	13421	11678

Michael C. Kerr over Gresham, 1,743.

III.

	Harrington.	Hunter.
Barthlm'w	2366	2156
Brown	1016	430
Jackson	2314	1500
Jennings	1283	1930
Jefferson	2246	2938
Lawrence	1428	1809
Monroe	1379	1589
Switzerl'd	1126	1496
Total	13158	13848

M. C. Hunter over Harrington, 690.

IV.

	Holman.	Grover.
Dearborn	2935	2239
Decatur	1953	2336
Franklin	2507	1537
Ohio	490	628
Ripley	2093	2180
Rush	1943	2132
Total	11921	11052

Wm. S. Holman over Grover, 869.

V.

	Bundy.	Julian.
Delaware	863	2159
Fayette	1016	1326
Henry	1261	2594
Randolph	1221	2947
Union	649	808
Wayne	2178	4032
Total	7188	13416

Geo. W. Julian over Bundy, 6,228.

VI.

	Lord.	Coburn.
Hancock	1474	1310
Hendricks	1253	2909
Johnson	2005	1618
Marion	5602	6785
Morgan	1455	2058
Shelby	2456	2039
Total	14245	16719

John Coburn over Lord 2,474.

VII.

	Claypool.	Washburne
Clay	1656	1422
Greene	1679	1756
Owen	1629	1439
Parke	1206	2260
Putnam	2388	2386
Sullivan	2220	1248
Vermillion	706	1183
Vigo	2874	3177
Total	14358	14871

H. D. Washburne over Claypool, 513.

VIII.

	Purdue.	Orth.
Boone	2196	2384
Carroll	1820	1801
Clinton	1699	1702
Fountain	2094	1812
Montgom'y	2610	2538
Tippecanoe	3345	3300
Warren	964	1396
Total	14728	14933

G. S. Orth over Purdue 205.

IX.

	Turpie.	Colfax.
Benton	375	512
Cass	2592	2219
Fulton	1338	1268
Jasper	359	754
Lake	676	1449
Laporte	2650	2962
Marshall	2213	1843
Miami	2080	2095
Newton	341	477
Porter	1254	763
Pulaski	824	626
Starke	315	295
St. Joseph	1898	2748
White	1158	1190
Total	18073	20221

S. Colfax over Turpie, 2,148.

X.

	Lowry.	Williams.
Allen	4944	2823
De Kalb	1724	1818
Elkhart	2329	2681
Kosciusko	2048	2662
La Grange	913	1796
Noble	1888	2500
Steuben	760	1811
Whitley	1536	1323
Total	16142	17414

William Williams over Lowry, 1,272.

XII.

	Snow.	Shanks.
Adams	1261	632
Blackford	605	522
Grant	1367	1832
Hamilton	1318	3154
Howard	1164	1960
Huntingd'n	1998	1873
Jay	1309	1408
Madison	2276	1771
Tipton	1182	934
Wabash	1372	2969
Wells	1416	1090
Total	15268	18145

J. P. C. Shanks over Snow, 2,877.

ILLINOIS.

COUNTIES.	Congress, 1866. Dick'y Dem.	Logan Rep.	Treasurer, 1866. Phillips. Dem.	Smith. Rep.	President, 1864. McClel'n Dem.	Lincoln. Rep.
Adams.....	4750	4091	4744	4107	4562	3496
Alexander..	942	631	944	632	881	722
Bond......	679	1352	676	1350	713	1154
Boone.....	165	1646	162	1653	242	1727
Brown.....	1270	907	1273	902	1318	718
Bureau.....	1376	3337	1379	3338	1798	3351
Calhoun....	541	316	546	311	562	311
Carroll.....	259	1655	258	1658	443	1903
Cass	1278	995	1280	992	1243	863
Champaign	1475	2360	1485	2346	1133	2116
Christian ..	1635	1501	1642	1498	1606	1043
Clark......	1393	1331	1396	1322	2237	1061
Clay......	1117	1245	1116	1252	1002	852
Clinton	1233	1242	1221	1242	1168	1110
Coles	1908	2436	1910	2428	1555	2210
Cook......	5650	15295	5506	15342	4351	18667
Crawford...	1209	998	1214	992	1371	822
Cumberl'd .	1062	797	1062	797	1134	591
De Kalb....	491	2554	485	2563	741	2985
De Witt....	1080	1484	1083	1484	1069	1271
Douglas....	649	924	652	926	774	993
Du Page....	527	1546	527	1550	774	1816
Edgar	1994	2025	1997	2020	1858	1683
Edwards....	324	764	327	761	330	636
Effingham..	1307	904	1307	903	1223	635
Fayette	1616	1468	1614	1467	1680	1054
Ford......	166	490	176	488	258	238
Franklin....	1049	863	1052	848	876	659
Fulton.....	3628	3712	3627	3722	3694	2991
Gallatin....	636	649	942	645	692	624
Greene.....	1961	1113	1971	1101	2249	978
Grundy	819	1536	822	1532	775	1151
Hamilton...	1133	602	1136	595	1145	382
Hancock....	3231	3287	3232	3291	2929	2655
Hardin.....	404	355	494	353	315	314
Henderson	941	1282	938	1286	877	1210
Henry	1170	3380	1161	3384	1414	3553
Iroquois....	955	1939	959	1936	843	1777
Jackson....	1474	1238	1476	1235	1203	783
Jasper.....	955	773	954	773	923	537
Jefferson ..	1533	888	1533	884	1487	649
Jersey.....	1407	965	1423	942	1546	817
Jo Daviess.	1418	2149	1416	2453	1722	2517
Johnson....	631	1173	630	1171	380	1230
Kane......	1052	3942	1022	3962	1482	4270
Kankakee..	440	1960	442	1914	564	2113
Kendall ...	300	1536	309	1533	470	1765
Knox......	1317	4314	1610	4313	1864	4245
Lake	645	2112	645	2116	873	2403
La Salle...	3183	5012	3170	5038	4515	5174
Laurence..	921	934	921	932	954	735
Lee.......	771	2172	764	2182	1173	2562
Livingston..	1017	2213	1090	2236	1100	1746
Logan.....	1539	2241	1551	2228	1371	1727
Macon.....	1745	2352	1749	2346	1516	1827
Macoupin..	2972	2762	2969	2760	2935	2274
Madison....	3441	3574	3455	3573	3287	3156
Marion	1835	1916	1898	1921	1678	1427
Marshall...	983	1690	980	1694	1403	1548
Mason	1253	1311	1262	1304	1253	1155
Massac	503	961	509	958	265	948
M'Donough	2423	2665	2424	2667	2171	2145
McHenry ..	682	2697	677	2698	1188	2951
McLean....	2566	4743	2466	4754	2582	4001
Menard....	1063	1048	1064	1062	1075	854
Mercer.....	1291	2020	1289	2022	1100	1759
Monroe....	1488	674	1495	670	1527	560
Montg'ry...	2133	1790	2125	1788	1960	1274
Morgan....	2578	2486	2572	2494	2354	2292
Moultrie...	878	713	830	711	829	549
Ogle......	989	2882	980	2902	1142	3239
Peoria.....	3616	3837	3619	3853	3739	3536
Perry......	806	1404	814	1397	718	1147
Piatt......	544	872	546	871	529	747
Pike.......	2968	2713	2969	2715	2857	2335
Pope......	525	1098	528	1088	333	1089
Pulaski....	563	564	507	561	534	601

	Dem.	Rep.	Dem.	Rep.	Dem.	Rep.
Putnam....	344	687	345	686	428	711
Randolph..	1809	1756	1811	1754	1727	1520
Richland...	1189	1237	1189	1238	987	889
Rock Island	1481	2631	1486	2634	1542	2091
Saline.....	988	942	987	940	818	765
Sangam'n..	4154	4073	4146	4678	3945	3565
Schuyler ..	1614	1382	1617	1368	1106	1614
Scott.......	1030	1033	1029	1036	910	873
Shelby	2142	1488	2149	1483	2297	1168
Stark......	585	1292	585	1293	613	1174
St. Clair...	2611	4451	2629	4429	2726	4207
Stephenson.	1767	2567	1770	2567	1928	2598
Tazewell...	2395	2312	2396	2319	2307	2147
Union......	1600	819	1593	819	1315	709
Vermillion.	1672	2766	1675	2722	1639	2546
Wabash....	736	689	741	683	679	516
Warren	1736	2682	1737	2684	1714	2306
Wash'gton.	1103	1662	1102	1626	1207	1244
Wayne	1271	1307	1281	1291	1147	937
White......	1486	988	1491	984	1336	774
Whitesides.	816	2998	796	3004	1033	2905
Will	2479	3444	2473	3457	2792	3343
Wiliamson.	1197	1245	1163	1251	1121	859
Winneb'go.	407	3375	399	3387	705	3969
Woodford..	1688	1552	1687	1553	1685	1270
Total.....	147058	203045	147267	203935	158730	18 949

There was no general election in Illinois in 1867; the results of the county elections, however, showed democratic gains, though neither party polled its full vote.

STATE OFFICERS—Governor, Richard J. Oglesby; Lieut. Governor, William Bross; Secretary of State, Sharon Tyndall; Auditor, Orlin H. Miner; Treasurer, James H. Beveridge; Supt. of Public Instruction, Newton Bateman.

STATE DEBT—Civil debt, $6,832,000; war debt, $790,000. Total, $7,622,000.

STATE LEGISLATURE, 1868.

	Senate.	House.	Joint Bal.
Republicans...............	15	55	70
Democrats...............	10	30	40
Rep. majority..........	5	25	30

CONGRESS, 1866.

Dist.	Dem.	Rep.
I.		Wallace. Judd.
Cook......	5667	15247

N. B. Judd over R. M. Wallace, 9580.

II.	Haines. Farnsworth.
Lake......	615	2111
McHenry ..	657	2681
Boone.....	159	1648
Winnebago	346	3336
De Kalb...	507	2519
Kane.....	1062	3890
Total.....	3346	16185

John F. Farnsworth over E. M. Haines, 12839.

III.	Turner. Washburn.
Jo Daviess.	1416	2433
Stephenson	1758	2552
Carroll....	252	1651
Ogle......	872	2552
Lee.......	789	2171
Whiteside.	819	2998
Total.....	5897	14657

E. B. Washburne over Thomas J. Turner, 8760.

IV	Thompson. Harding.
Adams.....	4749	4097
Hancock...	3232	3283
Warren	1723	2675
Henderson	902	1270
Mercer.....	1303	1992
Rock Island	1482	2630
Total	13391	15952

A. C. Harding over J. S. Thompson, 2561.

V.	Ramsey. Ingersoll.
Peoria.....	3608	3808
Knox......	1616	4313
Stark......	585	1280
Marshall...	966	1689
Putnam ...	345	687
Bureau....	1378	3314
Henry	1167	3346
Total.....	9665	18437

E. C. Ingersoll over Silas Ramsey, 8,772.

VI.	Harris. Cook.
Le Salle....	3105	5078
Grundy....	843	1507
Kendall....	305	1535
Du Page...	528	1545
Will......	2494	3440
Kankakee.	446	1910
Total.....	7721	14815

B. C. Cook over S. W. Harris, 7,094.

VII.	Black. Bromwell.
Macon.....	1764	2330
Pratt......	572	847
Champaign	1505	2330
Douglas..	653	926
Moultrie...	887	704
Coles.....	1920	2416
Cumberl'd.	1079	779
Edgar.....	2021	2001
Vermillion	1693	2697

Iroquois ...	989	1905
Ford	189	475
Total....	13272	17410

H. P. H. Bromwell over Chas. Black, 4,138.

VIII. — Fowler. / Cullum.

	Fowler.	Cullum.
Sangamon.	4142	4070
Logan....	1548	2228
De Witt....	1083	1483
McLean....	2561	4753
Tazewell ..	2406	2307
Woodford.	1687	1549
Livingston	1093	2233
Total....	14520	18623

S. M. Cullum over E. S. Fowler, 4103.

IX. — Ross. / Lippincott.

	Ross.	Lippincott.
Fulton....	3621	3716
Mason....	1257	1308
Menard....	1057	1054
Cass.......	1276	982
M'Donough	2425	2668
Schuyler..	1616	1380
Brown.....	1273	902
Pike.......	2791	2711
Total....	15496	14721

Lewis E. Ross over C. E. Lippincott, 775.

X. — Burr. / Case.

	Burr.	Case.
Bond......	678	1347
Morgan....	2556	2748
Scott......	1069	1014
Calhoun...	549	339
Jersey....	1416	942
Greene....	1972	1092
Macoupin .	2975	2760
Montgom'y	2131	1793
Christian.	1646	1496
Shelby....	2154	1482
Total..	17116	14743

A. G. Burr over Henry Case, 2,373.

XI. — Marshall. / Kitchell.

	Marshall.	Kitchell.
Marion....	1906	1915
Fayette....	1625	1465
Clay.......	1119	1254
Rickland..	1191	1226
Jasper.....	955	770
Clark......	1403	1323
Crawford..	1222	986
Lawrence.	919	931
Wayne....	1287	1287
Hamilton..	1136	591
Franklin..	1051	843
Jefferson..	1548	882
Effingham.	1306	905
Total....	16663	14378

S. S. Marshall over Ed. Kitchell, 2,290.

XII. — Morrison. / Baker.

	Morrison.	Baker.
Madison ..	3641	3546
Clinton....	1228	1226
Washing'n	1119	1644
Randolph..	1839	1729
Monroe....	1629	535
Total....	11956	12032

John Baker over Wm. R. Morrison, 2.076.

XIII. — Allen. / Raum.

	Allen.	Raum.
Alexander.	958	624
Pulaski....	493	566
Union......	1591	822
Johnson...	608	1159
Williamson	1187	1248
Jackson....	1462	1237
Perry......	793	1405
Massac....	495	960
Pope.......	519	1074
Hardin....	398	353
Saline.....	955	920
Gallatin...	918	615
White.....	1466	932
Edwards...	321	762
Wabash....	726	692
Total....	12890	13459

G. B. Raum over Wm. J. Allen, 569.

MICHIGAN.

COUNTIES.	Governor, 1866. Williams Dem.	Crapo Rep.	Regent, 1865. Wells Dem.	Walker Rep.	President, 1864. McClel'n Dem.	Lincoln Rep.
Allegan ...	1459	2496	388	1390	1543	1861
Alpena ...	130	125	34	97	71	116
Antrim ...	17	124	5	65	18	71
Barry	1090	2243	49	1316	1022	1632
Bay	737	713	355	246	584	462
Berrien ...	2347	3229	851	1751	2307	2554
Branch	1195	3276	87	1483	1465	3035
Calhoun ...	2163	4009	1219	2387	2525	3742
Cass	1445	2034	848	1223	1435	1765
Cheboygan.	82	41		9	64	23
Chippewa..	82	57			124	46
Clinton ...	1511	2102	159	949	1411	1524
Delta	101	74		47	31	24
Eaton	1439	2333	337	1319	1369	1848
Emmet.....					141	75
Genesee...	1977	3214	117	2089	2003	2743
G'd Trave'e	9	481		217	83	375
Gratiot....	482	888	56	440	396	571
Hillsdale ..	1658	4364	34	2572	1725	3805
Houghton..	937	368		83	978	380
Huron	332	505	24	377	337	360
Ingham	2050	2538	114	1454	1793	1792
Ionia	1295	2687	136	1437	1383	2205
Iosco......	103	121		35	43	57
Isabella ...	223	336		145	83	215
Jackson ...	3012	3410	1255	2087	2909	3002

	Dem.	Rep.	Dem.	Rep.	Dem.	Rep.
Kalamazoo	1678	3145	278	1916	2101	3151
Kent........	2698	4067	1893	2157	2966	3398
Keweenaw	326	394		109	391	295
Lapeer....	1268	1831	243	877	1347	1464
Leelenaw.	51	243	23	153	146	235
Lenawee..	3593	5639	191	3197	3632	4780
Livingston	2004	1968	1326	1255	1983	1604
Mackinac..	91	39			185	30
Macomb ..	2185	2461	172	1241	2177	2041
Manistee ..	1	271		81	70	145
Manitou ...					135	11
Marquette..	524	211		69	88	143
Mason.....	7	134		83	97	143
Mecoster ..	109	274		83	97	143
Menominee	21	116	3	83	23	58
Midland...	121	258		119	101	208
Monroe....	2085	2164	1194	1193	2331	1659
Montcalm..	511	911		483	443	595
Muskegon..	386	803			366	654
Newaygo ..	229	545	42	238	242	406
Oakland....	3839	4257	536	2413	3816	3709
Oceana....	203	600		282	177	356
Ontonagon.	380	226	273	294	454	252
Ottawa....	1395	1606	554	874	1536	1345
Saginaw...	1749	2339	411	733	1900	1731
Sanilac.....	298	925	8	493	318	753
Shiawassee	1451	1907	358	1035	1383	1412
St. Clair...	2105	2566	368	1320	2063	1808
St. Joseph..	1752	2898	218	1619	1796	2681
Tuscola....	355	1073	7	558	401	798
Van Buren.	1363	2507	710	1403	1400	1983
W'htenaw.	3688	3914	2722	2738	3836	3632
Wayne.....	6299	5054	1828	2104	7670	5946
Soldier's V't					2959	9402
Total....	67708	96746	19426	52334	74604	91521

STATE OFFICERS.—Governor, Henry H. Crapo; Lieut. Governor, Dwight May; Secretary of State, Oliver L. Spaulding; Treasurer, E. O. Grosvenor; Attorney General, William L. Stoughton; Auditor General, William Humphrey; Commissioner State Land Office, Benj. D. Pritchard; Supt. Public Instruction, Oramel Hosford.

STATE DEBT.—Interest bearing debt, $3,821,500,00; non-interest bearing, $797,42.70. Total, $3,901,242,70.

STATE LEGISLATURE—

	Senate.	House.	Joint Bal.
Republicans....	30	79	109
Democrats......	2	21	23
Rep. majority,	28	58	86

CONGRESS, 1866.

Dists. Dem.		Rep.		Rep. Maj.
1 J. L. Chipman..	13443	F. C. Beaman.	17319	3876
2 H. F. Severns...	1122?	C. Upson......	19263	8395
3 B. F. Granger...	12288	A. Blair......	16240	3952
4 J. B. Hutchins..	8154	T. W. Ferry...	15306	7152
5 W. L. Bancroft.	11664	R. E. Trowb'e.	14046	2382
6 J. K. Rose,......	10564	J. F. Driggs...	14603	4039

IOWA.

COUNTIES.	Judge Sup. Court, 1867. Craig Dem.	Beck Rep.	Governor, 1865. Benton Dem.	Stone Rep.	President, 1864. McClel'n Dem.	Lincoln Rep.
Adair......	108	237	98	162	60	141
Adams.....	135	310	111	184	76	225
Alamakee..	1311	1213	1270	1004	1363	1337
Appanoose.	1164	1345	986	1096	934	1089
Audubon...	92	79	66	52	56	31
Benton.....	762	1540	512	1050	564	1334
Blackhawk.	612	1405	373	1240	434	1761
Boone......	876	1082	608	566	468	477
Bremer....	483	999	217	725	259	847
Buchanan..	825	1395	583	947	614	587
Buena Vista	2	6			9	6
Butler.....	307	513	232	454	243	665
Calhoun....	51	83	41	18	24	16

COUNTIES.	Craig. Dem.	Beck. Rep.	Benton. Dem.	Stone. Rep.	McClel'n Dem.	Lincoln Rep.
Carroll	46	113	54	38	33	40
Cass	190	305	171	203	128	223
Cedar	1033	1837	760	1551	839	1828
CerroGordo	52	344	17	242	14	254
Cherokee	14	40	8	14	1	8
Chickasaw	331	758	419	501	310	684
Clarke	326	740	359	559	208	775
Clay	6	61		27	11	24
Clayton	1709	2553	1529	1633	1674	2054
Clinton	1662	2133	1091	1708	1413	2377
Crawford	119	134	58	56	18	53
Dallas	446	820	402	662	345	739
Davis	1221	1326	1072	1185	971	1287
Decatur	876	863	824	667	584	817
Delaware	890	1508	704	1182	634	1580
Des Moines	1880	2173	1609	1871	1539	2413
Dickinson	4	162	2	52	1	4
Dubuque	3340	1940	2842	1552	3375	2223
Emmet	19	112	2	35		42
Fayette	965	2104	740	1145	868	1691
Floyd	292	773	233	571	190	647
Franklin	55	397	85	243	63	271
Fremont	859	799	776	542	458	644
Greene	214	303	97	198	105	183
Grundy	7	277	24	134	19	217
Guthrie	399	455	279	329	297	371
Hamilton	120	465	79	283	81	299
Hancock	24	54	14	57	20	39
Hardin	399	1078	334	772	307	924
Harrison	588	694	437	357	31	401
Henry	860	2349	882	1886	67	2756
Howard	337	616	283	353	257	467
Humboldt	71	248	31	96	32	78
Ida	1	15	3	9		10
Iowa	992	1189	734	840	702	927
Jackson	1859	1730	1525	1587	1673	1958
Jasper	681	1814	1027	1304	775	1518
Jefferson	1311	1790	1086	1478	966	1759
Johnson	1928	1509	1547	1447		1917
Jones	1198	1753	839	1463	958	1839
Keokuk	1312	1472	1197	1306	996	1461
Kossuth	13	217	12	138	14	75
Lee	3078	2587	2865	2289	2283	3136
Linn	1169	2631	1230	2059	1087	2755
Louisa	698	1344	832	1114	560	1640
Lucas	668	788	516	553	396	729
Madison	744	1185	562	976	587	855
Mahaska	1340	2064	1188	1820	945	2382
Marion	1975	2064	1804	1634	1553	1970
Marshall		1388	375	1002	367	1790
Mills	516	631	243	432	237	615
Mitchell		747	119	606	108	642
Manona	134	268	138	115	88	126
Monroe	753	1096	654	880	592	1027
Montgom'y	189	251	113	174	91	169
Muscatine	1468	2071	1481	1678	1317	2236
O'Brien	3	6	5	2	5	5
Page	399		298	397	171	597
Palo Alto	56	39	48	6	44	33
Plymouth	5	50		23		19
Pocahontas	18	82	10	43	8	38
Polk	1659	2162	1468	1689	1147	1816
Pattawatt'e	942	816	435	490	364	58
Poweshiek	553	1049	393	805	461	947
Ringgold	204	436	152	336	76	405
Sac	34	111	40	36	22	51
Scott	1737	1846	1648	2081	1408	2851
Shelby	109	107	74	73	80	78
Sioux					3	1
Story	405	769	439	539	317	630
Tama	413	938	479	863	388	1027
Taylor	228	540	271	382	146	509
Union	301	363	179	233	181	214
Van Buren	1515	1881	1202	1565	1067	1885
Wapello	1790	1837	1446	1544	1275	1761
Warren	670	1320	756	1172	622	1457
Washing'n	1024	1824	988	1600	951	1942
Wayne	619	863	529	599	464	647
Webster	480	598	432	396	337	385
Winneb'go	1	147		83	14	42
Winnesh'k	528	1319	668	1144	868	1745
Woodbury	238	234	87	112	96	232
Worth	36	180	6	143	37	132
Wright	62	191	45	124	42	98
Sold'rs Vote				607	736	
Total	58880	90789	54070	70445	49260	87331

A Governor and other State officers were chosen in 1867, but as the vote is not canvassed until the 2d Wednesday in January, 1868, the returns could not be given in this issue of THE WORLD ALMANAC.

STATE OFFICERS.—Governor, Samuel Merrill; Lieut. Governor, John Scott; Secretary of State, Ed. Wright; Auditor, Jno. A. Elliott; Treasurer, Sam'l E. Rankin; Register of Land Office, C. C. Carpenter; Attorney General, Henry O'Connor.

STATE DEBT.—Civil debt, $322,295.75; war debt, $300,000.00. Total, $622,295.75.

STATE LEGISLATURE—

	Senate.	House.	JointBal.
Republicans	40	78	118
Democrats	8	17	25
People's Party	1	4	5
Rep. majority	31	57	88

CONGRESS, 1866.

Dists.	Dem.	Rep.
I.	Warren.	Wilson.
Davis	1117	1401
Des Moines	1758	2401
Henry	751	2543
Jefferson	1173	1807
Lee	2765	2795
Louisa	678	1521
Van Buren	1339	1909
Wash'gton	934	2029
Total	10515	16406

James F. Wilson over Warren, 5,891.

II.	Cook.	Price.
Cedar	950	2068
Clinton	1444	2420
Jackson	1760	1797
Jones	1015	1923
Linn	1217	2797
Muscatine	1426	2216
Scott	1408	3036
Total	9220	16257

Hiram Price over Cook, 7,037.

III.	Noble.	Allison.
Alamakee	1244	1209
Bremer	355	1049
Buchanan	712	1286
Chickasaw	342	743
Clayton	1615	2191
Delaware	796	1667
Dubuque	3121	2097
Fayette	866	1575
Floyd	261	835
Howard	229	429
Mitchell	187	738
Winnesh'k	742	1653
Total	10470	15472

Wm. B. Allison over Noble, 5,002.

IV.	Mackey.	Loughridge.
Appanoose	1001	1301
Benton	605	1544
Iowa	903	1139
Jasper	772	1812
Johnson	1484	1844
Keokuk	1287	1559
Mahaska	1284	2216
Marion	1805	2026
Monroe	733	1046
Poweshiek	447	1015
Tama	426	1042
Wapello	1642	1931
Total	12395	18475

Loughridge over Mackey 6080.

V.	Tuttle.	Dodge.
Adair	130	151
Adams	119	250
Audubon	77	79
Cass	160	236
Clarke	309	749
Dallas	421	839
Decatur	825	782
Fremont	812	667
Guthrie	317	427
Harrison	498	601
Lucas	543	731
Madison	638	1185
Mills	484	572
Montgom'y	149	216
Page	359	591
Polk	1495	2099
Pottawat'e	646	698
Ringgold	126	408
Shelby	96	93
Taylor	215	525
Union	199	308
Warren	685	1318
Wayne	535	771
Total	9898	14296

Grenville M. Dodge over Tuttle, 4398.

VI.	Thompson.	Hubbard.
B'k Hawk	516	1692
Boone	655	854
Buena V'ta	3	27
Butler	234	675
Calhoun	40	54
Carroll		88
Cerro G'do	48	301
Cherokee	8	23
Clay	16	74
Crawford	104	75
Dickinson	1	91
Emmett	16	93
Franklin	58	345
Greene	94	270
Grundy	12	255
Hamilton	100	395
Hancock	16	71
Hardin	437	1083

Humboldt..	42	193	Webster ...	471	559
Ida.......	6	6	Winnebago	2	98
Kossuth	5	149	Woodbury.	161	194
Marshall	354	1256	Worth	33	160
Monona....	134	211	Wright	49	183
O'Brien..	4	5			
Plymouth .	1	81	Total.....	3985	10030
Pocahontas	6	68	A. W. Hubbard over		
Sac	34	64	Thompson, 6,072.		
Story	808	387			

MISSOURI.

COUNTIES.	Supt. Public Schools, 1866.		Constitution, 1865.		President, 1864.	
	Williams. Dem.	Parker. Rep.	Ag'st Dem.	For Rep.	Mc-Clel'n Dem.	Lincoln. Rep.
Adair......	129	704	25	569	162	797
Andrew....	180	1079	126	781	60	1141
Atchison...	13	587	172	246	7	639
Audrain....	284	239	474	160	392	126
Barry	95	191	33	99	17	197
Barton	50	67				23
Bates......	96	216			13	27
Benton.....	275	600	88	309	21	574
Bollinger..	132	155			12	243
Boone......	631	135	1763	132	813	262
Buchanan..	1292	1447	789	866	813	1914
Butler.....	49	27				
Caldwell...	207	496	58	405	88	496
Callaway...			1630	146	965	274
Caraden...	32	355	42	290	1	468
C. Girard'n.	370	804	448	696	581	1213
Carroll....	460	669	304	291	113	285
Carter		10				
Cass.......	236	391	73	167	105	76
Cedar	15	352	12	202		297
Chariton...	564	530	68	236	2	363
Christian..	58	437	40	328	5	557
Clark......	132	1082	56	645	128	997
Clay	114	121	890	90	777	216
Clinton....	322	445	196	269	492	297
Cole.......	636	809	575	416	502	1256
Cooper	497	896	492	704	381	939
Crawford ..	382	329	295	170	307	297
Dade......	1	57	15	417	4	507
Dallas.....	84	488	40	362	12	243
Daviess....	345	795	43	564	286	775
De Kalb....	193	382	90	221	197	400
Dent......	96	145	37	52	1	107
Douglass...	3	261	1	31	2	189
Dunklin...	120					
Franklin...	907	1387	838	847	401	1717
Gasconade.	227	905	346	508	185	862
Gentry	345	597	79	396	281	525
Greene.....	372	1072	208	1059	346	2223
Grundy	102	839	43	645	17	933
Harrison...	279	1077	185	820	212	1252
Henry	252	472	34	365	233	465
Hickory ...	10	398	49	282	1	365
Holt.......	31	784	50	517	81	673
Howard....	960	200	750	265	6	534
Howell.....	16	61				
Iron.......	105	200	172	182	2	535
Jackson....	1004	868	694	428	557	602
Jasper	1	278			2	46
Jefferson..	771	771	489	452	323	915
Johnson....			67	592	224	832
Knox	344	647	197	541	348	669
Laclede....	272	271	119	258	50	659
Lafayette..	651	502	816	295	395	346
Lawrence..	182	484	156	317		833
Lewis	555	789	530	560	533	774
Lincoln....	483	480	367	409	357	542
Linn	444	754	213	594	135	907
Livingston.	487	692	155	431	497	442
Macon.....	664	956	328	742	23	1757
Madison...	157	169	303	71	14	240
Maries			332	81	244	215
Marion	640	822	547	646	375	828
McDonald..		101	1	29		26
Mercer....	123	944	35	770	3	1158
Miller	34	431	5	460	111	565

COUNTIES.	Dem.	Rep.	Ag'st.	For.	Dem.	Rep.
Mississippi.	438		334	22	257	108
Moniteau..	470	708	247	534	434	866
Monroe	240	163	926	74	597	158
Montgom'y	296	575	159	372	225	530
Morgan	373	457	77	282	264	348
New Madrid	371		477	45	9	99
Newton ...	20	357	13	11	1	212
Nodaway...	99	734	285	380	9	839
Oregon						
Osage	624	563	721	396	679	764
Ozark						38
Pemiscot...	134		122			
Perry	542	581	527	435	116	509
Pettis.....	490	694	334	253	396	879
Phelps	180	251	269	422	263	985
Pike	1245	983	1113	638	930	1143
Platte	781	653	821	410	882	496
Polk	190	695	106	644	5	870
Pulaski....	163	121	15	50	28	105
Putnam ...	33	1101	15	938	47	1292
Ralls	277	216	235	191	194	292
Randolph ..	1168	182	817	96	327	484
Ray	522	585	403	350	798	531
Reynolds...	137		20	1	20	7
Ripley.....						
St. Charles..	891	1239	1133	512	394	1438
St. Clair	1	318			125	1
St. Francois.	325	270	408	146	134	246
St. Genevi'e	394	178	213	172	217	423
St. Louis....	9231	12076	11248	5322	8883	14027
Saline	357	442	137	317	96	170
Schuyler ...	152	388	25	260	191	546
Scotland ...	549	655	162	404	533	612
Scott	236	259	142	131	186	155
Shannon...						
Shelby	200	475	164	283	216	366
Stoddard...	147	117	105	130	6	111
Stone	89	103	103	25		100
Sullivan...	254	764	140	540	52	1074
Taney	8	103				29
Texas	126	88			10	37
Vernon	189	46	106	11		
Warren	273	655	280	451	271	948
Washingt'n	575	296	699	167	239	788
Wayne.....	87	105	247	15	189	343
Webster....	259	407	163	292	192	533
Worth.....	194	277	106	167	121	346
Wright.....	41	192			2	65
Soldiers V't			1168	3995		
Total.....	40958	62187	41308	43670	31626	71676

STATE OFFICERS—Governor, Thomas C. Fletcher; Lieut. Governor, George Smith; Secretary of State, Francis Rodman; Attorney General, Robt. Wingate; Auditor, Alonzo Thompson; Treasurer, William Bishop.

STATE DEBT -$3,181,730,45.

STATE LEGISLATURE, 1868—

	Senate.	House.	Joint Bal.
Republicans	27	96	123
Democrats	6	36	42
Rep. majority	21	60	81

CONGRESS. 1867.

Election in Third District to fill vacancy occasioned by death of Thomas E. Noell.

	McCormick.	Chase.
Counties.	Dem.	Rep.
Dunklin ...	14	
Pemiscott ..	26	1
New Madrid	106	
Mississippi .	146	
Stoddard ...	49	77
Butler	43	28
Ripley		
Scott.......	95	58
Wayne......	57	79

	Dem.	Rep.
Reynolds....	63	11
Shannon....		
C. Girardeau	173	416
Bollinger ...	3	119
Madison....	89	109
Iron	73	119
Dent........	15	41
Perry	195	166
S. Genevieve	198	103
St. Francois.	223	121
Washington.	118	80
Carter.......		
Oregon	36	3
Total	1721	1531

James R. McCormick over Jas. H. Chase, 190.

CONGRESS, 1866.

Dist.	Dem.	Vote.	Rep.	Vote.	Maj.
1.	John Hogan..	6510	Wm. A. Pile.....	6728	218
2.	W. V. N. Bay..	6354	C. A. Newcombe	9564	3310
3.	Thos. E. Noell.	4637	A. Jackson	3571	1066
4.	Jno. S. Waddill	1929	Jno. J. Gravelly	6083	4154
5.	Thos. L. Price.	4084	Jos. W. McClurg	7617	3533
6.	Jas. H. Birch..	5391	Robt. T. Van Horn	4857	534
7.	G. H. Hawley.	3980	Benj. F. Loan....	10942	6962
8.	Jno. W. Glover.	6069	Jno. F. Benjamin.	7601	1532
9.	W. F. Switzler	4876	Geo. W. Anderson	4698	178

MINNESOTA.

COUNTIES.	Negro Suff., 1867.		Governor, 1867.		President, 1864.	
	No.	Yes.	Flandrau. Dem.	Marshall. Rep.	McClel'n Dem.	Lincoln. Rep.
Anoka.....	202	285	243	309	167	285
Benton	107	55	91	82	53	62
Blue Earth.	1168	1246	1079	1498	575	962
Brown	181	434	256	382	58	325
Carver	1146	401	1031	668	610	484
Chisago....	115	375	100	413	88	372
Dacota	1616	1115	1544	1241	1176	1176
Dodge	503	820	488	843	325	760
Douglass...	71	339	54	336		
Faribault..	371	721	301	919	150	642
Fillmore ..	1301	1573	1212	1801	1031	1642
Freeborn..	301	694	234	887	201	658
Goodhue...	952	1685	854	1949	658	1866
Hennepin..	1980	2485	2024	2662	1221	1711
Houston...	963	901	920	1099	635	796
Isanti	30	122	31	153	24	59
Jackson....	8	116	6	164		
Kanabec ...			9	10		
Kandiyohi.	11	57	10	60		
LeSeuer ...	1010	516	1051	619	812	495
Lake			17			
Lincoln....	2	31		32		
Manomin ..	33	1	83	1		
Martin	90	306	74	386	17	190
McLeod....	284	363	261	411	142	202
Meeker ...	259	346	230	403	84	115
Mille Lac..	60	60	49	82	20	51
Monaugal..	47	142	44	174		
Morrison..	141	31	132	43	50	35
Mower.....	418	577	321	733	214	637
Nicollet....	503	551	500	630	420	505
Olmstead..	1162	1757	1217	1910	829	1849
Pine	1	19		28	4	17
Pope	28	158	19	188		
Ramsey....	2210	1034	2064	1324	1421	1260
Redwood'..	13	63	11	74		
Renville ...	25	82	20	94		
Rice.......	1265	1346	1233	1424	667	1275
Scott......	1408	232	1359	404	1045	396
Sherburne..	120	117	131	157	78	108
Sibley.....	697	192	679	303	559	263
Stearns....	1384	662	1336	794	913	427
Steele	620	903	570	996	209	636
St. Louis...	11	28	13	28	5	39
Todd......	74	30	17	108	31	23
Wabashaw	1978	1620	3958	4045	635	1302
Waseca....	606	544	575	637	284	418
Washingt'n	639	621	602	674	502	781
Watonwan	53	92	35	120	5	38
Winona....	1953	1119	1910	1792	1032	1590
Wright.....	639	494	622	778	356	528
Total.....	28759	27461	29543	34887	17351	24966

STATE OFFICERS.—Governor, W. R. Marshall; Lieut. Governor, T. H. Armstrong; Secretary of State, H. C. Rogers; Treasurer, E. Munch; Attorney General, F. R. E. Cornell.

STATE DEBT.—Civil debt, $100,000; war debt, $100,000. Total, $200,000.

STATE LEGISLATURE—

	Senate.	House.	Joint Bal.
Republicans.	15	33.......	48
Democrats........	7	13..........	20
Rep. majority..	8	20.......	28

CONGRESS, 1866.

Dists.	Dem.	Rep.
	Jones.	Windom.
Blue Earth	647	1159
Brown	97	451
Dodge	171	636
Faribault..	201	1026
Fillmore..	729	1452
Freeborn		
Houston ...	710	1107
Jackson		118
LeSueur ...	787	500
Martin	7	337
Mower.....	142	572
Nicollet....	342	477
Olmstead..	540	1548
Redwood ...	2	56
Renville...	2	43
Rice........	595	1080
Scott......	849	330
Sibley.....	521	283
Steele	468	779
Waseca....	330	427
Watonwan	12	93
Winona...	878	1497
Total....	8021	13961

Wm. Windom over R. A. Jones, 5,940.

II.	Colville.	Donnelly.
Anoka.....	187	294
Benton....	96	48
Carver.....	633	489
Chisago....	67	342
Dakota	1024	1183
Douglass...	69	103
Goodhue...	475	1837
Hennepin..	1095	2008
Isanti	15	112
Kandiyohi.	6	34
Lincoln....		44
McLeod....	164	437
Manomin..	25	5
Mille Lac..	142	299
Monaugal...	42	57
Morrison...	102	91
Pine	81	82
Todd......	3	15
Pope	18	86
Ramsey....	1343	1048
St. Louis...	7	35
Sherburne.	96	128
Stearns....	943	580
Wabashaw	493	1419
Wash'gton.	372	651
Wright	254	595
Total....	7754	12022

Ignatius Donnelly over Wm. Colville, 4,268.

WISCONSIN.

COUNTIES.	Governor, 1867.		Governor, 1865.		President, 1864.	
	Tallmadge Dem.	Fairchild. Rep.	Hobart. Dem.	Fairchild. Rep.	McClel'n Dem.	Lincoln. Rep.
Adams.....	194	624	126	594	222	581
Ashland....	34	3	23	29	29	14
Bayfield....	9	12				
Brown.....	1217	815	846	447	730	1286
Buffalo....	388	708	211	523	284	597
Burnett....	6	41		27		
Calumet....	823	687	578	485	718	444
Chippewa..	361	309	223	200	293	205
Clarke.....	96	233	39	109	48	171
Columbia..	1603	2649	1087	2021	1483	2652
Crawford..	1007	845	581	517	786	711
Dane......	4217	4530	2660	3534	3811	4018
Dodge.....	4795	2804	3580	2702	4696	3226
Door	125	404	63	309	75	256
Douglass..	64	51	54	45	67	37
Dunn & Dal	282	679	257	417	251	506
Eau Claire..	467	662	312	422	362	515
Fon du Lac	3696	3789	2759	2871	3305	3484
Grant	1649	3095	1131	2577	1561	3247
Green	1137	2094	728	1552	1107	2017
Green Lake	640	1197	422	1027	508	1441
Iowa......	1604	1677	1051	1102	1424	1282
Jackson....	301	736	194	506	207	680
Jefferson..	3112	2344	2335	2003	2742	2157
Juneau	924	1030	556	627	687	776
Kewaunee..	549	268	383	122	753	157
Kenosha...	1088	1173	552	1035	879	1318
LaCrosse...	1183	1536	725	1127	904	1531
LaFayette..	1730	1526	1370	1213	1712	1471
LaPointe...			16	29	29	15
Manitowoc	2112	1247	1792	1013	2248	1179
Marathon..	618	90	499	112	527	136
Marquette..	748	445	580	446	647	437
Milwaukee.	7176	3500	5038	2271	6875	3175
Monroe ...	1061	1329	581	1006	650	1160
Oneonto...	262	576	241	352	178	291
Ontagamie.	1388	949	1007	739	989	651
Ozankee....	2042	230	1643	263	2050	243
Pepin	150	302	76	261	119	273
Pierce.....	387	829	238	540	326	656
Polk	117	224	112	205	107	176
Portage....	683	972	369	597	311	704
Racine.....	1629	2117	1152	1499	1644	2034
Richland ..	884	1166	636	967	652	1020
Rock	1830	4227	1122	3190	1532	4368

COUNTIES.	Tall-madge Dem.	Fair-child. Rep.	Ho-bart. Dem.	Fair-child. Rep.	Mc-Clel'n Dem.	Lin-coln. Rep.
St. Croix...	775	884	241	543	511	594
Sauk......	939	2060	750	1681	986	2076
Shawanaw.	148	145	116	138	97	134
Sheboygan	2079	1858	1689	1605	2185	1958
Trempeleau	165	622	47	415	130	573
Vernon....	384	1443	120	1164	451	1337
Walworth.	1286	3258	852	2890	1182	3455
Wash'ton .	2554	615	1369	539	2323	664
Waukesha.	2656	2303	2035	1939	2196	2010
Waupacca.	720	1294	492	1109	541	1139
Waushara.	313	908	261	1050	282	1053
Winnebago	2110	3161	1239	2180	1772	2926
Wood	352	282	259	223	248	247
Soldiers' v'e			277	1200	3291	14550
Total....	68873	73637	48330	58332	65684	83458

STATE OFFICERS.—Governor, Lucius Fairchild; Lieut. Governor, W. Spooner; Secretary of State, T. S. Allen; Treasurer, W. E. Smith; Attorney General, C. R. Gill; Controller, J. M. Rusk; Sup't. Public Instruction, A. J. Craig; Prison Commissioner, H. Cordier.

STATE DEBT.—Civil debt, $100,000; war debt, $2,179,057. Total, $2,279,057.00.

STATE LEGISLATURE, 1868—

	Senate.	House.	Joint Bal.
Republicans......	18	59....	77
Democrats........	15	41.....	56
Rep. majority...	3	18.....	21

CONGRESS, 1866.

Dist.	Dem.	Rep.
I.	Brown.	Paine.
Kenosha ..	776	1528
Milwaukee.	5304	4268
Racine	1028	2460
Walworth.	965	3875
Waukesha.	2205	2553
Total....	10298	14679

Halbert E. Paine over J. S. Brown, 4,381.

II.	Pease.	Hopkins.
Columbia..	1141	2840
Dane......	3903	4531
Jefferson ..	2796	2797
Rock......	991	3961
Total....	8838	14129

Benj. F. Hopkins over J. J. H. Pease, 5,291.

III.	Virgin.	Cobb.
Crawford..	919	968
Grant	1320	3197
Green.....	639	1994
Iowa......	1434	1766
La Fayette	1364	1790
Richland...	748	1258
Sauk	731	2033
Total....	7655	13006

Amasa Cobb over N. H. Virgin, 5,351.

IV.	Eldridge	Hatch.
Dodge	3879	2954
Fond du Lac	3013	3387
Ozaukee...	1559	183
Sheboygan	2061	2264
Washing'n.	2124	740
Total....	12636	10028

Chas. A. Eldridge over Orin Hatch, 2,608.

V.	Martin.	Sawyer.
Brown....	1318	982
Calumet..	690	852
Door.....	93	465
GreenLake	443	1488
Kewaunee.	330	403
Manitowoc	1891	1737
Marquette.	716	562
Oconto ...	256	449
Ontagamie	1179	1053
Shawanaw	140	212
Waupacca.	549	1448
Waushara.	251	1270
Winnebago	1491	3420
Total....	9347	14341

Philetus Sawyer over M. L. Martin, 4,994.

VI.	Park.	Washburne.
Adams....	180	640
Ashland....		12
Buffalo....	261	708
Burnett....		34
Chippewa.	342	341
Clark.....	61	188
Dallas....		7
Douglas...	58	71
Dunn.....	279	723
Eau Clarg.	341	625
Jackson...	155	633
Juneau....	855	959
La Crosse.	708	1525
La Pointe..		10
Marathon.	513	140
Monroe...	807	1403
Pepin.....	44	389
Pierce....	193	782
Polk.....	58	166
Portage...	543	885
St. Croix..	675	846
Trempleau.	30	623
Vernon....	238	1333
Wood.....	299	212
Total....	6640	13135

C. C. Washburne over G. L. Park, 6495.

NEBRASKA.

COUNTIES.	Governor, 1866.		Congress, 1866.		Constitution, 1866.	
	Morton Dem.	Butler. Rep.	Paddock. Dem.	Taffe. Rep.	For.	Ag'st.
Burt....	112	125	94	142	229	42
Buffalo....	32	10	16	11	1	41
Cedar	31	29	31	24	12	39
Cumming .	51	28	43	41	31	41
Cass......	343	375	398	573	233	480
Dixon.....	49	30	41	32	34	36
Dakota....	106	87	109	83	106	32
Douglas...	645	426	695	699	491	572
Dodge	33	110	49	147	96	45
Gage......	49	116	54	124	96	61
Hall......	27	10		46	2	29
Johnson...	76	121	45	131	108	69
Jones	2	50	11	45	32	13
Kearney...	28	22	80	14	21	7
L'eau qui C't	1	10	6			
Lancaster..	53	112	69	128	95	53
Lincoln....	36	16	134	18	30	20
Merrick....	8	16	8	26	16	8
Nemaha...	206	533	308	665	346	489
Otoe......	842	462	782	445	432	870
Platte.....	89	90	96	85	123	55
Pawnee....	32	238	44	239	233	31
Richardson.	419	487	473	564	503	373
Sarpy.....	235	106	210	147	109	231
Saunders...			39	49		
Seward....	14	28	16	13	23	24
Saline.....	50	11	68	44	5	54
Washingt'n	205	283	156	275	404	89
Soldiers' v'e	41	152			134	34
Total....	3948	4093	4072	4820	3938	3838

In October, 1866, an election was held for Representative to the 40th Congress and a Delegate to the same, the former to take his seat in case Nebraska should be admitted as a State into the Union. John Taffe, therefore, took his seat. The candidates for Delegate were J. S. Morton, (Dem.) and T. N. Marquette, (Rep.,) who received respectively 4101 and 4871 votes. George Francis Train ran for both Delegate and Member; he received 31 votes for the former office and 39 for the latter.

STATE OFFICERS.—Governor, David Butler; Secretary of State, Thomas P. Kennard; Auditor, John Gillespie; Treasurer, Aug. Kountze; Adjutant General, C. H. Gere.

STATE LEGISLATURE—

	Senate.	House.	Joint Bal.
Republicans......	9	28.....	37
Democrats........	4	11.....	15
Rep. majority..	5	17.....	22

NEVADA.

COUNTIES.	Governor, 1866.	
	Winters. Dem.	Blasdel. Rep.
Churchill	112	109
Douglas.....	75	269
Esmeralda ..	105	225
Humboldt...	120	188
Lyon......	266	494
Lander.....	745	795
Nye.......	249	280
Storey.....	1547	1782
Ormsby.....	286	457
Washoe.....	560	609
Total........	4065	5208

STATE OFFICERS.—Governor, H. G. Blasdel; Secretary of State, C. N. Noteware; Attorney-General, R. M. Clark; Treasurer, E. Rhoades.

STATE DEBT.—Civil Debt, $390,000; War Debt, $110,000. Total, $500,000.

STATE LEGISLATURE—

	Senate.	House.	Joint Bal.
Republicans	16	35	51
Democrats	3	3	6
Rep. majority	13	32	45

CONGRESS, 1866.

Dem.	Rep.
Mitchell......4195	Ashley......5047

Delos R. Ashley over Henry K. Mitchell, 852.

KANSAS.

COUNTIES.	Negro Suff., 1867.		Female Suff., 1867.		President, 1864.	
	Ag'st	For.	Ag'st.	For.	Mc-Clel'n Dem.	Lin-coln. Rep.
Allen	266	324	303	243	73	250
Anderson	259	258	275	218	37	256
Atchison	1161	412	1235	345	378	735
Bourbon	725	550	736	464	126	960
Brown	346	265	341	248	3	362
Butler	70	33	76	28	19	39
Chase	123	120	125	118	47	79
Cherokee	186	200	139	249		
Clay	53	47	58	39		
Coffee	434	239	359	299	124	307
Crawford	199	50	150	45		
Davis	383	183	364	167	65	153
Dickinson	95	89	140	24	20	42
Doniphan	1425	338	1390	358	19	1081
Douglass	1147	1017	1164	652	194	1353
Franklin	539	280	709	120	23	393
Greenwood	198	133	198	99	16	106
Jackson	445	173	387	162	76	300
Jefferson	1159	392	1188	335	178	855
Johnson	852	400	866	325	105	437
Labette	213	115	217	95		
Leavenw'th	2703	890	1775	1588	1371	2139
Linn	798	340	791	253	62	689
Lyon	273	503	565	209	69	487
Marion	58	13	59	16		
Marshall	421	167	410	160	59	260
Miami	865	486	970	243	80	614
Morris	212	48	203	66	98	70
Nemaha	421	251	427	237	30	341
Neosho	322	151	367	101		
Osage	143	207	238	121	21	167
Ottawa	27	44	32	34		
Pottawat'ie	456	226	501	155	35	213
Riley	277	351	378	218	50	220
Saline	219	162	233	112		
Shawnee	670	464	731	439	75	573
Wab'unsee	108	149	152	114	7	163
Wash'gton	118	39	143	19		93
Wilson	138	36	170	43		
Woodson	88	149	94	141	67	375
Wyandotte	826	159	798	168	190	285
Sold'rs Vote						1600
Total	19421	10483	19857	9070	3691	15691

In 1866 a Governor was elected, as follows: Crawford, (Rep.), 19,370; McDowell, 8,151. Vote for Member of Congress, 1866: Sidney Clarke, 19,252; C. W. Blair, 8,056; Clarke's majority 11,196.

STATE OFFICERS—S. J. Crawford, Governor; N. Green, Lieut. Governor; R. A. Baker, Secretary of State; J. R. Swallow, Auditor; M. Anderson, Treasurer; G. H. Hoyt, Attorney General; P. McVickar, Sup't Public Instruction.

STATE DEBT—$824,475.00

STATE LEGISLATURE, 1868—

	Senate.	House.	Joint Bal.
Republicans	19	31	50
Democrats	5	20	25
Rep. majority	14	11	25

WEST VIRGINIA.

COUNTIES.	Legislature, 1867.		Governor, 1866.		President, 1864.	
	Dem.	Rep.	Smith. Dem.	Bore-man. Rep.	Mc-Clel'n Dem.	Lin-coln. Rep.
Barbour	279	405	699	693	293	593
Berkeley	83	351	256	807		726
Boone	40	106	97	164		
Braxton			182	186		
Brooke	449	376	437	483	401	464
Cabell	134	192	165	305		191
Calhoun			109	95		
Clay	58	63	79	70		73
Doddridge	340	373	425	518		
Fayette			68	206		
Gilmer	78	72	158	165	34	244
Grant	25	94	25	315		
Greenbrier			202	126		
Hampshire			391	102	7	163
Hancock	328	384	326	425	297	424
Hardy	89	7	238	24		254
Harrison	895	976	981	1235	863	1323
Jackson	177	358	468	593	190	679
Jefferson	159	171	215	292	21	174
Kanawha	594	616	534	1011	26	1421
Lewis	401	363	182	266	443	649
Logan	47	74	23	59		
McDowell			7	82		
Marion			720	1039	511	1082
Marshall	813	983	666	1330	770	1470
Mason	966	900	874	1012	362	1346
Mercer	122	122	76	139		
Mineral	152	177	246	341		
Monong'lia	752	855	549	926	705	1321
Monroe			18	121		
Morgan			1	314		265
Nicholas	75	108	67	118		143
Ohio	1797	1091	2224	2081	2008	2138
Pendleton			62	224		211
Pleasants	282	205	258	272	215	267
Pocahontas			28	152		
Preston	587	981	534	1400	564	1612
Putnam	274	242	264	314	109	338
Raleigh			55	186		
Randolph	121	156	290	207	50	177
Ritchie	244	469	317	596	217	673
Roane	109	224	210	360	31	275
Taylor	656	573	619	796	349	785
Tucker			138	48	36	56
Tyler	452	593	458	615	320	709
Upshur	109	327	243	716	68	19
Wayne			163	224		
Webster			20	23		
Wetzel	520	221	708	356	756	329
Wirt	268	238	184	300	209	262
Wood	918	1228	818	1269	591	1496
Wyoming			81	101		
Total	13393	14674	17158	23802	10438	23152

In 1867 there was an election for members of the State Legislature, but not for State officers. We have received official returns from 36 counties, which are given in the above table; the vote of these counties in 1866 was: Dem., 14,943; Rep., 20,573.

STATE OFFICERS.—Governor, Arthur I. Boreman; Secretary of State, John S. Witcher; Auditor, Joseph M. McWhorter; Treasurer, Jacob H. Bristor.

STATE LEGISLATURE, 1868—

	Senate.	House.	Joint Bal.
Republicans	20	42	62
Democrats	2	14	16
Rep. majority	18	28	46

CONGRESS, 1866.

Dist.	Dem.	Rep.	Rep. maj.
1.	D. V. Johnson......8239	C. D. Hubbard...10001	1762
2.	E. W. Andrews.5190	B. H. Kitchen...8296	3106
3.	— Oley......3639	Dan'l Palsey... 5211	1572

VIRGINIA.

COUNTIES.	Registration, 1867.		Convention, 1867.			
			Against.		For.	
	White	Col'd	White	Col'd	White	Col'd
Accomac...	2058	1470	1327	3	35	1183
Alb'marle..	2310	2759	1499	29	97	2353
Alexandria.	1491	1933	838	8	193	1576
Alleghany..	484	93	163	5	52	53
Amelia....	494	1492	306	81	22	1359
Amherst....	1515	1371	984	15	160	1208
Ap'omatox.	759	903	453	3	33	839
Augusta...	3579	1362	1646	9	233	1024
Bath......	418	111	177	1	8	28
Bedford...	2408	2110	1556	22	120	1878
Bland.....	687	56	227		128	39
Botetourt..	1420	662	735	4	133	577
Brunswick..	775	1733	446	2	55	1647
Buck'gham.	1072	1799	709	12	58	1557
Buchanan..	463	5	55			69
Campbell...	2576	2978	2006	24	38	2587
Caroline...	1317	1402	1166	20	7	1241
Carroll....	1410	65	163	2	692	4
Chas. City.	309	658	83		93	585
Charlotte..	913	2080	555	20	74	1878
Chesterf'd.	1871	2018	1082		36	1972
Clarke....	763	378	514	3	19	340
Craig.....	448	47	181	6	44	14
Culpepper.	1005	896	849	17	17	809
Cumberl'd.	535	1331	345	1	26	1235
Dinwiddie.	705	1606	326	1	42	1483
Elizabeth C	361	1585	39		55	1427
Essex.....	576	1124	394	3	24	1026
Fairfax....	1400	1039	778	12	245	909
Fauquier...	1889	1299	1305	13	60	1128
Floyd.....	1360	189	95		613	159
Fluvanna..	884	970	686	19	64	857
Franklin...	2109	1091	491	11	497	900
Frederick..	2093	540	1001	5	431	477
Giles.....	829	139	257	2	12	9
Gloucester..	860	869	569	4	5	756
Goochland..	662	1519	364	1	8	1358
Grayson...	1289	128	170		447	106
Greene....	556	263	380	7	10	220
Greenesv'e..	303	720	192	1	22	672
Halifax....	1980	3402	582	11	577	2748
Hanover...	1504	1556	1003	2	63	1453
Henrico....	1229	1879	669	1	53	1606
Henry.....	1017	1006	126	3	368	902
Highland..	602	58	214	4	48	21
Isle of Wig't	871	656	401	2	303	613
James City.	226	492				
King&Qu'n	710	883	375	4	39	826
Ki'g George	456	439	351	3	9	393
K'g William	488	713	297	1	11	662
Lancaster..	362	487	256		6	472
Lee	1487	120	491		307	51
Loudon ...	2799	1007	1536	13	584	899
Louisa....	1122	1761	542	3	88	1593
Lunenburg.	726	1219	434	7	46	1124
Madison...	808	599	557	1	55	556
Mathews...	651	334	289		81	258
Mecklenb'g.	1275	2843	784	10	92	2623
Middlesex..	388	409	237		6	376
Montgom'y	1546	567	387		624	506
Nansemond	1084	1154	699		20	1056
Nelson....	1243	1208	753	17	48	1100
New Kent..	370	454	159	1	23	405
NorfolkCity	1910	2049	1130	2	446	1821
Norfolk Co. &Portsm'th	2738	3281	1090	1	309	2912
Northam'n.	556	1004	372	1	5	873
Northum'ld	648	451	363		84	434
Nottoway..	481	1448	161	32	43	1302
Orange ...	899	1081	649	2	45	984
Page	1248	190	232	3	185	121
Patrick....	1197	326	46		574	249
Petersbur'h	1516	2647	1177	5	59	2423
Pittsylva'a.	2768	3534	1054	42	314	2470
Powhatan.	451	1173	298	10	20	1118
PrincessA'e	870	931	561		84	843

COUNTIES.	White	Col'd	White	Col'd	White	Col'd
Prince Ed'd	709	1659	468	3	63	1518
Prince Geo.	535	1095	108	1	46	946
Prince Wm.	958	307	491	6	107	244
Pulaski....	693	366	286	1	39	295
Rappaha'k.	1007	479	564	2	69	443
Richm'd C'y	5392	6284	4712	11	145	5184
Richm'd Co.	591	489	273		91	475
Roanoke...	1030	650	427	2	119	571
Rockbridge	2171	1051	886	5	145	932
Rockingh'm	2881	431	1082	10	261	304
Russell....	1415	224	244	1	369	160
Scott......	1884	110	346	1	767	76
Shenando'h	2168	176	964	1	251	155
Smyth....	1283	319	700	8	160	228
Southam'n.	1124	1273	612		20	1242
Spottsylv'a.	1310	1026	1085	10	40	882
Stafford...	847	253	616	6	38	196
Surry.....	447	582	263	1	101	510
Sussex....	535	1104	290		32	1026
Tazewell...	1309	275	501	4	90	165
Warren....	656	197	406	3	31	172
Warwick...	135	291	15		2	258
Wash'gton.	2479	637	1142	5	454	498
W'tmorel'd.	625	663	360	3	27	596
Wise......	654	9	234		152	4
Wythe....	1581	480	569	3	585	406
York......	425	1188	115		20	987
Total.....	120101	105832	61249	638	14835	92507

The total number of registered voters was 225,933. The total number of votes cast on the question of holding a convention was 169,229, of which 107,342 were for a convention, and 61,887 against it.

The convention, which met at Richmond, Dec. 3, 1867, was composed of 105 delegates, of whom 76 were white and 29 were colored.

NORTH CAROLINA.

COUNTIES.	Registration, 1867.		Convention, 1867.	
	White	Col'd	Ag'st.	For.
Alamance........	1326	777		
Anson........	1081	1067	604	1182
Ashe........	1174	67		
Alleghany...	467	57		
Alexander..	799	130		
Beaufort...	1457	907		
Bertie......	963	1265		
Bladen....	1060	1135	389	1043
Brunswick..	755	734	343	813
Buncombe..	1622	403	421	1012
Burke.....	1015	431	230	792
Cabarrus...	1231	748	280	1042
Catawba...	1315	315	303	780
Carteret...	1126	721		
Caswell....	1105	1845		
Clay......	389	14		
Cleveland..	1390	373	392	898
Columbus..	744	681	505	577
Cumberland	1454	1421	859	1720
Craven....	1531	3108	585	3232
Camden....	593	405		*709
Chowan....	586	640	277	823
Cherokee...	826	31		
Caldwell...	997	209		
Chatham...	2466	1055	330	2116
Currituck..	919	381		
Davidson...	2134	679		
Duplin.....	1414	969	937	1055
Davie.....	863	484		
Edgecombe.	1194	2593		
Forsythe...	1311	437	29	1062
Franklin...	1100	1483	770	1460
Gaston....	1007	445	84	823
Granville...	1845	2662		
Greene....	690	692		
Guilford...	2457	1054	638	1766

COUNTIES.	White	Col'd	Ag'st.	For.
Gates....	734	468		
Haywood	818	80		
Harnett	830	521		
Henderson	814	191	56	598
Hyde	863	560		*175
Halifax	1095	3140	737	2543
Hertford	700	747	503	705
Iredell	1859	757		
Johnston	1704	881		
Jackson	767	56		
Jones	485	525		
Lenoir	904	1075	349	1134
Lincoln	836	407	283	677
Madison	932	55		*400
Martin	965	791		
McDowell	877	221	162	498
Macon	860	55		
Mecklenburg	1835	1645	447	1985
Moore	1348	558		
Montgomery	874	317		*744
Mitchell	735	53		
New Hanover	1736	2975	1081	2928
Northampton	1139	1810		
Nash	1048	869		
Orange	1956	1294		
Onslow	787	399		
Person	941	903	746	742
Pitt	1296	1500		
Pasquotank	757	849		*565
Perquimans	678	683		
Polk	474	120		
Richmond	991	1067		
Robeson	1509	1404		
Rowan	1913	454	540	2610
Rutherford	1459	452	74	1026
Randolph	2192	1054		
Rockingham	1421	1302		
Stanly	927	259	89	639
Sampson	1461	953	785	1129
Stokes	1248	397	96	548
Surry	1482	273		
Transylvania	459	69		
Tyrrell	595	246		*176
Union	1294	422	174	1059
Wake	2996	2862	662	4026
Washington	674	548		*400
Wilkes	2139	241		
Wilson	1021	897	582	884
Wayne	1453	1283	828	1272
Warren	803	2208	600	2200
Watanga	725	40		
Yadkin	1502	245		
Yancey	746	49		
Total	103060	71657	16818	49901

*Majority.

Full and official returns of the vote on holding a convention had not been received at the time that THE WORLD ALMANAC was put to press. The number of delegates elected was 120, of whom 107 were whites and 13 were colored.

DISTRICTS.	White	Col'd	White	Col'd	White	Col'd
Fairfield....	983	2451	7		4	2046
Georgeto'n	474	3177			5	2444
Greenville	2077	1485	320			1530
Hocry	1127	513	21		24	431
Kershaw	859	1765			22	1406
Lancaster	983	881	324			833
Laurens	1628	2372	5		4	2168
Lexington	1480	975				900
Marion	1837	1737			1	1472
Marlboro'	961	1207	6		214	1271
Newberry	1131	2251	11		30	1939
Orangeburg	1645	3371				238
Pickens	2075	653	9			749
Richland	1235	2812	24		14	1329
Spartanbu'g	2960	1462	190		510	1400
Sumter	1214	3457	10			3035
Union	800	1725				1746
Williams'g	1426	1893				1568
York	2006	2078	68	5		1773
Total....	46676	80714	1471	9	1167	59111

The official returns of the vote on holding a convention had not been declared at the time of putting THE WORLD ALMANAC to press; those given above are as full as could be obtained to date. The number of delegates elected to the convention was 124.

GEORGIA.

COUNTIES.	Registration, 1867.		Convention, 1867.	
	White	Col'd	Ag'st.	For.
Appling	453	94	40	114
Baldwin	595	1252	1	1080
Baker	284	999	11	812
Banks	522	149	14	401
Berrien	460	65		45
Bibb	1638	2399		1858
Brooks	504	874		617
Bryan	247	332		243
Bullock	554	235		40
Burke	791	2543	1	1781
Butts	543	422	7	437
Bartow	1689	658	66	1218
Calhoun	324	696	76	533
Camden	145	556	24	476
Campbell	1071	362	125	678
Carroll	1448	214	4	797
Catoosa	597	115	77	335
Chattahoochee	438	568		447
Charlton	160	53	15	67
Chattooga	920	210	28	317
Chatham	2398	4845		3922
Cherokee	1464	219	95	734
Clarke	861	1111	2	1140
Clay	414	453		393
Clayton	555	230	70	456
Clinch	406	210	23	348
Columbia	603	1780		1596
Coffee	356	99		237
Correta	1283	1315	353	1383
Cobb	1648	573	10	671
Colquitt	173	17	2	65
Crawford	548	755		488
Dade	441	34	109	82
Dawson	555	63	24	346
Decatur	1024	1115		997
De Kalb	1052	422	8	355
Dooley	867	791	5	690
Dougherty	388	2274		1804
Echols	161	60	7	85
Early	339	814	76	533
Effingham	494	339		238
Elbert	795	836		813
Emmanuel	554	216	74	206
Fannin	693	40	46	472
Fayette	785	380	155	546
Floyd	1554	899	5	967
Forsyth	1010	265	117	679

SOUTH CAROLINA.

DISTRICTS.	Registration, 1867.		Vote on Convention, 1867.			
			Against		For	
	White	Col'd	White	Col'd	White	Col'd
Abbeville	1722	3352		8		1960
Anderson	2052	1670	69			1364
Barnwell	1889	3719		5		2457
Beaufort	934	6273		120		4109
Berkley	982	8264		1		3825
Charleston	3653	5192		69		4827
Chester	1222	2198	199	4	5	1343
Chesterfield	817	1071	204		98	1092
Clarendon	754	1555	1		3	1264
Colleton	1449	3931	1			2775
Darlington	1572	2910			30	2845
Edgefield	2760	4367	1			5811

COUNTIES.	White	Col'd	Ag'st	For.
Franklin	815	225	34	460
Fulton	2506	1943	471	2118
Gilmer	886	33	12	567
Glasscock	342	172		182
Glynn	160	592		519
Gordon	1203	218	390	584
Greene	822	1434		1240
Gwinnett	1604	340	8	390
Habersham	723	155	7	511
Hall	1190	204	68	801
Hancock	746	1545		1350
Haralson	499	48		270
Hart	683	216	7	583
Harris	1114	1267		1145
Heard	753	382		569
Henry	1047	610	7	601
Houston	916	2596	1	1909
Irwin	194	38	1	107
Jackson	1060	604	167	923
Jasper	661	979		971
Jefferson	693	1273		1044
Johnson	273	147	4	123
Jones	473	1070		900
Laurens	677	635	16	523
Lee	356	1679		1200
Liberty	326	869	2	582
Lincoln	294	588		477
Lowndes	520	673		562
Lumpkin	750	115	146	431
Macon	639	1382		1232
Marion	667	649	1	555
Madison	456	229		223
M'Intosh	307	600		531
Meriwether	961	1272	85	1235
Miller	272	185		146
Milton	610	63	8	119
Mitchell	390	607		522
Monroe	1113	1663		1513
Montgomery	328	163	17	158
Morgan	579	1231		1154
Murray	848	127	128	648
Muscogee	1133	1900		1744
Newton	1308	955	2	890
Oglethorp	709	1095		937
Paulding	1021	130	109	811
Pickens	732	31	6	516
Pierce	180	201	2	165
Pike	958	833	3	859
Polk	794	395	7	503
Pulaski	879	1131	17	1092
Putnam	558	1171		1062
Quitman	308	401		318
Rabun	459	32	5	255
Randolph	838	1100	2	811
Richmond	2264	3262	2	3256
Schley	329	501		434
Screnen	654	916	13	574
Spaulding	731	840	422	825
Stewart	858	1510		1123
Sumter	975	1924		1608
Talbot	778	1256		1096
Taliaferro	386	563		526
Tatnall	456	165		
Taylor	618	506	2	468
Telfair	339	163	17	158
Terrell	601	864	90	609
Thomas	786	1540		1392
Towns	424	25	7	325
Troup	1118	1991		1872
Twiggs	522	999	6	893
Union	758	17	15	587
Upson	820	821	5	783
Walker	1184	298	109	82
Walton	1047	673		615
Warren	727	1221		1036
Ware	227	134	1	167
Washington	1261	1336		1313
Wayne	157	69	2	92
Webster	393	386		231
White	512	86	12	361
Whitfield	1175	277	169	1047
Wilcox	248	118		253

COUNTIES.	White	Col'd	Ag'st	For.
Wilkes	597	1349		1144
Wilkinson	911	869		680
Worth	329	194	11	66
Total	96262	95973	4256	95778

The Convention met at Atlanta Dec. 9, 1867; it was composed of 169 delegates, of whom 147 were whites and 22 were blacks.

REGISTERED VOTES IN THE CITIES.

	Whites.	Blacks.	Totals.
Savannah	2240	3091	5331
Augusta	1574	1777	3351
Macon	1353	1851	3204
Atlanta	1829	1653	3482
Columbus	635	653	1288
Total	7631	9025	16656

ALABAMA.

Dists.	COUNTIES.	Registration, 1867			Convention, 1867	
		White	Col'd	Total.	Ag'st.	For.
1	Mobile City	2671	4001	6672	3	4556
2	Mobile Co.	5333	969	1502		
3	Baldwin	1172	1386	2558		494
	Conecuh				25	754
4	Covington	1746	293	2039	129	82
	Coffee				217	288
5	Dale	2818	1248	4066	139	621
	Henry				150	810
6	Barbour	1848	3275	5123	102	2113
7	Bullock	3032	3926	6958	599	2483
	Pike				838	619
8	Crenshaw	2553	1615	4168	146	376
	Butler				17	1175
9	Clarke	1761	2783	4544	13	1035
	Monroe				81	1150
10	Wash'gtn	1270	1754	3024	8	285
	Choctaw				155	977
11	Marengo	939	4229	5168	28	3863
12	Wilcox	2094	2633	4727	339	2969
13	Dallas	1460	6870	8330	144	5602
14	Lowndes	721	3433	4654	11	3521
15	Montgom'ry	2110	6544	8654		5881
16	Macon	635	2660	3305	1	2089
17	Russell	2422	4657	7079	32	1774
	Lee				8	1789
18	Elmore	2114	2729	4843	1	1281
	Autauga				4	1462
19	Hale	624	6225	7849	31	3520
	Greene				104	2379
20	Perry	1114	4245	5359	99	3594
21	Sumter	961	3683	4634	2	3144
22	Pickens	695	2082	2777	74	1430
23	Tuscaloosa	1718	1672	3390	3	1955
24	Bibb	2161	1290	3451	14	777
	Shelby				50	1033
25	Coosa	1188	491	1679	45	876
26	Tallapoosa	2142	823	2965	255	765
27	Chambers	822	1996	2718	37	1380
28	Randolph	2352	302	2655	2	814
	Clay				46	488
29	Talladega	1117	1871	2988	273	1527
30	Jefferson	1286	434	1720	15	624
31	Walker	1344	64	1408	30	424
	Winston					295
32	Jones				15	444
	Fayette	1936	300	2236	30	530
	Marion				9	357
33	Blount	2648	498	3146	13	692
	St. Clair					604
34	Marshall	2177	355	2532	160	471
	Baine				144	538
35	Calhoun	2487	725	3212	450	600
	Cleburne				17	140

Dists.	COUNTIES.	White	Col'd.	Total.	Ag'st.	For.
36....	Cherokee }	1840	601	2441	110	436
	De Kalb. }				4	384
37....	Jackson....	2315	550	2865	85	983
38....	Madison....	2136	2634	4770	1	2483
39....	Morgan.. }	2066	1821	3887	47	895
	Limest'ne }				195	1177
40....	Lauderdale.	1494	972	2466	16	1009
41....	Lawrence..	1471	1124	2595	59	1264
42....	Franklin. }				8	559
	Colbert... }	1838	957	2795	54	729
	Total......	73746	93543	166289	5685	87672

The convention met at Montgomery Nov. 5, 1867, and adjourned Dec. 6, 1867; the State Constitution framed by it was to be submitted to the voters of the State Feb. 4, 1868. The convention was composed of 101 delegates, of whom 85 were whites and 16 colored.

FLORIDA.

COUNTIES.	Registration, 1867.			Convention, 1867.	
	White	Col'd.	Total.	Ag'st.	For.
Alachua..........	495	1265	1760		987
Baker	89	54	143		56
Bradford........	320	104	424		245
Brevard........	5	3	8		
Calhoun........	162	66	328		
Clay	187	86	273		80
Columbia......	477	516	993		465
Dade..........	13	2	15		
Duval..........	385	705	1090		726
Escambia......	333	619	952		593
Franklin.......	223	162	385		
Gadsden.......	648	1138	1786		1066
Hamilton......	402	321	723		232
Hernando......	225	168	393		
Hillsboro.......	211	87	298		
Holmes........	187	27	214		
Jackson.......	684	1169	1853		
Jefferson......	556	1747	2303		136
La Fayette	226	36	262		67
Leon..........	515	2666	3181		2424
Levy..........	206	72	278		85
Liberty.......	107	95	202		
Madison.......	606	1214	1820		1088
Marion........	484	1269	1753		963
Manatee.......	139	16	155		
Monroe........	292	201	493		217
Nassau........	160	317	477		
Orange........	179	27	206		
Polk..........	159	17	176		
Putnam........	228	197	425		115
Santa Rosa......	347	207	554		
St. John's.......	311	112	423		137
Sumter.........	147	78	225		
Suwanee........	257	259	516		172
Taylor........	181	30	211		
Volusia.......	121	29	150		
Wakulla.......	239	248	487		211
Walton........	379	50	429		
Washington....	266	62	328		
Total.......	11151	15541	26692		10065

The total vote on holding a convention was 13,993, thus divided: For a convention, 13,882; against it, 111. Number of delegates elected, 46.

LOUISIANA.

PARISHES.	Registration, 1867.			Conv., 1867.
	White	Col'd.	Total.	Total Vote.
Avoyelles..............	859	1228	2087	1574
Ascension.............	563	1769	2332	1686
Assumption	947	1603	2550	1536
East Baton Rouge	980	2835	3815	2779

PARISHES.	White	Col'd.	Total.	Total Conv.
West Baton Rouge	248	771	1019	672
Bienville............	823	940	1763	1121
Bossier.............	504	1938	2442	1610
Caddo..............	747	2894	3641	2478
Calcasieu...........	486	198	684	285
Caldwell............	435	387	822	472
Catahoula...........	491	904	1395	839
Claiborne...........	1296	1659	2955	1811
Concordia...........	103	2083	2186	1983
De Soto............	613	1686	2299	1502
East Feliciana.......	529	1674	2303	1398
West Feliciana.......	275	1689	1964	1585
Franklin............	405	579	984	516
Iberville............	509	2131	2640	2132
Jackson............	750	659	1409	944
Jefferson...........	1128	3723	4856	3371
Lafayette...........	817	755	1572	744
Lafourche..........	1255	1568	2823	1522
Livingston..........	618	302	920	404
Madison............	147	1821	1968	1447
Morehouse.........	494	1313	1807	1247
Natchitoches.......	686	2357	3043	2300
Orleans............	15342	14805	30147	12841
Ouachita...........	546	1533	2079	1485
Plaquemine........	361	1534	1895	1479
Point Coupée.......	508	2216	2724	2055
Rapides............	818	2902	3720	2556
Sabine.............	459	321	780	359
St. Bernard........	274	679	953	721
St. Charles.........	187	1368	1555	1224
St. Helena.........	503	674	1177	856
St. James..........	469	2039	2508	1959
St. John...........	480	1269	1749	1221
St. Landry..........	2020	3113	5133	2715
St. Martin..........	1073	1605	2678	1373
St. Mary...........	605	2071	2676	1864
St. Tammany.......	507	536	1043	680
Tensas............	147	2358	2505	1974
Terrebonne........	883	1567	2450	1564
Union.............	969	661	1630	865
Vermillion.........	590	242	832	402
Washington........	519	267	786	487
Winn.............	799	243	1042	1094
Total.........	45169	83249	128418	79174

Gen. Mower, in an order dated Oct. 21, 1867, announced that 75,083 votes had been cast for a convention and 4,006 against it. The number of delegates elected was 98, of whom 49 were whites and 49 colored. The convention met at New-Orleans, Nov. 23, 1867.

MISSISSIPPI.

COUNTIES.	Registration, 1867.		COUNTIES.	Registration, 1867.	
	White	Col'd.		White	Col'd.
Adams	729	3210	Jackson....	521	256
Amite......	681	993	Jasper.....	814	837
Attala......	1419	968	Jefferson...	541	1916
Bolivar.....	290	1126	Kemper....	951	199
Calhoun....	1097	304	Lafayette...	1464	949
Carroll.....	1496	2213	Lauderdale.	1285	1402
Chickasaw..	1495	1684	Lawrence...	981	892
Choctaw....	1774	620	Leak.......	874	442
Claiborne...	549	1977	Lee........	1904	898
Clarke.....	724	1105	Lowndes....	1120	4238
Coahoma...	254	875	Madison....	532	1782
Copiah.....	1173	1369	Marion.....	312	183
Covington..	400	201	Marshall....	1843	1899
Davis......	372	53	Monroe.....	1508	2790
De Soto....	1917	2254	Neshuba....	388	97
Franklin....	565	557	Newton.....	1022	591
Green......	214	97	Noxubee....	936	3344
Hancock....	564	259	Oktibbeha..	825	1461
Harrison....	568	305	Panola.....	637	586
Hinds......	1551	3620	Perry......	260	114
Holmes.....	962	615	Pontotoc...	1491	470
Issaquena..	224	1293	Pike.......	993	831
Itawamba..	1003	150	Rankin.....	1070	1190

COUNTIES.	White	Col'd	COUNTIES.	White	Col'd	COUNTIES.	White	Col'd	Ag'at.	For.
Scott......	765	461	Warren	1433	4794	Van Buren....	746	148	52	249
Simpson....	409	286	Wash'ton..	200	2031	Washington	1834	84	662	326
Smith	735	264	Wilkinson..	547	2274	White......	1279	155	539	184
Sunflower..	186	822	Winston ...	837	506	Woodruff...	673	354	*75	
T'lahatchie	168	189	Yalabusha..	1313	1746	Yell.......	831	131	111	344
Tippah	754	147	Yazoo......	1014	2816					
Tishomingo	2647	626				Total......	43170	23146	9506	21817
Tunica	198	597	Total.....	47434	62091					
Wayne....	353	459								

Gen. Ord, in his order of Dec. 5, 1867, designating Jan. 7, 1868, as the time for the convention to assemble at Jackson, stated that in consequence of "irregularities in the conduct of the election," it was "impracticable to promulgate at the present time the total vote of the State for and against a convention." The number of delegates elected to the convention was 100. In a subsequent order, dated Dec. 16, 1867, it was stated that the total vote was 76,016, of which 69,739 were for and 6,277 were against a convention.

ARKANSAS.

COUNTIES.	Registration, 1867. White	Registration, 1867. Col'd	Convention. 1867. Ag'st.	Convention. 1867. For.
Arkansas	495	1030	109	927
Ashley............	710	604	549	531
Benton...........	998	11	392	92
Bradley...........	908	368		*230
Calhoun..........	422	184	134	211
Carroll...........	767	277		178
Chicot............	268	894		
Clark.............	1112	464	400	635
Columbia.........	1313	740	594	970
Conway...........	934	146		*200
Craighead........	523	42		
Crawford.........	746	148	233	370
Crittenden........	245	505		
Cross.............	415	184		
Dallas............	638	337	326	374
Desha............	231	592		*425
Drew.............	1079	577	386	694
Franklin..........	740	107	198	285
Fulton............	297	9	17	73
Greene............	922	5		
Hempstead........	130?	1195		*372
Hot Spring........	923	102	121	363
Independence.....	1455	140	251	513
Izard.............	763	31		*8
Jackson...........	849	283		*30
Jefferson..........	1058	2738		*2546
Johnson...........	682	73	262	259
Lafayette.........	583	962	229	896
Lawrence.........	971	43	203	125
Little River.......	327	426		*221
Madison..........	709	10	57	323
Marion...........	382	9	167	150
Mississippi........	292	193		
Monroe	525	551		*290
Montgomery......	491	27	31	28
Newton...........	425	1		
Ouachita..........	1084	870	551	817
Perry.............	235	25	34	114
Phillips...........	955	2681	454	2178
Pike..............	489	76		
Poinsett..........	172	39		
Polk..............	392	1	51	111
Pope..............	741	94	91	433
Prairie...........	1071	512	513	457
Pulaski	1494	2402	419	2430
Randolph.........	818	59	219	105
Saline............	712	42	251	142
Scott.............	557	17		
Searcy............	574	1	20	235
Sebastian.........	1912	283	113	236
Sevier............	567	251	135	531
St. Francis........	964	464	150	393
Union	622	798		*192

The returns of the vote on holding a convention, as given above are not official; the latter could not be obtained in consequence of "irregularities in the conduct of the election," as stated by Gen. Ord in his order of Dec. 5, 1867, designating Jan. 7, 1868, as the day for the convention to assemble at Little Rock. In an order dated Dec. 21, 1867, Gen. Ord announced that 27,576 votes were cast for a convention and 13,558 against it, the total number of registered voters being 66,805. The number of delegates elected to the convention was 77.

TEXAS.

The only information at hand concerning it is contained in an order of Gen. Hancock, dated Dec. 18, 1867, to wit:—The election to be held on Feb. 10 to 14, 1868, inclusive; ninety delegates are to be elected; the total registration is 104,259; a revision of the registration is to be commenced fourteen days previous to the election.

IDAHO.

Del. Congress, 1566.

Counties.	Holbrook. Dem.	Kirkpatrick. Rep.
Ada	389	324
Alturas	160	160
Boise	1987	1298
Idaho	210	190
Nez Perce	155	230
Oneida	88	131
Owyhee	675	551
Shoshone	27	39
Total	3641	2923

E. D. Holbrook over Kirkpatrick, 718.

ARIZONA.

Del. to Congress, 1866.

Counties.	Bashford.	Poston.	Adams.
Mohave.................	27	65	89
Pima...................	526	89	
Pah-Ute................	141	1	
Yavapai................	226	217	48
Yuma..................	89	146	31
Total..................	1009	518	168

The present Legislature is about equally divided between Democrats and Republicans.

COLORADO.

The following is the official canvass of the vote for Delegates to Congress, as returned by the Territorial Board of Canvassers, though for sufficient reason, Gov. Alexander Cummings gave a certificate of Election to A. C. Hunt, the democratic candidate:

Geo. M. Chilcott, (Rep.) 3529
A. C. Hunt, (Dem.) 3421
Scattering................................ 46

In 1867 there was an election for members of the Legislature, at which 9,349 votes were polled, being an increase of 2,353 votes over the vote of 1866. The following is the political complexion of the Territorial Legislature:

	Council.	House.	Joint Bal.
Republicans........	9	17	26
Democrats	4	9	13
Rep. majority	5	8	13

UTAH.

An election for delegate to the 40th Congress was held February 4, 1867, at which 16,281 votes were polled; of these Wm. H. Hooper, the Mormon Candidate, received 16,176, and Wm. McGroarty, 105 votes. A large majority of the Legislature is Mormon.

DAKOTA.

Del. Congress, 1866.
Burleigh. Brookings.

Counties	Dem.	Rep.
Charles Mix	59	2
Clay	79	66
Bon Homme	17	14
Kitteon	103	
Todd	26	
Union	213	85
Yankton	96	87
Total	593	254

Walter A. Burleigh over Brookings, 339.

LEGISLATURE—

	Council.	House.	Joint Bal.
Democrats	13	18	31
Republicans	0	6	6
Dem. majority	13	12	25

MONTANA.

Del. Congress, 1867.
Cavanaugh. Sanders.

Counties.	Dem.	Rep.
Beaverhead	297	301
Chouteau	165	115
Deer Lodge	1298	1037
Edgerton	1632	1259
Gallatin	1037	633
Jefferson	368	286
Madison	1022	1125
Missoula	195	140
Total	6004	4896

James B. Cavanaugh over Wilber P. Sanders, 1,108.

LEGISLATURE—

	Council.	House.	Joint Bal.
Democrats	7	15	22
Republicans	0	1	1
Dem. majority	7	14	21

NEW MEXICO.

Del. Congress, 1867.
Clever. Chaves.

Counties.	Dem.	Rep.
Bernalillo	733	895
Dona Anna	563	763
Mora	2128	715
Santa Fe	780	780
San Miguel	130	2137
Santa Ana	662	296
Socorro	1497	573
Rio Cerriba	851	594
Taos	577	1937
Valencia		1123
Total	8891	6794

Clever over Chaves, 97.

TERRITORIES.

Territory.	Capital.	Governor.	Salary.
Arizona	Tucson	Rich'd C. McCormick	$3,000
Colorado	Denver	C'y.A. C. Hunt	1,500
Dakota	Yankton	Andrew J. Faulk	1,500
Idaho	Lewiston	Isaac L. Gibbs	2,500
Ind'nT'y	Tolequa	Lewis Downing	
Montana	Va. City	Green Clay Smith	
N Mexico	Santa Fe	Robert D. Mitchell	3,000
Utah	G S L City	Charles Durkee	2,500
Wash'gt'n	Olympia	Marshall F. Moore	3,000

* Appointed by the President in Dec., 1867, but unconfirmed by the Senate at the present date, Jan. 1, 1868.

THE ELECTORAL COLLEGE, 1868.

States.	Votes.
Alabama	8
Arkansas	5
California	5
Connecticut	6
Delaware	3
Florida	3
Georgia	9
Illinois	16
Indiana	13
Iowa	8
Kansas	3
Kentucky	11
Louisiana	7
Maine	7
Maryland	7
Massachusetts	12
Michigan	8
Minnesota	4
Mississippi	7
Missouri	11
Nebraska	3
Nevada	3
New Hampshire	5
New Jersey	7
New York	33
North Carolina	9
Ohio	21
Oregon	3
Pennsylvania	26
Rhode Island	4
South Carolina	6
Tennessee	10
Texas	6
Vermont	5
Virginia	10
West Virginia	5
Wisconsin	8

Total, (including all the States) 317
Total, (excluding Southern States) 247

Should Colorado be admitted to the Union as a State before the presidential election, it would be entitled to three electoral votes, making the total electoral vote 320, and without the Southern States, 250:

HOP STATISTICS.

The growth of hops in the United States has been as follows:

Year	1840.	1850.	1860.
Pounds	1,238,502	3,496,950	11,010,985
Bales	6,193	17,485	55,055

The estimated growth for 1867 was 19,000,000 pounds or 95,000 bales.

The growth of hops in the State of New York has been as follows:

1840.	447,259 pounds or	2,236 bales.
1850.	2,536,239 "	" 12,681 "
1855.	7,192,234 "	" 35,951 "
1860.	9,655,542 "	" 48,277 "
1865.	12,092,570 "	" 60,463 "

Number of acres in the State of New York planted with hops:

1854, 9,461 3-4 ; 1864, 23,417 3-4 ; 1865, 25,641 1-4. Average yield per acre in 1854, 1,017 pounds; in 1864, 466 pounds. Prices ranged in New York in fall of 1867 from 55 to 70 cents.

STATE GOVERNMENTS.

STATES.	CAPITALS.	GOVERNORS.	Term Exp'rs.	Sal'ry.	Legislature meets.	State election
Alabama........	Montgomery......					
Arkansas........	Little Rock......					
California........	Sacramento......	*Henry H. Haight	Jan....1872	$7000	1st. M. Dec.	1st. W.Sept
Connecticut......	Hartf'd&N.Hav'n	*Jas. E. English..	May...1868	1100	1st W.May.	1st.M. April
Delaware........	Dover..........	*Gove Saulsbury..	Jan....1871			
Florida..........	Tallahassee......					
Georgia..........	Milledgeville....					
Illinois..........	Springfield......	Rich'd J. Oglesby.	Jan....1869	1500	2d. M. Jan.	1st. Tu.Nov
Indiana..........	Indianapolis.....	Conrad Baker.....	Jan....1869	3000	1st. W. Jan.	2d. Tu. Oct.
Iowa............	Des Moines......	Sam'l Merrill.....	Jan....1870	2000	2d. M. Jan.	2d. Tu. Oct.
Kansas..........	Topeka..........	Sam'l J. Crawford	Jan....1869	2500	2d. Th.Jan.	1st. Tu.Nov
Kentucky........	Frankfort........	*J. W. Stevenson.	Sept...1871	2500	1st. M. Dec.	1st. M.Aug.
Louisiana........	Baton Rouge....					
Maine...........	Augusta........	J. L. Chamberlain	Jan....1869	1500	1st. W. Jan.	2d. M. Sept.
Maryland........	Annapolis.......	*Ogden Bowie....	Jan....1869			
Massachusetts....	Boston..........	Alex. H. Bullock.	Jan....1869	3500	1st.W. Jan.	1st. Tu.Nov
Michigan........	Lansing.........	Henry H. Crapo..	Jan....1869	1500	1st.W. Jan.	1st. Tu.Nov
Minnesota.......	St. Paul.........	Wm. R. Marshall.	Jan....1870	2500	1st.Tu.Jan.	1st. Tu.Nov
Missouri.........	Jefferson City...	Thos. C. Fletcher.	Jan....1869	2500	LastM.Dec	1st. Tu.Nov
Mississippi......	Jackson.........					
North Carolina..	Raleigh.........					
Nebraska........	Omaha..........	David Butler.....				
Nevada..........	Virginia City....	Henry G. Blasdel.	Jan....1871		1st. M. Jan.	1st. Tu.Nov
New Hampshire.	Concord.........	Walter Harriman	June...1868	1000	1st W.June	2 Tu.March
New Jersey......	Trenton.........	Marcus L. Ward..	Jan....1870	3000	2d. Tu.Jan.	1st.Tu. Nov
New York.......	Albany..........	Reuben E. Fenton	Jan....1869	4000	1st. Tu.Jan	1st.Tu. Nov
Ohio............	Columbus.......	Ruth'fd B. Hayes.	Jan....1870	1800	1st. M. Jan.	2d. Tu. Oct.
Oregon..........	Salem...........	Geo. L. Woods...	Sept...1870	1500	3d. M. Sept.	1st. M.June
Pennsylvania....	Harrisburg......	John W. Geary...	Jan....1869	3500	1st. Tu.Jan.	2d. Tu. Oct.
Rhode Island....	Newp't&Provid'e.	A. E. Burnside...	May...1868	1000	May & Jan.	1st W.April
South Carolina...	Columbia.......					
Tennessee........	Nashville.......	Wm. G. Brownlow	Oct....1869	3000	1st. M. Oct.	1st.Th. Aug
Texas...........	Austin..........					
Vermont........	Montpelier......	John B. Page.....	Oct....1868	1000	2d. Tu. Oct.	1st.Tu.Sept
Virginia.........	Richmond.......					
West Virginia....	Wheeling.......	Arthur I. Boreman	March.1869	2000	3d. Tu.Jan.	4th. Th.Oct
Wisconsin.......	Madison........	Lucius Fairchild..	Jan....1870	1200	2d. W. Jan.	1st. Tu.Nov

* Democrats.

POPULAR VOTE FOR PRESIDENT.

STATES.	1864.				1860.				1856.		
	Mc-Clellan Dem.	Lincoln. Rep.	Dem. Major'ity.	Rep. Major'ity.	Douglas. Dem.	Br'ken-ridge. Dem.	Bell. Union.	Lincoln. Rep.	Buchanan. Dem.	Fillmore. Am.	Fremont. Rep.
Alabama.........					13651	48831	27875		46739	28552	
Arkansas........					5227	28732	20094		21910	10787	
California........	43841	62134		18293	38516	34334	6817	39173	53365	36165	20691
Connecticut......	42285	44691		2406	15522	14641	3291	43792	34995	2615	42715
Delaware........	8767	8155	612		1023	7337	3864	3815	8004	6175	308
Florida..........					367	8543	5437		6358	4883	
Georgia..........					11590	51889	42886		56578	42228	
Illinois..........	158730	189496		30766	160215	2404	4913	172161	105298	37454	96200
Indiana..........	130233	150422		20189	115509	12295	5306	139033	118670	22386	94375
Iowa............	49596	89075		39479	55111	1048	1763	70409	36170	9180	43954
Kansas..........	3691	16441		12750							
Kentucky........	64301	27786	36515		25651	53143	66058	1364	74642	67416	314
Louisiana........					7825	22681	20204		22164	20709	
Maine...........	46992	68114		21122	26693	6368	2046	62811	39080	3325	67179
Maryland........	32739	40153		7414	5966	42482	41760	2294	39115	47460	281
Massachusetts....	48745	126742		77997	34372	5939	22331	106533	39287	19679	108515
Michigan........	74604	91521		16917	65057	805	405	88480	52136	1660	71762
Minnesota.......	17375	25060		7685	11920	748	62	22069			
Mississippi......					3253	40797	25040		35447	24196	
Missouri.........	31678	72750		41072	58801	31317	58372	17028	58164	48524	
Nevada..........	6594	9826		3232							
New Hampshire	32871	36400		3529	25881	2112	441	37519	32789	422	38345
New Jersey......	68024	60723	7301		62801			58324	46943	24115	28338
New York.......	361986	368735		6749	312510			362646	195878	124604	276007
North Carolina..					2701	48539	44990		48246	36886	
Ohio............	205568	265154		59586	187232	11403	12194	231610	170874	28126	187497
Oregon..........	8457	9888		1431	3951	5006	183	5270			
Pennsylvania....	276316	296391		20075	16765	178871	12776	268030	230772	82202	148272
Rhode Island....	8718	14349		5631	7707			12244	6680	1673	11467
South Carolina...			Electors chosen by the Legislature.								
Tennessee........					11350	64709	69274		73638	66178	
Texas...........						47548	15438		31169	15639	
Vermont........	13321	49419		29098	6349	218	1969	33808	10569	545	39563
Virginia.........					16290	74323	74681	1929	89706	60310	291
West Virginia....	10438	23152		12714							
Wisconsin.......	65884	83458		17574	65021	888	161	86110	52843	579	66090
Total............	**1811754**	**223035**	**44428**	**456709**	**1375157**	**847953**	**590631**	**1866452**	**1838229**	**874625**	**1342164**

Entered at the New York Post Office as Second Class Matter.

Vol. 2, No 14. THE WORLD SUPPLEMENT, January, 1893.

Issued Monthly by the Press Publishing Co., Pulitzer Bl'dg, New York

Yearly Subscription 35 cts.

PREFACE.

THE publication of THE WORLD ALMANAC for 1893 has been delayed somewhat beyond the customary time of issue by the difficulty experienced in obtaining the official returns in detail of the Presidential election in a number of States. The conditions of the late contest were unusual. The varying combinations of political parties on electoral, legislative, and local candidates in those States gave rise to disputes and recounts, consuming a great deal of time. The ALMANAC could have been issued earlier, with a large part of the election returns omitted and other returns hastily estimated, but it was believed that this would not be satisfactory to the users of this book, who are accustomed to look to it for completeness and accuracy in its presentation of statistics.

This issue of the ALMANAC has more pages than any of its predecessors, and the increase is due to the purpose to supply information upon all current matters of human interest. Foremost among them this year is the great international Exposition at Chicago. For the convenience of the many possessors of the ALMANAC who will visit the Western metropolis while the Exposition is open, a directory suited to the needs of strangers has been prepared, and with accompanying maps of Chicago and the Exposition grounds will be found in the volume. The ALMANAC contains also other features new to its readers. With the assistance of the Department of State, at Washington, a complete list of United States ministers to the principal countries of the world and of their ministers here, from the beginning of diplomatic intercourse to the present year, is printed for the first time. A history of the University Extension movement is given, and lovers of whist will find ample space devoted to their favorite pastime. There are several additional population tables, the latest outputs of the Census bureaus of the United States and the State of New York. The astronomical, religious, and educational departments and records of sports, to each of which special attention has always been given in this publication, have been further extended.

It was announced in the ALMANAC of last year that, in recognition of the growing interest among intelligent Americans in the affairs of foreign countries and the persons who are conspicuous in directing them, more space would hereafter be devoted to such matters, and particularly to Great Britain, its possessions and people, about which the newspapers of the day are making us almost as familiar as with our own affairs. In continuance of this plan the foreign department has been still further enlarged in this volume, the best authorities—Whitaker's admirable Almanack, the Statesman's Year Book, and the Almanach de Gotha—being drawn upon when needed.

In concluding, the editor repeats the assurance of last year, that THE WORLD ALMANAC, while grateful of the public appreciation, as evidenced in its annual sale of over 100,000 copies, is also mindful of the fallibility of the human brain and eye. Sources of information are sometimes at fault, and, typographically speaking, there are five million figures and letters in the ALMANAC. Errors are inevitable under such conditions. But the utmost that human endeavor can accomplish has been done to secure accuracy and completeness, and the editor can only reiterate his request that such errors and omissions as may be discovered will be kindly pointed out.

NEW YORK CITY, January, 1893.

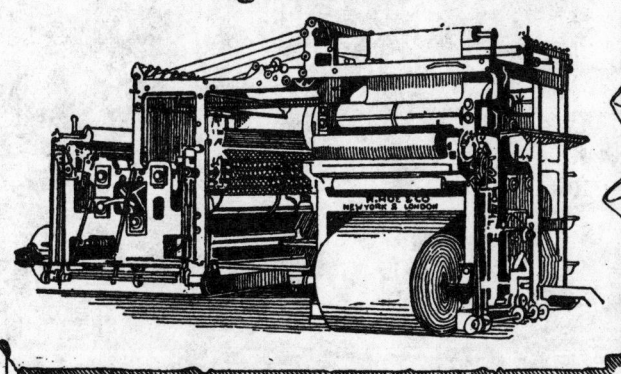

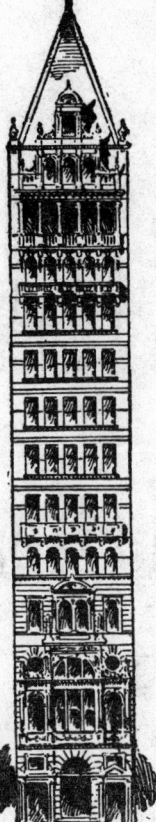

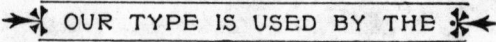

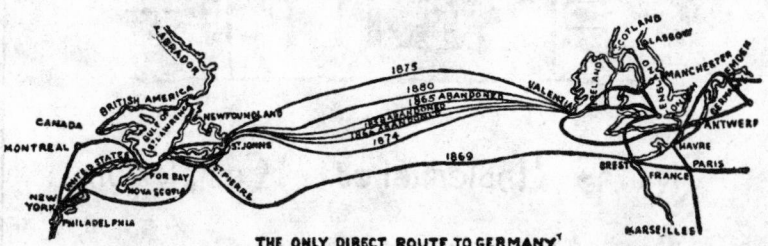

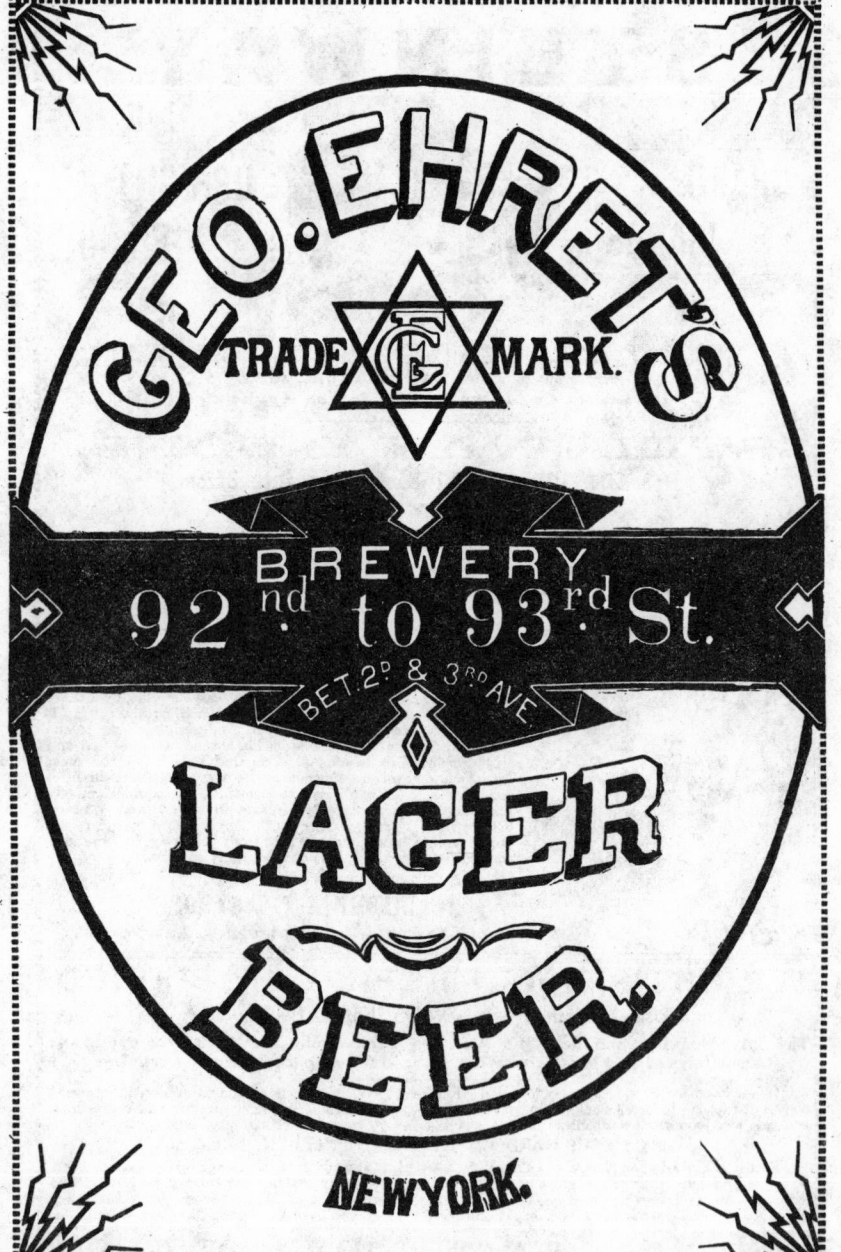

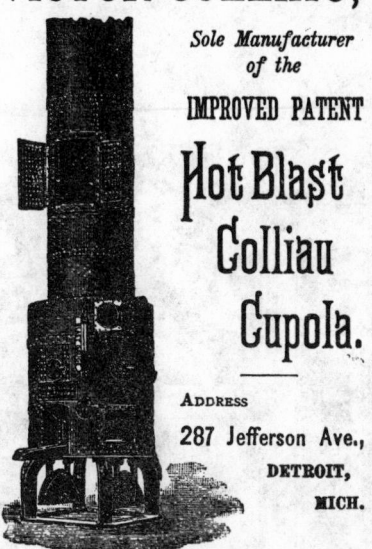

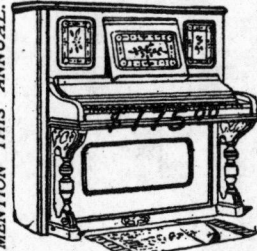

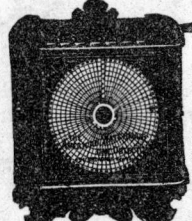

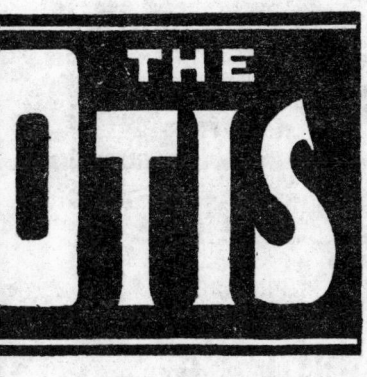 

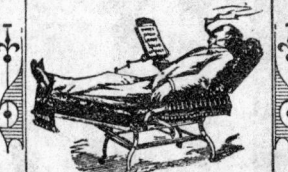
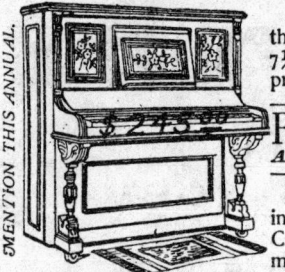

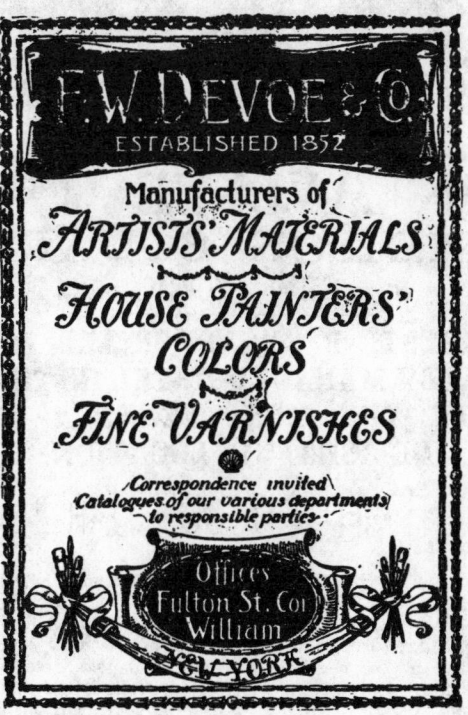

FIFTH AVENUE HOTEL,
MADISON SQUARE,
NEW YORK.

THE LARGEST, BEST APPOINTED AND MOST LIBERALLY MANAGED HOTEL IN THE CITY, WITH THE MOST CENTRAL AND DELIGHTFUL LOCATION.

A. B. DARLING.
CHARLES N. VILAS.
E. A. DARLING.
HIRAM HITCHCOCK.

HITCHCOCK, DARLING & CO.

THIS noble pile of white marble, Corinthian architecture, covering eighteen full city lots and accommodating one thousand guests, marks a place in the heart of the great City of New York, and an era in the history of the Nation's wealth and advancement. It is located in the centre of the City, upon the charming Madison Square and at the intersection of the two great streets, Broadway and Fifth Avenue, and convenient to the most important points of interest in the Metropolis.

Its patrons include the names of the most prominent men and women in America—The Presidents, hundreds of Government Officials, Senators, Congressmen, Judges, Army and Navy Officers, Divines, Physicians, Authors, and in fact all who have attained prominence and celebrity in public and private life, both at home and abroad; and the most distinguished Europeans of rank and title who have visited this country.

It has been the centre of all the great public occasions which the City has witnessed for thirty years.

Years have come and gone, new hotels have multiplied with innovations and features introduced to affect and influence patronage, but the Fifth Avenue is as new and fresh as the most recent hotel construction, with more liberal accommodations than any of them, and its well-earned reputation as the leading Hotel of the world is more and more assured.—*King's Handbook of the United States.*

SUGGESTIONS FOR THE WORLD ALMANAC 1894.

Comments and Suggestions are always in order, and will be highly appreciated by The Editor of The World Almanac,

New York.

Signed,_____

_____
Give address in full.

Agricultural Statistics.

GRAIN PRODUCTION OF THE UNITED STATES.

The following are the United States census reports of the productions of the principal cereals in the United States in the several census years, together with the reports of the U. S. Department of Agriculture for 1885-92.

Year.	Indian Corn.	Wheat.	Oats.	Barley.	Rye.	Buckwheat.
	Bushels.	*Bushels.*	*Bushels.*	*Bushels.*	*Bushels.*	*Bushels.*
1850	592,071,104	100,485,940	146,584,179	5,167,015	14,188,813	8,956,912
1860	838,792,742	173,104,924	172,643,185	15,825,898	21,101,380	17,571,818
1870	760,944,549	287,745,626	282,107,157	29,761,305	16,918,795	9,821,721
1880	1,754,861,535	459,479,503	407,858,900	44,113,495	19,831,595	11,817,327
1885	1,936,176,000	357,112,000	629,409,000	58,360,000	21,756,000	12,626,000
1886	1,665,441,000	457,218,000	624,134,000	59,428,000	24,489,000	11,869,000
1887	1,456,161,000	456,329,000	659,618,000	56,812,000	20,691,000	10,844,000
1888	1,987,790,000	415,868,000	701,735,000	63,884,593	28,412,011	12,000,000
1889	2,112,892,000	490,560,000	751,515,000	*65,000,000	*30,000,000	*11,000,000
1890	1,489,970,000	399,262,000	523,621,000	*63,000,000	*28,000,000	*11,000,000
1891	2,060,154,000	611,780,000	738,394,000	*75,000,000	*33,000,000	*12,000,000
1892	1,628,464,000	519,490,000	661,037,000	....	....	....

* Estimated by the Cincinnati *Price Current.*

In 1888 the production in the United States of hay was 41,454,458 tons; hops, 1,987,790,000 pounds; Irish potatoes, 201,984,140 bushels; cane sugar, 162,264 tons; maple sugar, 20,000 tons; tobacco, 565,794,264 pounds; peanuts, 2,600,000 bushels; wool, 265,000,000 pounds.

THE WHEAT AND RYE CROPS OF THE WORLD.

(1890-91).

Countries.	Wheat.	Rye.	Countries.	Wheat.	Rye.
Algeria	25,000,000	....	Italy	102,200,000	....
Argentine Rep. and Chile	35,000,000	....	India	235,000,000	....
Australasia	42,000,000	....	Netherlands	42,000,000	....
Austria	40,000,000	63,000,000	Portugal	8,400,000	....
Belgium	15,400,000	....	Roumania	64,000,000	....
Canada	61,000,000	....	Russia	186,200,000	539,000,000
Denmark	1,820,000	9,000,000	Servia	10,000,000	....
Egypt	10,000,000	....	Sweden and Norway	4,760,000	....
France	231,000,000	....	Switzerland	8,400,000	....
Germany	86,800,000	....	Spain	75,600,000	....
Great Britain	71,400,000	....	Turkey	21,000,000	....
Hungary	119,000,000	32,760,000	United States	600,000,000	33,000,000

The estimates for Europe were compiled from estimates mostly made by Consul-General Goldschmidt, of Vienna.

WHEAT HARVEST CALENDAR.

January—Australia, New-Zealand, Chile, Argentine Republic.

February and March—Upper Egypt, India.

April—Lower Egypt, India, Syria, Cyprus, Persia, Asia Minor, Mexico, Cuba.

May—Texas, Algeria, Central Asia, China, Japan, Morocco.

June—California, Oregon, Mississippi, Alabama, Georgia, North-Carolina, South-Carolina, Tennessee, Virginia, Kentucky, Kansas, Arkansas, Utah, Colorado, Missouri, Turkey, Greece, Italy, Spain, Portugal, South of France.

July—New-England, New-York, Pennsylvania, Ohio, Indiana, Michigan, Illinois, Iowa, Wisconsin, Southern Minnesota, Nebraska, Upper Canada, Roumania, Bulgaria, Austria-Hungary, South of Russia, Germany, Switzerland, South of England.

August—Central and Northern Minnesota, the Dakotas, Manitoba, Lower Canada, Colombia, Belgium, Holland, Great Britain, Denmark, Poland, Central Russia.

September and October—Scotland, Sweden, Norway, North of Russia.

November—Peru, South-Africa.

December—Burmah, New-South Wales.

The tables of wheat crop of the world in 1890, of the wheat harvest calendar and of prices of wheat in the Chicago market from 1860 to 1892 inclusive were compiled by Charles B. Murray, editor of the Cincinnati *Price Current.*

PRICES OF WHEAT (CHICAGO MARKET), 1860-92.

Years.	Months of Lowest Price.	Yearly Range of Prices.	Months of Highest Price.	Years.	Months of Lowest Price.	Yearly Range of Prices.	Months of Highest Price.
1860	December	66 @1.13	April.	1877	August	1.01½@1.76½	May.
1861	June and July.	55 @1.25	May.	1878	October	77 @1.14	April.
1862	January	65 @ 92½	August.	1879	January	81⅝@1.33⅛	December.
1863	August	80 @1.12½	December.	1880	August	86½@1.32	January.
1864	March	1.07 @2.26	June.	1881	January	95⅜@1.43¼	October.
1865	December	85 @1.55	January.	1882	December	91⅛@1.40	April and May
1866	February	77 @2.03	November.	1883	October	90 @1.13½	June.
1867	August	1.55 @2.85	May.	1884	December	69½@ 96	February.
1868	November	1.04½@2.20	July.	1885	March	73⅜@ 91¾	April.
1869	December,	76½@1.46	August.	1886	October	69⅜@ 84¾	January.
1870	April	73¼@1.31½	July. [Sept.	1887	August	66⅝@ 94¾	June.
1871	August	99½@1.32	Feb., April, and	1888	April	71⅛@*2.00	September.
1872	November	1.01 @1.61	August.	1889	June	75½@1.08¾	February.
1873	September	89 @1.46	July.	1890	February	74¼@1.08¼	August.
1874	October	81⅛@1.28	April.	1891	July	85 @1.16	April.
1875	February	83¼@1.30½	August.	1892	October	69⅛@ 91¾	February.
1876	July	83 @1.26¾	December.				

* The Hutchinson "corner" figure.

The Cotton Supply.

CROP OF THE UNITED STATES FOR SIXTY YEARS.

The following statements are furnished by the New York "Commercial and Financial Chronicle :"

Year.	Bales.	Year.	Bales.	Year.	Bales.	Year.	Bales.
1829........	870,415	1845........	2,394,503	1861........	3,656,006	1879........	5,073,531
1830........	976,845	1846........	2,100,537	1862 to 1865.	No record.	1880........	5,757,397
1831........	1,038,848	1847........	1,778,651	1866........	2,193,987	1881........	6,589,329
1832........	987,487	1848........	2,347,634	1867..	2,019,774	1882........	5,435,845
1833........	1,070,438	1849........	2,728.596	1868........	2,593,993	1883........	6,992,234
1834........	1,205,324	1850........	2,096,706	1869........	2,439,039	1884........	5,714,052
1835........	1,254,328	1851........	2,355,257	1870........	3,154 946	1885........	5,669,021
1836........	1,360,752	1852........	3,015,029	1871........	4 352,317	1886........	6,550,215
1837........	1,422,930	1853........	3,262,882	1872........	2,974,351	1887........	6,513.624
1838........	1,801,497	1854........	2,930,027	1873........	3,930,508	1888........	7,017,707
1839........	1,360,532	1855........	2,847,339	1874........	4,170,368	1889........	6,935,082
1840........	2,177,835	1856........	3,527,845	1875........	3,832,991	1890........	7,313,726
1841........	1,634,945	1857........	2,939,519	1876........	4,669,288	1891........	8,655,518
1842........	1,683,574	1858........	3,113,962	1877........	4,485,423	1892........	9,038,707
1843........	2,378,875	1859........	3,851,481	1878........	4,811,265		
1844........	2,030,409	1860........	4,669 770				

The returns are for the years ending September 1. The average net weight, per bale, is 440 pounds.

EXPORTS AND DOMESTIC CONSUMPTION OF AMERICAN COTTON.

	1891-92.	1890-91.	1889-90.	1888-89.	1887-88.	1886-87.	1885-86.	1884-85.
	Bales.	Bales.	Bales.	Bales.	Bales.	Bales.	Bales.	Bales.
Export to Europe.....	5,815,365	5,750,443	4,885,326	4,700,198	4,602,248	4,414,326	4,296,825	3,898,905
Consumption U. S., Canada, etc........	2,932,908	2,642,912	2,431,757	2,372,641	2,259,606	2,265,324	2,087,785	1,764,326
Total...	8,748,273	8,393,355	7,317,083	7,072,839	6,861,854	6,679,650	6,384,610	5,663,231

COTTON CONSUMPTION OF THE ENTIRE WORLD.

Consumption Bales, 400 lbs.	Great Britain.	Continent.	Total Europe.	Total United States.	Total World.
1880-81......................	3,572,000	2,956,000	6,528,000	2,118,000	8,640,000
1881-82......................	3,640,000	3,198,000	6,838,000	2,197,000	9,035,000
1882-83......................	3,744,000	3,380,000	7,124,000	2,375,000	9,499,000
1883-84......................	3,666,000	3,380,000	7,046,000	2,244,000	9,290,000
1884-85......................	3,433,000	3,255,000	6,688,000	1,909,000	8,597,000
1885-86......................	3,628,000	3,465,000	7,093,000	2,278,000	9,371,000
1886-87......................	3,694,000	3,640,000	7,334,000	2,423,000	9,757,000
1887-88......................	3,841,000	3,796,000	7,637,000	2,530,000	10,167,000
1888-89...	3,770,000	4,069,000	7,839,000	2,685,000	10,524,000
1889-90......................	4,034,000	4,290,000	8,324,000	2,731,000	11,055,000
1890-91......................	4,230,000	4,538,000	8,768,000	2,958,000	11,726,000
1891-92......................	4,977,000	4,524,000	8,501,000	3,290,000	11,791,000

SOURCES OF COTTON SUPPLY.

The following is the estimate of Ellison & Co. for 1892-93 :

	Total.		Total.
	Bales.		Bales.
America...........................	8,418,000	Brazils, W. I., etc...............	225,000
East India...........................	1,300,000	Total	10,566,000
Egypt...........................	570,000	Average weight...................	468
Smyrna...........................	53,000	Bales of 400 lbs	12,353,000

SPINDLES IN OPERATION.

	1892.	1891.	1890.	1889.	1888.	1887.
Great Britain.	45,350,000	44,750,000	43,750,000	43,500,000	42,740,000	42,740,000
Continent....	26,405,000	26,035,000	24,575,000	24,000,000	23,380,000	23,180,000
United States	15,277,000	14,781,000	14,550,000	14,175,000	13,525,000	13,500,000
East Indies ..	3,402,000	3,351,000	3,270,000	2,760,000	2,490,000	2,420,000
Total.......	90,434,000	88,917,000	86,145,000	84,435,000	82,135,000	81,840,000

Vine Cultivation in the United States.

THE Census Bureau provides the following table, showing the area and production of vineyards and native wine made, together with capital invested in the industries, in the year 1889-90:

States.	Area in Bearing Vines.	Market Value of Grapes per Ton.	Wine Made.	Market Value of Wine per Gallon.	States.	Area in Bearing Vines.	Market Value of Grapes per Ton.	Wine Made.	Market Value of Wine per Gallon.
	Acres.	Dollars.	Gallons.	Dollars.		Acres.	Dollars.	Gallons.	Dollars.
Arizona..........	1,000	16.50	25,000	1.00	North-Carolina ..	4,000	60.00	388,833	1.00
California........	155,272	17.66	14,626,000	0.19	Ohio............	28,087	57.00	1,934,833	0.56
Georgia.........	1,938	96.00	107,666	1.15	Tennessee.......	1,500	89.00	208,333	1.00
Illinois..........	3,750	54.00	250,000	1.00	Virginia.........	4,100	60.00	461,000	1.00
Indiana..........	3,850	67.00	224,500	1.00	Other States and				
Kansas..........	4,542	58.00	130,990	0.80	Territories. ...	45,000	60.00	1,875,000	1.00
Missouri........	10,000	50.00	1,250,000	0.56					
New-Mexico....	1,186	45.00	296,500	0.86	Total..........	307,575	....	24,306,905	....
New-York.......	43,350	70.00	2,528,250	0.50					

Since the census statistics were collected, the vineyard and wine-producing industries have sprung up in Florida, and promise to become as valuable and important as those of any other State of the Union.
The number of persons employed in these industries in 1889-90 was 200,780.

Sugar Production.

MULHALL gives the following estimates of the production of cane and beet sugar in the world :

YEAR.	Cane.	Beet.	Total.	YEAR.	Cane.	Beet.	Total.
	Tons.	Tons.	Tons.		Tons.	Tons.	Tons.
1840	1,100,000	50,000	1,150,000	1870	1,830,000	900,000	2,730,000
1850	1,200,000	200,000	1,400,000	1880	1,860,000	1,810,000	3,670,000
1860	1,830,000	400,000	2,200,000	1889	2,580,000	2,780,000	5,360,000

Bouchereau's statement of cane sugar and molasses production in the United States in 1890-91 was as follows : Louisiana production, 495,000,000 pounds ; other Southern States, 13,680,000 pounds ; total production of the United States in tons of 2,240 pounds, 227,089. Molasses, production of Louisiana, 25,000,000 gallons ; other Southern States, 4,200,000 gallons ; total gallons, 29,200,000. The imports of cane and beet sugar into the United States in 1891 amounted to 1,696,000 tons.
Mulhall quotes the *Bulletin Statistique's* estimate of the production of beet sugar in the United States of 337,000 tons annually.

Dairy Production and Consumption.

MULHALL gives the following figures of approximate production and consumption of butter and cheese, presumably for 1890 :

COUNTRIES.	Production.	CONSUMPTION.			COUNTRIES.	Production.	CONSUMPTION.		
		Domestic.	Imported.	Lbs. per Inhab.			Domestic.	Imported.	Lbs. per Inhab.
	Tons.	Tons.	Tons.			Tons.	Tons.	Tons.	
Austria..........	130,000	130,000	.....	7	Norway	10,000	10,000	3,000	14
Australia........	30,000	30,000	.....	17	Portugal........	6,000	6,000	1,000	3
Belgium	30,000	30,000	10,000	15	Russia..........	220,000	210,000	.....	5
Canada.........	100,000	50,000	.....	22	Sweden.........	40,000	25,000	.....	11
Denmark.......	60,000	20,000	.....	22	Switzerland.....	40,000	15,000	.....	11
France.........	160,000	145,000	.....	8	Spain	30,000	30,000	.....	3
Germany	200,000	185,000	.....	8	Turkey*.........	40,000	40,000	.....	9
Great Britain....	110,000	110,000	218,000	19	United States....	610,000	500,000	.....	20
Italy...........	50,000	50,000	10,000	4					
Netherlands.....	80,000	30,000	.....	15	Total..........	1,946,000	1,676,000	242,000	11

* Includes Roumania and Servia.

Flax, Hay, Hemp, and Potatoes.
UNITED STATES PRODUCTION.

FLAX.		Hay.		Hemp.		Potatoes.	
Acres, bushels....	1,318,698	Acres..........	38,591,903	Acres..........	25,054	Acres..........	1,162,195
Seed, bushels....	10,250,410	Crop, tons	46,643,094	Crop, tons	11,511	Crop, bushels..	201,783,000
Fibre, lbs........	241,389	Value..........	$408,499,565	Value..........	$1,102,602	Value..........	$89,276,830
Value...........	$10,436,228						

The flax and hemp statistics were reported by the census for the year 1889, the hay and potatoes by the Department of Agriculture for 1888.

The American Hog.

HOGS PACKED AND MARKETED, YEAR ENDING MARCH 1, 1892.

Cities.	Number of Hogs.	Cities.	Number of Hogs.	Cities.	Number of Hogs.
Chicago..	5,249,798	St. Paul............	276,246	Other Places East.....	2,771,000
Kansas City	1,813,066	Cedar Rapids.........	429,056	New-York Receipts....	
Omaha..........	1,288,772	Cleveland...........	303,282	Philadelphia Receipts.	} 3,684,000
St. Louis..........	664,188	Louisville...........	161,365	Baltimore Receipts....	
Indianapolis.........	607,002	Ottumwa............	241,600		
Milwaukee...........	576,563	Nebraska City.	197,423		
Sioux City..........	255,068	St. Joseph....	155,000	Total Hogs Packed	
Cincinnati...........	484,173	Other Places West ...	1,755,012	and Marketed......	20,912,000

DISTRIBUTION OF HOG PRODUCTS EXPORTED FROM THE UNITED STATES.

Countries.	Bacon, Pounds.	Hams, Pounds.	Pork, Pounds.	Total Meats.	Lard, Pounds.	Aggregate, 1890-91.	Aggregate, 1889-90.	Aggregate, 1888-89.
Gt. Brit. & Ireland.	413,850,146	68,084,482	23,086,647	505,021,275	158,561,052	663,582,327	682,996,218	466,809,774
France.............	31,970	33,305	184,400	249,675	58,123,323	58,372,998	44,682,739	29,407,921
Germany	5,773,738	455,775	2,460,912	8,690,455	106,278,235	114,968,690	119,891,320	50,060,699
Belgium.........	38,933,339	7,367,498	162,842	46,463,679	49,132,982	95,596,661	86,118,933	47,525,295
Netherlands.....	11,736,255	527,671	227,100	12,491,026	26,681,523	39,172,549	23,311,535	4,037,634
Denmark.........	2,017,879	23,400	....	2,041,279	13,025,375	15,066,654	14,860,462	11,404,546
Sweden & Norway.	7,912,422	39,625	122,400	8,074,447	2,147,671	10,222,118	7,571,237	3,934,683
Spain............	5,761	2,923	....	8,684	377,630	386,314	433,054	638,693
Italy.............	....	....	....	....	2,441,110	2,441,110	2,529,754	3,819,746
Cuba.............	5,423,621	2,141,208	547,160	8,111,989	32,054,107	40,166,096	40,122,362	36,315,383
Hayti...........	5,414	330,317	15,008,771	15,344,502	2,557,708	17,902,210	14,945,671	10,523,682
Porto Rico.......	1,066,038	258,725	3,546,000	4,870,763	3,075,060	7,945,823	7,388,384	6,728,826
British West Indies	627,600	580,263	8,231,119	9,238,982	2,333,143	11,572,125	10,953,709	11,360,797
Mexico...........	56,034	285,101	4,268	345,403	1,611,313	1,956,716	1,973,108	1,663,234
Brazil............	9,995,871	13,328	71,525	10,080,724	15,511,709	25,592,433	23,832,078	5,868,309
Colombia.	7,979	97,119	189,623	294,721	1,208,546	1,503,267	1,513,070	2,301,944
Venezuela	30,198	714,271	63,750	808,219	6,163,012	6,971,231	6,398,274	5,610,220
British Guiana....	140,427	83,275	2,615,918	2,839,650	352,758	3,192,408	5,315,850	4,020,842
Peru....'........	8,342	18,556	6,000	32,898	1,526,935	1,559,833	3,910,397	1,144,741
Quebec, Ont.,* etc.	16,229,074	2,390,150	12,629,422	31,218,646	5,204,496	36,453,142	32,940,649	59,758,083
Nova Scotia, etc..	70,331	40,970	3,340,479	3,451,780	224,305	3,676,085	9,211,524	2,077,100
Newfoundland, etc.	5,806	68,140	3,358,455	3,432,401	33,440	3,465,841	2,173,036	3,208,186
All other.........	747,312	1,054,006	5,460,513	7,261,831	9,718,494	16,980,325	16,290,058	14,298,143
Year to June 30..	514,675,557	84,410,108	81,317,364	680,403,029	498,343,927	1,178,746 956	1,159,363,422	782,578,481
Value	$37,404,989	$8,245,685	$4,787,343	$50,438,017	$34,414,323	$84,852,340	$84,265,768	$66,714,435

*Includes Manitoba, Northwest Territories, and British Columbia.

The tables of statistics of hog products were compiled by the C.ncinnati *Price Current*.

The Department of Agriculture reported the following farm animals in the United States in 1891 : Horses, 14,056,750, value, $941,823,222 ; mules, 2,296,532, value, $178,847,370 ; milch cows, 16,019,591, value, $346,397,900 ; oxen and other cattle, 36,875,648, value, $544,127,908 ; sheep, 43,431,136, value, $108,397,447 ; swine, 50,625,106, value, $210,193,923. Total value of farm animals, $2,329,787,770.

Production of Tobacco.

STATEMENT OF PRODUCTION IN THE UNITED STATES IN THE YEAR ENDING JANUARY 1, 1889.* FROM THE REPORT OF THE SECRETARY OF AGRICULTURE.

States.	Pounds.	Acres.	Value.	States.	Pounds.	Acres.	Value.
Arkansas..........	1,156,000	2,408	$80,909	Ohio...........	35,195,000	39,105	$2,745,171
Connecticut.......	9,603,000	6,136	1,248,369	Pennsylvania......	24,180,000	19,500	2,587,260
Illinois...........	2,947,000	4,648	223,959	Tennessee........	45,641,000	67,119	3,651,274
Indiana............	16,153,000	18,252	1,130,711	Virginia..........	64,034,000	127,052	3,842,052
Kentucky..........	283,300,000	323,409	· 21,247,971	West-Virginia.....	4,496,000	5,620	359,680
Maryland..........	14,017,000	33,775	770,914	Wisconsin.........	12,846,000	13,813	1,220,379
Massachusetts.....	3,893,000	2,464	486,640	Other States and			
Missouri..........	13,109,000	14,126	1,048,714	Territories........	2,976,000	6,613	312,464
New-York	6,488,000	6,179	778,554				
North-Carolina....	25,755,000	57,107	1,931,644	Total........	565,795,000	747,326	$43,666,665

The number of cigarettes manufactured in the United States in 1890-91 was, according to the Internal Revenue returns, 2,877,799,440.

The product of tobacco in Europe is nearly equal in quantity to the average production of the United States. Neumann-Spallart has usually made it about 500,000,000 pounds. Austria-Hungary produces about one third of it, Russia one tenth, Germany nearly as much, France about 35,000,000 pounds, and the other countries a small quantity. Europe can easily produce all the tobacco required, but two reasons are prominent for importation of tobacco from this country. It is very cheap, and it is very desirable for mixing with and fortifying European leaf. If it becomes dearer, a smaller quantity is purchased : if very much dearer, it would scarcely find sale at all. The production is regulated and limited by governmental edicts. Our exportation is not increasing ; the proportion of our crop exported is declining, and will continue to fall off as our population increases. Much the larger portion was formerly exported ; now the larger part is annually manufactured. * These are the latest returns published by the department.

Statistics of Wool in the United States.

Year Ending June 30.	Production.	Imports.	Total Production and Imports.	Domestic Wool Exported.	Foreign Wool Exported.	Total Wool Exported.	Retained for Home Consumption.	Per cent. Imported.
	Pounds.	Pounds.	Pounds.	Pounds.	Pounds.	Pounds.	Pounds.	Per cent.
1870........	162,000,000	49,230,199	211,230,199	152,892	1,710,053	1,862,945	209,367,254	23.3
1880........	232,500,000	128,131,747	360,631,747	191,551	3,648,520	3,840,071	356,791,676	35.5
1881........	240,000,000	55,904,236	295,904,236	71,455	5,507,534	5,578,989	290,385,247	18.9
1882........	272,000,000	67,861,744	339,861,744	116,179	3,831,836	3,948,015	335,913,729	20.0
1883........	290,000,000	70,575,478	360,575,478	64,474	4,010,043	4,074,517	356,500,961	19.7
1884........	300,000,000	78,350,651	378,350,651	10,393	2,304,701	2,315,093	396,035,558	20.8
1885........	308,000,000	70,596,170	378,595,170	88,006	3,115,339	3,203,345	375,392,825	18.8
1886........	302,000,000	129,084,958	431,084,958	2,138,080	6,534,426	8,672,506	422,412,452	30.6
1887........	285,000,000	114,038,030	399,038,030	257,940	6,728,292	6,986,232	392,051,998	29.1
1888........	269,000,000	113,558,753	382,558,753	22,164	4,359,731	4,381,895	378,176,858	30.0
1889........	265,000,000	126,487,929	391,487,729	141,576	3,263,094	3,404,670	388,083,059	31.7
1890........	276,000,000	105,431,285	381,431,285	231,042	3,288,467	3,519,509	377,911,776	30.2
1891........	285,000,000	129,303,648	414,303,648	291,922	2,638,123	2,930,045	411,373,603	31.2

The above was prepared by the Bureau of Statistics of the Treasury Department.

The census report for 1890 gives the following statistics of wool manufacture in the United States in 1890: Number of manufacturing establishments, 2,770; capital employed, $320,417,304; miscellaneous expenses, $19,547,200; average number of hands employed, males, 99,318, females, 106,112, children, 15,657, total, 221,087; total amount paid in wages, $76,768,871; cost of materials used, $203,095,642; value of products, $338,231,109.

THE WORLD'S PRODUCTION OF WOOL.

Countries.	Pounds.	Countries.	Pounds.	Countries.	Pounds.
Europe:		North America :		Afghanistan, Beluchistan, and Thibet	
Russia............	291,500,000	United States........	307,100,000	(exports to India)..	12,200,000
Great Britain & Irel'd	147,475,000	British N. A. Prov...	12,000,000	Asiatic Turkey......	8,300,000
France............	124,803,000	South America :		Mesopotamia.......	31,555,000
Spain....	66,138,000	Argentine Republic		Persia (exports to India)..	
Germany..........	54,894,000	(exports 1885)	376,700,000	dia)..............	3,470,000
Hungary..........	43,146,000	Brazil..............	1,875,000	Africa :	
Italy	21,385,000	Peru...............	6,700,000	Cape Colony & Natal	
Austria	11,155,000	Uruguay(exports1884)	42,000,000	(exports 1885)	128,681,600
Portugal	10,362,000	Australasia.........	550,000,000	Egypt.............	2,800,000
Belgium..........	4,409,000	Asia :		All other countries....	48,000,000
Sweden	3,307,000	British East Indies			
All other Europe.....	8,818,000	(exports 1885–86)...	72,000,000	Total production...	2,456,773,600
		Russia..............	66,000,000		
Total Europe.....	762,589,000				

This data is for 1891 except where otherwise stated. The statistics of this and the following table are from "The Wool Book," published by the National Association of Wool Manufacturers.

THE WORLD'S WOOL SUPPLY SINCE 1870.

The figures prior to 1891 are the estimates of the London Board of Trade.

Countries.	1870.	1880.	1891.	Countries.	1870.	1880.	1891.
	Pounds.	Pounds.	Pounds.		Pounds.	Pounds.	Pounds.
United Kingdom....	150,000,000	149,000,000	147,475,000	River Plate........	197,000,000	256,000,000	376,700,000
Cont. of Europe....	485,000,000	450,000,000	639,917,000	Other Countries....	69,000,000	133,000,000	294,900,000
North America	176,000,000	270,000,000	319,100,000				
Australasia........	175,000,000	308,000,000	550,000,000	G. Totals........	1,295,000,000	1,626,000,000	2,456,773,600
C. of Good Hope...	43,000,000	60,000,000	128,681,600				

SHEEP IN THE UNITED STATES IN 1891.

States:	Number.	States.	Number.	States:	Number.
Maine..............	547,670	Alabama............	274,788	Kansas.............	447,079
New-Hampshire.	183,183	Mississippi........	235,345	Nebraska...........	234,612
Vermont...........	351,249	Louisiana..........	113,931	California..........	3,712,310
Massachusetts.....	55,905	Texas..............	4,990,722	Oregon	2,431,759
Rhode-Island......	20,433	Arkansas...........	269,484	Nevada............	504,710
Connecticut.......	45,824	Tennessee.........	511,118	Colorado...........	1,819,569
New-York..........	1,393,583	West-Virginia......	518,827	Arizona...........	593,643
New-Jersey........	100,075	Kentucky..........	764,679	Dakota............	274,519
Pennsylvania......	1,039,505	Ohio..............	4,061,897	Idaho.............	501,978
Delaware..........	22,517	Michigan..........	2,263,240	Utah..............	2,089,337
Maryland..........	156,838	Indiana............	1,150,200	New-Mexico........	3,123,663
Virginia...........	444,563	Illinois............	770,993	Utah..............	2,055,900
North-Carolina....	398,226	Wisconsin.........	889,910	Washington........	673,060
South-Carolina....	98,970	Minnesota.........	330,649	Wyoming..........	1,119,110
Georgia...........	383,017	Iowa..............	452,025		
Florida............	111,455	Missouri...........	898,650	Total............	43,431,136

Record of Events in 1892.

Jan. 7. The Khedive of Egypt died.

Jan. 14. The Duke of Clarence, elder son of the Prince of Wales, died at Sandringham.

Jan. 14. Cardinal Manning died.

Jan. 25. Alice Mitchell, a Memphis young lady, murdered her friend, Freda Ward, in the streets of that city. She was tried, and pronounced insane July 30.

Jan. 25. Chile withdrew the offensive note by Minister Matta to the United States, and apologized for the Valparaiso riots.

Jan. 31. Spurgeon, the pulpit orator, died.

Feb. 1. The United States Supreme Court decided that James E. Boyd, Dem., was legally governor of Nebraska.

Feb. 2. Carlyle W. Harris was convicted in New-York of murdering his wife by poison. **Feb. 8,** he was sentenced to death.

Feb. 7. The Hotel Royal, New-York, was burned, with great loss of life.

Feb. 8 William H. Beers resigned the presidency of the New-York Life Insurance Company, and was succeeded by John A. McCall.

Feb. 14. Rev. Dr. Parkhurst denounced the New-York City officials as a "damnable pack of administrative blood-hounds."

Feb. 18. Edward P. Deacon, an American, shot and killed his wife's lover, M. Abeille, at Cannes, France.

Feb. 18. The French ministry were defeated on a religious question and resigned. M. Loubet formed a new ministry, Feb. 27.

Feb. 18. Lieut. Hetherington, U. S. N., killed a too persistent admirer of his wife, at Yokohama, Japan.

March 1. The United States Supreme Court affirmed the constitutionality of the McKinley Tariff act.

March 2. Ministerial crisis in Greece.

March 17. Tennyson's play of "The Foresters" was produced for the first time ; Daly's Theatre, New-York, being the place.

March 23. The Bar Association of New-York recommended the removal of Justice Maynard from the New-York Court of Appeals.

March 26. Extradition treaty between France and the United States was signed at Paris.

March 29. The Senate ratified the Behring Sea arbitration treaty without opposition.

April 12. A fire at Tokio, Japan, destroyed 6,000 houses.

April 12. The United States Government paid $25,000 indemnity to the families of the Italian subjects lynched at New-Orleans.

April 21. The United States invited other nations to a monetary conference.

April 19-24. Earthquake scares in California.

April 25. Cafe Very, Paris, was destroyed by dynamite.

April 27. William Astor died in Paris.

April 27. Corner-stone of the Grant Monument in New-York was laid by President Harrison.

April 28. The Grand Central Theatre, Philadelphia, was burned, with 12 lives lost.

April 29. Hurricane at Mauritius destroyed 1,000 lives.

April 30. Ferdinand Ward's term at Sing Sing Prison expired.

May 1. Conference of the Methodist Episcopal Church opened at Omaha.

May 2. Deeming, the wholesale murderer, was convicted at Melbourne, Australia. He was executed May 23.

May 2. The Actors' Fund Fair was opened in Madison Square Garden, New-York.

May 5. The Rudini ministry in Italy resigned.

May 12. Bridge across the Mississippi River at Memphis was opened with ceremonies.

May 13. An American steamer laden with grain for the starving Russians arrived at Riga.

May 18. A flood at Sioux City, Ia., caused great damage.

May 23. The golden wedding of the Danish king and queen was celebrated.

May 27. A mass-meeting at Cooper Union, New-York, endorsed Rev Dr. Parkhurst's crusade against vice.

May 27. A cyclone destroyed two towns in Kansas ; 31 persons were killed.

May 31. The Briggs heresy case was remanded by the Presbyterian General Assembly, at Portland, Ore., to the New-York Presbytery for trial.

June 4. Alden Fales, sixteen years old, was convicted of the murder of Thomas Haydon, at Newark, N. J.

June 28. The Twelfth Parliament of Victoria was dissolved. Elections for the new Parliament began.

June 28. The battleship Texas was launched at Norfolk, Va.

July 1. Inman steamer City of Chicago was wrecked on the Irish coast, near Cork.

July 6. A conflict between strikers at Homestead, Pa., and Pinkerton men resulted in 10 killed and many wounded.

July 9 Gov. Pattison of Pennsylvania ordered the State troops to Homestead to preserve order.

July 9. St. John's, Newfoundland, was nearly destroyed by fire.

July 9. The New-York Society of the Sons of the Revolution celebrated the reading of the Declaration of Independence, at White Plains, N. Y.

July 11. A false report of the death of William Waldorf Astor was cabled from London.

July 11. Ravachol, the anarchist and dynamiter, was guillotined at Paris.

July 11. There were bloody riots between union and non-union miners at Cœur d'Alene mines, Idaho.

July 12. An avalanche from Mount Blanc destroyed villages and 200 lives.

July 12. Cyrus W. Field died at New-York.

July 13. The Stewart Free Silver Coinage bill was defeated in the House of Representatives by 154 to 136.

July 23. Rev. Dr. Talmage visited the Czar.

July 23. H. C. Frick, manager of the Carnegie Steel Works, at Homestead, Pa., was shot by Berkman, an anarchist.

July 23. W K. Vanderbilt's yacht Alva was wrecked by collision on Nantucket shoals.

July 31. The Christopher Columbus celebrations began at Cadiz, Spain.

Aug. 1. The Honduras revolution ended.

Aug. 1. The German Emperor visited England.

RECORD OF EVENTS IN 1892—*Continued*.

Aug. 4. The new British Parliament was opened.

Aug. 4. Andrew J. Borden and his wife were murdered at Fall River, Mass. Their daughter, Lizzie Borden, was arrested on suspicion, Aug. 11.

Aug. 4. Lieut. Peary, Arctic explorer, and party arrived on their return, at McCormack Harbor.

Aug. 5. Congress appropriated $2,500,000 to be coined into memorial half dollars, in aid of the World's Columbian Fair at Chicago.

Aug. 11. A vote of "no confidence" in the Conservative ministry was carried in the House of Commons, 350 to 310.

Aug. 12. The Conservative ministry in Great Britain resigned. Mr. Gladstone formed a Liberal ministry.

Aug. 12. Switchmen's strike began at Buffalo, N. Y. Gov. Flower ordered the State troops there. The strike was a failure, declared off Aug. 24.

Aug. 15-30. Riotous miners at Coal Creek, Tenn., had conflicts with the Tennessee State troops.

Aug. 17. Nancy Hanks, at Chicago, lowered the trotting record to 2.07¾.

Aug. 20. President Harrison issued a proclamation retaliatory upon Canada, by establishing tolls on Sault Ste. Marie Canal.

Aug. 23. Gloucester, Mass., celebrated the 250th anniversary of its settlement.

Aug. 27. The Metropolitan Opera House, New-York, was almost wholly burned.

Sept 1. Lizzie Borden, at Fall River, Mass., was committed for the murder of her parents.

Sept. 1. To shut out the cholera, the United States Government proclaimed 20 days' quarantine for all European vessels.

Sept. 7. John L. Sullivan was knocked out by Corbett, in 21 rounds, at New-Orleans.

Sept. 13. A death from cholera occurred in New-York. The city was declared free of cholera after Sept. 19.

Sept. 13. Railroad from Joppa to Jerusalem was completed.

Sept. 19. Berkman, the anarchist assailant of H. C. Frick, was sentenced at Pittsburgh to 22 years' imprisonment.

Sept. 19, 20. Encampment of the Grand Army of the Republic at Washington. On the latter day there was a parade of 75,000 veterans.

Sept. 20. The Italian people celebrated the twenty-first anniversary of the unification of Italy.

Sept. 22. The centennial of the birth of the first republic was celebrated in France.

Sept. 29. Stuart Knill, a Roman Catholic, was elected Lord Mayor of London.

Oct. 1-6. German and Austrian army officers raced between Berlin and Vienna.

Oct. 2. At the school election at Faribault, Minn., Archbishop Ireland's plan of education in the public schools was voted down.

Oct. 5. The Dalton gang of robbers was nearly exterminated in a battle at Coffeyville, Kan.

Oct. 5. The triennial convention of the Protestant Episcopal Church began at Baltimore.

Oct. 5. The Venezuelan revolution triumphed in a battle won by Gen. Crespo.

Oct. 6. Tennyson died. He was buried in Westminster Abbey Oct. 12.

Oct. 10. Columbian celebrations at Huelva Spain.

Oct. 9-15. The discovery of America by Columbus was commemorated by a series of celebrations in New York, the military pageant occurring Oct. 12.

Oct. 11. The German and Austrian emperors had a fraternal conference at Vienna.

Oct. 17. The United States Supreme Court decided that the Michigan plan of choosing Presidential electors by Congressional districts was constitutional.

Oct. 20-23. There were magnificent ceremonies dedicatory of the Columbian World's Fair at Chicago. In Brooklyn, N. Y., there were extensive ceremonies.

Oct. 25. Mrs. Harrison, wife of the President, died at the White House.

Oct. 28. A great fire at Milwaukee burned over 26 acres. Loss, $5,000,000.

Oct. 28. Steamship Roumania, of the Anchor Line, was wrecked on the coast of Portugal, with a loss of over 100 lives.

Oct. 31. The Norfolk and Western Railroad was opened for traffic to Portsmouth, O.

Oct. 31. Celebrations in honor of Luther, at Wittenberg.

Nov. 8. Dynamite explosions caused by anarchists in Paris.

Nov. 11. Professor J. G. Schurman was installed as President of Cornell University.

Nov. 19. Conference of Roman Catholic Archbishops in New-York City.

Nov. 20. The Amalgamated Association declared the strike at Homestead at an end.

Nov. 22. The International Monetary Conference met in Brussels. It suspended its sessions Dec. 17, until May 13, 1893.

Nov. 25. Sir John Thompson succeeded Sir John Abbott as Canadian prime-minister, and chose a new ministry.

Nov. 25. The investigation of the Panama Canal scandal in France began.

Nov. 28. The Loubet ministry in France resigned on the Panama scandal issue. The Ribot ministry succeeded Dec. 5.

Dec. 2. Jay Gould died.

Dec. 2. Lizzie Borden was indicted at Fall River for the murder of her parents.

Dec. 8, 9. Police Superintendent Byrnes, of New-York, and Rev. Dr. Parkhurst published sharp reflections on each other.

Dec. 13. The Cincinnati Presbytery suspended Prof. Henry P. Smith, of Lane Theological Seminary, for heresy, 31 to 27.

Dec. 16. Charles de Lesseps was arrested for complicity in the Panama Canal frauds.

Dec. 23. Rev. Dr. McGlynn was restored to his priestly functions by the Papal delegate, Mgr. Satolli.

Dec. 23. Clemencean and Deroulede, the French political leaders, fought a bloodless duel.

Dec. 27. The corner-stone of the Protestant Episcopal Cathedral of St. John the Divine, in New-York, was laid.

Dec. 30. The New-York Presbytery dismissed the charges of heresy against Prof. Briggs, by majorities ranging from 7 to 21.

Public Debt of the United States.

OFFICIAL STATEMENT OF DECEMBER 1, 1892.

INTEREST-BEARING DEBT.

Funded loan of 1891...................... $25,364,500.00
Funded loan of 1907...................... 559,592,050.00
Refunding certificates 76,430.00

Aggregate of interest-bearing debt,
exclusive of United States bonds
issued to Pacific railroads......... $585,032,980.00

DEBT ON WHICH INTEREST HAS CEASED SINCE MATURITY.

Aggregate of debt on which interest has
ceased since maturity................. $2,432,015.26

DEBT BEARING NO INTEREST.

Legal-tender notes...................... $346,681,016.00
Old demand notes....................... 55,647.50
National bank notes:
Redemption account.................. 24,137,678.25
Fractional currency:
Less $8,375,934 estimated as lost or
destroyed, act of June 21, 1879.... 6,903,462.62

Aggregate of debt bearing no interest $377,777,804.37

CERTIFICATES AND NOTES ISSUED ON DEPOSITS OF COIN AND LEGAL-TENDER NOTES AND PURCHASES OF SILVER BULLION.

Gold certificates...................... $142,821,639.00
Silver certificates.................... 326,251,304.00
Currency certificates................. 8,500,000.00
Treasury notes of 1890 .... 120,796,713.00

Aggregate of certificates and Treasury notes, offset by cash in the
Treasury............................ $598,369,656.00

CLASSIFICATION OF DEBT DECEMBER 1, 1892.

Interest-bearing debt................... $585,032,980.00
Debt on which interest has ceased since
maturity................................. 2,432,015.26
Debt bearing no interest................. 377,777,804.37

Aggregate of interest and non-in-
terest bearing debt.................. $965,242,709.63
Certificates and Treasury notes offset by
an equal amount of cash in the Trea-
sury..................................... 598,369,656.00
Aggregate of debt, including certifi-
cates and Treasury notes........ $1,563,612,455.63

CASH IN THE TREASURY.

Gold certificates....................$142,821,639.00
Silver certificates........ 326,251,304.00
Currency certificates.... 8,500,000.00
Treasury notes of 1890... 120,796,713.00

                                    $598,369,656.00
Fund for redemption of
uncurrent National bank
notes............................ $5,855,215.24
Outstanding checks and
drafts 4,822,165.98
Disbursing officers' bal-
ances............................ 22,786,939.77
Agency accounts, etc 3,281,906.86

                                      36,776,227.85
Gold re-
serve... $100,000,000.00
Net cash
balance. 30,328,918.50

                                     130,328,918.50

Total.................................. $765,474,802.35
Cash balance in the Treasury, Novem-
ber 30, 1891........................... $130,328,918.50

Principal of the Public Debt.

Statement of outstanding Principal of the Public Debt of the United States on January 1 of each Year from 1791 to 1842, inclusive; and on July 1 of each Year from 1843 to 1886, inclusive; and on December 1 of each Year from 1887 to 1892, inclusive.

1791 Jan. 1	$75,463,476.52	1825 Jan. 1	$83,788,432.71	1859 July 1	$58,496,837.88
1792 "	77,217,924.66	1826 "	81,054,059.99	1860 "	64,842,287.88
1793 "	80,352,634.04	1827 "	73,987,357.20	1861 "	90,580,873.72
1794 "	78,427,404.77	1828 "	67,475,043.87	1862 "	524,176,412.13
1795 "	80,747,587.39	1829 "	58,421,413.67	1863 "	1,119,772,138.63
1796 "	83,762,172.07	1830 "	48,565,406.50	1864 "	1,815,784,370.57
1797 "	82,064,479.33	1831 "	39,123,191.68	1865 "	2,680,647,869.74
1798 "	79,228,529.12	1832 "	24,322,235.18	1866 "	2,773,236,173.69
1799 "	78,408,669.77	1833 "	7,001,698.83	1867 "	2,678,126,103.87
1800 "	82,976,294.35	1834 "	4,760,082.08	1868 "	2,611,687,851.19
1801 "	83,038,050.80	1835 "	37,513.05	1869 "	2,588,452,213.94
1802 "	86,712,632.25	1836 "	336,957.83	1870 "	2,480,672,427.81
1803 "	77,054,686.30	1837 "	3,308,124.07	1871 "	2,353,211,332.32
1804 "	86,427,120.88	1838 "	10,434,221.14	1872 "	2,253,251,328.78
1805 "	82,312,150.50	1839 "	3,573,343.82	1873 "	2,234,482,993.20
1806 "	75,723,270.66	1840 "	5,250,875.54	1874 "	2,251,690,468.43
1807 "	69,218,398.64	1841 "	13,594,480.73	1875 "	2,232,284,531.95
1808 "	65,196,317.97	1842 "	20,601,226.28	1876 "	2,180,395,067.15
1809 "	57,023,192.00	1843 July 1	32,742,922.00	1877 "	2,205,301,392.10
1810 "	53,173,217.52	1844 "	23,461,652.50	1878 "	2,256,205,892.53
1811 "	48,005,587.76	1845 "	15,925,303.01	1879 "	2,349,567,232.04
1812 "	45,209,737.90	1846 "	15,550,202.97	1880 "	2,128,791,054.63
1813 "	55,962,827.57	1847 "	38,826,534.77	1881 "	2,077,389,253.58
1814 "	81,487,846.24	1848 "	47,044,862.23	1882 "	1,926,688,678.03
1815 "	99,833,660.15	1849 "	63,061,858.69	1883 "	1,892,547,412.07
1816 "	127,334,933.74	1850 "	63,452,773.55	1884 "	1,838,904,607.57
1817 "	123,491,965.16	1851 "	68,304,796.02	1885 "	1,872,340,557.14
1818 "	103,466,633.83	1852 "	66,199,341.71	1886 "	1,783,438,607.78
1819 "	95,529,648.28	1853 "	59,803,117.70	Dec. 1	1,664,461,536.38
1820 "	91,015,566.15	1854 "	42,242,222.42	1888 "	1,680,917,706.23
1821 "	89,987,427.66	1855 "	35,586,858.56	1889 "	1,617,372,419.53
1822 "	93,546,676.98	1856 "	31,972,537.90	1890 "	1,549,296,126.48
1823 "	90,875,877.28	1857 "	28,699,831.85	1891 "	1,546,961,695.61
1824 "	90,269,777.77	1858 "	44,911,881.03	1892 "	1,563,612,455.63

Indebtedness of the States and Territories in 1890.

COMPILED FROM THE ELEVENTH UNITED STATES CENSUS.

GEOGRAPHICAL DIVISIONS.	TOTAL COMBINED DEBT LESS SINKING FUND	PER CAPITA OF COMBINED DEBT.		STATE DEBT.	COUNTY DEBT.	MUNICIPAL DEBT.	SCHOOL DISTRICT DEBT.
	1890.	1890.	1880.	1890.	1890.	1890.	1890.
North Atlantic............	$467,968,615	$26.89	$37.28	$25,140,357	$27,585,070	$405,572,083	$9,671,105
Maine....................	$15,600,777	$23.60	$35.81	$3,470,908	$434,346	$11,695,523	....
New-Hampshire..........	8,148,362	21.64	31.10	2,691,019	556,987	4,718,025	$182,331
Vermont.................	3,785,373	11.39	13.54	148,416	5,108	3,529,014	102,835
Massachusetts...........	81,550,027	36.42	51.55	7,267,349	4,051,830	70,230,848	....
Rhode-Island............	13,042,117	37.75	46.91	422,983	....	12,499,254	119,880
Connecticut.............	23,703,478	31.76	35.33	3,740,200	30,547	18,322,371	1,610,360
New-York................	201,763,217	33.61	43.06	2,308,230	10,936,638	187,348,163	1,170,186
New-Jersey..............	49,333,589	34.14	43.66	1,022,642	3,728,130	42,990,338	1,592,479
Pennsylvania............	71,041,675	13.51	25.03	4,068,610	7,841,484	54,238,547	4,893,034
South Atlantic............	165,107,113	18.64	22.10	89,652,873	7,825,561	67,610,380	18,299
Delaware................	$2,919,084	$17.32	$16.17	$887,573	618,400	1,413,111	....
Maryland................	42,175,408	40.46	44.31	8,434,368	893,776	32,847,264	....
District of Columbia......	19,781,050	85.86	126.66	19,781,050	....	....	....
Virginia.................	50,837,315	30.70	30.09	34,227,234	1,774,535	14,835,546	....
West-Virginia...........	2,532,460	3.32	2.65	184,511	1,197,462	1,132,188	$18,299
North-Carolina..........	11,117,445	6.87	12.83	7,703,100	1,514,600	1,899,745	....
South-Carolina..........	13,295,037	11.55	14.25	6,953,582	1,062,750	5,279,305	....
Georgia.................	20,272,095	11.03	12.74	10,449,542	429,380	9,393,173	....
Florida.................	2,176,619	5.56	9.89	1,031,913	334,658	810,048	....
North Central............	320,238,281	14.32	14.17	41,656,112	69,110,453	184,219,923	25,251,793
Ohio....................	$71,065,386	$19.35	$16.59	$7,135,806	$7,797,005	52,888,263	$3,244,312
Indiana.................	24,442,031	11.15	9.28	8,538,059	6,406,239	9,498,333	....
Illinois.................	41,841,619	10.94	15.07	1,184,907	11,016,350	26,456,905	3,183,397
Michigan................	16,941,928	8.09	7.36	5,308,294	1,529,681	8,510,439	1,865,497
Wisconsin...............	10,440,580	6.19	9.19	2,295,391	3,317,657	18,427,368	311,903
Minnesota...............	26,050,929	20.01	14.51	2 239,482	3,416,889	6,391,772	2,066,422
Iowa....................	11,275,319	5.90	5.01	11,759,832	10,240,082	28,092,193	1,221,223
Missouri................	51,557,568	19.24	2.57	769,769	3,728,261	711,665	1,465,551
North-Dakota............	3,842,790	21.03	3.5	703,709	1,372,261	711,665	1,055,095
South-Dakota............	6,613,707	20.11	8.82	871,600	2,441,334	1,197,520	2,103,253
Nebraska................	15,536,772	14.67	16.56	253,879	5,510,175	7,124,506	2,648,212
Kansas..................	40,629,022	28.47	15.97	1,119,658	14,805,052	18,617,384	6,086,928
South Central............	138,255,311	12.60	16.14	66,281,194	19,177,151	52,576,623	220,343
Kentucky................	$19,432,885	$10.46	$9.09	$1,671,133	$5,712,463	$11,880,417	$168,872
Tennessee...............	29,543,843	16.71	26.42	19,695,974	2,172,059	7,675,810	....
Alabama.................	18,930,867	12.51	14.26	12,413,196	1,433,321	5,084,350	....
Mississippi..............	6,011,347	4.66	4.38	3,503,009	1,230,299	1,278,039	....
Louisiana...............	33,335,497	29.80	45.60	16,008,585	177,798	17,149,114	....
Texas...................	20,172,063	9.02	7.34	4,317,515	6,891,714	8,928,852	33,982
Oklahoma...............	....	....	....	....	....	....	....
Arkansas................	10,828,809	9.60	13.37	8,671,782	1,559,497	580,041	17,489
Western.................	43,641,122	14.41	13.85	6,266,853	21,349,810	14,484,051	1,540,408
Montana.................	$2,918,893	$22.09	$19.54	$167,815	$2,004,513	614,519	$132,046
Wyoming................	1,647,381	27.14	9.88	320,000	1,083,790	243,591	....
Colorado................	8,411,027	20.41	18.67	599,851	4,601,588	2,955,962	253,626
New-Mexico.............	2,831,538	18.44	0.71	870,000	1,815,083	127,085	19,370
Arizona.................	2,937,971	49.28	9.33	757,159	1,954,414	200,165	26,233
Utah....................	767,501	3.69	0.81	....	49,859	717,642	....
Nevada..................	1,337,501	29.23	22.48	509,525	812,676	....	15,300
Idaho...................	1,594,333	18.89	7.05	218,493	1,234,987	29,211	111,642
Washington..............	3,145,658	9.00	3.19	300,000	1,507,786	1,046,510	291,362
Oregon.................	2,479,860	7.90	4.86	1,685	905,711	1,386,444	186,020
California...............	15,569,459	12.89	19.18	2,522,325	5,379,403	7,162,922	504,809
Total....................	$1,135,210,442	$18.13	$22.40	$228,997,389	$145,048,045	$724,463,060	$36,701,948

THE CARPET-BAG DEBTS OF THE SOUTHERN STATES.

The "carpet-bag" debts of the Southern States, under which some of them are still suffering, were created during the reconstruction period, when the South was at the mercy of adventurers from the North and the ranks of the negro population supported and protected by the Federal Government. These burdens on the helpless people aggregated in 1871 some $291,626,015, distributed among the reconstructed States as follows: Alabama, $52,761,917; Arkansas, $19,398,000; Florida, $15,797,587; Georgia, $42,560,500; Louisiana, $40,021,734; North-Carolina, $34,887,464; South-Carolina, $22,480,516; Texas, $14,930,000; Virginia, $47,090,866. It must be borne in mind that the debts of the Southern States contracted from 1861 to 1865 were repudiated by order of the Federal Government, so that the indebtedness above shown was due almost wholly to "carpet-bag" financiering.

Foreign Trade of the United States.

(Prepared for THE WORLD ALMANAC by the Bureau of Statistics of the Treasury Department.)

EXPORTS.

DOMESTIC MERCHANDISE AND SPECIE EXPORTED FROM THE UNITED STATES DURING THE FISCAL YEAR ENDED JUNE 30, 1892.

Articles.	Quantities.	Values.
Merchandise.		
Agricultural Implements......		$3,794,983
Animals....		36,498,221
Books. Maps, Engravings, and other Printed Matter......		1,943,228
Breadstuffs: Corn....bush.	75,451,849	41,590,460
" Wheat....bush.	157,280,351	161,399,132
" Wheat Flour bbls	15,196,769	75,362,283
" All other...		21,011,242
Carriages, Horse, and R. R. Cars......		3,264,435
Chemicals, Drugs, Dyes, and Medicines....		6,693,855
Clocks and Watches....		1,229,616
Coal: Anthracite....tons.	808,277	3,419,660
" Bituminous....tons.	1,700,496	5,229,498
Copper Ore....tons.	42,984	6,036,777
" Manufactures of....		7,226,392
Cotton, Unmanufactured..lbs.	2,935,219,811	258,461,241
" Manufactures of....		13,226,277
Fish...		4,522,763
Flax, Hemp, and Jute, Manufactures of....		1,998,663
Fruits, Apples, Green or Ripe. bbls.	938,743	2,407,956
Fruits and Nuts....		4,218,189
Furs and Fur Skins....		3,586,339
Hops....lbs.	12,604,686	2,420,502
Instruments for Scientific Purposes...		1,388,117
Iron and Steel, Manufactures of....		28,800,930
Leather, and Manufactures of.		12,084,781
Musical Instruments....		1,164,656

Articles.	Quantities.	Values.
Merchandise.		
Naval Stores....		$7,989,933
Oil Cake, Oil Cake Meal....lbs.	826,398,719	9,713,204
Oils: Animal....galls.	2,156,357	978,688
" Mineral, Crude....galls.	103,592,767	5,101,840
" Mineral, Refined or Manufactured....galls.		39,704,152
Oils, Vegetable....		5,334,955
Paper, and Manufactures of...		1,382,251
Paraffine, Paraffine Wax ..lbs.	64,998,867	3,965,263
Provisions, Beef Products....	468,521,159	34,436,169
" Hog Products·....	1,125,536,392	85,116,566
" Oleomargarine....	93,192,540	9,207,476
" Other Meat Products....		1,243,055
" Dairy Products...		10,358,893
Seeds: Clover....lbs.	19,532,411	1,696,671
" All other....		4,615,611
Spirits ....proof galls.	3,350,797	2,401,117
Sugar, Molasses, Syrup .galls.	9,343,214	1,057,216
" Refined....lbs.	14,604,608	665,477
Tobacco, Unmanufactured.lbs.	255,432,077	20,670,045
" Manufactures of.....		4,009,980
Vegetables....		1,808,145
Wood, and Manufactures of....		25,788,907
All other Articles....		29,416,741
Total Exports, Domestic Merchandise........ ...		1,015,732,011
Specie: Gold....		$43,321,351
" Silver....		16,765,067
Total Domestic Exports...		1,075,818,429

IMPORTS.

MERCHANDISE AND SPECIE IMPORTED INTO THE UNITED STATES DURING THE FISCAL YEAR ENDED JUNE 30, 1892.

Articles	Quantities.	Values.
Merchandise.		
Animals....		$4,251,616
Art Works....		2,336,668
Books, Maps, etc....		3,996,085
Bristles....lbs.	1,495,003	1,455,058
Breadstuffs....		4,031,408
Chemicals, Drugs, Dyes, and Medicines....		45,961,639
Clocks and Watches....		1,930,538
Coal, Bituminous....tons.	1,331,964	4,373,079
Coffee....lbs.	640,210,788	128,041,930
Cotton, Manufactures of....		28,323,841
Earthenware and China....		8,705,598
Fish....		4,585,450
Flax, Hemp, Jute, etc., and Manufactures of....		26,293,217
Fruits and Nuts....		20,943,906
Furs, and Manufactures of...		10,197,131
Glass and Glassware....		8,758,964
Hats and Bonnets....		1,897,190
Hides and Skins....		26,850,218
Hops....lbs.	2,506,224	885,701
India Rubber, and Manufactures of....		20,265,946
Iron and Steel, and Manufactures of.		31,520,564
Jewelry, and Manufactures of, Gold and Silver....		618,518
Lead, and Manufactures of....		3,653,378
Leather, and Manufactures of.		13,300,321

Articles.	Quantities.	Values.
Merchandise.		
Liquors, Spirituous and Malt..		4,660,455
Molasses....galls.	22,448,209	2,877,744
Musical Instruments....		1,031,485
Paints and Colors....		1,372,052
Paper, and Manufactures....		3,342,304
Paper Stock....		5,448,263
Precious Stones,and Imitations of, not set, including Diamonds, Rough or Uncut....		13,451,007
Salt....lbs.	470,151,826	713,901
Seeds....		2,264,837
Silk, Manufactures of....		31,172,894
" Unmanufactured....	8,834,049	25,059,325
Sugar ....lbs.	3,556,509,105	104,408,813
Tea....lbs.	90,079,039	14,372,222
Tin....lbs.	43,908,652	8,667,870
Tobacco, and Manufactures of.		13,258,474
Wines....		8,944,503
Wood, and Manufactures of....		19,846,438
Wool, and Manufactures of....		55,253,987
All other Articles....		107,375,924
Total Merchandise....		$827,402,462
Specie: Gold....		$49,699,454
" Silver....		19,955,086
Total Imports....		$897,057,002

FOREIGN TRADE OF THE UNITED STATES—Continued.
VALUE OF IMPORTS AND EXPORTS OF MERCHANDISE, 1873–92.

Year Ending June 30.	Exports. Domestic.	Exports. Foreign.	Total Exports.	Imports.	Total Exports and Imports.	Excess of Exports.	Excess of Imports.
1873....	$505,033,439	$17,446,483	$522,479,922	$642,136,210	$1,104,610,132	....	$119,656
1874....	569,433,421	16,849,619	586,283,040	567,406,342	1,153,689,352	$18,876,698	....
1875....	499,284,100	14,158,611	513,442,711	533,005,436	1,046,448,147	....	19,562,725
1876....	525,582,247	14,802,424	540,384,671	460,741,190	1,001,125,861	79,643,481	....
1877....	589,670,224	12,804,996	602,475,220	451,323,126	1,053,798,346	151,152,094	....
1878....	680,709,268	14,156,498	694,865,766	437,051,532	1,131,917,298	257,814,234	....
1879....	698,340,790	12,098,651	710,439,441	445,777,775	1,156,217,216	264,661,666	....
1880....	823,946,353	11,692,305	835,938,658	667,954,746	1,503,593,404	167,683,912	....
1881....	883,925,947	18,451,399	902,377,346	642,664,628	1,545,041,974	259,712,718	....
1882....	733,239,732	17,302,525	750,542,257	724,639,574	1,475,181,831	25,902,683	....
1883....	804,223,632	19,615,770	823,839,402	723,180,914	1,547,020,316	100,658,488	....
1884....	724,964,852	15,548,757	740,513,609	667,697,693	1,408,211,302	72,815,916	....
1885....	726,682,946	15,506,809	742,189,755	577,527,329	1,319,717,084	164,662,426	....
1886....	665,964,529	13,560,301	679,524,830	635,436,136	1,314,960,966	44,088,694	....
1887....	703,022,923	13,160,288	716,183,211	692,319,768	1,408,502,979	23,863,443	....
1888....	683,862,104	12,118,766	695,954,507	723,957,114	1,419,911,621	....	28,002,607
1889....	730,282,609	12,118,766	742,401,375	745,131,652	1,487,533,027	....	2,730,277
1890....	845,293,828	12,534,856	857,828,684	789,310,409	1,647,139,093	68,518,275	....
1891....	872,270,283	12,210,527	884,480,810	844,916,196	1,729,397,006	39,564,614	....
1892....	1,015,732,011	14,546,137	1,030,278,148	827,402,462	1,857,680,610	202,875,686	....

The imports and exports of specie are not included in the above table.

VALUE OF UNITED STATES EXPORTS OF MERCHANDISE TO AND IMPORTS OF MERCHANDISE FROM PRINCIPAL FOREIGN COUNTRIES, YEAR ENDING JUNE 30, 1892.

Countries.	Exports. Domestic.	Exports. Foreign.	Imports.	Countries.	Exports. Domestic.	Exports. Foreign.	Imports.
Argentine Rep...	$2,643,325	$284,163	$5,343,798	Hawaiian Islands	$3,662,018	$119,610	$8,075,882
Australasia, Brit.	11,246,474	140,203	8,492,306	Haïti..........	4,963,430	319,453	3,202,729
Austria-Hungary	1,485,233	42,747	7,718,565	Hong Kong.....	4,887,350	6,699	763,323
Belgium.........	47,713,121	1,071,906	10,273,061	Italy..........	14,223,947	93,835	22,161,617
Brazil..........	14,240,009	51,864	118,633,604	Japan..........	3,288,282	1,829	23,790,202
British E. Indies	3,674,141	166	24,773,107	Mexico.........	13,696,531	597,468	28,107,525
British W. Indies	7,995,185	135,072	12,440,132	Netherlands....	43,556,865	361,119	10,886,802
Canada, Dom. of	41,006,120	2,293,667	34,954,203	Peru..........	1,002,977	4,058	591,300
Centr'l Am.States	5,872,029	250,017	10,219,788	Puerto Rico...	2,808,631	47,372	3,248,007
Chile..........	3,533,342	11,365	3,487,159	Portugal.......	4,081,453	9,595	1,966,369
China..........	5,663,471	26	20,458,291	Russia & Posses.	6,812,779	35,262	5,246,797
Colombia.......	3,665,466	68,686	4,116,886	Santo Domingo.	984,188	35,262	2,293,748
Cuba..........	17,622,411	331,159	77,931,671	Spain..........	11,522,150	6,274	5,207,861
Danish W. Indies	610,843	4,080	362,078	Sweden & Norw'y	6,578,857	524	3,754,932
Denmark.......	8,358,881	11,795	228,545	Switzerland....	10,397	....	13,196,469
Dutch E. Indies.	1,372,035	....	6,914,743	Uruguay.......	907,067	31,963	2,480,596
France.........	97,896,132	1,230,575	68,554,793	Venezuela......	3,991,908	57,247	10,325,338
French W. Indies	1,950,403	32,100	29,828	All other Countr's	14,505,590	189,602	26,631,524
Germany.......	104,180,732	1,340,826	82,907,553	Total........	$1,015,732,011	$14,546,137	$827,402,462
Great Brit. & Ire.	493,957,868	5,357,464	156,300,881				
Greece.........	100,370	....	1,300,449				

𝔇ecline in the 𝔄merican 𝔠arrying 𝔗rade.

The following table shows the values of the imports and exports of the United States carried respectively in American and foreign vessels during each fiscal year from 1856 to 1892.

Year Ending June 30.	In American Vessels.	In Foreign Vessels.	Per cent. in American Vessels.	Year Ending June 30.	In American Vessels.	In Foreign Vessels.	Per cent in American Vessels.
1856....	$482,268,274	$159,336,576	75.2	1875....	$314,257,792	$884,788,517	26.1
1857....	510,331,027	213,519,796	70.5	1876....	311,076,171	813,354,987	27.7
1858....	447,191,304	160,066,267	73.7	1877....	316,660,281	859,920,536	26.9
1859....	465,741,381	229,816,211	66.9	1878....	313,050,906	876,991,129	26.3
1860....	507,247,757	255,040,793	66.5	1879....	272,015,692	911,269,232	21.0
1861....	381,516,788	203,478,278	65.2	1880....	258,346,577	1,224,265,434	17.4
1862....	217,695,418	218,015,296	50.0	1881....	250,586,470	1,269,002,983	16.5
1863....	241,872,471	343,056,031	41.4	1882....	227,229,745	1,212,978,769	15.8
1864....	184,061,486	485,793,548	27.5	1883....	240,420,500	1,258,506,924	16.0
1865....	167,402,872	437,010,124	27.7	1884....	233,699,035	1,127,798,109	17.2
1866....	325,711,861	685,226,691	32.2	1885....	194,865,743	1,079,518,566	15.3
1867....	297,834,904	581,330,403	33.9	1886....	197,349,503	1,073,911,113	15.5
1868....	297,981,573	550,546,074	35.1	1887....	194,356,746	1,165,194,508	14.3
1869....	289,956,772	586,492,012	33.1	1888....	190,857,473	1,174,697,321	14.0
1870....	352,969,401	638,927,488	35.6	1889....	203,805,108	1,217,063,541	14.3
1871....	353,664,172	755,822,576	31.9	1890....	202,451,086	1,371,116,744	12.9
1872....	345,331,101	839,346,362	29.2	1891....	206,459,725	1,450,081,087	12.5
1873....	346,306,592	966,722,651	26.4	1892....	220,173,735	1,564,558,808	12.3
1874....	350,451,994	939,206,106	27.2				

Gold and Silver Produced in the United States.

THE following estimate of the gold and silver produced in the United States, since the discovery of gold in California, is compiled from the official reports of the Director of the United States Mint:

Year.	Gold.	Silver.	Total.	Year.	Gold.	Silver.	Total.
1849	$40,000,000	$50,000	$40,050,000	1871	$43,500,000	$23,000,000	$66,500,000
1850	50,000,000	50,000	50,050,000	1872	36,000,000	28,750,000	64,750,000
1851	55,000,000	50,000	55,050,000	1873	36,000,000	35,750,000	71,750,000
1852	60,000,000	50,000	60,050,000	1874	33,490,902	37,324,594	70,815,496
1853	65,000,000	50,000	65,050,000	1875	33,467,856	31,727,560	65,195,416
1854	60,000,000	50,000	60,050,000	1876	39,929,166	38,783,016	78,712,182
1855	55,000,000	50,000	55,050,000	1877	46,897,390	39,793,573	86,690,963
1856	55,000,000	50,000	55,050,000	1878	51,206,360	45,281,385	96,487,745
1857	55,000,000	50,000	55,050,000	1879	38,899,858	40,812,132	79,711,990
1858	50,000,000	500,000	50,500,000	1880	36,000,000	38,450,000	74,450,000
1859	50,000,000	100,000	50,100,000	1881	34,700,000	43,000,000	77,700,000
1860	46,000,000	150,000	46,150,000	1882	32,500,000	46,800,000	79,300,000
1861	43,000,000	2,000,000	45,000,000	1883	30,000,000	46,200,000	76,200,000
1862	39,200,000	4,500,000	43,700,000	1884	30,800,000	48,800,000	79,600,000
1863	40,000,000	8,500,000	48,500,000	1885	31,800,000	51,600,000	83,400,000
1864	46,100,000	11,000,000	57,100,000	1886	35,000,000	51,000,000	86,000,000
1865	53,225,000	11,250,000	64,475,000	1887	33,000,000	53,357,000	86,357,000
1866	53,500,000	10,000,000	63,500,000	1888	33,175,000	59,195,000	92,370,000
1867	51,725,000	13,500,000	65,225,000	1889	32,800,000	64,646,000	97,446,000
1868	48,000,000	12,000,000	60,000,000	1890	32,845,000	70,464,000	103,309,000
1869	49,500,000	12,000,000	61,500,000	1891	33,175,000	75,416,565	108,591,565
1870	50,000,000	16,000,000	66,000,000				

Total Gold, $1,870,345,000. Silver, $1,072,721,565. Grand Total, 2,943,066,565.

The coinage at the United States Mint during the fiscal year which ended June 30, 1891, was as follows:

	Gold.	Silver Dollars.	Subsidiary Silver Coins.	Minor Coins.	Total.
Number of Pieces	1,414,154	36,232,802	18,560,371	63,340,550	119,547,877
Value	$24,172,203	$36,232,802	$2,039,218	$1,166,936	$63,611,159

STATEMENT OF DEPOSITS AT MINTS AND ASSAY OFFICES OF THE GOLD AND SILVER PRODUCED IN THE SEVERAL STATES FROM 1793 TO JUNE 30, 1891.

Locality.	Gold.	Silver.	Total.	Locality.	Gold	Silver	Total.
Alabama	$235,334.83	$134.08	$235,468.91	Penn	$1,138.34	$2,588.47	$3,726.81
Alaska	810,105.37	7,578.30	19,219,321.04	S. Carolina	1,908,676.79	2,668.51	1,911,345.30
Arizona	5,361,963.00	13,857,358.04	19,219,321.04	S. Dakota	39,423,766.21	917,262.60	40,341,028.81
California	757,713,300.94	4,097,079.65	761,810,380.59	Tennessee	89,747.45	12.27	89,759.72
Colorado	60,140,436.68	24,467,565.29	84,608,001.97	Texas	3,626.02	5,526.83	9,152.85
Georgia	8,895,835.72	5,393.39	8,901,229.11	Utah	1,142,713.54	19,576,538.48	20,719,252.02
Idaho	32,597,083.87	1,889,772.19	34,486,856.06	Vermont	85,598.21	49.94	85,648.15
Indiana	40.13		40.13	Virginia	1,743,100.86	392.40	1,743,493.26
Maine	5,638.20	22.00	5,660.20	Wash	627,178.16	6,671.77	633,849.93
Maryland	18,288.28	36.86	18,325.14	Wyoming	808,660.48	12,860.30	821,520.78
Mass		917.56	917.56	Other sources. }	40,938,815.41	42,685,179.70	83,623,995.11
Michigan	274,407.24	3,889,408.06	4,163,815.30				
Montana	67,118,541.81	16,556,225.39	83,674,767.20				
Nebraska	2,078.76	22.84	2,101.60	Total un- } refined. }	$1,086,634,436.15	$235,075,410.26	$1,321,709,846.41
Nevada	29,883,948.37	100,279,775.49	130,163,723.86				
N. H.	11,501.89	1.74	11,503.63	Refined } bullion. }	373,851,817.32	367,498,914.54	741,350,731.86
N. Mexico	4,595,031.94	6,676,169.03	11,271,200.97				
N. Carolina	11,604,867.79	57,874.36	11,662,742.15				
Oregon	20,593,009.86	80,324.72	20,673,334.58	G. Total	$1,460,486,253.47	$602,574,324.80	$2,063,060,578.27

Gold and Silver Production in 500 Years.

Countries.	Gold.			Silver.		
	Tons.	Value.	Ratio.	Tons.	Value.	Ratio.
Africa	740	$520,000,000	7.1			
Australia	1,840	1,290,000,000	17.8			
Austria	460	325,000,000	4.4	7,930	$305,000,000	4.1
Brazil	1,040	725,000,000	10.0			
Germany				8,470	325,000,000	4.4
Mexico				78,600	3,040,000,000	40.7
Peru, etc.				72,000	2,770,000,000	37.3
Russia	1,235	865,000,000	12.0	3,200	120,000,000	1.7
Spanish America	2,220	1,550,000,000	21.5			
United States	2,042	1,430,000,000	19.7	11,600	445,000,000	6.0
Other Countries	778	535,000,000	7.5	11,200	430,000,000	5.8
The World	10,355	$7,240,000,000	100.0	193,000	$7,435,000,000	100.0

The estimates in this table of gold and silver production for 500 years (1380-1880) are made by Mulhall.

Statistics of Savings Banks.

NUMBER OF DEPOSITORS, AMOUNT OF DEPOSITS, AND AVERAGE TO EACH DEPOSITOR, 1891-92.

STATES AND TERRITORIES.	Number of Depositors.	Amount of Deposits.	Average to each Depositor.	STATES AND TERRITORIES.	Number of Depositors.	Amount of Deposits.	Average to each Depositor.
Maine.............	146,668	$50,278,452	$342.80	Texas	1,950	$279,783	$143.48
New-Hampshire....	169,949	72,439,660	426.24	Arkansas.........	258	51,854	200.10
Vermont.........	80,740	24,674,742	305.60	Tennessee.........	*16,392	1,292,913	78.87
Massachusetts....	1,131,203	369,526,386	326.67	Ohio.............	84,779	33,895,078	399.80
Rhode-Island.......	136,648	66,276,157	485.01	Indiana............	15,418	3,754,622	243.52
Connecticut.......	317,925	122,582,160	385.57	Illinois............	*73,872	21,106,369	285.72
New-York.........	1,516,289	588,425,421	388.07	Michigan..........	180,391	36,950,573	204.88
New-Jersey	131,739	33,807,634	256.62	Wisconsin..........	948	138,926	146.59
Pennsylvania	248,471	65,233,993	262.54	Iowa..............	*71,687	26,115,384	364.29
Delaware..........	17,318	3,626,319	209.39	Minnesota..........	35,123	8,786,879	250.17
Maryland..........	142,135	41,977,868	295.34	Nebraska..........	....	....	....
District of Columbia	1,303	60,178	46.18	Colorado..........	*21,215	2,893,276	136.38
West-Virginia.....	8,426	473,848	56.22	California	*167,667	127,312,088	759.32
North-Carolina....	6,247	282,425	45.21	New-Mexico.......	900	149,449	166.05
South-Carolina....	21,397	4,225,459	197.48	Utah..............	*13,596	2,427,950	178.58
Georgia...........	4,569	572,523	125.30	Washington.......	*8,955	1,193,967	133.33
Florida...........	170	31,91	187.73				
Alabama..........	1,698	220,046	129.59	Total........	4,781,605	$1,712,769,026	358.20
Louisiana..........	5,557	1,695,732	305.15				

* Partially estimated.

SAVINGS BANKS, DEPOSITORS AND DEPOSITS IN THE UNITED STATES EVERY TEN YEARS SINCE 1820.

YEAR.	Number of Banks.	Number of Depositors.	Deposits.	YEAR.	Number of Banks.	Number of Depositors.	Deposits.
1820........	10	8,635	$1,138,576	1870........	517	1,630,846	$549,874,358
1830........	36	38,085	6,973,304	1880........	629	2,335,582	819,106,973
1840........	61	78,701	14,051,520	1890........	921	4,258,893	1,524,844,506
1850........	108	251,354	43,431,130	1891........	1,011	4,533,217	1,623,079,749
1860........	278	693,870	149,277,504	1892........	1,059	4,781,605	1,712,769,026

The above tables were compiled from the report of the Comptroller of the Treasury for 1892.

NUMBER OF DEPOSITORS AND AMOUNT OF DEPOSITS IN EUROPEAN COUNTRIES.

COUNTRIES.	Number of Depositors.	Amount of Deposits.	COUNTRIES.	Number of Depositors.	Amount of Deposits.
Austria..............	1,850,000	$613,000,000	Prussia..............	....	$720,000,000
Belgium and Netherlands.	310,000	82,000,000	Russia..............	200,000	36,000,000
France.................	4,150,000	559,000,000	Scandinavia........	1,600,000	220,000,000
Germany..............	5,000,000	....	Spain..............	....	10,000,000
Great Britain........	3,715,000	536,000,000	Switzerland........	1,600,000	118,500,000
Italy.................	1,970,000	346,000,000			

Manufactures.

THE United States Census Bureau has not yet reported the completed statistics of manufactures in the United States.

The following summary by Mulhall shows approximately the value of all manufactures in the world in one year, 1888:

COUNTRIES.	Textiles.	Hardware.	Clothing.	Beer & Spirits.	Leather.	Total Manufactures.*
Austria.............	$180,000,000	$75,000,000	$150,000,000	$115,000,000	$195,000,000	$1,265,000,000
Australia............	35,000,000	75,000,000	20,000,000	15,000,000	30,000,000	205,000,000
Belgium	80,000,000	85,000,000	60,000,000	65,000,000	30,000,000	510,000,000
Denmark	5,000,000	5,000,000	15,000,000	20,000,000	30,000,000	130,000,000
France	540,000,000	210,000,000	320,000,000	105,000,000	260,000,000	2,425,000,000
Germany.............	410,000,000	455,000,000	265,000,000	355,000,000	265,000,000	2,915,000,000
Great Britain........	850,000,000	775,000,000	330,000,000	375,000,000	210,000,000	4,100,000,000
Italy................	105,000,000	20,000,000	120,000,000	20,000,000	85,000,000	605,000,000
Netherlands............	15,000,000	5,000,000	30,000,000	25,000,000	30,000,000	175,000,000
Norway..............	5,000,000	5,000,000	10,000,000	15,000,000	20,000,000	95,000,000
Portugal.............	10,000,000	5,000,000	15,000,000	....	15,000,000	80,000,000
Russia...............	260,000,000	70,000,000	255,000,000	100,000,000	255,000,000	1,815,000,000
Spain...............	80,000,000	20,000,000	80,000,000	5,000,000	60,000,000	425,000,000
Sweden.............	10,000,000	30,000,000	30,000,000	10,000,000	40,000,000	250,000,000
Switzerland..........	55,000,000	10,000,000	15,000,000	10,000,000	10,000,000	160,000,000
United States..........	560,000,000	970,000,000	490,000,000	305,000,000	520,000,000	7,215,000,000
Total..............	$3,200,000,000	$2,815,000,000	$2,205,000,000	$1,560,000,000	$2,055,000,000	$22,370,000,000

The total valuation of manufactures in Canada by latest official returns was $425,000,000 for the year.
* Including sundry manufactures not enumerated in preceding columns.

Stock List and Sales of Leading Stocks in 1892.

OUTSTANDING STOCK, BONDED INDEBTEDNESS, AND MILEAGE, JANUARY 1, 1893.
HIGHEST AND LOWEST PRICES AND NUMBER OF SHARES SOLD ON THE NEW-YORK STOCK EXCHANGE IN 1892.

Stocks.	Stock Outstanding.	Bonded Indebtedness.	Mileage.	Date Payment Last Dividend Declared.	Rate per cent. Last Dividend.	Highest and Lowest, 1892.		Number Shares sold in 1892 N. Y. Stock Exchange.
Adams Express	$12,000,000	....	....	Dec. 1, 1892	2	155½	143⅛	6,007
American Cotton Oil Co. common	20,237,100	$3,790,000	...	....	..	47⅞	32½	595,837
American Cotton Oil Co. pref.	10,198,600		...	Dec. 1, 1892	3	87⅓	63½	177,560
American Express	18,000,000	....	....	Jan. 3, 1893	3	123½	116	6,720
American Sugar Refining Co.	25,000,000	....	....	Jan. 3, 1893	2½	115⅜	78½	4,664,622
American Sugar Refining Co. pref.	25,000,000	....	....		3½	107⅜	90	207,562
American Tobacco*	....	....	....	....	..	126	106	130,157
American Tobacco pref.	11,935,000	....	....	Nov. 1, 1892	2	115	90	22,961
Atchison, Topeka & Santa Fé	102,000,000	221,332,000	6,654	Nov. 15, 1888	½	46⅝	32⅜	3,853,644
Atlantic & Pacific	79,760,300	38,913,534	947	....	..	5⅞	3⅞	15,819
Baltimore & Ohio, common	16,025,000	42,467,000	3,226	Nov. 15, 1892	2½	101¼	92½	184,612
Buffalo, Rochester & Pittsburgh	6,000,000	8,091,000	....	....	..	44¾	34⅛	114,693
Canada Southern	15,000,000	19,573,601	359	Feb. 1, 1893	†1¼	64⅛	54¼	180,544
Canadian Pacific	65,000,000	47,956,686	5,767	Aug. 17, 1892	2½	94½	85¼	44,517
Central Pacific	68,000,000	61,144,000	1,360	Aug. 1, 1892	1	35	27⅛	13,011
Chesapeake & Ohio V. T. R.	57,192,900	37,002,000	952	....	..	28	21⅜	394,161
Chesapeake & Ohio 1st pref.	2,707,900			....	..	64½	59	100,836
Chesapeake & Ohio 2d pref.	3,329,200			....	..	44⅜	38⅛	142,619
Chicago & Alton	17,594,500	12,944,850	843	Dec. 1, 1892	2	154	139	3,776
Chicago, Burlington & Quincy	76,392,600	111,459,482	5,324	Dec. 15, 1892	1¼	110⅝	95	2,793,122
Chicago & East Illinois	6,197,800	11,538,000	436	Mar. 1, 1888	3	71¼	59	10,102
Chicago & East Illinois pref.	4,733,100			Jan. 2, 1893	1½	104	96¼	54,219
Chicago Gas Companies	25,000,000	20,440,000	....	Dec. 22, 1892	1½	99¼	71¾	3,610,254
Chicago, Milwaukee & St. Paul	46,027,261	127,286,000	5,721	Oct. 20, 1892	2	84⅝	75⅝	5,129,804
Chicago, Milwaukee & St. Paul pref.	24,364,900				3½	128⅞	119⅛	143,133
Chicago & Northwestern	38,948,700	114,062,500	4,273	Dec. 23, 1892	3	121⅞	110⅛	869,484
Chicago & Northwestern pref.	22,333,500			Dec. 23, 1892	1¾	147½	139	11,279
Chicago, Rock Island & Pacific	46,156,000	55,183,000	3,456	Nov. [illegible], 1892	1	94⅛	75½	2,247,603
Chicago, St. P., Minneap. & Omaha	21,403,293	24,564,846	1,481	....	..	54⅝	44	....
Chicago, St. P., Minneap. & O. pref.	12,646,833			Jan. 20, 1893	3½	123½	108½	....
Chicago Stock Yards common	6,141,800	10,000,000	....	Jan. 5, 1893	4	109¾	72	49,839
Citizens' Gas, Brooklyn	1,714,500	....	...	....	..	114⅛	94¼	50,042
Cleveland, Cin., Chic. & St. L.	28,000,000	48,031,730	1,686	Aug. 1, 1892	1½	75	57	463,696
Cleveland, Cin., Chic. & St. L. pref.	10,000,000			Jan. 2, 1893	1¼	99¼	91¾	8,693
Colorado Coal & Iron Company	10,000,000	3,101,000	....	....	..	43¾	28¼	....
Colorado Coal & Iron Dev. Co.	....	700,000	....	....	..	27¼	22⅞	14,300
Colorado Fuel & Iron	9,250,000	....	....	....	..	66⅞	60¼	34,677
Colorado Fuel & Iron pref.	2,000,000	....	....	....	..	115	99	1,198
Columbus, Hocking Val. & Toledo	11,696,300	15,703,000	325	Aug. 19, 1885	..	40	27	353,800
Columbus, Hocking Val. & Tol. pref.	2,000,000			Jan. 3, 1893	2½	80¾	66	27,720
Consolidated Gas Company	35,430,060	2,612,000	....	Dec. 15, 1892	1½	128	102	186,058
Delaware & Hudson Canal	30,000,000	9,829,000	852	Dec. 15, 1892	1¾	149½	122⅞	406,130
Delaware, Lackawanna & Western	26,200,000	3,674,000	893	Oct. 20, 1892	1¾	167½	138⅛	1,682,225
Denver & Rio Grande	38,000,000	42,867,500	1,610	....	..	19½	15	39,557
Denver & Rio Grande pref.	23,650,000			....	..	54⅝	45	302,666
Distilling & Cattle Feeding Co.	35,000,000	....	....	Jan. 3, 1893	1½	72½	44⅛	4,369,000
Duluth, South Shore & Atlantic	....	4,000,000	...	....	..	14⅜	6	170,427
Duluth, South Shore & Atlantic pref.	....		...	....	..	35½	14	102,406
East Tennessee, Va. & Ga.	27,500,000	37,460,000	1,896	....	..	9¾	3⅝	50,111
East Tennessee, Va. & Ga. 1st pref.	11,000,000			Nov. 30, 1891	2	51¾	22½	2,422
East Tennessee, Va. & Ga. 2d pref.	18,500,000			....	..	20	6½	70,677
Edison Electric Illuminating Co.	5,800,000	2,650,000	....	Nov. 1, 1892	1¼	115½	79⅞	32,151
Evansville & Terre Haute	3,000,000	3,855,000	....	Oct. 10, 1892	5	151	119½	49,024
General Electric Co.	30,284,000	4,000,000	....	Nov. 1, 1892	2	119⅞	104½	425,059
Great Northern pref.	20,000,000	....	3,005	Aug. 1, 1892	1¼	144	119	32,138
Green Bay, Winona & St. P. T. R.	8,000,000	5,381,000	215	....	..	15⅝	8¼	99,747
Green Bay, Win. & St. P. T. R. pref.	2,000,000		...	....	..	28	26¼	10,351
Illinois Central	42,095,000	29,618,500	2,275	Sept. 1, 1892	2½	110	95½	139,201
Iowa Central	8,199,856	6,300,000	510	....	..	15½	9	38,438
Iowa Central pref.	5,543,736			....	..	56¾	31	45,956
Laclede Gas	7,500,000	10,000,000	...	....	..	27¼	17¼	132,047
Laclede Gas pref.	2,500,000		...	....	..	74½	57½	30,628
Lake Erie & Western	11,840,000	7,250,000	725	....	..	27¾	20¼	334,079
Lake Erie & Western pref.	11,840,000			Nov. 15, 1892	1¼	80	69¼	201,646
Lake Shore & Michigan Southern	49,466,500	46,167,000	1,445	Feb. 1, 1893	3	140½	120	540,010
Long Island	12,000,000	11,885,405	344	Nov. 1, 1892	1¼	112	95	36,195
Louisville, Evansville & St. Louis	3,790,747	8,000,000	....	....	..	26	20	4,094
Louisville & Nashville	52,800,000	66,722,660	2,296	Aug. 1, 1892	2	84½	64¾	1,808,766
Louisville, New-Albany & Chicago	9,600,600	12,800,000	539	....	..	31	20½	490,375
Louisville, St. Louis & Texas	3,000,000	2,690,000	....	....	..	26¾	14½	38,275
Manhattan Consolidated	29,891,980	33,618,000	36¼	Jan. 3, 1893	1½	153½	104	623,379
Mexican Central	47,094,000	55,838,000	1,876	....	..	23¾	10	26,620
Michigan Central	18,738,204	21,745,000	1,595	Feb. 1, 1893	*2	117	102	71,515
Minneapolis & St. Louis	5,771,700	9,213,000	350	....	..	21¼	8	80,716
Minneapolis & St. Louis pref.	4,000,000			....	..	49⅛	18	92,249
Missouri, Kansas & Texas	47,000,000	60,000,000	1,672	....	..	20¾	13	66,975
Missouri, Kansas & Texas pref.	13,000,000			....	..	33⅛	24	236,299

STOCK LIST AND SALES OF LEADING STOCKS IN 1892—*Continued.*

Stocks.	Stock Outstanding.	Bonded Indebtedness.	Mileage.	Date Payment Last Dividend Declared.	Rate per cent. Last Div.	Highest and Lowest, 1892.	Number Shares sold in 1892. N. Y. Stock Exchange.
Missouri Pacific......	$47,432,850	$51,376,000	3,192	July 15, 1891	1	65¾ 53⅞	1,247,711
Mobile & Ohio........	5,320,600	16,339,230	687			42¼ 33	154,168
Morris & Essex.......	15,000,000	24,373,000	120	Jan. 2, 1890	3½	155 143⅜	5,052
Nashville, Chattanooga & St. Louis	10,000,000	12,904,000	810	Nov. 1, 1892	1¼	91 83	5,691
National Cordage Company........	10,000,000	....	}	Nov. 1, 1892	{ 3	142⅜ 91½	878,714
National Cordage pref.	5,000,000	....	}		{ 2	123¼ 100	245,529
National Lead*.......	14,905,400	....				51⅜ 30⅝	939,902
National Lead pref.	14,904,000	....		Dec. 15, 1892	1¾	99⅞ 81	230,626
National Linseed Oil	18,000,000	....		Aug. 1, 1891	½	45 27	112,408
National Starch	5,000,000	}	...			46½ 29¼	64,865
National Starch 1st pref.	3,000,000	} 3,837,000	...			106 100½	6,012
National Starch 2d pref.	2,500,000	}	...	Jan. 3, 1893	6	109 97	18,121
New-Jersey Central...	22,467,000	44,140,000	661	Nov. 1, 1892	1¾	145 111½	327,288
New-York Central & Hudson R.....	89,428,300	68,077,333	1,421	Jan. 16, 1893	1¼	119¼ 107⅝	308,106
New-York, Chicago & St. Louis.....	14,000,000	}				22½ 15½	53,043
New-York, Chic. & St. L. 1st pref.	5,000,000	} 19,575,000	513	Mar. 1, 1892	3	81½ 71⅜	10,124
New-York, Chicago & St. L. 2d pref.	11,000,000	}		....		45 32¾	26,390
New-York, Lake Erie & Western..	78,000,000	77,664,885	1,658			34¾ 23⅝	3,123,807
New-York, Lake Erie & West. pref.	8,536,900	}		Jan. 15, 1892	3	77½ 53½	204,284
New-York & New-England com...	19,798,000	16,386,000	361			59 30¾	4,187,275
New-York, New-Haven & Hartford	23,375,000	2,000,000	508	Jan. 1893	2½	255 224	4,605
New-York, Ontario & Western... ..	58,119,982	13,300,000	2 8			23⅝ 17½	....
New-York, Susquehanna & Western	13,000,000	}				20⅞ 10½	317,221
New-York, Susquehanna & West. pf	8,000,000	} 8,136,000	1⅗	Nov. 10, 1892	1¾	74 41½	139,967
Norfolk & Western.....	9,500,000	}				18 9	9,661
Norfolk & Western pref.	43,000,000	} 42,583,311	1,120	Oct. 28, 1892	1	56 37½	24,962
North American Company........	40,000,000	....				18⅞ 9⅞	363,966
Northern Pacific.....	49,000,000	122,482,500	5,199			26½ 15	200,016
Northern Pacific pref	36,599,405	}				72½ 44½	3,37,028
Ohio Southern........	3,840,000	4,620,000	140			55⅜ 19	77,158
Ohio & Mississippi....	20,000,000	15,730,000				24 19	9,672
Ontario Silver Mining.	15,000,000	....		Aug. 30, 1892	50c.	45¼ 15	7,810
Oregon Railway & Navigation..	24,000,000	22,844,000	863	Jan. 1, 1893	1½	91⅜ 70	11,931
Oregon Short Line & Utah Northern.	26,033,719	50,179,000	1,421			33⅝ 20¼	98,486
Pacific Mail.........	20,000,000	....		Sept. 15, 1887	1	40⅜ 25	186,024
Peoria, Decatur & Evansville....	8,400,000	4,845,000	256			22⅜ 15	53,387
Peoria & Eastern.....	10,000,000	13,603,000	341			15¾ 8	8,979
Philadelphia & Reading....	40,105,301	137,445,823	2,460			65 38	1,88,832
Pittsburgh, Cin., Chic. & St. L....	20,050,600	41,836,000	1,082	Oct. 25, 1892	2	30⅝ 18⅝	20,349
Pittsburgh, Cin., Chic. & St. L. pf.	22,373,500	}		Oct. 5, 1892	1¼	67⅜ 57¾	23,745
Pittsburgh, Fort Wayne & Chicago.	34,088,575	12,410,000	470			155 152	2,805
Pittsburgh & Western pref.	5,000,000	12,315,375	352			45⅜ 34	33,870
Pullman's Palace Car Company...	30,000,000	820,000		Nov. 15, 1892	2	200½ 184	53,130
Richmond & West Point Term'l....	70,000,000	16,565,000	}			17½ 6¾	427,746
Richmond & West Point pref....	5,000,000	}	...	July 15, 1891	2½	79 32	122,395
Rio Grande Western..	7,500,000	}				41 23	5,275
Rio Grande Western pref.	6,250,000	} 14,000,000	504	Feb. 1, 1893	1¾	74 22	9,829
Rome, Watertown & Ogdensburg..	8,768,100	10,773,800	629	Nov. 15, 1892	1¾	113½ 110	16,711
St. Louis Southwestern.	16,500,000	}				11⅜ 6	40,837
St. Louis Southwestern pref.....	20,000,000	} 26,000,000	1,227			23⅜ 11½	84,401
St. Paul & Duluth....	4,660,200	}		July 1887		48⅞ 39½	42,592
St. Paul & Duluth pref.	5,188,866	} 3,000,000	247	Sept. 1, 1892	3½	108 103	8,523
St. Paul, Minneapolis & Manitoba..	20,000,000	52,505,000	2.775	May 1, 1892	1½	116½ 112	32,992
Southern Pacific Co...	118,858,170	....	6,461			41¼ 33⅝	111,000
Tennessee, C. I. & R. R. Co......	9,000,000	} 4,860,000		May 15, 1887	1	50⅝ 31½	411,719
Tenn., C. I. & R. R. Co. pref.....	1,000,000	}	...	Jan. 15, 1893	4	109 92	4,414
Texas & Pacific......	38,710,900	50,000,000	1,499			14⅜ 7	166,821
Toledo, A. A. & North Michigan...	6,200,000	6,300,000	301			38⅝ 23	186,947
Union Pacific........	60,868,500	123,883,147	1,821	April 1, 1884	1¾	50¾ 35¾	2,153,975
Union Pacific, Denver & Gulf....	31,759,082	15,673,000	1,385			25 15½	94,853
United States Express.	10,000,000	....		Nov. 15, 1892	2	64 44	12,173
United States Rubber..	13,481,100	....				48¾ 38¾	46,990
Wabash.............	28,000,000	}				15⅜ 10	55,561
Wabash preferred.....	24,000,000	} 78,000,000	1,921	Nov. 5, 1881	1½	33½ 22½	411,544
Wells, Fargo & Co. Express	6,250,000	....		Jan. 16, 1893	4	148¾ 140	3,099
Western Union Telegraph....	100,000,000	14,801,364	....	Jan. 16, 1893	1¼	100⅞ 82	1,718,564
Wheeling & Lake Erie...	6,000,000	}				40¼ 19½	328,037
Wheeling & Lake Erie pref.	4,500,000	} 6,619,000	237	Nov. 15, 1892	1	80¼ 62	124,612
Wisconsin Central Co...	12,000,000	12,000,000	628			21½ 14⅞	16,889
Total	....	....		....		....	**76,992,000**
Total sales of unlisted stocks...							7,683,750

* Extra dividends of 1½ per cent. on Michigan Central and ½ per cent. on Canadian Southern, payable February 1, 1893.

The total sales of shares at the New-York Stock Exchange in 1892 were 78,215,748; in 1891 were 65,045,217; in 1890 were 56,126,365; in 1889 were 60,823,904; in 1888 were 62,845,772; in 1887 were 85,921,028; in 1886 were 102,852,804; in 1885, 90,920,707; in 1884, 96,865,325; in 1883, 96,037,905; in 1882, 113,720,655; in 1881, 113,392,685; in 1880, 97,200,000; and in 1879, 74,166,652. These statistics were partially compiled from Bradstreet's.

Importation of Spirits, Malt Liquors, and Wines

INTO THE UNITED STATES FROM 1885 TO 1891 INCLUSIVE.

QUANTITIES.

	1885.	1886.	1887.	1888.	1889.	1890.	1891.
MALT LIQUORS :							
In bottles or jugs..........galls.	869,224	968,320	1,015,582	1,126,771	1,151,065	1,188,851	1,265,934
Not in bottles or jugs........ "	1,189,900	1,287,873	1,276,513	1,390,123	1,373,616	1,491,179	1,817,043
SPIRITS, DISTILLED, AND SPIRITUOUS COMPOUNDS :							
Brandy..............proof galls.	503,945	432,611	421,141	416,899	400,089	461,257	443,278
All other............. " "	1,012,777	1,011,290	1,101,349	1,152,944	1,127,458	1,139,981	1,218,802
WINES :							
Still wines—							
In casks.................. galls.	3,419,532	3,787,420	3,383,593	3,333,322	3,078,554	3,485,792	3,860,502
In bottles...............doz.	239,321	258,153	253,132	284,174	260,026	329,604	348,666
Champagne and other sparkling. "	228,580	238,604	255,656	274,914	315,870	354,350	400,084

VALUES.

MALT LIQUORS...............	$1,097,184	$1,231,388	$1,255,164	$1,363,858	$1,361,990	$1,427,608	$1,765,702
SPIRITS, DISTILLED, AND SPIRITUOUS COMPOUNDS.......................	2,006,336	1,864,858	1,955,468	1,957,811	1,928,087	2,214,200	2,209,736
WINES...........	6,275,703	6,940,041	7,050,085	7,336,198	7,706,772	8,859,956	10,097,060

The value of champagne and other sparkling wines imported in 1890-91 was $5,615,872.

Production of Distilled Spirits.

(In the United States, stated in gallons. Prepared by the Internal Revenue Bureau.)

FISCAL YEARS ENDED JUNE 30.	Bourbon Whiskey.	Rye Whiskey.	Alcohol.	Rum.	High Wines.	Pure, Neutral, or Cologne Spirits.	Fruit Brandy.	Aggregate Production, including Miscellaneous.
1880........	15,414,148	6,341,991	21,631,009	2,439,301	15,210,389	20,657,975	129,086	91,378,417
1885........	12,277,750	5,328,043	13,436,916	2,081,165	3,235,889	27,104,382	312,197	76,405,074
1886........	19,318,819	7,842,540	11,247,877	1,799,952	2,396,248	26,638,581	329,679	81,849,260
1887........	17,015,034	7,313,640	10,337,035	1,857,223	2,410,923	27,066,219	673,610	79,433,446
1888........	7,463,609	5,879,600	11,075,639	1,891,246	1,916,436	29,475,913	864,704	71,688,188
1889........	21,960,784	8,749,768	10,939,135	1,471,054	1,029,495	30,439,354	952,358	91,133,550
1890........	32,474,784	13,355,577	11,354,448	1,657,808	555,572	34,022,619	1,137,649	111,101,738
1891........	29,931,415	14,345,389	12,260,821	1,784,312	1,007,070	35,356,126	1,223,725	117,186,114

Malt Liquors.

SALES IN PRINCIPAL CITIES OF THE UNITED STATES, 1891-92.

Cities.	Barrels.	Cities.	Barrels.	Cities.	Barrels.	Cities.	Barrels.
Albany, N. Y....	302,473	Cincinnati, O.....	1,222,905	New-Orleans, La.	257,418	S. Francisco, Cal.	569,976
Baltimore, Md...	559,401	Cleveland, O.....	443,985	New-York City...	4,573,019	St. Louis, Mo....	1,849,282
Boston, Mass...	987,361	Detroit, Mich	326,813	Philadelphia, Pa...	1,658,529	Syracuse, N. Y..	231,011
Brooklyn, N. Y..	1,788,285	Louisville, Ky...	214,233	Pittsburgh, Pa...	429,452	Toledo, O.......	273,349
Buffalo, N. Y....	602,310	Milwaukee, Wis..	2,066,592	Rochester, N. Y..	563,071	Troy, N. Y......	183,033
Chicago, Ill......	2,634,860	Newark, N. J....	1,103,840				

The *Brewers' Journal* of New-York, which furnishes the preceding table showing sales of malt liquors in cities of the United States, reports total sales of 30,021,079 barrels in United States in 1891.

The production of beer in the principal beer manufacturing countries of the world in 1891 was : Germany, 52,722,638 hectolitres (a hectolitre is equal to 26.414 gallons) ; Great Britain and Ireland, 52,707,460 hectolitres ; United States, 44,354,511 hectolitres ; Austria-Hungary, 15,079,705 hectolitres ; Belgium, 9,845,537 hectolitres ; France, 9,476,183 hectolitres ; Russia, 4,456,860 hectolitres ; Denmark, 2,185,600 hectolitres.

AVERAGE PERCENTAGE OF ALCOHOL IN WINES AND LIQUORS.

	Per cent.		Per cent.		Per cent.		Per cent.		Per cent.
Beer........	4.0	Tokay......	10.2	Claret......	13.3	Marsala........	20.2	Gin...............	51.6
Porter.......	4.5	Rhine......	11.0	Burgundy....	13.6	Madeira........	21.0	Brandy.........	53.4
Ale.........	7.4	Orange......	11.2	Malaga......	17.3	Port...........	23.2	Rum...........	53.7
Cider.......	8.6	Bordeaux ...	11.5	Canary......	18.8	Curaçoa.......	27.0	Whiskey, Irish	53.9
Perry.......	8.8	Hock.......	11.6	Sherry......	19.0	Aniseed........	33.0	Whiskey, Bourbon..	54.0
Elder	9.3	Gooseberry..	11.8	Vermouth....	19.0	Maraschino....	34.0	Whiskey, Rye....	54.0
Moselle.....	9.6	Champagne..	12.2	Malmsey	20.0	Chartreuse	43.0	Whiskey, Scotch	54.3

The percentage as above indicated is by volume. "Proof spirit" contains 49.24 per cent by weight, or 57.06 per cent by volume of absolute alcohol.

Mulhall gives the average percentage of alcohol in Burton's ale as 8.2 ; Bass's ale, 8.4 ; Edinburgh ale, 4.4 ; Guinness's ale, 6.8 ; London porter, 4.1 ; London beer 3.9 ; lager beer, 3.2.

The ratio of dipsomaniacs to all insane is as follows in several countries : Italy, 12 per cent ; France, 21 per cent ; United States, 26 per cent ; Scotland, 28 per cent.

Expectancy of life, drunk and sober: At age 20, drunk, 15 years ; sober, 44 years. At age 30, drunk, 14 years ; sober, 36 years. At age 40, drunk, 11 years ; sober, 29 years.

Qualifications for Voting in Each State of the Union.

(Communicated to THE WORLD ALMANAC and corrected to date by the Attorneys-General of the respective States.)

IN all the States except Wyoming the right to vote at general elections is restricted to males of 21 years of age and upward. Women are entitled to vote at school elections in several States. They are entitled by local law to full suffrage in the State of Wyoming. (See article entitled "Woman Suffrage.")

STATES.	Requirements as to Citizenship.	In State.	In County.	In Town.	In Precinct.	Persons Excluded from Suffrage.
		Previous Residence Required.				
Alabama.......	Citizen of United States or alien who has declared intention.	1 yr....	3 mo...	30 dys..	30 dys.	Convicted of treason or other crime punishable by imprisonment, idiots, or insane.
Arkansas*.....	Citizen of United States or alien who has declared intention.	1 yr....	6 mo...	....	30 dys.	Idiots, insane, convicted of felony, until pardoned.
California*. ...	Citizen by nativity, naturalization, or treaty of Queretaro.	1 yr....	90 dys..	....	30 dys.	Chinese, insane, embezzlers of public moneys, convicted of infamous crime.
Colorado.......	Citizen or alien who has declared intention 4 months previous to offering to vote.	6 mo...	90 dys..	10 dys..	10 dys.	Under guardianship, insane, idiots, or imprisoned.
Connecticut*.	Citizen of United States who can read Constitution or statutes.	1 yr....	....	6 mo...		Convicted of felony or theft.
Delaware*.....	Citizen and paying county tax after age 22.	1 yr....	1 mo...	....	15 dys.	Idiots, insane, paupers, felons.
Florida*.......	Citizen of United States or alien who has declared intention, who has paid capitation tax 2 years.	1 yr....	6 mo...	....	(a)	Insane, under guardianship, convicted of felony, or any infamous crime.
Georgia........	Citizen of the United States who has paid all his taxes since 1877.	1 yr....	6 mo...	....		Idiots, insane, convicted of crime punishable by imprisonment until pardoned.
Idaho.	Citizen of the United States...	6 mo...	30 dys..	....		Chinese, Indians, Mormons, felons, insane, election bribery.
Illinois*........	Citizen of the United States...	1 yr....	90 dys..	30 dys.	30 dys.	Convicted of crime punishable in penitentiary until pardoned and restored to rights.
Indiana*.......	Citizen of United States or alien who has declared intention and resided 1 year in United States and 6 months in State.	6 mo...	....	60 dys..	30 dys.	Convicted of crime and disfranchised by judgment of the court.
Iowa*...........	Citizen of the United States...	6 mo...	60 dys..	....	....	Idiots, insane, convicted of infamous crime, United States soldiers and marines not bona fide residents.
Kansas........	Citizen of United States or alien who has declared intention(a)	6 mo...	30 dys..	30 dys..	30 dys.	Idiots, insane, convicts, rebels not restored to citizenship, under guardianship, public embezzlers, bribed.
Kentucky......	Citizen of the United States...	2 yrs...	6 mo...	60 dys..	60 dys.	Convicted of treason, felony, bribery at election, idiots, insane.
Louisiana......	Citizen of United States or alien who has declared intention.	1 yr....	6 mo...	....	30 dys.	Idiots, insane, convicted of treason, embezzlement of public funds, all crime punishable by imprisonment in penitentiary.
Maine*........	Citizen of the United States...	3 mo...	3 mo...	3 mo...		Paupers, persons under guardianship, Indians not taxed, and in 1893 all new voters who cannot read the Constitution or write their own names.
Maryland*.....	Citizen of the United States...	1 yr....	6 mo...	....	....	A person over 21 yrs. convicted of larceny or other infamous crime, unless pardoned, persons under guardianship, as lunatics or non compos mentis.
Massachusetts .	Citizen who can read Constitution in English and write.	1 yr....	....	6 mo...	30 dys.	Paupers (except honorably discharged U. S. soldiers and sailors) and persons under guardianship.
Michigan*.....	Citizen or inhabitant who has declared intention under U.S. laws 6 months before election and lived in State 2½ years.	3 mo...	....	10 dys..	10 dys.	Indians, duellists and accessories.
Minnesota*....	Citizen of United States or alien who has declared intention, and civilized Indians (c).	4 mo.†	10 dys..	10 dys..	10 dys.	Convicted of treason or felony, unless pardoned, persons under guardianship or insane.
Mississippi*....	Citizen of the United States who can read or understand Constitution after January 1, 1892.	2 yrs...	1 yr....	1 yr....	1 yr.(b)	Insane, idiots, Indians not taxed, felons, persons who have not paid taxes.
Missouri*.	Citizen of United States or alien who has declared intention not less than one year or more than five before offering to vote.	1 yr....	60 dys..	60 dys..	....	U. S. soldiers and marines, paupers, criminals convicted once until pardoned, felons and violators of suffrage laws convicted a second time.

* Australian Ballot Law or a modification of it in force.   † And one year's residence in United States prior to voting.   (a) And females, in school and city elections.   (b) Clergymen are qualified after six months' residence in precinct.   (c) Women can vote in school elections.

States.	Requirements as to Citizenship.	Previous Residence Required.				Persons Excluded from Suffrage.
		In State.	In County.	In Town.	In Precinct.	
Montana *	Citizen of the United States...	1 yr...	30 dys.	......	......	Indians, felons, soldiers.
Nebraska*	Citizen of United States or alien who has declared intention thirty days prior to election.	6 mo..	40 dys.	10 dys.	10 dys.	Idiots, insane, convicted of treason or felony, unless pardoned, soldiers, sailors.
Nevada........	Citizen of the United States....	6 mo..	30 dys.	30 dys.	30 dys.	Idiots, insane, convicted of treason or felony, unamnestied Confederates who bore arms against the United States.
N. Hampshire*.	Inhabitants, native or naturalized.................	6 mo..	....	6 mo..	....	Paupers (except honorably discharged U. S. soldiers and sailors), persons excused from paying taxes at their own request.
New-Jersey*...	Citizen of the United States...	1 yr...	5 mo..	......	......	Idiots, insane paupers, persons convicted of crimes (unless pardoned), which exclude them from being witnesses.
New-York*.	Citizen who shall have been a citizen for ten days..........	1 yr..	4 mo..	30 dys.	30 dys.	Convicted of bribery or any infamous crime, unless sentenced to reformatory or pardoned, betters on result of any election at which they offer to vote, bribers for votes and the bribed.
North-Carolina.	Citizen of the United States...	1 yr...	90 dys.	......	......	Convicted of felony or other infamous crime, idiots, lunatics.
North-Dakota*.	Citizen of the United States, alien who has declared intention, and civilized Indian†..	1 yr...	6 mo..	......	90 dys.	United States soldiers and sailors, persons non compos mentis, and felons.
Ohio*..........	Citizen of the United States...	1 yr...	30 dys.	....	20 dys.	Felony until pardoned and restored to citizenship, idiots, insane.
Oregon*	Citizen of United States or alien who has declared intention one year preceding election.	6 mo..	....	......	......	Idiots, insane, convicted of felony, United States soldiers and sailors, Chinese.
Pennsylvania...	Citizen of the United States at least one month, and if 22 years old or more must have paid tax within two years.	1 yr‡..	....	......	2 mo..	Convicted of some offence whereby right of suffrage is forfeited, non-taxpayers.
Rhode-Island*..	Citizen of the United States.......	2 yrs..	....	6 mo..	....	Paupers, lunatics, persons non compos mentis, convicted of bribery or infamous crime until restored to right to vote under guardianship.
South-Carolina.	Citizen of the United States...	1 yr...	60 dys.	60 dys.	......	Convicted of treason, murder, or other infamous crime, duelling, paupers, insane, idiots.
South-Dakota* .	Citizen of the United States or alien who has declared intention.	6 mo.§	30 dys.	......	10 dys.	Under guardianship, idiots, insane, convicted of treason or felony, unless pardoned.
Tennessee*.....	Citizen of the United States....	1 yr...	6 mo..		(a)	Convicted of bribery or other infamous offence.
Texas..........	Citizen of United States	1 yr...	6 mo..	6 mo..	(a)	Idiots, lunatics, paupers convicted of felony, U. S. soldiers and seamen.
Vermont*.......	Citizen of the United States ...	1 yr..	3 mo..	3 mo..	3mo(b)	Unpardoned convicts and deserters from United States military or naval service during civil war, ex-Confederates.
Virginia	Citizen of the United States...	1 yr...	3 mo..	3 mo..	30 dys.	Idiots, lunatics, convicted of bribery at election, embezzlement of public funds, treason, felony and petty larceny, duellists and abettors, unless pardoned by Legislature.
Washington*...	Citizen of the United States...	1 yr..	90 dys.	30 dys.	30 dys.	Indians not taxed.
West-Virginia *.	Citizen of the State.............	1 yr...	60 dys.	....	(a)	Paupers, idiots, lunatics, convicted of treason, felony, or bribery at elections, U. S. soldier or sailor.
Wisconsin*.....	Citizen of United States or alien who has declared intention.	1 yr...	....	......	10 dys.	Insane, under guardianship, convicted of treason or felony, unless pardoned.
Wyoming*.....	Citizen of the United States, male or female.	1 yr...	60 dys.	......	......	Idiots, insane, felons, unable to read State Constitution.

For laws requiring Registration of Voters, see next page.

*Australian ballot law or a modification of it in force. † Indian must have several tribal relations two years next preceding the election. ‡ Or if, having previously been a qualified elector or native, he shall have removed and returned, then 6 months. § One year's residence in the United States prior to election required. (a) Actual residence in the precinct or district required. (b) If residing in State 1 year, a bona fide resident in precinct at time of registration may vote without previous residence in precinct.

Requirements Regarding the Registration of Voters.

(Continuation of "Qualifications for Voting," on preceding pages.)

THE registration of voters is required in the States of Alabama, California, Colorado, Connecticut, Florida, Idaho, Louisiana, Maryland, Massachusetts, Michigan, Minnesota, Mississippi, Nevada, New-Hampshire, New-Jersey, North-Carolina, Pennsylvania, South-Carolina, Vermont, Virginia, and Wyoming, and the territories of Arizona, New-Mexico, and Utah.

In Georgia registration is required in most counties by local law, and in South-Dakota in a few counties.

In Maine and Kentucky registration is required in cities, in Kansas in cities of the first and second class, in Iowa and Nebraska in cities of and over 2,500 inhabitants, in North-Dakota in cities of over 3,000 inhabitants, and in Ohio in cities of not less than 9,000 inhabitants.

In Illinois registration is required in Chicago and East St. Louis. Elsewhere a voter not registered may swear in his vote.

In Missouri it is required in cities of 100,000 inhabitants, and in Wisconsin in cities having 3,000 inhabitants and over. In New-York it is required in all cities and in all incorporated villages of over 7,000 inhabitants. In Rhode-Island non-taxpayers are required to register yearly before December 31. In Texas, cities of 10,000 or over may require registration.

The registration of voters is not required in the States of Delaware, Indiana, Kentucky, Oregon, South-Dakota, and Tennessee. It is prohibited in Arkansas and West-Virginia by constitutional provision.

Woman Suffrage.

THE following is a statement of the Woman Suffrage movement, corrected to January 1, 1893.

Wyoming.—Women have voted on the same terms with men since 1870. The convention in 1889 to form a State Constitution unanimously inserted a provision securing them suffrage. This Constitution was ratified by the voters at a special election by about three-fourths majority. Congress admitted the State July 10, 1890.

Washington.—Women voted in the Territory for five years, till excluded by a decision of the Territorial Supreme Court, which court was not elected by the people nor responsible to them. In adopting a State Constitution, the question of allowing women to vote was submitted separately to vote of the men. It was not carried. Many women claim that they were illegally excluded, and are seeking to regain suffrage.

Kansas.—Women have suffrage in all municipal elections. About 60,000 voted last year.

Utah.—Women voted in this Territory until excluded by the Edmunds law. They have organized in large numbers to demand the repeal of this law. The State Constitution of 1884 gave suffrage to women.

School suffrage exists, on various terms, in Arizona, Colorado, Delaware, Idaho, Illinois, Indiana, Kansas, Kentucky, Massachusetts, Michigan, Minnesota, Nebraska, New-Hampshire, New-Jersey, New-York, North-Dakota, Oklahoma, Oregon, South-Dakota, Texas, Vermont, Washington, and Wisconsin. Women can vote for trustees of the State University in Illinois and for county superintendents in Minnesota.

Montana.—The State Constitution guarantees women the power to vote on local taxation.

New-York.—Women can vote at waterworks elections, and on questions of local improvements; also for Assembly District School Commissioners in the rural districts once in three years.

Pennsylvania.—Women vote on local improvements, by signing or refusing to sign petitions.

New-Jersey.—Women can vote at elections for sewers and other improvements.

Southern States.—Delaware has municipal woman suffrage in Wilmington and many other places. Louisiana admits women to vote on the question of running railroads through parishes, Tennessee on incorporation of cities and annexation thereto, Mississippi on fence questions under the stock law, Arkansas and Missouri by signing or refusing to sign petitions on liquor license. Kentucky, widows whose children attend school vote. Texas women in many counties vote by signing or refusing to sign petitions for school officers.

Thirty-two States and Territories—a majority of the Union—have given women some form of suffrage.

Canada.—Women have municipal suffrage in every province, including the Northwest Territories. In Ontario they vote for all elective officers but members of the Legislature and Parliament.

Europe.—In England, Scotland, and Wales single and widowed women vote for all elective officers but one (member of Parliament) on like terms with men. The number of these voters is estimated at 2,000,000.

In Ireland women have municipal suffrage in Belfast; they vote for harbor boards in the seaports, and for poor-law guardians everywhere.

In France the women teachers elect members to sit in the "Department Councils of Instruction."

In Sweden their suffrage is about the same as in England; and they vote, too, indirectly for members of the House of Lords. In Norway they have school suffrage.

In Russia women, heads of households, vote for all elective officers and on all local questions.

In Austria they vote (by proxy) at elections for members of provincial and imperial Parliaments. In Hungary and all Austrian provinces they vote at local elections in person.

In Italy widows vote for members of Parliament. In Finland women vote for all elective officers.

In Prussia women vote (mostly by proxy) for township officers and members of provincial Diets.

In Roumania women vote (by proxy) at municipal elections.

In Belgium and Luxembourg widows have municipal suffrage.

Asia.—In British Burmah women taxpayers vote in the rural tracts.

In the Madras Presidency and the Bombay Presidency (Hindustan) they can do so in all municipalities.

The Russians are colonizing all their vast Asian possessions, and carry everywhere the "mir" or self-governing village, wherein women, heads of households, vote.

Africa.—Women have municipal suffrage in Cape Colony, which covers 1,000,000 square miles.

Australasia.—Municipal woman suffrage exists in New-Zealand, and the Legislature has declared that women shall vote for members of Parliament. Municipal suffrage exists in every province of Australia. The Parliament of South-Australia has declared for women voting at Parliamentary elections also.

Islands.—Iceland, in the North-Atlantic, the Isle of Man, between England and Ireland, Jersey, between England and France, and Pitcairn Island, in the South Pacific, have full woman suffrage. Tasmania, Sicily, Sardinia, Corsica, nearly 300 islands around Britain, the islands around Australia, Tasmania, and New-Zealand, and a number of islands elsewhere have various degrees of partial woman suffrage.

The New-York State Assembly passed, April 15, 1892, by 71 votes to 34, a bill urged since 1880, by Hamilton Willcox, fully enfranchising the women of the State. The majority of the Senate agreed to pass the bill, but the minority prevented a vote being taken.

This information respecting woman suffrage is furnished to THE WORLD ALMANAC by Mr. Hamilton Willcox, of New-York, author of "Freedom's Conquests; the Great Spread of Woman Suffrage through the World," and Chairman of the New-York State Executive Committee of the Woman Suffrage Party.

STATES AND TERRITORIES.	POPULAR VOTE.						ELECTORAL VOTE.		
	Cleveland, Dem.	Harrison, Rep.	Weaver, Peop.	Bidwell, Pro.	Wing, S. Lab.	Pluralities.	Cleveland, Dem.	Harrison, Rep.	Weaver, Peop.
Alabama	138,138	9,197	85,181	239	....	52,957 C	11	..	..
Arkansas	87,834	46,884	11,831	113	....	40,950 C	8	..	..
California	117,908	117,618	25,226	8,056	....	290 C	8	1	..
Colorado	....	38,620	53,584	1,638	....	14,964 W	..	..	4
Connecticut	82,395	77,025	806	4,025	329	5,370 C	6	..	..
Delaware	18,581	18,083	13	565	....	498 C	3	..	..
Florida	30,143	....	4,843	475	....	25,300 C	4	..	..
Georgia	129,361	48,305	42,937	988	....	81,056 C	13	..	..
Idaho	....	8,599	10,520	288	....	1,921 W	..	..	3
Illinois	426,281	399,288	22,207	25,870	. .	26,993 C	24	..	..
Indiana	262,740	255,615	22,208	13,050	....	7,125 C	15	..	..
Iowa	196,367	219,795	20,595	6,402	....	22,965 H	..	13	..
Kansas	....	157,237	163,111	4,539	....	5,874 W	..	..	10
Kentucky	175,461	135,441	23,500	6,442	....	40,020 C	13	..	..
Louisiana	87,922	13,282	13,281	....	....	61,359 C	8	..	..
Maine	48,044	62,923	2,381	3,062	....	14,979 H	..	6	..
Maryland	113,866	92,736	796	5,877	....	21,130 C	8	..	..
Massachusetts	176,813	202,814	3,210	7,539	649	26,001 H	..	15	..
Michigan	202,296	222,708	19,892	14,069	....	20,412 H	5	9	..
Minnesota	100,920	122,823	29,313	14,182	....	21,903 H*	..	9	..
Mississippi	40,237	1,406	10,256	910	....	29,981 C	9	..	..
Missouri	268,398	226,918	41,213	4,331	....	41,480 C	17	..	..
Montana	17,581	18,851	7,334	549	....	1,270 H	..	3	..
Nebraska	24,943	87,227	83,134	4,902	....	4,093 H	..	8	..
Nevada	714	2,811	7,264	89	....	4,453 W	..	..	3
New-Hampshire	42,081	45,658	292	1,297	....	3,547 H	..	4	..
New-Jersey	171,042	156,068	969	8,131	1,337	14,974 C	10	..	..
New-York	654,868	609,350	16,429	38,190	17,956	45,518 C	36	..	..
North-Carolina	132,951	100,342	44,736	2,636	....	32,609 C	11	..	..
North-Dakota	.. ..	17,519	17,700	899	....	181 W	1	1	1
Ohio	404,115	405,187	14,850	26,012	....	1,072 H	1	22	..
Oregon	14,243	35,002	*26,965	2,281	....	811 F†	..	3	1
Pennsylvania	452,264	516,011	8,714	25,123	898	63,767 H	..	32	..
Rhode-Island	24,335	26,972	228	1,654	....	2,637 H	..	4	..
South-Carolina	54,692	13,345	2,407	....	....	41,347 C	9	..	..
South-Dakota	9,081	34,888	26,544	....	....	8,344 H	..	4	..
Tennessee	138,874	100,331	23,477	4,851	....	38,543 C	12	..	..
Texas	239,148	81,444	99,688	2,165	....	139,460 C	15	..	..
Vermont	16,325	37,992	43	1,415	....	21,667 H	..	4	..
Virginia	163,977	113,262	12,275	2,738	....	50,715 C	12	..	..
Washington	29,802	36,460	19,165	2,542	....	6,658 H	..	4	..
West-Virginia	84,467	80,293	4,166	2,145	....	4 174 C	6	..	..
Wisconsin	177,335	170,791	9,909	13,132	....	6,544 C	12	..	..
Wyoming	....	8,454	7,722	530	....	732 H	..	3	..
Total	5,556,533	5,175,577	1,040,902	264,060	21,164	......	277	145	22

Popular Vote, Cleveland over Harrison **382,956**
Electoral Vote, Cleveland over Harrison **132**
Electoral Vote, Cleveland over Harrison and Weaver **110**
Total Popular Vote, 1892, Including Scattering, ... **12,110,636**

The total Democratic popular vote in 1888 was 5,538,233; in 1892 it was 5,556,533, an increase of 18,300 from 1888 to 1892. The total Republican vote in 1888 was 5,440,216; in 1892 it was 5,175,577, a decrease of 264,639 from 1888 to 1892.

In the States of Colorado, Idaho, Kansas, North-Dakota, and Wyoming the Democrats ran no electoral tickets, and voted for the People's Party electoral tickets for the purpose of taking those States from the Republicans. With a few exceptions they also voted for the People's Party electors in Nevada. In Louisiana the Republicans and People's Party united their vote, each nominating half of the eight candidates for electors, and in the table their aggregate popular vote is divided.

In five States the electoral vote was divided: in California and Ohio because the vote for the Cleveland and Harrison electors was so close; in Michigan because by act of Legislature each Congressional district voted separately for an elector; in Oregon because one of the four candidates for electors on the People's Party ticket was also on the Democratic ticket, the result being three Republicans and one People's Party elected; in North-Dakota because one of the two People's Party electors who were elected cast his vote for Cleveland, this causing the electoral vote of the State to be equally divided between Cleveland, Harrison, and Weaver. *Harrison over Fusion vote 14,182.

† In Oregon the highest vote for an elector was that cast for the one candidate who was on both the Democratic and People's Party tickets. He received 35,813 votes. The next highest vote was for a Republican candidate for elector, 35,002. This gave the Fusion candidate (who afterward voted for Weaver) a plurality of 811, and it so appears in the column of pluralities above.

The Federal Government.

President..........................GROVER CLEVELAND, of New-York, salary, $50,000
Vice-President ....ADLAI E. STEVENSON, of Illinois,   "   8,000

THE CABINET.

Arranged in the order of succession for the Presidency declared by Chapter 4, Acts of 49th Congress, 1st Session.*

Secretary of State—Walter Q. Gresham, of Ill.	*Postmaster-General*—Wilson S. Bissell, of N. Y.
Secretary Treasury—John G. Carlisle, of Ky.	*Secretary Navy*—Hilary A. Herbert, of Ala.
Secretary of War—Daniel S. Lamont, of N. Y.	*Secretary Interior*—Hoke Smith, of Ga.
Attorney-General—Richard Olney, of Mass.	*Secretary Agriculture*—J. S. Morton, of Neb.

The salaries of the Cabinet officers are $8,000 each.

THE DEPARTMENTS.

STATE DEPARTMENT.

Assistant Secretary—Josiah Quincy, Mass.	$4,500	*Ch. Consular Bureau*...	$2,100
Second Ass't Secretary—A. A. Adee, D. C.	3,500	*Ch.Indexes &Archives*—J.H.Haswell,N.Y.	2,100
Third Ass't Sec't'y—W. M. Grinnell, N. Y.	3,500	*Ch. Bureau Accounts*—F. J. Kieckhoefer.	2,100
Chief Clerk—Sevellon A. Brown, N. Y	2,750	*Ch. Bureau Rolls & Lib.*—A. H. Allen....	2,100
Ch. Dipl'tic B'reau—T. W. Cridler, W. Va.	2,100	*Ch. Bureau Statistics*—M. Scanlan, N. Y.	2,100

TREASURY DEPARTMENT.

Ass't Secretary—G. M. Lambertson, Neb.	$4,500	*Com. of Navigation*—E. C. O'Brien, N.Y..	$3,600
Assistant Secretary—Oliver L. Spaulding..	4,500	*First Comptroller*—A. C. Matthews, Ill...	5,000
Assistant Secretary—John H. Gear, Ia	4,500	*Second Comptroller*—B. F. Gilkeson, Pa..	5,000
Chief Clerk—Fred A. Stocks, Kan........	3,000	*Comp. of Customs*—Sam'l V. Holliday, Pa.	4,000
Ch. Appointment Div.—H. Kretz, Pa.....	2,750	*Dep. Comp. Customs.*—H. A. Lockwood...	2,250
Ch. Warrant Div.—W. F. Mclennan, N.Y.	3,000	*First Auditor*—E. P. Baldwin, Md........	3,600
Ch. Pub. Moneys Div.—E. B. Daskam, Ct..	2,500	*Second Auditor*—J. N. Patterson, N. H....	3,600
Ch. Customs Div.—J. M. Comstock, N. Y..	2,750	*Third Auditor*—W. H. Hart, Ind........	3,600
Ch.Loans&Cur.Div.—A. T. Huntington..	2,500	*Fourth Auditor*—John R. Lynch, Miss...	3,600
Ch.Stationery&Printing—A.L. Sturtevant	2,500	*Fifth Auditor*—Thos. Holcomb, Del......	3,600
Ch. Mails & Files—John Nichols.........	2,500	*Sixth Auditor*—Thomas B. Coulter, O....	3,600
Ch.Miscellaneous Div.—J. W. Thomson...	2,500	*Treasurer of U. S.*—E. H. Nebeker, Ind..	6,000
Sup.Insp.-Gen.ofSteamboats—J.A.Dumont	3,500	*Ass't Treasurer*—J. W. Whelpley, N. Y..	3,600
Director of Mint—Edward O. Leech, D. C.	4,500	*Register Treasury*—W. S. Rosecrans, Cal.	4,000
Government Actuary—W. Fewsmith.	2,250	*Assistant Register*—Henry H. Smith......	2,250
Ch. Bureau of Statistics—S. G. Brock, Mo.	3,000	*Comp. of Currency*—A. B. Hepburn, N. Y.	5,000
Supt. Life-Saving Service—S. I. Kimball.	4,000	*Com. of Internal Rev.*—J.W. Mason,W.Va.	6,000
Ch'm Lt.House Bd.—Rr. Ad. J. A. Greer.	5,000	*Dep. Com. Internal Rev.*—G. W. Wilson..	3,200
Supervis. Surg.-Gen.—Walter Wyman,Mo.	4,000	*Solicitor Internal Rev.*—Alphonso Hart, O.	4,500
Ch. Bur. Engraving—W. M. Meredith, Ill.	4,500	*Solicitor of Treasury*—W. P. Hepburn, Ia.	4,500
Supervising Architect—W. J. Edbrooke...	4,500	*Chief Secret Service*—A. L. Drummond....	3,500
Sup. U. S. Coast Survey—T. C. Mendenhall	6,000	*Supt. Immigration*—Herman Stump, Md.	4,000

WAR DEPARTMENT.

Assistant Secretary—L. A. Grant, Minn ..	$4,500	*Insp.-Gen.*—B.-Gen.J.C.Breckinridge,Ky.	$5,500
Chief Clerk—John Tweedale, Pa..........	2,750	*Chief Clerk*—Warren H. Orcutt.........	2,000
Disbursing Clerk—W. S. Yeatman, D. C..	2,000	*Q'rmaster-Gen.*—B.-Gen. R. N. Batchelder.	5,500
Inspector Records—Samuel Hodgkins.....	2,000	*Chief Clerk*—J. Z. Dare, D. C...........	2,000
Adjutant-Gen.—B.-Gen. R. Williams.......	5,500	*Paymaster-Gen.*—B -Gen. William Smith.	5,500
Chief Clerk—R. P. Thian, N. Y..........	2,000	*Chief Clerk*—G. D. Hanson, D.C........	2,000
Commis'y-Gen.—B.-Gen. B. DuBarry	5,500	*Ch.of Engineers*—B.-Gen. T. L.Casey,R.I.	5,500
Chief Clerk—W. A. De Caindry, Md......	2,000	*Chief Clerk*—William J. Warren, N. Y....	2,000
Surgeon-Gen.—B.-Gen. C. Sutherland, Pa.	5,500	*Officer Charge Pub.Bldg.*—Col.O.H.Ernst.	4,500
Ass't Surg. Gen.—Lt.-Col. J. S. Billings, O.	3,250	*Chief Clerk*—E. F. Concklin, N. Y........	2,100
Ass't Surg. Gen.—Lt.-Col.C.R.Greenleaf,O	3,250	*Gardener*—George H. Brown, D. C........	1,800
Ass't Surg. Gen.—Maj. C. Smart, N. Y....	3,250	*Chief of Ordnance*—B.-Gen. D. W. Flagler	5,500
Chief Clerk—Geo. A. Jones.............	2,000	*Chief Clerk*—John J. Cook, D.C.........	2,000
Judge Adv.-Gen.—Col. G. N. Lieber, N.Y.	5,500	*Chief Signal Officer*—B.-Gen. A.W. Greely.	5,500
Chief Clerk—J. N. Morrison, Mo.........	1,800		

* The Department of Agriculture was made an executive department and the Secretary of Agriculture made a Cabinet officer, after the passage of the Succession act of the 49th Congress.

THE FEDERAL GOVERNMENT—*Continued.*

NAVY DEPARTMENT.

Ass't Secretary—William McAdoo, N. J.. $4,500
Chief Clerk—John W. Hogg, Tenn.. 2,500
Judge Adv.-Gen.—Capt. S. C. Lemly.... 4,500
Registrar—W. P. Moran, Va.............. 2,000
Chief Docks & Yds.—Com. N. H. Farquhar 5,000
Chief Ordnance—Com. W. M. Folger..... 5,000
Chief Prov. & Cloth.—Pym. Gen. Edwin
Stewart... 5,000
Chief Medicine.—Surg. Gen. J. M. Browne 5,000
Chief Equipment—Capt. Geo. Dewey ... 5,000
Chief Construction—T. D. Wilson, N. Y.. 5,000

Chief Navigation—Com. F. M. Ramsay.. $5,000
Engineer in Chief—G. W. Melville, Pa.... 5,000
Pay Director—Gilbert E. Thornton, Mass. 4,000
Pres. Nav. Exam. Bd.—Rr. Ad. J. A.
Greer.................. ....
Sup.Naval Obs.—Capt. F. V. McNair...... 5,000
Supt. Nautical Alm.—Prof. S. Newcomb.. 3,500
Hydrographer—Lieut. Com. R. Clover.... 3,000
Pres.Naval Ret'g Bd.—Rr. Ad. J. A.Greer. 5,000
Hdqts. Marine Corps—Col.Chas.Heywood

POST-OFFICE DEPARTMENT.

Chief Clerk—W. B. Cooley, Pa.......... $2,500
First Ass't P. M. G.—(Vacant)......... 4,000
Second Ass't P. M. G.—J. Lowrie Bell.... 4,000
Third Ass't P. M. G.—A. D. Hazen, Pa... 4,000
Fourth Ass't P.M.G.—R. A. Maxwell, N.Y. 4,000

Sup't Foreign M.—N. M. Brooks, Pa..... $3,000
Sup't Money-Order.—C.F.McDonald,Mass. 3,500
Gen. Supt. Railway M. S.—Jas. E.White. 3,500
Supt. Dead Letter Office—D. P. Leibhardt. 2,500
Chief P. O. Inspct.—M. D. Wheeler...... 3,000

INTERIOR DEPARTMENT.

First Ass't Sec.—John M. Reynolds, Pa.. $4,500
Assistant Secretary—Wm. H. Sims, Miss.. 4,000
Chief Clerk—Edward M. Dawson, Md..... 2,750
Com. Land Office—S. W. Lamoreaux, Wis. 4,000
Ass't Commis.—E. A. Bowers, D. C....... 3,000
Commis Pensions—.................. 5,000
Com. Ind. Affairs—T. J. Morgan, R. I.... 4,000
Ass't Commis.—Robert V. Belt, Md... 3,000

Com. Patents—John S. Seymour, Ct..... $5,000
Ass't Commis.—Samuel T. Fisher, Mass... 3,000
Commis. Education—W. T. Harris, Mass.. 3,000
Commis. Railroads—Wade Hampton, S. C. 4,500
Supt. of Census—Robt. P. Porter, N. Y.... 6,000
Direc. Geol. Surv.—John W. Powell, Ill.. 6,000
Chief Clerk—H. C. Rizer................. 2,400

DEPARTMENT OF AGRICULTURE.

Assistant Secretary—Edwin Willits, Mich.. $4,500
Chief Clerk—Henry Casson 2,500
Chief Weather Bureau—M. W. Harring-
ton, Mich 4,500
Statistician—... 2,500
Chief Forestry—B. E. Fernow, N. Y...... 2,000
Entomologist—C. V. Riley, Mo........... 2,500

Chemist—Harvey W. Wiley, Ind........ $2,500
Ornithologist—C. H. Merriam, N. Y....... 2,500
Botanist—George Vasey, Ill.............. 2,500
Pomologist—H. E. Van Deman, Kan...... 2,500
Microscopist—Thomas Taylor, Mass...... 2,500
Chief Seed Div.—J. B. Peck............. 2,500

DEPARTMENT OF JUSTICE.

Attorney-General—Richard Olney, Mass.. $8,000
Solicitor-Gen.—Lawrence Maxwell, Jr., O. 7,000
Ass't Atty.-Gen.—W. A. Maury, D. C..... 5,000
Ass't Atty.-Gen.—John B. Cotton, Me 5,000
Ass't Atty.-Gen.—Ed. B. Whitney, N. Y .. 5,000
Ass't Atty.-Gen.—John I. Hall, Ga....... 5,000
Ass't Atty.-Gen.—James N. Tyner, Ind.... 4,000
Ass't. Atty.-Gen.—L. W. Colby 5,000

Solicitor State Dep.—W. D. Dabney, Va.. $3,500
Chief Clerk—Cecil Clay, W. Va........... 2,450
Solicitor Treasury—Felix A. Reeve, Tenn. 4,500
Solicitor Internal Rev.—Alphonso Hart, O. 4,500
Law Clerk—A. J. Bentley, O.............. 2,700
General Agent—Elijah C. Foster.......... 3,650
Appointment Clerk—Frank A. Branagan, O. 2,000
Att'y for Pardons—Charles F. Scott..... 2,400

Civil Service Commis.—Chas. Lyman, Ct. $3,500
Civil Service Commis.—T. Roosevelt, N.Y. 3,500
CivilService Commis.—G. D. Johnston,La. 3,500
Chief Examiner Civ.S.—W.H.Webster,Ct. 3,000
Secretary Civ. S.—John T. Doyle, N. Y.... 2,000
Commis. of Labor—C. D. Wright, Mass... 5,000
Chief Clerk of Lab.—O. W. Weaver, Mass. 2,500

Government Printer—Frank W. Palmer, Ill $4,500
Fish Commis.—Marshall McDonald....... none
.... 4,000
Librarian of Congress—A.R.Spofford,D.C. 4,000
Director, Bureau of Amer. Republics—
Wm. E. Curtis ....

INTERSTATE COMMERCE COMMISSION.

Commis.—Chairman,Wm. R. Morrison, Ill. $7,500
Commis.—Jas. W. McDill, Ia. 7,000
Commis.—Judson C. Clements, Ga....... 7,000

Commis.—Martin A. Knapp, N. Y........ $7,000
Commis.—Wheelock G. Veazey, Vt...... 7,000
Secretary, Edward A. Moseley, Mass...... 3,500

SMITHSONIAN INSTITUTE.

Presiding Officer, ex-officio — Grover Cleveland, President of the United States .
Chancellor—Melville W. Fuller, Chief-Justice of the United States.
Secretary—S. P. Langley, Pa............ None.   *Chief Clerk*—William J. Rhees, D. C..... $2,100
Assistant Secretary—G. B. Goode, Ct..... $4,000

INTERCONTINENTAL RAILWAY COMMISSION.
Commissioners for the United States.

President—A. J. Cassatt, Pa............. ...... *Commissioner*—R. C. Kerens, Mo.......... .....
Commissioner—Henry G. Davis, Md...... ......

INTERNATIONAL MONETARY CONFERENCE.
Delegates from the United States.

Senator—Wm. B. Allison, Ia.
Senator—John P. Jones, Nev.
Congressman—James B. McCreary, Ky.
Director of the Mint—E. O. Leech, D. C.
Pres. Brown Univ.—E. Benjamin Andrews, R. I.

Prof. Univ. of Pa.—Ronald P. Falkner, Pa.
Pres. Chase Nat. Bank.—H. W. Cannon, N. Y.
James T. Morgan, Thomas T. Keller, Thomas
W. Cridler.

Party Divisions

IN THE HOUSE OF REPRESENTATIVES; 52D AND 53D CONGRESSES.

STATES.	Fifty-second Congress.* Dem.	Rep.	Peop.	Fifty-third Congress. Dem.	Rep.	Peop.	STATES.	Fifty-second Congress.* Dem.	Rep.	Peop.	Fifty-third Congress. Dem.	Rep.	Peop.
Alabama	8	..	..	9	..	..	Nebraska	1	..	2	1	3	2
Arkansas	5	..	..	6	..	1	Nevada	..	1	..	..	..	1
California	2	4	..	4	3	..	N.H'mpshire	2	..	..	..	2	..
Colorado	..	..	..	..	..	2	New-Jersey†	4	2	..	6	2	..
Connecticut	3	1	..	3	1	..	New-York†	22	11	..	20	14	..
Delaware	1	..	..	1	..	..	N.Carolina	8	1	..	8	1	1
Florida	2	..	..	2	..	..	N. Dakota	..	1	..	..	..	..
Georgia	9	1	1	11	..	..	Ohio	14	7	..	11	10	..
Idaho	..	1	..	..	1	..	Oregon	..	1	..	..	2	..
Illinois	14	6	..	12	10	..	Penn	10	18	..	10	20	..
Indiana	11	2	..	11	2	..	R. Island	2	..	..	‡	..	..
Iowa	6	5	..	1	10	..	S. Carolina	7	..	..	7	..	..
Kansas	..	2	5	2	3	3	S. Dakota	..	2	..	..	2	..
Kentucky	10	1	..	10	1	..	Tennessee	8	2	..	8	2	..
Louisiana	6	..	..	6	..	..	Texas	11	..	..	13	..	..
Maine	..	4	..	..	4	..	Vermont	..	2	..	..	2	..
Maryland	6	..	..	6	..	..	Virginia	10	..	..	10	..	..
Mass	7	5	..	3	10	..	Washington	..	1	..	..	2	..
Michigan	7	4	..	5	7	..	W. Virginia	4	..	..	4	..	..
Minnesota	3	1	1	2	5	..	Wisconsin	8	1	..	6	4	..
Mississippi	7	..	..	7	..	..	Wyoming	..	1	..	..	1	..
Missouri	14	..	..	13	2	..	**Total†**	**233**	**88**	**9**	**220**	**126**	**8**
Montana	1	..	..	1	..	..							

* As constituted at the beginning of the second session.   † Vacancies, 2—one in New-Jersey by the death of Edward F. McDonald, Democrat; one in New-York by the resignation of Alfred C. Chapin, Democrat.   ‡ The Rhode-Island vacancies will be filled at the State election in April, 1893.

PARTY DIVISIONS IN CONGRESS SINCE THE FORMATION OF THE REPUBLICAN PARTY, IN 1856.

CONGRESSES.	Years.	SENATE. Dem.	Rep.	Amer.	Union.	Ind.	HOUSE OF REPRESENTATIVES. Dem.	Rep.	Amer.	Union.	Ind.
XXXV	1857-1859	39	20	5	..	..	131	92	14	..	..
XXXVI	1859-1861	38	26	2	..	..	101	113	23	..	..
XXXVII	1861-1863*	10	31	..	2	..	42	106	..	28	..
XXXVIII	1863-1865*	9	36	..	5	..	75	102	..	..	9
XXXIX	1865-1867	11	41	..	..	..	40	145	..	..	..
XL	1867-1869	11	42	..	..	..	49	143	..	..	..
XLI	1869-1871	11	58	..	..	..	78	151	..	..	..
XLII	1871-1873	17	57	..	..	..	103	138	..	..	5†
XLIII	1873-1875	20	47	..	..	7†	92	194	..	..	14
XLIV	1875-1877	29	43	..	..	2†	168	107	..	..	..
XLV	1877-1879	39	35	..	..	1†	151	142	..	..	..
XLVI	1879-1881	41	32	..	..	..	148	129	..	..	16‡
XLVII	1881-1883	38	37	..	..	1§	138	146	..	..	10‡
XLVIII	1883-1885	36	40||	..	..	..	198	124	..	..	1‡
XLIX	1885-1887	34	42	..	..	..	204	120	..	..	1‡
L	1887-1889	37	39	..	..	..	168	153	..	..	4
LI	1889-1891	37	39	..	..	..	159	166	..	..	..
LII	1891-1893	39	47	..	..	2¶	236	88	..	..	8¶
LIII	1893-1895	45	39	..	..	4¶	220	126	..	..	8¶

Parties as constituted at the beginning of each Congress are given. These figures were liable to change by contests for seats, etc.

* During the Civil War most of the Southern States were unrepresented in Congress.   † Liberal Republicans.   ‡ Greenbackers.   § David Davis, Independent, of Illinois. || Two Virginia Senators were Readjusters, and voted with the Republicans.   ¶ People's Party.

Acts of the Fifty=Second Congress. First Session.

DURING the first session of the Fifty-second Congress, which extended from December 7, 1891, to August 5, 1892, 9,835 bills and joint resolutions were introduced in the House of Representatives and 3,604 in the Senate. Of these 823 became laws, the remainder being either defeated, unreported from committee, or left on the calendar to be disposed of at the second session.

The principal bills and joint resolutions of a public nature which passed during the first session of the Fifty-second Congress were as follows:

Chapter 35. An act to protect exhibitors at the World's Fair from prosecution for exhibiting wares protected by American patents and trade marks.

Chapter 60. An act to prohibit the coming of Chinese into the United States.

Chapter 63. An act to encourage American ship-building. (Granting an American registry to two Inman ocean steamships on condition that two others be built by the company in the United States.)

Chapter 71. An act to authorize the establishment of a branch national bank on the World's Fair Grounds.

Chapter 117. An act appropriating $7,674,332 to supply pension deficiencies.

Chapter 140. An act to provide for opening a part of the Colville Indian Reservation in the State of Washington.

Chapter 237. An act accepting a bequest of $250,000 from General George W. Cullum, of New-York City, for a memorial hall at West Point, and providing for its erection.

Chapter 248. An act to enforce reciprocal commercial relations between the United States and Canada (the Retaliatory Act).

Chapter 277. An act granting pensions to the survivors of the Indian wars of 1832-42, known as the Black Hawk War, Creek War, Cherokee disturbances, and the Seminole War.

Chapter 312. An act establishing the "National Academy of Art" in the District of Columbia.

Chapter 328. An act to provide for the examination and promotion of enlisted men of the army to the grade of second lieutenant.

Chapter 352. An act limiting the work day of laborers and mechanics employed upon the public works of the United States or the District of Columbia to eight hours.

Chapter 374. An act changing the date for the dedication of the buildings of the World's Fair from October 12, 1892, to October 21, 1892.

Chapter 281. An act providing for 5,000,000 Columbian silver half dollars for medals and diplomas, and for the closing of the World's Fair on Sundays.

Joint Resolution No. 21. Authorized the President to invite certain governments to send delegates to the Pan-American Medical Congress.

Joint Resolution No. 22. Provided for an investigation relative to the "slums" of cities having 200,000 inhabitants and over.

Joint Resolution No. 25. Requested the loan of certain historical relics for the World's Fair from the Queen Regent of Spain, the city of Genoa, the Duke of Veragua, the descendants of Columbus, and others.

Joint Resolution No. 26. Authorized the Secretary of the Interior to prepare and send to the World's Fair models, drawings, etc., prepared or invented by women.

Joint Resolution No. 32. Extended an invitation to the King and Queen of Spain and the descendants of Columbus to participate in the World's Fair.

The Ballot Reform Movement.

Two States, through legislation in 1892, were added to the large number which now have, in one form or another, laws securing the secrecy of the ballot and protecting the voter from intimidation or the influence of bribery. Iowa adopted the Australian system, and Mississippi incorporated the secret ballot in her new code, the constitution prescribing an intelligence qualification for the suffrage. Maryland extended the operation of her secret ballot law of 1890 from the city of Baltimore to the whole State.

The following is a list of the States and Territories which have adopted new ballot laws, based more or less on the Australian system:

1888—Kentucky (applying only to Louisville), Massachusetts.

1889—Connecticut, Indiana, Michigan, Minnesota, Missouri, Montana, Rhode-Island, Tennessee, Wisconsin.

1890—Maryland (applying to Baltimore), New-Jersey, New-York, Oklahoma, Vermont, Washington, Wyoming.

1891—Arkansas, California, Delaware, Illinois, Maine, Nebraska, New-Hampshire, North-Dakota, Ohio, Pennsylvania, South-Dakota, Oregon, West-Virginia, Colorado.

1892—Iowa, Maryland (whole State), Mississippi.

FORM OF BALLOT.

The distinctive feature of the ballot practice in New-South-Wales is that the names of all the candidates being on one ticket, the names of persons for whom the voter does not wish to vote must be crossed off, a blue lead-pencil being provided for the purpose by the authorities, while there are clearly printed on the ticket, in red ink, directions as to how many candidates must be voted for.

Under the New-York and New-Jersey laws each party ticket is printed on a separate ballot. For straight voting, therefore, no marking is required. For the benefit mainly of the illiterate or blind, as claimed, the paster ballot is permitted in New-York.

In all the other States which have adopted the reform system of voting, the single or "blanket" ballot is used. All the names in nomination are printed on one sheet, the voter's choice to be indicated by marking. There are two methods used of grouping the names of the candidates. The Australian plan arranges the titles of the offices alphabetically, the names of the candidates, and usually their party connection, being attached.

The States which follow this plan with more or less variation in the form, but preserving the feature of alphabetical arrangement of titles of offices to be voted for, are California, Kentucky, Massachusetts, Minnesota, Montana, Nebraska, New-Hampshire, Oregon, Rhode-Island, Tennessee, Vermont, Washington, and Wyoming.

The other form groups all names and offices by parties. It is illustrated by the following diagram of a ballot:

Democratic.	Republican.	Prohibition.	People's.
O	O	O	O
For Governor.	*For Governor.*	*For Governor.*	*For Governor.*
☐ William Smith.	☐ Thomas Jones.	☐ John Brown.	☐ Henry Robinson.

The voter of a straight ticket marks a cross in the circle at the head of his ticket. The voter who scatter marks the squares opposite the names of all the candidates on the tickets.

The States and Territories which use this plan, with or without immaterial variations, are Delaware, Illinois, Indiana, Maine, Maryland, Missouri, Ohio, Wisconsin, and Oklahoma.

National Party Platforms of 1892.

NATIONAL DEMOCRATIC PLATFORM, ADOPTED AT CHICAGO, ILL., JUNE 22, 1892.

THE representatives of the Democratic Party of the United States, in National Convention assembled, do reaffirm their allegiance to the principles of the party as formulated by Jefferson and exemplified by the long and illustrious line of his successors in Democratic leadership, from Madison to Cleveland; we believe the public welfare demands that these principles be applied to the conduct of the Federal Government, through the accession to power of the party that advocates them; and we solemnly declare that the need of a return to these fundamental principles of free popular government, based on home-rule and individual liberty, was never more urgent than now, when the tendency to centralize all power at the Federal Capital has become a menace to the reserved rights of the States, that strikes at the very roots of our Government under the Constitution as framed by the fathers of the Republic.

The Force Bill.—We warn the people of our common country, jealous for the preservation of their free institutions, that the policy of Federal control of elections, to which the Republican Party has committed itself, is fraught with the gravest dangers, scarcely less momentous than would result from a revolution practically establishing a monarchy on the ruins of the Republic. It strikes at the North as well as the South and injures the colored citizen even more than the white; it means a horde of deputy marshals at every polling place, armed with Federal power, returning boards appointed and controlled by Federal authority; the outrage of the electoral rights of the people in the several States; the subjugation of the colored people to the control of the party in power and the revival of race antagonisms now happily abated, of the utmost peril to the safety and happiness of all—a measure deliberately and justly described by a leading Republican Senator as " the most infamous bill that ever crossed the threshold of the Senate." Such a policy, if sanctioned by law, would mean the dominance of a self-perpetuating oligarchy of office-holders, and the party first intrusted with its machinery could be dislodged from power only by an appeal to the reserved right of the people to resist oppression, which is inherent in all self-governing communities. Two years ago this revolutionary policy was emphatically condemned by the people at the polls; but, in contempt of that verdict, the Republican Party has defiantly declared, in its latest authoritative utterance, that its success in the coming election will mean the enactment of the Force bill and the usurpation of despotic control over the elections in all the States.

Believing that the preservation of Republican government in the United States is dependent upon the defeat of this policy of legalized force and fraud, we invite the support of all citizens who desire to see the Constitution maintained in its integrity with the laws pursuant |thereto which have given our country a hundred years of unexampled prosperity; and we pledge the Democratic Party, if it be intrusted with power, not only to the defeat of the Force bill, but also to relentless opposition to the Republican policy of profligate expenditure, which in the short space of two years squandered an enormous surplus and emptied an overflowing treasury, after piling new burdens of taxation upon the already overtaxed labor of the country.

Protection.—We denounce Republican protection as a fraud; a robbery of the great majority of the American people for the benefit of the few. We declare it to be a fundamental principle of the Democratic Party that the Federal Government has no constitutional power to impose and collect tariff duties, except for the purpose of revenue only, and we demand that the collection of such taxes shall be limited to the necessities of the Government when honestly and economically administered.

The McKinley Tariff.—We denounce the McKinley tariff law enacted by the Fifty-first Congress as the culminating atrocity of class legislation; we endorse the efforts made by the Democrats of the present Congress to modify its most oppressive features in the direction of free raw materials and cheaper manufactured goods that enter into general consumption; and we promise its repeal as one of the beneficent results that will follow the action of the people in intrusting power to the Democratic Party. Since the McKinley tariff went into operation there have been ten reductions of the wages of laboring men to one increase. We deny that there has been any increase of prosperity to the country since that tariff went into operation, and we point to the dulness and distress, the wage reductions and strikes in the iron trade as the best possible evidence that no such prosperity has resulted from the McKinley act.

The Mortgage Burden.—We call the attention of thoughtful Americans to the fact that after thirty years of restrictive taxes against the importation of foreign wealth in exchange for our agricultural surplus, the homes and farms of the country have become burdened with a real estate mortgage debt of over $2,500,000,000, exclusive of all other forms of indebtedness; that in one of the chief agricultural States of the West there appears a real estate mortgage debt averaging $165 per capita of the total population; and that similar conditions and tendencies are shown to exist in other agricultural exporting States. We denounce a policy which fosters no industry so much as it does that of the sheriff.

Reciprocity.—Trade interchange on the basis of reciprocal advantages to the countries participating is a time-honored doctrine of the Democratic faith, but we denounce the sham reciprocity which juggles with the people's desire for enlarged foreign markets and freer exchanges by pretending to establish closer trade relations for a country whose articles of export are almost exclusively agricultural products with other countries that are also agricultural, while erecting a custom-house barrier of prohibitive tariff taxes against the richest countries of the world that stand ready to take our entire surplus of products and to exchange therefor commodities which are necessaries and comforts of life among our own people.

Trusts.—We recognize in the Trusts and Combinations which are designed to enable capital to secure more than its just share of the joint product of capital and labor a natural consequence of the prohibitive taxes which prevent the free competition which is the life of honest trade, but believe their worst evils can be abated by law, and we demand the rigid enforcement of the laws made to prevent and control them, together with such further legislation in restraint of their abuses as experience may show to be necessary.

The Public Lands.—The Republican Party, while professing a policy of reserving the public land for small holdings by actual settlers, has given away the people's heritage, until now a few railroad and non-resident aliens, individual and corporate, possess a larger area than that of all our farms between the two seas. The last Democratic administration reversed the improvident and unwise policy of the Republican Party touching the public domain, and reclaimed from corporations and syndicates, alien and domestic, and restored to the people nearly one hundred millions (100,000,000) acres of valuable land to be sacredly held as homesteads for our citizens, and we pledge ourselves to continue this policy until every acre of land so unlawfully held shall be reclaimed and restored to the people.

Gold and Silver.—We denounce the Republican legislation known as the Sherman act of 1890 as a cowardly makeshift, fraught with possibilities of danger in the future, which should make all of its supporters, as well as its author, anxious for its speedy repeal. We hold to the use of both gold and silver as the standard money of the country, and to the coinage of both gold and silver without discriminating against either metal or charge for mintage, but the dollar unit of coinage of both metals must be of equal intrinsic and exchangeable value, or be adjusted through international agreement, or by such safeguards of legislation as shall ensure the maintenance of the parity of the two metals. and the equal power of every dollar at all times in the markets, and in payment of debt; and we demand that all paper currency shall be kept at par with and redeemable in such coin. We insist upon this policy as especially necessary for the protection of the farmers and laboring classes, the first and most defenceless victims of unstable money and a fluctuating currency.

Tax on State Banks.—We recommend that the prohibitory ten per cent tax on State bank issues be repealed.

Civil Service Reform.—Public office is a public trust. We reaffirm the declaration of the Democratic National Convention of 1876, for the reform of the civil service, and we call for the honest enforcement of all laws regulating the same. The nomination of a President as in the recent Republican Convention, by delegations composed largely of his appointees, holding office at his pleasure, is a scandalous satire upon free popular institutions, and a startling illustration of the methods by which a President may gratify his ambition. We denounce a policy under which the Federal office-holders usurp control of party conventions in the States, and we pledge the Democratic Party to reform these and all other abuses which threaten individual liberty and local self-government.

Our Foreign Policy.—The Democratic Party is the only party that has ever given the country a foreign policy consistent and vigorous, compelling respect abroad and inspiring confidence at home. While avoiding entangling alliances, it has aimed to cultivate friendly relations with other nations, and especially with our neighbors on the American continent, whose destiny is closely linked with our own, and we view with alarm the tendency to a policy of irritation and bluster which is liable at any time to confront us with the alternative of humiliation or war. We favor the maintenance of a navy strong enough for all purposes of national defence and to properly maintain the honor and dignity of the country abroad.

Sympathy with the Oppressed.—This country has always been the refuge of the oppressed from every land—exiles for conscience' sake—and in the spirit of the founders of our Government we condemn the oppression practised by the Russian Government upon its Lutheran and Jewish subjects, and we call upon our National Government, in the interest of justice and humanity, by all just and proper means, to use its prompt and best efforts to bring about a cessation of these cruel persecutions in the dominions of the Czar and to secure to the oppressed equal rights.

Irish Home Rule.—We tender our profound and earnest sympathy to those lovers of freedom who are struggling for home rule and the great cause of local self-government in Ireland.

Immigration.—We heartily approve all legitimate efforts to prevent the United States from being used as the dumping ground for the known criminals and professional paupers of Europe, and we demand the rigid enforcement of the laws against Chinese immigration or the importation of foreign workmen under contract, to degrade American labor and lessen its wages, but we condemn and denounce any and all attempts to restrict the immigration of the industrious and worthy of foreign lands.

Soldiers' Pensions.—This convention hereby renews the expression of appreciation of the patriotism of the soldiers and sailors of the Union in the war for its preservation, and we favor just and liberal pensions for all disabled Union soldiers, their widows and dependents, but we demand that the work of the Pension Office shall be done industriously, impartially, and honestly. We denounce the present administration of that office as incompetent, corrupt, disgraceful, and dishonest.

Improvement of Waterways.—The Federal Government should care for and improve the Mississippi River and other great waterways of the Republic, so as to secure for the interior States easy and cheap transportation to the tidewater. When any waterway of the Republic is of sufficient importance to demand the aid of the Government, such aid should be extended on a definite plan of continuous work until permanent improvement is secured.

The Nicaragua Canal.—For purposes of national defence and the promotion of commerce between the States, we recognize the early construction of the Nicaragua Canal and its protection against foreign control as of great importance to the United States.

The World's Columbian Fair.—Recognizing the World's Columbian Exposition as a national undertaking of vast importance, in which the General Government has invited the co-operation of all the powers of the world, and appreciating the acceptance by many of such powers of the invitation so extended, and the broad and liberal efforts being made by them to contribute to the grandeur of the undertaking, we are of opinion that Congress should make such necessary financial provision as shall be requisite to the maintenance of the national honor and public faith.

Freedom of Education.—Popular education being the only safe basis of popular suffrage, we recommend to the several States most liberal appropriations for the public schools. Free common schools are the nursery of good government, and they have always received the fostering care of the Democratic Party, which favors every means of increasing intelligence. Freedom of education, being an essential of civil and religious liberty, as well as a necessity of the development of intelligence. must not be interfered with under any pretext whatever. We are opposed to State interference with parental rights and rights of conscience in the education of children as an infringement of the fundamental Democratic doctrine that the largest individual liberty consistent with the rights of others insures the highest type of American citizenship and the best government.

Admission of Territories.—We approve the action of the present House of Representatives in passing bills for admitting into the Union as States of the Territories of New-Mexico and Arizona, and we favor the early admission of all the Territories having the necessary population and resources to entitle them to statehood, and while they remain territories we hold that the officials appointed to administer the government of any territory, together with the District of Columbia and Alaska, should be *bona fide* residents of the territory or district in which their duties are to be performed. The Democratic Party believes in home rule and the control of their own affairs by the people of the vicinage.

Protection of Railway Employés.—We favor legislation by Congress and State legislatures to protect the lives and limbs of railway employés and those of other hazardous transportation companies, and denounce the inactivity of the Republican Party, and particularly the Republican Senate, for causing the defeat of measures beneficial and protective to this class of wage workers.

Labor Evils.—We are in favor of the enactment by the States of laws for abolishing the notorious sweating system, for abolishing contract convict labor, and for prohibiting the employment in factories of children under fifteen years of age.

Sumptuary Laws.—We are opposed to all sumptuary law as an interference with the individual rights of the citizen.

A Change of Administration Demanded.—Upon this statement of principles and policies the Democratic Party asks the intelligent judgment of the American people. It asks a change of administration and a change of party, in order that there may be a change of system and a change of methods, thus assuring the maintenance unimpaired of institutions under which the Republic has grown great and powerful.

THE ORIGINAL TARIFF PLANK AS REPORTED BY THE COMMITTEE ON RESOLUTIONS.

The following is the first part of the third plank of the platform, as reported by the Committee on Resolutions. The clause of the third plank (entitled "Protection"), beginning with "We denounce" and closing with "economically administered," was substituted for it by the Convention by a vote of 564 to 342.

[III.—We reiterate the oft-repeated doctrines of the Democratic Party that the necessity of the Government is the only justification for taxation, and whenever a tax is unnecessary it is unjustifiable; that when Custom House taxation is levied upon articles of any kind produced in this country, the difference between the cost of labor here and labor abroad, when such a difference exists, fully measures any possible benefits to labor, and the enormous additional impositions of the existing tariff fall with crushing force upon our farmers and workingmen, and, for the mere advantage of the few whom it enriches, exacts from labor a grossly unjust share of the expenses of the Government, and we demand such a revision of the tariff laws as will remove their iniquitous inequalities, lighten their oppressions, and put them on a constitutional and equitable basis. But, in making reduction in taxes, it is not proposed to injure any domestic industries, but rather to promote their healthy growth. From the foundation of this Government, taxes collected at the Custom House have been the chief source of Federal revenue. Such they must continue to be. Moreover, many industries have come to rely upon legislation for successful continuance, so that any change of law must be at every step regardful of the labor and capital thus involved. The process of reform must be subject in the execution to this plain dictate of justice.]

NATIONAL REPUBLICAN PLATFORM, ADOPTED AT MINNEAPOLIS, MINN., JUNE 9, 1892.

The representatives of the Republicans of the United States, assembled in general convention on the shores of the Mississippi River, the everlasting bond of an indestructible Republic, whose most glorious chapter of history is the record of the Republican Party, congratulate their countrymen on the majestic march of the nation under the banners inscribed with the principles of our platform of 1888, vindicated by victory at the polls and prosperity in our fields, workshops, and mines, and make the following declaration of principles:

Protection.—We reaffirm the American doctrine of protection. We call attention to its growth abroad. We maintain that the prosperous condition of our country is largely due to the wise revenue legislation of the Republican Congress. We believe that all articles which cannot be produced in the United States, except luxuries, should be admitted free of duty, and that on all imports coming into competition with the products of American labor there should be levied duties equal to the difference between wages abroad and at home. We assert that the prices of manufactured articles of general consumption have been reduced under the operations of the Tariff act of 1890. We denounce the efforts of the Democratic majority of the House of Representatives to destroy our tariff laws by piecemeal, as manifested by their attacks upon wool, lead, and lead ores, the chief products of a number of States, and we ask the people for their judgment thereon.

Reciprocity.—We point to the success of the Republican policy of reciprocity, under which our export trade has vastly increased, and new and enlarged markets have been opened for the products of our farms and workshops. We remind the people of the bitter opposition of the Democratic Party to this practical business measure, and claim that, executed by a Republican administration, our present laws will eventually give us control of the trade of the world.

Gold and Silver Money.—The American people, from tradition and interest, favor bimetallism, and the Republican Party demands the use of both gold and silver as standard money, with restrictions and under such provisions, to be determined by legislation, as will secure the maintenance of the parity of values of the two metals, so that the purchasing and debt-paying power of the dollar, whether of silver, gold, or paper, shall be at all times equal. The interests of the producers of the country, its farmers and its workingmen, demand that every dollar, paper, or coin, issued by the Government, shall be as good as any other. We commend the wise and patriotic steps already taken by our Government to secure an international conference, to adopt such measures as will insure a parity of value between gold and silver for use as money throughout the world.

The Ballot.—We demand that every citizen of the United States shall be allowed to cast one free and unrestricted ballot in all public elections, and that such ballot shall be counted and returned as cast; that such laws shall be enacted and enforced as will secure to every citizen, be he rich or poor, native or foreign-born, white or black, this sovereign right guaranteed by the Constitution.

The Force Bill.—The free and honest popular ballot, the just and equal representation of all the people, as well as their just and equal protection under the laws, are the foundation of our Republican institutions, and the party will never relax its efforts until the integrity of the ballot and the purity of elections shall be fully guaranteed and protected in every State.

Southern Outrages.—We denounce the continued inhuman outrages perpetrated upon American citizens for political reasons in certain Southern States of the Union.

Extension of Commerce.—We favor the extension of our foreign commerce, the restoration of our mercantile marine by home-built ships and the creation of a navy for the protection of our national interests and the honor of our flag; the maintenance of the most friendly relations with all foreign powers; entangling alliances with none; and the protection of the rights of our fishermen.

The Monroe Doctrine.—We reaffirm our approval of the Monroe Doctrine and believe in the achievement of the manifest destiny of the Republic in its broadest sense.

Foreign Immigration.—We favor the re-enactment of more stringent laws and regulations for the restriction of criminal, pauper, and contract immigration.

Legislation for Employés.—We favor efficient legislation by Congress to protect the life and limbs of employés of transportation companies engaged in carrying on interstate commerce, and recommend legislation by the respective States that will protect employés engaged in State commerce, in mining and manufacturing.

Ireland and Russia.—The Republican Party has always been the champion of the oppressed, and recognizes the dignity of manhood, irrespective of faith, color, or nationality; it sympathizes with the cause of home rule in Ireland, and protests against the persecution of the Jews in Russia.

Education and Religion.—The ultimate reliance of free popular government is the intelligence of the people and the maintenance of freedom among men. We, therefore, declare anew our devotion to liberty of thought and conscience, of speech and press, and approve all agencies and instrumentalities which contribute to the education of the children of the land; but while insisting upon the fullest measure of religious liberty, we are opposed to any union of church and State.

Opposition to Trusts.—We reaffirm our opposition, declared in the Republican platform of 1888, to all combinations of capital organized in trusts or otherwise to control arbitrarily the condition of trade among our citizens. We heartily indorse the action already taken upon this subject, and ask for such further legislation as may be required to remedy any defects in existing laws, and to render their enforcement more complete and effective.

The Postal Service.—We approve the policy of extending to towns, villages, and rural communities the advantages of the free delivery service now enjoyed by the larger cities of the country, and reaffirm the declaration contained in the Republican platform of 1888, pledging the reduction of letter postage to one cent at the earliest possible moment consistent with the maintenance of the post-office department and the highest class of postal service.

Civil Service Reform.—We commend the spirit and evidence of reform in the civil service and the wise and consistent enforcement by the Republican Party of the laws regulating the same.

The Nicaragua Canal.—The construction of the Nicaragua Canal is of the highest importance to the American people, both as a measure of national defence and to build up and maintain American commerce, and it should be controlled by the United States Government.

Admission of the Territories.—We favor the admission of the remaining Territories at the earliest possible date, having due regard to the interests of the people of the Territories and of the United States. All the Federal officers appointed for the Territories should be selected from *bona fide* residents thereof, and the right of self-government should be accorded as far as practicable.

Cession of the Arid Public Lands.—We favor the cession, subject to the homestead laws, of the arid public lands, to the States and Territories in which they lie, under such congressional restrictions as to disposition, reclamation, and occupancy by settlers as will secure the maximum benefits to the people.

The World's Fair.—The World's Columbian Exposition is a great national undertaking, and Congress should promptly enact such reasonable legislation in aid thereof as will insure a discharge of the expenses and obligations incident thereto, and the attainment of results commensurate with the dignity and progress of the nation.

The Liquor Traffic.—We sympathize with all wise and legitimate efforts to lessen and prevent the evils of intemperance and promote morality.

Soldiers' Pensions.—Ever mindful of the service and sacrifices of the men who saved the life of the nation, we pledge anew to the veteran soldiers of the Republic a watchful care and recognition of their just claims upon a grateful people.

President Harrison's Administration.—We commend the able, patriotic, and thoroughly American administration of President Harrison. Under it the country has enjoyed remarkable prosperity, and the dignity and honor of the nation, at home and abroad, have been faithfully maintained, and we offer the record of pledges kept, as a guaranty of faithful performance in the future.

NATIONAL PROHIBITION PARTY PLATFORM, ADOPTED AT CINCINNATI, OHIO, JUNE 30, 1892.

The Prohibition Party, in National Convention assembled, acknowledging Almighty God as the source of all true government and His law as the standard to which all human enactments must conform to secure the blessings of peace and prosperity, presents the following declaration of principles:

The Liquor Traffic.—The liquor traffic is a foe to civilization, the arch enemy of popular government and a public nuisance. It is the citadel of the forces that corrupt politics, promote poverty and crime, degrade the nation's home life, thwart the will of the people, and deliver our country into the hands of rapacious class interests. All laws that under the guise of regulation legalize and protect this traffic or make the Government share in its ill-gotten gains are "vicious in principle and powerless as a remedy." We declare anew for the entire suppression of the manufacture, sale, importation, exportation and transportation of alcoholic liquors as a beverage by Federal and State legislation, and the full powers of the Government should be exerted to secure this result. Any party that fails to recognize the dominant nature of this issue in American politics is undeserving of the support of the people.

Woman Suffrage.—No citizen should be denied the right to vote on account of sex, and equal labor should receive equal wages without regard to sex.

Increased Issue of Money.—The money of the country should consist of gold, silver, and paper, and should be issued by the General Government only, and in sufficient quantities to meet the demands of business and give full opportunity for the employment of labor. To this end an increase in the volume of money is demanded, and no individual or corporation should be allowed to make any profit through its issue. It should be made a legal tender for the payment of all debts, public and private. Its volume should be fixed at a definite sum per capita and made to increase with our increase in population.

The Tariff.—Tariff should be levied only as a defence against foreign governments which levy tariff upon or bar out our products from their markets, revenue being incidental. The residue of means necessary to an economical administration of the Government should be raised by levying a burden on what the people possess instead of what they consume.

Government Control of Transportation and Telegraphs.—Railroad, telegraph, and other public corporations should be controlled by the Government in the interest of the people, and no higher charges allowed than necessary to give fair interest on the capital actually invested.

Foreign Immigration.—Foreign immigration has become a burden upon industry, one of the factors in depressing wages and causing discontent; therefore our immigration laws should be revised and strictly enforced. The time of residence for naturalization should be extended, and no naturalized person should be allowed to vote until one year after he becomes a citizen.

Alien Ownership of Land.—Non-resident aliens should not be allowed to acquire land in this country, and we favor the limitation of individual and corporate ownership of land. All unearned grants of land to railroad companies or other corporations should be reclaimed.

Lynch Law.—Years of inaction and treachery on the part of the Republican and Democratic parties have resulted in the present reign of mob law, and we demand that every citizen be protected in the right of trial by constitutional tribunals.

The Sabbath.—All men should be protected by law in their right to one day's rest in seven.

Arbitration in Labor Differences.—Arbitration is the wisest and most economical and humane method of settling national differences.

Speculation and Trusts.—Speculation in margins, the cornering of grain, money and products, and the formation of pools, trusts, and combinations for the arbitrary advancement of prices should be suppressed.

Soldiers' Pensions.—We pledge that the Prohibition Party, if elected to power, will ever grant just pensions to disabled veterans of the Union army and navy, their widows and orphans.

Public Schools.—We stand unequivocally for the American Public School, and opposed to any appropriation of public moneys for sectarian schools. We declare that only by united support of such common schools, taught in the English language, can we hope to become and remain a homogeneous and harmonious people.

Arraignment of Other Political Parties.—We arraign the Republican and Democratic Parties as false to the standards reared by their founders; as faithless to the principles of the illustrious leaders of the past to whom they do homage with the lips; as recreant to the "higher law," which is as inflexible in political affairs as in personal life; and as no longer embodying the aspirations of the American people or inviting the confidence of enlightened progressive patriotism. Their protest against the admission of "moral issues" into politics is a confession of their own moral degeneracy. The declaration of an eminent authority that municipal misrule is "the one conspicuous failure of American politics" follows as a natural consequence of such degeneracy, and is true alike of cities under Republican and Democratic control. Each accuses the other of extravagance in congressional appropriations, and both are alike guilty; each protests when out of power against the infraction of the civil-service laws, and each when in power violates those laws in letter and spirit; each professes fealty to the interests of the toiling masses, but both covertly truckle to the money power in their administration of public affairs. Even the tariff issue, as represented in the Democratic Mills bill and the Republican McKinley bill, is no longer treated by them as an issue upon great and divergent principles of government, but is a mere catering to different sectional and class interests. The attempt in many States to wrest the Australian ballot system from its true purpose, and to so deform it as to render it extremely difficult for new parties to exercise the right of suffrage, is an outrage upon popular government. The competition of both the parties for the vote of the slums, and their assiduous courting of the liquor power and subserviency to the money power, has resulted in placing those powers in the position of practical arbiters of the destinies of the nation. We renew our protest against these perilous tendencies, and invite all citizens to join us in the upbuilding of a party that has shown in five national campaigns ...at it prefers temporary defeat to an abandonment of the claims of justice, sobriety, personal rights and the protection of American homes.

Invitation to Party Fellowship.—Recognizing and declaring that prohibition of the liquor traffic has become the dominant issue in national politics, we invite to full party fellowship all those who on this one dominant issue are with us agreed, in the full belief that this party can and will remove sectional differences, promote national unity, and insure the best welfare of our entire land.

The World's Fair.—*Resolved*, That we favor a liberal appropriation by the Federal Government for the World's Columbian Exposition, but only on the condition that the sale of intoxicating drinks upon the Exposition grounds is prohibited, and that the Exposition be kept closed on Sunday.

NATIONAL PEOPLE'S PARTY PLATFORM, ADOPTED AT OMAHA, NEB., JULY 4, 1892.

Assembled upon the 116th anniversary of the Declaration of Independence, the People's Party of America, in their first national convention, invoking upon their action the blessing of Almighty God, put forth in the name and on behalf of the people of this country, the following preamble and declaration of principles:

PREAMBLE.

The conditions which surround us best justify our co-operation; we meet in the midst of a nation brought to the verge of moral, political, and material ruin. Corruption dominates the ballot-box, the Legislatures, the Congress, and touches even the ermine of the bench. The people are demoralized; most of the States have been compelled to isolate the voters at the polling places to prevent universal intimidation and bribery. The newspapers are largely subsidized or muzzled, public opinion silenced, business prostrated, homes covered with mortgages, labor impoverished, and the land concentrating in the hands of capitalists. The urban workmen are denied the right to organize for self-protection, imported pauperized labor beats down their wages, a hireling standing army, unrecognized by our laws, is established to shoot them down, and they are rapidly degenerating into European conditions. The fruits of the toil of millions are boldly stolen to build up colossal fortunes for a few, unprecedented in the history of mankind; and the possessors of those, in turn, despise the Republic and endanger liberty. From the same prolific womb of governmental injustice we breed the two great classes—tramps and millionaires.

The national power to create money is appropriated to enrich bondholders; a vast public debt payable in legal tender currency has been funded into gold-bearing bonds, thereby adding millions to the burdens of the people.

Silver, which has been accepted as coin since the dawn of history, has been demonetized to add to the purchasing power of gold by decreasing the value of all forms of property as well as human labor, and the supply of currency is purposely abridged to fatten usurers, bankrupt enterprise, and enslave industry. A vast conspiracy against mankind has been organized on two continents, and it is rapidly taking possession of the world. If not met and overthrown at once it forebodes terrible social convulsions, the destruction of civilization, or the establishment of an absolute despotism.

We have witnessed for more than a quarter of a century the struggles of the two great political parties for power and plunder, while grievous wrongs have been inflicted upon the suffering people. We charge that the controlling influences dominating both these parties have permitted the existing dreadful conditions to develop without serious effort to prevent or restrain them. Neither do they now promise us any substantial reform. They have agreed together to ignore, in the coming campaign, every issue but one. They propose to drown the outcries of a plundered people with the uproar of a sham battle over the tariff, so that capitalists, corporations, national banks, rings, trusts, watered stock, the demonetization of silver and the oppressions of the usurers may all be lost sight of. They propose to sacrifice our homes, lives, and children on the altar of mammon; to destroy the multitude in order to secure corruption funds from the millionaires.

Assembled on the anniversary of the birthday of the nation, and filled with the spirit of the grand general and chief who established our independence, we seek to restore the government of the Republic to the hands of "the plain people," with which class it originated. We assert our purposes to be identical with the purposes of the National Constitution ; to form a more perfect union and establish justice, insure domestic tranquillity, provide for the common defence, promote the general welfare, and secure the blessings of liberty for ourselves and our posterity.

We declare that this Republic can only endure as a free government while built upon the love of the whole people for each other and for the nation ; that it cannot be pinned together by bayonets ; that the civil war is over, and that every passion and resentment which grew out of it must die with it, and that we must be in fact, as we are in name, one united brotherhood of free men.

Our country finds itself confronted by conditions for which there is no precedent in the history of the world ; our annual agricultural productions amount to billions of dollars in value, which must, within a few weeks or months, be exchanged for billions of dollars' worth of commodities consumed in their production ; the existing currency supply is wholly inadequate to make this exchange ; the results are falling prices, the formation of combines and rings, the impoverishment of the producing class. We pledge ourselves that if given power we will labor to correct these evils by wise and reasonable legislation, in accordance with the terms of our platform.

We believe that the power of government—in other words, of the people—should be expanded (as in the case of the postal service) as rapidly and as far as the good sense of an intelligent people and the teachings of experience shall justify, to the end that oppression, injustice, and poverty shall eventually cease in the land.

While our sympathies as a party of reform are naturally upon the side of every proposition which will tend to make men intelligent, virtuous, and temperate, we nevertheless regard these questions, important as they are, as secondary to the great issues now pressing for solution, and upon which not only our individual prosperity but the very existence of free institutions depend ; and we ask all men to first help us to determine whether we are to have a republic to administer before we differ as to the conditions upon which it is to be administered, believing that the forces of reform this day organized will never cease to move forward until every wrong is remedied and equal rights and equal privileges securely established for all the men and women of this country.

PLATFORM.

We declare, therefore—

First.—That the union of the labor forces of the United States this day consummated shall be permanent and perpetual ; may its spirit enter into all hearts for the salvation of the Republic and the uplifting of mankind.

Second.—Wealth belongs to him who creates it, and every dollar taken from industry without an equivalent is robbery. "If any will not work, neither shall he eat." The interests of rural and civic labor are the same ; their enemies are identical.

Third.—We believe that the time has come when the railroad corporations will either own the people or the people must own the railroads, and should the government enter upon the work of owning and managing all railroads, we should favor an amendment to the Constitution by which all persons engaged in the government service shall be placed under a civil-service regulation of the most rigid character, so as to prevent the increase of the power of the national administration by the use of such additional government employés.

Finance.—We demand a national currency, safe, sound, and flexible, issued by the general government only, a full legal tender for all debts, public and private, and that without the use of banking corporations, a just, equitable, and efficient means of distribution direct to the people, at a tax not to exceed 2 per cent. per annum, to be provided as set forth in the sub-treasury plan of the Farmers' Alliance, or a better system ; also by payments in discharge of its obligations for public improvements.

1. We demand free and unlimited coinage of silver and gold at the present legal ratio of 16 to 1.
2. We demand that the amount of circulating medium be speedily increased to not less than $50 per capita.
3. We demand a graduated income tax.
4. We believe that the money of the country should be kept as much as possible in the hands of the people, and hence we demand that all State and national revenues shall be limited to the necessary expenses of the government, economically and honestly administered.
5. We demand that postal savings banks be established by the government for the safe deposit of the earnings of the people and to facilitate exchange.

Transportation.—Transportation being a means of exchange and a public necessity, the government should own and operate the railroads in the interest of the people. The telegraph, telephone, like the post-office system, being a necessity for the transmission of news, should be owned and operated by the government in the interest of the people.

Land.—The land, including all the natural sources of wealth, is the heritage of the people, and should not be monopolized for speculative purposes, and alien ownership of land should be prohibited. All land now held by railroads and other corporations in excess of their actual needs, and all lands now owned by aliens should be reclaimed by the government and held for actual settlers only.

EXPRESSION OF SENTIMENTS.

Your Committee on Platform and Resolutions beg leave unanimously to report the following :

Whereas, Other questions have been presented for our consideration, we hereby submit the following, not as a part of the Platform of the People's Party, but as resolutions expressive of the sentiment of this Convention :

1. *Resolved,* That we demand a free ballot and a fair count in all elections, and pledge ourselves to secure it to every legal voter without Federal intervention, through the adoption by the States of the unperverted Australian or secret ballot system.
2. *Resolved,* That the revenue derived from a graduated income tax should be applied to the reduction of the burden of taxation now levied upon the domestic industries of this country.
3. *Resolved,* That we pledge our support to fair and liberal pensions to ex-Union soldiers and sailors.
4. *Resolved,* That we condemn the fallacy of protecting American labor under the present system, which opens our ports to the pauper and criminal classes of the world and crowds out our wage-earners ; and we denounce the present ineffective laws against contract labor, and demand the further restriction of undesirable emigration.
5. *Resolved,* That we cordially sympathize with the efforts of organized workingmen to shorten the hours of labor, and demand a rigid enforcement of the existing eight-hour law on Government work, and ask that a penalty clause be added to the said law.
6. *Resolved,* That we regard the maintenance of a large standing army of mercenaries, known as the Pinkerton system, as a menace to our liberties, and we demand its abolition ; and we condemn the recent invasion of the Territory of Wyoming by the hired assassins of plutocracy, assisted by Federal officers.

7. *Resolved,* That we commend to the favorable consideration of the people and the reform press the legislative system known as the initiative and referendum.

8. *Resolved,* That we favor a constitutional provision limiting the office of President and Vice-President to one term, and providing for the election of Senators of the United States by a direct vote of the people.

9. *Resolved,* That we oppose any subsidy or national aid to any private corporation for any purpose.

10. *Resolved,* That this convention sympathizes with the Knights of Labor and their righteous contest with the tyrannical combine of clothing manufacturers of Rochester, and declare it to be the duty of all who hate tyranny and oppression to refuse to purchase the goods made by the said manufacturers, or to patronize any merchants who sell such goods.

SOCIALISTIC LABOR PARTY PLATFORM, ADOPTED AT CHICAGO, ILL., OCTOBER 12, 1889.*

The Socialist Labor Party of the United States, in convention assembled, reasserts the inalienable right of all men to life, liberty, and the pursuit of happiness.

With the founders of the American republic we hold that the purpose of government is to secure every citizen in the enjoyment of this right; but in the light of our social conditions we hold, furthermore, that no such right can be exercised under a system of economic inequality, essentially destructive of life, of liberty, and of happiness.

With the founders of this republic we hold that the true theory of politics is that the machinery of government must be owned and controlled by the whole people; but in the light of our industrial development we hold, furthermore, that the true theory of economics is that the machinery of production must likewise belong to the people in common.

To the obvious fact that our despotic system of economics is the direct opposite of our democratic system of politics, can plainly be traced the existence of a privileged class, the corruption of government by that class, the alienation of public property, public franchises and public functions to that class, and the abject dependence of the mightiest of nations upon that class. Again, through the perversion of democracy to the ends of plutocracy, labor is robbed of the wealth which it alone produces, is denied the means of self-employment, and, by compulsory idleness in wage-slavery, is even deprived of the necessaries of life. Human power and natural forces are thus wasted, that the plutocracy may rule. Ignorance and misery, with all their concomitant evils, are perpetuated, that the people may be kept in bondage. Science and invention are diverted from their humane purpose to the enslavement of women and children.

Against such a system the Socialistic Labor Party once more enters its protest. Once more it reiterates its fundamental declaration, that private property in the natural sources of production and in the instruments of labor is the obvious cause of all economic servitude and political dependence; and

Whereas, the time is fast coming when, in the natural course of social evolution, this system, through the destructive action of its failures and crises, on the one hand, and the constructive tendencies of its trusts and other capitalistic combinations, on the other hand, shall have worked out its own downfall; therefore, be it

Resolved, That we call upon the people to organize with a view to the substitution of the co-operative commonwealth for the present state of planless production, industrial war, and social disorder—a commonwealth in which every worker shall have the free exercise and full benefit of his faculties, multiplied by all the modern factors of civilization. We call upon them to unite with us in a mighty effort to gain by all practicable means the political power.

In the mean time, and with a view to immediate improvement in the condition of labor, we present the following "Demands:"

SOCIAL DEMANDS.

1. Reduction of the hours of labor in proportion to the progress of production.
2. The United States shall obtain possession of the railroads, canals, telegraphs, telephones, and all other means of public transportation and communication.
3. The municipalities to obtain possession of the local railroads, ferries, water-works, gas-works, electric plants, and all industries requiring municipal franchises.
4. The public lands to be declared inalienable. Revocation of all land grants to corporations or individuals, the conditions of which have not been complied with.
5. Legal incorporation by the States of local Trade Unions which have no national organization.
6. The United States to have the exclusive right to issue money.
7. Congressional legislation providing for the scientific management of forests and waterways, and prohibiting the waste of the natural resources of the country.
8. Inventions to be free to all; the inventors to be remunerated by the nation.
9. Progressive income tax and tax on inheritances; the smaller incomes to be exempt.
10. School education of all children under fourteen years of age to be compulsory, gratuitous, and accessible to all by public assistance in meals, clothing, books, etc., where necessary.
11. Repeal of all pauper, tramp, conspiracy, and sumptuary laws. Unabridged right of combination.
12. Official statistics concerning the condition of labor. Prohibition of the employment of children of school age and of the employment of female labor in occupations detrimental to health or morality. Abolition of the convict labor contract system.
13. All wages to be paid in lawful money of the United States. Equalization of women's wages with those of men where equal service is performed.
14. Laws for the protection of life and limb in all occupations, and an efficient employers' liability law

POLITICAL DEMANDS.

1. The people to have the right to propose laws and to vote upon all measures of importance, according to the Referendum principle.
2. Abolition of the Presidency, Vice-Presidency, and Senate of the United States. An Executive Board to be established, whose members are to be elected, and may at any time be recalled, by the House of Representatives as the only legislative body. The States and Municipalities to adopt corresponding amendments to their constitutions and statutes.
3. Municipal self-government.
4. Direct vote and secret ballots in all elections. Universal and equal right of suffrage, without regard to color, creed, or sex. Election days to be legal holidays. The principle of minority representation to be introduced.
5. All public officers to be subject to recall by their respective constituencies.
6. Uniform civil and criminal law throughout the United States. Administration of justice to be free of charge. Abolition of capital punishment.

---

* This platform, adopted by the Socialistic Labor Party in 1889, continued in force as a statement of the principles of the party, in the Presidential contest of 1892, and upon it the party candidates—Simon Wing, of Massachusetts, for President, and Charles H. Matchett, of New-York, for Vice-President—were voted for.

Labor Legislation.

EIGHT-HOUR LAWS.

Alabama.—Eight hours of labor constitute a day's work for a woman or a child under eighteen (18) years of age in a mechanical or manufacturing business.

California.—Eight hours of labor constitute a day's work, unless it is otherwise expressly stipulated by the parties to a contract. A stipulation that eight-hours' labor constitutes a day's work must be made a part of all contracts to which the State or any municipal corporation therein is a party. But in the case of drivers, conductors, and grip-men of street-cars for the carriage of passengers, a day's work consists of twelve hours. It is a misdemeanor for any person having a minor child under his control, either as ward or apprentice, to require such child to labor more than eight hours in any one day, except in vinicultural or horticultural pursuits, or in domestic or household occupations.

Connecticut.—Eight hours of labor constitute a lawful day's work, unless otherwise agreed.

Idaho.—Eight hours' actual work constitutes a lawful day's work on all State and municipal works.

Illinois.—Eight hours are a legal day's work in all mechanical employments, except on farms, and when otherwise agreed; does not apply to service by the day, week, or month, or prevent contracts for longer hours.

Indiana.—Eight hours of labor constitute a legal day's work for all classes of mechanics, workingmen, and laborers, excepting those engaged in agricultural and domestic labor. Overwork by agreement and for extra compensation is permitted.

Missouri.—Eight hours constitute a day's work, unless otherwise expressly stipulated by the parties to a contract. This does not apply to persons employed by the month, or to agricultural laborers or farm hands.

New-Mexico.—Eight hours of labor actually performed upon a mining claim constitute a day's work, the value of the same being fixed at four dollars.

New-York.—Eight hours constitute a day's work for mechanics, workingmen, and laborers, except in farm or domestic labor, but overwork for extra pay is permitted. The law applies to those employed by the State or municipality, or by persons contracting for State work.

Ohio.—Eight hours shall constitute a day's work in all engagements to labor in any mechanical, manufacturing, or mining business, unless otherwise expressly stipulated in the contract. But in case of conductors, engineers, firemen, brakemen, or trainmen of railroads, a day's work consists of ten hours.

Pennsylvania.—Eight hours, between rising and setting of sun, constitute a day's work in the absence of an agreement for longer time. The law does not apply to farm labor or to service by the year, month, etc.; but in case of employés of street railway companies a day's work consists of twelve hours.

Wisconsin.—In all engagements to labor in any manufacturing or mechanical business, where there is no express contract to the contrary, a day's work shall consist of eight hours; but the law does not apply to contracts for labor by the week, month, or year. In all manufactories, workshops, or other places used for mechanical or manufacturing purposes, the time of labor of children under the age of eighteen, and of women employed therein, shall not exceed eight hours in one day.

Wyoming.—Eight hours' actual work constitute a legal day's work in all mines and public works.

United States.—Eight hours shall constitute a day's work for all laborers, workmen, and mechanics who may be employed by or on behalf of the United States.

ANTI-BOYCOTTING AND ANTI-BLACKLISTING LAWS.

The States having laws prohibiting *boycotting* in terms are Illinois and Wisconsin.

The States having laws prohibiting *blacklisting* in terms are Colorado, Illinois, Indiana, Iowa, North-Dakota, and Wisconsin.

The following States have laws which may be fairly construed as prohibiting *boycotting:* Alabama, Connecticut, Georgia, Indiana, Maine, Michigan, Minnesota, Missouri, Montana, New-Hampshire, New-York, North-Dakota, Oregon, Rhode-Island, South-Dakota, Texas, and Vermont.

The following States have laws which may be fairly construed as prohibiting *blacklisting:* Georgia, Michigan, Minnesota, Montana, New-Hampshire, New-York, Oregon, Rhode-Island, South-Dakota, and Texas.

In New-York it is a misdemeanor for any employer to exact an agreement, either written or verbal, from an employé not to join or become a member of any labor organization, as a condition of employment.

THE WORLD ALMANAC is indebted to Commissioner Wright, of the U. S. Department of Labor, for the summary of eight hours, anti-boycotting and anti-blacklisting laws, and the following table.

LIST OF BUREAUS OF LABOR AND LABOR STATISTICS IN THE UNITED STATES.

TITLE OF BUREAU.	Where Located.	When Organized.	Chief Officer.	Title.
United States Department of Labor.....	Washington, D. C.	1885	Carroll D. Wright.....	Commissioner.
Bureau of Statistics of Labor...........	Boston, Mass.	1869	Horace G. Wadlin.....	Chief.
Bureau of Industrial Statistics...........	Harrisburg, Pa.	1872	Albert S. Bolles.......	Chief.
Bureau of Labor Statistics............	Hartford, Ct.	1873	Samuel M. Hotchkiss..	Commissioner.
Bureau of Labor Statistics............	Columbus, O.	1877	W. T. Lewis.	Commissioner.
Bureau of Statistics of Labor and Indust's	Trenton, N. J.	1878	James Bishop.........	Chief.
Bureau of Labor Statistics and Inspection	Jefferson City, Mo.	1876	Willard C. Hall.......	Commissioner.
Bureau of Labor Statistics	Springfield, Ill.	1879	John S. Lord.........	Secretary.
Bureau of Statistics.....	Indianapolis, Ind.	1879	William A. Peelle, Jr .	Chief.
Bureau of Labor Statistics............	Albany, N. Y.	1883	Charles F. Peck.......	Commissioner.
Bureau of Labor Statistics............	San Francisco, Cal.	1883	George S. Walts.......	Commissioner.
Bureau of Labor and Industrial Statistics.	Lansing, Mich.	1883	Henry A. Robinson ...	Commissioner.
Bureau of Labor Statistics............	Madison, Wis.	1883	J. Dobbs..............	Commissioner.
Bureau of Labor Statistics............	Des Moines, Ia.	1884	J. R. Sovereign.......	Commissioner.
Bureau of Statistics of Labor............	Baltimore, Md.	1884	A. B. Howard, Jr.....	Chief.
Bureau of Labor Statistics............	Topeka, Kan.	1885	Frank H. Betton......	Commissioner.
Bureau of Labor Statistics....	Providence, R. I.	1887	Almon K. Goodwin....	Commissioner.
Bureau of Labor and Industrial Statistics.	Lincoln, Neb.	1887	Philip Andres	Deputy Com.
Bureau of Labor Statistics	Raleigh, N. C.	1887	J. C. Scarborough....	Commissioner.
Bureau of Labor Statistics	Augusta, Me.	1887	Samuel W. Matthews..	Commissioner.
Bureau of Labor Statistics	St. Paul, Minn.	1887	L. G. Powers..........	Commissioner.
Bureau of Labor Statistics and Mines....	Denver, Col.	1887	Lester Bodine.........	Commissioner.
Department of Labor and Statistics......	Sioux Falls, S. D.	1890	R. A. Smith...........	Commissioner.
Department of Agriculture and Labor...	Bismarck, N. D.	1890	H. F. Helgesen........	Commissioner.
Bureau of Labor Statistics and Mines....	Nashville, Tenn.	1891	George W. Ford.......	Commissioner.

Naturalization Laws of the United States.

THE conditions under and the manner in which an alien may be admitted to become a citizen of the United States are prescribed by Sections 2165-74 of the Revised Statutes of the United States.

DECLARATION OF INTENTION.

The alien must declare upon oath before a circuit or district court of the United States, or a district or supreme court of the Territories, or a court of record of any of the States having common law jurisdiction, and a seal and clerk, two years at least prior to his admission, that it is, *bona fide*, his intention to become a citizen of the United States, and to renounce forever all allegiance and fidelity to any foreign prince or State, and particularly to the one of which he may be at the time a citizen or subject.

OATH ON APPLICATION FOR ADMISSION.

He must at the time of his application to be admitted declare on oath, before some one of the courts above specified, "that he will support the Constitution of the United States, and that he absolutely and entirely renounces and abjures all allegiance and fidelity to every foreign prince, potentate, State, or sovereignty, and particularly, by name, to the prince, potentate, State, or sovereignty of which he was before a citizen or subject," which proceedings must be recorded by the clerk of the court.

CONDITIONS FOR CITIZENSHIP.

If it shall appear to the satisfaction of the court to which the alien has applied that he has resided continuously within the United States for at least five years, and within the State or Territory where such court is at the time held one year at least; and that during that time "he has behaved as a man of good moral character, attached to the principles of the Constitution of the United States, and well disposed to the good order and happiness of the same," he will be admitted to citizenship.

TITLES OF NOBILITY.

If the applicant has borne any hereditary title or order of nobility, he must make an express renunciation of the same at the time of his application.

SOLDIERS.

Any alien of the age of twenty-one years and upward who has been in the armies of the United States, and has been honorably discharged therefrom, may become a citizen on his petition, without any previous declaration of intention, provided that he has resided in the United States at least one year previous to his application, and is of good moral character. (It is judicially decided that residence of one year in a particular State is not requisite.)

MINORS.

Any alien under the age of twenty-one years who has resided in the United States three years next preceding his arriving at that age, and who has continued to reside therein to the time he may make application to be admitted a citizen thereof, may, after he arrives at the age of twenty-one years, and after he has resided five years within the United States, including the three years of his minority, be admitted a citizen; but he must make a declaration on oath and prove to the satisfaction of the court that for two years next preceding it has been his *bona fide* intention to become a citizen.

CHILDREN OF NATURALIZED CITIZENS.

The children of persons who have been duly naturalized, being under the age of twenty-one years at the time of the naturalization of their parents, shall, if dwelling in the United States, be considered as citizens thereof.

CITIZENS' CHILDREN WHO ARE BORN ABROAD.

The children of persons who now are or have been citizens of the United States are, though born out of the limits and jurisdiction of the United States, considered as citizens thereof.

CHINESE.

The naturalization of Chinamen is expressly prohibited by Section 14, Chapter 126, Laws of 1882.

PROTECTION ABROAD TO NATURALIZED CITIZENS.

Section 2000 of the Revised Statutes of the United States declares that "all naturalized citizens of the United States while in foreign countries are entitled to and shall receive from this Government the same protection of persons and property which is accorded to native-born citizens."

THE RIGHT OF SUFFRAGE.

The right to vote comes from the State, and is a State Gift. Naturalization is a Federal right, and is a gift of the Union, not of any one State. In nearly one half the Union aliens (who have declared intentions) vote and have the right to vote equally with naturalized or native-born citizens. In the other half only actual citizens may vote. (See Table of Qualifications for Voting in each State, on another page.) The Federal naturalization laws apply to the whole Union alike, and provide that no alien may be naturalized until after five years' residence. Even after five years' residence and due naturalization he is not entitled to vote unless the laws of the State confer the privilege upon him, and he may vote in several States six months after landing, if he has declared his intention, under United States law, to become a citizen.

Facts About the Earth.

ACCORDING to Clark, the equatorial semi-diameter is 20,926,202 feet = 3963.296 miles, and the polar semi-diameter is 20,854,895 feet = 3950.738 miles. One degree of latitude at the pole = 69.407 miles. One degree of latitude at the equator = 68.704 miles.

POPULATION OF THE EARTH BY CONTINENTS.

(From Proceedings of the Royal Geographical Society for January, 1891.)

CONTINENTAL DIVISIONS.	Area in Square Miles.	INHABITANTS.		CONTINENTAL DIVISIONS.	Area in Square Miles.	INHABITANTS.	
		Number.	Per Sq. Mile.			Number.	Per Sq. Mile.
Africa........	11,514,000	127,000,000	11.0	Europe.......	3,555,000	380,200,000	106.9
America, N...	6,446,000	89,250,000	13.8	Polar Regions	4,888,800	300,000	0.7
America, S....	6,837,000	36,420,000	5.3				
Asia	14,710,000	850,000,000	57.7	Total	51,238,800	1,487,900,000	29.0
Australasia ..	3,288,000	4,730,000	1.4				

The above estimate was made by Ernest George Ravenstein, F.R.G.S., the geographer and statistician, and is for 1890.

An estimate of population of the earth, made by Drs. Wagner and Supan, editors of "Bevölkerung der Erde" (Perthes, Gotha, 1891), is as follows: Europe, 357,379,000; Asia, 825,954,000; Africa, 163,953,000; America, 121,713,000; Australia, 3,230,000; Oceanic Islands, 7,420,000; polar regions, 80,400. Total, 1,479,729,400. The estimate of area of the continents and islands by the same authorities is 52,821,684.

Ravenstein's estimate of the earth's fertile region, in square miles, is 28,269,200; steppe, 13,901,000; desert, 4,180,000; polar region, 4,888,800.

The population of the earth at the death of the Emperor Augustus, estimated by Bodio, was 54,000,000. The population of Europe hardly exceeded 50,000,000 before the fifteenth century.—*Mulhall.*

The area and cubic contents of the earth, according to the data of Clark, given above, are: Surface, 196,971,984 square miles; cubic contents, 259,944,035,515 cubic miles.

Murray (Challenger expedition) states the greatest depth of the Atlantic Ocean at 27,366 feet; Pacific Ocean, 30,000 feet; Indian Ocean, 18,582 feet; Southern Ocean, 25,200 feet; Arctic Ocean, 9,000 feet. The Atlantic Ocean has an area, in square miles, of 24,536,000; Pacific Ocean, 50,309,000; Indian Ocean, 17,084,000; Arctic Ocean, 4,781,000; Southern Ocean, 30,592,000. The highest mountain is believed to be Deodhunga, one of the Himalayas, 29,002 feet.

For population of the earth, according to creed, see RELIGIOUS STATISTICS.

POPULATION OF THE EARTH ACCORDING TO RACE.

(Estimate by John Bartholomew, F.R.G.S., Edinburgh.)

RACE.	Location.	Number.	RACE.	Location.	Number.
Indo-Germanic or Aryan	Europe, Persia, etc	545,500,000	Hottentot and Bushmen. Malay and Polynesian...	South-Africa... Australasia and Polynesia	150,000 35,000,000
Mongolian or Turanian...	Greater part of Asia	630,000,000	American Indian	North & South America......	15,000,000
Semitic or Hamitic......	North - Africa, Arabia......	65,000,000			
Negro and Bantu.... ...	Central Africa.	150,000,000	Total	....	1,440,650,000

The human family is subject to forty-five principal governments. As to their form, they may be classified as follows: *Absolute monarchies,* China, Madagascar, Morocco, Persia, Russia, Siam, Turkey; *Limited monarchies,* Austria-Hungary, Belgium, British Empire, Denmark, Germany, Greece, Hawaii, Italy, Japan, Netherlands, Portugal, Roumania, Servia, Spain and Sweden and Norway; *Republics,* Argentine Republic, Bolivia, Brazil, Chile, Colombia, Costa Rica, Ecuador, France, Guatemala, Hayti, Honduras, Mexico, Nicaragua, Orange Free State, Paraguay, Peru, Salvador, San Domingo, Switzerland, Transvaal, United States of America, Uruguay, Venezuela. Besides these are the undefined despotisms of Central and South Africa, and a few insignificant independent states.

The average duration of human life is about 33 years. One quarter of the people on the earth die before age 6, one half before age 16, and only about 1 person of each 100 born lives to age 65. The deaths are calculated at 67 per minute, 97,790 per day, and 35,639,835 per year; the births at 70 per minute, 100,800 per day, and 36,792,000 per year.

EUROPEAN LANGUAGES SPOKEN.

LANGUAGES.	NUMBER OF PERSONS SPOKEN BY.		PROPORTION OF THE WHOLE.		LANGUAGES.	NUMBER OF PERSONS SPOKEN BY.		PROPORTION OF THE WHOLE.	
	1801.	1890.	1801.	1890.		1801.	1890.	1801.	1890.
English	20,520,000	111,100,000	12.7	27.7	Portuguese........	7,480,000	13,000,000	4.7	3.2
French	31,450,000	51,200,000	19.4	12.7	Russian...........	30,770,000	75,000,000	19.0	18.7
German	30,320,000	75,200,000	18.7	18.7					
Italian	15,070,000	33,400,000	9.3	8.3	Total...........	161,800,000	401,700,000	100.0	100.0
Spanish	26,190,000	42,800,000	16.2	10.7					

These estimates by Mulhall (1891) exhibit the superior growth of the English language in the last ninety years.

𝕽𝖊𝖑𝖎𝖌𝖎𝖔𝖚𝖘 𝕾𝖙𝖆𝖙𝖎𝖘𝖙𝖎𝖈𝖘.

NUMBERS IN THE WORLD ACCORDING TO CREED.

The following estimates, by M. Fournier de Flaix, are the latest that have been made by a competent authority. (See Quarterly of the American Statistical Association for March, 1892.)

CREEDS.	No. of Followers.	CREEDS.	No. of Followers.
1 Christianity..................	477,088,158	5 Buddhism......................	147,900,000
2 Worship of Ancestors and Confucianism................	256,000,000	6 Taoism........................	43,000,000
		7 Shintoism.....................	14,000,000
3 Hindooism..................	190,000,000	8 Judaism......................	7,056,000
4 Mohammedanism......	176,834,372	9 Polytheism...................	117,681,669

CHRISTIANITY.

CHURCHES.	Total.	CHURCHES.	Total.
Catholic Church...................	230,866,533	Armenian Church................	1,690,000
Protestant Churches.............	143,237,625	Nestorians......................	80,000
Orthodox Greek Church.........	'98,016,000	Jacobites.......................	70,000
Church of Abyssinia.............	3,000,000		
Coptic Church...................	120,000		477,080,158

DISTRIBUTION OF SEMITIC ARYAN RACES.

GEOGRAPHICAL DIVISIONS.	CHRISTIANITY.			Mohammedanism.	Judaism.
	Catholic Church.	Protestant Churches.	Orthodox Churches.		
Europe.....................	160,165,000	80,812,000	89,196,000	6,629,000	6,456,000
America....................	58,393,882	57,294,014	....	....	....
Oceanica...................	6,574,481	2,724,781	....	24,699,787	....
Africa.....................	2,655,920	1,744,080	....	36,000,000	400,000
Asia.......................	3,007,250	662,750	8,820,000	109,535,585	200,000
Total........	230,866,533	143,237,625	98,016,000	176,834,372	7,056,000

RELIGIOUS DIVISIONS OF EUROPE.

COUNTRIES.	Catholic Church.	Protestant Churches.	Orthodox Church.	Jews.	Mohammedans.	Unclassified.
Russia......................	9,600,000	3,400,000	73,310,000	3,400,000	3,000,000	290,000
Germany....................	17,100,000	29,478,000	....	590,000	....	32,000
Austro-Hungary.............	31,100,000	3,900,000	3,100,000	1,700,000	....	100,000
France.....................	35,387,000	580,000	....	49,000	....	84,000
United Kingdom.............	6,500,000	30,100,000	....	100,000	....	500,000
Italy.......................	29,850,000	62,000	....	38,000	....	50,000
Spain......................	16,850,000	29,000	....	5,000	....	....
Belgium....................	5,880,000	15,000	....	3,000	....	2,000
Roumania..................	100,000	15,000	4,800,000	400,000	30,000	55,000
Ottoman Empire............	320,000	11,000	1,700,000	60,000	2,708,000	70,000
Netherlands................	1,545,000	2,756,000	....	83,000	....	16,000
Portugal...................	4,300,000	....	....	....	....	1,000
Sweden....................	1,000	4,698,000	....	2,000	....	1,000
Switzerland................	1,172,000	1,710,000	....	8,000	....	10,000
Denmark...................	3,000	2,089,000	....	4,000	....	4,000
Greece.....................	10,000	10,000	1,930,000	5,000	45,000	....
Servia.....................	6,000	1,000	1,973,000	5,000	15,000	....
Bulgaria...................	29,000	....	1,393,000	....	571,000	....
Norway....................	1,000	1,958,000	....	....	....	1,000
Roumelia..................	30,000	....	700,000	4,000	240,000	2,000
Montenegro................	5,000	....	290,000	....	....	1,000
Luxembourg............. ...	200,000	....	....	....	....	
Malta......................	160,000	....	....	....	....	
Gibraltar...................	16,000	....	....	....	....	
Total.................	160,165,000	80,812,000	89,196,000	6,456,000	6,629,000	1,219,000

ENGLISH-SPEAKING RELIGIOUS COMMUNITIES OF THE WORLD.

Episcopalians..................	23,250,000	Lutherans, etc....................	1,800,000
Methodists of all descriptions.....	18,150,000	Unitarians...	1,250,000
Roman Catholics...............	15,250,000	Minor Religious sects.............	4,000,000
Presbyterians of all descriptions...	11,150,000	Of no particular religion...........	14,000,000
Baptists of all descriptions........	9,000,000		
Congregationalists............ ...	5,500,000	English-speaking Population....	107,250,000
Free Thinkers.................	3,700,000		

A very large number, more than 10,000,000, of Hindus, Mohammedans, Buddhists, and others in the East also speak and read English.

The estimates in the last table are from Whitaker's (London) Almanack, 1892.

The Encyclopedia Britannica, last edition, makes a rough estimate of numbers of Protestants in the world speaking all civilized languages, and places the Lutherans at the head, with over 42,000,000 members (mostly in Germany and Scandinavia), and the Anglican Church second, with about 20,000,000 members.

Values of Foreign Coins in United States Money.

(Proclaimed by the Secretary of the Treasury, October 1, 1892.)

COUNTRY.	Standard.	Monetary Unit.	Value in U. S. Money.	Coins.
Argentine Republic..	Double*.	Peso.................	$0.96,5	Gold: Argentine ($4.82,4) and ½ Argentine. Silver: peso and divisions.
Austria-Hungary.....	Gold.....	Crown............	.20,3	Former system—Gold: 4 florins ($1.92,9), 8 florins ($3.85,8), ducat ($2.28,7), and 4 ducats ($9.15,8). Silver: 1 and 2 florins. Present system—Gold: 20 crowns ($4.05,2) and 10 crowns ($2.02,6).
Belgium............	Double..	Franc............	.19,3	Gold: 10 and 20 francs. Silver: 5 francs.
Bolivia.............	Silver...	Boliviano........	.61,6	Silver: Boliviano and divisions.
Brazil..............	Gold.....	Milreis..........	.54,6	Gold: 5, 10, and 20 milreis. Silver: ½, 1, and 2 milreis.
British N. America..	Gold.....	Dollar...........	1.00	
Central Amer. States.	Silver....	Peso.............	.61,6	Silver: peso and divisions.
Chile..............	Double..	Peso.............	.91,2	Gold: escudo ($1.82,4), doubloon ($4.56,1), and condor ($9.12,3). Silver: peso and divisions.
China.............	Silver...	Tael..{ Shanghai... Haikwan (Customs).	.91,0 / 1.01,3	
Colombia..........	Silver...	Peso.............	.61,6	Gold: condor ($9.64,7) and double-condor. Silver: peso.
Cuba..............	Double..	Peso.............	.92,6	Gold: doubloon ($5.01,7). Silver: peso.
Denmark...........	Gold.....	Crown...........	.26,8	Gold: 10 and 20 crowns.
Ecuador...........	Silver...	Sucre...........	.61,6	Gold: condor ($9.64,7) and double-condor. Silver: sucre and divisions.
Egypt.............	Gold.....	Pound (100 piastres)	4.94,3	Gold: pound (100 piastres), 5, 10, 20, and 50 piastres. Silver: 1, 2, 5, 10, and 20 piastres.
Finland............	Gold.....	Mark............	.19,3	Gold: 20 marks ($3.85,9), 10 marks ($1.93).
France............	Double..	Franc...........	.19,3	Gold: 5, 10, 20, 50, and 100 francs. Silver: 5 francs.
German Empire.....	Gold.....	Mark............	.23,8	Gold: 5, 10, and 20 marks.
Great Britain........	Gold.....	Pound sterling...	4.86,6½	Gold: Sovereign (pound sterling) and ½ sovereign.
Greece.	Double..	Drachma........	.19,3	Gold: 5, 10, 20, 50, and 100 drachmas. Silver: 5 drachmas.
Hayti.............	Double..	Gourde.........	.96,5	Silver: gourde.
India..............	Silver...	Rupee..........	.29,3	Gold: mohur ($7.10,5). Silver: rupee and divisions.
Italy..............	Double..	Lira...........	.19,3	Gold: 5, 10, 20, 50, and 100 liras. Silver: 5 liras.
Japan.............	Double†.	Yen..{ Gold.... Silver...	.99,7 / .66,4	Gold: 1, 2, 5, 10, and 20 yen. Silver: yen.
Liberia............	Gold.....	Dollar..........	1.00	
Mexico............	Silver...	Dollar..........	.66,9	Gold: dollar ($0.98,3), 2½, 5, 10, and 20 dollars. Silver: dollar (or peso) and divisions.
Netherlands.........	Double..	Florin..........	.40,2	Gold: 10 florins. Silver: ½, 1, and 2½ florins.
Newfoundland......	Gold.....	Dollar..........	1.01,4	Gold: 2 dollars ($2.02,7).
Norway...........	Gold.....	Crown..........	.26,8	Gold: 10 and 20 crowns.
Peru..............	Silver...	Sol............	.61,6	Silver: sol and divisions.
Portugal...........	Gold.....	Milreis.........	1.08	Gold: 1, 2, 5, and 10 milreis.
Russia............	Silver ..	Rouble..{ Gold.... Silver...	.77,2 / .49,2	Gold: imperial ($7.71,8), and ½ imperial ‡($3.86). Silver: ¼, ½, and 1 rouble.
Spain.............	Double..	Peseta..........	.19,3	Gold: 25 pesetas. Silver: 5 pesetas.
Sweden...........	Gold.....	Crown..........	.26,8	Gold: 10 and 20 crowns.
Switzerland........	Double..	Franc	.19,3	Gold: 5, 10, 20, 50, and 100 francs. Silver: 5 francs.
Tripoli............	Silver...	Mahbub of 20 piastres	.55,5	
Turkey............	Gold.....	Piastre.........	.04,4	Gold: 25, 50, 100, 250, and 500 piastres.
Venezuela ....,,	Silver...	Bolivar.........	.12,3	Gold: 5, 10, 20, 50, and 100 bolivars. Silver: 5 bolivars.

* Gold and silver.   † Gold the nominal standard. Silver practically the standard.   ‡ Coined since January 1, 1886. Old half-imperial —$3.98,6.

TABLE SHOWING THE VALUE OF FOREIGN COINS AND PAPER NOTES IN AMERICAN MONEY BASED UPON THE VALUES EXPRESSED IN THE ABOVE TABLE.

NUMBER.	British £ Sterling.	German Mark.	French Franc, Italian Lira.	Chinese Tael (Shanghai).	Dutch Florin.	Indian Rupee.	Russian Gold Rouble.	Austrian Crown.
1	$4.86,6½	$0.23.8	$0.19,3	$0.91	$0.40,2	$0.29.3	$0.77,2	$0.20,3
2	9.73-3	0.47,6	0.38,6	1.82	0.80,4	0.58,6	1.54,4	0.40,6
3	14.59.9½	0.71,4	0.57,9	2.73	1.20,6	0.87,9	2.31,6	0.60,9
4	19.46,6	0.95,2	0.77,2	3.64	1.60,8	1.17,2	3.08,8	0.81,2
5	24.33,2½	1.19	0.96,5	4.55	2.01,0	1.46,5	3.86	1.01,5
6	29.19,9	1.42,8	1.15,8	5.46	2.41,2	1.75,8	4.63,2	1.21,8
7	34.06,5½	1.66,6	1.35,1	6.37	2.81,4	2.05,1	5.40,4	1.42,1
8	38.93,2	1.90,4	1.54,4	7.28	3.21,6	2.34,4	6.17,6	1.62,4
9	43.79,8½	2.14,2	1.73,7	8.19	3.61,8	2.63,7	6.94,8	1.82,7
10	48.66,5	2.38	1.93	9.10	4.02	2.93	7.72	2.03
20	97.33	4.76	3.86	18.20	8.04	5.86	15.44	4.06
30	145.99,5	7.14	5.79	27.30	12.06	8.79	23.16	6.09
40	194.66	9.52	7.72	36.40	16.08	11.72	30.88	8.12
50	243.32,5	11.00	9.65	45.50	20.10	14.65	38.60	10.15
100	486,65	23.80	19.30	91.00	40.20	29.30	77.20	20.30

The Partition of Africa

BY THE NATIONS OF EUROPE AMONG THEMSELVES.

(Corrected to 1892.)

Divisions.	Area.	Population.	Inhabitants to a Square Mile.
BRITISH AFRICA:			
Gambia	2,700	50,000	19
Sierra Leone	15,000	300,000	20
Gold Coast	46,600	1,905,000	41
Lagos and Yoruba	21,100	3,000,000	142
Niger Territories and Oil Rivers*	269,500	17,500,000	65
British Guinea	354,900	23,755,000	67
Cape Colony (with Pondo Land and Walvisch Bay)...............	225,600	1,700,000	8
Basutoland.............	11,750	180,000	16
Natal.................	21,150	540,000	25
Zulu and Tonga Lands .	10,560	170,000	16
British Bechuanaland..	71,420	46,000	0.6
Bechuanaland Protectorate................	99,000	150,000	1.5
Zambezi, Nyassaland, etc	520,000	950,000	1.8
British South Africa..	959,480	3,736,000	4
Zanzibar and Pemba ...	985	165,000	167
Ibea, to 6° N. Latitude.	468,000	6,500,000	14
Rest to Egyptian Frontier...............	745,000	6,000,000	8
Northern Somal Coast..	40,000	200,000	5
Sokotra	1,382	10,000	8
British East Africa..	1,255,367	12,875,000	10
Mauritius, etc.........	*1,053	392,500	374
St. Helena, Ascension, and Tristan da Cunha.	126	5,600	45
Total British Africa..	2,570,926	40,764,100	16
FRENCH AFRICA:			
Tunis.................	44,800	1,500,000	33
Algeria...............	260,000	3,870,000	15
Sahara................	1,550,000	1,100,000	0.7
Senegambia (old possessions)	51,000	250,000	5
Gold and Benin Coasts.	7,500	250,000	33
Soudan and Guinea (remainder).............	531,500	10,500,000	20
French Congo (and Gabon).................	220,000	2,500,000	11
Obok (Bay of Tajura)..	7,700	70,000	9
Madagascar and dependencies..............	228,600	3,520,000	16
Comoros...............	760	63,000	84
Réunion...............	764	165,000	215
Total French Africa..	2,902,624	23,788,000	8

Divisions.	Area.	Population.	Inhabitants to a Square Mile.
PORTUGUESE AFRICA:			
Portuguese Guinea.....	11,600	150,000	13
Angola	517,200	3,500,000	7
Mozambique	310,000	1,500,000	5
Madeira...............	318	134,000	421
Cape Verde Islands....	1,400	111,000	75
St. Thomé and Principé.	417	21,000	50
Tot. Port'gu'se Africa.	841,025	5,416,000	6
SPANISH AFRICA:			
Tetuan, etc. (Morocco).	27	16,000	592
Sahara	200,000	100,000	0.5
Canaries	2,940	288,000	98
Gulf of Guinea†	800	33,000	41
Total Spanish Africa.	203,767	437,000	2
GERMAN AFRICA:			
Togoland (Slave Coast)	16,000	650,000	40
Camarons (Kamerun)..	130,000	2,600,000	20
South-West Africa	322,000	200,000	0.6
East Africa(with Mafia)	354,000	2,500,000	7
Total German Africa	822,000	5,950,000	7
ITALIAN AFRICA:			
Eritrea................	52,000	300,000	6
Abyssinia.............	195,000	4,500,000	23
Somal, Galla, etc......	355,300	1,500,000	4
Total Italian Africa..	602,000	6,300,000	10
SUMMARY:			
British Africa.........	2,570,926	40,764,100	16
French Africa.........	2,902,624	23,788,000	8
Portuguese Africa.....	841,025	5,416,000	6
Spanish Africa........	203,767	437,000	2
German Africa........	822,000	5,950,000	7
Italian Africa........	602,000	6,300,000	10
Congo State (Belgian)..	865,400	15,600,000	18
Boer Republics.......	162,640	888,000	5
Swazi Land...........	6,370	61,000	10
Liberia...............	37,000	1,000,000	27
Turkish (Egypt and Tripoli).............	836,000	7,980,000	10
Unappropriated........	1,584,398	‡22,000,900	14
Great Lakes...........	80,350	....	..
Total Africa.........	11,514,500	130,185,000	11

This table is from "The Statesman's Year Book," for which it was prepared by E. G. Ravenstein, F.R.G.S. The population estimates are for January 1, 1892.

* Inclusive of Sokoto (121,000 square miles, 9,800,000 inhabitants) and Gando (98,500 square miles, 66,000,000 inhabitants), with Borgu and territories tributary to Sokoto on the north.
† This includes Fernando Po, Annobom, Corisco, and Cape S. Juan.
‡ Unappropriated Africa includes Morocco (219,000 square miles, 6,000,000 inhabitants), Bornu, with Kanem (80,000 square miles, 5,100,000 inhabitants), Wadai (172,000 square miles, 2,600,000 inhabitants), Bagirmi (71,000 square miles, 1,500,000 inhabitants), etc.

African exploration began, in a systematic way, with Mungo Park's first expedition in 1795. On his second expedition, in 1804, he died. From Burckhardt's expedition, in 1812, to Livingstone's, beginning in 1840, there was no important undertaking. Dr. Livingstone's second journey was begun in 1858; Du Chaillu's, 1856 and 1863; Sir Samuel Baker's, 1864 and 1870. Stanley's expedition to find Livingstone was in 1871; to explore the Congo and the great lakes, 1875-77; to relieve Emin, 1887-89.

Indebtedness of Nations.

COMPILED FROM THE ELEVENTH UNITED STATES CENSUS.

Countries.	Debt Less Sinking Fund, 1890.	Debt per Capita.	Countries.	Debt Less Sinking Fund, 1890.	Debt per Capita.
Argentine Republic.........	$284,867,069	$70.40	Bermudas................	$41,864	$2.69
Austria-Hungary.........	*2,866,339,539	70.84	Canada.................	237,533,212	47.51
Belgium................	380,504,099	63.10	Fiji..................	678,800	5.41
Bolivia................	14,763,307	12.38	New-South Wales.....	233,289,245	214.87
Brazil................	585,345,927	41.80	New-Zealand.........	184,898,305	298.01
Chile................	85,192,339	31.96	Queensland.........	129,204,750	333.46
Colombia................	63,451,583	16.36	South-Australia.....	102,177,500	321.00
Denmark................	33,004,722	15.66	Tasmania..........	22,335,345	147.46
France................	4,440,793,398	116.35	Victoria..........	179,614,005	161.63
Madagascar......	2,827,900	0.81	Western Australia..	6,509,736	150.23
Tunis................	34,881,500	23.25	Greece.............	107,306,518	49.06
German Empire........	77,577,719	1.57	Guatemala..........	10,825,836	7.59
Alsace-Lorraine....	3,837,373	2.39	Hayti..............	13,500,000	14.06
Baden.............	71,165,252	42.95	Hawaii.............	2,302,235	26.57
Bavaria.........	335,593,105	60.03	Honduras..........	63,394,267	146.77
Bremen.............	16,217,400	89.94	Italy..............	2,324,826,329	76.06
Brunswick.........	4,876,174	12.10	Japan..............	305,727,816	7.83
Hamburg.........	59,202,946	94.85	Liberia...........	972,000	0.91
Hesse.............	7,562,763	7.60	Mexico.............	113,606,675	9.98
Lippe.............	220,725	1.72	Montenegro........	740,200	3.14
Lübeck.............	3,295,709	43.10	Netherlands.......	430,589,858	95.56
Oldenburg.........	9,211,095	25.95	Dutch East Indies.	18,381,509	0.64
Prussia.........	1,109,384,127	37.03	Nicaragua.........	1,711,206	4.28
Reuss, E. B........	70,687	1.13	Norway............	13,973,752	7.13
Reuss, Y. B........	63,540	0.53	Paraguay..........	19,633,013	59.56
Saxe-Weimar.......	425,862	1.31	Peru..............	382,175,655	145.77
Saxony.............	143,897,747	41.11	Roumania..........	180,145,800	32.75
Schaumburg-Lippe...	150,000	3.83	Russia............	3,491,018,074	30.79
Saxe-Altenburg.....	158,853	0.93	Salvador..........	6,013,300	9.05
Saxe Coburg-Gotha..	955,311	4.63	Santo Domingo.....	9,865,256	16.17
Saxe-Meiningen.....	2,550,698	11.39	Servia............	60,811,330	30.20
Schwarzburg-Rudolstadt..	743,800	8.67	Spain.............	1,251,453,696	73.85
Schwarzb'rg-Sondershausen	842,631	11.16	Sweden............	64,220,807	13.53
Waldeck.........	568,200	9.92	Switzerland.......	10,912,925	3.72
Würtemberg.........	107,735,500	52.93	Turkey............	821,000,000	37.20
Great Britain and Ireland....	3,350,719,563	87.79	Egypt.............	517,278,200	75.88
Ceylon.............	11,184,400	3.86	United States.....	915,962,112	14.63
India.............	†881,003,592	3.27	Venezuela.........	22,517,437	11.00
Cape of Good Hope.........	110,817,720	77.56			
Mauritius.........	8,464,662	22.92	Total..............	$27,396,055,389	......
Natal.............	22,028,424	45.76			

* In these amounts there is included debt of Hungary for 1880, $536,051,184; for 1890, $837,928,836. Florin reckoned at 50 cents.   † Inclusive of floating debt, but exclusive of annuities, whose capitalized value is estimated by good authority to be not less than $2,000,000,000.   ‡ The rupee is reckoned at 50 cents. Its exchange value in 1890 was about 35 cents, making the actual face value of the debt about 30 per cent less than stated.

Assessed Valuation of Real and Personal Property.

States and Territories.	Total Assessed Valuation. Census of 1890.		Assessed Valuation Per Capita.		States and Territories.	Total Assessed Valuation. Census of 1890.		Assessed Valuation Per Capita.	
	1880.	1890.	1880.	1890		1880.	1890.	1880.	1890.
Alabama....	$122,867,228	$197,080,441	97.32	130.26	Nebraska.....	$90,585,782	$184,770,305	$200.23	$174.49
Arizona....	9,270,214	21,434,707	229.23	309.52	Nevada......	29,291,459	24,663,385	470.42	538.99
Arkansas...	86,409,364	172,408,497	107.67	152.82	N. Hampshire	164,755,181	252,722,016	474.81	671.19
California...	584,578,036	1,071,102,327	676.05	886.58	New-Jersey..	572,518,361	688,309,187	506.15	476.39
Colorado...	74,471,693	188,911,325	383.23	458.30	New-Mexico .	11,363,406	46,041,010	95.04	299.70
Connecticut	327,177,385	358,913,906	525.42	480.95	New-York....	2,651,940,000	3,775,325,938	521.74	629.45
Delaware...	59,951,643	74,134,401	408.92	439.09	N. Carolina.	156,100,202	212,697,287	111.52	131.46
Dist. of Col.	99,401,787	153,307,541	559.62	605.42	North-Dakota	8,786,572	78,394,536	238.06	429.04
Florida....	30,938,309	76,926,938	114.80	196 53	Ohio........	1,534,360,508	1,778,138,457	479.78	484.20
Georgia....	239,472,599	377,366,784	155.28	205.39	Oregon......	52,522,084	166,025,731	300.52	529.14
Idaho.....	6,440,876	25,581,305	197.51	303.15	Pennsylvania	1,683,459,016	2,592,841,032	393.07	493.12
Illinois....	786,616,394	727,416,252	255.57	190.11	Rhode-Island.	252,536,673	321,764,503	913.23	931.28
Indiana....	727,815,131	782,872,126	367.90	357.08	S. Carolina.	133,561,135	*132,182,698	134.15	114.83
Iowa......	398,671,251	478,318,248	245.39	250.18	South-Dakota	11,534,958	131,592,587	117.38	400.21
Kansas....	160,891,689	290,593,711	161.52	203.63	Tennessee...	211,778,538	347,510,103	137.31	196.61
Kentucky...	350,563,971	512,015,506	212.63	275.80	Texas.......	320,364,515	695,842,320	201.27	311.27
Louisiana..	160,162,439	234,320,780	170.40	209.48	Utah........	24,775,279	104,758,750	172.00	503.88
Maine.....	235,978,716	309,129,101	363.94	467.61	Vermont....	86,806,775	161,551,328	261.24	485.98
Maryland..	497,307,675	482,184,824	531.91	462.58	Virginia....	308,455,135	362,422,741	203.93	218.86
M'ss'ch's'tts	1,584,756,802	2,154,134,626	888.77	962.12	Washington..	23,810,693	124,795,449	316.99	357.18
Michigan..	517,666,359	945,450,000	316.24	451.53	W. Virginia.	139,622,705	169,927,587	225.76	222.77
Minnesota..	258,028,687	588,531,743	330.48	450.68	Wisconsin...	438,971,751	592,890,019	333.69	351.47
Mississippi.	110,628,129	157,518,906	97.76	122.15	Wyoming....	13,621,829	31,431,495	655.24	517.77
Missouri...	532,795,801	786,343,753	255.71	293.50					
Montana...	18,609,802	106,392,892	475.24	805.04	Total......	$16,902,993,543	$24,249,585,804	$337.01	$387.62

* Disputed by the Comptroller-General of the State, who reports that the assessed valuation in 1890 was $150,602,457, showing an increase in the decade of over $17,500,000.

Statistics of the Countries of the World.

Countries.	Population.	Sq. Miles.	Capitals.	Countries.	Population.	Sq. Miles.	Capitals.
British Empire*	378,946,973	12,208,506	London.	Italy	29,699,785	110,665	Rome.
China	303,241,960	4,468,750	Peking.	Italy and Colonies	34,970,785	425,765	Rome.
Russian Empire	108,787,244	8,457,289	St.Petersb'rg	Abyssinia	4,500,000	189,000	
France and Colonies	59,666,967	3,127,856	Paris.	Eritrea	660,000	56,100	
France	38,218,903	204,177	Paris.	Somal Coast	210,000	70,000	
Colonies	21,448,064	2,923,679		Spain	17,550,216	196,173	Madrid.
Algeria	3,870,000	260,000	Algiers.	Spain and Cols.	28,911,609	603,076	Madrid.
Senegal, etc	183,237	580,000	St. Louis.	Spanish Africa	437,000	203,767	
Tunis	1,500,000	45,000	Tunis.	Philippine Isl'ds	9,500,000	114,326	Manilla.
Cayenne	26,502	46,697	Cayenne.	Brazil	14,000,000	3,219,000	Rio de J'n'iro
Cambodia	1,500,000	32,254	Saigon.	Mexico	11,632,924	751,700	Mexico.
Cochin-China	1,223,000	13,692		Corea	10,519,000	85,000	Seoul.
Tonquin	12,000,000	60,000	Hanoi.	Cuba	1,521,684	43,220	Havana.
New-Caledonia	62,752	7,624	Noumea.	Porto Rico	784,709	3,550	San Juan.
Tahiti	12,800	462		Congo State	8,000,000	802,000	
Sahara	1,100,000	1,550,000		Persia	7,653,600	636,000	Teheran.
United States	62,622,250	3,602,990	Washington.	Portugal	4,708,178	34,038	Lisbon.
German Empire†	49,421,064	211,108	Berlin.	Portugal & Cols.	11,073,681	951,785	Lisbon.
Prussia	29,957,302	134,467	Berlin.	Port. Africa	5,416,000	841,025	
Bavaria	5,589,382	29,291	Munich.	Port. Asia	847,503	7,923	
Saxony	3,500,513	5,789	Dresden.	Sweden and Nor.	6,774,409	298,974	Stockholm.
Würtemberg	2,035,443	7,531	Stuttgart.	Morocco	6,500,000	314,000	Fez.
Baden	1,656,817	5,803	Karlsruhe.	Belgium	6,030,043	11,373	Brussels.
Alsace-Lorraine	1,603,987	5,602	Strasburg.	Siam	5,700,000	280,550	Bangkok.
Hesse	956,170	2,965	Darmstadt.	Roumania	5,376,000	46,314	Bucharest.
Meckl.-Schwerin	575,140	5,137	Schwerin.	Argentine Repub.	4,200,000	1,095,013	Buenos A'res
Hamburg	622,530	158		Colombia	4,000,000	331,420	Bogotá.
Brunswick	372,580	1,425	Brunswick.	Afghanistan	4,000,000	279,000	Cabul.
Oldenburg	341,250	2,479	Oldenburg.	Madagascar	3,500,000	230,000	Ant'n'narivo
Saxe-Weimar	313,668	1,387	Weimar.	Peru	2,970,000	405,040	Lima.
Anhalt	247,603	906	Dessau.	Switzerland	2,933,334	15,981	Berne.
Saxe-Meiningen	214,697	953	Meiningen.	Chile	2,665,926	256,860	Santiago.
Saxe-Coburg-Gotha	198,717	760	Gotha.	Bolivia	2,300,000	472,000	La Paz.
Bremen	180,443	99		Greece	2,187,208	24,977	Athens.
Saxe-Altenburg	161,129	511	Altenburg.	Denmark	2,172,205	14,780	Copenhagen.
Lippe	123,262	472	Detmold.	Denmark & Cols.	2,288,193	101,403	Copenhagen.
Reuss(younger line)	112,118	319	Gera.	Iceland	72,445	39,756	Rejkjavik.
Meckl.-Strelitz	98,371	1,131	Neu Strelitz.	Greenland	9,780	46,740	Godthaab.
Schwarzburg-Rud.	83,939	363	Rudolstadt.	West Indies	33,763	118	
Schwarzburg-Son.	73,023	333	S'nd'rsh'usen	Venezuela	2,121,988	566,159	Caracas.
Lubeck	76,435	115		Servia	2,096,043	18,757	Belgrade.
Waldeck	56,565	433	Arolsen.	Nepaul	2,000,000	56,800	Khatmandu.
Reuss (elder line)	53,787	122	Greiz.	Oman	1,600,000	81,000	Muscat.
Schaumburg-Lippe	37,204	131	Buckeburg.	Guatemala	1,427,116	46,774	N.Guatemala
German Africa	5,950,000	822,000		Ecuador	1,146,000	144,000	Quito.
Austro-Hung.Empire	41,827,700	201,591	Vienna.	Liberia	1,050,000	14,000	Monrovia.
Japan	39,607,234	147,669	Tokio.	Transvaal	800,000	110,193	Pretoria.
Netherlands	4,450,870	12,680	The Hague.	Uruguay	700,000	72,112	Montevideo.
Netherlands and Cols.	33,042,238	778,187	The Hague.	Khiva	700,000	22,320	Khiva.
Borneo	1,073,500	203,714		Salvador	651,130	7,228	San Salvador
Celebes	2,000,000	72,000		Hayti	550,000	29,830	P. au. Prince
Java	21,974,161	50,848	Batavia.	Paraguay	476,000	145,000	Asuncion.
Molaccas	353,000	42,420	Amboyns.	Honduras	431,917	42,658	Tegucigalpa.
New-Guinea	200,000	150,755		Nicaragua	400,000	51,660	Managua.
Sumatra	2,750,000	170,744		Dominican Repub.	350,000	20,596	San Domingo.
Surinam	57,141	46,060	Paramaribo.	Montenegro	245,380	3,486	Cettinje.
Turkish Empire	33,559,787	1,652,533	C'nst'ntin'ple	Costa Rica	213,785	19,985	San José.
European Turkey	4,790,000	63,850		Orange Free State.	133,518	41,484	Bloemfontein
Asiatic Turkey	16,133,900	729,170		Hawaii	86,647	6,587	Honolulu.
Tripoli	1,000,000	398,873	Tripoli.				
Bulgaria	3,154,375	37,860	Sofia.				
Egypt	6,817,265	400,000	Cairo.				

* These estimates of the population and area of the British Empire include the recently acquired great possessions in Africa (see "Partition of Africa"). For statistics in detail see tabular page entitled "The British Empire."   † In Europe ; the late acquisitions in Africa and elsewhere are given below separately.

Foreigners in Various Countries.

Countries.	Number.	Per cent of Population.	Countries.	Number.	Per cent of Population.	Countries.	Number.	Per cent of Population.
Argentine Republic*	600,000	14.68	Egypt§	90,886	1.34	Japan**	9,063	0.02
Austria	155,471	0.66	France	1,101,728	2.87	Roumania	89,000	1.82
Belgium	98,000	1.96	Germany†	434,525	0.94	Russia	148,000	.21
Brazil	243,000	2.04	Great Britain and Ireland	127,000	0.36	Spain	41,000	.26
Chile‡	87,077	3.45	Greece¶	31,969	1.62	Switzerland	238,313	8.17
China‡	8,107		Holland**	47,888	1.06	Sweden and Norway	17,000	.27
Denmark	54,000	2.84	Italy	261,000	1.02	UnitedStates††	9,249,547	14.90

* In 1887.   † In 1885.   ‡ In 1890.   § In 1882.   ‖ In 1891.   ¶ In 1879.   ** In 1889.   †† Census of 1890.

Largest Cities of the Earth.
POPULATION ACCORDING TO THE LATEST OFFICIAL CENSUSES.

Cities	Census Year	Population.	Cities.	Census Year	Population.	Cities.	Census Year	Population.
London	1891	4,231,431	Prague	1889	304,000	Kieff, Russia	1891	183,640
Paris	1891	2,447,957	San Francisco	1890	298,997	Cawnpore, India	1891	182,310
New-York (State)*	1892	1,801,739	Cincinnati	1890	296,908	Newark, U.S	1890	181,830
Canton	est.	1,600,000	Coiogne	1890	281,273	Toronto	1891	181,220
Berlin	1890	1,579,244	Kioto, Japan	1890	279,792	Rangoon	1891	181,210
Tokio, Japan	1890	1,389,684	Buffalo (State)*	1892	278,796	Bagdad, Turkey	est.	180,000
Vienna	1890	1,364,548	Dresden	1890	276,085	Tabriz, Persia	est.	180,000
Philadelphia(municip)	1892	1,142,653	Lucknow	1891	272,590	Frankfort	1890	179,850
Chicago†	189c	1,099,850	Barcelona	1887	272,481	Montevideo‡	est.	175,000
Brooklyn (State)*	1892	957,103	Palermo	1890	267,416	Valencia	1886	170,763
St. Petersburg	189c	956,226	Cleveland	1890	261,353	Hanover	1890	165,499
Constantinople	188:	873,565	Edinburgh	1891	261,261	Minneapolis	1890	164,738
Calcutta	1891	840,130	Belfast	1891	255,896	Jersey City	1890	163,003
Bombay	1891	804,470	Dublin	1891	254,709	Nagoya	1890	162,767
Moscow	1885	753,469	Bordeaux	1891	252,415	Konigsburg	1890	161,528
Glasgow	1891	565,714	Seoul, Corea	est.	250,000	Louisville	1890	161,129
Buenos Ayres	1891	561,160	Lisbon	1878	246,343	The Hague	1890	160,531
Naples	1890	530,872	Stockholm	1890	246,154	Manila	est.	160,000
Liverpool	1891	517,951	New-Orleans	1890	242,039	Patna	est.	160,000
Budapest	1890	506,384	Pittsburgh	1890	238,617	Portsmouth, Eng	1891	159,255
Manchester	1891	505,343	Santiago, Chile	1885	236,412	Trieste	1890	158,344
Peking, China	est.	500,000	Washington	1890	230,392	Venice	1890	158,019
Melbourne	1891	488,999	Antwerp	1891	227,225	Dundee	1891	155,640
Brussels‡	1891	482,268	Alexandria	1882	227,064	Ghent	1890	153,740
Osaka, Japan	1890	476,271	Benares	1891	222,420	Toulouse	1891	149,791
Madrid	1887	472,228	Bucharest	1876	221,805	Liege	1891	149,789
Warsaw	1891	465,272	Bristol, Eng.	1891	221,665	Rochester, U.S. (State)*	1892	144,834
St. Louis	1890	451,770	Hong Kong	1891	221,441	Dusseldorf	1890	144,682
Madras	1891	449,950	Montreal	1891	216,650	Altona	1890	143,249
Boston	1890	448,477	Bradford, Eng.	1891	216,361	Seville	1887	143,182
Baltimore	1890	434,439	Nottingham, Eng.	1891	211,984	Nuremberg	1890	142,403
Birmingham	1891	429,171	Teheran, Persia	est.	210,000	Leicester, Eng.	1891	142,051
Rome	1890	423,217	Rotterdam	1890	209,136	Omaha	1890	140,452
Amsterdam	1890	417,539	Genoa	1890	206,485	Stuttgart	1890	139,659
Lyons	1891	416,029	Detroit	1890	205,876	Chemnitz	1890	138,955
Milan	1890	414,551	Milwaukee	1890	204,468	Kobe	1890	135,639
Rio de Janeiro§	1888	406,958	Magdeburg	1890	202,235	Malaga	1887	134,016
Marseilles	1891	403,749	Lille	1891	201,211	St. Etienne	1891	133,443
Hyderabad, India	1891	392,730	Damascus	est.	200,000	St. Paul, Minn.	1890	133,156
Sydney	1891	386,400	Hull, Eng.	1891	199,991	Kansas City	1890	132,716
Cairo	1882	368,108	Havana	1888	198,261	Providence	1890	132,146
Leeds	1891	367,506	Salford, Eng.	1891	198,136	Lemberg	1890	128,419
Shanghai	est.	355,000	Riga, Russia	1888	195,668	Elberfeld	1890	125,830
Leipzig	1890	353,272	Delhi	1891	193,580	Lodz, Russia	1890	125,227
Munich	1890	348,317	Florence	1890	191,453	Bremen	1890	124,887
Breslau	1890	335,174	Pernambuco	est.	190,000	Strassburg	1890	123,545
Mexico	1890	329,535	Kharkoff, Russia	1888	188,469	Saratoff, Russia	1888	123,410
Sheffield	1891	324,243	Smyrna	1885	186,510	Nantes	1891	122,750
Hamburg	1890	323,923	Newcastle	1891	186,345	Yokohama	1890	121,985
Turin	1890	320,808				Danzig	1890	120,459
Odessa	1890	313,687	Prague	1890	184,109	Kirshineff, Russia	1888	120,074
Copenhagen	1890	312,387						

* New-York State census of 1892. † A school census taken in Chicago in 1892 revealed an estimated population of upward of 1,400,000. ‡ Including suburbs. § Official estimate. The statistics of population of largest cities of the earth other than those of the United States have been taken mainly from the "Statesman's Year-Book" for 1892.

Note.—The population of Chinese cities other than Canton, Peking, and Shanghai is omitted, because reports respecting it are utterly untrustworthy. There are forty or more Chinese cities whose inhabitants are numbered by rumor at from 200,000 to 1,000,000 each, but no official censuses have ever been taken; and setting aside consideration of the Oriental tendency to exaggeration, there is reason to believe that the estimates of population in many instances covered districts of country bearing the same names as the cities, instead of definite municipalities.

TRADE OF PRINCIPAL NATIONS.

Countries.	Imports.	Exports.	Countries.	Imports.	Exports.
Gt. Britain and Ireland	$2,040,356,186	$1,278,123,338	China	$144,886,568	$99,344,707
Germany	1,461,172,500	1,234,675,250	Argentine Republic	142,241,000	100,819,000
France	1,090,400,000	968,000,000	Canada	121,858,241	96,749,149
United States*	844,916,196	872,270,283	New South Wales	113,075,020	110,229,685
Belgium	637,832,003	589,030,368	Victoria	114,770,075	66,331,110
Netherlands	519,900,000	435,012,800	Sweden (1889)	101,780,280	81,405,750
India	309,902,525	337,756,736	Turkey (1889)	94,686,854	68,275,934
Russia	208,042,000	351,984,000	Denmark	82,898,370	63,136,260
Austria-Hungary	207,698,000	262,270,000	Japan	81,670,354	55,791,847
Italy (including gold)..	263,227,687	179,189,051	Roumania	72,558,200	55,191,600
Spain	188,227,585	187,551,977	Mexico (1889)	47,000,000	62,499,388
Switzerland	200,328,130	145,014,562	Norway	56,337,903	35,396,055
Brazil	143,055,000	174,802,100	Portugal (1883)	51,819,853	35,592,238

These statistics are for 1890, and are exclusive of specie, except when otherwise specified. * For 1891.

Heads of the Governments of the World.

JANUARY 1, 1893.

Country.	Official Head.	Title.	Born.	Acceded.
Abyssinia	Menelik	Emperor	....	March 12, 1889
Afghanistan	Abdur Rahman Khan	Amir	1845	1880
Annam	Bun-Lan	King	1879	Jan. 30, 1889
Argentine Republic	Dr. Luis Saenz Pena	President	....	Oct. 12, 1892
Austria-Hungary	Francis Joseph	Emperor	Aug. 18, 1830	Dec. 2, 1848
Baluchistan	Mir Khodâdâd	Khan	....	1856
Belgium	Leopold II	King	April 9, 1835	Dec. 10, 1865
Bokhara	Seid Abdul Ahad	Amir	....	Nov. 12, 1885
Bolivia	Aniceto Arce	President	....	Aug. 15, 1888
Borneo	Hasim Jalilal Alam Akamaldin	Sultan	....	May 1885
Brazil, United States of	Floriano Peixoto	President	....	Nov. 23, 1891
Bulgaria	Ferdinand of Saxe-Coburg	Prince	Feb. 26, 1861	Aug. 11, 1887
Chile	Admiral Jorge Montt	President	1847	Nov. 6, 1891
China	Kuang Hsü	Emperor	Aug. 15, 1871	Jan. 12, 1875
Colombia, United States of	Rafael Nuñez	President	....	Aug. 7, 1886
Congo Free State	Leopold	Sovereign	April 5, 1835	April 30, 1885
Corea	Li Hung	King	July 25, 1851	Jan. 1864
Costa Rica	J. J. Rodriguez	President	....	May 8, 1890
Denmark	Christian IX	King	April 8, 1818	Nov. 15, 1863
Dominican Republic	General Ulises Heureaux	President	....	Sept. 1, 1886
Ecuador	Luis Cordero	President	....	July 1, 1892
Egypt	Abbas Pacha	Khédive	July 14, 1874	Jan. 8, 1892
France	Marie François Sadi Carnot	President	Aug. 11, 1837	Dec. 3, 1887
Germany	William II	Emperor	} Jan. 27, 1859	June 15, 1888
Prussia	William II	King		
Bavaria	Otto	King	April 27, 1848	June 13, 1886
Saxony	Albert	King	April 23, 1828	Oct. 29, 1873
Wurtemberg	William II	King	Feb. 25, 1848	Oct. 16, 1891
Baden	Frederick I	Grand Duke	Sept. 9, 1826	Sept. 5, 1856
Hesse	Louis V	Grand Duke	Nov. 25, 1868	March 13, 1892
Anhalt	Frederick	Duke	April 29, 1831	May 22, 1871
Brunswick	Prince Albrecht	Regent	May 8, 1837	Oct. 21, 1885
Mecklenburg-Schwerin	Frederick Francis III	Grand Duke	March 19, 1851	April 15, 1883
Mecklenburg-Strelitz	Frederick William	Grand Duke	Oct. 17, 1819	Sept. 6, 1860
Oldenburg	Peter	Grand Duke	July 8, 1827	Feb. 27, 1853
Saxe-Altenburg	Ernest	Grand Duke	Sept. 16, 1826	Aug. 3, 1853
Saxe-Coburg and Gotha	Ernest II	Duke	June 21, 1818	Jan. 29, 1844
Saxe-Meiningen	George II	Duke	April 2, 1826	Sept. 20, 1866
Saxe-Weimar	Charles Alexander	Grand Duke	June 24, 1818	June 8, 1853
Waldeck-Pyrmont	George Victor	Prince	Jan. 14, 1831	May 15, 1845
Great Britain and Ireland	Victoria	Queen	May 24, 1819	June 20, 1837
Greece	George I	King	Dec. 24, 1845	Oct. 31, 1863
Guatemala	General José Maria Reina Barrios	President	....	March 15, 1892
Hawaii	Liliuokolani	Queen	Sept. 2, 1838	Jan. 19, 1891
Hayti	General L. M. F. Hippolyte	President	....	Oct. 17, 1889
Honduras	General Leiva	President	....	Dec. 1, 1891
Italy	Humbert	King	March 14, 1844	Jan. 9, 1878
Japan	Mutsu Hito	Emperor	Nov. 3, 1852	Feb. 13, 1867
Khiva	Seid Mehemed	Rehim	....	1868
Liberia	J. J. Cheeseman	President	....	Jan. 7, 1892
Luxemburg	Adolph (Duke of Nassau)	Grand Duke	July 24, 1817	Nov. 23, 1890
Madagascar	Ranavalona III	Queen	1861	July 13, 1883
Mexico	General Porfirio Diaz	President	....	Dec. 1, 1888
Monaco	Albert	Prince	Nov. 13, 1848	Sept. 10, 1889
Montenegro	Nicholas	Prince	Oct. 7, 1841	Aug. 14, 1860
Morocco	Mulai Hassan	Sultan	1831	Sept. 20, 1873
Netherlands	Wilhelmina (a minor)	Queen	Aug. 31, 1880	Nov. 23, 1890
Nicaragua	Dr. Roberto Sacasa	President	....	March 1, 1891
Oman	Seyyid Feysal bin Turkee	Sultan	....	June 4, 1888
Orange Free State	F. W. Reitz	President	....	Jan. 1889
Paraguay	Juan G. Gonzalez	President	....	Sept. 25, 1890
Persia	Nasir-ed-Din	Shah	July 18, 1831	Sept. 10, 1848
Peru	Remigio Morales Bermudez	President	....	Aug. 10, 1890
Portugal	Charles I	King	Sept. 28, 1863	Oct. 19, 1889
Roumania	Charles	King	April 20, 1839	March 26, 1881
Russia	Alexander III	Emperor	March 10, 1845	March 1, 1881
Salvador	General Carlos Ezeta	President	....	Sept. 11, 1890
Samoa	Malietoa	King	....	Dec. 5, 1889
Sarawak	Sir Charles Johnson Brooke	Raja	June 3, 1829	1868
Servia	Alexander I. (a minor)	King	Aug. 14, 1876	March 6, 1889
Siam	Phrabat Somdet Phra Yühua	King	Sept. 21, 1853	Oct. 1, 1868
Spain	Alphonso XIII. (a minor)	King	May 17, 1886	May 17, 1886
Sweden and Norway	Oscar II	King	Jan. 21, 1829	Sept. 18, 1872
Switzerland	Dr. Charles Emmanuel Schenck	President	....	Dec. 15, 1892
Transvaal	S. J. Paul Krüger	President	....	May 8, 1888
Tunis	Sidi Ali Pasha	Bey	1817	Oct. 28, 1882
Turkey	Abdul Hamid II	Sultan	Sept. 22, 1842	Aug. 31, 1876
United States of America	Benjamin Harrison	President	Aug. 20, 1833	March 4, 1889
Uruguay	Julio Herrera y Obes	President	....	March 1, 1890
Venezuela	General Joaquin Crespo	President	....	Oct. 10, 1892
Zanzibar	Seyyid Ali	Sultan	....	Feb. 13, 1890

Sovereigns of Europe.

ARRANGED ACCORDING TO THE DATES OF THEIR ACCESSION TO THE THRONE.

SOVEREIGNS.	Accession.	Age at Accession.
Victoria, Queen of Great Britain, etc.....	1837	18
Ernest II., Duke of Saxe-Coburg-Gotha...	1844	26
George Victor, Prince of Waldeck	1845	14
Francis Joseph, Emperor of Austria.....	1848	18
Frederick, Grand Duke, Baden.....	1852	25
Peter, Grand Duke, Oldenburg.....	1853	25
Charles, Grand Duke, Saxe-Weimar.....	1853	35
Ernest, Duke, Saxe-Altenburg.....	1853	26
John II., Prince of Liechtenstein......	1858	18
Henry XXII., Prince of Reuss (Elder line)	1859	13
Nicholas, Prince, Montenegro.....	1860	19
Frederick William, Grand Duke of Mecklenburg-Strelitz.....	1860	40
Adolphus, Prince of Schaumburg-Lippe..	1860	43
George I., King of the Greeks.....	1863	17
Christian IX., King of Denmark.....	1863	45
Leopold II., King of the Belgians......	1865	30
Charles, King of Roumania.....	1866	26
George II., Duke, Saxe-Meiningen......	1866	40
Henry XIV., Prince of Reuss (Younger line)......	1867	35
Frederick, Duke, Anhalt.....	1871	40
Oscar II., King of Sweden.....	1872	43
Albert, King of Saxony.....	1873	45
Waldemar, Prince of Lippe-Detmold.....	1875	51
Abdul, Hamid, Sultan of Turkey......	1876	33
Humbert I., King of Italy......	1878	34
Leo XIII., Pope.....	1878	68
Charles, Prince of Schwarzburg-Sondershausen.....	188.	49
Alexander III., Emperor of Russia.....	1881	36
Frederick III., Grand Duke, Mecklenburg-Schwerin.....	1883	32
Alphonso XIII., King of Spain.	1886	..
Otho I., King of Bavaria.....	1886	38
William II., German Emperor.....	1888	29
Alexander I., King of Servia.....	1889	13
Albert, Prince of Monaco.....	1889	41
Charles I., King of Portugal.....	1889	26
Gunther, Prince of Schwarzburg-Rudolstadt.....	1890	38
Adolphus, Grand Duke, Luxemburg.....	1890	73
Wilhelmina, Queen of Netherlands.....	1890	10
William, King of Würtemberg.....	1891	43
Ernest Louis, Grand Duke of Hesse.....	1892	23

ARRANGED ACCORDING TO THEIR RESPECTIVE AGES.

SOVEREIGNS.	Year of Birth.	Age Jan. 1, 1893. (y. m. d.)
Leo XIII., Pope.....	1810	82 9 29
Adolphus, Grand Duke of Luxemburg..	1817	75 5 7
Adolphus, Prince of Schaumburg-Lippe	1817	75 5 ..
Christian IX., King of Denmark.....	1818	74 8 22
Ernest II., Duke, Saxe-Coburg-Gotha...	1818	74 6 9
Charles, Grand Duke, Saxe-Weimar...	1818	74 6 6
Victoria, Queen of Great Britain......	1819	73 7 7
Frederick William, Grand Duke of Mecklenburg-Strelitz.....	1819	73 2 13
Waldemar, Prince of Lippe-Detmold...	1824	68 6 12
George II., Duke, Saxe-Meiningen.....	1826	65 8 28
Frederick, Grand Duke, Baden.....	1826	66 3 21
Ernest, Duke, Saxe-Altenburg.....	1825	66 3 14
Peter, Grand Duke, Oldenburg.....	1827	65 5 23
Albert, King of Saxony.....	1828	64 8 7
Oscar II., King of Sweden.....	1829	63 11 10
Charles, Prince of Schwarzburg-Sondershausen.....	1830	62 4 24
Francis Joseph, Emperor of Austria ...	1830	62 4 13
George Victor, Prince of Waldeck.....	1831	61 11 17
Frederick, Duke, Anhalt.....	1831	61 8 2
Henry XIV., Prince of Reuss (Younger line)......	1832	60 7 3
Leopold II., King of the Belgians.....	1835	57 8 21
Charles, King of Roumania.....	1839	53 8 19
John II., Prince of Liechtenstein.....	1840	52 2 26
Nicholas, Prince of Montenegro.....	1841	52 2 3
Abdul Hamid, Sultan.....	1842	50 3 8
Humbert I., King of Italy.....	1844	48 9 17
Alexander III., Emperor of Russia.....	1845	47 9 20
George I., King of the Greeks.....	1845	47 0 7
Henry XXII., Prince of Reuss (Eld. line)	1846	45 9 3
William, King of Würtemberg	1848	44 10 3
Otho, King of Bavaria.....	1848	44 8 4
Albert, Prince of Monaco.....	1848	44 1 19
Frederick III., Grand Duke, Mecklenburg-Schwerin.....	1851	41 9 12
Gunther, Prince of Schwarzburg Rudolstadt.....	....	40 4 9
William III., German Emperor.....	1859	32 11 4
Charles I., King of Portugal.....	1863	29 3 4
Ernest Louis, Grand Duke of Hesse....	1858	24 1 6
Alexander I., King of Servia.....	1876	16 4 18
Wilhelmina, Queen of Netherlands....	1880	12 4 1
Alphonso XIII., King of Spain.....	1886	6 7 14

The royal and imperial personages who died in 1892 were the Archduke Charles of Austria-Tuscany, Princess Louise of Bavaria, Count of Trapani of the Sicilian Bourbons, the British Duke of Clarence and Avondale, the reigning Grand Duke Louis IV., of Hesse, the Dowager Grand Duchess of Mecklenburg-Schwerin, Olga, the Dowager Queen of Würtemberg, and the Grand Duke Constantine of Russia.

COST OF THE BRITISH ROYAL FAMILY.

THE annuities paid by the British people to the royal family for its support are as follows: The Queen, $1,925,000; Prince of Wales, $200,000; Princess of Wales, $50,000; Crown Empress Frederick of Germany, $40,000; Duke of Edinburgh, $125,000; Princess Christian, $30,000; Princess Louise, $30,000; Duke of Connaught, $125,000; Princess Beatrice, $30,000; Duke of Cambridge (the Queen's cousin), $60,000; Duchess of Teck (the Queen's cousin), $25,000; Duchess of Albany, $30,000; Duchess of Mecklenburg-Strelitz (the Queen's cousin), $15,000; children of the Prince of Wales, $180,000. Total, $2,895,000. The Queen also receives the revenues of the Duchy of Lancaster. During recent years these have amounted to about $250,000 per annum. When the royal children marry dowries are usually provided for them. The last of the Queen's children to marry, Princess Beatrice, received $150,000 as dowry from the British people, by Parliamentary grant.

CIVIL LISTS OF EUROPEAN SOVEREIGNS.

Austria-Hungary, Emperor of, $3,875,000.
Bavaria, King of, $1,412,000.
Belgium, King of, $660,000.
Denmark, King of, $227,775; and Crown Prince, $33,330.
Greece, King of, $260,000, including $20,000 a year each from Great Britain, France, and Russia.
Netherlands, King of, $250,000, also a large revenue from domains, and $62,500 for royal family, courts, and palaces.
Italy, King of, $2,858,000, of which $180,000 for family.
Norway and Sweden, King of, $575,525.
Portugal, King of, $634,440.

Prussia, King of, $3,852,770; also a vast amount of private property, castles, forests, and estates, out of which the court expenditure and royal family are paid.
Roumania, King of, $237,000.
Russia, Czar of, has private estates of more than 1,000,000 square miles of cultivated land and forests, besides gold and other mines in Siberia. The annual income has been estimated at about $12,000,000.
Saxony, King of, $735,000.
Servia, King of, $240,000.
Spain, King of, $1,400,000, besides $600,000 for family.
Würtemberg, King of, $449,050.—*Barker's Facts.*

Order of Succession to the British Throne.

THE following is the order of succession to the British throne (January, 1893) to the last of the living descendants of George III. Failing all these the succession would fall to the other descendants of the preceding British kings, going backward in regular order. Every future new birth among the descendants of Victoria and George III. in the line below takes its relative place therein.

DESCENDANTS OF QUEEN VICTORIA.

1. The Prince of Wales, son.
2. The Duke of York, grandson.
3. Duchess of Fife, granddaughter.
4. The Lady Alexandra Duff, great-granddaughter.
5. Princess Victoria of Wales, granddaughter.
6. Princess Maud of Wales, granddaughter.
7. The Duke of Edinburgh, son.
8. Prince Alfred of Edinburgh, grandson.
9. Princess Marie of Edinburgh, Crown Princess of Roumania, granddaughter.
10. Princess Victoria Melita of Edinburgh, granddaughter.
11. Princess Alexandra of Edinburgh, granddaughter.|
12. Princess Beatrice of Edinburgh, granddaughter.
13. The Duke of Connaught, son.
14. Prince Arthur of Connaught, grandson.
15. Princess Margaret of Connaught, granddaughter.
16. Princess Victoria Patricia of Connaught, granddaughter.
17. The Duke of Albany, grandson.
18. Princess Alice of Albany, granddaughter.
19. The Empress Frederick of Germany, daughter.
20. The German Emperor, grandson.
21. The Crown Prince of Prussia, great-grandson.
22. Prince William Frederick of Prussia, great-grandson.
23. Prince Adalbert of Prussia, great-grandson.
24. Prince August of Prussia, great-grandson.
25. Prince Oscar of Prussia, great-grandson.
26. Prince Joachim Franz Humbert of Prussia, great-grandson.
27. Princess Victoria of Prussia, great-granddaughter.
28. Prince Henry of Prussia, grandson.
29. Prince Waldemar of Prussia, great-grandson.
30. The Hereditary Princess of Saxe-Meiningen, granddaughter.
31. Princess Feodora of Saxe-Meiningen, great-granddaughter.
32. Princess Frederika of Prussia, granddaughter.
33. The Crown Princess of Greece, granddaughter.
34. Prince George of Greece, great-grandson.
35. Princess Margarete of Prussia, granddaughter.
36. The Grand Duke of Hesse, grandson.
37. Prince of Battenberg, son of the preceding, great-great-grandson.
38. Princess Victoria Alberta of Battenberg, granddaughter.
39. Princess Victoria Alice of Battenberg, great-granddaughter.
40. Princess Louise Alexandra of Battenberg, great-granddaughter.
41. The Grand Duchess Sergius of Russia, granddaughter.
42. Princess Henry of Prussia (wife of No. 28), granddaughter.
43. Princess Victoria Alice Helena of Hesse, granddaughter.
44. Princess Christian of Schleswig-Holstein, daughter.
45. Prince Christian Victor of Schleswig-Holstein, grandson.
46. Prince Albert of Schleswig-Holstein, grandson.
47. Princess Victoria of Schleswig-Holstein, granddaughter.
48. Princess Franziska of Schleswig-Holstein, granddaughter.
49. The Marchioness of Lorne, daughter.
50. Princess Beatrice (Princess Henry of Battenberg), daughter.
51. Prince Alexander Albert of Battenberg, grandson.
52. Prince Leopold of Battenberg, grandson.
53. Prince Donald of Battenberg, grandson.
54. Princess Victoria Eugenie of Battenberg, granddaughter.

DESCENDANTS OF KING GEORGE III.

55. The Duke of Cumberland, great-grandson.
56. Prince George of Cumberland, great-great-grandson.
57. Prince Christian of Cumberland, great-great-grandson.
58. Prince Ernest of Cumberland, great-great-grandson.
59. Princess Mary of Cumberland great-great-granddaughter.
60. Princess Alexandra of Cumberland, great-great-granddaughter.
61. Princess Olga of Cumberland, great-great-granddaughter.
62. Princess Frederica of Hanover (Baroness von Pawel Rammingen), great-granddaughter.
63. Princess Mary Ernestina of Hanover, great-granddaughter.
64. The Duke of Cambridge, grandson.
65. The Grand Duchess of Mecklenburg-Strelitz, granddaughter.
66. The Hereditary Grand Duke of Mecklenburg, great-grandson.
67. Prince Frederick George of Mecklenburg, great-grandson.
68. Princess Victoria Mary of Mecklenburg, great-granddaughter.
69. Princess Augusta of Mecklenburg, great-granddaughter.
70. The Duchess of Teck, granddaughter.
71. Prince Adolphus of Teck, great-grandson.
72. Prince Francis of Teck, great-grandson.
73. Prince Alexander of Teck, great-grandson.
74. Princess May, who was betrothed to the late Duke of Clarence, eldest son of the Prince of Wales, great-granddaughter.

The above, originally prepared by the *St. James's Gazette*, of London, has been corrected to January, 1893.

PRECEDING SUCCESSION TO THE THRONE.

In the year 1066, Harold, the last of the Saxon kings, being slain in battle, William the Conqueror, as he was afterward called, seized the throne by right of conquest, and the succession passed from him to his second son, William, and then to his third son, Henry I. On the death of the latter a war ensued between his granddaughter Matilda and his nephew Stephen, which resulted in favor of the latter. On Stephen's death the crown reverted to Matilda's son, Henry II., who was succeeded by his second son, Richard I. He dying without children, Henry's fourth son, John, succeeded, who was followed by his son, Henry III. He in turn was followed by his eldest son, Edward I., who was in succession followed by his son and grandson, Edward II. and Edward III. The son of Edward III. dying in his father's lifetime, a grandson, Richard II., succeeded, and in his reign were sown the seeds of the Wars of the Roses, which were afterward to bear such ill fruit.

Richard II. was deposed by Henry IV., who was the eldest son of a younger brother of his father. Henry IV. was succeeded by his son, Henry V., and he by his son, Henry VI., who was deposed by Edward IV., who claimed the throne by right of descent from Lionel, third son of Edward III., and who was an elder brother of John of Gaunt, the father of Henry IV. Edward IV. was succeeded by his son, Edward V., who died an infant, and then by his brother, Richard III., who was slain in the battle of Bosworth Field, fought between him and Henry Tudor, great-great-grandson of John of Gaunt, by his third wife, Katherine Swynford. Henry ascended the throne under the title of Henry VII., and married Elizabeth, the daughter of Edward IV., and thus united the two houses of York and Lancaster and put an end to the Wars of the Roses.

Henry VII. was followed by his son, Henry VIII., who was succeeded in turn by his three children, Edward VI., Mary I., and Elizabeth, at whose death the crown fell to James VI. of Scotland, who was great-grandson of Margaret, eldest daughter of Henry VII. of England, and who ascended the throne of England under the title of James I. On his death his third son ascended as Charles I., but he was beheaded in 1649 by Cromwell, who was made Protector until his death in 1660, when the eldest son of Charles came to the throne as Charles II., and he was followed by his brother, James II. The latter abdicated in 1688, and was succeeded by a nephew, who had married the eldest daughter of James, and the two reigned under their joint names as William III. and Mary II.

On their death James II.'s second daughter, Anne, ascended, and she dying childless the crown fell to the Elector of Hanover, who was grandson of Elizabeth, daughter of James I. of England. This prince, George I., was succeeded by his son, George II., who was succeeded by his grandson, George III. After a longer reign than any previous English monarch, this king was succeeded by his eldest son, George IV., and by his third son, William IV., both of whom dying childless, the crown fell to the present sovereign, Victoria, only child of Edward, fourth son of George III., who ascended the throne in 1837.

The British Empire.

THE UNITED KINGDOM.

Countries.	Area in Sq. Miles.	How Acquired by England.	Date.	Population, 1891.
England	50,823	....	....	27,499,984
Wales	7,363	Conquest	1282	1,501,034
Scotland	29,820	Union	1603	4,033,103
Ireland	32,531	Conquest	1172	4,706,448
Islands	295	....	....	147,870
Total	120,832			37,888,153

COLONIES AND DEPENDENCIES.

Countries.	Area in Sq. Miles.	How Acquired by England.	Date.	Population, 1891.
Europe:				
Gibraltar	2	Conquest	1704	25,000
Malta, etc.	122	Treaty cession	1814	164,000
Asia:				
India (including Burma)	1,800,258	Conquest...... Transfer from East India Co.	Begun 1757 1858	284,652,330
Ceylon	25,365	Treaty cession	1801	3,008,239
Cyprus	3,584	Convention with Turkey	1878	187,000
Aden and Socotra	3,070	(Aden) Conquest	1839	44,000
Straits Settlements	1,500	Treaty cession	1785–1824	506,577
Hong Kong	30½	Treaty cession	1841	221,441
Labuan	31	Treaty cession	1846	5,853
British North Borneo	31,000	Cession to Company	1877	150,000
Africa:				
Cape Colony	225,600	Treaty cession	1588, 1814	1,700,000
Natal	21,150	Annexation	1843	543,913
St. Helena	47	Conquest	1673	4,116
Ascension	38	Annexation	1815	200
Sierra Leone	15,000	Settlement	1787	300,000
British Guinea, Gold Coast, etc.	339,900	Treaty cession	1872	23,455,000
Mauritius, etc.	1,063	Conquest and cession	1810, 1814	392,500
British South and East Africa	1,989,247	Conquest and cession	1870–1890	14,911,000
America:				
Canada Proper	370,488	Conquest	1759–60	
New-Brunswick	27,174	Treaty cession	1763	
Nova Scotia	20,907	Conquest	1627	
Manitoba	60,520	Settlement	1813	5,000,000
British Columbia, etc.	341,305	Transfer to Crown	1858	
Northwest Territories	3,257,500	Charter to Company	1670	
Prince Edward Island	2,133	Conquest	1745	
Newfoundland	42,200	Treaty cession	1713	198,000
British Guiana	76,000	Conquest and cession	1803–1814	282,000
British Honduras	7,562	Conquest	1798	28,000
Jamaica	4,193	Conquest	1655	581,000
Trinidad and Tobago	1,754	Conquest	1797	205,000
Barbadoes	166	Settlement	1605	172,000
Bahamas	5,794	Settlement	1629	48,000
Bermuda	41	Settlement	1612	16,000
Other Islands	8,742			255,000
Australasia:				
New South Wales	310,700	Settlement	1788	1,122,000
Victoria	87,884	Settlement	1832	1,105,000
South-Australia	903,690	Settlement	1836	325,000
Queensland	668,497	Settlement	1824	407,000
Western Australia	1,060,000	Settlement	1828	44,000
Tasmania	26,215	Settlement	1803	152,000
New-Zealand	104,032	Purchase	1845	621,000
Fiji	7,423	Cession from the Natives	1874	125,000
New-Guinea (British)	234,768	Annexation	1884	150,000

Estimates of area and present population are by Whitaker except for British Africa and the late accessions there, which are corrected by Ravenstein's figures (see "Partition of Africa"), and India by McKeltie's figures. The entire population of the empire, according to these estimates, is 378,946,973, and the total area, 12,208,506. The East Indian possessions extend over a territory larger than the continent of Europe without Russia; but the North American possessions are greater still; and, inclusive of Hudson's Bay and the great lakes, have a larger area than the whole of Europe. British Africa and Australasia are the next possessions in size.

Wars of the United States.

STATEMENT OF THE NUMBER OF UNITED STATES TROOPS ENGAGED.

Wars.	From—	To—	Regulars.	Militia and Volunteers.	Total.
War of the Revolution	April 19, 1775	April 11, 1783	130,711	164,080	309,781
Northwestern Indian Wars	Sept. 19, 1790	Aug. 3, 1795	......	......	8,983
War with France	July 9, 1798	Sept. 30, 1800	......	......	*4,593
War with Tripoli	June 10, 1801	June 4, 1805	......	......	*3,330
Creek Indian War	July 27, 1813	Aug. 9, 1814	600	13,181	13,781
War of 1812 with Great Britain	June 18, 1812	Feb. 17, 1815	85,000	471,622	576,622
Seminole Indian War	Nov. 20, 1817	Oct. 21, 1818	1,000	6,911	7,911
Black Hawk Indian War	April 21, 1831	Sept. 31, 1832	1,339	5,126	6,465
Cherokee disturbance or removal	1836	1837	......	9,494	9,494
Creek Indian War or disturbance	May 5, 1836	Sept. 30, 1837	935	12,483	13,418
Florida Indian War	Dec. 23, 1835	Aug. 14, 1843	11,169	29,953	41,122
Aroostook disturbance	1836	1839	......	1,500	1,500
War with Mexico	April 24, 1846	July 4, 1848	30,954	73,776	112,230
Apache, Navajo, and Utah War	1849	1855	1,500	1,061	2,561
Seminole Indian War	1856	1858	......	3,687	3,687
Civil War†	1861	1865	......	......	2,772,408

* Naval forces engaged.   † The number of troops on the Confederate side was about 600,000.

Soldiers' Homes.

LOCATIONS OF HOMES FOR DISABLED UNITED STATES SOLDIERS AND SAILORS, AND REGULATIONS FOR ADMISSION TO THEM.

NATIONAL HOME FOR DISABLED VOLUNTEER SOLDIERS.

President of the Board of Managers..............General William B. Franklin, Hartford, Conn.
Secretary...General M. T. McMahon, 41 Park Row, New York City.

BRANCHES OF THE NATIONAL HOME.

Branches.	Location.	No. of Members.	Branches.	Location.	No. of Members.
Central	Dayton, O.	4,548	Pacific	Santa Monica, Cal.	652
Northwestern	Milwaukee, Wis	1,976	Marion	Marion, Ind	770
Eastern	Togus, Me.	1,533			
Southern	Hampton, Va	2,070	Total		14,193
Western	Leavenworth, Kan	2,044			

Above is average number present in National Home for year ending June 30, 1892. Total number cared for in National Home during same period, 23,521.

NOTIFICATION.

The Board of Managers of the National Home for Disabled Volunteer Soldiers informs the disabled soldiers and sailors of the United States that Homes have been established, at the places above named, for all such as are unable to earn a living by labor. All the ordinary comforts of a home are provided. Chapels for religious services; halls for concerts, lectures, etc.; hospitals with experienced surgeons and nurses; libraries and reading rooms; amusement halls; post and telegraph offices; stores, etc. Good behavior ensures kind treatment.

Soldiers and sailors are especially informed that the Home is neither an hospital nor almshouse, but a home, where subsistence, quarters, clothing, religious instruction, employment when possible, and amusements are provided by the Government of the United States. The provision is not a charity, but is a reward to the brave and deserving, and IS THEIR RIGHT, to be forfeited only by bad conduct at the Home or conviction of heinous crimes. A soldier or sailor desiring admission may apply by letter to either of the managers, whereupon a blank application will be sent to him, and if he be found duly qualified, transportation will be furnished; or he can apply personally or by letter at the branch nearest to his place of residence.

REQUIREMENTS FOR ADMISSION.

1. An honorable discharge from the United States Service.
2. Disability which prevents the applicant from earning his living by labor.
3. Applicants for admission will be required to stipulate and agree to abide by all the rules and regulations made by the Board of Managers, or by its order; to perform all duties required of them, and to obey all the lawful orders of the officers of the Home. Attention is called to the fact, that by the law establishing the Home the members are made subject to the Rules and Articles of War, and will be governed thereby in the same manner as if they were in the army of the United States.
4. A soldier or sailor must forward with his application for admission his Discharge Paper, and when he is a pensioner, his Pension Certificate, and if he has been a member of a State Home, his discharge from that Home, before his application will be considered; which papers will be retained at the branch to which the applicant is admitted, to be kept there for him, and returned to him when he is discharged. This rule is adopted to prevent the loss of such papers and certificates, and to hinder fraudulent practices; and no application will be considered unless these papers are sent with it. If the original discharge does not exist, a copy of discharge, certified by the War or Navy Department or by the Adjutant-General of the State, must accompany the application.

Soldiers or sailors whose pensions exceed $16 the month are not eligible to the Home unless the reasons are peculiar, and are explained to the manager and are satisfactory to him. Those who have been members of State Homes must have been discharged from those Homes at least six months before they can be admitted to a branch of the National Home, except by a vote of the Board of Managers. Applicants are requested to conform strictly to the above requirements.

The Civil War of 1861-65.

NUMBER OF MEN IN THE UNION ARMY FURNISHED BY EACH STATE AND TERRITORY, FROM APRIL 15, 1861, TO CLOSE OF WAR.

STATES AND TERRITORIES.	Number of Men Furnished.	Aggregate Reduced to a Three Years' Standing.	STATES AND TERRITORIES.	Number of Men Furnished.	Aggregate Reduced to a Three Years' Standing.
Alabama	2,556	1,611	New-York	448,850	392,270
Arkansas	8,289	7,836	North-Carolina	3,156	3,156
California	15,725	15,725	Ohio	313,180	240,514
Colorado	4,903	3,697	Oregon	1,810	1,773
Connecticut	55,864	50,623	Pennsylvania	337,926	265,517
Delaware	12,284	10,322	Rhode-Island	23,236	17,866
Florida	1,290	1,290	South-Carolina	.....	.....
Georgia	.....	.....	Tennessee	31,092	26,394
Illinois	259,092	214,133	Texas	1,965	1,632
Indiana	196,363	153,576	Vermont	33,288	29,068
Iowa	76,242	68,630	Virginia	.....	.....
Kansas	20,149	18,706	West-Virginia	32,068	27,714
Kentucky	75,760	70,832	Wisconsin	91,327	79,260
Louisiana	5,224	4,654	Dakota	206	206
Maine	70,107	56,776	District of Columbia	16,534	1,506
Maryland	46,638	41,275	Indian Territory	3,530	3,530
Massachusetts	146,730	124,104	Montana	.....	.....
Michigan	87,364	80,111	New-Mexico	6,561	4,432
Minnesota	24,020	19,693	Utah	.....	.....
Mississippi	545	545	Washington	964	964
Missouri	109,111	86,530	U. S. Army	.....	.....
Nebraska	3,157	2,175	U. S. Volunteers	.....	.....
Nevada	1,080	1,080	U. S. Colored Troops	93,441	91,789
New-Hampshire	33,937	30,849			
New-Jersey	76,814	57,908	Total	2,778,304	2,326,168

The number of casualties in the volunteer and regular armies of the United States, during the war of 1861-65, according to a statement prepared by the Adjutant-General's office, was as follows : Killed in battle, 67,058 ; died of wounds, 43,012 ; died of disease, 199,720 ; other causes, such as accidents, murder, Confederate prisons, etc., 40,154 ; total died, 349,944 ; total deserted, 199,105. Number of soldiers in the Confederate service who died of wounds or disease (partial statement), 133,821. Deserted (partial statement), 104,428. Number of United States troops captured during the war, 212,608 ; Confederate troops captured, 476,169. Number of United States troops paroled on the field, 16,431 ; Confederate troops paroled on the field, 248,599. Number of United States troops who died while prisoners, 30,156 ; Confederate troops who died while prisoners, 30,152.

THE GREAT BATTLES OF THE CIVIL WAR.

(From " Regimental Losses in the American Civil War," by William F. Fox, Lieutenant-Colonel, U.S.V.) As to the loss in the Union armies, the greatest battles in the war were :

DATE.	Battle.	Killed.	Wounded.*	Missing.	Aggregate.
July 1-3, 1863	Gettysburg	3,070	14,497	5,434	23,001
May 8-18, 1864	Spottsylvania	2,725	13,413	2,258	18,399
May 5-7, 1864	Wilderness	2,246	12,037	3,383	17,666
September 17, 1862	Antietam†	2,108	9,549	753	12,410
May 1-3, 1863	Chancellorsville	1,606	9,762	5,919	17,287
September 19-20, 1863	Chickamauga	1,656	9,749	4,774	16,179
June 1-4, 1864	Cold Harbor	1,844	9,077	1,816	12,737
December 11-14, 1862	Fredericksburg	1,284	9,600	1,769	12,653
August 28-30, 1862	Manassas‡	1,747	8,452	4,263	14,462
April 6-7, 1862	Shiloh	1,754	8,408	2,885	13,047
December 31, 1862	Stone's River§	1,730	7,802	3,717	13,249
June 15-19, 1864	Petersburg (assault)	1,688	8,513	1,185	11,386

* Wounded in these and the following returns includes mortally wounded.
† Not including South Mountain or Crampton's Gap.
‡ Including Chantilly, Rappahannock, Bristol Station, and Bull Run Bridge.
§ Including Knob Gap and losses on January 1 and 2, 1863.

The Union losses at Bull Run (first Manassas), July 21, 1861, were: killed, 470 ; wounded, 1,071 ; captured and missing, 1,793 ; aggregate, 3,334.

The Confederate losses in particular engagements were as follows: Bull Run (first Manassas), July 21, 1861, killed, 387 ; wounded, 1,582 ; captured and missing, 13 ; aggregate, 1,982. Fort Donelson, Tenn., Feb. 14-16, 1862, killed, 466 ; wounded, 1,534 ; captured and missing, 13,829 ; aggregate, 15,829. Shiloh, Tenn., April 6-7, 1862, killed, 1,723 ; wounded, 8,012 ; captured and missing, 959 ; aggregate, 10,694. Seven Days' Battle, Virginia, June 25-July 1, 1862, killed, 3,478 ; wounded, 16,261 ; captured and missing, 875 ; aggregate, 20,614. Second Manassas, Aug. 21-Sept. 2, killed, 1,481 ; wounded and missing, 7,627 ; captured and missing, 9,197. Antietam campaign, Sept. 12-20, 1862, killed, 1,886 ; wounded, 9,348 ; captured and missing, 1,367 ; aggregate, 12,601. Fredericksburg, Dec. 13, 1862, killed, 596 ; wounded, 4,068 ; captured and missing, 651 ; aggregate, 5,315. Stone's River, Tenn., Dec. 31, 1862, killed, 1,294 ; wounded, 7,045 ; captured and missing, 1,027 ; aggregate, 10,266. Chancellorsville, May 1-4, 1863, killed, 1,665 ; wounded, 9,081 ; captured and missing, 2,018 ; aggregate, 12,764. Gettysburg, July 1-3, 1863, killed, 2,592 ; wounded, 12,706 ; captured and missing, 5,150 ; aggregate, 20,448. Chickamauga, Sept. 19-20, 1863, killed, 2,268 ; wounded, 13,613 ; captured and missing, 1,090 ; aggregate, 16,971.

" Gettysburg was the greatest battle of the war ; Antietam the bloodiest. The largest army was assembled by the Confederates at the seven days' fight ; by the Unionists at the Wilderness."

Living Confederate Generals.

JANUARY 1, 1893.

During the Civil War there were 408 persons commissioned as generals of the several grades in the Confederate Army. Of these, less than 164 are now living—twenty-seven years after the close of the war.

General W. L. Cabell, of Dallas, Tex., has prepared a following list of survivors, together with their present places of residence, when known. It has been revised by him for THE WORLD ALMANAC, and has had the advantage of further suggestion by General Marcus J. Wright, agent for the collection of Confederate statistics for the War Department, and Mr. A. E. Allen, of Trenton, N. J.

GENERALS.

Peter Gustave T. Beauregard, New-Orleans, La.
Edmund Kirby Smith, Sewanee, Tenn.

LIEUTENANT-GENERALS.

Stephen D. Lee, Starkville, Miss.
James Longstreet, Gainesville, Ga.
Jubal A. Early, Lynchburg, Va.
Simon B. Buckner, Frankfort, Ky.
Joseph Wheeler, Wheeler, Ala.
Alexander P. Stewart, Chickamauga, Ga.
Wade Hampton, Columbia, S. C.
John B. Gordon, Atlanta, Ga.

MAJOR-GENERALS.

Gustavus W. Smith, New-York.
LaFayette McLaws, Savannah, Ga.
S. G. French, Winter Park, Fla.
John H. Forney, Jenifer, Ala.
Dabney H. Maury, Richmond, Va.
Henry Heth, Antietam Battle Field Survey.
J. L. Kemper, Orange Court House, Va.
Robert F. Hoke, Raleigh, N. C.
Fitzhugh Lee, Glasgow, Va.
W. B. Bate, U. S. Senate.
J. B. Kershaw, Camden, S. C.
M. C. Butler, U. S. Senate.
E. C. Walthall, U. S. Senate.
L. L. Lomax, Washington, D. C.
P. M. B. Young, Cartersville, Ga.
T. L. Rosser, Charlottesville, Va.
W. W. Allen, Montgomery, Ala.
S. B. Maxey, Paris, Tex.
William Mahone, Petersburg, Va.
G. W. Custis Lee, Lexington, Va.
William B. Tallaferro, Gloucester, Va.
John G. Walker, Washington, D. C.
William T. Martin, Natchez, Miss.
C. J. Polignac, Orleans, France.
E. M. Law, Yorkville, S. C.
James F. Fagan, Little Rock, Ark.
Richard Gatlin, Fort Smith, Ark.
Matt Ransom, U. S. Senate.
J. A. Smith, Jackson, Miss.
William H. Forney, Jacksonville, Ala.

BRIGADIER-GENERALS.

George T. Anderson, Anniston, Ala.
Frank C. Armstrong, Washington, D. C.
E. P. Alexander, Savannah, Ga.
Arthur S. Bagby, Texas.
Laurence S. Baker, Suffolk, Va.
Pinckney D. Bowles, Alabama.
Rufus Barringer, Charlotte, N. C.
Seth M. Barton, Fredericksburg, Va.
John Bratton, White Oak, S. C.
J. L. Brent Baltimore, Md.
C. A. Battle, Alabama.
R. L. T. Beale, Hague, Va.
Hamilton P. Bee, San Antonio, Tex.
W. R. Boggs, Winston, N. C.
Tyree H. Bell, Tennessee.
William L. Cabell, Dallas, Tex.
E. Capers, Columbia, S. C.
James R. Chalmers, Vicksburg, Miss.

BRIGADIER-GENERALS—Continued.

Thomas L. Clingman, Asheville, N. C.
George B. Cosby, Sacramento, Cal.
Francis M. Cockrell, U. S. Senate.
A. H. Colquitt, U. S. Senate.
R. E. Colston, Washington, D. C.
Phil Cook, Atlanta, Ga.
M. D. Corse, Alexandria, Va.
Alexander W. Campbell, Jackson, Tenn.
John B. Clark, Jr., Rockville, Md.
Alfred Cumming, Augusta, Ga.
X. B. DeBray, Austin, Tex.
William R. Cox, Raleigh, N. C.
Joseph Davis, Mississippi City, Miss.
H. B. Davidson, California.
T. P. Dockery, Arkansas.
Basil W. Duke, Louisville, Ky.
John Echols, Louisville, Ky.
C. A. Evans, Atlanta, Ga.
Samuel W. Ferguson, Greenville, Miss.
J. J. Finley, Florida.
D. M. Frost, St. Louis, Mo.
Richard M. Gano, Dallas, Tex.
James Z. George, Jackson, Miss.
William L. Gardner, Memphis, Tenn.
G. W. Gordon, Memphis, Tenn.
D. C. Govan, Arkansas.
Johnson Hagood, Barnwell, S. C.
George P. Harrison, Sr., Auburn, Ala.
A. T. Hawthorne, Atlanta, Ga.
J. F. Holtzclaw, Montgomery, Ala.
Eppa Hunton, U. S. Senator, Warrenton, Va.
William P. Hardeman, Austin, Tex.
N. H. Harris, Vicksburg, Miss.
George B. Hodge, Kentucky.
Louis Hobert, Breaux, La.
J. D. Imboden, Southwest Virginia.
Henry R. Jackson, Savannah, Ga.
William H. Jackson, Nashville, Tenn.
Bradley T. Johnson, Baltimore, Md.
A. R. Johnson, Texas.
George D. Johnston, Civil Service Commissioner, Washington, D. C.
Robert D. Johnston, Birmingham, Ala.
J. D. Kennedy, Camden, S. C.
William H. King, Austin, Tex.
William W. Kirkland, New-York.
James H. Lane, North-Carolina.
A. R. Lawton, Savannah, Ga.
T. M. Logan, Richmond, Va.
Robert Lowry, Jackson, Miss.
Joseph H. Lewis, Frankfort, Ky.
W. H. Lewis, Tarboro, N. C.
William McComb, Gordonsville, Va.
Samuel McGowan, Abbeville, S. C.
E. McNair, Hattisburg, Miss.
John T. Morgan, U. S. Senate.
T. T. Mumford, Uniontown. Ala.
George Manney, Nashville, Tenn.
B. McGlathan, Savannah, Ga.
John McCausland, Mason C. H., W. Va.
Henry E. McCulloch, Seguin, Tex.
W. R. Miles, Mississippi.
William Miller, Florida.
John C. Moore, Texas.

LIVING CONFEDERATE GENERALS—*Continued.*

BRIGADIER-GENERALS—*Continued.*

Francis T. Nichols, New-Orleans, La.
R. L. Page, Norfolk, Va.
W. H. Payne, Warrenton, Va.
W. F. Perry, Glendale, Ky.
Roger A. Pryor, New-York City.
C. W. Phyfer, Mississippi.
W. H. Parsons, Philadelphia, Pa.
N. B. Pearce, Gainesville, Tex.
E. W. Pettus, Selma, Ala.
W. A. Quarles, Clarkesville, Tenn.
B. H. Robertson, Washington, D. C.
F. H. Robertson, Waco, Tex.
George W. Rains, Augusta, Ga.
Daniel Ruggles, Fredericksburg, Va.
Charles A. Ronald, Blacksburg, Va.
D. H. Reynolds, Arkansas City, Ark.
William P. Roberts, Raleigh, N. C.
L. S. Ross, College Station, Tex.
Jake Sharp, Jackson, Miss.
Joe Shelby, Carthage, Mo.
Charles M. Shelly, Birmingham, Ala.
James E. Slaughter, Washington, D. C.

BRIGADIER-GENERALS—*Continued.*

F. A. Shoup, Sewanee, Tenn.
Thomas B. Smith. Nashville, Tenn.
G. M. Sorrell, Savannah, Ga.
George H. Stewart, Baltimore, Md.
Marcellus A. Stovall, Augusta, Ga.
Edward L. Thomas, Washington, D. C.
W. R. Terry, Richmond, Va.
J. C. Tappan, Helena, Ark.
Robert B. Vance, Asheville, N. C.
A. J. Vaughan, Memphis, Tenn
James A. Walker, Wytheville, Va.
D. A. Weisger, Richmond, Va.
G. C. Wharton, New River, Va.
Marcus J. Wright, Washington, D. C.
G. J. Wright, Griffin, Ga.
W. S. Walker, Florida.
H. H. Walker, New-York.
W. H. Wallace, Columbia, S. C.
T. N. Waul, Galveston, Tex.
John S. Williams, Mount Sterling, Ky.
Zebulon York, Baton Rouge, La.

Mount Vernon Ladies' Association.

THE Washington estate at Mount Vernon, Va., is under the care and direction of the Mount Vernon Ladies' Association of the Union. The founder of the association, in 1854, was Miss Ann Pamela Cunningham, of South-Carolina. She was the first Regent, and was succeeded in 1873 in that position by Mrs. MacAllister Laughton. She died in 1892, and the present Regent is Mrs. Justine Van Rensselaer Townsend, of New-York (a great granddaughter of General Philip Schuyler). The Vice-Regents are as follows: Mrs. M. J. M. Sweat, Me.; Mrs. Cornelius L. King, Vt.; Miss Alice M. Longfellow, Mass.; Mrs. A. R. Winder, N. H.; Mrs. Susan E. J. Hudson, Ct.; Miss Comegys, Del.; Mrs. Mary T. Barnes, D. C.; Mrs. Emma R. Ball, Va.; Mrs. Ella B. Washington, W. Va.; Mrs. Letitia H. Walker, N. C.; Mrs. Lucy H. Pickens, S. C.; Mrs. Georgia Page Wilder, Ga.; Mrs. Martha Mitchell, Wis.; Mrs. Ida A. Richardson, La.; Mrs. Elizabeth A. Rathbone, Mich.; Mrs. Mary T. Leiter, Ill.; Mrs. Woodward, Ky.; Mrs. Jenny M. Ward, Kan.; Mrs. Rebecca B. Flandrau, Minn.; Mrs. Alice Hill, Col.; Mrs. Phœbe A. Hearst, Cal.; Mrs. Baker. Fla.

The advisory committee is composed of Judge J. P. Comegys, of Delaware; Mr. Justice Field, of the Supreme Court; T. N. McCarter, LL.D., of New-Jersey; President J. C. Welling, of Columbian University, D. C., and George W. Childs, of Philadelphia. The resident Superintendent at Mount Vernon is Harrison H. Dodge.

Military Societies of the United States.

COLONIAL AND INDIAN WARS, 1607-1775.

Founded.	Title.	Membership.
1892	Society of Colonial Wars	230

WAR OF THE REVOLUTION, 1775-1883.

1783	Order of the Cincinnati	432
1876	Society of Sons of the Revolution	2,732
1889	Society of Sons of the American Revolution	3,000

WAR WITH GREAT BRITAIN, 1812-1815.

1854	Society of the War of 1812*	264
1890	Society of the War of 1812 in the State of New-York†	184

WAR WITH MEXICO, 1846-1848.

1847	Aztec Club	200

CIVIL WAR, 1861-1865.

1865	Military Order of the Loyal Legion	10,264
1866	Grand Army of the Republic	398,000
1880	Sons of Veterans, U. S. A.	100,000
1884	Union Veteran Legion	10,000
1887	National Association of Naval Veterans	7,000
1891	Naval Legion of the United States	3,000
1889	Association of United Confederate Veterans	40,000
1888	Regular Army and Navy Union‡	7,000

By joint resolution of Congress, approved September 25, 1890, "the distinctive badges adopted by military societies of men who served in the War of the Revolution, the War of 1812, the Mexican War, and the War of the Rebellion, respectively, may be worn upon all occasions of ceremony by officers and enlisted men of the United States, who are members of said organizations in their own right." This resolution practically makes all societies of the character indicated in the resolution military societies of the United States, to be recognized as such by civil and military authorities at home and abroad.

* Not organized originally as a military society.   † Organized as a military society by veterans of the war and descendants of soldiers and sailors participating therein.   ‡ This society does not limit membership to participators in the Civil War.

The State Militia of the States of the Union.

STRENGTH OF THE NATIONAL GUARD AND OF THE AVAILABLE ARMS-BEARING POPULATION OF EACH OF THE STATES AND TERRITORIES.

Compiled for The World Almanac from records in the War Department up to October 1, 1892, by Lieutenant W. R. Hamilton, Fifth Artillery, U. S. A.

States and Territories.	Infantry.	Cavalry.	Artillery.	Total Commissioned	Total Enlisted.	Available for Service.*	States and Territories.	Infantry.	Cavalry.	Artillery.	Total Commissioned	Total Enlisted.	Available for Service.*
Alabama	2,320	324	122	287	2,479	160,000	Nebraska	1,813	51	92	92	1,864	115,000
Arizona	288	....	....	20	268	15,500	Nevada	462	....	71	54	479	11,960
Arkansas	2,200	122	....	209	2,113	125,000	N. Hampshire	880	53	67	105	895	34,000
California	3,311	60	856	392	3,835	141,000	New-Jersey	3,260	....	117	278	3,099	254,000
Colorado	781	....	....	75	706	86,000	New-Mexico	365	387	....	72	680	31,000
Connecticut	3,022	....	67	242	2,847	90,800	New-York	12,589	103	371	726	12,337	700,000
Delaware	488	118	....	60	546	38,000	N. Carolina	1,864	36	....	246	1,736	225,000
D.of Columbia	860	81	43	155	829	42,000	North-Dakota	431	....	....	58	373	37,200
Florida	921	642	40	120	1,483	47,700	Ohio	4,123	62	521	372	4,334	600,000
Georgia	2,974	51	142	389	2,678	205,000	Oregon	1,120	73	50	135	1,108	44,370
Idaho	311	....	....	27	286	10,500	Pennsylvania	7,603	173	254	596	7,524	693,000
Illinois	3,428	63	160	329	3,322	544,000	Rhode-Island	1,120	91	64	142	1,733	47,000
Indiana	1,766	31	175	177	1,795	453,000	S. Carolina	2,925	1,360	521	521	4,385	116,000
Iowa	2,466	52	40	215	2,343	233,000	South-Dakota	421	....	....	42	379	61,200
Kansas	2,923	70	50	259	2,884	226,500	Tennessee	1,260	38	311	144	1,463	263,700
Kentucky	1,020	47	43	74	1,046	385,000	Texas	2,842	119	111	337	2,825	301,560
Louisiana	1,244	160	249	113	1,540	138,500	Vermont	711	....	....	75	636	44,200
Maine	987	....	....	81	906	97,500	Virginia	2,222	326	198	225	2,521	220,000
Maryland	1,871	....	63	182	1,752	125,000	Washington	907	98	....	106	909	61,700
Massachusetts	4,615	221	429	417	4,948	339,700	West-Virginia	872	....	....	90	782	90,000
Michigan	2,341	....	....	107	2,234	315,500	Wisconsin	2,113	70	55	195	2,043	287,000
Minnesota	1,690	....	113	152	1,651	154,000	Wyoming	298	....	....	17	281	13,000
Mississippi	2,230	326	172	191	2,637	140,000	*Totals	86,570	4,574	4,234	9,099	95,378	9,144,590
Missouri	1,420	43	116	140	1,439	350,000							
Montana	442	123	51	60	556	32,500							

* Total number of men available for military service in the United States.

Naval Militia.

By act of Congress, 1888, the maritime States were authorized to organize naval battalions. Massachusetts, New-York, California, North-Carolina, and a few other States have taken advantage of this law to create these battalions. The Naval Reserve Artillery of the State of New-York is a part of the State Militia, and is regularly mustered in as such. Its commander is Jacob W. Miller, Lieutenant-Commander, and it is composed of four batteries, each commanded by a lieutenant. There are about 350 men in the force.

The duty of the Naval Militia in time of war will be to man the coast and harbor defence vessels, thus leaving free the regular force to carry on offensive operations at sea. The Naval Militia will also operate in boat squadrons with torpedoes against any hostile fleet in our waters. The New-York Naval Militia is composed of a very high grade of volunteers—merchants, professional men, and others of like social position being the material. The principal officers are graduates of the Annapolis Naval Academy. The drills in summer take place in vessels of war in the harbor.

Navies of Asia.

	China.	Japan.	India.	Siam.		China.	Japan.	India.	Siam.
Armored Vessels	5	5	....	1	Guns of Same	53	11	6	8
Guns of Same	31	56	Troop Ships.	22	Transports	4	7	1	....
Unarmored Vessels	26	30	5	5	Other Vessels	41	47 Dispatch Boats.	5 Inland Steamers.	11
Guns of Same	231	318	22	22					
Torpedo Boats, No. 1	22	22	7	....	Floating Batteries	6	3	4	....
" No. 2	9	4	....	....	Guns of Same	18	7	15	....
Armored Gunboats	1	1	....	....	Training Ships	....	3	....	....
Guns of Same	1	8	....	....	Guns of Same	....	33	....	....
Unarmored Gunboats	24	3	2	4	Officers and Men	9,500	6,000	1,300	700

Armies of Asia.

	China.	Japan.	India.	Siam.	Persia.		China.	Japan.	India.	Siam.	Persia.
Infantry	400,000	86,920	186,572*	13,000	16,000	Irregulars	1,200,000	......	......	150,000	200,000
Cavalry	83,000	4,378	12,000*	......	8,700	Totals	1,683,000	97,798	214,872*	163,000	224,700
Artillery	......	6,500	16,300*	......	......						
Guns	292	420	490*	86	......						

* Includes British forces (white) with native troops serving under both white and native officers.

Death Roll of 1892.

Age at death is given in parenthesis ; vocation, place, cause, and time of death when known follow.

Adams, John Couch (72), astronomer, England, Jan.24.

Agnew, D. Hayes, M.D. (74), surgeon, Philadelphia, Pa., Mar. 22.

Airy, Sir George B. (90), late Astronomer Royal, Jan. 2.

Anderledy, Anthony M., general of the Jesuits, Rome, Italy, Jan. 19.

Arago, Alfred (77), French painter, Paris, Feb. 4.

Arago, Etienne (90), French dramatist, Mar. 6.

Astor, William (63), millionaire, Paris, France, pneumonia, April 25.

Atkins, Hiram (85), journalist and Democratic Party leader, Montpelier, Vt., Oct. 1.

Barbour, John S. (72), United States Senator from Virginia, Washington, D. C., May 14.

Barnum, Henry A. (60), United States Brigadier-General in the Civil War, and prominent public man, New-York City, pneumonia, Jan. 29.

Beach, Moses S., veteran journalist, former proprietor of the New-York *Sun*, Peekskill, N. Y., July 25.

Bedell, Gregory T., D.D. (75), Protestant Episcopal Bishop of Ohio, New-York City, Mar. 11.

Bermudez, Edward (60), late Chief Justice of Louisiana, New-Orleans, July 22.

Blaine, Emmons (35), son of James G. Blaine, Chicago, inflammation of the bowels, June 18.

Bodenstedt, Frederick M. (73), German author, Berlin, April 19.

Bomford, James V. (80), ex-Brigadier-General, U.S.A., Elizabeth, N. J., paralysis of the heart, Jan. 6.

Booth, Newton (67), ex-Governor of California, Sacramento, Cal. July 14.

Bowditch, Henry I. (84), physician and author, Salem, Mass.

Bradford, William (70), painter of Arctic scenery, New-York City, apoplexy, April 25.

Bradley, Joseph P. (79), Associate Justice United States Supreme Court, Washington, D. C., Jan. 22.

Bramwell, Baron—George W. W.—(84), British jurist, May 11.

Brice, Benjamin W. (86), Major-General U. S. A., retired, Washington, D. C.

Brisbin, James S. (55), ex-Brigadier-General U. S. A., Philadelphia, Pa., bronchitis, Jan. 14.

Brucke, Ernest Wilhelm (73), German physiologist, Berlin, Jan. 7.

Bryson, Andrew (69), Rear-Admiral U. S. N., Washington, D. C., Feb. 7.

Bungay, George W. (74), author and journalist, Bloomfield, N. J., July 10.

Caird, Sir James (75), England, agricultural statistician, Feb. 9.

Cambriels, Albert (76), French general, Jan. 5.

Campbell, Sir Alexander (70), Canadian statesman, Toronto, May 24.

Carpenter, Alfred (66), sanitary reformer, England, Jan. 20.

Castleton, Kate, actress, Providence, R. I., July 10.

Cathcart, George R. (49), book publisher, Newport, R. I., heart disease, June 27.

Charles Salvator (52), Archduke of Austria, Vienna, the grippe, Jan. 18.

Child, Theodore, author, died in Persia, in November.

Chimay, Prince Joseph de (56), Belgian statesman, Mar. 29.

Cialdini, Enrico (81), Italian general and statesman, died in Italy in September.

Clarence and Avondale, Duke of—Albert Victor Christian Edward — (28), elder son of the Prince of Wales, Jan. 14.

Clark, Myron H. (86), ex-Governor of New-York, Canandaigua, N. Y., Aug. 23.

Comstock, George F. (81), jurist, Syracuse, N. Y., Sept. 27.

Conner, William M. (60), turfman and New-York hotel proprietor, St. Louis, Mo., dropsy, Feb. 17.

Constantine, Grand Duke of Russia (64), second son of Emperor Nicholas I., commander of the Russian Navy, Jan. 25.

Cook, Thomas (84), founder of tourist system, Leicester, England, July 19.

Cooke, Rose Terry (65), author, Pittsfield, Mass., pneumonia, July 18.

Cranch, Christopher P. (79), painter, Boston, Mass., Jan. 20.

Cremieux, Hector J. (64), French dramatic author, Paris, suicide, Sept. 29.

Cullum, George W. (83), Major-General U. S. A., retired, New-York City, pneumonia, Feb. 28.

Curtis, George William (68), author, journalist, orator, Staten-Island, N. Y., dropsy, Aug. 31.

Cutting, Hiram A. (60), scientist, Lunenburgh, Vt., apoplexy, April 18.

Daboll, William S. (35), actor, Holliston, Mass., suicide, Aug. 22.

Da Fonseca, Gen. Deodora (65), first President of the Republic of Brazil, Aug. 23.

DeBreau, Jean L. A. Quatrefages (82), French naturalist, June 7.

De la Gravière, Jurien (79), Vice-Admiral and member of the Institute of France, Mar. 6.

Denning, Edward J. (52), New-York dry-goods merchant, New-York City, heart failure, Oct. 22.

Dent, Frederick T. (72), ex-Brigadier-General U. S. A., and brother-in-law of General Grant, Denver, Col., dropsy, Dec. 23.

Denver James W. (75), ex-Governor of Kansas, ex-Brigadier-General U. S. A. (The city of Denver was named after him), Washington, D. C., Aug. 9.

Dillon, Sidney (80), ex-President of the Union Pacific Railroad, New-York City, June 9.

Dougherty, Daniel, orator and lawyer, Philadelphia, Sept. 5.

Douglas, John H., M.D. (65), physician (he was General Grant's last physician), New-York City, Oct. 2.

Drake, Charles D. (81), ex-Chief Justice of the United States Court of Claims, Washington, D. C., April 1.

Dwight, Theodore W., jurist and professor of law, New-York City, June 29.

Edwards, Amelia B., novelist and Egyptologist, England, April 16.

Eyre, Sophie (40), actress, Naples, Italy, heart disease, Nov. 5.

Failly, Pierre L. C. de (82), French general, Paris, Nov. 15.

Farley, Frederick A., D.D. (91), oldest alumnus of Harvard University, Unitarian clergyman, Brooklyn, N. Y., March 24.

Field, Charles W. (64), ex-Confederate Major-General, Washington, D. C., Bright's disease, April 10.

Field, Cyrus W. (73), financier, founder of the Atlantic cable enterprise, New-York City, general debility, July 11.

Flower, Charles Edward, Shakespearian scholar, Stratford-on-Avon, May 3.

Franz, Robert (77), German song-writer, Oct. 24.

Freeman, Edward A. (69), historian, Alicante, Spain, small-pox, March 16.

Gardner, Henry J., ex-Governor of Massachusetts, Milton, Mass., July 21.

Garrison, William D. (54), hotel proprietor, New-York City, heart disease, Dec. 2.

Gibson, Randall L. (60), United States Senator from Louisiana, Hot Springs, Ark., Dec. 15.

Gilmore, Patrick Sarsfield (61), bandmaster, St. Louis, Mo., heart disease, Sept. 24.

Gisborne, F. N. (68), electrician, Ottawa, Canada, Aug. 30.

Gould, Jay (56), millionaire railroad magnate, New-York City, consumption, Dec. 2.

Grant, Robert (78), astronomer, Glasgow, Scotland, Nov. 1.

Guiraud, Ernest (55), composer, Paris, May 7.

Hampden (Lord), Sir Henry Bouverie Brand (78), ex-Speaker of the House of Commons, Brighton, Eng., March 15.

Hardinge, Sir Arthur E. (64), British soldier (one of the 500 at Balaclava), July 15.

Harris, Charles L. (38), actor, Chicago, Oct. 22.

Harrison, Caroline Scott (58), wife of President Harrison, Washington, D. C., consumption, Oct. 25.

Herve, Florimond (67), composer, Paris, asthma, Nov. 5.

DEATH ROLL OF 1892—Continued.

Hesse, Louis IV. (54), Grand Duke of Darmstadt, March 13.

Hoey, John (67), expressman, New-York City, Bright's disease, Nov. 14.

Holden, William W. (74), ex-Governor of North-Carolina, Raleigh, March 1.

Howard, H., Cardinal (63), Rome, Sept. 16.

Hoyt, Henry M. (62), ex-Governor of Pennsylvania, Wilkesbarre, Pa., rheumatic gout, Dec. 1.

Hubner, Joseph A., Baron (81), Austrian diplomatist, Vienna, July 30.

Hunt, Thomas Sterry (66), chemist and geologist, New-York, heart disease, Feb. 12.

Hunt, Wilson G. (89), capitalist, New-York City, Dec. 7.

Husted, James W. (58), New-York politician, Peekskill, N. Y., Bright's disease, Sept. 25.

Jaffray, Edward S. (76), dry-goods merchant, New-York, April 23.

Judd, Orrin B. (76), religious journalist and author, Brooklyn, N. Y., Jan. 12.

Junker, Wilhelm (51), naturalist and African explorer, St. Petersburg, Feb. 13.

Kendall, Henry, D.D. (77), Presbyterian clergyman, East-Bloomfield, N. Y., Sept. 11.

Kennedy, Anthony (82), ex-United States Senator from Maryland, Annapolis, Md., July 31.

Kernan, Francis, ex-United States Senator from New-York, Utica, N. Y., Sept. 7.

Kimball, Richard B. (76), author, New-York City, Dec. 28.

Klapka, George (72), ex-Hungarian General under Kossuth, Hungary, May 16.

Knox, John J. (64), ex-Comptroller of the Treasury, New-York City, pneumonia, Feb. 9.

Knight, George S., actor, Philadelphia, Pa., paralysis, Jan. 14.

Kountze, Augustus, banker, New-York, April 30

Lavelaye, Emile L. V. de (69), political economist, Liege, the grippe, Jan. 3.

Lavigere, Charles Martial, Cardinal Archbishop of Carthage, Algiers, Nov. 26.

Leidy, Joseph (69), physician and naturalist, Philadelphia, Pa., April 29.

Lemoinne, John Emile (77), French statesman, Dec. 14.

Leslie, Fred. (37), actor and singer, London, Eng., typhoid fever, Dec. 7.

Littlejohn, Dewitt C. (74), politician, ex-Speaker of the New-York Assembly, Oswego, N. Y., Oct. 27.

Longfellow, Samuel (73), Unitarian clergyman and brother of the poet, Portland, Me., Oct. 3.

Lortie, Pierre Marcelin (71), classical bookbinder, Paris May 9.

Lowe, E. Louis (72), lawyer, ex-Governor of Maryland, Brooklyn, N. Y., Aug. 23.

Lovering, Joseph (78), Harvard professor of divinity, Cambridge, Mass., Jan. 18.

Mackenzie, Sir Morell (65), laryngologist and surgeon, London, bronchitis, Feb. 3.

Mackenzie, Alexander (70), Canadian statesman, Toronto, April 17.

Manning, Henry Edward (84), Cardinal, London, Jan. 14.

Marlborough, Duke of — George Charles Spencer Churchill—(51), Woodstock, Eng., Nov. 9.

Manchester, Duke of—George Victor Drogo Montagu —(39), Ireland, Aug. 18.

Marmier, Xavier (83), French litterateur, Oct. 11.

McCready, Benjamin W. (80), physician, New-York City, Aug. 9.

McKenna, Cecil Stanley (48), journalist, Jan. 3.

Mecklenburg-Schwerin (89), Alexandrine, Dowager, Grand Duchess of, April 21.

Meigs, Montgomery (76), Major-General U. S. A., retired, Washington, D. C., Jan. 2.

Mermillod, Gasper (68), Cardinal, Berne, Switzerland, Feb. 23.

Merrimon, Augustus S. (62), Chief-Justice of the Supreme Court of North-Carolina, Raleigh, N. C., Nov. 15.

Milbank, Harry Vane, society man, noted as a duellist, Switzerland, Oct. 24.

Morgan, George W. (69), organist and composer, Tacoma, Wash., July 10.

Moore, D. D. T. (72), writer on agriculture, editor of the *Rural New-Yorker*, New-York City, June 4.

Moore, George Henry (69), bibliographer, librarian of Lenox Library, New-York City, pneumonia, May 5.

Moore, J. Solomon (71), writer on political economy, New-York City, paralysis, March 5.

Morse, Leopold, Massachusetts politician, Boston, Mass., apoplexy, Dec. 15.

Neafie, Andrew Jackson (82), veteran actor, New-York City, April 24.

Newberry, John S. (70), Professor of Geology at Columbia College, New-Haven, Ct., Dec. 7.

Osgood, James R. (56), American book publisher, London, Eng., May 18.

Peck, William Guy (72), Professor of Mathematics and Astronomy at Columbia College, Greenwich, Ct., Bright's disease, Feb. 7.

Pelly, General Sir Lewis (67), diplomatist, London, April 22.

Pierrepont, Edwards (79), ex-United States Minister to Great Britain, New-York City, cerebral hemorrhage, March 6.

Polk, Leonidas L. (55), President of the Farmer's Alliance, Washington, D. C., June 11.

Pollard, Josephine (50), author, New-York City, Aug. 15.

Pope, John (69), Major-General U. S. A., retired, Sandusky, O., Sept. 23.

Porter, John K. (73), lawyer, Waterford, N. Y., Apr. 11.

Porter, Noah (81), ex-President of Yale University, New-Haven, Conn., the grippe, March 4.

Rangabé, Alexander R. (81), Greek statesman and scholar, Jan. 10.

Reinach, Baron J. (56), French financier, involved in the Panama Canal scandal, Paris, Nov. 18.

Renan, Joseph Ernest (69), philologist and author, Paris, pneumonia, Oct. 2.

Robinson, William E., Brooklyn journalist, Jan. 23.

Rousset, Camille F. M. (71), historian, France, Oct. 20.

Rose, Ernestine (82), woman-suffragist agitator, Brighton, Eng., Aug. 3.

Roxburghe, Duke of—James Henry Robert Innes-Ker—(53), England, Oct. 3.

Rogers, Randolph (62), sculptor, Rome, Italy, pulmonitis, Jan. 15.

Rodgers, Christopher R. P. (73), Rear-Admiral U.S.N., Washington, D. C., heart disease, Jan. 8.

Rooney, "Pat" (41), Irish comedian, New-York City, pneumonia, March 28

Roemer, Jean (77), linguist, New-York City, Sept. 1.

Ruggles, William B. (65), lawyer and journalist, Albany, N. Y., heart failure, Jan. 4.

Ruger, William C. (68), Chief Judge of the New-York Court of Appeals, Syracuse, N. Y., inflammation of the stomach, Jan. 14.

Saulisbury, Willard (72), ex-United States Senator from Delaware, Dover, Del., heart failure, April 6.

Saxe-Weimar, Prince Gustave of (65), Austrian Field Marshal, Jan. 5.

Schaus, William (71), New-York City, heart failure, Dec. 29.

Schwatka, Frederick (43), Arctic explorer, Portland, Ore., Nov. 2.

Scott, John Witherspoon (92), Presbyterian clergyman and father-in-law of President Harrison, Washington, D. C., general debility, Nov. 29.

Shea, John D. Gilmary (68), Roman Catholic historian and journalist, Elizabeth, N. J., cancer, Feb. 22.

Sherbrooke, Viscount — Robert Lowe — (81), English statesman, London, July 27.

Siemens, Ernest W. (76), electrician, Berlin, Dec. 6.

Simeoni, John (76), Cardinal, Prefect General of the Propaganda, Rome, Jan. 14.

Sistare, George K. (50), financier, New-York City, suicide, July 1.

Smith, Roswell (63), publisher of the *Century Magazine*, New-York City, Bright's disease, April 19.

Spurgeon, Charles H. (58), pulpit orator, Mentone, Italy, Bright's disease, Jan. 30.

Storrs, Augustus (75), Brooklyn public-spirited citizen, Willimantic, Conn., paralysis, March 3.

Strakosch, Max (57), opera manager and composer, New-York City, paralysis, March 17.

Stuart, Mary Macrae (81), widow of Robert L. Stuart, philanthropist, New-York City, Dec. 31, 1891.

DEATH ROLL OF 1892—*Continued.*

Sutherland, Duke of—George Granville W. S. Gower—Dunrobin Castle, Scotland, pneumonia, Sept. 22.

Sweeny, Thomas W. (72), Brigadier-General U. S. A., retired, Astoria, N. Y., April 10.

Swinton, William (59), author, New-York City, apoplexy, Oct. 23.

Tennyson, Alfred, Lord Tennyson (82), poet, Aldworth, England, Oct. 6.

Tewfik, Pacha, Khedive of Egypt (40), Cairo, Egypt, heart disease, Jan. 7.

Teissereno de Bort, Pierre (78), French statesman, Paris, July 29.

Trebelli-Bettini, Zelia (54), August 17, opera singer, died in France.

Trollope, Thomas A. (82), novelist, Clifton, England, Nov 11.

Trapani, Count of (65), son of the ex-King Francis I. of Naples, Paris, Sept. 25.

Ullman, Daniel (83), ex-Major-General U. S. A., Nyack, N. Y., Sept. 20.

Vermilye, Jacob D. (75), financier, New-York City, heart failure, Jan. 1.

Warren, George Henry (69), financier, New-York City, April 8.

Watts, Thomas H. (73), ex-Governor of Alabama, Sept. 16.

Wallis, Sir Provo W. P. (100), Senior Admiral of the British Navy, England, February 14.

Weaver, John G. (81), proprietor of the Ocean House at Newport, R. I., Newport, R. I., paralysis, Aug. 10.

Whittier, John Greenleaf (85), poet, Sept. 7.

Whitman, Walt (73), poet, Camden, N. J., general debility, March 26.

Withers, David D. (70), turfman, New-York City, Bright's disease, Feb. 18.

Wyant, Alexander H. (56), landscape painter, New-York City, paresis, Nov. 29.

Würtemberg, Olga, Dowager Queen of, Oct. 30.

Yeamans, Emily (32), actress, New-York City, Feb. 28.

The Irish National Federation of America.

President, Dr. Thomas Addis Emmet : *Secretary*, James S. Coleman ; *Corresponding Secretary*, Joseph P. Ryan ; *Treasurer*, Eugene Kelly.

Founded in New-York in 1891 by the Irish National Party of which Justin McCarthy is leader. Headquarters, Room 22, Cooper Union.

The Irish National League.

FOUNDED in 1880, and represents the Parnellite Party, as now organized in Ireland. Officers : *President*, Daniel Riordan ; *First Vice-President*, John J. Murphy ; *Second Vice-President*, John W. Quigley ; *Secretary*, Laurence F. Fullam ; *Financial Secretary*, John W. Nolan ; *Treasurer*, Roderick J. Kennedy. Headquarters, 1911 Third Avenue, New-York.

New=York Commission for the Promotion of Uniformity of Legislation in the United States.

Commissioners.—Henry R. Beekman, *President ;* Irving Browne and William L. Snyder.

This commission was the first appointed by any State for the promotion of uniform legislation It originated by an act drafted by Albert E. Henschel, who is Secretary of the New-York commission. The States which have appointed similar commissions are : Pennsylvania, New-Jersey, Massachusetts, Delaware, Mississippi, Georgia, and Michigan.

Two conferences have been held, one on August 24, 25, 1891, at Sartoga Springs, the other on November 15, 1892, in the city New-York. The office of the Secretary is 214 Broadway.

Nationalism.

THE following statement of the principles of "Nationalism," public interest in which was awakened by Mr. Bellamy's novel of "Looking Backward," is from the pen of Edward S. Huntington, Secretary of the Boston Nationalist Club :

"The Nationalists, seeing the inevitable evolutionary inclinations toward association and combination in all business enterprises, as illustrated in the huge trusts and syndicates of our present age, believe in the wisdom of forming, eventually, one grand industrial association for the benefit of the whole people. The Nationalists advocate the gradual assumption by the municipal, State and national governments of all public duties now performed by private corporations. They demand that the load of oppression by monopolies shall be lifted from the shoulders of our American citizens.

"Nationalism offers for public consideration the following measures of reform : 1. The governmental control of all telegraphs, telephones and express companies. 2. The nationalization of all railroads. 3. The public ownership of all coal-mines, oil and gas wells now in operation or hereafter discovered. 4. The municipal control of all lighting, heating and street car service, or such other town or city duties as are now discharged by private companies.

"It is understood, of course, that all these monopolies and large industries which come into national, State or municipal control shall be carried on for use and not for profit. The hours of labor will be more reasonable, and a more humane treatment of all workers established.

"In the change of industries from private to public control, the Nationalists aim at no confiscation. The holders of valuable securities in any property taken by the public shall either receive fair dividends on such investments, or they shall be reimbursed outright at a fair estimate of the real value of such possessions.

"One of the chief reforms insisted upon by the Nationalists is that children shall be given an education till the age of 17 years, and this education shall be compulsory. They propose that the present limit of the school age (14 years) shall be raised, year by year, as rapidly as public sentiment will allow, and in cases of poverty partial State support shall be given to such children while attending school ; child labor in factories and mines shall be absolutely prohibited by the most stringent laws."

Population of the United States,

AT EACH CENSUS FROM 1790 TO 1890.

(Compiled from the Reports of the Superintendents of the Census.)

STATES AND TERRITORIES.	1810.	1820.	1830.	1840.	1850.	1860.	1870.	1880.	1890.
Alabama.........		127,901	309,527	590,756	771,623	964,201	996,992	1,262,505	1,513,017
Arizona..........							9,658	40,440	59,620
Arkansas.........		14,255	30,388	97,574	209,897	435,450	484,471	802,525	1,128,179
California........					92,597	379,994	560,247	864,694	1,208,130
Colorado.........						34,277	39,864	194,327	419,198
Connecticut......	261,942	275,148	297,675	309,978	370,792	460,147	537,454	622,700	746,258
Dakota...........						4,837	14,181	135,177	
Delaware.........	72,674	72,749	76,748	78,085	91,532	112,216	125,015	146,608	168,493
Dist. of Columbia	24,023	32,039	39,834	43,712	51,687	75,080	131,700	177,624	230,392
Florida...........			34,730	54,477	87,445	140,424	187,748	269,493	391,422
Georgia..........	252,433	340,985	516,823	691,392	906,185	1,057,286	1,184,109	1,542,180	1,837,353
Idaho............							14,999	32,610	84,385
Illinois...........	12,282	55,162	157,445	476,183	851,470	1,711,951	2,539,891	3,077,871	3,826,351
Indiana..........	24,520	147,178	343,031	685,866	988,416	1,350,428	1,680,637	1,978,301	2,192,404
Iowa.............				43,112	192,214	674,913	1,194,020	1,624,615	1,911,895
Kansas...........						107,206	364,399	996,096	1,427,096
Kentucky........	406,511	564,135	687,917	779,828	982,405	1,155,684	1,321,011	1,648,690	1,858,635
Louisiana........	76,556	152,923	215,739	352,411	517,762	708,002	726,915	939,946	1,118,587
Maine............	*228,705	298,269	399,455	501,793	583,169	628,279	626,915	648,936	661,086
Maryland.........	380,546	407,350	447,040	470,019	583,034	687,049	780,894	934,943	1,042,390
Massachusetts....	472,040	523,159	610,408	737,699	994,514	1,231,066	1,457,351	1,783,085	2,238,943
Michigan.........	4,762	8,705	31,639	212,267	397,654	749,113	1,184,059	1,636,937	2,093,889
Minnesota........					6,077	172,023	439,706	780,773	1,301,826
Mississippi.......	40,352	75,448	136,621	375,651	606,526	791,305	827,922	1,131,597	1,289,600
Missouri.........	20,845	66,557	140,455	383,702	682,044	1,182,012	1,721,295	2,168,380	2,679,184
Montana..........							20,595	39,159	132,159
Nebraska.........						28,841	122,993	452,402	1,058,910
Nevada...........						6,857	42,491	62,266	45,761
New-Hampshire...	214,460	244,022	269,328	284,574	317,976	326,073	318,300	346,991	376,530
New-Jersey.......	245,562	277,426	320,823	373,306	489,555	672,035	906,096	1,131,116	1,444,933
New-Mexico......					61,547	93,516	91,874	119,565	153,593
New-York........	959,049	1,372,111	1,918,608	2,428,921	3,097,394	3,880,735	4,382,759	5,082,871	5,997,853
North-Carolina...	555,500	638,829	737,987	753,419	869,039	992,622	1,071,361	1,399,750	1,617,947
North-Dakota....									182,719
Ohio.............	230,760	581,295	937,903	1,519,467	1,980,329	2,339,511	2,665,260	3,198,062	3,672,316
Oklahoma........									61,834
Oregon..........					13,294	52,465	90,923	174,768	313,767
Pennsylvania.....	810,091	1,047,507	1,348,233	1,724,033	2,311,786	2,906,215	3,521,951	4,282,891	5,258,014
Rhode-Island.....	76,931	83,015	97,199	108,830	147,545	174,620	217,353	276,531	345,506
South-Carolina...	415,115	502,741	581,185	594,398	668,507	703,708	705,606	995,577	1,151,149
South-Dakota....									328,808
Tennessee.......	261,727	422,771	681,904	829,210	1,002,717	1,109,801	1,258,520	1,542,359	1,767,518
Texas............					212,592	604,215	818,579	1,591,749	2,235,523
Utah.............					11,380	40,273	86,786	143,963	207,905
Vermont.........	217,895	235,966	280,652	291,948	314,120	315,098	330,551	332,286	332,422
Virginia..........	974,600	1,065,116	1,211,405	1,239,797	1,421,661	1,596,318	1,225,163	1,512,565	1,655,980
Washington......						11,594	23,955	75,116	349,390
West-Virginia....							442,014	618,457	762,704
Wisconsin........				30,945	305,391	775,881	1,054,670	1,315,497	1,686,880
Wyoming.........							9,118	20,789	60,705
Total........	7,239,881	9,633,822	12,866,020	17,069,453	23,191,876	31,443,321	38,558,371	50,155,783	62,622,250

The inhabitants of Alaska and the Indian Territory are not included in the above. The population of Alaska in 1890 was 30,329; of the Indian Territory, 179,321. Total population of the United States in 1890, 62,830,361.

POPULATION: CENSUS OF 1790.—Connecticut, 237,916; Delaware, 59,096; Georgia, 82,548; Kentucky, 73,677; Maine,* 96,540; Maryland, 319,728; Massachusetts, 378,787; New-Hampshire, 141,885; New-Jersey, 184,139; New-York, 393,751; Pennsylvania, 434,373; Rhode-Island, 68,825; South-Carolina, 249,072; Tennessee, 35,691; Vermont, 85,425; Virginia, 747,610. Total, U. S., 3,589,063.

POPULATION: CENSUS OF 1800.—Connecticut, 251,002; Delaware, 64,273; District of Columbia, 14,093; Georgia, 162,686; Indiana, 5,641; Kentucky, 220,955; Maine,* 151,719; Maryland, 341,548; Massachusetts, 422,845; Mississippi, 8,850; New-Hampshire, 183,858; New-Jersey, 211,149; New-York, 589,051; North-Carolina, 478,103; Ohio, 45,365; Pennsylvania, 602,365; Rhode-Island, 69,122; South-Carolina, 345,591; Tennessee, 105,602; Vermont, 154,465; Virginia, 880,200. Total, U. S., 5,308,483.

POPULATION PRIOR TO 1790 (according to Bancroft), 1688, 200,000; 1714, 434,600; 1727, 580,000; 1750, 1,260,-000; 1754, 1,425,000; 1760, 1,695,000; 1770, 2,312,000; 1780, 2,945,000 (2,383,000 white, 562,000 colored).

* Maine was a part of Massachusetts until its admission into the Union in 1820.

Population of the United States.

ACCORDING TO SEX, NATIVITY, AND RACE.

(Compiled from the Reports of the Census of 1890.)

STATES AND TERRITORIES.	Total Population.	SEX.		NATIVITY.		RACE.			
		Male.	Female.	Native Born.	Foreign Born.	Total Whites.	Native Born Whites.	Foreign Born Whites.	Colored.
Alabama	1,513,017	757,456	755,561	1,498,240	14,777	833,718	819,114	14,604	679,299
Arizona	59,620	36,571	23,049	40,825	18,795	55,580	38,117	17,463	4,040
Arkansas	1,128,179	585,755	542,424	1,113,915	14,264	818,752	804,658	14,094	309,427
California	1,208,130	700,059	508,071	841,821	366,309	1,111,672	818,119	293,553	96,458
Colorado	419,198	245,247	166,951	328,208	83,990	404,468	321,962	* 82,506	7,730
Connecticut	746,258	369,538	376,720	562,657	183,601	733,438	550,283	183,155	12,820
Delaware	168,493	85,573	82,920	155,332	13,161	140,006	126,970	13,096	28,427
Dist. of Columbia	230,392	109,584	120,808	211,622	18,770	154,695	136,178	18,517	75,697
Florida	391,422	201,947	189,475	368,490	22,932	224,949	205,771	18,178	166,473
Georgia	1,837,353	919,925	917,428	1,825,216	12,137	978,357	966,465	11,862	858,996
Idaho	84,385	51,290	33,095	66,929	17,456	82,018	66,554	15,464	2,367
Illinois	3,826,351	1,972,308	1,854,043	2,984,004	842,347	3,768,472	2,927,497	840,975	57,879
Indiana	2,192,404	1,118,347	1,074,057	2,046,199	146,205	2,146,736	2,000,733	146,003	45,668
Iowa	1,911,896	994,453	917,443	1,587,827	324,069	1,901,086	1,577,154	323,932	10,810
Kansas	1,427,096	752,112	674,984	1,279,258	147,838	1,376,553	1,228,923	147,630	50,543
Kentucky	1,858,635	942,758	915,877	1,799,279	59,356	1,590,462	1,531,222	59,240	268,173
Louisiana	1,118,587	559,350	559,237	1,068,840	49,747	558,395	509,555	48,840	560,192
Maine	661,086	332,590	328,496	582,125	78,961	659,263	580,568	78,695	1,823
Maryland	1,042,390	515,691	526,699	948,094	94,296	826,493	732,706	93,787	215,897
Massachusetts	2,238,943	1,087,709	1,151,234	1,581,806	657,137	2,215,373	1,561,870	653,503	23,570
Michigan	2,093,889	1,091,780	1,002,109	1,550,009	543,880	2,072,884	1,531,283	541,601	21,005
Minnesota	1,301,826	695,321	606,505	834,470	467,356	1,296,159	829,102	467,057	5,667
Mississippi	1,289,600	649,687	639,913	1,281,648	7,952	544,851	537,127	7,724	744,749
Missouri	2,679,184	1,385,238	1,293,946	2,444,315	234,869	2,528,458	2,294,176	234,282	150,726
Montana	132,159	87,882	44,277	89,063	43,096	127,271	86,941	40,330	4,888
Nebraska	1,058,910	572,824	486,086	856,368	202,542	1,046,888	844,644	202,244	12,022
Nevada	45,761	29,214	16,547	31,055	14,706	39,084	27,190	11,894	6,677
New Hampshire	376,530	186,566	189,964	304,190	72,340	375,840	303,614	72,196	690
New Jersey	1,444,933	720,819	724,114	1,115,978	328,975	1,396,581	1,068,590	327,985	48,352
New Mexico	153,593	83,055	70,538	142,334	11,259	142,719	131,859	10,860	10,874
New York	5,997,853	2,976,893	3,020,960	4,426,803	1,571,050	5,923,952	4,358,260	1,565,692	73,901
North Carolina	1,617,947	799,149	818,798	1,614,245	3,702	1,655,382	1,051,720	3,662	562,565
North Dakota	182,719	101,590	81,129	101,258	81,461	182,123	100,775	81,348	596
Ohio	3,672,316	1,855,736	1,816,580	3,213,023	459,293	3,584,805	3,126,252	458,553	87,511
Oklahoma	61,834	34,733	27,101	59,094	2,740	58,826	56,117	2,709	3,008
Oregon	313,767	181,840	131,927	256,450	57,317	301,758	253,936	47,822	12,009
Pennsylvania	5,258,014	2,666,331	2,591,683	4,412,294	845,720	5,148,257	4,304,668	843,589	109,757
Rhode Island	345,506	168,025	177,481	239,201	106,305	337,859	231,832	106,027	7,647
South Carolina	1,151,149	572,337	578,812	1,144,879	6,270	462,008	455,865	6,143	689,141
South Dakota	328,808	180,250	148,558	237,753	91,055	327,290	236,447	90,843	1,518
Tennessee	1,767,518	891,585	875,933	1,747,489	20,029	1,336,637	1,316,738	19,899	430,881
Texas	2,235,523	1,172,553	1,062,970	2,082,567	152,956	1,745,935	1,594,466	151,469	489,588
Utah	207,905	110,463	97,442	154,841	53,064	205,899	153,766	52,133	2,006
Vermont	332,422	169,327	163,095	288,334	44,088	331,218	287,394	44,024	1,004
Virginia	1,655,980	824,278	831,702	1,637,606	18,374	1,020,122	1,001,933	18,189	635,858
Washington	349,390	217,562	131,828	259,385	90,005	340,513	254,319	86,194	8,877
West Virginia	762,794	390,285	372,509	743,911	18,883	730,077	711,225	18,852	32,717
Wisconsin	1,686,880	874,951	811,929	1,167,681	519,199	1,680,473	1,161,484	518,989	6,407
Wyoming	60,705	39,343	21,362	45,792	14,913	59,275	44,845	14,430	1,430
Total	62,622,250	32,067,880	30,554,370	53,372,703	9,249,547	54,983,890	45,862,023	9,121,867	7,638,360

CENTRE OF POPULATION IN THE UNITED STATES.

DATE.	N. Lat.		W. Long.		POSITION OF CENTRE OF POPULATION. Approximate Location by Important Towns.	Westward Movement during Preceding Decade.
	°	′	°	′		Miles.
1790	39	16.5	76	11.2	23 miles east of Baltimore, Md	
1800	39	16.1	76	56.5	18 miles west of Baltimore, Md	41
1810	39	11.5	77	37.2	40 miles N. W. by west of Washington, D. C.	36
1820	39	5.7	78	33.0	16 miles north of Woodstock, Va	50
1830	38	57.9	79	16.9	19 miles W. S. W. of Moorefield, West Va.	39
1840	39	2.0	80	18.0	16 miles south of Clarksburgh, West Va	55
1850	38	59.0	81	19.0	23 miles S. E. of Parkersburgh, West Va.	55
1860	39	0.4	82	48.8	20 miles south of Chillicothe, O.	81
1870	39	12.0	83	35.7	48 miles E. by N. of Cincinnati, O.	42
1880	39	4.1	84	39.7	8 miles W. by S. of Cincinnati, O.	58
1890	39	11.9	85	32.9	20 miles east of Columbus, Ind.	48
					Total	505

This table was prepared by the Census Office.

Population of the United States

BY VOTING, SCHOOL, AND MILITIA AGES.

(Compiled from the Reports of the Census of 1890.)

STATES AND TERRITORIES	VOTING AGES—MALES, 21 YEARS AND OVER.					PERCENTAGE.		SCHOOL AGES.	MILITIA AGES.
	Total.	Native Born.	Foreign Born.	Whites.	Colored.	Native.	Foreign.	Total Population, 5 to 20 years old.	Total Population, Males.
Alabama	324,822	316,697	8,125	184,059	140,763	97.50	2.50	639,494	265,025
Arizona	23,696	13,665	10,031	21,160	2,536	57.67	42.33	18,284	19,226
Arkansas	257,868	249,608	8,260	188,296	69,572	96.80	3.20	476,185	214,708
California	462,289	230,154	232,135	390,228	72,061	49.79	50.21	360,289	343,001
Colorado	164,920	114,580	50,340	161,015	3,905	69.48	30.52	113,150	163,865
Connecticut	224,092	145,673	78,419	220,116	3,976	65.01	34.99	221,245	186,076
Delaware	47,559	41,407	6,152	40,007	7,552	87.06	12.94	57,496	47,623
District of Col.	64,505	55,263	9,242	46,159	18,346	85.67	14.33	74,176	57,604
Florida	96,213	85,561	10,652	58,068	38,145	88.93	11.07	155,676	79,604
Georgia	398,122	391,168	6,954	219,094	179,028	98.25	1.75	771,027	336,295
Idaho	31,490	19,785	11,705	29,525	1,965	62.83	37.17	27,257	24,688
Illinois	1,072,663	682,346	390,317	1,054,463	18,200	63.61	36.39	1,323,090	852,635
Indiana	595,066	521,708	73,358	581,987	13,079	87.67	12.33	785,172	455,823
Iowa	520,332	364,662	155,670	517,006	3,326	70.08	29.92	701,182	299,687
Kansas	383,231	310,166	73,065	370,688	12,543	80.93	19.07	540,170	295,364
Kentucky	450,792	420,976	29,816	387,371	63,421	93.39	6.61	727,061	361,137
Louisiana	250,563	225,212	25,351	130,743	119,815	89.88	10.12	455,234	205,215
Maine	201,241	170,771	30,470	200,609	632	84.86	15.14	201,851	133,169
Maryland	270,738	228,149	42,589	218,843	51,895	84.27	15.73	370,892	205,816
Massachusetts	665,009	407,915	257,094	657,042	7,967	61.34	38.66	650,870	499,312
Michigan	617,445	369,128	248,317	615,445	2,000	59.78	40.22	703,684	462,765
Minnesota	376,036	154,727	221,309	374,027	2,009	41.15	58.85	454,804	304,268
Mississippi	271,080	266,049	5,031	120,611	150,469	98.14	1.86	559,101	228,764
Missouri	705,718	584,981	120,737	667,451	38,267	82.89	17.11	1,008,935	566,448
Montana	65,415	35,442	29,973	61,948	3,467	54.18	45.82	30,240	55,490
Nebraska	301,500	205,625	95,875	297,281	4,219	68.20	31.80	384,255	255,665
Nevada	20,951	10,181	10,770	17,002	3,949	48.59	51.41	12,391	14,606
N. Hampshire	118,135	92,088	26,047	117,889	246	77.95	22.05	106,611	79,878
New-Jersey	413,530	268,483	145,047	398,966	14,564	64.92	35.08	464,992	313,683
New-Mexico	44,951	38,194	6,757	41,478	3,473	84.97	15.03	52,543	36,665
New-York	1,769,649	1,084,187	685,462	1,745,418	24,231	61.27	38.73	1,836,935	1,325,619
North-Car'lina	342,653	340,572	2,081	233,307	109,346	99.39	0.61	673,405	273,834
North-Dakota	55,959	19,645	36,314	55,769	190	35.11	64.89	59,324	48,608
Ohio	1,016,464	797,623	218,841	990,542	25,922	78.47	21.53	1,271,031	767,975
Oklahoma	19,161	17,502	1,659	18,238	923	91.34	8.66	21,642	15,084
Oregon	111,744	74,329	37,415	102,113	9,631	66.52	33.48	103,365	88,049
Pennsylvania	1,461,869	1,064,429	397,440	1,426,996	34,873	72.81	27.19	1,791,710	1,140,476
Rhode-Island	100,017	59,832	40,185	97,756	2,261	59.82	40.18	105,534	75,317
South-Car'lina	235,606	232,200	3,406	102,657	132,949	98.55	1.45	501,393	196,059
South-Dakota	96,765	53,851	42,914	96,177	588	55.65	44.35	113,900	79,219
Tennessee	402,476	391,429	11,047	310,014	92,462	97.26	2.74	720,872	324,214
Texas	535,942	460,694	75,248	434,010	101,932	85.96	14.04	924,142	447,413
Utah	54,471	29,946	24,525	53,235	1,236	54.98	45.02	79,937	45,139
Vermont	101,697	82,011	19,686	101,369	328	80.64	19.36	101,457	67,203
Virginia	378,782	367,469	11,313	248,035	130,747	97.01	2.99	671,779	295,340
Washington	146,918	88,968	57,950	141,934	4,984	60.66	39.44	97,863	124,800
West-Virginia	181,400	171,611	9,789	172,198	9,202	94.60	5.40	305,669	147,334
Wisconsin	461,722	217,338	244,384	459,893	1,829	47.07	52.93	603,846	347,469
Wyoming	27,044	17,852	9,192	26,050	994	66.01	33.99	10,291	24,614
Total	16,940,311	12,591,852	4,348,459	15,199,856	1,740,455	74.33	25.67	22,447,392	13,230,168

COLORED POPULATION OF THE UNITED STATES IN 1890 ACCORDING TO RACE.—Persons of African descent, 7,470,040; Chinese, 107,475; Japanese, 2,039; civilized Indians, 58,806. Total, 7,698,360.

PERSONS OF AFRICAN DESCENT CLASSIFIED.—Blacks, 6,337,980; mulattoes, 956,989; quadroons, 105,135; octoroons, 69,936. Total, 7,470,040.

Mississippi contained the largest number of pure negroes—657,393—and Virginia the next largest number—621,781; Virginia contained the largest number of mulattoes, quadroons, and octoroons—122,441, and Louisiana the next largest number—90,953.

ALIENS SPEAKING ENGLISH.—Classifying alien population according to their ability to speak English, 791,876, or 68.25 per cent, can speak the English language, and 368,338, or 31.75 per cent, cannot. The States showing the highest percentages of aliens who cannot speak the English language are: Arizona, 65.81 per cent; Texas, 60.54 per cent; New-Mexico, 54.31 per cent; Oregon, 50.48 per cent; California, 43.43 per cent; Florida, 43.14 per cent; Wisconsin, 42.23 per cent; Pennsylvania, 41.40 per cent, and Idaho, 40.53 per cent.

MALE AND FEMALE CHILDREN OF SCHOOL AGE.—Total number of white males from five to twenty years old inclusive, 9,655,372; colored, 1,587,328. Total number of white females of same ages, 9,595,193; colored, 1,609,499.

Population of the United States.

(Compiled from the Reports of the Census of 1890.)

WHITE AND NEGRO POPULATION OF THE SOUTH.

GROWTH of the population by decades in the territory now covered by the sixteen Southern States of Alabama, Arkansas, Delaware, Florida, Georgia, Kentucky, Louisiana, Maryland, Mississippi, Missouri, North-Carolina, South-Carolina, Tennessee, Texas, Virginia and West-Virginia, and the District of Columbia.

YEARS.	White.	Colored.	YEARS.	White.	Colored.	YEARS.	White.	Colored.
1790......	1,271,488	689,884	1830......	3,660,758	2,187,545	1870......	9,466,353	4,538,883
1800......	1,702,980	918,336	1840......	4,632,530	2,701,901	1880.....	12,578,253	6,099,253
1810......	2,208,785	1,272,119	1850......	6,222,418	3,442,238	1890......	15,549,358	6,898,806
1820......	2,831,560	1,653,240	1860......	8,097,462	4,215,614			

The table shows that the whites increased faster than the blacks in the last decade. In 1890 there were in the 16 Southern States and the District of Columbia 6,898,806 colored inhabitants, and in 1880, 6,099,253. The colored element increased during the decade at the rate of 13.1 per cent. The white population of these States in 1890 numbered 15,549,358, and in 1880, 12,578,253. They increased during the decade at the rate of 23.6 per cent, or nearly twice as rapidly as the colored element.

DISTRIBUTION OF TOTAL POPULATION IN ACCORDANCE WITH ALTITUDE.

Altitude, ft.	Pop.	Altitude, ft.	Pop.	Altitude, ft.	Pop.	Altitude, ft.	Pop.
0 to 100...	10,387,000	1,500 to 2,000...	2,354,000	5,000 to 6,000...	487,000	9,000 to 10,000...	39,000
100 to 500...	13,838,000	2,000 to 3,000...	1,154,000	6,000 to 7,000...	161,000	Above 10,000...	10,000
500 to 1,000...	23,947,000	3,000 to 4,000...	381,000	7,000 to 8,000...	94,000		
1,000 to 1,500...	9,431,000	4,000 to 5,000...	296,000	8,000 to 9,000...	43,000		

DISTRIBUTION IN ACCORDANCE WITH TOPOGRAPHIC FEATURES.

Regions.	Pop.	Regions.	Pop.	Regions.	Pop.
Coast Swamps..........	1,809,000	Lake..............	3,578,000	Plateau................	110,000
Atlantic Plain............	8,784,000	Ozark Mountain......	1,041,000	Basin..............	403,000
Piedmont............	7,858,000	Alluvial Mississippi R..	885,000	Columbian Mesas...	219,000
New-England Hills......	2,290,000	Prairie................	13,048,000	Sierra Nevada......	146,000
Appalachian Mountain...	2,849,000	Great Plains..........	737,000	Pacific Valley........	435,000
Cumberland-Allegheny..	5,749,000	North Rocky Mountains.	153,000	Cascade Range..........	179,000
Interior timbered........	11,292,000	South Rocky Mountains.	247,000	Coast Ranges.........	810,000

The American Indian.

(Population in 1890 as reported by the census.)

Arizona..........	16,740	Kansas............	1,437	Pueblos.......... 8,278	Utah.............. 2,489
California........	15,283	Louisiana........	132	New-York...... 28	Washington..... 10,837
Colorado........	1,034	Maine............	140	Six Nations...... 5,304	Wisconsin........ 8,896
Connecticut.....	24	Massachusetts...	145	North-Carolina.. 2,885	Wyoming........ 1,806
Florida..........	215	Michigan........	6,991	Cherokees........ 2,885	War Department
Georgia..........	2	Minnesota........	7,065	North-Dakota... 7,952	Apaches, Mt.
Idaho............	3,909	Mississippi........	1,404	Oklahoma........ 5,689	Vernon bar-
Illinois...........	1	Missouri..........	14	Oregon.......... 4,282	racks........... 384
Indiana..........	71	Montana..........	10,573	South-Dakota... 19,845	Indians in prison. 184
Indian Territory.	8,708	Nebraska........	3,864	Tennessee........ 10	
Five Civ. Tribes.	66,289	Nevada..........	4,956	Texas.......... 258	Total.......... 249,273
Iowa............	397	New-Mexico.....	20,521		

INDIAN POPULATION IN DETAIL.

The total Indian population of the United States, exclusive of Alaska, but including 32,567 counted in the general census, being the taxed or taxable Indians, numbers 249,273. The following table gives the division of the Indians in detail:

Indians on reservations or at schools, under control of the Indian office (not taxed or taxable).......... 133,382
Indians incidentally under the Indian office, and self-supporting:
    The five civilized tribes, Indians and colored: Cherokees, 29,599 ; Chickasaws, 7,182 ; Choctaws, 14,397 ; Creeks, 14,632 ; Seminoles, 2,561 ; total, 68,371. Total Indians, 52,065 ; total colored Indian citizens and claimants, 14,224 ; grand total, 66,289.
Pueblos of New-Mexico... 8,278
Six Nations, Saint Regis and other Indians of New-York.. 5,304
Eastern Cherokees of North-Carolina... 2,885
Indians taxed or taxable, and self-sustaining citizens, counted in the general census (98 per cent not on reservations)... 32,567
Indians under control of the War Department, prisoners of war (Apaches at Mount Vernon barracks).. 384
Indians in State or Territorial prisons 184

    Total.. 249,273

Population of Cities of the United States.

ONE HUNDRED PRINCIPAL CITIES IN 1890 IN THE ORDER OF THEIR RANK.

CENSUS OF 1890.

City	Pop.	City	Pop.	City	Pop.
New-York City ..... {*1,710,715 / †1,515,301		Toledo, O	81,434	Utica, N. Y	44,007
Chicago, Ill	1,099,850	Richmond, Va	81,388	Hoboken, N. J	43,648
Philadelphia, Pa	1,046,964	New-Haven, Ct	81,298	Savannah, Ga	43,189
Brooklyn, N. Y ..... {‡853,945 / †806,343		Paterson, N. J	78,347	Seattle, Wash	42,837
St. Louis, Mo	451,770	Lowell, Mass	77,696	Peoria, Ill	41,024
Boston, Mass	448,477	Nashville, Tenn	76,168	New-Bedford, Mass	40,733
Baltimore, Md	434,439	Scranton, Pa	75,215	Erie, Pa	40,634
San Francisco, Cal	298,997	Fall River, Mass	74,398	Somerville, Mass	40,152
Cincinnati, O	296,908	Cambridge, Mass	70,028	Harrisburg, Pa	39,385
Cleveland, O	261,353	Atlanta, Ga	65,533	Kansas City, Kan	38,316
Buffalo, N. Y	255,664	Memphis, Tenn	64,495	Dallas, Tex	38,067
New-Orleans, La	242,039	Wilmington, Del	61,431	Sioux City, Ia	37,806
Pittsburgh, Pa	238,617	Dayton, O	61,220	Elizabeth, N. J	37,764
Washington, D. C	230,392	Troy, N. Y	60,956	Wilkesbarre, Pa	37,718
Detroit, Mich	205,876	Grand Rapids, Mich	60,278	San Antonio, Tex	37,673
Milwaukee, Wis	204,468	Reading, Pa	58,661	Covington, Ky	37,371
Newark, N. J	181,830	Camden, N. J	58,313	Portland, Me	36,425
Minneapolis, Minn. ...	164,738	Trenton, N. J	57,458	Tacoma, Wash	36,006
Jersey City, N. J	163,003	Lynn, Mass	55,727	Holyoke, Mass	35,637
Louisville, Ky	161,129	Lincoln, Neb	55,154	Fort Wayne, Ind	35,393
Omaha, Neb	140,452	Charleston, S. C	54,955	Binghamton, N. Y	35,005
Rochester, N. Y	133,896	Hartford, Ct	53,230	Norfolk, Va	34,871
St. Paul, Minn	133,156	St. Joseph, Mo	52,324	Wheeling, W. Va	34,522
Kansas City, Mo .....§	132,716	Evansville, Ind	50,756	Augusta, Ga	33,300*
Providence, R. I	132,146	Los Angeles, Cal	50,395	Youngstown, O	33,220
Denver, Col	106,713	Des Moines, Ia	50,093	Duluth, Minn	33,115
Indianapolis, Ind	105,436	Bridgeport, Ct	48,866	Yonkers, N. Y	32,033
Allegheny, Pa	105,287	Oakland, Cal	48,682	Lancaster, Pa	32,011
Albany, N. Y	94,923	Portland, Ore	46,385	Springfield, O	31,895
Columbus, O	88,150	Saginaw, Mich	46,322	Quincy, Ill	31,494
Syracuse, N. Y	88,143	Salt Lake City, Utah.....	44,843	Mobile, Ala	31,076
Worcester, Mass	84,655	Lawrence, Mass	44,654	Topeka, Kan	31,007
		Springfield, Mass	44,179	Elmira, N. Y	30,893
		Manchester, N. H	44,126	Salem, Mass	30,801

* Municipal census of October, 1890. For population of New-York State cities by the State enumeration of 1892, see page 430. By the municipal census of 1892, Philadelphia has 1,142,653 inhabitants.
† Federal census of June, 1890.   ‡ Municipal census of November, 1890.
§ Includes 13,048 population, which by recent decision of Missouri State Supreme Court is now outside the limits of Kansas City.

POPULATION OF ALL OTHER PLACES IN THE UNITED STATES HAVING 5,000 POPULATION AND OVER.

Place	Pop.	Place	Pop.	Place	Pop.	Place	Pop.
Adams, Mass	9,213	Auburn, Me	11,250	Brattleboro, Vt	6,862	Charlotte, N. C	11,557
Adrian, Mich	8,756	Auburn, N. Y	25,858	Brazil, Ind	5,905	Charlottesville, Va..	5,591
Akron, O	27,601	Augusta, Me	10,527	Brenham, Tex	5,209	Chattanooga, Tenn .	29,100
Alameda, Cal	11,165	Aurora, Ill	19,688	Bridgeton, N. J	11,424	Cheboygan, Miss....	6,235
Albina, Ore	5,129	Austin, Tex	14,575	Bristol, Pa	6,553	Chelsea, Mass	27,909
Alexandria, Va	14,339	Bangor, Me	19,103	Bristol, R. I	5,478	Chester, Pa	20,226
Allentown, Pa	25,228	Batavia, N. Y	7,221	Brockton, Mass	27,294	Cheyenne, Wyo	11,600
Alliance, O	7,607	Baton Rouge, La ..	10,478	Brookline, Mass	12,103	Chicopee, Mass	14,050
Alpena, Mich	11,283	Battle Creek, Mich .	13,197	Brownsville, Tex....	6,134	Chillicothe, Mo	5,717
Alton, Ill	10,294	Bay City, Mich	27,839	Brunswick, Ga	8,459	Chillicothe, O	11,288
Altoona, Pa	30,337	Bayonne, N. J	19,033	Brunswick, Me	6,012	Chippewa Falls, Wis.	8,670
Americus, Ga	6,398	Beatrice, Neb	13,836	Bucyrus, O	5,974	Circleville, O	6,546
Amesbury, Mass	9,798	Beaver Falls, Pa....	9,735	Burlington, Ia	22,565	Claremont, N. H....	5,565
Amsterdam, N. Y..	17,336	Bellaire, O	9,934	Burlington, N. J	7,264	Clarksville, Tenn ..	7,924
Anderson, Ind	10,741	Beloit, Wis	6,315	Burlington, Vt	14,590	Clinton, Ia	13,619
Annapolis, Md	7,604	Berkeley, Cal	5,101	Burrillville, R. I	5,492	Clinton, Mass	10,424
Ann Arbor, Mich ..	9,431	Belleville, Ill	15,361	Butler, Pa	8,734	Cohoes, N. Y	22,509
Anniston, Ala	5,629	Bethlehem, Pa	6,762	Butte, Mont	10,723	Colchester, Vt	5,143
Ansonia, Ct	10,342	Beverly, Mass	10,821	Cairo, Ill	10,324	Coldwater, Mich	5,247
Appleton, Wis	11,869	Biddeford, Me	14,443	Calais, Me	7,290	College Point, N. Y.	6,127
Arkansas, Kan	8,347	Big Rapids, Mich...	5,303	Canandaigua, N. Y.	5,868	Colorado Spr'gs, Col.	11,140
Arlington, Mass	5,629	Birmingham, Ala...	26,178	Canton Ill	5,604	Columbia, Pa	10,599
Asheville, N. C	10,235	Blackstone, Mass...	6,138	Canton, O	26,189	Columbia, S. C	15,353
Ashland, Pa	7,346	Bloomington, Ill....	20,484	Cape Elizabeth, Me.	5,459	Columbia, Tenn	5,370
Ashland, Wis	9,956	Boone, Ia	6,520	Carbondale, Pa	10,833	Columbus, Ga	17,303
Ashtabula, O	8,338	Bowling Green, Ky.	7,803	Carlisle, Pa	7,620	Columbus, Ind	6,719
Aspen, Col	5,108	Braddock, Pa	8,561	Carthage, Mo	7,981	Concord, N. H	17,004
Astoria, Ore	6,184	Bradford, Pa	10,514	Cedar Rapids, Ia ..	18,020	Connellsville, Pa ..	5,629
Atchison, Kan	13,963	Brainerd, Minn	5,703	Chambersburg, Pa..	7,863	Conshohocken, Pa..	5,470
Athens, Ga	8,639			Champaign, Ill	5,839	Corning, N. Y	8,550
Atlantic, N. J	13,055					Corry, Pa	5,677
Attleboro, Mass	7,577			Charleston, W. Va..	6,742	Corsicana, Tex	6,285

POPULATION OF PLACES IN THE UNITED STATES—*Continued.*

Place	Population
Cortland, N. Y.	8,590
Council Bluffs, Ia.	21,474
Coventry, R. I.	5,068
Cranston, R. I.	8,099
Crawfordsville, Ind.	6,089
Creston, Ia.	7,200
Cumberland, Md.	12,729
Cumberland, R. I.	8,090
Danbury, Ct.	16,552
Danvers, Mass.	7,454
Danville, Pa.	7,998
Danville, Ill.	11,491
Danville, Va.	10,305
Davenport, Ia.	26,872
Decatur, Ill.	16,841
Dedham, Mass.	7,123
Deering, Me.	5,353
Defiance, O.	7,694
Delaware, O.	8,224
Denison, Tex.	10,958
Derby, Ct.	5,969
Dixon, Ill.	5,161
Dover, N. H.	12,790
Dubuque, Ia.	30,311
Dunkirk, N. Y.	9,416
Durham, N. C.	5,485
East-Liverpool, O.	10,956
Easton, Pa.	14,481
East-Portland, Ore.	10,532
East-Provid'ce, R. I.	8,422
East-St. Louis, Ill.	15,169
Eau Claire, Wis.	17,415
Edgewater, N. J.	14,265
Elgin, Ill.	17,823
Elkhart, Ind.	11,360
El Paso, Tex.	10,338
Elyria, O.	5,611
Emporia, Kan.	7,551
Enfield, Ct.	7,199
Escanaba, Mich.	6,808
Everett, Mass.	11,068
Fargo, N. D.	5,664
Faribault, Minn.	6,520
Findlay, O.	18,553
Fitchburg, Mass.	22,037
Flint, Mich.	9,803
Florence, Ala.	6,012
Flushing, N. Y.	8,436
Fond du Lac, Wis.	12,024
Fort Madison, Ia.	7,901
Fort Scott, Kan.	11,946
Fort Smith, Ark.	11,311
Fort Worth, Tex.	23,076
Fostoria, O.	7,070
Framingham, Mass.	9,239
Frankfort, Ind.	5,919
Franklin, Pa.	6,221
Frederick, Md.	8,163
Freeport, Ill.	10,189
Fremont, Neb.	6,747
Fremont, O.	7,141
Fresno, Cal.	10,818
Gainesville, Tex.	6,594
Galena, Ill.	5,635
Galesburg, Ill.	15,264
Galion, O.	6,326
Galveston, Tex.	29,084
Gardiner, Me.	5,491
Gardner, Mass.	8,424
Geneva, N. Y.	7,557
Glens Falls, N. Y.	9,509
Gloucester, Mass.	24,651
Gloucester, N. J.	6,564
Gloversville, N. Y.	13,864
Goshen, Ind.	6,033
Grafton, Mass.	5,002
Grand Haven, Mich.	5,023
Grand Island, Neb.	7,536
Green Bay, Wis.	9,069
Greenbush, N. Y.	7,301
Greenfield, Mass.	5,252
Greenville, O.	5,473
Greenville, S. C.	8,607
Greenville, Miss.	6,658
Greenwich, Ct.	10,131
Groton, Ct.	5,539
Hackensack, N. J.	6,004
Hagerstown, Md.	10,118
Hamilton, O.	17,565
Hammond, Ind.	5,428
Hannibal, Mo.	12,857
Harrison, N. J.	8,338
Hastings, Neb.	13,584
Haverhill, Mass.	27,412
Haverstraw, N. Y.	5,070
Hazleton, Pa.	11,872
Helena, Ark.	5,189
Helena, Mont.	13,834
Henderson, Ky.	8,835
Highlands, Col.	5,161
Homestead, Pa.	7,911
Hoosick Falls, N. Y.	7,014
Hopkinsville, Ky.	5,833
Hornellsville, N. Y.	10,996
Hot Springs, Ark.	8,086
Houston, Tex.	27,557
Hudson, N. Y.	9,970
Huntingdon, Pa.	5,729
Huntington, Ind.	7,328
Huntington, W. Va.	10,108
Huntsville, Ala.	7,995
Hutchinson, Kan.	8,682
Hyde Park, Mass.	10,193
Independence, Mo.	6,380
Iowa City, Ia.	7,016
Ironton, O.	10,939
Ironwood, Mich.	7,745
Ishpeming, Mich.	11,197
Ithaca, N. Y.	11,079
Jackson, Mich.	20,798
Jackson, Miss.	5,920
Jackson, Tenn.	10,039
Jacksonville, Fla.	17,201
Jacksonville, Ill.	12,935
Jamaica, N. Y.	5,361
Jamestown, N. Y.	16,038
Jamesville, Wis.	10,836
Jefferson City, Mo.	6,742
Jeffersonville, Ind.	10,666
Johnston, R. I.	9,778
Johnstown, Pa.	21,805
Johnstown, N. Y.	7,768
Joliet, Ill.	23,264
Joplin, Mo.	9,943
Kalamazoo, Mich.	17,853
Kankakee, Ill.	9,025
Kearney, Neb.	8,074
Keene, N. H.	7,446
Kenosha, Wis.	6,532
Kenton, O.	5,557
Keokuk, Ia.	14,101
Key-West, Fla.	18,080
Killingly, Ct.	7,027
Kingston, N. Y.	21,261
Knoxville, Tenn.	22,535
Kokomo, Ind.	8,261
Laconia, N. H.	6,143
La Crosse, Wis.	25,090
Lafayette, Ind.	16,243
Lancaster, O.	7,555
Lansing, Mich.	13,102
Lansingburgh, N. Y.	10,550
Laporte, Ind.	7,126
Laramie, Wyo.	6,388
Laredo, Tex.	11,319
La Salle, Ill.	9,855
Lawrence, Kan.	9,997
Leadville, Col.	10,384
Leavenworth, Kan.	19,768
Lebanon, Pa.	14,664
Leominster, Mass.	7,269
Lewiston, Me.	21,701
Lexington, Ky.	21,567
Lima, O.	15,981
Lincoln, Ill.	6,725
Lincoln, R. I.	20,355
Litchfield, Ill.	5,811
Little Falls, N. Y.	8,783
Little Rock, Ark.	25,874
Lockhaven, Pa.	7,358
Lockport, N. Y.	16,038
Logansport, Ind.	13,328
Long Branch, N. J.	7,231
Long Isl'd City, N.Y.	30,506
Louisiana, Mo.	5,090
Ludington, Mich.	7,517
Lynchburg, Va.	19,709
Lyons, Ia.	5,799
McKeesport, Pa.	20,741
Macon, Ga.	22,746
Madison, Ind.	8,936
Madison, Wis.	13,426
Mahanoy, Pa.	11,286
Malden, Mass.	23,031
Malone, N. Y.	4,986
Manchester, Va.	9,246
Manchester, Ct.	8,222
Manistee, Mich.	12,812
Manitowoc, Wis.	7,710
Mankato, Minn.	8,838
Mansfield, O.	13,473
Marblehead, Mass.	8,202
Marietta, O.	8,273
Marinette, Wis.	11,523
Marion, Ind.	8,769
Marion, O.	8,327
Marlboro, Mass.	13,805
Marquette, Mich.	9,093
Marshall, Ia.	8,914
Marshall, Tex.	7,207
Martinsburg, W. Va.	7,226
Martin's Ferry, O.	6,250
Massillon, O.	10,092
Mattoon, Ill.	6,833
Maysville, Ky.	5,358
Meadville, Pa.	9,520
Medford, Mass.	11,070
Melrose, Mass.	8,519
Menominee, Mich.	10,630
Menomonie, Wis.	5,491
Meriden, Ct.	21,652
Meridian, Miss.	10,624
Merrill, Wis.	6,809
Michigan City, Ind.	10,776
Middleboro, Mass.	6,065
Middletown, Pa.	5,080
Middletown, Ct.	9,013
Middletown, N. Y.	11,977
Middletown, O.	7,681
Milford, Mass.	8,780
Millville, N. J.	10,002
Milton, Pa.	5,317
Moberly, Mo.	8,215
Moline, Ill.	12,000
Monmouth, Ill.	5,936
Monroe, Mich.	5,258
Montgomery, Ala.	21,883
Morristown, N. J.	8,156
Mount Carmel, Pa.	8,254
Mount Vernon, O.	6,027
Mount Vernon, N.Y.	10,830
Muncie, Ind.	11,345
Muscatine, Ia.	11,454
Muskegon, Mich.	22,702
Nanticoke, Pa.	10,044
Nashua, N. H.	19,311
Natchez, Miss.	10,101
Natick, Mass.	9,118
Naugatuck, Ct.	6,218
Nebraska City, Neb.	11,494
Neenah, Wis.	5,083
Negaunee, Mich.	6,078
Nevada, Mo.	7,262
New-Albany, Ind.	21,059
Newark, O.	14,270
Newbern, N. C.	7,843
New-Brighton, Pa.	5,616
New-Brighton, N.Y.	16,423
New-Britain, Ct.	16,519
N. Brunswick, N.J.	18,603
Newburgh, N. Y.	23,087
Newburyport, Mass.	13,947
Newcastle, Pa.	11,600
New-London, Ct.	13,757
Newport, Ky.	24,918
Newport, R. I.	19,457
New-Rochelle, N.Y.	8,217
Newton, Kan.	5,605
Newton, Mass.	24,379
Niagara Falls, N. Y.	5,502
Norristown, Pa.	19,791
North-Adams, Mass.	16,074
Northampton, Mass.	14,990
N. Attleboro, Mass.	6,727
Norwalk, O.	7,195
Norwalk, Ct.	17,747
Norwich, Ct.	16,156
Norwich, N. Y.	5,212
Oconto, Wis.	5,219
Ogden, Utah.	14,889
Ogdensburg, N. Y.	11,662
Oil City, Pa.	10,932
Oldtown, Me.	5,312
Olean, N. Y.	7,358
Oneida, N. Y.	6,083
Oneonta, N. Y.	6,272
Orange, N. J.	18,844
Oshkosh, Wis.	22,836
Oskaloosa, Ia.	6,558
Oswego, N. Y.	21,842
Ottawa, Ill.	9,985
Ottawa, Kan.	6,248
Ottumwa, Ia.	14,001
Owensboro, Ky.	9,837
Owosso, Mich.	6,564
Paducah, Ky.	12,797
Palestine, Tex.	5,838
Palmer, Mass.	6,520
Pana, Ill.	5,077
Paris, Tex.	8,254
Parkersburg, W.Va.	8,408
Parsons, Kan.	6,736
Passaic, N. J.	13,028
Pawtucket, R. I.	27,633
Peabody, Mass.	10,158
Peekskill, N. Y.	9,676
Pekin, Ill.	6,347
Pensacola, Fla.	11,750
Perth Amboy, N.J.	9,512
Peru, Ill.	5,550
Peru, Ind.	7,028
Petersburg, Va.	22,680
Phillipsburg, N. J.	8,644
Phoenixville, Pa.	8,514
Pine Bluff, Ark.	9,952
Piqua, O.	9,090
Pittsburg, Kan.	6,697
Pittsfield, Mass.	17,281
Pittston, Pa.	10,302
Plainfield, N. J.	11,267
Plattsburg, N. Y.	7,010
Plattsmouth, Neb.	8,392
Plymouth, Pa.	9,344
Plymouth, Mass.	7,314
Pontiac, Mich.	6,200
Portage, Wis.	5,143
Port Chester, N. Y.	5,274
Port Huron, Mich.	13,543
Port Jervis, N. Y.	9,327
Port Richmond, N.Y.	6,290
Portsmouth, N. H.	9,827
Portsmouth, O.	12,394
Portsmouth, Va.	13,268
Pottstown, Pa.	13,285
Pottsville, Pa.	14,117
Poughkeepsie, N.Y.	22,206
Provo, Utah.	5,159
Pueblo, Col.	24,558
Putnam, Ct.	6,512
Quincy, Mass.	16,723
Racine, Wis.	21,014
Rahway, N. J.	7,105
Raleigh, N. C.	12,678
Red Wing, Minn.	6,294
Revere, Mass.	5,668
Richmond, Ind.	16,608
Richmond, Ky.	5,073
Roanoke, Va.	16,159
Rochester, Minn.	5,321
Rochester, N. H.	7,396
Rockford, Ill.	23,584
Rock Island, Ill.	13,634
Rockland, Me.	8,174

POPULATION OF PLACES IN THE UNITED STATES—*Continued.*

Rockland, Mass	5,213	Sing Sing, N. Y	9,352	Tiffin, O............	10,801	Watertown, Mass...	7,073
Rome, Ga..........	6,957	Sioux Falls, S. D....	10,177	Titusville, Pa.......	8,073	Waterville, Me	7,107
Rome, N. Y........	14,991	Skowhegan, Me.....	5,068	Tonawanda, N. Y .	7,145	Waukegan, Ill......	4,915
Rutland, Vt........	11,760	Somersworth, N. H.	6,207	Torrington, Ct.....	6,048	Waukesha, Wis.....	6,321
Saco, Me..........	6,075	South Bend, Ind....	21,819	Trenton, Mo.......	5,039	Wausau, Wis.......	9,253
Sacramento, Cal....	26,386	S. Bethlehem, Pa...	10,302	Trinidad, Col	5,523	Webb, Mo	5,043
St. Albans, Vt......	7,771	Southbridge, Mass..	7,655	Tucson, Ariz.......	5,150	Webster, Mass.....	7,031
St. Charles, Mo	6,161	Southington, Ct.....	5,501	Tyler, Tex.........	6,908	Wellsville, O.......	5,247
St. Cloud, Minn	7,686	S. Kingstown, R. I..	6,231	Union, N. J	10,643	West Bay, Mich....	12,981
St. Johnsbury, Vt..	6,567	South Omaha, Neb..	8,062	Uniontown, Pa	6,359	Westboro, Mass ...	5,195
Salem, N. J	5,516	Spartanburg, S. C..	5,544	Urbana, O.........	6,510	Westbrook, Me	6,632
Salem, O...........	5,780	Spencer, Mass	8,747	Vallejo, Cal.......	6,343	West Chester, Pa...	8,028
Salina, Kan........	6,149	Spokane, Wash.....	19,922	Valparaiso, Ind....	5,090	Westerly, R. I	6,813
San Diego, Cal.....	16,159	Springfield, Ill.....	24,963	Van Wert, O	5,512	Westfield, Mass....	9,805
Sandusky, O........	18,471	Springfield, Mo	21,850	Vernon, Ct........	8,808	W. Springfield, Mass.	5,077
San José, Cal......	18,060	Stamford, Ct.......	15,700	Vicksburg, Miss	13,373	West Troy, N. Y...	12,967
Santa Barbara, Cal..	5,864	Staunton, Va.......	6,975	Vincennes, Ind.....	8,853	Weymouth, Mass ...	10,866
Santa Cruz, Cal....	5,596	Steelton, Pa.......	9,250	Virginia City, Nev..	8,511	Wichita, Kan......	23,853
Santa Fé, N. M.....	6,185	Sterling, Ill........	5,824	Wabash, Ind.......	5,105	Williamsport, Pa...	27,132
Santa Rosa, Cal....	5,220	Steubenville, O.....	13,394	Waco, Tex........	14,445	Wilmington, N. C..	20,056
Saratoga Spr'gs,N.Y	11,975	Stevens Point, Wis..	7,866	Wakefield, Mass....	6,982	Winchester, Va.....	5,196
S. Ste Marie, Mich.	5,760	Stillwater, Minn....	11,260	Wallingford, Ct....	6,584	Winchester, Ct.....	6,183
Schenectady, N. Y.	19,902	Stockton, Cal......	14,424	Waltham, Mass.....	18,707	Winfield, Kan......	5,184
Sedalia, Mo........	14,068	Stoneham, Mass ...	6,155	Ware, Mass........	7,329	Winona, Minn.....	18,208
Selma, Ala........	7,622	Stonington, Ct.....	7,184	Warren, O	5,973	Winston, N. C.....	8,018
Seneca Falls, N. Y.	6,116	Streator, Ill........	11,414	Warwick, R. I......	17,761	Woburn, Mass.....	13,499
Seymour, Ind......	5,337	Sunbury, Pa.......	5,930	Washington, Pa ...	7,063	Woonsocket, R. I...	20,830
Shamokin, Pa......	14,403	Superior, Wis......	11,983	Washington, Ind ...	6,064	Wooster, O........	5,901
Sharon, Pa........	7,459	Tamaqua, Pa	6,054	Washington, O	5,742	Xenia, O..........	7,301
Sheboygan, Wis	16,359	Tampa, Fla........	5,532	Waterbury, Ct.....	28,646	York, Pa..........	20,793
Shelbyville, Ind	5,451	Taunton, Mass.....	25,448	Waterloo, Ia.......	6,674	Ypsilanti, Mich	6,129
Shenandoah, Pa ...	15,944	Terre Haute, Ind...	30,217	Watertown, N. Y...	14,725	Zanesville, O.......	21,009
Sherman, Tex......	7,335	Thomasville, Ga....	5,514	Watertown, Wis....	8,755		
Shreveport, La.....	11,979	Thompson, Ct	5,480				

There are, according to the census of 1890, in the United States 3,715 cities and villages having over 1,000 inhabitants each. There are 7 having 400,000 inhabitants, and over 21 having 100,000 and under 400,000 ; 30 having 50,000 and under 100,000 ; 66 having 25,000 and under 50,000 ; 92 having 15,000 and under 25,000 ; 138 having 10,000 and under 15,000, and 94 having 8,000 and under 10,000.

Population of the State of New=York

BY COUNTIES, ACCORDING TO THE STATE ENUMERATION MADE IN 1892.

COUNTIES.	Total Inhabitants.	Total Citizens.	Total Aliens.	COUNTIES.	Total Inhabitants.	Total Citizens.	Total Aliens.
Albany.......	167,289	156,748	10,541	Onondaga	150,808	142,058	8,750
Allegany.....	43,131	42,644	487	Ontario	48,718	46,974	1,744
Broome.....	62,793	61,591	1,202	Orange	97,760	93,271	4,489
Cattaraugus..	61,774	59,700	2,074	Orleans	30,762	28,732	2,030
Cayuga	62,816	60,579	2,237	Oswego	70 970	69,023	1,947
Chautauqua ..	78,900	73,884	5,016	Otsego......	50,361	49,862	499
Chemung	47,223	45,845	1,378	Putnam	14,230	13,325	905
Chenango ...	37,602	37,121	481	Queens	141,805	123,974	17,831
Clinton	46,601	44,518	2,083	Rensselaer...	128,923	121,679	7,244
Columbia.....	45,205	43,990	1,215	Richmond....	53,452	46,592	6,860
Cortland	28,271	27,955	316	Rockland	33,726	31,325	2,401
Delaware.....	45,488	44,985	503	St. Lawrence.	86,254	80,679	5,575
Dutchess.....	78,342	75,078	3,264	Saratoga	57,301	54,909	2,392
Erie.........	347,328	304,713	42,615	Schenectady .	34,194	31,630	2,564
Essex	33,110	32,092	1,018	Schoharie ...	28,815	28,668	147
Franklin.....	39,817	37,025	2,792	Schuyler	16,861	16,326	535
Fulton.......	38,478	37,285	1,193	Seneca	26,542	25,928	614
Genesee	33,436	32,328	1,108	Steuben	82,468	81,400	1,068
Greene......	31,141	30,843	298	Suffolk	63,572	58,872	4,700
Hamilton	5,216	4,784	432	Sullivan.....	31,860	31,438	422
Herkimer....	47,491	45,769	1,722	Tioga	29,675	29,365	310
Jefferson.....	70,358	66,245	4,113	Tompkins ...	33,612	33,159	453
Kings.......	995,276	868,983	126,293	Ulster	87,652	85,392	2,260
Lewis.......	30,248	29,414	834	Warren......	28,618	28,157	461
Livingston ...	37,010	35,448	1,562	Washington..	46,458	45,144	1,314
Madison	42,206	41,674	532	Wayne......	48,262	46,538	1,724
Monroe	200,056	181,230	18,826	Westchester..	145,106	129,224	15,882
Montgomery .	46,081	43,831	2,250	Wyoming ...	31,218	30,253	965
New-York ...	1,801,739	1,423,984	377,755	Yates........	20,801	20,316	485
Niagara.....	64,378	59,161	5,217				
Oneida.......	123,756	117,205	6,551	Total	6,513,344	5,790,865	722,479

Immigration into the United States, 1820-1892.

YEAR.	Total Alien Passengers.	YEAR.	Total Alien Passengers.	YEAR.	Total Immigrants.	YEAR.	Total Immigrants.
1820	8,385	1840	84,066	1860	150,237	1879	177,826
1821	9,127	1841	80,289	1861	89,724	1880	457,257
1822	6,911	1842	104,565	1862	89,007	1881	669,431
1823	6,354	1843	52,496	1863	174,524	1882	788,992
1824	7,912	1844	78,615	1864	193,195	1883	603,322
1825	10,199	1845	114,371	1865	247,453	1884	518,592
1826	10,837	1846	154,416	1866	103,594	1885	395,346
1827	18,875	1847	234,968	Fiscal Year ending June 30		1886	334,203
1828	27,382	1848	226,527	1867	298,967	1887	490,109
1829	22,520	1849	297,024	1868	282,189	1888	546,889
1830	23,322	1850	369,986	1869	352,569	1889	444,427
1831	22,633	1851	379,466	1870	387,203	1890	455,302
1832	60,482	1852	371,603	1871	321,350	1891	560,319
1833	58,640	1853	368,645	1872	404,806	1892	623,084
1834	65,365	1854	427,833	1873	459,803		
1835	45,374	1855	200,877	1874	313,339	Total	*16,004,093
1836	76,224	1856	195,857	1875	227,498		
1837	79,340	1857	246,945	1876	169,986	From 1789 to 1820,	
1838	38,914	1858	119,501	1877	141,857	estimated	250,000
1839	68,069	1859	118,616	1878	138,469		

Of the whole number of immigrants in the fiscal year ending June 30, 1891, 533,164 came through the customs district of New-York ; 41,995 through Baltimore ; 36,149 through Boston ; 28,120 through Philadelphia, and 10,115 through San Francisco.

The reported occupations of immigrants who arrived during the year ending June 30, 1890, were as follows : Laborers, 139,365 ; farmers, 29,296 ; servants, 28,625 ; carpenters, 3,776 ; miners, 3,745 ; clerks, 3,653 ; tailors, 3,879 ; shoemakers, 2,232 ; blacksmiths, 1,792. The total number of professional immigrants was 3,236 ; of skilled laborers, 44,540 ; of miscellaneous, 211,756.

* Immigrants from the British North American possessions and Mexico are not included since July 1, 1885.

NATIONALITY OF IMMIGRANTS BY DECADES, 1841 to 1890.
(Compiled by the Superintendent of the Census.)

COUNTRIES.	1841 to 1850.	1851 to 1860.	1861 to 1870.	1871 to 1880.	1881 to 1890.
England	32,092	247,125	251,288	440,961	649,052
Ireland	780,719	914,119	456,593	444,589	655,381
Scotland	3,712	38,331	44,681	88,925	149,856
Wales	1,261	6,319	4,642	6,779	11,990
Great Britain, not specified	229,979	132,199	349,766	7,908	147
Total United Kingdom	1,047,763	1,338,093	1,106,970	989,163	1,466,426
Austria	......	......	9,398	69,558	226,020
Belgium	5,074	4,738	7,416	7,278	17,506
Denmark	539	3,749	17,885	34,577	88,108
France	77,262	76,358	37,749	73,301	50,460
Germany	434,626	951,667	822,007	757,698	1,452,952
Hungary	......	......	448	13,475	127,678
Italy	1,870	9,231	12,982	60,830	307,095
Netherlands	8,251	10,789	9,539	17,236	53,701
Norway and Sweden	13,903	20,931	117,798	220,488	560,483
Russia and Poland	656	1,621	5,047	54,606	265,064
Spain and Portugal	2,759	10,353	9,047	9,767	5,564
Switzerland	4,644	25,011	23,839	31,722	81,987
All other countries in Europe	155	116	234	1,265	22,770
Total Europe	1,597,502	2,452,657	2,180,399	2,346,964	4,725,814
China	35	41,397	68,050	122,436	59,995*
Total Asia	82	41,458	68,444	123,068	63,932
Africa	55	210	324	221	375*
Canada	41,723	59,309	184,713	430,210	392,802†
Mexico	3,271	3,078	2,380	5,164	1,913†
Central America	368	449	96	229?	1,646
South America	3,579	1,224	1,443	1,125	
West Indies	13,528	10,660	9,698	14,461	26,487*‡
Total America	62,469	74,720	198,336	451,216	422,848
All other countries	53,143	29,169	19,249	23,226	25,759
Aggregate	1,713,251	2,598,214	2,466,752	2,944,695	5,238,728

* Not given in 1890. † Reports discontinued after 1885. ‡ Includes Central and South America for 1889.
As the reports for British North American Provinces and for Mexico have been discontinued since 1885 by the Treasury Department, the figures here represented only cover five years of the decade. An estimate based upon the immigration of the years from 1881 to 1885, inclusive, would give 785,604 to British North America for the decade from 1881 to 1890, and 3,826 to Mexico, making the aggregate for America 817,563, instead of 422,848.
Mulhall estimates the number of individuals who emigrated from Europe in 72 years, 1816 to 1888, at 27,205,-000. Of these, 15,000,000 came to the United States.

Postal Information.

(Revised December, 1892, at the New-York Post-Office, for THE WORLD ALMANAC.*)*

DOMESTIC RATES OF POSTAGE.

ALL mailable matter for transmission by the United States mails within the United States is divided into four classes, under the following regulations :

FIRST-CLASS MATTER.

This class includes letters, postal cards, and anything sealed or otherwise closed against inspection, or anything containing writing not allowed as an accompaniment to printed matter under class three.

Rates of letter postage to any part of the United States, *two cents per ounce qr fraction thereof.*

Rates on local or drop letters at free delivery offices, two cents per ounce or fraction thereof. At offices where there is no free delivery by carriers, one cent per ounce or fraction thereof.

Rates on postal cards, one cent. Nothing must be added or attached to a postal card, except that a printed address slip may be pasted on the address side. The addition of anything else subjects the card to letter postage. A card containing any offensive dun or any scurrilous or indecent communication will not be forwarded. Nothing but the address must be placed on the face, or stamped side.

Rates on specially delivered letters, ten cents on each letter in *addition* to the regular postage. This entitles the letter to immediate delivery by special messenger. Special delivery stamps are sold at post-offices, and must be affixed to such letters. An ordinary ten-cent stamp affixed to a letter will *not* entitle it to special delivery. The delivery, at carrier offices, extends to the limits of the carrier routes. At non-carrier offices it extends to one mile from the post-office. Postmasters are not obliged to deliver beyond these limits, and letters addressed to places beyond must await delivery in the usual way, notwithstanding the special delivery stamp.

Prepayment by stamps invariably required. Postage on all letters should be *fully* prepaid, but if prepaid one full rate and no more, they will be forwarded, and the amount of deficient postage collected on delivery ; if wholly unpaid, or prepaid with less than one full rate, and deposited at a post-office, the addressee will be notified to remit postage ; and if he fails to do so, they will be sent to the Dead Letter Office ; but they will be returned to the sender if he is located at the place of mailing, and if his address be printed or written upon them.

Letter rates are charged on all productions by the typewriter or manifold process.

Letters (but no other class of mail matter) will be returned to the sender free, if a request to that effect is printed or written on the envelope. There is no limit of weight for first-class matter.

Prepaid letters will be reforwarded from one post-office to another upon the written request of the person addressed, without additional charge for postage. The direction on forwarded letters may be changed as many times as may be necessary to reach the person addressed.

SECOND-CLASS MATTER.

This class includes all newspapers, periodicals, or matter exclusively in print and regularly issued at stated intervals as frequently as four times a year, from a known office of publication or news agency, to actual subscribers or news agents, and transient newspapers and publications of this character mailed by persons other than publishers.

Rates of postage to publishers, *one cent a pound or fractional part thereof,* prepaid by special stamps. Publications designed primarily for advertising or free circulation, or not having a legitimate list of subscribers, are excluded from the pound rate, and pay third-class rates.

Publications sent to actual subscribers in the county where published are free, unless mailed for local delivery at a letter-carrier office.

Rates of postage on transient newspapers, magazines, or periodicals, *one cent for each four ounces or fraction thereof.* It should be observed that the rate is one cent for each four ounces, not one cent for each paper. Second-class matter will be entitled to special delivery when special delivery ten-cent stamps are affixed in addition to the regular postage.

Transient second-class matter must be so wrapped as to enable the postmaster to inspect it. The sender's name and address may be written in them, but any other writing subjects the matter to letter postage. The name and address of the sender may also be written on the wrapper.

THIRD-CLASS MATTER.

Mail matter of the third class includes printed books, pamphlets, engravings, circulars (in print or by the hectograph, electric pen or similar process), and other matter wholly in print, proof-sheets, corrected proof-sheets, and manuscript copy accompanying the same.

The rate on matter of this class is *one cent for each two ounces or fraction thereof.*

Manuscript unaccompanied by proof-sheets must pay letter rates.

Third-class matter must admit of easy inspection, otherwise it will be charged letter rates on delivery. It must be fully prepaid, or it will not be forwarded. Its wrapper must bear no writing or printing except the name and address of the sender and a return request.

The limit of weight is four pounds, except single books in separate packages, on which the weight is not limited. It is entitled, like matter of the other classes, to special delivery when special delivery stamps are affixed in addition to the regular postage.

The name and address of the sender, preceded by the word "from," may be written upon the package, and a simple manuscript dedication may appear in a book or upon the article enclosed.

Rates of Postage to Foreign Countries.

COUNTRIES NOT OF THE UNIVERSAL POSTAL UNION.

Countries.	Letters, per ½ oz.	News-papers, per 2 oz.	Countries.	Letters, per ½ oz.	News-papers, per 2 oz.
Ascension	10	2	Morocco (except Spanish posses-		
Cape Colony	10	2	sions)	10	2
China, via Brindisi	10	2	Orange Free State	10	2
Comoro Islands	5	1*	St. Helena	10	2
Madagascar (except French Sta-					
tions), British mail	10	2			

Registration allowed on all mail matter to South African Colonies and States, 10 cents. * Per 2 ounces.
Prepayment to all of above places compulsory.

ALL COUNTRIES EXCEPT THE ABOVE ARE IN THE UNIVERSAL POSTAL UNION, within which the rates of postage (except as to Canada and Mexico) are as follows:

Letters, per 15 grams (½ ounce), prepayment optional. (See paragraph "Unpaid Letters," preceding page.) .... 5 cents.
Postal cards, each .... 2 cents.
Newspapers and other printed matter, per 2 ounces.. 1 cent.
Commercial papers. { Packets not in excess of 10 ounces.. 5 cents.
{ Packets in excess of 10 ounces, for each 2 ounces, or fraction thereof........... 1 cent.
Samples of merchandise. { Packets not in excess of 4 ounces .... 2 cents.
{ Packets in excess of 4 ounces, for each 2 ounces, or fraction thereof...... 1 cent.
Registration fee on letters or other articles.. 10 cents.

All correspondence other than letters must be prepaid, at least partially. For Parcels Post to certain West India Islands, and Central and South American States, see preceding page.

CANADA.

Letters, per ounce, prepayment compulsory.. 2 cents.
Postal cards, each... 1 cent.
Newspapers, per 4 ounces.. 1 cent.
Merchandise and samples of merchandise, not exceeding 4 pounds, per ounce .... 1 cent.
Commercial papers, same as to other Postal Union countries.
Registration fee .... 10 cents.

Any article of correspondence may be registered. Packages of merchandise are subject to the regulations of either country to prevent violations of the revenue laws; must not be closed against inspection, and must be so wrapped and enclosed as to be easily examined. No sealed packages other than letters in their usual and ordinary form may be sent by mail to Canada.

MEXICO.

Letters, newspapers, and printed matter are now carried between the United States and Mexico at same rates as in the United States. Samples are 1 cent for 2 ounces; limit of weight, 8¾ ounces. Merchandise, other than samples, may only be sent by Parcels Post. No sealed packages other than letters in their usual and ordinary form may be sent by mail to Mexico, nor any package over 4 pounds 6 ounces in weight.

SAMPLES.

By special agreement between the United States and France, Great Britain, Belgium, Switzerland, the Argentine Republic, Italy, Hawaiian kingdom, Egypt, and the British Colonies, except India, Canada, and the Australian Colonies, Austria, and Hungary, packets of samples of merchandise are admissible in the mails between the two countries, up to 350 grams (12 oz.) in weight, and the following dimensions apply : all Postal Union countries: 30 centimeters (12 inches) in length, 20 centimeters (8 inches) in width, and 10 centimeters (4 inches) in depth, or if they are in the form of a roll, 12 inches in length and 6 inches in diameter.

Distances from New=York.

POSTAL ROUTE DISTANCES OF VARIOUS CITIES FROM THE CITY OF NEW-YORK. PRE-PARED BY THE FOREIGN MAILS DIVISION OF THE POST-OFFICE DEPARTMENT.

	Miles.		Miles.
Adelaide, via San Francisco	12,845	Honolulu, via San Francisco	5,645
Alexandria, via London	6,150	Liverpool	3,540
Amsterdam " "	3,085	London, via Queenstown	3,740
Athens, via London	5,655	Madrid, via London	4,925
Bahia, Brazil	5,870	Melbourne, via San Francisco	12,265
Berlin, via London	4,385	Mexico City (Railroad)	3,750
Bombay " "	9,765	Panama	2,355
Buenos Ayres	8,045	Paris	4,020
Calcutta, via London	11,120	Rio de Janeiro	6,730
Cape Town, via London	11,245	Rome, via London	5,030
Constantinople, via London	5,810	St. Petersburg, via London	5,370
Florence, via London	4,800	Shanghai, via San Francisco	9,920
Glasgow	3,375	Stockholm, via London	4,975
Greytown, via New-Orleans	2,810	Sydney, via San Francisco	11,570
Halifax, N. S	645	Valparaiso, via Panama	5,910
Havana	1,400	Vienna, via London	4,740
Hong Kong, via San Francisco	10,590	Yokohama, via San Francisco	8,725

Review of Scientific Progress During the Year 1892.

ASTRONOMY.

Among the astronomical discoveries of the year 1892 none possesses more interest or created more surprise to astronomers and scientific men generally than that made at the Lick Observatory on September 9 by Mr. E. E. Barnard, who has added a fifth satellite to the well-known four satellites of Jupiter. The latter were discovered by Galileo on January 7, 1610, and although this planet has been most carefully observed ever since, no evidence of a fifth satellite was found until the planet was scrutinized by Mr. Barnard with the great Lick refractor. This fifth satellite is so near the planet and so minute that it is an exceedingly difficult object to see even with the Lick telescope; indeed, there is some doubt as to whether or not it has been seen at any other observatory. There are, however, not more than six or seven telescopes in the world capable of showing it. Its distance from Jupiter's centre is about 112,400 miles—considerably less than half the distance of our Moon—its period of revolution, 11 hours, 50 minutes, and it is estimated to be about the thirteenth magnitude.

Several asteroids have been discovered during the year, but some of them have been subsequently identified with those previously discovered. The number of these bodies is now so great that ephemerides of them cannot be prepared to give their position beforehand, and consequently many of them are practically lost. Eight comets have been detected, all of them telescopic and of little or no importance. One of them—Holmes's comet—was mistaken for the lost comet of Biela, whose nearest approach to the earth, on or about the 27th November, was predicted to be attended with a meteoric shower, which, however, did not take place so far as at present known. The planet Mars passed its most favorable opposition in August, and was most carefully observed at the Lick and other observatories, with the view of determining its chief physical features. Certain markings, consisting of long, narrow, and nearly parallel lines, which have hitherto been regarded as huge canals constructed by the Martians for commercial purposes, are now considered to be parallel mountain ridges set in the sea; and the nearly circular island called Hellas by astronomers, which was supposed to be intersected by a great canal, is now believed to be a large lake or sea, with a high, narrow mountain range dividing it into two nearly equal portions. In fact, recent observations have nearly reversed the character of the surface as hitherto believed; the dark portions now being regarded as land and the bright parts water. Mars possesses all the conditions necessary for the existence of animal and vegetable life—an atmosphere, land and water, and a succession of the seasons similar to our own—but as to its being or having been inhabited by rational beings like ourselves science has no means of determining, much less of communicating with the inhabitants, if there are any.

CHEMISTRY.

An extensive series of experiments, with the view of determining the physical and chemical properties of the element Fluorine, has shown that the element is a greenish-yellow gas having a density of 1.265 compared with air and its atomic weight, 19.05. It is not liquefied at a temperature of $-95°$ C. in a bottle of solid carbon dioxide; it combines with hydrogen with explosion at as low a temperature as $-23°$ C., but does not unite with oxygen even at 500° C.

A method for the production of ozone in large quantities for commercial purposes has been devised. Ozone is especially valuable as a disinfectant and for the sterilization of water.

An instrument, by means of which the mass of a given gas is given directly from a single reading of its volume, has been invented by Japp, who has given it the name of Gravi-volumeter. It is a modification of the gas-volumeter of Lunge. Experiments on liquid oxygen and liquid air show that the former, when seen in bulk, is of a pale blue color, boils at $-180°$ C., and is a non-conductor of electricity. When liquid oxygen is interposed in the path of a beam of light, its absorption spectrum shows clearly the lines A and B of the solar spectrum, which lines, as already known, are due to absorption by the oxygen of the atmosphere. By accelerating the evaporation of liquid oxygen by reducing the pressure, common air—a mixture of oxygen and nitrogen—is liquefied in an open test-tube under atmospheric pressure. Common air is liquefied at a much lower temperature than oxygen, is clearer, fumes less, and boils less violently. On evaporating liquid air, the nitrogen boils off before the oxygen.

The industrial production of liquid carbon dioxide in large quantities has been successfully carried out in Germany and France. In the former country its chief use is in the manufacture of beer, and in the latter for the preparation of salicylic acid by the reaction of liquid carbon dioxide on sodium phenol. It is also employed in making aërated waters, filtering wines, and other purposes.

Some success has been attained in photographing natural colors. Brilliant photographs of spectra have been produced, all the colors appearing at once after an exposure of about twenty or thirty seconds. The plates on which these photographs were taken were prepared by depositing on them films of albumen bromide of silver, rendered orthochromatic by azalin and cyanin. In order to photograph the complex colors that adorn natural objects, it only remains to perfect the orthochromatism of the plate and to increase its sensitiveness. An extensive series of experiments have been made to determine whether pure gases raised to a high temperature emit light rays or not, and the result has been contrary to what has hitherto been believed. It has been shown that oxygen, carbon dioxide, nitrogen, and hydrogen do not emit light rays when heated to 1500° C. The hypothesis that a gas can be made luminous through mere rise of temperature cannot be established experimentally, and therefore it may be safely stated that comets must shine from reflected light, and not from any intrinsic light of their own.

GEOLOGY.

Numerous researches in geology have been successfully carried on by our own Geological Survey, and also by foreign geologists. Among the chief geological contributions of the year may be mentioned "The Tenth Annual Report of the United States Geological Survey," which contains valuable monographs on the history, geological structure, and economic value of the region of the Great Dismal Swamp; on the structure and formation of the iron beds in Michigan and Wisconsin; on the discovery of a new hot spring area on the east side of the Yellowstone, and on many other subjects of general and local interest.

"The Stratigraphy of the Bituminous Coal Fields of Pennsylvania, Ohio, and West-Virginia," by J. C. White, of the United State Geological Survey, is a valuable contribution to the geology of this interesting and valuable region. "The Annual Report of the Geological Survey of Arkansas," by the State Geologist; "The Distribution of the Upturned Cretaceous Beds of Canada," by Dr. Dawson; "The History of Volcanic Action in the Area of the British Islands," by A. Geikie; "Report on the Petroleum Natural Gas and Asphalt Rock of Western Kentucky;" "The Geological Survey of Alabama," are contributions of a very high order of merit, and add very materially to our knowledge of these regions.

EXPLORATION.

An exploration of the Coral Islands off New-Guinea, and of the Tonga or Friendly Islands, makes known for the first time the chief geological and other features of these remote and interesting localities. The latter is remarkable for the great depth of the surrounding sea, depths of 28,000 feet having been found in the vicinity.

REVIEW OF SCIENTIFIC PROGRESS—*Continued.*

SCIENTIFIC LITERATURE.

A very valuable contribution to science has been issued by the Government of India on the Fauna of British India, including Ceylon and Burma. Among the other valuable scientific publications of the year "The Advanced Course on Physics," by Professor George F. Barker, of the University of Pennsylvania, stands in the foremost rank.

"The Outlines of Theoretical Chemistry," by Lothar Meyer, gives a very clear discussion of the various topics which come within this branch of science. "The Principles of Chemistry," by Mendeléeff, translated from the Russian, by Greenway, is another work of rare merit, its treatment of the subject being both profound and far-reaching; and an "Introduction to the Mathematical Theory of Electricity," by W. T. A. Emtage, is an excellent introduction to the mathematical side of the subjects of electricity and magnetism.

During the year 1892 we have to deplore the loss to science of many of its most distinguished votaries. The list of those who have passed away—many of them at a very advanced age—is unusually long. Their places can hardly be filled for many years to come. In our own country we mourn the loss of Lovering, Hunt, Rutherfurd, and Sereno Watson, and in Europe, Airy, Adams, Sir A. C. Ramsay, Mosely, Carpenter, Dr. F. Von Roemer, Admiral Mouchez, Sir Richard Owen, and De Gasparis.

National Academy of Sciences.

OFFICERS.

President—Professor O. C. Marsh, New-Haven, Ct.
Vice-President—General Francis A. Walker, Boston, Mass.
Foreign Secretary—Wolcott Gibbs, Newport, R. I.
Home Secretary—Asaph Hall, U. S. N., Washington, D. C.
Treasurer—Dr. John S. Billings, U. S. A., Washington, D. C.
Council—George J. Brush, New-Haven, Ct.; Benjamin A. Gould, Cambridge, Mass.; Thomas C. Mendenhall, Washington, D. C.; Professor Simon Newcomb, Washington, D. C.; Ira Remsen, Baltimore, Md.; Samuel P. Langley, Washington, D. C., and the officers of the National Academy.

The National Academy of Sciences was incorporated by act of Congress, March 3, 1863. The charter provides that "the Academy shall, whenever called upon by any department of the Government, investigate, examine, experiment, and report upon any subject of science or art; the actual expense of such investigations, examinations, experiments, and reports to be paid from appropriations which may be made for the purpose." The Academy is composed at present of 91 members, 3 honorary members, and 24 foreign associates.

American Social Science Association.

OFFICERS.

President—H. L. Wayland, Philadelphia, Pa.
First Vice-President—Andrew Dickson White, Ithaca, N. Y.
Vice-Presidents—Francis Wayland, New-Haven, Ct.; Daniel C. Gilman, Baltimore, Md.; William T. Harris, Washington, D. C.; Carroll D. Wright, Washington, D. C.; Mrs. John E. Lodge, Boston, Mass.; Lucy M. Browne, M.D., Brooklyn, N. Y.; Mrs. Caroline H. Dall, Washington, D. C.; E. Benjamin Andrews, Providence, R. I.; John Eaton, Washington, D. C.; Grace Peckham, M.D., New-York; Henry B. Baker, Lansing, Mich.; Dorman B. Eaton, New-York; Henry Villard, New-York; H. Holbrook Curtis, M.D., New-York; John M. Gregory, Washington, D. C.; R. A. Holland, St. Louis, Mo.
General Secretary—F. B. Sanborn, Concord, Mass.
Treasurer—Anson Phelps Stokes, 45 Cedar Street, New-York.
The next meeting of the Association will be held at Saratoga Springs, N. Y., September, 1893.

American Association for the Advancement of Science.

OFFICERS.

President—William Harkness, Washington, D. C.
Vice-Presidents—A—Mathematics and Astronomy, C. L. Doolittle, South Bethlehem, Pa.; B—Physics, E. L. Nichols, Ithaca, N. Y.; C—Chemistry, Edward Hart, Easton, Pa.; D—Mechanical Science and Engineering, S. W. Robinson, Columbus, Ohio; E—Geology and Geography, Charles D. Walcott, Washington, D. C.; F—Zoology, Henry F. Osborn, New-York; G—Botany, Charles E. Bessey, Lincoln, Neb.; H—Anthropology, J. Owen Dorsey, Tacoma, Md.; I—Economic Science and Statistics, William H. Brewer, New-Haven, Ct.
Permanent Secretary—F. W. Putnam, Cambridge (office Salem), Mass.
General Secretary—T. H. Norton, Cincinnati, Ohio.
Secretary of the Council—H. L. Fairchild, Rochester, N. Y.
Treasurer—William Lilly, Mauch Chunk, Pa.
Auditor—Thomas Meehan, Germantown, Pa.

American Statistical Association.

OFFICERS.

President—Francis A. Walker, Ph.D., LL.D.
Vice-Presidents—George C. Shattuck, M.D.; Hamilton A. Hill, A.M.; Hon. Carroll D. Wright; Richmond M. Smith, A.M.; Hon. Horace G. Wadlin.
Corresponding Secretary—Edward Atkinson, LL.D.
Treasurer—John S. Clark, Esq., 7 Park Street, Boston, Mass.
Secretary and Librarian—Davis R. Dewey, Ph.D., Institute of Technology, Boston, Mass.
Counsellors—John Ward Dean, A.M.; Samuel W. Abbott, M.D.; S. N. D. North, Esq.
Committee on Publication—Davis R. Dewey, Ph.D.; Walter C. Wright, Esq.; Roland P. Falkner, Ph.D.
Committee on Finance—Hamilton A. Hill, A.M.; Lyman Mason, A.M.; George O. Carpenter, Esq. *Committee on Library*—Hon. Julius L. Clarke; Rev. Robert C. Waterston; Samuel A. Green, A.M., M.D.

𝔐oonlight 𝔈hart, 1893.

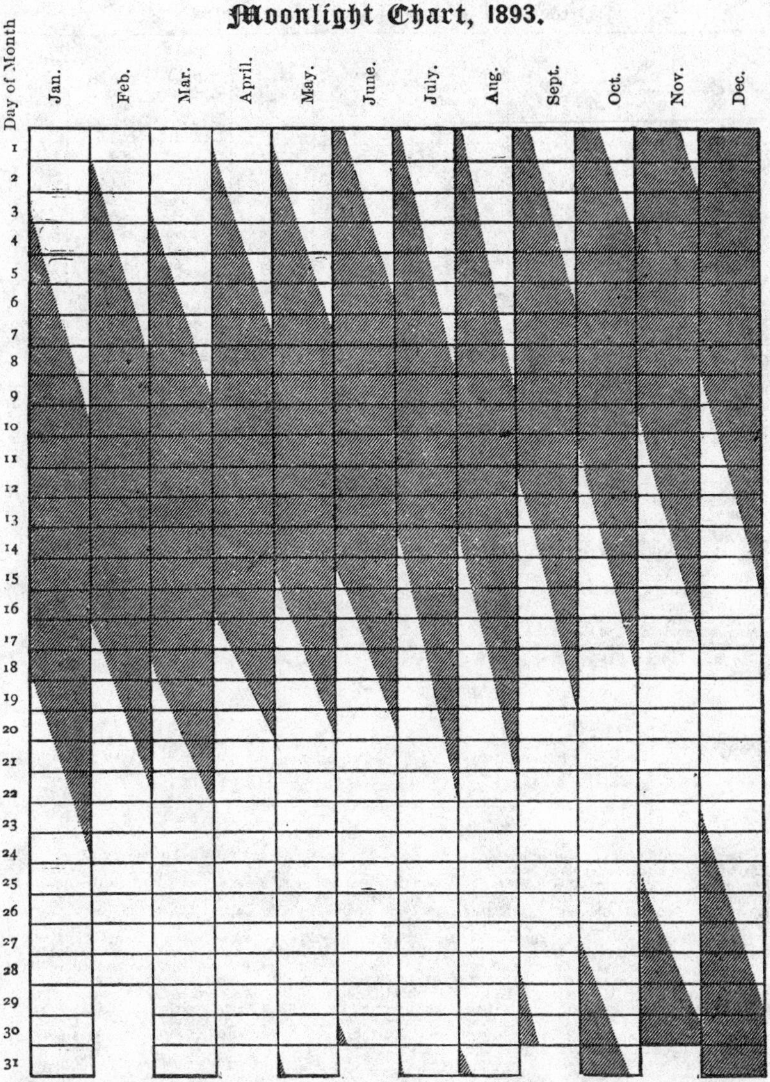

EXPLANATION.—The *white* spaces indicate the amount of moonlight each evening (from sunset to midnight). January 3, February 1, etc., are the last evenings when the moon *rises* during twilight; January 10, February 8, etc., are the first days on which the moon *rises* after midnight; January 19, February 17, etc., are the first evenings when the new moon is visible; January 25, February 22, etc., are the first days when the moon *sets* after midnight.

Principal Elements of the Solar System.

NAME.	Mean Distance, From Sun Millions of Miles.	Sidereal Period, Days.	Orbit Veloc- ity, Miles per Second.	Mean Diameter, Miles.	Mass. Earth = 1.	Volume. Earth = 1.	Density. Earth = 1.	Gravity at Sur- face. Earth = 1.
Sun	....	....	....	866,400	331100	1310000	0.25	27.65
Mercury...	36.0	87.969	23 to 35	3,030	0.125	0.056	2.23	0.85
Venus.....	67.2	224.701	21.9	7,700	0.78	0.92	0.86	0.83
Earth	92.9	365.256	18.5	7,918	0.00	1.00	1.00	1.00
Mars......	141.5	686.950	15.0	4,230	0.107	0.152	0.72	0.38
Jupiter ...	483.3	4332.58	8.1	86,500	316.0	1309	0.24	2.65
Saturn.....	886.0	10759.22	6.0	71,000	94.9	721	0.13	1.18
Uranus.....	1781.9	30686.82	4.2	31,900	14.7	65	0.22	0.91
Neptune....	2791.6	60181.11	3.4	34,800	17.1	85	0.20	0.88

The number of asteroids discovered up to present date is 330. A number of these small planets have not been observed since their discovery, and are practically lost. Consequently it is now some-times a matter of doubt, until the elements have been computed, if the supposed new planet is really new, or only an old one rediscovered.

It is supposed that a Centauri, one of the brightest stars of the Southern Hemisphere, is the nearest of the fixed stars to the earth. The researches on its parallax by Henderson and Maclear gave it for its distance from the earth, in round numbers, 20,000,000,000,000 of miles. At the incon-ceivably rapid rate at which light is propagated through space, it would require three years and three months to reach the earth from this star.—*Whitaker.*

Chronological Cycles.

Dominical Letter.................	A	Lunar Cycle, or Golden Number. 13	Roman Indiction 6
Epact	12	Solar Cycle........ 26	Julian Period.............. 6606

Morning Stars.

MERCURY. January 1 to February 16; March 31 to June 4; August 8 to September 20; November 26 to end of the year.
VENUS. January 1 to May 2.
MARS. September 4 to end of the year.
JUPITER. April 27 to November 18.
SATURN. January 1 to March 29; October 8 to end of year.

Evening Stars.

MERCURY. February 16 to March 31; June 4 to August 8; September 20 to November 26.
VENUS. May 2 to end of year.
MARS. January 1 to September 4.
JUPITER. January 1 to April 27; November 18 to end of year.
SATURN. March 29 to October 8.

The Seasons.

			D.	H.	M.	
The Sun enters Aries,	Spring begins	March	20	4	12.3 A.M.	} New-York *Mean Time.*
" " " Cancer,	Summer begins	June	21	12	8.3 A.M.	
" " " Libra,	Autumn begins	September	22	2	59.3 P.M.	
" " " Capricornus,	Winter begins	December	21	8	57.2 A.M.	

Standard Time.

PRIMARILY, for the convenience of the railroads, a standard of time was established by mutual agreement in 1883, by which trains are run and local time regulated. According to this system, the United States, extending from 65° to 125° west longitude, is divided into four time sections, each of 15° of longitude, exactly equivalent to one hour. The first (eastern) section includes all territory between the Atlantic coast and an irregular line drawn from Detroit to Charleston, S. C., the latter being its most southern point. The second (central) section includes all territory between the last-named line and an irregular line from Bismarck, N. D., to the mouth of the Rio Grande. The third (mountain) section includes all territory between the last-named line and nearly the western borders of Idaho, Utah and Arizona. The fourth (Pacific) section covers the rest of the country to the Pacific coast. Standard time is uniform inside each of these sections, and the time of each section differs from that next to it by exactly one hour. Thus at 12 noon in New-York City (eastern time), the time at Chicago (central time) is 11 o'clock A.M.; at Denver (mountain time), 10 o'clock A.M.; and at San Francisco (Pacific time), 9 o'clock A.M. Standard time is 16 minutes slower at Boston than true local time, 4 minutes slower at New-York, 8 minutes faster at Washington, 19 minutes faster at Charleston, 28 minutes slower at Detroit, 18 minutes faster at Kansas City, 10 minutes slower at Chicago, 1 minute faster at St. Louis, 28 minutes faster at Salt Lake City, and 10 minutes faster at San Francisco.

The Ancient and Modern Year.

THE Athenians began the year in June, the Macedonians in September, the Romans first in March and afterward in January, the Persians on August 11, the ancient Mexicans on February 23, the Mohammedans in July.

The Chinese year, which begins early in February, is similar to the Mohammedan in having 12 months of 29 and 30 days alternately; but in every nineteen years there are seven years which have 13 months. This is not quite correct, and the Chinese have therefore formed a cycle of 60 years, in which period 22 intercalary months occur.

American Whist.

THE LAWS OF WHIST AS ADOPTED BY THE AMERICAN WHIST CONGRESS, NEW-YORK, JULY 19-23, 1892.

SCORING.

1. A game consists of seven points, each trick above six counting one. The value of the game is determined by deducting the loser's score from seven.

FORMING THE TABLE.

2. Those first in the room have the preference. If by reason of two or more arriving at the same time more than four assemble, the preference among the last comers is determined by cutting, a lower cut giving the preference over all cutting higher. A complete table consists of six. The four having the preference play.

3. If two players cut intermediate cards of equal value they cut again, and the lower of the new cut plays with the original lowest.

4. If three players cut cards of equal value they cut again. If the fourth has cut the highest card the lowest two of the new cut are partners, and the lowest deals. If the fourth has cut the lowest card he deals, and the highest two of the new cut are partners.

5. At the end of the game, if there are more than four belonging to the table, a sufficient number of the players retire to admit those awaiting their turn to play. In determining which players remain in, those who have played a less number of consecutive games have the preference over all who have played a greater number; between two or more who have played an equal number the preference is determined by cutting, a lower cut giving the preference over all cutting higher.

6. To entitle one to enter a table he must declare his intention to do so before any one of the players has cut for the purpose of commencing a new game or of cutting out.

CUTTING.

7. In cutting, the ace is the lowest card. All must cut from the same pack. If the player exposes more than one card he must cut again. Drawing cards from the outspread pack may be resorted to in place of cutting.

SHUFFLING.

8. Before every deal the cards must be shuffled. When two packs are used the dealer's partner must collect and shuffle the cards for the ensuing deal and place them at his right hand. In all cases the dealer may shuffle last.

9. The pack must not be shuffled during the play of a hand, nor so as to expose the face of any card.

CUTTING TO THE DEALER.

10. The dealer must present the pack to his right-hand adversary to be cut; the adversary must take a portion from the top of the pack and place it toward the centre of the table; at least four cards must be left in each packet; the dealer must reunite the packets by placing the one not removed in cutting upon the other.

11. If in cutting or in reuniting the separate packets a card is exposed, the pack must be reshuffled and cut; if there is any confusion of the cards or doubt as to the place where the pack was separated, there must be a new cut.

12. If the dealer reshuffles the cards after they have been properly cut he loses his deal.

DEALING.

13. When the pack has been properly cut and reunited the dealer must distribute the cards one at a time to each player in regular rotation, beginning at his left. The last, which is the trump card, must be turned up before the dealer. At the end of the hand, or when the deal is lost, the deal passes to the player next to the dealer on his left, and so on to each in turn.

14. There must be a new deal by the same dealer :
I. If any card except the last is faced in the pack.
II. If during the deal or during the play of the hand the pack is proved incorrect or imperfect, but any prior score made with that pack shall stand.

15. If, during the deal, a card is exposed, the side not in fault may demand a new deal, provided neither of that side has touched a card. If a new deal does not take place the exposed card cannot be called.

16. Any one dealing out of turn or with his adversaries' cards may be stopped before the trump card is turned, after which the deal is valid and the cards, if changed, so remain.

MISDEALING.

17. It is a misdeal:
I. If the dealer omits to have the pack cut and his adversaries discover the error before the trump card is turned and before looking at any of their cards.
II. If he deals a card incorrectly and fails to correct the error before dealing another.
III. If he counts the cards on the table or in the remainder of the pack.
IV. If, having a perfect pack, he does not deal to each player the proper number of cards, and the error is discovered before all have played to the first trick.
V. If he looks at the trump card before the deal is completed.
VI. If he places the trump card face downward upon his own or any other player's cards.
A misdeal loses the deal unless during the deal either of the adversaries touches the cards, or in any other manner interrupts the dealer.

THE TRUMP CARD.

18. The dealer must leave the trump card face upward on the table until it is his turn to play to the first trick. If left on the table until after the second trick has been turned and quitted, it

AMERICAN WHIST—*Continued.*

becomes an exposed card. After it has been lawfully taken up it must not be named, and any player naming it is liable to have his highest or his lowest trump called by either adversary. A player may, however, ask what the trump suit is.

IRREGULARITIES IN THE HANDS.

19. If at any time after all have played to the first trick, the pack being perfect, a player is found to have either more or less than his correct number of cards, and his adversaries have their right number, the latter, upon the discovery of such surplus or deficiency, may consult, and shall have the choice:

I. To have a new deal; or
II. To have the hand played out; in which case the surplus or missing card or cards are not taken into account.

If either of the adversaries also has more or less than his correct number there must be a new deal.

If any player has a surplus card by reason of an omission to play to a trick, his adversaries can exercise the foregoing privilege only after he has played to the trick following the one in which such omission occurred.

EXPOSED CARDS.

20. The following are exposed cards:
I. Every card faced upon the table otherwise than in the regular course of play, but not including a card led out of turn.
II. Every card thrown with the one led or played to the current trick. The player must indicate the one led or played.
III. Every card so held by a player that his partner admits that he has seen any portion of its face.
IV. All the cards in a hand so lowered or held by a player that his partner admits that he has seen the hand.
V. Every card named by the player holding it.

21. All exposed cards are liable to be called by either adversary, must be left face upward on the table, and must not be taken into the player's hand again. A player must lead or play them when they are called, provided he can do so without revoking. The call may be repeated until the card is played. A player cannot be prevented from leading or playing a card liable to be called; if he can get rid of it in the course of play no penalty remains.

22. If a player leads a card better than any his adversaries hold of the suit, and then leads one or more other cards without waiting for his partner to play, the latter may be called upon by either adversary to take the first trick, and the other cards thus improperly played are exposed cards; it makes no difference whether he plays them one after the other or throws them all on the table together; after the first card is played the others are exposed.

23. A player having an exposed card must not play until the adversaries have stated whether or not they wish to call it. If he plays another card without so waiting, such card is an exposed card.

LEADING OUT OF TURN.

24. If any player leads out of turn or before the preceding trick has been turned and quitted, a suit may be called from him or his partner when it is next the turn of either of them to lead. The penalty can be enforced only by the adversary on the right of the player from whom a suit can lawfully be called.

If a player so called on to lead a suit has none of it, or if all have played to the false lead, no penalty can be enforced. If all have not played to the trick, the cards erroneously played to such false lead cannot be called, and must be taken back.

PLAYING OUT OF TURN.

25. If the third hand plays before the second the fourth hand may also play before the second.

26. If the third hand has not played and the fourth hand plays before the second, the latter may be called upon by the third hand to play his highest or lowest card of the suit led, or, if he has none, to trump or not to trump the trick.

REVOKING.

27. A revoke is a renounce in error not corrected in time. A player renounces in error when, holding one or more cards of the suit led, he plays a card of a different suit.

28. A renounce in error may be corrected by the player making it before the trick in which it occurs has been turned and quitted, unless either he or his partner, whether in his right turn or otherwise, has led or played to the following trick, or unless his partner has asked whether or not he has any of the suit renounced.

29. If a player corrects his mistake in time to save a revoke the card improperly played by him becomes an exposed card. Any player or players who have played after him may withdraw their cards and substitute others; the cards so withdrawn are not liable to be called.

30. The penalty for revoking is the transfer of two tricks from the revoking side to their adversaries. It can be claimed for as many revokes as occur during the hand. The revoking side cannot win the game in that hand; if both sides revoke neither can win the game in that hand.

31. The revoking player and his partner may require the hand in which the revoke has been made to be played out, if the revoke loses them the game; they nevertheless score all points made by them up to the score of six.

32. At the end of a hand the claimants of a revoke may search all the tricks. If the cards have been mixed the claim may be urged and proved if possible; but no proof is necessary and the

AMERICAN WHIST—*Continued.*

revoke is established if after it has been claimed the accused player or his partner mixes the cards before they have been examined to the satisfaction of the adversaries.

33. The revoke can be claimed at any time before the cards have been presented and cut for the following deal, but not thereafter.

MISCELLANEOUS.

34. If a player is lawfully called upon to play the highest or lowest of a suit or to trump or not to trump a trick, or to lead a suit, and unnecessarily fails to comply, he is liable to the same penalty as if he had revoked.

35. Any one during the play of a trick and before the cards have been touched for the purpose of gathering them together may demand that the players draw their cards.

36. If any one, prior to his partner playing, calls attention in any manner to the trick or to the score, the adversary last to play to the trick may require the offender's partner to play his highest or lowest of the suit led, or, if he has none, to trump or not to trump the trick.

37. In all cases where a penalty has been incurred the offender must await the decision of the adversary entitled to exact it. If the wrong adversary demands a penalty, or a wrong penalty is demanded, none can be enforced.

38. When a trick has been turned and quitted it must not again be seen until after the hand has been played. A violation of this law subjects the offender's side to the same penalty as in case of a lead out of turn.

39. If any player says, "I can win the rest," "The rest are ours," "We have the game," or words to that effect, his partner's hand must be laid upon the table and treated as exposed cards.

40. League clubs may adopt any rule requiring or permitting methods of scoring or of forming the table different from those above prescribed.

THE AMERICAN WHIST LEAGUE.
OFFICERS.

President, Eugene S. Elliott, Milwaukee, Wis.
Vice-President, J. M. Walton, Philadelphia, Pa.
Recording Secretary W. H. Barney, Providence, R. I.
Corresponding Secretary, Theodore Schwartz, Chicago, Ill.
Treasurer, C. A. Chapin, Milwaukee, Wis.

Directors: A. G. Safford, Washington, D. C.; H. A. Mandell, Detroit, Mich.; N. B. Trist, New-Orleans, La.; E. LeRoy Smith, Albany, N. Y.; T. C. Orndorff, Worcester, Mass.; J. H. Briggs, Minneapolis, Minn.; H. S. Stevens, Chicago, Ill.; C. H. Keyes, Pasadena, Cal.; Geo. W. Carr, New-York, N. Y.; C. D. P. Hamilton, Easton, Pa.

WHIST LEADS.

CARDS AT HEAD OF SUIT.	NUMBER OF CARDS IN SUIT.				
	3	4	5	6	7
A. K. Q. J		K.-J.	J.-A.	J.-K.	J.-Q.
A. K. Q	K.-Q.	K.-Q.	Q.-A.	Q.-K.	**
A. K. (plain)...........	K.-A.	K.-A.	A.-K.	*	*
A. K. J. (trumps).......	K.-A.	K.-A.	A.-K.	A.-K.	A.-K.
A. K. (trumps)........	K.-A.	4th.	4th.	4th.	A.-K.
A. Q. J. 10		A.-10	A.-J.	*	*
A. Q. J	A.-Q.	A.-Q.	A.-J.	*	*
A. (plain)	A. (1)	4th-A.	A.-4th.	*	*
A. (trumps)...	A.	4th-A.	4th-A.	4th-A.	A.-4th.
K. Q. J. 10		K.-10.	J.-K.	J.-Q.	**
K. Q. J	K.-Q.	K.-J.	J.-K.	J.-Q.	**
K. Q. (plain)...........	K.-Q.	K. (2)	Q. (3)	*	*
K. Q. 10 (trumps)......	K.-Q.	K. (2)	Q. (3)	Q. (3)	Q. (3)
K. Q. (trumps)........	K.-Q.	4th.	4th.	4th.	Q. (3)
K. J. 10	10-K.	10. (4)	10. (4)	*	*
K	K. (1)	4th.	4th	*	*
Q. J. 10. 9		Q.-9.	Q.-10.	*	*
Q. J. 10	Q.-J.	Q.-J.	Q.-10.	*	*
Q. J	Q.-J.	4th.	4th.	*	*
Q	Q. (1)	4th.	4th.	*	*
J. 10. 9. 8. (trumps)....		J.-8.	J.-9.	*	*
J. 10. 9. (trumps).......	J.-10	J.-10.	J.-9.	*	*
All other cards	Best.	4th.	4th.	*	*

* Lead as in a five-card suit.   ** Lead as in a six-card suit.   (1) If partner has not shown strength in suit, lead lowest.   (2) If K. wins, follow with original 4th best.   (3) If Q. wins, follow with 4th best remaining in hand.   (4) If 10 wins, follow with original 4th best. If A. falls and Q. does not, follow with K. If Q. falls, follow with K. from four, with J. from more.

"Whist leads" was compiled from the nineteenth edition of "Cavendish," for the American Whist League.

Chess.

THE PRIZE PROBLEMS OF 1892.*

NEW-YORK CHESS ASSOCIATION.
Black.

NEW-YORK CHESS ASSOCIATION.
Black.

White.
White to play and mate in two moves.

White.
White to play and mate in two moves.

1892 was a notable year in the annals of the royal game and chronicled many important events. Showalter opened the new year by wresting the United States championship from Max Judd, of St. Louis, who had defeated him in a previous match. In the return meeting, which terminated in January, 1892, Showalter won by the score of 7 to 4. He was then challenged by S. Lipschutz, of the Manhattan Club of New-York, who won the United States championship by the decisive score of 7 to 1. The return match, involving the championship of the world, began January 1, between Steinitz and Tschigorin, at Havana, and was won by the former by the score of 10 to 8 and 5 draws.

Meetings were held as usual in many of the States on Washington's Birthday. At the fourteenth annual meeting of the New-York State Association thirty-two masters participated, and the chief honors were divided among Messrs. Hodges, Olley, Delmar, and Eccles, Messrs. Halpern, Ferris, and De Visser winning the prizes for problem-solving. At the midsummer meeting, Voight won the first prize, and Hodges, who holds the championship, defeated Delmar in a set match by five straight wins. S. Lisner, of Hoboken, won the New-Jersey championship at the annual meeting, held at Newark. S. N. Cunningham won the Rhode-Island championship at the Providence meeting, and G. L. Curtis carried off the Ohio honors at Toledo.

The summer meeting of the Indiana Association was held at Kokomo, and was won by H. C. Brown, but at the December meeting, held at Logansport, the championship was won by Otto Ballar, and an exhibition match, which was played between Showalter and Lasker, resulted in a tie, and will be decided by a set match of seven games, for a stake of $1,500.

The first meeting of the Texas Chess Association was held at San Antonio, and resulted in a tie for chief honors between Messrs. Ford and Norton.

Team matches were played by telegraph between the Manhattan Club of New-York and the New-Orleans Club, the former winning by the score of 6½ to 3½. The City Club of New-York lost to the Brooklyn Club in a team match by the score of 14½ to 9½, but defeated the Juniors, of Philadelphia, 6 to 4.

The National Tournament in London closed March 18, the winners being: Lasker, 9; Mason, 7½; Loman, 7; Bird and Locock, 6½. Lasker won the London Master's Tournament in April, and then won set matches against Blackburne, Bird, and other masters, without suffering a single defeat. He then challenged Dr. Tarrash, who, for the fourth time in succession, had carried off the international honors of the German Association held at Dresden. Tarrash declined to play upon the grounds that Lasker had not won his spurs in an international contest.

Lasker arrived in the United States on October 6, 1892, and played a series of exhibition games against the leading players of the most prominent clubs throughout the United States. It has been computed that he lost but twenty-five games out of nearly four hundred, but the result cannot be accepted as an international test, as he has yet to meet our best players in set matches.

The intercollegiate tournament for a $500 trophy began in New-York on December 27, between representative champions selected from the different colleges, and terminated on January 2, 1893, Columbia winning by the score of 9 to 3, Edward Hymes winning six straights, and his associate, Edward Libaire, four. Harvard secured second place, with a score of 7½ to 4½. The Harvard players were Sidney M. Ballou and George B. Wilson. The Yale champions, Arthur Bumstead and Alburn E. Skinner, won 5 to 7. Samuel Dickey and Boyd R. Ewing, of Princeton, scored 2½ to 9½. Tournaments will be held in the colleges during the year to select representative champions, who will compete in the annual contest for the intercollegiate championship which will be held each year in the city of New-York to determine which college shall hold the trophy for the ensuing year. At present the competition is limited to Columbia, Harvard, Yale, and Princeton, but after the year 1895 all the colleges of the United States will enter the lists.

William Steinitz, who has held the world's chess championship for upward of twenty years without the loss of a single match, has officially announced his retirement from active match play, and declined defies which were issued in behalf of Dr. Tarrash and E. Lasker.

* By S. Loyd.

THE AMERICAN TURF—RECORD OF BEST PERFORMANCES—*Continued.*

With Running Mate.

Distance.	Name.	Place.	Date.	Time.		
1 mile	H. B. Winship*	Narragansett, R. I	Aug. 1, 1884	......	......	2.06
PACING—IN HARNESS.						
1 mile	Mascot	Terre Haute, Ind	Sept. 29, 1892	......	......	2.04
1 " in a race	Mascot	Terre Haute, Ind	Sept. 29, 1892	......	......	2.04
1 " best three heats	Mascot	Columbus, Ind	Sept. 24, 1892	2.08¼	2.07	2.07¾
1 " by a yearling	Belle Acton*	Wichita, Kan	Sept. 29, 1892	......	......	2.21¼
1 " by a two-year old	Ouline*	Lyons, Neb	Oct. 14, 1892	......	......	2.11
1 " by a three-year old	Manager*	Independence, Iowa	Sept. 19, 1891	......	......	2.11½
1 " by a four-year old	William Wood*	Stockton, Cal	Oct. 29, 1892	......	......	2.07
1 " by a five-year old	Storm	Nashville, Tenn.	Oct. 22, 1892	......	......	2.08¼
1 " best by a mare	Vinette	Terre Haute, Ind	Sept. 29, 1892	......	......	2.09¼
1 " best by a stallion in a race	Guy	Terre Haute, Ind	Sept. 29, 1892	......	......	2.06¾
1 " by a stallion against time	Direct*	Nashville, Tenn	Nov. 8, 1892	......	......	2.05½
2 miles	Defiance ... / Longfellow	Sacramento, Cal	Sept. 26, 1872	......	......	4.47¾
3 " in a race	James K. Polk	Centreville, L. I	Sept. 13, 1847	......	......	7.44
3 "	Joe Jefferson*	Knoxville, Iowa	Nov. 6, 1891	......	......	7.33¼
4 "	Joe Jefferson*	Knoxville, Iowa	Nov. 13, 1891	......	......	10.10
5 " in a race	Fisherman	San Francisco, Cal	Dec. 19, 1874	......	......	13.03½
PACING—TO WAGON.						
1 mile	Roy Wilkes*	Independence, Iowa	Oct. 30, 1891	......	......	2.13
1 mile in a race	Johnston	Detroit, Mich	July 21, 1887	......	......	2.14½
2 miles	Young America	......	......	......	......	4.58½
3 "	Longfellow	Sacramento, Cal	Sept. 7, 1869	......	......	7.53
4 "	Longfellow	San Francisco, Cal	Dec. 31, 1869	......	......	10.42½
5 " in a race	Lady St. Clair	San Francisco, Cal	Dec. 11, 1874	......	......	12.54¾
Fastest 3 heats	Johnston	St. Paul, Minn	Sept. 16, 1887	2.16¼	2.15¼	2.15¼
Under Saddle.						
1 mile	Johnston*	Cleveland, Ohio	Aug. 3, 1888	......	......	2.13
2 miles	James K. Polk. / Roanoke	Philadelphia, Pa	June 20, 1850	......	......	4.57½
3 "	Oneida Chief	Hoboken, N. J	Aug. 15, 1843	......	......	7.44
By a Team.						
1 mile	Daisy D. and Silver Tail	East Saginaw, Mich*	July 15, 1887	......	......	2.18½
With a Running Mate.						
1 mile	Westmont	Chicago, Ill	July 10, 1884	......	......	2.01¾

* Against time.

The English Derby.

THE Derby was first run on May 4th, 1780; it was then a dash of a mile, and was won by Sir Charles Banbury's Diomed, by Florizel. In 1799 he was imported into the United States, and to him can be traced nearly all the best of the American racing families. In 1784 the distance was increased to a mile and a half, and the weights raised to 115 pounds for colts and 112 pounds for fillies. The present course was first used in 1872. In 1884 the weights were raised to 126 pounds for colts and 121 pounds for fillies. The winners since 1867 were:

Year.	Owner and Winner.	Sire.	Subs.	Starters.	Time.	Second.
1867	Mr. H. Chaplin's Hermit	Newminster	256	30	2.52	Marksman.
1868	Sir J. Hawley's Blue Gown	Beadsman	262	18	2.43 1-2	King Alfred.
1869	Mr. J. Johnstone's Pretender	Adventurer	247	22	2.52 1-2	Pero Gomez.
1870	Lord Falmouth's Kingcraft	King Tom	252	15	2.45	Palmerston.
1871	Baron Rothschild's Favonius	Parmesan	209	17	2.50	Albert Victor. / King of the Forest.
1872	Mr. Savile's Cremorne	Parmesan	191	23	2.45 1-2	Pell Mell.
1873	Mr. Merry's Doncaster	Stockwell	201	12	2.50	Gang Forward. / Kaiser.
1874	Mr. Cartwright's George Frederick.	Marsyas	212	20	2.46	Couronne de Fer.
1875	Prince Batthyany's Galopin	Vedette	199	18	2.48	Claremont.
1876	Mr. A. Battazzi's Kisber	Buccaneer	226	15	2.44	Forerunner.
1877	Lord Falmouth's Silvio	Blair Athol	245	17	2.50	Glen Arthur.
1878	Mr. Crawfurd's Sefton	Speculum	231	22	2.56	Insulaire.
1879	Mr. Acton's Sir Bevys	Favonius	278	23	3.02	Palmbearer.
1880	Duke of Westminster's Bend Or	Doncaster	257	19	2.46	Robert the Devil.
1881	Mr. P. Lorillard's Iroquois	Leamington	242	15	2.50	Peregrine.
1882	Duke of Westminster's Shotover	Hermit	198	14	2.45 3-5	Quicklime.
1883	Sir F. Johnstone's St. Blaise	Hermit	215	11	2.48 2-5	Highland Chief.
1884	Mr. J. Hammond's St. Gatien / Sir J. Willoughby's Harvester	Rotherhill or The Rover. / Stirling	189	15	2.46 1-5	......
1885	Lord Hasting's Melton	Master Kildare	189	12	2.44 1-5	Paradox.
1886	Duke of Westminster's Ormonde	Bend Or	199	9	2.45 3-5	The Bard.
1887	Mr. Abington's Merry Hampton	Hampton	190	11	2.43	The Baron.
1888	Duke of Portland's Ayrshire	Hampton	158	9	2.42 1-5	Crowberry.
1889	Duke of Portland's Donovan	Galopin	169	13	2.44 2-5	Miguel.
1890	Sir James Miller's Sainfoin	Springfield	233	8	2.49 1-4	Le Nord.
1891	Sir F. Johnson's br. c. Common	Isonomy	203	11	2.56 4-5	Gouverneur.
1892	Lord Bradford's ch. c. Sir Hugo	Wisdom	259	13	2.44	La Flèche.

Game Laws.

NEW-YORK.

THESE are the regulations of the new game law of May 5, 1892, and in force January 1, 1893. *Changes are liable during year.*

Deer.—Open season in Kings, Queens, and Suffolk Counties and Long Island Sound from November 10 to 16; elsewhere, from August 16 to October 31; but absolutely prohibited in Ulster, Greene, Sullivan, and Delaware Counties till August 16, 1897. Taking alive for breeding in State deer parks permitted at any time anywhere. Only two can be killed or taken alive by anybody each season. Fawns must never be killed or caught. No traps, salt licks, or other devices can be made or used. Dogs can be used in Sullivan County from October 1 to November 30; in Kings, Queens, and Suffolk Counties and Long Island Sound from November 10 to 16; elsewhere, from September 11 to October 10, but never in St. Lawrence, Delaware, Greene, or Ulster Counties. Any one may shoot dogs so used at other times. Can be sold only from August 16 to November 14, and possessed only from August 16 to October 31. Only one carcass killed in New-York may be transported when accompanied by owner. Crusting or the shooting or capturing of yarded deer forbidden.

Moose, Caribou, and Antelope.—Hunting, killing, possession, or sale absolutely forbidden.

Hares and Rabbits.—Open season in Kings, Queens, and Suffolk Counties and Long Island Sound from November 1 to December 31; elsewhere, any time.

Black and Gray Squirrels.—Open season in Kings, Queens, and Suffolk Counties and Long Island Sound from November 1 to December 31; elsewhere, from September 1 to December 31.

Web-Footed Wild Fowl.—Except wild geese and brant. Open season in Kings, Queens, and Suffolk Counties and Long Island Sound from October 1 to April 30; elsewhere, from September 1 to April 30. Hours limited to from dawn to sunset.

Quail.—Open season from November 1 to December 31; but on Robbin's Island, while belonging to the Robbins Island Club, from October 15 to January 31. Killing or possession forbidden for five years in Genesee, Wyoming, Orleans, Livingston, Monroe, Cayuga, Seneca, Wayne, Tompkins, Tioga, Onondaga, Ontario, Steuben, and Cortland Counties. Can be sold from November 1 to January 31, and possessed from November 1 to December 31. Cannot be snared, trapped, or netted.

Partridge, all Grouse, and Woodcock.—Open season in Kings, Queens, and Suffolk Counties and Long Island Sound from November 1 to December 31; elsewhere, from August 15 to December 31. Can be sold in above counties from November 1 to January 31; elsewhere, from August 15 to January 31, and possessed in above counties from November 1 to December 31; elsewhere, from August 15 to December 31. Transportation allowed only when with owner. No partridge or grouse can be snared, trapped, or netted.

Robins.—Must never be killed.

Wild Birds.—Must never be killed, except English sparrow, crane, hawk, crow, raven, crow-blackbird, common blackbirds, or kingfishers.

Bass.—Black and Oswego; open season from June 1 to December 31, but in Lake George from August 1 to December 31, and in Black Lake, St. Lawrence County, from May 6 to December 31. Black bass must be eight inches long.

Muskallonge.—Open season from June 1 to December 31.

Pike.—Open season always, save in Susquehanna and tributaries from November 1 to May 30.

Salmon.—Open season from March 1 to August 15. Must be eighteen inches long.

Salmon Trout and Land-locked Salmon.—Open season in Kings, Queens, and Suffolk Counties and Long Island Sound from April 1 to September 30; elsewhere, in inland waters, May 1 to September 30. Salmon trout can be sold if not caught during closed season, and be possessed from May 1 to September 30. Must not be molested while spawning. Transportation allowed only when with owner.

Shad and Herring.—Open season in Rondout Creek, and Hudson and Delaware Rivers from March 15 to June 15 (netting then permitted, save from sunset Saturdays to sunrise Mondays). Nets forbidden north of dam at Troy. Open season elsewhere always.

Trout.—Open season in Kings, Queens, and Suffolk Counties and Long Island Sound, in Spring Brook Creek (in Monroe and Livingston Counties), from April 1 to August 31, and in Lake George from May 1 to August 31; elsewhere, from April 15 to August 31. Must be six inches long. Must not be molested while spawning. Transportation allowed only when with owner.

Shooting on Sunday, fishing within fifty rods of State fisheries and fishways, drawing off water to catch fish, pollution of waters, and stocking of the Adirondack waters with any fish except of the salmon and trout families, fishing through the ice in waters inhabited by trout, salmon trout, or land-locked salmon, prohibited. Salmon, black bass, trout, salmon trout, pike, and perch caught in nets, in fishing for other fish in the Hudson River, must be cast back.

PENNSYLVANIA.

BIRDS AND ANIMALS.	Open Season.	FISH.	Open Season.
Turkeys	Oct. 15 to Jan. 1	Wall-eyed Pike	June 1 to Jan. 1
Ducks	Sept. 1 to May 1	Salmon or Speckled Trout	April 1 to Aug. 1
Plover	July 15 to Jan. 1	Shad (with nets)	Jan. 1 to June 20
Woodcock	July 4 to Jan. 1	Lake Trout	Jan. 1 to Sept. 30
Quail	Nov. 1 to Dec. 15	Pickerel	June 1 to Dec. 31
Ruffed Grouse or Pheasant	Oct. 1 to Jan. 1	Black and Rock Bass	May 30 to Jan. 1
Rail and Reed Bird	Sept. 1 to Dec. 1	Delaware River Shad, above Trenton,	
Snipe and Wild Pigeons	Any time.	fishing with nets prohibited from	Jan. 1 to June 15
Elk and Deer	Oct. 1 to Dec. 15	Below Trenton	June 15 to July 10
Squirrels	Sept. 1 to Jan. 1	Hunting and fishing on Sunday unlawful.	
Hares and Rabbits	Nov. 1 to Jan. 1		

NEW-JERSEY.

	Open Season.		Open Season.
Ruffed Grouse	Sept. 30 to Dec. 16	Gray and Black Squirrel	Sept. 14 to Dec. 16
Quail	Oct. 31 to Dec. 16	Fox Squirrel	Aug. 31 to Jan. 1
Woodcock	July and Sept. 30 to Dec. 16	Rabbit and Hare	Oct. 31 to Dec. 16
Upland Plover	July 31 to Dec. 16	Deer	Oct. 31 to Dec. 1
English Snipe	Mar. 1 to April 31, Sept. 30 to Dec. 16	Salmon Trout	Mar. 1 to Oct. 1
Prairie Chicken	Oct. 31 to Jan. 1	Brook Trout	Mar. 31 to July 15
Reed and Rail Bird and Marsh Hen	Aug. 25 to Dec. 16	Black and Oswego Bass	May 29 to Dec. 1
Wood Duck	Aug. 31 to Jan. 1	Pickerel and Pike	April 30 to Mar. 1

In all the States there is a penalty of from $5 to $50 for killing song-birds.

American Turf Events of 1892.

Jan. 1. The first race of the year was run at Guttenburg, N. J., and was won by Eugene Leigh's b. f. Ma Belle, by imp. Charaxus, 113 pounds, Martin up, at 5 to 2; Beaverhead stable's Comet was second, and A. J. Carlin's Houston, third; five furlongs in 1.02.

Jan. 4. Racing at Guttenburg was postponed on account of bad weather.

Jan. 5. The Board of Control appointed James Rowe starter at the Board of Control tracks. Jockey Garrison received his license.

Jan. 6. THE WORLD exclusively announced the entries in the Suburban and Brooklyn Handicaps.

Jan. 6. Racing was again postponed at Guttenburg on account of bad weather.

Jan. 8. Toano, 116 pounds, H. Penny up, ran 4½ furlongs at Guttenburg in 0.54, a new record.

Jan. 12. J. Malcolm Forbes, of Boston, bought Arion, 3 years old, by Electioneer, from Senator Leland Stanford, at a price reported to be $150,000.

Jan. 13. The big mid-winter sales of trotters began in New-York City.

Jan. 16. Guttenburg bookmakers were arrested on warrants sworn out by the Law and Order Society.

Jan. 31. M. F. Dwyer's Longstreet was assigned top weight in the Brooklyn Handicap, 128 pounds; D. T. Pulsefer's Tenny, second weight, 127 pounds, and M. F. Dwyer's Kingston, third weight, 125 pounds. Longstreet was also given top weight in the Suburban, 132 pounds; Tenny and Kingston, second, 129 pounds each, and Eon, third, 124 pounds.

Feb. 19. Longstreet and Kingston were declared from the Suburban Handicap.

Feb. 24. The New-York, Coney-Island, and Brooklyn Jockey Clubs agreed to set apart some of their racing dates for the use of the Monmouth Park Association.

Feb. 28. Foxhall, winner of the Cambridgeshire and Cesarewitch in 1881, arrived in New-York after a stormy voyage.

March 4. La Grippe ch. h., 5, by Luke Blackburn-Longitude, fell at Guttenburg in a race, and was killed.

March 12. Jockey Blakely was ruled off at Guttenburg for pulling Benefit.

March 17. Jockey Snyder was ruled off at Guttenburg for pulling Forty in the Shamrock Stakes.

March 18. Jockey Cook was found riding Gyda with an electrical spur at Guttenburg. A rule was passed prohibiting a jockey from using anything in the future but whip and spur.

April 7. The Board of Control refused to accept the entries of the owner of any horse trained on the Winter race tracks.

May 11. Bashford Manor's b. c. Azra, by Reform-Albia (Clayton), won the Kentucky Derby; E. Corrigan's Huron (Britton), second, and E. Corrigan's Phil Dwyer (Overton), third. Time, 2.41½.

May 16. Green Morris' b. h. Judge Morrow, 5, by Vagabond-Moonlight, 116 pounds (A. Covington), won the Brooklyn Handicap; Wolcott and Campbell's Pessarra, 4, 115 pounds, was second, and J. A. and A. H. Morris' Russell, 4, 114 pounds, was third. Time, 2.08¾.

May 26. Oneck stable's b. c. Sir Walter, by Midlothian-La Scala (Garrison), won the Great American; F. A. Ehret's Don Alonzo, second, and J. Ruppert, Jr.'s Ajax, third. Time, 1.01¼.

May 30. Wolcott and Campbell's b. h. Pessarra, 4, by Pizarro-Sister Monica, 117 pounds (Taral), won the Metropolitan Handicap; Rancocas stable's Locohatchee, second; L. L. Lorillard's Sleipner, third. Time, 1.54.

June 11. Oneck stable's b. c. Sir Walter, 2, by Midlothian-La Scala, 118 pounds (Taral), won the Great Eclipse Stakes; F. A. Ehret's Don Alonzo, second, and Gideon and Daly's Dr. Rice, third. Time, 1.15½.

June 18. Marcus Daly's b. c. Montana, 4, by Ban Fox-Imported Queen, 115 pounds (Garrison), won the Suburban; W. J. Spiers' Major Domo, 115 pounds, second; Rancocas stable's Lamplighter, 104, third. Time, 2.07 2-5.

June 20. The Board of Control revoked the license of A. F. Van Ness.

July 2. Marcus Daly's Tammany, 3, by Iroquois-Tullahoma, 119 pounds (Garrison), won the Realization; J. E. Pepper and Co.'s The Pepper was second; L. Stewart's Patron, third. Time, 2.51 2-5.

July 4. The Monmouth Park race track was reopened, and 30,000 people saw the racing.

July 5. The Law and Order Society of Monmouth County arrested the bookmakers at Monmouth Park.

July 6. Brighton Beach race track began a war on the New-York pool rooms.

July 8. The fight between the pool rooms and Brighton Beach was settled.

July 9. Marcus Daly's Tammany, 122 pounds (Garrison), won the Lorillard; The Pepper, second; Bashford Manor's Azra, third. Time, 2.20½.

July 13. Jockey William Martin and owner Eugene Leigh were ruled off the Brighton Beach track because of the running of Ma Belle.

Aug. 10. F. A. Ehret's b. c. Don Alonzo, 118 pounds (Sloane), won the Junior Champion; Blemton stable's Lady Violet, second; Gideon and Daly's Dr. Rice, third. Time, 1.12½. Brown and Rogers' b. c. Lamplighter, 3, by Spendthrift-Torchlight, won the Champion Stakes; M. F. Dwyer's Banquet, second; Rancocas stable's Locahatchee, third. Time, 2.32¾.

Aug. 13. Rancocas stable's b. m. Kildeer, 4, by Darebin-Loulanier, 91 pounds, ran a mile at Monmouth Park, straight course, in 1.37¼.

Aug. 27. F. Van Ness' Morello, by Eolus-Cerise, 118 pounds (W. Hayward), won the Futurity; Blemton stable's Lady Violet, second; J. R. Keene's St. Blaise-Belladonna colt, third. Time, 1.12 1-5.

Sept. 7. The license of C. Oxx, owner of the horse Watterson, was revoked by the Board of Control.

Sept. 10. Blemton stable's b. f. Lady Violet, by St. Blaise-Lady Primrose, 125 pounds (Garrison), won the Great Eastern Handicap; F. A. Ehret's Sir Francis, second; same stable's Don Alonzo, third. Time, 1.10 1-5.

Sept. 23. War Path, Ha' Penny, and John Cavanagh fell at the Gravesend track, and were killed.

Sept. 28. Nancy Hanks trotted on a regulation track at Terre Haute, Ind., drawing a pneumatic tire sulky, in 2.04.

Oct. 1. F. A. Ehret's ch. c. Sir Francis, by Mr. Pickwick-Thora, 118½ pounds (Garrison), won the Matron Stakes; Boyle and Littlefield's Miss Maud, second; W. Donohue's Panique-Rebecca Rowett colt, third. Time, 1.10.

Oct. 10. Wm. Barricks' Dr. Hasbrouck, 4, by Sir Modred-Sweetbriar, 122 pounds (Doggett), ran five furlongs in 0.57; Rancocas stable's Yemen, 3, by Alarm-Hira, 105½ pounds, ran six furlongs in 1.09¾; both on the straight track at Morris Park.

Oct. 11. M. F. Dwyer's b. c. Nomad, 3, by Wildidle-Amelia, 119 pounds (Taral), ran 1.5-16 miles in 2.15 at Morris Park.

Oct. 16. THE WORLD published a complete list of the winning owners of the Eastern Turf.

Oct. 17. The sale of the Algeria stud was begun, eighty head selling for $117,000.

Oct. 19. Imported Rayon d'Or was sold to August Belmont for $32,000.

Nov. 1. W. O'B. McDonough, of San Francisco, Cal., bought Ormonde for $150,000.

Weight-Throwing Records.

PERFORMANCE.	Thrower.	Distance. Ft.	In.
Putting 16-lb. shot..........	Geo. R. Gray......	46	7¾
Putting 21-lb. shot..........	Geo. R. Gray......	39	1⅛
Putting 20-lb. shot..........	Geo. R. Gray......	38	7⅛
Putting 24-lb. shot..........	Geo. R. Gray......	33	11¾
Throwing 16-lb. hammer...	J. S. Mitchell......	145	¾

PERFORMANCE.	Thrower.	Distance. Ft.	In.
Throwing 21-lb. hammer...	C. Queckberner.	90	3
Throwing 56-lb. weight for height....................	J. S. Mitchell..	15	2
Throwing 56-lb. weight for distance..................	J. S. Mitchell..	35	6⅛

University Boat=Racing.

INTERNATIONAL RACING.

1869, August 17. Oxford (Eng.) four beat Harvard (Am.) four over the Putney-Mortlake course on the Thames by three clear lengths. Time, 22.17.

1876, September 1. Yale four beat Columbia four at the Centennial Regatta, rowed over a mile and a half course on the Schuylkill, in 9.10¾ ; Columbia, 9.21. A four from First Trinity College, Cambridge, Eng., was entered, but withdrew by reason of illness of one of the four.

1878, a Columbia College four won the Visitors' Challenge Cup at Henley Regatta, Eng., in 8.42.

HARVARD AND YALE UNIVERSITY EIGHTS.

The Harvard and Yale University "eights" have rowed as follows—distance, four miles straight :

Date.	Course.	Winner.	Time.	Loser.	Time.
June 30, 1876......	Springfield, Mass.	Yale........	22.02	Harvard....	22.33
June 30, 1877......	" "	Harvard....	24.36	Yale......	24.44
June 28, 1878......	New-London, Ct.	"	20.44¾	"	21.29
June 27, 1879......	" "	"	22.15	"	23.58
July 1, 1880......	" "	Yale........	24.27	Harvard....	25.09
July 1, 1881......	" "	"	22.13	"	22.19
June 30, 1882......	" "	Harvard....	20.47	Yale......	20.50½
June 28, 1883......	" "	"	24.26	"	25.59
June 26, 1884......	" "	Yale........	20.31	Harvard....	20.46
June 26, 1885......	" "	Harvard....	25.15½	Yale......	26.30
July 2, 1886......	" "	Yale........	20.41¼	Harvard....	21.05¾
July 1, 1887......	" "	"	22.56	"	23.10½
June 29, 1888......	" "	"	20.10	"	21.24
June 29, 1889......	" "	"	21.30	"	21.55
June 27, 1890......	" "	"	21.29	"	21.40
June 26, 1891......	" "	Harvard....	21.23	Yale......	21.57
July 1, 1892......	" "	Yale........	20.48	Harvard....	21.42½

HARVARD AND YALE—PREVIOUS RACES.

Previous races in which Harvard and Yale have rowed are summarized as follows :

1852, August 3. Lake Winipiseogee, Centre Harbor, N. H., two miles straight to windward, in eight-oared barges, class of 1853, Oneida, of Harvard, beat Halcyon, of Yale, two lengths.

1855, July 21. Connecticut River, at Springfield, three miles with a turn, in barges Iris (eight-oared) and Y.Y. (four-oared), of Harvard, beat Nereid and Nautilus (both sixes), of Yale. Allowances, eleven seconds per oar. Time : Iris, 22 m. ; Y.Y., 22.03 ; Nereid, 23.38, and Nautilus, 24.38.

1858, no race. George E. Dunham, stroke of the Yale crew, was drowned at Springfield, six days, before the race, in a collision while at practice.

1859, July 26. Lake Quinsigamond, Worcester, Mass., three miles with a turn, Harvard shell, 19.18 ; Yale shell, 20.18. Harvard lapstreak, Avon, 21.13 ; Brown lapstreak, Atalanta, 24.40. Same course, July 27, in Citizen's regatta, Yale shell, 19.14 ; Harvard, 19.16.

1860, July 24. Lake Quinsigamond, Harvard, 18.53 ; Yale, 19.05 ; Brown, 21.15.

There were no further races until 1864, when they were renewed by University six-oared crews, at three miles with a turn, and with the following results :

Date.	Course.	Winner.	Time.	Loser.	Time.
July 29, 1864......	Lake Quinsigamond	Yale..... ..	19.01	Harvard....	19.43½
July 28, 1865......	" "	"	17.42½	"	18.09
July 27, 1866......	" "	Harvard....	18.43	Yale........	19.10
July 19, 1867......	" "	"	18.13	"	19.25½
July 24, 1868......	At Worcester, Mass.	"	17.48½	"	18 38½
July 23, 1869......	Lake Quinsigamond	"	18.02	"	18.11
July 22, 1870......	Lake Saltonstall	.....	(Foul)	"	Disq.

In 1871 was begun what were then known as the Inter-University Races, in which Harvard and Yale were contestants.

1871, July 21. At Springfield, three miles straight, Massachusetts Agricultural, 16.46½ ; Harvard, 17.23½ ; Brown, 17.47½.

1872, July 24. At Springfield, same course, Amherst, 16.33 ; Harvard, 16.57 ; Amherst Agricultural, 17.10 ; Bowdoin, 17.31 ; Williams, 17.59 ; Yale, 18.13.

1873, July 17. At Springfield, same course, Yale, 16.59 ; Wesleyan, 17.09 ; Harvard, 17.36½ ; Amherst, 17.40 ; Dartmouth, 18.07 ; Columbia, 18.16 ; Massachusetts Agricultural, 18.26½ ; Cornell, 18.32 ; Bowdoin, 18.49½ ; Trinity, 19.32 ; and Williams, 19.45.

1874, July 18. At Saratoga, N. Y., three miles straight, Columbia, 16.42 ; Wesleyan, 16.50 ; Harvard, 16.54 ; Williams, 17.08 ; Cornell, 17.31 ; Dartmouth, 18.00 ; Trinity, 18.23 ; Princeton, 18.38 ; Yale fouled and withdrawn.

1875, July 14. At Saratoga, N. Y., Cornell, 16.53½ ; Columbia, 17.04½ ; Harvard, 17.05 ; Dartmouth, 17.10½ ; Wesleyan, 17.13½ ; Yale, 17.14½ ; Amherst, 17.29½ ; Brown, 17.33½ ; Williams, 17.43½ ; Bowdoin, 17.50½ ; Hamilton and Union not timed ; Princeton withdrawn.

1876, July 19. At Saratoga, N. Y., Cornell, 17.01½ ; Harvard, 17.05½ ; Columbia, 17.08½ ; Union, 17.27½ ; Wesleyan, 17.58½ ; Princeton, 18.10. Yale refused to enter, but rowed Harvard an eight-oared race as above.

Baseball Records.

CHAMPIONSHIP OF AMERICA.

From 1884 to 1890, inclusive, the winners of the respective pennants of the National League and American Association played a post-season series for the championship of America. This series was omitted in 1891, owing to strained relations between the two bodies. In 1892 the Bostons and Clevelands, the winners of the first and second divisions of the League's season, played for the championship. The results:

Year.	Contesting Teams.	Results of Series.					
1884	Providence vs. Metropolitans	Providence	3	Metropolitans	0	Drawn	0
1885	Chicago vs. St. Louis	Chicago	3	St. Louis	3	Drawn	1
1886	Chicago vs. St. Louis	Chicago	2	St. Louis	4	Drawn	0
1887	Detroit vs. St. Louis	Detroit	11	St. Louis	4	Drawn	0
1888	New-York vs. St. Louis	New-York	6	St. Louis	4	Drawn	0
1889	New-York vs. St. Louis	New-York	6	Brooklyn	3	Drawn	0
1890	Brooklyn vs. Louisville	Brooklyn	3	Louisville	3	Drawn	1
1891	No games played.						
1892	Boston vs. Cleveland	Boston	5	Cleveland	0	Drawn	1

THE NATIONAL LEAGUE.

The record of the champion team of the National League, together with the name of the leading batter each year, since its organization, is as follows:

Year.	Champion Club.	Won.	Lost.	Average.	Champion Batter.	Club.	Average.
1876	Chicago	52	14	.788	Barnes	Chicago	.403
1877	Boston	31	17	.648	White	Boston	.385
1878	Boston	41	19	.707	Dalrymple	Milwaukee	.356
1879	Providence	55	23	.705	Anson	Chicago	.407
1880	Chicago	67	17	.798	Gore	Chicago	.365
1881	Chicago	56	28	.667	Anson	Chicago	.399
1882	Chicago	55	29	.655	Brouthers	Buffalo	.367
1883	Boston	63	35	.643	Brouthers	Buffalo	.371
1884	Providence	84	28	.750	O'Rourke	Buffalo	.350
1885	Chicago	87	25	.776	Connor	New-York	.371
1886	Chicago	90	34	.725	Kelly	Chicago	.388
1887	Detroit	79	45	.637	Maul	Philadelphia	.343
1888	New-York	84	47	.641	Anson	Chicago	.343
1889	New-York	83	43	.659	Brouthers	Boston	.313
1890	Brooklyn	86	43	.667	Luby	Chicago	.342
1891	Boston	87	51	.630	Hamilton	Philadelphia	.338
1892 (a)	Boston	52	22	.703	} Brouthers	Brooklyn	.335
1892 (b)	Cleveland	53	23	.697			

(a) and (b) represent the first and second divisions of the championship season.

The catcher's record of continuous games played was broken in 1890 by Charles Zimmer, of the Cleveland Club, who caught in 110 consecutive championship games.

The cities which have been represented at different times in the National League are Chicago, Boston, New-York, Philadelphia, Pittsburgh, Cleveland, Indianapolis, Washington, Detroit, St. Louis, Kansas City, Providence, Buffalo, Troy, Worcester, Cincinnati, Brooklyn, Syracuse, Milwaukee, Baltimore, Hartford, and Louisville. Boston and Chicago have been in the League every year since its organization.

THE AMERICAN ASSOCIATION.

The American Association was organized in 1882. In December, 1891, it was merged with the National League. Its record follows:

Year.	Champion Club.	Won.	Lost.	Average.	Champion Batter.	Club.	Average.
1882	Cincinnati	54	26	.673	Browning	Louisville	....
1883	Athletic	66	32	.673	Mansell	St. Louis	.357
1884	Metropolitan	75	32	.701	Esterbrook	Metropolitan	.405
1885	St. Louis	79	33	.705	Browning	Louisville	.367
1886	St. Louis	93	46	.669	Orr	Metropolitan	.346
1887	St. Louis	95	40	.704	O'Neil	St. Louis	.492*
1888	St. Louis	92	43	.681	O'Neil	St. Louis	.392
1889	Brooklyn	93	44	.679	Tucker	Baltimore	.375
1890	Louisville	87	44	.664	Goodall	Louisville	.492
1891	Boston	93	42	.689	No official record.		

* Bases on balls were credited as base hits in the records of 1887.

BASEBALL RECORDS—*Continued.*

RESULT OF THE LEAGUE SEASON OF 1892.

FIRST DIVISION.
HOW THE CLUBS FINISHED.

CLUBS.	Won.	Lost.	Played	Postponed.	Average.
Boston	52	22	74	3	.703
Brooklyn	51	26	77	0	.662
Philadelphia	46	30	76	1	.605
Cincinnati	44	31	75	2	.587
Cleveland	40	33	73	4	.548
Pittsburgh	37	39	76	1	.487
Washington	35	41	76	1	.461
Chicago	31	39	70	7	.443
St. Louis	31	42	73	4	.425
New-York	31	43	74	3	.419
Louisville	30	47	77	0	.390
Baltimore	20	55	75	2	.267

SECOND DIVISION.
HOW THE CLUBS FINISHED.

CLUBS.	Won.	Lost.	Played	Postponed.	Average.
Cleveland	53	23	76	1	.697
Boston	50	26	76	1	.658
Brooklyn	44	33	77	1	.571
Pittsburgh	43	34	77	0	.558
Philadelphia	41	36	77	0	.532
New-York	40	37	77	0	.519
Chicago	39	37	76	1	.513
Cincinnati	38	37	75	2	.507
Louisville	33	42	75	2	.440
Baltimore	26	46	72	5	.361
St. Louis	25	52	77	0	.325
Washington	23	52	75	2	.307

RECORD OF GAMES PLAYED.

WINNING CLUBS.	Boston.	Brooklyn.	Philadelphia.	Cincinnati.	Cleveland.	Pittsburgh.	Washington.	Chicago.	St. Louis.	New-York.	Louisville.	Baltimore.
Boston	—	4	2	4	5	4	6	5	3	6	6	7
Brooklyn	3	—	3	4	4	6	5	5	3	4	5	7
Philadelphia	4	4	—	4	2	5	4	5	3	7	5	
Cincinnati	2	3	3	—	3	1	5	0	5	5	5	
Cleveland	2	1	5	4	—	4	2	3	4	6	6	
Pittsburgh	2	1	2	6	3	—	2	3	4	5	3	6
Washington	1	2	3	2	5	5	—	1	4	3	5	
Chicago	2	2	2	0	2	4	6	—	3	5	2	3
St. Louis	4	4	1	3	3	3	2	2	—	2	3	
New-York	1	3	4	2	2	2	2	4		—	5	4
Louisville	1	2	0	2	1	4	4	5	5	2	—	
Baltimore	0	0	2	2	1	1	2	4	3	3		—

RECORD OF GAMES PLAYED.

WINNING CLUBS.	Cleveland.	Boston.	Brooklyn.	Pittsburgh.	Philadelphia.	New-York.	Chicago.	Cincinnati.	Louisville.	Baltimore.	St. Louis.	Washington.
Cleveland	—	4	5	3	5	4	6	5	7	5	5	4
Boston	3	—	5	4	5	5	4	6	6	4	5	5
Brooklyn	2	2	—	4	0	3	2	4	6	5	6	5
Pittsburgh	4	4	3	—	4	5	2	4	3	5	6	4
Philadelphia	2	3	1	3	—	4	4	5	3	5	4	5
New-York	3	2	4	2	1	—	2	4	5	5	4	7
Chicago	1	2	2	3	3	5	—	6	3	4	4	6
Cincinnati	2	2	3	2	3	1	1	—	2	5	5	6
Louisville	0	1	3	4	4	2	4	4	—	3	4	4
Baltimore	1	0	3	4	2	2	1	3	2	—	3	4
St. Louis	2	3	1	1	3	2	3	0	1	3	—	4
Washington	3	2	3	2	3	0	1	1	2	4	2	—

In 1884 the Association circuit embraced twelve clubs. It was considered too unwieldy, and reduced to eight the following winter.

Since its organization the following clubs have held membership in the American Association: St. Louis, Cincinnati, Louisville, Athletic, Allegheny (Pittsburgh), Baltimore, Metropolitan, Columbus, Toledo, Brooklyn, Indianapolis, Washington, Virginia (Richmond), Cleveland, Kansas City, Syracuse, Rochester, Milwaukee, and Boston.

AMATEUR BASEBALL LEAGUE.

The Staten Island Athletic Club won the Amateur League championship. The New-Jersey Athletic Club rejoined the League in 1892.

AMERICAN COLLEGE BASEBALL ASSOCIATION.
NEW-ENGLAND.

Dartmouth won the championship from Amherst and Williams. The scores made in the championship games in the season of 1892 follow.

May 6—Williams vs. Dartmouth, at Williamstown, 3-0.
May 7—Williams vs. Dartmouth, at Williamstown, 5-4.
May 18—Dartmouth vs. Amherst, at Amherst, 4-2.
May 19—Dartmouth vs. Amherst, at Amherst, 6-1.
June 3—Dartmouth vs. Williams, at Hanover, ?-0.
June 4—Dartmouth vs. Williams at Hanover, 4-0.
June 8—Amherst vs. Williams, at Amherst, 11-6.
June 10—Dartmouth vs. Amherst, at Hanover, 4-2.
June 11—Dartmouth vs. Amherst, at Hanover, 8-1.
June 15—Amherst vs. Williams, at Williamstown, 6-3.
June 18—Amherst vs. Williams, at Amherst, 4-1.
June 21—Williams vs. Amherst, at Williamstown, 4-2.

INTERCOLLEGIATE BASEBALL.

The Intercollegiate League has varied in membership almost every year since its organization. The record since 1880 shows the following winners:

1880—Princeton.	1883—Yale.	1886—Yale.	1889—Yale.
1881—Yale.	1884—Yale.	1887—Yale.	1890—Yale.
1882—Yale.	1885—Harvard.	1888—Yale.	1891—Princeton.

1892—Yale and Harvard a tie.

BASEBALL RECORDS—*Continued.*

Harvard and Princeton did not play in 1890, and in 1891 neither Yale nor Princeton played against Harvard, Yale refusing because of Harvard's attitude toward Princeton. In December, 1891, Harvard and Princeton agreed to resume baseball contests.

Yale and Harvard each won a majority of games from Princeton in 1892, and broke even in their own series. Harvard's challenge for a deciding game was declined on diplomatic grounds. The record for the year follows:

YALE-PRINCETON SERIES.

May 29—at New-Haven—Yale, 1; Princeton, 0. June 11—at Princeton—Yale, 3; Princeton, 1. June 18—at New-York—Princeton, 12; Yale, 2.

HARVARD-PRINCETON SERIES.

May 7—at Princeton—Harvard, 11; Princeton, 5. May 30—at Cambridge—Harvard, 9; Princeton, 4.

YALE-HARVARD SERIES.

June 29—at Cambridge—Harvard, 5; Yale, 0. June 28—at New-Haven—Yale, 4; Harvard, 3.

LONG DISTANCE THROWING RECORDS.

October 15, 1872—John Hatfield, of the Mutuals, threw the ball 133 yards, 1 foot, 7½ inches, at the Union Grounds, Brooklyn.

September 9, 1882—Ed. Williamson, of Chicago, threw the ball 132 yards, 1 foot, at the Chicago Grounds.

October 12, 1884—Ed. Crane, of the Boston Unions, topped the record with a throw of 135 yards, 1 foot, ½ inch, at Cincinnati.

Ed. Williamson won the Cincinnati competition in 1888, with a throw of 133 yards, 11 inches.

The shortest 9-inning game on record was played on the Excelsior Grounds, Brooklyn, May, 1861, by the Excelsior and Field clubs; time, 50 minutes.

The longest game on record was played at Boston, May 11, 1877. The Manchester and Harvard College teams played 24 innings; score, 0 to 0.

The longest championship game on record was played at Tacoma, May 16, 1891, between the Tacoma and Seattle teams. The Tacomas won in 22 innings; score, 6 to 5.

Harry Berthrong's record of 14 2-5 seconds, for running around the bases, made at Washington, in 1868, is still the standard.

IMPORTANT BASEBALL EVENTS.

1876—Organization of the National League.

1882—Organization of the American Association.

1884—First baseball war, caused by the organization of the Union Association, under the leadership of Henry V. Lucas. The new Association was no match for the older bodies, and went to pieces before the season ended.

1890—Players League organized. Its object was to conduct baseball on broader principles than those of the League and Association. The competition was disastrous to both sides, and at the conclusion of the playing season the new League was dismembered by the superior diplomacy of the old magnates.

1891—American Association withdrew from the new National Agreement and opened warfare against the National League. In December the two bodies met at Indianapolis, and the Association went out of existence, four of its clubs (St. Louis, Louisville, Baltimore, and Washington) being added to the League circuit. The other four were bought out.

1892—The League decided to divide the championship season into two halves, the winner of the first to play the winner of the second in a final series. Boston and Cleveland were the respective winners, the former taking the final series in five straight games. The scheme did not meet with great favor, and was abolished at the annual meeting at Chicago, November 17 and 18.

Canoeing.

The thirteenth annual meet of the American Canoe Association was held in August, 1892, at Willsborough Point, Lake Champlain, N. Y. The results of the races follow:

Record Sailing Race, five miles—Won by G. Gray, Vesper Canoe Club, in 56 minutes, 16 seconds.

Novice Sailing Race, three miles—Won by W. T. Foote, Jr., in 47 minutes, 50 seconds.

Paddling Half Mile—Won by J. Knapp, of Springfield, Mass.

Single Blade, Open Canoe, Paddling, half mile—Won by E. C. Archibald.

Half Mile Tandem Race—Won by Springfield Club in 3 minutes, 52 seconds.

Trophy Sailing Race, six miles—Won by Paul Butler, Vesper Club, in 1 hour, 30 minutes, 30 seconds.

Trophy Paddling Race, one mile—Won by E. C. Knapp, Springfield Club, in 7 minutes, 56 seconds.

Combined Paddling and Sailing Race, half miles alternately, distance three miles—Won by E. C. Knapp in 44 minutes.

Cruising Race, three miles—Won by H. L. Quick.

Club Sailing Race, three miles—Won by Vesper Boat Club in 29 minutes, 30 seconds.

Pecowsic Cup Sailing Race, four and a half miles—Won by T. S. Oxholm, Yonkers, in 45 minutes, 47 seconds.

Upset Paddling Race—Won by L. R. Palmer, Ianthe Canoe Club.

Hurry-Scurry Race—Won by T. E. Barrington.

Upset Paddling and Manœuvring Race—Won by C. E. Archibald.

The New York Canoe Club's Challenge Cup Sailing Races, June 21 and 22, were won by T. S. Oxholm, Yonkers Canoe Club, in the canoe Glenwood.

Football Records.

SHORTLY after the close of the football season of 1891 the prospects for a renewal of the Harvard-Princeton contests seemed excellent. These colleges had not met on the football field since 1889, when Harvard withdrew from the Intercollegiate Association because of a controversy with Princeton, the latter being charged with playing professionals on its team. In December, 1891, representatives of Harvard and Princeton met in New-York for the purpose of healing the breach, but they could not agree upon a plan which should be satisfactory to both. Harvard subsequently made a proposition to Princeton, which the latter would not accept.

Harvard offered to play Princeton in New-York on Thanksgiving Day in 1892, and in New-England on a Saturday in 1893. Princeton declined, and made a counter proposition, which gave Harvard the option of re-entering the Intercollegiate Association or arranging a game with Princeton for any Saturday in November, 1892, to be played in or near New-York. Princeton's loyalty to Yale and the Intercollegiate Association precluded its acceptance of Harvard's offer to play in New-York, Thanksgiving Day. Harvard, in turn, declined Princeton's proposition, and there the matter was dropped, although great pressure was brought to bear on Harvard to agree to terms.

Yale stands in a peculiar position in the mean time. It is bound by a contract to play a game with Harvard at Springfield each fall, and, being a member of the Intercollegiate Association, is called upon to play two hard games with Princeton and Pennsylvania respectively. Harvard has only one hard game to play, and Princeton two. Yale is, therefore, naturally anxious to have the Harvard-Princeton contests resumed, so as to equalize matters.

The football season of 1892 was marked by several sensational features. The most notable of these was the victory of the University of Pennsylvania over Princeton at Philadelphia, November 5th. The result of that game placed the Pennsylvania team second in the Intercollegiate race. The victory was entirely unexpected, for although it was generally conceded that Pennsylvania was stronger than ever before and Princeton weaker than usual, no one looked for a Princeton defeat. An impression to the effect that Princeton thus lost its right to play Yale Thanksgiving Day, 1892, in New-York, became general. This was erroneous, because while the constitution of the Association provides that the leading two colleges of one year shall play in or near New-York the next, it does not specify any date.

Wesleyan's poor showing in the race caused rumors at the close of the season that the Middletown college would be dropped. Wesleyan set all these rumors at rest by resigning early in December. Cornell is anxious to fill the vacancy, believing that it will be able to hold its own. The success achieved by the Cornell team in 1891 and 1892 entitles it to be classed in the front rank, but it remains to be seen whether Yale, Princeton, and Pennsylvania will agree to admit it as a member of the Intercollegiate Association.

INTERCOLLEGIATE FOOTBALL ASSOCIATION.

The records of the first eight years of the Intercollegiate Football Association are summarized in the following table, which shows the number of games won by each college each year:

	1877.	1878.	1879.	1880.	1881.	1882.	1883.	1884.
Yale	2	2	0	2	2	3	2	3
Princeton	2	3	1	2	1	1	1	3
Harvard	1	1	0	1	1	2	0	2
Columbia	0	0	—	0	0	0	0	0

* Columbia was dropped in 1884.

The Association was reorganized in 1885, with the following members: Yale, Princeton, Harvard, University of Pennsylvania, and Wesleyan. The record from that year to date follows:

	1885.	1886.	1887.	1888.	1889.	1890.	1891.	1892.
Yale	2	3	4	4	3	3	3	3
Princeton	3	3	2	3	4	2	2	1
Harvard	0	2	3	2	*	—	—	—
University of Pennsylvania	0	1	0	1	2	1	1	2
Wesleyan	1	0	1	0	1	0	0	0

* Harvard withdrew from the Intercollegiate Association late in 1889, but has played an independent game with Yale at Springfield, Mass., each year since. These games resulted as follows:

1890—Harvard, 12; Yale, 6.   1891—Yale, 10; Harvard, 0.
1892—Yale, 6; Harvard, 0.

In the subjoined table the record of the Intercollegiate Association for the season of 1892 is shown:

	Yale.	University of Pennsylvania.	Princeton.	Wesleyan.	Won.	Points Scored.	Opponents.
Yale		1	1	1	3	114	0
University of Pennsylvania	0		1	1	2	40	32
Princeton	0	0		1	1	64	18
Wesleyan	0	0	0		0	0	168
Lost	0	1	2	3	..	..	..

The scores of the above games, together with the dates and places where they were played, follow:

October 29—New-York—Princeton, 60; Wesleyan, 0.
November 5—Philadelphia—University of Pennsylvania, 6, Princeton, 4.
November 5—New-Haven—Yale, 74; Wesleyan, 0.
November 12—New-York—Yale, 28; University of Pennsylvania, 0.
November 24—New-York—Yale, 12; Princeton, 0.
November 24—Philadelphia—University of Pennsylvania, 34; Wesleyan, 0.

FOOTBALL RECORDS—*Continued*.

The scores of the Yale-Harvard, Yale-Princeton, and Harvard-Princeton games, since the present system of scoring was adopted, are here given:

YALE-HARVARD.

1883—Yale, 23; Harvard, 2.
1884—Yale, 52; Harvard, 0.
1885—No game played.
1886—Yale, 29; Harvard, 4.
1887—Yale, 17; Harvard, 8.

1888—Harvard forfeited.
1889—Yale, 6; Harvard, 0.
1890—Harvard, 12; Yale, 6.
1891—Yale, 10; Harvard, 0.
1892—Yale, 6; Harvard, 0.

YALE-PRINCETON.

1883—Yale, 6; Princeton, 0.
*1884—Yale, 6; Princeton, 4.
1885—Princeton, 6; Yale, 5.
*1886—Yale, 4; Princeton, 0.
1887—Yale, 12; Princeton, 0.

1888—Yale, 10; Princeton, 0.
1889—Princeton, 10; Yale, 0.
†1890—Yale, 32; Princeton, 0.
1891—Yale, 19; Princeton, 0.
1892—Yale, 12; Princeton, 0.

* Game unfinished.
† Largest score ever made against Princeton.

HARVARD-PRINCETON.

1883—Princeton, 26; Harvard, 7.
1884—Princeton, 34; Harvard, 6.
1886—Princeton, 12; Harvard, 0.

1887—Harvard, 12; Princeton, 0.
1888—Princeton, 18; Harvard, 6.
1889—Princeton, 41; Harvard, 15.

AMERICAN COLLEGE FOOTBALL ASSOCIATION (NEW-ENGLAND).

The championship was fought for by three colleges—Amherst, Dartmouth, and Williams. Amherst won with a clean record of victories. The scores follow:

November 5—Dartmouth, 24; Williams, 12. | November 12—Amherst, 30; Dartmouth, 2.
November 18—Amherst, 60; Williams, 0.

AMERICAN FOOTBALL UNION.

The Crescent Athletic Club won the championship of the American Football Union for the fourth time in succession. Scores of games played:

October 29—At Orange—Crescent Athletic Club, 14; Orange Athletic Club, 0.
November 5—At Orange—Orange Athletic Club, 18; New-York Athletic Club, 6.
November 20—At Brooklyn—Crescent Athletic Club, 20; New-York Athletic Club, 0.

ARMY AND NAVY SERIES.

The series of games between the Military Academy and Naval Academy, which began in 1890, has aroused almost as great general interest throughout the country as the contests between Yale and Harvard, and Yale and Princeton. The Naval Cadets took the lead this year, the record standing two victories to one in their favor. It was feared for a time last fall that the authorities would not permit the Military Cadets to play this year, but the necessary consent was given, and the game was played at West Point, Saturday, November 26ht. The record follows:

1890—At West Point—Naval Academy, 24; Military Academy, 0.
1891—At Annapolis—Military Academy, 32; Naval Academy, 16.
1892—At West Point—Naval Academy, 12; Military Academy, 4.

LOCAL SCHOOL CHAMPIONSHIPS.

Cutler School won the championship of the Interscholastic League, which was made up of Cutler, Dwight, Berkeley, Harvard, and Columbia schools.

The championship of the Interscholastic League of schools north of Fifty-eighth Street went to Hamilton Institute. These schools comprise the league: Hamilton, Columbia Institute and Barnard, Condon and Dr. Sachs's schools.

Lawn Tennis Records.

F. H. HOVEY won the all-comers tournament at Newport in August, 1892. He was then defeated by O. S. Campbell for the championship.

O. S. Campbell and R. P. Huntington, Jr., defeated V. G. and E. L. Hall for the championship in doubles.

CHAMPIONSHIPS—SINGLES.

America—O. S. Campbell.
Ladies'—Miss M. E. Cahill.
Western—S. T. Chase.
Pacific Coast—W. H. Taylor, Jr.
Tropical States—C. A. Grinstead.
Southern—E. L. Hall.

Canada—F. H. Hovey.
English—Wilfred Badelley.
New-England—E. L. Hall.
New-York State—W. P. Knapp.
Middle States—Richard Stevens.
North-Western—V. M. Elting.

CHAMPIONSHIPS—DOUBLES.

America—O. S. Campbell and R. P. Huntington, Jr.
Ladies'—Miss M. E. Cahill and Miss A. M. McKinley.
English—E. W. Lewis and H. S. Barlow.
Canada—F. H. Hovey and H. G. Bixby.
Eastern—V. G. and E. L. Hall.

Western—J. W. Carber and J. H. Ryerson.
Pacific Coast—H. H. Haight and C. P. Hubbard.
New England—E. L. Hall and A. E. Wright.
Mixed Doubles—Miss M. E. Cahill and Clarence Hobart.

Cricket Records.

THE game of cricket during the season of 1892 gained much in popularity, and the increase in the standard of play throughout the United States was very noticeable. The clubs of New-York City and neighborhood played a series of games for the championship of the Metropolitan District, which the Berkeley Club won. The following is the record:

SECTION I.

	Played.	Won.	Lost.	Drawn.	Per Cent.
Berkeley......................................	10	7	2	1	.777
New-Jersey A. C............................	10	5	3	2	.625
Staten Island...............................	10	4	3	3	.571
Manhattan...................................	10	4	6	0	.400
Brooklyn.....................................	10	3	5	2	.375
Paterson......................................	10	3	7	0	.300

SECTION II.

	Played.	Won.	Lost.	Drawn.	Per Cent.
Newark..	12	11	1	0	.916
New-York.....................................	12	7	5	0	.583
Harlem..	12	7	5	0	.583
Sons of St. George.........................	12	6	5	1	.545
Kings County................................	12	4	6	2	.400
South-Brooklyn.............................	12	2	8	2	.200
St. George's A. C...........................	12	2	9	1	.181

TOUR OF THE IRISH TEAM.

A team of Irish gentlemen played between September 5 and October 5, 1892, a series of eight matches, of which they won four, lost two, and had two drawn. The team was made up as follows: M. Gavin, A. Penny, W. Vint, J. M. Meldon (captain), B. Hamilton, J. W. Hynes, F. F. Kilkelly, E. K. Thompson, C. G. Green, C. L. Johnson, T. I. Considine, W. F. Thompson, and D. Rutledge. The record:

Sept. 5 and 6. At Boston, Fifteen of New England, 120 and 6 (no wickets); Irish Team, 84 and 41.
Sept. 9 and 10. At Lowell, Fourteen of Massachusetts, 74 and 115; Irish Team, 156 and 34 (6 wickets).
Sept. 12 and 13. At Toronto, All Canada, 107; Irish Team, 131 and 10 (2 wickets).
Sept. 17, 19 and 20. At Staten Island, All New-York, 225 and 164; Irish Team, 187 and 203 (6 wickets).
Sept. 23, 24, 26 and 27. At Manheim, All Philadelphia, 123 and 164; Irish Team, 175 and 239.
Sept. 28 and 29. At Baltimore, All Baltimore, 158 and 52; Irish Team, 247.
Sept. 30, Oct. 1 and 3. At Philadelphia, All Philadelphia, 157 and 181; Irish Team, 122 and 193.
Oct. 3, 4 and 5. At Philadelphia, All Philadelphia, 133; Irish Team, 168 and 133 (8 wickets).

THE INTER-CITY LEAGUE.

First Round.—Philadelphia beat Baltimore; Boston beat New-York; Pittsburgh beat Detroit.
Second Round.—Philadelphia beat Boston; Chicago beat Pittsburgh.
Championship.—Between Philadelphia and Chicago, unplayed.

ENGLISH CRICKET RECORDS.

The highest total ever made in any match is 920, obtained by the Orleans Club against the Rickling Green Club, at Rickling Green, in August, 1882.
The highest individual score ever made in any match is 485, by Mr. A. E. Stoddart, for the Hampstead Club against the Stoics, in August, 1886.
The highest total ever obtained in a first-class match is 803, by the Non-Smokers against the Smokers, on the East Melbourne Ground in Australia, in March, 1887.
The highest total ever made in a first-class match in England is 703, obtained by Cambridge University against Sussex, at Brighton, in June, 1890.
The highest total ever obtained in a first-class county match is 698, by Surrey against Sussex, at the Oval, in August, 1888.—*Barker's Facts for 1892.*

Bicycling Records.

AMERICAN AMATEUR, ORDINARY.				ENGLISH AMATEUR, ORDINARY.		
MILES.	Time.	Names.	Dates.	Time.	Names.	Dates
	H. M. S.			H. M. S.		
¼	.. .. 33 4-5	A. A. Zimmerman...	Sept. 9, 1891	.. .. 35 4-5	F. J. Archer............	June 21, 1890
½	.. 1 10 3-5	A. A. Zimmerman...	Sept. 9, 1891	.. 1 12 2-5	W. Lambley............	July 11, 1891
¾	.. 1 55 1-5	W. A. Rowe...........	Oct. 26, 1885	.. 1 51 4-5	F. J. Osmond..........	July 15, 1890
1	.. 2 22 1-5	C. M. Murphy.........	July 5, 1892	.. 2 21 3-5	F. J. Osmond..........	Aug. 29. 1892
2	.. 5 21 2-5	W. A. Rowe...........	Oct. 23, 1885	.. 5 12 1-5	F. J. Osmond..........	July 15, 1890
3	.. 8 07 2-5	W. A. Rowe...........	Oct. 19, 1885	.. 8 03 2-5	W. Lambley............	Sept. 10, 1891
4	.. 11 11 4-5	W. A. Rowe...........	Oct. 19, 1885	.. 10 51 1-5	W. Lambley............	Sept. 10, 1891
5	.. 13 51 3-5	A. B. Rich.............	Sept. 15, 1890	.. 13 44 1-5	W. Lambley............	Sept. 10, 1891
6	.. 16 55 3-5	W. A. Rowe...........	Oct. 19, 1885	.. 16 35	B. W. Atlee.............	Sept. 2, 1891
7	.. 19 47 2-5	W. A. Rowe...........	Oct. 19, 1885	.. 19 20 4-5	B. W. Atlee.............	Sept. 2, 1891
8	.. 22 41 4-5	W. A. Rowe...........	Oct. 19, 1885	.. 22 14 1-5	B. W. Atlee.............	Sept. 2, 1891
9	.. 25 41 2-5	W. A. Rowe...........	Oct. 19, 1885	.. 25 01 1-5	B. W. Atlee.............	Sept. 2, 1891
10	.. 28 37 4-5	W. A. Rowe...........	Oct. 19, 1885	.. 27 55 1-5	B. W. Atlee.............	Sept. 2, 1891

Fly=Casting Records.

THESE casts were made at the National Rod and Reel Association tournaments held at Central Park, New-York, and the statement of records was contributed to THE WORLD ALMANAC by Mr. A. N. Cheney, of Glens Falls, N. Y.

Light Rod Contest (rods not to exceed five ounces in weight): Reuben C. Leonard, 95 feet, made 1888.

Single-Handed Fly Casting, Amateur: R. C. Leonard, 85 feet, made 1882; R. B. Lawrence, 85 feet, made 1888.

Switch Fly-Casting: H. W. Hawes, 102 feet, made 1887.

Single-Handed Fly Casting, Expert: R. C. Leonard, 102½ feet, made 1888.

Salmon Casting: H. W. Hawes, 138 feet, made 1888.

Minnow Casting for Black Bass: A. F. Dressel, average of five casts, 137 feet, made 1888; Sidney Fry made an average of 140 4-5 feet in 5 casts, but failing in accuracy, yielded first place to Mr. Dressel.

Striped Bass Casting (Light): H. W. Hawes, average of five casts, 129 6-10 feet, made 1884.

Striped Bass Casting (Heavy): W. H. Wood, average of 5 casts, 246 5-10 feet, made 1889. Longest single cast, same class as above, W. H. Wood, 250 feet, made 1885.

Fly Casting for Black Bass: James L. Breese, 90 feet, made 1889.

ENGLISH FLY AND BAIT-CASTING RECORDS.

(These records were compiled by Mr. A. N. Cheney for THE WORLD ALMANAC.)

SALMON FLY CASTING, AMATEUR.

Major John P. Traherne.................*135 feet	Mr. Reuben Wood (of Syracuse, N. Y.)........108 feet
Mr. George M. Kelson............................111 feet	

SALMON FLY CASTING, SCOTCH PROFESSIONAL.

J. Stevens..126 feet

TROUT FLY CASTING—SINGLE-HANDED ROD.

Mr. P. D. Mallock.................................†92 feet	Mr. R. B. Marston, } tie...................... ‡74 feet
Mr. Reuben Wood (of Syracuse, N. Y.)... 82 ft. 6 in.	Mr. Hyde Clark, }

NOTTINGHAM BAIT-CASTING, AMATEUR.§

Mr. H. W. Little.......................176 feet, 3 inches

THAMES BAIT-CASTING, AMATEUR.‖

Mr. R. Gillson...........................190 feet, 7 inches

LONGEST CAST HEAVY (3-OUNCE) SINKER.

Mr. Hobden...216 feet

* This distance was made by measuring the line after the cast, and is not considered as good as Mr. Kelson's which was made by measuring to the point where the fly struck on the water, as was Mr. Wood's.

† This distance was made by measuring the line after casting.

‡ This cast of Messrs. Marston and Clark is given in English reports as the best, but for some unknown reason Mr. Wood's cast of 82 feet, 6 inches, and Mr. George M. Kelson's cast of 81 feet, have been entirely overlooked, although both are records at an international tournament.

§ In Nottingham casting the cast is made from the reel, as is done in America.

‖ In Thames casting the line is coiled at the feet of the caster.

Jumping Records.

PERFORMANCE.	Jumper.	Distance.	PERFORMANCE.	Jumper.	Distance.
		Ft. In.			Ft. In.
Running high jump........	M. F. Sweeney..	6 4¼	Standing hop, step and jump..	J. W. Rich....	29 11
Running broad jump........	C. S. Reber....	23 6½	Running hop, step and jump..	E. W. Goff....	47 1
Standing high jump........	A. P. Schwaner	5 3¼	Pole vault for height.........	W. Rodenbaugh	11 5¾
Standing broad jump........	A. P. Schwaner	10 9¾	Pole vault for distance.........	A. H. Green...	26 4¾
Three standing broad jumps	M. W. Ford....	34 4½			

Lacrosse.

THE lacrosse season of 1892 terminated in a very unsatisfactory manner as far as the Amateur Athletic Union champion contests were concerned. In the Spring it was decided that each association of the A. A. U. should arrange a distinct series of games, and then the association winners should play for the championship in the Fall.

The Metropolitan, Atlantic and New-England Associations entered teams. No games were played in the last-named organization. There was trouble in the Metropolitan from the start. And so many charges of professionalism and violations of the rules were made that all the games played were thrown out. In the Atlantic Association the team of the Athletic Club of the Schuylkill Navy won first honors, and so was given the A. A. U. championship by default.

Pugilism.

CHAMPIONSHIP BATTLES.

SINCE the memorable battle in New-Orleans, when the colors of John L. Sullivan were lowered by the young and exceedingly agile Californian, James J. Corbett, the question as to whether the latter won the championship of the world or of America has been discussed thousands of times. John L. Sullivan was the recognized champion of the world, and that title, therefore, belongs to his conqueror. Dating back to the fight between Tom Allen, champion at that time of this country, and Joe Goss, who occupied a like position in the English ring, it is found that the world's championship was in dispute. It was for this title that these champions battled, and Goss was the victor. Paddy Ryan challenged Goss, and they fought also for the world's championship. Ryan won. The battle between Sullivan and Ryan in Mississippi City, on February 7, 1882, is still fresh in the memories of men who follow the sport.

From the time he defeated Ryan, the Boston pugilist met scores of aspirants for his title, and was successful in defeating them all until he met Charles Mitchell, near Chantilly, France, on March 10, 1888. Mitchell got a draw with the champion. It is quite clear, therefore, that Corbett in defeating Sullivan fairly won the championship of the world.

Here is a list of the various class championships and their holders:

HEAVYWEIGHT.—Champion of the world, James J. Corbett.
   Champion of Australia, Peter Jackson.
   Champion of England, Peter Jackson.
MIDDLEWEIGHTS.—Champion of America, Bob Fitzsimmons.
   Champion of Australia, Bob Fitzsimmons.
   Champion of England, Jim Hall.
LIGHTWEIGHTS.—Champion of America, Jack McAuliffe.
   Champion of England, Dick Burge.
FEATHERWEIGHTS.—Champion of the world, George Dixon.

PUGILISTIC HAPPENINGS OF 1892.

A record of the important glove contests which have taken place in the United States, Great Britain, and Australia:

Jan. 2. Joe Goddard defeated Ned Ryan in four rounds, Melbourne Athletic Club. Purse, $750.

Jan. 2. Peter Maher's backers deposited $5,000 with THE WORLD, and challenged John L. Sullivan to fight for $10,000 a side and the championship.

Jan. 12. Billy Plimmer, of England, and "Kid" Hogan, of Brooklyn, fought an eight-round draw, Clermont Avenue Rink, Brooklyn. Gate receipts.

Jan. 21. George Siddons defeated Tommy Warren, Metropolitan Club, New-Orleans, in nine rounds. Purse, $1,500.

Jan. 21. Peter Maher and Bob Fitzsimmons matched to fight on March 2, Olympic Club, New-Orleans. Purse, $10,000.

Jan. 27. Cal McCarthy defeated Tom Callaghan, Olympic Club, New-Orleans, in fifteen rounds. Purse, $2,000.

Feb. 25. Jimmy Lynch defeated Walter Halligan in seven rounds, Clermont Avenue Rink, Brooklyn. Gate receipts.

March 1. Danny Needham defeated young Jack Burke, 10 rounds, Metropolitan Club, New-Orleans. Purse, $2,500.

March 2. Bob Fitzsimmons defeated Peter Maher, Olympic Club, New-Orleans, in twelve rounds. Purse, $10,000, of which $1,000 went to the loser.

March 15. John L. Sullivan and James J. Corbett matched for $10,000 a side and a purse of $25,000. The articles were signed at THE WORLD office.

April 27. Johnny Van Heest defeated George Siddons in seven rounds, Metropolitan Club, New-Orleans. Purse, $1,500.

May 9. Billy Plimmer defeated Tommy Kelly in ten rounds, Coney-Island Athletic Club. Purse, $1,500.

May 16. George Godfrey defeated Joe Lannon in four rounds, Coney-Island Athletic Club. Purse, $3,000.

May 30. Peter Jackson defeated Frank P. Slavin in ten rounds, National Sporting Club, London. Purse, $10,000.

May 30. Bobby Burns defeated Cal McCarthy, eight rounds, Coney-Island Athletic Club. Purse, $1,800.

June 2. Jack Slavin defeated Con. Riordan in nineteen rounds, Ormonde Club, London. Purse, $1,250.

June 22. Jack McAuliffe defeated Billy Frazier, three rounds, Manhattan Athletic Club. Purse, $500.

June 27. George Dixon defeated Fred Johnson, of England, in fourteen rounds, Coney-Island Athletic Club. Purse, $5,000.

July 1. Joe Goddard, of Australia, defeated Joe McAuliffe in fourteen rounds, Pacific Athletic Club, San Francisco. Purse, $5,000.

July 25. George Dawson, of Australia, defeated Danny Needham, twenty-nine rounds, California Athletic Club. Purse, $2,000.

Aug. 8. George Siddons and Eddie Pierce fought a draw, forty-one rounds, Coney-Island Athletic Club. Purse, $1,200.

Aug. 20. Jim Hall defeated Ted Pritchard in four rounds, at Brighton, England. $5,000 a side.

Sept. 5. Jack McAuliffe defeated Billy Myer in fifteen rounds, Olympic Club, New-Orleans. $5,000 a side, $10,000 purse.

Sept. 6. George Dixon defeated Jack Skelly, of Brooklyn, in eight rounds, Olympic Club, New-Orleans. Purse, $7,500 and $5,000 a side.

Sept. 7. James J. Corbett defeated John L. Sullivan in 21 rounds, Olympic Club, New-Orleans, for $10,000 a side, a purse of $25,000, and the championship of the world.

Sept. 20. Billy Smith defeated Billy Maber, Pastime Club, Portland, Ore., in twenty-five rounds. Purse, $1,000.

Sept. 25. Johnny Griffin, of Braintree, Mass., defeated Jimmy Lynch in five rounds, Coney-Island Athletic Club. Purse, $2,500.

Oct. 31. Joe Choynski defeated George Godfrey in fifteen rounds, Coney-Island Athletic Club. Purse, $5,000.

Nov. 28. Martin Costello, of Buffalo, and "Alec" Greggains, of San Francisco, fought an eighty round draw, Coney-Island Athletic Club. Purse, $2,500.

Dec. 8. Joe Goddard defeated Peter Maher in the third round, Coney-Island Athletic Club. Purse, $7,500, of which $1,000 went to the loser.

Dec. 12. Jim Hall and Bob Fitzsimmons signed articles at THE WORLD office to fight on March 8, 1893, at the Crescent City Athletic Club, New-Orleans, for a purse of $40,000, of which $2500 goes to the loser.

Dec. 28. Billy Plimmer defeated Joe McGrath in eight rounds, at the Coney Island Athletic Club. Purse, $2,500.

Railroad Statistics.

MILEAGE, ASSETS, LIABILITIES, EARNINGS, EXPENDITURES, AND TRAFFIC OF RAILROADS IN THE UNITED STATES.

Mileage of Railroads...............	167,845.56	Miles of Railroad Operated...........	152,689
Side Tracks and Sidings...............	46,683.39	Passenger Train Mileage...............	320,712,013
		Freight " "	403,541,969
Total Track...................	214,528.95	Mixed " "	16,948,394
Steel Rails in Track	174,775.14	Total...........................	831,202,376
Iron Rails in Track	39,753.81	Passengers Carried...................	556,015,802
Locomotive Engines, Number.........	33,563	Passenger Mileage...................	13,316,925,239
Cars, Passenger...................	23,083	Tons of Freight Moved...............	704,398,609
" Baggage, Mail, etc...............	7,368	Freight Mileage...................	81,210,154,523
" Freight...................	1,110,286		
		Traffic Earnings.	
Total Cars...................	1,140,737	Passengers...........................	$290,799,696
Liabilities.		Freight.............................	754,185,910
		Miscellaneous.......................	80,549,209
Capital Stock...................	$4,751,750,408		
Bonded Debt...................	5,178,821,989	Total...........................	$1,138,024,459
Unfunded Debt...................	345,102,632		
Current Accounts...................	374,051,161	Net Earnings.......................	$356,227,883
Total Liabilities...................	$10,649,726,280	Total Available Revenue............	$457,504,066
Assets.		*Payments.*	
Cost of Railroad and Equipment......	$8,927,571,592	Rentals, Tolls, etc...................	$64,255,732
Real Estate, Stocks, Bonds, and other		Interest on Bonds...................	225,339,413
Investments...................	1,588,590,522	Other Interest......................	5,920,397
Other Assets...................	233,862,243	Dividends on Stock.................	90,719,757
Current Accounts...................	241,399,182	Miscellaneous.......................	31,018,045
Total Assets...................	$10,991,423,539	Total Payments...................	$417,253,344
Excess of Assets over Liabilities....	$341,697,259	Total Surplus...................	$40,250,722

The above table and the one following were compiled from "Poor's Manual of the Railroads of the United States for 1892."

COMPARATIVE STATISTICS OF RAILROADS IN THE UNITED STATES, 1879-91.

YEAR ENDING.	Capital Stock.	Miles Line Worked.	Funded Debt.	Gross Earnings.	Net Earnings.	Interest Paid.	Dividends Paid.
1879......	$2,395,647,293	79,009	$2,319,489,172	$525,620,577	$216,544,999	$112,237,515	$61,681,470
1880......	2,708,673,375	82,146	2,530,874,943	613,733,616	255,557,555	107,866,328	77,115,371
1881......	3,177,375,179	92,971	2,878,423,606	701,780,082	272,406,787	128,587,302	93,344,190
1882......	3,511,035,824	104,971	3,235,543,323	770,209,899	280,316,606	154,295,380	102,031,534
1883......	3,708,060,583	110,414	3,500,879,914	823,772,924	293,367,285	175,139,064	102,052,584
1884......	3,762,616,686	115,672	3,669,115,772	770,683,908	268,106,258	176,694,302	93,203,853
1885......	3,817,697,831	123,320	3,765,727,066	765,310,419	266,488,993	189,426,035	77,672,105
1886......	3,999,508,508	125,185	3,882,966,330	829,940,830	300,603,564	189,036,304	81,644,138
1887......	4,191,562,029	137,028	4,186,943,116	931,385,154	334,989,119	203,790,352	91,573,458
1888......	4,438,411,342	145,341	4,624,035,023	950,622,008	297,363,677	205,280,052	78,943,041
1889......	4,495,099,318	152,689	4,828,365,771	992,856,856	318,125,339	211,171,279	79,532,803
1890......	4,640,239,578	163,420	5,105,902,025	1,097,847,428	343,921,318	229,101,144	83,863,632
1891......	4,809,176,651	164,324	5,235,295,074	1,138,024,459	356,209,880	231,259,810	90,719,757

INTERSTATE COMMERCE COMMISSION STATISTICS.

A synopsis of the "Statistics of Railways in the United States," for the year ending June 30, 1891, specially prepared from the fourth annual report of the Interstate Commerce Commission (December 12, 1892) by its statistician. The returns are slightly later than those by Poor, in the preceding tables.

Railway mileage in the United States on June 30, 1891, 168,402 miles. This figure indicates the length of single track mileage, the total mileage of all tracks being 216,149 miles. The length of single track per 100 square miles of territory, exclusive of Alaska, was 5.67 miles, and the length of track per 10,000 inhabitants was 26.29 miles. No country in Europe, Sweden alone excepted, has 10 miles of line per 10,000 inhabitants; while here only two States have less.

The increase in railway mileage during the year was 4,805.69 miles, the smallest for several years. The greatest activity in railway building seems to have been in the Southern States.

There were on June 30, 1891, 1,785 railway corporations, of which 889 were independent, 747 subsidiary, and 149 private lines. Sixteen roads were abandoned during the year, and 92 roads disappeared by purchase, merger, or consolidation. The tendency toward consolidation is clearly indicated. On June 30, 1891, there were 42 companies, each controlling more than a mileage in excess of 1,000 miles of road, and nearly one half of the mileage of the country is the property of these 42 companies. Eighty railway companies have a gross revenue of over $3,000,000 each, and control 69.48 per cent of the total mileage of the country.

The total number of locomotives was 32,139, an increase of 1,999 during the year, and the total number of cars was 1,215,611, an increase of 45,044. The increase in equipment has not proceeded as rapidly as the increase in train brakes and automatic couplers. Yet at the present rate it will be many years before the total equipment of railways will be fitted with safety devices. The number of railway men employed during the year was 784,285, an increase of 34,984. The number of railway men in proportion to the total population was 1 to 87 inhabitants in 1889; 1 to 84 in 1890; and 1 to 82 in 1891.

Railroad Accidents in the United States.

YEARS.	Number Accidents.	Number Killed.	Number Injured.	PER 100 ACCIDENTS.	
				Killed.	Injured.
1880	1,078	315	1,172	29.2	108.7
1881	1,458	414	1,597	28.4	109.0
1882	1,365	380	1,588	27.5	116.8
1883	1,619	474	1,954	29.2	120.7
1884	1,191	389	1,760	32.6	147.7
1885	1,217	307	1,538	25.2	144.6
1886	1,211	401	1,433	33.0	108.0
1887	1,491	656	1,946	43.0	130.5
1888	1,935	667	2,207	34.4	114.0
1889	1,569	492	1,772	31.3	112.3
1890	2,146	806	2,812	37.5	131.0
1891	2,444	790	2,685	32.3	109.8

The above covers only casualties caused by accidents to, not accidents caused by walking on or crossing tracks or falling from trains in motion. These statistics, as well as those in the table which follows, were compiled from press reports by the New-York *Railroad Gazette*.

CAUSES OF ACCIDENTS TO TRAINS.

STATISTICS OF FIVE YEARS.

	1887.	1888.	1889.	1890.	1891.		1887.	1888.	1889.	1890.	1891.
COLLISIONS:											
Rear	362	404	379	495	555	Negligence in operating.	74	117	92	108	144
Butting	309	311	360	323	284	Unforeseen obstructions.	129	152	131	194	192
Crossing & Miscellaneous	29	89	110	222	298	Unexplained	243	385	296	377	439
Total Collisions	700	804	749	1,041	1,137	Total derailment	705	1,032	759	1,004	1,204
DERAILMENTS:						Accidents without collision or derailment*..	86	86	61	101	103
Defects of road	152	189	120	167	214						
Defects of equipment	100	148	120	158	215	Grand total	1,491	1,935	1,569	2,146	2,444

* Such as boiler explosions and broken wheels.

Railroad Speed.

ONE mile.—The fastest time on record as having been made by a locomotive for one mile is 37 seconds, which is at the rate of 97.3 miles an hour. This was made by a regular train on the Central Railroad of New-Jersey, going east, between Fanwood and Westfield, N. J., on November 18, 1892. The engine was one of Vauclain's four-cylinder compound locomotives, and the train consisted of four cars. The grade of the road was descending, at the rate of 32 feet a mile.

Two miles.—The mile next following the one above mentioned was traversed in 38 seconds, making a record of 96 miles an hour.

Five miles.—On the same trip, a distance of five miles, between Somerton and Parkland, Pa., on the Philadelphia and Reading, was made in 3 minutes 25 seconds, or at the rate of 87.8 miles an hour.

Twelve miles.—All of the above are "world records." A rate of 86 miles an hour has been recorded on the Northeastern of England, but not for any specified distance. The fastest time made by an American train for 12 miles was on the Philadelphia and Reading Railroad, August 27, 1891, 12 miles, Jenkintown to the Delaware River, in 8 minutes, 42½ seconds, being at the average rate of 82.7 miles an hour. The train was composed of an engine, tender, and three cars, all weighing 169 tons.

The fastest long-distance run was on the New-York Central Railroad, September 14, 1891, from New-York City to East Buffalo, 436½ miles, in 425 minutes, 14 seconds, actual time, or 439½ minutes, including three stops. Average speed, including stops, 61.56 miles an hour.

The Jarrett and Palmer special theatrical train, Jersey City to San Francisco, June, 1886, made the fastest time between the two oceans—3 days, 7 hours, 39 minutes and 16 seconds.

The fastest regular trains in the United States, for a short distance, are believed to be those between Washington and Baltimore, on the Baltimore and Ohio Railroad, 40 miles in 45 minutes, a speed of 53.33 miles an hour. The run from Washington to New-York, 225.3 miles, is made in 5 hours. Deducting 12 minutes for the Jersey City Ferry and 10 minutes for the Canton Ferry, the rate of speed is 48.6 miles per hour. The "Congressional Limited," on the Pennsylvania Railroad, also makes the run in 5 hours, 5 minutes, but the distance is 227 miles.

The fastest regular train in the world for a long distance is the Empire State express, on the New-York Central and Hudson River road, which runs from New-York via Albany to Buffalo in 8 hours, 40 minutes. The distance is 439 miles, making the rate through 50.7 miles an hour. This includes two stops of five minutes (Albany and Syracuse) and two of two minutes (Utica and Rochester).

The quickest run between New-York and Washington was made on the Pennsylvania Railroad, November 28, 1891, by a special train, in 4 hours, 11 minutes, making the running time, exclusive of stops, 56¾ miles an hour. This beat the time of the "Aunt Jack" train, made by the Madison Square Theatre Company, March 10, 1890, which was 4 hours, 18 minutes each way, going and return.

The Production of Books.

AMERICAN AND IMPORTED PUBLICATIONS IN 1888, 1889, 1890, AND 1891 RECORDED BY "THE PUBLISHERS' WEEKLY," NOT INCLUDING GOVERNMENT WORKS AND THE PRODUCTIONS OF THE MINOR CHEAP LIBRARIES.

Divisions.	1888.	1889.	1890.	1891.	Divisions.	1888.	1889.	1890.	1891.
Fiction	874	942	1,118	1,105	Biography, Memoirs	217	178	218	211
Law	335	410	458	348	Fine Arts and Illus. Books.	250	171	135	228
Juvenile Books	410	388	408	460	Physical and Math. Science	56	96	93	97
Literary History and Miscel.	291	144	183	251	Useful Arts	124	129	133	106
Theology and Religion.	482	363	467	528	Sports and Amusements	46	43	82	79
Education, Language	413	319	399	355	Domestic and Rural	39	44	29	71
Poetry and the Drama	280	171	168	193	Humor and Satire	47	25	42	26
History	144	110	153	124	Mental and Moral Philos	18	28	11	39
Medical Science, Hygiene.	151	157	117	108					
Social and Political Science.	227	157	183	197	Total	4,631	4,014	4,559	4,665
Description, Travel	194	139	162	139					

Many of the American productions are reprints of English works.

BRITISH PUBLICATIONS FROM 1888 TO 1891 INCLUSIVE.

Divisions.	1888. New Books.	1888. New Eds.	1889. New Books.	1889. New Eds.	1890. New Books.	1890. New Eds.	1891. New Books.	1891. New Eds.
Theology, Sermons, Biblical, etc	748	164	630	134	555	153	520	107
Educational, Classical and Philological	630	149	557	124	615	88	587	107
Juvenile Works and Tales	357	113	418	93	443	95	348	99
Novels, Tales and other Fiction	929	385	1,040	364	881	323	896	320
Law, Jurisprudence, etc	115	57	66	40	40	39	61	48
Political and Social Economy, Trade and Commerce	111	24	110	16	87	22	105	31
Art, Sciences and Illustrated Works	184	69	112	34	54	19	85	31
Voyages, Travels, Geographical Research	224	73	203	57	188	69	203	68
History, Biography, etc	377	109	310	114	294	97	328	85
Poetry and the Drama	163	68	133	54	114	74	146	55
Year-Books and Serials in Volumes	324	3	342	4	318	1	310	6
Medicine, Surgery, etc	126	73	133	49	143	50	120	55
Belles-Lettres, Essays, Monographs, etc	165	224	157	183	171	191	131	123
Miscellaneous, including Pamphlets, not Sermons	507	120	483	107	511	100	589	142
	4,960	1,631	4,694	1,373	4,414	1,321	4,429	1,277
		4,960		4,694		4,414		4,429
		6,591		6,067		5,735		5,706

Bible Statistics.

THE following statement is on the authority of a communication published in *Notes and Queries* (London). It is represented to be the fruits of three years' labor by the indefatigable Dr. Horne, and is given by him in his introduction to the study of the Scriptures. The basis is an old English Bible of the King James version.

OLD TESTAMENT.—Number of books, 39; chapters, 929; verses, 23,214; words, 593,493; letters, 2,728,100.

NEW TESTAMENT.—Number of books, 27; chapters, 260; verses, 7,959; words, 181, 253; letters, 838,380.

THE BIBLE.—Total number of books, 66; chapters, 1,189; verses, 31,173; words, 773,746; letters, 3,566,480.

APOCRYPHA.—Number of books, 14; chapters, 183; verses, 6,031; words, 125,185.

OLD TESTAMENT.—The middle book of the Old Testament is Proverbs. The middle chapter is Job 29. The middle verse is 2 Chronicles 20, between verses 17 and 18. The shortest book is Obadiah. The shortest verse is 1 Chronicles 1 : 25. The word "and " occurs 35,543 times. Ezra 7 : 21 contains all the letters of our alphabet. The word " Selah" occurs 73 times and only in the poetical books. 2 Kings 19 and Isaiah 37 are alike. The Book of Esther does not contain the words God or Lord. The last two verses of 2 Chronicles and the opening verses of the Book of Ezra are alike. Ezra 2 and Nehemiah 7 are alike. There are nearly 30 books mentioned, but not found in the Bible, consisting of civil records and other ancient writings now nearly all lost. About 26 of these are alluded to in the Old Testament.

NEW TESTAMENT.—The middle book is 2 Thessalonians. The middle chapter is between Romans 13 and 14. The middle verse is Acts 17: 17. The smallest book is 2 John. The smallest verse is John 11 : 35. The word "and " occurs 10.684 times. The name Jesus occurs nearly 700 times in the Gospels and Acts, and in the Epistles less than 70 times. The name Christ alone occurs about 60 times in the Gospels and Acts, and in about 240 times in the Epistles and Revelation. The term Jesus Christ occurs 5 times in the Gospels.

THE BIBLE.—The middle book is Micah. The middle (and smallest) chapter is Psalm 117. The middle verse is Psalm 118 : 8. The middle line is 2 Chronicles 4 : 16 the largest book is that of the Psalms ; the largest chapter is Psalm 119. The word Jehovah (or Lord) occurs 6,855 times. The word "and " occurs 46,227 times. The number of authors of the Bible is 50. The Bible was not until modern times divided into chapters and verses. The division of chapters has been attributed to Lanfrank, Archbishop of Canterbury, in the reign of William I.; but the real author of this division was Cardinal Hugo de Sancto-Caro, about 1236. The number of languages on earth is estimated at 3,000 ; the Bible or parts of it have been rendered into only about 180. The first English translation complete of the Bible was by Wickliffe in 1380. The first American edition was printed in Boston in 1752.

The Stage.

BIRTHPLACES AND BIRTH YEARS OF DRAMATIC AND MUSICAL PEOPLE.

Name.	Birthplace.	Born.	Name.	Birthplace.	Born.
Albani, Emma	Chambly, Canada.	1851	Janauschek, Francesca	Prague, Austria	1830
Albaugh, John W.	Baltimore, Md	1837	Janisch, Antonie	Vienna, Austria	1850
Aldrich, Louis	Mid-ocean	1843	Jefferson, Joseph	Philadelphia, Pa	1829
Anderson, Mary	Sacramento, Cal	1859	Karl, Tom	Dublin, Ireland	1849
Archer, Belle	Easton, Pa	1860	Kendal, Mrs. W. H	Lincolnshire, Eng.	1849
Arditi, Luigi	Piedmont, Italy	1822	Keene, Thomas W	New-York City	1840
Bandmann, Daniel E	Cassel, Germany	1839	Kellogg, Clara Louise	Sumterville, S. C.	1842
Bangs, Frank C	Alexandria, Va	1836	Kelcey, Herbert H. L	London, Eng	1855
Barnabce, H. C.	Portsmouth, N. H.	1833	Langtry, Lily	St. Helens, Jersey.	1852
Barrett, Wilson	Essex, Eng	1846	Lewis, James	Troy, N. Y	1839
Barron, Charles	Boston, Mass	1841	Lucca, Pauline	Vienna, Austria	1842
Barrymore, Maurice	India	1847	Mackaye, Steele	Buffalo, N. Y	1843
Bateman, Isabel	Cincinnati, O	1854	Maddern, Minnie	New-Orleans, La.	1865
Bateman, Kate	Baltimore, Md	1842	Mansfield, Richard	Heligoland, Ger	1857
Bellew, Kyrle	London	1845	Mantell, Robert B	Ayrshire, Scotland	1854
Bernard-Beere, Mrs.	Norwich, Eng	1859	Marius, C. D	Paris, France	1850
Bell, Digby	Milwaukee, Wis	1851	Marlowe, Julia	Cincinnati, O	1870
Bernhardt, Sarah	Paris	1844	Martinot, Sadie	Yonkers, N. Y	1857
Boniface, George C	New-York City	1832	Mather, Margaret	Detroit, Mich	1861
Booth, Agnes	Australia	1843	Mayo, Frank	Massachusetts	1839
Booth, Edwin	Belair, Md	1833	Mitchell, Maggie	New-York City	1832
Bowers, Mrs. D. P	Stamford, Conn	1830	Modjeska, Helena	Cracow, Poland	1844
Buchanan, Virginia	Cincinnati, O	1846	Mordaunt, Frank	Burlington, Vt	1841
Burgess, Neil	Boston, Mass	1846	Morris, Clara	Cleveland, O	1846
Burroughs, Marie	San Francisco	1866	Murphy, Joseph	Brooklyn, N. Y	1839
Campanini, Italo	Parma, Italy	1846	Nilsson, Christine	Wederslof, Sweden	1843
Carey, Eleanor	Chile, S. A	1852	O'Neil, James	Ireland	1849
Cayvan, Georgia	Maine	1858	Pastor, Tony	New-York	1837
Chanfrau, Mrs. F. S	Philadelphia, Pa	1837	Patti, Adelina	Madrid	1843
Clarke, George	Brooklyn, N. Y	1840	Pixley, Annie	New-York City	1856
Clarke, John S	Baltimore, Md	1835	Plympton, Eben	Boston, Mass	1850
Claxton, Kate	New-York City	1848	Ponisi, Madame	Huddersfield, Eng.	1825
Cody, William F	Scott Co., Iowa	1845	Proctor, Joseph	Marlboro', Mass	1816
Coghlan, Rose	Peterboro, Eng	1853	Rankin, A. McKee	Sandwich, Canada.	1844
Coquelin, Benôit C	Boulogne, France	1841	Reed, Roland	Philadelphia, Pa	1852
Couldock, Charles W	London, Eng	1815	Rehan, Ada	Limerick, Ireland	1860
Crabtree, Lotta	New-York City	1847	Rhea, Mlle	Brussels	1855
Crane, William H	Leicester, Mass	1845	Ristori, Adelaide	Cividale, Italy	1821
Daly, Augustin	North-Carolina	1838	Robinson, Frederick	London, Eng	1832
Damrosch, Walter J	Breslau, Prussia.	1862	Robson, Stuart	Annapolis, Md	1836
Davenport, Fanny	London, Eng	1850	Rossi, Ernesto	Leghorn, Italy	1829
D'Arville, Camille	Holland	1861	Roze, Marie	Paris	1846
De Bellville, Frederick	France	1844	Russell, Lillian	Clinton, Ia	1860
Dickinson, Anna	Philadelphia, Pa	1842	Russell, Sol Smith	Brunswick, Mo	1848
Dillon, Louise	Savannah, Ga	1857	Salvini, Tommaso	Milan, Italy	1830
Dixey, Henry E	Boston, Mass	1859	Scanlan, William J	Springfield, Mass.	1856
Drew, John	Philadelphia, Pa	1853	Scott-Siddons, Mrs.	India	1844
Drew, Mrs. John, Sr.	England	1818	Sothern, Edward H	England	1864
Illsler, Effie	Philadelphia, Pa	1858	Stanhope, Adelaide	Paris, France	1858
Eytinge, Rose	Philadelphia, Pa	1837	Stanley, Alma Stuart	Jersey, Eng	1860
Fawcett, Owen	London, Eng	1838	Stevenson, Charles A	Dublin, Ireland	1842
Florence, Mrs. W. J	New-York City	1846	Stoddart, J. H	Yorkshire, Eng	1827
Germon, Effie	Augusta, Ga	1845	Studley, John B	Boston, Mass	1832
Gerster, Etelka	Kaschau, Hungary	1857	Sully, Mounet	France	1841
Gilbert, Mrs. G. H	Rochdale, Eng	1820	Tearle, Osmond	Plymouth, Eng	1852
Goodwin, Nat C	Boston, Mass	1857	Terris, William	London, Eng	1840
Hall, Josephine	E. Greenwich, R. I.	1868	Terry, Ellen	Coventry, Eng	1848
Hading, Jane	Marseilles, France.	1861	Thompson, Charlotte	Bradford, Eng	1843
Harrigan, Edward	New-York City	1845	Thompson, Denman	Girard, Pa	1833
Harrison, Maud	England	1858	Thompson, Lydia	London, Eng	1838
Hauk, Minnie	New-Orleans, La.	1853	Thursby, Emma	Brooklyn, N. Y	1857
Haworth, Joseph S	Providence, R. I.	1855	Toole, John L	London, Eng	1833
Henley, E. J	England	1852	Tree, Beerbohm	England	1846
Heron, Bijou	New-York City	1863	Turner, Carrie	St. Charles, Iowa.	1862
Holland, E. M	New-York City	1848	Vezin, Hermann	Philadelphia, Pa	1829
Hill, Charles Barton	Dover, Eng	1828	Vokes, Rosina	London, Eng	1854
Hilliard, Robert S	Brooklyn	1860	Warde, Frederick	Wadington, Eng	1851
Hopper, De Wolf	New-York	1862	Wheatcroft, Nelson	London, Eng	1852
Irving, Henry	Keinton, Eng	1838	Wilson, Francis	Philadelphia, Pa	1865
James, Louis	Tremont, Ill	1842	Willard, E. S	Wales	1850

Statistics of Crime and Pauperism.

(Compiled from United States Census Bulletins, 1890.)
PENITENTIARY CONVICTS OF THE UNITED STATES IN 1890.

UNITED STATES.	Aggregate	WHITE.								Colored.
		Total.	Native.					Foreign Born.	Nativity Unknown.	
			Total.	Parents Native.	One Parent Foreign.	Parents Foreign.	One or both Parents Unknown.			
Total.........	45,233	30,546	23,094	12,842	1,747	6,584	1,921	7,267	185	14,687

PRISONERS IN COUNTY JAILS, JUNE 1, 1890.

| Total........... | 19,538 | 13,961 | 9,684 | 5,265 | 629 | 2,734 | 1,056 | 3,765 | 512 | 5,577 |

INMATES OF JUVENILE REFORMATORIES OF THE UNITED STATES IN 1890.

| Total........... | 14,846 | 12,903 | 11,078 | 3,245 | 963 | 3,965 | 2,905 | 1,405 | 420 | 1,943 |

ALMSHOUSE PAUPERS IN THE UNITED STATES IN 1890.

| Total......... | 73,045 | 66,578 | 36,656 | 21,519 | 949 | 3,580 | 10,608 | 27,648 | 2,274 | 6,467 |

PAUPERISM IN FOREIGN COUNTRIES.

1890. Public paupers in England and Wales, 787,545 ; Ireland, 107,774 ; France, 290,000 ; Germany, 320,000 ; Russia, 350,000 ; Austria, 290,000 ; Italy, 270,000.

HOMICIDE IN THE UNITED STATES.

The census bulletin presenting statistics of homicide in the United States in 1890 was prepared by Frederick H. Wines, special agent on pauperism and crime. The following is the summing up of the results of his investigations :

Of 82,329 prisoners in the United States June 1, 1890, the number charged with homicide was 7,386, or 8.97 per cent.

Omitting 35 who were charged with double crimes, 6,958 of them (or 94.65 per cent) were men, and 293 (or 5.35 per cent) were women.

As to color, 4,425 were white, 2,739 negroes, 94 Chinese, 1 Japanese, and 92 Indians.

As to the nativity of the 4,425 whites, 3,157 were born in the United States, 1,213 were foreign born, and the birthplace of 55 is unknown.

A careful and accurate inquiry into the parentage of those born in the United States results in the mathematical conclusion that 56.14 per cent of homicide committed by white men and women is chargeable to the native white element of the population, and 43.86 per cent to the foreign element. On the same scale of 4,614 to 3,605, the negro contribution to homicide is represented by 5,478.

More than one half of the foreign-born whites are unnaturalized, and nearly one fifth are unable to speak the English language.

In respect to age, prisoners charged with homicide range from 11 to 86 years. One sixth of them are under 24 years, and more than one half under 33 years of age. Their average age is 34 years and 193 days. The lowest averages are among the Indians, 30 years and 180 days, and the negroes, 30 years and 279 days. The highest are among the Chinese, 37 years and 246 days, and the foreign-born whites, 41 years and 159 days. The average age of women charged with homicide is 32 years and 216 days. The ages at which homicide was committed are estimated to be at least 5 years below the averages here stated.

Nearly one half of this group of prisoners were found to be unmarried. The number of unmarried was 3,615 ; married, 2,715 ; widowed, 703 ; divorced. 144.

The percentage of those who can both read and write is 61.73 ; of those who can read only, 4.84 ; of those who can do neither, 33.43. Of the negroes, more than one half can neither read nor write ; of the Indians, nearly two thirds. The percentage of illiteracy among the foreign born is nearly or quite three times as great as that among the native whites.

The number who have received a higher education is 253, or 3.44 per cent.

More than four fifths have no trade. The foreign born and their children have much more generally acquired a trade than the native whites, and the native whites than the negroes.

The occupations of 6,546 prior to incarceration have been ascertained, and are grouped as follows : professional, 102 ; official, 38 ; agricultural, 1,893 ; lumber, 29 ; mining, 212 ; fisheries, 19 ; trade and commerce, 173 ; transportation, 380 ; manufactures and mechanical industries, 1,086 ; personal service, 690 ; unskilled labor, 2,253 ; miscellaneous, 21.

The number employed at the time of their arrest was 5,659 ; unemployed, 1,225 ; unknown, 467.

The habits of 973, in respect of use of intoxicating liquors, are not stated. The remaining 6,378 are classed as follows : total abstainers, 1,282 ; occasional or moderate drinkers, 3,829 ; drunkards, 1,267.

The number arrested and imprisoned in the State of their residence, was 6,268 ; out of the State, 861.

Four hundred and sixty-three had served as soldiers in the Civil War, 224 were federal prisoners, 534 were known to have served a previous term of imprisonment.

As to their physical condition, 6,149 were in good health, 600 ill, 283 insane, 24 blind, 14 deaf and dumb, 18 idiots, and 263 crippled.

CAPITAL PUNISHMENT.

The only States in which the death penalty is forbidden by law are Rhode-Island, Michigan and Wisconsin. In Rhode-Island, the only alternative is imprisonment for life.

Murderous Nations.

ITALY takes the lead of European nations, with an average annual crop of murders of 2,470, a ratio per 10,000 deaths of 29.4 ; Spain follows, with a ratio of 23.8, and 1,200 murders ; Austria, ratio of 8.8, and 600 murders ; France, ratio of 8.0, and 662 murders ; England, ratio of 7.1, and 377 murders.

In England, in the reign of Henry VIII., there were 71,400 persons hanged or beheaded ; in one year 300 beggars were executed for soliciting alms. In 1820 no less than 46 persons were hanged in England for forging Bank of England notes, some of which were afterward asserted to be good. Capital punishment was abolished in Italy in 1875, and murders increased 42 per cent. (Compiled from Mulhall.)

Mortality in the United States

IN THE CENSUS YEAR 1889-90.
(Prepared for THE WORLD ALMANAC by the Census Office.)

STATES AND TERRITORIES.	Total Deaths.	WHITE.* Native Born.	WHITE.* Foreign Born.	Colored.	UNDER FIVE YEARS OF AGE. White.	UNDER FIVE YEARS OF AGE. Colored.	STATES AND TERRITORIES.	Total Deaths.	WHITE.* Native Born.	WHITE.* Foreign Born.	Colored.	UNDER FIVE YEARS OF AGE. White.	UNDER FIVE YEARS OF AGE. Colored.
Alabama..	20,898	9,215	320	10,591	3,880	3,847	Nevada....	434	217	181	20	69	3
Arizona...	573	301	169	30	130	3	New-Ham.	7,074	5,704	849	17	1,809	3
Arkansas..	14,391	10,089	274	3,627	3,874	1,168	New-J'sey.	30,344	22,227	6,339	1,344	11,829	642
California.	17,703	10,605	5,286	1,281	4,234	119	New-Mex..	2,522	2,234	107	29	1,014	4
Colorado..	5,453	3,929	921	86	1,875	32	New-York.	123,117	85,592	33,146	1,903	43,580	715
Conn'ticut	14,470	10,733	3,182	309	4,188	106	North-Car.	18,420	10,886	69	7,234	4,021	2,680
Delaware..	3,107	2,060	241	695	805	282	North-Dak.	1,716	1,067	593	4	763	1
D. of Col..	5,955	2,512	522	2,893	1,054	1,437	Ohio......	49,844	38,494	8,151	2,000	15,395	655
Florida...	4,145	2,108	176	1,806	726	642	Oklahoma.	352	302	15	20	133	6
Georgia...	21,174	9,356	269	10,971	3,667	4,321	Oregon ...	2,575	1,959	386	38	636	5
Idaho.....	711	522	105	34	216	2	Penn'va'ia.	73,530	50,401	12,648	2,383	24,824	932
Illinois...	53,123	39,336	11,650	1,031	20,795	340	R'de-Is'nd.	7,559	5,344	1,939	224	2,627	73
Indiana....	24,180	20,505	2,185	862	7,317	298	South-Car.	15,495	4,730	178	10,448	1,767	3,786
Iowa......	17,521	13,381	3,221	162	5,187	54	South-Dak.	2,705	1,869	733	11	1,001	3
Kansas....	12,018	9,593	1,321	701	4,278	258	Tennessee.	23,854	15,229	428	7,573	5,363	2,754
Kentucky.	23,877	17,446	1,177	4,479	6,789	1,572	Texas.....	26,478	18,096	1,841	5,190	7,042	1,938
Louisiana.	16,354	6,953	1,494	7,716	3,094	2,592	Utah......	2,118	1,488	574	11	837	2
Maine.....	10,044	8,590	1,161	34	1,835	8	Vermont...	5,425	4,556	575	13	1,154	3
Maryland.	18,000	11,279	2,012	4,421	5,346	1,981	Virginia...	23,232	11,600	400	10,819	3,937	3,999
Mas'ch'ts	45,112	32,747	11,327	630	15,109	237	Wash'ton..	2,695	1,750	512	65	834	14
Michigan..	25,016	18,117	5,746	412	8,267	127	West-Vir..	8,275	7,223	328	519	2,724	178
Minnesota	15,488	10,389	4,775	98	6,375	35	Wisconsin.	18,662	11,508	6,493	101	6,014	24
Missi'si'pi.	14,899	5,834	177	8,560	2,095	2,896	Wyoming..	414	258	95	7	127	....
Missouri..	32,435	24,499	4,005	2,794	11,390	1,105							
Montana..	1,012	625	272	26	258	6	Total....	†872,944	596,055	140,075	114,313	264,784	41,911
Nebraska..	8,445	6,591	1,451	91	3,570	33							

* Including birthplace unknown ; total number, 22,501. † Exclusive of Indians on Reservations.

CAUSES OF DEATHS.

STATES AND TERRITORIES.	Scarlet Fever.	Measles.	Whooping Cough.	Diphtheria, Croup.	Enteric Fever.	Malarial Fever.	Diarrhoeal Diseases.	Cancer, Tumors.	Consumption.	Pneumonia.	Puerperal Diseases.
Alabama	23	496	182	448	874	1,030	2,069	331	2,163	1,585	423
Arizona	11	14	1	26	15	30	34	9	68	70	11
Arkansas	25	87	116	420	590	1,527	1,176	154	1,209	1,591	342
California	55	76	105	538	479	153	763	567	2,889	1,526	137
Colorado	69	66	38	382	417	38	394	73	489	686	107
Connecticut	81	43	110	717	331	191	1,148	412	1,743	1,344	95
Delaware	18	31	10	163	102	28	284	59	476	268	27
District of Columbia	18	6	30	192	200	98	592	115	827	484	45
Florida	10	68	60	54	163	287	397	81	377	251	119
Georgia	8	440	89	553	1,000	937	2,353	340	2,155	1,738	426
Idaho	31	5	7	45	46	11	36	16	36	83	13
Illinois	412	314	359	3,501	1,700	731	4,970	1,262	5,698	4,912	676
Indiana	217	257	310	899	1,071	386	1,823	636	3,504	1,701	*344
Iowa	226	187	185	1,502	366	216	1,152	545	1,832	1,377	296
Kansas	105	207	207	644	375	400	948	286	1,368	948	220
Kentucky	107	513	539	1,115	1,046	514	1,671	412	3,538	1,924	298
Louisiana	16	239	128	382	319	1,204	1,153	285	1,516	1,213	270
Maine	36	14	96	288	305	32	322	461	1,477	958	98
Maryland	91	272	139	528	517	221	145	446	2,315	1,453	178
Massachusetts	194	97	365	2,212	827	115	3,731	1,497	5,981	3,965	284
Michigan	249	282	178	1,557	686	373	2,115	795	2,747	1,830	420
Minnesota	282	158	77	1,176	489	30	1,528	376	1,532	1,219	281
Mississippi	15	456	275	315	521	1,273	1,198	209	1,433	1,447	335
Missouri	283	513	410	1,377	1,072	1,013	2,430	717	3,559	3,300	493
Montana	55	5	2	48	47	2	54	14	55	154	23
Nebraska	142	111	120	808	338	95	886	182	604	649	168
Nevada	2	1	1	16	8	10	17	14	35	68	6
New-Hampshire	20	16	37	326	139	20	567	262	729	624	41
New-Jersey	207	183	376	1,516	684	274	2,522	687	3,388	2,674	207
New-Mexico	36	3	17	678	49	72	80	21	97	189	57
New-York	956	757	1,081	5,653	1,715	953	11,347	3,186	14,851	12,945	872
North-Carolina	34	158	139	657	920	604	2,535	303	2,212	1,332	307
North-Dakota	41	19	16	145	81	23	199	24	167	111	37
Ohio	408	714	555	2,523	1,587	472	3,396	1,497	6,393	3,626	534
Oklahoma	3	1	3	12	10	29	42	4	21	27	12
Oregon	20	25	17	159	149	30	144	66	305	218	49

MORTALITY IN THE UNITED STATES—*Continued.*

STATES AND TERRITORIES.	Scarlet Fever.	Measles.	Whooping Cough.	Diphtheria, Croup.	Enteric Fever.	Malarial Fever.	Diarrheal Diseases.	Cancer, Tumors.	Consumption.	Pneumonia.	Puerperal Diseases.
Pennsylvania........	776	676	517	4,360	2,836	328	5,642	1,926	7,689	6,535	604
Rhode-Island........	35	119	102	283	150	59	714	218	921	574	56
South-Carolina......	21	145	96	331	551	740	1,609	213	2,112	1,164	278
South-Dakota......	49	35	41	254	132	19	246	54	208	281	74
Tennessee	71	306	244	757	1,083	1,020	2,143	343	3,637	1,892	372
Texas..............	45	468	260	628	1,026	2,102	2,434	369	2,059	2,533	612
Utah..............	40	2	14	292	95	37	157	31	62	230	70
Vermont	21	20	16	277	124	14	331	252	661	552	55
Virginia	46	344	299	781	757	616	2,197	410	3,050	1,710	330
Washington........	55	46	22	190	232	59	189	42	278	226	50
West-Virginia......	33	109	238	424	429	74	672	151	1,143	500	115
Wisconsin..........	216	128	105	1,221	350	76	1,400	632	2,015	1,549	336
Wyoming..........	16	2	....	33	27	1	27	2	18	45	9
Total	5,960	9,228	8,354	41,536	27,033	18,565	74,576	20,978	101,645	76,291	11,232

STATISTICS OF DEATHS IN TWENTY-FIVE PRINCIPAL CITIES IN THE CENSUS YEAR 1889-1890. PREPARED FOR "THE WORLD ALMANAC" BY THE CENSUS OFFICE.

25 PRINCIPAL CITIES.	Total Deaths.	WHITE. Native-Born.	WHITE. Foreign-Born.	Colored.	PRINCIPAL CAUSES. Scarlet Fever.	Diphtheria and Croup.	Enteric Fever.	Malarial Fever.	Diarrheal Diseases.	Consumption.	Pneumonia.
New-York, N. Y.....	43,378	27,141	14,747	962	366	1,870	348	243	4,565	5,871	5,112
Chicago, Ill.........	23,162	15,923	6,597	346	202	1,545	794	111	2,797	1,935	2,032
Philadelphia, Pa....	23,738	16,837	5,360	1,309	187	844	770	60	1,602	2,927	1,959
Brooklyn, N. Y.....	20,593	14,146	5,990	383	154	1,366	194	207	1,890	2,325	2,261
St. Louis, Mo.......	8,645	5,300	2,356	935	121	279	145	229	535	834	639
Boston, Mass.......	11,117	7,299	3,462	286	33	638	174	12	893	1,685	1,127
Baltimore, Md......	10,752	6,616	1,609	2,450	59	243	202	122	1,334	1,273	878
San Francisco, Cal ..	7,060	3,677	2,573	681	20	176	166	28	262	1,131	684
Cincinnati, O........	6,640	4,437	1,807	386	23	489	151	29	418	832	624
Cleveland, O........	5,736	4,140	1,444	96	56	385	164	41	535	415	492
Buffalo, N. Y.......	5,087	3,502	1,503	40	28	220	80	24	597	476	409
New-Orleans, La	6,875	3,198	1,294	2,367	2	156	45	292	713	832	342
Pittsburgh, Pa.......	5,206	3,549	1,376	232	71	452	304	16	460	356	584
Washington, D. C ...	5,955	2,512	522	2,893	18	192	200	98	592	827	484
Detroit, Mich.......	4,203	2,871	1,135	81	40	360	40	35	474	334	295
Milwaukee, Wis.....	3,942	2,576	1,286	12	24	270	61	2	368	376	292
Newark, N. J........	5,280	3,737	1,316	190	56	314	181	45	460	594	462
Minneapolis, Minn..	2,440	1,765	598	26	32	179	94	2	257	252	205
Jersey City, N. J....	4,484	3,117	1,264	66	21	312	134	47	324	443	528
Louisville, Ky.......	3,514	1,962	606	917	21	80	122	23	173	453	281
Omaha, Neb.........	1,597	1,002	269	44	5	144	63	17	125	95	128
Rochester, N. Y.....	2,323	1,526	715	4	1	61	53	12	244	286	248
St. Paul, Minn.......	2,240	1,641	526	36	34	139	92	2	303	167	159
Kansas City, Mo ...	2,553	1,643	323	469	18	72	53	54	191	238	246
Providence, R. I......	2,955	2,032	778	141	12	124	53	38	220	401	244

𝔅𝔲𝔰𝔦𝔫𝔢𝔰𝔰 𝔉𝔞𝔦𝔩𝔲𝔯𝔢𝔰 𝔦𝔫 𝔱𝔥𝔢 𝔘𝔫𝔦𝔱𝔢𝔡 𝔖𝔱𝔞𝔱𝔢𝔰.
CLASSIFIED AS TO CAUSES.

FAILURES DUE TO	No. 1891.	No. 1890.	Assets. 1891.	Assets. 1890.	Liabilities. 1891.	Liabilities. 1890.	PERCENTAGE. No. 1891.	Liabilities. 1891.	No. 1890.	Liabilities. 1890.
Incompetence.........	2,021	2,005	$8,563,259	$10,656,524	$16,268,941	$21,545,326	16.3	8.4	18.8	12.3
Inexperience	592	611	4,077,785	1,951,933	6,021,670	3,662,065	4.7	3.1	5.7	2.1
Lack of capital	4,869	4,052	34,572,098	23,571,043	61,716,157	45,818,944	39.2	32.0	37.9	26.1
Unwise credits.......	509	502	5,389,382	3,965,650	9,223,319	7,204,055	4.1	4.7	4.7	4.2
Failures of others....	279	257	8,723,326	9,745,954	16,195,080	20,799,648	2.7	12.1	5.6	11.2
Extravagance........	251	232	1,399,991	1,265,670	2,584,181	2,626,381	3.0	1.0	3.6	1.4
Neglect	383	390	1,049,640	1,223,198	2,070,709	2,411,302	2.0	1.3	2.1	1.5
Competition	199	246	929,215	1,235,549	1,859,352	2,191,551	7.0	6.8	3.9	3.9
Disaster (com. crisis).	2,075	1,358	21,959,012	28,637,846	40,736,054	42,650,814	16.5	21.1	12.7	24.3
Speculation	341	63	12,198,055	8,917,424	23,356,718	19,616,481	2.2	8.3	2.4	11.9
Fraud...............	875	416	4,031,237	1,604,828	13,139,819	6,612,069	1.6	0.9	2.3	1.2
Totals..............	12,394	10,673	$102,893,000	$92,775,625	$193,178,000	$175,032,836	100.00	100.00	100.00	100.00

The statistics of business failures were furnished by "Bradstreet's."

Marriage Laws.

(These tables have been specially revised to present date.)

States and Territories.	Age of Consent. Male.	Age of Consent. Female.	Prohibited Degrees.	Void Marriages.	Voidable Marriages.	Licenses. If Required (d).	Licenses. Age to Entitle to (e). Male.	Licenses. Age to Entitle to (e). Female.
Alabama.....	17 (b)	14 (b)	Ancestors, descendants, brothers, sisters, uncles, aunts, nephews, nieces, step-relatives.	Prohibited degrees, white with negro blood.	Under age of consent.	Yes	21 (f)	18
Arizona......	18 (b)	16 (b)	Ancestors, descendants, brothers, sisters, uncles, aunts, nephews, nieces, first cousins.	Prohibited degrees, white with negro or Mongolian.	Under age of consent.	......	..	..
Arkansas	17 (b)	14 (b)	Same as Arizona.....	Prohibited degrees, bigamous, under age of consent, white with negro blood.	Insane, incapacity, consent obtained by fraud or force (h).	Yes	21	18
California....	18 (b)	15 (b)	Ancestors, descendants, brothers, sisters, uncles, aunts, nephews, nieces.	Prohibited degrees, bigamous, white with negro blood.	Under age of consent if no cohabitation since attaining such age, insane or idiot, incapacity, force or fraud if no voluntary cohabitation, bigamous, when either party had married while other was absent and unheard of for over five years.	Yes	21	18
Colorado ...	14 (a)	12	Same as California...	Same as California.....	....	Yes	21	18
Connecticut..	14 (a) (b)	12 (a) (b)	Same as Alabama, except that restriction as to step-relatives does not extend beyond step-mother, step-daughter, step-father, or step-son.	Prohibited degrees, and those solemnized by persons not having authority.	....	Yes	21	21
Delaware....	14 (a)	12	Same as Alabama, and great-nephews and nieces.	Same as California, and those not properly solemnized.	Insane or idiot...	Yes	21	18
Dist. of Colu.	14	12	Same as Maryland..	Same as Maryland.....	....	Yes	21 (g)	16 (g)
Florida	14 (a)	12	" Within the Levitical degrees."	Bigamous, and white with negro blood.	....	Yes	21	21
Georgia......	17	14	" Within the Levitical degrees" and step-relatives.	Prohibited degrees, bigamous, insane when married, physically incompetent, white with negro blood, force or fraud, under age of consent.	....	Yes	21	18
Idaho........	18	18	Same as California...	Same as California....	Same as Calif'a.	No	..	..
Illinois.......	17	14	Same as Arizona......	Prohibited degrees, and insane or idiot when married.	....	Yes	21	21
Indiana	18	16	Same as Arizona......	Same as California, and also insane or idiot when married.	Under age of consent.	Yes	21	18
Iowa.........	16	14	Same as Alabama...	Prohibited degrees and bigamous............	Same as Indiana.	Yes	21	18
Kansas.......	15	12	Same as Arizona......	Prohibited degrees	Same as Indiana.	Yes	..	..
Kentucky....	14	12	Same as Delaware....	Prohibited degrees, bigamous, insane or idiot when married, physically incompetent, white with negro blood; not solemnized according to law.	Under age of consent if no cohabitation since attaining age, consent obtained by fraud or force.	Yes	21 (d)	21
Louisiana....	14	12	Same as California.	Bigamous............	Consent obtained by fraud or force if no cohabitation before suit.	Yes	21	21
Maine........	14 (a) (b)	12	Same as Alabama.....	Prohibited degrees, bigamous, insane or idiot when married.	....	Yes	21	18
Maryland....	14 (a)	12 (c)	Same as Alabama....	Same as California.....	....	Yes	21 (g) (m)	16 (g) (m)

MARRIAGE LAWS—Continued.

States. AND Territories.	Age of Consent. Male.	Age of Consent. Female.	Prohibited Degrees.	Void Marriages.	Voidable Marriages.	Licenses. If Required (d).	Licenses. Age to Entitle to (e). Male.	Licenses. Age to Entitle to (e). Female.
Massachusetts.	14 (a) (b)	12 (a) (b)	Same as Alabama.....	Prohibited degrees, bigamous, under age of consent, if parties separate during such nonage and do not cohabit afterwards, insane or idiot when married, when parties leave the State to contract contrary to laws of Mass., and return to reside.	....	Yes	21	18
Michigan....	18	16	Same as Alabama.....	Same as Mass., force or fraud.	Same as California.	Yes	..	..
Minnesota...	18	15	Same as California...	Prohibited degrees, bigamous.	Under age of consent if no cohabitation since attaining such age, insane, force or fraud, woman unchaste before marriage unknown to husband.	Yes	21	18
Mississippi...	14 (a)	12	Same as Alabama....	Same as California.....	Insane or idiot when married unknown to others.	Yes	21	18
Missouri.....	15	12	Same as Arizona.....	Same as California.....	....	Yes	21	18
Montana....	18	16	Same as Arizona.....	Same as Iowa.........	....	Yes	21	18
Nebraska.....	18	16	Same as California....	Same as Indiana.......	Same as Ky......	Yes	21	18
Nevada......	18 (b)	16 (b)	Same as Arizona......	Prohibited degrees, bigamous, white with negro blood, Indian or Mongolian.	Same as Minnesota.	Yes	21	18
New - Hampshire.	14	12	Same as Alabama, and also first cousins.	Same as Minnesota....	....	Yes	..	..
New-Jersey.	14 (a)	12 (k)	Same as Alabama.....	Bigamous and physically incompetent.	....	No	..	..
New-Mexico.	18	15 (k)	Same as California....	Prohibited degrees and under age.	....	No	..	..
New-York...	18	16	Ancestors, descendants, brothers and sisters.	Prohibited degrees, bigamous, and imprisonment for life.	Same as California, and under age of consent, but only when contracted without consent of parent, force or fraud.	....	..	..
North - Carolina.	16	14	Same as California....	Prohibited degrees, bigamous, under age of consent, insane when married, physically incompetent, white with negro or Indian and negro with Indian	....	Yes	18	18
North - Dakota.	18	16	Same as Arizona......	Prohibited degrees, bigamous.	Incapable from physical causes, consent obtained by force or fraud.	No	..	..
Ohio.........	18	16	Same as Arizona.....	Same as Iowa, and under age of consent unless ratified by cohabitation after such age, idiot when married.	....	Yes	21 (m)	18
Oklahoma...	18	15	Same as Arizona, and step-father and step-daughter, step-mother and step-son.	Prohibited degrees, bigamous.	Consent obtained by fraud or force, incapable from physical causes, under age of consent, idiot or insane.	No	..	..
Oregon.......	18	15	Same as California....	Bigamous, prohibited degrees, white with negro, Indian or Mongolian.	Same as Minnesota.	Yes	21	18

MARRIAGE LAWS—*Continued.*

STATES AND TERRITORIES.	AGE OF CONSENT. Male.	AGE OF CONSENT. Female.	Prohibited Degrees.	Void Marriages.	Voidable Marriages.	LICENSES. If Required (d).	LICENSES. Age to Entitle to (e). Male.	LICENSES. Age to Entitle to (e). Female.
Pennsylvania	14 (a)	12	Same as Alabama.....	Same as Iowa..........	Where obtained by force or fraud and no subsequent cohabitation, or where either has been sentenced for two years or more for felony.	Yes	21	21
Rhode-Island	14 (a) (b)	12	Same as Alabama ; Jews may marry within degrees allowed by their religion.	Prohibited degrees, bigamous, and insane when married.	....	Yes	21	18
South - Carolina.	14 (a)	12 (c)	Same as Alabama.....	Bigamous, insane when married, white with negro or Indian blood.	Consent obtained by fraud or force, or if either party for any cause was not aware that a marriage was being entered into, if marriage not consummated afterward.	....	.	..
South - Dakota.	18	15	Same as Arizona, and step-father with step-daughter, step-mother with step son.	Prohibited degrees, bigamous.	Incapacity, consent obtained by force or fra'd	Yes	21	21
Tennessee...	14 (a)	12	Same as Alabama.....	Bigamous, white with negro blood.	Insane when married, duress, under age of consent, consent obtained by fraud unless afterwards made valid by cohabitation.	Yes	..	..
Texas........	16	14	Same as Alabama.....	White with negro, bigamous, prohibited degrees.	Physical incapacity, or any impediment making contract void.	Yes	21	18
Utah.........	14	12	Same as California...	Bigamous, mixed blood (African or Chinese), under age of consent, and those not solemnized before authorized person.	Force or fraud, where male was under 16 and female under 14, and parents did not consent and marriage was not subsequently ratified by cohabitation.	Yes	21	18
Vermont.....	14 (a) (b)	12 (b)	Same as Alabama.....	Same as Iowa	Same as California and force or fraud.	Yes	21	18
Virginia.	14	12	Same as Alabama.....	Bigamous, under age of consent without cohabitation, white with negro.	Prohibited degrees, insane or idiot, physical incapacity.	Yes	21	21
Wash'ton (i).	21	18	Same as Arizona......	Same as South-Dakota.	Same as Minn....	Yes	21	18
West - Virginia.	14	12	Same as Alabama.....	Prohibited degrees, underage, insane, incapacity, white with negro, former spouse living.	....	Yes	21	21
Wisconsin...	18	15	Same as California....	Prohibited degrees, bigamous, insane when married, imprisonment for life.	Same as Kentucky.	....	21	18
Wyoming...	18	16	Same as Arizona......	Prohibited degrees, bigamous, insane, idiot when married.	Same as Kentucky.	Yes	21	21

(a) As at common law ; no statutory mention.   (b) Consent of parents required if under age.   (c) Consent of parents required by females under sixteen.   (d) A marriage without a license is nevertheless valid ; the person solemnizing it is punished.   (e) Without parental consent.   (f) Parties under 21 years must give $200 bonds that no lawful impediment exists.   (g) Unless parents consent to less, but not under age of consent.   (h) Forced marriage is punishable by death to the male participant.   (i) Under Territorial laws.   (k) Must have consent of parents if male is under 21 and female under 18.   (m) Unless banns are published in some church.

MARRIAGE LAWS—*Continued.*

NOTE TO TABLES ON THE THREE PRECEDING PAGES.

Marriage is a civil contract between a man over 14 and a woman over 12 joined on the one side, and the State on the other. To make it valid, it must have the consent both of the State and of the persons. It has, necessarily, the consent of the State, for that is given in advance to everybody not idiots or of near kin, of the ages mentioned—14 and 12. The consent of the parties is taken for granted, unless proof to the contrary is shown. *It never needs the consent of the parent.* But the contract—valid while it lasts—if challenged, may be terminated by the State formally withdrawing its consent, if the consent of either of the parties to enter into such a contract with it, having been temporarily entrusted to the parent, cannot be given or obtained by them. It is their own consent that is lacking, not the parent's. No rule or regulation of State law concerning marriage applies to a civil contract, which any two citizens may freely enter into with the State at any time and under any circumstances. All rules and regulations affect the personal conduct of the parties during ceremonies outside of the contract. No possible violation of any State law, rule, or regulation concerning marriage can, of itself, make void a contract once entered into between a State and two citizens, and no punishment inflicted for such violation of the law can affect the validity of the marriage. These are questions between the State and single individuals. The State cannot punish one person for a crime committed by another.

Marriage is a double, not a single contract: 1. A private contract between the two persons; 2. a public contract between the State and the two persons joined. With the private contract between the two persons the State cannot interfere. They may make any changes or modifications they like at any time; this is none of its business. But no private contract they may enter into and no modification of the private contract they entered into can affect their joint public contract with the State; and no public contract (which is the marriage) once made between two persons and the State can be changed, altered, or amended by them without the consent of the State through its courts; nor can it be changed, altered, or amended by the State without the consent of at least one of the parties to the marriage. No marriage is illegal until so declared by a court; and no person can be legally freed from a marriage contract except by a court or by death or conviction for felony. Ceremonies and sacraments are parts of the private contract between the persons, and all rules and regulations concerning licenses, banns, age, and the like are a part of them; but they form no part of the public contract between the parties and the State, which is the only marriage the law recognizes, although the public contract must be made a part of the ceremony. No sacrament or ceremony alone can marry a man and woman. It is their contract with the State which alone marries them. In other words, the mutual consent of the parties, if legally marriageable, to be married constitutes marriage in the eyes of the law, though the statutory requirements as to licenses, banns, ceremonies, and age are not complied with by them. The neglect to comply may be punishable, but it does not, usually, invalidate the marriage.

Divorce Laws.

CAUSES FOR ABSOLUTE DIVORCE IN THE UNITED STATES.

The violation of the marriage vow is cause for divorce in all the States and Territories having divorce laws.

Alabama.—Voluntary abandonment for two years; imprisonment in penitentiary for two years on a sentence for seven years or more; crime against nature; habitual drunkenness after marriage and physical incapacity. To the husband, when wife was with child at time of marriage without knowledge of or by husband; to wife, where husband has committed actual violence on her person, attended with danger to life or health. Chancellor in making decree may decide whether defendant shall marry again or not.

Required residence in State, one year; but if the application is made on ground of desertion a residence of three years must be proven.

Arizona.—Excesses or cruel treatment by personal violence or otherwise; abandonment for six months; habitual intemperance; wilful neglect on part of husband to provide; conviction of felony.

Required residence, six months; either party may marry again.

Arkansas.—Wilful desertion one year; conviction of felony or other infamous crime; physical incapacity; habitual drunkenness one year; cruel and barbarous treatment as to endanger life; indignities to the person such as to render condition intolerable; permanently or incurably insane.

Required residence, one year; either party may remarry.

California.—Extreme cruelty; wilful desertion, neglect, and habitual drunkenness, either continued for one year; conviction of felony.

Previous residence, one year; either can remarry.

Colorado.—Wilful desertion one year, or has departed from State without intention of returning; physical incapacity; failure on part of husband to provide for wife for one year; habitual drunkenness one year; extreme cruelty; conviction of felony.

Previous residence, one year Either may remarry.

Connecticut.—Fraudulent contract; wilful desertion for three years, with total neglect of duty; absent seven years unheard of; habitual intemperance; intolerable cruelty; sentence to imprisonment for life; any infamous crime involving a violation of conjugal duty and punishable by imprisonment in State prison. Either party may remarry. Previous residence required, three years.

Delaware.—Desertion three years; habitual drunkenness; physical incapacity; extreme cruelty; conviction of felony; parties married under age; fraud and force in procuring marriage; wilful neglect of husband to provide for wife for three years.

Either party may remarry, but party guilty of adultery shall not* marry the person with whom crime was committed. No statutory provision as to previous residence.

District of Columbia.—Insanity at marriage; incapacity; habitual drunkenness; cruel and abusive treatment endangering life or health; wilful desertion for two years. Divorces from bed and board may be granted for cruel treatment and reasonable apprehension of bodily harm.

Residence of two years required. No statutory provision as to remarrying.

Florida.—Extreme cruelty; habitual indulgence in violent and ungovernable temper; physical incapacity; habitual intemperance for one year; wilful, obstinate, and continued desertion for one year; also to any person who has been a resident of Florida for two years whose husband or wife has procured a divorce in any other State or country.

Previous residence required, two years. Either party can marry.

Georgia.—Mental incapacity at time of marriage; physical incapacity; force, menaces, threats, duress, and fraud in procuring marriage; wife with child at time of marriage not by or with knowledge of husband; wilful desertion three years; conviction for offence involving moral turpitude, and under which party has been sentenced to two years or longer; cruel treatment; habitual intoxication. Concurrent verdict of two juries at different terms of court are necessary in procuring a divorce.

No statutory provision as to previous residence or remarrying.

Idaho.—Extreme cruelty; wilful desertion, wilful neglect, and habitual intemperance, each for one year; conviction of felony; physical incapacity.

Residence required, six months; either party may remarry.

DIVORCE LAWS—*Continued.*

Illinois.—Wilful desertion two years; attempt by either party on life of the other; extreme and repeated cruelty; physical incapacity; conviction of felony or other infamous crime.

Residence required, one year. No statutory provision as to remarriage.

Indiana.—Incapacity at time of marriage; abandonment two years; cruel and inhuman treatment; habitual drunkenness; failure of husband to support wife for two years; conviction of infamous crime.

Previous residence, two years; either party may marry.

Iowa.—Wilful desertion two years; conviction of felony; habitual drunkenness contracted after marriage; inhuman treatment such as to endanger life; wife with child at time of marriage not by or with knowledge of husband; physical incapacity; insanity at time of marriage.

Previous residence, one year. No statutory provision as to remarriage.

Kansas.—Abandonment one year; physical incapacity; wife with child at time of marriage not by or with knowledge of husband; extreme cruelty; fraudulent contract; habitual drunkenness; gross neglect of duty; conviction of and imprisonment for felony.

Residence required, one year; parties may remarry at once unless appeal is taken, and then not until 30 days after final judgment on the appeal.

Kentucky.—Living apart without cohabitation for five years; physical incapacity; abandonment for one year; condemnation for felony; concealment of immoral disease; force, duress, or fraud in obtaining marriage; uniting with religious society which forbids husband and wife to cohabit. Also to wife, for husband's confirmed habits of intoxication, with neglect to provide, and habitually behaving toward her in such cruel and inhuman manner as to destroy her peace and happiness; cruel beating or injury, indicating an outrageous temper and endangering her life; also to husband for pregnancy of wife at time of marriage not by him or with his knowledge; habitual drunkenness on her part of not less than one year.

Either party may remarry; residence required, one year.

Louisiana.—Habitual intemperance excess; cruel treatment or outrages, if of such a nature as to render living together insupportable; condemnation to an ignominious punishment; desertion for five years, having been summoned to return within one year of filing petition; fugitive from justice; attempt on life of the other. No divorce shall be granted except for adultery, except a decree of separation shall have been previously had and parties have lived apart one year.

On divorce for adultery the guilty party shall not marry the person with whom crime was committed, woman cannot remarry for ten months after marriage is dissolved; no statutory provision as to previous residence.

Maine.—Extreme cruelty; utter desertion for three years; gross and confirmed habits of intoxication; physical incapacity; cruel and abusive treatment; failure of husband to provide for wife; sentence of imprisonment for life.

Previous residence, one year; either party may marry.

Maryland.—Any cause which would render marriage void *ab-initio;* abandonment three years; woman guilty before marriage of illicit carnal intercourse unknown to husband; physical incapacity.

Residence required, two years. Where divorce is for adultery, court may decree that guilty party shall not marry during life of the other.

Massachusetts.—Extreme cruelty; utter desertion for three years; gross and confirmed habits of intoxication with liquors, by opium, or other drugs; cruel and abusive treatment; husband wantonly and cruelly refusing to provide for wife; where either party has joined religious society that professes to believe relation of husband and wife unlawful, and has continued with that society for three years, refusing for that time to cohabit; sentenced to hard labor for life or five years or more, and physical incapacity.

Previous residence where parties have resided together in State, three years; otherwise five years; guilty party cannot marry for two years.

Michigan.—Imprisonment for life or three years or more; physical incapacity; desertion for two years; habitual drunkenness; where either party has obtained a divorce in another State; neglect by husband to provide.

Court may order that guilty party shall not marry for a term not exceeding two years; previous residence of one year required.

Minnesota.—Cruel and inhuman treatment; sentence to State prison; physical incapacity; wilful desertion three years; habitual drunkenness one year.

Either party may remarry; residence required, one year.

Mississippi.—Sentenced to penitentiary; wilful desertion two years; habitual drunkenness; habitual cruel and inhuman treatment; physical incapacity; pregnancy of wife at time of marriage not by or with knowledge of husband; insanity or idiocy at time of marriage unknown to other.

Previous residence, one year; court may decree that guilty party shall not remarry.

Missouri.—Absent without cause for one year; conviction of felony or infamous crime; habitual drunkenness for one year; cruel or barbarous treatment as to endanger life; indignities as to render condition intolerable; husband guilty of such conduct as to constitute him a vagrant; conviction of crime or felony prior to marriage unknown to the other; incapacity; wife pregnant at time of marriage not by or with knowledge of husband.

One year's residence required. Either party may remarry.

Montana.—Desertion one year; husband wilfully deserting wife and departing from State without intention of returning; habitual drunkenness for one year; extreme cruelty; incapacity; conviction of felony or infamous crime.

One year's residence required; no statutory provision as to remarriage.

Nebraska.—Sentenced to imprisonment for life or for three years or more; wilful desertion for two years; habitual drunkard; extreme cruelty; utter desertion for two years; physical incapacity; neglect on part of husband to provide.

Residence required, six months; neither party can marry within time allowed for appeal, nor before final judgment, if appeal is taken.

Nevada.—Wilful desertion for one year; conviction of felony or infamous crime; habitual gross drunkenness; physical incapacity at time of marriage, continued to date of petition; extreme cruelty; neglect of husband to provide for one year.

Either party may remarry; residence of six months required.

New-Hampshire.—Extreme cruelty; conviction of crime and imprisonment for one year; where either has treated the other so seriously as to injure health or endanger reason; absence three years unheard of; habitual drunkenness three years; physical incapacity; where either has joined any society which professes to believe the relation of husband and wife unlawful, and refusal to cohabit with the other for six months; desertion for three years with refusal to cohabit, desertion for three years with refusal to support; where wife has resided out of State ten years without his consent without returning to claim her marital rights; where the wife of an alien has resided in the State three years and her husband has left the United States with intention of becoming a citizen of another country, not having made any suitable provision for her support; one or the other of the parties must be a resident of the State one year, unless both parties were domiciled in State when action was commenced, or the defendant was served with process in State, the plaintiff being domiciled therein.

Either party can remarry.

DIVORCE LAWS—*Continued.*

New-Jersey.—Wilful, continued, and obstinate desertion for two years; physical incapacity; extreme cruelty. Required residence, three years. No statutory provision as to remarriage.

New-Mexico.—Cruel or inhuman treatment; abandonment; habitual drunkenness; neglect on part of husband to provide. Required residence, six months.

New-York.—No absolute divorce is granted except for adultery; the following marriages are voidable: woman under age of sixteen when married without consent of parent or guardian; consent obtained by fraud, force, or duress; physical incapacity; idiot or insane.

Required residence, one year; where marriage is annulled for any of the above causes, either may remarry, but on absolute divorce granted for adultery, the guilty party shall not marry during life of the other, with these exceptions, this prohibition is not extra-territorial, and if the guilty party marries out of the State, in accordance with the laws of the State in which the marriage is solemnized, the marriage will be held good in New-York [see case of Van Voorhis *vs.* Brintnall, 86, N. Y. Reports 18]. The guilty party *may* also be permitted by the New-York court to marry again upon proving that the other party has remarried, that five years have elapsed since the divorce, and that his conduct has been uniformly good during that time.

North-Carolina.—Wife with child at marriage not by or with knowledge of husband; to wife, if husband is indicted for felony and flees from the State and does not return for one year; also to the husband, if wife refuses sexual relations with him for twelve months. Divorces from bed and board are granted for abandonment, maliciously turning the other out of doors; physical incapacity; cruel or barbarous treatment endangering life; indignities to the person as to render condition intolerable; habitual drunkenness.

Residence required, two years. On absolute divorce, either party may remarry.

North-Dakota.—Extreme cruelty; wilful desertion; wilful neglect and habitual intemperance; each continued for one year; conviction of felony.

Residence required, ninety days. Guilty party cannot marry during lifetime of the other.

Ohio.—Wilful absence for three years; extreme cruelty; physical incapacity; fraudulent contract; gross neglect of duty; habitual drunkenness for three years; imprisonment in penitentiary; divorce procured by either party in another State. Residence required, one year. Either party may remarry.

Oklahoma.—Extreme cruelty; wilful desertion; wilful neglect; habitual intemperance, each continued one year; conviction of felony. Residence required, ninety days. Either party may remarry.

Oregon.—Conviction of felony; habitual, gross drunkenness for one year; wilful desertion for one year; physical incapacity; cruel and inhuman treatment or personal indignities, rendering life burdensome.

Residence required, one year; neither party can marry until after expiration of time for appeal, and in case of appeal not until after judgment on the appeal.

Pennsylvania.—Wilful and malicious desertion for two years, or where husband has by cruel and abusive treatment endangered his wife's life or offered such indignities to her person as to render her condition intolerable and life burdensome, and thereby forced her to withdraw from his home and family; where wife, by cruel and barbarous treatment, renders condition of husband intolerable; physical incapacity; fraud, force, or coercion in obtaining marriage; conviction of felony and sentence for two or more years.

Residence of one year required. Either party can remarry.

Rhode-Island.—Any case where marriage was void or voidable by law; where either party is for crime deemed civilly dead, or from absence or other circumstances presumed to be dead; physical incapacity; extreme cruelty; wilful desertion for five years or for a shorter time, in discretion of court; continued drunkenness; neglect or refusal on part of husband to suitably provide for the wife, or for any other gross misbehavior and wickedness in either of the parties repugnant to or in violation of the marriage covenant.

Residence of one year required. No statutory provision as to remarriage.

South-Carolina.—(No divorce laws.)

South-Dakota.—(Same as North-Dakota.)

Tennessee.—Wilful or malicious desertion for two years; conviction of infamous crime; conviction for felony and sentenced to penitentiary; attempting life of the other; physical incapacity; refusal on part of wife to move into this State, and wilfully absenting herself from husband for two years; woman pregnant at time of marriage not by and without the knowledge of the husband; habitual drunkenness.

Divorces from bed and board are granted for cruel and inhuman treatment to wife; indignities to her person, rendering her condition intolerable and forced her to withdraw; abandoned her or turned her out of doors, and refused or neglected to provide for her.

Two years' residence required. On absolute divorce either party may marry, but on divorce for adultery the guilty party shall not marry the party with whom crime was committed during lifetime of the other.

Texas.—Excesses; cruel treatment or outrages, if of such a nature as to render living together insupportable; adultery; desertion for three years; conviction of felony and imprisonment in State prison.

Residence of six months required; either party may marry.

Utah.—Wilful desertion more than one year; wilful neglect to provide for wife; habitual drunkenness; conviction of felony; physical incapacity; cruel treatment to extent of causing great bodily injury or great mental distress. One year's residence required; either party may again marry.

Vermont.—Sentence to hard labor in State prison for life or three years or more; intolerable severity; wilful desertion three years, or absence seven years unheard of; husband grossly, wantonly, and cruelly neglecting to provide for wife; fraud or force in marriage, or either party under age of consent; parties must have lived together in the State.

Petitioner must reside at least one year in State; guilty party shall not marry for three years.

Virginia.—Sentenced to confinement in penitentiary; conviction of infamous offence before marriage unknown to the other; fugitive from justice for two years; wilful desertion for five years; wife with child at marriage not by or with knowledge of husband; wife a prostitute before marriage unknown to husband, and physical incapacity. Divorces from bed and board are granted for cruelty; reasonable apprehension of bodily harm; abandonment or desertion. Court may decree that guilty party shall not marry again without permission of court; residence of one year required.

Washington.—Consent to marriage obtained by fraud or force; abandonment one year; cruel treatment or personal indignities rendering life burdensome; habitual drunkenness, or neglect or refusal to provide; imprisonment in penitentiary or any other cause deemed by the court sufficient; chronic mania or dementia of either party for ten years. Residence of one year required; either party may marry again.

West-Virginia.—Confinement in penitentiary; infamous crime prior to marriage unknown to the other; wilful desertion for three years; wife with child at marriage not by or with knowledge of husband; wife immoral before marriage unknown to husband; husband notoriously licentious, and physical incapacity. Divorces from bed and board are granted for cruel and inhuman treatment; reasonable apprehension of bodily harm; abandonment; desertion; habitual drunkenness.

Residence of one year required. No statutory provision as to remarriage.

Wisconsin.—Imprisonment for life or three or more years; physical incapacity; wilful desertion for one year; cruel and inhuman treatment by personal violence; habitual drunkenness for one year; where the parties have voluntarily lived apart five years; neglect to provide. One year's residence required; either party can remarry.

DIVORCE LAWS—*Continued.*

Wyoming.—Conviction of felony and sentenced therefor ; wilful desertion for one year ; habitual drunken-ness ; neglect on part of husband to provide for one year ; such indignities as to render condition intolerable ; husband guilty of such conduct as to constitute him a vagrant ; physical incapacity ; conviction of felony or infamous crime before marriage without the other's knowledge ; wife with child at marriage not by or with knowledge of husband.
Residence of six months required ; no statutory provision as to remarrying.

The courts of every State, and particularly of New-York, are very jealous of their jurisdiction, and generally refuse to recognize as valid a divorce against one of the citizens of the State by the court of another State, unless both parties to the suit were subject at the time to the jurisdiction of the court granting the divorce.
Kansas courts grant divorces for the reason that the applicant's husband or wife has obtained a divorce in another State and the applicant has been forbidden to remarry. If a wife in New-York obtains a divorce from her husband, and he is forbidden to remarry, he may go to Kansas and obtain a divorce on that ground. If his wife contests the case, or can be served with the papers in Kansas, so that she is brought under the jurisdic-tion of the Kansas court, the courts of New-York must recognize the divorce as valid, and cannot punish the hus-band for remarrying in New-York.
New-York permits polygamy and polyandry in certain cases. Desertion for five years, without knowledge that the deserter is living, permits the one deserted to marry again ; and the second marriage is valid, though the deserter returns. The second marriage may be declared void, but only from the date of the decree, by a court of competent jurisdiction, upon proper petition ; but if no such petition is made, and all parties are satisfied, one husband may live in lawful wedlock with two or more wives, or one wife with two or more husbands. The children will inherit, and both wives will be entitled to dower.
According to the Divorce Statistics for twenty years ending 1886, collected by Labor Commissioner Wright, the number of divorces in the United States in that period was 328,716, of which 129,382 were of couples with children, and 57,524 of couples without. The causes were : desertion, 126,676 ; adultery, 67,686 ; cruelty, 51,595 ; drunkenness, 13,866 ; neglect to provide, 7,955.

Barrenness, Illegitimacy, and Childbirth.

BARRENNESS.—One woman in 20, one man in 30 are barren—that is, 4 per cent of population. It is found that one marriage in 20 is barren, say 5 per cent. Among the nobility of England, 21 per cent have no children, owing to intermarriage of cousins, no less than 4½ per cent of the present nobility being married to cousins.—*Mulhall.*
CHILDBIRTH, DEATHS IN.—The average for 20 years in England and Wales has been 32 per 10,000 births—that is, 1½ per cent of all mothers die sooner or later in childbirth.—*Mulhall.*
ILLEGITIMACY.—Percentage of illegitimate births to total births : Greece, 1.6 ; Ireland, 2.3 ; Russia, 3.1 ; Netherlands, 3.5 ; England, 4.5 ; Switzerland, 4.6 ; Canada, 5.0 ; Spain and Portugal, 5.5 ; Italy, 6.8 ; Belgium, 7.0 ; United States, 7.0 ; France, 7.2 ; Germany, 8.4 ; Norway, 8.5 ; Scotland, 8.9 ; Sweden, 10.2 ; Denmark, 11.2 ; Austria, 12.9.—*Mulhall.*
FECUNDITY.—In "Statistique Humaine de la France," M. J. Bertillon presents the following table show-ing that the French are the least prolific and the Germans the most prolific people of Europe. Number of chil-dren born alive annually per 1,000 women of 15 to 50 years : France, 102 ; Ireland, 114 ; Belgium, 127 ; England, 136 ; Netherlands, 137 ; Spain, 141 ; Prussia, 150 ; Bavaria, 156. Aristotle mentions a woman who had 5 children at a birth four times successively ; Menage one who had 21 children in seven years. The Empress Catherine received a Russian woman in 1757 who had had 57 children, all of whom were then living, having been born thus : 16 in four confinements, 21 in seven confinements, 20 in ten confinements, or in all 57 children in 21 confine-ments. This woman's husband married again, and his second wife had 15 children in 7 confinements. Fedor Vassileff, of Moscow (1782), had 83 children living when pensioned by the Czar. He had 69 children by his first wife at 27 births. Lucas Saez, who was living in Spain in 1883, then had 197 descendants. Mrs. George Hirsch, of Dallas, Tex., is reported, November, 1888, of having been confined of 6 children, 4 being boys and 2 girls. (The above was compiled from Mulhall.) On September 12, 1892, the wife of Charles Billings, in Ashe County, N. C., gave birth to 6 boys, all living.
FATAL HOURS IN ILLNESS.—A writer in the *Quarterly Review*, several years ago, undertook to in-vestigate the popular notion that there are certain hours during the twenty-four more fatal to life than others. He ascertained the hour of death in 2,880 instances of all ages from a mixed population, and from deaths occur-ring during a period of several years. The *maximum* hour of death is from 5 to 6 o'clock A.M., when it is 40 per cent above the average ; and the *minimum* during the hours from 9 till 11 o'clock in the evening, when it is 6¼ per cent below the average. Thus the least mortality is during midday hours—namely, from 10 till 3 o'clock ; the greatest during early morning hours, from 3 till 6 o'clock. Fishermen say that the times of the ebb and flow of the tides are always critical hours with invalids.—*Barker's Facts.*

Suicides.

In European cities the number of suicides per 100,000 inhabitants is as follows : Paris, 42 ; Lyons, 29 ; St. Petersburg, 7 ; Moscow, 11 ; Berlin, 36 ; Vienna, 28 ; London, 23 ; Rome, 8 ; Milan, 6 ; Madrid, 3 ; Genoa, 31 ; Brussels, 15 ; Amsterdam, 14 ; Lisbon, 2 ; Christiania, 9 ; Stockholm, 27 ; Constantinople, 12 ; Geneva, 11 ; Dresden, 51. Madrid and Lisbon show the lowest, Dresden the highest figure.
The average annual suicide rate in countries of the world per 100,000 persons living is given by Barker as follows : Saxony, 31.1 ; Denmark, 25.8 ; Schleswig-Holstein, 24.0 ; Austria, 21.2 ; Switzerland, 20.2 ; France, 15.7 ; German Empire, 14.3 ; Hanover, 14.0 ; Queensland, 13.5 ; Prussia, 13.3 ; Victoria, 11.5 New-South Wales, 9.3 ; Bavaria, 9.1 ; New-Zealand, 9.0 ; South-Australia, 8.9 ; Sweden, 8.1 ; Norway, 7.5 ; Belgium, 6.9 ; England and Wales, 6.9 ; Tasmania, 5.3 ; Hungary, 5.2 ; Scotland, 4.0 ; Italy, 3.7 ; Netherlands, 3.6 ; United States, 3.5 ; Russia, 2.9 ; Ireland, 1.7 ; Spain, 1.4.
The causes of suicide in European countries are reported as follows : Of 100 suicides : madness, delirium, 18 per cent ; alchoholism, 11 ; vice, crime, 19 ; different diseases, 2 ; moral sufferings, 6 ; family matters, 4 ; poverty, want, 4 ; loss of intellect, 14 ; consequence of crimes, 3 ; unknown reasons, 19.
The number of suicides in the United States, five years, 1882–87, was 8,226. Insanity was the principal cause, shooting the favorite method. 5,386 acts of suicide were committed in the day, and 2,419 in the night. Summer was the favorite season, June the favorite month, and the 11th the favorite day of the month.
The month in which the largest number of suicides occurs is July.

Weather Signals

OF THE WEATHER BUREAU, U. S. DEPARTMENT OF AGRICULTURE.

The Weather Bureau furnishes, when practicable, for the benefit of the general public and those interests dependent to a greater or less extent upon weather conditions, the "Forecasts" which are prepared at that office daily, at 10 A.M. and 10 P.M., for the following day. These weather forecasts are telegraphed to observers at stations of the Weather Bureau, railway officials, and many others, and are so worded as to be readily communicated to the public by means of flags or steam whistles. The flags adopted for this purpose are five in number, and of the form and dimensions indicated below:

EXPLANATION OF FLAG SIGNALS.

No. 1. White Flag.	No. 2. Blue Flag.	No. 3. White and Blue Flag.	No. 4. Black Triangular Flag.	No. 5. White Flag with black square in centre.

Clear or fair weather.	Rain or snow.	Local rains.	Temperature signal.	Cold wave.

Number 1, white flag, six feet square, indicates clear or fair weather. Number 2, blue flag, six feet square, indicates rain or snow. Number 3, white and blue flag (parallel bars of white and blue), six feet square, indicates that local rains or showers will occur, and that the rainfall will not be general. Number 4, black triangular flag, four feet at the base and six feet in length, always refers to temperature; when placed above numbers 1, 2, or 3 it indicates warmer weather; when placed below numbers 1, 2, or 3 it indicates colder weather; when not displayed, the indications are that the temperature will remain stationary, or that the change in temperature will not vary more than four degrees from the temperature of the same hour of the preceding day from March to October, inclusive, and not more than six degrees for the remaining months of the year. Number 5, white flag, six feet square, with black square in centre, indicates the approach of a *sudden* and *decided* fall in temperature. This signal is not to be displayed unless it is expected that the temperature will fall to forty-two degrees, or lower, and is usually ordered at least twenty-four hours in advance of the cold wave. When number 5 is displayed, number 4 is always omitted.

A special storm flag, red with black square in centre (not shown above), is prescribed for use in North and South-Dakota, Minnesota (except at Lake stations), Iowa, Nebraska, and Wyoming, to indicate high winds, accompanied by snow, with temperature below freezing.

When displayed on poles, the signals should be arranged to read downward; when displayed from horizontal supports, a small streamer should be attached to indicate the point from which the signals are to be read.

INTERPRETATION OF DISPLAYS.

No. 1, alone, indicates fair weather, stationary temperature.
No. 2, alone, indicates rain or snow, stationary temperature.
No. 3, alone, indicates local rain, stationary temperature.
No. 1, with No. 4 above it, indicates fair weather, warmer.
No. 1, with No. 4 below it, indicates fair weather, colder.
No. 2, with No. 4 above it, indicates warmer weather, rain or snow.
No. 2, with No. 4 below it, indicates colder weather, rain or snow.
No. 3, with No. 4 above it, indicates warmer weather with local rains.
No. 3, with No. 4 below it, indicates colder weather with local rains.
No. 1, with No. 5 above it, indicates fair weather, cold wave.
No. 2, with No. 5 above it, indicates wet weather, cold wave.

Communications with reference to the display of these symbols and signals should be addressed to the Director of the State Service in which the station is located or to the Chief of the Weather Bureau, Washington, D. C. (For wind signals, see next page.)

The several States, with headquarters, in which State Weather Services are in operation are:

Alabama, Auburn.	Md., Baltimore (for Del. also).	Ohio, Columbus.
Arizona, Tucson.	Mass., Boston (for New England).	Oklahoma, Oklahoma City.
Arkansas, Little Rock.	Michigan, Detroit.	Oregon, Portland or Oswego.
California, Sacramento.	Minnesota, Minneapolis.	Pennsylvania, Philadelphia
Colorado, Denver.	Mississippi, University.	South-Carolina, Columbia.
Florida, Jacksonville.	Missouri, Columbia.	South-Dakota, Huron.
Georgia, Atlanta.	Montana, Helena.	Tennessee, Nashville.
Idaho, Idaho Falls.	Nebraska, Crete.	Texas, Galveston.
Illinois, Springfield.	Nevada, Carson City.	Utah, Salt Lake City.
Ind., Indianapolis or Lafayette.	New-Jersey, New-Brunswick.	Virginia, Lynchburgh.
Iowa, Des Moines.	New-Mexico, Santa Fé.	Washington, Olympia.
Kansas, Topeka.	New-York, Ithaca.	West-Virginia, Parkersburgh.
Kentucky, Louisville.	North-Carolina, Raleigh.	Wisconsin, Milwaukee.
Louisiana, New Orleans.	North-Dakota, Bismarck.	Wyoming, Cheyenne.

The Public Lands of the United States.

(Prepared for THE WORLD ALMANAC by the General Land Office, December, 1892.)

THE following is a tabular statement showing the number of acres of public lands surveyed in the following land States and Territories up to June 30, 1892; also the total area of the public domain remaining unsurveyed within the same.

LAND STATES AND TERRITORIES.	AREAS OF PUBLIC LANDS IN STATES AND TERRITORIES.		Number of Acres of Public Lands Surveyed up to June 30, 1892.	Total Area Remaining Unsurveyed up to June 30, 1892.	LAND STATES AND TERRITORIES.	AREAS OF PUBLIC LANDS IN STATES AND TERRITORIES.		Number of Acres of Public Lands Surveyed up to June 30, 1892.	Total Area Remaining Unsurveyed up to June 30, 1892.
	Acres.	Square Miles.				Acres.	Square Miles.		
Alabama. .	32,462,115	50,722	32,462,115	......	Nevada....	71,737,600	112,090	33,619,543	38,118,087
Arkansas . .	33,410,063	52,203	33,410,063	......	N. Dakota.	45,561,600	71,190	†25,018,232	20,543,368
California..	100,992,640	157,801	72,036,471	28,356,169	Ohio	25,581,976	39,972	25,581,976	......
Colorado...	66,880,000	104,500	60,207,932	6,672,068	Oregon	60,975,360	95,274	41,101,029	19,874,331
Florida	37,931,520	59,268	30,830,657	7,100,863	S. Dakota.	50,643,200	79,130	33,557,389	17,085,811
Illinois....	35,465,093	55,414	35,465,093	......	Wisconsin .	34,511,360	53,924	34,511,360	......
Indiana ...	21,637,760	33,809	21,637,760	......	Washing'tn	44,796,160	69,994	22,364,100	22,432,060
Iowa.......	35,228,800	55,045	35,228,800	......	Wyoming..	62,645,120	97,883	48,856,379	13,788,741
Idaho......	55,228,160	86,294	11,482,966	43,745,194	Alaska.....	369,529,600	577,390	......	369,529,600
Kansas	51,770,240	80,891	51,770,240	......	Arizona....	72,906,240	113,916	15,306,123	57,600,117
Louisiana..	28,731,090	44,893	27,164,766	1,566,324	Indian Ter.	*25,840,640	40,376	10,800,640	15,040,000
Michigan...	36,128,640	56,451	36,128,640	......	N. Mexico.	77,568,640	121,201	48,859,849	28,708,791
Minnesota.	53,459,840	83,531	43,684,161	9,775,679	Oklahoma.	*18,234,080	28,647	15,996,644	2,237,436
Mississippi.	30,179,840	47,156	30,179,840	......	Utah.......	54,064,640	84,476	15,124,187	38,940,453
Missouri...	41,836,931	65,370	41,836,931	......					
Montana...	92,016,640	143,776	21,823,758	70,192,882	Total	1,815,424,388	2,836,757	1,003,904,151	‡811,520,237
Nebraska..	47,468,800	74,170	47,256,537	212,263					

* The figures given for Indian Territory include the area of the Cherokee Outlet, which is 9,790 square miles, or 6,265,600 acres. Those for Oklahoma Territory include the area of the former Public-Land Strip, 5,738 square miles, or 3,672,320 acres.

† This area includes 572,775 acres of land surveyed under contracts made with the United States Surveyor-General of South-Dakota, and reported by him prior to the establishment of the district and office of United States Surveyor-General of North-Dakota.

‡ This estimate is of a very general nature, and affords no index to the disposable volume of land remaining, nor the amount available for agricultural purposes. It includes Indian and other public reservations, unsurveyed private land claims, as well as surveyed private land claims, in the district of Arizona, California, Colorado, and New-Mexico; the sixteenth and thirty-sixth sections reserved for common schools; unsurveyed lands embraced in railroad, swamp land, and other grants; the great mountain areas; the areas of unsurveyed rivers and lakes, and large areas wholly unproductive and unavailable for ordinary purposes. The area of land in the unsurveyed portion of the public domain suitable for homes and subject to settlement under the laws of the United States is of comparatively small proportions.

PUBLIC LANDS VACANT AND SUBJECT TO ENTRY IN THE PUBLIC-LAND STATES AND TERRITORIES, JUNE 30, 1892.

STATES AND TERRITORIES.	Surveyed Land.	Unsurveyed Land.	Total Area.	STATES AND TERRITORIES.	Surveyed Land.	Unsurveyed Land.	Total Area.
	Acres.	Acres.	Acres.		Acres.	Acres.	Acres.
Alabama.	807,947	....	807,947	Montana	11,842,217	62,715,926	74,558,143
Arizona..........	11,925,460	42,683,071	54,608,531	Nebraska.........	10,674,332	125,000	10,799,332
Arkansas.........	5,091,313	....	5,091,313	Nevada...........	29,958,237	12,427,497	42,385,734
California.........	34,970,286	15,161,955	50,132,241	New-Mexico......	39,333,082	15,387,781	54,720,863
Colorado.........	36,858,798	5,139,579	41,998,377	North-Dakota.....	6,425,985	13,074,570	19,500,555
Florida..........	2,007,157	799,430	2,806,587	Oklahoma	6,324,863	....	6,324,863
Idaho............	4,422,571	29,802,578	34,225,149	Oregon	24,166,334	14,269,539	38,435,873
Iowa.............	....	....	....	South-Dakota ...	6,182,216	6,824,180	13,006,396
Kansas..........	734,080	....	734,080	Utah.............	7,024,133	28,207,333	35,231,466
Louisiana........	1,071,129	101,389	1,172,518	Washington......	5,079,567	14,018,853	19,098,420
Michigan.........	724,232	....	724,232	Wisconsin........	871,087	....	871,087
Minnesota........	2,767,971	3,742,640	6,510,611	Wyoming.........	38,611,739	13,413,509	52,055,248
Mississippi.......	978,418	....	978,418				
Missouri.........	808,799	....	808,799	Total... .	289,691,953	277,894,830	*567,586,783

* This aggregate is exclusive of Ohio, Indiana, and Illinois, in which, if any public land remains, it consists of a few small isolated tracts; it is exclusive of the Cherokee Strip, containing 8,044,644 acres, and all other lands owned or claimed by the Indians in the Indian Territory west of the ninety-sixth degree of longitude, contemplated to be made a part of the public domain by the fourteenth section of the act of March 2, 1889 (25 United States Statutes, 1,005), and it is also exclusive of Alaska, containing 577,390 square miles, or 369,529,600 acres, of which not more than 1,000 acres have been entered under the mineral laws, and includes 356,659 acres of mineral land in Nevada, in addition to the quantities given under the head surveyed land and unsurveyed land in the foregoing table.

TABLE SHOWING MINIMUM COST OF INSURANCE OF LIVES FROM YEAR TO YEAR WITHOUT EXPENSES.

Age.	TABLE OF MORTALITY BASED ON AMERICAN EXPERIENCE.			Amount that will Insure $1,000 for One Year at Each Age from 10 to 95.	Age.	TABLE OF MORTALITY BASED ON AMERICAN EXPERIENCE.			Amount that will Insure $1,000 for One Year at Each Age from 10 to 95.
	Number Living.	Number Dying.	Expectation of Life.			Number Living.	Number Dying.	Expectation of Life.	
10	100,000	749	48.72	$7.48	53	66,797	1,091	18.79	$16.33
11	99,251	746	48.08	7.51	54	65,706	1,143	18.09	17.40
12	98,505	743	47.44	7.73	55	64,563	1,199	17.40	18.57
13	97,762	740	46.82	7.57	56	63,364	1,260	16.72	19.89
14	97,022	737	46.16	7.60	57	62,104	1,325	16.05	21.34
15	96,285	735	45.50	7.63	58	60,779	1,394	15.39	22.93
16	95,550	732	44.85	7.66	59	59,385	1,468	14.74	24.72
17	94,818	729	44.19	7.69	60	57,717	1,546	14.09	26.69
18	94,089	727	43.53	7.72	61	56,371	1,628	13.47	28.87
19	93,362	725	42.87	7.76	62	54,743	1,713	12.86	31.29
20	92,637	723	42.20	7.81	63	53,030	1,800	12.26	33.94
21	91,914	722	41.53	7.86	64	51,230	1,889	11.68	36.87
22	91,192	721	40.85	7.91	65	49,341	1,980	11.10	40.13
23	90,471	720	40.17	7.95	66	47,361	2,070	10.54	43.70
24	89,751	719	39.49	8.02	67	45,291	2,158	10.00	47.64
25	89,032	718	38.81	8.07	68	43,133	2,243	9.48	52.00
26	88,314	718	38.11	8.13	69	40,890	2,321	8.89	56.75
27	87,596	718	37.43	8.19	70	38,569	2,391	8.48	61.98
28	86,878	718	36.73	8.27	71	36,178	2,448	8.00	67.66
29	86,160	719	36.03	8.34	72	33,740	2,487	7.54	73.73
30	85,441	720	35.33	8.42	73	31,243	2,505	7.10	80.17
31	84,721	721	34.62	8.51	74	28,738	2,501	6.68	87.03
32	84,000	723	33.92	8.61	75	26,237	2,476	6.28	94.37
33	83,277	726	33.21	8.71	76	23,761	2,431	5.88	102.31
34	82,551	729	32.50	8.83	77	21,330	2,369	5.48	111.06
35	81,822	732	31.78	8.95	78	18,961	2,291	5.10	120.82
36	81,090	737	31.07	9.09	79	16,670	2,196	4.74	131.73
37	80,353	742	30.35	9.24	80	14,474	2,091	4.39	144.46
38	79,611	749	29.62	9.40	81	12,383	1,964	4.04	158.60
39	78,862	756	28.90	9.58	82	10,419	1,816	3.71	147.30
40	78,106	765	28.18	9.79	83	8,603	1,648	3.30	191.56
41	77,341	774	27.45	10.01	84	6,955	1,470	3.08	211.36
42	76,567	785	26.72	10.25	85	5,485	1,292	2.77	235.55
43	75,782	797	25.99	10.52	86	4,193	1,114	2.47	205.68
44	74,985	812	25.27	10.83	87	3,079	933	2.19	303.02
45	74,173	828	24.54	11.16	88	2,146	744	1.93	346.69
46	73,345	848	23.80	11.55	89	1,402	555	1.69	395.86
47	72,497	870	23.08	11.99	90	847	385	1.42	454.54
48	71,627	896	22.36	12.51	91	462	246	1.19	532.47
49	70,731	927	21.63	13.10	92	216	137	.98	634.26
50	69,804	962	21.91	13.77	93	79	58	.80	734.18
51	68,842	1,001	20.20	14.53	94	21	18	.64	857.14
52	67,841	1,044	19.49	15.39	95	3	3	.50	1,000.00

This table shows the cost for an annual insurance of $1,000 at each age from ten to ninety-five. The life insurance companies level this annually increasing cost so as to make a larger portion payable in the younger ages, and a corresponding reduction later. The assessment or natural premium companies rely upon getting each year the cost of the year's insurance.

PREMIUM RECEIPTS FROM AND PAYMENTS TO POLICY-HOLDERS AND RESIDUE TO THEIR CREDIT IN LEADING AMERICAN LIFE INSURANCE COMPANIES FROM THE ORGANIZATION OF EACH.

COMPANIES.	Total Amount Received for Premiums from Organization to Jan. 1, 1892.	Total Paid Policy-holders.	Amount Invested for Policy-holders Jan. 1, 1892.	COMPANIES.	Total Amount Received for Premiums from Organization to Jan. 1, 1892.	Total Paid Policy-holders.	Amount Invested for Policy-holders Jan. 1, 1892.
Ætna......	$98,581,952	$78,174,882	$37,393,086	N. E. Mut.	$64,396,238	$52,648,606	$21,946,691
Berkshire..	15,504,927	11,291,604	5,078,071	New-York.	271,843,495	155,295,004	125,947,291
Brooklyn ..	9,092,639	11,305,553	4,381,591	No'western	94,677,745	56,960,643	48,808,880
Com. Alli..	641,447	326,188	276,820	PacificM...	7,806,122	4,744,622	2,358,714
Conn. Mut.	168,763,703	151,650,762	59,728,546	Penn. Mut.	41,447,486	27,044,866	18,431,984
Equitable..	294,895,192	158,357,477	133,231,785	Phœnix Mu	38,239,755	31,404,078	10,033,576
Germania..	40,377,721	26,284,572	16,673,743	Prov. Sav..	8,238,032	5,445,580	960,238
Home......	20,018,327	13,886,876	7,593,930	Prov. L.&T	31,401,199	13,917,908	20,839,364
J. Hancock	19,547,663	11,305,553	4,381,591	Prudential.	30,084,533	9,066,756	6,889,674
Manhattan.	40,300,189	32,047,584	12,870,200	State Mut..	13,763,415	8,281,832	7,153,638
Mass. Mut.	32,552,615	21,370,464	12,239,520	Travelers ..	16,846,814	6,009,401	11,506,503
Metr'p'lit'n	63,961,502	27,237,178	13,626,948	Union Cen.	16,971,663	6,451,108	7,879,959
Mich. Mut.	8,395,407	3,860,264	3,427,238	Union Mut.	32,371,221	25,737,950	6,297,555
Mut. Benf.	139,254,424	118,724,809	48,924,829	United Sta.	23,251,367	15,889,004	6,706,886
Mutual....	422,503,232	327,079,635	158,124,245	Washing'tn	31,887,753	20,635,554	11,409,924

This table of life insurance receipts and payments was compiled from returns printed in the New-York "Spectator."

The Fire Waste.

ANNUAL PROPERTY LOSSES IN THE UNITED STATES BY FIRES—1875-92.

Years.	Aggregate Property Loss.	Aggregate Insurance Loss.	Years.	Aggregate Property Loss.	Aggregate Insurance Loss.
1875	$78,102,285	$39,325,400	1885	$102,818,796	$57,430,789
1876	64,630,600	34,374,500	1886	104,924,750	60,506,567
1877	68,265,800	37,398,900	1887	120,283,055	69,659,508
1878	64,315,900	36,575,900	1888	110,885,665	63,965,724
1879	77,703,700	44,464,700	1889	123,046,833	73,679,465
1880	74,643,400	42,525,000	1890	108,993,792	65,015,465
1881	81,280,900	44,641,900	1891	143,704,967	90,576,918
1882	84,505,024	48,875,131	1892	132,621,311	79,215,291
1883	100,149,228	54,808,664			
1884	110,008,611	60,679,818	Total 18 years	$1,760,944,617	$1,003,722,557

The figures in the above table, from 1875 to 1891 inclusive, are taken from the *Chronicle* Fire Tables.

The waste by fires in the United States during the past five years has averaged $112,000,000 annually. To this must be added the expense of maintaining fire-extinguishing departments and appliances and of conducting insurance companies, to obtain an estimate of what the people pay out on account of fire.

The principal reported causes of fires, and the number of fires from each cause, in 1891, as compiled by the *Chronicle*, were as follows: Incendiarism, 2,602; defective flues, 1,439; sparks (not locomotive), 672; matches, 865; explosions of lamps and lanterns, 849; stoves, 552; lightning, 457; spontaneous combustion, 383; forest and prairie fires, 165; lamp and lantern accidents, 323; locomotive sparks, 309; cigars, cigarettes, and tobacco pipes, 286; friction in machinery, 196; gas-jets, 291; engines and boilers, stationary, 168; furnaces, 170; fire-crackers, 87; ashes and hot coals, 147; candles, 125; electric wires and lights, 116; explosions (oil and gas stoves), 302; ignition (grease, oil, etc.), 151; tramps, 106. There were 7,803 fires classified as "not reported," and 3,322 as "unknown."

HUMAN BEINGS AND ANIMALS BURNED TO DEATH IN SIX YEARS.

The following compilation in the *Chronicle* Fire Tables gives the number of human lives and those of animals destroyed in fires in the United States in five years, 1883-88 inclusive.

Years.	Human Beings.	Horses.	Cattle.	Other Animals.	Years.	Human Beings.	Horses.	Cattle.	Other Animals.
1883	447	2,171	1,183	5,981	1887	662	4,733	1,802	3,012
1884	384	2,114	1,230	3,926	1888	447	2,171	1,183	5,981
1885	491	1,973	1,161	4,077					
1886	344	2,241	2,281	8,142	Total	2,975	15,405	8,840	31,119

AVERAGE ANNUAL PROPERTY LOSS BY FIRE IN FOREIGN COUNTRIES.

Countries.	Average Annual Loss.	Cost per Inhabitant.	Ratio of Insured Property. Per Cent.	Countries.	Average Annual Loss.	Cost per Inhabitant.	Ratio of Insured Property. Per Cent.
Austria	$17,500,000	$0.50	..	Italy	$5,000,000	$0.17	..
Belgium	2,600,000	0.47	43	Netherlands	2,000,000	0.50	..
Canada	10,500,000	2.30	44	Russia	70,000,000	0.85	9
France	15,500,000	0.42	75	Scandinavia	6,500,000	0.80	..
Germany	31,000,000	0.67	74	Spain	2,500,000	0.15	..
Gt. Britain & Ireland	45,000,000	1.37	46				

This table of average annual property loss by fire in foreign countries is compiled from Mulhall's statement.

FIRES IN PRINCIPAL AMERICAN CITIES IN 1891.

Cities.	No. of Alarms.	No. of Fires.	Total Loss Thereon.	Total Insurance Thereon.	Total Insurance Loss Thereon.	No. of Incendiary Fires.	No. of Fires to 1,000 Pop.	Per cent. of Total Loss to Pop.
New-York	4,199	3,805	$6,959,650	$80,813,298	$6,234,706	33	2.08	$3.86
Chicago, Ill	4,349	3,247	3,053,874	22,029,520	3,292,046	63	2.68	2.44
Philadelphia, Pa	1,296	1,287		20,689,281	2,676,363	..	1.22	....
Brooklyn, N. Y	1,491	1,433	1,608,591	5,920,626	....	32	1.68	1.89
Boston, Mass	1,015	606	1,511,674	10,447,876	1,388,877	34	1.35	....
St. Louis, Mo	1,055	1,313	2,717,080	9,659,181	2,662,431	..	2.42	5.00
Baltimore, Md	493	428	2,989,612	625,097	....	..	.89	1.69
Cincinnati, O	700	....	1,704,649	....	1,370,142	..	....	5.37
Cleveland, O	986	895	1,225,774	3,224,248	872,926	55	3.31	4.53
New-Orleans, La	287	417					1.66	..
Washington, D. C	191	....	165,803	84,993	....	..	....	.69
Newark, N. J	263	284	212,341	2,418,920	160,421	6	1.53	1.14
Jersey City, N. J	386	386	394,773	....	369,785	7	2.36	2.42
Omaha, Neb	226	208	267,855				1.48	1.90
Providence, R. I	497	419	151,126	1,070,988	107,312	..	3.12	1.13
Rochester N. Y	189	189	....	1,429,057	111,566	10	1.41	....
Kansas City, Mo	545	474	217,076	3,527,561	194,729	21	3.64	1.66
Richmond, Va	131	131	196,190	809,617	....	12	1.45	2.17
Worcester, Mass	339	291	137,531	778,661	77,776	17	3.23	1.52
Atlanta, Ga	56	118	151,426	1,178,250			1.58	2.01

Electrical Statistics.

It is estimated that about $900,000,000, at the beginning of 1893, is invested in electrical industry in the United States, distributed as follows: Telegraph companies, $150,000,000; telephone companies, $100,000,000; electric lighting and power companies, $350,000,000; electrical supply companies, $100,000,000; and electric railway companies, $200,000,000.

THE WESTERN UNION TELEGRAPH COMPANY.

Statement exhibiting the mileage of lines operated, number of offices, number of messages sent, receipts, expenses, and profits for 1866, 1870, 1875, and 1880, and each year from 1885 to 1892 inclusive.

Year.	Miles of Poles and Cables.	Miles of Wire.	Offices.	Messages.	Receipts.	Expenses.	Profits.
1866....	37,380	75,686	2,250	....	....	....	....
1870....	54,109	112,191	3,972	9,157,646	$7,138,737.96	$4,910,772.42	$2,227,965.54
1875....	72,833	179,496	6,565	17,153,710	9,561,574.60	6,335,414.77	3,229,157.83
1880....	85,645	233,534	9,077	29,215,509	12,782,894.53	6,948,956.74	5,833,937.79
1885....	147,500	462,283	14,184	42,096,583	17,706,833.71	12,005,909.58	5,700,924.13
1886....	151,832	489,607	15,142	43,289,807	16,298,638.55	12,378,783.42	3,919,855.13
1887....	156,814	524,641	15,658	47,394,530	17,191,909.95	13,154,628.54	4,037,281.41
1888....	171,375	616,248	17,241	51,463,955	19,711,164.12	14,640,592.18	5,070,571.94
1889....	178,754	647,697	18,470	54,108,326	20,783,194.07	14,565,152.61	6,218,041.46
1890....	183,917	678,997	19,382	55,878,762	22,387,028.91	15,074,303.81	7,312,725.10
1891....	187,981	715,591	20,098	59,148,313	23,034,326.59	16,428,741.84	6,605,584.75
1892....	189,576	739,105	20,700	62,387,298	23,706,404.72	16,307,857.10	7,398,547.62

GROWTH OF THE TELEGRAPH SERVICE IN THE WORLD.

Number of messages, 1870: Russia, 2,716,300; Norway, 466,700; Sweden, 590,300; Denmark, 513,623; Germany, 8,207,800; Holland, 1,837,800; Belgium, 1,998,800; France, 5,663,800; Switzerland, 1,629,235; Spain, 1,050,000; Italy, 2,189,000; Austria, 3,388,249; Hungary, 1,489,000; United States, 9,157,646; Great Britain and Ireland, 9,650,000.

Number of messages, 1890: Russia, 9,949,405; Norway, 1,453,932; Sweden, 1,755,000; Denmark, 1,502,965; Germany, 25,847,836; Holland, 4,285,516; Belgium, 5,312,295; France, 28,094,000; Switzerland, 3,695,988; Spain, 4,084,704; Italy, 8,175,870; Austria, 9,081,631; Hungary, 4,464,277; United States, 60,000,000; Great Britain and Ireland, 66,409,000.

The average toll per message in 1868 was 104.7; in 1889 was 31.2; in 1890 was 32.4; in 1891 was 32.5; in 1892 was 31.6. The average cost per message to the company in 1868 was 63.4; in 1889 was 22.4; in 1890 was 22.7; in 1891 was 23.2 in 1892 was 22.3.

TELEPHONE STATISTICS.

The following are the latest statistics made public by the American Bell Telephone Company, which practically monopolizes the telephone business in the United States.

	1890.	1891.	1892.		1890.	1891.	1892.
Exchanges..................	757	774	788	Miles of wire submarine..	603	779	1,029
Branch offices.............	471	467	509	Total miles of wire.......	193,213	240,412	266,456
Miles of wire on poles.......	154,009	171,498	180,139	Total circuits..........	156,780	173,665	186,462
Miles of wire on buildings...	11,484	13,445	14,954	Total employes.........	6,758	7,845	8,376
Miles of wire underground..	27,117	54,690	70,334	Total subscribers.........	185,003	202,931	216,017

The number of instruments in the hands of licensees under rental at the beginning of 1892 was 512,407. The number of exchange connections daily in the United States is 1,584,712, or a total per year of over 500,000,000. The average number of daily calls per subscriber is 7.33. The company received in rental of telephones in 1892 $3,127,783. It paid its stockholders in dividends in 1892, $1,320,646. The capital of the company is $15,000,000. The Bell Telephone and its subsidiary companies represent about $80,000,000 of capital; the Long Distance Telephone Company about $5,000,000.

ELECTRIC RAILWAYS IN THE UNITED STATES.

States.	No. Roads.	Capital Stock.	Miles.	States.	No. Roads.	Capital Stock.	Miles.
Alabama...............	2	$3,175,000	22	Montana.............	4	$1,150,000	39
Arkansas.............	2	800,000	29	Nebraska.............	6	6,880,0.0	122
California.............	8	5,200,000	89	New-Hampshire.....	2	250,000	14
Colorado....	7	2,970,000	121	New-Jersey..........	8	2,485,000	50
Connecticut...........	3	270,000	8	New-York...........	33	13,337,000	375
Delaware.............	1	500,000	12	North-Carolina.......	5	575,000	24
District of Columbia....	3	700,000	26	Ohio.................	34	14,962,000	392
Georgia...............	9	2,550,000	98	Oregon..............	6	1,860,000	51
Illinois...............	24	6,055,000	204	Pennsylvania.......	40	11,560,000	2.3
Indiana...............	10	1,933,000	74	Rhode-Island........	1	100,000	4
Iowa.................	16	8,360,000	177	South-Dakota........	1	100,000	7
Kansas...............	7	3,100,000	74	Tennessee...........	9	5,200,000	171
Kentucky.............	5	2,000,000	59	Texas	21	7,488,673	219
Louisiana.............	1	100,000	5	Utah	2	600,000	10
Maine................	3	520,000	28	Virginia.............	9	3,576,000	82
Maryland.............	3	680,000	12	Washington..........	19	6,600,000	172
Massachusetts........	27	8,830,000	210	West-Virginia........	2	246,000	13
Michigan.............	19	3,695,300	120	Wisconsin...........	7	3,280,000	70
Minnesota............	6	11,350,000	252				
Missouri..............	20	12,050,000	205	Total.................	385	$155,087,973	3,980

These statistics of electrical railways were furnished by *Electrical Industries*.

Statistics of Education.

UNIVERSITIES AND COLLEGES OF LIBERAL ARTS IN THE UNITED STATES.
(Prepared for THE WORLD ALMANAC by the United States Bureau of Education.)

STATES AND TERRITORIES, 1891	Institutions	Professors and Instructors.				Students.					Volumes in Libraries.
		Preparatory Departments.	Collegiate Departments.	Professional Departments.	Total Number.	Preparatory Departments.	Collegiate Departments.	Graduate Departments.	Professional Departments.	Total Number.	
North Atlantic Division.											
Maine	3	..	37	16	52	.	510	..	102	612	89,117
New-Hampshire	1	..	18	17	48	..	256	..	98	462	72,000
Vermont	2	..	32	20	50	..	239	..	203	442	58,766
Massachusetts	9	33	236	204	548	292	2,720	302	1,179	4,827	571,150
Rhode-Island	1	.	35	.	35	..	326	26	....	352	70,000
Connecticut	3	..	99	62	193	..	1,204	18	318	2,031	278,501
New-York	23	119	423	245	831	2,534	4,465	467	2,365	10,859	636,552
New-Jersey	5	5	109	4	114	72	1,101	103	37	1,354	108,662
Pennsylvania	26	100	329	140	540	1,485	3,298	171	1,246	6,833	317,080
South Atlantic Division.											
Delaware	1	..	8	.	8	.	81	..	....	81	4,500
Maryland	10	52	155	3	171	532	889	276	84	1,885	126,907
District of Columbia	4	29	37	98	170	303	228	..	1,075	1,86	68,000
Virginia	7	22	87	17	116	195	1,079	6	307	1,593	134,050
West-Virginia	2	8	25	3	34	146	263	2	26	421	6,200
North-Carolina	11	44	83	18	126	865	1,019	17	234	2,407	72,100
South-Carolina	9	26	74	7	91	353	626	13	61	1,364	54,000
Georgia	7	16	49	18	101	291	726	5	185	2,152	49,300
Florida	4	26	31	..	36	463	82	..	....	545	7,240
South Central Division.											
Kentucky	13	42	91	24	145	904	1,244	5	361	2,514	55,910
Tennessee	24	117	187	120	368	2,214	2,336	49	957	6,094	100,531
Alabama	7	13	70	4	89	809	887	4	30	1,730	36,200
Mississippi	5	14	38	7	52	377	416	20	47	1,086	22,950
Louisiana	10	48	106	46	205	747	928	16	513	3,821	124,600
Texas	12	48	95	9	150	1,595	1,648	4	149	3,546	25,606
Arkansas	5	14	23	..	44	413	258	..	50	1,082	6,650
North Central Division.											
Ohio	37	248	350	147	717	4,389	4,029	258	1,264	12,190	303,272
Indiana	15	80	186	49	318	1,634	1,897	56	337	4,281	148,100
Illinois	28	218	288	189	629	3,854	2,701	530	2,336	10,472	177,173
Michigan	11	66	164	61	281	1,239	2,148	102	1,343	5,354	153,427
Wisconsin	9	54	135	25	160	677	1,372	56	316	2,602	94,900
Minnesota	11	71	132	92	250	856	1,125	51	493	2,991	53,221
Iowa	22	125	200	78	387	2,796	2,000	62	739	7,042	110,297
Missouri	27	152	232	17	342	2,506	2,007	51	267	5,791	134,015
North-Dakota	3	14	16	1	21	103	38	..	1	232	5,700
South-Dakota	6	58	47	.	65	559	133	..	....	1,008	10,539
Nebraska	8	53	78	39	143	857	457	32	78	1,801	33,360
Kansas	16	78	140	5	218	1,787	942	25	83	3,945	62,832
Western Division.											
Montana	1	6	6	..	15	71	13	..	....	127	1,200
Wyoming	1	7	8	..	15	39	13	..	....	75	2,300
Colorado	4	34	41	33	110	322	132	4	52	1,160	20,944
Utah	1	9	8	..	20	95	17	..	....	335	10,000
Nevada	1	4	8	..	10	115	48	..	....	193	1,932
Washington	4	20	19	1	32	381	73	..	4	656	7,700
Oregon	6	16	31	49	86	472	376	..	123	1,127	16,600
California	14	62	153	101	314	1,453	1,186	32	387	3,308	99,412
Total N. Atlantic Div	73	257	1,318	708	2,411	4,483	14,118	1,187	5,548	27,802	2,201,228
" S. Atlantic Div	56	223	519	164	846	3,248	4,993	319	1,972	12,316	522,207
" S. Central Div	76	296	610	210	1,053	7,059	7,717	98	2,107	19,873	372,447
" N. Central Div	193	1,217	1,968	703	3,541	21,347	18,849	1,223	7,257	57,742	1,296,842
" Western Div	32	158	274	184	611	2,948	1,858	36	566	6,951	160,088
" **United States**	430	2,151	4,719	1,969	8,472	39,085	47,535	2,863	17,450	124,684	4,542,900

American College Cheers.

THIS collection of college cheers has been made by THE WORLD ALMANAC, by correspondence with officials of the respective institutions, and revised to 1893. It is believed to be the largest collection ever published.

Alabama Polytechnic.—"'Rah-'rah-'ree—Rah-'rah-'ree—Ala-bam-a—A. M. C.!"

Alfred University.—"Rah, Rah, Zip, Rah, Boom! Alfred University. Give her room!"

Allegheny.—"Al-le-ghe-ny, rah boom!"

Amherst.—"Rah; 'rah-'rah; 'Rah; 'rah-'rah; Am-h-e-r-s-t!"

Antioch.—"Hobble, gobble! Razzle, dazzle! Zip, Boom, Ah! Antioch! Antioch! Rah! Rah! Rah!"

Baker University.—"B. A. Baker! Rah! Rah! Rah!"

Beloit.—"O-Y-Ya-Ya-Ya-B-L-O-I-T!"

Bethany (W. Va.).—"Hi! Yi! Yi! Rah! Rah! Rah! Yah! Hoo! Bethany!"

Bethany (Kan.).—"Rah! Rah! Beth-any! Bra! Rah! Rah!"

Boston University.—"Boston, Boston, B-B-B-Boston, 'Varsity, 'Varsity, Rah! Rah!! Rah!!!"

Bowdoin.—"B-o-w-d-o-i-n 'Rah, 'Rah, 'Rah!"

Brown University.—"Rah, Rah! Rah, Rah! Rah, Rah! Brown!!"

Buchtel.—"Ye-ho! Ye-he! Ye-hesa! Hisa! Wow wow! Buchtel!"

Bucknell University.—"Rah, 'rah ru, Bucknell, B. U., Wah-hu-hu-wah! bang!"

Butler University.—"B! U! Hurrah! B. U. Hurrah! Boomlah! Butler! 'Rah! 'Rah! 'Rah!"

Carleton.—"C-A-R-L-E-T-O-N-'Rah! 'Rah! 'Rah!"

Central (Kansas).—"Rock, Chalk! Jayhawk C. C. we be!"

Central University (Pella, Ia.).—"Central Central ra, ra, ra! 'Varsity 'Varsity ha, ha, ha! Iowa, Iowa, wa, wa, wa! Maxima pro patria, ra, ra ra!"

Central University (Richmond, Ky.).—"Hip, Hip, Hip, Hi Yi C-U-R-K-Y.!"

Centre.—"Rackity-cax! Co-ax! Co-ax! (twice) Hurrah! Hurrah! Centre! Centre! Rah! Rah!"

Colby University.—"C-O-L-B-Y! Rah! Rah! Rah!"

Colgate University.—"Rah! Rah! Colgate! Zip Boom Ah!"

College of the City of New York.—"Rah 'Rah 'Rah, C. C. N. Y.!"

Colorado.—"Rah, rah, rah! Pike's Peak or Bust! Colorado College! Yell we must!"

Columbia.—"H'ray! h'ray! h'ray! C-o-l-u-m-b-i-a!"

Columbian University.—"Orange and Blue! Orange and Blue! Rah, rah! Rah, rah! Columbian!"

Cornell (Iowa).—"Zip-siss-boom, Cah-Cah-nell, C-C-Tiger-la, Zip-siss hurrah!"

Cornell University.—"Cornell! I Yell! Yell! Yell! Cornell!"

Cumberland University.—"Roo, rah! Roo, rah! Roo, rah, rau! Roo, rah! Roo, rah! Cum-ber-land!"

Dartmouth.—"Wah, who, wah! wah who wah! da-didi, Dartmouth! wah who wah!"

Davidson.—"Rah-rah-rah-Run-Run-Run-Pink and Blue, Da-vid-son!"

Denison University.—"Heike! Heike! D-E-N-I-S-O-N! Denison! Denison!"

De Pauw University.—"Rip, rah, hoo! D-P-U! Rip, Saw! Boom, Baw! Rah, rah! Rah, rah! De Pauw!"

Des Moines.—"Three times three! Rah, rah, rah! Rah, rah, rah! Des Moines!"

Detroit.—"Red and white! (twice) Detroit College! Our Delight! Rah, rah, rah! Hurrah!" (thrice).

Dickinson.—"Rip-rah-bus-bis—Dickinsoniensis—Tiger!"

Earlham.—"Rah : 'rah, 'rah : ri, ro, rem ; E-A-R-L-H-A-M ; thee, thou! 'rah!!!!!"

Elmira.—"Rah! Rah! Rah! Elmira! Elmira College! Rah! Rah! Rah!"

Emory and Henry.—"Rah, rah, rah! Siss, boom, ah! Emory-Henry! Wah-hoo-wah!"

Erskine.—"Rebel yell."

Eureka.—"Hip, Hip! Hurrah! Eu-re-kah!"

Franklin.—"Franklin! Hurrah, hurrah! We're her men! Boom-rang! Boom-rang! Wahoo, hoo, wah! Franklin! Wah, wah, wah!"

Franklin and Marshall.—"Hullabaloo, bala! (twice) Way-up! Way-up! F. and M.! Nevonia!"

Furman University.—"Rah, rah! Rah, rah! Rah, rah, ree! Furman! Furman! Universitee!"

Geneva.—"Geneva! Rah, rah, rah, rah! (twice) Roo, rah, roo, rah! Geneva, Geneva! Rah, roo, rah!"

Grand Traverse.—"Kala, kala, kala! Sst, boom, gah! Benzo, Benzo, Benzon-iah! Whooo!"

Griswold.—"G-R-I-S-W-O-L-D! Rah! rah! rah!"

Hamline University.—"Ho! Ho'! Ho!!! Ham-le-u-ne Vers-te. Rah! Re! Hooray!"

Hamilton.—"Rah! 'rah! 'rah! Hamilton! Zip 'rah boom!"

Hampden-Sidney.—"Hoop la hi—Hoopla-he—hoopla—hoopla! H-S-C!"

Hanover.—"Han, Han, Han-O-Ver!"

Harvard University.—"Rah rah rah! rah rah rah! rah rah rah—Harvard!"

Haverford.—"Yo-Yo-Yo—Yo-Yo-Yo—Yo-Yo-Yo—Hav-er-ford!"

Heidelberg University.—"Killi-killick! Rah, rah, Zik, zik! Ha! Ha! Yi! Hoo! Barn! Zoo! Heidelberg!"

Hillsdale.—"Hallabaloo, wahoo! Hallabaloo, wahoo! Hoo-wah, wah-hoo! Hillsdale!"

Hiram.—"Rah, Rah, Rah; Rah, Rah, Rah! Hiram, Hiram; Zip, Boom, Rah!"

Hobart.—"Hip, Hobart! Hip, Hobart! Hip, Ho! Hip, Ho! Hip Hobart!"

Howard (Ala.).—"Zip, Za, Boom! Rip, Rah, Ree! Ah! there! Howard College! H! Yi! Kee!"

Illinois.—"I-L-L-I-N-O-I-S! Illinois!"

Iowa College.—"Rah, rah, rah! Boom, Tee, Ray! Iowa College! I-O-Ay!"

Iowa State College.—"Hip ha! Rip Ra! Peda balloo ballee! Huzza! Zip boom! I. A. C.!"

Iowa State University.—"Hi! Hi! Hi! S. U. I.! Giddy, Giddy, Uni! U. N. I.!"

Iowa Wesleyan University.—"Rah, rah, rah! Hip, hi, hoo! I-O-U!"

Kansas Wesleyan University.—"Psi, Chi! Ye sons of Wesley! Rip, rah, roar!"

Kenyon.—"Heika! Heika! Ken-yon! Ken-yon! Ken-yon!"

Knox.—"Zip rah! Boom rah! Knox-i-ae! Knox-i-a! Knox! Knox! KNOX!"

Lafayette.—"Rah! Rah! Rah! Tiger Lafayette!"

Lawrence University.—"Rah, rah, rah! L-A-W-R-E-N-C-E! Rah, rah, rah!"

Lehigh University.—"Hoo, 'rah 'ray! Hoo, 'rah 'ray! Ray 'ray 'ray, Lehigh!"

Leland Stanford, Jr., University.—"Wah, Hoo! Wah Hoo! L. S. J. U.! *Stanford!!*"

Lenox.—"Rah, rah, rah! Zip, zip, zip! Hip, hi, ho! X-O-N-E-L! Lenox!"

Lincoln University.—"Ki-yi-mockli-on, Ra-ha—Lincoln!"

Lombard University.—"Rah, re, ri, ro! Ring, ching, bang! Lombard! Lombard! Zip, boom, bang!"

Macalister.—"Rah, rah, rah! Macalister! Great North Western! Rah, rah, rah!"

McKendree.—"Rah, rah, rah! Hoop, hi, he! Rip, boom! Zip, boom! McKendree!"

Maine State.—"M. S. C. Rah! Rah! Rah! M. S. C. Rah! Rah! Rah! M. S. C. Rah! Rah! Rah! Tiger!"

Manhattan.—"Rah! Rah! Rah! Ma-n—h-a-t—t-a-n, Manhattan!"

Maryville.—"Howee, how! Chilhowee! Maryville, Maryville, Tennessee!"

Mercer University.—"Rah, rah, rah! Un-I-V! Siss, boom, ba! Ver-Si-Tee! Mercer!"

Miami University.—"Rah—Rah—Rah—M-I-A-M-I—Mi-am-i, Miami!"

Middlebury.—"Midd', Midd', Middlebury! 'rah, 'rah, 'rah!"

AMERICAN COLLEGE CHEERS—Continued.

Mississippi Agricultural.—"Ray, raw, ree! Ray, raw, ree! A. and M: C.!"
Mt. St. Mary's.—"Rah! Rah, Rah, Sis! Boom, Bah! Mount St. Mary's Ha! Ha! Ha!"
Muhlenberg.—"Rah 'Rah 'Rah 'Rah, Muhlenberg!"
Norwich University.—"Rah! Rah! Rah! Old N. U.! N.U., N. U., N. U.!"
Notre Dame.—"Reh! reh! reh! U. N. D., N. D. U.; reh! reh! reh!"
Nevada State University.—"Wa-hoo, N. S. U.! Rah, rah, rah! Varsity!"
Oberlin.—"Hi!-O!-Hi!-O!-Hi!-O!-Hi! Hi! O! Hi! O-ber-lin!"
Ohio State University.—"Wahoo, Wahoo, Rip, Zip, Baz, Zoo, I yell, I yell, for *O. S. U.!*"
Ohio University.—"Wah-hoo, wah-hoo, Rip, rah. O-U-O-hi-O U! followed by three cheers!"
Ohio Wesleyan University.—"O-wee-wi-wow! Ala-ka-zu-ki-zow! Ra-zi-zi-zow! Viva, viva! O. W. U.!"
Olivet.—"Wha, whoo, wha! Wha, whoo, wha! Olivet! Olivet! Rah, rah, rah!"
Park.—"P-A-R-K! Rah, rah, rah! Siss, boom, ah! Booma-lacka, booma-lacka! Boom! Park! Boom!"
Pennsylvania College.—"Rah, Rah, Rah, Rah, Rah, Penn-syl-va-ni-a!"
Polytechnic Institute (Brooklyn).—"Rah! Rah! Rah! P. O. L. Y. Tiger!"
Princeton.—"Hooray, Hooray, Hooray, Tiger-Sis-Boom-ah!" Princeton!"
Racine.—"Rah, rah, rah! Racine!"
Randolph-Macon College.—"Rip, rah, rah! rip rah rah!! Randolph-Macon, Virginia!"
Rensselaer Polytechnic Institute.—"Rah, rah, rah! Rah, rah, rah! Rensselaer!"
Richmond.—"Rah, rah, rah! R-C-V! Rip, rap! Rah, Tah! Siss, Bum, Bee!"
Ripon.—"R-I! Ri! P-O-N! Rah, de, kah! Rah, rah, rah! Ripon!"
Rollins.—"R-O-L-L-I-N-S! Rol, rol, rol! Rol, rol, rol! Rol, rol, rol, Rollins!"
Rutgers.—"Rah! 'rah! 'rah! bow-wow-wow! Rutgers!"
San Joaquin Valley.—"Hip, Hip! Hoop, Hi! S-J-V-C! Hi, Ho, Heen! San Joaquin! Hoop, Hip, Hi!"
Seton Hall.—"Rah! Rah! Rah! S-E-T-O-N-I-A, Ha! Ha! Ha!"
Shurtleff.—"Shurtleff! Shurtleff! Rah, rah, rah! Tiger! Sic 'em! Bum, yah, yah!"
Stevens Institute of Technology.—"Boomrah! Boomrah! Boomrah Stevens!"
St. Francis Xavier.—"Rah, Rah, Rah, X-A-V-I-E-R!"
St. John's (Md.).—"Rah, rah, rah. Rah, rah, rah! Rah, rah, rah! St. John's!"
St. Lawrence University.—"Rah Rah Rah, Rah rah rah, Rah rah rah, Laurentia!"
St. Stephens.—"Rah! Rah! Rah! St. Stephens!"
Syracuse University.—"Hip-hoo-rah! Hip-hoo-rah! Syracuse! Syracuse! Rah-rah-rah!"
Swarthmore.—"Rah, Rah! Rah Rah Rah! Rah Rah! Rah Rah Rah! Swarthmore!"
Tabor.—"We-wah-ka! Tabor! Tabor! I-O-Ah!"
Trinity, Hartford.—"Rah! 'rah! 'rah! Trin-i-ty! boom-'rah! boom-'rah! Trin-i-ty!"
Tufts.—"Rah, 'rah, 'rah! 'rah, 'rah, 'rah! Tufts!"
Union.—"Rah! Rah! Rah! U-N-I-O-N-Hikah! Hikah! Hikah!"
University of Alabama.—"Rah, hoo, ree! Universitee! Rah, hoo! Wah, hoo! A, C. U.!"
University of California.—"Ha-Ha-Ha-California—U. C. Berk-lee Zip-Boom-ah!"
University of Cincinnati.—"Rah, rah, rah! Rah, rah, rah! Rah, Mack! Rah, Mick! Rah, McMicken!"
Univ. of Col.—"U-U-U- of C. V-V-Varsity, U-U-U- of C. V-V-Varsity. *S-i-8-8-8-8* Boom COLORADO!"
University of Denver.—"U, U, U, of D, Den-ver, Ver-si-tee!"
University of Georgia.—"Rah-Rah-Rah! Rah-Rah-Rah! Rah-Rah! *Georgia!*"
University of Illinois.—"Rah-hoo-rah, Zip boom ah! Hip-zoo, rah zoo, Jimmy, blow your bazoo. Ip-sidi-iki, U. of I. Champaign!. !"
University of Kansas.—"Rock-Chalk-Jay-Hawk K. U.!"
Univ. of Mich.—"U. of M. Hurrah! Hurrah! Hōō-ráh! Hōō-ráh! Michigan! Michigan! ráh! ráh! ráh!"
University of Minnesota.—"Rah, rah, rah, Ski-U-mah—Minne-So-ta!"
University of Mississippi.—"Rah, rah, Riss, Riss, University of Miss. Hip! Hip! Hurrah!"
University of Missouri.—"Rah, rah, rah! Missouri! U-S-U-niversitee! Hoorah, hirah, Yessiree!"
University of Nashville.—"Rah, rah, rah! U N! U-N! Rah, rah, rah!"
University of Nebraska.—"U, U, U, N-I-Ver-Ver-Ver-Sit-Y-Oh My!!"
University of North-Carolina.—"Rah! Rah!! Rah!!! White and Blue! Vive-la! Vive-la N. C. U.!"
University of Notre Dame.—"Rah, rah, rah! Nostra Domina!"
Univ. of Penn.—"Hoo-rah! Hoo-rah! Hoo-rah! Penn-syl-va-ni-ah! H'ray! H'ray! H'ray! Penn-syl-va-nl-â!"
University of Rochester.—"Hoi, hoi, hoi! Rah, rah, rah! Rochester!"
University of South-Dakota.—"Da-ko-tâ, Da-ko-ta, U-ni-vee of Da-ko-tâ. Hurrah! Hurrah! Hurrah!"
University of the City of New-York.—"Rah, Rah, Rah, N. Y. U. Siss! Boom!! Ah!!!
Univ. of Tenn.—"U. of T.! Rah, rah! Rah, rah! (twice) Hoorah! Hoorah! Tennessee! Tennessee! Rah, rah, rah!"
Univ. of Texas.—"Hullabaloo! Hooray, hooray! (twice) Hooray! Hooray! Varsity! Varsity! U.! T.! A.!"
University of the Pacific.—"Hi, ho, he! Old U-P! P-A-C-I! F-I-C!"
University of the South.—"Rah 'Rah Ree, Varsity! Hey-ip-hey-ip, Se-wa-nee!"
University of Vermont.—"Rah, 'rah, 'rah! 'rah, 'rah, 'rah! U. V. M.! 'rah, 'rah!"
University of Virginia.—"Rah-rah-rah, Uni-v! Rah-rah-rah, Var-si-tee! Vir-gin-i-a!"
Univ. of Washington.—"U. of W.! Hiah, hiah! U. of W.! siah, siah! Skookum, skookum! Wash-ing-ton!"
University of Wisconsin.—"U-Rah-Rah-Wis-con-sin!" repeated three times with a Tiger.
University of Wooster.—"Rah, 'rah,'rah! 'Rah, 'rah, 'rah! 'Rah, 'rah,'rah! Wooster-rr!"
Upper Iowa University.—"Hi, hi! Hi, ky! Yah, wah! Hoo, wah! U. I. Varsity! Zip, boom, rah!"
Vanderbilt University.—"Vanderbilt, Rah, Rah, Rah! Whiz Boom! Zip-boom, Rah, Rah, Rah!"
Wabash.—"Wah-Hoo-Wah, Wah Hoo Wah, Wah Hoo Wah Hoo W-a-bash!"
Wake Forest.—"Rah! Rah! Rah! Rah, rah, rah! Rah, rah, rah! Wake Forest!"
Washburn.—"Rah, rah rah! Rah, rah, rah! Rah, rah, rah! W-a-s-h-b-u-r-n!"
Wash. and Jefferson.—"Wich-i-Koâx, Ko-âx, Koâx! Wich-i-Koax, Koax, Koax! W. J. W. J. Boom!"
Washington and Lee.—"Chick-a-go-runk! go-runk! go-ru¹k! ha, ho, hi, ho! Wash-ing-ton and Lee!"
Wellesley.†—"Tra, la, la, la! Tra, la, la, la! Tra, la, la, la! la, la, la! W-E-L-L-E-S-L-E-Y! Welles-ley!"
Wesleyan.—"Rah! Rah! Rah! Rah! Wesleyana! Rah! Rah! Rah! Rah!"
Western Maryland.—"Rah, rah, rah! Rah, rah, ree! Rah, rah, hullabaloo! W-M-C! Rah!"
Western Reserve.—"Rah! Rah! Rah! Biff! Bum! Bah! a la 'delbert, Rah! Rah! Rah!"
Western University of Pennsylvania.—"Allegenee-genack-genack! Hooray! Wup!"
Westminster (Fulton, Mo.).—"Rah! Rah! Rah! Oh! yes. Sir! Vive-la, Vive-la, West-min-ster!"
Williams College.—"Rah! Rah! Rah! yums, yams, yums! Will-yums!"
Wilmington.—"Rah, rah! Wilmington! Wilmington! Oh!"
*Yale University.**—"Rah, Rah, Rah! Rah, Rah, Rah! Rah, Rah, Rah! Yale!

---

* The difference between the cheers of Harvard and Yale lies in the length of time it takes to give them. Harvard's cheer is long and deep; Yale's quick and sharp.   † The Wellesley girls sing their cheer.

Statistics of American College Fraternities.

GENERAL FRATERNITIES.

	Name.	Member-ship.	Active Chapters.	Inactive Chapters.	Houses or Halls Owned.	Where Founded.	When Founded.
ΑΔΦ	Alpha Delta Phi.........	6,236	19	8	7	Hamilton.	1832
ΑΤΩ	Alpha Tau Omega........	2,061	35	21	1	V. M. I.*	1865
ΒΘΠ	Beta Theta Pi............	6,995	60	19	1	Miami.	1839
ΧΦ	Chi Phi	3,147	21	23	1	Princeton.	1854
ΧΨ	Chi Psi..................	2,930	16	9	5	Union.	1841
ΔΚΕ	Delta Kappa Epsilon....	10,353	34	13	9	Yale.	1844
ΔΦ	Delta Phi...............	2,205	11	4	2	Union.	1827
ΔΨ	Delta Psi................	2,504	9	10	8	Columbia.	1847
ΔΤΔ	Delta Tau Delta.........	4,044	39	26	—	Bethany.	1860
ΔΥ	Delta Upsilon............	4,871	26	6	7	Williams.	1834
ΚΑ	Kappa Alpha........	997	4	2	3	Union.	1825
ΚΑ(s)	Kappa Alpha (Southern).	2,057	26	12	—	Wash. & Lee.	1867
ΚΣ	Kappa Sigma............	2,048	22	20	—	Virginia.	1867
ΦΑΧ	Phi Alpha Chi	†200	3	4	—	——	——
ΦΔΘ	Phi Delta Theta........	6,803	66	17	1	Miami.	1848
ΦΓΔ	Phi Gamma Delta........	4,244	40	23	—	Jefferson.	1848
ΦΚΨ	Phi Kappa Psi.....	5,302	35	16	1	Jefferson.	1852
ΦΚΣ	Phi Kappa Sigma	1,878	11	15	1	U. of Pa.	1850
ΦΘΨ	Phi Theta Psi............	†170	3	—	—	——	——
ΠΚΑ	Pi Kappa Alpha.........	310	4	7	—	U. of Va.	1868
ΨΥ	Psi Upsilon..............	7,124	17	2	5	Union.	1833
ΣΑΕ	Sigma Alpha Epsilon....	2,342	31	33	—	Alabama.	1856
ΣΧ	Sigma Chi.......	3,999	38	21	—	Miami.	1855
ΣΝ	Sigma Nu................	971	20	7	—	V. M. I.*	1869
ΣΦ	Sigma Phi...............	1,820	7	2	6	Union.	1827
ΤΔΣ	Tau Delta Sigma.........	61	3	—	—	U. of South.	1889
ΘΔΧ	Theta Delta Chi	2,817	18	17	2	Union.	1847
ΖΨ	Zeta Psi.................	3,590	20	10	4	N. Y. U.	1846
	Total..	92,279	638	353	64		

LADIES' FRATERNITIES.

ΛΒΓ	Lambda Beta Gamma....	212	2	—	—	Oxford, Miss.	1881
ΛΦ	Alpha Phi..	348	5	—	1	Syracuse.	1872
ΒΣΟ	Beta Sigma Omicron.....	11	1	—	—	Missouri.	1889
ΔΔΔ	Delta Delta Delta........	190	5	—	—	Boston.	1889
ΔΓ	Delta Gamma............	632	12	9	—	Mississippi.	1872
ΓΦΒ	Gamma Phi Beta........	272	5	—	—	Syracuse.	1874
ΚΑΘ	Kappa Alpha Theta......	1,180	20	6	—	De Pauw.	1870
ΚΚΓ	Kappa Kappa Gamma ..	1,523	22	9	—	Monmouth.	1870
ΠΒΦ	Pi Beta Phi	1,344	19	8	—	Monmouth.	1867
ΣΚ	Sigma Kappa...........	91	1	—	—	Colby.	1874
ΡΕΟ	Rho Epsilon Omicron..	†1,500	5	—	—	Iowa.	
	Total................. ..	7,303	97	32	1		

There are 16 professional fraternities founded by the professional schools attached to colleges, and these number 45 active chapters and 3,364 members. But a part of these members also belong to the general fraternities.

There are also 17 local fraternities, or one college societies, which number in the aggregate 3,876 members.

SUMMARY.

	Members.	Active Chapters.	Inactive Chapters	Houses or Halls.
General Fraternities	92,279	638	353	64
Ladies' Fraternities............	7,303	97	32	1
Professional Fraternities.......	3,364	45	3	—
Local Fraternities....	3,876	17	—	5
Total	106,822	797	388	70

* Virginia Military Institute. † Estimated.

These tables are from a work on "American College Fraternities," by William Raimond Baird, and are reprinted with the permission of the author. The statistics of membership are the latest that have been gathered.

University Extension.

THE popular educational movement known as University Extension was started by the University of Cambridge in 1872. In that year Professor Stuart gave a course of lectures before various women's clubs in the north of England. The popular favor which his lectures instantly won encouraged him to repeat them before various audiences of different character and make-up in all parts of the country. The necessity of varying his treatment of the subject to suit hearers of widely different minds, training, and experience, led him to develop a special system of teaching. Briefly, this includes a series of lectures upon some not too extended subject in history, literature, or science. The presentation is clear, concise, suggestive, aiming to take advantage of the mental maturity of the audience, and making this supply, as far as possible, the lack of special preparation in the particular field. Each lecture was followed up by Professor Stuart with a conference for further discussion and explanation. Definite references were given to the best books on the subject, and those following the courses were encouraged to well-directed reading, which was in turn made more helpful by reviews and written exercises. An examination at the end of the lecture series was made by Professor Stuart, at once a stimulus to study and a test of results accomplished. This carefully evolved plan of work offered to busy men and women, even in the smaller towns and villages, full opportunities of instruction by enthusiastic, scholarly men. The growth of the movement was constant both under the direction of Cambridge University, and later under the direction of Oxford and of the London Society for University Extension. During the past season of 1892 nearly eighty thousand students followed courses under these auspices.

The movement was introduced into the United States in 1890 by the American Society for the Extension of University Teaching, founded in Philadelphia by Provost William Pepper of the University of Pennsylvania. Mr. Richard G. Moulton, of the Cambridge University Extension staff, gave invaluable help during the first year, as did Secretary Michael E. Sadler and Professor Halford J. Mackinder, of Oxford, during the second winter. The first season of 1890-91 saw the establishment of twenty-three "centres" in and near Philadelphia, at which more than forty courses of lectures were given to an average attendance of nearly ten thousand. In the winter of 1891-92 the number of centres was increased to sixty, with a like increase in the number of lectures and of hearers. Through the "circuit" of five or six towns, which joined in engaging the same lecturer, even the points most distant from university towns were enabled to share the benefits of the movement. The growth of the work led the American Society to engage the entire time of the most successful Extension lecturers, and in securing Edward T. Devine and Henry W. Rolfe, it has formed the nucleus of a permanent staff.

A same need of more workers in this field has been met by the establishment in Philadelphia of a seminary for the training of University Extension lecturers and organizers, which was opened on October 1, 1892, with a faculty made up from the most distinguished professors of Haverford, Swarthmore, Drexel, and the University of Pennsylvania, under the direction of Professor Edmund J. James, the President of the American Society. The Seminary is distinctly a place for advanced study, and its members are largely graduates of the leading American universities.

More than a hundred American colleges have, from the first, co-operated in the work of the American Society. Through this joint action and common experience, a well-developed plan has been evolved by which institutions of learning in all parts of the country are now enabled to share for themselves in the benefits of the movement and to extend them still further to others. Any college or university may join in three ways in the work of University Extension as directed by the American Society.

1. A college desiring to engage directly in Extension teaching may avail itself of the resources at the disposal of the Society to arouse interest in the subject and to inform the public as to the scope and methods of the work. For this purpose efficient aid is found in the circulars of the Society, the addresses delivered at its meetings, and the syllabi prepared by its lecturers.

) 2. A college or university may co-operate more closely with the Society by using the latter's organizers to form centres near the institutions, which shall be supplied with lecturers from its own faculty. For these centres a special joint certificate will be issued by the American Society and the Extension department of such institutions.

3. Still another form of co-operation will be carried out as far as practicable. The American Society is willing, so far as the circumstances of the work under its immediate care may permit, to send its staff lecturers to any locality to engage in work under the auspices of any college or university which chooses to avail itself of their services; the lecturers to be for the time being members of the Extension staff of the respective institution; provided that the work be carried on according to plans approved by the Society. This will enable an institution to secure at small expense, for the organization of its Extension work, all the experience at the disposal of the Society.

The movement has spread from Philadelphia as a centre to all parts of the United States. In Rhode-Island, Brown University has been active in the work. In Connecticut, representatives of Yale, Wesleyan, Trinity, and Hartford Theological are on the executive committee of the State Branch of the American Society. In New-York, an appropriation of $10,000 by the Legislature has enabled the University of the State through its secretary, Mr. Melvil Dewey, to organize centres in many important towns and cities. Rutgers College in New-Jersey has been especially active in offering scientific courses for the farmer of that State.

The most promising field in the West is Wisconsin, where the faculty of the State University has formed an Extension Department, under the direction of Mr. Lyman P. Powell. The Chicago Society for University Extension, formed by the Northwestern, Chicago, Illinois, and Indiana Universities, is pushing the work in the Mississippi Valley, while farther west the Universities of Kansas, Colorado, and California have conducted many courses. The annual conferences in Philadelphia during the Christmas holidays have attracted hundreds of workers.

UNIVERSITY EXTENSION.—*Continued.*

A monthly Journal of the American Society is published, and provides full information as to the system, cost of membership, etc. There is also a "Handbook of University Extension," edited by George J. James, General Secretary of the American Society. The motto of the system is "Help people to help themselves." Instead of obliging the student always to come to the university, the university proposes, in addition to its home work, to go out to the people.

A Shakespearian Table.

PROFESSOR ROLFE, the Shakespearian scholar, has counted the lines which the principal characters in Shakespeare's plays have to speak. His rule was to consider parts of lines, beginnings and endings of speeches as full lines. This is the result:

	Lines to Speak.		Lines to Speak.		Lines to Speak.
Hamlet	1,569	Macbeth	705	Mistress Page	361
Richard III	1,161	Cleopatra	670	Viola	353
Iago	1,117	Prospero	665	Julia (" Two Gentlemen")	323
Othello	888	Romeo	618	Volumnia	315
Coriolanus	886	Petruchio	585	Beatrice	309
Timon	863	Touchstone	516	Lady Macbeth	261
Antony (Cleopatra's)	829	Imogen	541	Katherine(in" The Shrew")	220
Lear	770	Helen (" All's Well")	479	Miranda (" Tempest")	142
Richard II	755	Isabella	426	Perdita	128
Brutus	727	Desdemona	389	Cordelia	115

Henry V., as king and prince (in " Henry IV." and " Henry V."), has 1,087 lines to speak, and Falstaff, in both parts of " Henry IV." and " Henry V." and in the " Merry Wives," has 1,895.

Chautauqua Literary and Scientific Circle.

President .... Lewis Miller, Akron, Ohio.

Chancellor ....Bishop John H. Vincent, Buffalo.		*General Secretary* .. A. M. Martin, Pittsburgh.
Principal ....Dr. Jesse L. Hurlbut, Chautauqua.		*Office Secretary*....Miss K. F. Kimball, Buffalo.

The Chautauqua Literary and Scientific Circle was organized in 1878 at the instance of Lewis Miller. Its purpose is to promote habits of reading and study in nature, art, science, and in secular and sacred literature, in connection with the routine of daily life; to give college graduates a review of the college course; to secure for those whose educational advantages have been limited the college student's general outlook upon the world and life, and to develop the habit of close, connected, persistent thinking.

It endeavors to encourage individual study in lines and by text-books which shall be indicated; by local circles for mutual help and encouragement in such studies; by summer courses of lectures and "students' sessions" at Chautauqua, and by written reports of each year's work.

Any person may join the circle upon payment of the annual membership fee, which is fifty cents. No entrance examination is necessary. Persons may enter for one year, but the full course is four years, after which the graduate receives a diploma. The course of studies is directed from the centre of the circle, and may be pursued at home and in the local circles. Attendance at the summer meetings at Chautauqua, N. Y., is urged, but is not imperative. Application for membership should be made to John H. Vincent, Chancellor, Buffalo, N. Y.

There are over fifty Chautauqua assemblies in the United States, Canada, Great Britain, Japan, India, South-America, Australasia, and South-Africa, with a membership of a half million persons. All are modelled in organization and methods upon the original Chautauqua Assembly, but are independent in management.

A Catholic Chautauqua or summer school has been established at New-London, Conn., under the auspices of distinguished clergymen and laymen, and the first meetings were held from July 30 to August 14, 1892. The following were the officers of the first year: Rev. Morgan M. Sheedy, president, Pittsburgh, Pa.; Rev. P. A. Halpin, S. J., first vice-president, New-York; John H. Haaren, second vice-president, Brooklyn, N. Y.; Mrs. A. T. Toomey, third vice-president, Washington, D. C.; Warren E. Mosher, secretary and treasurer, Youngstown, Ohio; Rev. Thomas McMillan, C. S. P., chairman of General Council, New-York; Rev. Joseph H. McMahon, chairman of Board of Studies, New-York; George E. Hardy, chairman Committee on Entertainment, New-York; William J. Moran, chairman Committee on Arrangements, New-York; Rev. John F. Mullany, financial committee for Northern and Western New-York, Syracuse, N. Y.; John P. Brophy, financial committee, New-York; G. P. Lathrop, Esq., chairman Local Committee, New-London, Conn.

The Faribault System of Education.

THIS compromise between the common school system and the parochial system of the Roman Catholic Church of the United States is the device of Dr. Ireland, the Roman Catholic Bishop of Minnesota, and may be briefly described as follows: In the town of Faribault, Minn., the Catholic Church had built a parochial school, in which the Sisters of the Order of St. Dominic were teachers. The school was in a very precarious condition, and, in order to keep it in existence, Archbishop Ireland, about two years ago, proposed to the Board of Education of that town to sell them the schoolhouse for the sum of $1, if they would guarantee to keep the same teachers and be responsible for their pay. The transaction was closed with the agreement that no religious services were to be held, that religion was not to be taught, and that all crucifixes and other emblems of Catholicity were to be taken away There is a catechism class after school hours for such pupils as wish to benefit themselves by the religious training given by the Sisters, but it is treated entirely as a separate arrangement. The plan has met with much opposition from Catholic clergymen and laymen, but it has its advocates also and has been provisionally tolerated by the Propaganda at Rome.

The Famous Old People of 1893.

(Age at the last birthday is given. The list was made up January 1, 1893.)

Age.

94. Sir James Bacon, jurist.

90. Louis Kossuth, Rev. Dr. William H. Furness.

89. Earl Grey, statesman.

88. Neal Dow, prohibitionist; Field Marshal Sir Patrick Grant.

87. Ferdinand de Lesseps, David Dudley Field, Francis William Newman, James Martineau, philosopher; Barthelemy-Sainte-Hilaire, statesman; George Müller, orphanage founder.

84. Hamilton Fish, Marshal MacMahon, Robert C. Winthrop.

83. William Ewart Gladstone, Oliver Wendell Holmes, Marshal Canrobert, Cassius M. Clay, Hugh Mc-Culloch, Professor Blackie, Admiral Keppel, R. N.; Frances Anne Kemble.

82. Pope Leo XIII., ex-Senator Payne, Senator Morrill, Lord Armstrong, gunmaker.

81. Ex-President McCosh, of Princeton College; General Cialdini, of Italy; Bishop Colenso, Professor Bunsen, chemist.

80. Samuel Smiles, biographer; Harriet Beecher Stowe.

79. Sir H. Bessemer, inventor; Professor Dana, geologist; ex-Senator Thurman.

78. Ernest Curtius, Greek scholar; Verdi, the composer; Duc de Nemours, Baroness Burdett-Coutts.

77. Bismarck, Rawlinson, the historian; General Jubal A. Early, N. P. Banks, C. W. Couldock, comedian; Sir Henry Parkes, Australian statesman; Elizabeth Cady Stanton.

76. Justice Field, Senator Dawes, M. Leon Say, the financier; Rev. Newman Hall; Daniel Huntington, painter; Philip James Bailey, poet; Sir James Caird, political economist; Gustav Freytag, novelist; Parke Godwin, Russell Sage.

75. Professor Mommsen, historian; King Christian of Denmark, Dr. Brown-Sequard, Sir Alexander Galt, Canadian statesman; Sir John Gilbert, R. A.; Sir Joseph Hooker, botanist; Sir Austin Layard, Professor Jowett, Senator John M. Palmer.

74. General Beauregard, ex-Senator Evarts, Lucy Stone, Froude, historian; Gounod, composer; Prince de Joinville, ex-Senator Hampton, Professor Bain, Bishop A. C. Coxe, Baron Reuter, news-gatherer; Mrs. John Drew, comedienne.

73. Queen Victoria, ex-Prime Minister Crispi, General Longstreet, John Ruskin, Lord Playfair, Duke of Cambridge; Prince Hohenlohe, statesman; Sir Monier-Williams, Sanscrit scholar; W. W. Story, author and sculptor; Julia Ward Howe.

72. Herbert Spencer, John Tenniel, cartoonist · Professor John Tyndall, De Giers, Russian statesman; Florence Nightingale, Mrs. G. H. Gilbert, comedienne; Jean Ingelow, poet; Princess Mathilde Bonaparte, General Rosecrans, Susan B. Anthony, Justice Blatchford.

71. Lord Coleridge, Lord Chief Justice of England; Professor Virchow, Duc de Broglie, Sir Samuel W. Baker, William H. Russell, journalist; Rev. Dr. Storrs, Sir Charles Tupper, Ristori, tragic actress; Professor Helmholtz, physiologist; Dr. Temple, Bishop of London; Sims Reeves, singer.

70. Duc d'Aumale, Rosa Bonheur, Francis Galton, Got, French comedian; Edward Everett Hale, ex-President Hayes, Professor Pasteur, chemist; Professor Alfred R. Wallace, Abram S. Hewitt, Rev. Henry M. Field.

69. Duke of Argyll, Thomas Wentworth Higginson, Thomas Hughes, Max Müller, Senator Sherman, Professor Goldwin Smith, ex-Speaker Grow.

68. Alexander Dumas (fils), Professor Huggins, astronomer; Eastman Johnson, painter; Vice-President Morton, George Macdonald, novelist; Senator Stanford, Senator Colquitt.

67. Sir William Aitken, pathologist; Professor Charcot, Professor Huxley, Justice Lamar, Professor March, philologist; R. D. Blackmore, novelist.

66. Karl Blind, Earl of Derby, Marquis of Dufferin, ex-Empress Eugenie, Senator Hoar, M Waddington, French statesman; Senator Hawley.

65. Sir William Harcourt, statesman; Père Hyacinthe, Professor St. George Mivart, Sagasta, Spanish statesman; Professor Whitney, philologist; J. H. Stoddart, comedian; Senator Voorhees.

---

64. Sir Henry James, lawyer; De Freycinet, French statesman; ex-Senator Edmunds, General Gourko, Russian commander; Ibsen, dramatist; Mrs. Oliphant, novelist; George Augustus Sala, Henri Taine, literary critic; Jules Verne, Count Tolstoi, Justice Gray, of the Supreme Court; King Albert, of Saxony.

63. General Booth, Salvation Army leader; George W. Childs, Joseph Jefferson, comedian; Sir John Millais R.A.; Carl Schurz, Senator Allison, Senator Cullom, King Oscar, of Sweden.

62. James G. Blaine, Hans Von Bülow, President Diaz, of Mexico; Emperor Francis Joseph, ex Queen Isabella, ex-Khedive Ismail, Sir Frederick Leighton, R.A.; Rev. Joseph Parker, English pulpit orator; James Payn, novelist; Rubinstein, pianist; Marquis of Salisbury, British premier; Salvini, tragedian; Secretary Tracy, Madame Janauschek, actress; General Oliver O. Howard, Mrs. D. P. Bowers, actress.

61. Chancellor Von Caprivi, Archdeacon Farrar, General Galiffet, French soldier; President Gilman, of Johns Hopkins; George J. Goschen, British statesman; Frederick Harrison, positivist; Henry Labouchère, journalist; Professor Marsh, of Yale, palæontologist; Henri Rochefort, Victorien Sardou, General Schofield, Edmund Yates.

60. General Lord Roberts, British Army; Rev. Dr. Talmage, Maggie Mitchell, actress; Sir Edwin Arnold, poet; Castelar, Spanish statesman, Professor William Crooks, Jules Ferry, Senator Gordon of Georgia; General Ignatieff.

At what age does one become "old"? Five centuries ago a man was old at fifty. But the hale and hearty gentleman of to-day who has just turned sixty would probably protest against being classed among old people, even if famous. That his susceptibilities may not be wounded, therefore, a separating dash has been discreetly introduced after age sixty-five.

The Epworth League.

THE following statistics and statement of the purposes of the organization were prepared for THE WORLD ALMANAC by Mr. Robert R. Doherty, Vice-President of the Epworth League.

OFFICERS OF THE EPWORTH LEAGUE.—*President*, Bishop James N. FitzGerald, New-Orleans, La.; *Vice-Presidents:* Department of Spiritual Work, W. W. Cooper, St. Joseph, Mich.; Department of Mercy and Help, Rev. W. I. Haven, 85 Lexington Street, East Boston, Mass.; Department of Literary Work, R. R. Doherty, 150 Fifth Avenue, New-York; Department of Social Work, Rev. H. C. Jennings, Red Wing, Minn.; *General Secretary*, Rev. William N. Brodbeck, 57 Washington Street, Chicago; *General Treasurer*, Charles E. Piper, Chicago. The Central Office of the Epworth League is located at 57 Washington Street, Chicago.

The Epworth League was formed in May, 1889, by the union of five general (Methodist) societies of young people, which had under their united jurisdiction about 1,500 local societies or "chapters," and about 60,000 members. By vigorous effort the united society has now (December, 1892) 8,888 chapters and an aggregate membership of over 440,000.

Its purpose is to promote intelligent and loyal piety in the young members and friends of the church, to aid them in religious development, and to train them in works of mercy and help. Its constitution provides for development along social, intellectual, and religious lines. Its essential features are the weekly prayer-meeting, the "intellectual" and "mercy and help" departments, and its harmony with the officiary of the church.

It has a weekly organ, the *Epworth Herald*, edited by Dr Joseph F. Berry, with a circulation of 50,000. There are no salaried officers, except the General Secretary, the organization being entirely voluntary, and no assessments on local chapters. The incidental expenses thus far have been paid by voluntary contributions.

The following table shows the total number of chapters composing the organization by States and Territories:

STATES.	No. of Chapters.	STATES.	No. of Chapters.	STATES.	No. of Chapters.	STATES.	No. of Chapters.
Alabama	15	Iowa	648	New-Hampshire	68	Tennessee	65
Arizona	3	Kansas	471	New-Jersey	327	Texas	41
Arkansas	11	Kentucky	53	New-Mexico	7	Utah	2
California	158	Louisiana	12	New-York	1,020	Vermont	100
Colorado	52	Maine	134	North-Carolina	6	Virginia	10
Connecticut	85	Maryland	144	North-Dakota	47	Washington	69
Delaware	40	Massachusetts	303	Ohio	944	West-Virginia	68
Dist. of Columbia	16	Michigan	488	Oklahoma Terr.	9	Wisconsin	259
Florida	10	Minnesota	206	Oregon	52	Wyoming	6
Georgia	20	Mississippi	34	Pennsylvania	750	Foreign	29
Idaho	7	Missouri	198	Rhode-Island	31		
Illinois	866	Montana	20	South-Carolina	21	Total	8,888
Indiana	580	Nebraska	270	South-Dakota	97	Tot. Membership	444,000
Indian Territory	1	Nevada	2				

The Theosophical Society.

THE following information about this organization was prepared by William Q. Judge, General Secretary of the American section:

The Theosophical Society has been in existence seventeen years, having been founded in New-York in November, 1875, with the following objects:

First.—To form a nucleus of a UNIVERSAL BROTHERHOOD OF HUMANITY, without distinction of race, creed, caste, sex, color.

Second.—To promote the study of Aryan and other Eastern literatures, religions, and sciences, and demonstrate the importance of that study.

Third.—To investigate unexplained laws of nature and the psychical powers latent in man.

The Society appeals for support and encouragement to all who truly love their fellow-men and desire the eradication of the evils caused by the barriers raised by race, creed, or color, which have so long impeded human progress; to all scholars, to all sincere lovers of TRUTH, *wheresoever it may be found*, and to all philosophers, alike in the East and in the West; and lastly, to all who aspire to higher and better things than the mere pleasures and interests of a worldly life, and are prepared to make the sacrifices by which alone a knowledge of them can be attained.

The Society represents no particular creed, is entirely unsectarian, and includes professors of all faiths. No person's religious beliefs are interfered with, and all that is exacted from each member is the same toleration of the views of others which he desires them to exhibit toward his own. The Society, as a body, eschews politics and all subjects outside its declared sphere of work, the rules stringently forbidding members to compromise its strict neutrality in these matters.

As a condition precedent to membership, belief in and adherence to the first of the above-named objects is required; as to the other two, members may pursue them or not, as they see fit. The act of joining the Society, therefore, carries with it no obligation whatever to profess belief in either the practicability of presently realizing the brotherhood of mankind, or in the superior value of Aryan over modern science, or the existence of occult powers latent in man. It implies only intellectual sympathy in the attempt to disseminate tolerant and brotherly feelings, to discover as much truth as can be uncovered by diligent study and careful experimentation, and to essay the formation of a nucleus of a universal brotherhood.

The headquarters are at Adyar, a suburb of Madras, where the Society has a property of twenty-seven acres and extensive buildings, including one for the Oriental Library and a spacious hall wherein the General Council meets annually in convention, on December 27.

Many branches of the Society have been formed in various parts of the world, and new ones are constantly being organized. Each branch frames its own by-laws and manages its own local business without interference from headquarters; provided only that the fundamental rules of the Society are not violated. All branches in America and the West Indies are under the jurisdiction of the American section; those in Europe, India, Ceylon, etc., are under the jurisdiction of the General Convention held in India. Each section is autonomous.

The President of the Society is Colonel Henry S. Olcott, in India; the Vice-President, William Q. Judge (also General Secretary American section), 144 Madison Avenue, New-York.

Throughout the world there are about 250 branches. The American section includes at this date the 68 branches in the United States, which are located in most of the principal cities and in many of the smaller towns. Addresses may be obtained from the General Secretary. Inquirers and applicants can address him at the address given above, enclosing a stamp, and will receive from him further information or application blanks. The American headquarters are at 144 Madison Avenue, New-York, where a Theosophical meeting is held each Tuesday evening.

Freemasonry.

THE DEGREES IN MASONRY.

Lodge.

1. Entered Apprentice.
2. Fellow Craftsman.
3. Master Mason.

YORK RITE.	SCOTTISH RITE.		
Chapter. 4. Mark Master. 5. Past Master. 6. Most Excellent Master. 7. Royal Arch Mason. *Council.* 8. Royal Master. 9. Select Master. 10. Super Excellent Master *Commandery.* 11. Red Cross Knight. 12. Knight Templar. 13. Knight of Malta.	*Lodge of Perfection.* 4. Secret Master. 5. Perfect Master. 6. Intimate Secretary. 7. Provost and Judge. 8. Intendant of the Building. 9. Elect of Nine. 10. Elect of Fifteen. 11. Sublime Knight Elect. 12. Grand Master Architect 13. Knight of the Ninth Arch. 14. Grand Elect, Perfect and Sublime Mason. *Councils of Princes of Jerusalem.* 15. Knight of the East or Sword.	*Councils of Princes of Jerusalem (Continued).* 16. Prince of Jerusalem. *Chapters of Rose Croix.* 17. Knight of the East and West. 18. Knight of the Rose Croix de H.R.D.M. *Consistories of Sublime Princes of the Royal Secret.* 19. Grand Pontiff. 20. Master Ad Vitam. 21. Patriarch Noachite. 22. Prince of Libanus. 23. Chief of the Tabernacle. 24. Prince of the Tabernacle.	*Consistories of Sublime Princes of the Royal Secret (Continued).* 25. Knight of the Brazen Serpent. 26. Prince of Mercy. 27. Commander of the Temple. 28. Knight of the Sun. 29. Knight of St. Andrew. 30. Grand Elect Knight, K.H., or Knight of the Black and White Eagle 31. Grand Inspector Inquisitor Commander. 32. Sublime Prince of the Royal Secret. 33. Sovereign Grand Inspector General of the 33d and Last Degree.

MASONIC GRAND LODGES IN THE UNITED STATES AND BRITISH AMERICA.

GRANDLODGES.	No. Members, 1891.	Grand Secretaries.	GRANDLODGES.	No. Members, 1891.	Grand Secretaries.
Alabama.....	10,448	G. A. Joiner, Montg'm'ry	Nebraska	9,717	W. R. Bowen, Omaha.
Arizona......	451	J. M. Ormsby, Tucson.	Nevada	991	C. N. Noteware, Carson.
Arkansas	13,191	F. Hempstead, Little R'ck	N. Brunswick	1,851	E. J. Wetmore, St.John
British Colum	726	W. J. Quinlan, Victoria.	N. Hampshire	8,542	G. P. Cleaves, Concord.
California....	16,262	G. Johnson,SanFrancisco	New-Jersey...	14,320	T.H.R.Redway,Trenton
Canada.......	20,892	J. J. Mason, Hamilton.	Mew-Mexico	696	A. A. Keen, Las Vegas.
Colorado.....	5,719	Ed. C. Parmalee, Pueblo.	New-York ...	77,923	E.L.M.Ehlers, N Y.City
Connecticut..	15,641	J. K. Wheeler, Hartford.	N. Carolina..	10,513	D. W. Bain, Raleigh.
Delaware.....	1,787	B. F. Bartram, Wilmi'gt'n	North-Dakota	1,594	T. J. Wilder, Casselton.
Dist.of Colum	4,202	W. R. Singleton, Wash.	Nova Scotia..	2,904	William Ross, Halifax.
Florida.......	3,910	W.A.McLean,J'cks'nville	Ohio.........	35,603	J. H. Bromwell, Cinn.
Georgia......	14,703	A. M. Wolihin, Macon.	Oregon.......	3,918	S. F. Chadwick, Salem.
Idaho	825	J. H. Wickersham, Boisé.	Pennsylvania	42,412	M. Nisbet, Philadelphia
Illinois	43,930	Loyal L. Munn, Freeport.	Pr. Ed. Island	509	B.W. Higgs,Charlottet'n
Indiana......	24,776	W. H. Smith,Indianapolis	Quebec......	3,060	J. H. Issacson, Montre'l
Indian Terr..	1,570	J. S. Murrow, Atoka.	Rhode-Island	4,177	E. Baker, Providencé.
Iowa	22,525	T. S. Parvin, Ced. Rapids	S. Carolina..	6,058	C. Inglesby, Charleston
Kansas	18,426	J. H. Brown, Kansas City	South-Dakota	3,565	C. T. McCoy, Aberdeen.
Kentucky....	16,465	H. B. Grant, Louisville.	Tennessee ...	17,329	J. Frizzell, Nashville.
Louisiana	4,590	R. Lambert, New-Orleans.	Texas	23,193	W. F. Swain, Houston.
Maine	20,968	Stephen Berry, Portland.	Utah	544	C. Diehl, Salt Lake City.
Manitoba	1,878	W. G. Scott, Winnipeg.	Vermont.....	8,658	W.G.Reynolds,Burlgt'n
Maryland....	5,868	J. H Medairy, Baltimore.	Virginia......	10,574	W. B. Isaacs, Richm'nd.
Massach'setts	31,786	S. D. Nickerson, Boston.	Washington..	3,649	T. M. Reed, Olympia.
Michigan....	33,098	J. S. Conover, Coldwater	W. Virginia..	4,258	G.W. Atkinson, Wh'l'g.
Minnesota ...	12,830	T. Montgomery, St. Paul.	Wisconsin....	13,899	J.W. Laflin, Milwaukee.
Mississippi .	8,950	J. L. Power, Jackson.	Wyoming	708	W.L.Kuykendall,Cheyn
Missouri.....	28,816	J. D. Vincil, St. Louis.			
Montana.....	2,007	Cornelius Hedges, Helena	Total	698,402	

The returns of the Grand Lodges of the United States and British America for 1891-92 were as follows : Whole number of members, 698,402 ; raised, 43,345 ; admissions and restorations, 22,549 ; withdrawals, 20,086 ; expulsions and suspensions, 717 ; suspensions for non-payment of dues, 14,113 ; deaths, 10,242. Net gain in membership over preceding year, 23,693.

These Grand Lodges are in full affiliation with the English Grand Lodge, of which the Prince of Wales is Grand Master, and the Grand Lodges of Ireland, Scotland, Cuba, Peru, South Australia, New-South Wales, and Victoria, and also with the Masons of Germany and Austria. They are not in affiliation and do not correspond with the Masons of France. Freemasonry is under the ban of the Church in Spain, Italy, and other Catholic countries, and the membership is small and scattered.

Odd Fellowship.

SOVEREIGN GRAND LODGE OF THE INDEPENDENT ORDER OF ODD FELLOWS.

OFFICERS.

Grand Sire—Charles T. Campbell.
Deputy Grand Sire—John W. Stebbins.
Grand Secretary—Theo. A. Ross (Columbus, O.).
Grand Treasurer—Isaac A. Sheppard.

Grand Chaplain—Rev. J. W. Venable.
Grand Marshal—Walter G. Dye.
Grand Guardian—J. S. Tyson.
Grand Messenger—R. Alexander.

GRAND LODGES AND MEMBERSHIP.
(Reported to the Annual Communication in 1892.)

JURISDICTION.	No. of Members.	JURISDICTION.	No. of Members.	JURISDICTION.	No. of Members.
Alabama	2,741	Maine	19,599	Oregon	5,186
Arizona	607	Manitoba	1,668	Pennsylvania	101,258
Arkansas	3,607	Maryland	8,651	Quebec	1,209
British Columbia	1,430	Massachusetts	43,187	Rhode-Island	6,277
California	29,393	Michigan	23,399	South-Carolina	704
Colorado	6,638	Minnesota	11,633	South-Dakota	3,321
Connecticut	13,768	Mississippi	1,253	Switzerland	259
Delaware	2,871	Missouri	21,140	Tennessee	4,365
Denmark	2,085	Montana	2,231	Texas	5,743
Dist. of Columbia	1,824	Nebraska	7,718	Utah	1,338
Florida	782	Nevada	1,570	Vermont	3,517
Georgia	4,869	New-Hampshire	11,297	Virginia	5,171
Idaho	1,489	New-Jersey	23,043	Washington	5,800
Illinois	42,725	New-Mexico	717	West-Virginia	6,358
Indiana	36,475	New-York	58,529	Wisconsin	16,060
Iowa	27,931	North-Carolina	3,465	Wyoming	770
Kansas	19,226	North-Dakota	1,433		
Kentucky	8,000	Ohio	58,651	Total	696,008
Louisiana	1,123	Ontario	18,390		
L. Prov., B.N.A.	3,434				

The membership of the Independent Order of Odd Fellows, which includes the German Grand Lodges, is 698,533. The American organization is not in affiliation with an English order entitled the Manchester Unity Odd Fellows, who number 769,503.

The Encampment branch of the Independent Order of Odd Fellows numbers 123,061 members; Rebekah lodges, sisters, 73,238; brothers, 81,682; Chevaliers of the Patriarchs Militant, 25,000. The next meeting of the Sovereign Grand Lodge will be at Milwaukee, Wis., on September 25, 1893.

The total relief paid by the Independent Order of Odd Fellows, year ending December 31, 1891, was $3,064,720.80; brothers relieved, 82,603; widowed families relieved, 5,683; paid for relief of brothers, $1,905,943.75; for widowed families, $145,990.27; education of orphans, $23,610; burying the dead, $505,058.53.

Independent Order of Good Templars.

THE RIGHT WORTHY GRAND LODGE.

R. W. G. Templar—Dr. Oronhyatekha, Toronto, Can.
R. W. G. Counsellor—Edw. Wavrinsky, Sweden.
R. W. G. V. Templar—Miss Schreiner, South Africa.
R. W. G. S. J. Templar—Mrs. A. A. Brookbank, Ind.
R. W. G. Secretary—B. F. Parker, Milwaukee, Wis.
R. W. G. Treasurer—W. M. Jones, Rochester, N. Y.

R. W. G. Chaplain—Rev. M. B. Hogg, Ireland.
R. W. G. Marshal—A. J. Leonard, Kasauli, India.
R. W. G. D. Marshal—Mrs. A. A. Minnick, Neb.
R. W. G. Guard—Mrs. A. J. Pyle, Virginia.
R. W. G. Sentinel—F. J. Merchant, Queensland.
R. W. G. Messenger—Lars O. Jensen, Norway.

The last report of the R. W. G. Secretary returned the number of grand lodges in the world as 100, and the membership as 410,996. The membership of the juvenile branch was 159,106. The Good Templars, which is a beneficial order, based on total abstinence, are organized in nearly every State of the Union, England, Ireland, Scotland, Wales, Germany, Denmark, Sweden and Norway, Canada, West Indies, East, West, and South Africa, Australia, New-Zealand, British India, Iceland, and other countries. All persons becoming members of the Order are required to subscribe to the following pledge: "That they will never make, buy, sell, use, furnish, nor cause to be furnished to others, as a beverage, any spirituous or malt liquors, wine, or cider, and will discountenance the manufacture and sale thereof in all proper ways." The Right Worthy Grand Lodge will hold its next biennial meeting at Des Moines, Ia., in June, 1893.

Order of the Sons of Temperance.

NATIONAL DIVISION OF NORTH AMERICA.

M. W. Patriarch—Charles A. Everett, St. John, N. B.
M. W. Associate—W. H. Armstrong, Milford, Pa.
M. W. Scribe—Benj. R. Jewett, South Hampton, N.Y.
M. W. Treasurer—James H. Roberts, Boston, Mass.

M. W. Chaplain—Rev. G. W. Fisher Pownal, P. E. I.
M. W. Conductor—Mrs. C. B. Searles, Cleveland, O.
M. W. Sentinel—P. A. Cummings, Asheville, N. C.
Supt. Y. P. Work—F. M. Bradley, Washington, D. C.

The Order of the Sons of Temperance was organized in the city of New-York, September 29, 1842. It is composed of subordinate Grand and National Divisions. It has four National Divisions—one for North America, one for Great Britain and Ireland, and two for Australia. In the course of its existence it has had several hundred thousand members on its rolls. Its present membership in North America is 67,603, of which 36,668 are in the United States. Its fundamental principle is total abstinence from all intoxicating liquors. Its next convention will be held in Chicago, in June, 1893.

INFORMATION ABOUT THE CITY OF NEW YORK.

In the following pages, information of daily interest to citizens and visitors about the City of New-York is given, the subjects, for convenience of reference, being arranged alphabetically. This information is of the date of January 1, 1893, but it must be borne in mind that changes in an active community like that of New-York are continuously going on, and that accuracy in details can only be guaranteed for the date of issue of the ALMANAC.

Amusements.
OPERA HOUSES AND THEATRES.

Name.	Location.	Proprietors or Managers.	Seating Capacity.*	Prices of Admission.	Performance Begins. P. M.
Abbey's Theatre†	Broadway and 38th St	Henry E. Abbey	1,800	$1.00, 75c., 50c	8.15, mat. 2.
Academy of Music	E. 14th St. and Irving Pl.	Gilmore & Tompkins	2,900	$1.00, 75c., 50c	8.15, mat. 2.
Amberg Theatre	E. 15th St. and Irving Pl.	Gustav Amberg	1,200	1.50, 1.00, 75c., 50c	8.15, mat. 2.
American Theatre†	8th Ave., n. 42d St	T. H. French	1,800		
Berkeley Lyceum	W. 44th St., n. 5th Ave.	F. H. Sargent	500		
Bijou Theatre	Broadway, n. 31st St	J. W. Rosenquest	1,500	1.50, 1.00, 75c., 50c	8.10, mat.2.
Broadway Theatre	Broadway and 41st St	T. H. French	1,850	1.50, 1.00, 75c., 50c	8, mat. 2.
Columbus Theatre	E. 125th St., n. Lex. Ave	Oscar Hammerstein	2,000	1.00, 75c., 50c., 35c	8.15, mat. 2.
Casino	Broadway and 39th St	Rudolph Aronson	1,600	2.00, 1.50, 1.00, 50c	8.15, mat. 2.
Daly's Theatre	Broadway and 30th St	Augustin Daly	1,400	2.00, 1.50, 1.00, 75c., 50c.	8.15, mat. 2.
Empire Theatre†	40th St. and Broadway	F. W. Sanger	1,100		
Fifth Ave. Theatre	Broadway and 28th St	Henry C. Miner	1,700	1.50, 1.00, 75c., 50c	8, mat. 2.
Fourteenth St. Th.	W. 14th St., n 6th Ave	J. W. Rosenquest	1,700	1.50, 1.00, 75c., 50c	8, mat. 2.
Garden Theatre	Madison Ave., 27th St	T. H. French	1,800	1.50, 1.00, 75c., 50c	8, mat. 2.
Grand Opera House	W. 23d St. and 8th Ave	T. H. French	2,000	1.00, 75c., 50c	8, mat. 2.
Harlem Op. House.	W. 125th St., n. 7th Ave	Oscar Hammerstein	2,000	1.50, 1.25, 1.00, 75c., 50c	8.15, mat. 2
Harlem Theatre	E. 125th St., n. 3d Ave		1,400	30c., 20c., 10c	8, mat. 2.
Harrigan's Theatre	W. 36th St., n. 6th Ave.	M. W. Hanley	1,100	1.50, 1.00, 75c	8, mat. 2.
Herrmann's Th	Broadway, n. 29th St	A. Herrmann	700	1.50, 1.00, 75c., 50c	8.15, mat. 2.
Hoyt's Madison Sq.	W. 24th St., n. B'way	Hoyt & Thomas	800	1.50, 1.00, 75c., 50c	8.30, mat. 2.
Lex. Ave. Op. House	3d Ave., n. 58th St		1,400		8.
London Theatre	235 Bowery	James Donaldson	1,800	75c., 50c., 35c., 15c	8, mat. 2.
Lyceum Theatre	4th Ave., n. 23d St	Daniel Frohman	2,700	$1.50, 1.00, 75c	8.15, mat. 2.
Manhatt'n Op. H'se.	W. 34th St., n. B'way	Oscar Hammerstein	2,500	2.00, 1.50, 50c	8, mat. 2.
Metrop'litan Op. H‡	B'way, 39th and 40th Sts.		3,045		
Miner's Bowery Th.	Bowery, n. Broome St	H. C. Miner	2,000	75c., 50c., 25c	8, mat. 3.
Miner's 8th Ave. Th.	8th Ave., n. 23d St	H. C. Miner	1,000	75c., 50c., 35c., 25c	8, mat. 2.
National Theatre	118 Bowery		1,500		
Niblo's Garden	Broadway, n. Prince St.	A. C. Comstock	3,000	75c., 50c., 25c., 15c	8, mat. 2.
Olympic Theatre	3d Ave. and 130th St		1,000		8.
Palmer's Theatre	Broadway and 30th St	A. M. Palmer	1,100	$1.50, 1.00, 50c	8.15, mat. 2.
Park Theatre	Broadway and 35th St	William M. Dunlevy	1,300	1.50, 1.00, 75c., 50c	8.15, mat. 2.
People's Theatre	199 Bowery	H. C. Miner	2,200	1.00, 75c., 50c., 25c	8, mat. 2.
Proctor's Theatre	W. 23d St., n. 6th Ave	Proctor & Turner	1,700	$1.50, 1.00, 75c., 50c	8.15, mat. 2.
Standard Theatre	Broadway, n. 33d St	J. M. Hill	1,400	1.50, 1.00, 75c., 50c	8.15, mat. 2.
Star Theatre	Broadway and 13th St	Theodore Moss	2,000	1.50, 1.00, 50c	8.15, mat. 2.
Thalia Theatre	Bowery, n. Canal St	C. & T. H. Rosenfeld	2,000	1.50, 1.25, 1.00, 75c., 50c	8.15, mat. 2.
Third Ave. Theatre	3d Ave. and 30th St	H. R. Jacobs	2,500	75c., 50c., 35c., 25c	8, mat. 2.
Tony Pastor's Th.	E. 14th St., n. 3d Ave	Tony Pastor	900	$1.50, 1.00, 75c., 50c	8, mat. 2.
Union Sq. Theatre.	E. 14th St., n. Broadway	J. M. Hill	1,200	1.50, 1.00, 75c., 50c	8.15, mat. 2.
Union Theatre	W. 8th St., n. Broadway.		800		8.
Windsor Theatre	Bowery, n Canal St	F. B. Murtha	1,800	75c., 50c., 35c., 25.	8, mat. 2.

* Seating capacity is given, but there is usually standing room in addition for a large number of persons.
† These houses are now (January 1) being built. Theatre-goers should consult the daily papers as to time performance begins, as it varies in some houses with the nature of the attractions. ‡ The interior of this house was destroyed by fire August 27, 1892, and arrangements for rebuilding are pending.

MUSIC HALLS.

Name.	Managers.	Location.	Seating Capacity.
Chickering Hall	E. H. Colell	5th Ave. and 18th St	1,250
Eden Musée	E. G. Graham	W. 23d St., bet. Broadway and 6th Ave	1,000
Hardman Hall	Hardman & Peck	5th Ave. and 19th St	500
Imperial Music Hall	J. M. McDonough	Broadway and 29th St	1,100
Koster & Bial's	Koster & Bial	W. 23d St., W. of 6th Ave	1,000
Lenox Lyceum	E. Ferrero	E. 59th St. and Madison Ave	2,000
Lyric Hall		6th Ave., near 42d St	800
Madison Square Garden.	T. H. French	Madison Ave., 26th and 27th Sts	10,000
Music Hall (Carnagie)	Morris Reno	W. 57th St., near 7th Ave	2,000

Musical entertainments are sometimes given in halls customarily used for other purposes, such as the hall of the Cooper Union, the hall of the Masonic Temple, Tammany Hall, Clarendon Hall, 114 East 13th Street, and the Germania Assembly Rooms, on the Bowery.

There are, in addition, a large number of music halls patronized by our German population, in which refreshments are served, the most notable of which are the Atlantic Garden, on the Bowery, near Canal Street, and the Fourteenth Street Music Hall, near Third Avenue.

INFORMATION ABOUT CHICAGO.

INFORMATION for the convenience of visitors to Chicago during the World's Columbian Exposition is given in the following pages. No attempt has been made to print a full directory of the institutions of the great Western metropolis ; only such details are presented as will be useful to strangers, and for them this *résumé* is intended.

GENERAL FACTS.

Area of Chicago, 185 square miles. It is 24 miles long and 10 miles wide. Distant 911 miles from New-York and 2,417 miles from the Pacific coast. Mean annual temperature in 1891, 48.70 degrees ; mean annual precipitation, 35.55 inches. Death rate, 20.25 per 1,000 population (May, 1892), which is very low. Population by census of 1890, 1,099,850 ; estimated population, January 1, 1892, 1,375,335 ; by school census of 1892 it reached 1,428,318. Vote for President, 1892, Cleveland, Dem., 136,525 ; Harrison, Rep., 100,851. Democratic plurality, 35,674.

Amusements.

THEATRES.

Name.	Location.	Name.	Location.
Academy of Music...........	83 S. Halsted St.	Haymarket Theatre........	167 W. Madison St.
Alhambra...................	State St.and Archer Ave.	Hooley's Theatre............	149 Randolph St.
Auditorium.................	Wabash Ave.& Congress St.	Lyceum Theatre..........	54 Desplaines St.
		Madison Street Theatre.....	83 Madison St.
Central Music Hall..........	State and Randolph Sts.	McVicker's Theatre.........	82 Madison St.
Chicago Opera House........	Washington & Clark Sts.	Olympic Theatre	46 Clark St..
Clark Street Theatre........	Kinzie & N. Clark Sts.	Park Theatre................	325 State St.
Columbia Theatre............	110 Monroe St.	Paris Gaieties......	131 Michigan Ave.
Criterion Theatre............	274 Sedgwick St.	People's Theatre....	339 State St.
German Opera House........	103 Randolph St.	Standard Theatre....	169 S. Halsted St.
Grand Opera House.........	87 Clark St.	Waverly Theatre............	454 W. Madison St.
Halsted Street Theatre......	Halsted & W. Harrison Sts.	Windsor Theatre............	468 N. Clark St.
Havlin's Theatre............	Wabash Ave. & 19th St.	Timmerman's Opera House.	Stewart Ave and 63d St.

MUSEUMS, ETC.—Eden Musée, wax works, curios, etc., 227 Wabash Ave.; Cyclorama of the Battle of Gettysburg, Wabash Ave., near Hubbard Court ; Cyclorama of the Chicago Fire, Michigan Ave. and Monroe St.; Libby Prison Museum (the old Libby Prison, which was moved from Richmond in 1889 and opened as a National War Museum), Wabash Ave. and 15th St. ; John Brown's Fort (the Harper's Ferry, Va., engine house removed to Chicago and filled with ante-bellum relics), Wabash Ave., between 13th and 14th Sts.

DIME MUSEUMS.—Kohl & Middleton's South Side, 146 S. Clark St.; Globe, State St., near Harrison St. ; Epsean's New, Randolph St., near Clark St.

Art.

THE Art Institute, at Michigan Ave. and Van Buren St., contains the only public art gallery. The land and building, which is of brown stone, cost $300,000. Six galleries occupy a floor space of nearly 5,000 feet, and can accommodate 500 pictures. The Art Institute School, the principal art school of Chicago, is located in this building, where the Fortnightly Club, the Chicago Women's Club, the Chicago Literary Club, the Chicago Architectural Sketch Club, and the Chicago Society of Decorative Art also have quarters. Admission to the exhibits is free all day Saturdays and four hours on Sundays.

The collections of the Illinois Art Association, in the rooms of the Illinois Club, 154 Ashland Boulevard ; the Vincennes Gallery of Fine Arts, 3841 Vincennes Ave., and the galleries of the Illinois Club, the Chicago Club, the Marquette Club, the Calumet Club, the Union League Club, and Mr. Charles T. Yerkes, 3201 Michigan Ave., are well worth inspection, if the tourist can secure permission.

Asylums and Benevolent Institutions.

American Educational and Aid Association (Children's Home Society of Chicago), office, 230 La Salle St.

Armour Mission, Butterfield and 33d Sts.

Bethany Home, for old people and children of working women, 1029 W. Monroe St.

Bureau of Justice secures justice for the helpless, 149 La Salle St.

Chicago Children's Hospital, 214 Humboldt Boulevard.

Chicago Daily News Fresh Air Fund, contributions received at 123 Fifth Ave.; South Side Sanitarium at foot of 22d St.

Chicago Free Kindergarten Association.

Chicago Nursery and Half Orphan Asylum, Burlington St., south of Centre St.

Chicago Orphan Asylum, 2228 Michigan Ave.

Chicago Policlinic, a mission. 174 Chicago Ave.

Chicago Relief and Aid Society, La Salle St., between Lake and Randolph Sts.

Church Home for Aged Persons, 4327 Ellis Ave.

Convalescents' Home, just organized.

Danish Lutheran Orphans' Home, Maplewood (on Western division, Northwestern Railroad).

Erring Woman's Refuge, Indiana Ave., between 50th and 51st Sts.

Foundlings' Home, Wood St. and Ogden Pl.

German Old People's Home, Harlem (via. Wisconsin Central Railroad).

Good Samaritan Society, Industrial Home at 151 Lincoln Ave.

Guardian Angel Orphan Asylum, Rosehill.

Hebrew Charity Association.

The Electoral Vote.

THE following is the electoral vote of the States as based upon the Apportionment Act of February 7, 1891:

STATES.	Electoral Votes.	STATES.	Electoral Votes.	STATES.	Electoral Votes.
Alabama........	11	Maryland......	8	Pennsylvania.	32
Arkansas.....	8	Massachusetts	15	Rhode-Island.	4
California.....	9	Michigan......	14	S. Carolina. ...	9
Colorado......	4	Minnesota....	9	S. Dakota......	4
Connecticut..	6	Mississippi....	9	Tennessee.....	12
Delaware......	3	Missouri......	17	Texas.......	15
Florida........	4	Montana......	3	Vermont.......	4
Georgia........	13	Nebraska.......	8	Virginia......	12
Idaho....... ..	3	Nevada.......	3	Washington...	4
Illinois..........	24	N. Hampshire.	4	W. Virginia...	6
Indiana........	15	New-Jersey..	10	Wisconsin.....	12
Iowa..........	13	New-York....	36	Wyoming......	3
Kansas........	10	N. Carolina..	11		
Kentucky......	13	N. Dakota......	3	Total........	444
Louisiana.....	8	Ohio.	23		
Maine..........	6	Oregon......	4		

Electoral votes necessary to a choice.................................223

Universities of Great Britain and Ireland.

FOUNDED.	Names.	Chancellors.	No of Colleges.	Instructors.	Undergraduates, 1890.
1494......	Aberdeen...............	Duke of Richmond and Gordon...	1	35	909
1257......	Cambridge..............	Duke of Devonshire........	19	150	3,029
1831......	Durham.................	None.................	1	13	225
1591......	Dublin.................	Earl of Rosse.............	1	74	1,196
1582......	Edinburgh..............	Arthur J. Balfour..........	1	103	3,576
1450......	Glasgow................	Earl of Stair.............	1	61	2,165
1836......	London.................	Earl of Derby............	1	110	1,200
1274......	Oxford.................	Marquis of Salisbury.......	23	84	3,212
1411......	St. Andrews............	Duke of Argyll...........	2	16	208

Membership of Fraternal Organizations.

ACCORDING to the latest reports of the supreme bodies of these organizations to THE WORLD ALMANAC, the membership of the principal fraternal organizations in the United States and Canada is as follows:

Free Masons.............................	698,402	Royal Templars of Temperance.................	39,829
Odd Fellows.............................	696,008	Order of Chosen Friends...................	38,652
Knights of Pythias......................	357,924	Catholic Mutual Benefit Association.........	38,000
Ancient Order of United Workmen......	298,158	Benevolent and Protective Order of Elks......	35,000
Improved Order of Red Men..............	139,127	Catholic Benevolent Legion...	30,157
Knights of Honor.......................	135,126	Ancient Order of Foresters.................	28,434
Royal Arcanum..........................	132,284	Independent Order of B'nai B'rith.........	26,000
Junior Order of United American Mechanics.	107,491	Brotherhood of Railroad Trainmen...........	25,000
Ancient Order of Hibernians in America.	100,000	Catholic Knights of America...............	23,000
Ancient Order of Foresters of America.	98,608	Order of United Friends.................	21,521
Knights of the Maccabees................	96,338	Order of the Golden Cross...............	19,560
Knights and Ladies of Honor............	73,000	United Order of Pilgrim Fathers.........	15,690
Modern Woodmen of America............	68,667	Ancient Order of Druids.................	14,500
Sons of Temperance.....................	67,603	Royal Society of Good Fellows...........	11,055
American Legion of Honor...............	61,355	Smaller Organizations not reported...........	173,629
Order of United American Mechanics........	50,464		
Equitable Aid Union....................	46,100	Total................................	3,707,947
National Union..........................	41,265		

None of the so-called endowment assessment concerns, of which the "Iron Hall" and "Order of Tonti" are the type, are included in the above, which are genuine fraternal societies.

Murders and Hangings in 1892.

THE number of murders and homicides in the United States reported in the newspapers during the year 1892 was 6,791, classified by causes as follows: quarrels, 2,037; liquor, 748; unknown, 769; jealousy, 513; by highwaymen, 376; infanticide, 314; resisting arrest, 240; highwaymen killed, 148; self-defence, 81; insanity, 111; outrages, 28; strikes, 82; riots, 6.

The number of legal executions during the year was 107, as compared with 123 in 1891 and 102 in 1890. The executions in the several States and Territories were as follows: Alabama, 3; Arkansas, 9; Connecticut, 2; Georgia, 14; Illinois, 3; Kentucky, 10; Louisiana, 4; Maryland, 1; Mississippi, 2; Missouri, 2; Montana, 1; Nebraska, 1; New-York, 5; New-Jersey, 3; North-Carolina, 4; Ohio, 3; Oregon, 2; Pennsylvania, 4; South-Carolina, 5; South-Dakota, 1; Tennessee, 4; Texas, 10; Vermont, 1; Virginia, 5; West-Virginia, 2; Washington, 2; Wyoming, 1; New-Mexico, 1; Indian Territory, 2. Of the total number, 57 were whites, 47 negroes, 1 Chinaman, 2 Indians, and 4 women. From the annual compilation in the Chicago *Tribune*.

Transportation of the Mails, Average Time.

THE Post-Office Department reports the average time occupied per trip by mail steamers of the transatlantic service, during the fiscal year ended June 30, 1892, as follows:

NEW-YORK TO LONDON AND PARIS.

STEAMERS.	Trips.	Average time occupied per trip (hours).	STEAMERS.	Trips.	Average time occupied per trip (hours).	STEAMERS.	Trips.	Average time occupied per trip (hours).	STEAMERS.	Trips.	Average time occupied per trip (hours).
Fürst Bismarck....	9	171.3	City of Paris......	11	182.4	Saale............	10	208.0	Bothnia...........	2	277.7
Columbia.........	8	175.3	City of Berlin...	10	235.7	Trave............	11	208.4	Alaska...........	4	214.0
Normannia.......	9	177.1	City of Chicago...	11	246.5	Kaiser Wilhelm II	2	212.0	Arizona..........	2	224.3
Augusta Victoria..	7	185.7	Havel............	12	182.8	Eider............	5	215.3	La Touraine ...	9	198.5
Teutonic..........	13	175.5	Spree............	11	182.8	Elbe.............	9	227.9	La Bourgogne ...	10	202.4
Majestic..........	13	178.8	Lahn............	10	189.2	Umbria...........	12	184.5	La Champagne..	10	204.5
Germanic.........	11	212.6	Hamilton...	11	201.9	Etruria...........	13	184.7	La Gascogne.....	9	205.6
Britannic.........	10	216.0	Werra..........	3	201.9	Servia...........	11	210.6	La Bretagne.....	9	207.3
Adriatic..........	2	260.5	Fulda..........	3	204.1	Aurania	13	211.0	La Normandie ...	5	226.0
City of New-York.	10	179.4	Aller............	10	205.0	Gallia...........	1	226.0			
			Ems.............	13	205.8						

The number of hours stated shows the time elapsing between the actual receipt of the mails on board the steamers and their delivery at the Post-Office in London or Paris.

Curling Records.

MATCH.	Medal.	Last Played.	No. of Rinks.	Location.	Winner.	Medal Holder.
North vs. South of Scotland...	Dalrymple.	Jan. 28, 1892·	9	New-York ...	North........	Pres. Peattie.
Scotch vs. Other Nations.	McLintock.	Feb. 11, 1890.	7	St. Paul....	Scotch......	J. C. Myron.
International (2 rinks)...	Gordon	Feb. 11, 1891.	2	Montreal ...	Canada	W. Wilson.
Champion Rink.............	Gordon	Jan. 21, 1892.	9	New-York ...	John O'Groat	George Oag.
Scotch vs. American........	Patterson..	Feb. 22, 1889.	9	New-York ...	Scotch	John Patterson.
New-York vs. New-Jersey...	Hamilton..	Jan. 14, 1886.	12	Paterson....	New-York ...	Rob. Kellock.
Masonic, Pyramid vs. Templar	Honor	March 5, 1892.	5	Hoboken....	Templar ...	J. B. Gillie.
Stonecutters vs. Stonesetters..	Alpha......	Jan. 27, 1892.	7	New-York ...	Stonesetters..	Geo. Manson.
United States vs. Canada......	Honor	Jan. 8, 1892.	33	Toronto......	Canada......	Pres. Badenach
New-York State vs. Granite, Toronto..................	Honor	Jan. 9, 1892.	12	Toronto......	Granite, Tor.	A. H. Wright.

Billiard Records.

Three-Ball Straight Rail.—Highest run on record, 1,531, on a 5x10 table, by Maurice Vignaux, at Paris, April 10-14, 1880, against George F. Slosson. Harvey McKenna, the celebrated rail player, who died November 4, 1889, in New-York, and Jacob Schaefer have made higher runs on a 4½x9 table, but the 5x10 is the only recognized table for records of the present day. The best average at the three-ball straight-rail game on a 5x10 table is 333⅓, by Jacob Schaeffer, at Music Hall, Chicago, May 15, 1879.

Cushion Carroms.—Highest run, 77, on a 5x10 table, by William Sexton, at Tammany Hall, New-York, December 19, 1881, against Jacob Schaefer. Best average, 10 in 200 points, on a 5x10 table, by Jacob Schaefer, at Chicago, November 10, 1887.

Champion's Game.—(Corner play barred.) Highest run on record (18 by 38-inch lines), 398 on a 5x10 table, by George F. Slosson, at Paris, January 30 to February 3, 1882, against Maurice Vignaux. Slosson also made the best average on record in this match, 38 36-78 in 3,000 points up.

Balk-Line Game.—Highest run, at the 8-inch balk-line game, 329 on a 5x10 table, by Maurice Vignaux, at Paris, January, 1884.

Highest run at the 14-inch balk-line game, 230, on a 5x10 table, by Jacob Schaefer, at Cosmopolitan Hall, New-York, March 8-13, 1886, against Vignaux.

Best average at the 14-inch balk-line, 75, by Maurice Vignaux, at Chicago, November, 1885.

BILLIARD EVENTS IN 1892.

January 22—at New-York. Jacob Schaefer defeated George Slosson, 14-inch balk-line game, for $500 a side and the championship trophy. Scores: Schaefer, 800; Slosson, 592. Averages: Schaefer, 23 9-17; Slosson, 17 31-33. Best runs: Schaefer, 155; Slosson, 110.

March 19—at Chicago. Frank C. Ives defeated Jacob Schaefer, 14-inch balk-line game, for $500 a side and the championship trophy. Scores: Ives, 800; Schaefer, 499. Averages: Ives, 16 16-49; Schaefer, 10 19-48. Best runs: Ives, 95; Schaefer, 45.

May 21—at Chicago. Frank C. Ives defeated George Slosson, 14-inch balk-line game for $500 a side and the championship trophy. Scores: Ives, 800; Slosson, 488. Averages: Ives, 26⅔; Slosson, 16 4-19. Best runs: Ives, 142; Slosson, 120.

December 20 and 21—at Paris. Maurice Vignaux defeated Jacob Schaefer, 600 points a night, 14-inch balk-line game, $1,000 a side. Scores: Vignaux, 1,200; Schaefer, 982. Averages: Vignaux, 37½; Schaefer, 30 11-16. Best runs: Vignaux, 136; Schaefer, 127.

Easter Sundays.

A TABLE SHOWING THE DATE OF EASTER SUNDAY IN EACH YEAR OF THE NINETEENTH CENTURY.

1801—April 5.	1821—April 22.	1841—April 11.	1861—March 31.	1881—April 17.
1802—April 18.	1822—April 7.	1842—March 27.	1862—April 20.	1882—April 9.
1803—April 10.	1823—March 30.	1843—April 16.	1863—April 5.	1883—March 25.
1804—April 1.	1824—April 18.	1844—April 7.	1864—March 27.	1884—April 13.
1805—April 14.	1825—April 3.	1845—March 23.	1865—April 16.	1885—April 5.
1806—April 6.	1826—March 26.	1846—April 12.	1866—April 1.	1886—April 25.
1807—March 29.	1827—April 15.	1847—April 4.	1867—April 21.	1887—April 10.
1808—April 17.	1828—April 6.	1848—April 23.	1868—April 12.	1888—April 1.
1809—April 2.	1829—April 19.	1849—April 8.	1869—March 28.	1889—April 21.
1810—April 22.	1830—April 11.	1850—March 31.	1870—April 17.	1890—April 6.
1811—April 14.	1831—April 3.	1851—April 20.	1871—April 9.	1891—March 29.
1812—March 29.	1832—April 22.	1852—April 11.	1872—March 31.	1892—April 17.
1813—April 18.	1833—April 7.	1853—March 27.	1873—April 13.	1893—April 2.
1814—April 10.	1834—March 30.	1854—April 16.	1874—April 5.	1894—March 25.
1815—March 26.	1835—April 19.	1855—April 8.	1875—March 28.	1895—April 14.
1816—April 14.	1836—April 3.	1856—March 23.	1876—April 16.	1896—April 5.
1817—April 6.	1837—March 26.	1857—April 12.	1877—April 1.	1897—April 18.
1818—March 22.	1838—April 15.	1858—April 4.	1878—April 21.	1898—April 10.
1819—April 11.	1839—March 31.	1859—April 24.	1879—April 13.	1899—April 2.
1820—April 2.	1840—April 19.	1860—April 8.	1880—March 28.	1900—April 15.

Bell Time on Shipboard.

Time, A.M.		Time, A.M.		Time, A.M.	
1 Bell	12.30	1 Bell	4.30	1 Bell	8.30
2 Bells	1.00	2 Bells	5.00	2 Bells	9.00
3 "	1.30	3 "	5.30	3 "	9.30
4 "	2.00	4 "	6.00	4 "	10.00
5 "	2.30	5 "	6.30	5 "	10.30
6 "	3.00	6 "	7.00	6 "	11.00
7 "	3.30	7 "	7.30	7 "	11.30
8 "	4.00	8 "	8.00	8 "	Noon

Time, P.M.		Time, P.M.		Time, P.M.	
1 Bell	12.30	1 Bell	4.30	1 Bell	8.30
2 Bells	1.00	2 Bells	5.00	2 Bells	9.00
3 "	1.30	3 "	5.30	3 "	9.30
4 "	2.00	4 "	6.00	4 "	10.00
5 "	2.30	5 Bell	6.30	5 "	10.30
6 "	3.00	6 Bells	7.00	6 "	11.00
7 "	3.30	7 "	7.30	7 "	11.30
8 "	4.00	8 "	8.00	8 "	Midnight

On shipboard, for purposes of discipline and to divide the watch fairly, the crew is mustered in two divisions: the Starboard (right side, looking toward the head), and the Port (left). The day commences at noon, and is thus divided: Afternoon Watch, noon to 4 P.M.; First Dog Watch, 4 P.M. to 6 P.M.; Second Dog Watch, 6 P.M. to 8 P.M.; First Watch, 8 P.M. to midnight; Middle Watch, 12 A.M. to 4 A.M.; Morning Watch, 4 A.M. to 8 A.M.; Forenoon Watch, 8 A.M. to noon. This makes seven WATCHES, which enables the crew to keep them alternately, as the Watch which comes on duty at noon one day has the afternoon next day, and the men who have only four hours' rest one night have eight hours the next. This is the reason for having Dog Watches, which are made by dividing the hours between 4 P.M. and 8 P.M. into two Watches. Time is kept by means of "Bells," although sometimes there is but one Bell on the ship.—*Whitaker.*

The French Revolutionary Era.

IN September, 1793, the convention decreed that the common era should be abolished in all civil affairs, and that the new French era should begin on September 22, 1792, the day of the true autumnal equinox, and that each succeeding year should begin at the midnight of the day on which the true autumnal equinox falls. The year was divided into twelve months of 30 days each. In ordinary years there were five extra days, from the 17th to the 21st of our September, and at the end of every fourth year was a sixth complementary day. This reckoning was first used on November 22, 1793, and was continued until December 31, 1805, when it was discontinued, and the Gregorian calendar, used throughout the rest of Europe, was resumed. The following were the dates for the year 1804, the last complete year of this style of reckoning:

Vendémiaire	(Vintage),	Sept. 23 to Oct. 22.	Germinal	(Budding), Mar. 22 to April 21.
Brumaire	(Foggy),	Oct. 23 to Nov. 22.	Floréal	(Flowery), April 21 to May 20.
Frimaire	(Sleety),	Nov. 22 to Dec. 21.	Prairial	(Pasture), May 21 to June 20.
Nivôse	(Snowy),	Dec. 22 to Jan. 21.	Messidor	(Harvest), June 20 to July 19.
Pluviôse	(Rainy),	Jan. 21 to Feb. 20.	Thermidor	(Hot), July 20 to Aug. 19.
Ventôse	(Windy),	Feb. 20 to Mar. 19.	Fructidor	(Fruit), Aug. 19 to Sept. 18.

The months were divided into three decades of ten days each, but to make up the 365, five were added at the end of September: Primidi, dedicated to Virtue; Duodi, to Genius; Tridi, to Labor; Quartidi, to Opinion; and Quintidi, to Rewards. To Leap Year, called Olympic, a sixth day, September 22 or 23, Sextidi, "the day of the Revolution," was added.

The current French names of the months are: Janvier (January), Février (February), Mars (March), Avril (April), Mai (May), Juin (June), Juillet (July), Août (August), Septembre (September), Octobre (October), Novembre (November), Décembre (December).

The days of the week are: Dimanche (Sunday), Lundi (Monday), Mardi (Tuesday), Mercredi (Wednesday), Jeudi (Thursday), Vendredi (Friday), Samedi (Saturday).

The World
Almanac

1943

and
Book of Facts
58th YEAR OF ISSUE
PUBLISHED BY THE

New York World-Telegram
A SCRIPPS—HOWARD NEWSPAPER

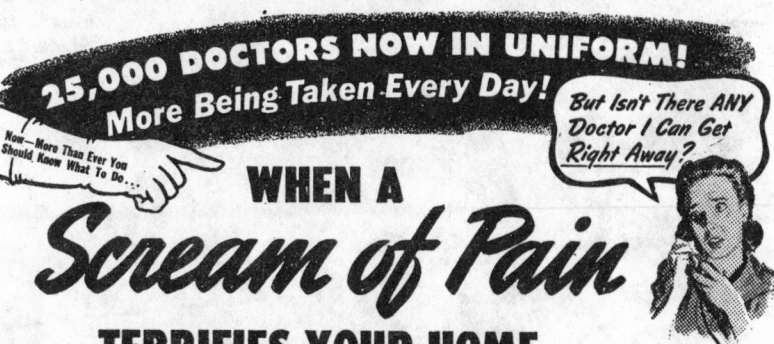
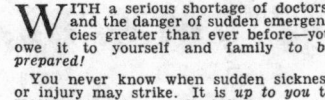

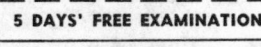
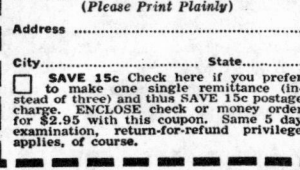

Which of These Mistakes in English Do YOU Make?

Sherwin Cody's remarkable invention has enabled more than 100,000 people to correct their mistakes in English. Only 15 minutes a day required to improve your speech and writing.

MANY persons say, "Did you hear from him today?" They should say, "Have you heard from him today?" Some spell "calendar" "calender" or "calander." Still others say "between you and I" instead of "between you and me." It is astonishing how often "who" is used for "whom," and how frequently the simplest words are mispronounced. Few know whether to spell certain words with one or two "c's" or "m's" or "r's," or with "ie" or "ei." Most persons use only common words—colorless, flat, ordinary. Their speech and their letters are lifeless, monotonous, humdrum.

Every time they talk or write they show themselves lacking in the essential points of English.

Wonderful New Invention

For many years Mr. Cody studied the problem of creating instinctive habits of using good English. After countless experiments he finally invented a simple method by which you can acquire a better command of the English language in only 15 minutes a day. Now you can stop making the mistakes which have been hurting you. Mr. Cody's students have secured more improvement in five weeks than previously had been obtained by other pupils in two years!

Learn by Habit—Not by Rules

Under old methods rules are memorized, but correct habits are not formed. Finally the rules themselves are forgotten. The new Sherwin Cody method provides for the formation of correct habits by calling to your attention constantly only the *mistakes you yourself make.*

One of the wonderful things about Mr. Cody's course is the speed with which

these habit-forming practice drills can be carried out. You can write the answers to fifty questions in 15 minutes and correct your work in 5 minutes more. The drudgery and work of copying have been ended by Mr. Cody!

SHERWIN CODY

You concentrate always on your own mistakes until it becomes "second nature" to speak and write correctly.

FREE—Book On English

A new book explaining Mr. Cody's remarkable method is ready. If you are ever embarrassed by mistakes in grammar, spelling, punctuation, pronunciation, or if you cannot instantly command the exact words with which to express your ideas, this new free book, "How You Can Master Good English—in 15 Minutes a Day," will prove a revelation to you. Send the coupon or a letter or postal card for it now. No agent will call. SHERWIN CODY SCHOOL OF ENGLISH, 63 Searle Building, Rochester, N. Y.

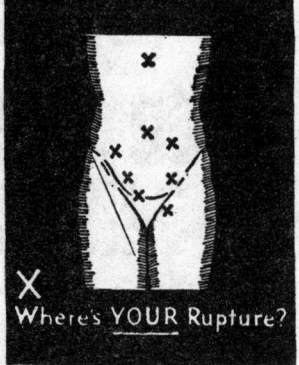

INTERNAL BATHS END YEARS OF DISTRESS

Baffled at 47 — Feels Like a Young Man at 77

Imagine how thrilling it must be for a man, feeling half-sick, half-alive for years, suddenly to find himself restored to new happiness and vitality. How wonderful he must feel to realize at last he may be able to say good-bye to the headaches, biliousness, sluggishness, that all-in feeling, due to chronic constipation suffered through many years.

But such a man was Leopold Aul, and as explained in his own words: "One day when I was feeling especially bad and as nervous as a cat, I met an old friend of mine. He noticed how fagged out I looked and how rapidly I seemed to be aging. 'Why don't you take Internal Baths?' he asked. 'They did wonders for me.'"

What Is An Internal Bath?

Thereupon Mr. Aul began investigating Internal Baths. He found a bona-fide Internal Bath to be the administration into the lower intestine of pure warm water—Nature's greatest cleansing agent—to which is added J.B.L. Cleansing Powder. Through the use of the J.B.L. Cascade four quarts of the cleansing solution may be sent gently swirling throughout the entire length of the colon. In fifteen minutes your impacted colon is thoroughly cleansed of its whole foul mass; the putrefying, delayed waste is loosened and washed away. Often the relief is immense—often a new sense of vigor and well-being sweeps over you.

Naturally, Mr. Aul did buy a J.B.L. Cascade. It proved a turning point in his life. Gone, according to his testimony, was the worry and distress that had hitherto over-shadowed his whole life, sapped his ambition.

Send for This Free Booklet

Investigate yourself the merits of Internal Bathing. Simply fill in and mail this coupon and receive, absolutely FREE, your copy of "Why We Should Bathe Internally." This instructive 24-page booklet may open your eyes to many surprising facts about constipation and its many attributed ills; reveals, too, how many thousands of Internal Bathers have gained new health and vigor through this drugless treatment.

Read Mr. Aul's Astounding Letter

"I am now 77 years young, have owned a Cascade for over thirty years. When I first started using the J.B.L. Cascade I was a victim of constipation and at my wits' end as to what to do about it. Tried most everything that was recommended and prescribed for me for years without results. I now feel that Internal Bathing was responsible for bringing back my health and for keeping it ever since. I use the Cascade occasionally now, but I would not part with it for $1,000. Have sincerely recommended it to every one suffering from the ill effects of constipation."

Leopold Aul
1505 Bushwick Ave., Brooklyn, N. Y.

● ● ● ● ●

I would like to thank you kindly for your letter of Dec. 7th and the interest which you showed in my case. I have used the Cascade for a little over a month now and feel like a different person. My husband has also received great benefit from it. I do regret that I did not hear of the Cascade many years ago.

Mrs. Oliver Roylance
R. D. No. 1, Waterford, N. Y.

● ● ● ● ●

Upon receiving my Cascade I followed direction closely. I have used it for a little over a month and have already found it to be very helpful. I wish every person who is being troubled with constipation could afford to own a Cascade. To me it is a big asset. It is helping me and I know it would help them.

Mr. Edward G. Turnau
215 Irving Street, Toledo, Ohio

● ● ● ● ●

I would not take ten times the price for it. Don't see how I ever got along without a J.B.L. Cascade. My health is much better and still improving. I was terribly constipated, nervous, bloated, etc. I can truthfully say that the Cascade has helped me from the very first. I thoroughly enjoy it now and am enjoying my meals—everything tastes so good.

Mrs. Roy Brown, c/o A. Fiske
3929 Bronson Blvd., Kalamazoo, Mich.

MAIL YOUR COUPON TODAY

Tyrrell's Hygienic Institute, Inc.
152 West 65th Street, Dept. W.A.43
New York, N. Y.

Send me, without cost or obligation, your illustrated book on intestinal ills and the proper use of the famous Internal Bath—"Why We Should Bathe Internally."

Name.....................................

Street....................................

City........................ State...........

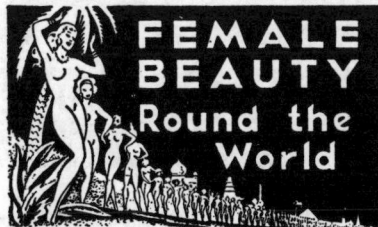

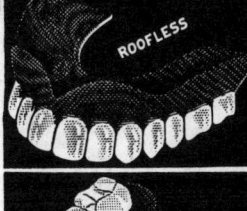
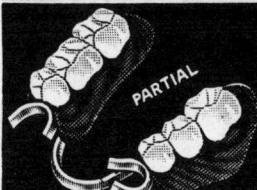

New York World-Telegram

THE WORLD ALMANAC

AND

BOOK OF FACTS

FOR

1943

EDITED BY

E. EASTMAN IRVINE

Fifty-eighth Year of Publication

PUBLISHED ANNUALLY BY

THE NEW YORK WORLD-TELEGRAM

A SCRIPPS-HOWARD NEWSPAPER

125 Barclay Street, New York City

WORLD WAR II
Review of Fighting in the Third Year

The Axis powers failed to gain their objectives in the third year of World War II, and early in the fourth year the initiative passed to the United Nations as a 1,500-mile offensive opened in North Africa and in Egypt and Libya. Military observers viewed this action as a possible forerunner of a second front against the Axis in Europe once the Mediterranean was cleared and the extensive system of airfields was made available for bombing raids by the Allies.

In the Russian campaign the Germans stalled before Stalingrad after five months of fighting and the Russians had taken the offensive there and west of Moscow. The German drive for the Caucasus and the rich oil fields of the region also fell short at another large cost in men.

The United States held the balance of power in the Southwest Pacific and turned to the offensive against the Japanese. American forces had established on the Solomon Islands a base for operations. In New Guinea the United Nations forces battled the Japanese for possession and to block any attempt to cut the supply lines to Australia or to take the island continent.

The United States established and maintained a defense line from the Aleutians in Alaska to Hawaii and down through the Pacific to Australia.

In the Occupied Countries the subjugated peoples were constantly on the "offensive" committing acts of sabotage against munitions plants and transportation centers. The threat of revolt was present in these countries and large forces of the Axis were held immobile there to cope with possible outbreaks.

United Nations forces also were active in Burma to regain territory lost there early in 1942 to the Japanese who destroyed the value of the Burma road as a munitions traffic artery to China. The Chinese also were on the offensive against the Japanese striking for the coastal points from which Allied planes, including many from the United States, might strike against Japan proper in bombing raids.

One predominating factor in the United Nations gaining the initiative was the supply of war materials furnished by the United States. From American factories to the battle fronts in all parts of the world there was poured a stream of airplanes, tanks, trucks and armored equipment, all of which gave an excellent account of their capabilities. United States soldiers, sailors and marines, also were on fronts throughout the world doing their share against the Axis.

President Roosevelt, in an address read in New York City (Nov. 17, 1942) at the New York Herald Tribune Forum, said: "It would seem that the turning point of this war has at last been reached. But this is no time for exultation. There is no time for anything but fighting and working to win."

Observers in Washington found it the most significant expression of official opinion about the war since Pearl Harbor. All the news from the Solomon Islands, from New Guinea, from North Africa and from Russia had contributed to the feeling that the power of the United Nations at last was being brought to bear against the Axis and the power of the Axis was on the wane.

After his return to Washington from a nationwide trip, President Roosevelt said (Oct. 12, 1942) in a radio broadcast: "The strength of the United Nations is on the upgrade in this war. The Axis leaders, on the other hand, know by now that they have already reached their full strength, and that their steadily mounting losses in men and material cannot be fully replaced. Germany and Japan are already realizing what the inevitable result will be when the total strength of the United Nations hits them—at additional places on the earth's surface."

In an earlier fireside chat to the nation (Sept. 7, 1942), President Roosevelt closed: "This is the toughest war of all time. We need not leave it to the historians of the future to answer the question whether we are tough enough to meet this unprecedented challenge. We can give the answer now. The answer is, 'Yes.'"

After news of the new British offensive in Egypt and Libya and the American landing in North Africa, Prime Minister Churchill commented (Nov. 10, 1942): "No, this is not the end. It is not even the beginning to the end. But it is, perhaps, the end of the beginning."

In this address Mr. Churchill gave credit to President Roosevelt as the author of the North African offensive in these words: "The President of the United States, who is the Commander-in-Chief of the armed forces of America, is the auth of this mighty undertaking and in all of it I ha' been his acting and ardent lieutenant."

Field Marshal Jan Christian Smuts, Prim Minister of South Africa, before an extraordinar, meeting of the Lords and Commons in London (Oct. 21, 1942) said that the defensive phase of the war had ended and that the day of the offensive had dawned.

Marshal Smuts was one of the architects of victory in World War I and is highly esteemed as a grand strategist. He believes that the war may be ended in 1944, but adds that 1943 will see the heaviest fighting.

There follows a summary of the fighting on the various fronts in the global war.

The Pacific Front—The Japanese made a sneak attack on Pearl Harbor, Hawaii (Dec. 7, 1941), an action that brought the United States into World War II. The Japanese followed with a smashing offensive into the Allied countries in the Southwest Pacific. There fell rapidly to the Japanese the Philippines, Malaya—including Singapore—the Netherlands East Indies, parts of the British East Indies and Hong Kong. Singapore at the tip of the Malayan Peninsula, was believed impregnable and commanded the trade routes of the East Indies. Japanese troops were landed in the Solomon Islands, in New Guinea and in New Britain to prepare bases and airfields for attacks against the United Nations and to control the Southwest Pacific with its trade routes and rich supplies of war materials. Australia faced the peril of invasion and there were air attacks against the country from the new Japanese bases.

In the first five months of their headlong drive, the Japanese seized and occupied an area one-third the size of the United States. It was not until May, 1942, that they were checked in the naval engagement in the Coral Sea. In this engagement the Japanese lost 11 ships with 12 damaged; the United States three and none damaged. The Japanese later moved their fleet eastward against Midway and were defeated again. The losses this time were 10 Japanese ships sunk, and 8 damaged; the United States two sunk, none damaged. From then on it became the task of the United States to roll back the Japanese and to regain some of the lands they had seized. In August the United States opened a combined land and sea offensive. United States Marines invaded Tulagi and Guadalcanal in the Solomons. Marines seized an airport in the jungle, renamed it Henderson Field and prepared it as a base for their attacks. To the Japanese, Guadalcanal represented a jumping off place for new conquests; to the United States it represented a defense against further Japanese advances and a starting point in the task of depriving the Japanese of their conquests from the winter and spring. It was possible from the Solomons to link a chain of "stepping" islands to reach Rabaul in New Britain and place the forces of the United Nations on the flank of the Japanese positions north of Australia.

The Japanese Navy disputed the advance of the Marines and sought to drive them out but failed. The Marines consolidated their positions as the Japanese Navy and Army attacked. Late in August a Japanese armada was turned back by United States naval and air forces. Small raiding parties of Japanese were repelled on Guadalcanal and possession by the Marines grew more secure. Attempts were made by the Japanese to land reinforcements in transports and small boats but there was a heavy loss in these maneuvers. The Japanese struck again in September; the Marines held and the Japanese losses were considerable. The Japanese tried again the next month, and, despite damage to their transports by American planes, landed sizable reinforcements.

The showdown came in November when one of the greatest naval battles since Jutland in World War I was fought. The Japanese were defeated with the loss of 28 ships and ten damaged, and retreated to the north still under attack from American planes and ships. The United States losses were nine ships, two cruisers and seven destroyers. Air power played a dominant part in the victory but the bulk of the damage was accomplished by gun salvos of the American warships who outfought the enemy in slashing engagements. The naval victory cleared away one threat overhanging the American positions in the Solomons and New Guinea where a land campaign was being waged to drive the enemy from that island and their bases for air attacks on Australia. The

The Southwest Pacific War Area

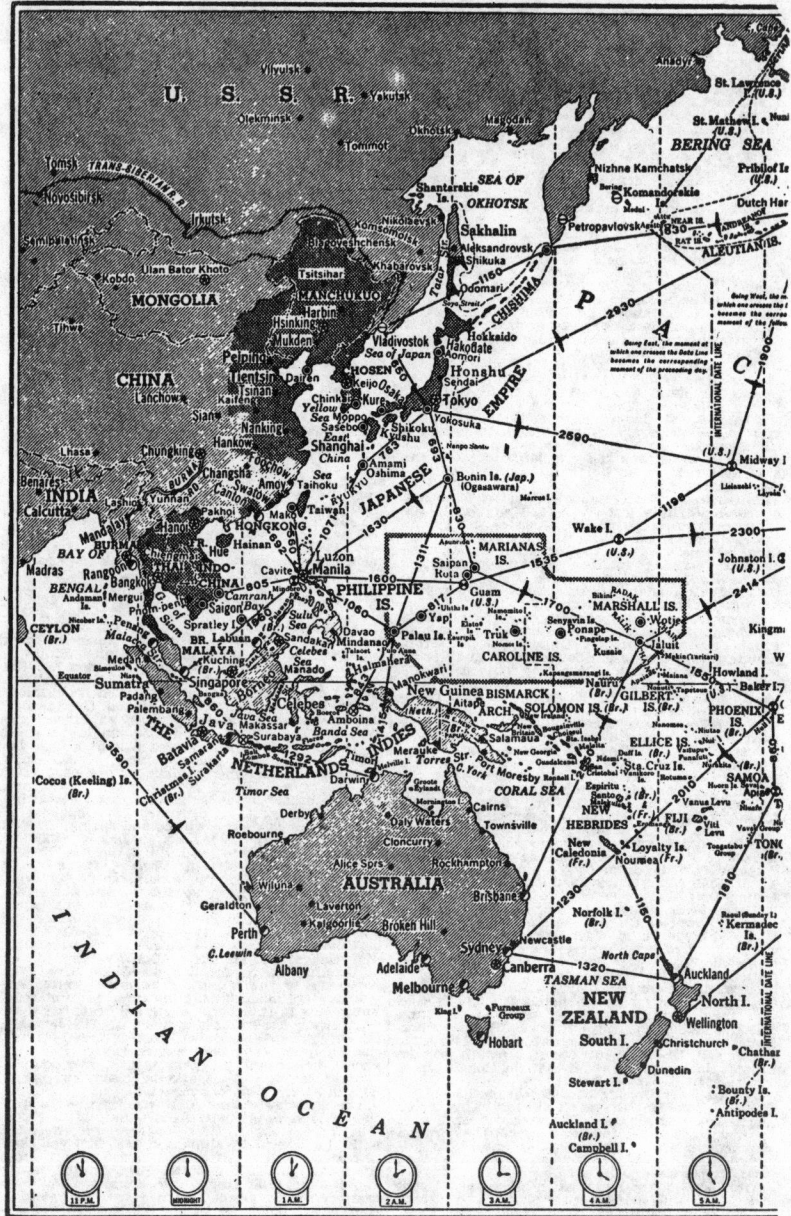

American command in the battle of the Solomons operated through Admiral William F. Halsey and General Douglas MacArthur, in charge of the United Nations Armies in the Southwest Pacific.

Coincident with the fighting in the Solomons, American and Australian units were occupied in driving the Japanese from New Guinea. The Japanese moved against Port Moresby, but half way across the island they were checked by the MacArthur forces and later driven back to the sea. They were reinforced again despite heavy losses.

As part of the general offensive in the Southwest Pacific, American troops operated from bases

The Southwest Pacific War Area

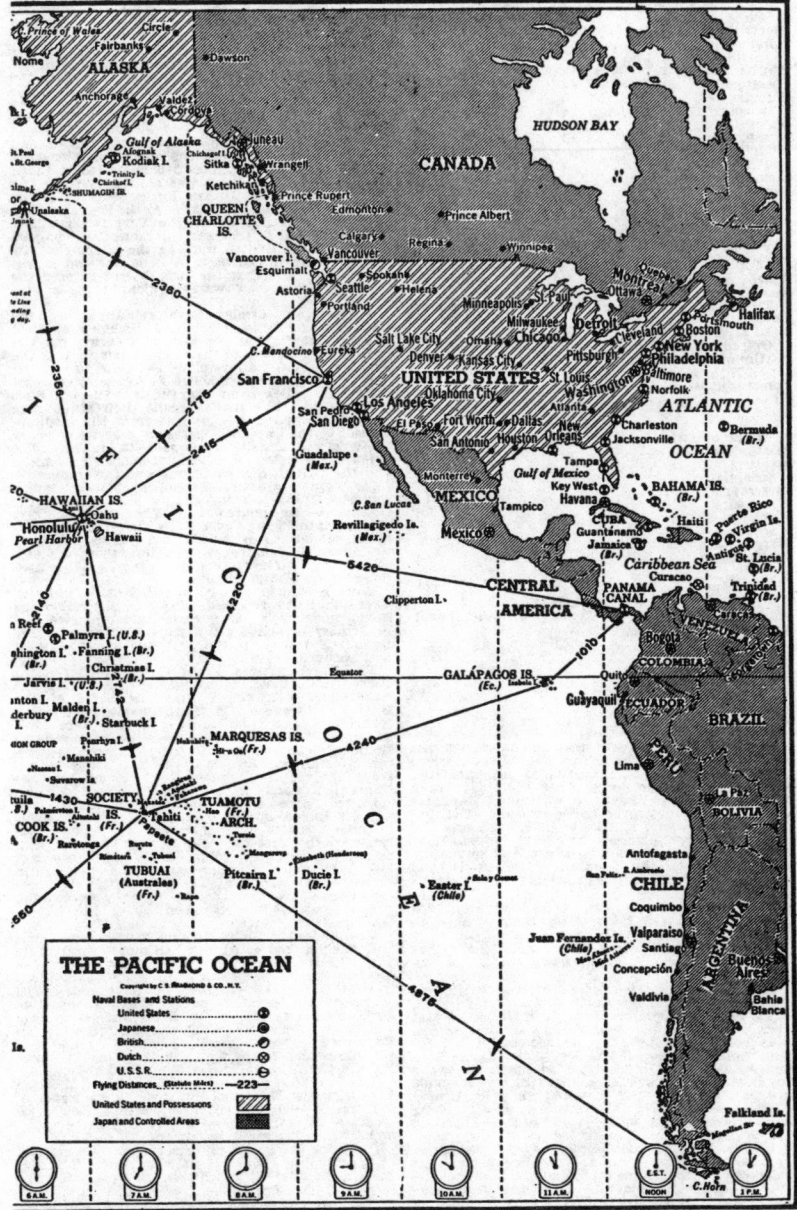

THE PACIFIC OCEAN

Copyright by C. S. HAMMOND & CO., N.Y.

Naval Bases and Stations

United States
Japanese
British
Dutch
U.S.S.R.

Flying Distances (Statute Miles) ——223—

United States and Possessions
Japan and Controlled Areas

on the New Hebrides, New Caledonia and the Fiji Islands. Armed American forces also operated from New Zealand.

Frank Knox, secretary of the Navy, told the War Congress of American Industry meeting in New York City (Dec. 2, 1942) that the comparative losses in men in the fighting in the Southwest Pacific had been at the rate of five to one in favor of this country. He estimated Army and Navy losses at 50,000 in killed and missing.

There follows a United Press compilation of all United States and Japanese ship losses since Pearl Harbor.

| | UNITED STATES | | | JAPAN | | |
	Sunk	Dam-aged	Total	Sunk	Dam-aged	Total
Battleships.	1	9	2	2	9	11
Aircraft carriers.	4	..	4	6	9	15
Cruisers....	7	6	13	21	70	91
Destroyers..	21	5	26	39	49	88
Submarines..	5	..	5	7	7	14
Transports..	4	..	4	53	46	99
Fleet tankers...	3	..	3	19	8	27
Supply ships	..	..	..	65	31	96
Gunboats...	5	..	5	9	3	12
Armed auxiliaries	..	..	..	2	..	2
Miscella-neous....	12	1	14	23	27	50
Totals...	62	21	76	246	259	505

*For the purposes of this table Japanese ships listed in communiques as "probably sunk" are combined with those listed as "probably damaged."

The Navy communique (Dec. 2) added five more ships, including a Japanese destroyer, as having been sunk and two others damaged.

United States and Japanese naval losses in the battle of the Solomons since that fight started Aug. 7 through Nov. 15, as announced in navy communiques:

JAPANESE LOSSES

Type of Ship	Sunk	Probably Sunk	Dam-aged	Total
Battleships.........	1	..	4	5
Cruisers.........	6	..	28	34
Carriers.........	..	..	4	4
Destroyers.........	13	3	19	35
Transports.........	11	1	6	18
Tankers-tenders...	..	..	3	3
Cargo.........	..	..	4	4
Cargo transports...	4	..	..	4
Unidentified.........	..	..	4	4
Totals.........	35	4	72	111

AMERICAN LOSSES

Type of Ship	Sunk	Damaged	Total
Cruisers.................	5	1	6
Aircraft carriers........	2	..	2
Destroyers..............	12	3	15
Transports..............	1	..	1
Auxiliary transports.....	3	..	3
Fleet tug..............	1	..	1
Total...............	24	4	28

Japanese losses do not include announcements from General MacArthur's Australian headquarters of damage inflicted by aircraft from his command. Nor do they include Secretary of the Navy Frank Knox's statement that two additional Japanese cruisers and a destroyer had been sunk (Oct. 11-12) in the second battle of Savo Island. His statement (never placed in any Navy communique) would add those ships to the sunk column, and eliminate one cruiser from the damaged list and a destroyer from the "probably sunk" classification.

In comparing American and Japanese ships damaged it should be recalled that damage to American ships generally is not announced.

There have been some losses, not listed, since the main Solomons Island battle in minor engagements.

The United States established a defense line running from the Aleutian Islands, off Alaska, down to Hawaii and on through to the Southwest Pacific to guard the supply lines to that sector.

Early in June the Japanese occupied the three westernmost islands of the Aleutians—Kiska, Attu and Agattu, 1,300 miles from Alaska and toward the Siberian Peninsula of Kamchatka. The islands are on the great circle route from the United States to Japan and their strategic location long has been recognized but only at Dutch Harbor had the United States constructed a military base. Other harbors in the desolate wastes remained undeveloped. The United States countered the Japanese stroke with naval and air raids. Throughout the summer, when the notoriously bad Aleutians weather permitted there were air attacks on the Japanese positions. Big Army planes dumped tons and tons of bombs on Kiska.

Early in October, United States forces occupied the Andreanof Islands in the Aleutians, and Army aircraft, including Flying Fortresses, began using the new fields to attack the Japanese on the other islands. The Andreanof Islands are only 125 miles east of Kiska, the main Japanese base in the Aleutians. These air attacks against the Japanese continued throughout October. Early in the month it was reported they had quit Attu and Agattu and no activity was observed on Kiska. Later, after another bombing raid, it was reported that the Japanese were back on Kiska and Attu.

Egyptian-Libyan Front—British and Axis armies fought for two years across the sands and desert wastes of Libya and Egypt to gain control of the transport lines of the Mediterranean and the traffic routes of the Suez Canal. The Italian army opened the campaign (1940) and pushed the British 70 miles into Egypt. The Italian force halted and the British, reinforced with planes, tanks and armored equipment, took the offensive. The drive carried the British armies 340 miles inside Libya in 1941 and again there was a halt. Within two months the Fascist Italian forces returned to the offensive and before it had ended the British troops had been driven back to the Egyptian frontier. Before the end of the year the tables had changed again and the British were on the offensive. The Italians were forced back to Benghazi and it was the second time that the British had entered the place in the seesaw warfare along the Mediterranean.

The Italian armies were reinforced by the Germans and General Erwin Rommel (later Field Marshal) undertook the task of clearing out the British and driving to the Suez. Early in 1942 the Rommel forces had retaken Benghazi, swept on and by mid-year had reached El Alamein, approximately 75 miles from Alexandria with the Suez just beyond. The British made their stand here and established a defense line from the Mediterranean to the Qattara depression, a series of below sea-level salt marshes impassable to an army. The defense line extended over approximately 40 miles and the British held it throughout the summer.

Meanwhile American supplies, planes, tanks, armored trucks—all superior to that used by the Germans—had poured in. The United States shipped into Egypt "over 1,000 planes, many hundreds of tanks, of which more than 500 were mediums, 200,000 trucks, and hundreds of pieces of artillery." The shipments to the Egyptian area had a value of $636,952,000.

Rommel tried the reinforced British lines in August but was repulsed. Early in September the Allies smashed a large scale Axis offensive and in October launched a full scale drive that cleared Rommel's forces from Egypt and pursued them into western Libya.

The North African Front—The United Nations opened an offensive in North Africa early in November, 1942, timed with the drive of the British Army against Marshal Rommel's retreating forces in Egypt and Libya. It was part of a gigantic pincers movement from the East and the West to clear the Axis forces from the Mediterranean and establish bases for a possible second front against the "underbelly" (Prime Minister Churchill's word) of the Axis European domain.

United States troops, supported by British sea and air forces, landed on the Atlantic and Mediterranean coasts of French Africa. Algiers surrendered the first day, but Oran and Casablanca held out and fighting followed. Oran fell two days later and tank columns stormed and warships bombarded Casablanca. Three days after the landing Casablanca surrendered and Morocco and Algeria passed into the control of the United Nations.

Meanwhile the American and British forces that had disembarked at Algiers had moved on Tunisia with Bizerte, once the French Gibraltar of the Mediterranean, and Tunis, their immediate objectives. The Axis opposed the move and landed forces by air transport on the Tunisian coast to fight for the system of air fields and ports from which an offensive against the Axis in southern Europe could be launched. It was in Tunisia that the American troops met the Germans in battle for the first time since 1918 in World War I.

The armada used for landing the American Expeditionary Force in North Africa consisted of 850 vessels—500 transports protected by 350 naval craft of all types. It was called the "greatest amphibious operation in history."

Plans for the grand pincers movement were laid in Washington (June, 1942) when Prime Minister Churchill conferred with President Roosevelt. The men met in the White House to discuss "the earliest maximum concentration of Allied power upon the enemy." Out of that meeting came the decision for the campaign that was held as the greatest secret of the war until the attack was launched.

It was necessary to keep the Germans confused and uncertain as to the timing and place of the attack. A war of nerves was waged against the Axis. Misleading information was released and it was soon discovered that Hitler and his collaborationists in France were confused. They knew a blow was coming but did not know where. When the British unleashed their army in Egypt against Marshal Rommel the Axis was surprised by the strength of the artillery and the air arms. Even while the armada was being gathered to land the forces in North Africa, Hitler complained of the difficulty of divining the plans of military "idiots and drunkards" who were his opponents.

Vice Admiral Jean Francois Darlan, commander of all the Vichy armed forces, was made political leader under authority of Gen. Eisenhower of the areas taken by the United Nations. As the campaign progressed he announced that Dakar, the French West African port dominating the Allied sea lanes from the bulge where Africa is closest to Brazil and a possible base for attacks against the South American continent, had gone over to the United Nations. In Europe the Germans completed the occupation of all France but in Africa French forces shifted to the United Nations and fought with these forces. But France was taken nominally into a military alliance with Hitler and Mussolini.

The French later scuttled their fleet of 62 warships in Toulon harbor to prevent the ships from falling into the hands of Hitler and the Nazi forces, scrapping the last vestige of the Franco-German armistice, raced into Toulon and seized the post. Three French submarines were reported to have escaped.

The Russian Front—There was fighting along most of the 1,800 miles of Russian front extending from the Arctic to the Black Sea. The chief offensive was directed at the southern end of the line where the Germans massed an estimated 1,500,000 troops for a drive on Stalingrad, an important manufacturing city of Russia, and control of the Volga river, a vital traffic artery. Twinned with this offensive was another drive into the Caucasus to wrest control of the oil fields from the Russians at the same time cutting their supply of fuel and replenishing the dwindling reserves of the Nazis.

The German staff allotted three weeks for this task, and assisting the 100 divisions of troops were 2,000 planes, 2,000 guns and thousands of tanks. For more than three months the Germans hammered at Stalingrad, fought in the suburbs, in the city's streets, in factories and in the halls of buildings. The Germans expended hundreds of thousands of men and masses of material but when the chill winds of winter raced down upon the steppes into Stalingrad the Russians still held. As winter fastened its grip on the section the Russians started an offensive of their own, aimed to trap the stalled German armies. Russian forces timed another offensive near Rzhev, west of Moscow.

The offensive into the Caucasus had fared slightly better, but the Nazi objectives were not attained. The Germans drove through Crimea, captured Sevastopol and pushed on to the Maikop oil fields. There their progress was slowed and the rich oil fields of the Caucasus—at Grozny and Baku—remained in the hands of the Russians, still beyond the armies of Hitler and his intention. Once again winter came whistling down the steppes and the German drive stalled.

August, September, October and a major part of November had been used up by the Germans; hundreds of thousands of men, masses of tanks, guns, trucks and armored cars had been sacrificed without achieving the goal of the 1942 offensive.

When the German drive stalled at Stalingrad, coincident with the opening of the Allied offensive in North Africa, the Russians were quick to open an attack to win back the strategic points that had given the Germans command around the city. This offensive was timed with another to the north around Rzhev where it was the Russian plan to capture the keystone to the German defenses there and cause the whole line to fall back. The German defensive lines were pierced at many points as winted closed down and hampered the Nazis in the movement of men and machines of war.

The Germans, in their war against Russia, killed, captured, wounded or destroyed numerous Russian armies and inflicted casualties running into the hundreds of thousands. The Germans occupied roughly 700,000 square miles of Russia, less than 9 per cent of Russian territory. The German vanguard penetrated 950 miles into Russia and occupied a territory once populated by 77,000,000 persons, mostly workers. Some were killed and others fled to other Soviet areas. The Ukraine-Dombas industrial area was occupied by the Germans. They also held the Maikop oil fields

with their relatively small output of 43,750 barrels a day (about 7 per cent of the Russian production.) The Germans also gained part of the Northern Caucasus but they had not reached the Caspian Sea and the oil fields.

Economic experts said that the best the Nazis could show for their efforts was not positive gain but the advantage of having deprived Russia of vital war materials. Germany received little from the overrun wheat lands and other agricultural areas and the armament industry received little or nothing from the coal, iron and steel producing areas. Not one barrel of oil had gone to Germany and these experts said the Soviet scorched earth policy, an acute German labor shortage and inadequate transportation facilities had made it impossible for Hitler to realize on the Eastern conquests.

In the fighting in the north the Germans neutralized the Leningrad industrial area and seized many of the lesser manufacturing areas at Kiev, Minsk and elsewhere, depriving the Russians of industrial cities and areas that at the start of the war were producing some 25 to 50 per cent of the total industrial output. The Germans also occupied mineral producing areas that, at the war's start, provided about 60 per cent of the Russian iron ore, 7 per cent of the petroleum, 60 to 90 per cent of the aluminum, 30 to 55 per cent of the power output, 35 per cent of the manganese and one-half to two-thirds of the coal.

The great Moscow industrial area, which once accounted for the major share of Russian production and still was the most important in the production of aircraft and automotive equipment, remained intact. To the east new factories were being constructed or coming into war production. Russia was still producing, her supply routes not cut, her industry not broken down.

Along the Finnish border there was minor fighting and in the north the chief activities of the Germans were aimed at blocking the landing of supplies from the Allies for Russia.

Richard K. Law, Parliamentary Under-Secretary for Foreign Affairs, told Commons in London (Nov. 12, 1942) that in the preceding twelve months there had been dispatched to Russia by Great Britain and the United States 3,052 planes, 4,084 tanks, 30,031 vehicles, 831,000 tons of machine tools and metals, 42,000 tons of aviation and other gasoline and 66,000 tons of fuel oil—all by the northern convoy route. Law said his figures represented supplies dispatched—not necessarily delivered and added that losses had been heavy but that the "great bulk" of materials had reached their destination.

Burma-China Front—In the Far East, Japan took advantage of her starting momentum to roll up Allied land power from New Guinea to the borders of India. The chief goal of the offensive was to cut the Burma road, the munitions supply line of the United Nations to China in her effort to regain some of the territory seized by the Japanese in five years of warfare. Once this goal had been attained, the Japanese forces stopped. The Allies were not idle, however, for they established a new supply line and through it there were sent sufficient amounts of munitions to arm the Chinese in continuing their offensives against the invader.

The Japanese drive carried the forces of Nippon to Rangoon, Mandalay, through Burma to the borders of India. With the Japanese in control of Rangoon, a shift in the supply line was made and munitions for China were unloaded at India's ports and then shipped across northern India to await delivery to China by the Army's small but rapidly expanding ferrying command and the China Aviation Corporation's growing air line. By mid-1942 thousands of tons of war material had been delivered to China each month and some of it had been used on the Japanese in attacks on their war centers.

Brig. Gen. Claire L. Chennault took over command of the American air task force and prepared to open a front against the Japanese to regain the old Burma road supply line. The action was largely in the air and American flyers established a ratio of eight Japanese planes downed to each American lost. These planes struck from the Burma Road of Free China and unloaded tons of explosives on Japanese bases.

Coincident with this fighting, Brig. Gen. Caleb V. Haynes of the United States Air Forces arrived in India to direct the American task force there. Generalissimo Chiang Kai-shek declared the Chinese were shifting from the defensive to the offensive and had prepared an attack to carry the Chinese to the coast.

For day-by-day developments in the war see War Chronology, beginning on page 52.

The Mediterranean War Area

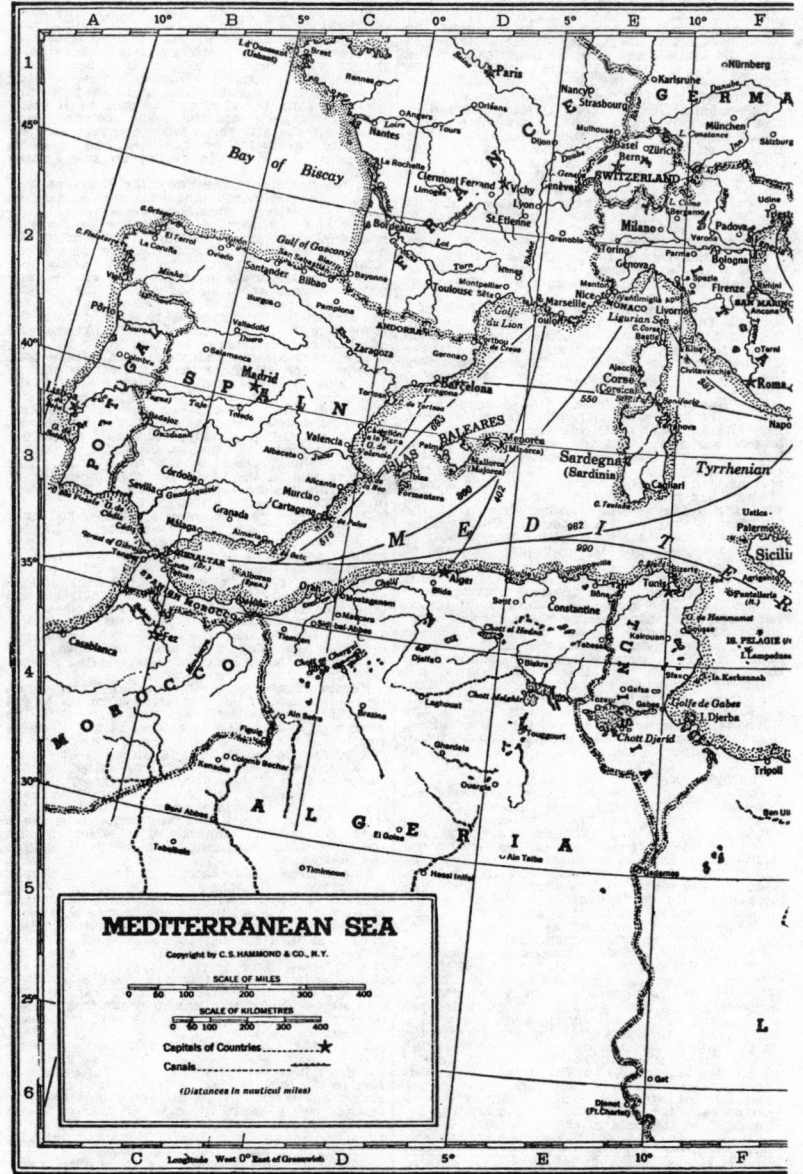

Bomber Crosses Atlantic in 6 Hours 40 Minutes

An American-built four-engined Liberator (Consolidated) bomber flew 2,200 miles from Newfoundland to Great Britain in 6 hours 40 minutes, the Ferry Command announced (April 2, 1942) in London. The new time eclipsed by exactly one hour the trans-Atlantic flight record set three months earlier by a British pilot. The Liberator pilot averaged 330 miles an hour. The Bomber Command said the record was the result of "a combination of the qualities of the airplane, an exceptional tail wind and magnificent aviation."

The Mediterranean War Area

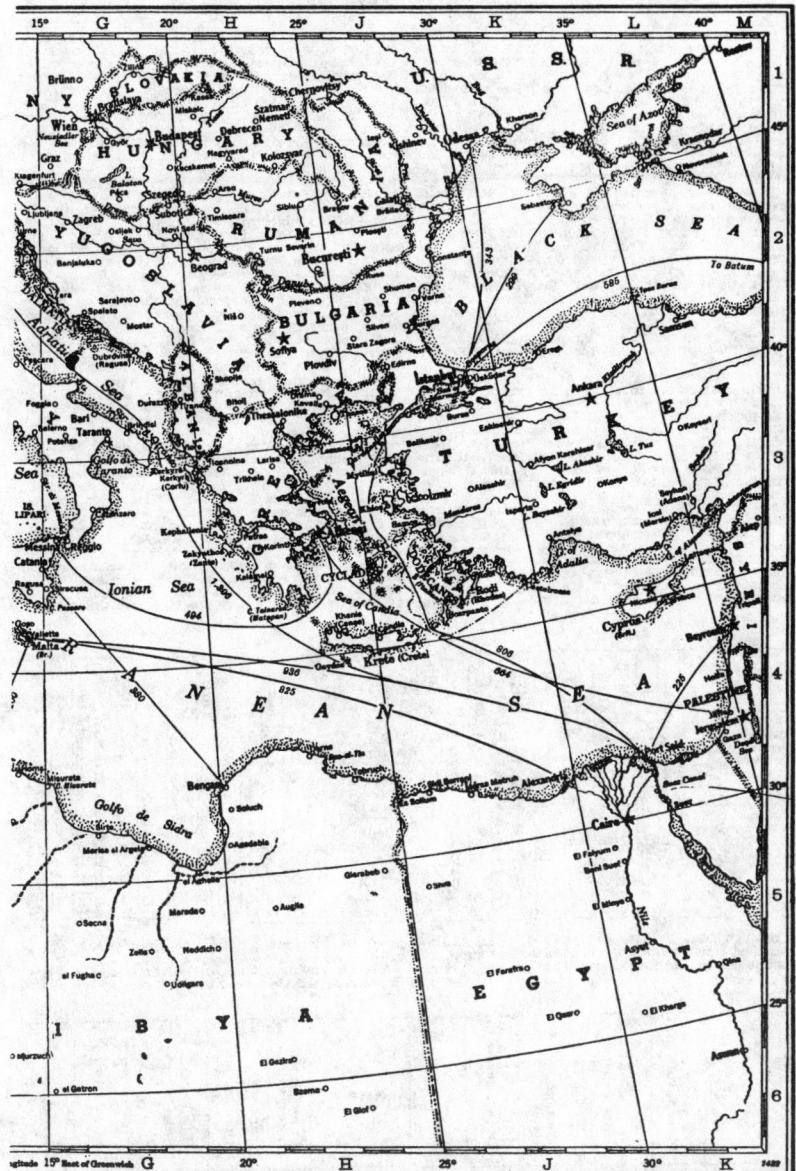

Match Flare in Blackout Visible to Flier Mile High

The flare of a single match lighted in a blacked-out area strikes the eyes of an airplane pilot at an elevation of a mile "like a powerful searchlight beam," Major R. F. Breckinridge, chairman of the engineer board at Fort Belvoir, Va., and camouflage expert of the War Department, told an audience of 500 representatives of vital industries in Philadelphia (Feb. 20, 1942) at a meeting in Franklin Institute. Major Breckinridge said that in some instances the flare of a match had been observed by a flier from a height of approximately five miles. He said the results were obtained in tests made over New Jersey and Ohio.

The Submarine War

The Axis powers shifted their submarine warfare to the western Atlantic early in 1942 and in ten months the loss of more than 500 vessels of the United Nations was reported. The attacks ranged from a point in the St. Lawrence River, 220 miles from the city of Quebec, through the Gulf of St. Lawrence, along the north Atlantic coast of the United States—at times within sight of New York City—south to the Caribbean and then on to the Brazilian coast. Axis submarines also toured the Gulf of Mexico and sank ships at the mouth of the Mississippi River.

When the strategists of the United States and Great Britain had devised plans to combat the U-boats and had reduced the sinkings from a high of 111 in June to 11 in October, submarines returned eastward. The loss of U-boats in the constant battle being waged from the surface and the air also was a factor in their departing the coastal waters of the United States. Small new-model U-boats, fought to a standstill in the North Atlantic, shifted their operations against Allied shipping to 'lanes along the bulge of West Africa. The focal point was Cape Palmas in Liberia, just west of the border of then Vichy-controlled French West Africa. The Cape juts to the sea at the extreme southwestern corner of the African bulge and the waters are ideal hunting ground because steamships bound north and south around Africa must pass through there. The area is well removed from the British naval stations at Freetown and Takorddi. The route also was used by Great Britain to carry supplies to the Near East with the Mediterranean life line menaced by the German and Italian planes and surface craft in addition to submarines.

One result of the submarine campaign in the western Atlantic waters was to add Brazil to the list of nations declaring war against Germany and Italy. Brazil acted after she had lost ships by torpedoing in the waters off her own shores.

American ships in convoy with war supplies to Russia and on their way to Murmansk often were under heavy U-boat and air attack through the Arctic Ocean for days at a time. Convoys of transports were reported hunted by wolf packs of U-boats but protecting destroyers and planes fought the submarines and saved the convoys. Herbert Morrison, British Home Secretary, reported (Nov. 1, 1942) that more than 20,000 convoys had been escorted in which 199 of every 200 vessels reached port.

Minor submarine activity was reported off the west coast of the United States. The activities of these submarines—presumably Japanese—were off the California, Washington and Oregon coasts—caused little damage. Japanese submarines were reported by the Axis Powers as active in the Indian Ocean late in 1942.

A. V. Alexander, First Lord of the British Admiralty, speaking in London on the third anniversary of the outbreak of the war, said that new methods and new devices were making life "doubly dangerous" for Nazi submarine crews. July and August, he said, had seen the destruction of the largest numbers of U-boats since the war began. Many others, he asserted, had been put out of action for months. The Daily Mail of London estimated that one out of every two U-boats that put to sea was attacked and that most of them could be claimed as "damaged." The paper said that the Coastal Command of the R. A. F. had made a "remarkable number of attacks," especially in the Bay of Biscay where the main U-boat bases were said to be.

Mr. Alexander reported (Oct. 20, 1942) that 530 Axis submarines had been sunk or damaged since the start of the war. "We have actual records of attacks which resulted in the sinking or damaging of 530 submarines," he said. "This does not include attacks made by the Soviets but includes partial reports of attacks by Americans." Mr. Alexander increased (Nov. 10, 1942) the number damaged or sunk submarines to 570.

There follows a compilation of the Associated Press of Allied and neutral nation ship losses from Dec. 7, 1941, through October, 1942, with actual sinking dates used where officially announced:

	Jan.	Feb.	March	April	May	June	July	Aug.	Sept.	Oct.	Totals		Jan.	Feb.	March	April	May	June	July	Aug.	Sept.	Oct.	Totals
United States..	5	11	24	28	39	46	23	10	9	6	201	Cuba.........	0	0	0	0	0	1	2	0	0	3
Great Britain...	5	6	8	3	21	19	10	12	6	2	92	Argentina.....	0	0	0	0	0	1	0	0	0	1
Norway.......	7	1	5	6	10	12	4	3	1	0	49	Colombia......	0	0	0	0	1	0	0	0	0	1
Panama.......	2	2	2	3	5	8	2	3	2	2	31	Belgium.......	0	0	0	0	1	0	0	0	0	1
Brazil.........	0	1	2	1	2	2	3	6	2	0	19	Portugal......	0	0	0	0	1	0	0	0	0	1
Netherlands...	0	0	1	2	6	4	1	2	0	0	16	Chile.........	0	0	0	0	1	0	0	0	0	1
Greece........	1	2	2	1	2	0	1	1	0	0	10	Uruguay......	0	0	0	0	0	0	1	0	0	1
Sweden.......	0	1	0	1	2	1	0	2	0	0	7	Russia........	0	0	0	0	0	0	1	0	0	1
Honduras.....	0	0	1	0	2	2	1	0	0	0	6	Spain.........	0	0	0	0	0	0	0	1	0	1
Latvia........	1	0	0	1	1	2	0	1	0	0	6	Poland........	0	0	0	0	0	0	1	0	0	1
Mexico.......	0	0	0	0	2	2	1	0	1	0	6	Egypt.........	0	0	0	0	0	0	1	0	0	1
Yugoslavia....	0	0	1	0	4	0	0	1	0	0	6	Unidentified										
Dominican Rep.	0	0	0	0	2	1	1	0	0	0	4	Allied.......	0	3	3	3	7	3	1	4	4	1	29
Nicaragua.....	0	0	0	0	1	1	1	0	0	0	3	Totals.....	21	27	50	49	102	111	51	49	27	11	498

Between Dec. 7, 1941, and Jan. 11, 1942, 23 unidentified merchantmen were reported sunk by submarines in the Caribbean. Since exact sinking or announcement dates were undisclosed, these are not listed.

The following "box score" lists sea warfare losses reported through Nov. 7, 1942:

Nation	Sunk by subs, planes, warships	Mines	Other causes or unknown	Tonnage	Known dead	Missing	Nation	Sunk by subs, planes, warships	Mines	Other causes or unknown	Tonnage	Known dead	Missing
Sweden.....	1	0	0	5,842	0	0	United States	3	0	0	*	53	1
Britain.....	2	0	0	*5,244	6	0	Total....	13	0	0	13,647	72	1
Norway....	1	0	0	2,561	0	0	Previously						
Axis.......	1	0	0	*	0	0	reported	2,539	291	807	10,479,878	44,256	18,038
Italian.....	2	0	0	*	0	0	Grand total	2,552	291	807	10,493,525	44,328	18,039
Panama....	1	0	0	*	13	0							
Allied......	2	0	0	*	0	0							

*Tonnages on 1 British, 1 Axis, 2 Italian, 1 Panamanian, 2 Allied and 3 United States ships unknown.

WINNING CLUBS.	Cleveland.	Boston.	Brooklyn.	Pittsburgh.	Philadelphia.	New-York.	Cincinnati.	Louisville.	Baltimore.	St. Louis.	Washington.
Cleveland	–	4	5	3	5	4	6	5	7	5	4
Boston	3	–	5	3	4	5	5	4	6	6	5
Brooklyn	2	2	–	4	6	3	5	2	4	5	6
Pittsburgh	4	4	3	–	4	5	4	3	3	5	4
Philadelphia	2	3	1	3	–	6	4	3	5	4	4
New-York	3	2	4	2	1	–	2	4	5	5	7
Chicago	2	2	3	3	3	5	–	6	3	2	4
Cincinnati	2	3	5	4	2	1	–	2	5	6	4
Louisville	0	1	3	4	4	2	4	–	3	4	4
Baltimore	1	0	2	4	2	2	2	3	–	4	4
St. Louis	2	3	1	1	3	2	0	1	3	–	3
Washington	3	2	2	3	2	0	1	2	3	2	4	–

1888—Yale, 10 ; Princeton, o.
1889—Princeton, 10 ; Yale, o.
†1890—Yale, 32 ; Princeton, o.
1891—Yale, 19 ; Princeton, o.
1892—Yale, 12 ; Princeton, o.

𝕭𝖚𝖘𝖎𝖓𝖊𝖘𝖘 𝕱𝖆𝖎𝖑𝖚𝖗𝖊𝖘 𝖎𝖓 𝖙𝖍𝖊 𝖀𝖓𝖎𝖙𝖊𝖉 𝕾𝖙𝖆𝖙𝖊𝖘.

𝕭𝖆𝖗𝖗𝖊𝖓𝖓𝖊𝖘𝖘, 𝕴𝖑𝖑𝖊𝖌𝖎𝖙𝖎𝖒𝖆𝖈𝖞, 𝖆𝖓𝖉 𝕮𝖍𝖎𝖑𝖉𝖇𝖎𝖗𝖙𝖍.

THE BRITISH EMPIRE
Area and Population

Source: Areas are Government figures; population data are latest census figures or latest official estimates

	Area, Sq. M.	Population		Area, Sq. M.	Population
UNITED KINGDOM...	94,279	46,213,169	Tristan da Cunha......	12	165
England			Seychelles Island......	156	32,150
(ex. Monmouthshire)	50,328	37,354,917	Mauritius Island......	720	420,861
Wales			Dependencies.........	89	12,144
(Inc. Monmouthshire)	8,012	2,593,014			
Scotland.............	30,405	4,842,980	NORTH AMERICA....	3,847,597	11,312,240
Northern Ireland......	5,238	1,279,745	Canada.............	3,694,863	11,419,896
Isle of Man.........	221	49,308	Alberta...........	255,285	788,893
Channel Islands.......	75	93,205	British Columbia..	366,255	809,203
			Manitoba.........	246,512	722,447
EUROPE (Other).......	27,261	3,278,767	New Brunswick....	27,985	453,377
Ireland-Eire..........	27,137	2,989,700	Nova Scotia.......	21,068	573,190
Gibraltar............	2	20,399	Ontario..........	412,582	3,756,632
Malta...............	122	268,668	Prince Edward Island..	2,184	99,919
ASIA................	1,951,348	358,793,631	Quebec...........	594,534	3,319,640
India...............	1,808,679	352,837,778	Saskatchewan......	251,700	887,747
British Provinces....	1,318,346	289,491,241	Yukon...........	207,076	4,687
Native States, etc....	490,333	63,346,537	Northwest Territories..	1,309,682	10.661
Aden (Prot. and Perim)	112,000	48,338	Newfoundland........	42,734	300,000
Socotra.............	1,400	12,000	Labrador...........	110,000	4,716
Bahrein Islands.......	250	120,000			
Cyprus..............	3,572	383,967	CENTRAL AMERICA		
Ceylon..............	25,332	5,312,548	British Honduras......	8,598	59,965
Maldive Islands.....	115	79,000	WEST INDIES, etc.....	12,835	2,399,316
British Malaya.......	51,172	5,566,778	Bermuda.........	19	32,086
Straits Settlements...	1,356	1,435,895	Bahamas..........	4,404	68,903
Federated Malay States	27,540	2,212,052	Barbados.........	166	198,203
Other Malay States....	22,276	1,918,831	Jamaica..........	4,450	1,223,241
British North Borneo..	29,500	270,223	Turks and Caicos Isl'ds	166	5,300
Brunei..............	2,226	30,135	Cayman Islands.....	104	6,182
Sarawak.............	50,000	490,585	Leeward Islands......	727	93,130
Hong Kong and Ter....	391	1,050,256	Windward Islands.....	821	262,006
Palestine (M.).......	10,429	1,568,664	Trinidad.........	1,862	484,907
AFRICA.............	3,810,009	63,378,513	Tobago...........	116	25,358
Union of South Africa	472,550	9,979,000	SOUTH AMERICA.....	95,098	350,472
Cape of Good Hope..	277,169	3,635,100	British Guiana.......	89,480	346,982
Natal.............	35,284	2,018,000	Falkland Islands and		
Orange Free State...	49,647	790,800	South Georgia....	5,618	3,490
Transvaal.........	110,450	3,535,100			
S. W. Africa (M.)....	317,725	314,194	AUSTRALASIA........	3,263,196	9,706,116
British South Africa..	734,074	3,815,104	Australia..........	2,974,581	7,137,000*
Basutoland........	11,716	562,411	New South Wales...	309,433	2,770,348
Bechuanaland Prot....	275,000	265,756	Victoria.........	87,884	1,887,278
Northern Rhodesia...	290,320	1,381,829	Queensland.......	670,500	1,015,927
Southern Rhodesia...	150,333	1,448,393	South Australia.....	380,070	597,045
Swaziland..........	6,705	156,715	West Australia.....	975,920	465,916
British East Africa...	716,315	14,319,245	Tasmania.........	26,215	241,576
Kenya Col. and Prot...	224,960	3,534,862	Northern Territory..	523,620	6,973
Uganda Protectorate...	93,981	3,829,705	Capital Territory...	939	12,263
Tanganyika (M.)......	360,000	5,270,484	Papua, Territory of....	90,540	338,822
Nyasaland..........	37,374	1,684,194	New Guinea (M.).....	93,000	668,871
Zanzibar Protectorate..	1,020	235,428	New Zealand..........	103,934	1,640,901
Somaliland Prot.......	68,000	344,700	Western Samoa (M.).	1,133	62,391
British West Africa...	542,931	27,735,964	Nauru (M.).........	8	3,460
Nigeria...........	372,559	20,641,814	OCEANIA.............	388,279	436,691
Cameroons (M.)......	34,081	868,637	Fiji Colony........	7,083	220,787
Gold Coast........	91,483	3,962,520	Tonga Island Prot....	256	34,130
Togoland (M.)......	13,041	391,473	Gilbert and Ellice Isl'ds	180	32,838
Sierra Leone.......	27,699	1,672,000	Brit. Solomon Isl. Prot.	375,000	94,105
Gambia............	4,068	199,520	New Hebrides......	5,700	54,531
Anglo-Egypt, Soudan..	969,600	6,342,477	Other Pacific Islands...	60	300
Ascension Island......	34	169			
St. Helena............	47	4,710	BRITISH EMPIRE.....	13,655,393	495,928,880

*Breakdown not available.
(M) British Mandate. The Anglo-Egyptian Soudan and the New Hebrides are Co-dominions.

POPULATION OF THE UNITED KINGDOM, 1801-1931

Census Year	England and Wales	Scotland	Ireland	Total for United Kingdom		
				Males	Females	Total
1801.........	8,892,536	1,608,420				
1821.........	12,000,236	2,091,521	6,801,827	10 174,868	10,718,716	20,893,584
1841.........	15,914,148	2,620,184	8,196,597	13,060,497	13,670,432	26,730,929
1861.........	20,066,224	3,062,294	5,798,967	14,063,477	14,864,008	28,927,485
1871.........	22,712,266	3,360,018	5,412,377	15,301,830	16,182,831	31,484,661
1881.........	25,974,439	3,735,573	5,174,836	16,972,654	17,912,194	34,884,848
1891.........	29,002,525	4,025,647	4,704,750	18,314,571	19,418,351	37,732,922
1901.........	32,527,843	4,472,103	4,458,775	20,102,408	21,356,313	41,458,721
1911.........	36,070,492	4,760,904	4,390,219	21,946,495	23,275,120	45,221,615
1921.........	37,885,242	4,882,288	No census.	*20,430,623	*22,336,907	*42,767,530
1931.........	39,947,031	4,842,544	4,229,124	*21,464,711	*23,325,774	*44,790,485

*The 1921 and 1931 figures for males and females and total (last three columns) exclude Ireland.
By the census, 1936, Ireland-Eire has 2,965,854 population, 1,518,807 males and 1,447,047 females.
Northern Ireland (census of 1937) has 1,279,745—623,308 males, and 656,437 females. Total for Ireland, 4,245,599.

Government of Great Britain

The British Empire covers about one-fourth (13,499,557 square miles) of the world's habitable land surface. Its population in the aggregate, according to the latest census and official estimates, is some 15 millions more than one-fourth of the inhabitants of the world—a total of 504,683,246.

The Capital of this vast empire is London. The census (1931) returned the population of the metropolitan district of London as 8,202,818, an increase of 9.7% since 1921, and the County of London (registration and administrative district) contained in it as 4,470,814. The area of the City of London is 675 acres; the County of London 74,-850 acres; Greater London 443,455 acres.

The Ruling Sovereign is George VI, third of the House of Windsor, whose title is "by the Grace of God, King of Great Britain and Ireland and of the British Dominions Beyond the Seas, Defender of the Faith, Emperor of India." He was born (Dec. 14, 1895), son of the late King George V., who died (Jan. 20, 1936) and Queen Mary, daughter of the late H. S. H. Duke of Teck and H. R. H. Princess Mary of Cambridge. He succeeded to the throne on the abdication of his brother, Edward VIII. (Dec. 10, 1936).

The King, as Prince Albert, Duke of York, married in Westminster Abbey (April 7, 1923), Lady Elizabeth Bowes-Lyon (born 1900), daughter of the Earl of Strathmore and Kinghorne. They have two children: Princess Elizabeth Alexandra Mary (born Apr. 21, 1926), heir-apparent, and Princess Margaret Rose (born Aug. 21, 1930).

The children of the late King George V. besides the present sovereign are: H. R. H. Prince Edward Albert, formerly King Edward VIII, created Duke of Windsor (Dec. 12, 1936) (born June 23, 1894), married Mrs. Wallis Warfield (June 3, 1937); H. R. H. Princess Mary, Princess Royal (born April 25, 1897), married Viscount Lascelles, K. G., son of the Earl of Harewood (Feb. 28, 1922) and who succeeded to the title on the death of his father (Oct. 6, 1929)—issue, George Henry Hubert, Viscount Lascelles (born Feb. 7, 1923), and the Hon. Gerald Davis (born Aug. 21, 1924); H. R. H. Prince Henry (born March 31, 1900), created Duke of Gloucester (March 31, 1928), married (Nov. 6, 1935) Lady Alice Montagu-Douglas-Scott, daughter of the Duke and Duchess of Buccleuch and Queensberry (issue, William Henry Andrew Frederick (born Dec. 18, 1941); H. R. H. Prince George (born Dec. 20, 1902), created Duke of Kent (Oct. 9, 1934), married (Nov. 29, 1934) Princess Mariana, daughter of Prince and Princess Nicholas of Greece (issue, Prince Edward, born Oct. 9, 1935); Alexandra Helen Elizabeth Olga Christabel (born Dec. 25, 1936); Michael, George Charles, Franklin (born July 4, 1942). The Duke of Kent was killed in an airplane accident in Scotland (Aug. 25, 1942).

Parliament is the legislative governing body for the empire. It consists of two Houses. The **House of Lords** is made up of the peers of the United Kingdom, to wit: the Royal Dukes, the Archbishops, the Dukes, the Marquises, the Earls, the Viscounts, 24 Bishops, and the Barons; also 28 Irish peers elected for life; and 16 Scottish peers elected for the duration of Parliament. The full membership of the House of Lords consists of about 740 members but the voting strength is about 720.

The House of Commons numbers 615 members elected by direct ballot. Of this House, England has 492 members; Wales, 36; Scotland, 74; and Northern Ireland, 13. Clergymen of the Church of England, ministers of the Church of Scotland and Roman Catholic clergymen are disqualified from sitting as members, also certain Government officers, Sheriffs, and Government contractors. Women have had the right to vote since 1918 and are eligible to Parliament.

The popular vote in the last two general elections, and the seats won, were as follows:

| | Oct., 1931 | | Nov., 1935 | |
| | Pop. | | Pop. | |
Government	Vote	Seats	Vote	Seats
Conservative....	11,907,875	471	10,488,626	387
Nat. Labor.....	342,480	13	339,811	8
Liberal Nat'l...	809,102	35	866,624	33
National........	90,000	3	97,271	3
Total........	**13,149,457**	**522**	**11,792,332**	**431**
Opposition				
Labor..........	6,648,023	52	8,325,260	154
Ind. Labor.....	100,000	3	139,517	4
Liberal (Samuel)	1,405,102	33	1,377,962	17
Ind. Lib. (Ll. G.)	106,106	4	65,150	4
Communist......	75,000	0	27,117	1
Independent....	100,000	3	274,499	4
Total........	**8,434,231**	**95**	**10,209,505**	**184**

The Statute of Westminster passed by the House of Commons (Nov. 24, 1931) gave formal ratification to the declarations of the Imperial Conferences (1926 and 1930), which were participated in by the United Kingdom of Great Britain and Northern Ireland, and the Prime Ministers of the Dominion of Canada, the Commonwealth of Australia, the Dominion of New Zealand, the Union of South Africa, the Irish Free State and the Dominion of Newfoundland.

The Conference (1926) defined the Dominions as "autonomous Communities within the British Empire, equal in status, in no way subordinate one to another in any aspect of their domestic or foreign affairs, though united by a common allegiance to the Crown, and freely associated as members of the British Commonwealth of Nations. . . . Every self-governing member of the Empire is master of its destiny. In fact, if not always in form, it is subject to no more compulsion whatever."

The Government, formed May 10, 1940, with the changes March 19, 1942, follows:

Position and Date of Appointment	WAR CABINET	Party	Date of Birth
Prime Minister, First Lord of the Treasury, and Minister of Defense (May 10, 1940)............................	Winston Churchill	C.	Nov. 30, 1874
Lord President of the Council (Oct. 3, 1940).................	Sir John Anderson	Nat.	July 8, 1882
Lord Privy Seal, and Leader of House of Commons (Feb. 19, 1942).......................................	Sir Stafford Cripps	.....	April 24, 1889
Minister of Production (March 12, 1942)..................	Oliver Lyttelton	C.	1893
Secretary of State for Foreign Affairs (Dec. 22, 1940).......	Anthony Eden	C.	June 12, 1897
Minister of Labour and National Service (May 10, 1940).....	Ernest Bevin	Lab.	1884
Secretary of State for Dominion Affairs, and Deputy Prime Minister (Feb. 19, 1942)............................	C. R. Attlee	Lab.	Jan. 3, 1883
Minister of State—Middle East (March 19, 1942)............	Richard G. Casey	Australia	1890

The following are Ministers of Cabinet rank, but are not members of the War Cabinet, although in peacetime they would be in the Cabinet.

MINISTERS

Position	Ministers	Position	Ministers
Admiralty..............	A. V. Alexander (Lab.)	Information...............	Brendan Bracken (C.)
Agriculture...........	R. S. Hudson (C.)	Law Officers:	
Air..................	Sir Archibald Sinclair (L.)	Attorney-General......	Sir Donald Somervell (C.)
Aircraft Production........	Col. J. J. Llewellin (C.)	Solicitor-General.......	David Maxwell Fyfe (C.)
Burma.............	Leopold S. Amery (C.)	Lord Chancellor.......	Viscount Simon (Lib.-Nat.)
Chancellor of Exchequer....	Sir Kingsley Wood (C.)	Paymaster-General.......	Sir Wm. A. Jowitt (Lab.)
Colonies, and Leader of	Viscount Cranborne (C.)	Pensions...........	Sir Walter J. Womersley (C.)
the House of Lords.....	(Baron Cecil of Essendon)	Post Office..............	W. S. Morrison (C.)
Duchy of Lancaster.......	Alfred Duff Cooper (C.)	Scotland...........	Thomas Johnston (Lab.)
Economic Warfare............	Lord Selborne (C.)	Supply.........	Sir Andrew R. Duncan (Nat.)
Education............	Richard Austen Butler (C.)	Trade................	Hugh Dalton (Lab.)
Food................	Lord Woolton (Non-party)	War................	Sir James Grigg
Health...........	Ernest Brown (Lib. Nat.)	War Transport.........	Lord Leathers (Non-party)
Home Office and Home		Work and Buildings, and First	
Security............	Herbert Morrison (Lab.)	Commissioner for Works........	Lord Portal (C.)
India.............	Leopold S. Amery (C.)		

C.—Conservative; L.—Liberal; Lab.—Labor; Lib.-Nat.—Liberal Nationalist; Nat.—National.

The executive government is vested nominally in the Crown, but in actual practice in a committee of Ministers, known as the Cabinet. The existence of the Cabinet is dependent on the support of the majority in the House of Commons. The Prime Minister, who is also First Lord of the Treasury, receives a salary of £10,000 a year. His colleagues are appointed on his recommendations and he dispenses the major portion of the patronage of the Crown.

BUDGETS OF GREAT BRITAIN FOR 30 YEARS

Year End'g Mar31	Revenues £.	Expendit's £.	Year End'g Mar31	Revenues £.	Expendit's £.	Year End'g Mar31	Revenues £.	Expendit's £.
1914	198,242,897	197,492,969	1924	837,169,284	788,840,211	1934	809,379,149	778,231,289
1915	226,694,080	560,473,533	1925	799,435,595	795,776,711	1935	804,629,050	797,067,170
1916	336,766,825	1,559,158,377	1926	812,061,658	826,099,778	1936	844,775,143	841,834,441
1917	573,427,582	2,198,112,710	1927	805,701,233	842,395,027	1937	896,596,194	902,193,385
1918	707,234,565	2,696,221,405	1928	842,824,465	838,563,341	1938	872,580,000	938,046,000
1919	889,020,825	2,579,301,188	1929	836,434,988	818,040,523	1939	927,285,000	1,024,804,000
1920	1,339,571,381	1,665,772,928	1930	814,970,280	829,493,543	1940	1,025,192,000	1,032,217,000
1921	1,425,984,666	1,195,427,877	1931	857,760,934	881,036,905	1941	1,408,867,000	3,884,288,000
1922	1,124,879,873	1,079,186,627	1932	851,482,281	851,117,944	1942	2,074,057,000	4,775,694,000
1923	914,012,452	812,496,604	1933	827,031,184	859,310,173	1943	*2,469,100,000	*5,286,479,000

*Estimates. Expenditures do not include value of supplies from the United States under Lease-Lend. Sir Kingsley Wood, Chancellor of the Exchequer, in submitting a vote of credit for £1,000,000,000, informed the House of Commons (Sept. 9, 1942) that this brought the total amount of credits asked in the fiscal year to £3,000,000,000 and to £11,050,000,000 since the start of the war. He said that in recent weeks war costs had averaged £12,250,000 a day made up of £102,500,000 for the supply and fighting forces and an additional £2,000,000 for miscellaneous items. Sir Kingsley said the daily expenditure ranged from £8,000,000 to £12,000,000 and that the total budget (1940-1941) had mounted from £3,884,000,000 to £5,286,000,000. He added that taxation which had accounted for 33 per cent of the British expenditure (1940-1941) was carrying 45 per cent of the load (1942).

Sir Kingsley put the grand total of expenditures for the 1943 fiscal year at about £6,500,000,000. Allowing for non-budgetary receipts, including the sale of foreign investments and contributions from Canada, the Chancellor took £4,500,000,000 as the amount to be provided by votes of credit. Expenditures (1943 fiscal year) made no provision for lend-lease aid from the United States running at the time (April, 1942) at the rate of approximately £100,000,000 a month.

PUBLIC DEBT OF GREAT BRITAIN

March 31	£.	March 31	£.	March 31	£.	March 31	£.
1915	1,161,951,702	1922	7,720,532,214	1929	7,716,024,047	1936	7,796,056,000
1916	2,189,838,245	1923	7,812,562,525	1930	7,469,060,000	1937	7,797,229,544
1917	4,063,644,983	1924	7,707,537,545	1931	7,413,278,000	1938	8,026,127,000
1918	5,921,095,819	1925	7,665,880,405	1932	7,433,942,880	1939	8,163,289,000
1919	7,481,050,442	1926	7,633,722,152	1933	7,644,952,000	1940	8,931,459,000
1920	7,875,641,961	1927	7,652,687,904	1934	7,822,330,000	1941	11,398,000,000
1921	7,623,097,128	1928	7,714,084,295	1935	7,800,565,000	1942	14,070,000,000

BRITISH PRIME MINISTERS FOR 100 YEARS

Viscount Melbourne....1835	William Ewart Gladstone....1868	Herbert Henry Asquith....1908
Sir Robert Peel....1841	Earl of Beaconsfield....1874	H. H. Asquith (Coalition)....1915
Lord John Russell....1846	Mr. Gladstone....1880	David Lloyd George....1916
Earl of Derby....1852	Marquis of Salisbury....1885	Andrew Bonar Law....1922
Earl of Aberdeen....1852	Mr. Gladstone....1886	Stanley Baldwin....1923
Viscount Palmerston....1855	Marquis of Salisbury....1886	J. Ramsay MacDonald....1924
Earl of Derby....1858	Mr. Gladstone....1892	Stanley Baldwin....1924
Viscount Palmerston....1859	Earl of Rosebery....1894	J. Ramsay MacDonald....1929
Earl Russell....1865	Marquis of Salisbury....1895	Stanley Baldwin....1935
Earl of Derby....1866	Arthur James Balfour....1902	Neville Chamberlain....1937
Benjamin Disraeli....1868	Sir H. Campbell-Bannerman....1905	Winston Churchill....1940

The Imperial Conference (1930) adopted the report of its committee which had been studying the methods of sweeping away all possible limitation on Dominion freedom and drafted the Statute of Westminster. This declares that no act of the British Parliament thereafter passed shall extend to a Dominion unless the Dominion itself has requested and consented to the enactment; it repeals so far as it concerned them the Colonial Laws Validity Act (1865) which made void any legislation by a Dominion Parliament which conflicted with an act of the British Parliament; and it declares that a Dominion Parliament has full power to make laws with extra-territorial effect—that is, to control, as do independent states, the acts of their nationals beyond Dominion territory.

The United Kingdom

Capital, London—Area, 94,279 square miles—Population (1931 and 1939 for Northern Ireland), 46,213,169

The United Kingdom, or British Isles, lie off the northwest corner of Europe, with the North Atlantic Ocean on the north and west, the North Sea on the east and the English Channel separating it from the mainland on the south. The Straits of Dover, 18 miles wide, divide it from France. The northern end of Scotland lies due west from the southern end of Norway.

The climate of the British Isles is equable, mild and somewhat warmer than that of the continent opposite, because of the Gulf Stream modifying the temperature, which is mean at 48 degrees. Rainfall is abundant, averaging 35 inches annually, but is seldom heavy at a given time, so that the precipitation covers longer periods, and fogs often prevail in many parts, "London Fog," holding much soot in suspension, being particularly dense at times.

The coastline is tortuous, giving very many harbors for shipping, and numerous rivers up which deep sea craft may go.

The soil is of varied natural fertility. It is more sterile in the north, notwithstanding the figures show that the Scotch have attained a relatively high per acre production by intensive cultivation.

But centuries of tillage have made necessary elaborate and large use of artificial fertilizers.

The prevalent precipitation of moisture, together with the mild climate, has induced profuse growth of vegetation of all sorts. The Isles were naturally covered with forests, which have been largely cut off to accommodate so large a population on so small an area with an average of 504.7 to the square mile.

The United Kingdom is a fascinating country, with its varied topography; its hills and valleys, moors and heaths; buzzing industries and quiet countrysides; narrow winding streets and modern motor parkways; quaint fishing villages leaning back against steep cliffs. Its history may be read in ancient castles, towers, battle sites and monuments. Traces of every important period in its life may still be seen in cities or in isolated sections of the country.

London, for years the chief metropolis of the world, retains its ancient atmosphere—its historic Houses of Parliament—its famous Tower built by William the Conqueror in the eleventh century, where noted figures in English history were tortured and put to death. In London, also, is St. Paul's Cathedral on Ludgate Hill, "the parish church of the British Empire"; and Westminster Abbey, where every English monarch has been crowned since William the Conqueror in 1066 and where lie buried kings and queens and many persons who have made the grade in English history or letters. The chapel of Henry VII is the finest example in England of Tudor Gothic and contains the tomb of Mary Queen of Scots. The House of Lords—in which may be seen the double royal throne (the King's chair is slightly higher than the Queen's)—and the House of Commons, are open to visitors without charge on Saturdays from 10 A. M. to 3:30 P. M. Many of these landmarks have been damaged by German bombings during the war.

Although Buckingham Palace is designated the town residence of the King, it is at St. James's Palace (built by Henry VIII) that a new King is proclaimed and foreign ambassadors are still "accredited to the "Court of Saint James."

In the center of London are five parks—St. James's, Green Park, Hyde Park, Kensington Gardens and Regent's Park: the first four adjoin each other: here the well-to-do ride their horses, and all London comes out to take the air, to exercise the children or the dogs or to listen to the band. In Regent's Park there is an open-air theater. St. James's Park was made by Henry VIII as a private deer park, so were Kensington Gardens and Hyde Park.

There are more traditional ceremonies alive in peace time London than in any other city in the world; and clothes of every period from the fifteenth century to the present day are worn as regular costume.

The "Yeomen of the Guard" at the Tower of London are in Tudor dress; the band of the Life Guards wears the uniform of Stuart days; the learned judges in the neighborhood of the Law Courts or the Inns of Court wear full-bottomed wigs and gowns of the late seventeenth century, while "learned counsel" who plead before them are in the fashion of the eighteenth. The green livery and black top-hats of the bank messengers are only one of many examples of the nineteenth century.

A famous military ceremony known as "Trooping the Color"- is performed on the Horse Guards' Parade. The precision and pageantry of this occasion are only equalled by another display of pageantry, the famous Aldershot Military Tattoo, which, though it takes place 30 miles out of the Capital, is definitely an event of the London season. The State Opening of Parliament, usually in the beginning of November, when the King rides in his gilded state coach preceded by an escort of Life Guards along streets lined with guardsmen, from Buckingham Palace to the Houses of Parliament, is an unequalled piece of pageantry.

Despite the lack of plan London is a city of great beauty, not only for its parks, river and monuments but for the peculiar effect of the Portland stone, its most characteristic building material. This stone where beaten by the weather turns almost as white as marble, while on the other surfaces its coat is black with smoke. Thus London is a city of light and shade; and there are few more beautiful city vistas in the world than Whitehall on an afternoon in spring.

The whole of England abounds in sites of historic interest. The "Shakespeare Country" is about 80 miles from London in the county of Warwickshire. It lies at the very gates of the industrial Midlands. Here is Birmingham, England's "Second City," where the automobile and the jewelry come from. The city library boasts the biggest Shakespearean collection in the world. At Stratford-on-Avon one can still see the house where Shakespeare was born, the house to which he retired, his burial place in the parish church, and innumerable other records and relics of his life. The Shakespeare Memorial Theater, built by funds subscribed from Britain and the United States, is an interesting example of modern architecture.

Only a few miles from Stratford is Leamington Spa, which rose on the fame of its saline springs to become one of the best-known and most attractive spas in the country. Nathaniel Hawthorne lived here; George Elliot laid the scenes of all her novels in the neighborhood. Sulgrave Manor, the home of Washington's ancestors, is within easy reach.

Canterbury, 53 miles southeast of London, where St. Augustine founded a Benedictine monastery (597), is the ecclesiastical capital of England, famous all the world over for its magnificent cathedral, and as the See of the Church of England's spiritual head, the Archbishop of Canterbury. The stone steps leading to the shrine have grooves in them, made by praying knees of thousands upon thousands of pilgrims who have visited the church since long before the time of Chaucer, whose Canterbury Tales form one of the masterpieces of literature.

The lakes and highlands of Scotland are noted for their beauty and have been made the subject of poetry and song. Edinburgh, the capital, is an attractive city of gray old streets, wide classic squares; spires, pinnacles and turrets contesting with one another in a sort of confusion. Points of interest to the tourist include Edinburgh castle overlooking the city; the house where John Knox lived; Holyrood Palace where the Stuart kings and queens lived out their ill-fated lives, and Princes Street. Not far from Edinburgh are Loch Lomond and Loch Katrine in the Trossach country, made famous by Sir Walter Scott.

The border country is a loose term describing the greater part of 100 miles which separates Edinburgh from the English border line. It is a land soft green and brown in color, of rounded hills, a land of shepherds with huge flocks. The border has had the stormiest history in all Britain, expressed today in the terms of castles. The abbeys of Melrose, Jedburgh and Dryburgh are roofless and ruined because of battles long ago. Here the English and Scots fought their battles, the great Border clans fought both sides and filled their stables and barns with their neighbors' cattle and horses. This is the country of Sir Walter Scott, a "Borderer" himself, whose house in Abbotsford still stands and who is buried in Dryburgh Abbey.

On the east coast of Scotland about half-way between Edinburgh and Dundee is situated the city of St. Andrews, the birthplace of golf.

The Protestant Episcopal is the Established Church of England, of which the King is the supreme governor, possessing the right to nominate to the vacant archbishoprics and bishoprics. There are two archbishops (of Canterbury and York), 41 bishops and 39 suffragan bishops.

A recent summary of the active membership of certain churches in England, Wales, Channel Islands and the Isle of Man showed:

Anglicans	2,294,000
Methodists	1,262,596
Congregationalists	494,199
Baptists	383,373
Calvinistic Methodists	261,287
Presbyterians	81,715
Quakers	19,000
Christian Scientists	14,000
Wesleyan Reform Union	13,198
Independent Methodists	10,388
Moravians	3,210
Roman Catholics	*2,361,504

*For England and Wales.

POPULATION OF CITIES OF OVER 100,000 IN GREAT BRITAIN, 1931 CENSUS

Cities	Population	Cities	Population	Cities	Population
London (Greater)	8,202,818	Portsmouth	252,421	Oldham	140,309
City and Administrative County of London	4,470,814	Leicester	239,169	Middlesborough	138,274
		Croydon	233,032	Wolverhampton	133,212
Glasgow	1,088,417	Cardiff	223,589	Walthamstow	132,965
Birmingham	1,002,603	Salford	223,442	Ilford	131,046
Liverpool	855,688	Plymouth	208,182	Leyton	128,317
Manchester	766,278	Sunderland	185,870	Norwich	126,207
Sheffield	511.742	Willesden	184,410	Stockport	125,505
Leeds	482,809	Bolton	177,235	Blackburn	122,695
Edinburgh	438,998	Southampton	176,025	Gateshead	122,379
Belfast (1926)	425,156	Dundee	175,583	Southend-on-Sea	120,093
Bristol	397,012	Aberdeen	167,259	Preston	119,001
Dublin (1926)	316.471	Coventry	167.046	Ealing	117,688
Hull	311,366	Swansea	164,797	Bournemouth	116,780
Bradford	298.041	Tottenham	157.748	Hendon	115,682
West Ham	294.278	Birkenhead	147,803	Huddersfield	113,475
Newcastle-on-Tyne	283,156	Brighton	147,426	South Shields	113,452
Stoke-on-Trent	276,639	East Ham	142,460	St. Helen's	106.793
Nottingham	268.801	Derby	142,406	Walsall	103,059
		Rhondda	141,344	Blackpool	101,543

The Lord Mayor of London is Sir Samuel George Joseph.

The Established Church of Scotland is Presbyterian with 1,285,011 members as compared with 61,547 Episcopalians and 614,021 Roman Catholics.

There are about 300,000 Jews in the United Kingdom with approximately 300 synagogues.

The total number of emigrants of British origin to places other than Europe from (1853-1938) was 16,710,072.

The net excess of emigrants from the United Kingdom and Northern Ireland over immigrants (1930) was 23,540; (1931) it was 8,831. Emigration for four years to non-European countries was:

	1935	1936	1937	1938
United States	1,261	1,638	2,423	1,992
Canada	1,707	2,281	2,850	3,367
Australia	3,747	4,096	4,122	5,427
New Zealand	1,206	1,462	1,981	2,425
South Africa	4,136	6,015	5,577	6,003
Indian and Ceylon	4,873	6,160	5,632	5,540

England, Wales, Scotland, the Isle of Man and the Channel Islands have a total land area of 56,343,000 agricultural acres, divided (1939) as follows:

	Grazing	Pasture	Arable
England	3,794,000	13,550,000	8,397,000
Wales	1,812,000	2,159,000	538,000
Scotland	10,465,000	1,623,000	2,935,000
Isle of Man	41,000	23,000	53,000

The aggregate number of holdings in Great Britain (1939) is: From 1 to 5 Acres, 77,773; from 5 to 50 acres, 193,977; from 50 to 300 acres, 149,969; more than 300 acres, 14,235.

The principal agricultural products are wheat, barley, oats, beans, peas, potatoes, turnips, swedes, mangold and hay.

Great Britain imports about four-fifths of the breadstuffs and fruits she consumes; one half of the meat, eggs and dairy products, and one third of the fish and vegetables.

The country is rich in mineral resources. There are huge deposits of coal, the annual output approximates $900,000,000 in value. The yearly production of limestone, igneous rock and iron ore is valued in the neighborhood of $15,000,000 each. Other important minerals, in the order of their value, are—gravel and sand; clay and shale; slate; sandstone; salt; China clay; fireclay; chalk; gypsum; oil shale; lead ore; tin, ore; ganister and silica rock; Potters' clay; moulding and Pig-bed sand; barytes and witherite; and dolomite.

Great Britain's strength is largely in manufacturing, mining and trade. The key industries with their approximate annual peace time output in American dollars are—food, drink and tobacco, $3,163,815,000; engineering, shipbuilding and vehicles. $2,366,195,000; textiles, $2,220,000,000; public utilities, $1,700,000,000; iron and steel, $1,400,000,000; chemicals, $950,000,000; building and contracting, $935,000,000; paper and printing, $900,000,000; clothing, $860,000,000; non-ferrous metals, $520,000,000; clay and building materials, $425,000,000; timber, $340,000,000; leather, $165,000,000. Textiles, woollen and worsted tissues, iron and steel, machinery and vehicles (including locomotives and shipping) are the key industries supplying the bulk of the exports.

TONNAGE AT BRITISH HOME PORTS

The net tonnage of the British and foreign vessels in foreign trade that entered and cleared with cargoes at the ports of the United Kingdom during recent years was:

Year	Entered With Cargoes			Cleared With Cargoes		
	British	Foreign	Total	British	Foreign	Total
	Tons	Tons	Tons	Tons	Tons	Tons
1930	40,785,000	22,925,000	63,716,000	42,619,000	23,234,000	65,853,000
1931	38,195,000	22,080,000	60,275,000	38,165,000	20,175,000	58,340,000
1932	35,521,000	20,549,000	56,070,000	34,850,000	20,591,000	55,441,000
1933	35,363,892	25,064,297	60,428,199	33,856,000	21,796,000	55,653,000
1934	36,127,000	26,542,000	62,669,000	33,798,662	22,290,908	56,089,570
1935	36,111,000	27,581,000	63,629,000	34,302,032	23,091,865	57,321,896
1936	38,055,000	29,360,000	67,415,000	34,302,000	22,516,000	56,818,000
1937	39,289,000	31,130,000	70,420,000	35,893,000	25,407,000	61,390,000
1938	38,909,000	29,463,000	68,372,000	34,511,000	24,370,000	58,881,000

The merchant marine of Great Britain, July 1, 1939, was composed of 6,722 steam and motor ships of 17,891,134 gross tonnage, and 289 sailing vessels of 93,024 gross tonnage; total, 7,009 vessels of 17,984,158 tonnage.

United States ships with cargoes entering British ports totaled 3,118,798 tons in 1938, 3,302,661 (1937), 3,085,763 (1936), 3,004,000 (1935), 2,549,000 (1934).

Great Britain's principal peace time imports in the order of their monetary value are—food and drink; wood and timber; non-ferrous metals and manufactures; wool and woollen rags; raw cotton and cotton waste; oils, fats and resins; hides and skins; machinery; iron and steel manufactures; non-ferrous ores and scrap; tobacco; paper and cardboard; chemicals, drugs, dyes and colors; iron ore and scrap; rubber.

The chief domestic exports are—cotton yarns, manufactures and other textiles; machinery; iron and steel manufactures; vehicles including ships and aircraft; coal; food and drink; chemicals, drugs, dyes and colors; electrical goods and apparatus; wearing apparel; earthenware and glass; cutlery, hardware, implements; wool and woollen rags.

The most important colonial re-exports (that is, materials imported from the colonies and dominions and re-exported from Great Britain) are, in the order of their monetary value—wool and woollen rags; non-ferrous metals and manufactures; hides and skins; food and drink; rubber; oil, fat, resin manufactures; raw cotton and cotton waste; leather, machinery, cutlery, hardware, implements; non-ferrous ores and scrap; woollen, worsted yarns and manufactures.

DISTRIBUTION OF GREAT BRITAIN'S TRADE, 1938

Country	Imp.	Exp.	Country	Imp.	Exp.	Country	Imp.	Exp.
British—	%	%	Foreign—	%	%	Foreign—	%	%
Eire	2.49	4.30	United States	12.81	4.35	Japan	0.71	0.44
Canada	8.53	4.78	Argentina	4.19	4.11	Poland	1.04	1.14
Australia	7.84	8.11	Germany	3.28	4.36	Baltic States	1.06	1.01
New Zealand	5.09	4.09	Denmark	4.11	3.35	China	0.73	0.86
Un. of S. Africa	1.59	8.39	France	2.57	3.21	Italy	0.79	1.21
Rest of Africa	3.05	4.32	Netherlands	3.19	2.79	Switzerland	0.80	0.74
British Malaya	1.32	2.36	Sweden	2.67	2.49	Dutch E. Indies	0.69	0.77
India, Ceylon	7.43	8.48	Belgium	2.02	1.75	Spain	0.62	0.73
West Indies, etc.	1.25	1.67	Finland	2.09	1.17	Rumania	0.42	0.29
			U.S.S.R.	2.12	1.37			
Tot. Brit. (incl. those not enumerated)	40.39	49.87	Egypt	1.26	1.84	Tot. Foreign(incl. those not enumerated)	59.61	50.13
			Norway	1.20	1.61			
			Brazil	0.84	1.10			

There are four railway systems in the United Kingdom with a total mileage of 20,080. Public highways extend for 179,630 miles.

The Government leased (1941) the country's railroads for a fixed annual rental of £43,000,000 to avoid any increase in rail and freight charges. The agreement operates from Jan. 1, 1941, retroactively, for the duration of the war and for at least one year thereafter.

The telephone service is a part of the postal system. The number of telephones in Great Britain (1940) was 3,338,929. London in its exchange area had 1,155,093 telephones.

British civilian aircraft flew 5,000,000 miles and carried nearly 30,000,000 airmail letters in 1940.

Social welfare legislation is well advanced in Great Britain. The National Health Insurance Acts (1936-38), the Unemployment Insurance Acts (1935-36), the Old Age Pensions Act (1936) and the Widows', Orphans' and Old Age Contributory Pensions Act (1936-41) make provision for compulsory insurance against sickness and unemployment; and for pensions for widows, orphans and the aged.

The minimum age of entry into unemployment insurance for boys and girls was lowered from 16 years to 14 (the age at which the juvenile is no longer required to attend school) (Sept. 3, 1934) insurance was extended to cover agricultural workers; it was estimated to cover about 700,000 males and 50,000 females.

The most celebrated of British universities are Oxford and Cambridge, each with colleges founded in the thirteenth century, and inextricably intertwined in the fabric of English history. But there are many others in England, London, Durham, Manchester, Birmingham, Liverpool, Leeds, Sheffield, Bristol, and Reading (1926); in Scotland, St. Andrews, Edinburgh, Glasgow and Aberdeen; and one in Wales. Elementary education is compulsory from five to 14 years of age.

The monetary unit of Great Britain is the pound sterling with an average value of $4.03.

The armed land forces of Great Britain prior to 1939 were composed of the Regular Army, the Territorial Army and the Reserve Forces. The Regular Army, commonly known as the British Army, serves at home and also overseas. The Territorial Army, corresponding to the National Guard in the United States, serves only at home in peace time, but has been asked to serve overseas in war time.

Conscription was adopted (April 27, 1939) and provides six months of training after which the conscript has the option of entering the Territorial Army for a period of three and a half years. Those who decline are registered in the Regular Army Reserve. The Reserve Forces consist of the Army Reserve—men who have completed their service in the Regular Army—the Supplementary Reserve of Officers and the Supplementary Re-

serve, the Militia and the Territorial Reserves.

Parliament passed (May 22, 1940) the Emergency Powers Defense Bill that gives the Government the right to conscript every person and every penny in the realm for the duration of the war.

The national conscription bill provides for compulsory national service by women, 20 to 31 years old, and for men, 18½ to 50 years old. Girls, 16 and 17 years old are registered and listed for training.

The Navy is undergoing a vast expansion program but the additional construction has not been announced in detail although it is known to be large. The estimates (1939-1940) provided for a personnel of 145,000 by March 31, 1940, not including the Royal Marine Police. Reserves total 70,000. For 1940 the total naval personnel, including the mobilized reserves, was estimated officially to be 250,000, but this figure has since been increased.

The Royal Air Force consists of the Royal Air Force, the Air Force Reserve, the Auxiliary Air Force, the Air Training Corps and the Women's Auxiliary Air Force.

The establishment of the Royal Air Force (1939-1940) was 118,000 exclusive of those serving in India. The British Empire Training Plan provides for the training of 20,000 pilots a year. The recruits are drawn from Great Britain, Australia, New Zealand and other parts of the Empire and are trained in Canada. The plan was reported (1940) as far ahead of schedule. To Civil Aviation there was allotted (1939-1940) £4,787,000 to provide expansion and improved equipment for the Empire Mail Service and the establishment of an interisland service in the West Indies. Subsidies also were given to light airplane clubs and for the development of gliding.

NORTHERN IRELAND
(ULSTER)

Six of the nine counties of Ulster, the northeast corner of Ireland, constitute Northern Ireland, with the parliamentary boroughs of Belfast, and Londonderry; they are Antrim, Armagh, Down, Londonderry, Fermanagh and Tyrone. The country has a population (census of 1937) of 1,279,745 and an area of 5,238 square miles.

Although it has its own Parliament, Northern Ireland is politically a part of the United Kingdom. The Prime Minister is John Millar Andrews. The Governor is the Duke of Abercorn (appointed 1922). Belfast is the capital.

The finest scenery in Northern Ireland is to be found on or close to the coast line. From Belfast there runs northward along the coast of the county of Antrim the "Corniche" of Northern Ireland, a perfectly engineered road running for nearly 100 miles, walled off by sheer green and white cliffs on the landward side.

The Antrim road takes the visitor to the most famous of the sights of Northern Ireland, the Giant's Causeway, which consists of a perfect honeycomb of stone columns, 40,000 in all, each having the shape of a polygon or hexagon. How these stones came to be cut to such exact mathematical shapes is still a mystery unsolved by geologists. Along the north coast, at the head of a long inlet of the sea, Lough Foyle, is the city of Londonderry. Lough Erne with its 40 islands is one of the most famous of lakes, and Lough Neagh the largest in the British Isles.

A separate parliamentary and executive government for Northern Ireland was established (1920) and "contracted out" of the newly established

Irish Free State (Dec. 1922). The Parliament consists of a Senate of 26, and House of Commons of 52, both elected with power to legislate in local matters except such as are of Imperial concern or specifically reserved to the Imperial Parliament. Northern Ireland returns 13 members to the House of Commons.

The bulk of the taxation is imposed and collected by the Imperial authorities, which makes certain deductions and remits the remainder to the local exchequer. The British pound is the monetary unit. The budget (1941-1942) estimated receipts at £16,374,000 and expenditures at £16,-297,000.

Northern Ireland is preponderantly Protestant. The religious population follows: Roman Catholics, 428,290; Presbyterians, 390,931; Protestant Episcopalians, 345,474; Methodists, 55,135; other sects, 59,915. Elementary education is compulsory. The Queens University of Belfast (founded in 1849) is a well-known institution of higher learning.

Agriculture—particularly the raising of flax and live stock—is an important undertaking. The principal crops include wheat, oats, barley, potatoes, turnips, fruit and hay. Mineral wealth is confined primarily to chalk, clay, fireclay, flint, gravel and sand, granite, igneous rock, limestone, rock salt, sandstone and diatomite.

Linen weaving and shipbuilding are the chief industries. The manufacturing of linen gives direct employment to about 70,000 persons, the number of spindles being 875,000. Ropes and twines, clothing, aircraft, tobacco, soaps, aerated waters, hosiery and underwear are other important products.

Ireland
(EIRE)
Capital, Dublin—Area, 27,137 square miles—Population (1941) 2,989,700

Ireland, an island in the Atlantic Ocean near the European mainland and separated from Great Britain by St. George's Channel, the Irish Sea and the North Channel, is a picturesque country consisting mainly of a central plateau surrounded by isolated groups of hills and mountains. The coast is much indented by the sea, affording many inlets and coves. Because of a luxurious growth of rich green vegetation, Ireland has been called the "Emerald Isle." The prevailing winds are westerly, conducing to a climate generally mild and moist. The mean annual temperature ranges from 48 degrees in the north to 52 degrees in the south. Dublin has an average temperature of 39 in the coldest month and 60 in the warmest. There are numerous lakes (called loughs), the best known of which are situated in Killarney. The most important river is the Shannon, about 200 miles long. Some mountains attain an altitude in excess of 3,000 ft. Wildlife is scarce, and there are no known snakes existent.

A point of interest to visitors is an old castle in the village of Blarney, four miles northwest of Cork, built on a limestone rock on the site of an older stronghold erected (1446) by Cormac M'Carthy. Some 20 feet from the top of the castle is a famous stone called the Blarney Stone which, according to tradition, invests great powers of persuasion on those who kiss it.

Ireland, or Eire, is a sovereign independent state associated for certain purposes with the British Commonwealth of Nations. The Dublin government exercises jurisdiction over the three southern provinces of the island—Leinster, Munster and Connaught and three counties—Cavan, Donegal and Monaghan, of the province of Ulster. (This area became known as the Irish Free State (1922) but has been redesignated "Eire", the Gaelic name for Ireland under the new constitution (effective, Dec. 29, 1937). The Constitution applies to the whole of Ireland, but it provides that, pending the re-integration of the national territory, the laws enacted by the Parliament established by the Constitution shall have the same area and extent of application as those of the Irish Free State.

The government of Eire is bicameral with a President elected directly by the people for a term of seven years; a House of Representatives called Dail Eireann; and a Senate (Seanad Eireann). The Senate consists of 60 members, eleven of whom are appointed by the Taoiseach (Prime Minister), who is the Head of Government. Of the remaining 49, the universities elect six and the balance are elected from five panels of candidates established on a vocational basis, representing the following public services and interests—(1) National Language and Culture, Literature, Art, Education and other professional interests that may be defined by law from time to time; (2) Agriculture and allied interests, and fisheries; (3) Labor, whether organized or unorganized; (4) Industry and commerce, including banking, finance, accountancy, engineering and architecture; (5) Public administration and social services, including voluntary social activities.

The Dail Eireann consists of 138 members elected by the people.

The Senate considers and amends legislation but has no veto power. The Government exercises the executive power. The President, on the advice of the Taoiseach, summons and dissolves Dail Eireann. He signs and promulgates laws; and (on the nomination of Dail Eireann) appoints the Prime Minister and other members of the government. The supreme command of the Defense Forces is vested in him.

The President of Ireland is Douglas Hyde, elected without opposition (May 4, 1938), Eamon de Valera was re-elected Prime Minister (June 30, 1938).

Under the terms of a treaty concluded (April 25, 1938) with Ireland, Great Britain surrendered her treaty rights over the Irish ports of Cobh (Queenstown), Bere Haven and Lough Swilly "together with the buildings, magazines, emplacements, instruments and fixed armaments" at those ports The agreement also provided for the payment of £10,000,000 by Ireland as the final settlement of all the outstanding financial matters between the two countries and for an adjustment of the tariff duties, which for three years had curtailed Anglo-Irish trade.

The population of Eire has declined in recent years because of emigration. Roman Catholic is the prevailing religion with an enrollment of 2,773,120. Other chief sects are: Protestant Episcopal, 145,030; Presbyterian, 28,067; Methodist, 9,649.

The population of Dublin, with its four suburban districts, has increased from 383,076 (1911) to an estimated 482,300 (mid-1939). Other cities and their population (1936) are: Cork, 80,765; Limerick, 41,061; Waterford, 27,968.

The country is chiefly agricultural, the ranking crops being wheat, oats, barley, rye, potatoes, turnips, mangels, sugar beets, cabbage, flax and hay.

The chief industries (1940) with the production in pounds follow: grain milling, 13,087,994; bread, flour, confectionery, biscuits, etc., 5,235,246; butter, cheese, margarine, condensed milk, 7,104,729; bacon curing, 8,534,636; brewing, 8,365,694; malting, 482,733; sugar, sugar confectionery, jam making, 9,239,688; tobacco, 8,808,685; women's readymade clothing, 1,356,291; woolen and worsteds, 2,286,911; wood furniture and upholstery, 804,825; soap and candles, 690,966; timber, 1,842,213; distilling, 505,164; bricks, glass, cement and monumental masonry, 1,456,386; assembly, construction and repair of vehicles, 2,113,028; metals, 1,-948,195; engineering and implements, 1,149,325; linen, cotton, jute and canvas, 2,290,001; boot and shoe, 2,211,179; hosiery, 1,645,196; paper making and manufactured stationery, 1,326,315; electricity utilities, 1,999,215; printing, publishing and book binding, 2,672,473.

Elementary education is free and compulsory, and the Irish language is a required study in all national schools. The National University of Ireland (founded 1908), comprising the Constituent Colleges of Dublin, Cork and Galway, and Trinity College, Dublin (founded 1591) are institutions of higher learning.

There is maintained a defense force of approximately 25,000, including the permanent force, reserves and volunteers. There is an air corps and a coastal patrol service of two motor torpedo boats. Defense expenditures (1941-1942) were £8,383,556.

The monetary unit is the Irish pound which has the same value as the British pound. Revenues (1941-1942) were estimated at £35,630,000 and expenditures at £40,172,000.

British European Possessions

Gibraltar, the rock at the southernmost point of the Iberian Peninsula, guards the entrance to the Mediterranean. The width of the strait dividing Europe from Africa is 14 miles. The Rock has been in British possession since 1713. It has been elaborated, tunneled and armed until it is considered impregnable. A large and secure harbor has been constructed at its foot. As a naval base its position is of the greatest strategic importance. The Rock is 2¾ miles long, ¾ of a mile wide and 1,396 ft. in height; the area is nearly two square miles; a narrow isthmus connects it with the Spanish mainland.

The fixed population (estimated, 1939) is 20,399. The natives are mostly Roman Catholics. Education is compulsory between five and 14 years of age. The monetary unit is the pound sterling, but Spanish money circulates freely.

Gibraltar is a Crown Colony and the Governor and Commander-in-Chief is Lieut. Gen. F. N. Mason MacFarlane.

Malta, an island 17 miles long by eight wide and 58 miles due south of Sicily in the Mediterranean Sea and about 180 miles from the African coast, has had centuries of stormy history. It was annexed to the British Empire (1814) following the Napoleonic wars and has been greatly strengthened and made into a base for repair and refitment for the British fleet. The harbor of Valletta has been improved with a breakwater, but it is not large. The area of the island is 95 square miles. The neighboring island of Gozo has an area of 27 square miles which with Comino, one square mile, brings the total for the group to 122 square miles. The civil population (1939) is 268,668.

The George Cross was conferred on Malta (April 16, 1942) at a time when it was under almost daily bombing by Axis forces by King George in the following message: "To honor the brave people I award the George Cross to the island fortress of Malta to bear witness to the heroism and devotion that will long be famous in history."

Farming is the prime industry, chief crops being wheat, barley, potatoes, onions, beans, vegetables and fruits. Trade is chiefly with Great Britain.

The Governor and Commander-in-Chief is General Viscount Gort.

India

Capital, New Delhi—Area, 1,808,679 square miles—Population (1931) 352,837,778

The name India describes the central peninsula of southern Asia, south of the Himalayas, reaching eastward to Siam, French Indo-China and China. It is bounded on the north by Afghanistan, Nepal, Bhutan and Thibet; on the south by the Bay of Bengal, the Indian Ocean and the Arabian Sea; on the west by the Indian Ocean, the Arabian Sea, Persia and Afghanistan. Its territory is as large as that of the United States east of the Rocky Mountain States. Burma was separated from India politically (April 1, 1937).

The climate ranges from the extremely hot in the southeast to cooler elevations of the northwest mountains, the whole being tropical in general character. The highest point in the world is Mt. Everest, 29,141 ft., in the Himalayas, between India and China.

Approximately 20% of the area is forested, among the timber products being sandalwood, teak, ironwood, deodar, satinwood, date palm, cocoanut, sago, banyan and acacia.

The country is essentially agricultural, 70% of the people living therefrom. The most important crop is tea and engages the daily employment of nearly a million persons. Other principal agricultural products are: rice, coffee, wheat, sugar cane, cotton, jute, linseed, mustard, sesamum, castor seed, groundnut and rubber. Corn, barley, tobacco and indigo are also grown.

India has an unusually wide range of minerals and was famous for its riches even before the time of Marco Polo. The country has yielded much gold, silver, diamonds and rubies to the western world. The most important minerals today are coal, petroleum, gold, lead, manganese, salt, silver, tin, mica, copper, tungsten, iron and zinc.

The chief industry, after agriculture, is the weaving of cotton cloths, followed by silk rearing and weaving, shawl and carpet weaving, wood-carving and metal-working.

CITIES OVER 200,000

The cities of above 200,000 inhabitants with their population (census of 1931) are:

City	Pop.	City	Pop.
Calcutta (with		Bagalore	306,470
suburbs)	1,485,582	Lucknow	274,659
Calcutta proper	1,161,410	Amritsar	264,840
Bombay	1,161,383	Karachi	263,565
Madras	647,230	Cawnpore	243,755
Hyderabad	466,894	Poona	233,885
Delhi	447,442	Agra	229,764
Lahore	429,747	Nagpur	215,165
Ahmedabad	313,789	Benares	205,315

The census (1941) gives Greater Calcutta 2,109,-000 and Bombay 1,486,971.

In British India (1939) there were 211,192 "recognized" educational institutions with 13,911,172 scholars; and 19,354 "unrecognized" schools with 597,443 scholars. There are 16 universities. The percentage of illiteracy in the nation is high.

Christian missionaries, Catholic and Protestant, exceed 6,000 in number. They conduct more than 12,000 "recognized" schools, operate more than 200 hospitals and many centers for welfare work.

There are more than 45 races speaking 200 languages, 2,400 castes and tribes, and 700 feudatory states. Each cult, caste and tribe adheres strongly to its religious beliefs and social rules, many of them with fanaticism. The religious population (census of 1931) follows—Hindus, 239,195,140; Muslims, 77,677,545; Buddhists, 12,786,806; Tribal, 8,280,347; Christians, 6,296,763; Sikhs, 4,335,771; Jains, 1,252,105; Zoroastrians, 109,752; Jews, 24,141.

The Legislative Assembly (Sept. 1929), by a large majority, enacted a law, introduced by a Hindu member, raising the minimum age for marriage of girls to 14 years and the age of consent to 16.

Units of the British Regular Army, the Indian Army, Auxiliary and Territorial Forces, the Indian Army Reserve, the Royal Indian Navy, the Indian State Forces, the Royal Air Force and the Indian Air Force form the defense. Members of the British Regular Army in Indian service are paid by India. The Auxiliary Force is composed of persons of British extraction and is subject to call for local service. The Indian Territorial Force comprises provincial and urban battalions and a University Training Corps, all subject to general service. The Indian Army Reserve comprises reservists of all arms. The Indian States maintain the Indian State Forces and are trained by British officers. The strength of the Indian Army (1942) was estimated at 1,000,000. The Royal Indian Navy consists of five escort vessels, a survey boat, patrol ship and trawler.

In London the governmental affairs of India are handled by the Secretary of State for India. At New Delhi, the capital of India, there is a British governor-general and, under the Government of India Act (1935), two native legislative chambers, the Council of State and the House of Assembly. The former consists of 58 representatives of British India, the majority of whom are elected on a franchise of some 100,000 persons, and the remainder of whom are appointed by the native rulers. The Assembly consists of 141 representatives, 39 nominated of whom 26 are officials and 102 are elected.

The India Act establishes a federation embracing British India and the Native States with a wide measure of autonomy for some of the provinces. These provinces are: Bengal, Bombay, Madras, Assam, Bihar, Orissa, Punjab, Sind, Central Provinces, United Provinces, and Northwest Provinces. Delhi has, like Washington, a separate administration. Each Province has a Governor appointed by the King, a Cabinet and Legislature set up on similar lines except that in Assam, Orissa, Punjab, Central Provinces and United Provinces there is only one chamber.

The native states of India have always enjoyed local autonomy. Only in matters affecting India as a whole such posts and telegraphs, customs and currency, have they been subject to British law. The British Viceroy and Governor-General of India is the Marquess of Linlithgow (born Sept. 24, 1887).

Gold is hoarded in India by all classes of people, as a reserve against famine. The wealthy princes have accumulated enormous sums.

The monetary unit is the rupee with an average value of $.30. The budget (1942-1943) estimates revenue at 1,400,000,000 rupees and expenditures 1,870,700,000 rupees.

Sikkim is a state of India in the Himalayas, south from Thibet. The area is 2,818 square miles, and population (1931) 109,808, composed of Bhutias, Lepchas and Nepalese. It is governed by a Maharajah under a a British protectorate. Cereals, fruits and woolen cloth are the products.

The Andaman Islands, 204 in number, are in the Bay of Bengal, 120 miles from the mainland of Burma. Area is 2,508 square miles, and population (1941) 21,483 (aborigines not counted). Timber wealth is large. The islands have been used as a penal colony for life and long-term convicts, but this is being discontinued. There were (1940) 6,069 convicts. The natives are pygmy, jungle dwellers, expert with spear and arrow and savage. Japanese forces occupied the islands (March, 1942).

The Nicobar Islands, 75 miles from Andaman Islands, have 635 square miles of area and a population (1931) of 9,481. Japan announced (July 1, 1942) occupation of the islands.

BRITISH AND NATIVE STATES IN INDIA, INCLUDING BURMA

British Provinces	Area in Sq. M.	Pop. 1931	Native States and Agencies	Area in Sq. M.	Pop. 1931
Ajmer-Merwara	2,711	560,292	Baroda State	8,164	2,443,007
Andamans and Nicobars	3,143	29,463	Central India Agency	51,597	6,632,790
Assam	67,334	9,247,857	Cochin State	1,480	1,205,016
Baluchistan	82,955	868,617	Gwalior State	26,367	3,523,070
Bengal	134,635	51,087,338	Hyderabad State	82,698	14,436,148
Bihar and Orissa	111,702	42,329,583	Jammu & Kashmir State	84,516	3,646,243
Bombay Presidency	151,673	26,398,997	Mysore State	29,326	6,557,302
Aden	80	51,478	Punjab States Agency	31,241	4,472,218
Burma	233,492	14,667,146	Rajputana Agency	129,059	11,225,712
Central Provinces & Berar	131,095	17,990,937	Sikkim State	2,818	109,808
Coorg	1,593	163,327	Travancore State	7,625	$5,095,973
Delhi	573	636,246	Western India States Agency	35,442	3,999,250
Madras	143,870	47,193,602			
North-West Frontier Province	36,356	4,684,364	Total States	490,333	63,346,537
Punjab	105,020	24,018,639	Total Provinces	1,318,346	289,491,241
United Provinces	112,191	49,614,833			
			Total India	1,808,679	352,837,778
Total Provinces	1,318,346	289,491,241			

Burma

Burma is bounded on the north by Thibet and China, on the East by China and Siam, on the south by the Bay of Bengal, and on the west by the Bay of Bengal and the Provinces of Bengal and Assam of British India. Since the first Burma war (1826) it has been administered as part of British India.

Under the Government of India Act of 1935, Burma, which had long sought release, was detached from British India (April 1, 1937), made a Crown Colony, and received a constitution of her own. Under the new law, there was a Senate of 36 members and a House of Representatives of 132 members.

The area of Burma (including the Shan States) is 261,610 square miles; population (1931) was 14,-667,146. About 85% are Buddhists. Rangoon is the capital. Japanese forces occupied Rangoon (March 9, 1942).

The Irrawaddy River is navigable for 900 miles and its tributary, the Chindwin, for 300.

The principal products are teakwood, tin, silver and petroleum.

British Malaya

STRAITS SETTLEMENTS

The Straits Settlements, formerly a Crown Colony of which Singapore, an island 27 miles long by 14 wide, area, 225 square miles, is the capital and chief port. Singapore just misses being the southernmost point of Asia by a half-mile water channel. The Johore Causeway joins it with the mainland and affords through train service between Bangkok and Singapore. It is at the funnel point of the Strait of Malacca, which extends between the Malay Peninsula and the island of Sumatra, the great water highway between India and China. The area is 1,356 square miles; the population (1941) was estimated at 1,435,895.

Singapore was occupied by Japanese forces (Feb. 15, 1942) in the conquest of Malaya.

Singapore has a polyglot population of more than 600,000, of which 80 per cent is Chinese. The port was served by 80 steamship lines and annually was host to 30,000 ships. The city had magnificent banks, modern office buildings and stately Government palaces.

Three-fourths of the tin and three-fifths of the rubber used in the United States came from British Malaya. One of the richest tin deposits is in the Kinta valley in the state of Perak. The Malay States are the chief source of tin in the world. The British introduced rubber trees into British Malaya about fifty years ago from seed smuggled out of Brazil and rubber trees practically cover the Malay States.

The four Federated Malay States are situated on the Malay Peninsula are: Perak, area, 7,980 square miles; Selangor, 3,160 square miles; Negri Sembilan, 2,580 square miles; Pahang, 13,820 square miles; total, 27,540 square miles; population (estimated (1941) 2,212,052.

Rubber and tin are the chief products, others being coconuts, rice, tapioca, sugar, pepper, camphor and nepah and oil palm.

The Unfederated Malay States are Johore, Kedan, Perlis, Kalantan and Trengganu. Their area aggregates 22,276 square miles, and population (estimated 1939) of 1,918,831. Johore is a protectorate of Great Britain (since 1885), the others were transferred from Siam to Great Britain by treaty (1909). Each state is under a native sultan with a British adviser. Rubber is the chief product. Rice and copra also are exported.

British North Borneo has 29,500 square miles area, with 270,223 population (census, 1931), chiefly Mohammedans on the seacoast, and aboriginal tribes inland.

Exports are mainly timber, sago, rice, gum, and the tropical products.

The British governor of North Borneo, Brunei and Sarawak is the High Commissioner of British Malaya.

Brunei has been since 1888 a protected sultanate on the north side of the Island of Borneo, between Sarawak and British North Borneo. Its area is about 2,226 square miles, and population (census of 1931), 30,135, of which 60 were Europeans. Japanese forces occupied Brunei (Jan., 1942).

Sarawak, the land of the white Rajah, is along the northwest coast of Borneo, between the mountains and the China Sea. Its coast line is 400 miles long and its area 50,000 square miles. Its population is estimated at 490,585. The capital is Kuching. The chief exports are sago, pepper, gold, plantation rubber, petroleum. Japanese forces occupied Sarawak (Dec., 1941).

Other British Asiatic Possessions

Aden, a peninsula on the Arabian coast, is at the southern end of the Red Sea, and has 75 square miles of area, in Aden proper, and 112,000 square miles including protectorate areas. It is a Crown Colony. The population, including Perim (5 square miles), an island in the Red Sea, in 1931, was 48,338, mostly Mohammedans. It is the principal commercial center for the Arabian peninsula.

Manufacturing is chiefly of cigarettes and salt. Aden is a free port, an important coaling station, and has an excellent harbor.

Socrotra is an island off the African coast under British protection, attached to Aden. Area in all is 1,400 square miles, and population 12,000, mostly engaged in livestock husbandry.

Ceylon, a Crown Colony since 1802, is an island off the southern tip of India, in the Indian Ocean, with 25,332 square miles of area and a population (1931) of 5,312,548.

Tea and rubber are the chief products.

The Maldive Islands, with an area of 115 square miles, are 400 miles southwest from Ceylon, with 79,000 population (1931 census), almost all Mohammedans. Coconuts, millet, fruit and nuts are the products.

British Hong Kong is a Crown Colony (acquired in 1841) and lies at the mouth of the Canton River 60 miles from Canton. The island is 11 miles long, with an area of 32 square miles; including the new territory, Kowloon, on the mainland, the area of the colony is 391 square miles. The population (estimated (1938) is 1,050,256, non-Chinese numbering 23,096. Chinese refugees (not counted) number approximately 750,000.

Hong Kong was a British station of strategic value, commercially as well as naval.

It is the gateway between the east and the west, and one of the greatest trans-shipment ports in the world. Hong Kong was occupied by Japanese forces (Dec. 25, 1941) after a 16-day siege.

The Hong Kong dollar varied with the price of silver with an average value fo $.25.

Cyprus is an island, third largest in the Mediterranean Sea, 40 miles south of Asia Minor and 60 miles west of Syria, and 240 miles north of Egypt. Its area is 3,572 sq. m., and population (estimated, 1940) of 383,967. It has been administered by England since 1878, under an agreement with Turkey; it was annexed (Nov. 5, 1914).

The natives, dissatisfied with their status as a Crown Colony, asked permission (1931) to join Greece. This was refused. There was a rising against the Government (Oct. 1931) which was put down by troops from Egypt. The legislative council was suspended and legislative powers conferred on the Governor-in-Council.

Four-fifths of the inhabitants are Greek Christians, and nearly all the remainder are Turkish Mohammedans. More than half are illiterate. Turkish customs, laws and weights and measures are in use; Cyprus has known more alien governments even than Palestine.

The island is agricultural, with wheat, barley, vetches, oats, olives, and cotton as chief products. Thirty per cent of the land is cultivated.

Nicosia is the capital. The chief ports are Limassol, Larnaca and Famagusta.

The budget (1941) estimates revenues of £965,-146 and expenditures of £1,075,872. Cyprus has contributed annually (since 1928) £10,000 to Imperial defense.

Union of South Africa

Capital, Pretoria—Area, 472,550 square miles—Population (est. 1939), 10,160,000

The Union of South Africa, a Dominion within the British Commonwealth of Nations, was formed (1910) and includes the former Colonies of the Cape of Good Hope, Natal, the Transvaal and the Orange Free State. The former German territory of South West Africa is administered by the Union under Mandate from the League of Nations.

The legislative power of the Union is vested in the Parliament of the Union, consisting of the King, the Senate and the House of Assembly. There is an elected Provincial Council in each of the four Provinces. The Governor-General is Sir Patrick Duncan (appointed 1936). The Prime Minister is Gen. Jan Christian Smuts (appointed 1939). The High Commissioner in the Union for His

Majesty's Government in the United Kingdom and His Majesty's High Commissioner for Basutoland, the Bechuanaland Protectorate and Swaziland is S. F. Waterson (appointed Sept. 19, 1939).

The population (1937) and area in square miles of the four provinces comprising the Union of South Africa follow:

| | | Area | |
Province	Pop.	Sq. Mi.	Capital
Transvaal	3,535,100	110,450	Pretoria
C. of Good Hope	3,635,100	277,169	Cape Town
Orange Fr. State	790,800	49,647	Bloemfontein
Natal	2,018,000	35,284	Pietermaritzburg

The capital of the Union is Pretoria although the Union's Legislature meets in Cape Town.

South Africa is the richest gold and diamond

country in the world. Nearly 35% of the world's supply of gold originates there, the gold industry providing work for 361,459 persons, or 81.89% of the employed population.

Coal, copper and tin are also important. Other minerals are iron, lead, lime, manganese, platinum, salt, talc, chrome, mica, graphite, beryl.

Production of gold, by fine ounces, for five years, was (1935), 12,603,000; (1936), 11,378,000; (1937), 14,002,000; (1938), 12,161,392; (1939), 12,821,507.

Production of diamonds, by carats, for five years, (1935), 676,722; (1936), 623,923; (1937), 1,030,434; (1938), 1,238,608; (1939), 1,249,828.

The defense system makes every European citizen between 17 and 60 years of age, eligible for military duty in time of war. Those between 17 and 25 are obligated to undergo training in the Coast Garrison Force, the Active Citizen Force, the Royal Naval Volunteer Force, or a Rifle Association, over a period of four years. The Rifle Association provides for training in the handling of a rifle for those between 21 and 25 years.

The Transvaal and Natal have land suitable for growing cotton. Corn is an important crop, and its export due to great variations in production is handled on a quota system. Wheat and fruit are also grown.

There are five universities—Cape Town, Stellenbosch, South Africa, Witwatersrand and Pretoria, and five constituent colleges, with an average enrollment exceeding 9,000 students.

The monetary unit is the South Africa pound with an average value of $4.03. The budget (1941-1942) estimated revenues of £73,640,000, and expenditures of £101,799,000.

South-West Africa, formerly German territory (annexed 1884), occupies the Atlantic Coast from the Orange River to Angola. It was conquered by the armed forces of the Union in the World War (July 9, 1915). It is now administered by the Union under a Mandate from the League of Nations (dated Dec. 17, 1920).

It covers an area of 317,725 square miles and the native population (1936) is 314,194, with 30,677 Europeans.

It is a very healthful climate, dry and temperate with variety as the country rises to mountainous elevations inland. It is ideal as a stock-raising country. Minerals represent 20% to 30% of the exports.

British East Africa

Kenya, crown colony and protectorate, extends from the Indian Ocean northeast to Italian Somaliland, north to Ethiopia, west to Uganda, and south to Tanganyika; its boundaries are the Umba, Juba and Uganda Rivers. Its area is 224,960 square miles, and population (estimated 1940) of 3,534,862, largely native.

In the northeast, stretching across the Equator, there is a tract of 200,000 square miles lying at an elevation of more than 4,000 ft., with a climate like that of California, vast rolling plains, crossed by rivers, dotted with lakes, where cotton and rubber can be grown, and two crops a year of food staples. Experts report that enough cotton can be grown there to make the British textile industry independent of American supply. It is unexploited, occupied only by roving natives and thronged with wild game. White men can live there in health as nowhere else in Central Africa.

The Europeans of Kenya passed laws reserving the highlands for white settlement, restricting the natives to the lowlands and less healthful regions. Nairobi, a famous center for big game hunting, is the capital. Government revenue (1940) was £4,111,412, expenditures £4,064,465.

The Uganda Protectorate lies to the west of Kenya with the Anglo-Egyptian Soudan on the north, Belgian Congo on the west, and Tanganyika on the south. Its territory includes part of the Victoria Nyanza, Lake Kiogu and Lake Salisbury, also the Nile from Victoria Nyanza to the Soudan. Uganda has an estimated elephant population of 20,000, or one elephant to every 175 inhabitants.

The game warden reported 1,500 elephants killed (1938).

Its area is 93,381 square miles, including 13,680 square miles of water. The population is estimated at 3,829,705, largely native. The country is well advanced in civilization. Government revenues (1940) were £1,870,915; expenditures £2,056,543.

Tanganyika was formerly German East Africa, and was taken by the British (1918), the Urundi and Ruanda districts going to Belgium, and the "Kionga Triangle" to Mozambique (Portuguese East Africa). It reaches from the coast to Lake Tanganyika and from Lake Nyasa to Victoria Nyanza. It is administered under a mandate from the League of Nations, by a Governor.

The area is 360,000 square miles, and population (estimated 1939) 5,270,484.

The western part of Tanganyika is a paradise for big game. There are many huge extinct craters, about 125 in number, west of the gorilla country, Kilimanjaro; that of Ngoro Ngoro is surrounded by escarpments 2,000 ft. high, is 35 miles wide and crowded with game.

Government revenue (1941) was estimated at £2,126,789, expenditures £2,472,753.

The principal products are sisal, cotton, coffee, ground nuts, hides and skin, beeswax and ivory.

Nyasaland Protectorate (until 1907 British Central Africa) is situated on the southern and western shores of Lake Nyasa and extends as far as the Zambesi river. Its area is 37,374 square miles with a population (1940) of 1,684,194. Tea and tobacco are cultivated.

British South Africa

Southern Rhodesia lies in the central part of South Africa, extending from the Transvaal Province northward to the Zambesi River, with Portuguese East Africa on the east and Portuguese West Africa and Bechuanaland on the west. It has an area of 150,333 square miles. Population is estimated (1941) was 1,448,393 and includes 62,330 Europeans. The country is rich in gold reefs and other minerals, but has proved to be an ideal agricultural country, especially adapted to European settlers. Salisbury is the capital.

The Victoria Falls in Southern Rhodesia on the Zambesi River are the greatest natural spectacle in South Africa. They are a mile wide and from 250 to nearly 350 ft. high.

The two Rhodesias, Southern and Northern, were under the administration of the British South Africa Company from 1898 until they became Crown colonies (1923) and (1924) respectively.

Corn, cotton, tobacco are grown. The output of gold, coal, chrome and asbestos is considerable. Government revenues (1941-1942) are estimated at £6,058,000; expenditures £8,582,749.

Northern Rhodesia, was taken over by the British government from the British South Africa Company (1924) and established as a Crown Colony. The capital is Lusaka.

Its area is 290,320 square miles extending north from the Zambesi river to the Belgian Congo and Tanganyika Territory. The country is mostly high plateau covered with thin forest and suitable for farming and grazing. The population was estimated (1940) at 1,381,829, of whom 15,188 were Europeans. The budget (1941) estimated revenues of £2,431,054 and expenditures of £2,147,172.

The country is rich in minerals, particularly copper, zinc, cobalt, gold, vanadium and manganese.

Basutoland, with 11,716 square miles, and a population (1936) of 562,411, lies in South Africa northeast from the Cape of Good Hope Province on an elevated plateau. Stock raising is most important. Products are wool, wheat, cereals. The territory is governed by a Resident Commissioner under the High Commissioner for South Africa.

It is a reservation set apart for the natives of South Africa. White people are not permitted to own land. The budget (1939-1940) estimated revenues of £420,963 and expenditures of £396,371.

Bechuanaland, area, 275,000 squares miles, land population (census, 1936), 265,756, is in the middle of Southern Africa, between South-West Africa and the Union of South Africa and Rhodesia. It is undeveloped, but cattle growing and agriculture have gained momentum, and the livestock already totals more than 600,000 head. The budget (1941-1942) estimated revenues of £237,007 and expenditures of £240,059.

Swaziland, with 6,705 square miles, and a population (census, 1936) of 156,715, lies at the southeast side of the Transvaal, in South Africa, and produces chiefly tobacco, corn, vegetables, sweet potatoes, and livestock. Some gold is yielded. The country is undeveloped. The budget (1939-1940) estimated revenues of £109,756 and expenditures of £159,812.

British West Africa

Nigeria lies in Western Africa, between Cameroon and Dahomey (French) on the Gulf of Guinea. The hinterland stretches back 600 miles to French West Africa. The tin, lead and iron ore industries are old and valuable. Railroad development has been rapid because of the mines. The chief exports are, besides tin, palm oil, palm kernels, cotton lint, cocoa, hides and skins. Revenues (1939-1940) were £6,113,126; expenditures £6,498,566.

Nigeria has an area of 372,559 square miles and a population (1939) of 20,641,814.

British Cameroons, 34,081 square miles and 868,-637 population, lies between British Nigeria and the French Congo in Western Africa. It is part of the former German colony Kamerun, the eastern and larger part of which went to France after the World War. It is a region of fertile soils, and progress is rapid toward building up valuable agricultural production—cloves, vanilla, ginger, pepper and palm oil. Ivory is an important product.

The seat of Government is Bueca and the administrator is the Governor of Nigeria.

Gambia is a British Protectorate in western Africa consisting of the island of St. Mary at the mouth of the Gambia River which flows through the French colony, Senegal. The British protectorate consists of a six-mile wide strip of territory on each side of the river, and extends northeast for 200 miles from the coast. The river is navigable for ocean-going steamers for a considerable distance at all seasons. The colony and protectorate have a total area of 4,068 square miles and a population (1931) of 199,520. Bathurst, on St. Mary's Island, is the capital. The Governor is Sir Wilfred T. Southorn (appointed, 1936). Revenues (1939) were £151,744; expenditures £205,889.

Sierra Leone lies on the west coast of Africa for 180 miles, between French Guinea and Liberia. In its capital, Freetown, it has the greatest seaport in West Africa, with an excellent harbor and a naval coaling station. The colony has been in British possession since 1767. The hinterland forms the British protectorate of Sierra Leone, which extends inland about 180 miles. The area of the colony and protectorate is 27,699 square miles; the population (1931) was 1,672,000.

The principal products are ginger, palm kernels, gold and diamonds.

Revenue (1940) was £1,139,131; expenditures were £951,999.

The Gold Coast lies along the Gulf of Guinea for 334 miles. Its area is 78,802 square miles; the population (1940) was 3,962,520. The French Ivory Coast is on the west and on the east is Togoland, formerly a German colony, and now divided by mandate of the League of Nations between Great Britain and France. The French portion, albeit 21,100 square miles, is attached for administrative purposes to Dahomey in the east, and the British, 13,041 square miles to the Gold Coast. Accra is the capital.

Under its administration also falls Ashanti, due north of the Gold Coast, and the Northern Territories, due north of Ashanti. These countries have enormous wealth in their forests, and the cultivation of cacao and rubber is being fostered. The chief exports are cacao, gold and diamonds.

Government revenues (1940-1941) were £5,143,028; expenditures £5,152,286.

There is a railway from Seccondee to Kumasi and a line from Accra to Kumasi.

Togoland, area 13,041 square miles, population (1940) 391,473, is under British Mandate administered by the Gold Coast, which it adjoins to the east.

Minor African Possessions

Zanzibar is an island of 640 square miles, 23 miles off the eastern coast of Africa, having 137,741 population (census, 1931). Lord Salisbury (1890) traded Heligoland in the North Sea with Germany for it.

It is governed by a Sultan, Seyyid Khalifa Ibn Harub, but is administered by a British resident. The island of Pemba, 30 miles to the northeast, area 380 square miles, is included in the Government. The population of the Protectorate (census, 1931) is 235,428. The people are mostly Mohammedans.

The chief industry is the production of cloves, the islands of Zanzibar and Pemba yielding the bulk of the world's supply. It is estimated that there are on both islands 48,000 acres, with 4,750,-000 trees devoted to that product, the average output of the last 20 seasons being 17,940,000 pounds, and 5,200,000 pounds of clove stems. Cocoanuts and copra are important exports. Pottery, coir fiber, rope, soap, oil, jewelry and mats are the principal manufactures. Government revenue (1940) was £465,260; expenditures £523,627.

Mauritius, an island in the Indian Ocean, 500 miles east from Madagascar, has 720 square miles, and population (1940) of 420,861. Port Louis is the capital and chief seaport.

Chief exports are sugar, copra, poonac, aloe fiber and rum. Trade is principally with Great Britain, Canada, India, Hong Kong, Union of South Africa, France, Madagascar and Reunion Islands. Government revenue (1940-1941) was estimated at 18,342,170 rupees, expenditures 18,815,561. The rupee has an average value of $.36.

Seychelles and tributary dependencies include 101 islands of 156 square miles, and a population (estimated, 1940) of 32,150, lying in the Indian Ocean near Mauritius. The capital is Victoria, a port with a coaling station. Cocoanuts are the chief product, followed by cinnamon, patchouli, mangrove bark, the yolk of birds' eggs, and phosphate. Government revenue (1940) was 694,029 rupees, expenditures 711,781. The rupee has an average value of $.36.

Somaliland, a protectorate, with 68,000 square miles, and 344,700 population, mostly Mohammedans, is in Northwest Africa, on the Gulf of Aden, with Ethiopia to the south and west and Italian Somaliland on the east. The chief town is Berbera, and the products skins, resin, gum, cattle and sheep.

St. Helena, the island made famous by the exile of the Emperor Napoleon, is 1,200 miles off the west coast of Africa, has 47 square miles and population (estimated, 1940) of 4,710. Fruits, nuts, timber, flax, lace making (flax the chief) are the industries. It is an important naval coaling station, and, although volcanic and small, has great strategic value.

Ascension, an island of volcanic origin, 34 square miles in area, 700 miles northwest of St. Helena, is noted for its sea turtles. Population (1941) was 169.

Tristan da Cunha, a group of islands of volcanic origin, 12 square miles in area, half way between the Cape and South America, difficult for boats to reach because of its rugged shores, forms one of the loneliest places on the globe. About 165 persons, descendants of shipwrecked sailors, and soldiers from St. Helena, get a rude livelihood there. The island produces apples and peaches. Sheep, geese and bullocks are reared and there are plenty of fish, but potatoes are the chief diet. Efforts to get them to leave have been fruitless.

Australia

Capital, Canberra—Area, 2,974,581 square miles—Population (1941), 7,137,000

Australia, itself a continent, is situated between 10° 41' and 39° 8', or including Tasmania 43° 39' south latitude and 113° 9' to 153° 39' east longitude in the Pacific Ocean, with the Indian Ocean on the west, and the Southern Ocean on the south.

The states and territories of the Commonwealth with their areas and populations are:

	Area sq. mi.	Population
New South Wales	309,433	2,770,348
Victoria	87,884	1,887,278
Queensland	670,500	1,015,927
South Australia	380,070	597,045
Western Australia	975,920	465,916
Tasmania	26,215	241,576
Northern Territory	523,620	6,973
Australian Capital Territory	939	12,263

The state capitals are: New South Wales, Sydney; Victoria, Melbourne; Queensland, Brisbane; South Australia, Adelaide; Western Australia, Perth; Tasmania, Hobart.

In eastern Australia mountains rise to about 7,000 ft. altitude. The central portion extends westward in rolling plains until higher elevations are reached along the west coast. The Murray River, rising on the slopes of the mountains, is navigable inland for 2,000 miles. The climate is temperate in the south, and tropical in the north.

Australia is the habitat of strange flora and fauna. The koala, or living Teddy Bear, may be seen in parks near the cities and in the "bush." He is a soft bundle of fur about 20 to 25 pounds in weight when fully grown. He never drinks, obtaining enough moisture from the young eucalyptus leaves on which he lives.

The platypus, a combination of fish, bird and animal which is equally at home in the water or on land, is one of only two creatures known to science which lay eggs and nourish their young with milk. The other is the Australian echidna or ant-eating porcupine.

There are many other strange creatures—the wombat, which burrows deeply; the Tasmanian devil and wolf; the dingo and the spotted native cat; the mole that is blind, deaf and dumb; barking and cycling lizards and house-building rodents. Birds of brilliant plumage are numerous. Parrots, red green and yellow, fly in flocks.

In the far north, wild buffalo roam where few white men live; and wild ducks and geese swarm over lagoons and lakes in flocks of almost unbelievable size.

In the north, too, are to be seen the best specimens of the aboriginal tribes. They are the most primitive of all peoples, entirely nomadic, making fire with sticks, throwing boomerangs, and killing kangaroos and other game with spears. Except in the far region of the "Never Never" land, the aborigines are quite harmless.

Australia has been settled for 150 years. The Commonwealth was proclaimed (Jan. 1, 1901). It enjoys Dominion status and is governed on the Federal plan with a Parliament consisting of a Senate and a House of Representatives.

The British Governor General is Lord Gowrie (born July 6, 1872), who took office (Jan. 23, 1936). The Prime Minister is John Curtin (Labor Party).

Seats held in the lower House by the various parties (1941): United Australia, 24; Country, 14; Federal Labor, 36, giving the Coalition Government a majority of two. In the Senate the line-up is Coalition 19, Labor 17.

Primarily an agricultural country, Australia is the greatest wool-producing country in the world. Important crops are wheat, oats, barley, corn, hay, potatoes, sugar cane, sugar beets, grapes and fruits.

The country yields gold, silver, lead, copper, tin and coal.

Education is free and compulsory. There are six universities—one in each of the State capitals. Church of England claims 44.4% of the population, the remainder being distributed as follows —Roman Catholic, 22.3%; Presbyterian, 12.3%; and Methodist, 11.8%.

Military training for all males between the ages of 18 and 26 years was compulsory (1911 to 1929) but from Nov. 1, 1929, enlistment on a voluntary basis was adopted. Compulsory training, however, was again introduced (1940). All men between the ages of 18 and 60 must register for military service. Since the outbreak of the war the strength of the Defense Forces has been greatly increased. The Royal Australian Air Force has been greatly enlarged to complete a Home Defense organization of 19 squadrons and to cope with Australia's share of the Empire Air scheme.

An emergency powers bill (1940) gave the Government the right to mobilize all national resources with the exception of conscription for overseas service. Australia is engaged in a defense program costing £453,000,000 over a period of three years. Defense expenditures (1941-1942) were £353,000,000 and are expected (1942-1943) to exceed £400,000,000.

The strength of the military forces (Jan. 1, 1939) was 42,895, including Permanent Forces, organized for peace time duties, to prepare for defense and to form the basis for the technical services.

Australia also maintains a Navy, two 10,000-ton cruisers, three of 7,000 tons, one of 5,100 tons with several minor craft (Jan. 1, 1940). The active service personnel (1939) was 5,170 but this has been vastly increased since the start of the war. Additional destroyers and mine sweepers are being constructed in the naval expansion program.

The monetary unit is the Australian pound with an average value of $3.21. The budget (1941-1942) estimated revenues at £185,000,000 and normal expenditures of £324,965,000.

Pension acts provide for payments of old age and invalid pensions, including the blind, the unemployed, victims of tuberculosis and in some cases to dependents of former soldiers. A Maternity Act provides for the payment of pensions for every livable child born in Australia.

The Australian Government Trade Commissioner in the United States is L. R. MacGregor, C. B. E., 630 Fifth Ave., New York City.

AUSTRALIAN TERRITORIES

Papua, or British New Guinea, is the southeastern part of the Island of New Guinea north from Australia. Its area is estimated at 90,540 square miles with an estimated native population of 338,822.

The European population (1940) was 1,822. Queensland annexed the territory (1883) but control was taken over by the Federal Government of Australia (1906).

The Commonwealth Government pays an annual subsidy—£42,500. Revenues (1940-1941) were £189,518; expenditures £189,297. The chief exports are copra, gold, rubber and desiccated cocoanut.

Territory of New Guinea, formerly German New Guinea, the northeast quarter of the island, was placed by the League of Nations after the war under mandate to Australia. It includes the **Bismarck Archipelago,** 19,200 square miles, and the former **German Solomon Islands,** 4,100 square miles. The total area of the mandated territory is about 93,000 square miles, with a native population estimated roughly at 668,871. The white population was 6,498 (June 30, 1939).

Norfolk Island was taken over by the Government of the Commonwealth of Australia (1913). It has an area of 8,528 acres and a population of 983. The soil is very fertile and is suitable for the cultivation of citrus fruits, bananas and coffee.

Nauru Island, formerly German, was mandated by the League of Nations to the British Empire. Its area is about eight square miles; its population is 3,460. It has valuable phosphate deposits.

New Zealand

Capital, Wellington—Area, 103,934 square miles—Population (1940), 1,640,901

The main islands of New Zealand, a self-governing British Dominion of the South Pacific Ocean, lie between the parallels of 34° and 48° and the meridians of 166° and 179° east longitude, about 1,200 miles to the eastward of Australia. Including the remote islands in the north and the Ross Dependency in the far south, the reach of New Zealand is from the tropics to Antarctica.

New Zealand comprises **North Island,** 44,281 square miles; **South Island,** 58,092 square miles; **Stewart Island,** 670 square miles; **Chatham Islands,** 372 square miles. Both the North and South Islands slightly exceed 500 miles in length. Cook Strait, separating the two islands, is only 16 miles in width at its narrowest part.

Additional islands within the geographical boundaries of New Zealand are Campbell Island, Solander Island, the Three Kings, Auckland, Antipodes, Bounty, and Snares Islands (a total area of 307 square miles). Islands annexed to New Zealand are the Cook Islands, Kermadec Islands, Niue Island, and certain other small islands in the Pacific (a total area of 212 square miles), so that the actual New Zealand aggregate is 103,934 square miles.

The territory of Western Samoa, including chiefly the large islands of Savaii (703 square miles) and Upolu (430 square miles) is administered by New Zealand under mandate of the League of Nations. New Zealand is also associated with Great Britain and Australia in the mandate for the administration of the very valuable phosphate island of Nauru. The control of Tokelau or Union Islands, formerly part of the Gilbert and Ellice Islands colony, was transferred to New Zealand (1926).

New Zealand was discovered (1642) by Abel Janszoon Tasman, a Dutch navigator, and its coasts were explored by Capt. James Cook (1769-1770). British sovereignty was proclaimed (1840) with organized settlement commencing in the same year. Representative institutions were granted (1853) and (1907) the Colony became a Dominion. The capital is Wellington.

The Maoris (the native race) are Polynesians of high intelligence, their forebears having migrated from the Eastern Pacific several centuries ago. They numbered 90,980 (March 31, 1940).

New Zealand has a remarkable diversity of landscape—plains, downs and broad valleys, extensive tracts of hills and mountains, numerous rivers and many lakes. The Sutherland Waterfalls, with a drop of 1,900 ft., is one of the tallest and most beautiful in the world. The climate ranges from the sub-tropical in the north to the mildly temperate in the south. The country has the second lowest death rate, and the lowest infant mortality rate, in the world.

The central plateau of the North Island possesses thermal attractions renowned for their scenic and healing properties, while the surrounding streams and lakes provide trout fishing of world fame. Off the northern peninsula rod and reel sea fishing has resulted in several world records.

The South Island of New Zealand presents scenery of a totally different nature from that of the North. The great range of the Southern Alps (highest point, Mt. Cook, 12,349 ft.) stretches from end to end of the Island and forms the eastern side; on the western side the towering mountain slopes crowd in upon the coastline, their glaciers and snow-fields being easily accessible from the densely forested foothills.

New Zealand enjoys Dominion status within the British Empire and is governed by a Governor-General, representing the King of Great Britain and the British Dominions, and a General Assembly consisting of a Legislative Council and a House of Representatives. The Governor-General is Sir Cyril L. N. Newall (appointed 1941). Membership of the Legislative Council is achieved by nomination for a 7-year term, and of the House of Representatives by election on a universal franchise for a 3-year term. The Prime Minister is Peter Fraser.

A War Administration of 13 members was formed (June 24, 1942) but all members of the Labor Government, not appointed to the War Administration, continue to hold their existing posts. The Government has seven representatives in the War Administration and the Opposition six. An electoral truce for the war and a year thereafter was negotiated the same day.

The political complexion of the House of Representatives (elected Oct. 15, 1938) follows—Labor, 52; National, 24; Independents, 4.

New Zealand is primarily a farming country. For decades the sheep held supremacy in value of exports (wool, meat, tallow, pelts, etc.) by a large margin, but during recent years dairy products, butter and cheese have taken first place on occasions. Two-thirds of the surface of the country is suitable for farming.

Compulsory military service at home and abroad applies to all males more than 16 years old with conscription for foreign service which is restricted to the 21-41 age group. The man power is enrolled in the general reserve. The air force continued on the voluntary basis.

There were (1941) 3,570 miles of government-owned and 198 miles of privately owned railways.

Commercial air service at home reported (1941) 9,808 hours flown, 1,070,292 miles flown, 42,452 passengers carried, 133,838 lbs. of mail carried and 204,513 lbs. of freight. On overseas service (1941) there were 4,091 hours flown, 594,720 miles flown, 2,411 passengers carried, 128,913 lbs. of mail and 38,102 lbs. of freight.

A general social insurance law, modifying and extending the former pension laws, became effective (April, 1939). The act provided for superannuation and old age and invalidity benefits, widows' and orphans' benefits, family allowances, sickness and accident benefits, unemployment benefits, and a national health service. All persons 16 years of age and more are required to be registered and to pay the registration fee and a charge on salaries, wages and other income. The Government and New Zealand Corporations also contribute to the general operating fund. A national free medicine plan went into effect (May, 1941).

Pensions (1941) cost £10,500,000, medical and hospital benefits £2,500,000 and administrative costs were £500,000. Revenue under the social security tax was £11,000,000 and although the social security fund received £3,500,000 credit from general taxation, it had almost the same sum left in credit at the end of the year.

The monetary unit is the New Zealand pound with an average value of $3.25. Government revenues (1941-1942) are estimated at £39,296,000 and expenditures at £39,212,000.

Foreign trade (1941-1942) recorded exports of more than £69,000,000 and imports of £50,000,000.

Western Samoa was German Samoa, which included Savaii and Upolu, the two largest of the Samoan Islands in the western Pacific, and was occupied by the British (Aug. 29, 1914). This territory was assigned as a mandate from the League of Nations to New Zealand (1920).

Savaii is 48 miles by 25 miles and has an area of about 703 square miles. Upolu has an area of about 430 square miles. Both are mountainous, fertile and well watered. The population (1941) of the two aggregated 62,391. The chief exports are copra, bananas and cocoa.

The Union or Tokelau Islands, formerly part of the Gilbert and Ellice Islands Colony, were transferred to the jurisdiction of New Zealand (1926). The area of the three clusters of islets is four square miles, and population (1941), 1,380.

British Oceania

Fiji Islands are from 200 to 250 in number, with an area of 7,083 square miles, and a population (1940) of 220,787 (4,287 Europeans). They are situated in the South Pacific Ocean, due east of northern Australia.

The larger islands are mountainous, reaching altitudes of 4,000 ft., with one peak of 5,000. The southern islands contain dense forests with many valuable woods. The inlands are very fertile and well watered. The climate is for the tropics comparatively cool; the temperature seldom rising above 90°, or falling below 60°, and the rainfall is abundant.

The islands form a British Crown Colony. The capital is Suva.

Bananas, coconuts, maize, sugar cane, rice and tobacco are the principal products.

The budget (1940) estimated revenues at £938,282 and expenditures at £947,721.

In Fiji, according to Dr. Dorothy M. Spencer of the University of Pennsylvania, the human head is held to be sacred and it is an insult to reach above the head of another person.

Tonga Islands, or Friendly Islands, form a protectorate, with an area of 256 square miles, and a population (1939) of 34,130. The native Queen is Salote Tubou, who succeeded her father George II (April 12, 1938). Government revenue (1939-1940) was £56,867, expenditures £69,687.

The British Solomon Islands, a protectorate, number 15 large islands and four groups of small islands, with a total area of about 375,000 sq. m., and a population (1931) of 94,105, of which 497 are Europeans. Exports are chiefly copra and ivory nuts. Government revenue (1940-1941) was £51,-320, expenditures £65,848.

Gilbert and Ellice Islands Colony. The group of islands in the Colony was proclaimed a Protectorate (1892) and, at the request of the native Governments, was annexed (Nov. 10, 1915) as the Gilbert and Ellice Islands Colony. The Colony includes the Ellice Islands, Fanning, Washington and Ocean Islands, Christmas Islands (annexed by Great Britain, 1888, and included in the Colony, Nov. 1919), which is the largest atoll in the Pacific, the Phoenix Group and the Gilbert Islands. The total area is 180 square miles and the population (1938) 32,838. Exports are chiefly of copra and phosphates. Government revenue (1939-1940) was £64,846, expenditures £79,453.

The Gilbert Islands were occupied by the Japanese (Dec. 1941).

Pitcairn Island is situate in the Pacific, equidistant from America and Australia. The Island was discovered (1767) by Carteret but was not inhabited until 23 years later when the mutineers of the Bounty landed there. Their existence became known (1808) when ships visited the Island and gave assistance to the mutineers and their Otaheite women. The population became too large for the resources of the Island and the mutineers and their women, 192 in all, moved (1856) to Norfolk Island. Forty returned later to Pitcairn and the population increased (1879) to 90. The area is two square miles and population (1941) 193. It is a British Colony by settlement and was brought (1898) within the jurisdiction of the High Commissioner of the Western Pacific.

British South American Possessions
GUIANA

British Guiana is on the north shore of South America, with Venezuela on the west, Dutch Guiana on the east, and Brazil on the south. It is a Crown Colony administered by a governor and a small elected legislative body. The area is 89,480 square miles; the population (estimated 1940) 346,982. Georgetown is the capital.

There are many beautiful waterfalls in British Guiana, including Kukenaam, which has been generally conceded to be the tallest in the world with a drop of 2,000 ft. Dr. Paul Arthur Zahl, research associate at Haskins Laboratory, Schenectady, N. Y., reported (May 11, 1938) the discovery (May 8) of a waterfalls of 3,500 ft. in the Karanang River in the heart of Guiana's richest diamond area, 80 miles northeast of Mt. Roraima. Another famous waterfalls—Kaiteur—is noted for its scenic splendor.

Much of British Guiana is jungle land. but there are extensive deposits of gold, diamonds, manganese, mica and bauxite. Timber is also an important export, besides sugar, rice, rum, molasses, balata, charcoal and copra.

A site on the Demarara River, 25 miles from the sea, was leased (1940) to the United States for a defense base.

The budget (1940) estimated revenues at £1,452,-974 and expenditures £1,498,657.

The Falkland Islands lie 300 miles east of the Strait of Magellan at the southern end of South America. Their main value is in their strategic location, although there are large sheep farms and whaling interests.

There are more than 100 islands in the group. The area is 4,618 square miles; the population (estimated 1940) was 2,785. Wool is the chief export.

Although Great Britain has held possession of the Islands since 1834, Argentina refuses to renounce her claim of ownership.

South Georgia is a whaling station. Its area is 1,000 square miles. The population (estimated 1939) consists of 705. Whale produce is the principal export.

Canada

(DOMINION OF CANADA)

Capital, Ottawa—Area, 3,694,863 square miles—Population (1941), 11, 419,896

The boundaries of Canada are: On the east, Baffin Bay, Labrador, the Gulf of St. Lawrence and the Atlantic: on the south, the Atlantic, Maine, New Hampshire, Vermont, New York, the St. Lawrence and the Great Lakes, Minnesota, North Dakota, Montana, Idaho, Washington and the Juan de Fuca Strait; and on the West, Alaska and the Pacific Ocean. Canada includes all the Arctic islands in an area beginning half-way between Greenland and Baffin and extending westward to 141° longitude, which coincides approximately with the Alaskan border. Altogether, Canada has 24,500 miles of coastline. The 4,000-mile boundary between Canada and the United States has been unfortified for more than one hundred years.

The country has an extremely varied topography —mountains in the West, then foothills and prairies, the barrens north of Lake Superior, the open lands of Ontario, the rocky Laurentian district in Quebec, with the fertile Eastern Townships to the south of it, and then plains sloping down to sea level in the East; the mountains of New England extend north into Canada, where they attain to practically the same height as in the United States.

Lakes, large and small, abound in Canada. Some of them exceed in size the famed Great Lakes on the United States border.

Great Bear Lake in the Canadian Northwest Territory, is larger than Erie by 1,550 square miles and larger than Ontario by 3,950 square miles. Great Slave Lake is nearly the size of Great Bear. Lake Winnipeg in Manitoba is about 2,000 square miles larger than Lake Ontario. Eleven Canadian lakes are above 1,100 square miles in extent. The lakes wholly within Canada are of high importance to transportation and fisheries, climate and sport.

The once common misconception that Canada is almost Arctic has been nearly dispelled. The climate of the southern parts of Canada corresponds to that of the northern States. The mean annual temperature is 49° at Victoria; 34° at Winnipeg; 44° at Toronto; 40° at Fredericton; and 44° Fahrenheit at Yarmouth. These figures show only slight variations from West to East, but the extremes are much greater in the prairie and eastern provinces than in British Columbia.

Like the United States, Canada is a federation with provincial governments similar on the whole to the State governments of the United States, and with Ottawa corresponding to Washington, D. C., as the chief legislative, executive and judicial seat of the country. The members of the Senate are nominated for life by summons of the Governor-General. The House of Commons is elected directly by the people for terms of five years.

The House of Commons elected March 26, 1940, stands:

Liberals, 177; Conservatives, 40; Independent-Conservative, 1; Cooperative Commonwealth Federation, 8; New Democracy, 10; Unity, 1; Independent, 1; Lib.-Prog., 3; Ind.-Lib., 3; vacant, 1. Total 245.

The Communist party and the National Unity (Fascist) party were outlawed with fourteen other organizations (June 5, 1940) under the Defense of Canada regulations.

The Governor-General of Canada is the Earl of Athlone (born April 14, 1874). He took office June 21, 1940.

The Dominion Cabinet in order of precedence follows:

Prime Minister, President of the Privy Council, Secretary of State for External Affairs—W. L. Mackenzie King.

Minister without Portfolio—J. K. King.

Minister of Mines and Resources—Thomas Alexander Crerar.

Minister of Justice and Attorney General of Canada—Louis St. Laurent.

Minister of Public Works and Transport—Alphonse Fournier.

Minister of National Defense—James L. Ralston.

Minister of Pensions and National Health—Ian Alastair Mackenzie.

Associate Minister of National Defense and Minister of National Defense for Air—Charles Gavan Power.

Minister of Finance—James Lorimer Ilsley.

Minister of Fisheries—Ernest Bertrand.

Minister of Munitions and Supply—Clarence Decatur Howe.

Minister of Agriculture—James Garfield Gardiner.

Minister of Labor—Humphrey Mitchell.

Minister of Trade and Commerce—James A. MacKinnon.

Secretary of State—Norman Alexander McLarty.

Minister of National Revenue—Colin W. Gibson.

Postmaster General—William Pate Mulock.

Minister of National Defense for Naval Services—Angus L. Macdonald.

Minister of National War Services—Maj. Gen. L. R. LaFleche.

The British High Commissioner to Canada is Malcom MacDonald.

Canada is largely agricultural, although manufacturing industries now dominate the economic life of the nation. The principal crops are wheat, oats, barley, rye, flaxseed, potatoes, roots, tobacco, and corn. Dairy and fruit products are enormous. The wool yield is considerable. Fishing is a huge commercial enterprise, and fresh and canned varieties are an important export. The chief kinds of fish marketed are salmon, lobsters, cod, herring, halibut, white fish, sardines, haddock, pickerel, trout and pilchards. Furs are a prolific source of income and the fox, mink, muskrat, beaver, raccoon, marten, and fisher are raised commercially on large farms. Hydroelectric power is extensive.

The country is rich in minerals, particularly gold, although deposits of copper, lead, nickel, platinum, silver, zinc, coal, natural gas and petroleum are mined. Canada leads the world in production of asbestos.

The most important manufactures and their gross value (1940) were:

Iron and its products	$906,000,000
Wood and paper	751,000,000
Vegetable products	738,000,000
Textile products	547,000,000
Animal products	546,000,000
Non-ferrous metal products	541,000,000
Non-metallic minerals	256,000,000
Chemicals and allied products	194,000,000
Miscellaneous industries	50,000,000

The St. Lawrence River is navigable to ocean-going vessels for 600 miles, as far as Montreal, which is by virtue of its Great Lakes connections and its proximity to London and Liverpool, one of the greatest grain exporting harbors on the continent. The Port of Montreal has nine miles of deep-draft wharf, capable of accommodating 100 large ocean steamers.

Of the railways in Canada, the Canadian Pacific is the great privately owned corporation. The Canadian National Railway System operates practically all other important lines in the Dominion.

Canada (Jan. 1, 1941) had 222,580 telephones in Government systems and 1,238,450 in private companies, a total of 1,461,030 being 12.8 to every 100 persons, and 3.31 of the world's telephones. The number of licensed radio receiving sets (March 31, 1942) was 1,615,473.

There was completed (1941) a highway from Halifax to Vancouver, a distance of 4,190 miles, at a cost estimated between $75,000,000 and $100,-000,000. The highway provides a motorist a means of travel from Halifax to Vancouver without passing through the United States on a road that has no grade in excess of five per cent and no curve in excess of four degrees. The road provides an east-west artery for military uses and opens a vast virgin territory.

In two years Canadian Airways (a part of the Canadian Pacific Railway Air Services) operated 3,067 round trips on its services between Victoria and Vancouver. Since the service started (March 1, 1939) the company's planes have flown 1,017,112 passenger miles and carried more than 100,000 pounds of mail. Revenue miles flown (1941) were 11,800,661. The number of revenue passengers increased from 137,690 (1940) to 193,097 (1941) and revenue freight carried rose from 12,899,998 pounds to 14,804,681. Mail carried increased from 2,737,122 pounds (1940) to 3,388,634 (1941).

The monetary unit of Canada is the dollar. As from Sept. 16, 1939, buying and selling rates for the U. S. Dollar, as set by the Foreign Exchange Control Board, were $1.10-$1.11, respectively.

The Bank of Canada was incorporated as a central bank by Act of Parliament (1934). It capital stock then fixed at $500,000 was increased (June 18, 1936) to $10,000,000 of which $100,000 Class B shares were issued to the Dominion of Canada at par. The rest (Class A shares of $50 each) were sold to the public and the maximum holding permitted to one person is 50 shares. Directors, officers or employees of the chartered banks may not hold shares of the Bank. Shares may be held only by British subjects ordinarily resident in Canada, or by corporations controlled by such persons. The Bank became (Aug. 15, 1938) a wholly government-owned institution, the capital being reduced to $5,000,000.

The statement of Aug. 31, 1942 showed assets and liabilities of $885,656,426.

Canada—with its great stretches of virgin timberland, its rolling hills and skyscraping mountains; its many lakes and streams and rivers; its odd villages, customs and picturesque peoples—has become the vacationland of thousands of American tourists. It is reached by many highways.

Ontario's attractions include its great variety of developed summer resorts, its extensive fishing and hunting areas and its multitude of lakes and rivers. Quebec's are its old-world atmosphere, its historical traditions and its diversified scenery. Nova Scotia and New Brunswick offer moose hunting and salmon fishing, sailing and surf bathing. In the Bay of Chaleur, which New Brunswick shares with Quebec's famous Gaspe Peninsula, the tourist finds the warmest sea water north of New York.

Western Alberta and Eastern British Columbia have the Rockies, which means mountain climbing, canoe and pack trail trips and matchless scenery. The Yukon has the midnight sun and unexcelled sport for the hunter of big game and game fish. The Northwest Territories have become popular among Americans, some of whom camp and canoe on the Mackenzie River, 300 miles beyond the Arctic Circle.

Among Canada's greatest tourist attractions are her national parks, consisting of approximately 29,704 square miles of outstanding scenic beauty. They conserve wild life under natural conditions, preserve in its primitive state the grandeur of scenic regions and commemorate persons and events of especial importance in the nation's history. They may be divided into three groups: the scenic and recreational parks of the Rockies, Selkirks and prairies and Eastern Canada; the wild animal parks; and the national historic parks.

The first group includes Banff, Jasper and Waterton Lakes Parks in Alberta; Kootenay, Yoho, Glacier and Mount Revelstoke Parks in British Columbia; Prince Albert Park in Saskatchewan; and Riding Mountain Park in Manitoba. In Ontario there are three smaller recreational parks, Point Pelee, Georgian Bay Islands and the St. Lawrence Islands Park. Recent additions to the system of recreational parks are the Cape Breton Highlands Park in Nova Scotia and a shore-line park area on the northern coast of Prince Edward Island.

The wild animal parks include Elk Island Park

in Alberta, noted for its large herd of buffalo, and Nemiskam Park, also in Alberta, which is a sanctuary for prong-horned antelope. Fort Anne Park in Nova Scotia and Fort Beausejour in New Brunswick are the outstanding historic parks.

In Nova Scotia is the Evangeline country, the land of Acadian memories. Here are found the largest aggregation of apple orchards in the British Dominions. Grand Pre, made classic ground by Longfellow's "Evangeline," attracts visitors from all over the world to see Evangeline Park, established on the site of the original Acadian village, with its ancient well still intact, its old willows still surviving. A replica of the original Acadian church houses relics of the first settlers and in the gardens are flowers brought from the ancestral homes of the leaders of the Acadian pioneers.

Automobiles entering Canada for touring purposes are shown in the following table:

	1941	1940	1939
Maritime Provinces	498,014	635,191	786,236
Quebec	372,892	359,299	456,613
Ontario	2,546,320	2,178,508	2,701,780
Manitoba	43,691	51,087	59,913
Saskatchewan	24,225	23,438	23,439
Alberta	23,594	24,578	24,272
British Columbia	150,209	135,251	160,563
Total	3,658,945	3,407,353	4,212,816

Five distinct white races are represented in Nova Scotia: English, Scottish, French-Canadian, Irish and Hanoverian, all holding to many traits of their forefathers. The Acadians, first white settlers, from Normandy and Brittany, cling to their own customs and traditions, thus making a contact with the long ago. The Hanoverians settled largely in Lunenburg and today their descendants, skilled sailors and fishermen, possess one of the finest fishing fleets in the world. The Highland Scots settled in Cape Breton Island. Pictou and Antigonish counties, and their descendants reserve the kilt and plaid for ceremonial occasions and cherish the Gaelic language of their forebears.

Ancient Quebec, only walled city in North America, sitting in a gigantic amphitheater of hills, former capital of the Dominion, is one of the oldest cities in America (founded in 1608), with elongated, crooked streets, turreted battlements, casemented windows and other medieval aspects. Some points of interest to the tourist are: the Fortifications, comprising the Citadel, on a promontory 350 ft. high; the Enclosing Wall, two miles long; the three City Gates, part of the city's old defense system; the Battlefields Park, site of the Battle of the Plains of Abraham (1759); Wolfe's Cove, with its goat-path up the cliff, scaled by British soldiers for the Battle of the Plains; Dufferin Terrace, world-famed boardwalk overlooking the St. Lawrence; Montmorency Park, location of Canada's first House of Parliament; the Ramparts, with their ancient cannon; Avenue des Braves, Ste. Foy Park, where the last clash between the British and the French occurred; Notre Dame des Victoires Church, built in 1688.

Two miles outside of the village of Beaupre, on Highway 15, stands the shrine of Ste. Anne de Beaupre, founded (1650) by storm-wearied Breton sailors and today one of the most famous places in the world. It is the home of countless miracles and is annually visited by thousands of pilgrims. A chapel erected by the sailors to Ste. Anne in thanksgiving for their deliverance is still carefully preserved.

The census (1931) gave the religious population as follows:

Roman Catholics	4,098,734
United Church	2,017,375
Anglicans	1,635,615
Presbyterians	870,728
Baptists	443,341
Lutherans	394,194
Greek Catholics	186,654
Jews	155,614
Greek Orthodox	102,389
Miscellaneous creeds*	456,100
Not given	16,042
Total	10,376,786

*Includes pagans.

The population of the chief Canadian cities, 1941 census, follows:

Montreal	890,234	Ottawa	150,861	London	77,105	St. John, N. B.	50,084
Toronto	657,612	Quebec	147,908	Halifax	69,326	Victoria	42,907
Vancouver	271,597	Windsor, Ont.	104,415	Verdun, P. Q.	66,503	Saskatoon	42,320
Winnipeg	217,994	Edmonton	92,404	Regina	57,389	Three Rivers	41,811
Hamilton	164,719	Calgary	87,267				

Canadian Statistics

Source: S. A. Cudmore, Dominion Statistician; revised figures are given for 1911 to agree with boundary changes made in 1912.

LAND AND FRESH WATER AREA, AND POPULATION BY PROVINCES

Provinces, Territories	Capitals	Area in Square Miles			Population		
		Land	Water	Total	1921	1931	1941
Prince Edward	Charlottetown	2,184	.....	2,184	88,615	88,038	99,919
Nova Scotia	Halifax	20,743	325	21,068	523,837	512,846	573,190
New Brunswick	Fredericton	27,473	512	27,985	387,876	408,219	453,377
Quebec	Quebec	523,534	71,000	594,534	2,360,665	2,874,255	3,319,640
Ontario	Toronto	363,282	49,300	412,582	2,933,662	3,431,683	3,756,632
Manitoba	Winnipeg	219,723	26,789	246,512	610,118	700,139	722,447
Saskatchewan	Regina	237,975	13,725	251,700	757,510	921,785	887,747
Alberta	Edmonton	248,800	6,485	255,285	588,454	731,605	788,893
British Columbia	Victoria	359,279	6,976	366,255	524,582	694,263	809,203
Yukon Territory	Dawson	205,346	1,730	207,076	4,157	4,230	4,687
Northwest Territories	.....	1,258,217	51,465	1,309,682	7,988	9,723	10,661
Total		3,466,556	228,307	3,694,863	8,787,949	10,376,786	11,419,896

Of the population (1931) there were 5,374,541 males and 5,002,245 females; population per square mile, 3.0. Of the males, 3,179,444 were single, 2,033,240 were married, 148,954 were widowed, 4,049 were divorced, and 8,854 were not given. Of the females, 2,771,968 were single, 1,937,950 were married, 288,641 were widowed, 3,392 were divorced, and 294 were not given.

Of the total population (1931) of 10,376,786, 5,381,071 were of British; and 2,927,990 of French origin. There remain 2,067,725, comprehending the following main classes: German, 473,544; Scandinavian, 228,049; Ukrainian, 225,113; Hebrew, 156,726; Dutch, 148,962; Polish, 145,503; Italian, 98,173; Russian, 88,148; Austrian, 48,639; Chinese, 46,519; Finnish, 43,885; Hungarian, 40,582; Bulgarian and Roumanian, 32,216; Belgian, 27,585; Japanese, 23,342.

Owing to the Labrador Boundary Award, the area of Canada was reduced (1927) by 112,400 square miles—106,970 square miles of land and 5,430 square miles of water.

CANADIAN IMMIGRATION

Year (Fiscal)	From United Kingdm	From United States	From Other Count.	Total	Year (Fiscal)	From United Kingdm	From United States	From Other Count.	Total
1910	59,790	91,048	45,206	196,044	1927	49,784	21,025	73,180	143,989
1912	138,121	114,326	82,406	334,853	1928	50,872	25,007	75,721	151,600
1913	150,542	119,418	112,881	382,841	1929	58,880	30,560	78,283	167,723
1914	142,622	89,892	134,726	367,240	1930	64,082	30,727	68,479	163,288
1915	43,276	41,768	41,734	126,778	1931	27,584	24,280	36,359	88,223
1916	8,664	25,853	2,936	37,453	1932	7,088	14,297	4,367	25,752
1917	8,282	51,143	5,703	65,128	1933	3,097	13,196	3,489	19,782
1918	3,178	58,185	4,582	65,915	1934	2,260	7,740	3,903	13,903
1919	9,914	31,955	7,073	48,942	1935	2,198	5,960	3,978	12,136
1920	59,603	40,728	8,077	108,408	1936	2,049	5,121	3,933	11,103
1921	74,262	38,310	26,156	138,728	1937	2,264	5,113	4,646	12,023
1922	39,020	21,670	21,634	82,324	1938	2,972	5,643	7,030	15,645
1923	34,508	16,566	16,372	67,446	1939	3,373	5,663	8,092	17,128
1924	72,919	17,211	55,120	145,250	1940	3,566	5,748	6,891	16,205
1925	53,178	15,818	42,366	111,362	1941	3,104	7,443	949	11,496
1926	37,030	18,778	40,256	96,064	1942	2,182	6,311	372	8,865

The Canadian fiscal year since 1907 ends with March 31.

CHIEF SOURCES OF REVENUE—CONSOLIDATED FUND ONLY

Year Ending Mar. 31	War Tax Revenue			Customs	Excise	Post Office	Public Works and Canals	Dominion Lands	Int. Rec'd from Invest.	Total Rec'pts
	Income Tax	Sales, etc.	Other Taxes							
	$1,000	$1,000	$1,000	$1,000	$1,000	$1,000	$1,000	$1,000	$1,000	$1,000
1923	59,712	106,483	15,441	118,056	35,762	29,017	1,229	2,348	16,465	394,615
1924	54,204	120,676	7,156	121,501	38,182	28,865	1,400	2,282	11,916	396,838
1925	56,248	85,811	5,105	108,147	38,603	28,783	1,391	2,390	11,332	346,834
1926	55,572	98,097	3,627	127,355	42,924	30,335	1,416	2,804	8,535	380,746
1927	47,386	105,613	3,168	141,969	48,513	29,069	1,502	3,327	8,559	398,696
1928	56,571	90,223	3,525	156,986	57,401	31,563	1,809	3,689	10,938	422,718
1929	59,422	83,007	2,600	187,206	63,685	30,612	1,690	4,070	12,228	455,464
1930	69,021	63,409	1,656	179,430	65,036	33,345	1,505	4,139	13,515	441,412
1931	71,048	34,735	1,538	131,209	57,747	30,212	1,444	1,655	10,421	349,487
1932	61,254	59,606	1,405	104,133	48,655	32,235	1,336	485	9,330	329,709
1933	62,067	52,192	2,154	76,073	37,834	30,928	1,119	459	11,221	306,637
1934	61,399	106,576	2,077	66,305	35,494	30,893	1,232	419	11,148	324,062
1935	66,808	112,192	5,692	76,562	43,190	31,248	1,092	516	10,963	358,475
1936	82,710	112,733	3,455	74,005	44,410	32,508	1,141	458	10,614	372,222
1937	102,365	152,473	1,984	83,771	45,957	34,275	1,278	478	11,231	445,029
1938	120,366	180,819	1,974	93,456	52,037	35,546	2,184	540	13,120	510,298
1939	142,026	161,711	1,905	78,751	51,314	35,288	1,020	680	13,163	498,017
1940	134,449	166,028	1,875	104,301	61,032	36,729	1,068	676	13,393	541,616
1941	248,143[1]	284,167	25,865	130,757	88,608	40,383	[2]	[2]	14,911	859,755
1942	510,243	453,425	144,762	142,392	110,091	44,994			25,826	1,463,824

Note—The total includes other unenumerated items.

INSURANCE IN FORCE IN CANADA—DOMINION COMPANIES

Life—In Force at End of Year				Fire—At Risk at End of Year			
	Dollars		Dollars		Dollars		Dollars
1923	3,433,508,673	1933	6,247,625,974	1923	7,224,475,267	1933	9,008,262,736
1924	3,763,996,472	1934	6,220,725,929	1924	7,583,297,899	1934	8,804,840,676
1925	4,159,019,848	1935	6,259,158,404	1925	8,051,444,136	1935	8,782,698,099
1926	4,610,196,334	1936	6,403,037,477	1926	8,287,732,966	1936	9,248,273,260
1927	5,044,408,834	1937	6,541,625,046	1927	8,761,579,512	1937	9,773,324,476
1928	5,607,645,623	1938	6,630,183,594	1928	6,020,513,839	1938	9,953,905,417
1929	6,157,262,207	1939	6,776,262,587	1929	9,431,169,592	1939	10,200,346,551
1930	6,492,283,194	1940	6,975,318,346	1930	9,672,996,917	1940	10,737,568,226
1931	6,622,267,793			1931	9,544,641,293	1941	11,391,929,823
1932	6,471,608,546			1932	9,301,747,991		

[1] National defense tax ($106,637,000), shown under income tax; excess profits tax ($135,168,000), shown under "other taxes." [2] Net now shown separately in preliminary statement.

CANADIAN BANKING STATISTICS

Year (a)	Chartered Banks				P. O. and Gov. Savings Bank Depos. (c)
	Paid Up Capital	Assets	Liabilities(b)	Deposits	
	Dollars	Dollars	Dollars	Dollars	Dollars
1930	144,560,874	3,237,073,853	3,214,730,383	2,516,611,587	26,086,036
1931	144,674,853	3,066,018,472	3,048,304,073	2,422,834,828	24,750,227
1932	144,500,000	2,869,429,779	2,852,649,789	2,256,639,530	23,919,677
1933	144,500,000	2,831,393,641	2,819,684,260	2,236,841,539	23,920,915
1934	144,916,667	2,837,919,961	2,826,241,267	2,274,607,936	23,158,919
1935	145,500,000	2,956,577,704	2,946,200,352	2,426,760,923	22,547,006
1936	145,500,000	3,144,506,755	3,134,122,223	2,614,895,597	22,047,287
1937	145,500,000	3,317,087,132	3,304,971,653	2,775,530,413	21,879,593
1938	145,500,000	3,348,708,580	3,335,934,905	2,823,686,934	22,587,233
1939	145,500,000	3,591,564,586	3,577,601,099	3,060,859,111	23,045,576
1940	145,500,000	3,707,316,459	3,690,354,825	3,179,523,062	23,100,118
1941	145,500,000	4,008,381,256	3,991,287,347	3,464,781,844	22,176,633
1942	145,500,000(d)	4,194,549,584(d)	4,176,908,568(d)	3,626,907,190(d)	21,671,413

(a) Average of the 12 monthly statements for each year. (b) Includes liabilities to shareholders.
(c) Figures are as Mar. 31. (d) Figures are as at June 30.

CHIEF CONSOLIDATED AND TOTAL EXPENDITURES

Fiscal Year	Interest on Public Debt	Old Age Pensions	Nat'l Defense	Pensions, War, Milit'ry & Civil	Post Office	Total, Ordin'ry Exp'nditure	Capital Exp'nditure	Special Exp'nditure	Gov't Owned Enterprises	Grand Total Exp'nditure
	$1,000	$1,000	$1,000	$1,000	$1,000	$1,000	$1,000	$1,000	$1,000	$1,000
1935	138,533	14,942	13,920	43,786	30,252	359,700	7,107	60,659	50,136	478,106
1936	134,549	16,764	16,593	43,337	31,437	372,539	6,544	102,047	50,940	532,585
1937	137,410	21,149	21,678	43,356	31,906	387,112	3,491	78,003	44,218	532,060
1938	132,117	28,653	32,760	42,823	33,762	414,891	4,430	68,534	44,833	534,408
1939	127,996	29,044	34,432	42,793	35,455	413,832	5,424	71,895	58,943	553,063
1940	129,315	29,977	13,189[1]	42,869	36,726	398,323	7,030	207,404	42,079	680,794
1941	139,179	29,912	194[1]	42,196	38,700	390,620	3,358	794,914	18,182	1,249,601
1942	155,018	29,612	260[1]	41,244	41,502	444,778	3,430	1,403,650	1,214	1,885,066

Note—The National Defense expenditures include Militia, Naval Service, Air Force (covering also Civil Government air operations. Railway and Canals include Collection and Income. The total includes other unenumerated items.

[1]Since Sept. 1, 1939, nearly all National Defence expenditure, including administration, has been charged under the War appropriation classified as Special Expenditures.

ASSETS, NET DEBT, AND PER CAPITA TAXATION

Year Ending March 31	Assets	Net Debt	Per Capita Taxation	Year Ending March 31	Assets	Net Debt	Per Capita Taxation
	Dollars	Dollars	Dollars		Dollars	Dollars	Dollars
1935	359,845,411	2,846,110,958	27.84	1939	485,761,502	3,152,559,314	38.51
1936	425,843,510	3,006,100,517	28.77	1940	687,976,735	3,271,259,647	40.95
1937	458,568,937	3,083,952,202	34.76	1941	1,362,707,671	3,648,691,449	68.09
1938	438,570,044	3,101,667,570	40.03	1942	....	4,045,221,161	119.17

INDUSTRIAL AND COMMERCIAL FAILURES IN CANADA
Source: Dun and Bradstreet, Incorporated

Year and Province	Manufacturing		Wholesale Trade		Retail Trade		Construction		Commercial Service		Total Totals	
	No.	Liabilities	No.	Liabilities	No.	Liabilities	No.	Liabilities	No.	Liabilities	No.	Liabilities
		$'000		$'000		$'000		$'000		$'000		$'000
Totals, 1935	285	5,044	65	1,249	879	5,202	58	689	80	910	1,367	13,094
Totals, 1936	260	4,459	63	1,454	806	4,331	37	574	72	496	1,238	11,314
Totals, 1937	190	2,875	51	925	630	3,041	33	228	48	357	952	7,426
Totals, 1938	225	4,760	55	1,229	699	4,464	39	267	31	316	1,049	11,036
Totals, 1939	234	3,829	77	1,293	874	4,946	53	793	61	774	1,299	11,635
Totals, 1940	197	3,482	72	1,128	774	3,949	56	569	59	450	1,158	9,578
1941												
P. E. Island	Nil	—	Nil	—	6	22	Nil	—	Nil	—	6	22
Nova Scotia	1	65	2	19	17	99	1	2	Nil	—	21	185
New Brunswick	Nil	—	1	6	17	138	Nil	—	Nil	—	18	144
Quebec	83	1,579	22	226	279	1,453	35	315	30	198	449	3,771
Ontario	32	650	12	164	132	718	16	174	8	129	200	1,835
Manitoba	3	8	1	8	37	189	2	25	Nil	—	43	230
Saskatchewan	4	24	1	3	96	346	Nil	—	2	10	103	383
Alberta	3	50	1	1	20	91	Nil	—	Nil	—	24	142
Brit. Columbia	4	41	2	112	10	65	1	3	1	26	18	247
Totals, 1941	130	2,419	42	539	614	3,118	55	519	41	364	882	6,959

CANADIAN RAILWAY STATISTICS

Year (Cal.)	Trackage	Investment	Passengers	Freight	Gross Earnings	Operating Expenses
		Dollars	Numbers	Short Tons	Dollars	Dollars
1930	56,585	3,328,208,911	34,698,767	115,229,511	454,231,650	380,723,411
1931	56,851	3,382,047,218	26,396,812	85,993,206	358,549,382	321,025,588
1932	57,004	3,386,165,100	21,099,582	67,722,105	293,390,415	256,668,375
1933	56,679	3,365,464,255	19,172,193	57,364,025	270,278,276	233,133,108
1934	56,519	3,379,233,796	20,530,718	68,036,505	300,837,816	251,999,667
1935	57,171	3,307,616,904	20,084,185	69,141,100	310,107,155	263,942,899
1936	56,692	3,301,033,373[1]	20,497,616	75,846,566	334,768,557	283,345,968
1937	56,833	3,072,460,924[1]	22,038,709	82,220,374	355,103,271	300,652,548
1938	56,760	3,094,704,775	20,911,196	76,175,305	336,833,400	295,705,638
1939	56,601	3,095,939,284	20,482,296	84,631,122	367,179,095	304,373,285
1940	56,533	3,159,573,547	21,969,871	97,947,541	429,142,659	335,287,503

[1]Revised.

Figures of capital for the last 9 years include advances of Dominion Government to Canadian National for operating expenses, interest charges and stock acquired by Dominion Government which at time of acquiring had relatively little value, also cost of constructing Government lines.

The single track mileage of the Canadian Pacific Railway (1940) was 17,153. The other principal railways are now, in pursuance of the government policy of nationalization, included in the Canadian National Railway System, which has a trackage (1940) of 21,848 miles.

U. S.-CANADA MERCHANDISE TRADE IN DOLLARS

Calendar year	Exports to U. S.			Imports from U. S.
	Canadian	Foreign	Total	
1920	555,337,289	26,071,180	581,408,469	921,235,401
1921	323,101,184	11,871,437	334,972,621	555,091,001
1922	336,202,309	11,415,052	347,617,361	509,909,469
1923	409,517,195	10,811,013	420,328,208	610,354,278
1924	384,611,743	10,012,304	394,624,047	524,473,366
1925	441,002,198	9,854,766	450,856,964	578,575,073
1926	457,877,594	12,686,575	470,564,169	668,747,247
1927	466,887,149	16,963,393	483,850,542	706,683,861
1928	481,531,086	21,158,661	502,689,747	825,651,549
1929	492,685,606	22,652,175	515,337,781	893,585,482
1930	373,424,236	16,487,858	389,912,094	653,676,496
1931	240,196,849	9,603,772	249,800,621	393,775,289
1932	158,705,050	6,316,726	165,021,776	263,549,346
1933	168,242,840	4,712,124	172,954,964	217,291,498
1934	218,597,071	5,426,186	224,023,257	293,779,813
1935	261,685,372	11,434,232	273,119,604	312,416,604
1936	333,916,949	10,869,594	344,786,543	369,141,513
1937	360,012,143	12,208,624	372,220,767	490,504,978
1938	270,461,189	8,296,737	278,757,926	424,730,567
1939	380,392,047	9,361,551	389,753,598	496,898,466
1940	442,984,157	8,959,511	451,943,668	744,231,156

War time restrictions preclude the publication of trade figures for 1941.

EXTERNAL TRADE OF CANADA, CALENDAR YEARS 1919-39.
(Merchandise only)

Year	Imports			Exports		
	Dutiable	Free	Total	Canadian Produce	Foreign Produce	Total
	Dollars	Dollars	Dollars	Dollars	Dollars	Dollars
1920	890,847,353	446,073,668	1,336,921,021	1,268,014,533	30,147,672	1,298,162,205
1921	546,863,395	252,615,088	799,478,483	777,149,296	13,994,461	791,143,757
1922	513,330,771	249,078,538	762,409,309	880,408,645	13,815,268	894,223,913
1923	594,098,589	308,931,926	903,030,515	1,002,401,467	13,584,849	1,015,986,316
1924	528,912,305	279,232,265	808,144,573	1,029,699,449	12,553,718	1,042,253,167
1925	561,061,127	329,132,221	890,193,348	1,239,554,207	12,111,941	1,251,666,148
1926	642,448,478	365,893,433	1,008,341,911	1,261,241,525	15,357,292	1,276,598,817
1927	696,253,024	390,864,906	1,087,117,930	1,210,596,998	20,445,231	1,231,042,229
1928	788,271,150	434,046,766	1,222,317,916	1,339,409,562	24,378,794	1,363,788,456
1929	849,114,653	449,878,039	1,298,992,692	1,152,416,330	25,926,117	1,178,342,447
1930	647,230,123	361,249,346	1,008,479,479	863,683,761	19,463,987	883,147,748
1931	416,179,513	211,918,873	628,098,386	587,653,440	11,907,020	599,560,460
1932	288,425,260	164,188,997	452,614,257	489,883,112	8,030,485	497,913,597
1933	235,195,782	166,018,529	401,214,311	529,449,529	6,034,260	535,483,789
1934	295,566,101	217,903,396	513,469,497	649,314,236	6,991,992	656,306,228
1935	306,913,652	243,400,899	550,314,551	724,977,459	12,958,420	737,935,879
1936	350,903,936	284,286,908	635,190,844	937,824,933	12,684,319	950,509,252
1937	436,327,558	372,568,767	808,896,325	997,366,918	14,754,862	1,012,121,780
1938	379,095,355	298,355,999	677,451,354	837,583,917	11,100,216	848,684,133
1939	427,470,633	323,584,901	751,055,534	924,926,104	10,995,609	935,921,713
1940	582,937,741	499,012,978	1,081,950,719	1,178,954,420	14,263,172	1,193,217,592

Wartime restrictions preclude the publication of trade figures for 1941.

The quantity and value of gold produced in Canada (1941) were the largest ever recorded in the history of the Canadian mining industry. The amount from all primary sources, totaling 5,351,689 fine ounces value at $206,040,026, compared with 5,311,145 valued at $204,479,083 (1940). Virtually all Canada's newly mined bullion is sold to the Dominion Government through the Royal Canadian Mint in Ottawa or the Assay Office in Vancouver.

Merchandise imports from United Kingdom		Merchandise exports to United Kingdom (Canadian produce only)	
	Dollars		Dollars
1920	231,487,979	1920	341,167,883
1921	123,149,776	1921	308,866,522
1922	136,859,352	1922	374,751,894
1923	154,478,720	1923	360,782,279
1924	148,891,714	1924	387,180,147
1925	162,118,705	1925	492,136,981
1926	164,707,111	1926	459,225,468
1927	182,620,421	1927	409,546,331
1928	190,756,736	1928	446,128,667
1929	194,777,650	1929	290,294,564
1930	162,632,466	1930	235,213,959
1931	109,468,081	1931	170,597,455
1932	93,508,143	1932	178,171,680
1933	97,878,232	1933	210,697,224
1934	113,415,984	1934	270,491,857
1935	116,670,227	1935	303,500,846
1936	122,971,264	1936	395,351,950
1937	147,291,551	1937	402,062,094
1938	119,292,430	1938	339,688,685
1939	114,007,409	1939	328,099,242
1940	161,216,352	1940	508,095,949

AGRICULTURAL WEALTH AND REVENUE OF CANADA

	1939	1940	1941		1939	1940	1941
	$1,000	$1,000	$1,000		$1,000	$1,000	$1,000
Current value of farm capital.............	4,496,668	4,482,223	4,689,656	Farm animals........	218,385	268,679	335,945
Net value of agricul. production........	826,390	885,115	914,601	Poultry and eggs.....	60,829	67,135	76,428
				Fruits and vegetables.	56,804	58,463	69,410
				Tobacco............	19,444	10,470	18,464
Gross value of agricul. production........	1,204,940	1,265,112	1,379,386	Maple products......	3,444	4,210	3,561
				Wool..............	1,827	2,703	3,263
Field crops........	685,839	676,682	647,850	Honey.............	2,616	2,584	3,276
Milk production....	145,883	164,132	206,543				

At the outbreak of the war (1939) Canada was a relatively weak military power, but since then has expanded and modernized her armed forces. Since the beginning of the war Canada has diverted more and more of her resources, both human and material, into her war effort. Expenditures on the war from its beginning to March 31, 1942, were given by the Minister of Finance as $2,299,841,000. Direct war expenditures (1942-1943) are estimated at $1,340,000,000.

Canada extended (1942) by six years the age limits within which single men may be called to service. The limits are 20 to 40 years instead of 21 to 35 as formerly. Men married after July 15, 1940, are considered single for purposes of call-up regulations. A plebiscite (April 27, 1942) released the Government from its pledge not to conscript Canadian manpower for overseas military service. Col. J. L. Ralston, Minister of National Defense, disclosed in London (Oct. 13, 1942) that "well over 500,000" Canadians were on active service. The men were taken to London by the convoy system without the loss of a man. The Canadian Army (as of Oct. 13, 1942) included 335,000 officers and men available for general service. Col. Ralston placed the strength of the Royal Canadian Air Force at 130,000 and fighting over occupied Europe, the Middle and the Far East.

Approximately 340,000 Canadians were serving (July 1, 1942) in the active armed services at home and abroad. They enlisted on a voluntary basis and will go wherever called.

Government control of labor became effective (Sept. 1, 1942) through the Director of National Service working in cooperation with the Ministry of Labor and the National Defense Department.

The Royal Canadian Navy went into action when Canada declared war. At the outbreak of the war the strength of the Navy was approximately 3,600 men with 13 ships of all kinds. The mobilized strength has since passed 41,000 and it musters more than 400 vessels including destroyers, armed merchant cruisers, corvettes, mine sweepers and smaller craft.

The personnel of the rapidly growing Royal Canadian Air Force was approximately 115,000 (July 1, 1942).

The Dominion Government maintains a constabulary called the Royal Canadian Mounted Police, once known as the Northwest Mounted Police. The force is responsible for the enforcement of the laws against smuggling by land, sea or air, the suppression of traffic in narcotic drugs, enforcement of the migratory birds convention act, and assists the Mines and Resources and Fisheries and other government departments in executing the provisions of their acts and sometimes assists in the administrative duties. The strength of the force had grown (1940) to 4,300. There is a reserve strength of 300. The means of transport consist of horses, automobiles, sleigh dogs and police dogs.

Newfoundland

Capital, St. John's—Area, 42,734 square miles—Population (est. 1940), 300,000

Newfoundland, at the eastern end of British America, is an island in the Atlantic Ocean. It is separated from Canada by the Straits of Belle Isle, the Gulf of St. Lawrence and the Cabot Strait.

Newfoundland is the oldest English Colony. Discovered by John Cabot (June 24, 1497) (Cape Bonavista) (August, 1583), formally occupied by Sir Humphrey Gilbert, and by the Treaty of Utrecht, (1713) acknowledged to the British. A Governor was appointed (1728). The French also had a station on the island and there were frequent disputes with the British over fishing rights. The dispute was settled (1904).

Although Newfoundland had enjoyed the status of a Dominion since the World War, a Royal Commission of Inquiry, headed by Lord Amulree (appointed Feb. 22, 1933) to investigate the desperate financial state into which it had fallen, recommended that the Dominion rights be relinquished until it again became self-supporting. The action was precipitated by Newfoundland's inability to meet the service charges on its debt of about $90,-000,000. The Royal Commission's recommendations were approved by the Newfoundland Parliament (Dec. 2, 1933).

The British House of Commons later put into effect the financial provision of the Commission's report and agreed to meet Newfoundland's budget deficits. Holders of Newfoundland bonds (other than about £3,500,000 of pre-war loans) were offered the right to exchange for new 3% 10-30 year Sterling stock guaranteed, both as to principal and interest, by the United Kingdom.

The Parliament was suspended during the emergency and full legislative and executive power was vested in the Governor, acting on the advice of a Commission of six, three appointed by the United Kingdom and three by Newfoundland. This Royal Commission, which took office (Feb. 16, 1934) consists of the following—Governor and Commander-in-Chief, Vice-Admiral Sir Humphrey Thomas Walwyn; Commissioners (Newfoundland) J. Alex Winter, Lewis Edward Emerson, Sir John Charles Puddester; (United Kingdom), Sir Wilfrid Woods, Ira Wild and Peter Douglas Haig Dunn.

The principal industries are fishing, lumber, minerals and manufactures. Huge deposits of iron ore have been found on Bell Island in Conception Bay. Copper, pyrites, coal, gold, silver, and lead are other minerals.

Government receipts (1942-1943) were estimated at $13,647,400; expenditures, $12,798,900. These figures are for nine months ending March 31, 1943. Sites on Newfoundland were leased to the United States (1940) for use as defense bases.

Labrador, the most easterly part of the American continent, comprising 110,000 square miles and a population of 4,716, is under the jurisdiction of Newfoundland. It has 850 miles of coast line and 800 of its inhabitants are Eskimos. The rest are fishermen of British descent. The interior is heavily timbered and reputed to be rich in minerals, but is largely unexplored. The United States established (1941) a protective outpost in Labrador.

British West Indies and other possessions

JAMAICA

Jamaica is situated in the Caribbean Sea, 90 miles south of Cuba, and is the largest and most valuable of the British West Indies. It has an area of 4,450 square miles and population (estimated, 1941) 1,223,241, (about 20,000 whites). Attached to Jamaica for administrative purposes are the Turks and Caicos Islands (population, 5,300; area, 226 square miles), and Cayman Island (population, 6,182; area, 104 square miles). The capital of Jamaica is Kingston. The British Governor is Sir Arthur Frederick Richards (appointed June 14, 1938).

The climate has attractions for winter tourists. It is estimated 65 to 75 per cent of the tourists are American. The island figures largely in the history of the Buccaneers of the West Indies before and during the time of Sir Henry Morgan, once its Governor. The old haunt of the pirate, Port Royal, at the entrance of the harbor, was destroyed and sunk (1692) under the sea by an earthquake.

The principal products are sugar-cane, logwood, coffee, bananas, rum, coconuts, ginger, cocoa, pimento, oranges and cigars. Trade is chiefly with the United States and Great Britain.

A site on Portland Bight was leased (1940) to the United States for a naval base.

Estimated revenue (1940-1941) was £3,201,164, expenditures £3,431,756.

BERMUDA

Bermuda is a group of 360 small islands of coral formation, about 20 inhabited, in the Atlantic Ocean, 677 miles southeast of New York and 580 miles east of North Carolina. It was settled (1609) by a party of colonists under Sir George Somers, who were headed for Virginia, but were wrecked on the islands. The area is 19 square miles; the population (estimated, 1940) was 32,086. Hamilton is the capital.

The Governor is Viscount Knollys (appointed Aug. 27, 1941).

Conscription for home defense with men between the ages of 18 and 36 was ordered (June, 1940).

Bermuda is a colony with representative government; its parliament dates from Aug. 1, 1620. The assembly of 36 members is elected, there being about 2,691 electors (freeholders). There is also an Executive Council of seven members and a Legislative Council of nine members, both councils appointed by the Crown.

The budget (1940) estimated revenues at £394,035 and expenditures £411,811.

The island, a perennial garden, with a dozen winter hotels and famous beaches, is a favorite winter resort for Americans. Effective (July 8, 1940) passports were required for entry into Bermuda. There are no taxes on real estate, incomes or inheritance. The currency, weights and measures are British.

Once autoless, the island now permits doctors to operate automobiles for professional use.

Sites on the island were granted to the United States (1940) for use as a naval base.

OTHER POSSESSIONS

Barbados is the most eastern of the Windward Islands, in the West Indies, lying out in the Atlantic at 13° north latitude. Its area is 166 square miles; the population (estimated, 1941) was 198,203. Bridgetown is the capital.

Of the total 106,470 acres, 66,000 are tilled, producing chiefly sugar, cotton, and tamarinds. Molasses and rum are manufactured. Imports are heaviest from United States and exports heaviest to Canada. Governmental receipts (1941-1942) were estimated at £530,761; expenditures £624,883.

Trinidad, with an area of 1,862 square miles and a population (estimated, 1941) 484,907, is the most southerly of the West Indies. It lies off the north coast of South America. Attached to it for administrative purposes is the island of Tobago, the population and area of which are 25,358 and 116 square miles respectively. The capital is Port au Spain. Trade is heaviest, both import and export, with the United States. Of 1,192,844 acres on the island of Trinidad, 348,850 are cultivated. Products are mostly asphalt, oil, with derivatives therefrom. The great asphalt lake, 114 acres in extent, on the island is immensely valuable and seems inexhaustible.

Sites on the island were leased to the United States (1940) for a naval base.

The Governor is Captain Sir Bede Clifford (appointed March 24, 1942).

The Bahama Islands number 20, part of them uninhabited, and are in the Atlantic Ocean, off the coast of America. Nassau, on the Island of New Providence, near the Florida coast, is an attractive winter resort for Americans. The area is 4,404 square miles; the population (estimated, 1939) is 68,903. Nassau is the capital.

A site on the island of Mayaguana was leased (1940) to the United States for use as a naval base.

Sponges and sisal are the chief sources of revenue. Fruit growing is being developed. Trade with the United States is three times as heavy as with any other country. The budget (1940) estimated revenues at £404,192 and expenditures £441,557.

The Governor General is the Duke of Windsor.

The Windward Islands lie at the eastern side of the Caribbean Sea, west from Martinique. They are Grenada and the Grenadines, St. Vincent and St. Lucia. Each has its own local Government. The total area is 821 square miles (Grenada, 133; St. Vincent, 150; St. Lucia, 233; Dominica, 305). The population is 262,006; (Grenada) (1921) 90,085; St. Vincent (1931) 47,961; St. Lucia (1940) 71,222; Dominica (1940) 52,738. St. George's on Grenada Island is the capital.

The chief products are arrowroot, cotton, copra, sugar, molasses, rum, cocoa, peanuts, cassava, limes, fruit, vegetables and spices. The cotton grown on Sea Island is considered the best in the world. St. Vincent is famous for its arrowroot.

Dominica was transferred (Jan. 1, 1940) from the Leeward to the Windward Islands and since has been governed as a separate colony.

A site at Gros Islet Bay was leased (1940) to the United States for a naval base.

The Leeward Islands, of the West Indies, situated southeast of Puerto Rico, are part of the Lesser Antilles. They comprise the islands of Antigua, Barbuda, Redonda, St. Christopher, Nevis, Anguilla, Dominica, Montserrat, Sombrero, and the British Virgin Islands. The area is 727 square miles; population (estimated 1940) is 93,130.

The principal products are sugar and molasses (Antigua and St. Kitts), cotton (Montserrat, St. Kitts, Nevis and Virgin Islands), limes and fruits, tomatoes and onions (Montserrat), cocoanuts (Nevis), tobacco and cigars (Virgin Islands), and salt (Anguilla and St. Kitts).

A site near Partain Harbor, Antigua, was leased to the United States (1940) for use as a naval base.

British Honduras is situated in Central America, on the Caribbean Sea, south of Yucatan, and produces chiefly tropical fruits, mahogany, logwood, chicle, and cedar, much of which comes to the United States.

Its area is 8,598 square miles, and population, (estimated, 1941) was 59,965. Belize, population 16,687, is the capital.

Government receipts (1940) were $1,756,523; expenditures $1,684,139.

OTHER FOREIGN COUNTRIES

Afghanistan

Capital, Kabul—Area, 250,000 square miles—Population, estimated, 12,000,000

Afghanistan occupies a mountainous country in Asia between 61° and 75° east longitude and 29° and 38° 20′ north latitude. Its extreme breadth northeast to southwest is about 700 miles, and from the Herat frontier on the west to the Khyber Pass on the east it is 600 miles. It is bounded on the north by the Turkoman S.S.R. of the U.S.S.R., on the east by British India, on the south by Baluchistan (British India), and on the west by Iran. The elevation is generally over 4,000 ft. There are three great river basins, the Oxus and the Kabul in the northeast, and the Helmund, which runs southwest through the middle of the country.

Towering above Kabul are the Hindo-Kush Mountains, 15,000 and 16,000 ft. high and reaching 25,425 ft. 100 or 200 miles to the east. Trade to India flows through the famous Khyber Pass from Kabul to Peshawur.

Afghanistan has been called "the land of rocks and stones and sanguinary feuds." Its people are nearly all Mohammedans. The Durani have been the dominant race for 200 years, the Tajiks, aborigines, being cultivators and traders. Along the frontier are warlike and independent tribes of Pathans. The languages spoken are Pushtu and Persian. The predominant religion is Islam.

It is almost exclusively an agricultural country, with two harvests a year. The fat-tailed sheep is native to the country, furnishing the Afghans their chief meat diet while the fat of its immense tail is a substitute for butter. The apple, pear, almond, peach, quince, apricot, plum, cherry, pomegranate, grape, fig, and mulberry are profuse.\ The castor-oil plant, madder, and the asafoetida plant abound. Wool and skins are the main articles of export, together with fruits, nuts and ghi. The imports are textiles, metals and hardware, leather goods, tea and sugar. The chief trade is with India, Russia and Iran. Copper, lead and iron are found in the country.

There are no railroads in the country. Merchandise is transported on camel or pony back along the seven important trade routes. The chief trade route is through Khyber pass. There is a university in Kabul (established 1932).

The government is constitutional monarchy and the laws and customs those of Islam. Legislative power is vested in a Parliament consisting of the King; a Senate of 45 members appointed for life by the King; and a National Assembly of 109 elected members. The reigning King is Mohammed Zahir Shah (born 1914). He married (Nov. 7, 1931) his cousin, Umairah, daughter of Sirdar Ahmed Shah

Chile

(REPUBLICA DE CHILE)

Capital, Santiago—Area, 296,717 square miles—Population (1940), 5,000,782

The Republic of Chile lies on the west coast of South America, occupying the strip of land between the Andes and the South Pacific, from Peru to Diego Ramerez Island 55°59'S., having an extreme length of about 2,620 miles, with a coast line of 2,900 miles. The average breadth north of 40° is 100 miles.

The Andes have many lofty peaks, notably Aconagua (altitude 23,080 ft.), on the Chilean-Argentine boundary, the highest peak in the Americas, Corcoputi (22,162 ft.), El Muerto (21,227 ft.), the Baya (19,993 ft.), the Guallatiri (19,882 ft.) From 1907 to 1924 there were 12,694 earthquakes, an average of two daily.

Easter Island 2,000 miles west of Chile, with its hundreds of stone figures, and the two Juan Fernandez Islands, less than 500 miles west, are national parks of the Chilean Government.

The land in the north part is arid, but two provinces there, Tarapaca and Antofagasta, produced 95% of the world's nitrate supply until the process of obtaining nitrate from the air was made commercially profitable. There are 152 nitrate works in all (1938) but only about 25 are in actual operation producing about 100,000 metric tons a month. About 70% of the world's supply of iodine is a by-product of Chilean nitrate oficinas. Chile is the world's second largest producer of copper. The provinces of Atacama and Coquimbo have enormous iron deposits estimated at a billion tons. South of Valparaiso are large beds of coal, the reserve estimated at two billion tons. Other minerals are gold, silver, cobalt, zinc, manganese, borate, salt, sulphur, marble and onyx.

Agriculture is an important industry. There are many large dairy farms. Wheat, barley, oats, beans, lentils, apples, melons, peaches, plums, nectarines, peas and potatoes are grown in abundance. Chile ranks seventh among wine producing countries.

Manufacturing industries have developed greatly during the last ten years. With the creation (1939) of the Corporacion de Fomento de la Produccion (Corporation for the Promotion of Production) with a capital of $40,000,000, production of agriculture and manufactures has vastly increased.

Chilean imports consist mainly of machinery,

petroleum, sugar, newsprint, automobiles, coffee, tea and maté and textiles. Besides minerals and wool the exports are chiefly meats, barley, oats, beans, lentils and fresh fruits.

The population is almost entirely of European origin; there are about 30,000 Araucans (natives) in the Andes and an indeterminate number of nomadic Fuegans in Tierra del Fuego.

Magallanes (former Punta Arenas), in the Straits of Magellan, is the southernmost city in the world, and the center of a flourishing sheep industry.

Valparaiso, chief seaport, was founded (1536) and Santiago, the capital, three hours inland, is five years younger. The latter has two universities and a National Library.

Chile has about 6,000 miles of railroads, over half being state owned. An electric railroad connects Valparaiso with Santiago, 117 miles.

Education is free and (since 1920) compulsory. There is a government university and a Catholic University in Santiago. The Roman Catholic religion is dominant though not maintained by the state (since 1925) and all religions are protected. The language is Spanish.

All able-bodied citizens from 19 years to 45 are liable for army service. Service in the active Army is for 12 years and with the second reserve to the end of the 45th year. The strength of the Army approximates 20,000 officers and men. The Navy consists of one battleship, one armored cruiser and two protected cruisers, eight destroyers, nine submarines and auxiliary vessels. The personnel is 8,000 men in normal times. There is an Air Service of four brigades.

Chile threw off the Spanish yoke (1810-18).

Under the constitution (1925), the President is elected for six years, the 45 senators for eight, and 143 deputies for four, all by direct popular vote. The President is Juan Antonio Rios (born Nov. 10, 1888) who was elected to a full six-year term (Feb. 1, 1942) succeeding Pedro Aguirre Cerda, who died Nov. 25, 1941. All male persons, 21 years of age or more, and able to read and write, have suffrage.

The monetary unit is the peso with an average value of $.315. The budget (1942) is estimated to balance at 3,000,000,000 pesos.

China

(CHUNG-HUA MIN-KUO, i. e. REPUBLIC OF CHINA)

Capital (temporary) Chungking—Area, including outlying territories, 4,314,097 square miles; China proper, 2,279,134 square miles—Population (est. 1936), 457,835,475

China, with a history reaching back to 2205 B. C., occupies a territory in the eastern part of Asia about one-third larger than continental United States. To the north lie Siberia and Manchukuo; to the west Russian Turkestan; to the southwest and south the well-nigh impassable barrier of the Himalayas forms the Thibetan-Indian frontier. French Indo-China borders it on the south; and the China Sea and Yellow Sea on the east separate it from the Philippines, Formosa (now Japanese), the Japanese Empire and Korea. The country is of rolling topography, rising to high elevation in the north in the Kinghan and Tarbagatai Mountains in Mongolia; the Himalayan and Kunlun Mountains in the southwest, in Thibet, and the Hinghan Mountains of Manchuria. Its length from north to south is 1,860 miles, and its breadth from east to west is about 1,500 miles.

China Proper—China has 28 provinces and two special territories (Outer Mongolia and Thibet). China Proper, which includes 24 provinces (excepting Li'aoning, Kirin, Heilungkiang and Sinkiang) occupies the fertile southeastern part of the country, an area nearly twice the size of the United States east of the Mississippi. There the population on the generally accepted estimates has a density of 174 to the square mile. China Proper is one of the best watered countries of the world. From the mountains on the west four great rivers run in general course stretching for hundreds of miles along the ocean and inland for 300 miles. These rivers, the Yangtze, the Yellow, the Si kiang and the Hanho, drain four-fifths of the country.

The Province of Kiangsu, in which Shanghai is situated, having about 36,469,321 people in 41,818 square miles, is the most densely populated political unit in the world.

China has all the important religions of the world, but none of its own. Confucianism and Taoism are considered by the Chinese not as religions, but as political philosophies and teach-

ings. Buddhism was introduced from India and has the most followers, though its influence is declining. Mohammedanism and Christianity came from Europe. It is estimated that there are 48,-000,000 Mohammedans with more than 42,000 mosques, and 2,624,166 Catholics and 618,600 Protestants.

China is essentially agricultural. Wheat, barley, corn, kaoliang, and millet and other cereals, with peas and beans, are produced in the north; rice, sugar and indigo in the south. Rice is the staple food of the Chinese. Fruit is grown in abundance. Fibre crops are important and include abutilon, hemp, jute, ramie and flax. Cotton is produced mostly in the Yangtze and Yellow River valleys. Tea is cultivated principally in the west and south. One of the most important industries of China is silk culture. It has flourished 4,000 years. Livestock is raised in large numbers.

Cotton, wool and silk manufacture are important industries, especially in Shanghai and Canton, although native looms are found in most Chinese dwellings. In recent years flour and rice milling has become extensive; also tanning and cement and glass manufacture.

China is one of the foremost coal countries in the world, with reserves estimated at 243,669,000,-000 tons. Other minerals are iron ore, tin, antimony, wolfram, molybdenum, bismuth and salt. Oil wells are worked in South Manchuria and Kansu. The oldest iron industry in the world is in Shansi.

Shanghai, China's commercial and industrial capital, is situated on the left bank of the Whangpoo River, 12 miles above its mouth at Woosung. It is in the Yangtze delta. It occupies the most strategic position economically of any city in China.

The Shanghai Municipal area (population, Census of 1935, 3,489,998), is made up of the International Settlement administered by the Shanghai Municipal Council (population, 1,007,868); the

French Concession, administered by a Council under the French Consul General (population, 496,-536), and the Municipality of Greater Shanghai, a purely Chinese administrated municipality (population, 1,986,358). The International Settlement stretches along the Whangpoo River between Chapei and the French concession and contains the interests of 12 nations, the chief business buildings and houses 30,000 foreign nationals. Before the outbreak of hostilities (Aug. 1937) the Japanese residents numbered 28,000 of whom 18,000 resided in Chapei, and Japanese property interests were estimated as worth $189,500,000 gold.

The National Government at Chungking is responsible to the Kuomintang, or National People's Party, which came into power (1925). The supreme authority of the Kuomintang is vested in the National Congress, delegates to which are elected by provincial and other local party headquarters. The incumbent Central Executive Committee and the Central Supervisory Committee were elected by the Fifth Congress (1935). They have 260 full and reserve members, constituting the highest organs in between the national congresses, which meet on the average of once every two years.

The Central Executive Committee can decide any matter in regard to party and government affairs, pending revision by the National Congress. It elects the chairman of the National Government, presidents and vice-presidents of the Executive, Legislative, Judicial, Examination and Control Yuan, all responsible to the Central Executive Committee pending the promulgation of a constitution.

The Political Committee, also known as the Central Political Council, once was a most powerful body. It was created (1925) to supervise the Government, the latter being appointed by the party. According to its organic law, the chairman, vice-chairman and from 19 to 25 are appointed by the Central Executive Committee from among its members and members of the Central Supervisory Committee. It has the power to discuss and decide principles of legislation, administrative programs, major military and government projects, financial schemes including budgets, and the appointment and dismissal of high government officials. All laws promulgated by the National Government in recent years were first passed in principle by the Political Committee. The latter also has the power to intervene or restrict the activities of, the five Yuan in the exercise of their respective functions. In this way, in prewar days, the Political Committee, was the highest organ in the Chinese political structure serving as a link between the party and the Government.

Since the start of the war the name and organization of the Political Committee have undergone many changes. In August, 1937, the National Defense Council, which hitherto had been in charge of the discussion and decision of matters relating to the national defense, was elevated to be the Supreme National Defense Council. Soon its functions in many respects resembled those of the Political Committee. The standing committee (Nov. 11, 1937) ordered that pending conclusion of the war the functions of the Political Committee should be absorbed by the Supreme National Defense Council. In reality, however, this new Defense Council was scarcely more than a reduced Political Committee. Besides being the highest organ to direct government policy in time of war, it was also the final voice in the determination of government policy.

In February, 1937, the Defense Council was further changed into the Supreme National Defense Committee. It bears the same mandate as its predecessor, namely to act for the Political Committee for the duration of the war. In addition it has the power to direct all party, government and military organs. In other words it not only decides upon but also executes policy.

The Constitution, promulgated (May, 1936) entrusts the Government to five Yuan, executive, legislative, judicial, examination and censor. The Executive Yuan, in point of actual importance, by far exceeds that of the other four Yuan. It is often likened to a responsible cabinet. The Executive Yuan is responsible to the party and not to any representative assembly. In regard to important administrative programs or plans, the Executive Yuan has no power to decide by itself. They have to be approved first by the Supreme National Defense Council. As at present constituted the Executive Yuan has three divisions, namely the Secretariat, the Political Affairs Department, and the Economic Council. Then it has the following principal organs: Ministries: Interior, Foreign Affairs, Military Affairs, Finance, Education, Economic Affairs, Communications, Social Affairs, Agriculture and Forestry, Food, Health

Administration, Relief Commission, Mongolian and Thibetan Affairs Commission, Overseas Chinese Affairs Commission. There are also several smaller organizations.

The Legislative Yuan is not a parliamentary assembly. First, its members are appointed or dismissed by the National Government upon recommendation of the Legislative Yuan president. Second, though it has the power to decide laws, budgets, amnesty, declaration of war, conclusion of peace and other international affairs. Its power is very much restricted, formerly by the Political Committee and now by the Supreme National Defense Council. The Legislative Yuan may have from forty-nine to ninety-nine members. Ordinarily, it has five committees of law codification, foreign relations, finance, economic affairs and military affairs.

The Judicial Yuan has four units. They are the Ministry of Justice, the Supreme Court, the Administrative Court and the Commission for the Disciplinary Punishment of Public Functionaries.

Under the Examination Yuan are the Ministry of Personnel and the Examination Commission.

The Control Yuan may have from 29 to 49 members. Its principal functions are impeachment and auditing. The former is exercised by members of the Yuan, while the latter is exercised through the Ministry of Audit.

The National Military Council is directly under the National Government. It directs, on behalf of the chairman of the National Government, the military powers pertaining to him as head of a Chinese state. The council has assumed great importance since the Japanese invasion of Manchuria in 1931 and especially since the outbreak of the war in 1937.

The Kuomintang has an administrative machinery of its own. Under the Central Executive Committee are four divisions: the Secretariat, the Organization Board, the Information Board and the Overseas Board.

The National Government was first organized in July 1925 in Canton with only three ministries, in charge of military affairs, foreign affairs and finance. Later, it grew to sixteen units. They were all directly under the National Government which was then actually functioning actively. Following the unification of the country and the establishment of the capital in Nanking in 1928, the present system of five Yuan took shape. In May 1931 the People's Convention was held in Nanking. It adopted a Provisional Constitution for the period of political tutelage. Then the fourth National Kuomintang Congress decided to change the existing government structure. A new organic law of the National Government was drafted in accordance with the resolution and promulgated on December 31, 1931.

The National Government itself has three divisions: First, the chairman of the National Government, the State Council with thirty members, and the civil affairs, military affairs, and comptroller-general's departments; second, the five Yuan and the ministries and commissions under them; third, organs directly under the National Government, of which the most important one is the National Military Council.

Both the chairman of the National Government and all state councillors, like the presidents and vice-presidents of the five Yuan, are elected by the Central Executive Committee of the Kuomintang. The chairman of the National Government is the titular head of the state.

The President of the National Government is Lin Shen.

The Cabinet of Ministers follows:

President of the Executive Yuan—Gen. Chiang Kai-shek.

Minister of Finance—Dr. H. H. Kung.
Minister of Foreign Affairs—Dr. T. V. Soong.
Minister of War—Gen. Ho Ying-chin.
Minister of Navy—Admiral Chen Shao-kuan.
Minister of Economics—Gong Wenhao.
Minister of Publicity—Wang Shih-chieh.
Minister of Education—Chen Li-Foo
Minister of Interior—Ho Chien.
Minister of Communications—Chang Kia-ngau.
Minister of Agriculture and Forestry—Admiral Shen Hunglieh.

The Japanese have been extending their power over China for the past 50 years, since the Sino-Japanese war of 1894. Korea was annexed (1910); Manchuria (1931-32). The border province of Jehol was cut off as a buffer state (1933). Kwantung army troops came through (1935) the Great Wall north of Peiping from Jehol into the province of Chahar which lies between Jehol and Mongolia. The principal Chinese officials in Peiping and Tientsin and in Hopei and Chahar provinces were turned out and replaced by new men acceptable to the Japanese leaders. In effect Chahar was made a demilitarized zone by June of 1935.

Japan set up (1937) a so-called independent government in Peiping, called "The Provisional Government of the Republic of China" and (1938) established a second regime "The New Reformed Government of the Republic of China" at Nanking. Japan announced (1938) that it would establish two chartered companies to exploit China. These are the North China Exploitation Company with a capital of 350,000,000 yen and the Central China Development Company with a capital of 100,000,000 yen.

Fighting broke out between China and Japan (July 7, 1937) and since then large areas of the coastal provinces have been occupied by the Japanese invaders.

The Japanese established (1940) at Nanking a so-called central government under Wang-Ching-wei, dedicated to end the war and establish a new economic relationship.

China began conscripting (July, 1942) 6,000,000 new soldiers to swell her total of trained fighters to 26,000,000. Gen. Cheng Cheh-yuen announced the increase would be achieved by drafting men between the ages of 18 and 40 and that wealthy classes no longer would have the privilege of paying money instead of sending their sons to war. The armed forces at the time exceeded 20,-000,000 with 5,000,000 in active service as regular troops, 15,000,000 in training or in reserve units and 800,000 operating as guerrillas in Japanese-occupied areas. By August, 1942, 11,129,576 able bodied Chinese had been conscripted.

Chief exports are animal products, oils, tallow, wax, seeds, raw cotton, raw silk, hides, skin, leather, tea, chemicals, metals, minerals, piece goods, paper, cereals, beans and peas. The imports include cotton, wool, metals, fishery products, tobacco, chemicals, dyes, paints, coal, coke, machinery and armaments. Trade is principally with the United States, Japan, Germany and Great Britain.

Chinese Industrial Cooperatives have more than 2,000 units with a capital investment of 30,000,000 yuan and are producing goods valued at more than 9,000,000 yuan monthly.

Since the abolition of the civil service examination in 1905, the education system in China has been modelled after the American system. Education is not yet compulsory, but the Chinese Government has tried its best to make it as popular as possible among the people. The administration is under the Central, Provincial and District Government authorities, but many schools are still under private maintenance, especially the missionary schools.

Prior to the Sino-Japanese war, there were more than three thousand middle schools (high schools) with about 540,000 students, and 108 institutions of higher learning with about 42,000 students. Since the war many schools have been destroyed by the Japanese or uprooted and removed thousands of miles to the interior from their original sites.

Illiteracy is still high, but is being reduced through mass education movement for adults.

China has a national Army which gets its recruits through a system of compulsory citizenship service for a period of three years. There is also the regular Army with voluntary and obligatory service for six years and with extended service up to the age of 40 years. Recruits must be between the ages of 20 and 25. The Chinese Navy, since the war with Japan, is practically non-existent and was undergoing a reorganization when hostilities opened.

The monetary unit is the yuan. It was valued (1935) at 29½ cents American currency, but since the Sino-Japanese war the yuan has steadily declined in value to between five and six cents in American currency.

MONGOLIA

Mongolia, although nominally of China, was somewhat shaken loose from Chinese adherence during the world war. Outer Mongolia is a republic, but it is recognized by Russia as under Chinese suzerainty. It is bounded on the north by Siberia, on the south by Sinkiang, on the southwest by Turkestan, on the east by China Proper and Manchuria. Its area is about 622,744 square miles; the population is about 850,000.

Inner Mongolia (1928) declared its allegiance to National Government of China, but (April 23, 1934) under pressure of Japanese militarists, set up an autonomous government in Pailingmiao to handle local affairs. Outer Mongolia governs itself on the Soviet model.

The chief means of transportation is by caravan but in recent years motor truck and steamboat lines have been established.

Tannu-Tuva, the northwest portion, about 64,000 sq. m. with a population of about 65,000 also governs itself on a Soviet model as a U.S.S.R. protectorate.

There is little agriculture, the great plains between the Tarbagatai and Kinghan Mountains being desert, with camels, horses and sheep as principal interests. The religion of the people is Buddhist Lamaism.

Chief exports are livestock and animal products. Foreign trade is backed by Soviet capital and the chief trading unit is the Mongo Central Cooperative Society.

SINKIANG (Chinese Turkestan)

Sinkiang, known as the New Dominion, comprises Chinese Turkestan, Kulja and Kashgaria. There are Turks, Mohammedans and Chinese residents there. Along the Kashgar and Yarkand Rivers there is much irrigation, and cereals, fruits and vegetables are grown with wool, cotton and silk production. Ili is the chief town. The population of Sinkiang is estimated at 1,200,000 and its area at 633,802 square miles.

It is from Sinkiang that much of the jade comes. In view of its propinquity to Soviet Russia this province, especially economically, has been under the influence of the Russians.

THIBET

Thibet, in Western China, is a country little known, situated between the Himalaya and Kwen-lun Mountains, and hithmerto practically shut to strangers. The trade is with India mostly, being carried on through lofty passes, some of which are 14,000 to 18,000 ft. high, which are impassable in winter. China's hold on Thibet was visibly loosened when the revolution (1911) broke in China. The Thibetans expelled the Chinese garrisons. But since the establishment of the National Government (1927) a great deal has been accomplished to bring Thibet closer under the influence of the Chinese Government. The capital is Lhasa. The area of Thibet is 349,419 square miles with wide areas unexplored. Population is estimated at 3,-000,000. Some recent estimates place it as high as 6,000,000 and as low as 700,000.

A 6-year-old peasant boy—Ling-ehr-la-mu-tan-chu—was enthroned (Feb. 22, 1940) in Potala Palace, Lhasa, as the 14th Dalai Lama, chief civil and religious ruler of Thibet. Supposedly the child—born of a peasant family in Kokonor Province in China and taken to Lhasa by Thibetan monks—was born at the exact moment the 13th Dalai Lama stopped breathing (Dec. 17, 1933). Until the new Dalai Lama is 18 years old the head Lama of Reting Lamasery will rule the forbidden land.

The religion is Lamaism, a modified form of Buddhism.

The highest grade musk is obtained from the muskdeer, now becoming very scarce in Tsarung mountains in Southeastern Thibet.

Colombia

(LA REPUBLICA DE COLOMBIA)

Capital, Bogota—Area, 448,794 square miles—Population (1942), 9,523,200

The Republic of Colombia, situated in the extreme northwest of South America, extends up the Isthmus of Panama to the Republic of Panama. It has a coast line of 782 miles on the Pacific Ocean, and 1056 miles on the Caribbean Sea. It has as neighbors Venezuela and Brazil on the east, and Ecuador and Peru on the south.

Three great ranges of the Andes, the Western, Central and Eastern Cordilleras, run through the country from north to south. The eastern range consists mostly of high table lands, cool and healthful, the most densely populated part of the country. The Magdalena River, in the east, rises in the high Andes and flows north into the Caribbean Sea, 12 miles from Barranquilla.

Finland

(SUOMEN TASAVALTA)

Capital, Helsinki—Area, 134,588 square miles—Population (1938), 3,863,753

Finland formed part of the Kingdom of Sweden from 1154 to 1809, when it became an autonomous Grand Duchy of the Russian Empire. It declared its independence (Dec. 6, 1917), established a Provisional Government, and became a republic (1919). Finland is bounded on the north by Norway, on the east by Russia, on the south by the Gulf of Finland, and on the west by the Gulf of Bothnia, Sweden and Norway.

Finland was attacked by the Union of Soviet Socialist Republics (Nov. 30, 1939) and was forced to make peace after three months of fighting. Through the peace (March, 1940) Finland ceded to the U.S.S.R. 16,173 square miles of territory with a population of 450,000 which had be be settled in the rest of the war-torn country. All the lost territory was recovered (1941) in the war between Germany and the U.S.S.R. with Finland lined up with the Axis. The resettlement of refugees from Karelia on their conquered land is progressing although complicated by the virtual loss of all overseas trade by the war.

Finland, after the downfall of the Czar, had representative government restored to her by a Provisional Government. Following the Bolshevist coup d'etat the Diet and Senate (Dec. 6, 1917) proclaimed the independence of the republic. Civil war between the "Reds" and "Whites" followed. With German intervention, the "Reds" were defeated and driven back into Russia in two battles (April, 1918) and the German troops went home in December of that year. The Finnish Diet resolved (July 17, 1919) to establish a republic, and a peace treaty acknowledging the independence of Finland was signed with Russia at Dorpat (Oct. 14, 1920).

The lake and canal waterways are navigable for 3,000 miles. Notable are the mighty Imatra rapids of the river Vuokski, having in a channel about 25 yards wide an aggregate fall of about 72 feet in a distance of 1,400 yards and a volume (the greatest in Europe) of between 480 and 700 cubic meters per second, discharging ultimately into Lake Ladoga.

Although extending far north into extremely cold latitudes, with rugged climate and topography, Finland is an agricultural country. Lumber is the most important industry. The principal crops are rye, barley, oats, potatoes and hay. Other chief industries in the order of their importance are paper and pulp; iron and mechanical works; textiles; leather, rubber and fur; and chemicals.

Imports are mostly metals and metal goods; machinery; minerals and earths; textiles; colonial produce and spices; oils, fats, and waxes; means of transport; cereals; spinning materials. Exports, in order of their value, are pulp and paper; timber and manufactures of wood; food obtained from animals; metals and metal goods; leather, hides, furs; minerals, ores, and products from same; yarn and ropes; matches, ammunition, and other explosives; machinery; resins and tars; textiles.

The cooperative system has worked throughout Finland for nearly 40 years with marked success. There are (1939) more than 7,000 cooperatives with a total membership exceeding 900,000 and they handle about 25% of the retail trade and 40% of the wholesale.

Universal military service prevails from 17 years to 60. Males reaching 21 are summoned to service for a period of approximately a year for training. The conscript then remains in the first reserve until 40 years old. The second reserve is comprised of those between the ages of 40 and 60, conscripts who are considered unfit for active service and youths between 17 and 21, not yet enrolled as conscripts. There is also an Air Force and a Coast Defense. The Civic Guards, approximately 100,000, also are a part of the national defense.

The Evangelical Lutheran Church is the state religion, although there is absolutely free worship. There are three universities—one in Helsinki and two in Turku.

The President is chosen for six years by an Electoral College of 300 chosen by direct vote; he appoints the Cabinet. The President is Risto Ryti, (born 1889) who was elected (1940) after the resignation of Kyosti Kallio.

In the general election (July, 1939) the Government coalition bloc, composed of Laborites, Agrarians and Liberals, increased its majority in the Diet from 143 to 149. Of the opposition parties the Conservatives gained three seats while the Swedish party, representing the minority population, lost three. Fascists and Nazis operating in the Patriotic National League lost seven of their 14 seats. The voting system is devised for proportional representation.

The monetary unit is the mark with an average value of $.02. The budget (1942) is estimated to balance at 11,100,000,000 marks.

France

Capital, Paris—(War) Vichy—Area, 212,659 square miles—Population (1936), 41,907,056

France, a republic for 70 years and now an authoritarian state, has for neighbors on the north Belgium and Luxemburg. On the east Germany lies beyond the Rhine, the boundary; the Jura Mountains and Lake Geneva separate it from Switzerland, and the Graian Alps and the Maritime Alps from Italy. On the south is the Mediterranean Sea and Spain, with the Pyrenees for the boundary line. On the west lie the Bay of Biscay and the North Atlantic Ocean, and on the north again the English Channel and the Straits of Dover separate it from England. From north to south its length is about 600 miles, and from the western extremity near Brest to Strasbourg on the Rhine it is about 560 miles wide. The coastline on the north is 700 miles long; along the Atlantic and the Bay of Biscay, 865; on the Mediterranean, 384 miles.

It has the highest mountain in Europe west of the Caucasus, Mont Blanc (15,781 ft.). On the French side of the Pyrenees are several peaks exceeding 10,000 ft. in height.

In the south-central part of France is the so-called Central Plateau, which is bordered on its southeastern side by rugged mountain ranges, beginning with the Cevennes, which ascend from the Rhone Valley and reach a height of 5,584 ft. in Mont Lozere, and on its northwestern side by the Monts d'Auvergne which attain an altitude of 6,000 ft. Further it is bordered by the hills of Burgundy and Cote d'Or. Still further north are the Vosges, which run parallel with the Rhine; their crest formed the boundary line between France and Germany before World War I. Thence the wooded highlands of the Argonne and the Ardennes bear off to the frontier. The western and northwestern part of France consists of fertile plains save for the hills of Normandy and the picturesque rocky coast of Brittany.

On the North Sea and the Channel are the seaports of Dunkirk, Calais and Boulogne, with the great port of Havre at the mouth of the Seine, and Cherbourg, an important naval base, between Cape Hague and Cape Barfleur. In the extreme northwestern projection, sheltered by Cape St. Mathieu, is the roadstead of Brest, the great naval station. Further down the coast is Lorient, St. Nazaire, at the mouth of the Loire, with Nantes further up the river, Rochefort and La Rochelle. Up the estuary of the Garonne is the important port of Bordeaux, fourth city of the republic; and at the mouth of the Adour, in the extreme southwest corner, is Bayonne with its neighboring seaside resort of Biarritz. On the Mediterranean coast, which on the west is low, with lagoons and sand dunes, there is no great port till the mouths of the Rhone are passed and Marseilles, the second city of the country, is reached. Beyond is the great naval base, Toulon, and from there by Nice and Monaco to the Italian frontier and beyond runs the beautiful Riviera—the Cote d'Azur.

France, country of arts, letters and science, is also a land of festivals and gaiety. There are historical pageants elaborately presented in beautiful settings, such as Versailles, St. Germain, and in some of the many gardens in Paris.

France possesses 1,300 thermal springs and 120 health resorts. Spas are scattered through the mountain ranges, notably in Savoy, the Massif Central and the Vosges, Alps, Pyrenees and the Jura, as well as in the lower slopes of Normandy, Touraine, Provence and many other localities. Along the 1,900 miles of French coast bordering on two seas and an ocean, there are more than 900 bathing beaches.

Much of the history of France may be read in her art. The prehistoric remains at Les Eyzies in Dordogne, the caves of Monestan in Ariege, the dolmens and menhirs of Brittany, the arenas of Arles and Nimes, all speak eloquently of ancient are. Traces of the Merovingian period are to be found in Aix-en-Provence, Frejus and Poitiers; masterpieces of the Romanesque and Gothic abound throughout France; the Renaissance and seventeenth century are especially well represented by the world-famous chateaux and their gardens, among which Villandry, Versailles, Vaux, Sceaux and Saint-Cloud are particularly famous. Other famous castles are Chantilly, St. Germain-en-Laye, Fontainebleau, and the Grand and Petit Trianon. The magnificent public buildings and charming private mansions built during the eighteenth and nineteenth centuries in Paris, Abbeville, Nantes, Tours, Orleans and Bordeaux excite the admiration of tourist and native alike.

Throughout France there are many famous museums including the world-renowned Louvre, the Carnavalet and others in Paris. The country is noted for beautiful churches and cathedrals, particularly in Paris, Amiens, Beauvais, Reims, Chartres, Rouen, Poitiers, Bourges, Strasbourg, Albi and Arles. The chateaux of France, especially those of the Loire, are well known. Amboise, Blois, Luynes, Chenonceaux, Chambord, Sully, Langeais, Cheverny, Chinon, Loches, Azay-le-Rideau, have been available to tourist inspection for the past few years. Carcassonne is known for its old fortified walls.

There are many popular winter resorts scattered in mountains of the Vosges, the Jura, the Alps and the Pyrenees.

France has four important rivers, the Seine, the Loire, the Garonne and the Rhone, the left bank of the Rhine from Basle, Switzerland, to Lauterbourg, and a dozen others, all of great value because of canalization, which binds them together. The waterways total 7,543 miles in length, of which canals cover 3,031.

France became an authoritarian state in the swift current of martial and political events that culminated (1940) in France signing an armistice with Germany and Italy. A single political party was created (Aug. 31, 1940) under the direction of Marshal Henri Philippe Petain, who had succeeded to the head of the Government. The war with Germany saw many rapid changes in cabinets that year. Premier Edouard Daladier with his cabinet resigned (March 20, 1940) and was succeeded by Paul Reynaud. The Reynaud cabinet served until its resignation (June 16, 1940) when Marshal Petain was named Premier and immediately declared for peace. This was the beginning of the end of the Third Republic.

The German Army had entered Paris following its occupation of Holland, Luxemburg, and northern France. The invasion of the Low Countries began (May 10, 1940) and within a month the Germans had seized these lands and had overrun northern France. German troops entered Paris (June 14, 1940) and the Government moved to Bordeaux. The cabinet by a vote of 13 to 11, agreed to ask Germany for an armistice. The cabinet, the last under the Constitution of 1875, resigned and President Lebrun asked Marshal Petain to take the helm. There followed the armistice negotiations. The compact with Germany was signed (June 22, 1940); the one with Italy two days later. The German Army at the time occupied three-fifths of France.

The Government moved to Vichy (July 2) and Parliament voted (July 9) full powers to Marshal Petain to establish a new constitution. The vote in the Chamber of Deputies was 395 to 3 and in the Senate 225 to 1.

The members of the Chamber of Deputies and the Senate met in National Assembly (July 10) and passed by a vote of 395 to 3 a Constitutional Law, giving to Marshal Petain the power to promulgate "through one or more Acts a new Constitution for the French State", based on the rights of "labor, family and the fatherland", to be ratified by the Nation and applied by the Assemblies to be created. This "Constitutional Law" was adopted by a vote of 569 to 80, with 17 members absent.

By virtue of the power vested in him Marshal Petain issued seven decrees under the heading of Constitutional Acts.

Under Act No. 1 (July 11), Marshal Petain assumed the functions of Chief of the French State, heretofore held by Albert Lebrun as President of the French Republic. President Lebrun did not officially resign but retired. It was assumed that the publication of this act automatically entailed the abolition of the function of the President of the French Republic.

Under Act No. 2 (July 11) The powers of Marshal Petain are defined.

As Chief Executive he will:
Appoint and remove Secretaries of State who will be responsible only to him;
Promulgate laws and enforce their execution;
Fill all civil and military positions for which no

other method of choice has been provided by law;
Command the armed forces;
Exercise the right of pardon and amnesty;
Negotiate and ratify treaties;
Receive envoys of foreign powers who shall be accredited to him;
Have the right to declare martial law in one or more parts of the land;
He shall not have the power to declare war without the previous assent of the Legislative Assemblies.
Temporarily he shall also exercise legislative power:
Until the formation of new assemblies;
After such formation, in case of foreign tension or grave internal crisis.

Under Act No. 3 (July 11) The Senate and Chamber of Deputies will continue to exist until there have been formed the Assemblies provided for by the Constitutional Law of July 10; the Senate and Chamber of Deputies are adjourned until further order and hereafter will be convened only on the call of the Head of the State; article 1 of the Constitutional Law of July 16, 1875, is repealed.

Under Act No. 4 (July 12) M. Pierre Laval was appointed successor to Marshal Petain in case the change was made necessary by events.

Under Act No. 5 (July 30) A Supreme Court of Justice was created as a permanent body to pass judgment upon such ministers or high officials as have failed in their duty, particularly during the events that brought about the passage from peace to war prior to September, 1939, and upon individuals guilty of attempts against the security of the State.

Under Act No. 6 (Dec. 1) The deposition of Parliamentarians was decreed henceforth by the Chief of the French State and not by the Parliament.

Under Act No. 7 (Jan. 21, 1941) All members of the Government and high officials of the Civil Service are required to swear allegiance to Marshal Petain personally and are responsible to him.

The Cabinet was reorganized (Sept. 6, 1940) with Laval as Deputy Prime Minister and later Minister of Foreign Affairs. Marshal Petain "for high reasons of internal policy" (Dec. 12) dismissed Laval and abolished the office of Vice Premier. At the same time he named Pierre Etienne Flandin Foreign Minister. Flandin resigned his post (Feb. 9, 1941) and Admiral Jean Francois Darlan was named his successor. The following day Marshal Petain designated Admiral Darlan as his successor as Chief of the French State should circumstances make the succession necessary.

Marshal Petain appointed (Jan. 22, 1941) a National Council of 192 members to advise with him and to share with him the duties of directing the French State.

A New Government was formed (April 14, 1942) by Petain, Darlan and Laval, with the latter participating in the Cabinet and with Darlan continuing as successor to the Chief of State. The New Government follows:

Chief of State—Marshal Petain.
Chief of Government and Minister of Foreign Affairs, Interior and Propaganda—Pierre Laval.
Minister of State Without Portfolio Attached to the Chief of State—Lucien Romier.
Minister of Justice—Joseph Barthelemy.
Minister of Finance—Pierre Cathala.
Minister of Agriculture and Food Supply—Max Bonnafous.
Education—Abel Bonnard.

SECRETARIES OF STATE

Attached to Laval—Fernand de Brinon, Admiral Rene Platon.
Internal Administration (Ministry of the Interior)—Georges Hilaire.
Police—Robert Bousquet.
Information—Paul Marion.
Colonies—Jules Brevie.
War—Gen. Eugene Bridoux.
Navy—Vice Admiral Paul Auphand.
Air—Gen. Jean Jennekyn.
Industrial Production—Jean Bichelonne.
Labor—Hubert Lagardelle.
Communications—Robert Gribrat.
Health—Dr. Raymond Grasset.

OTHERS

Delegate General for French-German Economic Relations—Jacques Barnaurd.
Commissioner General for Sports—Joseph Pascot.
Charging that the Government had capitulated to Germany before it had exhausted all means of existence, Gen. Charles J. de Gaulle organized (June 23, 1940) a Provisional French National Committee. London recognized "Gen. de Gaulle

(June 28) as leader of all Free Frenchmen, wherever they may be, who rally to him in support of the Allied cause. "French colonies supporting the Free French movement are French Equatorial Africa, New Caledonia, Oceania, French Cameroons, French East Indies, French West Indies and French India. Gen. de Gaulle formed a Council of Defense of the French Empire to "exercise all the powers of a Government of War in the name of France on all territories where fighting against the enemies of France continues or will sooner or later be resumed." De Gaulle announced (Sept. 25, 1941) a Free French Council to serve under his presidency as a provisional government until they can hand over their functions to a constitutionally representative French Government.

The National Council (created 1941) by Marshal Petain to frame a new Constitution was scrapped (1942). Lucien Romier, Minister of State who represented the Government on the council, said that it would be reorganized "with a view of establishing contact between the Government and the population through the intermediary of local and national representatives.

French railways, totalling 26,417 miles, and formerly owned and operated under seven great railway systems, two of which were state-owned, were merged (Jan. 1, 1938) into one French National Railway system, the Société Nationale des Chemins de Fer Francais.

Agriculturally, France is a country of small farms, the average unit being 24 acres. The French peasant is a frugal individual and grows most of what he eats. The land is suited to a variety of products the most important of which from a commercial standpoint are wheat, mixed corn, rye, barley, oats, potatoes and beets. A great diversity of fruits are grown, chiefly apples and pears, plums, peaches, apricots, nuts and cherries. The fishing industry is extensive. The government assists financially in the culture of silk.

The country is rich in minerals, and the basins of Pas de Calais and Lorraine are noted for their huge coal deposits. Subterranean products, besides coal, include lignite, iron ore, bauxite, pyrites, mineral oils, auriferous ore, asphalt, rock salt and potash salts. The iron ore deposits in Eastern France and the bauxite deposits in Central France are among the richest in the world.

Manufactures occupy a predominant position in the economic life of the nation, and chief among these are the making of chemicals, silk and cotton textiles, perfumes and iron products.

France imports more wine than she exports. France imported (1938) from the colonies 18,566,231 metric quintals and from foreign countries 198,093, metric quintals. Exports (1938) to the colonies were 311,636 metric quintals and to foreign countries 875,186.

The principal imports in peace time in the order of their monetary value are coal and coke, wines, wool, vegetable oils and seeds, cotton, cereals, fruit (fresh and dried), machinery, coffee, copper, skins, hides, rice, timber. The order of exports, according to value, was machinery, iron and steel, wool, cotton cloth, silk cloth, chemicals, minerals, motor cars, wines, skins and hides, paper, sugar, spirits, precious and semi-precious stones, wool thread, fruits (dried and fresh), drugs, medicines, perfumes, soaps, cotton thread, timber.

Alsace-Lorraine, returned by Germany to France at the end of the World War, had a population (1921 census) of 1,709,749. The census (1921) returned the total population of enlarged France as 39,209,706, a loss of 395,474 over the previous census (1911). France, always an attractive country to foreigners, counted as residents (1911) 1,132,696, and (1921) 1,417,357 in the pre-war territory and 1,550,459, comprising Alsace-Lorraine, an increase of foreigners of 284,661. According to these figures the decrease of French citizens between 1911 and 1921 was, for pre-war territory, 2,389,884, or, counting the return of Alsace-Lorraine, 813,237.

The number of foreigners in France (1936 census) was 2,453,507, a decrease of approximately 400,000 over 1932. The number of households (1936 census) was 13,145,184, occupying 9,109,687 houses.

France is in the vanguard in the matter of social welfare legislation. Both employers and employees contribute to the old-age pension fund. There is also compulsory social insurance against illness, maternity, disablement and death. The legislation has been continued by the French State.

The French State repealed (Sept., 1940) the famous laws (1904) which nominally denied the right to teach to all religious organizations. This law was for a long time regarded as one of the most important pieces of legislation passed by the Third Republic in its struggle against clericalism. It was not too rigidly enforced, however, especially after the World War of 1914-1918, but schools conducted by religious groups were nevertheless illegal. From now on, religious orders will be allowed to resume their teaching under the official control and authority of the Ministry of Education.

Primary instruction is free and compulsory. The public schools form the University of France with an enrollment (1937-1938) of 5,436,554 pupils in 81,500 schools. There are 17 universities in the country.

The University of Paris was founded around 1150-1170 and the University of Montpellier existed as a School of Medicine at the beginning of the twelfth century. A faculty of jurisprudence was created in the latter part of the century. The University of Toulouse also was founded in the twelfth century.

The country is predominantly Roman Catholic, only about a million persons adhering to the Protestant faith. The state recognizes no religion and tolerates all. The monks of the Grand Chartreuse were permitted by decree (March 4, 1941) to return to France where they receive official recognition.

France, as a Republic, was governed under constitutional law adopted (1875) and modified (1875-1884-1885-1889). Legislative power rested in a Senate and Chamber of Deputies, with the Deputies elected by manhood suffrage every four years. The Senators were elected for nine years, one third retiring every three years; the election was indirect and made by an electoral body in each district made up of delegates chosen in the municipal council of each commune, and of Deputies, councillor-generals and district councillors in each department.

The two Houses united as a National Assembly, elected by absolute majority a President of the Republic to serve seven years, meeting immediately whenever a vacancy occurred. The President selected a Cabinet of Ministers, generally from the two Chambers, but was permitted to go outside the membership. In practice the President summoned a leader who could obtain a majority in the Chambers in support of his policies as President of the Council (Premier) and he made up his list of Ministers and submitted it for approval to the two Houses. The number of portfolios varied. Each Minister was responsible to the Chambers for his acts and the Ministry as a whole was responsible for the general policy of the Government.

The unit of local Government was the commune. Each commune elected by general suffrage a municipal council which in turn elected a Mayor, who is both a representative of the commune, the agent of the central Government and the head of the police. Each Department had representatives of all Ministries and was placed under a prefect nominated by the Government and having wide functions. The system continues under the French State.

The tenure of office of the Premier was subject to the will of the Chamber of Deputies. If the Chamber refused him a vote of confidence, he tendered his resignation and another Premier was named by the President.

The last elected President of France was Albert Lebrun (1932-1939). He was born (Aug. 29, 1871) and elected (May 10, 1932) to succeed Paul Doumer, who was assassinated (May 5, 1932). Lebrun was reelected (April 5, 1939) by the National Assembly.

In a letter addressed to Marshal Petain and his Chief of Government, M. Laval, Jules Jeanneney, president of the Senate, and Edouard Herriot, president of the Chamber of Deputies, protested the order of Marshal Petain in decreeing the dissolution of the permanent staffs of the Houses of Parliament, putting the final, formal seal of death on the Third Republic. The parliamentary chieftains protested against what they called Marshal Petain's violation of his solemn promises to limit his powers and against any move to enter the war against the United Nations. The letter said in part: "In July, 1940, to obtain a vote of full powers by the National Assembly you promised through Pierre Laval that the chambers would not be suppressed. Your Constitution Act of July 11, 1940, stipulated that the Senate and the Chamber should continue until new assemblies provided by the new Constitution were ready. But by the same act you adjourned the chambers and decreed that they could meet again only when you convoked them."

The unit of currency is the franc, stabilized (Feb. 29, 1940) at 21 milligrammes of fine gold.

The budget (1942) anticipates revenues of 80,000,-000,000 francs and expenditures of 138,500,000,000.

The French Army was divided into the Metropolitan and the Colonial armies. The peace establishment Metropolitan army (1938-1939) consists of an active army of 491,000, of whom 421,000 are for home defense and 70,000 a mobile reserve for overseas garrisons. The conscript served two years in the active army, and is available thereafter for a period of 26 years.

The Navy consisted (1941) of seven battleships, two of which were disabled at Oran and Dakar, two manned by Free French forces in British ports and one demilitarized at Alexandria, Egypt; one aircraft carrier, immobilized at Martinique; 18 cruisers, of which four were demilitarized at Alexandria and one immobilized at Martinique; 47 sloops and other ships of which the Free French had at least nine; 50 destroyers of which five were with the Free French or demobilized at Alexandria; 67 submarines of which four were with the Free French or were demilitarized at Alexandria, and minor craft. At the time of the armistice the Navy personnel was approximately 85,000 officers and men.

The terms of the armistice provided that all naval units, except some left to guard the empire, be recalled to specified ports and placed under German or Italian control. Germany declared it would not use the French fleet against Great Britain.

The armistice terms deprived France of all military aircraft at home but there is an Air Force Overseas.

The armistice provided for the demobilization of all naval, air and military forces, with the exception of police troops of which a force of 100,000 was permitted.

All French youth in their twenties, the former military age, must enroll for six months in the compulsory National Service organization instead of the army, which, under the terms imposed by Germany, must be recruited entirely from volunteers.

France constructed a system of fortifications, known as the Maginot line, extending 125 miles along the Franco-German frontier from Switzerland to Luxemburg. Later the line was extended along the Franco-Belgian border to the North Sea. It is estimated that the original Maginot line and the extension cost $500,000,000. The extension was constructed after the declaration of war by France against Germany (1939) and was not as formidable as the original line which took five years to build.

Trenches linked a series of casemates—shellproof vaults with embrasures through which artillery and machine guns might be fired—from one to 16 miles apart. From this chain, which included an elaborate system of subterranean barracks connected by tunnels, army officers believed a continuous barrage might be laid down along the frontier. The line was so constructed that troops were hidden from enemy view and protected by the fortifications against bombardment.

Defense against gas was provided by a special process; electric machinery maintained in the interior an atmospheric pressure slightly higher than the exterior pressure. Gunners laid their fire by following the indications on a dial, controlled by an artillery officers in a hermetically sealed armored chamber, who viewed the outside world through panoramic telescopes. Telephone lines were built through concrete slabs or buried underground. The fortifications contained miles of barracks with passages lighted by electricity. Every precaution was taken to make the line habitable for months. Tons of concrete and steel for more obstacles, traps, pits, trenches, gun emplacements and field fortifications of all kinds as well as concrete casements and block houses were added (1940) to the line.

The German army in the Battle of France cut through all except a few miles of the rear of the line (June 16, 1940) and the French withdrew virtually all of the 500,000 in the line. Later it was reported that the Germans had destroyed the line so far as its military value was concerned. Germany began to dismantle the line (1941) and the land was subdivided into small farms and handed down to peasant families under a system established in Germany.

More than one-third of the French merchant fleet has been lost or destroyed since 1938, according to an article published (1942) in The Merchant Marine Journal. The fleet in 1938 numbered 643 ships of 1,000 tons or more, divided as follows: 133 liners, 412 freighters, 28 fruit ships and 69 tankers.

French Colonies

	Sq. Mi.	Population		Sq. Mi.	Population
IN ASIA			**IN AFRICA**		
Syria & Lebanon (Mandate)	57,900	3,630,000	Morocco (Protectorate)....	162,120	6,242,706
French India..............	196	323,500	Algeria...................	847,552	7,234,684
French Indo-China........	286,000	23,853,295	Tunis....................	48,313	2,608,313
			French West Africa........	1,818,698	14,944,830
Total in Asia..........	344,096	27,806,795	Togoland (Mandate)........	21,893	780,497
IN AMERICA			Cameroon (Mandate)......	166,489	2,516,623
St. Pierre and Miquelon....	93	3,916	French Equatorial Africa..	959,256	3,418,066
Guadeloupe..............	583	304,209	Reunion..................	970	208,858
Martinique..............	385	246,712	Madagascar..............	241,094 }	3,797,936
French Guiana and Inini...	65,041	30,906	Commoro................	790	
			French Somaliland........	8,492	44,240
Total in America......	66,102	585,743			
IN OCEANIA			**Total in Africa..........**	4,275,667	41,796,753
New Caledonia, etc........	8,548	53,245			
Tahiti, etc...............	1,520	39,920	**Grand total in all colonies.**	4,695,933	70,282,456
Total in Oceania.......	10,068	93,165			

•The Petain Government announced (Sept. 30, 1940) that it would retain full military and civilian control of all French Colonies and Protectorates.

ALGERIA
(L'Algerie)

Algeria is in the northern part of Africa, extending for 650 miles along the Mediterranean Sea, between Tunis on the east and Morocco on the west. Both neighbors are French protectorates. The northern territory extends inland approximately 350 miles; beyond, the four southern territories extend southward indefinitely into the Sahara Desert, merging into French West Africa. On the coast is an area, the Tell, from 50 to 100 miles wide, of very fertile plains with valleys running out from the hills, mainly owned by Europeans, which is cultivated scientifically. Behind the Tell is the tableland of the Shat with an elevation of 3,000 ft., arid, or covered with salt lakes and swamp. The two chains of the Atlas Mountains, reaching to altitudes of 7,000 ft., divide the country from the Sahara. Algeria has a population (1936) of 7,234,684; and area of 847,500 square miles. The capital is Algiers. The natives are Moslems.

The Northern Territory, area 80,117 square miles, is divided into three departments: Algiers, population, 2,240,911; Oran, 1,623,356; and Constantine, 2,727,766. Each department sends one senator and three deputies to the National Assembly which alone has the right to legislate for Algeria.

An army corps of the Metropolitan army (the XIXth) was stationed in Algeria. It included the Foreign Legion; six regiments of Zouaves; six regiments of cavalry (Chasseurs d'Afrique); six of field, and one of heavy, artillery, the battalion of engineers and one regiment of the flying corps; 12 regiments of Algerian Tirailleurs, and six regiments of Spahis (Arab cavalry). The strength of the garrison at Algiers and Tunis (1937) was 3,003 officers and 82,722 men. The Air Corps had 2,280 of all ranks in 5 groups. French and British fleets fought a battle at the naval base of Oran (July 4, 1940) after the signing of the armistice.

Nationals must serve two years with the army and then may be called up as reservists in case of mobilization.

Agricultural products include wheat, barley, oats, corn, potatoes, artichokes, flax and tobacco. Wine and olive oil are produced. Dates, pomegranates and figs grow abundantly. Cattle grazing is the chief agricultural pursuit. There are large deposits of iron, zinc, lead, mercury, copper and antimony.

The principal imports are textiles, machines, automobiles, petroleum, sugar, coal, iron and steel, cereals and coffee. Exports consist chiefly of wines, cereals, sheep, olive oil, esparto, spirits. Trade is mainly with France.

The unit of currency is the French franc. Gov-ernmental revenues (1940) were estimated at 2,526,128,968 francs; expenditures at 2,525,778,285.

The Southern Territory, area 767,435 square miles, forms a separate colony under military command which acts with the authority of a governor and has a separate budget. The Southern Territory has a population (1936) of 642,651.

TUNIS
(Afrikiya; Tunisie)

Tunis, one of the former Barbary states under the suzerainty of Turkey, is situate on the northern coast of Africa, with the Mediterranean Sea on the north and east, Italian Libya on the southeast, the Sahara Desert on the south and Algeria on the west. The capital is Tunis. The country has an area of 48,313 square miles and a population (1936) of 2,608,313. The native population is composed of Arabs and Bedouins.

The French were obliged to send a military force into the country (1881) to protect Algeria from the raids of the Khroumer tribes, which resulted in a treaty (signed May 12, 1881) placing Tunis under the protectorate of France.

The native ruler of Tunis is Sidi Ahmed Bey (born 1862).

The army of occupation consists of 25,000 men with 1,150 officers.

There are large fertile valleys in the mountainous north, excellent land for fruit culture in the northeast peninsula, high tablelands and pastures in the center, and famous oases and gardens in the south, where dates grow in profusion. The chief industry is agriculture, and wheat, barley, oats, olives, grapes and dates are produced in abundance, besides almonds, oranges, lemons, shaddocks, pistachios, alfa grass, henna and cork. Lead, iron, phosphate and zinc are the most important minerals.

Textiles, manufactured metals, and minerals comprise the chief imports; agricultural products, olive oil, and minerals are the principal exports. Government receipts (1940) were 811,198,000 francs; expenditures 810,954,000.

(For information on the French protectorate of Morocco, see Morocco.)

FRENCH WEST AFRICA

French West Africa reaches from the Atlantic Ocean at about 17° west longitude across Africa to the Soudan at about 15° east longitude and from the southern desert boundaries of Morocco, Algeria, Tunis and Italian Libya to the Gulf of Guinea and the indeterminate boundary of French Equatorial Africa. It has been formed by consolidation of seven colonies.

The population included 26,614 Europeans. The capital, Dakar, has about 40,000 population. The governmental budget for 1938 was estimated to balance at 1,126,264,486 francs.

The colonies export fruits, palm nuts and oil, rubber, cotton, cacao, timber, and peanuts. The chief imports are foodstuffs, textiles, machinery

and hardware, and spirits. Trade is mainly with France.

Colony	Sq. M.	Pop., 1937
Senegal, incl. Dakar Dist.	77,790	1,666,374
Mauritania	323,310	370,764
French Guinea	96,886	2,065,527
Ivory Coast	184,174	3,981,459
Dahomey	43,232	1,289,128
French Sudan	590,966	3,635,073
Niger	499,410	1,809,576
Dakar and dependencies	60	126,929
Total	1,818,698	14,944,830

The general budget (1939) balanced at 349,000,000 francs.

FRENCH EQUATORIAL AFRICA
(French Congo)

French Equatorial Africa is in the heart of Africa and has a seacoast on the South Atlantic Ocean between Spanish Guinea and the Belgian Congo.

Its other neighbors are the Cameroons, Anglo-Egyptian Soudan, Libya, French West Africa and Nigeria. French acquisition began (1841) and its territory has since been extended by exploration and occupation. That part (107,270 square miles) ceded to Germany as compensation for acknowledgment of the Morocco protectorate (1911) was restored to France in the Treaty of Versailles and incorporated in this territory. The capital is Brazzaville. The constituent colonies are:

Colony	Sq. M.	Pop., 1931
Gabun	93,218	408,516
Middle Congo	166,069	744,503
Ubangi-Shari	238,767	833,041
Chad	461,202	1,432,006
Total	959,256	3,418,066

Europeans number 4,949.

There are 300,000 square miles of tropical forests, rich in timber, but the output as yet is only wild rubber, and palm oil and ivory. Copper, lead and zinc are found. Commerce is chiefly with France. The general budget (1938) was balanced at 224,-629,000 francs.

The Government is in control of the Free French and received recognition from the United States (April 4, 1942).

CAMEROON AND TOGOLAND

Cameroon is that part of the former German Colony Kamerun (captured Feb., 1916). It consists of 166,489 square miles and was allotted to France as a Mandate by the Treaty of Versailles. It was constituted an autonomous territory by decree (March, 1921). It is governed by a Commissioner. The capital is Yaounde. Its population (1938) is 2,516,623, including 3,106 Europeans.

The colony has two seaports, Douala and Kibri. Its chief products are palm oil, ground nuts, almonds, hides, cacao and ivory. Trade is principally with France.

The Government is in control of the Free French and received recognition from the United States (April 4, 1942).

Of Togoland, the only German colony that was self-supporting, France received 21,893 square miles, about two-thirds. It is attached to French Dahomey, and is a mandated territory with a population of 780,497.

The local budget (1939) balanced at 50,354,000 francs; in addition there was a railroad budget of 12,889,000 francs.

FRENCH SOMALILAND

French Somaliland lies between Eritrea (Italian), Ethiopia and British Somaliland and is separated by the Straits of Bab-el-Mandeb from Aden (British).

The area is 8,492 square miles and population (1936), 44,240; the capital is Jibuti (population,

14,870), its port on the Gulf of Aden, acquired (1862) but not developed until 1884. The budget (1939) balanced at 26,000,000 francs.

The colony has few industries, but hides, coffee and ivory are exported. Jibuti is connected with Addis Ababa by railroad and much of Ethiopia's commerce passes through it.

MADAGASCAR

Madagascar, an island off the east coast of Africa from which it is separated by the Mozambique Channel (240 miles wide at its narrowest part), is about 980 miles long and 360 miles wide at its greatest breadth. Its area is 241,094 square miles; its population (1936, including Mayotte and Comoro Islands) 3,797,936. The capital is Tananarivo.

To Madagascar is attached for government the prosperous archipelago of the Comoro Islands with an area in all of about 790 square miles, and with, in 1931, 130,253 inhabitants.

Madagascar came under a French protectorate (1885) and was declared a French colony (1896). More than 3,000,000 acres are under cultivation, the chief crops being rice, manioc, beans, vanilla, corn, coffee, cloves, tobacco, sugar cane and cocoa. The forests are rich in cabinet and tanning wood, raffia, resins, gums and beeswax.

Agriculture and stock-raising are the chief industries. Minerals found include graphite, mica, phosphates, gold and radium.

The estimated budget (1939) balanced at 343,660,-000 francs.

British forces, acting in behalf of the United Nations, occupied the naval base of Diego Suarez (May 7, 1942). This was extended later to complete occupation of the island.

REUNION

Reunion is in fact an integral part of France, as it is represented in Parliament at Paris by a Senator and two Deputies. It is an island in the Indian Ocean, about 420 miles east of Madagascar, and has belonged to France since 1643. The area is 970 square miles; the population (1936), 208,858,

of whom 203,319 are of French extraction. The chief products are sugar, rum, coffee, manioc, tapioca, vanilla and spices. The chief imports are rice and cereals. Trade is principally with France. The budget (1937) balanced at 61,620,700 francs.

FRENCH INDIA

The French possessions in India lie along the Coromandel coast, on the Bay of Bengal, in the southeastern part, to the north of the island of Ceylon. The most important is Pondicherry, established by the French East Indian Company (1674), which, after changing hands eight times, finally rested in the control of France (1814). The colonies are divided in five dependencies: Pondicherry, population (1941), 204,653; Karikal, 60,055; Chan-

dernagor, 38,284; Mahe, 14,092; Yanaon, 5,711. The colonies send one Senator and one Deputy to Parliament at Paris. Agriculture is the chief industry and oil seed the chief export. Pondicherry has five cotton mills.

The total population of French India is 304,680; the area is 196 square miles. Pondicherry is the capital The budget (1941) balanced at 2,940,769 rupees.

FRENCH INDO-CHINA

	Area	Population
Cochin-China	26,476 sq. mi.	4,615,968
Annam	56,973 sq. mi.	6,211,228
Cambodia	67,550 sq. mi.	3,046,432
Tonkin	40,530 sq. mi.	9,264,309
Laos	89,320 sq. mi.	1,023,314
Kwangchow	325 sq. mi.	300,000
Total	**281,174 sq. mi.**	**24,461,251**

French Indo-China, situated in the southeastern part of Asia with China on the north, Siam on the west and the Gulf of Tonkin and the South China Sea on the east and south, comprises five states, as shown above. The population includes about 42,000 Europeans. The capital is Hanoi, Tonkin.

Under the terms of settlement (1941) of a border dispute, French Indo-China ceded 21,750 square

miles to Thailand. Cambodia yielded 16,887 square miles and Laos 4,863.

French Indo-China was placed under the armed protection of Japan (1941) according to an agreement reached by the French Government (Vichy) and Japan. Under the terms of the accord Japan occupied military and navy bases in Indo-China.

The whole country was under a Governor-General with a Secretary-General and a superior Council, and each state had a head, that of the colony being a Governor, and those of the protectorates being called Residents Superior. There was a common budget for Indo-China, which (1940) balanced at 134,678,870 plastres. The piastre was stabilized (1926) at 10 francs (39.2 cents gold).

The chief exports are rice, rubber, fish, coal, pepper, cattle and hides, corn, zinc and tin. The principal imports are cotton and silk tissues, metal goods, kerosene and motor cars.

GUADELOUPE

Guadeloupe, consisting of two large islands, Basse-Terre and Grande Terre, separated by a narrow channel, and five smaller islands, is a group of the Windward Islands in the West Indies, between Antigua and Dominica. They have been in the possession of France since 1634 and are represented in Parliament at Paris by a Senator and two Deputies. The government consists of a Gov-

ernor and an elected Council. The soil is very productive. The area of the entire group of islands is 583 square miles; population (1936) is 304,209. Basse-Terre is the capital. The budget (1939) balanced at 86,608,979.

The principal exports are sugar, coffee, rum, cacao, vanilla, bananas. Trade is mainly with France.

MARTINIQUE

Martinique, one of the Windward Islands, in the West Indies, has been a possession of France since 1635. It is represented in the French Parliament by a Senator and two Deputies. It is administered by a Governor, a General Council, and elective Municipal Councils. In Martinique is located the famous volcano, Mt. Pelee, which in eruption on (May 8, 1902) destroyed the city of St. Pierre with all its 40,000 inhabitants. The island is the birth-

place of the Empress Josephine.

Martinique has a population (1936) of 246,712, and an area of 385 square miles. The capital is Fort-de-France.

The chief exports are sugar, rum, bananas, pineapples and cocoa beans. Trade is mainly with France. The franc is the monetary unit. The governmental budget (1937) was balanced at 101,-100,000 francs.

ST. PIERRE AND MIQUELON

St. Pierre and Miquelon are two groups of rocky barren islands close to the southwestern coast of Newfoundland, inhabited by fishermen. Townships were abolished (July 18, 1935) and an administrator, assisted by a council, rules the islands. The exports are chiefly cod, dried and fresh, and other fish products. Imports consist of textiles, salt, wines, foodstuffs and meat. A regular boat service is maintained with North Sydney and Halifax. A telegraph cable connects St. Pierre with

Europe and the American continent. The French franc, is the medium of exchange. The budget (1940) was balanced at 13,738,690 francs.

The St. Pierre group has an area of 10 square miles; Miquelon, 83 square miles. The population is—St. Pierre: 3,396; Miquelon: 520; total: 3,916. The capital is St. Pierre.

Free French forces occupied the islands (Dec. 24, 1941). A plebiscite, held later, voted: for Free French, 783; for collaboration with the Axis powers, 14; voided ballots, 215.

FRENCH GUIANA

French Guiana is on the north coast of South America on the Atlantic Ocean, with Dutch Guiana on the west and Brazil on the east and south. The country has lost heavily in population in the last several decades, the census of 1911 returning 49,009 inhabitants as compared with 30,906 in 1936 (including the hinterland of Inini, separated territorially from Guiana July 6, 1930). The area of Guiana is 34,740 square miles. The area of Inini is 30,301 square miles. Guiana sends one Deputy to the Chamber at Paris. The colony has a Governor and a Council General of 16 elected members.

France has a famous penal colony there since 1885, known as Devil's Island. It has (1938) nearly 6,000 prisoners. The capital is Cayenne.

Immense forests of rich timber cover the territory. Very little of the land is cultivated. The principal crops are rice, corn, manioc, cocoa, bananas, and sugar cane. Placer gold mining is the most important industry. Exports comprise cocoa, bananas, various woods, gold, fish glue, rum, rosewood essence, balata and hides. Trade is chiefly with France.

The franc is the monetary unit. The budget (1938) balanced at 17,704,755 francs.

OCEANIA—TAHITI

The French possessions, widely scattered in the southern Pacific Ocean, were grouped together (1903) as one homogeneous colony under one Governor, with headquarters at Papeete, Tahiti, one of the Society Islands. The other groups are the Marquesas, the Tuamoti Group, the Leeward Islands, the Gambier, the Tubuai, and Rapa Islands. Tahiti is picturesque and mountainous with a productive coastland bearing cocoanut, banana' and orange trees, sugar-cane, vanilla and other tropical fruits. Preparation of copra, sugar and rum are the chief industries. Trade is largely with France.

The area of the islands administered at Tahiti is 1,520 square miles; the population is 39,920.

New Caledonia, with an area of 8,548 square miles and a population (census of 1936) of 53,245, is 248 miles long and has an average breadth of 31 miles. It is about half way between Australia and the Fiji Islands. Its dependencies are: The Isle of Pines, the Wallis Archipelago, the Loyalty Islands, the Huon Islands, Fortuna, and Alofi. The group was acquired by France (1854), and " penal colony was maintained on Nou Island until 1896.

The Colony is administered by a Governor and an elective council general. It is under control of the Free French, assisted by United States forces. Noumea is the capital.

Mining is the chief industry. Chrome, cobalt, nickel, iron and manganese abound. Other minerals found are antimony, mercury, cinnabar, silver, gold, lead and copper. Agricultural products include coffee, copra, cotton, manioc (cassava), corn, tobacco, bananas and pineapples.

The New Hebrides, 250 miles northeast of New Caledonia and 500 miles west of Fiji, is a group with an aggregate area of 5,700 square miles, having a native population estimated at about 60,000, and a white population. (1930): British, 219; French, 931. The group has been a condominium since 1906 and administered jointly by High Commissioners of France and Great Britain. Chief products are copra, cotton, cacao and coffee.

Germany
(DEUTSCHES REICH)

Capital, Berlin—Area, 225,256 square miles—Population (census, 1939), 79,375,281. (The area and population data include Austria and the Sudetenland.)

The German Reich, as it is called officially, is situated in the heart of Europe. It is bounded on the north by the North Sea, Denmark and the Baltic; on the east by Poland, Lithuania, Czechoslovakia and Hungary; on the south by Czechoslovakia, Yugoslavia, Switzerland and Italy, and on the west by France, Luxemburg, Belgium, Holland, Switzerland and Liechtenstein.

The climate of Germany is quite mild in summer and rather cold in winter, as in all western Europe. The soil is not naturally fertile, being largely a glacial plain over which the action of the ice moved much sand: it has always demanded unusual artificial fertilization. The land is heavily wooded. Forestry is far advanced, perhaps more perfected as a science than in any other country. The Black Forest of Germany is famed for its timber and as a resort. The highest mountains are the Bavarian and Austrian Alps in the south. The northern part is a plain sloping to the north and west.

The longest river within the Reich until recently was the Oder, whose length is 515 miles. Only 402 miles of the Danube lay within German territory until the addition of 217 miles of the Austrian Danube made this historical and romantic old river the longest.

The census (1939) gives Germany a population of 79,375,281, not including Bohemia and Moravia, Danzig and Memel. The census reported 38,812,032 males and 40,764,726 females (the total does not accord with the official population figures.) The Government announced the density of population had increased from 339.2 inhabitants per square mile (1933) to 352.3 and that the population of the old Reich, excluding the Saar, Austria, Sudetenland, Bohemia and Moravia and Memelland had increased about 3,200,000 or more than 4 per cent since 1933. The census disclosed 1,048 women for each 1,000 men and that more male babies than female were being born in the Reich.

The census also revealed that there remained in the Reich 330,892 fullblooded Jews; 72,733 half-breed Jews and 42,811 quarterbreeds. These figures are from the Old Reich and include Austria and the Sudetenland, but not Bohemia and Moravia. Of the Jews counted it was said that 88.1 were German subjects and 11.9 foreigners and stateless.

Through its union with Austria the Reich acquired four new neighbors—Italy, Yugoslavia, Hungary and Liechtenstein. The Austro-German frontier of 500 miles has been abolished, but the Reich has gained frontiers on the south aggregating 1,300 miles. South of Lake Constance, the Rhine now forms the boundary between Switzerland and the Reich, while at the point where the Inn River flows out of the Lower Engadine Valley, the frontiers of Germany, Italy and Switzerland join in a sort of triangle. It was the German absorption of Austria with the latter's frontage on southern Czechoslovakia that gave the Reich a pincers hold on the Czech republic, thus opening the way to the annexation of the Sudetenland.

Vienna, the former capital of Austria, is now the second city of Germany, ranking next to Berlin and ahead of Hamburg. To the 60 large German cities with populations of more than 100,000 there are now added Graz and Linz. Former Czechoslovakia cities awarded to the Reich in the four-power accord (Sept. 1938) include Karlsbad, a famous health resort and porcelain center; Komotau, noted for its zinc production, and Reichtenberg, a textile town.

World War I cost Germany 27,275 square miles and 6,471,581 in population. It lost Alsace-Lorraine, returned to France, 5,604 square miles, and 1,874,014 population; Eupen and Malmedy, ceded to Belgium, 386 square miles, and 60,924 population; part of Eastern and Upper Silesia, ceded to Poland, 17,787 square miles, and 3,853,354 population; Memel, ceded to the Allies, 1,057 square miles, and 140,746 population; Danzig, made a free city, 794 square miles, and 330,252 population; Schleswig northern zone, ceded to Denmark by the plebiscite, 1,537. square miles, and 166,895 population; part of Upper Silesia, ceded to Czecho-Slovakia, 110 square miles, and 45,395 population.

The Saar Basin, area 738 square miles, was separated from Germany after World War I and administered by the League of Nations through a commission. The French had the sole right to work the coal mines for 15 years in recompense for the destruction of the coal mines in North of France. The Saar, which by a vote of 477,119 to 48,637 (Jan. 13, 1935) declared its desire to rejoin Germany, was returned to the Reich by the League (March 1, 1935.)

The plebiscite in Upper Silesia (March, 1921) resulted in a majority for retention in the Reich, but, notwithstanding, that territory of 1,255 square miles with a population of 891,669 was annexed by Poland.

The Ruhr, seized and held by France and Belgium under the "sanctions" of the Treaty of Versailles (Jan. 11, 1923) and extended subsequently, is a territory of approximately 965 square miles with 4,000,000 inhabitants. It was evacuated (Oct. 14, 1925.)

Following an ultimatum from Berlin, Dr. Kurt von Schuschnigg, Chancellor of Austria, resigned (March 11, 1938) and was succeeded by the Austrian Nazi leader, Arthur Seyss-Inquart. Seyss-Inquart immediately asked the Reich to send troops to help in preserving order, and some 50,000 highly armed and mechanized forces crossed the border.

Chancellor Adolf Hitler entered Austria (March 12, 1938) and in a speech before a great throng at Linz proclaimed the unity of the country with Germany. He was preceded by large forces of troops which occupied important cities, a detachment going to the capital and another to Brenner Pass on the Italian frontier. Schuschnigg was placed under arrest. Austria was formally incorporated into the Reich (March 13, 1938). President Wilhelm Miklas was forced out of office and Hitler appointed Seyss-Inquart Statthalter (governor).

The absorption of Austria into Germany has not been recognized by the United States.

The Sudeten area of Czechoslovakia was annexed by Germany (Oct. 1, 1938) following an agreement to that effect signed in Munich (Sept. 29, 1938) by Great Britain, France, Italy and Germany and accepted by Czechoslovakia (Sept. 30). The agreement further called for a plebiscite on affiliation with Germany to be held in other disputed areas of Czechoslovakia which the Nazis claimed were predominantly German. The signatories were Neville Chamberlain, Edouard Daladier, Benito Mussolini and Adolf Hitler, representing Great Britain, France, Italy and Germany respectively. Their meeting climaxed a 15-day international crisis in which all the great European powers mobilized for war.

The British Government announced (Aug. 5, 1942) that the Munich agreement had been repudiated and that the fixing of post-war frontiers of Czechoslovakia will not be influenced by changes made since the pact was signed.

Bohemia and Moravia (area 28,717 sq. mi., population 10,897,000) were occupied by Germany (March, 1938). See Index, Czechoslovakia.

Memel (area 1,099 sq. mi.; population 152,000) the chief port of Lithuania, since absorbed by Soviet Russia, was returned to the Reich (March, 1939) on a demand of the Reich based on the self determination of the peoples. Memel was detached from East Prussia, Germany, by the treaty of Versailles and awarded to Lithuania. The harbor of Memel, unlike other Baltic ports, never freezes. Shortly after the occupation of Memel, the area was fortified by Germany.

Danzig (area 754 sq. m.; population 415,000) was absorbed by the Reich in the war against Poland (1939). See Index Danzig.

German troops occupied Poland (1939): see Index, Poland.

Eupen and Malmedy were incorporated into the Reich (1940) by order of Hitler. German forces occupied Denmark and invaded Norway the same year. German troops occupied Holland, Belgium and Luxemburg (1940) and Germany mastered

France the same year with the signing of the armistice.

The land area and population of the States of the Reich (census, 1939) follow:

States of the Reich	Land area Sq. Miles	Pop.
Prussia	113,575	41,762,040
Bavaria	30,054	8,280,090
Wurttemberg	7,532	2,907,166
Mecklenberg	6,069	910,826
Baden	5,818	2,518,103
Saxony	5,789	5,206,861
Thuringia	4,541	1,760,595
Hesse	2,969	1,469,909
Oldenburg	2,083	582,400
Brunswick	1,418	599,208
Anhalt	893	436,213
Lippe	469	188,598
Hamburg	288	1,682,220
Schaumburg-Lippe	131	54,162
Bremen	99	400,086
Saarland	743	863,736
German Reich	182,471	*69,622,213
Austria	34,064	7,009,014
Sudetenland	8,721	2,945,261
Greater Germany	225,256	79,576,488

*The official count of the 1939 census was announced as 79,375,281.

The census (1939) revealed 39,792,000 gainfully employed in Germany (including the Saar, Austria and Sudetenland but not Memeland), of which 34,269,000 were in the old Reich. This was an increase of 29.6 per cent over 1933. The distribution (1939) according to occupation follows:

Occupation	Wage earners Millions	Per cent of total	Male Millions	Female Millions
Agriculture and forestry	10.85	27.3	4.91	5.94
Industry, handicraft....	16.50	41.5	12.67	3.83
Trade service..........	6.85	17.2	4.46	2.39
Public service.........	4.07	10.2	2.82	1.25
Household service......	1.52	3.8	0.01	1.51
Total.............	39.79	100.0	24.87	14.92

The Free State of Waldeck was absorbed by Prussia (April 1, 1929). The Free States of Mecklenburg-Schwerin and Mecklenburg-Strelitz were united as Mecklenburg (Jan. 1, 1934).

There are 29 universities in Germany including the University of Vienna (founded in 1356) and Heidelberg (founded in 1386). There is compulsory military training in Nazi storm detachments and a one-year term of manual labor for all male undergraduates. Elementary education is compulsory.

When the German Emperor abdicated and fled to Holland (Nov., 1918) the self-constituted Council of People's Commissioners took over the government and proclaimed a republic. A call was issued for the election of a National Assembly. It met at Weimar (Feb. 6, 1919) and elected Friedrich Ebert President of the republic (Feb. 11). His term was extended to June 30, 1925.

The National Assembly adopted a Constitution (July 31, 1919). It was known as the Weimar Constitution.

Ebert died (Feb. 28, 1925) and was succeeded by Field Marshal Paul von Hindenburg (re-elected 1932). In this election Hindenburg received 19,-359,642 votes to Adolf Hitler's 13,417,460.

The result of the election (March 5, 1933) as compared with the election (Nov. 6, 1932), is shown in the following table:

Parties of the Right	March, 1933 Vote	Seats	Nov., 1932 Vote	Seats
Nation'l Socialists.	17,269,629	288	11,737,185	196
Nationalists......	3,133,938	52	3,235,896	51
People's Party....	432,234	2	660,672	11
Agrarians........	47,723	...	64,004	1
Totals........	**20,883,524**	**342**	**15,697,757**	**262**
Republican Parties				
Germ'n Soc'l Dem.	7,177,294	120	7,251,410	121
Catholic Centre...	4,423,319	74	4,100,603	70
Bavarian People's.	1,073,815	18	1,156,841	20
Chris.Soc.People's	384,146	4	413,144	5
State Party......	333,619	5	338,542	2
Economic Party...	....	...	110,343	1
Peasants' Party...	114,237	2	149,005	3
Wurtt. Farmers...	83,828	1	96,859	2
Totals........	**13,590,258**	**224**	**13,685,747**	**224**
Extreme Left				
Communists.....	4,845,651	81	5,980,240	100
Grand total...	**39,319,433**	**647**	**35,363,744**	**583**

The Nazi vote increased by 5,532,544, 44% of the total, and the 288 seats which they won, in combination with the 52 seats of the Nationalists, gave them an absolute majority of the Reichstag. Hitler became Chancellor.

The new Reichstag promptly passed an Enabling Act by which absolute power was conferred on Chancellor Hitler and his cabinet. The Reichstag continued (Jan. 31, 1937) the Enabling Act until April 1, 1941. Deriving authority from this act, Hitler has completely personalized government in Germany. He has absolute control of all activities throughout the country—political, economic, industrial, commercial, cultural. Freedom of speech and of the press has been abolished. Equality before the law applies only to Aryans, the only people in Germany who have full citizenship rights which are restricted by the Gestapo (secret police).

The Cabinet follows:

Fuehrer and Chancellor—Adolf Hitler (born April 20, 1889 in Braunau, Austria.)

Ministers:

Interior—Heinrich Lammers.
Foreign Affairs—Joachim von Ribbentrop.
Defense—Adolf Hitler.
Munitions—Albert Speer.
Finance—Ludwig Count Schwerin von Krosigk.
Food and Agriculture—Herbert Backe.
Economic Affairs—Dr. Walther Funk.
Labor—Franz Seldte.
Posts—Dr. Wilhelm Ohnesorge.
Transport—Dr. Dorpmueller.
Aviation—Reich Marshal Hermann Goering.
Justice—Dr. Otto Georg Thierack.
Learning and Education—B. Rust.
National Enlightenment and Propaganda—Dr. Joseph Goebbels.

Ministers without Portfolio:
Dr. Hanns Frank, Dr. Hjalmar Schacht, Dr. Heinrich Lammers, Dr. Otto Meissner and Konstantin Count von Neurath.

Goering became war-time economic dictator of Germany (Jan. 4, 1940) by taking control of every branch of industry and commerce directly or indirectly connected with the nation's war economy. Goering assumed most of the powers held by Dr. Funk as minister of economic affairs. Goering formed a "general council" to direct and coordinate production, distribution and consumption. Subordinated to him are several cabinet members. Included in the "council" are several high army and Nazi party officials.

The National Socialist German Labor Party, to give its full name, though familiarly known as Nazis, was founded (1920) in Munich by Hitler (then 31 years old). Austrian-born, he had served throughout the war in the German Army and in consequence had lost his Austrian citizenship. He later obtained German citizenship and took the oath to support the constitution when the State of Brunswick (Feb. 22, 1932) gave him a position in its diplomatic service.

The Nazis were a small group, anti-Semitic, with vague socialist leanings but strongly opposed to the Social Democrats and the Republican Constitution of the Reich. With Hitler and Gen. Ludendorf as leaders, it staged the so-called "Beer Hall Putsch" in Munich (Nov. 8-9, 1923). This proved abortive and Hitler was sentenced to five years imprisonment—a sentence soon quashed. The party was reorganized but was reduced by internal dissensions to insignificance. In the Reichstag election (1924) the party joined with a party called Movement for German Racial Freedom and the combination won 32 seats. But the next year the Nazis cut loose and reorganized again. The economic crisis and widespread discontent gave Hitler, a magnetic speaker, renewed opportunity. The growth of the Nazis is shown in the following table.

Election	Date	Popular Vote	Seats
Reichstag	May 20, 1928	809,541	12
Reichstag	Sept. 14, 1930	6,406,397	107
Presidential 1st B.	Mar. 10, 1932	11,341,119	...
Presidential 2d B.	Apr. 10, 1932	13,417,460	...
Reichstag	July 31, 1932	13,732,777	230
Reichstag	Nov. 6, 1932	11,737,185	196
Reichstag	Mar. 5, 1933	17,269,629	288

To crush an incipient revolt against him by the radicals headed by Capt. Roehm, Chief of Staff of the Storm Troops (S. A.), Hitler (June 30, 1934) flew from Berlin to Munich and arrested Roehm in his own house. Roehm, Heines and Karl Ernest, head of the Berlin brown shirts, with others were shot. In Berlin Goering's special police with the Nazi Schutz Staffel (the black shirt elite of the storm troops) in carrying out their part of the "purge" shot ex-Chancellor Gen. von Schleicher and his wife while "resisting arrest," also the adjutant and two secretaries of Vice Chancellor von Papen (later sent to Austria as Minister after the murder of Dollfuss, and then to Turkey), Dr. Erich Klausener, head of the Catholic Action Society, and several others. When Hitler justified the "purge" before the Reichstag (July 13) he gave the number of dead as 77.

President von Hindenberg died (Aug. 2, 1934), the day after the Cabinet adopted a decree uniting the office of Reich President with that of Reich Chancellor to take effect after his death.

The result of the plebiscite (Aug. 19, 1934) as compared with the vote at the plebiscite (Nov. 12, 1933) when the Reich approved of the government's withdrawal from the League of Nations and the General Disarmament Conference, follows:

	August, 1934	November, 1933
Electorate	45,473,635	45,146,277
Total votes cast	43,529,710	43,460,529
For Hitler	38,362,763	40,609,247
Against	4,294,654	2,101,000
Invalid	872,296	750,282

Hitler got 88.1% of the August vote. He got 93.5% of the vote in November.

In the plebiscite (March 29, 1936) on his foreign policy, Hitler was credited with 44,409,523 votes out of 44,952,476 votes cast, being 98.5% of the eligible voters.

Prussia's autonomous rights as a Federated State were wiped out (Feb. 6, 1933) by decree of President von Hindenburg. Hitler took personal control with Goering as Minister of the Interior in command of the police and later as Premier. Bavaria's premier was thrown out by storm troopers (March 9) and Wurttemberg, Saxony, Baden, Hesse, Schaumberg-Lippe and Bremen likewise came under control.

The nine other states had either purely Nazi governments or coalition governments dominated by Nazis.

The President was empowered on nomination by the Chancellor, to appoint the Governors (Statthalters) of the 17 States.

The anti-Semitic campaign carried on ruthlessly by Storm troopers by boycotts and violence resulted in the arrest and detention of 80.000 to 90,000 Jews, and more than 90,000 Jews fled the country, mostly in poverty. Sweeping laws ousted nearly all Jews from the professions and the public service and from the universities, also from the German Labor Front and even the Chess League. A "non-Aryan" was defined as "a person descended particularly from Jewish parents or grandparents."

All Jewish cultural activities, it was decreed, must be united in one officially recognized Jewish Cultural Organization to which directly or through one of its affiliated societies all non-Aryan doctors, writers and actors must belong in order to exercise their profession.

The number of German grammar schools and pupils decreased (1939), schools at the rate of 0.7 per cent and pupils 1.4. In the old Reich territory, exclusive of Austria, the Sudeten provinces and the former Polish territories, there were (1939) 50,592 schools and 186,582 classes and 7,503,195 pupils, taught by 177,303 teachers. For every 10,000 population there were 7.3 schools, 1,078 pupils and 25.4 teachers. There was an average of 40.3 pupils to a class and 42.4 pupils to a teacher. For every 100 girls there were 101.2 boys, which is regarded as the average relationship.

The decrease in the number of Jewish pupils (1939) was 80 per cent of the 1938 total. There were 2,008 Jewish pupils attending grammar schools (1939) as against 10,069 (1938). Including private schools there were (1939) 8,962 Jewish pupils as against 19,913 the previous year.

In Austria the count (1939) showed 4,721 public schools with 657,000 pupils; the Sudeten provinces counted 2,957 schools and 274,000 pupils.

The government sought (1934) to bring the various Lutheran churches into a single German Evangelical Church under the direction of a pro-Nazi bishop and, failing in this, promulgated a law (Sept. 24, 1935) giving absolute powers in church matters to the Minister for Church Affairs. In the course of the conflict more than 700 Lutheran pastors were arrested. Conflict with the Roman Catholic Church developed over control of education of youth organizations, the administration of which was guaranteed to the Church under the terms of the German-Vatican concordat of July 20, 1933.

The budget law contains no figures since none has been issued since 1935. It presents this blanket order:

"The Reich Minister of Finance is authorized, in agreement with competent Reich ministers, to allot to the respective Reich administrations the necessary working funds and to determine their utilization." The budget decree is signed by Chancellor Hitler and Count Lutz Schwerin von Krosigk, Finance Minister.

Germany does not report officially its expenditures, although the Government does make public its revenues. The following table from Foreign Commerce Weekly, published by the United States Department of Commerce, gives Germany's financial conditon:

(Amounts in millions of reichsmarks)

Fiscal years	Disclosed indebtedness At end of period	Increase during period	Tax receipts	Total amount available for expenditures during period	Fiscal years	Disclosed indebtedness At end of period	Increase during period	Tax receipts	Total amount available for expenditures during period
1933-1934	11,793	103	6,846	6,949	1939-1940	52,060	21,383	23,580	44,963
1934-1935	12,452	659	8,223	8,882		60,145	8,085	6,067	14,152
1935-1936	14,372	1,920	9,654	11,574		69,721	9,577	7,351	16,928
1936-1937	17,570	1,686	11,492	13,178		³79,000	⁴9,279	6,987	16,266
1937-1938	19,098	3,040	13,964	17,004	1939-1940	³79,000	44,488	38,764	83,252
1938-1939	30,676	11,578	17,710	29,288					

NATIONAL INCOME [1]
(Amounts in millions of reichsmarks)

Year	Amount	Year	Amount	Year	Amount
1933............	46,500	1935............	58,600	1937............	71,000
1934............	52,700	1936............	64,900	1938............	79,700

[1] Estimates of Reich Statistical Office.
[2] Estimate for Old Reich; estimate for the Great Reich is 88,000,000,000 reichsmarks.
[3] Estimate of Herr Reinhardt; actual figure for end of November was 76,980,000 reichsmarks.
[4] On the basis of estimate mentioned in footnote 3.

The German national debt is increasing by 4,000,000,000 marks a month, according to the Reichsbank balances of March 31, 1942. The long-term debts of the Reich were 70,833,000,000 marks, against 64,239,000,000 on Dec. 31, 1941. To that must be added a floating debt that has increased from 60,637,000,000 marks on Dec. 31, 1941, to 66,859,000,000 March 31, 1942. Written in German currency are 69,600,000,000 marks of long-term debts, while 61,106,000,000 marks of floating debt are in treasury bills bearing no interest.

Although taxation has reached its highest limits, the German national debt is, therefore, mounting at an average of 4,000,000,000 marks a month, due to the cost of the war. The German national income is estimated at 115,000,000,000 marks annually, of which the State takes roughly one-half in taxes.

The banknote circulation has risen from 6,260,-000,000 marks in 1938 to more than 20,000,000,000 at present. That rise is only partly explained by the extension of the Reich's annexation of Austria and the occupation of Bohemia-Moravia and Poland, since at least the latter two had their own notes in crowns and zloty.

The Reichstag voted to Chancellor Hitler (April 26, 1942) full powers to "demand of every one the discharge of his duties or to cashier any one from his post or office if I consider that he has failed in his duty, regardless of who he may be or what acquired right he may have." The assembly voted assent by standing but no dissent vote was asked.

Chancellor Hitler appointed Dr. Thierack Reich Minister of Justice (Aug. 24, 1942). The decree appointing Thierack authorized him to "build up a National Socialist (Nazi) administration of justice and to take all measures required." The decree specifically authorized him to "deviate from existing law." Hitler, as Germany's supreme arbiter of justice, ordered Dr. Thierack to act "according to instructions and general directions by himself in agreement with Reich Minister of Interior Heinrich Lammers."

In an address to the Reichstag (April 26) Hitler warned judges to act with greater severity or to face removal. At the same time he assumed complete power over the lives of the German people, whom he informed that "in war time we recognize no talk of 'established rights!' "

The Nazi government has endeavored to assure the country's economic self-sufficiency by producing synthetic substitutes for many of the necessaries of life. To conserve Germany's few natural resources, the public has been encouraged to salvage anything that industry might use, from old razor blades to dog bones. Storm troopers, the Hitler Youth, and school children everywhere are mobilized in the service, with 150,000 boys and girls from Berlin alone. Bottle caps and toothpaste containers are wanted for light metals; human hair for felt and cardboard manufacture and carpets; bones for fodder, fats, fertilizer and glue. Coffee grounds yield wax and resin and a powder useful in filling dolls and pillows. Garbage is steamed and sterilized and used as hog feed.

To conserve tin, foods are packed in transparent plastic containers. The scientists have made a wool substitute from a mixture of fish albumen and cellulose; also from casein, a milk derivative and from German beech wood. Sugar is extracted from wood. "Pumpkin milk" competes with cow's milk; potato starch is used in bread; and "fish sausage" vies with the real thing.

The unit of currency is the Reichsmark. It averages around forty cents in value in United States money.

Germany has had social insurance since 1883 and the law makes mandatory the insurance of workingmen against sickness (including maternity), accidents, unemployment, old age and infirmity. Workers pay two-thirds of the contributions to the State and employers one-third.

The network of motor highways spreading over Germany—Reichsautobahnen as they are called—is one of the marvels of modern engineering. They are completely free from obstructions and fast motoring on them is not hindered either by passing through villages, level crossings or cross-roads. Two lines of traffic are separated by a verge of 16½ ft. wide planted with grass or bushes. Hence

there is a special roadway 24½ ft. wide for traffic in each direction on which three cars can travel abreast. There is also a firm embankment 6½ ft wide on the outer side of each roadway. The average total width of a Reich motor road is 78½ ft.

Entering and leaving the roads can be done only at certain points which are provided at average intervals of from 12½ to 15½ miles. At these points of entry it is also possible to turn by using special bridges.

By the end of 1938 approximately 2,000 miles of these roads were completed and more were under construction. It is planned to add 750 miles of new roads each year. The roads are used in the movement of troops throughout the Reich.

National motor roads construction and maintenance (1939) involved an expenditure of 1,120,-800,000 marks, an increase of 152,000,000 marks over the preceding year. Construction costs proper (1939) were 921,300,000 marks with contingent expenditures set at 199,500,000 marks.

Air operations in Germany during 1941 were increased by a third over 1940, despite the decreased number of airplanes available because of war, according to the European press. Total air operations reached 6,900,000 air kilometers, while paid transportation services amounted to 9,300,000 kilometer tons, a 50 percent increase over 1940, it is stated. This volume of paid transportation services approximates that of 1937. Wartime conditions caused a restriction of passenger traffic in favor of freight and postal traffic, though 111,000 paying air passengers were carried during 1941.

Agriculture is a highly specialized industry although the ground is not naturally fertile and requires much artificial fertilizer. Some of the more important crops are wheat, rye, barley, oats, potatoes, sugar beets and hay. Other commercial products are tobacco, grapes, hops, apples, pears, plums, cherries, apricots, peaches and walnuts.

The principal minerals are coal, lignite, iron, zinc. lead, copper, salt, potash, petroleum.

The Ruhr and Saarland are the chief seat of iron and steel production, though the industry is carried on to a lesser degree in the Sieg, Lahn and Dill districts and along the lower Rhine and in Westphalia. Berlin is the center of the electrical industry. Bavaria, Rhenish Prussia and Prussian Saxony lead in the manufacture of chemicals; Saxony in textiles; Silesia and Westphalia in linen. Cotton goods are made in Saxony, Westphalia, Wurttemberg and Bavaria; woollens in Saxony, Brandenburg, Rhenish Prussia and Baden. Beetroot sugar is manufactured in Prussia (chiefly in the provinces of Saxony, Silesia, Hanover and Pomerania). Potash is produced in Prussian Saxony, Thuringia and Hanover; glass, porcelain and earthenware in Bavaria, Thuringia, Silesia, Brandenburg and Saxony; clocks and woodenware in Baden, Wurttemberg and Bavaria; and beer in Bavaria.

The German merchant marine (1939) had 2,466 ships of 4,492,708 gross tonnage, compared with 5,459,296 tons (1914).

Chancellor Hitler (March 16, 1935) reintroduced compulsory military service and increased the peace basis of the Army to 36 divisions in 12 corps, probably about 600,000 men. inclusive of police troops. By the Versailles treaty, Germany was allowed an army of 100,000, in which the soldiers were enlisted for 12 years and the officers for 20.

The Army was increased by one corps (1938) and two more were added with the absorption of Austria into the Reich. There has been a vast increase in the size of the Army with the War in Europe and its true size has not been made public.

The new army law, (May 21, 1935) provides for one year of active training of all ablebodied, non-Jewish Germans between the ages of 18 and 45, with active military service beginning at 20. The trained soldier then passes into the Reserve until he is 35, then becomes a member of the Landwehr from 36 to 45. From 1813 to 1892 the term of active service was three years, and from 1892 to 1919, two years; however, the present one-year term follows compulsory service in the labor camps.

The Air Force, under control of the Air Ministry, was organized (1939, before the outbreak of war) into seven groups, including one in Austria, with 60 squadrons each of 12 aircraft in commission and to have more than 2,000 reserve aircraft. The Air Force has been increased vastly since the War in Europe and the true facts as to its size have not been made available.

By assuming the cabinet post of Minister of Defense (Feb. 4, 1938) Chancellor Hitler became supreme commander of all the armed forces of the Reich.

Conscription of all German youth between the ages of 10 and 18 for service in the Hitler Youth was decreed (April 5, 1939) by Chancellor Hitler. By this decree the Hitler Youth gets exclusive charge of the "physical, mental and moral education of the entire German youth within the Reich territory outside of the home and school." The decree abrogates voluntary membership and implements the Hitler Youth Law (Dec. 1, 1936) which declared "the entire German youth within the territory of the Reich is comprised in the Hitler Youth." The principle of voluntary membership was in force then. There were within the confines of the Reich (1939) approximately 11,-750,000 boys and girls between the ages of 10 and 18 and the Hitler Youth membership was given as 7,000,000. As a result of the new decree all German males, excluding the unworthy and unfit, begin compulsory service on reaching 10 and are discharged only on death. From the Hitler Youth they go to the Labor Service, then to the army, then into the armed reserve and Reich Warriors League, in all of which they are under constant supervision.

Facing the Maginot Line of France, Germany has constructed a similar series of fortifications along the eastern shore of the Rhine from Switzerland to Luxemburg. The line, originally known as the Siegfried Line and West Wall and later changed to "Limes Germanicus" by Hitler, is built of steel and concrete with tank traps with pillboxes of slightly more flexible construction than those in the Maginot Line.

The labor code (effective May 1, 1934), definitely eliminates collective wage agreements and substitutes the fixing of wage scales for the individual enterprises. Manufacturers failing to comply with the national economic policy may be deprived under the law of their managerial rights.

Dr. Friederich Syrup, Secretary of State in the Reich's Ministry of Labor, announced (July 6, 1942) that the number of foreign workers employed in various capacities in Germany had reached a total of 2,500,000. Women farmhands constituted a heavy percentage of this army of foreign laborers, most of them, he reports, coming from the newly occupied territories in the East.

The influx of workers from France, Belgium, the Netherlands, and even Spain also continued unabated, he said. Before the war the number of foreign workers in Germany amounted to 500,000.

The principal German imports in the order of their value on the last available returns are—wool, raw cotton, iron ore, mineral oil, wheat, coffee, butter, fruit, coal, timber and copper ore. The chief exports are—coal, iron and steel, dyes, pharmaceuticals, paper, copperware, glass and glassware, leather, silk and rayon, cotton goods, woollen goods.

The Reich-owned railway system began a four-year replacement program (1939) costing 3,500,-000,000 marks to include the purchase of 10,000 passenger cars, 112,000 freight cars and 17,300 automobile trailers. An additional 620,000,000 marks were added to the replacement budget (1939). The Reich had (1938) 42,299 miles of railroad. Germany also has vast inland waterways of some 7,000 miles (1938).

The rolling stock of the Reich Railways is reported by the Foreign Commerce Weekly of the United States Department of Commerce (Feb. 1, 1941) as follows:

Item	1935	1938
Locomotives	20,663	24,200
Motorized cars	1,561	1,990
Passenger cars	63,793	76,000
Express cars	20,317	28,400
Freight cars	580,151	640,000
Closed cars	212,272	274,000
Railway service cars	16,484	19,000

Greece
(KINGDOM OF HELLAS)
Capital, Athens—Area, 50,257 square miles—Population (est. 1939) 7,108,814

Greece occupies the southern peninsula of the Balkans, stretching down into the Mediterranean Sea, with the Ionian Sea on the west and the Aegean Sea on the east. On the northwest lies Albania, on the north Yugo-Slavia and Bulgaria, and on the northeast Turkey. Pindus Mountains with many spurs, a continuation of the Balkans, run through the country from north to south. Gulfs and bays are many.

The authentic history of Greece begins (776 B. C.) although the country obtained its greatest glory and power in the fifth century B. C. It became a province of the Roman Empire (46 B. C.,) of the Byzantine Empire (395 A. D.) and was conquered by the Turks in 1456. Greece won its war of independence (1821-1829) and became a kingdom under the guarantee of Great Britain, France and Russia.

Greece fought (1912) with the other Balkan states against Turkey for the liberation of Greek territories under Turkish domination and allied with the Serbs (1913) an attack by Bulgaria. During World War I, Greece fought by the side of the Allies against Germany and Bulgaria. Greece attempted unsuccessfully (1920-1923) to liberate Greek populations in Asia Minor. This war against Turkey was terminated (1923) by the Treaty of Lausanne under the terms of which 1,-500,000 Greeks in Asia Minor were transplanted to Greece.

The Greek National Assembly (1925) voted the overthrow of the monarchy and the establishment of a republic, which lasted for ten years, or until a plebiscite (Nov. 3, 1935) restored the throne to George II, King of the Hellenes, who had fled Greece during an uprising against him (Dec. 18, 1923). Gen. John Metaxas became premier (Aug. 4, 1936). Metaxas tried to fashion a Fascist state with large expenditures for rearmament.

Greece was occupied (1941) by Germans, Italians and Bulgarians after having defeated the Italians and later resisted German aggression.

Italy sent an ultimatum, demanding complete capitulation, to Greece (Oct. 20, 1940) and when it was rejected Italians marched from Albania into Greece. Within six months the Italians had been driven out of Greece and Greek forces occupied large sections of Albania. Germany launched (April 6, 1941) an attack on Greece and forced the Greek army to capitulate two weeks later. German troops marched into Athens (April 27) and set up a puppet government under Gen. George Tsolakoglu.

King George and the Government, headed by Prime Minister Emmanuel Tsouderous, escaped the country and established a Government-in-Exile in London. Greece now maintains in the Middle East armed forces which are fighting the Axis on land, on sea and in the air.

A son, heir to the throne, was born (June 2, 1940) to Crown Princess Frederika. Greece's King is childless and his brother, Prince Paul, to whom the son was born, is next in line of succession. Prince Paul and the Crown Princess also have two daughters (one born Nov. 2, 1938, and the other May 11, 1942).

Military service was compulsory between the ages of 21 and 50. Service was for two years in the Army followed by nine years in the first reserve and teight in the second. About 50,000 recruits were called up each year. The Greek Navy comprises light craft, and is serving with the Allied forces at sea. Greece created (1929) an air force of ten groups, each of three flights of four aircraft.

Greece proper is chiefly agricultural, with little manufacturing. Only one-fifth of the total area is arable; 13,350,000 of the total of 16,074,000 acres are covered by mountains and lakes and rivers. The forests have been denuded, but reforestation is going on; they cover 5,944,059 acres of which 4,121,119 are state-owned. The chief agricultural products are wheat, rye, barley, oats, corn, tobacco, olives, lemons, oranges, mandarins, apples, pears, figs and nuts. The principal minerals are iron, zinc, lignite and salt.

Greek Orthodox is the State church. Education is compulsory. There are two universities in Athens, and one in Thessaloniki.

The rocky promontory of Mount Athos (121 square miles), is occupied by 20 monasteries of the Greek Orthodox Church, each a sort of little republic in itself. The monks number 4,800. No females are allowed to enter the territory, which has been granted a constitution by the Greek government, receiving autonomous powers as a monastic republic under Greek sovereignty, but with an appointed Greek Governor.

the election of a Chamber of Deputies. A Constitutional Monarchy, hereditary in the family of King Feisal, was created with a Senate of 20 members nominated by the King for eight years and a Chamber of Deputies of 150 members, elected by suffrage. The Prime Minister is appointed by the king and (if acceptable himself) selects a cabinet agreeable to the legislature.

A pro-British Government was set up (June 3, 1941) under Prime Minister Jamil al-Midfai after a revolt had been crushed and the insurgent leaders had fled to Iran. Jamil al-Midfai resigned (Sept. 21, 1941) and was succeeded by Nuri es-Said.

The Iraq army numbers 50,000 in normal times. Military service is compulsory between the ages of 20 and 25.

A treaty with Great Britain was signed at Bagdad (June 30, 1930). By it the British mandatory rights were formally renounced and the independence of Iraq recognized.

The monetary unit is the dinar, equal to about $4 in American money. The government's receipts (1939-1940) were 6,093,054 dinars, exclusive of oil royalties totaling 2,054,503; expenditures were 6,369,148, exclusive of capital works expenditures amounting to 2,232,916 dinars.

The principal imports in the order of their monetary value are iron and steel; cotton piece goods; machinery and tools; silk and rayon goods; sugar; tea; vehicles; and woollen piece-goods. Exports, in order, are (besides petroleum) dates, barley, wool, wheat, hides, skins and sheep guts. The chief sources of imports are Great Britain, Japan, India, Germany, United States and Iran, respectively. Exports are consigned mainly to Great Britain, United States, India and Iran.

Italy
(REGNO d'ITALIA)
Capital, Rome—Area, 119,800 square miles—Population (1941) 45,354,000

The Kingdom of Italy occupies the entire Italian peninsula, stretching from the Alps southeast into the Mediterranean, with the islands of Sicily, Sardinia, Elba and about 70 smaller ones. On the east is the Adriatic Sea, which it dominates; on the south, the Mediterranean, on the west between the mainland and Sicily and Sardinia is the Tyrrhenian Sea, and further north the Ligurian Sea. The Maritime Alps on the west separate it from France, the Swiss Alps in the north from Switzerland, and the Dolomite Alps from Germany (Austria), and the Carnac and Julian Alps on the east from Yugo-Slavia. The great plain shut in by these huge mountains, and the Ligurian Apennines, and watered by the River Po (220 miles long) and the Adige, shared by the departments, Piedmont, Lombardy, Emilia and Venetia, stretches across the top from the Maritime Alps to the head of the Adriatic. The Ligurian Mountains, circling the Gulf of Genoa, run down the middle of the peninsula as the Apennines, with many summits like Monte Cimone (altitude 7,103 ft.) in the northern part, and the Gran Sasso d'Italia (9,560 ft.) in Central Italy nearing the western coastline in Campagna and continuing down (with altitudes of about 6,000 ft.), through the southern province, Calabria, to the "toe of the boot" at Cap Spartivento. Across the narrow Strait of Messina the mountain range continues through the Island of Sicily with its famous volcano, Mt. Etna (altitude 10,755 ft.) having a record of more than 120 eruptions. The active volcano, Mt. Vesuvius (altitude about 4,300 ft.), with a record of 50 known eruptions, rises to an altitude of more than 4,000 ft. on the Bay of Naples, and north of the Strait of Messina is the island volcano of Stromboli (3,022 ft.)

The length of the peninsula is 760 miles, while its breadth nowhere exceeds 150 miles and does not generally measure more than 100 miles. Italy is slightly larger than New England and New York and has more than twice their population.

Two rivers, having the greatest historic importance, rise in the Apennines, and flow west to the sea—the Tiber, which moves through Rome, and the Arno, which waters the Florentine plain. Between the spurs of the Alps lie seven beautiful Italian lakes, especially noteworthy being Como, Lugano, Maggiore and Garda, the largest. Both Maggiore and Garda are more than 30 miles long.

The Adriatic coastline is flat and has five ports of major importance, Trieste, Venice, Ancona, Bari and Brindisi. Trento and Trieste, which formed the "Italia Irredenta," were annexed to Italy as a result of the World War. Fiume, after a bitter quarrel, was annexed (1924) through the inspiration and efforts of Gabriel D'Annunzio, Italy's famed poet and soldier. Its annexation was acknowledged by Yugoslavia (April 5, 1925) in a treaty which also granted Hungary free port rights in Fiume.

The climate of Italy is sunny, although northern Italy has a cold winter; snow is rarely seen in Naples, and olives, oranges, lemons, figs, cotton, almonds, and pomegranates flourish in southern Italy. The soil is fertile. Italy, though drained before the war by emigration, is one of the most densely populated states in Europe, having a population of 371-2 (1939) to the square mile.

It is a country of immense interest to the tourist, with its lively landscape and picturesque people, its masterpieces of ancient, medieval and modern art. Here are awe-inspiring works of Michelangelo, Leonardo da Vinci and Raphael, in churches and galleries that look back through the centuries. The glory that was ancient Rome may still be seen in the Catacombs and Coliseum.

St. Peter's Church—a masterpiece of architecture and the mecca of Christian pilgrimages for hundreds of years—is the largest church in the world; and the Vatican, the home of Roman Catholicism, the largest residence extant.

The Governments of Italy and of Germany reached an accord (Dec. 31, 1939) whereby the German population of the former Austrian provinces got the option of remaining in Italy, after accepting Italian citizenship, or of emigrating to the Reich. Of the 229,500 who were present in the area, 166,488 decided in favor of emigration; 27,712 preferred to remain in Italy as Italian citizens; and 35,300 did not turn in a ballot and therefore, according to the terms of the agreement, acquired Italian nationality. The exodus, which is still under way, is taking place at the rate of 200/300 individuals per day and, according to the prearranged schedule, should be completed by December, 1942.

After the occupation of Yugoslavia (April, 1941) Italy annexed the province of Lubiana. Furthermore, Croatia, an ethnical unit of Yugoslavia, was declared an independent kingdom. Prince of Spoleto, of the Italian royal family of Savoy, was given the crown under the title of King Aimone. A customs and monetary union between Italy and Croatia was established. Italy also placed under her own sovereignty several islands along the Dalmatian coast.

The religion of the great majority is Roman Catholic, the census of 1936 returning 41,017,369 Catholics (99.6%), 83,618 Protestant, 47,825 Jews.

Italy has 26 universities, with ten of them dating from the 13th century or the first years of the 14th. Famous among these are Bologna (founded 1200); Genoa (1243); Naples (1224); Padua (1222); Pisa (1338); Rome (1303), and Turin (1404). Primary education is compulsory between the ages of six and 14. Much progress has been made in combating illiteracy, especially in the southern provinces.

Agriculture is the chief industry, with an area (1939) comprising 70,548,131 acres with 8,756,848 engaged in it (1936). The principal crops are wheat, barley, oats, rye, corn, rice, beans, potatoes, sugar beets, grapes and olives.. Dairy farming and cheese making are important in Northern Italy.

Italy is not rich in mineral deposits, and is especially lacking in coal, although she is a large producer of sulphur, chiefly in the volcanic regions of Sicily. Other minerals are iron, manganese, mercury, lead, zinc, antimony and bauxite.

The largest and most important industry, aside from agriculture, is the manufacture of textiles. Silk culture is carried on extensively in Lombardy, Piedmont and Venetia. Other principal manufactures are chemicals (sulphuric acid, superphosphate and copper phosphate); sugar; cheese, and macaroni.

It is estimated that Italy has water power sites that would yield 9,000,000 horsepower, but only one half of this has been harnessed.

Italy's principal exports in the order of their monetary value are—vegetables and fruit; cotton; vehicles; artificial silk; cereals and roots; wool and hair; hemp, linen and jute; stones, earths and minerals; silk; machines and apparatus; dairy products; iron and steel. Imports, in order, are—stones, earths and minerals; cereals, roots; mineral oils; iron and steel; wool and hair; machines and apparatus; seeds and fruits; copper; skins and furs; paper and cardboard.

Air travel is greatly developed in Italy with the aviation companies subsidized by the State.

Divided, dismembered even for centuries, Italy began to take shape as a unity when, following the war of 1859, Lombardy, by the peace of Zurich, came under the crown of King Victor Emmanuel

II, of Sardinia of the house of Savoy. By plebiscite (1860) Parma, Modena, the Romagna and Tuscany joined, to be followed at once by Sicily and Naples, and by The Marches and Umbria. The first Italian Parliament assembled (February, 1861) and (March 17, 1861) declared Victor Emmanuel King of Italy. Mantua and Venetia were added (1866), an outcome of the Austro-Prussian war. The Papal States were taken possession of by Italian troops (Sept. 20, 1870) after the withdrawal of the French garrison in the Franco-Prussian war (see Index, VATICAN CITY), and by plebiscite (Oct. 2) were annexed to the kingdom, thereby rounding out United Italy. The Papal States were Marches, Romaqua and Umbria, which were annexed previously. What was occupied in 1870 was the city of Rome and environments, long known as the "Patrimony of St. Peter."

Since the advent of Fascism, the government of Italy has consisted of a Sovereign, a Senate and a Chamber of Deputies, whose activities have all been subordinate to the Grand Council of Fascism. (A decree signed by the Grand Council (Oct. 8, 1938) effective (March, 1939), abolishes the Chamber of Deputies and substitutes a Chamber of Fasces and Corporations composed exclusively of government and Fascist party appointees, without benefit of election. Laws passed by the new Chamber are transmitted to Premier Mussolini in his capacity the Duce of Fascism and head of the State, and he submits them to the King for his signature).

The Senate—whose members are appointed for life by the King—is composed of princes of the royal house and persons of fame in science, literature or in a pursuit particularly beneficial to the nation. The number (1939) was 543.

The Chamber of Deputies—the most democratic of the Fascist governmental agencies—contained 400 members, elected for five years. Candidates for the Chamber were proposed by the "National Syndicate Confederation" (representing labor and industry jointly), and by several other associations of a national character, including the representatives of the judiciary. Candidates were presented to the electorate for acceptance or rejection only after the Grand Council had first approved of them.

The Grand Council of Fascism is composed of the original leaders of the Black Shirt party, ministers and other high dignitaries of the government, and of an undetermined number of members appointed by the Premier for a term of three years. The Council co-ordinates the work of the Sovereign, the Senate and the Chamber, and has absolute power in questions of a constitutional nature.

The King of Italy is Victor Emmanuel III (born Nov. 11, 1869), who succeeded his father, King Humbert I (July 29, 1900). He married Helena, daughter of Nicholas, King of Montenegro (Oct. 24, 1896). The Crown Prince, Humbert, Prince of Piedmont (born Sept. 15, 1904), and was married (Jan. 8, 1930) to Princess Maria Jose of Belgium (born Aug. 4, 1906). They have a daughter, Princess Maria Pia, (born Sept. 24, 1934), and a son, Victor-Emmanuel, Prince of Naples (born Feb. 13, 1937), a daughter, Maria Gabriella (born Feb. 24, 1940).

The daughters of the King and Queen of Italy are—Princess Yolanda (born June 1, 1901), married (April 9, 1923) Capt. Count Carlo Calvi di Bergolo; Princess Mafalda (born Nov. 19, 1902), married Prince Philip of Hesse (Sept. 23, 1925); Princess Giovanna (born Nov. 13, 1907), married (Oct. 25, 1930) King Boris III of Bulgaria; and Princess Marie (born Dec. 26, 1914), married (Jan. 23, 1939) Prince Louis of Bourbon-Parma.

The Italian Cabinet follows:

Prime Minister, Chief of the Government and Minister of the Interior, of War, of the Navy, of the air and Justice—Benito Mussolini.
Minister of State—Alfred Dallolio.
Minister of Italian Africa—Ottilio Teruzzi.
Foreign Affairs, Count Galeazzo Ciano di Cortellazzo.
Corporations, Renato Ricci.
National Education, Giuseppe Bottai.
Agriculture and Forests, Giuseppe Pareschi.
Finance, Count Paolo Thaon di Revel.
Justice, Count Dino Grandi.
Communications, Giovanni Host Venturi.
Popular Culture, Alessandro Pavolini.

Public Works, Aldo Vidussoni.
Trade and International Payments, Raffael Riccardi.
Minister-Secretary of Fascist Party, Aldo Vidussoni.

Premier Mussolini announced (May 7, 1942) a new codification of Italian law and himself as Lord Chief Justice. By decree of Premier Mussolini (June 14, 1942) civil service was placed under military rule.

The original Fascisti—called Black Shirts because of their garb—were a group of ex-soldiers (150 in number) organized (March 23, 1919) into an association against Communism and Socialism by Benito Mussolini, himself an ex-Socialist and former newspaper editor, who had fought and been wounded in the World War. The organization grew in numbers and power until (Oct. 24, 1922), following a general strike (Aug. 22, 1922) and chaotic conditions in the capital, it marched on Rome and in a bloodless revolution took over the government at the invitation of the King.

As leader of the Fascisti and head of the government, Mussolini, the son of a poor Socialist blacksmith and school teacher mother, has acquired dictatorial powers over the life of the country. The Fascist party exercises virtual control over every private and public activity of the nation. Industry, labor, agriculture, commerce, the professions, the arts, the press—all are controlled by the Fascisti.

Under the terms of a decree issued by the Fascist Grand Council (Oct. 6, 1938) no Italian is permitted to marry a Jew, whether or not the Jew is a citizen of Italy, and no Italian is allowed to marry a foreigner unless the marriage is specifically approved by the Ministry of Interior Affairs.

The Fascist party membership (as of Oct. 28, 1939) follows:

Fasces (Fasce di Combattimento) 2,633,514.
Women groups (Fasci Femminili) 774,181.
University Group (Gruppi Universitari) 105,383.
Youth Organizations (Gioventù Italiana del Littorio) 7,891,547, divided as follows:

BOYS

4-5 Figli della Lupa, 1,546,389.
6-14 Balilla, 1,746,560.
14-18 Avanguardisti, 906,785.
18-21 Giovani Fascisti, 1,176,798.

GIRLS

Piccole Italiane, 1,622,766.
Giovani Italiane, 441,254.
Giovani Fasciste, 450,995.

The teachers in all Italian schools, both men and women, are ordered to wear the uniform of officers of either the Balilla or the Fascist militia. In secondary schools and colleges, army officers in uniform now occupy the platforms of teachers during the period of compulsory military courses (military history, military mathematics, war geography and tactics and manoeuvres) prescribed by a decree (Sept. 18, 1934). No student can be promoted or graduated unless he has satisfactorily completed his military course.

Military service is compulsory between the ages of 21 and 55: The normal period of training service in all branches is 18 months, after which the recruits are transferred to the reserve where they remain until 55. Military expenditures (1941-1942) are estimated at 12,210,400,000 lire for all three services.

The metropolitan Army had a peace time strength of 260,000. When Italy entered the war (Italy declared war on Great Britain, June 11, 1940) the Army was estimated at 64 divisions, consisting of 51 infantry, 5 Alpini or mountain, three mobile, two armored and three motorized divisions. The Carabinieri or military police are recruited from the Army by voluntary enlistment and (1938) had a strength of 52,000.

The Royal Italian Air Force consisted (1940) of four commands for the Home Air zone and separate commands for Sicily, Sardinia, Aegean Islands, Libya and Italian East Africa. The Naval Air Force consists of reconnaisance groups, all carried on ships.

The monetary unit is the lira with an average value of $.0526.

The budget (1942-1943) estimates receipts of 35,425,000,000 lire and expenditures of 43,825,-000,000.

Italian Colonies

ERITREA

Italy's colonial venture in Africa began (1870) when the port of Assab, in the extreme southern part of Eritrea, was purchased. Lagging interest was revived (1885), when the colonial project was vigorously pushed. An effort to establish a protectorate over Abyssinia (now called Ethiopia) was made in (1889) but was upset by King Menelek, who, with an army of 80,000, annihilated a force of 12,000 Italians at the Battle of Adowa (1896). Eritrea was constituted a colony (1890).

Eritrea stretches for 670 miles along the African coast of the Red Sea from Cape Kasar to Cape Dumereh. To the west it is bordered by the Soudan, on the south by Ethiopia, and French Somaliland, a small section of which bordering on the Gulf of Eden was transferred to Italy by France (1935) when an interest in the railroad from Djibouti to Addis Ababa was also transferred to her. The total area (1931) was 15,754 square miles and the population 600,573, including 4,188 Italians. The Italian government (June 1, 1936) transferred the districts of Tigry (Tigrai), Danakilland (Dancalia) and Haussa (Aussa), all formerly a part of Ethiopia, to Eritrea.

Eritrea was occupied by British Colonial Forces (April, 1940).

The lowlands along the coast are hot and malarial, but the uplands are cool, sometimes cold. Irrigation is necessary to supplement rainfall for the crops, and the soil is poor. Agriculture and stock raising are the chief industries. There is a railroad 75 miles long connecting the seaport Massawa (population, 12,277) with the capital, Asmara (altitude 7,765 ft.), thence 65 miles to

Cheren, thence 53 miles to Agordat. It is being constructed to Tessenei to open up a cotton-growing district. Gold is mined in Hamassen and petroleum is found but there has been as yet no development. The monetary unit is the Italian lira.

Italian Somaliland (area, 194,000 square miles; population, (est. 1936) 1,300,000) extends along the Indian Ocean from the Gulf of Aden to the Juba River. The coastline extending in a north-east-southwest direction, is 1,100 miles long, with no indentation of importance.

Italian Somaliland was occupied by British Colonial forces (April, 1940).

Italian Somaliland is the source of half the world's supply of incense. Other exports are oil, gum, hides, kapok, resin, and ivory. The principal imports are cottons, sugar, rice, tea, coffee, iron, machinery and timber. The Italian lira is the monetary unit. The budget (1935-36) showed receipts of 70,750,000 lire, including a contribution of 47,190,000 from the Italian Government; expenditures were 70,750,000, of which 29,960,000 defrayed military expenses.

LIBYA
(Libia Italiana)

Italian Libya in North Africa extends along the Mediterranean Sea from Egypt on the East to Tunis (French) and Algeria on the West. On the south Libya extends to Algeria, to French West Africa and the Soudan. Libya for administrative and military purposes is divided into four provinces (Tripoli, Misurata, Benghazi and Derne) and into a military territory in the South having jurisdiction over the southern sections of the four provinces. The area of the territory is estimated at 679,358 square miles with a population (1939) of 888,401. The capitals are Tripoli and Benghazi.

Tripoli, formerly one of the Barbary States and independent (since 1714) was reconquered by Turkey (1835). During the Turko-Italian war (1911-12) Italy proclaimed the annexation of Tripoli, which was recognized by the great powers in the Treaty of Ouchy (Oct. 18, 1912). The oasis of Jarabub, on the eastern side of Cirenaica, was ceded to Italy by Egypt (1926).

The legislative power is reserved to Rome, and the governors have purely administrative functions. Italian courts have final jurisdiction.

The prevailing religion is Mohammedan, and Arabic is generally spoken.

The country is rather barren, but has date palm

orchards, olive groves, lemon, almond and fig trees, and vineyards. Other products include tobacco, matting, carpets, leather articles, and fabrics embroidered with gold and silver.

The Italian lira is the monetary unit. Governmental receipts and expenditures (1939-1940) were balanced at 600,115,000 lire.

Fourteen **Aegean Isles** were occupied by Italy during the war of 1912 with Turkey and though claimed by Greece have been retained by Italy. Rhodes has been fortified. The area is 1,035 square miles, and population 140,848. Rhodes (population, 27,466) is the capital. It is heavily fortified and was made (1935) into a hospital and munitions center.

Tientsin, an Italian concession (since June 7, 1902) lies on the left bank of Pei-Ho and consists of about 130 acres with a population (1936) of 7,953 (Chinese, 7,411; Italians, 358; other Europeans, 184).

The **Island of Saseno**, in the entrance to Vallona Bay (Albania), is three miles long and 1.25 miles wide. It is occupied by marines of the Royal Italian Navy and natives. There is a radio station and a small harbor at St. Nicholas which is used by small fishing ships.

Japan
(NIPPON)

Capital, Tokyo—Area (Japan Proper) 148,756 square miles; (Empire of Japan) 260,770—Population (Japan Proper) (est. 1939) 72,875,800; (Empire of Japan) (Census 1940) 105,226,101.

The island empire of Japan lies in the north Pacific Ocean off the coast of China and Siberia from 21° 46' north latitude, the southern point of Formost (Taiwan), due east of Hong Kong, to 50° 55' north latitude, the last of the Kurile Islands, a few miles south of Kamchatka. It includes also the southern half of the island of Sakhalin, and the ancient Kingdom of Korea (annexed Aug. 22, 1910) on the mainland. Japan also holds the Kwantung peninsula (Port Arthur and Dairen) on a 99-year lease, and has the mandate for the Marshall, Caroline, Ladrone and Pelew Islands, former German possessions in the Pacific.

The southernmost island is subtropical; the northernmost subarctic. Were the empire stretched out in the Atlantic off the coast of the United States at the same latitudes, Formosa would lie across Cuba and Southern Florida, Tokio would be due east of Norfolk, Hakodate due east of New York, and Sakhalin would be athwart Newfoundland with the northernmost island, Paramushir, off Labrador.

While nominally an independent State, Manchukuo (formerly Manchuria, a Chinese province) is in reality a Japanese possession with Nipponese advisers in practical control of the government.

The Japanese coast is deeply indented, its coast line measuring 17,150 miles. Few places in Japan are far removed from the mountains or really distant from the sea. The northern islands are a continuation of the Russian Karafuto chain running down through Yezo and the mainland. The continuation of the Kuentin mountain range of China appears in the southern islands, the ranges meeting in the grand Japanese Alps. In the vast transverse fissure crossing the mainland from the Sea of Japan to the Pacific rises a group of volcanoes, mostly extinct or dormant, with the majestic sacred mountain Fujiyama lifting its white cone 60 miles west of Tokyo to an altitude of 12,425 ft. The

earthquake zone—where the average is said to be four slight ones a day, with serious ones every six or seven years—has its greatest center along the Pacific Coast near the Bay of Tokyo.

Tokyo (1939) had an estimated population of 7,094,600. The city absorbed (Oct. 1, 1932) 82 suburban boroughs and villages, increasing its area 214 square miles (137,190 acres).

Separating the islands of Shikoku and Kiushiu from the mainland is the famous Inland Sea, opening both into the Sea of Japan and the Pacific. It is 255 miles long and 56 wide, with a coast line of 700 miles and a surface expanse of 1,325 square miles.

Heavy snowfalls are frequent on the Japan Sea slopes of the mountains of Yezo, while the Pacific side, by which flows the Japan Current, enjoys pleasing winter weather. There is an abundant rainfall. The streams are short, swift and often unruly, of little value for transportation, yet offering a vast but as yet little developed supply of hydroelectric power.

Myriads of waterfalls add their charm to the magnificent scenery. The "Splendor of the Sun" at Nikko makes an unbroken plunge of 350 ft. There are a thousand mineral springs.

Three-fourths of the mountain land is uncultivable, and the soil of the rest is only moderately fertile, yet by intensive cultivation, hard work and great frugality more than half the people wrest their living from the soil. There is a rich supply of fish of many kinds in the sea, and fish is a staple diet.

About three-fifths of the arable land is cultivated by small peasant proprietors, the rest by tenants. More than half the land is used for growing rice, the chief food of the country. Wheat, barley, rye, tobacco, tea, beans, peaches, pears, apples, grapes, persimmons and mandarins are also produced. Mulberry trees are widely grown, and the annual output of silk is huge (three-fourths of the world's total). The country possesses a variety of minerals including gold, silver, copper, lead, zinc, iron, chromite, white arsenic, coal, sulphur, salt and petroleum.

After agriculture and the making of silk, the principal industries are the manufacture of woolens, cottons, paper, pottery, vegetable oil, leather and matting. The chief imports in the order of their monetary value are—raw cotton, wool, wrought iron, mineral oil, machinery, beans, crude rubber, wood, iron ore and coal. Exports comprise, in order, cotton tissues, raw silk, rayon cloth, machinery, canned goods, silk tissues, knitted goods, potteries, wrought iron, cotton yarns, toys and vegetable oil.

Japan's trade (1939) was distributed among these nations in the following order: Imports—United States, Manchukuo, British India, China and Germany. Exports—Manchukuo, United States China, British India, and Netherlands Indies.

There were 67 ports open to foreign trade, the most important being Yokohama, Kobe and Osaka on the Pacific Coast of the main island, and Niigata on the Japan Sea Coast, the port of trans-shipment for Vladivostok.

The monetary unit is the yen with an average value of $.2344.

The budget (1941-1942), including war expenditures, is 13,875,000,000 yen, of which 7,574,000,000 yen must be borrowed. The extraordinary war expenditures, including the "affair in China," is 4,880,000,000.

The cabinet, at a special meeting (July 12, 1941) decided on an extension of government control over finance, industry, production and distribution in line with the wartime planned economy. A capital mobilization plan is to be formulated each year on the "composite basis of the total production of the nation's economy." Available capital is to be allocated "rationally" under government control.

Japan put herself on a full economic war footing (Aug. 11, 1941) by invoking the terms of the general mobilization act of 1938. This act provides a parallel, in an economic sense, of military mobilization. It confers on the Government unlimited power to draft man power for industry and to draft all economic resources. The act virtually permits all constitutional checks on executive action to be set aside.

The government of Japan rests in an Emperor and an Imperial Diet consisting of a House of Peers and a House of Representatives. There are 404 members of the House of Peers composed of princes, marquises, counts, viscounts, barons and persons of great distinction or wealth. The 466 members of the House of Representatives are elected by direct suffrage for terms of four years. The Emperor exercises complete executive power with the advice and assistance of Cabinet Ministers appointed by him and responsible to him, and (in important matters of State) with the help of a Privy Council. The Emperor exercises legislative power with the consent of the Imperial Diet. He may declare war, conclude peace and consummate treaties; and give sanction to legislation enacted by the Houses of the Diet, in either of which it may originate, and he may dissolve, prorogue, open and close the Diet.

The Emperor is Hirohito (the 124th of his line, born April 29, 1901). He succeeded his father, Yoshihito (Dec. 26, 1926); was crowned (Nov. 10-14, 1928); constituted Regent (Nov. 25, 1921) because of his father's ill health; was married (Jan. 26, 1924) to Princess Nagako Kuni. The Crown Prince is Akihito Tsugu No Miya (born Dec. 23, 1933). Other children are Princess Shigeko (born Dec. 6, 1925), Princess Kazuko (born Sept. 30, 1929), Princess Atsuko (born March 7, 1931), Princess Masahito (born Nov. 28, 1935). A daughter, the sixth child, was born (March 2, 1939) and christened Takako Suganomiya (pure and noble princess). She is known as Princess Suga.

The Emperor has three brothers—Prince Yasuhito Chicibu (born June 25, 1902), married Miss Setsu Matsudarra (Sept. 28, 1929); Prince Nobuhito Takamatsu (born Jan. 3, 1905), married Princess Kikuko Tokugawa, granddaughter of the last of the Shogun of Japan (Feb. 4, 1930), and Prince Takahito (born Dec. 2, 1915).

The succession to the throne is fixed by Imperial House Law upon the male descendants; in case of failure of direct descendants, the throne passes to the nearest prince and his descendants.
The Cabinet follows:

Premier, War Minister—Hideki Tojo.
Foreign Minister—Masayuki Tani.
Navy—Admiral Shigetaro Shimada.
Railways and Communications—Vice Admiral Ken Terashima.
Finance—Okinobu Kaya.
State—Kazuo Aoki.
Commerce and Industry—Shinsuke Kishi.

Welfare—Lieut. Gen. Chikahiko Koizumi.
Justice—Michiyo Iwamura.
Agriculture—Hiroyasu Ino.
Education—Kunikhiko Hashida.
Ministers Without Portfolio—Maj. Gen. Teiichi Suzuki, Kaubro Arouki.
Home—Michio Yusawa.
State, Without Portfolio—Kiaburo Ando.

As scion of one of Japan's five noblest houses, Prince Konoye is exempt from personal criticism sometimes directed at premiers.

Japan has no State religion and all faiths are tolerated. The principal forms of religion are Shintoism with 13 sects and Buddhism with 12 sects. There are 110,431 Shinto shrines, 106,634 Buddhist temples and 2,104 Christian Churches. The Roman Catholics have an archbishop and three suffragan bishops.

Shinto—the ancient religion, or "Way of the Gods"—embodies the strong nationalist concepts. It was long partially dormant after the official introduction of Buddhism from Korea and China, in 552, but eventually was revived and became stronger than ever with the overthrow of Japanese feudalism and the 1868 restoration of the Imperial House.

As with many of the material skills and arts of Western civilization, Japan adapted to her own psychology and customs the imported religious thought of the continental East. Thus modified forms of Buddhism and Confucianism were combined with native Shinto worship. At one time, Shinto and Buddhism were joined in a "double religion," their priests presiding over the same altars. The two faiths were later officially separated, but the Japanese people still practice both, using different temples and separate family altars.

To Westerners, Shinto and Buddhism present certain fundamental contradictions, which do not seem to disturb the Japanese, since the two religions are believed to serve different functions. Shinto, for example, has been called a belief in the past, Buddhism one for the future. Shinto (or Sinto in modern Japanese spelling) is traditionally conservative, while Buddhism is associated with social progress and advances in education, arts and crafts. Simplicity is the chief feature of Shinto architecture and worship; intricate decoration and philosophical thought characterize the Buddhist way.

Students say that Shinto, strictly speaking, is a religion only in the sense of popular worship. It is "a veneration of the Imperial forebears and an observance of festivities and rites in memory of the nation's heroes." Its followers seem to regard sin as a matter of personal defilement, to be cleansed through ritual, rather than an offense against an ideal. Purity, especially body cleanliness, is essential.

Unlike the one-god religions of Christianity, Mohammedanism, and Judaism, Shinto has countless deities, including 8,000,000 Nature gods. They range from the simplest objects of Nature and everyday life, such as trees, rivers, mountains, and the family rice pot, to the "Great Heaven Shining Deity," or Sun Goddess.

Personal ancestors are deified, as well as those of the Imperial line. So are outstanding local and national individuals and families who are considered to have made contributions to Japanese progress and prestige. The Emperor himself is believed to be a direct descendant of the Sun Goddess.

The war hero who gives his life in battle wins a special place of reverence, for to the Japanese, as one proverb puts it, "the cherry is the best of flowers; the soldier the best of men." The Shinto cult, however, in accepting a belief in eternal spirit existence, conceives no particular paradise or hell. The Japanese soldier, therefore, may be deified, but he is not promised a luxurious and delight-filled heaven such as the faithful Mohammedan warrior believes will be his reward.

Elementary education is compulsory. There are six imperial universities, as follows—Tokyo, (founded 1877), Kyoto ((1897), Tohoku at Sendai (1907), Kyusho at Fukuoka (1910), Hokkaido at Sapporo (1918) and Osaka (1931). Illiteracy is only 10% in the nation. English is the language of commerce and a required study in the high schools.

There were in Japan (1935) 4,759 libraries of 12,318,600 volumes.

Military service is compulsory and universal, liability beginning at the age of 17, though active service commences at 20. Conscripts are divided into two classes—the "fit" and the "absolutely fit." Actual service is for two years with five years and four months in first line of reserve and 12 years and eight months in second line reserve and home defense. Liability continues to the age of 40.

KOREA
(Chosen)

Korea is an ancient kingdom with a history extending back to the 12th century B. C., and known in recent centuries as the "Hermit Kingdom." It occupies a peninsula in northeastern Asia dividing the Yellow Sea from the Sea of Japan. The boundaries on the mainland are the Yalu River and the Tamean Rivers. Its coastline is more than 6,000 miles long. Southern Manchuria lies along its northwest frontier for 500 miles and it touches Siberia for a few miles, a scant 100 miles from Vladivostok, in the extreme northeast. Situated between that Russian port and Port Arthur, then a Russian leasehold and subject to diplomatic control and penetration by Russia, Korea became to Japan "a dagger pointed at her heart"—the chief immediate cause of the Russo-Japanese War of 1904-1905. After this war the "complete independence" of Korea that had been recognized in the treaty following Sino-Japanese War of 1894-1895 (which also was for the control of Korea) gave way to a recognition by Russia of Japan's paramount interest in Korea. Japan continued her military occupation of the country, and (Aug. 22, 1910), annexed Korea outright.

The area of Korea is 85,246 square miles; the population (1939) was 22,633,857.

Confucianism, Buddhism and Shintoism are the chief religions and Christianity has grown greatly. Many modern schools have been established by the Japanese. There is a university in Seoul (Keijo), the capital.

The country is mountainous, especially in the north, where the forests are of great value, and there is much mineral wealth awaiting development. The climate is dry and bracing. The mulberry tree thrives, 60,000 acres being planted with them. Silkworm culture has been much encouraged by the Japanese and the quality of the cocoons improved. Some 786,000 families are engaged in the industry. Rice is an important crop. The cultivation of tobacco is also fostered. Barley, wheat and beans also are grown.

There has been considerable development of cotton spinning, cotton, silk and rayon weaving industries in recent years. Fertilizer and chemical works have been developed; also cement, paper, pottery, electric bulbs and enamelled ironwares.

Mining concessions covering 270,000 acres, mostly gold-bearing, which had been in the hands of about 15 foreign corporations (four American) and individuals (four Americans) before annexation are respected, but the law of April 1, 1916, prohibits foreigners from acquiring mining rights. Silver, zinc, copper, lead, iron, tungsten, graphite, anthracite coal and kaolin are present.

Trade is chiefly with Japan. The principal imports are cotton goods, iron, machinery, silk and rayon, timber, mineral oil, millet, sugar, paper, flour, fertilizers and coal. The main exports are rice, beans, copper, iron and silk.

The monetary unit is the Japanese yen. The budget (1941-1942) is estimated to balance at 1,012,577 yen.

KWANTUNG

Kwantung is the southern part of the Liaotung peninsula, the southernmost portion of Manchuria, which has the Bay of Korea on the east, the Yellow Sea to the south and the Liaotung Gulf on the west. Japan has taken it as spoils of war from China by the Treaty of Shimonoseki but was forced to turn it back by diplomatic pressure from Russia, Germany and France. Russia then leased it for 25 years from China, and constructed the strongly fortified city of Port Arthur and the nearby commercial ice-free port of Dalny (now Darien), the capital. The area is 1,438 square miles; the population (Oct. 1, 1935), 1,656,726.

Japan took Port Arthur by siege (1905), and at the close of the Russo-Japanese War took over the lease in the Treaty of Portsmouth (1905). The lease was extended (May, 1915) to 99 years by China.

Kwantung by Imperial Ordinance (April 12, 1919) has a civil government superseding the former military government.

Darien is the chief seaport of Manchuria and the southern terminus of the South Manchurian Railroad, which connects with the Peiping and Korean lines at Mukden and with the Trans-Siberian at Changchun, now Hsinching.

Manufactured salt is the chief product of the territory, and the salt deposits are enormous. Principal agricultural products are corn, millet, beans, wheat, buckwheat, rice, tobacco and hemp. Trade is mostly with Japan and China, about 40% with the former and 25% with the latter. A Japanese governor rules the territory.

The budget (1938-1939) was estimated to balance at 23,021,024 yen.

FORMOSA
(Taiwan)

Formosa is an island lying between the Philippines on the south and Japan to the north, with the China Sea on the west and the Pacific Ocean on the east. A range of mountains from north to south forms the backbone of the island (highest peak, Mt. Niitaka, 14,500 ft.); the eastern half is exceedingly steep and craggy, but the western slope is flat, fertile and well cultivated, yielding two rice crops a year. The temperature rarely falls below 96° F. Rain is abundant. The area is 13,880 square miles; the population (Oct. 1, 1935), 5,212,426. Taihoku is the capital.

Besides rice, the principal agricultural products are tea, sugar, sweet potatoes, ramie, jute, turmeric and camphor. Minerals include gold, silver, copper and coal. Trade is mainly with Japan.

Formosa was ceded by China (1895) after the Sino-Japanese War and Japan has made it a source of profit. Japanese colonists were encouraged, schools established, railroads built, telegraph and telephone lines laid, harbors improved, industries aided and much done in public works. The aborigines, who in the north are savage headhunters, gave much trouble, and the government (1910) began a thorough subjugation program.

The monetary unit is the Japanese yen. The governmental budget (1938-1939) was estimated to balance at 183,014,971 yen.

The Pescadores (Pheng-hu), a group of islands with an area of 50 square miles and a population of about 60,000, are between Taiwan and the coast of China, by whom they were ceded to Japan in 1895. The islands are under the government of Taiwan.

Japanese Sakhalin (Karafuto) is the southern half of the island of that name, below the 50th parallel, which was ceded by Russia (Oct. 1905) in the Treaty of Portsmouth. The area is 13,930 square miles, and the population, (Oct. 1, 1935) was 331,949. The country is mountainous, and primeval forests cover 70% of the land. Coal output is considerable. Fisheries are important. In an effort to colonize the island, 9,988 families, numbering 42,683 persons, have been placed on the land.

The budget (1939) was balanced at 46,747,712 yen.

Japanese Mandates in the Pacific extend for 1,200 miles north from the equator and for about 2,500 miles from east to west. The total area of land in this immense expanse of sea is only 829 square miles. The islands, formerly German possessions number 623; the groups are the Marianne or Ladrone (except Guam, U. S.), population, 44,-205 (1935); the Marshall Islands, consisting of 33 coral atolls, population, 10,439, and the Caroline Islands, population, 30,915. The chief islands in the group are Ponape, Yap and Parao. Each group has a language of its own. The principal resources are phosphorous ores (chiefly in the Carolines), cocoanut and copra. The seat of government is in Paro (Palaou) in the Carolines.

Japan opened a commercial air service from Yokahoma to Palaou in the South Sea mandated islands (April 6, 1939). The distance is 2,595 miles, with a halt at Saipan. The flying time is approximately 15 hours.

The budget (1937-1938) was estimated to balance at 8,682,482 yen.

The Spratly Islands, seven in number and consisting of 247 acres of coral reefs in the South China Sea, 700 miles southwest of Manila, P. I., were annexed by Japan (March 31, 1939). The annexation was extended (April 18) when Japan included the entire group of reefs and inlets in the South China Sea, 300 miles long, in her plans. The islands are about 700 miles south of Hainan, an important island off the coast of French-Indo China, 500 miles west of the northern Philippines. The islands are about 300 miles from French-Indo China, 350 miles southward from British Sarawak and 600 miles from the great British naval base at Singapore.

France occupied the islands (1933), making the first formal claim to their ownership since discovery (1867). Previously Britain had regarded the islands as British. Japan protested, implying a claim to sovereignty because Japanese traders had tried to exploit the phosphate deposits (1925). The islands have no great commercial value but might be useful as an observation station in a Far Eastern war or as a ship or air base.

totaled about 710,224 square miles, with about 21,273,900 of population.

In Asia, a part of Armenia has adopted a Soviet government and is at least in harmonious agreement with Soviet Russia. Syria passed under the mandate of France, later was proclaimed a Republic, and was occupied by Great Britain (1941). Mesopotamia has been created the independent kingdom of the Iran; Palestine has come under the mandate of Great Britain; and Arabia has asserted its independence, and is now the Kingdom of Saudi Arabia.

Turkey in Europe is now bounded on the north by the Black Sea, Bulgaria and the Caucasus; on the east by the Caucasus and Persia; on the south by Iraq, Syria and the Mediterranean Sea; on the west by Bulgaria, Greece and the Aegean Sea.

Under the Treaty of Sevres (Aug. 10, 1920), imposed on Turkey after World War I, various divisions of her territory were made and a neutral zone was set up on either shore of the Dardanelles, the Sea of Marmora, and the Hellespont.

The Sanjak of Alexandria set up (Jan. 1, 1925) as part of the State of Syria became an independent province known as the Hatay Republic under a treaty concluded (June, 1938) between France and Turkey. Its capital is Antioch. Hatay was ceded to Turkey by France (June 23, 1939) in a mutual assistance pact.

The real power in the Turkish Empire was seized by the Grand National Assembly and a responsible Ministry set up by the Nationalists at Ankara, in Anatolia, which was the most genuinely Turkish section of the old Ottoman Empire, after the last Chamber of Deputies, sitting at Constantinople, was dissolved (April 11, 1920). The Assembly declared that Mohammed VI was deposed as Sultan, and the Sultanate abolished. It declared (March 2, 1924) that his successor as Caliph, Abdul Medjid II, was deposed as Caliph (spiritual head of Islam) and that the Caliphate was vested in the Assembly.

Turkey (April 10, 1936) asked of the eight powers signatory to the Treaty of Lausanne for its revision so that she might remilitarize the Straits of the Dardanelles and the Bosphorus. The powers consented at a meeting in Montreaux, Switzerland (June 20).

A constitution replacing the Fundamental Law of 1921 was adopted (Oct., 1925). It provided for a single legislative National Assembly of 283 Deputies elected on a basis of one to each 50,000 people by males over 18. This provision was changed (Dec. 14, 1934) when the franchise was given to women and the age of both men and women made 22 years, and the ratio changed to one for 40,000. The Assembly elected for four years (March 26, 1939) has 429 members including 12 women.

The National Assembly elects the President of the Republic for a four-year term from among its members. In 15 years a steady flow of legislation has been enacted to Westernize the country. By tacit omission polygamy and slavery were abolished,

civil marriages were made obligatory and registration of marriages was ordered. The Gregorian calendar was adopted, the 24-hour clock, and the metric system. All Turks were ordered to adopt family names. The fez was outlawed and most of the younger women discarded the veil and with it the old custom of seclusion. The Assembly (May 28, 1935) made Sunday the weekly day of rest throughout Turkey in place of Friday, the traditional Mohammedan Sabbath.

Islam is no longer recognized as the State religion, but the vast majority of the Turkish population is Moslem.. Turkish has been substituted for the liturgical language in all mosques. The law forbids the wearing of clerical garb except in places of worship during Divine service.

Education is compulsory, free and secular between the ages of 7 and 16. There are primary, intermediate, secondary and vocational schools with universities in Istanbul and Ankara.

Mustapha Kemal Ataturk (Chief Turk), president of Turkey, died (Nov. 10, 1938) and Gen. Ismet Inonu (Nov. 11) was elected to succeed him. A new cabinet was formed (Jan. 25, 1939) with only five of the twelve ministers who held office at the time of the death of Kemal Ataturk. The new cabinet re-elected Ismet Inonu. The Premier is Sukru Saracoglu.

Military service is compulsory with terms of three years in the Army and the same period in the Navy. Subjects are called up at the age of 20 and the liability conitnues for 26 years. Since the outbreak of the war, the Army has been maintained at approximately war strength, which is 500,000 or more. Complete mobilization would put 2,000,000 under the colors.

The Turkish Air Force has been strengthened since 1940, when it had approximately 400 first line planes. The present strength is not divulged, although the personnel is close to 10,000.

Reorganization of the Navy, started before the war, continues and the effective fleet comprises one battle cruiser, two cruisers, two gunboats and miscellaneous small craft. The effective strength is approximately 800 officers and 4,000 men.

Turkey adopted (1935) a Five-year plan for industrialization of the country and the next year adopted a second Five-year plan for mining and electrification.

Agriculture is the chief industry of the Turks, products being tobacco, which goes to almost all world marts; cereals, cotton, figs, nuts, fruits of almost all varieties, opium and gums. About 20 million acres are in forests.

Turkey has large mineral resources, not yet developed, including chrome ore, zinc, manganese, antimony, copper, borax, emery, asphalt, meerschaum, some coal and lignite, salt, some gold and silver, and petroleum on lands bordering the Marmora Sea.

The monetary unit is the piaster with an average value of $.80. Budget estimates (1942-1943) are receipts 394,328,340 Turkish pounds; expenditures, 394,326,938. A pound equals 100 piasters.

Union of Soviet Socialist Republics

(RUSSIA)

Capital, Moscow—Area, 8,819,791 square miles—Population (est. 1940), 192,695,710. (The area and population data include the Baltic Republics, occupied Poland and lands returned by Rumania to the U. S. S. R.)

The Union of Soviet Socialist Republics—in area the largest country in the world—stretches across two continents from the North Pacific Ocean to the Gulf of Finland. It occupies the northern part of Asia and the eastern half of Europe, from the Arctic to the Black Sea. Its western borders brush against Finland, the Baltic Sea, Germany (Poland), Hungary and Rumania. On the south it is bounded by Rumania, the Black Sea, Turkey, Iran, Afghanistan, China, Mongol People's Republic and Manchukuo.

The vast territory of the U. S. S. R., one-sixth of the earth's land surface, contains every phase of climate, except the distinctly tropical, and a varied topography. The European portion is a vast low plain with the Ural mountains on its eastern edge, the Crimean and Caucasian mountains on the south and southeast. The Urals, separating the European from the Asiatic portions of the country, stretch north and south for 2,500 miles. The Asiatic portion of the U. S. S. R. also consists largely of an immense plain, with mountain ranges on its eastern and southern borders.

The rivers are important as actual or potential channels of commerce. In the European section these include the Dnieper, flowing into the Black Sea, and the Volga and the Ural, flowing into the Caspian Sea. The Asiatic section is drained by three great rivers, the Ob, the Yenisei and the Lena, each over 2500 miles long, flowing into the

Arctic Ocean, and contains several large rivers in the south, including the Amur, which flows into the Pacific Ocean. The northern rivers and the Arctic coastline of 4,000 miles have been opened to navigation during recent years.

The area of the Soviet Union contains virtually every material natural resource of modern civilization—minerals of all kinds, base and precious; every variety of timber, except tropical; every character of cereal, vegetable and fruit lands. About 38% of the territory of the Soviet Union is timber area, 3,124,360 square miles. Land potentially suitable for agriculture is estimated at upwards of 1,037,400,000 acres, of which about one-eighth is now under cultivation. Potential hydraulic resources are estimated at 280,000,000 kilowatts.

Known mineral resources include: coal, peat, oil, iron ore, manganese, copper, zinc and lead.

The capital of this vast country is Moscow, a city of great charm, called the nerve center of the Soviet Union. Its lofty modern structures tower over quaint remnants of Czarist Russia; and ancient winding streets enter unexpectedly into spacious squares with shining Metro stations, fresh flower-beds and trees. Here is the famous Kremlin, the citadel of Moscow enclosing the former palace of the Czar.

Leningrad (formerly St. Petersburg and Petrograd), situated on the delta of the Neva River and spread out over many islands, is the center of science and research in the U. S. S. R. It is a city of museums and palaces, including the "Museum of the Revolution," the pre-war Winter Palace, the Palace of Count Stroganoff, built by Rastrelli, the Catherine and Alexander Palaces at Puskin, and the terraced fountains and palaces of Peterhof. Priceless paintings of Rubens, Valesquez and Titian adorn the walls of the Hermitage Museum.

Kiev, the 1,000-year-old capital of the Ukrainian U. S. S. R. is a busy industrial city and the scientific center of the Ukrainian Republic. The ancient Kiev-Perchersky Monastery, now converted into a historical museum, presents an outstanding example of medieval Slavonic architecture.

The Crimea is called the vacationland of the Soviet Union. Shining palaces of the former aristocracy, now sanatoria for the people, contrast with the picturesque villages of the Crimeans, a mixture of Tartar, Turk and Russian. The highway from Sevastopol along the shores of the Black Sea looks on a steadily-changing panorama of mountains and flourishing valleys studded with quaint Tartar villages. The highway winds past Yalta, Alupka, Mischor, Massandra, Gurzuf—a chain of health resorts washed by the warm waters of the Black Sea.

The Caucasus is the most scenic part of the Soviet Union. It is a land of ever-varying scenery where glaciers alternate with sub-tropical vegetation, a land where medieval mountain hamlets are just a few hours' ride from great power stations. The stretch of coast between the Caucasus Mountain Range and the sea is known as the "Black Sea Riviera"; Sochi, Matsesta, Cagry, Sukhum and Batum are some of the famous resort towns.

The new Soviet constitution (adopted Dec. 5, 1936), replacing that of 1924, divided the country into eleven Union Republics, each with its separate government for local affairs, patterned on the Union Government. A twelfth Union Republic, the Karelo-Finnish, was formed (1940), followed by the Moldavian, the thirteenth; the Lithuanian, the fourteenth; the Latvian, the fifteenth, and the Estonian, the sixteenth, all in the same year. The Russian Soviet Federated Socialist Republic, with nearly two-thirds of the entire population of the Union and upwards of three-fourths of the area, is the largest and most important of the Union Republics. A list of the Union Republics, with areas and populations, follows:

	Area, Sq. Mi.	Pop.
Russian S. F. S. R.	6,368,768	109,278,614
Ukrainian S. S. R.	170,978	38,960,221
Byelorussian S. S. R. (White Russia)	49,022	10,367,976
Armenian S. S. R.	11,580	1,281,599
Georgian S. S. R.	26,865	3,542,289
Azerbaijan S. S. R.	32,956	3,209,727
Uzbek S. S. F. R.	66,392	6,282,446
Turkmen S. S. R.	17,384	1,253,985
Tadjik S. S. R.	55,040	1,485,091
Kazakh S. S. R.	1,047,797	6,145,937
Kirghiz S. S. R.	75,926	1,459,301
Karelo Finnish S. S. R	16,173	469,100
Moldavian S. S. R.	19,176	3,464,952
Lithuanian S. S. R.	22,959	2,879,070
Latvian S. S. R.	25,402	1,950,502
Estonian S. S. R.	18,353	1,134,000
Total U. S. S. R.	8,819,791	183,736,286

The twelfth (in part), thirteenth, fourteenth, fifteenth and sixteenth Union Republics were occupied by German and Finnish forces (1941) in the war between U. S. S. R. and the Reich.

Large sections of White Russia, the Ukraine and parts of the Byelorussian and Moldavian Republics also were occupied by the Axis forces, including the section of Poland awarded to Russia in the German-Soviet partition.

The census (1939) gives 18.6 per cent of the population (Arctic regions not included) as below the age of 7, and 41 per cent between the ages of 15 and 39, with 6.6 more than 60 years old. It gives 81.2 per cent of the population as literate, or 90.8 per cent of the men and 72.6 per cent of the women. Illiteracy was to have been entirely cleared up by the completion of the second five-year plan at the end of January, 1938. [In 1926, literacy of the population of the Soviet Union above the age of 9 was put at 51 per cent.]

As to education, 8.86 per cent of the population was found to have secondary school training and 0.64 per cent university training.

By nationality Russians made up 58.41 per cent of the population of 170,000,000 in the Soviet Union, Ukrainians 16.56 per cent and White Russians 3.11 per cent. Jews, of whom there were 3,020,141 in the Soviet Union, made up 1.78 per cent and the Germans, numbering 1,423,534, or 0.84 per cent.

There were forty-nine recognized nationalities, plus more than 1,800,000 persons of other national groups.

The constitution (1936) provides for universal direct suffrage with the secret ballot. The first election under the new constitution was held (Dec. 12, 1937) when 90,319,346 persons recorded their vote, or 96.5 per cent of the total voting population of the U. S. S. R.

The autonomous republics, each of which is represented by eleven deputies in the Council of Nationalities, form the most important of the various subdivisions of the Union Republics.

The population (1939 census) was announced by the Government as 170,467,186, including 81,-664,981 men and 88,802,205 women, a total gain of 15.9 per cent over the 1926 figures. A movement toward the cities was indicated in an urban population (1939) of 32.9 compared with (1926) 17.9. After the re-union of Western Ukraine and Western Byelorussia, the population of the U. S. S. R. increased to 183,267,000. The creation of the Karelo-Finnish, Moldavian, Lithuanian, Latvia and Estonian Republics increased the population to 192,695,710.

The Russian Soviet Socialist Federated Republic (Soviet Russia proper), contains nearly 70% of the population of the Soviet Union and includes 78% of its territory. Its territories stretch from the Estonian, Latvian and Finnish borders and the White Russian and Ukrainian lines on the west, to the shores of the Pacific Ocean, and from the Arctic Ocean on the north to the shores of the Black and Caspian seas and the borders of Kazakh S. S. R., Mongolia and Manchuria on the south. The capital is Moscow.

Byelorussian Soviet Socialist Republic (White Russia), was proclaimed Jan. 1, 1919. Under the Czars Byelorussia was the pale of settlement of the Jewish population. It suffered greatly from periodical pogroms and from inter-racial struggles. Between 1914 and 1920 it was a field for military operations. The racial composition is Byelorussians 80.6%; Jews, 10%; others, Russians, Ukrainians, Poles. Minsk is the capital with a population of 238,772 (1939).

The country is agricultural. Much of the land is marshy, but modern drainage methods have increased the arable area. Principal crops are flax, grain and potatoes. Chief industries include woodworking, matches, linen, paper, leather, oil pressing, glass.

The Ukrainian Soviet Socialist Republic is the most densely populated of the Constituent Republics. It borders on the Black Sea, with Germany, Hungary and Rumania on the west and southwest. The northern part of Bukowina was added to the Ukraine S. S. R. (1940) when the country was returned to the U. S. S. R. by Rumania. The capital is Kiev, population (1939) 846,293.

Of the population 80% are Ukrainians, 9.5% Russians, 5.4% Jews, 1.6% Poles, and 3.5% Greeks, Bulgarians, Rumanians, Gypsies. There are also about 800,000 Ukrainians living in other portions of the Soviet Union.

The Ukraine contains the famous black soil belt, the chief wheat-producing section of the Soviet Union. Sugar beets and oil seeds are important crops and livestock breeding is rapidly advancing. In the Donetz Basin the Ukraine has a huge storage of coal, iron and other metals. Here are produced 54.1% of the coal mined in the country, 59.1% of the iron and a large proportion of the manganese. There are heavily developed chemical and dye industries and salt mines. Electric power development is making rapid advances and in the rural districts more than 200,000 farms are supplied with current.

The largest hydro-electric development in Europe, constructed on the Dnieper River and known as the Lenin Hydroelectric Station, with an ultimate capacity of 558,000 kilowatts, was dynamited (1941) by Russia during the war with Germany.

The three Soviet Socialist Republics of Azerbaijan, Armenia and Georgia were formed under the new Constitution (1936) by a splitting-up of the Transcaucasian Federation.

Azerbaijan has in the vicinity of Baku the most important oil fields in the U. S. S. R. Its natural wealth includes deposits of pyrites, barites and fossil copal, as well as zinc, silver, gold, copper, tin vanadium and molybdenum. Establishment of large irrigation projects during recent years has made cotton growing important of recent years a high quality Egyptian type cotton has been grown. Three-fifths of the population is composed of Azerbaijanians, a Turkish people. Georgia, in western Transcaucasus, contains the largest manganese mines in the world. There are rich timber resources. Large coal deposits have recently been discovered. Output of industrial machinery has become important of recent years. Grain and wine grapes are principal crops. The population includes two-thirds Georgians. Mountainous **Armenia** with its arid valleys has been transformed by irrigation of recent years into a country of orchards and vineyards, of cotton and tobacco plantations. Copper and lead mining have been developed and a diversified industry has grown up. The population is 85% Armenian.

The Uzbek Soviet Socialist Republic and the Turkmen Soviet Socialist Republic in Central Asia were organized (1924). The Uzbek Republic contains the finest cotton lands in the Soviet Union. A high quality caracul fur is produced for export. Its mineral wealth includes coal, sulphur, copper and oil. In the Turkmen Republic principal crops are cotton, grain and oil seeds. Mineral wealth includes oil, coal, sulphur, barite, lime gypsum. The Kara Kum desert occupies four-fifths of the territory.

Tajikistan, in the extreme south of Central Asia, bordering on Afghanistan and China, was raised from an autonomous republic in Uzbekistan to a federal republic (1929). It is a land of high mountains traversed by narrow valleys. Cotton and grain are principal crops. Mineral wealth includes lead, zinc, silver, cadmium, uranium vanadium, molybdenum.

The Kazakh Soviet Socialist Republic and the Kirghiz Soviet Socialist Republic, respective capitals Alma Ata and Frunze, were organized under the constitution (1936) from portions of the Russian Republic. The Kazakh Republic has great oil deposits in the Ural-Emba district and its coal deposits in the Karaganda coal basin form the third largest coal basin in the country. There are rich deposits of copper, lead and other nonferrous metals. Agricultural output includes grain, wheat and livestock. Mineral resources of the Kirghiz Republic include coal, oil, lead, zinc, copper, gold, silver and tin. Crops include wheat. rice, sugar beets, tobacco. kendyr and fruits.

The Karelo-Finnish Soviet Socialist Republic was formed from the territory of the former Karelian Autonomous Soviet Socialist Republic and partly from the territory ceded to the U. S. S. R. by the peace treaty with Finland at the close of the war. Seventy per cent of the territory is covered by woods (pine and other). The population is mainly Karelians, Finns and Russians. The mineral resources are copper, lead, zinc, silver and iron. The territory has 26,000 small lakes and includes the two largest lakes in Europe, Ladoga and Onega.

The Moldavian Soviet Socialist Republic was created from the territory of the former Moldavian Autonomous Republic and Bessarabia, which was returned to the U. S. S. R. by Rumania. Sections of Bessarabia had been taken from Russia at the close of World War I.

The Lithuanian Soviet Socialist Republic was voted into the U. S. S. R. (1940). Elections were held and a Communist dominated Parliament was chosen. The vote showed 99.19 per cent for the Working People's Bloc. Ballots were cast by 1,386,569 persons. The new Parliament proclaimed Lithuania a Soviet Socialist Republic (July 21) and asked for incorporation into the U. S. S. R., which was granted by the Supreme Soviet (Aug. 3). The capital is Vilna.

The Latvian Soviet Socialist Republic was established (1940). A new Parliament, dominated by the Communist party was chosen (July 14) at the elections. The vote showed 97.6 for the one-party Communist ticket. The new Parliament proclaimed Latvia a Soviet Republic (July 21) and asked for incorporation in the Union of Socialist Soviet Republics, which the Supreme Soviet granted Aug. 5). The capital is Riga.

The Estonian Soviet Socialist Republic was created (1940). A new Parliament with a Communist majority was elected (July 14), the Communist ticket—the only in the field—receiving 92.9 per cent of the vote. The new Parliament proclaimed Latvia a Soviet Republic (July 21) and asked for incorporation into the U. S. S. R., which was granted (Aug. 6) by vote of the Supreme Soviet. The capital is Tallinn.

The incorporation of the Lithuanian, Latvian and Estonian Soviet Socialist Republics into the U. S. S. R. has not been recognized by the United States.

Under the constitution (1936), the supreme organ of state power is the Supreme Soviet of the U. S. S. R. (replacing the All-Union Congress of Soviets), meeting regularly twice a year and elected for a period of four years. The Supreme Soviet consists of two legislative chambers with equal rights, viz: the Soviet of the Union, elected on the basis of one deputy per 300,000 population (647 deputies, an increase from 569 caused by the

addition of the Latvian, Lithuanian, Estonian, Karelo-Finnish and Moldavian Soviet Socialist Republics and additions to the Ukrainian and Byelorussian Soviet Socialist Republics); the Council of Nationalities, consisting of 25 delegates selected by the Supreme Soviet of each Union Republic, 11 from each of the 19 autonomous republics, and five from each autonomous province 713, an increase from 574 caused by the addition of the new Republics). In case of disagreement between the two Chambers, a conciliation commission is provided, and if its decision fails to bring agreement the Soviet is dissolved and new elections fixed.

The two Chambers in joint session elect a Presidium consisting of a president, sixteen vice-presidents and 24 members, which have wide administrative powers between sessions of the Supreme Soviet, including ratification of treaties and declaration of a state of war. The Presidium supervises the work of the Council of People's Commissars, selected by the Supreme Soviet, which acts as the executive and administrative organ of the State. In addition to a president and vice-president, the Soviet has commissar members, heads of the federal commissariats of defense, foreign affairs, foreign trade, railways, water transport, communications, sea transport, ferrous metallurgy, non-ferrous metallurgy, chemical industry, aviation, shipbuilding, armaments, munitions, heavy machine-building, medium machine-building, and general machine-building, navy, procurement, construction, electric industry, and electric power stations, coal industry, fuel industry.

Commissariats common to both federal government and the Union Republics are: food industry, fish industry, meat and dairy, light industry, textile industry, timber, state grain and livestock farms, finance, home trade, home affairs, justice, health, building materials industry, agriculture.

The remaining seven members of the Council are the chairman of: The State Planning Commission, the Committees on Art, Higher Education, Geology, Radio Broadcasting and Radiofication, Cinema Industry. There are in addition six economic councils attached to the Council of Peoples' Commissariats.

The highest judicial organ is the Supreme Court, which, with the Special Courts, are elected by the Supreme Council for five-year terms.

Land and natural resources are held in trust by the Government for the general population, though collective farms may hold their land under a system of perpetual leasehold. Natural resources are exploited by state trusts. The transport system, as well as posts, telephones and telegraphs, are operated as Government departments. Industry is conducted almost wholly by state enterprises, the output of private industries having declined to a fraction of one per cent of the industrial production. Some industrial enterprises are conducted by the cooperatives.

The Communist Party is the only legalized political organization in the Soviet Union, though non-party candidates are freely elected to public office. The party's directive body is the Central Committee, elected by the membership at the party congresses. The Committee selects a small executive body, the Political Bureau, which by virtue of its position of party leadership, makes decisions on policy which are followed by the Government.

A list of People's Commissariats (All-Union) of the Union of Soviet Socialist Republics follows:

Chairman of the Council of People's Commissars —Joseph V. Stalin, who is also chairman of the State Committee for Defense.

Foreign Affairs and Vice Premier—Viacheslav M. Molotov.

Foreign Trade—Anastase L. Mikoyan.
Railways—Alexander Khrulev.
Communications—Ivan T. Peresipkin.
Sea Transport—Semen S. Dukelsky.
River Transport—Zosim A. Shashkov.
Fuel Industry—M. Sedin.
Electric Industry—V. V. Bogatyrev.
Electric Power Stations—A. I. Letkov.
Ferrous Metallurgy—Ivan T. Tevosyan.
Chemical Industry—Mikhail Pervukhin.
Aviation Industry—A. J. Shakhurin.
Shipbuilding Industry—I. Nosenko.
Munitions—Boris L. Vannikov.
Armaments—Dmitri Ustinov.
Heavy Machine Building—Kazakov.
Medium Machine Building—V. A. Malyshev.
General Machine Building—Peter I. Parshin.
Navy—Nikolai G. Kuznetsov.
Procurement—V. A. Donskoy.
Construction—Semen Z. Ginzburg.
Coal Industry—Vasily V. Vakhrushev.

A list of the People's Commissariats (All-Union and Union Republic) of the Union of Soviet Socialist Republics follows:

Food Industry—Vasili P. Zotov.
Fish Industry—A. Ishkov.
Meat and Dairy Industry—Pavel V. Smirnov.
Light Industry—Sergei G. Lukin.
Textile Industry—I. Akimov.
Timber Industry—F. Sergeyev.
Agriculture—Ivan A. Benediktov.
State Grain and Livestock Farms—Pavel P. Lobanov.
Finance—Arseni G. Zverev.
Trade—Alexander B. Lubimov.
N. K. V. D. (Home Affairs)—Lavrenti P. Beria.
Justice—Nikolai M. Richkov.
Public Health—Georgi A. Miterev.
Building Materials Industry—Leonid A. Sosnin.
Red Fleet—Pytor Shirshov.
Chairman of the State Planning Commission of the U. S. S. R.—Maxim Z. Saburov.
Chairman of the Administration of the State Bank of the U. S. S. R.—N. K. Sokolov.
Chairman of Commissariat for Soviet Control—Lev Mekhlis.
Chairman of the Supreme Court of the U. S. S. R.—Ivan T. Golyakov.
Procurer of the U. S. S. R.—V. M. Bochkov.
Chairman of the Committee on High Education—Sergie V. Kaftanov.

Officers of the Supreme Soviet:
Chairman of the Presidium—Mikhail I. Kalinin.
President of the Soviet of the Union—A. A. Andreyev.
President of the Soviet of Nationalities—J. M. Shvernik.

Joseph Stalin is a deputy to the Supreme Soviet of the U. S. S. R., a member of the Military Council of the Supreme Soviet, and General Secretary of the Communist Party of the U. S. S. R., in addition to being Premier and Defense Commissar. Stalin also is Commander-in-Chief of the Army. A Committee for State Defense was formed (July 1, 1941) with Stalin as Chairman. The other members are Marshal Klementi E. Voroshilov, Lavrenti P. Beria and Georgi M. Malenkov.

Members of the Political Bureau (March, 1939) as elected at the eighteenth congress of the Communist Party of the Soviet Union are—Andreyev, Khruschev, Stalin, Kaganovich, Mikoyan, Voroshilov, Kalinin, Molotov, Zhdanov, and five candidates: L. Beria, N. Shvernik, N. Voznesensky, G. Malenkov and A. Shcherbakov.

There were organized (April 17, 1940) six new economic councils attached to the Council of People's Commissars, to coordinate the activities of the corresponding commissariats. These councils, with chairmen, are:
Metallurgy and Chemistry—N. I. Bulganin.
Machine-building—V. A. Malyshev.
Defense Industry—N. A. Voznesensky.
Fuel and Electro-Industry—M. G. Pervukhin.
Consumers Goods—A. N. Kosygin.
Agriculture and Procurement—M. Benediktov.

Education in the Soviet Union is a charge against the various Union Republics and the local budgets, with the exception that higher education is conducted on a federal basis.

Universal compulsory education for children, introduced for a four-year period (1930), has since been extended to seven years.

In the course of the first and second Five-Year Plans new alphabets were adopted for 50 of the minor nationalities that had never before possessed a written language. In most cases the Latin alphabet was adapted.

Appropriations for the cultural needs of the population (1941) were 47,803,000,000 rubles. The number of pupils in elementary and secondary schools (1941-1942) was 36,200,000 and 13,500 secondary and elementary schools were opened (1940). Thirty more colleges and universities also were opened in that year, bringing the total to 781 with a registration of approximately 600,000. A system of tuition was introduced (1940) in the secondary schools and higher educational institutions. Heretofore tuition had been free.

There were (1940) 9,000 newspapers with an aggregate circulation of 38,000,000. The number of public libraries increased from 40,300 (1933-1934) to 245,000 (1941). The number of portable libraries, which serve the people in the remote districts, increased (1941) to 144,000. The portable libraries delivered 30,000,000 books and magazines to their readers in a single year. The number of volumes in the public libraries (1941) was estimated at 1,500,000,000.

The Government announced (Aug. 13, 1941) that there were 8,338 churches, mosques and synagogues in the country.

Military training begins in the schools at the age of 12 when elementary courses are given for two hours each week. Pre-war military training follows and at the age of 16 compulsory service begins and continues to the age of 50. No reliable figures on the strength of the Red Army are available but Commissar Voroshilov said (1939) that the Army numbered 2,500,000. At the start of the war between Russia and Germany it was estimated that the U. S. S. R. had mobilized that number and this figure has been increased as the war has progressed.

The Soviet Navy has been undergoing reconstruction since 1940 and the process is expected to be completed (1943). Canals have been widened for the passage of capital ships from the White Sea into the Gulf of Finland and the Baltic sea. Naval bases have been reconstructed and at Vladivostok, there have been stationed 60 submarines, half of them of the ocean-going type and an equal number of speedy motor torpedo boats. The Navy (1940) consisted of three battleships, all launched (1911) and since refitted; seven cruisers, one launched (1905), three (1915), one (1916), one (1936), and one (1937). There were under construction (1938) 23 destroyers, 134 submarines, 18 torpedo boats. 130 motor torpedo boats, several mine layers, mine sweeping trawlers and miscellaneous craft.

The Navy is distributed in four fleets, Baltic, Black sea, Pacific and Northern. The Pacific fleet alone has more than 100 submarines and warships. not including smaller surface craft.

Admiral Nikolai G. Kuznetsov, Commissar of the Navy, announced (July 27, 1940) that Russia would add 168 warships to her fleet (1940-1941). He said the fleet was increased (1939) by 112 ships, large and small torpedo cutters included. "In 1940," he added, "we will get 168—that is a 50 per cent increase. If you consider the tonnage of 1939 as 100 per cent, in 1940 the tonnage will be 200 per cent."

According to a decree of the Council of People's Commissars (Sept. 29, 1935) consumers' cooperative organizations in the cities were discontinued and their property and trade transferred to the People's Commissariat of Trade of the U. S. S. R.

A system of planned development, embracing not only the entire economic field, but all cultural, scientific and public health activity as well, is in operation in the U. S. S. R. This has taken the form of a series of Five-Year Plans, with intermediate annual schedules. The Soviet Union completed (Dec. 31, 1937) its second Five-Year Plan and embarked on a third.

Under the first Plan (completed at the end of 1932) broad bases for heavy industry were established and mass-production was organized in many lines. Many large-scale regional power plants were constructed. Agriculture was completely reorganized on a collectivist basis. Under the second Plan these gains were extended and an improved economic coordination was attained. An important factor on the credit side was the rehabilitation and improvement of rail transport along with wide extension of the waterways system. The opening to navigation of the Northeast Passage and the development of the Soviet Arctic were also notable accomplishments. During the first Plan, 51,000,000,000 rubles was expended on new capital construction; during the second Plan two and a half times that amount. The industrial output was increased 119% during the first Plan; during the second Plan an additional increase of 121% (April 1, 1937—four years and three months of the second Five-Year Plan) was registered. Grain production increased 40 per cent under the second Plan. Industrial output in 1928 was 232.7% that of 1913; and in 1932 was 358.9% that of 1913.

The first year of each Five-Year Plan is usually taken as a test year. The schedule (1938) called for an increase in the output of industry of 15.5% and commensurate gains in other lines.

The annual output of Soviet industry has shown a six-fold increase during the past decade, the period of the first two Five-Year Plans. The increase (1937) was 13%. This was considerably below the schedule of increase for the year, owing to a decided lag in output during the summer and fall. The program (1938) called for an increase in output of 15.5% and the construction of 147 new large enterprises in heavy industry. The U. S. S. R. during the second Five-Year Plan took first place among the European countries in industrial production.

Nikolai Voznesensky, at the time Vice Chairman of the Council of People's Commissars and chairman of the State Planning Commission, told the 18th conference of the Communist party in Moscow (Feb. 19, 1941) that, taking the 1929 level of production as 100, he rated Russia's 1940 production at 534. He also reported that in three years of the Third Five-Year Plan, Russia's national income increased by 29,500,000,000 rubles for a total income of 125,500,000,000 in 1940. The State Planning Commission was directed to draw up a 15-year plan "to surpass capitalistic countries" in industrial production. The plan is to be designed to speed up production in pig iron, steel, fuel, electricity, machinery and consumer goods industries.

All large-scale industry in the U.S.S.R. is state-owned or operated by cooperative organizations. The state industries, which include all of the more important enterprises, account for more than 99.97% of the total industrial output of the country. They are operated under the supervision of the industrial commissariats. There are only a few scattered private industrial enterprises.

The Government ordered (June 26, 1940) new working hours throughout the country. Workers who had a five-day, 35-hour week had to sacrifice it for a six-day week of 48 hours. The six-day week was suspended and the seven-day week restored. Workers in branches working a six-hour day are required to work seven; those who worked seven are required to work eight hours. The work period of those on an eight-hour day is not changed. Industry was put on an overtime basis during the war with Germany.

The five-day working week was a feature of the changes wrought by the Revolution. Soviet trade unions urged the change to a longer work day and work weeks and the Government adopted the suggestion.

The Government drafts annually from 800,000 to 1,000,000 youths between 14 and 17 years for industrial training after which they work for the State for four consecutive years.

Before the revolution agricultural methods were extremely primitive. More than 60 per cent of the arable land was held by the imperial family, churches, large estates and "kulaks," the remainder being parcelled out among some 16,000,000 peasant households whose average holding—divided into three strips—was less than 14 acres. Grain area of collective farms increased from 187,500,000 acres (1933) to 230,000,000 acres (1938). Grain area of individual peasant farmers dropped in this period from 38,794,000 acres to 1,482,600 acres, or 0.6 per cent of the total grain area.

The revolution released much new land for the peasants, but over a decade passed before the Soviet Government was able to effect a general change in the set-up. The drive for collectivization began (1928-29) and today the bulk of the agricultural output as represented by large-scale, mechanized collective farms in which the peasant holdings are pooled. There were 243,000 collective farms (1941), operated by 18,800,000 households. Individual holdings were still worked by 1,400,000 peasant families. A number of large farms, most of which serve as agricultural laboratories and experiment stations, are operated directly by the State. Cash incomes in collective farms of rubles (1933), 5,662,000,000; (1937), 14,180,000,000; (1939), 18,300,000,000.

The backbone of mechanization in Soviet agriculture is furnished by the machine and tractor stations, each of which serves collective farms within its area. These stations operated (1940) 523,000 tractors and 182,000 combines.

The length of airlines in the U. S. S. R. (1940) was approximately 100,000 miles. Transport aviation carried (1939) 307,000 passengers, 11,500 tons of mail and 39,654 tons of cargo. By the end of the Third Five-Year Plan it is expected 450,000 persons will be carried annually.

Electric power development and operation in the Soviet Union is conducted under a unified system on a single technical and organizational foundation. Under this system a series of large regional power plants serves the principal industrial and mining sections of the country. High voltage grid networks covering wide areas link the regional plants. There are some 75 regional plants in operation, furnishing three-fourths of the country's power supply.

The budget reflects the economic progress of the Soviet Union because of the high degree of socialization of the nation. The first "firm" budget (1923-1924) balanced at 2,317,600,000 rubles.

Budgets (in thousands of rubles) for the last four years follow:

	Receipts	Expenditures
1938	127,571,000	124,000,000
1939	156,097,000	156,097,000
1940	183,955,000	183,955,000
1941	222,375,000	216,052,000

The budget (1941) provided for the expenditure of 57,000,000,000 rubles for capital construction. The defense appropriation (1941) was 78,002,000,000 rubles, a four-fold increase in four years.

The nominal value of the ruble is 19 cents, but accurate conversion into American money figures is impossible because of the lack of an open market.

The number of workers (1940) was 30,400,000 and the estimate (1941) was 31,600,000. The wage fund (1940) was 161,000,000,000 rubles and the estimate (1941) 175,000,000,000. State and Cooperative retail trade reached a value of 174,500,000,000 rubles (1940), with an estimate of 197,000,000,000 (1941).

Here are the figures on daily output in tons:

	1940	1937
Coal	467,000	370,000
Oil with gas	97-98,000	84-86,000
Rg. iron	46-47,000	40,000
Steel	58-59,000	50-51,000

The volume of capital investments in the national economy (1940) reached nearly 38,000,000,000 rubles, and for the three years of the third Five-Year Plan reached 108,000,000,000 rubles. During these three years 2,900 new factories, plants, power stations and other industrial plants were put into operation. The average annual growth of production during these three years was 13%.

Industrial production in rubles was:

1937	1940	1941 (Plan))
95,500,000,000	137,500,000,000	162,000,000,000

The State Bank is the center of the banking system. It has a monopoly of short term loan operations and it is the only bank of issue. It also finances the bulk of the foreign trade operations. Other banks are the Prombank (Industrial Bank), which finances capital construction in state industries; the Selkhozbank (Agricultural Bank), which finances capital investments in socialized agriculture; the Vsekobank (All-Union Cooperative Bank), which finances capital construction for cooperative organizations except housing cooperatives, and the Tsekombank (Central Bank for Public Utilities), which finances municipal public utilities, housing projects and the building of new cities.

Soviet currency has circulation only within the Soviet Union, both exports and imports thereof being prohibited by law. All payments abroad are made in gold or foreign currency. Gold mining has increased rapidly of recent years and the Soviet Union is said to stand second among the nations in gold production. No official figures for output are given.

The Soviet Government exercises a monopoly of foreign trade, under the Commissariat for Foreign Trade, and both exports and imports are regulated in accordance with the country's system of planned economy. The Commissariat maintains trading bureaus in foreign countries. In addition some of the large industrial syndicates buy equipment abroad under the supervision of the Commissariat.

Uruguay

(REPUBLICA ORIENTAL DEL URUGUAY)

Capital, Montevideo—Area, 72,153 square miles—Population (Jan. 1, 1938), 2,146,545

Uruguay, the smallest and one of the most advanced Republics in South America, is bounded on the north and east by Brazil, on the south by the South Atlantic Ocean and the River Plata, and on the west by Argentina, the boundary line being the River Uruguay, which is navigable from the Plata to Salto, 200 miles north. Lying between latitudes 30° and 35° south and consisting of rolling grassy plains, it enjoys an extraordinarily healthy climate with a uniform temperature. More than 2,150,000 acres are under cultivation. The chief products are wheat, corn, oats, linseed, tobacco and olives. Wine making is a large industry.

The new constitution presented by the Constituent Assembly of 284 members who were elected (June 25, 1933) was adopted by a plebiscite (April 19, 1934). It provides for a Chamber of Deputies of 99 members elected by the Provinces according to population, and a Senate of 30 members elected by the nation as a whole, 15 being from the party polling the largest vote and 15 from the party with the next largest vote. Suffrage is universal and compulsory, failure to vote being punishable by fine. Foreigners may become naturalized without losing their former citizenship.

The President, Senators and Deputies have four-year terms. The President appoints a Cabinet of nine from the parties which have a majority in Parliament. President and Ministers are subject to votes of censure. The President is Gen. Alfredo Baldomir (elected March 27, 1938).

President Baldomir dissolved Congress (Feb. 21, 1942) and appointed a Council of State to act.

Much of the Uruguayan code of advanced social legislation was written into the constitution, which provides for old-age pensions, child welfare, State care of mothers, free medical attention for the poor, workmen's accident insurance, cheap dwell-

Population of Important Foreign Cities

Source: Latest census figures and latest official estimates

City	Country	Pop.
Adelaide	Australia	325,000
Agra	India	284,189
Ahmedabad	India	313,789
Alexandria	Egypt	685,736
Algiers	Algeria	252,321
Altona	Germany	241,970
Amritsar	India	264,840
Amsterdam	Holland	793,526
Amoy	China	234,159
Antwerp	Belgium	273,317
Archangel	U.S.S.R.	281,000
Astrakhan	U.S.S.R.	254,000
Athens	Greece	652,385
Auckland	N. Zealand	223,760
Avellaneda	Argentina	386,000
Bagdad	Iraq	499,410
Bahia	Brazil	363,726
Baku	U.S.S.R.	809,347
Bangalore	India	306,470
Bangkok	Thailand	931,170
Barcelona	Spain	2,301,164
Batavia	Java	437,000
Belfast	Ireland	438,112
Belem (Para)	Brazil	303,740
Belgrade	Yugoslavia	405,000
Benares	India	263,100
Berlin, Gr'tr.	Germany	4,332,242
Birmingham	England	1,029,700
Bochum	Germany	303,288
Bogota	Colombia	395,300
Bologna	Italy	318,444
Bombay	India	1,486,971
Bordeaux	France	258,348
Bradford	England	289,510
Bremen	Germany	342,113
Breslau	Germany	615,006
Brisbane	Australia	335,520
Bristol	England	415,100
Brno	Cz'choslov.	264,925
Brunswick	Germany	201,306
Brus'ls,G'tr	Belgium	912,774
Bucharest	Rumania	648,162
Budapest G't'r	Hungary	1,162,800
Buenos Aires	Argentina	2,505,332
Cairo	Egypt	1,307,422
Calcutta	India	1,485,582
Canton	China	861,024
Cape Town	U.S. of Afr.	173,412
Caracas	Venezuela	377,434
Cardiff	Wales	224,850
Catania	Italy	244,972
Cawnpore	India	243,753
Changsha	China	606,972
Chemnitz	Germany	334,563
Cheliabinsk	U.S.S.R.	273,000
Chungking	China	635,000
Cologne	Germany	768,426
Colombo	Ceylon	284,155
Copenhagen	Denmark	843,168
Cordoba	Argentina	288,916
Cracow	Poland	254,600
Croydon	England	242,300
Dairen	Kwantung	282,665
Danzig	Free State	415,000
Delhi	India	447,442
Dne'p'tr'vsk	U.S.S.R.	500,662
Dortmund	Germany	537,000
Dresden	Germany	625,174
Dublin	Ireland	482,300
Duisburg	Germany	431,256
Dusseldorf	Germany	539,905
Edinburgh	Scotland	470,000
Erivan	U.S.S.R.	200,000
Essen	Germany	659,871
Firenze	Italy	322,535
Florence	Italy	354,975
Foochow	China	322,725
Frankfort	Germany	546,649
Fukuoka	Japan	322,000
Fushun	Manch'k'o	295,036
Geis'nk'ch'n	Germany	313,003
Genoa	Italy	659,665
Glasgow	Scotland	1,131,800
Gorky	U.S.S.R.	644,116
Gothenburg	Sweden	281,301
Graz	Germany	210,175
The Hague	Holland	495,185
Hakodate	Japan	226,500
Halle	Germany	220,364
Hamburg	Germany	1,682,220
Hanchow	China	506,930
Hankow	China	777,993
Hanover	Germany	472,527
Harbin	Manch'k'o	330,436
Havana	Cuba	568,913
Helsinki	Finland	304,965
Hiroshima	Japan	340,100
Hong Kong	China	1,050,256
Howrah	India	224,873
Hsinking	Manch'k'o	415,264
Hull	England	319,400
Hyderabad	India	466,894
Irkutsk	U.S.S.R.	243,000
Istanbul	Turkey	883,599
Ivanove-Voznesensk	U.S.S.R.	285,000
Johan'sburg	U. S. of Afr	257,671
Kalinin	U.S.S.R.	216,000
Kaiyuan	Manch'k'o	317,520
Karachi	India	263,565
Kassel	Germany	217,085
Kazan	U.S.S.R.	402,200
Kharkov	U.S.S.R.	833,432
Kiel	Germany	272,311
Kiev	U.S.S.R.	846,293
Kobe	Japan	1,006,100
Konigsberg	Germany	368,433
Kuibishev	U.S.S.R.	390,000
Kure	Japan	262,300
Kyoto	Japan	1,177,200
Lahore	India	429,747
La Paz	Bolivia	250,000
La Plata	Argentina	268,000
Leeds	England	491,880
Leicester	England	262,900
Leipzig	Germany	701,606
Lemberg (Lwow)	Poland	317,700
Leningrad	U.S.S.R.	3,191,304
Lille	France	200,575
Lima	Peru	520,528
Lisbon	Portugal	594,390
Liverpool	England	836,300
Lodz	Poland	665,200
Lond'n,Gr'tr	England	8,700,000
Lucknow	India	274,659
Lwow (Lemberg)	Poland	317,700
Lyons	France	570,622
Madras	India	647,230
Madrid	Spain	1,725,504
Magdeburg	Germany	334,358
Manchester	England	736,500
Mannheim	Germany	283,801
Marseilles	France	914,232
Mariupol	U.S.S.R.	222,000
Melbourne	Australia	1,076,700
Mexico City	Mexico	1,754,355
Milan	Italy	1,219,240
Minsk	U.S.S.R.	239,000
Montevideo	Uruguay	770,000
Montreal	Canada	890,234
Moscow	U.S.S.R.	4,137,018
Mukden	Manch'k'o	863,515
Munich	Germany	828,325
Nagasaki	Japan	230,800
Nagoya	Japan	1,249,100
Nagpur	India	215,165
Nanking	China	1,019,148
Naples	Italy	925,325
Newcastle	England	290,400
Nice	France	241,916
Ningpo	China	218,774
Nottingham	England	278,800
Novosibirsk	U.S.S.R.	278,000
Nurnberg	Germany	430,851
Odessa	U.S.S.R.	604,223
Omsk	U.S.S.R.	281,000
Oporto	Portugal	232,280
Osaka, Gr'tr	Japan	3,394,200
Oslo	Norway	253,124
Palermo	Italy	434,311
Para (Belem)	Brazil	303,740
Paris	France	2,829,746
Paris, G't'r.	France	4,933,855
Peiping	China	1,556,364
Perm	U.S.S.R.	255,000
Pernambuco (Recife)	Brazil	510,102
Perth	Australia	228,000
Piraeus	Greece	328,299
Plymouth	England	210,460
Poona	India	233,885
Porto Alegre	Brazil	321,628
Portsmouth	England	256,200
Poznan	Poland	268,800
Prague (Praha)	Cz'choslov.	848,823
Rangoon	Burma	400,415
Recife (Pern'buco)	Brazil	510,102
Riga	Latvia	393,211
Rio Janeiro	Brazil	1,711,466
Rome	Italy	1,348,700
Rosario	Argentina	516,668
Rostov	U.S.S.R.	520,700
Rotterdam	Holland	612,372
Salford	England	201,800
Saloniki	Greece	236,524
Santiago	Chile	829,830
Sao Paulo	Brazil	1,151,249
Saratov	U.S.S.R.	376,000
Sendai	Japan	219,547
Seoul	Korea	706,396
Sevilla	Spain	250,501
Shanghai	China	3,489,998
Sheffield	England	518,200
Shizuoka	Japan	200,737
Singapore	Straits Set.	769,216
Soerabaya	Dutch E. I.	313,000
Sofia	Bulgaria	287,095
Soochow	China	260,000
Stalingrad	U.S.S.R.	445,000
Stalino	U.S.S.R.	462,000
Stettin	Germany	268,915
Stockholm	Sweden	590,543
Stoke-on-T.	England	272,800
Stuttgart	Germany	459,538
Sverdlovsk	U.S.S.R.	426,000
Sydney	Australia	1,310,530
Tabriz	Iran	219,000
Taihoku	Formosa	274,157
Tashkent	U.S.S.R.	585,005
Tehran	Iran	540,087
Tientsin	China	1,292,025
Tiflis	U.S.S.R.	519,175
Tokyo,G't'r.	Japan	7,904,600
Toronto	Canada	657,612
Toulouse	France	213,220
Trieste	Italy	261,368
Tsingtao	China	514,769
Tula	U.S.S.R.	272,000
Tunis	Tunisia	219,578
Turin	Italy	698,096
Ufa	U.S.S.R.	246,000
Valencia	Spain	399,061
Valparaiso	Chile	343,635
Vancouver	Canada	271,597
Venice	Italy	285,833
Vienna	Germany	1,918,462
Vladivostok	U.S.S.R.	206,000
Voronezh	U.S.S.R.	327,000
Voroshilov-grad	U.S.S.R.	213,000
Wanhsein	China	210,837
Warsaw	Poland	1,265,700
Wenchow	China	631,276
West Ham	England	299,500
Winnipeg	Canada	217,994
Wuppertal	Germany	398,099
Yaroslovl	U.S.S.R.	298,000
Yawata	Japan	243,500
Yokohama	Japan	866,200
Zaporozhie	U.S.S.R.	289,000
Zurich	Switzerl'd	333,800

Becomes War Widow Twice Within Six Months

Mrs. Dorothy Murphy Hamilton Mahoney, 26, became a war widow for the second time within six months (Sept. 22, 1942) when she received word that her husband, a naval flight instructor, had perished when the training plane in which he was flying burst into flames and crashed with a student pilot near Pasco, Wash. Her first husband, Lieut. Frank Hamilton, 23, was killed in an airplane accident when training as an army bombardier at Midland, Tex. (April, 1942). Mrs. Hamilton returned to her home in St. Paul, Minn., where she met Ensign Francis T. Mahoney, her husband's best friend, whom she married later.

Population and Area of Foreign States and Countries

Source: Latest official sources and news dispatches

Country or State	Continent	Government or Ruling Power	Area, Square Miles	Population	Capital or Chief City
Aden and Prot.	Asia	British Empire	112,000	48,338	Aden
Aegean Islands	Europe	Italy	1,035	140,848	Rhodes
Afghanistan	Asia	Kingdom	250,000	12,000,000	Kabul
Albania	Europe	Italy	10,629	1,003,124	Tirana
Alberta	No. America	British Empire	255,285	788,893	Edmonton
Algeria	Africa	France	847,552	7,234,684	Algiers
Andorra	Europe	Fr.-Sp. Protect.	191	5,231	Andorra
Angola	Africa	Portugal	481,226	3,484,300	Loanda
Anhalt	Europe	Germany	893	436,213	Dessau
Annam	Asia	French Protect.	56,973	6,211,228	Hue
Antigua	West Indies	British Empire	108	34,523	St. John
Arabia	Asia		1,000,000	10,000,000	
Arabia, Saudi	Asia	Kingdom	350,000	5,250,000	Mecca
Argentina	So. America	Republic	1,078,278	13,518,239	Buenos Aires
Armenia	Asia	Soviet Republic	11,580	1,281,599	Erivan
Assam (India)	Asia	British Empire	67,334	9,247,857	Shillong
Australia	Oceania	British Empire	2,974,581	7,137,000	Canberra
Austria	Europe	Germany	34,064	7,009,014	Vienna
Aust.-Hung. (pre-war)	Europe	Emp. & King.	261,259	49,880,000	Vienna
Azerbaijan	Asia	Russian Soviet	32,956	3,209,727	Baku
Azores	No. Atlantic	Portugal	922	232,012	Ponta Delgada
Baden	Europe	Germany	5,818	2,518,103	Karlsruhe
Bahamas	West Indies	British Empire	4,404	68,903	Nassau
Bahrein Islands	Asia	Emirate	250	120,000	Manama
Balearic Isles	Europe	Spain	1,935	376,733	Palma
Bali and Lombok	Asia	Netherlands	3,973	1,802,683	Buleleng
Baluchistan	Asia	British Empire	134,638	868,617	Quetta
Bangka	Asia	Netherlands	4,610	205,363	Batavia
Barbados	West Indies	British Empire	166	198,203	Bridgetown
Baroda (India)	Asia	Semi-Indep'd't	8,164	2,443,007	Baroda
Basutoland	Africa	British Empire	11,716	562,411	Meseru
Bavaria	Europe	Germany	30,054	8,280,090	Munich
Bechuanaland	Africa	British Protect.	275,000	265,756	Serowe
Belgium	Europe	Kingdom	11,755	8,386,553	Brussels
Bengal (India)	Asia	British Empire	82,955	51,087,338	Calcutta
Bermuda	No. America	British Empire	19	32,086	Hamilton
Bhutan	Asia	British Protect.	18,000	300,000	Punakha
Bihar and Orissa	Asia	British Empire	111,702	42,329,583	Patna
Billiton	Asia	Netherlands	1,866	73,429	Batavia
Bismarck Islands	Oceania	Australia	90,000	666,000	Rabaul
Bohemia-Moravia	Europe	German Prot.	28,717	10,897,000	Prague (Praha)
Bolivia	So. America	Republic	537,792	3,426,296	La Paz
Bombay (Presidency)	Asia	British Empire	151,593	26,347,509	Bombay
Bombay (prov.)	Asia	British Empire	77,221	18,190,000	Bombay
Borneo (Brit. North)	Asia	British Empire	29,500	270,223	Sandakan
Borneo (Dutch)	Asia	Netherlands	208,285	2,168,661	Banjermasin
Bosnia, Herzegovina	Europe	Yugoslavia	19,768	1,889,929	Sarajevo
Brazil	So. America	Republic	3,275,510	41,356,605	Rio de Janeiro
Bremen	Europe	Germany	99	400,086	Bremen
British Columbia	No. America	British Empire	366,255	809,203	Victoria
British Empire		Empire	13,655,393	495,928,880	London
Brunei	Asia	British Protect.	2,226	30,135	Brunei
Brunswick	Europe	Germany	1,418	599,208	Brunswick
Bulgaria	Europe	Kingdom	42,808	6,549,664	Sofia
Burma (India)	Asia	British Empire	261,610	14,667,146	Rangoon
Cambodia	Asia	French Protect.	67,550	3,046,432	Pnom-penh
Cameroon (French)	Africa	French Mand'te	166,489	2,516,623	Yaounda
Cameroons (British)	Africa	British Mand'te.	34,081	868,637	Buea
Canada	No. America	British Empire	3,694,863	11,419,896	Ottawa
Canary Isles	No. Atlantic	Spain	2,807	564,873	Santa Cruz
Cape of Good Hope	Africa	British Empire	277,169	3,635,100	Cape Town
Cape Verde Isles	Africa	Portugal	1,557	174,403	Porto Grande
Cayman Islands	West Indies	British Empire	104	6,182	Georgetown
Celebes	Asia	Netherlands	72,886	4,231,906	Macassar
Ceylon	Asia	British Empire	25,332	5,312,548	Colombo
Chad Colony	Africa	France	461,202	1,432,006	Fort Lamy
Channel Islands	Europe	British Empire	75	93,205	St. Heliers
Chile	So. America	Republic	296,717	5,000,782	Santiago
China (ex. Manchukuo)	Asia	Republic	2,279,134	422,707,868	Chungking (temp.)
China (all)	Asia	Republic	4,314,097	457,835,475	Chungking (temp.)
Chosen (Korea)	Asia	Japan	85,228	22,899,038	Seoul (Keijo)
Cochin-China	Asia	French Colony	26,476	4,615,968	Saigon
Colombia	So. America	Republic	448,794	9,523,200	Bogota
Congo (Belgian)	Africa	Belgium	902,082	10,356,191	Kinshasa
Congo (French)	Africa	France	959,256	3,423,015	Brazzaville
Corsica	Europe	France	3,367	289,890	Ajaccio
Costa Rica	Cent. Amer.	Republic	23,000	656,129	San Jose
Crete	Europe	Greece	3,330	345,149	Candia
Croatia-Slovenia	Europe	Yugo-Slavia	16,920	2,739,593	Zagaret (Agram)
Cuba	West Indies	Republic	44,164	4,199,952	Havana
Curacao	So. America	Netherlands	403	90,870	Willemstad
Cyprus	Asia	British Empire	3,572	383,967	Nicosia
Cyrenaica	Africa	Italy	73,000	164,607	Bengazi
Czecho-Slovakia	Europe	Republic	54,244	15,247,000	Prague (Praha)
Dahomey	Africa	France	43,232	1,289,128	Porto Noro
Dalmatia	Europe	Yugoslavia	4,916	621,429	Ragusa
Danzig	Europe	Free City	754	415,000	Danzig
Denmark	Europe	Kingdom	16,575	3,805,000	Copenhagen
Dominican Republic	West Indies	Republic	19,322	1,616,561	Trujillo Cuidad
Ecuador	So. America	Republic	275,936	3,200,000	Quito
Egypt	Africa	Kingdom	383,000	15,920,703	Cairo
Eire (see Ireland)					
England (in. Monmouthshire)	Europe	British Empire	50,328	37,354,917	London

Country or State	Continent	Government or Ruling Power	Area Square Miles	Population	Capital or Chief City
Eritrea	Africa	Italy	15,754	600,573	Asmara
Estonia	Europe	U.S.S.R.	18,353	1,134,000	Tallinn (Reval)
Ethiopia (Abyssinia)	Africa	Italy	350,000	12,100,000	Addis Ababa
Faroe Isles	Europe	Denmark	540	25,744	Thornshawn
Falkland Isles & South Georgia	So. America	British Empire	5,618	3,490	Stanley
Fiji Islands	Oceania	British Empire	7,083	220,787	Suva
Finland	Europe	Republic	134,588	3,863,753	Helsinki
Formosa (Taiwan)	Asia	Japan	13,880	5,212,426	Taihoku
France	Europe	Republic	212,659	41,907,056	Paris, Vichy, (War)
French Equat. Africa	Africa	France	959,256	3,418,066	Brazzaville
French India	Asia	France	196	323,295	Pondicherry
French Indo-China	Asia	France	281,174	24,461,251	Hanoi
French West Africa	Africa	France	1,818,698	14,944,830	Dakar
Friendly Islands, (see Tonga)					
Gabun	Africa	France	93,218	408,516	Libreville
Gambia	Africa	British Empire	4,068	199,520	Bathurst
Georgia	Europe	U.S.S.R.	26,865	3,542,289	Tiflis
Germany	Europe	Republic	225,226	79,375,281	Berlin
Gibraltar	Europe	British Empire	2	20,399	Gibraltar
Goa	Asia	Portugal	1,537	601,000	New Goa
Gold Coast	Africa	British Empire	91,843	3,962,520	Accra
Greece	Europe	Republic	50,257	7,108,814	Athens
Greenland	No. America	Denmark	736,518	18,000	Godthaab
Guadeloupe	West Indies	France	583	304,209	Pointe-a-Pitre
Guatemala	Cent. Amer	Republic	45,452	3,284,000	Guatemala
Guiana, British	So. America	British Empire	89,843	346,982	Georgetown
Netherland	So. America	Netherlands	54,291	171,396	Paramaribo
French	So. America	France	65,041	30,906	Cayenne
Guinea, French	Africa	France	96,866	2,065,527	Konakry
Portuguese	Africa	Portugal	13,944	415,220	Bissau
Spanish	Africa	Spain	10,036	140,000	Santa Isabei
Hamburg	Europe	Germany	288	1,682,220	Hamburg
Haiti	West Indies	Republic	10,204	3,000,000	Port-au-Prince
Hejaz	Asia	Kingdom	150,000	1,500,000	Mecca
Hesse	Europe	Germany	2,969	1,469,909	Darmstadt
Holland (see Netherlands)					
Honduras	Cent. Amer	Republic	44,275	1,105,504	Tegucigalpa
Honduras, British	Cent. Amer	British Empire	8,598	59,965	Belize
Hong Kong & Territory	Asia	British Empire	391	1,050,256	Victoria
Hungary	Europe	Kingdom	66,409	14,733,000	Budapest
Hyderabad	Asia	Semi-Indep'd't	82,698	14,436,148	Hyderabad
Iceland	No. Atlantic	Kingdom	39,709	121,618	Reykjavik
India	Asia	British Empire	1,808,679	352,837,778	Delhi
(British)	Asia	British Empire	1,318,346	289,491,241	Delhi
(Native States)	Asia	British Empire	490,333	63,346,537	
Indo-China	Asia	France	281,174	23,853,429	Hanoi
Iran (Persia)	Asia	Kingdom	628,000	15,055,115	Teheran
Iraq (Mesopotamia)	Asia	Kingdom	140,000	5,000,000	Bagdad
Ireland	Europe	British Empire	27,137	2,989,700	Dublin
Ireland, North. (Ulster)	Europe	British Empire	5,238	1,279,745	Belfast
Isle of Man	Europe	British Empire	221	49,308	Douglas
Italy	Europe	Kingdom	119,800	45,354,000	Rome
Italian East Africa (see Eritrea, Ethiopia, Somaliland)					
Ivory Coast	Africa	France	184,174	3,981,459	Bingerville
Jamaica	West Indies	British Empire	4,450	1,223,241	Kingston
Japan (Proper)	Asia	Empire	148,756	72,875,800	Tokio
Japanese Empire	Asia	Empire	260,770	105,226,101	Tokio
Java and Madura	Asia	Netherlands	51,032	41,718,364	Batavia
Johore	Asia	British Empire	7,500	613,500	Johore Bahru
Kashmir (India)	Asia	Semi-Indep'd't	84,516	3,646,243	Srinagar
Kazakh	Asia	U.S.S.R.	1,047,797	6,145,937	Alma-Ata
Kenya and Prot	Africa	British Empire	224,960	3,534,862	Nairobi
Kirghiz	Asia	U.S.S.R.	75,926	1,459,301	Frunze
Korea	Asia	Japanese	85,246	22,633,587	Seoul (Keijo)
Kuwait	Asia	Sultanate	1,950	50,000	Kuwait
Kwang Chau Wan	Asia	French Lease	325	300,000	Kwangchow
Kwantung	Asia	Japanese Lease	1,438	1,656,726	Dairen
Labrador	No. America	British Empire	110,000	4,716	
Laos	Asia	French Protect	89,320	1,023,314	Piabang
Latvia	Europe	U.S.S.R.	25,402	1,950,502	Riga
Lebanon	Asia	Beirut	3,600	592,812	Beirut
Leeward Islands	West Indies	British Empire	727	93,130	Antigua
Liberia	Africa	Republic	45,000	1,500,000	Monrovia
Libya	Africa	Italy	679,358	888,401	Tripoli, Benghazi
Liechtenstein	Europe	Principality	65	188,598	Vaduz
Lippe	Europe	Germany	469	11,102	Detmold
Lithuania	Europe	U.S.S.R.	22,959	2,879,070	Vilna
Lubeck	Europe	Germany	115	136,413	Lubeck
Luxemburg	Europe	Grand Duchy	999	301,000	Luxemburg
Macao	Asia	Portugal	6	340,260	Macao
Madagascar	Africa	France	241,094	3,797,936	Tananarivo
Madeira	Africa	Portugal	314	211,610	Funchal
Madras (India)	Asia	Semi-Indep'd't	143,870	47,193,602	Madras
Malay States, Fed	Asia	British Protect	27,540	2,212,052	Perak
Malay States, Unfed	Asia	British Protect	22,276	1,918,831	Johore
Malta	Europe	British Empire	122	268,668	Valletta
Manchukuo	Asia	Semi-Independ't	503,013	36,949,972	Hsinking
Manitoba	No. America	British Empire	246,512	722,447	Winnipeg
Martinique	West Indies	France	385	246,712	Fort de France
Mauritania	Africa	France	323,310	370,764	St. Louis
Mauritius	Africa	British Empire	720	420,861	Port Louis
Mechlenburg	Europe	Germany	6,069	910,826	Schwerin
Memel	Europe	Germany	1,099	152,000	Memel
Mesopotamia (see Iraq)					
Mexico	No. America	Republic	763,944	19,473,741	Mexico City
Middle Congo	Africa	France	166,096	744,503	Brazzaville
Miquelon	No. America	France	83	520	St. Pierre
Moldavia	Europe	U.S.S.R.	12	615,000	Tiraspol

Country or State	Continent	Government or Ruling Power	Area, Square Miles	Population	Capital or Chief City
Molucca Isles	Asia	Netherlands	30,168	427,211	Ternate
Monaco	Europe	Principality	7,99	23,973	Monaco
Mongolia	Asia	China	622,744	850,000	Urga
Moravia	Europe	German	6,533	2,332,522	Brno
Morocco (French)	Africa	French Protect.	213,350	7,093,720	Rabat
Morocco (Spanish)	Africa	Spanish Protect.	18,350	795,202	Tetuan
Morocco (Intern. Zone)	Africa	Intern. Protect.	225	60,000	Tangier
Mozambique	Africa	Portugal	297,654	4,995,750	Lourenco-Marques
Mysore (India)	Asia	Semi-Indep'd't	29,326	6,557,302	Bangalore
Natal	Africa	British Empire	35,284	2,018,000	Pietermaritzburg
Nejd The	Asia	Kingdom	175,000	3,000,000	Kidayah
Nepal	Asia	Kingdom	54,000	5,600,000	Kathmandu
Netherlands	Europe	Kingdom	12,704	8,728,569	Amsterdam
Netherland Indies	Asia	Netherlands	735,168	67,000,000	Batavia
New Brunswick	No. America	British Empire	27,985	453,377	Fredericton
New Caledonia	Australasia	France	8,548	53,245	Noumea
Newfoundland	No. America	British Empire	42,734	300,000	St. John's
New Guinea, British	Oceania	British Mandate	93,000	668,871	Salamaua
New Hebrides (Isl.)	Australasia	Fr. & Brit. Prot.	5,790	54,531	Vila
New South Wales	Australia	British Empire	309,433	2,770,348	Sydney
New Zealand	Australasia	British Empire	103,934	1,640,901	Wellington
Nicaragua	Cent. Amer.	Republic	60,000	1,380,287	Managua
Niger	Africa	France	499,410	1,809,576	Niamey
Nigeria	Africa	British Empire	372,559	20,641,814	Lagos
Northern Ireland	Europe	British Empire	5,238	1,279,745	Belfast
Northern Territory	Australia	British Empire	523,620	6,973	Darwin
N. W. Territory	No. America	British Empire	1,309,682	10,661	Regina
Norway	Europe	Kingdom	124,556	2,937,000	Oslo
Nova Scotia	No. America	British Empire	21,068	573,190	Halifax
Nyasaland Prot.	Africa	British Empire	37,374	1,684,194	Berera
Oldenburg	Europe	Germany	2,083	582,400	Oldenburg
Oman	Asia	Kingdom	82,000	500,000	Muscat
Ontario	No. America	British Empire	412,582	3,756,632	Toronto
Orange Free State	Africa	British Empire	49,647	790,800	Bloemfontein
Orkney Isles	Europe	British Empire	392	21,600	Kirkwall
Palestine	Asia	British Mandate	10,429	1,568,664	Jerusalem
Panama	So. America	Republic	33,667	635,836	Panama
Papua	Oceania	British Empire	90,540	338,822	Port Moresby
Paraguay	So. America	Republic	174,854	1,014,773	Asuncion
Persia (see Iran)					
Peru	So. America	Republic	532,000	7,023,111	Lima
Poland (inc. Teschen)	Europe	Republic	150,470	34,775,698	Warsaw
Portugal	Europe	Republic	35,582	7,539,484	Lisbon
Prince Edward Isl.	No. America	British Empire	2,184	99,919	Charlottetown
Principe & St. Thomas	Africa	Portugal	597	48,809	Santa Cruz
Prussia	Europe	Germany	113,575	41,762,040	Berlin
Punjab, India	Asia	Semi-Indep'd't	105,020	24,018,639	Lahore
Quebec	No. America	British Empire	594,534	3,319,640	Quebec
Queensland	Australia	British Empire	670,500	1,015,927	Brisbane
Rajputana	Asia	British Empire	129,059	11,225,712	Jaipur
Reunion	Indian Ocean	France	970	208,858	St. Pierre
Rhodesia, Northern	Africa	British Empire	290,320	1,381,829	Lusaka
Rhodesia, Southern	Africa	British Empire	150,333	1,448,393	Salisbury
Riau-Lingga Arch.	Asia	Netherlands	12,234	298,225	....
Rumania	Europe	Kingdom	74,214	13,291,000	Bucharest
Russia (see U.S.S.R.)					
Russia (pre-war)	Europe-Asia	Empire	8,764,586	182,182,600	St. Petersburg
Saarland	Europe	Germany	743	863,736	Saarbrucken
St. Helena	Africa	British Empire	47	4,710	Jamestown
St. Pierre Islands	No. America	France	10	3,396	St. Pierre
Sakhalin Island (So.)	Asia	Japan	13,930	331,949	....
Salvador	Cent. Amer.	Republic	13,173	1,744,535	San Salvador
Samoa, Western	Oceania	British Mandate	1,133	62,391	Apia
San Marino	Europe	Republic	38	14,545	San Marino
Sarawak	Asia	British Empire	50,000	490,585	Kirching
Sardinia	Europe	Italy	9,301	1,034,206	Cagliari
Saskatchewan	No. America	British Empire	251,700	887,747	Regina
Saxony	Europe	Germany	5,789	5,206,861	Dresden
Schaumburg-Lippe	Europe	Germany	131	54,162	Buckeburg
Scotland	Europe	British Empire	30,405	4,842,980	Edinburgh
Senegal	Africa	France	77,790	1,666,371	St. Louis
Serbia (pre-war)	Europe	Yugo-Slavia	18,650	2,911,701	Belgrade
Seychelles Islands	Africa	British Empire	156	32,150	Victoria
Shetland Isles	Europe	British Empire	550	20,500	Lerwick
Siam (see Thailand)					
Sicily	Europe	Italy	9,926	4,000,078	Palermo
Sierra Leone	Africa	British Empire	27,699	1,672,000	Freetown
Sikkim (India)	Asia	Semi-Indep'd't	2,818	109,808	Ili
Sinkiang (Chinese Turkestan)	Asia	China	633,802	1,200,000	....
Slovakia	Europe	Republic	14,836	2,450,096	Bratislava
Slovenia	Europe	Yugo-Slavia	6,253	1,055,464	Zagreb
Society Isles, etc.	Oceania	France	1,520	39,970	Papeete
Solomon Islands, Brit.	Oceania	British Protect.	375,000	94,105	....
Somaliland, British	Africa	British Empire	68,000	344,700	Berbera
French	Africa	France	8,492	44,240	Jibuti
Italian	Africa	Italy	194,000	1,300,000	Mogadisho
Soudan, Ang.-Egyptian	Africa	British Empire	969,600	6,342,477	Khartoum
South Australia	Australia	British Empire	380,070	597,043	Adelaide
South West Africa	Africa	British Mandate	317,725	314,194	Windhoek
Spain	Europe	Republic	196,697	25,878,000	Madrid
Spitzbergen	Europe	Norway	24,290	2,700	Longyearbyen
Straits Settlements	Asia	British Empire	1,356	1,435,895	Singapore
Sudan (French)	Africa	France	590,966	3,635,073	Bamako
Sudetenland	Europe	Germany	8,721	2,945,261	Reichenberg
Sumatra	Asia	Netherlands	164,143	7,677,826	Batavia
Swaziland	Africa	British Empire	6,705	156,715	Mbabane
Sweden	Europe	Kingdom	173,347	6,406,474	Stockholm
Switzerland	Europe	Republic	15,737	4,260,719	Berne

Country or State	Continent	Government or Ruling Power	Area, Square Miles	Population	Capital or Chief City
Syria and the Lebanon	Asia	French Mandate	57,900	3,630,000	Beirut
Tadzhik	Asia	U.S.S.R.	55,040	1,485,091	Stalinabad
Tanganyika	Africa	British Mandate	360,000	5,270,484	Dar-es-Salaam
Tangier	Africa	Internationalized	225	60,000	Tangier
Tasmania	Australasia	British Empire	26,215	241,576	Hobart
Thailand (Siam)	Asia	Kingdom	200,148	15,718,000	Bangkok
Thuringia	Europe	Germany	4,541	1,760,595	Weimar
Thibet	Asia	China	463,200	3,000,000	Lhasa
Timor Arch	Asia	Portugal	7,330	463,796	Dilly
Tobago	West Indies	British Empire	114	25,358	Port of Spain
Togoland	Africa	French Mandate	21,893	780,497	Lome
Togoland	Africa	British Mandate	13,041	391,473	Lome
Tonga (Friendly) Isl	Oceania	British Protect	256	34,130	Nukualofa
Tonkin	Asia	French Protect	40,530	9,264,309	Hanoi
Transjordan	Asia	Palestine	34,740	300,000	Amman
Transvaal	Africa	British Empire	110,450	3,535,100	Pretoria
Trinidad	West Indies	British Empire	1,862	484,907	Port au Spain
Tunis	Africa	France	48,313	2,608,313	Tunis
Turkey	Europe-Asia	Republic	294,416	17,869,901	Ankara
Turkey (pre-war)	Europe-Asia	Sultanate	710,224	21,273,900	Constantinople
Turkoman	Asia	U.S.S.R.	171,384	12,253,985	Ashkhabad
Turks & Caicos Islands	West Indies	British Empire	166	5,300	Grand Turk.
U.S.S.R.	Europe-Asia	Soviet Republic	8,819,791	183,736,286	Moscow
Uganda Prot	Africa	British	93,381	3,829,705	Entebbe
Ulster (see Ireland, Northern)					
Ukraine	Europe	U.S.S.R.	170,978	38,960,221	Kiev
Union of So. Africa	Africa	British Empire	472,550	9,979,000	Pretoria
United Kingdom	Europe	Kingdom	94,279	46,213,169	London
Uruguay	So. America	Republic	72,153	2,146,545	Montevideo
Uzbek	Asia	U.S.S.R.	66,392	6,282,446	Tashkent
Vatican City, State of	Europe	Papal State	.16	1,025	Vatican City
Venezuela	So. America	Republic	352,170	3,492,747	Caracas
Victoria	Australia	British Empire	87,884	1,887,278	Melbourne
Wales	Europe	British Empire	8,012	2,593,014	Cardiff
West Australia	Australia	British Empire	975,920	465,916	Perth
White Russia	Europe	U.S.S.R.	49,022	10,367,976	Minsk
Windward Islands	West Indies	British Empire	821	262,006	St. George's
Wurttemberg	Europe	Germany	7,532	2,907,166	Stuttgart
Yemen	Asia	Kingdom	75,000	3,500,000	Sanaa
Yugoslavia	Europe	Kingdom	95,558	16,200,000	Belgrade
Yukon	No. America	British Empire	207,076	4,687	Dawson
Zanzibar	Africa	British Empire	1,020	235,428	Zanzibar

The Berlin-Rome-Tokyo Axis

Germany, Japan and Italy signed in Berlin (Sept. 27, 1940) a ten-year military and economic treaty—the Treaty of Berlin—by which they pooled their totalitarian armaments and pledged to help one another against the United States if one of them becomes involved with America. The official English translation of the treaty follows:

The governments of Germany, Italy and Japan, considering it as a condition precedent of any lasting peace that all nations of the world be given each its own proper place, have decided to stand by and cooperate with one another in regard to their efforts in Greater East Asia and regions of Europe respectively wherein it is their prime purpose to establish and maintain a new order of things calculated to promote the mutual prosperity and welfare of the peoples concerned.

Furthermore, it is the desire of the three governments to extend cooperation to such nations in other spheres of the world as may be inclined to put fourth endeavors along lines similar to their own, in order that their ultimate aspirations for world peace may be realized.

Accordingly, the governments of Germany, Italy and Japan have agreed as follows:

Article One—Japan recognizes and respects the leadership of Germany and Italy in establishment of a new order in Europe.

Article Two—Germany and Italy recognize and respect the leadership of Japan in the establishment of a new order in Greater East Asia.

Article Three—Germany, Italy and Japan agree to cooperate in their efforts on aforesaid lines. They further undertake to assist one another with all political, economic and military means when one of the three contracting powers is attacked by a power at present not involved in the European war or in the Chinese-Japanese conflict.

Article Four—With the view to implementing the present pact, joint technical commissions, members which are to be appointed by the respective governments of Germany, Italy and Japan, will meet without delay.

Article Five—Germany, Italy and Japan affirm that the aforesaid terms do not in any way affect the political status which exists at present as between each of the three contracting parties and Soviet Russia.

Article Six—The present pact shall come into effect immediately upon signature and shall remain in force ten years from the date of its coming into force. At the proper time before expiration of said term the high contracting parties shall at the request of any of them enter into negotiations for its renewal.

In faith whereof, the undersigned, duly authorized by their respective governments, have signed this pact and have affixed hereto their signatures.

Done in triplicate at Berlin, the 27th day of September, 1940, in the eighteenth year of the Fascist era, corresponding to the 27th day of the ninth month of the fifteenth year of Showa [the reign of Emperor Hirohito].

Hungary joined the Axis (Nov. 20, 1940), Rumania (Nov. 23) and Slovakia (Nov. 24). Bulgaria signed as a member (March 1, 1941). Yugoslavia attached its signature (March 25) with the provision that Axis troops should not march through the country and that its sovereignty and territorial integrity should be respected. The regime that signed the pact with the Axis was overthrown two days later and the new Cabinet did not ratify the agreement. The subjugation of Yugoslavia by the Axis powers followed. Croatia, carved from a part of vanquished Yugoslavia, joined the Axis (June 15, 1941) in a ceremony in Venice.

Bomb Nazis, Fly to Canada in 25 Hours

Five Canadian airmen bombed Saarbruecken, Germany (Sept. 2, 1942) and flew back to England. There they changed planes and started for Canada, landing at Ottawa (a few minutes after midnight of Sept. 3) to be greeted by Prime Minister Mackenzie King. Premier King said that their time table was: Took off from British airfield 11 P.M., Sept. 1, dropped bombs on Saarbruecken 2:21 A.M., Sept. 2, landed in England at 5:45 A.M., took off across the Atlantic at 6:45 A.M., and landed at Ottawa a few minutes after midnight (Sept. 3).

Noted Americans of the Past

Source: Biographical Records

(See also Presidents, and wives, Vice-Presidents, U. S. Supreme Court Justices, Ambassadors, Signers of the Declaration of Independence, Actors, Composers, Singers, Painters, etc.)

B.	D.	Name	Occupation	B.	D.	Name	Occupation
1883	1916	Abbe, Cleveland	Meteorologist	1782	1850	Calhoun, John C.	Sen., V. Pres.
1851	1928	Abbe, Robert	Surg. Radium	1843	1888	Campbell, Bartley	Dramatist
1803	1879	Abbot, Jacob	Juv. Fiction	1837	1909	Canfield, James H.	Educator
1835	1922	Abbott, Lyman	Preacher	1863	1941	Cannon, Annie J.	Astronomer
1807	1886	Adams, Charles F.	Statesman	1835	1919	Carnegie, Andrew	Iron Master
1835	1915	Adams, Charles F.	Historian	1737	1832	Carroll, Charles	Statesman
1838	1918	Adams, Henry	Hist. Biog.	1809	1868	Carson, Kit (Chris.)	Scout
1722	1803	Adams, Samuel	Gov., Patriot	1782	1866	Cass, Lewis	Sen., Cabinet
1822	1897	Adams, William T.	Juv. Fiction	1813	1879	Chamberlain, Joshua L.	Soldier
1860	1935	Addams, Jane	Civic Worker	1813	1879	Chandler, Zach.	Sen., Cabinet
1807	1873	Agassiz, Louis J. R.	Scientist	1780	1842	Channing, William E.	Theol.Reform
1799	1888	Alcott, A. Bronson	Philosophy	1829	1894	Childs, Geo. W.	Newspaper
1832	1888	Alcott, Louisa May	Fiction	1799	1859	Choate, Rufus	Lawyer
1836	1919	Alden, Henry M.	Ed. Mag.	1832	1917	Choate, Joseph H.	Lawyer
1841	1915	Aldrich, Nelson W.	U. S. Senator	1752	1818	Clark, Geo. Rogers	Soldier
1836	1907	Aldrich, Thos. Bailey	Fiction	1770	1838	Clark William	Explorer
1834	1899	Alger, Horatio	Juv. Fiction	1854	1916	Clarke, James P.	Gov., Sen.
1737	1789	Allen, Ethan	Patriot	1777	1852	Clay, Henry	Sen., Cabinet
1849	1925	Allen, James Lane	Fiction	1796	1856	Clayton, John M.	Law., State.
1803	1879	Allen, William	Gov., Sen.	1835	1910	Clemens, Samuel L.	Humorist
1758	1808	Ames, Fisher	Lawyer	1769	1828	Clinton, DeWitt	Sen. Gov.
1804	1873	Ames, Oakes	Credit Mobil.	1739	1812	Clinton, George	V.P., Gov.,
1844	1917	Anderson, Elisha B.	Educator	1845	1917	Cody, William F.	Scout
1818	1867	Andrew, John A.	War Gov.	1792	1865	Collamer, Jacob	Jur., P. M. G.
1841	1935	Andrus, John E.	Financier	1829	1888	Conkling, Roscoe	U.S. Senator
1829	1916	Angell, James B.	Educ., Diplo.	1830	1886	Cooke, John Esten	Fiction
1797	1867	Anthon, Charles	Educator	1865	1940	Cook, Dr. F. A.	Polar Explorer
1820	1906	Anthony, Susan B.	Suffrage	1789	1851	Cooper, J. Fenimore	Fiction
1832	1901	Armour, Philip D.	Meat Packer	1791	1883	Cooper, Peter	Merch., Phil.
1745	1816	Asbury, Francis	Bishop	1824	1889	Cox, S. S. (Sunset)	Congressm'n
1763	1848	Astor, John Jacob	Merchant	1867	1906	Craigie, Pearl M. (John Oliver Hobbes)	Fiction
1830	1908	Astor, William	Landowner				
1792	1875	Astor, William B.	Landowner	1870	1900	Crane, Stephen	Fiction
1847	1919	Astor, Wm. Waldorf	Landowner	1845	1909	Crawford, F. Marion	Fiction
1780	1851	Audubon, John James	Naturalist	1787	1863	Crittenden, John J.	U.S. Senator
1799	1836	Austin, Stephen F.	Texas Founder	1841	1922	Croker, Richard	Politics
1859	1912	Aycock, Charles B.	Gov., Educ.	1825	1903	Curry, J. L. M.	Diplomat
1823	1888	Baird, Spencer F.	Zoologist	1850	1933	Curtis, Cyrus H. K.	Publisher
1871	1937	Baker, Newton D.	Sec. War	1812	1894	Curtis, Geo. Ticknor	Historian
1771	1852	Ballou, Hosea	Preacher	1824	1892	Curtis, Geo. Wm.	Essayist
1761	1851	Baldwin, Simeon	Jurist	1839	1876	Custer, Geo. A.	Soldier
1800	1891	Bancroft, George	Historian	1819	1897	Dana, Chas. A.	Newspaper
1816	1894	Banks, Nathaniel P.	Soldier	1813	1895	Dana, James Dwight	Geologist
1754	1812	Barlow, Joel	Poet	1820	1882	Dana, John Cotton	Librarian
1810	1891	Barnum, Phineas T.	Showman	1787	1879	Dana, Richard Henry	Poet, Essayist
1821	1912	Barton, Clara H.	Red Cr's F'd'r	1815	1882	Dana, Richard Henry, Jr.	Author. Law
1827	1911	Bascom, John	Educator	1857	1938	Darrow, Clarence	Law
1767	1815	Bayard, James A. Sr.	U.S. Senator	1808	1889	Davis, Jefferson	Confed. Pres.
1799	1880	Bayard, James A. Jr.	U.S. Senator	1864	1916	Davis, Richard Harding	Fiction
1828	1898	Bayard, Thomas F.	Sec. St'te, Sen.	1855	1926	Debs, Eugene V.	Socialist
1785	1853	Beaumont, William	Army Surg.	1779	1820	Decatur, Stephen	Naval
1813	1887	Beecher, Henry Ward	Preacher	1834	1928	Depew, Chauncey M.	Orator
1775	1863	Beecher, Lyman	Preacher	1838	1917	Dewey, George, Admiral	Naval
1847	1922	Bell, Alexander G.	Inventor	1756	1834	DeWitt, Simeon	Geographer
1850	1898	Bellamy, Edward	Author	1849	1925	deYoung, M. H.	Newspaper
1816	1890	Belmont, August	Banker	1830	1886	Dickinson, Emily	Poetry
1853	1919	Belmont, August	Subway Bldr.	1732	1803	Dickinson, John	Statesman
1811	1884	Benjamin, Judah P.	Lawyer	1835	1905	Dodge, Mary E. Mapes	Author, Ed.
1795	1872	Bennett, James Gordon	Newspaper	1634	1715	Dongan, Thomas	Statesman
1841	1918	Bennett, J. G., Jr.	Newspaper	1819	1893	Doubleday, Arthur	Soldier,baseb'.
1782	1858	Benton, Thomas H.	Statesman	1813	1861	Douglas, Stephen A.	Statesman
1862	1927	Beveridge, Albert J.	U.S. Senator	1817	1895	Douglass, Fred (Negro)	Publicist
1842	1914	Bierce, Ambrose	Fiction	1804	1897	Dow, Neal	Prohibitionist
1830	1893	Blaine, James G.	Statesman	1795	1820	Drake, Jos. Rodman	Poet, Phys.
1821	1875	Blair, Francis P.	Sold., Edit.	1811	1882	Draper, John W.	Chem. Hist.
1858	1941	Blumenthal, George	Financier	1826	1893	Drexel, Anthony J.	Banker
1735	1820	Boone, Daniel	Hunter	1872	1906	Dunbar, Paul Laurence	Poet
1865	1939	Borah, William E.	U. S. Senator	1739	1817	duPont, Pierre S.	Powder M'f'r
1773	1838	Bowditch, Nathaniel	Mathematic.	1803	1865	Dupont, Samuel F., Adm.	Naval
1826	1874	Bowles, Samuel II	Journalist	1861	1938	Duryea, Charles E.	Auto Inv.
1847	1910	Bowne, Borden P.	Theologian	1820	1887	Eads, James B.	Engineer
1848	1895	Boyesen, Hjalmar H.	Fiction	1854	1932	Eastman, George.	Inventor
1863	1932	Bradford, Gamaliel	Biographer	1821	1910	Eddy, Mary Baker	Christ. Scien.
1613	1672	Bradstreet, Anne	Poetry	1847	1931	Edison, Thos. Alva	Inventor
1823	1896	Brady, Matthew B.	Photographer	1703	1758	Edwards, Jonathan	Theologian
1760	1806	Breckenridge, John	Statesman	1837	1902	Eggleston, Edward	Fiction
1837	1904	Breckenridge, W. C. P.	Confederate	1834	1926	Eliot, Charles W.	Educator
1567	1644	Brewster, William	Pilgr. Father	1604	1690	Eliot, John.	Missionary
1864	1936	Brisbane, Arthur	Editor	1803	1882	Emerson, Ralph Waldo.	Essayist
1835	1893	Brooks, Phillips	Preacher	1803	1889	Ericsson, John.	Inventor
1848	1908	Brooks, William K.	Biologist	1818	1901	Evarts, William M.	Statesman
1711	1810	Brown, Chas. Brockden	Fiction	1818	1901	Everett, Edward.	Statesman
1800	1859	Brown, John	Abolitionist	1794	1865	Farragut.DavidG.,Adm.	Naval
1805	1877	Brownlow, William G.	"Parson"	1801	1870	Faunce, William H. P.	Educator
1803	1873	Brownson, Orestes A.	Author	1859	1930	Fessenden, William P.	U.S. Sen.
1860	1925	Bryan, William J.	Statesman	1806	1869	Field, Cyrus W.	Atlantic cable
1794	1878	Bryant, William C.	Poet, Editor	1819	1892	Field, Eugene	Poet
1582	1658	Bulkeley, Peter	Preacher	1850	1895	Field, Marshall	Merchant
1855	1896	Bunner, Henry Cuyler	Humor	1835	1906	Field, Stephen J.	Jurist
1849	1926	Burbank, Luther	Botanist	1816	1899	Fields, James T.	Biography
1820	1870	Burlingame, Anson	Diplomat	1830	1881	Finley, John H.	Educ., Editor
1837	1921	Burroughs, John	Naturalist	1863	1940	Fiske, John	Historian
1818	1893	Butler, Benjamin F.	Law, Soldier	1842	1901	Fitch, Clyde	Drama
1844	1925	Cable, George W.	Fiction	1865	1909	Fitch, John	Inventor
1751	1823	Cabot, George.	U.S. Senator	1743	1798		

B.	D.	Name	Occupation	B.	D.	Name	Occupation
1865	1902	Ford, Paul Leicester....	Fiction, Hist.	1831	1885	Jackson, Helen Hunt...	Fiction
1826	1864	Foster, Stephen C.....	Ballads	1824	1863	Jackson (Stonewall), T.J.	Soldier
1862	1919	Freeman, Mary E. W...	Fiction	1843	1916	James, Henry........	Fiction
1813	1890	Fremont, John C......	Explorer	1842	1910	James, William......	Philosophy
1752	1832	Freneau, Philip	Poetry	1795	1885	Jervis, John B.......	Civ. Eng.
1860	1915	Frohman, Charles.....	Theater Prod.	1849	1909	Jewett, Sarah Orne....	Fiction
1851	1940	Frohman, Daniel	Theater Prod.	1811	1891	Jones, George.......	Newspaper
1830	1911	Frye, William P......	U.S. Senator	1747	1792	Jones, John Paul.....	Naval
1810	1850	Fuller, Sara Marg.....	Author	1788	1850	Judson, Adoniram.....	Missionary
1765	1815	Fulton, Robert.......	Inventor	1849	1927	Judson, Harry P......	Educator
1874	1938	Gale, Zona	Fiction	1776	1865	Jumel, Mme. (Betsy	
1761	1849	Gallatin, Albert.......	Statesman			Bowen)...........	Patriot
1787	1851	Gallaudet, Thomas H..	Educator	1843	1926	Kohler, Kaufmann.....	Rabbi, Educa.
1805	1879	Garrison, W. Lloyd....	Abolitionist	1820	1867	Kane, Elisha K.......	Explorer
1818	1903	Gatling, Richard J.....	Gun Invent.	1815	1862	Kearny, Philip........	Soldier
1839	1897	George, Henry........	Economist	1837	1932	Keen, William W......	Surgeon
1826	1897	George, James L......	Sold.,Jur.,Sen.	1813	1901	Kellogg, Elijah.......	Author
1844	1909	Gilder, Richard W.....	Poet, Editor	1856	1937	Kellogg, Frank B......	Sec. State
1831	1908	Gilman, Daniel C......	Educator	1848	1893	Kenna, John E........	Sold., Sen.
1750	1831	Girard, Stephen......	Merchant	1795	1870	Kennedy, John P......	Fiction
1827	1911	Glick, George W......	Gov., Sold.	1763	1847	Kent, James.........	Jurist
1831	1902	Godkin, Edwin L......	Newsp. Editor	1780	1843	Key, Francis Scott....	Poet
1809	1879	Goelet, Robert.......	Landowner	1886	1918	Kilmer, Joyce........	Poet
1846	1897	Goelet, Ogden........	Landowner	1824	1864	King, Rev. Thos. Starr..	Patriot
1858	1928	Goethals,Maj.-Gen.G.W.	Canal Eng.	1768	1852	King, William.......	Gov., Fin.
1850	1924	Gompers, Samuel.....	Labor Leader	1813	1894	Kirkwood, Samuel J...	Sen., Gov.,
1793	1860	Goodrich,S.G.(P.Parley)	Author				Dip.
1800	1860	Goodyear, Charles.....	Inventor	1750	1806	Knox, Henry.........	Soldier (Rev.)
1839	1906	Gorman, Arthur Pue...	Politics	1848	1909	Laffan, William......	Newspaper
1803	1855	Gorrie, Dr. John. .`...	Inventor	1855	1925	La Follette, Robert M...	Statesman
1836	1892	Gould, Jay...........	Railways	1834	1906	Langley, Samuel P	Astronomer
1851	1889	Grady, Henry W.......	Journalist	1842	1881	Lanier, Sidney.......	Poet
1810	1888	Gray, Asa...........	Botanist	1885	1933	Lardner, Ring W......	Humorist
1835	1901	Gray, Elisha.........	Inventor	1850	1925	Lawson, Victor F......	Newspaper
1811	1872	Greeley, Horace......	Newspaper	1849	1887	Lazarus, Emma......	Poet. Novel.
1844	1935	Greely, Gen. A. W....	Sold., Explo.	1823	1901	Leconte, Joseph......	Geologist
1846	1935	Green, Anna Katharine		1758	1818	Lee, Henry..........	Soldier (Rev.)
		(Mrs. Charles Rohlfs).	Fiction	1732	1794	Lee, Rich. Henry.....	Statesman
1834	1900	Green, Henrietta (Hetty)	Finance	1807	1870	Lee, Robert E........	Soldier
1742	1786	Greene, Nathaniel.....	Soldier	1823	1891	Leidy, Joseph........	Scientist
1872	1926	Greenway, Gen. John C.	Engineer	1824	1903	Leland, Chas. Godfrey..	Poet
1861	1920	Guiney, Louise Imogene.	Poetry	1774	1809	Lewis, Meriwether....	Explorer
1822	1909	Hale, Edward Everett...	Essayist	1764	1836	Livingston, Edward....	Statesman
1755	1776	Hale, Nathan........	Patriot	1746	1813	Livingston, Robt. R....	Statesman
1788	1879	Hale, Sarah J........	Poet Auth.	1833	1888	Locke, David R.......	Humor
1844	1924	Hall, Granville S......	Psychologist	1850	1924	Lodge, Henry Cabot...	Statesman
1790	1867	Halleck, Fitz-Greene...	Poet	1725	1792	Logan, John.........	Indian Chief
1829	1908	Halstead, Murat......	Journalist	1876	1916	London, Jack........	Fiction
1757	1804	Hamilton, Alexander...	Statesman	1815	1878	Long, Dr. Crawford W..	Anaesthesia
1830	1896	Hamilton, Gail (Mary		1807	1882	Longfellow, Henry W...	Poet
		Abigail Dodge)......	Fiction	1850	1933	Lord, Chester S.......	Newsp. Ed.
1811	1900	Hamlin, Cyrus........	Coll. Found'r	1796	1867	Lorillard, Peter......	Tobacco M'f'r
1809	1891	Hamlin, Hannibal.....	Vice Pres.,Gov	1833	1901	Lorillard, Pierre......	Tobacco M'f'r
1818	1902	Hampton, Wade......	Sold.,Statesm.	1813	1891	Lossing, Benson J.....	History
1824	1886	Hancock, W. S........	Soldier	1838	1915	Lounsbury, T. R.......	Essayist
1837	1904	Hanna, Mark.........	Iron, Politic.	1802	1837	Lovejoy, Elijah J......	Newsp. Editor
1820	1899	Harlan, James.......	Sen., Cabinet	1850	1916	Low, Seth...........	Mayor,Educ.
1795	1865	Harper, James.......	Publisher	1874	1925	Lowell, Amy.........	Poet
1797	1875	Harper, John........	Publisher	1819	1891	Lowell, Jas. Russell....	Poet
1856	1906	Harper, William R.....	Educator	1797	1849	Lyon, Mary..........	Educator
1837	1909	Harriman, Edward H...	Financier	1845	1916	Mabie, Hamilton W....	Author
1843	1908	Harris, Joel C........	Humor	1861	1908	MacDowell, Edward A..	Composer
1839	1902	Harte, Francis Bret....	Fiction	1831	1902	Mackay, John W	Mine Owner
1607	1638	Harvard, John.......	Univ. Found.	1863	1941	McAdoo, William G...	Fin., States.
1839	1897	Havemeyer, Theo. A...	Sugar M'f'r	1809	1884	McCormick, Cyrus H...	Inventor
1804	1864	Hawthorne, Nathaniel..	Fiction	1808	1895	McCulloch, Hugh.....	Sec. Treas'y
1838	1905	Hay, John...........	Statesman	1771	1830	McDowell, Ephraim....	Physician
1832	1881	Hayes, Isaac I........	Explorer	1800	1873	McGuffey, William H...	Educator
1830	1886	Hayne, Paul Hamilton..	Poet	1757	1811	McIntyre, Samuel.....	Woodcarver
1791	1839	Hayne, Robert Y......	Statesman	1816	1890	McLean, Washington...	Journalist
1850	1904	Hearn, Lafcadio......	Essayist	1852	1932	McMaster, John Bache.	Historian
1799	1878	Henry, Joseph........	Inventor	1796	1859	Mann, Horace........	Educator
1736	1799	Henry, Patrick.......	Statesman	1733	1795	Marion, Francis......	Soldier (Rev.)
1859	1924	Herbert, Victor.......	Composer	1852	1940	Markham, Edwin......	Poet
1748	1830	Hicks, Elias.........	Quaker	1801	1882	Marsh, George P......	Lawy. Dipl.
1843	1910	Hill, David B........	U.S. Senator	1856	1929	Marshall, Louis.......	Lawyer
1838	1916	Hill, James J........	Railroads	1725	1792	Mason, George.......	Statesman
1869	1933	Hillquit, Morris......	Socialist	1663	1728	Mather, Cotton.......	Preacher
1809	1894	Holmes, Oliver W.....	Poet, Essayist	1638	1723	Mather, Increase......	Educator
1841	1935	Holmes, Oliver W.....	Jurist	1852	1892	Matthews, J. Brander..	Writer
1814	1879	Hooker, Joseph.......	Soldier	1806	1873	Maury, Matthew F.....	Hydrographer
1718	1802	Hopkins, Esek, Com...	Naval	1823	1899	Medill, Joseph M.....	Newsp. Editor
1795	1873	Hopkins, Johns.......	Univ. Found.	1855	1937	Mellon, Andrew W....	Fin., Industr.
1802	1887	Hopkins, Mark.......	Educator	1819	1891	Melville, Herman.....	Adventure
1770	1842	Hopkinson, Joseph....	Poet	1849	1922	Miller, Charles R.....	Newspaper
1822	1885	Hough, Franklin B	Forester	1841	1913	Miller, Joaquin......	Poet
1858	1938	House, Edward.......	Diplomat	1825	1910	Mills, Darius........	Finance
1793	1863	Houston, Sam........	Sold., States.	1822	1908	Mitchell, Donald G....	Essayist
1864	1900	Hovey, Richard.......	Poet	1852	1927	Mitchell, Edward P....	Editor
1842	1908	Howard, Bronson.....	Drama	1818	1889	Mitchell, Maria.......	Astronomer
1830	1909	Howard, Oliver O......	Soldier	1829	1914	Mitchell, Silas Weir...	Fiction
1819	1867	Howe, Elias.........	Inventor	1737	1775	Montgomery, Richard...	Soldier (Rev.)
1819	1910	Howe, Julia Ward.....	Poet	1837	1899	Moody, Dwight L......	Preacher
1837	1920	Howells, William D....	Fiction	1869	1910	Moody, William Vaughn	Drama,Poetry
1859	1921	Huneker, James Gibbons	Essayist	1837	1913	Morgan, J. Pierpont...	Banker
1796	1859	Hunt, Walter........	Inventor	1813	1890	Morgan, Junius S.....	Banker
1821	1900	Huntington, C. P......	Railways	1838	1923	Morley, Edward W.....	Chemist
1590	1643	Hutchinson, Anne.....	Preacher	1802	1864	Morris, George P......	Poet
1833	1900	Ingalls, John James...	Sen., orator	1752	1816	Morris, Gouverneur....	Statesman
1833	1899	Ingersoll, Robert G....	Agnostic	1832	1902	Morton, J. S.........	Gov. Cabinet
1783	1859	Irving, Washington....	Fiction. Hist.	1791	1872	Morse, Samuel F. B....	Inventor

B.	D.	Name	Occupation	B.	D.	Name	Occupation
1823	1877	Morton, Oliver P.	Gov., Sen.	1813	1883	Sims, J Marion	Surgeon
1819	1868	Morton, William T. G.	Surgeon	1806	1870	Simms, W. Gilmore	Fiction
1742	1818	Moses, Isaac	Revol. fin.	1850	1928	Sloane, Wm. M	History
1814	1877	Motley, John	History	1824	1893	Smith, Gen. E. Kirby	Sold., Educ.
1793	1880	Mott, Lucretia	Reformer	1838	1915	Smith, F. Hopkinson	Fiction
1764	1807	Muhlenberg, Rev.J.P.G.	Sold., Congr	1797	1874	Smith, Gerrit	Abolitionist
1838	1914	Muir, Jonn	Naturalist	1580	1631	Smith, Capt. John	Explorer
1854	1925	Munsey, Frank A	Newspaper	1815	1877	Smith Hy. Boynton	Educator
1858	1924	Murphy, Charles F	Politics	1805	1844	Smith, Joseph	Morm'nPr'pht
1850	1922	Murfree Mary N. (C. E.Craddock)	Fiction	1808	1895	Smith, Rev. S. F	Nat'l Anthem
1841	1915	Nelson, William R	Journalist	1854	1932	Sousa, John Philip	Bandmaster
1835	1909	Newcomb, Simon	Astronomer	1775	1821	Spalding, Lyman	Physician
1870	1902	Norris, Frank	Fiction	1824	1893	—Stanford, Leland	Fin., Benef.
1827	1908	Norton, Charles Eliot	Essayist	1816	1902	Stanton, Elizabeth C	Suffragist
1811	1886	Noyes, John H	Oneida Comm	1728	1822	Stark, John	Soldier (Rev.)
1850	1896	Nye, Wilson	Humor	1833	1908	Stedman, Edmund C	Poet
1858	1935	Ochs, Adolph S	Newspapers	1812	1883	Stephens, A. H	Confed. V. P.
1856	1937	Ogden, Rollo	Journalist	1826	1876	Stewart, Alexander T	Merchant
1856	1935	Older, Fremont	Editor	1730	1781	Stockton, Richard	Rev. Patriot
1849	1919	Osler, William	Surgeon	1825	1903	Stoddard, Rich. Henry	Poet
1810	1850	Ossolli, Margaret Fuller	Essayist	1818	1893	Stone, Lucy	Reformer
1855	1918	Page, Walter H	Diarist	1848	1929	Stone, Melville E.	Founder A. P.
1737	1809	Paine, Thomas	Statesman	1811	1896	Stowe, Harriet Beecher	Fiction
1855	1902	Palmer, Alice F	Educator	1848	1931	Straus, Nathan	Philanth'pist
1810	1860	Parker, Rev. Theodore	Abolitionist	1850	1926	Straus, Oscar S	Diplomat
1842	1933	Parkhurst, Rev. C. H.	Reformer	1740	1795	Sullivan, John	Soldier (Rev.)
1823	1893	Parkman, Francis	History	1859	1918	Sullivan, John L	Pugilist
1791	1852	Payne, John Howard	Poet	1843	1923	Sulzberger, Mayer	Jurist
1779	1860	Paulding, J. K	Fic., Poetry	1811	1874	Sumner, Charles	Statesman
1795	1860	Peabody, George	Philanthropist	1734	1832	Sumter, Thomas	Soldier
1852	1938	Peabody, George F	Fin., Benef.	1871	1935	Sunday, Rev. Wil'm A	Evangelist
1856	1920	Peary, Robert E., Adm.	Explorer	1803	1880	Sutter, John A	Colonizer
1644	1718	Penn, William	Founder	1849	1909	Tabb, John B	Poetry
1860	1921	Penrose, Boise	Politics	1856	1929	Taggart, Thomas	Politics
1830	1905	Perry, Arthur L	Economist	1832	1902	Talmage, T. de Witt	Preacher
1785	1819	Perry, Oliver Hazard	Nav. Hero	1825	1878	Taylor, Bayard	Travel
1844	1911	Phelps-Ward, Eliz S.	Fiction	1806	1882	Taylor, Moses	Merchant
1867	1911	Phillips, David Graham	Novelist	1768	1813	Tecumseh (Indian)	Chief
1811	1884	Phillips, Wendell	Abolitionist	1836	1894	Thaxter, Celia	Poet
1739	1817	Pickens, Andrew	Soldier	1785	1872	Thayer, Sylvanus	Sold. Educ.
1814	1899	Pierpont, Francis H	Governor	1835	1905	Thomas, Theodore	Musician
1785	1866	Pierpont, Rev. John	Hymn-writer	1853	1937	Thomson, Elihu	Inventor
1779	1813	Pike, Zebulon M.	Soldier, Expl.	1817	1862	Thoreau, Henry D	Philos., Nat.
1746	1825	Pinckney, Charles C	Sold., Statesm.	1791	1871	Ticknor, George	History
1809	1849	Poe, Edgar Allan	Poet, Fiction	1814	1886	Tilden, Samuel J	Statesman
1867	1910	Porter, W. S. (O. Henry)	Fiction	1847	1918	Tillman, Benjamin R	Politics
1761	1807	Preble, Edward, Comm.	Naval	1740	1809	Trumbull, Jonathan	Statesman
1790	1859	Prescott, William H	History	1823	1878	Tweed, William M	Politician
1794	1860	Preston, William C	U.S. Senator	1830	1894	Vance, Zebulon B	Gov., Sen.
1847	1911	Pulitzer, Joseph	Newspaper	1794	1877	Vanderbilt, Cornelius	Ships, Railw'y
1831	1897	Pullman, George M.	Inventor	1843	1899	Vanderbilt, Cornelius	Railways
1898	1937	Putnam, Amelia Earhart	Aviator	1821	1885	Vanderbilt, Wm. H.	Railways
1718	1790	Putnam, Israel	Soldier	1849	1920	Vanderbilt, Wm. K.	Railways
1853	1904	Quay, Matt	Politics	1852	1933	Van Dyke, Rev. Henry	Poet, Educ.
1773	1833	Randolph, John	Statesman	1835	1900	Villard, Henry	Editor
1820	1869	Raymond, Henry J.	Newspaper	1864	1938	Vizetelly, F. H.	Etymologist
1822	1872	Read, Thos. Buchanan	Poet	1827	1905	Wallace, Lew	Sold., Dram.
1851	1902	Reed, Walter	Physician	1838	1922	Wanamaker, John	Merchant
1837	1912	Reid, Whitelaw	Journalist	1871	1937	Warburg, Felix M.	Banker
1846	1927	Remsen, Ira	Chemist	1727	1800	Ward, Artemas	Soldier (Rev.)
1735	1818	Revere, Paul (Apollos Rivoire)	Patriot	1834	1867	Ward, Artemus (Charles Farrar Browne)	Humor
1848	1927	Rhodes, James Ford	History	1831	1862	Ward, Frederick T	Soldier
1817	1894	Rice, Henry M	Sen., Pioneer	1841	1913	Ward, Lester F	Philosopher
1849	1914	Riis, Jacob A	Writer	1829	1900	Warner, Chas. Dudley	Essayist
1854	1916	Riley, J. Whitcomb	Poet	1830	1882	Warren, Gouvern K	Soldier (Rev.)
1869	1935	Robinson, Edwin A	Poet	1740	1775	Warren, Joseph	Soldier (Rev.)
1839	1937	Rockefeller, John D	Fin., Philan.	1858	1915	Washington, Booker T	Negro Educ.
1845	1937	Root, Elihu	Statesman	1840	1921	Watterson, Henry	Journalist
1834	1913	Rose, Uriah M	Jurist, Dip.	1745	1796	Wayne, Anthony	Soldier (Rev.)
1862	1932	Rosenwald, Julius	Merch. Phil	1782	1852	Webster, Daniel	Sen., Orator
1855	1916	Royce, Josiah	Philosopher	1758	1843	Webster, Noah	Dictionary
1743	1839	Rumsey, James	Steamboat	1797	1882	Weed, Thurlow	Journalist
1745	1813	Rush, Benjamin	Physician	1828	1898	Wells, David A	Economist
1780	1859	Rush, Richard	Statesman	1846	1914	Westinghouse, George	Inventor
1740	1785	Salmon, Haym	Patriot	1836	1906	Wheeler, Gen. Joseph	Soldier
1856	1921	Saltus, Edgar E.	Fiction	1832	1918	White, Andrew D	Educ.Diplom.
1818	1887	Saxe, John Godfrey	Poet	1834	1916	White, Horace V	Journalist
1847	1920	Schiff, Jacob Henry	Financier	1836	1906	White, Stanford	Architect
1829	1906	Schurz, Carl	Statesman	1802	1847	Whitman, Marcellus	Oreg. Explor.
1733	1804	Schuyler, Philip	Soldier (Rev.)	1819	1892	Whitman, Walt	Poet
1786	1866	Scott, Winfield	Soldier	1765	1825	Whitney, Eli	Inventor
1854	1926	Scripps, Edward W	Newspapers	1841	1904	Whitney, William C	St. Railways
1895	1938	Scripps, Robert P	Newspapers	1827	1894	Whitney, William D	Ed. Dict.
1838	1902	Scudder, Horace E	Ed. All. M.	1807	1892	Whittier, John Greenleaf	Poet
1729	1796	Seabury, Samuel	P. E. Bishop	1884	1921	Whittlesey, Charles W	Soldier
1888	1916	Seeger, Alan	Poet	1856	1923	Wiggin, Kate D	Fiction
1770	1843	Sequoyah (Cherokee)	Ind. leader	1798	1877	Wilkes, Lieut. Chas	Polar Explor.
1713	1784	Serra, Junipero	Missionary	1787	1870	Willard, Emma	Educator
1774	1821	Seton, Elizabeth (Bayley)	Educator	1839	1898	Willard, Frances E	Prohibitionist
1745	1815	Sevier, John	Sold., Gov.	1854	1932	Williams, John Sharp	Politics
1801	1872	Seward, William H	Statesman	1599	1683	Williams, Rev. Roger	Founder
1823	1897	Sheldon, Edward A	Educator	1806	1867	Willis, Nathaniel P	Essayist
1850	1911	Shepard, Edward M	Law. Reform	1588	1649	Winthrop, John	Gov. Conserv.
1823	1900	Sherman, John	Statesman	1828	1861	Winthrop, Theodore	Fiction
1831	1888	Sheridan, Phillip	Soldier	1785	1842	Woodworth, Samuel	Poet, Dram.
1820	1891	Sherman, William T	Soldier	1720	1772	Woolman, John	Religion
1810	1879	Shields, James	Sold., Sen.Gov.	1848	1894	Woolson, Constance F	Fiction
1836	1904	Shoup, Col. George L.	Gov., Sen.	1852	1919	Woolworth, Frank	Merchant
1791	1865	Sigourney, Lydia H	Poet	1801	1877	Young, Brigham	Morm'n Lead.
				1697	1746	Zenger, John P	Journalist

American Painters

Source: Biographical Records

B.	D.	Name	B.	D.	Name	B.	D.	Name
1852	1911	Abbey, Edwin A.	1838	1928	Gay, Edward	1741	1827	Peale, Chas. W.
1856	1915	Alexander, John W.	1823	1880	Gifford, S. R.	1778	1860	Peale, Rembrandt
1849	1924	Allen, Thomas	1834	1918	Griswold, C. C.	1831	1914	Pearce, Charles S.
1779	1843	Allston, Washington	1861	1927	Grover, Oliver Dennett	1857	1923	Potter, Edward C.
1814	1893	Beard, Jas. H.	1865	1931	Hale, Philip L.	1853	1911	Pyle, Howard
1825	1900	Beard, William H.	1792	1866	Harding, Chester	1868	1929	Quinn, Edmond T.
1852	1917	Beckwith, J. Carroll	1854	1929	Harrison, L. Birge	1858	1916	Ranger, Henry W.
1882	1925	Bellows, George W.	1828	1901	Hart, James M.	1850	1914	Ream, Vinnie
1828	1902	Bierstadt, Albert	1860	1935	Hassam, Childe	1862	1929	Reid, Robert
1847	1919	Blakelock, Ralph A.	1872	1930	Hawthorne, Charles W.	1861	1909	Remington, Frederic
1848	1936	Blashfield, Edwin H.	1813	1894	Healy, G. P. A.	1854	1922	Rice, William M. J.
1857	1903	Blum, Robert F.	1839	1917	Hennessy, William J.	1833	1905	Richards, William T.
1868	1923	Bohm, Max	1865	1929	Henri, Robert	1852	1896	Robinson, Theodore
1833	1905	Boughton, George H.	1823	1890	Hicks, Thomas	1847	1917	Ryder, Albert P.
1827	1892	Bradford, William	1836	1910	Homer, Winslow	1856	1918	Sargent, John S.
1832	1918	Brevoort, J. R.	1840	1895	Hovenden, Thomas	1843	1924	Sartain, William
1847	1928	Bridgman, F. A.	1844	1929	Howe, William H.	1859	1926	Sewell, Amanda B.
1814	1889	Brown, George L.	1824	1879	Hunt, William M.	1860	1924	Sewell, Robert V. V.
1859	1920	Browne, Charles Francis	1816	1906	Huntington, Daniel	1871	1922	Shardy, Henry M.
1855	1941	Brush, George de Forest	1801	1846	Inman, Henry	1832	1928	Shattuck, Aaron
1811	1893	Casilaer, John W.	1825	1894	Inness, George	1838	1910	Shirlaw, Walter
1843	1926	Cassatt, Mary	1854	1926	Inness, George, jr.	1858	1920	Smedley, William T.
1796	1872	Catlin, George	1855	1914	Isham, Samuel	1847	1926	Steele, Theodore C.
1860	1925	Chapman, Carlton T.	1780	1838	Jarvis, John W.	1835	1922	Story, George H.
1849	1916	Chase, William M.	1824	1906	Johnson, Eastman	1856	1919	Story, Julian
1826	1900	Church, F. E.	1848	1927	Jones, H. Bolton	1830	1901	Strauss, Raphael
1842	1924	Church, Fred'k Stuart	1818	1872	Kensett, J. F.	1755	1828	Stuart, Gilbert
1855	1925	Coffin, Wm. A.	1835	1910	La Farge, John	1783	1872	Sully, Thomas
1801	1848	Cole, Thos.	1849	1909	Lathrop, Francis	1861	1930	Symons, Gardner
1840	1928	Coleman, Charles C.	1816	1868	Leutze, E.	1849	1921	Thayer, Abbott H.
1832	1920	Colman, Samuel	1880	1940	Lie, Jonas	1848	1933	Tiffany, Louis C.
1737	1815	Copley, John S.	1849	1920	Lippincott, William H.	1756	1843	Trumbull, John
1856	1919	Cox, Kenyon	1852	1924	Loomis, Chester	1849	1925	Tryon, Dwight N.
1849	1924	Craig, Thomas B.	1867	1933	Luks, George B.	1850	1918	Turner, C. Y.
1845	1918	Crownshield, Fred'k	1860	1929	MacEwen, Walter	1853	1902	Twachtman, John H.
1843	1909	Currier, J. Frank	1836	1897	Martin, Homer	1776	1852	Vanderlyn, John
1833	1927	Dana, W. P. W.	1813	1894	Matteson, T.	1857	1920	Van Laer, Alexander T.
1853	1929	Dannat, William T.	1843	1923	Maynard, George W.	1836	1923	Vedder, Elihu
1862	1928	Davies, Arthur B.	1828	1891	McEntee, J.	1856	1935	Volk, Stephen A. D.
1856	1933	Davis, Charles H.	1860	1932	Melchers, Gari	1855	1935	Vos, Hubert
1861	1918	Day, Frank Miles	1858	1925	Metcalf, Willard L.	1783	1861	Waldo, Samuel L.
1858	1923	De Camp, Joseph R.	1842	1922	Miller, Charles H.	1843	1929	Walker, Henry O.
1847	1935	Dielman, Frederick	1846	1912	Millet, Francis D.	1861	1940	Waugh, Fred'k J.
1876	1935	Dodge, William De L.	1855	1930	Moeller, Louis	1856	1928	Webb, J. Louis
1856	1926	Drake, Will H.	1829	1901	Moran, Edward	1849	1903	Weeks, Edwin L.
1796	1886	Durand, A. B.	1863	1935	Moran, Percy	1852	1917	Weir, J. Alden
1848	1919	Duveneck, Frank	1837	1926	Moran, Thomas	1841	1926	Weir, John F.
1844	1916	Eakins, Thomas	1791	1872	Morse, Samuel F. B.	1803	1889	Weir, Rob. W.
1845	1921	Earle, Lawrence C.	1858	1928	Mowbray, H. Siddons	1738	1820	West, Benjamin
1812	1868	Elliott, Chas. L.	1853	1921	Murphy, J. Francis	1874	1929	Wetherill, E. Kent K.
1852	1926	Foster, Ben.	1847	1918	Nicoll, J. C.	1833	1903	Whistler, J. A. M.
1808	1884	Freeman, James E.	1835	1907	Noble, Thomas S.	1820	1910	Whittredge, Worthingt'n
1822	1884	Fuller, George	1811	1885	Page, William	1823	1903	Wood, Thomas W.
1867	1934	Fuller, Henry B.	1869	1941	Paxton, William McG.	1836	1892	Wyant, Alexander H.
1765	1815	Fulton, Robert	1845	1917	Peabody, Robert S.	1830	1923	Yewell, George H.

Whistler was born at Lowell, Mass., but most of his life was spent in Europe.

AMERICAN ETCHERS, ENGRAVERS, ILLUSTRATORS

B.	D.	Name	B.	D.	Name	B.	D.	Name
1842	1909	Bush, Charles G.	1866	1925	Keller, Arthur I.	1857	1926	Pennell, Joseph
1856	1909	Bacher, Otto Henry	1838	1895	Keppler, Joseph	1861	1933	Platt, Charles A.
1845	1926	Cassatt, Mary	1866	1924	Macdonald, Arthur N.	1853	1911	Pyle, Howard
1776	1820	Charley, William	1872	1934	McCay, Winsor	1761	1817	Savage, Edward
1852	1931	Cole, Timothy	1858	1938	McDougall, Walt	1807	1885	Smillie, James
1822	1888	Darley, Felix O. C.	1860	1919	Mielatz, C. F. Wm.	1833	1909	Smillie, James D.
1796	1886	Durand, Asher Brown	1869	1935	Mielziner, Leo	1867	1924	Watt, William G.
1851	1928	Frost, Arthur B.	1874	1940	Mora, F. Louis	1834	1903	Whistler, J. A. M.
1851	1906	French, Edwin D.	1840	1902	Nast, Thomas	1852	1916	Wolf, Henry
1876	1925	Haskell, Ernest	1863	1928	Outcalt, Richard F.	1792	1859	Yeager, Joseph
1849	1935	Hodson, William F.	1741	1827	Peale, Charles W.	1862	1935	Zimmerman, Eugene

AMERICAN ARCHITECTS

B.	D.	Name	B.	D.	Name	B.	D.	Name
1836	1918	Armstrong, D. Maitland	1859	1934	Gilbert, Cass.	1822	1903	Olmsted, Fred'k L.
1866	1924	Bacon, Henry	1869	1923	Goodhue, Bertram C.	1845	1917	Peabody, Robert S.
1871	1925	Barber, Donn	1847	1918	Hardenbergh, Henry J.	1837	1913	Post, George B.
1857	1925	Brunner, Arnold W.	1860	1929	Hastings, Thomas	1838	1886	Richardson, Henry H.
1763	1844	Bulfinch, Charles	1847	1909	McKim, Charles F.	1836	1909	Sturgis, Russell
1858	1911	Carrere, John M.	1846	1928	Mead, William R.	1862	1925	Trowbridge, Samuel B. P.
1846	1916	Cook, Walter	1781	1855	Mills, Robert	1853	1906	White, Stanford

AMERICAN SCULPTORS

B.	D.	Name	B.	D.	Name	B.	D.	Name
1819	1911	Ball, Thomas	1790	1852	Frazee, John	1844	1920	O'Donovan, William
1863	1938	Barnard, George Grey	1850	1931	French, Daniel C.	1870	1935	Paulding, John
1865	1925	Bartlett, Paul W.	1862	1929	Grafly, Charles	1805	1873	Powers, Hiram
1867	1915	Bitter, Karl T.	1805	1852	Greenough, Horatio	1867	1917	Pratt, Bela
1871	1941	Borglum, Gutzon	1830	1908	Hosmer, Harriet	1868	1929	Quinn, Edmond T.
1868	1922	Borglum, Solon H.	1868	1925	Jaegers, Albert	1829	1904	Rogers, John
1871	1924	Brenner, Victor D.	1843	1907	Kemeys, Edward	1848	1907	St. Gaudens, Augustus
1865	1919	Brooks, Richard E.	1863	1937	MacMonnies, Fred. W.	1871	1922	Shrady, Henry M.
1814	1886	Brown, Henry K.	1871	1935	Lukeman, Henry A	1830	1910	Ward, J. Q. A.
1857	1935	Bush-Brown, H. K.	1858	1927	Marling, Philip	1725	1785	Wright (Lovell) Patience
1860	1920	Clark, Thomas S.	1873	1940	O'Connor, Andrew			

Noted Men and Women of Great Britain

Source: Biographical Records

B.	D.	Name	Subject
1764	1831	Abernethy, John	Surgeon.
1672	1719	Addison, Joseph	Essays.
1805	1882	Ainsworth, W. H.	Novelist.
1721	1770	Akenside, Mark	Poet.
1861	1936	Allenby, Viscount	Sold.Admin'tr.
1832	1904	Arnold, Edwin	Poet.
1822	1888	Arnold, Matthew	Poet.
1515	1568	Ascham, Roger	Philosophy.
1852	1928	Asquith, Herbert H.	Statesman.
1775	1817	Austen, Jane	Fiction.
1561	1626	Bacon, Francis	Essays.
1214	1294	Bacon, Roger	Philos. Sci.
1781	1843	Bagot, Charles	Diplomat.
1763	1851	Baillie, Joanna	Poet.
1848	1930	Balfour, Arthur J.	Statesman.
1860	1937	Barrie, James M.	Fiction.
1615	1691	Baxter, Richard	Religion.
1584	1616	Beaumont, Francis	Drama.
1117	1170	Becket, Thomas à	Archbishop.
673	735	Bede, the Venerable	Historian.
1748	1832	Bentham, Jeremy	Political.
1662	1742	Bentley, Richard	Scholar.
1685	1753	Berkeley, George	Bishop.
1847	1933	Besant, Annie	Theosophist.
1723	1780	Blackstone, William	Law.
1829	1912	Booth, Gen. William	Religion.
1740	1795	Boswell, James	Biography.
1844	1930	Bridges, Robert	Poet.
1811	1889	Bright, John	Economist.
1816	1855	Brontë, Charlotte	Fiction.
1778	1868	Brougham, Sir Henry	Historian.
1806	1861	Browning, Elizabeth B.	Poet.
1812	1889	Browning, Robert	Poet.
1838	1922	Bryce, James	History.
1628	1688	Bunyan, John	Religion.
1729	1797	Burke, Edmund	Essays.
1759	1796	Burns, Robert	Poet.
1612	1680	Butler, Samuel	Poet.
1774	1839	Butler, Samuel	Bishop.
1788	1824	Byron (Geo. Gordon)	Poet.
1777	1844	Campbell, Thomas	Poet.
1770	1827	Canning, George	Statesman.
1795	1881	Carlyle, Thomas	History.
1421	1491	Caxton, William	Printer.
1863	1937	Chamberlain, Sir Austen	Statesman.
1836	1914	Chamberlain, Joseph	Statesman.
1869	1940	Chamberlain, Neville	Statesman.
1328	1400	Chaucer, Geoffrey	Poet.
1694	1773	Chesterfield, Earl of	Letters.
1725	1774	Clive, Robert	Sold. Statesm.
1762	1835	Cobbett, William	Essayist.
1804	1865	Cobden, Richard	Economist.
1772	1834	Coleridge, S. T.	Poet.
1670	1729	Congreve, William	Drama.
1728	1779	Cook, James	Discoverer.
1731	1800	Cowper, William	Poet.
1489	1556	Cranmer, Thomas	Archbishop
1599	1658	Cromwell, Oliver	Protector.
1809	1882	Darwin, Charles	Evolution
1731	1802	Darwin, Erasmus	Poet.
1606	1668	Davenant, Sir William	Drama, Poet.
1593	1669	Davidson, William	Chemist.
1661	1731	Defoe, Daniel	Fiction.
1785	1859	De Quincey, Thomas	Essays.
1812	1870	Dickens, Charles	Fiction.
1804	1881	Disraeli, Benjamin	Statesman.
1573	1631	Donne, Rev. John	Poet.
1540	1596	Drake, Sir Francis	Explorer.
1563	1631	Drayton, Michael	Poet.
1631	1700	Dryden, John	Poet.
1856	1934	Elgar, Edward	Composer.
1819	1880	Eliot, G. (Marion Evans)	Fiction.
1805	1869	Epps, John	Homeop.
1620	1706	Evelyn, John	Poet.
1791	1867	Faraday, Michael	Scientist.
1707	1754	Fielding, Henry	Fiction.
1459	1535	Fisher, Rev. John	Martyr.
1624	1691	Fox, George	Quaker.
1517	1587	Fox, John	Theologian
1786	1847	Franklin, John	Explorer.
1535	1594	Frobisher, Martin	Discoverer
1685	1732	Gay, John	Fables.
1836	1911	Gilbert, W. S.	Drama.
1737	1794	Gibbon, Edward	History.
1809	1898	Gladstone, William E.	Statesman.
1728	1774	Goldsmith, Oliver	Poet.
1320	1402	Gower, John	Poet.
1746	1820	Grattan, Henry	Orator.
1716	1771	Gray, Thomas	Poet.
1856	1925	Haggard, Rider	Novelist.
1777	1859	Hallam, Henry	History.
1594	1643	Hampden, John	Patriot.
1840	1928	Hardy, Thomas	Fiction.Poetry
1831	1923	Harrison, Frederic	Positivist.
1880	1941	Harty, Hamilton	Composer.
1795	1857	Havelock, Henry	Soldier.

B.	D.	Name	Subject
1778	1830	Hazlitt, William	Essayist.
1578	1657	Harvey, William	Physician.
1732	1818	Hastings, Warren	Sold. Gov.
1783	1826	Heber, Reginald	Poet, Preach.
1793	1835	Hemans, Felicia	Poet.
1591	1674	Herrick, Robert	Poet.
1792	1871	Herschel, John	Astronomer.
1738	1822	Herschel, William	Astronomer.
1795	1879	Hill, Rowland	Postal Ref.
1588	1679	Hobbes, Thomas	Philosopher.
1770	1835	Hogg, James	Poet.
1798	1845	Hood, Thomas	Poet.
1726	1799	Howe, Richard	Naval.
	1611	Hudson, Henry	Discoverer.
1711	1776	Hume, David	Hist., Philos.
1825	1895	Huxley, Thos. Henry	Scientist.
1859	1935	Jellicoe, Earl	Admiral.
1803	1857	Jerrold, Douglas W.	Dramatist.
1709	1784	Johnson, Samuel	Dictionary.
1574	1637	Jonson, Ben	Drama.
1573	1652	Jones, Inigo	Architect.
1796	1821	Keats, John	Poet.
1865	1936	Kipling, Rudyard	Fiction.
1775	1834	Lamb, Charles	Essays.
1775	1864	Landor, Walter S.	Poet.
1330	1400	Langland, William	Poet.
1491	1555	Latimer, Hugh	Religion.
1838	1903	Lecky, W. E. H.	History.
1632	1704	Locke, John	Philosophy.
1827	1912	Lister, Joseph	Surgeon.
1803	1873	Lytton, E. Bulwer	Fiction.
1800	1859	Macaulay, Thomas B.	Historian.
1866	1937	MacDonald, J. Ramsay	Statesman.
1808	1892	Manning, Henry E.	Religion.
1650	1722	Marlborough, Duke of	Soldier.
1564	1593	Marlowe, Christopher	Drama.
1621	1678	Marvell, Andrew	Poet.
1584	1640	Massinger, Philip	Drama.
1831	1879	Maxwell, Jas. Clerk	Physicist.
1828	1909	Meredith, George	Novelist.
1806	1873	Mill, J. Stuart	Economics.
1608	1674	Milton, John	Poet.
1779	1852	Moore, Thomas	Poet.
1480	1535	More, Sir Thomas	Economics.
1635	1688	Morgan, Henry	Buccaneer.
1838	1923	Morley, John	Biography.
1550	1617	Napier, John	Mathemat.
1758	1805	Nelson, Lord	Admiral.
1801	1890	Newman, John Henry	Religion.
1642	1727	Newton, Sir Isaac	Philosopher
1820	1910	Nightingale, Florence	Nurse, Sanit
1771	1858	Owen, Robert	Socialist.
1632	1703	Pepys, Samuel	Diarist.
1759	1806	Pitt, William	Statesman
1708	1778	Pitt, Wm.E. of Chatham	Statesman.
1688	1744	Pope, Alexander	Poet.
1664	1721	Prior, Matthew	Poet.
1658	1695	Purcell, Henry	Musician.
1592	1644	Quarles, Francis	Poet.
1552	1618	Raleigh, Sir Walter	History.
1814	1884	Reade, Charles	Fiction.
1860	1935	Reading, Marquess of	Jurist, Dipl.
1772	1823	Ricardo, David	Economist.
1689	1761	Richardson, Samuel	Fiction.
1832	1914	Roberts, Earl	Soldier.
1721	1793	Robertson, William	Historian.
1763	1855	Rogers, Samuel	Poet.
1847	1929	Rosebery, Earl of	Biography.
1800	1862	Ross, James C.	Discoverer.
1828	1862	Rossetti, D. Gabriel	Poet, Art.
1819	1900	Ruskin, John	Art Critic.
1830	1903	Salisbury, Marquess	Statesman.
1868	1912	Scott, Robert F.	Discoverer.
1771	1832	Scott, Sir Walter	Fiction.
1874	1922	Shackleton, Ernest H.	Explorer.
1564	1616	Shakespeare, William	Drama.
1792	1822	Shelley, Percy Bysshe	Poet.
1751	1816	Sheridan, Richard B.	Drama.
1554	1586	Sidney, Sir Philip	Poet, Hist.
1723	1790	Smith, Adam	Economics
1580	1631	Smith, Capt. John	Colonizer.
1771	1845	Smith, Sydney	Essays.
1721	1771	Smollett, Tobias	Fiction.
1774	1843	Southey, Robert	Poet.
1820	1903	Spencer, Herbert	Science.
1552	1599	Spenser, Edmund	Poet.
1672	1729	Steele, Richard	Essays.
1713	1768	Sterne, Lawrence	Fiction.
1781	1848	Stephenson, George	Engineer.
1850	1894	Stevenson, Robert Louis	Fiction.
1525	1605	Stow, John	Historian.
1842	1900	Sullivan, Arthur S.	Composer.
1667	1745	Swift, Jonathan	Fiction.
1837	1909	Swinburne, Algernon C.	Poet.
1613	1667	Taylor, Jeremy	Religion.
1809	1892	Tennyson, Alfred	Poet.

B.	D.	Name	Subject	B.	D.	Name	Subject
1811	1863	Thackeray, W. M	Fiction	1707	1788	Wesley, Charles	Preacher.
1700	1748	Thomson, James	Poet.	1703	1791	Wesley, John	Philos.
1815	1882	Trollope, Anthony	Fiction.	1787	1863	Whately, Rev. Richard.	Preacher.
1484	1536	Tyndale, William	Religion.	1714	1770	Whitefield, George	Theology.
1820	1893	Tyndall, John	Scientific.	1324	1384	Wickliffe, Rev. John	Abolitionist
1822	1913	Wallace, Alfred R	Scientist.	1759	1833	Wilberforce, William	Religion.
1676	1745	Walpole, Robert	Statesman.	1802	1865	Wiseman, Nicholas P	Poet.
1593	1683	Walton, Izaak	Angling.	1770	1850	Wordsworth, William	Architect.
1858	1935	Watson, Sir William	Poet.	1632	1723	Wren, Christopher	Drama.
1736	1819	Watt, James	Engineer.	1640	1715	Wycherly, William	Religion
1674	1748	Watts, Isaac	Hymns.	1324	1384	Wyckliffe, John	Poet.
1769	1852	Wellington, Duke of	Soldier.	1684	1765	Young, Edward	Preacher.

Poets-Laureate of England
Source: Official Records

There is no authentic record of the origin of the office of Poet-Laureate of England. According to Warton, there was a Versificator Regis, or King's Poet, in the reign of Henry III, (1216-1272), and he was paid 100 shillings a year. Geoffrey Chaucer (1328-1400) assumed the title of Poet-Laureate, and in 1389 got a royal grant of a yearly allowance of wine. In the reign of Edward IV, (1461-1483) John Kay held the post. Under Henry VII, (1485-1509) Andrew Bernard was the Poet-Laureate, and was succeeded under Henry VIII, (1509-1547) by John Skelton. Next came Edmund Spenser, who died in 1599; then Samuel Daniel, who died in 1619, and then Ben Jonson (app't'd 1619). Sir William D'Avenant was appointed in 1638. John

Dryden was appointed in 1670 but was deposed at the Revolution. The others, with the date of appointment, when known, have been: Thomas Shadwell, 1689; Nahum Tate, 1692; Nicholas Rowe, 1715; the Rev. Laurence Eusden, 1718; Colly Cibber, 1730; William Whitehead, 1758, on the refusal of Gray; Rev. Thomas Warton, 1785, on the refusal of Mason; Henry J. Pye, 1790; Robert Southey, 1813, on the refusal of Sir Walter Scott; William Wordsworth, 1843; Alfred Tennyson, 1850; Alfred Austin, 1896; Robert Bridges, 1913 (died April 21, 1930); John Masefield, 1930.

D'Avenant was the godson (and considered by some the natural son) of William Shakespeare. He was 10 years old when Shakespeare died.

Noted Painters of Great Britain
Source: Biographical Records

B.	D.	Name	B.	D.	Name	B.	D.	Name
1836	1912	Alma-Tadema, SirLawr.	1817	1897	Gilbert, Sir John	1835	1910	Orchardson, Sir W. Q.
1734	1808	Beauclerk, Lady Diana	1841	1917	Henry, C. N.	1878	1931	Orpen, Sir William
1833	1898	Burne-Jones, Sir Edw.	1697	1764	Hogarth, William	1839	1893	Pettie, John
1781	1841	Chantrey, Sir F. L.	1758	1810	Hoppner, John	1884	1937	Philpot, Glyn W.
1850	1934	Collier, John	1827	1910	Hunt, W. Holman	1836	1919	Poynter, Sir E. J., Bt.
1776	1837	Constable, John	1874	1937	Jamieson, Alexander	1756	1823	Raeburn, Sir Henry
1803	1902	Cooper, Thos. Sidney	1802	1873	Landseer, Sir Edwin	1723	1792	Reynolds, Sir Joshua
1793	1865	Eastlake, Sir Charles L.	1856	1941	Lavery, Sir John	1734	1802	Romney, George
1872	1932	Eland, John S.	1769	1830	Lawrence, Sir Thomas	1828	1882	Rossetti, D. G.
1787	1849	Etty, William	1830	1896	Leighton, Fred'k, Lord	1854	1935	Stokes, A.
1846	1935	Farquharson, Joseph	1794	1859	Leslie, Charles R.	1775	1851	Turner, J. M. W.
1755	1826	Flaxman, John	1864	1941	Llewellyn, Sir William	1817	1904	Watts, Geo. F.
1825	1899	Foster, Myles Birket	1806	1870	Maclise, Daniel	1775	1856	Westmacott, Sir R.
1727	1788	Gainsborough, Thos.	1829	1896	Millais, Sir J. E.	1785	1841	Wilkie, Sir David
1790	1866	Gibson, John	1849	1933	Murray, Sir D.	1852	1931	Wyllie, W. L.

Flemish and Dutch Painters
Source: Biographical Records

B.	D.	Name	B.	D.	Name	B.	D.	Name
1460	1516	Bosch, Hieronymus	1593	1678	Jordaens, Jacob	1582	1649	Teniers, David (Elder)
1410	1475	Bouts, Dirk	1460	1531	Matsys, Quentin	1610	1694	Teniers, David
1525	1569	Breugel, de Oude	1435	1495	Memling, Hans	1440	1482	Vander Goes, H.
1568	1625	Breugel, Jan	1610	1685	Ostade, Adr. Van	1400	1458	Vander Weyden
1605	1638	Brouwer, Adriaen	1625	1654	Potter, Paul	1633	1707	Van de Velde, Willem
1605	1691	Cuyp, Albert	1607	1699	Rembrandt Van Rijn*	1599	1641	Van Dyck, Anthony
1613	1680	Douw, Gerard	1833	1898	Rops, Felicien	1366	1426	Van Eyck, Hubert
1614	1654	Fabricius, Carel	1577	1640	Rubens, Peter Paul	1386	1440	Van Eyck, Jan
1584	1666	Hals, Frans	1625	1681	Ruysdael, Jacob	1596	1656	Van Goyen, Jan
1638	1709	Hobbema, Meindert	1626	1679	Steen, Jan	1494	1533	Van Leyden, Lucas
1632	1681	Hoogh, Pieter de	1828	1906	Stevens, Alfred	1632	1675	Vermeer Van Delft, Ja

*Rembrandt was his first name, Van Rijn his family name.

Spanish Authors
Source: Biographical Records

Born	Died	Name	Subject	Born	Died	Name	Subject
1180	1246	Berceo, Gonzalo de	Poet.	1600	1681	Calderón de la Barca, Pedro	
1282	1348	Juan Manuel	Prose.			Henao de la Barreda y Iraño	Dramatist
1332	1458	Lopez de Ayala, Pedro	Poet.	1760	1828	Fernández de Moratin,	
1398	1458	Lopez de Mendoza, Iñigo				Leandro	Dramatist
		Marques de Santillana	Poet.	1772	1857	Quintana, Manuel Jose	Poet.
1440	1479	Manrique, Jorge	Poet.	1796	1877	Fernan Caballero (Cecilia	
	1510	Rojas, Fernando de	Dramatist.			Bohl de Faber)	Novelist
1493	1542	Boscán (or Boscá) Almo-		1803	1839	Heredia y Campuzano, Jose	Poet.
		gaver, Juan	Poet.	1817	1893	Zorrilla y Moral, José	Poet.
1503	1536	Garcilaso de la Vega	Poet.	1817	1901	Campoamor y Campoosorio,	
1503	1541	Valdés, Juan de	Philosopher.			Ramon de	Poet.
1510	1566	Rueda, Lope de	Dramatist.	1824	1905	Valera y Alcalá Galiano,	Novelist.
1528	1591	León, Luis de	Poet, Prose.	1833	1891	Alarcon, Pedro Antonio de	
1533	1594	Ercilla y Zuniga, Alonso de	Poet			(Mexican)	Novelist.
1547	1616	Cervantes de Saavedra,		1833	1906	Pereda, Jose Maria de	Novelist.
		Miguel de	Novelist.	1836	1870	Becquer, Gustavo Adolfo	Poet.
1561	1627	Góngora y Argote, Luis de	Poet.	1843	1920	Perez Galdos, Genito	Novelist.
1562	1635	Vega Carpio, Lope Felix de	Dramatist.	1852	1921	Pardo Bazan, Emilia	Novelist.
1579	1644	Velez de Guevara, Luis	Novelist.	1853	1938	Armando Palacio Valdes	Novelist
1580	1639	Ruiz de Alarcón Juan	Dramatist.	1867	1916	Dario Ruben, (Nicaraguan)	Poet.
1580	1645	Quevedo y Villegoro, Francisco Gómez de	Poet, Prose.	1867	1928	Blasco Ibanez, Vicente	Novelist.

Noted French Personages
Source: Biographical Records

Born	Died	Name	Subject	Born	Died	Name	Subject
1079	1142	Abelard, Pierre........	Philosophy	1790	1869	Lamartine, Alphonse de.	Poetry.
1820	1889	Augier, (Emile).......	Drama.	1743	1794	Lavoisier, Antoine L....	Chemist.
1799	1850	Balzac, Honore......	Fiction.	1621	1695	La Fontaine, Jean de....	Fables.
1594	1654	Balzac, Jean L. G.......	Morals.	1818	1894	Le Comte de Lisle.....	Poetry.
1823	1891	Banville, Theodore de..	Poetry.	1853	1914	Lemaitre, Jules.........	Literature.
1862	1923	Barres, Maurice......	Literature	1668	1747	Le Sage, A. R.........	Fiction.
1473	1524	Bayard, Pierre T......	Knight	1850	1923	Loti, Pierre..........	Fiction.
1821	1867	Beaudelaire, Charles...	Poetry	1635	1719	Maintenon (Mme. de)...	Letters.
1732	1799	Beaumarchais, P......	Drama.	1555	1628	Malherbe............	Poetry.
1780	1857	Beranger, Pierre......	Poetry	1688	1763	Marivaux, Pierre......	Drama.
1859	1941	Bergson, Henri......	Philos.	1637	1675	Marquette, Jacque.....	Explorer.
1827	1907	Berthelot, Marcelin...	Science.	1850	1893	Maupassant, Guy de....	Fiction.
1636	1711	Boileau, Nicolas......	Poetry.	1803	1870	Merimee, Prosper......	Fiction.
1769	1821	Bonaparte, Napoleon..	Soldier	1798	1874	Michelet, Jules........	History.
1825	1901	Bornier, Henri de......	Drama.	1796	1884	Mignet..............	History.
1627	1704	Bossuet, Jacques B......	Religion.	1622	1673	Moliere, Jean B.......	Drama.
1852	1935	Bourget, Paul........	Fiction.	1533	1592	Montaigne, Michael de..	Essays.
1845	1921	Boutroux, Emile......	Philosophy.	1689	1755	Montesquieu, Charles de	Morals.
1867	1926	Boylesve, René........	Fiction.	1810	1857	Musset, Alfred de......	Poetry.
1755	1826	Brillat-Savarin........	Gastronomist	1739	1794	Necker, (Mme.)........	Morals.
1707	1788	Buffon, George L......	Nat. History	1839	1903	Paris, Gaston.........	Literature.
1509	1564	Calvin, Jean........	Religion.	1623	1662	Pascal, Blaise........	Essays.
1845	1935	Cambon, Jules M....	Diplomat	1822	1895	Pasteur, Louis........	Science.
1857	1922	Capus.............	Drama.	1848	1932	Pau, Paul G...........	Soldier
1491	1557	Cartier, Jacques......	Navigator	1624	1693	Pellisson............	History.
1570	1635	Champlain, Samuel de..	Explorer.	1769	1828	Picard..............	Drama.
1541	1603	Charron, Pierre......	Morals.	1854	1912	Poincare, Henri.......	Science.
1768	1848	Chateaubriand, Fr....	Philosophy	1860	1934	Poincare, Raymond....	Statesman
1762	1794	Chenier, André......	Poetry.	1814	1867	Ponsara.............	Drama.
1786	1889	Chevreud, Michael....	Chemist.	1849	1930	Porto-Riche, de.......	Drama.
1619	1683	Colbert, Jean B.......	Statesman.	1697	1765	Prévost (l'abbe).......	Fiction.
1445	1509	Comines, Philip......	History.	1803	1875	Quinet, Edgard.......	History.
1798	1857	Compte, Auguste......	Philosophy.	1495	1553	Rabelais, Francois.....	Stories.
1621	1686	Conde, Prince de......	Soldier.	1639	1699	Racine, Jean.........	Drama.
1743	1794	Condorcet, Marquis de..	Philosophy.	1875	1937	Ravel, Maurice.......	Music.
1767	1830	Constant, Benjamin...	Literature.	1573	1613	Regnier, Mathurin.....	Poetry.
1842	1908	Coppée, Francois......	Poetry.	1823	1893	Renan, Ernest........	Religion.
1606	1684	Corneille, Pierre......	Drama.	1585	1642	Richelieu, Cardinal....	Statesman.
1792	1867	Cousin, Victor......	Metaphysics	1849	1926	Richepin, Jean........	Poetry.
1674	1762	Crebillon...........	Poetry.	1613	1680	Rochefoucauld, Duc de la	Morals.
1854	1928	Curel, Francois de....	Drama.	1661	1741	Rollin, Charles........	History.
1769	1832	Cuvier, George L......	Nat. History	1524	1585	Ronsard, Pierre de.....	Poet.
1840	1897	Daudet, Alphonse......	Fiction.	1868	1918	Rostand, Edmond......	Poetry.
1596	1650	Descartes, Rene......	Philosophy.	1760	1836	Rouget de Lisle.......	Literature.
1713	1784	Diderot, Denis......	Encyclopedia.	1712	1778	Rousseau, Jean J......	Philos.
1860	1935	Dreyfus, Col. Alfred...	Soldier.	1616	1703	Saint-Evremond.......	Literature.
1803	1870	Dumas, Alexander....	Fiction.	1737	1814	Saint Pierre Bernardin..	Fiction.
1824	1895	Dumas, Alexander, Jr...	Drama.	1675	1755	Saint-Simon..........	History.
1651	1715	Fenelon, Francois de S..	Relig., Liter.	1804	1869	Sainte-Beuve.........	Criticism.
1821	1890	Feuillet, Octave......	Fiction.	1567	1622	Sales (St. Francois de)..	Relig., Liter
1821	1880	Flaubert, Gustave.....	Novelist.	1804	1876	Sand, George.........	Fiction.
1851	1929	Foch, Ferdinand......	Soldier	1831	1908	Sardou, Victorien......	Drama.
1844	1924	France, Anatole.......	Fiction.	1696	1750	Saxe, Maurice de......	Soldier.
1337	1410	Froissart, Jean........	Chronicles	1791	1861	Scribe, Eugene........	Drama.
1838	1882	Gambetta, Leon......	Statesman.	1626	1696	Sevigne (Mme. de)....	Letters.
1811	1872	Gautier, Theophile....	Poetry.	1766	1817	Stael, Mme de........	Author.
1892	1896	Goncourt, Edmond de.	Literature	1804	1857	Sue, Eugene..........	Fiction.
1830	1870	Goncourt, Jules de.....	Literature.	1839	1907	Sully-Prudhomme.....	Poetry.
1787	1874	Guizot, Francois......	History.	1828	1893	Taine, Hippolyte A.....	History.
1560	1631	Hardy, Alexandre.....	Poetry, Dr.	1795	1856	Thierry, Augustin.....	History.
1851	1935	Hennique, Leon......	Dram., Fict.	1797	1877	Thiers, Adolphe.......	History.
1842	1905	Heredia, Joseph M. de.	Poetry.	1805	1859	Tocqueville, A. C. de...	History.
1857	1915	Hervieu..............	Drama.	1611	1675	Turenne, Vicomte de...	Soldier.
1802	1885	Hugo, Victor.......	Poetry, Fict.	1828	1905	Verne, Jules..........	Fiction.
1848	1907	Huvsmans, Joris K.....	Fiction.	1799	1863	Vigny, Alfred de......	Poetry.
1852	1931	Joffre, Joseph J. C.....	Soldier	1431	1484	Villon, (Corbier) Francois	Poetry.
1753	1800	Kleber, Jean B........	Soldier.	1598	1648	Voiture..............	Poetry.
1530	1563	La Boétie, Etienne de..	Morals.	1694	1778	Voltaire, (F. M. Arouet).	Fict., Religion
1645	1696	La Bruyere, Jean D.....	Morals.	1840	1902	Zola, Emile..........	Fiction.

George Sand, novelist and dramatist, was the daughter of Lieut. Maurice de Saxe and his wife, Sophie, daughter of a Paris pool room keeper. When 17 she was married to Baron Dudevant, by whom she had 2 children. Her real name, she said, was Armandine Lucile Aurore Dupin.

French Painters
Source: Biographical Records

B.	D.	Name	B.	D.	Name	B.	D.	Name
1836	1904	Bartholdi, F. A.	1833	1883	Dore, Gustave	1815	1875	Millet, J. F.
1848	1884	Bastien-Lepage, J.	1811	1889	Dupre, Jules	1594	1665	Poussin, Nicholas
1822	1899	Bonheur, Rosa	1852	1931	Forain, Jean L.	1758	1823	Prudhon, Pierre
1825	1905	Bouguereau, W.	1820	1876	Fromentin, Eugene	1824	1898	Puvis de Chavannes
1851	1933	Carrier-Belleuse, P.	1770	1837	Gerard, F.	1841	1919	Renoir, P. A.
1845	1902	Constant, Benj.	1824	1904	Gerome, J. L.	1840	1917	Rodin, Auguste
1796	1875	Corot, J. B. C.	1628	1715	Girardon, Fr.	1812	1867	Rousseau, P. E. T.
1819	1877	Courbet, Gustave	1839	1883	Goupil, Jules A.	1795	1858	Scheffer, Ary
1817	1878	Daubigny, C. F.	1725	1805	Greuze, J. B.	1863	1935	Signac, Paul
1748	1825	David, Louis J.	1741	1828	Houdon, J. A.	1813	1865	Troyon, Constant
1783	1856	David d'Angers, P. J.	1780	1867	Ingres, J. A. D.	1758	1835	Vernet, Carle
1834	1917	Degas, H. G. E.	1755	1841	Lebrun, Marie	1714	1789	Vernet, Claude J.
1799	1863	Delacroix, Eugene	1798	1880	Lemaire, Ph. H.	1789	1863	Vernet, Horace
1797	1856	Delaroche, Paul	1600	1682	Lorrain, Claude	1868	1940	Vuillard, Edouard
1807	1876	Diaz de la Pena, N. V.	1815	1891	Meissonier, J. L. E.	1684	1721	Watteau, Antoine

Bartholdi was the sculptor who made the Liberty Statue now in N. Y. Harbor.

Noted Germanic Personages
Source: Biographical Records; * indicates Austrian

Born	Died	Name	Subject	Born	Died	Name	Subject
1840	1905	Abbe, Ernst	Physicist	1812	1887	Krupp, Alfred	Industry
1207	1280	Albertus, Magnus	Scientist	1827	1891	Lagarde, Paul de	Patriot
1769	1860	Arndt, Ernst Moritz	Poet, Patriot	1741	1801	Lavater, Johann K.	Essays
1686	1739	Asam, Cosmos D.	Architect	1881	1919	Lehmbruck, Wilhelm	Sculpture
1692	1750	Asam, Egid Quirin	Architect	1844	1900	Leibl, Wilhelm	Painter
1685	1750	Bach, Johann Sebastian	Music	1646	1716	Leibnitz, Gottfried. von	Philosophy
1476	1545	Baldung, Hans	Painter	1729	1781	Lessing, Gotthold E.	Drama, Critic
1770	1827	Beethoven, Ludwig von	Music	1847	1935	Liebermann, Max	Painter
1844	1929	Benz, Carl	Engineer	1803	1873	Liebig, Justus von	Chemistry
1836	1907	Bergmann, Ernst von	Surgeon	1844	1909	Liliencron, Detlev von	Poet
1815	1898	Bismarck, Otto von	Statesman	1848	1896	Lilienthal, Otto	Aeronautics
1742	1819	Bluecher, Gebhart L.	Soldier	1811	1886	Liszt, Franz	Music
1827	1901	Boecklin, Arnold	Painter	1865	1937	Ludendorff, Erich	Soldier
1831	1910	Bodelschwingh,Fried.von	Religion,Edu.	1483	1546	Luther, Martin	Religion
1575	1624	Boehme, Jakob	Mystic	1837	1887	Marees, Hans von	Painter
1771	1848	Boyen, Hermann von	Soldier	1818	1883	Marx, Karl	Soc. Economy
1833	1897	Brahms, Johannes	Music	1260	1327	Meister. Eckehart	Mystic, Phil.
1829	1884	Brehm, Alfred	Zoologist	1497	1560	Melanchthon. Philipp	Reformer
1778	1842	Brentano, Clemens	Poet	1440	1494	Memling, Hans	Painter
1824	1896	Bruckner, Anton*	Music	1822	1884	Mendel, Gregor	Science
1811	1899	Bunsen, Robert	Physicist	1815	1905	Menzel, Adolf von	Painter
1473	1531	Burkmair, Hans	Painter	1733	1815	Mesmer, Friedrich A	Magnetism
1832	1908	Busch, Wilhelm	Poet, Painter	1800	1891	Moltke, Helmuth v.	Soldier
1754	1798	Carstens, Jakob A.	Painter	1804	1875	Moerike, Eduard.	Poet
1726	1801	Chodowiecki, Daniel	Painter	1817	1908	Mommsen, Theodor.	History
1740	1815	Claudius, Matthias	Poet	1756	1791	Mozart, Wolfang A*.	Music
1780	1831	Clausewitz, Carl von	Military	1844	1900	Nietzsche, Friedrich.	Philosophy
1783	1867	Cornelius, Peter	Painter	1853	1932	Ostwald, Wilhelm	Chemist
1472	1553	Cranach, Lucas	Painter	1789	1869	Overbeck, Friedrich	Painter
1834	1900	Daimler, Gottlieb	Engineer	1796	1835	Platen, August Graf von.	Poet
1606	1695	Derfflinger, Georg	Soldier	1831	1910	Raabe, Wilhelm	Novelist
1858	1913	Diesel, Rudolf	Engineer	1795	1886	Ranke, Leopold von.	History
1797	1848	Droste-Huelshoff, A. von	Poetess	1867	1922	Rathenau, Walther	Statesman
1471	1528	Duerer, Albrecht	Painter	1777	1857	Rauch, Christian.	Sculpture
1861	1935	Duisberg, Carl	Chemist	1873	1916	Reger, Max	Music
1854	1915	Ehrlich, Paul	Science	1816	1859	Rethel, Alfred.	Painter
1788	1857	Eichendorff, Joseph	Poet	1810	1874	Reuter, Fritz	Poet
1170	1220	Eschenbach, Wolfram von	Poet	1803	1884	Richter, Ludwig	Painter
1861	1922	Falkenhayn, Erich von	Soldier	1468	1531	Riemenschneider, Tilman	Sculpture
1829	1880	Feuerbach, Anselm	Painter	1875	1926	Rilke, Rainer Maria.	Poet
1762	1814	Fichte, Johann G	Philosophy	1845	1923	Roentgen, Wilhelm K.	Physics
1656	1723	Fischer von Erlach, J. B.	Architect	1788	1866	Rueckert, Friedrich.	Poet
1819	1898	Fontane, Theodor.	Novelist	1777	1810	Runge, Philipp O.	Painter
1816	1895	Freytag, Gustav	Novelist	1494	1576	Sachs, Hans	Poet
1774	1840	Friedrich, Kaspar David.	Painter	1779	1861	Savigny, Friedrich K.	Jurist
1782	1852	Froebel, Friedrich	Educator	1663	1736	Savoyen, Eugen von	Soldier
1777	1855	Gauss, Karl F.	Mathematics	1764	1850	Schadow, Johann G.	Sculpture
1868	1933	George, Stefan	Poet	1755	1813	Scharnhorst, G. I. D.	Soldier
1607	1676	Gerhardt, Paul	Poet	1775	1854	Schelling, Friedrich W.	Philosophy
1714	1787	Gluck, Christopher W.	Music	1759	1805	Schiller, Friedrich.	Drama, Poet
1760	1831	Gneisenau, August	Soldier	1781	1841	Schinkel, Karl Friedrich	Architect
1776	1848	Goerres, Joseph von	Writer	1767	1845	Schlegel, August W.	Poet, Transl't
1749	1832	Goethe, Johann W. von	Poet, Drama.	1768	1834	Schleiermacher, Friedrich	Philosophy
1801	1836	Grabbe, Christopher D.	Drama	1833	1913	Schlieffen, Alfred von.	Soldier
1791	1872	Grillparzer, Franz*	Drama	1822	1890	Schliemann. Heinrich.	Archaeology
1785	1863	Grimm, Jakob	Essays, Fict.	1862	1931	Schnitzler, Arthur*	Drama, Nov.
1786	1859	Grimm, Wilhelm	Essays, Fict.	1445	1488	Schongauer, Martin	Painter
1503	1529	Gruenewald, Matthias.	Painter	1788	1866	Schopenhauer, Arthur.	Philosophy
1400	1468	Gutenberg, Johannes	Inventor	1797	1828	Schubert, Franz*	Music
1834	1919	Haeckel, Ernst	Philos., Scien.	1810	1856	Schumann, Robert.	Music
1685	1759	Haendel, Georg Friedrich	Music	1804	1871	Schwind, Moritz von.	Painter
1844	1919	Hagenbeck, Carl	Zoologist	1816	1892	Siemens, Werner von.	Physicist
1730	1788	Hamann, Johann G	Philosopher	1868	1932	Slevogt, Max	Painter
1851	1930	Harnack, Adolf von	Religion	1861	1914	Spee, Maximilian	Admiral
1732	1809	Haydn, Joseph*	Music	1635	1701	Starhemberg, Ernst R*.	Soldier
1813	1863	Hebbel, Friedrich	Drama	1757	1831	Stein, Karl von	Statesman
1760	1826	Hebel, Johann Peter	Poet	1831	1897	Stephan, Heinrich von.	Postmaster
1770	1831	Hegel, Georg W. F.	Philosophy	1805	1868	Stifter, Adalbert*	Novelist
1797	1856	Heine, Heinrich	Poet	1817	1888	Storm, Theodor.	Poet
1821	1894	Helmholtz, Hermann von	Physics	1455	1533	Stoss, Veit	Sculpture
1744	1803	Herder, Johann G. von	Writer	1825	1899	Strauss, Johann*.	Music
1847	1921	Hildebrand, Adolf von.	Sculpture	1857	1928	Sudermann, Hermann.	Drama, Nov.
1847	1934	Hindenburg, Paul von	Soldier	1839	1924	Thoma, Hans.	Painter
1852	1925	Hoetzendorf,FranzC.von	Soldier	1842	1926	Thyssen, August.	Industry
1776	1822	Hoffmann, Ernst T. A.	Poet	1849	1930	Tirpitz, Alfred von.	Admiral
1767	1810	Hofer, Andreas*	Patriot	1834	1896	Treitschke, Heinrich von.	History
1497	1543	Holbein, Hans	Painter	1848	1911	Uhde, Fritz von	Painter
1770	1843	Hoelderlin, Friedrich	Poet	1787	1862	Uhland, Ludwig	Poet
1769	1859	Humboldt, Alexander von	Scientist	1821	1902	Virchow, Rudolf.	Physician
1767	1835	Humboldt, W. von	Scientist	1455	1529	Vischer, Peter.	Sculpture
1488	1523	Hutten, Ulrich von.	Religion	1751	1826	Voss, Johann H.	Poet,Transl't
1778	1852	Jahn, Friedrich Ludwig	Patriot	1165	1230	Walther v. d. Vogelweide	Poet
1763	1825	Jean, Paul	Novelist	1813	1883	Wagner, Richard.	Music
1859	1935	Junkers, Hugo	Engineer	1583	1634	Wallenstein, Albrecht von	Soldier
1832	1912	Justi, Carl	Art, Critic	1873	1934	Wassermann, Jakob.	Novelist
1724	1804	Kant, Immanuel	Philosophy	1786	1826	Weber, Karl Maria von.	Music
1784	1864	Klenze, Leo von	Architect	1733	1772	Wieland, Christoph M.	Poet
1571	1630	Kepler, Johannes	Astronomy	1853	1905	Wissmann, Hermann von	Explorer
1777	1811	Kleist, Heinrich von.	Drama, Nov.	1860	1903	Wolf, Hugo.	Music
1724	1803	Klopstock, Frederick G.	Poetry	1832	1920	Wundt, Wilhelm.	Philosophy
1843	1910	Koch, Robert.	Physician	1759	1830	York, Hans D L .	Soldier
1791	1813	Koerner, Karl Theodor.	Poet, Patriot	1838	1917	Zeppelin, Ferdin'd G von	Aeronaut
1440	1507	Krafft, Adam.	Sculpture	1859		Zimmermann, A. F. M.	Diplomat

Kopernicus, Nikolaus (Nicholas) Copernicus (Prussian or Polish), astronomer, born 1473; died 1543. German unless with * indicating Austrian.

Illustrious Men of Italy

Source: Casa Italiana Records, Columbia University. C—Approximate time.

Born	Died	Name	Subject	Born	Died	Name	Subject
1407	1472	Alberti, Leon Battista....	Auth-Arch.	1469	1527	Machiavelli, Nicolo......	Author
1749	1803	Alfieri, Vittorio..........	Auth-Dram.	1628	1694	Malpighi, Marcello.......	Bio. Scient.
1265	1321	Alighieri, Dante.........	Poet	1431	1506	Mantegna, Andrea......	Painter
1487	1531	Andrea del Sarto (Andrea Vannucchi)....	Painter	1447	1516	Manuzio, Aldo...........	Scholar
1387	1455	Fra Angelico (Il Beato) (Fra Giovanni da Fiesole)	Painter	1785	1873	Manzoni, Alessandro.....	Author
1492	1556	Aretino, Pietro...........	Author	1874	1937	Marconi, Guglielmo......	Wireless Inv.
1474	1533	Ariosto, Ludovico.......	Poet-Satirist	c1401	1443	Massaccio, Tommaso Guidi	Painter
1776	1856	Avogadro, Amedeo......	Scientist	1805	1872	Mazzini, Giuseppe.......	Author
1485	c1560	Bandello, Matteo........	Author	1798	1854	Melloni, Macedonio......	Physicist
1738	1794	Beccaria, Cesare.........	Writer	1698	1782	Metastasio, Pietro Trapassi	Poet
1430	1516	Bellini, Giovanni.........	Painter	1568	1649	Monteverdi, Claudio.....	Composer
1801	1835	Bellini, Vincenzo.........	Composer	1682	1771	Morgagni, Giovanni Battista.............	Anatomist
1598	1680	Bernini, Giovanni Lorenzo	Sculptor	1784	1840	Paganini, Nicolo........	Comp.-Viol.
1313	1375	Boccaccio, Giovanni......	Author	1524	1594	Palestrina, Giovanni Pier Luigi, detto..........	Composer
1434	1494	Boiardo, Matteo Maria...	Author	1729	1779	Parini, Giuseppe.........	Composer
1447	1510	Botticelli, Alessandro....	Painter	1855	1912	Pascoli, Giovanni.......	Poet
1566	1645	Bracciolini, Francesco....	Author	1710	1736	Pergolese, Giovanni Battista.............	Composer
1444	1514	Bramante, Francesco......	Architect	XVI	Cent.	Peri, Jacopo.............	Mus.-Dram.
1377	1444	Brunelleschi, Filippo.....	Arch.-Sculp.	1446	1524	Perugino, Pietro Vannucci, detto..........	Painter
1369	1444	Bruni, Leonardo..........	Author	1304	1374	Petrarca, Francesco......	Auth.-Schol
1550	1600	Bruno, Giordano..........	Philosopher	1746	1826	Piazzi, Giuseppe.........	Astronom.
1475	1564	Buonarotti, Michelangelo.	Paint.-Arch.	1416	1492	Piero della Francesca.....	Painter
1420	1498	Cabotto, Giovanni.......	Navig-Expl.	1454	1513	Pinturicchio.............	Painter
1477	1557	Cabotto, Sebastiano......	Navig-Expl.	1205	1278	Pisano, Niccolo..........	Auth.-Sculp. Architect
1697	1767	Canaletto (Antonio Canale)	Painter	1454	1494	Poliziano, Angelo.......	Author
1757	1822	Canova, Antonio.........	Sculptor	1254	1325	Polo, Marco.............	Explorer
1568	1639	Campanella, Tommaso...	Philosopher	1432	1484	Pulci, Luigi.............	Author
1836	1907	Carducci, Giosuè........	Poet-Critic	1371	1438	Della Quercia, Jacopo....	Sculptor
1478	1529	Castiglione, Baldesar....	Author	1483	1537	Raffaello, Sanzio........	Painter
1810	1861	Cavour, Camillo (Conte).	Statesman	1626	1694	Redi, Francesco.........	Natur.-Auth
1500	1571	Cellini, Benvenuto.......	Sculptor	1615	1673	Rosa, Salvator..........	Painter
1240	1302	Cimabue, Giovanni......	Painter	1792	1868	Rossini, Gioacchino.....	Composer
1451	1506	Colombo, Cristoforo.....	Navig-Expl.	1452	1498	Savonarola, Fra Girolamo	Auth.-Pre'r
1494	1534	Coreggio, Antonio Allegri, detto..............	Painter	1649	1725	Scarlatti, Alessandro.....	Composer
1830	1903	Cremona, Luigi..........	Mathemat.	1683	1757	Scarlatti, Domenico......	Composer
1863	1938	Dannunzio, Gabrielle.....	Poet, Soldier	1735	1757	Schiaparelli, Giovanni Virginio.............	Astronom.
1400	1482	Della Robbia, Lucca......	Sculptor	1818	1878	Secchi, Angelo..........	Astr.-Math
1818	1883	De Sanctis, Francesco....	Critic	1827	1884	Sella, Quintino..........	Hydr. Eng.
1616	1686	Dolci, Carlo.............	Painter	1441	1523	Signorelli, Luca.........	Painter
1386	1446	Donatello (Donato di Betto Bardi)........	Sculptor	1729	1799	Spallanzani, Lazzaro.....	Scientist
1433	1499	Ficino, Marsilio..........	Scholar	1664	1728	Stradivarius, Antonio....	Viol.-maker
1398	1481	Filelfo, Francesco........	Scholar	1692	1770	Tartini, Giuseppe.......	Violinist
1842	1911	Fogazzaro, Antonio......	Author	1544	1595	Tasso, Torquato.........	Author
1778	1827	Foscolo, Ugo............	Poet	1696	1770	Tiepolo, Gian Battista....	Painter
1564	1642	Galilei, Galileo..........	Astronom.	1512	1594	Tintoretto, Giacomo Robusti.............	Painter
1737	1798	Galvani, Luigi...........	Scientist	1477	1576	Tiziano, Veccellio.......	Painter
1807	1882	Garibaldi, Giuseppe......	Sold.-Patr.	1608	1649	Torricelli, Evangelista....	Math.-Phys Scientist
1378	1455	Ghiberti, Lorenzo........	Sculptor	1398	1482	Toscanelli, Paolo del Pozzo	Geog.-Astr.
1449	1494	Ghirlandaio, Domenico...	Painter	1396	1476	Uccello, Paolo, Paolo di Dono, detto..........	Painter
1477	1511	Giorgione, Giorgio Barbarelli...........	Painter	1512	1574	Vasari, Giorgio.........	Auth.-Paint.
1276	1336	Giotto, Angelo Bondone..	Painter	c1480	c1527	Verazzano, Giovanni da..	Explorer
1809	1850	Giusti, Giuseppe.........	Poet	1813	1901	Verdi, Giuseppe.........	Composer
1707	1793	Goldoni, Carlo...........	Playwright	1528	1588	Veronese, Paolo Caliari, detto..........	Painter
1713	1786	Gozzi, Gasparo..........	Author	1435	1488	Verocchio, Andrea.......	Paint-Sculp.
1420	1497	Gozzoli, Benozzo........	Painter	1451	1512	Vespucci, Amerigo.......	Explorer
1483	1540	Guicciardini, Giovanni...	Author	1670	1744	Vico, Giovanni Battista...	Auth.-Phil.
:1630	c1695	Guarnerius, Andrea.....	Violin-makers	1745	1827	Volta, Alessandro........	Elec. Discov
1683	1745	Guarnerius, Giuseppe....		1861	1940	Zocchi, Arnaldo.........	Sculptor
1424	1504	Landino, Cristofero......	Scholar				
1175	?	Leonardo da Pisa........	Mathemat				
1452	1519	Leonardo da Vinci.......	Paint.-Sculp				
1822	1837	Leopardi, Giacomo.......	Author-Poet				
1406	1469	Lippi, Filippo...........	Painter				
1449	1492	Lorenzo de' Medici (Lorenzo Il Magnifico)..	Auth.-Poet, Patr.-States				

Leonardo da Vinci's "Mona Lisa" is said to have been posed by Isabella d'Este, the Marchioness of Mantua, about 1504. The picture was stolen from the Louvre Gallery, Paris, but was returned. Leonardo, or Lionardo, was born in Vinci, near Empoli, Italy, and died in Cloux, near Amboise, France. He settled in France in 1516, by invitation of Francis I.

The art of painting is said to have been introduced in Rome from Etruria by Quintus Fabius, 291 B.C. After the death of Augustus no painter of eminence appeared for several ages. Ludius was the last, about 14 A.D. Painting on canvas was known in Rome as early as 66 A.D. Cimabue, of Florence, is regarded the first in rank in the restoration of painting in Italy.

Spanish Painters

Source: Biographical Records

B.	D.	Name	B.	D.	Name	B.	D.	Name
1786	1827	Alvarez, Don Jose	1630	1691	Leal Valdes, Juan	1624	1700	Roldan, Pedro
1601	1667	Cano, Alonzo	1815	1894	Madrazo, Federico	1520	1590	Sanchez Coello, Alonso
1641	1685	Carreno de Miranda, Juan	1509	1586	Morales, Luis de (El Divino Morales)	1863	1923	Sorolla y Bastida, J.
1600	1680	Espinosa, Jacinto Jeronimo de	1618	1682	Murillo, B. E.	1548	1625	Theotocopuli, Domenico (El Greco)
1746	1828	Goya y Lucientes, F.	1551	1609	Pantoja de la Cruz, Juan	1599	1660	Velasquez, Diego
1838	1874	Fortuny, Mariano	1597	1628	Ribalta, Francisco de	1598	1662	Zurbaran, Franc.
			1588	1656	Ribera, Jose			

Illustrious Men and Women of Russia

Sources: Biographical Records

Born	Died	Name	Subject	Born	Died	Name	Subject
1817	1900	Aivazovsky, Ivan K....	Painter	1865	1942	Merezhkovsky, Dimitri S.........	Author
1791	1859	Aksakov, Sergei T.....	Author	1842	1904	Mikhailovsky, Nicholas.	Critic
1871	1919	Andreyev, Leonid N...	Author	1845	1900	Muraviev, Michael N...	Statesman
1843	1902	Antokolsky, Mark M...	Sculptor	1835	1881	Mussorgsky, Modest P..	Composer
1671	1728	Apraksin, Feodor M....	Statesman	1862	1887	Nadson, Semen Y......	Poet
1841	1893	Apukhtin, Alexei N....	Poet	1821	1877	Nekrasov, Nicholas A..	Poet
1861	1906	Arensky, Anton S......	Composer	1848	1936	Nemirovitch-Danchenko, Vasili I.........	Author
1846	1924	Arkhangelsky, Alex. A.	Composer	1824	1861	Nikitin, Ivan S........	Poet
1765	1812	Bagration, Peter I....	Soldier	1605	1681	Nikon (Nikita Minin)..	Patriarch
1866 ?	1924	Bakst, Leon S.........	Painter	1744	1818	Novikov, Nicholas I....	Statesman
1836	1910	Balakirev, Mily A.....	Composer	1737	1808	Orlov, Alexei G., Count	Soldier
1746	1819	Baranov, Alexander A.	Statesman	1823	1886	Ostrovsky, Alexander...	Dramatist
1761	1818	Barclay de Tolly, M. A.	Soldier	1743	1817	Oushakov, Feodor F....	Admiral
1860	1884	Bashkirtseva, Maria.....	Author; Painter	1860	1941	Paderewski, Ignace Jan	Polish Statesman, Pianist
1857	1927	Bekhterev, Vladimir M.	Neuropatholog.	1718	1783	Panin, Nikita I........	Statesman
1811	1848	Belinsky, Vissarion G..	Critic	1849	1936	Pavlov, Ivan P	Physiologist
1779	1852	Bellingshausen, Faddei..	Explorer	1885	1931	Pavlova, Anna M......	Dancer
1870	1928	Benois, Alex. N......	Painter	1822	1910	Petipa, Marius I.......	Ballet-master
1681	1741	Bering, Vitus J.......	Explorer	1810	1881	Pirogov, Nicholas I.....	Surgeon
1829	1897	Bestuzhev-Ryumin, K..	Historian	1820	1881	Pisemsky, Alexei F.....	Author
1880	1921	Blok, Alexander A.....	Poet	1857	1918	Plekhanov, Georgi V ...	Writer
1834	1887	Borodin, Alexander P...	Composer	1859	1905	Popov, Alexander S....	Inventor
1751	1825	Bortnyansky, Dimitri..	Composer	1739	1791	Potemkin, G. A., Prince	Statesman
1799	1852	Brullov, Karl P	Painter	1839	1888	Przhevalsky, Nicholas..	Explorer
1873	1938	Chaliapin, Feodor I....	Singer	1799	1837	Pushkin, Alexander S...	Poet
1835	1918	Cui, César A	Composer	1866	1920	Rebikov, Vladimir I....	Composer
1801	1872	Dal, Vladimir I.......	Lexicographer	1844	1930	Repin, Ilya Y.........	Painter
1813	1869	Dargomizhsky, Alex. ...	Composer	1844	1908	Rimsky-Korsakov, N....	Composer
1744	1810	Dashkova, Ekaterina R.	Littérateur	1856	1919	Rozanov, Vasil V	Author
1743	1816	Derzhavin, Gavrila R...	Poet	1848	1909	Rozhestvensky, Zinovi	Admiral
1872	1929	Diaghilev, Sergei P.....	Ballet Producer	1829	1894	Rubinstein, Anton G ...	Composer
1821	1881	Dostoyevsky, Feodor M.	Author	1835	1881	Rubinstein, Nicholas G.	Musician
1560?	1633	Filaret (Feo. Romanov)	Patriarch	1370	1430	Rublyov, Andrei.......	Ikons Painter
1745	1792	Fonvizin, Denis I ...	Author	1725	1796	Rumyantsev-Zadunaisky, Peter A., Count.	Statesman
1865	1936	Glazunov, Alexander K.	Composer	1854	1915	Savina, Maria G.......	Actress
1803	1857	Glinka, Michael I......	Composer	1871	1915	Scriabin, Alexander N..	Composer
1809	1852	Gogol, Nicholas V.....	Author	1763	1831	Senyavin, Dimitri N...	Admiral
1870	1940	Goldman, Emma......	Anarchist	1820	1871	Serov, Alexander N....	Composer
1862	1916	Golitzin, Boris, Prince.	Physicist	1865	1911	Serov, Valentin A......	Painter
1643	1714	Golitzin, Vasil, Prince.	Statesman	1788	1863	Shchepkin, Michael S..	Actor
1776	1831	Golovnin, Vasil M......	Admiral	1652	1719	Sheremetev, Boris, count	Soldier
1812	1891	Goncharov, Ivan A.....	Author	1844	1918	Sheremetev, Serg., count	Historian
1868	1936	Gorky, Maxim.........	Author	1814	1861	Shevchenko, Taras.....	Ukraine's Poet
1795	1829	Griboyedov, Alex. S....	Dramatist	1831	1898	Shishkin, Ivan I.......	Painter
1853	1934	Grot, Konstantin Y....	Lexicographer	1843	1882	Skobelev, Michael D....	Soldier
1780	1853	Haas, Feodor P........	Philanthropist	1820	1879	Soloviev, Sergei M	Historian
1812	1870	Herzen, Alexander I....	Author	1853	1900	Soloviev, Vladimir M...	Philosopher
1859	1935	Ippolitov-Ivanov, M ...	Composer	1772	1839	Speransky. Mich.,Count	Statesman
1766	1826	Karamzin, Nicholas M.	Historian	1863	1938	Stanislavsky, Konst. S.	Actor
1818	1882	Kaufman, Konstantin.	Statesman	1863	1911	Stolypin, Peter A.......	Statesman
1783	1836	Kiprensky, Orest A.....	Painter	1848	1916	Surikov, Vasili I.......	Painter
1841	1911	Klyuchevsky, Vasily ...	Historian	1834	1912	Suvorin, Alexei S.......	Editor; Author
1874	1920	Kolchak, Alexander V..	Statesman	1729	1800	Suvorov, Alexander V..	Soldier
1809	1842	Koltsov, Alexei V......	Poet	1843	1923	Tagantsev, Nicholas S..	Jurist
1844	1927	Koni, Anatoli F.......	Jurist	1856	1915	Taneyev, Sergei I......	Composer
1853	1921	Korolenko, Vladimir G.	Author	1750	1795	Tatishchev, Vasili N....	Historian
1817	1885	Kostomarov, Nicholas..	Historian	1860	1904	Tchekhov, Anton P	Author
1850	1891	Kovalevskaya, Sophia..	Mathematician	1875	1911	Tolstoy, Alexei, Count.	Author
1842	1921	Kropotkin, Peter, Prince	Geographer	1828	1910	Tolstoy, Lev N., Count.	Author
1770	1846	Krusenstern, A. J. von.	Admiral	1776	1857	Tropinin, Vasili A	Painter
1768	1844	Krylov, Ivan A........	Fabulist	1879	1940	Trotsky, Leon (Lev Bronstein).......	Revolutionist
1870	1938	Kuprin, Alexander I....	Author	1866	1938	Trubetskoy, Paolo P...	Sculptor
1878	1927	Kustodiyev, Boris M...	Painter	1840	1893	Tschaikovsky, Peter I..	Composer
1745	1813	Kutuzov, M. L., Prince.	Soldier	1818	1883	Turgenev, Ivan S......	Author
1870	1924	Lenin, Vladimir I.....	Statesman	1848	1926	Vasnetsov, Viktor M...	Painter
1814	1841	Lermontov, Michael Y.	Poet	1842	1904	Vereshchagin, Vasili....	Painter
1831	1895	Leskov, Nicholas S....	Author	1782	1856	Vorontsov,Mich.,Count	Soldier
1861	1900	Levitan, Isaak I.......	Painter	1794	1832	Vorontsov, Semen,count	Statesman
1793	1856	Lobachevsky, Nicholas.	Mathematician	1856	1910	Vrubel, Michael A.P...	Painter
1711c.	1765	Lomonosov, Michael V.	Scientist	1849	1915	Witte, Sergei Y., Count.	Statesman
1855	1914	Lyadov, Anatol K......	Composer	1847	1894	Yablochkov, Paul N....	Inventor
1857	1918	Lyapunov, Alexand'r M.	Mathematician	1847	1921	Zhukovsky, Nicholas E.	Mathematician
1821	1897	Maikov, Apollon N	Poet	1783	1852	Zhukovsky, Vas.li A....	Poet
1848	1904	Makarov, Stepan O.....	Admiral				
1845	1916	Mechnikov, Ilya I......	Biologist				
1819	1883	Melnikov, Paul I.......	Author				
1834	1907	Mendeleyev, Dimitri I.	Chemist				
1663?	1729	Menshikov, Alex. D...	Statesman				

Turkish (Sultans) Rulers Since 1481

Source: Historical Records

(1481) Bajazet II, son.
(1512) Selim I, son.
(1520) Solyman II, the Magnificent, son.
(1566) Selim II, son.
(1574) Amurath III, killed his brothers.
(1595) Mahommed III, son. Killed his brothers.
(1603) Ahmed I, son.
(1617) Mustapha I, brother; (1622) strangled.
(1618) Osman II, nephew, strangled.
(1623) Amurath IV, brother of Osman II.
(1640) Ibrahim, brother; strangled.
(1648) Mahommed IV, son.
(1687) Solyman III, brother.
(1691) Ahmed II.
(1695) Mustapha II, son of Mahomet IV.
(1703) Ahmed III, brother.

(1730) Mahommed V (Mahmud I).
(1754) Osman III, brother.
(1757) Mustapha III, brother.
(1774) Abdul Ahmed (Hamid I) (Ahmed IV).
(1789) Selim III, son of Mustapha III.
(1807) Mustapha IV.
(1808) Mahomet VI, brother.
(1839) Abdul Medjid, son.
(1861) Abdul-Aziz, brother.
(1876) Amurath V (Murad) deposed.
(1876) Abdul Hamid II, brother.
(1909) Mohammed V.
(1918) Mohammed VI.
In 1923 Mustapha Kemal Pasha was elected President, with the title Ataturk. He died in 1938 and was succeeded by Gen. Ismet Inonu.

3

Norwegian Authors
Source: Biographical Records

B.	D.	Name	Subject	B.	D.	Name	Subject
1813	1896	Aasen, Ivar............	Poet	1849	1906	Kielland, A. L.........	Fiction.
1866	1920	Andersen, Tryggve.....	Fiction.	1865	1926	Kinck, Hans E........	Fict., Drama.
1832	1910	Bjornson, B...........	Poet, Drama.	1870	1924	Kjaer, Nils..........	Fict., Drama.
1833	1907	Bugge, Sophus........	Folklore	1833	1908	Lie, Jonas...........	Fiction.
1853	1930	Bull, Jacob B.........	Fiction.	1810	1863	Munch, P. A.........	History.
1851	1921	Garborg, Arne........	Fiction.	1835	1918	Sars, J. E...........	History.
1857	1929	Helberg, Gunnar......	Drama.	1846	1905	Skram, Amalie.......	Fiction.
1684	1754	Holberg, Ludvig......	Drama, Hist.	1807	1874	Welhaven, J. S. C....	Poet.
1828	1906	Ibsen, Henrik........	Drama.	1808	1845	Wergeland, Henrik....	Poet, Drama

Swedish Authors
Source: Biographical Records

B.	D.	Name	Subject	B.	D.	Name	Subject
1793	1866	Almquist, C. J. L.....	Fiction	1843	1921	Montelius, Oscar.......	Hist., Archael.
1859	1927	Arrhenius, Svante A...	Chemist	1842	1919	Retzius, Gustaf.......	Anthropology
1740	1795	Bellman, C. M........	Poet	1630	1702	Rudbeck Olof........	Medicine
1779	1848	Berzelius, Jakob......	Chemist	1804	1877	Runeberg, J. L.......	Poet
1801	1865	Bremer, Fredrika.....	Fiction	1828	1895	Rydberg, Viktor......	Poet, Phil.
1860	1911	Froding, Gustaf......	Poet	1793	1823	Stagnelius, E. J	Poet
1783	1847	Geijer, E. G.........	Poet, Hist.	1598	1672	Stiernhielm, Georg...	Poet, Phil.
1860	1925	Hansson, Ola........	Poet, Fict.	1849	1912	Strindberg, August...	Drama, Fict.
1864	1930	Karlfeldt, Erik Axel...	Poet	1688	1772	Swedenborg, Emanuel..	Philosopher
1858	1940	Lagerlof, Selma......	Fiction	1782	1846	Tegner, Esaias.......	Poet
1707	1778	Linne, Carl von.......	Botanist				

Noted Swiss Personages
Source: Biographical Records

B.	D.	Name	Subject	B.	D.	Name	Subject
1807	1873	Agassiz, Louis........	Scientist	1825	1898	Meyer, Conrad F.......	Poet, Novelist
1815	1887	Bachnofen, Johann....	Jurist	1493	1541	Paracelsus, Theophrastus.	Science
1808	1881	Bluntschli, Jon. Kaspar..	Jurist	1746	1827	Pestalozzi, Johann H......	Educator
1818	1898	Burkhardt, Jakob.....	History	1712	1778	Rousseau, Jean Jacques...	Essays
1509	1564	Calvin, Jean.........	Religion	1740	1799	Saussure, Benedict.......	Geology
1787	1875	Dufour, William Henri..	Soldier	1465	1522	Schiner, Mathias.......	Religion
1828	1910	Dunant, Henri........	Phil., Founder of Red Cross	1845	1924	Spitteler, Karl........	Poetry
				1766	1817	Stael, Madame de....	Fiction
1848	1931	Forel, Auguste.......	Sociology	1799	1846	Toepffer, Rodolphe....	Writer
1745	1832	Fussli, Heinrich......	History	1797	1847	Vinet, Alexandre.....	Poetry, Phil.
1797	1854	Gotthelf, Jeremias....	Fiction	1417	1490	Von Flue, Nikolas....	Patriot
1708	1777	Haller, Albrecht von...	Physician	1825	1899	Welti, Emile........	Jurist
1819	1890	Keller, Gottfried......	Poet, Novelist	1484	1531	Zwingli, Ulrich.......	Religion

Swiss Painters
Source: Biographical Records

B.	D.	Name	B.	D.	Name	B.	D.	Name
1831	1910	Anker, Albert	1741	1825	Füssli (Fusely), J. H.	1828	1905	Koller. Rudolf
1828	1890	Bocion, F. L. D.	1813	1871	Girardet, Charles	1702	1798	Liotard, Jean Etienne
1827	1901	Boecklin, Arnold	1806	1874	Gleyre, Charles	1794	1835	Robert, Leopold
1850	1921	Burnand, Eugene	1736	1813	Graff, Anton	1858	1899	Segantini, Giovanni
1810	1864	Calame, Alexandre	1853	1918	Hodier, Ferdinand	1862	1912	Welti, Albert
1802	1877	Diday, Francois						

Sculptor (1820–1891) Vela, Vicenso

Ancient Authors, Greek (B. C. years are in bold face.)
Source: Historical Records

B.	D.	Name.	Subj.	B.	D.	Name.	Subj.	B.	D.	Name.	Subj.
389	**314**	Aeschines........	Orat.	**450**	...	Empedocles........	Philos.	**207**	**122**	Polybius........	Hist.
525	**456**	Aeschylus........	Dram.	...	**118**	Epictetus........	Stoic.	**570**	**500**	Pythagoras......	Philos.
...	**550**	Aesop............	Tales	**342**	**270**	Epicurus........	Philos.	**600**	...	Sappho..........	Poet.
563	**478**	Anacreon........	Poet	**480**	**406**	Euripides........	Dram.	**556**	**469**	Simonides.......	Poet
500	**428**	Anaxagoras.....	Philos.	**576**	**480**	Heraclitus........	Philos.	**495**	**405**	Sophocles.......	Drama
287	**212**	Archimedes.....	Physi.	**484**	**424**	Herodotus.......	Hist.	...	**63**	**24**	Strabo.........	Geog.
448	**380**	Aristophanes.....	Dram.	...	**735**	Hesiod..........	Poet.	**600**	**540**	Thales..........	Philos.
384	**322**	Aristotle........	Philos.	**460**	**377**	Hippocrates.....	Medic.	**530**	**460**	Themistocles....	Philos.
...	**194**	Athenaeus......	Antiq.	**962**	**927**	Homer..........	Poet.	...	**255**	Theocritus......	Poet.
460	**370**	Democritus......	Philos.	**436**	**338**	Isocrates........	Orat.	**382**	**287**	Theophrastus....	Philos.
310	**240**	Callimachus.....	Poet.	**342**	**292**	Menander.......	Dram.	**471**	**401**	Thucydides.....	Hist.
382	**322**	Demosthenes....	Orat.	**522**	**443**	Pindar..........	Poet.	**280**	...	Timon..........	Philos.
50	**13**	Diodorus........	Hist.	**429**	**347**	Plato...........	Philos.	**490**	...	Zeno...........	Philos
...	**7**	Dionysius.......	Hist.	**49**	**120**	Plutarch........	Biog.	**430**	**357**	Xenophon......	Hist.

Ancient Authors, Latin (B. C. years are in light face)
Source: Historical Records

B.	D.	Name	Subj.	B.	D.	Name	Subj.	B.	D.	Name	Subj.
330	390	Ammianus, M ...	Hist.	59	17	Livy...........	Hist.	35	95	Quintilian.......	Critic.
125	200	Apuleius........	Satir.	38	65	Lucan..........	Poet.	86	34	Sallust.........	Hist.
130	175	Aulus Gellius....	Satir.	180	103	Lucilius........	Satir.	5	65	Seneca.........	Moral.
475	524	Boethius........	Philos.	96	52	Lucretius.......	Philos.	25	100	Silius..........	Poet.
102	44	Caesar, Julius...	Hist.	43	104	Martial........	Poet.	61	96	Status.........	Poet.
232	147	Cato, the Elder...	Orat.	100	30	Nepos.........	Hist.	70	160	Suetonius......	Biog.
87	54	Catullus........	Poet.	43	18	Ovid..........	Poet.	55	117	Tacitus........	Hist.
107	43	Cicero..........	Orat.	34	62	Persius........	Satir.	185	159	Terence........	Dram.
365	408	Claudian........	Poet.	254	184	Plautus........	Dram	54	18	Tibullus.......	Poet.
65	8	Horace.........	Poet.	23	79	Pliny..........	Natur.	70	19	Vergil.........	Poet.
60	140	Juvenal........	Satir.	62	113	Pliny the Youn'r.	Essays	70	16	Vitruvius......	Arch.

Tacitus, the son-in-law of Agricola, left an account of the German people, based on his own travels and partly on Caesar and other authorities. He was famous as an orator and historian.

Amendments to the Nationality Act

(Passed by the 77th Congress)

Section 701. Notwithstanding the provisions of sections 303 and 326 of this Act, any person not a citizen, regardless of age, who has served or hereafter serves honorably in the military or naval forces of the United States during the present war and who, having been lawfully admitted to the United States, including its Territories and possessions, shall have been at the time of his enlistment or induction a resident thereof, may be naturalized upon compliance with all the requirements of the naturalization laws except that (1) no declaration of intention and no period of residence within the United States or any State shall be required; (2) the petition for naturalization may be filed in any court having naturalization jurisdiction regardless of the residence of the petitioner; (3) the petitioner shall not be required to speak the English language, sign his petition in his own handwriting, or meet any educational test; and (4) no fee shall be charged or collected for making, filing, or docketing the petition for naturalization, or for the final hearing thereon, or for the certification of naturalization, if issued:

Provided, however, That (1) there shall be included in the petition the affidavits of at least two credible witnesses, citizens of the United States, stating that each such witness personally knows the petitioner to be a person of good moral character, attached to the principles of the Constitution of the United States, and well disposed to the good order and happiness of the United States, (2) the service of the petitioner in the military or naval forces of the United States shall be proved by affidavits, forming part of the petition, of at least two citizens of the United States, members or former members during the present war of the military or naval forces of the noncommissioned or warrant officer grade or higher (who may be the witnesses described in clause (1) of this proviso) or by a duly authenticated copy of the record of the executive department having custody of the record of petitioner's service, showing that the petitioner is or was during the present war a member serving honorably in such armed forces, and (3) the petition shall be filed not later than one year after the termination of the effective period of those titles of the Second War Powers Act, 1942, for which the effective period as specified in the last title thereof.

The petitioner may be naturalized immediately if prior to the filing of the petition the petitioner and the witnesses required by the foregoing proviso shall have appeared before and been examined by a representative of the Immigration and Naturalization Service.

Section 702. During the present war, any person entitled to naturalization under section 701 of this Act, who while serving honorably in the military or naval forces of the United States is not within the jurisdiction of any court authorized to naturalize aliens, may be naturalized in accordance with all the applicable provisions of section 701 without appearing before a naturalization court.

The petition for naturalization of any petitioner under this section shall be made and sworn to before, and filed with, a representative of the Immigration and Naturalization Service designated by the Commissioner or a Deputy Commissioner.

Amendment to Nationalize Ex-Alien Soldiers

Section 323. A person who, while a citizen of the United States and during the first or second World War, entered the military or naval service of any country at war with a country with which the United States was or is at war, who has lost citizenship of the United States by reason of any oath or obligation taken for the purpose of entering such service, or by reason of entering or serving in such armed forces, and who intends to reside permanently in the United States, may be naturalized by taking before any naturalization court specified in subsection (a) of section 301, the oaths prescribed by section 335.

Any such person who has lost citizenship of the United States during the second World War may, if he so desires, be naturalized by taking, before any diplomatic or consular officer of the United States abroad, the oaths prescribed by section 335.

For the purposes of this section, the second World War shall be deemed to have commenced on Sept. 1, 1939, and shall continue until such time as the United States shall cease to be in a state of war.

Certified copies of such oath shall be sent by such diplomatic or consular officer or such court to the Department of State and to the Department of Justice.

1917-1918 Draft Records Are Proof of Birth

The cards of 24,000,000 men who signed for the draft registration in 1917 and 1918 were transferred from the War Department archives to the Census Bureau where they are available as a source of evidence for individuals who have no birth certificates.

The records, according to Director J. C. Capt of the Bureau, contain age and place of birth and citizenship information of all first World War draft registrants.

An applicant may have 1917-18 draft records searched by furnishing the Census Bureau with his name, date and place of birth, permanent residence at time of registration, name of the place where registered and $1. For a photostatic copy of the draft card the fee is $2, and for a certification under seal, $3.

Information on age and place of birth also may be obtained from census of population records on file in the Census Bureau. Unlike information from the draft records, which can be furnished to any-one, these individual census records are confidential and can be released only on the written authorization of individuals to whom they relate.

During the 1941-1942 fiscal year the Census Bureau made 726,500 searches in response to requests.

Acceptance of Conditional War Gifts to U. S.

A 1942 law, signed by the President, provides that—To further the war program of the United States, the Secretary of the Treasury is authorized to accept or reject on behalf of the United States any gift of money or other property, real or personal, or services, made on condition that it be used for a particular war purpose. He may convert into money at the best terms available, any such gift of property other than money.

The Secretary of the Treasury, in order to effectuate the purposes for which gifts accepted under this title are made, shall from time to time allocate the money in such special deposit account to such of the various appropriations available for the purchase of war material and the furtherance of the war program of the United States as in his judgment will best effectuate the intent of the donors, and such money is hereby appropriated and shall be available for expenditure for the purposes of the appropriations to which allocated.

Holds His Breath for 20 Minutes, 5 Seconds

In the interest of science, Eugene J. Frechette, Jr., a 20-year-old student at Wesleyan University, Middletown, Conn., stopped breathing (March 6, 1942) for 20 minutes and five seconds, setting a record. The test was made in a laboratory to demonstrate the capacity of human endurance and to prove that reflex action eventually would force a person to breathe even against his wish. The laboratory technique calls for the subject to over-breathe for three minutes and then to exhale three deep breaths of pure oxygen. After that the subject, who receives no other special chemical aid, sits as quietly as possible without breathing. Prechette said in describing his sensations: "You feel as if you were dying."

Foundation is created are the promotion of elee-mosynary, philanthropic and charitable means of any all of the means of human progress, whether they be for the benefit of religious, charitable, benevolent or education institutions or public benefactions of whatsoever name or nature." The discretion of the Trustees regarding disposition of the income from the Fund, for purposes indicated, shall not be questioned, except for a flagrant abuse thereof.

The Daniel and Florence Guggenheim Foundation, New York City, has for its objects "the promotion, through charitable and benevolent activities, the well-being of mankind throughout the world."

W. K. Kellogg Foundation, Battle Creek, Mich. Purpose: To advance the health, education and well-being of children without regard to race, creed or geographical boundary." The present program is made up of national and international health promotion activities, the granting of fellowships and administration of the Michigan Community Health Project which involves seven counties in southwestern Michigan.

The New York Foundation was incorporated in 1909. Its objects, for which the income may be expended, are "to receive and maintain a fund or funds and to apply the income thereof to altruistic purposes, charitable, benevolent, educational or otherwise within the United States of America, as the Trustees may determine."

Phelps-Stokes Fund, of New York City, incorporated in 1911, to improve housing conditions in New York City and to encourage practical education for handicapped people.

The Alfred P. Sloan Foundation is confining its present activities to the field of economic education. Within this field it makes grant-in-aid to fully accredited educational institutions of recognized standing to carry out specific projects. Among its current beneficiaries are: The University of Chicago for its Round Table of the Air; New York University for its Film Library; the Public Affairs Committee of New York for its pamphlet series; the University of Pennsylvania for its Tax Institute; Massachusetts Institute of Technology and

the University of Denver for special groups of sponsored fellowships; the Universities of Kentucky, Florida, and Vermont for experiments in applied economics.

The Cleveland Foundation, a community trust, is an agency organized for the permanent administration of funds placed in trust for public educational or charitable purposes for benefit of inhabitants of Cleveland and vicinity and other communities within Ohio as designated by donors. Illustrative purposes are: assisting public charitable or educational institutions; promoting scientific research for the advancement of human knowledge and the alleviation of human suffering; providing scholarships to young men or women of slender means; care of the sick, aged and helpless; care of needy men, women and children; improvement of living and working condition; providing facilities for public recreation; promotion of social and domestic hygiene, promotion of sanitation and measures for the prevention of disease; research into the causes of ignorance, poverty, crime and vice.

The Henry C. Frick Educational Commission was set up in 1909 in Pittsburgh with an original fund of $250,000, later increased to $2,500,000, by Henry C. Frick for improvement of the teaching in Pittsburgh public schools. Assets at last report were $2,825,530 and the amount expended $1,449,293.

The A. W. Mellon Educational and Charitable Trust, of Pittsburgh, Pa., founded by Andrew W. Mellon in a deed of trust dated Dec. 30, 1930, with an indenture dated June 6, 1935, is to be administered and operated exclusively for the benefit of such religious, charitable, scientific, literary and educational purposes as shall be in furtherance of the public welfare and tend to promote the well-doing and well-being of mankind, or for the use of the United States, any state, territory, or any political subdivision thereof, or the District of Columbia, for such exclusively public purposes as the Trustees shall determine.

The Chicago Community Trust, like similar trusts, was established not for profit but for better conservation and use of charitable trust funds.

Estimated U. S. Population, Jan. 1, 1942

Source: United States Bureau of the Census

The latest estimate of the population of continental United States, as of Jan. 1, 1942—133,965,000—"subject to still further revision" was announced by the Bureau of the Census on Sept. 28, 1942.

Age and Year	All Classes			Age and Year	All Classes		
	Total	Male	Female		Total	Male	Female
1942				1942			
All ages....	133,965,237	67,106,274	66,858,963	40 to 44......	8,953,908	4,472,144	4,481,764
Under 5......	11,237,440	5,719,782	5,517,658	45 to 49......	8,351,544	4,224,375	4,127,169
5 to 9......	10,516,686	5,334,004	5,182,682	50 to 54......	7,518,671	3,856,852	3,661,819
10 to 14......	11,392,588	5,779,059	5,613,529	55 to 59......	6,153,328	3,161,863	2,991,465
15 to 19......	12,244,278	6,165,968	6,078,310	60 to 64......	4,865,762	2,464,717	2,401,045
20 to 24......	11,850,326	5,852,927	5,997,399	65 to 69......	3,883,197	1,925,886	1,957,311
25 to 29......	11,242,505	5,507,266	5,735,239	70 to 74......	2,797,937	1,367,278	1,430,659
30 to 34......	10,505,183	5,179,837	5,325,346	75 and over...	2,719,375	1,271,887	1,447,488
35 to 39......	9,732,509	4,822,429	4,910,080	Median age...	29.3	29.3	29.4

Whites, by the above estimate, numbered 120,-215,770 (males, 60,356; females, 59,859,051). Non-whites, 13,749,467 (males, 6,749,555; females,

6,999,912).

The estimated total population, May 1, 1940, to Dec. 1, 1941, by months, was as follows—

Dec. 1, 1941........133,858,168	May	1, 1941......132,994,513	Nov.	1, 1940........132,463,919
Nov. 1, 1941........133,759,588	April	1, 1941......132,895,847	Oct.	1, 1940........132,357,331
Oct. 1, 1941........133,643,259	March	1, 1941......132,802,335	Sept.	1, 1940........132,229,400
Sept. 1, 1941........133,507,547	Feb.	1, 1941......132,719,387	Aug.	1, 1940........132,087,447
Aug. 1, 1941........133,360,787	Jan.	1, 1941......132,637,933	July	1, 1940........131,970,224
July 1, 1941........133,217,064			June	1, 1940........131,858,325
June 1, 1941........133,098,802	Dec.	1, 1940......132,550,825	May	1, 1940........131,756,967

Other population estimates are on page 469.

American Mother of the Year

Source: The Golden Rule Foundation Mothers' Committee; 60 East 42nd St., New York City

The American Mother is selected annually from nominations sent to the committee. The choice is based on these requirements; she must be a successful mother, as evidenced by the character and achievements of her children; she must embody those traits most highly regarded in mothers—courage, moral strength, patience, affection, kindness, understanding, homemaking ability; she must have a sense of social and world relationships and must have been active in her own community betterment or in some other service for public benefit.

Year	Name	Home
1935	Mrs. Fletcher M. Johnson	Gainesville, Ga.
1936	Mrs. James R. Smith	Claremont, Calif.
1937	Mrs. Carl R. Gray	Omaha, Neb.
1938	Mrs. Grace Noll Crowell	Dallas, Tex.
1939	Mrs. Elias Compton	Wooster, Ohio.
1940	Mrs. Charles H. Mayo	Rochester, Minn.
1941	Mrs. Dena Shelby Diehl	Danville, Ky.
1942	Mrs. William N. Berry	Greensboro, N. C.

The Mothers' Day paraphrase of the Golden Rule reads:

"Whatsoever ye would that others should do for your Mother if she were in need, and whatsoever your Mother would do for the needy if she had the opportunity, do in Her Name and in Her Honor for other Mothers and their children, victims of the wars in Europe and Asia, or present-day maladjustments in our own land."

Population by Race and Nativity for Cities of 100,000 or More: 1940

Source: United States Bureau of the Census

City	White Total	White Native	White Foreign born	Negro	Percent of total Native white	Percent of total Foreign-born white	Percent of total Negro
Akron, Ohio	232,482	207,062	25,420	12,260	84.6	10.4	5.0
Albany, N. Y.	127,564	112,386	15,178	2,929	86.1	11.6	2.2
Atlanta, Ga.	197,686	193,393	4,293	104,533	64.0	1.4	34.6
Baltimore, Md.	692,705	631,736	60,969	165,843	73.5	7.1	19.3
Birmingham, Ala.	158,622	154,197	4,425	108,938	57.6	1.7	40.7
Boston, Mass.	745,466	564,602	180,864	23,679	73.2	23.5	3.1
Bridgeport, Conn.	143,314	109,883	33,431	3,767	74.7	22.7	2.6
Buffalo, N. Y.	557,618	465,829	91,789	17,694	80.9	15.9	3.1
Cambridge, Mass.	105,855	81,297	24,558	4,858	73.3	22.1	4.4
Camden, N. J.	104,995	89,999	14,996	12,478	76.6	12.8	10.6
Canton, Ohio	104,319	93,250	11,069	4,041	86.0	10.2	3.7
Charlotte, N. C.	69,475	68,583	892	31,403	68.0	0.9	31.1
Chattanooga, Tenn.	91,742	90,628	1,114	36,404	70.7	0.9	28.4
Chicago, Ill.	3,114,564	2,441,859	672,705	277,731	71.9	19.8	8.2
Cincinnati, Ohio	399,853	374,063	25,790	55,593	82.1	5.7	12.2
Cleveland, Ohio	793,417	614,234	179,183	84,504	69.9	20.4	9.6
Columbus, Ohio	270,183	258,256	11,927	35,765	84.4	3.9	11.7
Dallas, Texas	244,246	236,891	7,355	50,407	80.4	2.5	17.1
Dayton, Ohio	190,414	181,085	9,329	20,273	85.9	4.4	9.6
Denver, Colo.	313,810	289,053	24,757	7,836	89.7	7.7	2.4
Des Moines, Iowa	153,426	145,952	7,474	6,360	91.3	4.7	4.0
Detroit, Mich.	1,472,662	1,151,998	320,664	149,119	71.0	19.8	9.2
Duluth, Minn.	100,659	81,327	19,332	314	80.5	19.1	0.3
Elizabeth, N. J.	104,910	82,305	22,605	4,941	74.9	20.6	4.5
Erie, Pa.	115,565	101,995	13,570	1,375	87.2	11.6	1.2
Fall River, Mass.	114,909	90,337	24,572	402	78.3	21.3	0.3
Flint, Mich.	144,858	129,013	15,845	6,599	85.1	10.5	4.4
Fort Wayne, Ind.	115,877	111,468	4,409	2,517	94.1	3.7	2.1
Fort Worth, Texas	152,345	148,805	3,540	25,254	83.8	2.0	14.2
Gary, Ind.	91,246	73,976	17,270	20,394	66.2	15.5	18.3
Grand Rapids, Mich.	161,567	141,220	20,347	2,660	86.0	12.4	1.6
Hartford, Conn.	159,119	122,514	36,605	7,090	73.7	22.0	4.3
Houston, Texas	297,959	282,646	15,313	86,302	73.5	4.0	22.4
Indianapolis, Ind.	335,755	325,200	10,555	51,142	84.0	2.7	13.2
Jacksonville, Fla.	111,247	107,275	3,972	61,782	62.0	2.3	35.7
Jersey City, N. J.	287,598	234,438	53,160	13,416	77.8	17.7	4.5
Kansas City, Kans.	100,390	93,818	6,572	21,033	77.2	5.4	17.3
Kansas City, Mo.	357,346	338,007	19,339	41,574	84.7	4.8	10.4
Knoxville, Tenn.	95,474	94,742	732	16,694	84.9	0.7	14.4
Long Beach, Calif.	162,582	150,150	12,432	610	91.4	7.6	0.4
Los Angeles, Calif.	1,406,430	1,191,182	215,248	63,774	79.2	14.3	4.2
Louisville, Ky.	271,867	265,666	6,201	47,158	83.3	1.9	14.8
Lowell, Mass.	101,252	81,834	19,418	94	80.7	19.2	0.1
Memphis, Tenn.	171,406	166,938	4,468	121,498	57.0	1.5	41.5
Miami, Fla.	135,192	122,675	12,517	36,857	71.3	7.3	21.4
Milwaukee, Wis.	578,177	494,368	83,809	8,821	84.2	14.3	1.5
Minneapolis, Minn.	487,099	422,950	64,149	4,646	85.9	13.0	0.9
Nashville, Tenn.	120,072	118,550	1,522	47,318	70.8	0.9	28.3
Newark, N. J.	383,534	293,188	90,346	45,760	68.2	21.0	10.6
New Bedford, Mass.	105,927	76,304	29,623	4,297	69.2	26.8	3.9
New Haven, Conn.	154,262	121,872	32,390	6,235	75.9	20.2	3.9
New Orleans, La.	344,775	330,080	14,695	149,034	66.7	3.0	30.1
New York, N. Y.	6,977,501	4,897,481	2,080,020	458,444	65.7	27.9	6.1
Bronx	1,370,319	909,843	460,476	23,529	65.2	33.0	1.7
Brooklyn Borough	2,587,951	1,820,313	767,638	107,263	67.5	28.4	4.0
Manhattan Borough	1,577,625	1,037,428	540,197	298,365	54.9	28.6	15.8
Queens Borough	1,270,731	994,143	276,588	25,890	76.6	21.3	2.0
Richmond Borough	170,875	135,754	35,121	5,397	77.8	20.1	1.9
Norfolk, Va.	98,248	94,591	3,657	45,893	65.5	2.5	31.8
Oakland, Calif.	287,936	245,275	42,661	8,462	81.2	14.1	2.8
Oklahoma City, Okla.	184,715	181,897	2,818	19,344	89.0	1.4	9.5
Omaha, Nebr.	211,640	189,329	22,311	12,015	84.6	10.0	5.4
Paterson, N. J.	135,300	101,212	34,088	4,268	72.5	24.4	3.1
Peoria, Ill.	102,202	96,738	5,464	2,826	92.1	5.2	2.7
Philadelphia, Pa.	1,678,577	1,388,252	290,325	250,880	71.9	15.0	13.0
Pittsburgh, Pa.	609,236	524,630	84,606	62,216	78.1	12.6	9.3
Portland, Oreg.	299,707	261,099	38,608	1,931	85.5	12.6	0.6
Providence, R. I.	246,904	195,696	51,208	6,388	77.2	20.2	2.5
Reading, Pa.	108,646	100,785	7,861	1,905	91.2	7.1	1.7
Richmond, Va.	131,706	128,293	3,413	61,251	66.5	1.8	31.7
Rochester, N. Y.	321,554	261,447	60,107	3,262	80.5	18.5	1.0
Sacramento, Calif.	99,808	87,664	12,144	1,468	82.7	11.5	1.4
St. Louis, Mo.	706,794	647,388	59,406	108,765	79.3	7.3	13.3
St. Paul, Minn.	283,399	249,787	33,612	4,139	86.8	11.7	1.4
Salt Lake City, Utah	148,699	135,359	13,340	694	90.3	8.9	0.5
San Antonio, Texas	234,022	205,985	28,037	19,235	81.1	11.0	7.6
San Diego, Calif.	196,946	177,417	19,529	4,143	87.3	9.6	2.0
San Francisco, Calif.	602,701	472,430	130,271	4,846	74.5	20.5	0.8
Scranton, Pa.	139,647	121,267	18,380	754	86.4	13.1	0.5
Seattle, Wash.	354,101	294,489	59,612	3,789	80.0	16.2	1.0
Somerville, Mass.	101,887	78,032	23,855	262	76.4	23.3	0.3
South Bend, Ind.	97,662	86,785	10,877	3,555	85.7	10.7	3.5
Spokane, Wash.	120,897	108,142	12,755	644	88.6	10.5	0.5
Springfield, Mass.	146,361	119,623	26,738	3,144	80.0	17.9	2.1
Syracuse, N. Y.	203,640	176,090	27,550	2,082	85.5	13.4	1.0
Tacoma, Wash.	107,611	91,757	15,854	650	83.9	14.5	20.6
Tampa, Fla.	85,043	73,961	11,082	23,331	68.2	10.2	1.5
Toledo, Ohio	267,589	242,842	24,747	14,597	86.0	8.8	5.2

City	White				Percent of total		
	Total	Native	Foreign born	Negro	Native white	Foreign-born white	Negro
Trenton, N. J.	115,357	93,501	21,856	9,308	75.0	17.5	7.5
Tulsa, Okla.	126,352	124,178	2,174	15,151	87.4	1.5	10.7
Utica, N. Y.	99,989	82,649	17,340	514	82.2	17.3	0.5
Washington, D. C.	474,326	440,312	34,014	187,266	66.4	5.1	28.2
Wichita, Kans.	109,186	107,032	2,154	5,686	93.1	1.9	4.9
Wilmington, Del.	98,175	87,694	10,481	14,256	77.9	9.3	12.7
Worcester, Mass.	192,263	152,272	39,991	1,353	78.6	20.6	0.7
Yonkers, N. Y.	138,441	109,784	28,657	4,108	77.0	20.1	2.9
Youngstown, Ohio	153,056	126,385	26,671	14,615	75.4	15.9	8.7

POPULATION BY RACE AND NATIVITY FOR PLACES OF 50,000 TO 100,000: 1940

Urban place	White		Negro	Urban place	White		Negro
	Native	Foreign born			Native	Foreign born	
Alabama:				**Mississippi:**			
Mobile	48,134	1,472	29,046	Jackson	37,493	358	24,226
Montgomery	42,955	592	34,535	**Missouri:**			
Arizona:				St. Joseph	69,914	2,755	3,029
Phoenix	56,276	4,097	4,263	Springfield	58,797	635	1,804
Arkansas:				**Nebraska:**			
Little Rock	64,950	964	22,103	Lincoln	76,099	5,064	794
California:				**New Hampshire:**			
Berkeley	69,510	10,757	3,395	Manchester	60,239	17,396	23
Fresno	48,686	8,328	2,002	**New Jersey:**			
Glendale	76,000	5,992	68	Atlantic City	40,152	8,195	15,668
Pasadena	67,602	9,135	3,929	Bayonne	60,213	17,206	1,754
San Jose	58,341	9,065	291	East Orange	54,433	8,540	5,950
Santa Monica	45,299	6,392	1,265	Hoboken	35,961	13,858	260
Stockton	42,571	7,061	875	Irvington	43,799	11,438	69
Colorado:				Passaic	41,645	17,720	2,003
Pueblo	46,315	4,344	1,381	Union City	41,976	14,148	29
Connecticut:				**New York:**			
New Britain	51,296	17,054	334	Binghamton	68,569	8,990	740
Waterbury	74,944	22,315	2,015	Mount Vernon	49,410	12,779	5,103
Florida:				New Rochelle	41,156	10,951	6,228
St. Petersburg	45,271	3,523	11,982	Niagara Falls	57,206	19,734	975
Georgia:				Schenectady	71,423	15,414	688
Augusta	38,135	556	27,004	Troy	62,124	7,554	612
Columbus	35,518	286	17,453	**North Carolina:**			
Macon	31,887	366	25,604	Asheville	37,078	795	13,435
Savannah	50,844	1,856	43,237	Durham	36,436	404	13,347
Illinois:				Greensboro	42,468	500	16,348
Cicero	49,332	15,366	7	Winston-Salem	43,431	358	36,018
Decatur	55,408	1,797	2,098	**Ohio:**			
East St. Louis	55,228	3,553	16,798	Cleveland Heights	46,524	7,934	511
Evanston	52,088	7,210	6,026	Hamilton	46,989	1,541	2,052
Oak Park	59,578	6,297	98	Lakewood	61,398	7,643	91
Rockford	69,737	13,689	1,190	Springfield	60,799	1,553	8,293
Springfield	67,507	4,615	3,357	**Pennsylvania:**			
Indiana:				Allentown	88,670	7,854	378
East Chicago	36,165	12,338	6,101	Altoona	74,718	4,754	735
Evansville	89,015	1,179	6,862	Bethlehem	49,674	8,167	638
Hammond	61,152	8,372	637	Chester	42,563	6,539	10,162
Terre Haute	57,405	1,887	3,398	Harrisburg	73,325	3,284	7,263
Iowa:				Johnstown	57,803	7,290	1,560
Cedar Rapids	57,583	3,869	663	Lancaster	57,605	2,226	1,503
Davenport	61,058	4,177	801	McKeesport	44,427	8,725	2,184
Sioux City	74,773	6,587	871	Upper Darby township	52,562	8,884	413
Waterloo	48,185	2,052	1,498	Wilkes-Barre	74,464	10,929	836
Kansas:				York	53,292	988	2,427
Topeka	59,809	2,287	5,679	**Rhode Island:**			
Kentucky:				Pawtucket	58,390	17,092	286
Covington	57,692	1,166	3,154	**South Carolina:**			
Louisiana:				Charleston	38,189	1,299	31,765
Shreveport	60,686	1,460	35,975	Columbia	39,683	508	22,195
Maine:				**Texas:**			
Portland	63,425	9,844	325	Amarillo	48,251	649	2,761
Massachusetts:				Austin	70,029	2,996	14,861
Brockton	50,281	11,514	506	Beaumont	38,704	1,401	18,921
Holyoke	41,579	12,067	94	Corpus Christi	49,718	3,024	4,545
Lawrence	61,234	22,939	122	El Paso	72,350	21,973	2,188
Lynn	76,267	21,047	744	Galveston	40,842	4,511	15,432
Malden	44,592	12,922	479	Waco	43,572	1,372	11,025
Medford	50,654	11,766	648	**Virginia:**			
Newton	58,127	11,034	680	Arlington County[1]	50,397	1,601	5,032
Quincy	61,078	14,687	17	Portsmouth	30,507	761	19,338
Michigan:				Roanoke	55,766	706	12,812
Dearborn	49,938	13,557	35	**West Virginia:**			
Highland Park	38,706	10,769	1,292	Charleston	59,279	1,608	7,011
Kalamazoo	48,159	4,802	1,117	Huntington	73,350	972	4,498
Lansing	71,903	5,184	1,638	Wheeling	55,183	4,003	1,897
Pontiac	57,158	6,630	2,794	**Wisconsin:**			
Saginaw	70,896	8,488	3,315	Madison	62,519	4,528	365
				Racine	55,621	11,120	432

[1] Classified as urban under special rule.

The most rapid decline in population per household during the period between 1930 and 1940 took place in the urban areas, where households were smallest at the beginning of the decade.

Urban areas showed a drop of 9.0 percent in population per household.

The figures for whites closely resemble those for the total population, because white households represent the great majority of persons in each region. On the average, non-white households were somewhat larger than white households in all regions.

Country of Birth of Foreign-Born Whites, 1940

Source: United States Bureau of the Census

	Austria	Cz'ch-slov.	Den-mark	Eng-land	Fin-land	France	Ger-many	Greece	Hun-gary	Irel'd (Eire)	Italy
Alabama.....	292	363	129	1,191	43	327	1,530	759	280	308	1,699
Arizona.....	415	126	284	1,687	189	242	1,117	336	136	523	715
Arkansas....	309	288	103	513	11	152	2,023	238	73	225	791
California...	16,260	5,063	19,726	73,345	7,798	17,696	71,727	12,421	8,401	27,631	100,911
Colorado....	3,226	1,036	1,843	4,706	414	786	7,017	1,049	666	2,120	8,352
Connecticut.	9,568	8,205	2,532	17,366	1,815	2,291	19,625	3,041	9,993	23,837	81,373
Delaware...	407	144	94	1,134	71	125	1,209	342	193	1,274	3,464
Dist. of Col.	879	265	259	2,665	138	719	3,390	1,863	412	2,326	4,913
Florida.....	1,828	700	1,070	7,985	461	1,153	7,080	1,643	1,444	1,751	5,138
Georgia.....	264	49	80	1,073	71	244	1,424	981	169	417	536
Idaho.......	542	373	1,244	2,252	658	271	2,533	345	102	466	892
Illinois.....	36,604	54,914	13,869	36,966	3,331	7,233	138,023	18,428	21,311	41,947	98,244
Indiana.....	4,405	5,782	768	5,562	195	1,459	18,784	3,747	7,733	2,657	6,309
Iowa........	1,558	5,552	10,977	5,961	59	892	35,540	1,535	325	2,671	3,461
Kansas......	2,115	1,783	1,098	3,136	24	789	10,870	439	280	1,197	1,654
Kentucky....	431	122	65	1,075	30	380	4,630	435	417	892	1,302
Louisiana...	434	228	241	1,215	74	1,840	2,574	505	393	691	9,849
Maine........	186	264	655	3,558	1,195	219	722	772	45	2,688	2,268
Maryland....	2,879	2,645	393	4,531	392	724	14,372	1,686	1,404	3,007	10,119
Mass........	6,772	1,734	2,342	58,438	10,696	4,688	16,531	15,208	1,113	103,388	114,362
Michigan....	17,918	12,725	5,441	47,728	21,151	3,364	59,783	8,989	20,593	8,905	40,631
Minnesota...	7,217	7,163	10,655	6,375	20,152	882	42,047	1,761	1,697	3,530	5,628
Mississippi..	108	40	120	316	42	152	585	286	57	161	1,294
Missouri.....	6,498	3,271	1,116	5,363	91	1,534	27,882	2,183	3,481	5,582	13,168
Montana.....	1,941	1,082	1,901	4,134	2,042	457	4,401	681	379	2,618	2,265
Nebraska....	1,647	9,880	7,030	2,538	34	307	21,657	718	418	1,514	3,201
Nevada.....	198	28	443	755	147	537	733	359	42	324	2,258
N.Hampshire	418	58	122	3,151	1,156	230	1,306	2,945	65	3,320	1,687
New Jersey..	34,195	18,075	5,069	39,316	2,156	7,352	87,692	5,288	33,816	35,830	169,063
New Mexico.	251	94	80	504	67	218	813	346	72	164	1,148
New York...	172,347	41,798	14,304	117,370	15,101	26,373	316,844	34,800	75,254	205,323	584,075
N. Carolina..	171	55	63	1,088	9	149	916	1,114	86	211	445
N. Dakota...	1,278	1,211	2,058	970	540	160	6,876	251	882	528	80
Ohio........	27,536	45,134	1,806	30,472	4,337	3,767	66,373	10,058	49,185	12,816	65,453
Oklahoma...	628	1,258	318	1,323	24	421	4,032	499	155	371	893
Oregon......	2,097	1,169	3,013	6,385	4,343	799	9,883	1,267	512	2,194	4,083
Pennsylvania	86,520	59,394	2,151	55,346	1,600	6,965	80,111	10,510	36,046	46,331	197,281
Rhode Island	1,455	145	224	18,858	504	1,611	2,726	987	174	10,099	28,851
S. Carolina..	124	24	45	447	20	87	570	713	32	132	175
S. Dakota...	625	1,593	3,721	1,410	556	125	8,304	263	164	573	238
Tennessee...	288	92	93	966	22	152	1,477	562	209	326	1,734
Texas.......	3,023	9,171	1,117	5,046	173	1,233	17,970	1,773	737	2,302	5,451
Utah........	465	65	3,155	7,190	309	184	3,353	1,882	78	362	2,189
Vermont....	261	158	122	1,378	443	137	494	185	169	904	2,339
Virginia.....	595	706	303	2,792	73	386	2,353	1,270	577	690	1,843
Washington..	4,373	1,424	5,739	16,206	9,199	1,482	15,470	2,476	637	3,758	8,853
West Virginia	2,664	1,572	59	2,440	109	399	2,197	1,915	3,221	455	10,691
Wisconsin...	14,880	12,654	9,507	6,259	4,715	961	88,808	2,636	6,444	2,236	11,086
Wyoming....	811	296	625	1,490	430	276	1,392	759	156	456	1,215
Total....	**479,906**	**319,971**	**138,175**	**621,975**	**117,210**	**102,930**	**1,237,772**	**163,252**	**290,228**	**572,031**	**1,623,580**

COUNTRY OF BIRTH OF FOREIGN-BORN WHITES

States	Norway	Poland	Russia	Sweden	States	Norway	Poland	Russia	Sweden
Alabama....	156	423	858	422	Nevada....	162	73	108	368
Arizona.....	221	294	682	582	N. Hamp...	344	3,250	1,667	1,320
Arkansas...	64	298	354	194	N. Jersey...	5,803	77,782	55,407	9,956
California...	15,324	14,735	51,758	34,899	N. Mexico..	83	135	190	175
Colorado...	948	1,796	11,185	5,844	New York...	37,169	281,080	436,028	48,317
Connecticut.	1,659	39,755	23,787	14,532	N. Carolina.	69	307	696	153
Delaware...	113	2,515	1,281	243	N. Dakota..	21,637	1,194	17,351	5,846
Dist. of Col.	264	2,019	6,038	580	Ohio.......	1,404	50,959	27,668	5,843
Florida.....	1,036	2,003	5,524	2,548	Oklahoma..	183	867	2,626	538
Georgia.....	86	915	2,016	180	Oregon......	6,129	1,431	5,981	8,498
Idaho......	1,637	166	1,113	2,974	Pa.........	2,259	117,319	95,803	11,571
Illinois.....	21,508	138,700	74,454	79,906	R. I.......	427	6,032	5,580	4,662
Indiana.....	599	14,257	4,126	3,565	S. Carolina.	57	405	536	82
Iowa.......	8,642	1,284	3,671	11,406	S. Dakota..	8,708	486	6,468	4,361
Kansas.....	523	1,426	6,401	4,540	Tennessee...	92	945	1,499	199
Kentucky...	61	621	1,326	165	Texas......	1,169	3,681	5,104	3,046
Louisiana...	383	581	1,190	316	Utah.......	1,166	135	286	2,832
Maine......	433	1,264	2,107	1,359	Vermont....	89	1,258	630	790
Maryland...	573	9,817	15,832	634	Virginia....	329	1,104	2,795	410
Mass.......	4,481	53,783	64,575	28,128	Washington.	26,489	3,119	8,598	26,993
Michigan....	5,345	96,826	32,229	17,436	W. Virginia.	51	4,245	1,811	230
Minnesota..	52,025	10,755	10,684	67,161	Wisconsin...	23,211	31,487	15,114	13,697
Mississippi..	46	216	412	156	Wyoming...	536	447	1,325	1,353
Missouri....	439	6,789	12,745	2,683					
Montana....	6,896	770	4,084	4,032	**Total....**	**262,088**	**993,479**	**1,040,884**	**445,070**
Nebraska...	1,060	3,130	9,181	9,435					

Foreign-born white persons from other countries not named above were enumerated in the 1940 census. Australia, 10,998; Azores, 25,751; Belgium, 53,958; Bulgaria, 8,888; Canada-French, 273,366; Canada-other, 770,753; Cuba and other West Indies, 30,534; Northern Ireland, 106,416; Latvia, 18,636; Lithuania, 165,771; Luxemburg, 6,886; Mexico, 377,433; Netherlands, 110,064; Newfoundland, 21,361; Palestine and Syria, 57,906; Portugal, 62,347; Rumania, 115,940; Scotland, 279,321; Spain, 47,707; Switzerland, 88,293; Turkey in Europe, 4,412; Turkey in Asia, 52,479; Wales, 35,360; Yugoslavia, 161,093; Central and South America, 36,408. Total all countries, 11,419,138.

Foreign-Born White, by Country of Birth, by Sex

Source: United States Bureau of the Census

Country of Birth	Both Sexes 1940	Both Sexes 1930	Male 1940	Male 1930	Female 1940	Female 1930
All countries................	11,419,138	13,983,405	6,011,015	7,502,491	5,408,123	6,480,914
England......................	621,975	808,684	310,299	412,072	311,676	396,612
Scotland.....................	279,321	354,323	139,019	181,654	140,302	172,669
Wales........................	35,360	60,205	18,692	32,189	16,668	28,016
Northern Ireland.............	106,416	178,832	47,827	81,088	58,589	97,744
Irish Free State (Eire).......	572,031	744,810	244,092	324,841	327,939	419,969
Norway.......................	262,088	347,852	145,621	196,349	116,467	151,503
Sweden.......................	445,070	595,250	245,469	333,623	199,601	261,627
Denmark......................	138,175	179,474	83,825	109,975	54,350	69,499
Netherlands..................	111,064	133,133	64,777	77,574	46,287	55,559
Belgium......................	53,958	64,194	29,279	35,265	24,679	28,929
Switzerland..................	88,293	113,010	49,612	64,833	38,681	48,177
France.......................	102,930	135,265	47,387	66,181	55,543	69,084
Germany......................	1,237,772	1,608,814	638,022	843,136	599,750	765,678
Poland.......................	993,479	1,268,583	523,543	681,425	469,936	587,158
Czechoslovakia...............	319,971	491,638	161,838	255,485	158,133	236,153
Austria......................	479,906	370,914	248,304	193,636	231,602	177,278
Hungary......................	290,228	274,450	144,354	139,828	145,874	134,622
Yugoslavia...................	161,093	211,416	97,781	131,351	63,312	80,065
Russia (U.S.S.R.)............	1,040,884	1,153,624	548,216	612,962	492,668	540,662
Lithuania....................	165,771	193,606	91,601	110,969	74,170	82,637
Latvia.......................	18,636	20,673	9,897	11,061	8,739	9,612
Finland......................	117,210	142,478	60,770	77,059	56,440	65,419
Rumania......................	115,940	146,393	61,596	78,685	54,344	67,708
Bulgaria.....................	8,888	9,399	6,858	7,587	2,030	1,812
Turkey in Europe.............	4,412	2,257	2,757	1,269	1,655	988
Greece.......................	163,252	174,526	117,324	129,101	45,928	45,425
Italy........................	1,623,580	1,790,424	935,139	1,042,621	688,441	747,803
Spain........................	47,707	59,033	32,770	42,528	14,937	16,505
Portugal.....................	62,347	69,993	36,143	42,318	26,204	27,675
Other Europe.................	26,101	31,379	16,595	20,019	9,506	11,360
Palestine and Syria..........	57,906	63,362	32,895	36,144	25,011	27,218
Turkey in Asia...............	52,479	46,651	30,721	28,117	21,758	18,534
Other Asia...................	39,524	47,567	23,694	29,145	15,830	18,422
Canada—French................	273,366	370,852	133,576	187,523	139,790	183,329
Canada—other.................	770,753	907,660	351,730	429,623	419,023	478,037
Mexico.......................	377,433	639,017	197,965	360,332	179,468	278,685
Cuba and other West Indies...	30,534	31,600	15,918	17,226	14,616	14,374
Central and South America....	36,408	38,124	19,929	22,270	16,479	15,854
Australia....................	10,998	12,720	5,522	6,656	5,476	6,064

POPULATION, MALE AND FEMALE, CHIEF U. S. CITIES, 1940

Source: United States Bureau of the Census

Cities 100,000 or More	Total Male	Total Female	White Male	White Female	Cities 100,000 or More	Total Male	Total Female	White Male	White Female
Akron, Ohio.	121,529	123,262	115,436	117,046	Minneapolis.	234,542	257,828	231,726	255,373
Albany.....	62,864	67,713	61,352	66,212	Newark.....	213,840	215,920	191,749	191,785
Atlanta, Ga.	139,331	162,957	93,254	104,432	N. Bedford..	53,401	56,940	51,100	54,827
Baltimore...	422,916	436,184	341,806	350,899	New Haven.	78,333	82,272	75,285	78,977
Birmingham	127,420	140,163	76,916	81,706	New Orleans	234,277	260,260	164,966	179,809
Boston.....	373,147	397,669	360,552	384,914	New York...	3,676,293	3,778,702	3,455,003	3,522,498
Bridgeport..	73,188	73,933	71,272	72,042	Norfolk, Va.	72,949	71,383	50,978	47,270
Buffalo.....	283,767	292,134	274,633	282,985	Oakland....	149,227	152,936	141,584	146,352
Cambridge..	52,479	58,400	50,076	55,779	Okla. City..	98,774	105,650	89,418	95,297
Camden.....	58,802	58,734	52,574	52,421	Omaha......	108,750	115,094	102,712	108,928
Canton.....	54,285	54,116	52,251	52,068	Paterson....	69,505	70,151	67,371	67,929
Charlotte...	47,662	53,237	33,338	36,137	Peoria, Ill...	51,832	53,255	50,360	51,842
Chattanooga	61,246	66,917	44,202	47,540	Philadelphia	942,550	988,784	822,266	856,311
Chicago, Ill.	1,681,665	1,715,143	1,547,490	1,567,074	Pittsburgh..	330,007	341,652	298,791	310,445
Cincinnati..	217,082	238,528	190,388	209,465	Portland....	149,135	156,259	145,776	153,931
Cleveland...	438,346	439,990	396,930	396,487	Providence..	121,797	131,707	118,555	128,349
Columbus...	148,971	157,116	130,812	139,371	Reading, Pa.	53,954	56,614	52,969	55,677
Dallas, Tex.	139,759	154,975	116,450	127,796	Richmond...	90,220	102,822	62,032	69,674
Dayton.....	103,358	107,360	93,370	97,044	Rochester...	157,574	167,401	155,867	165,687
Denver.....	155,635	166,777	151,582	162,228	Sacramento.	53,496	52,462	50,130	49,678
Des Moines.	75,879	83,940	72,779	80,649	St. Louis....	391,798	424,250	339,697	367,097
Detroit.....	827,499	795,953	751,817	720,845	St. Paul....	137,561	150,175	135,348	148,051
Duluth.....	50,586	50,479	50,355	50,304	Salt Lake C.	73,229	76,705	72,511	76,188
Elizabeth...	54,878	55,034	52,390	52,520	San Antonio.	123,508	130,346	114,441	119,581
Erie, Pa....	58,082	58,873	57,372	58,193	San Diego...	103,638	99,703	100,200	96,746
Fall River..	55,542	59,886	55,222	59,687	S. Francisco.	322,441	312,095	301,692	301,009
Flint, Mich.	75,976	75,567	72,684	72,174	Scranton....	68,593	71,811	68,184	71,463
Fort Wayne.	56,915	61,495	55,699	60,178	Seattle.....	183,526	184,776	174,997	179,104
Fort Worth.	85,061	92,601	73,234	79,111	Somerville..	49,332	52,845	49,184	52,703
Gary, Ind...	58,075	53,644	47,916	43,330	South Bend.	50,228	51,040	48,443	49,219
Gd. Rapids.	79,418	84,874	78,085	83,482	Spokane....	60,416	61,585	59,809	61,088
Hartford....	80,509	85,758	77,040	82,079	Springfield..	72,246	77,308	70,703	75,658
Houston.....	188,318	196,196	147,650	150,309	Syracuse....	100,296	105,671	99,152	104,458
Indianapolis	185,461	201,511	161,046	174,709	Tacoma.....	55,038	54,370	54,078	53,533
Jacksonville.	82,798	90,267	53,972	57,275	Tampa, Fla.	52,442	55,949	41,377	43,666
Jersey City..	149,703	151,470	143,176	144,422	Toledo, Ohio	140,001	142,348	132,738	134,851
Kansas City.	59,432	62,026	49,534	50,856	Trenton....	62,175	62,522	57,452	57,905
Kan.C., Mo.	190,117	209,061	170,184	187,162	Tulsa, Okla.	68,187	73,970	60,925	65,427
Knoxville...	52,708	58,872	45,263	50,211	Utica, N. Y.	48,857	51,661	48,575	51,414
Long Beach..	77,593	86,678	76,619	85,963	Washington..	317,522	345,569	227,748	246,578
Los Angeles.	734,135	770,142	683,075	723,355	Wichita....	54,996	59,970	52,199	56,987
Louisville...	152,267	166,810	129,971	141,896	Wilmington.	55,494	57,010	48,474	49,701
Lowell......	49,016	52,373	48,927	52,325	Worcester...	94,455	99,239	93,753	98,510
Memphis....	139,238	153,704	84,230	88,976	Yonkers....	69,991	72,607	68,127	70,314
Miami, Fla..	84,587	87,585	66,864	68,328	Youngstown	84,652	83,068	77,223	75,833
Milwaukee..	289,118	298,354	284,340	293,837					

United States German-Italian-Spanish, Mother Tongue Population

Source: United States Bureau of the Census; 1940 returns

GERMAN

STATES	Total	Foreign born	Native of foreign or mixed parentage	Native of native parentage	STATES	Total	Foreign born	Native of foreign) or mixed parentage	Native of native parentage
Alabama....	4,120	1,820	1,660	640	Nebraska...	133,260	28,240	80,420	24,600
Arizona....	3,980	1,240	2,240	500	Nevada....	2,120	740	1,180	200
Arkansas...	9,100	2,920	4,560	1,620	New Hamp..	3,100	1,640	1,400	60
California..	222,700	99,840	106,060	16,800	New Jersey.	209,220	107,480	93,320	8,420
Colorado...	48,840	14,980	29,460	4,400	New Mex...	3,300	1,100	1,640	560
Connecticut.	49,160	25,220	22,940	1,000	New York..	652,120	384,940	248,060	19,120
Delaware...	3,620	1,420	1,660	540	No. Dakota.	123,700	23,660	74,540	25,500
Dist. of Col..	8,540	3,560	3,920	1,060	Ohio.......	328,820	90,320	165,180	73,320
Florida.....	17,280	9,020	6,700	1,560	Oklahoma..	29,440	6,320	15,380	7,740
Georgia....	3,540	1,580	1,560	400	Oregon.....	48,980	18,700	25,520	4,760
Idaho......	14,140	4,180	8,160	1,800	Penn.......	407,120	109,840	156,780	140,500
Illinois.....	486,600	173,700	249,340	63,560	R. I.......	5,580	3,180	2,280	120
Indiana.....	123,600	20,380	54,940	48,280	So. Dakota.	83,160	14,140	48,660	20,360
Iowa.......	200,220	36,680	119,180	44,360	Tennessee..	5,540	1,900	2,800	840
Kansas.....	109,920	17,340	61,140	31,440	Texas......	159,100	21,000	67,040	71,060
Kentucky...	22,060	5,200	13,680	3,180	Utah......	7,720	4,480	2,920	320
Louisiana...	9,820	2,860	5,640	1,320	Virginia...	6,320	2,660	2,720	940
Maryland...	39,760	13,980	21,460	4,320	Washington.	67,060	24,580	37,140	5,340
Mass.......	35,540	19,480	15,160	900	W. Virginia.	10,620	3,600	5,880	1,140
Michigan...	230,220	77,000	123,140	30,080	Wisconsin..	506,000	104,700	273,220	128,080
Minnesota..	293,560	49,700	160,780	83,080	Wyoming...	7,460	2,480	4,500	480
Missouri....	173,220	37,080	88,900	47,240					
Montana...	32,600	10,420	19,400	2,780	Total....	4,949,780	1,589,040	2,435,700	925,040

ITALIAN

STATES	Total	Foreign born	Native of foreign or mixed parentage	Native of native parentage	STATES	Total	Foreign born	Native of foreign) or mixed parentage	Native of native parentage
Alabama...	3,800	1,440	2,000	360	Nebraska...	7,920	2,480	5,180	260
Arkansas...	2,220	820	1,240	160	Nevada....	4,560	2,220	2,220	120
California..	215,200	101,440	105,760	8,000	New Hamp..	4,060	1,660	2,280	120
Colorado...	21,040	8,180	12,000	860	New Jersey.	406,740	162,000	231,740	13,000
Connecticut.	200,420	75,980	119,860	4,580	New Mex...	2,860	1,140	1,560	160
Delaware...	9,440	3,780	5,100	560	New York..	1,302,860	562,040	703,820	37,000
Dist. of Col.	10,100	4,740	4,640	720	Ohio.......	148,800	62,280	81,360	5,160
Florida.....	10,360	4,600	4,700	1,060	Oregon.....	7,780	3,880	3,400	500
Illinois.....	219,320	94,520	119,060	5,740	Penn.......	500,480	191,020	288,820	20,640
Indiana.....	12,320	5,960	5,920	440	R. I.......	79,480	27,920	49,060	2,500
Iowa.......	7,060	3,460	3,460	140	Tennessee..	3,880	1,620	2,000	260
Kansas.....	4,000	1,620	2,220	160	Texas......	14,840	4,940	7,880	2,020
Kentucky...	2,240	1,020	1,040	180	Utah......	4,460	2,080	2,300	80
Louisiana...	31,940	9,080	18,460	4,400	Vermont...	5,660	2,340	3,160	160
Maine......	5,320	2,280	2,940	100	Virginia...	3,600	1,480	1,840	280
Maryland...	23,060	9,040	12,600	1,420	Washington.	17,200	9,120	7,540	540
Mass.......	272,240	110,400	155,220	6,620	W. Virginia.	25,740	10,180	14,520	1,040
Michigan...	87,540	38,480	46,220	2,840	Wisconsin..	27,600	10,200	16,580	820
Minnesota..	12,860	5,520	6,900	440	Wyoming...	3,060	1,520	1,480	60
Mississippi.	3,200	1,100	1,980	120					
Missouri....	29,460	12,040	16,420	1,000	Total....	3,766,820	1,561,100	2,080,680	125,040
Montana...	4,320	1,900	2,320	100					

SPANISH

STATES	Total	Foreign born	Native of foreign or mixed parentage	Native of native parentage	STATES	Total	Foreign born	Native of foreign) or mixed parentage	Native of native parentage
Arizona....	101,880	24,140	50,140	27,600	Nebraska...	5,500	1,840	3,200	460
California..	416,140	136,700	215,740	63,700	Nevada....	3,060	1,380	1,440	240
Colorado...	92,540	6,640	14,100	71,800	New Jersey.	6,940	4,180	2,160	600
Florida.....	25,100	8,220	11,900	4,980	New Mex...	221,740	7,820	21,100	192,820
Idaho......	2,720	1,300	1,280	140	New York..	129,260	39,500	21,740	68,020
Illinois.....	23,940	10,700	12,060	1,180	Ohio.......	5,540	3,020	2,000	520
Indiana.....	5,560	2,320	2,420	820	Oklahoma..	4,220	1,020	2,300	900
Iowa.......	3,320	1,360	1,880	80	Penn.......	7,360	4,140	2,560	660
Kansas.....	13,060	4,580	7,760	720	Texas......	738,440	148,140	318,220	272,080
Louisiana...	5,640	1,900	1,220	2,520	Utah......	2,580	780	980	820
Mass.......	2,220	1,360	660	200	Washington.	2,400	920	1,120	360
Michigan...	11,860	4,600	5,500	1,760	W: Virginia.	2,000	1,100	800	100
Minnesota..	3,300	1,300	1,600	400	Wyoming...	6,140	1,520	1,940	2,680
Missouri....	5,100	2,020	2,680	400					
Montana...	2,240	720	1,080	440	Total....	1,861,400	428,360	714,060	718,980

Figures show only for States having 2,000 persons or more of German, Italian and Spanish mother tongue.

U. S. Population by Age Groups, 1900-1980

Source: United States Bureau of the Census

Figures 1945-1980 are estimates.

Year	Total Population	14 Years or Less	15-24 Years	25 Years or Over	Percent			
					All Ages	14 Years or Less	15-24 Years	25 Years or Over
1900...........	75,994,575	26,124,985	14,891,105	*34,978,485	100.0	34.4	19.6	46.0
1910...........	91,972,266	29,499,136	18,120,587	*44,352,543	100.0	32.1	19.7	48.2
1920...........	105,710,620	33,612,442	18,707,577	*53,390,601	100.0	31.8	17.7	50.5
1930...........	122,775,046	36,056,876	22,422,493	*64,295,677	100.0	29.4	18.3	52.4
1940...........	131,669,275	33,114,698	23,908,014	74,646,563	100.0	25.1	18.2	56.7
1945...........	136,448,000	32,150,000	24,058,000	80,239,000	100.0	23.6	17.6	58.8
1950...........	140,561,000	32,442,000	22,279,000	85,841,000	100.0	23.1	15.9	61.1
1955...........	144,093,000	32,321,000	21,287,000	90,485,000	100.0	22.4	14.8	62.8
1960...........	146,987,000	31,694,000	21,601,000	93,692,000	100.0	21.6	14.7	63.7
1965...........	149,341,000	30,840,000	21,771,000	96,730,000	100.0	20.7	14.6	64.8

Japanese Population Under the U. S. Flag, 1940

Source: United States Bureau of the Census

Area	Total	Citizens	Aliens	Area	Total	Citizens	Aliens
U.S. and all possessions....	......	......	113,874	Guam............	326	288	38
U.S. and possess, exclusive of Philippines and military and naval services..	285,448	200,631	84,817	Hawaii..........	157,905	120,552	37,353
				Panama Canal Zone....	1	......	1
Continental U.S........	126,947	79,642	47,305	Puerto Rico......	2	......	2
Territ. and possess., excl. of				Virgin Islands of U.S....	......	......	......
Philippines.............	158,501	120,989	37,512	The Philippines......	......	......	29,057
Alaska..............	263	149	114	Military and naval serv., etc., abroad......	......	......	......
American Samoa.......	4	......	4				

Where there are no figures, they were not available.

JAPANESE POPULATION, 1940, BY STATES

State	Total	Citizens	Aliens	State	Total	Citizens	Aliens	State	Total	Citizens	Aliens
Alabama....	21	14	7	Maine.......	5	4	1	Ohio........	163	100	63
Arizona.....	632	412	220	Maryland...	36	17	19	Oklahoma...	57	41	16
Arkansas....	3	1	2	Mass........	158	71	87	Oregon......	4,071	2,454	1,617
California...	93,717	60,148	33,569	Michigan....	139	68	71	Pennsylvania	224	113	111
Colorado....	2,734	1,869	865	Minnesota...	51	28	23	Rhode Island	6	1	5
Connecticut.	164	54	110	Mississippi..	1	......	1	S. Carolina..	33	28	5
Delaware...	22	19	3	Missouri.....	74	38	36	So. Dakota..	19	11	8
Dist. of Col..	68	35	33	Montana.....	508	281	227	Tennessee..	12	5	7
Florida......	154	64	90	Nebraska....	480	323	157	Texas.......	458	291	167
Georgia.....	31	11	20	Nevada.....	470	225	245	Utah........	2,210	1,381	829
Idaho......	1,191	765	426	New H'shire.	4	3	1	Vermont....	3	2	1
Illinois......	462	233	229	New Jersey..	298	164	134	Virginia.....	74	45	29
Indiana.....	29	20	9	New Mexico.	186	114	72	Washington..	14,565	8,882	5,683
Iowa.......	29	24	5	New York...	2,538	766	1,772	W. Virginia..	3	1	2
Kansas.....	19	9	10	N. Carolina..	21	19	......	Wisconsin...	23	17	6
Kentucky...	9	5	4	N. Dakota...	83	43	40	Wyoming....	643	390	253
Louisiana...	46	33	13								

JAPANESE POPULATION, 1940, IN SELECTED CITIES

City	Total Japanese:	Japanese born in U.S. or its territories and possessions: (Citizens)	Foreign-born Japanese: (Aliens)	City	Total Japanese:	Japanese born in U.S. or its territories and possessions: (Citizens)	Foreign-born Japanese: (Aliens)
Los Angeles, Cal..	23,321	14,595	8,726	Tacoma, Wash...	877	532	345
Seattle, Wash....	6,975	4,099	2,876	San Diego, Calif...	828	501	327
San Francisco, Cal.	5,280	3,004	2,276	Fresno, Calif.....	797	517	280
Sacramento, Cal..	2,879	1,905	974	Pasadena, Calif...	795	480	315
New York City....	2,087	631	1,456	Alameda, Calif....	700	454	246
Oakland, Calif....	1,790	1,135	655	Long Beach, Calif..	696	452	244
Portland, Ore....	1,680	955	725	Belvedere towns'p			
Berkeley, Calif...	1,319	859	460	(Los Angeles Co.,)	605	391	214
Stockton, Calif...	1,259	772	487	Gardena, Calif....	509	350	159
Torrance, Calif...	1,189	781	408				

UNITED STATES NEGRO POPULATION, 1940

State	Number	State	Number	State	Number	State	Number
Alabama.....	983,290	Iowa.........	16,694	Nevada......	664	S. Dakota....	474
Arizona.....	14,993	Kansas.......	65,138	N. Hampshire.	414	Tennessee...,	508,736
Arkansas....	482,578	Kentucky....	214,031	New Jersey...	226,973	Texas.......	924,391
California...	124,306	Louisiana....	849,303	New Mexico..	4,672	Utah........	1,235
Colorado....	12,176	Maine.......	1,304	New York....	571,221	Vermont.....	384
Connecticut..	32,992	Maryland....	301,931	N. Carolina..	981,298	Virginia.....	661,449
Delaware....	35,876	Massachusetts	55,391	N. Dakota...	201	Washington...	7,424
Dist. of Col..	187,266	Michigan....	208,345	Ohio........	339,461	West Virginia.	117,754
Florida......	514,198	Minnesota...	9,928	Oklahoma...	168,849	Wisconsin ...	12,158
Georgia.....	1,084,927	Mississippi...	1,074,578	Oregon......	2,565	Wyoming.....	956
Idaho.......	595	Missouri.....	244,386	Pennsylvania.	470,172		
Illinois......	387,446	Montana.....	1,120	Rhode Island.	11,024		
Indiana.....	121,916	Nebraska....	14,171	S. Carolina...	814,164	Total.....	12,865,518

Population, other races (1940)—American Indian, 333,969; Chinese, 77,504; Japanese, 126,947; Filipino, 45,563; Hindus, 2,405; Koreans, 1,711; other, 788.

U. S. Population—Native, Foreign, Negro

Race, nativity, and region	1940			1930			Males per 100 females	
	Total	Male	Female	Total	Male	Female	1940	1930
United States:								
All classes.....	131,669,275	66,061,592	65,607,683	122,775,046	62,137,080	60,637,966	100.7	102.5
White.........	118,214,870	59,448,548	58,766,322	110,286,740	55,922,528	54,364,212	101.2	102.9
Native......	106,795,732	53,437,533	53,358,199	96,303,335	48,420,037	47,883,298	100.1	101.1
Foreign born.	11,419,138	6,011,015	5,408,123	13,983,405	7,502,491	6,480,914	111.1	115.8
Negro........	12,865,518	6,269,038	6,596,480	11,891,143	5,855,669	6,035,474	95.0	97.0
Other races....	588,887	344,006	244,881	597,163	358,883	238,280	140.5	150.6
Regions:								
The north......	76,120,109	38,133,112	37,986,997	73,021,791	36,903,563	36,117,628	100.4	102.2
The south......	41,665,901	20,794,906	20,870,995	37,857,633	19,015,060	18,842,573	99.6	100.9
The west......	13,883,265	7,133,574	6,749,691	11,896,222	6,218,457	5,677,765	105.7	109.5

Jewish People Here and Abroad, 1938

Source: Compilations from latest available data, by the American Jewish Committee, and the Jewish Statistical Bureau of the Synagogue Council of America, H. S. Linfield, director

JEWS IN THE WORLD, BY COUNTRIES

The American Jewish Committee, which gives the figures in the table below, estimated the Jewish population of the world, in 1939, as follows: Europe, 8,939,608; Africa, 598,339; Asia, 839,809; Australasia, 27,016; the Americas, 5,283,487; world total—15,688,259.

Country	Jews	Country	Jews	Country	Jews	Country	Jews
Abyssinia.....	51,000	Egypt........	72,550	Malta........	35	Russia (U. S.	
Aden & Perim.	4,151	Estonia.......	4,302	Mexico.......	20,000	S. R.).....	3,020,141
Afghanistan...	5,000	Finland.......	1,755	Morocco (Fr.)	161,312	Saar Basin....	3,117
Alaska.......	600	France........	240,000	Morocco (Sp.)	12,918	S. W. Africa...	200
Albania......	204	Germany......	240,000	Netherlands...	156,817	Spain........	4,000
Algeria......	110,127	Gibraltar.....	886	New Zealand..	2,653	Surinam (D.G.)	799
Arabia.......	25,000	Gt. Brit. & N.		Norway......	1,359	Sweden......	6,653
Argentina....	260,000	Ireland......	300,000	Palestine.....	424,373	Switzerland...	17,973
Australia.....	23,553	Greece.......	72,791	Panama......	74	Syria & Leban.	26,051
Austria......	191,408	Guiana (Brit.).	1,786	Panama C. Z..	25	Tanganyika...	10
Belgium......	60,000	Haiti........	150	Paraguay.....	1,200	Tangier Zone..	7,000
Brazil.......	40,000	Hawaii.......	310	Persia.......	40,000	Trans-Cauca-	
Brit. Malaya..	703	Hong Kong...	250	Peru........	1,500	sian Rep....	62,194
Bulgaria.....	48,398	Hungary......	444,567	Phillipine Is...	500	Transjordan..	200
Canada......	155,614	India........	24,141	Poland.......	3,113,900	Tunisia......	59,485
Chile.......	3,697	Indo-Ch'a (F.).	1,000	Porto Rico...	200	Turkmenistan.	2,041
China.......	19,850	Iraq........	90,970	Portugal.....	1,200	Turkey......	78,730
Colombia....	2,045	Irish F. State..	3,686	Portug'se E. A.	100	Ukraine.....	1,574,428
Congo (Belg.).	177	Italy........	47,825	Rhodesia (No.)	426	Un. of S. Africa	90,662
Crimea......	45,926	Jamaica.....	2,000	Rhodesia (So.)	2,021	United States.	4,770,647
Cuba........	7,800	Japan.......	200	Roumania....	900,000	Uruguay.....	12,000
Curacao.....	566	Jugoslavia....	68,405	Russia (R. S.		UzbekistanRep	37,834
Cyprus......	75	Kenya.......	305	F. S. R.) in		Venezuela....	882
Czechoslovakia	356,830	Latvia.......	93,479	Asia........	49,571	Virgin Islands.	62
Danzig......	10,448	Libya.......	30,046	Russia (R. S.		White Russia..	407,059
Denmark.....	5,690	Lithuania....	155,125	F. S. R.) in			
Dom. Rep....	756	Luxemburg...	3,144	Europe.....	539,272		

JEWISH PEOPLE IN CHIEF FOREIGN CITIES

Amsterdam, 65,558; Bagdad, 42,799; Berlin, 95,000; Bucharest, 50,000; Budapest, 204,371. Buenos Aires, 120,000; Cairo, 38,100; Cracow, 45,828; Czernowitz, 43,555; Haifa, 58,000; Istanbul, 47,173; Jassy, 45,000; Jerusalem, 79,000; Kharkov, 81,139; Kiev, 140,256; Kiskinev, 80,000; Leningrad; 84,503; Lodz, 191,720; London, 233,991; Lwow, 75,316; Manchester, 37,500; Minsk, 53,686; Montreal, 57,710; Moscow, 131,747; Odessa, 153,243. Paris, 175,000; Prague, 35,463; Riga, 43,558; Salonica, 55,250; Tel-Aviv, 130,300; Toronto, 45,205; Vienna, 178,034; Warsaw, 333,354; Wilno, 54,596.

JEWISH POPULATION IN THE UNITED STATES 1877-1937

Year and Division	Popula-tion	Jews	Per Ct.	% Distrib. Tot.	% Distrib. Jews	Year and Division	Popula-tion	Jews	Per Ct.	% Distrib. Tot.	% Distrib. Jews
North—						1917.....	30,983,045	155,251	0.5	29.89	4.59
1877.....	30,428,480	174,930	0.57	69.69	76.36	1927.....	34,531,618	225,940	0.65	29.23	5.35
1897.....	46,945,468	748,000	1.59	65.11	79.76	1937.....	38,324,000	229,049	0.59	.....	.....
1907.....	55,761,703	1,622,000	2.91	62.61	91.28						
1917.....	63,835,562	3,126,394	4.89	61.59	92.25	**West—**					
1927.....	72,710,620	3,821,045	5.25	61.54	90.39	1877.....	1,338,708	21,465	1.6	3.07	9.37
1937.....	78,302,000	4,322,276	5.52	.....	.....	1897.....	4,046,917	62,300	1.44	5.61	6.64
						1907.....	5,844,500	64,700	1.11	6.57	3.64
South—						1917.....	8,821,866	107,306	1.22	8.52	3.16
1877.....	11,894,780	32,692	0.27	27.24	14.27	1927.....	10,898,407	181,044	1.66	9.23	4.26
1897.....	21,113,735	127,500	0.64	29.28	13.60	1937.....	12,631,000	219,322	1.73	.....	.....
1907.....	27,180,855	90,185	0.33	30.62	5.08						

The regional division above follows that of the United States Census Bureau, except that Delaware, Maryland and the District of Columbia are here not considered as parts of the South but of the North, a change introduced ten years ago to meet the requirements of the distribution of the Jews.

The 1936 U. S. Census of religious denominations gave the number of members of Jewish congregations as 4,641,184, as against 4,081,242 in 1926, the figures for 1926 representing all Jews in communities having congregations.

The United States religious census of 1906 credited the Jews with 101,457 heads of families, principally male heads, and the census of 1916 fixed the number of heads of families (including seat holders and other contributors) but admittedly incomplete, at 357,135.

There were Jews in the original American colonies before 1650. In New York, then New Amsterdam, there were Jews in 1654, and in the fall of that year a company of Jewish refugees arrived from Brazil, and settled in the colony.

The Congregation Sheerith Israel (Remnant of Israel) was founded in 1656. The first minister was Saul Moreno (Brown) who came from Newport, R. I., and the synagogue was on Mill St., now South William St.

DISTRIBUTION OF THE JEWS IN THE CITY OF NEW YORK BY BOROUGHS, 1937

Borough	Jews	Per Cent of Jews to Tot.	Distrib. of Jews	Borough	Jews	Per Cent of Jews to Tot.	Distrib. of Jews
Bronx......	592,185	43.87	29.10	Queens.....	107,855	8.77	5.30
Brooklyn...	974,765	37.05	47.90	Richmond..	9,185	5.47	0.45
Manhattan.	351,037	18.76	17.25	Total....	2,035,000	28.08	100.00

New York—Buffalo, 21,800; Albany, 9,400; Rochester, 23,400; Syracuse, 14,500; Mt. Vernon, 9,300; Yonkers, 7,200.

New Jersey—Newark, 73,000; Paterson, 24,000; Jersey City, 21,600; Trenton, 9,650; Atlantic City, New Jersey, 12,800.

Jews in other American cities—Baltimore, 73,000; Boston, 118,000; Chicago, 363,000; Cleveland, 90,000; Detroit, 90,000; Los Angeles, 82,000; Philadelphia, 293,000; Pittsburgh, 52,000; St. Louis, 51,000.

Church Members in the United States in 1936 by States

(Source: United States Bureau of the Census)

STATES	1936 Total Members	1936 Exclusive of Jews	STATES	1936 Total Members	1936 Exclusive of Jews
Alabama	1,138,472	1,128,337	Nevada	27,881	27,636
Arizona	165,020	163,540	New Hampshire	237,736	234,740
Arkansas	570,219	565,995	New Jersey	2,357,432	2,099,671
California	1,928,439	1,776,843	New Mexico	243,936	243,383
Colorado	355,272	335,156	New York	7,150,501	4,953,083
Connecticut	1,050,927	960,313	North Carolina	1,274,722	1,270,011
Delaware	112,785	106,493	North Dakota	315,659	314,126
Dist. of Col	271,724	253,374	Ohio	2,934,248	2,758,306
Florida	555,317	536,548	Oklahoma	587,425	582,029
Georgia	1,264,287	1,244,742	Oregon	249,275	238,413
Idaho	178,316	178,016	Pennsylvania	5,412,246	4,988,303
Illinois	3,556,852	3,179,043	Rhode Island	473,361	446,050
Indiana	1,350,288	1,324,794	South Carolina	710,163	705,755
Iowa	1,086,989	1,075,101	South Dakota	278,567	277,962
Kansas	691,438	686,178	Tennessee	918,809	895,534
Kentucky	913,482	897,143	Texas	2,298,966	2,254,996
Louisiana	1,136,123	1,122,659	Utah	372,699	369,989
Maine	313,353	304,967	Vermont	169,792	168,065
Maryland	751,600	676,375	Virginia	1,017,531	993,967
Massachusetts	2,609,101	2,351,107	Washington	367,261	350,142
Michigan	1,786,839	1,687,473	West Virginia	491,607	486,216
Minnesota	1,352,662	1,313,502	Wisconsin	1,605,820	1,568,445
Mississippi	780,864	777,967	Wyoming	67,770	67,080
Missouri	1,392,860	1,309,502			
Montana	160,138	159,442	Total	55,807,366	51,166,182
Nebraska	566,806	553,884			

Of the total membership—less 10,029,328 whose sex was not reported—20,131,413 were males; 25,646,625 were females.
Members of urban churches numbered 38,519,170; rural, 17,084,410.
The membership by ages—less 11,215,915 who did not report—was: 13 years and over, 36,739,178; under 13 years, 7,852,273.
In the 162,233 churches reporting, there were 18,389,001 Sunday School scholars.

Church Members in 50 Cities, 1936, 1926

(Source: United States Bureau of the Census)

City	Members, 1936	Members, 1926	City	Members, 1936	Members, 1926
New York	4,245,907	4,079,501	Houston, Tex	154,260	103,372
Chicago	1,796,156	1,629,425	Toledo, Ohio	147,884	140,543
Philadelphia	1,205,694	1,163,131	Columbus, Ohio	139,836	133,113
Detroit	655,320	755,572	Denver	119,097	115,346
Los Angeles	427,348	326,446	Oakland, Calif	104,014	82,461
Cleveland	518,042	510,125	St. Paul	164,581	154,258
St. Louis	416,057	527,132	Atlanta	152,083	122,855
Baltimore	434,720	436,498	Dallas, Tex	119,446	102,631
Boston	520,708	513,649	Birmingham, Ala	109,945	125,253
Pittsburgh	451,389	430,337	Akron, Ohio	104,373	86,815
San Francisco	262,368	229,073	Memphis, Tenn	138,083	107,084
Milwaukee	319,766	274,620	Providence, R. I	198,983	182,205
Buffalo	378,425	351,907	San Antonio, Tex	134,338	103,511
Washington	271,724	238,871	Omaha, Nebr	104,029	101,680
Minneapolis	206,377	188,538	Syracuse, N. Y	126,873	125,391
New Orleans	264,370	276,490	Dayton, Ohio	90,385	86,377
Cincinnati	202,425	199,581	Worcester, Mass	130,161	130,763
Newark, N. J	322,671	266,146	Oklahoma City	65,250	47,057
Kansas City, Mo	168,120	157,957	Richmond, Va	111,147	109,055
Seattle	103,641	110,238	Youngstown, Ohio	110,557	89,663
Indianapolis	174,036	153,152	Grand Rapids, Mich	84,902	78,271
Rochester, N. Y	195,247	178,340	Hartford, Conn	116,951	116,620
Jersey City	265,340	190,112	Fort Worth, Tex	68,623	80,880
Louisville, Ky	185,862	169,434	New Haven, Conn	124,600	124,162
Portland, Oreg	98,155	95,743	Flint, Mich	46,092	31,130

RELIGIOUS POPULATION OF THE WORLD

Sect	No. Amer.	So. Amer.	Europe	Asia	Africa	Oceania	Total
Catholics:							
Roman	47,056,724	60,836,143	203,944,823	9,213,413	6,866,072	10,468,764	338,385,939
Orthodox	1,208,157		112,447,669	8,106,071	5,868,089		127,629,986
Protestants	38,998,467	657,481	81,767,054	4,422,777	2,782,864	6,372,250	135,000,893
Total	87,263,348	61,493,624	398,159,546	21,742,261	15,517,025	16,841,014	601,016,818
Jews	4,409,712	226,958	9,372,666	572,930	542,869	26,954	15,192,089
Mohammedans	1,400		5,672,225	138,299,194	55,538,211	21,467,868	220,978,848
Others	79,020,577	22,134,607	137,981,585	956,607,018	76,301,961	46,868,506	1,318,914,254
Total	83,431,689	22,361,565	153,026,476	1,095,479,092	132,383,041	68,363,328	1,555,085,191
Grand total	170,695,037	83,855,189	551,186,022	1,117,221,353	147,900,066	85,204,342	2,156,102,009

Orthodox (Eastern) Catholics includes Russian, Greek, Albanian, Bulgarian, Rumanian, Serbian, Syrian, Armenian and Coptic Catholics.
Roman Catholics include also Polish Catholics and Old Catholic Churches.
Jews include Jews by race not necessarily by religion.
Others includes Philosophic and heathen religions, unchurched, unclassified and unknown.

The National Catholic Welfare Conference

Source: An Official of the Organization

The National Catholic Welfare Conference was organized in 1919 as a common agency acting under the bishops to promote the welfare of the Catholics of the United States. The Conference has for its incorporated purposes "unifying, coordinating and organizing the Catholic people of the United States in works of education, social welfare, immigrant aid and other activities." The Conference comprises the following departments and bureaus:

Executive — Bureaus maintained: Information, Immigration, National Center Confraternity of Christian Doctrine, Publications, Business and Auditing, Family Life, and Catholic Action, monthly publication, N. C. W. C.

Youth—Facilitates exchange of information regarding the philosophy, organization, and program-content of Catholic youth organizations; promotes the National Catholic Youth Council, the federating agency for all existing, approved Catholic youth groups; contacts and evaluates national governmental and non-governmental youth organizations and youth servicing organizations.

Education—Divisions: Statistics and Information, Teachers' Registration, Library.

Press—Serves the Catholic press in the United States and abroad with regular news, features, editorial and pictorial services.

Social Action—Covers the fields of Industrial Relations, International Affairs, Civic Education, Social Welfare, and Rural Life.

Legal—Serves as a clearing house of information on Federal, State and local legislation.

Lay Organizations—Includes the National Council of Catholic Men and the National Council of Catholic Women, which maintain at N. C. W. C. headquarters permanent representations in the interests of the Catholic laity. These councils function through some 5,700 affiliated societies—national, State, diocesan, district, local and parish; also through units of the councils in many of the dioceses.

Catholic Action Study—Devoted to research and reports as to pronouncements, methods, programs and achievements in the work of Catholic Action at home and abroad.

The N. C. C. M. maintains at its national headquarters a Catholic Evidence Bureau and a Catholic Radio Bureau; and sponsors a weekly nation-wide radio Catholic Hour over the network of the National Broadcasting Company.

The N. C. C. W. maintains in Washington, D. C., the National Catholic School of Social Service.

N. C. W. C. Administrative Board—Most Rev. Edward Mooney, Archbishop of Detroit, chairman of the Administrative Board and episcopal chairman of the Executive Department; Most Rev. Samuel A. Stritch, Archbishop of Chicago, vice chairman and treasurer of the Administrative Board; Most Rev. Francis J. Spellman, Archbishop of New York, secretary of the Administrative Board; Most Rev. John F. Noll, Bishop of Fort Wayne, episcopal chairman of the Department of Lay Organizations; Most Rev. John Gregory Murray, Archbishop of St. Paul, episcopal chairman, Department of Catholic Action Study; Most Rev. Hugh C. Boyle, Bishop of Pittsburgh, episcopal chairman of the Legal Department; Most Rev. Edwin V. O'Hara, Bishop of Kansas City and episcopal chairman of the Social Action Department; Most Rev. John Mark Gannon, Bishop of Erie, episcopal chairman of the Press Department; and the Most Rev. John A. Duffy, Bishop of Buffalo, episcopal chairman of the Youth Department; and Most Rev. John T. McNicholas, O.P., Archbishop of Cincinnati, episcopal chairman of the Department of Education.

Assistant Bishops, Administrative Board—Most Rev. Emmet M. Walsh, Bishop of Charleston; Most Rev. Richard O. Gerow, Bishop of Natchez; Most Rev. Karl J. Alter, Bishop of Toledo; Most Rev. Thomas K. Gorman, Bishop of Reno; Most Rev. Walter A. Foery, Bishop of Syracuse; and Most Rev. Charles Hubert LeBlond, Bishop of St. Joseph; Most Rev. John B. Peterson, D.D., Bishop of Manchester; Most Rev. John F. O'Hara, Military Delegate; Most Rev. William D. O'Brien, Auxiliary Bishop of Chicago; and Most Rev. Aloisius J. Muench, Bishop of Fargo.

Administrative Board, The Right Rev. Msgr. Michael J. Ready, General Secretary; Rev. Howard J. Carroll, S.T.D., Asst. Gen. Sec.

Under the N.C.W.C. Episcopal Committee on Motion Pictures (Most Rev. John T. McNicholas, O.P., Archbishop of Cincinnati, chairman; Most Rev. John J. Cantwell, Archbishop of Los Angeles; Most Rev. Hugh C. Boyle, Bishop of Pittsburgh; Most Rev. John F. Noll, Bishop of Fort Wayne, and Most Rev. Stephen J. Donahue, Auxiliary Bishop of New York) there functions the Legion of Decency, organized for the purpose of securing for the public wholesome screen entertainment. One of the means towards the accomplishment of this end is the publishing of a weekly classification of current films. The Legion of Decency has its National Office in the Archdiocese of New York—Address: 485 Madison Ave., New York City, N. Y. The executive secretary is Rev. John J. McClafferty.

Bulgarians, Hungarians and Rumanians in U. S., 1940

Figures based on Alien Registration of 1940, subject to revision.

	Bul-garian	Hun-garian	Ru-manian		Bul-garian	Hun-garian	Ru-manian
Alabama..........	13	124	26	New Jersey........	46	12,978	1,098
Arizona..........	9	42	17	New Mexico.......	10	21	15
Arkansas.........	6	33	11	New York.........	546	26,312	12,126
California........	328	2,823	1,417	North Carolina....	4	43	13
Colorado.........	129	221	72	North Dakota.....	6	70	65
Connecticut......	14	5,137	301	Ohio.............	765	20,429	3,695
Delaware.........	0	71	25	Oklahoma........	76	50	13
Dist. of Col......	9	131	73	Oregon..........	88	212	112
Florida...........	32	452	146	Pennsylvania.....	221	15,157	2,936
Georgia..........	2	45	35	Rhode Island.....	34	53	82
Idaho............	19	36	12	South Carolina....	0	17	7
Illinois...........	426	7,954	3,107	South Dakota.....	20	57	20
Indiana..........	183	3,223	748	Tennessee........	1	57	27
Iowa.............	70	146	43	Texas............	33	243	124
Kansas...........	13	65	42	Utah............	18	36	10
Kentucky........	18	314	43	Vermont.........	0	76	2
Louisiana........	25	191	36	Virginia..........	7	317	39
Maine...........	4	28	6	Washington.......	134	272	100
Maryland........	7	655	241	West Virginia.....	87	2,390	191
Massachusetts....	47	427	445	Wisconsin........	47	2,227	230
Michigan.........	721	10,726	3,185	Wyoming........	23	45	10
Minnesota.......	80	538	388	Alaska...........	6	6	3
Mississippi.......	2	37	3	Hawaii..........	0	4	3
Missouri.........	63	1,871	636	Puerto Rico......	0	10	2
Montana.........	73	99	68	Virgin Islands.....	0	0	1
Nebraska........	13	144	80				
Nevada..........	4	15	7	**Total**...........	**4,491**	**116,696**	**32,164**
New Hampshire...	5	34	10				

SPORTING EVENTS OF 1942 AND RECORDS
St. Louis Cardinals Win 1942 World Series From New York Yankees

The St. Louis Cardinals, champions of the National League, defeated the New York Yankees, champions of the American League, in the 1942 World Series, four games to one.

COMPOSITE BOX SCORE OF FIVE GAMES
NEW YORK YANKEES

	g.	ab.	r.	h.	tb.	2b.	3b.	hr.	bb.	so.	sb.	Bat. avg.	po.	a.	e.	tc.	Fldg. avg.
Rizzuto, ss	5	21	2	8	11	0	0	1	2	1	2	.381	15	14	1	30	.967
Rolfe, 3b	4	17	5	6	8	2	0	0	1	2	0	.353	3	5	0	8	1.000
Crosetti, 3b	1	3	0	0	0	0	0	0	0	1	0	.000	1	1	0	2	1.000
Cullenbine, rf	5	19	3	5	6	1	0	0	1	2	1	.263	6	0	0	6	1.000
DiMaggio, cf	5	21	3	7	7	0	0	0	1	0	0	.333	20	0	0	20	1.000
Keller, lf	5	20	2	4	10	0	0	2	1	3	0	.200	12	1	0	13	1.000
Gordon, 2b	5	21	1	2	3	1	0	0	7	0	0	.095	11	12	0	23	1.000
Dickey, c	5	19	1	5	5	0	0	0	1	0	0	.263	25	1	1	27	.963
Hassett, 1b	3	9	1	3	4	1	0	0	0	1	0	.333	15	1	1	17	.941
Priddy, 3b-1b	3	10	0	1	2	1	0	0	1	0	0	.100	22	4	1	27	.963
*Ruffing, p	4	9	0	2	2	0	0	0	0	2	0	.222	0	1	0	1	1.000
**Selkirk	1	1	0	0	0	0	0	0	0	0	0	.000	0	0	0	0	.000
Bonham, p	2	2	0	0	0	0	0	0	1	0	0	.000	0	2	0	2	1.000
Chandler, p	2	2	0	0	0	0	0	0	0	1	0	.000	2	2	0	4	1.000
Stainback	2	0	0	0	0	0	0	0	0	0	0	.000	0	0	0	0	.000
Breuer, p	1	0	0	0	0	0	0	0	0	0	0	.000	0	1	1	0	.000
Turner, p	1	0	0	0	0	0	0	0	0	1	0	.000	0	0	0	0	.000
Borowy, p	1	1	0	0	0	0	0	0	0	0	0	.000	0	1	0	1	1.000
Donald, p	1	2	0	0	0	0	0	0	0	1	0	.000	0	0	0	0	.000
††Rosar	1	1	0	1	1	0	0	0	0	0	0	1.000	0	0	0	0	.000
Total		178	18	44	59	6	0	3	22	3		.247	132	45	5	182	.973

*Batted for Bonham, ninth inning, second game; for Chandler, eighth inning, third game. **Batted for Ruffing, ninth inning, fifth game. †Ran for Dickey, ninth inning, second game; for Dickey, ninth inning, fifth game. ††Batted for Bonham, ninth inning, fourth game.

ST. LOUIS CARDINALS

	g.	ab.	r.	h.	tb.	2b.	3b.	hr.	bb.	so.	sb.	Bat. avg.	po.	a.	e.	tc.	Fldg. avg.
Brown, 2b	5	20	2	6	6	0	0	0	3	0	0	.300	6	16	3	25	.880
T. Moore, cf	5	17	2	5	6	1	0	0	2	3	0	.294	15	0	0	15	1.000
Slaughter, rf	5	19	3	5	9	1	0	1	3	2	0	.263	9	1	1	11	.909
Musial, lf	5	18	2	4	5	1	0	0	4	0	0	.222	13	0	0	13	1.000
W. Cooper, c	5	21	3	6	7	1	0	0	0	1	0	.286	24	2	1	27	.963
Hopp, 1b	5	17	3	3	3	0	0	0	1	5	0	.176	46	3	1	50	.980
Kurowski, 3b	5	15	3	4	9	0	1	1	2	0	0	.267	7	4	1	12	.917
Marion, ss	5	18	2	2	4	0	1	0	1	2	0	.111	13	16	0	29	1.000
Beazley, p	2	5	1	1	1	0	0	0	0	1	0	.200	0	1	0	1	1.000
M. Cooper, p	2	7	0	1	1	0	0	0	0	5	0	.143	2	0	1	3	.667
Gumbert, p	2	1	0	1	1	0	0	0	0	0	0	1.000	0	1	2	3	.333
Lanier, p	1	1	0	0	0	0	0	0	1	0	0	.000	0	0	0	0	.000
*Walker	2	1	1	0	0	0	0	0	0	0	0	.000	0	0	0	0	.000
**Sanders	1	1	0	1	1	0	0	0	0	0	0	1.000	0	0	0	0	.000
†O'Dea	1	1	0	0	0	0	0	0	0	0	0	.000	0	0	0	0	.000
††Crespi	1	0	1	0	0	0	0	0	0	0	0	.000	0	0	0	0	.000
White, p	1	2	0	0	0	0	0	0	0	0	0	.000	0	0	0	0	.000
Pollet, p	1	0	0	0	0	0	0	0	0	0	0	.000	0	0	0	0	.000
Total		163	23	39	53	4	2	2	17	19	0	.239	135	45	10	190	.947

*Batted for Gumbert, eighth inning, first game. **Batted for Kurowski, ninth inning, first game; for Pollett, seventh inning, fourth game. †Batted for Lanier, ninth inning, first game. ††Ran for O'Dea, ninth inning, first game.

COMPOSITE SCORE BY INNINGS

New York Yankees	2	0	0	2	1	5	0	6	2—18		
St. Louis Cardinals	2	0	1	7	0	1	3	1	8—23		

Earned runs—New York, 13; St. Louis, 22. Runs batted in—Keller 5, W. Cooper 4, Kurowski 5, Marion 3, T. Moore 2, Musial 2, M. Cooper 2, Cullenbine 2, DiMaggio 3, Hassett 2, Brown, Slaughter, 2, Lanier, O'Dea, Priddy, Rizzuto. Left on bases—Cardinals 32, Yankees 34. Double plays—Brown, Marion and Hopp; Keller and Dickey; Marion and Brown; Gordon, Rizzuto and Priddy; Hopp, Marion and Brown. Sacrifices—T. Moore 3, Cullenbine, White, Hopp 2, Kurowski. Umpires—Summers and Hubbard (A. L.), Barr and Magerkurth (N. L.). Times of games—2:35, 1:57, 2:30, 2:28, 1:58.

PITCHING RECORDS
ST. LOUIS

Pitcher	g.	cg.	ip.	h.	r.	er.	bb.	so.	wp.	hb.	w.	l.	pct.	er av.
Beazley	2	2	18	17	5	5	3	6	0	0	2	0	1.000	2.50
White	1	1	9	6	0	0	6	6	0	0	1	0	1.000	0.00
M. Cooper	2	0	13	17	10	8	4	9	0	0	0	1	.000	5.54
Gumbert	2	0	⅔	0	0	0	0	0	0	0	0	0	.000	0.00
Lanier	2	0	4⅓	3	2	0	1	0	0	0	1	0	1.000	0.00
Pollet	1	0	⅓	0	0	0	0	0	0	0	0	0	.000	0.00

NEW YORK

Pitcher	g.	cg.	ip.	h.	r.	er.	bb.	so.	wp.	hb.	w.	l.	pct.	er av.
Ruffing	2	1	17⅔	14	8	8	7	11	0	0	1	1	.500	4.00
Bonham	2	1	11	9	4	5	3	3	0	0	0	1	.000	3.27
Chandler	2	0	8⅓	5	1	1	3	0	0	0	1	0	1.000	1.13
Borowy	1	0	3	6	6	6	3	1	0	0	0	1	.000	18.00
Breuer	1	0	2	0	0	0	1	0	0	0	0	0	.000	0.00
Turner	1	0	1	0	0	0	0	1	0	0	0	0	.000	0.00
Donald	1	0	3	3	2	2	2	1	0	0	0	0	.000	6.00

How Players Shared World Series Money

Yr.	G.	Winning Players'	Share	Losing Players'	Share	Yr.	G.	Winning Players'	Share	Losing Players'	Share
1929	5	Philadelphia..	$5,620	Chicago.....	$3,782	1936	6	Yankees......	$6,430	Giants......	$4,656
1930	6	Philadelphia.	5,785	Cardinals..	3,875	1937	5	Yankees......	6,471	Giants......	4,489
1931	7	Cardinals....	4,467	Athletics..	3,023	1938	4	Yankees.....	5,783	Cubs.......	4,674
1932	4	Yankees.....	5,232	Cubs.......	4,244	1939	4	Yankees.....	5,614	Reds.......	4,283
1933	5	Giants	4,257	Senators..	3,020	1940	7	Reds........	5,803	Tigers......	3,531
1934	7	Cardinals....	5,389	Tigers......	3,354	1941	5	Yankees.....	5,943	Dodgers.....	4,829
1935	6	Tigers	6,545	Cubs.......	4,198	1942	5	Cardinals....	6,192	Yankees.....	3,351

The Yankees voted 33¾ shares and $6,600 in gratuities; the Cardinals 28 full and five one-fifths shares and gratuities.

BASEBALL WORLD CHAMPIONSHIPS—1903-1942

Yr.	Winners	Won	Losers	Won	Yr.	Winners	Won	Losers	Won
1903	Boston, A. L...	5	Pittsb'gh, N. L..	3	1923	N. Y., A. L.....	4	N. Y., N. L.....	2
1904	N. Y., N. L. re	fused	play Boston,A.L.		1924	Wash., A. L....	4	N. Y., N. L.....	3
1905	N. Y., N. L....	4	Phila., A. L....	1	1925	Pittsb'gh, N. L.	4	Wash., A. L....	3
1906	Chicago, A. L..	4	Chicago, N. L..	2	1926	St. Louis, N. L..	4	N. Y., A. L.....	3
1907	Chicago, N. L..	4	Detroit, A. L...	0	1927	N. Y., A. L.....	4	Pitts., N. L....	0
1908	Chicago, N. L..	4	Detroit, A. L...	1	1928	N. Y., A. L.....	4	S. Louis, N. L..	0
1909	Pittsb'gh, N. L.	4	Detroit, A. L...	3	1929	Phila., A. L....	4	Chicago, N. L..	1
1910	Phila., A. L....	4	Chicago, N. L..	1	1930	Phila., A. L....	4	St. Louis, N. L..	2
1911	Phila., A. L....	4	N. Y., N. L.....	2	1931	St. Louis, N. L..	4	Phila., A. L....	3
1912	Boston, A. L...	4	N. Y., N. L.....	3	1932	N. Y., A. L.....	4	Chicago, N. L..	0
1913	Phila., A. L....	4	N. Y., N. L.....	1	1933	N. Y., N. L.....	4	Wash., A. L....	1
1914	Boston, N. L...	4	Phila., A. L....	0	1934	St. Louis, N. L..	4	Detroit, A. L...	3
1915	Boston, A. L...	4	Phila., N. L....	1	1935	Detroit, A. L...	4	Chicago, N. L..	2
1916	Boston, A. L...	4	B'klyn, N. L....	1	1936	N. Y., A. L.....	4	N. Y., N. L.....	2
1917	Chicago, A. L..	4	N. Y., N. L.....	2	1937	N. Y., A. L.....	4	N. Y., N. L.....	1
1918	Boston, A. L...	4	Chicago, N. L..	2	1938	N. Y., A. L.....	4	Chicago, N. L..	0
1919	Cincin., N. L..	5	Chicago, A. L..	3	1939	N. Y., A. L.....	4	Cincinnati, N.L.	0
1920	Clevel'd, A. L..	5	B'klyn, N. L....	2	1940	Cinc., N. L.....	4	Detroit, A. L...	3
1921	N. Y., N. L....	5	N. Y., A. L.....	3	1941	N. Y., A. L.....	4	B'klyn, N. L....	1
1922	N. Y., N. L....	4	N. Y., A. L.....	0	1942	St. Louis, N. L..	4	N. Y. A. L.....	1

WORLD SERIES RECEIPTS AND ATTENDANCE SINCE 1921

Yr.	Clubs	G	Atten.	Recpts.	Yr.	Clubs	G	Atten.	Recpts.
1921	N. Y., N. L.-N. Y., A. L.	8	269,976	$900,233	1932	N. Y., A. L.-Chicago, N. L.	4	191,998	$713,377
1922	N. Y., N. L.-N. Y., A. L.	5	185,947	605,475	1933	N. Y., N. L.-Wash., A. L.	5	163,076	679,365
1923	N. Y., A. L.-N. Y., N. L.	6	301,430	1,063,815	1934	S. L., N. L.-Detr., A. L.	7	281,510	1,128,995
1924	Wash., A. L.-N. Y., N. L.	7	283,665	1,093,104	1935	Detroit, A. L.-Chic., N. L.	6	286,672	1,173,794
1925	Pitts., N. L.-Wash., A. L.	7	282,848	1,182,854	1936	N. Y., A. L.-N. Y., N. L.	6	302,924	1,304,399
1926	St. L., N. L.-N. Y., A. L.	7	328,051	1,207,864	1937	N. Y., A. L.-N. Y., N. L.	5	238,142	1,085,994
1927	N. Y., A. L.-Pitts., N. L.	4	201,105	783,217	1938	N. Y., A. L.-Chicago, N. L.	4	200,833	851,166
1928	N. Y., A. L.-St. Louis, N.L.	4	199,072	777,290	1939	N.Y., A. L.-Cin'nati, N. L.	4	183,849	845,329
1929	Phil., A. L.-Chic., N. L...	5	190,490	859,484	1940	Cinc., N. L.-Detroit, A. L.	7	281,842*	1,322,328
1930	Phila.,A.L.-St.Louis, N.L.	6	212,619	953,772	1941	N. Y., A. L.-B'klyn, N. L.	5	235,773	1,107,762
1931	St. Louis, N.L.-Phila.,A. L.	7	231,587	1,030,723	1942	St. Louis, N.L.-N.Y., A. L.	5	276,717*	1,105,249

*Does not include broadcast rights.

1942—U. S. O. share $362,926.65. United Service Organizations received the entire $100,000 from the sale of the radio rights (not included in gross receipts) and 49 per cent of the receipts from the third and fourth games. U. S. O. also would have received all receipts from the sixth and seventh games if they had been played. Players shared only in the first four games. Commissioner, leagues and clubs shared in first and second games and received all receipts of fifth game. Seventy per cent of the players' share in the first four games go to the competing teams on a 60-40 basis. The remaining 30 per cent goes to the first division clubs in each league. The 1942 pool was $427,579.41 with the 70 per cent for the two clubs $299,304.59. Of this $179,582.75 went to the Cardinals. The Brooklyn Dodgers, runners-up in the National League, and the Boston Red Sox, runners-up in the American League, each received $32,068.46 to divide among the players. The New York Giants and the St. Louis Browns, third place teams in their leagues, drew down $21,378.97 each, and the fourth place teams, Cincinnati and Cleveland, received $10,689.49 each.

Pitchers Who Have Won 300 Big League Games

	Yrs.	W.	L.	PC.		Yrs.	W.	L.	PC.
Denton T. (Cy) Young........	22	511	315	.617	John Clarkson..................	11	327	*	.618
Walter Johnson...............	21	414	276	.600	Eddie Plank...................	17	324	190	.630
Grover Alexander	20	373	208	.640	Charles Radbourne............	11	310	191	.619
Christy Mathewson...........	17	372	189	.663	Mickey Welch.................	13	301	*	*
Charles A. (Kid) Nichols......	15	360	204	.638	Anthony Mulane...............	13	302	*	*
Tim Keefe	14	342	*	*	Robert M. Grove..............	17	300	138	.685

*No record.

Longest Games Played in the Major Leagues

NATIONAL LEAGUE—26 INNINGS, Boston, May 1, 1920

Brooklyn ....0 0 0 0 1 0 0 0 0 0 0 0 0 0 0 0 0 0 0 0 0 0 0 0 0 0—1 9 2
Boston. ....0 0 0 0 1 0 0 0 0 0 0 0 0 0 0 0 0 0 0 0 0 0 0 0 0 0—1 15 2
Game called on account of darkness after 3 hours and 50 minutes play.
Batteries—Cadore and Elliott; Oeschger and Gowdy.

AMERICAN LEAGUE—24 INNINGS, Boston, Sept. 1, 1906

Philadelphia ....1 0 0 0 0 0 0 0 0 0 0 0 0 0 0 0 0 0 0 0 0 0 0 3—4 16 2
Boston ....0 0 0 0 1 0 0 0 0 0 0 0 0 0 0 0 0 0 0 0 0 0 0 0—1 15 1
Time of game 4 hours 47 minutes.
Batteries—Coombs and Powers; Harris and Carrigan and Criger.

American League Wins 1942 All-Star Game, 3 to 1

The tenth annual All-Star game between the American and the National Leagues was played in the Polo Grounds, New York City (July 6, 1942). The game was won by the American League, 3 to 1. The game, scheduled for 6:30 P. M., did not start until 7:20 because of rain and was played entirely under the lights. Two home runs in the first inning off Mort Cooper—one by Lou Boudreau and the other by Rudy York—accounted for three American League runs. The National League made its score in the eighth inning when Mickey Owen hit a home run off Alton Benton.

AMERICAN LEAGUE

	ab.	r.	h.	tb.	2b.	3b.	hr.	sh.	sb.	bb.	so.	po.	a.	e.
Boudreau, Cleveland, ss...	4	1	1	4	0	0	1	0	0	0	0	4	5	0
Henrich, New York, rf....	4	1	1	2	1	0	0	0	0	0	1	2	0	0
Williams, Boston, lf.....	4	0	1	1	0	0	0	0	0	0	0	0	0	0
J. DiMaggio, New York, cf	4	0	2	2	0	0	0	0	0	0	0	2	0	0
York, Detroit, 1b........	4	1	1	4	0	0	1	0	0	0	1	11	3	0
Gordon, New York, 2b....	4	0	0	0	0	0	0	0	0	0	3	1	4	0
Keltner, Cleveland, 3b....	4	0	0	0	0	0	0	0	0	0	1	0	1	0
Tebbetts, Detroit, c......	4	0	0	0	0	0	0	0	0	0	2	4	1	0
Chandler, New York, p...	1	0	0	0	0	0	0	0	0	0	0	3	1	0
aJohnson, Philadelphia....	1	0	1	1	0	0	0	0	0	0	0	0	0	0
Benton, Detroit, p.......	1	0	0	0	0	0	0	0	0	0	0	0	1	0
Total.................	35	3	7	14	1	0	2	0	0	0	8	27	16	0

NATIONAL LEAGUE

	ab.	r.	h.	tb.	2b.	3b.	hr.	sh.	sb.	bb.	so.	po.	a.	e.
Brown, St. Louis, 2b......	2	0	0	0	0	0	0	0	0	0	0	1	0	1
Herman, Brooklyn, 2b.....	1	0	0	0	0	0	0	0	0	0	0	0	0	0
Vaughan, Brooklyn, 3b.....	2	0	0	0	0	0	0	0	0	1	0	1	2	0
Elliott, Pittsburgh, 3b.....	1	0	1	1	0	0	0	0	0	0	0	1	2	0
Reiser, Brooklyn, cf......	3	0	1	1	0	0	0	0	0	0	0	3	0	0
Moore, St. Louis, cf.....	1	0	0	0	0	0	0	0	0	0	0	1	0	0
Mize, New York, 1b......	2	0	0	0	0	0	0	0	0	0	0	3	0	0
F.McCormick,Cincinnati,1b	2	0	0	0	0	0	0	0	0	0	0	3	0	0
Ott, New York, rf......	4	0	0	0	0	0	0	0	0	2	1	0	0	0
Medwick, Brooklyn, lf....	2	0	0	0	0	0	0	0	0	0	0	1	0	0
Slaughter, St. Louis, lf....	2	0	1	1	0	0	0	0	0	0	0	1	0	0
W. Cooper, St. Louis, c....	2	0	1	1	0	0	0	0	0	0	0	7	0	0
Lombardi, Boston, c......	1	0	0	0	0	0	0	0	0	1	0	2	0	0
Miller, Boston, ss........	2	0	0	0	0	0	0	0	0	0	1	2	1	0
Reese, Brooklyn, ss.......	1	0	0	0	0	0	0	0	0	0	0	0	1	0
M. Cooper, St. Louis, p....	0	0	0	0	0	0	0	0	0	0	0	0	0	0
bMarshall, New York.....	1	0	0	0	0	0	0	0	0	0	0	0	0	0
Vander Meer, Cincinnati, p	1	0	0	0	0	0	0	0	0	0	1	0	1	0
cLitwhiler, Philadelphia...	0	0	0	0	0	0	0	0	0	0	0	0	0	0
Passeau, Chicago, p.......	1	1	1	4	0	0	1	0	0	0	0	0	0	0
dOwen, Brooklyn.........	1	1	1	4	0	0	1	0	0	0	0	0	0	0
Walters, Cincinnati, p.....	0	0	0	0	0	0	0	0	0	0	0	0	0	0
Total.................	31	1	6	9	0	0	1	0	0	2	3	27	7	1

a Batted for Chandler in fifth. b Batted for M. Cooper in third. c Batted for Vander Meer in sixth. d Batted for Passeau in eighth.

SCORE BY INNINGS

American League..............................	3	0	0	0	0	0	0	0	0	0—3
National League..............................	0	0	0	0	0	0	0	0	1	0—1

Runs batted in—Boudreau, York 2, Owen. **Earned runs**—American League, 3; National League, 1. **Left on bases**—American League, 5; National League, 6. **Double plays**—Gordon, Boudreau and York; Boudreau and York. **Struck out**—By M. Cooper 2 (Gordon, Tebbets); by Vander Meer 4 (York, Gordon 2, Henrich); by Passeau 1 (Tebbetts); by Walters 1 (Keltner); by Chandler 2 (Ott, Miller); by Benton 1 (Ott). **Bases on balls**—Off Benton 2 (Vaughan, Lombardi). **Hits**—Off Chandler 2 in 4 innings; Benton 4 in 5 innings; M. Cooper 4 in 3 innings; Vander Meer 2 in 3 innings; Passeau 1 in 2 innings; Walters 0 in 1 inning. **Hit by pitcher**—By Chandler (Brown). **Passed ball**—Tebbetts. **Winning pitcher**—Chandler. **Losing pitcher**—M. Cooper. **Umpires**—Ballanfant (N.L.), Stewart (A.L.), Barlick (N.L.) and McGowan (A.L.). **Time—of game**—2:07. **Attendance**—33,694.

Most Valuable Player Awards

NATIONAL LEAGUE

Year	Player	Club
1924—Dazzy Vance		Brooklyn
1925—Rogers Hornsby		St. Louis
1926—Bob O'Farrell		St. Louis
1927—Paul Waner		Pittsburgh
1928—Jim Bottomley		St. Louis
1929—Rogers Hornsby		Chicago
1930—No award.		
1931—Frankie Frisch		St. Louis
1932—Chuck Klein		Philadelphia
1933—Carl Hubbell		New York
1934—Dizzy Dean		St. Louis
1935—Gabby Hartnett		Chicago
1936—Carl Hubbell		New York
1937—Joe Medwick		St. Louis
1938—Ernie Lombardi		Cincinnati
1939—Bucky Walters		Cincinnati
1940—Frank McCormick		Cincinnati
1941—Dolph Camilli		Brooklyn
1942—Mort Cooper		St. Louis

AMERICAN LEAGUE

Year	Player	Club
1924—Walter Johnson		Washington
1925—Roger Peckinpaugh		Washington
1926—George Burns		Cleveland
1927—Lou Gehrig		New York
1928—Mickey Cochrane		Philadelphia
1929—No award		
1930—No award		
1931—Lefty Grove		Philadelphia
1932—Jimmy Foxx		Philadelphia
1933—Jimmy Foxx		Philadelphia
1934—Mickey Cochrane		Detroit
1935—Hank Greenberg		Detroit
1936—Lou Gehrig		New York
1937—Charley Gehringer		Detroit
1938—Jimmy Foxx		Boston
1939—Joe DiMaggio		New York
1940—Hank Greenberg		Detroit
1941—Joe DiMaggio		New York
1942—Joe Gordon		New York

American Legion Junior Baseball World Champions

1933—Chicago, Ill.	1936—Spartanburg, S. C.	1939—Omaha, Neb.	1941—San Diego, Calif.
1934—Cumberland, Md.	1937—Lynn, Mass.	1940—Albemarle, N. C.	1942—Los Angeles, Calif.
1935—Gastonia, N. C.	1938—San Diego, Calif.		

Boxing Results in 1942

Space permits the recording of only the more important bouts. The results are as appearing in public prints and the Almanac assumes no responsibility for the data.

Date	Winner	Loser	Rds.	Place	Date	Winner	Loser	Rds.	Place
Jan. 9	J. Louis	B. Baer	1	New York	June 4	F. Zivic	R. Shank	10	Minneapol
Jan. 10	R. Toles	G. Lovell	5	Buenos Aires	June 4	L. Salica	K. Lindsay	10	Vancouver
Jan. 12	M. Bettina	M. Brown	10	Pittsburgh	June 9	H. Bobo	B. Smith	2	Toledo
Jan. 12	B. Conn	H. Cooper	12	Toledo	June 15	E. Rightmire	E. Peters	10	Sioux City
Jan. 13	J. Bivins	B. Soose	10	Cleveland	June 20	F. Mills	L. Harvey	2	London
Jan. 16	R. Robinson	F. Zivic	10	New York	June 23	M. Bettina	H. Bobo	10	Cleveland
Jan. 20	B. Pastor	C. Villar	10	Washing'tn	June 24	H. Armstrong	S. Rangel	10	Oakland
Jan. 27	T. Maurello	G. Barlund	7	New York	June 27	A. Heuser	W. Neusel	12	Hamburg
Feb. 3	L. Savold	N. Beech	4	Washing'tn	June 29	N. Rubio	F. Zivic	10	Newark
Feb. 5	H. Jeffra	B. Speary	10	Toronto	June 29	A. Stolz	B. Banks	10	Baltimore
Feb. 3	C. Wright	R. Lemos	6	Los Angeles	July 3	R. Shank	H. Armstrong	10	Newark
Feb. 9	F. Zivic	R.Carrabantes	10	Pittsburgh	July 7	S. Angott	B. Montgomery	12	Philadel.
Feb. 10	L. Franklin	A. Reiss	1	Toledo	July 10	L. Salica	N. Corum	10	San Jose, Calif.
Feb. 13	B. Conn	T. Zale	12	New York					
Feb. 15	M. Servo	S. Jenkins	10	Philadel.	July 13	C. Wright	L.Transparenti	4	Baltimore
Feb. 24	J. Wilson	C. Garcia	10	Los Angeles	July 20	J. Paterson	F. Petrin	2	London
Feb. 24	B. Pastor	L. Franklin	8	Cleveland	July 20	H. Armstrong	J. Ybarra	3	Sacramento
Feb. 27	A. Stolz	A. Ruffin	12	New York	July 21	L. Savold	B. Poland	9	Toledo
Feb. 27	T. Motisi	F. Zivic	10	Chicago	July 23	T. Mauriello	C. Burman	9	New York
Mar. 2	T. Young	J. Wilson	8	New York	July 23	C. Constantino	P. Hernandez	12	New York
Mar. 2	C. Rico	M. Belloise	7	New York					
Mar. 2	K. Overlin	E. Charles	10	Cincinnati	Aug. 1	R. Robinson	S. Angott	10	New York
Mar. 2	T. Thompson	P. Valentino	9	San Franc.	Aug. 3	H. Armstrong	A. Spoldi	7	San Franc.
Mar. 3	P. Scalzo	N. Litfen	8	New York	Aug. 6	A. Stolz	C. Wright	10	New York
Mar. 6	S. Angott	B. Montgomery	12	New York	Aug. 7	M. Ortiz	L. Salica	12	Hollywood
Mar. 9	F. Zivic	T. Jannazzo	5	Pittsburgh	Aug. 13	B. Montgomery	B. Ruffin	10	New York
Mar.11	J. Bivins	G. Lesnevich	10	Cleveland	Aug. 13	H. Armstrong	J. Burke	10	Ogden, Ut.
Mar.10	G. Dorazio	L. Brooks	10	Philadel.	Aug. 17	H. Armstrong	R. Ramirez	8	Oakland
Mar.11	K. Overlin	P. Mahoney	10	Buffalo	Aug. 27	R. Robinson	T. Motisi	1	Chicago
May 3	R. Toles	A. Lovell		Buenos Aires	Aug. 27	C. Wright	J. Marinelli	2	Detroit
Mar.23	T. Maurello	H. Cooper	3	New York	Sept.14	H. Armstrong	L. Rodak	8	San Franc.
Mar.20	R. Robinson	N. Rubio	7	New York	Sept.15	J. Bivins	T. Mauriello	10	Cleveland
Mar.23	L. Savold	W. Cross	9	Newark	Sept.21	F. Zivic	J. Walker	10	Philadel.
Mar.27	M. Kaplan	L. Jenkins	10	Boston	Sept.22	L. Savold	J. Flynn	4	Akron
Mar.27	J. Louis	A. Simon	6	New York	Sept.29	S. Angott	A. Soldi	10	New Orleans
Mar.30	H. Bobo	L. Franklin	1	Pittsburgh	Sept.30	H. Armstrong	E. Turner	4	Oakland
Mar.31	M. Bettina	G. Dorazio	10	Philadel.	Sept.30	H. Matthews	A. Hostak	10	Seattle
Apr. 4	F. Apostoli	J. Mulli	2	New York	Oct. 2	J. Robinson	L. Motta	10	New York
Apr. 6	V. Bybee	C. White	10	San Franc.	Oct. 6	M. Shapiro	B. Montgomery	10	Philadel.
Apr. 7	J. Hatcher	P. Scalzo	8	New York	Oct. 6	M. Belloise	J. Forte	8	Philadel.
Apr. 10	M. Bettina	B. Beckwith	10	Chicago	Oct. 13	C. Wright	C. Cuebas	4	Hartford
Apr. 13	F. Zivic	M. Berger	10	Pittsburgh	Oct. 18	C. Wright	H. Vasquez	8	New Haven
Apr. 17	R. Robinson	H. Dubs	6	Detroit	Oct. 19	R. Robinson	I. Junnazzo	8	Philadel.
Apr. 17	B. Pastor	J. Bivins	10	Cleveland	Oct. 20	J. Bivins	B. Pastor	10	Cleveland
Apr. 17	C. Chavez	L. Salica	10	Hollywood	Oct. 27	H. Armstrong	F. Zivic	10	San Franc.
Apr. 20	T. Maurello	E. Eatman	5	Bridgeport	Oct. 30	T. Mauriello	L. Savold	10	New York
Apr. 23	R. Shank	F. Zivic	10	Minneapol.	Nov. 3	M. Berger	E. Robinson	8	New York
May 3	R. Toles	A. Godoy	12	Buenos Aires	Nov. 6	R. Robinson	V. Dellecurti	10	New York
May 7	A. Spencer	B. McCoy	5	San Franc.	Nov. 6	L. Nova	E. Nordham	4	Portl'd, O.
May 7	C. Wright	C. Constantino	8	New York	Nov. 9	J. Wilson	B. Miller	8	New York
May 13	J. Byrd	L. Jenkins	10	Hot Springs	Nov. 9	L. Brooks	T. Musto	12	Chicago
May 15	S. Angott	H. Stolz	15	New York	Nov. 9	M. Belloise	R. Garcia	10	Providence
May 20	A. Christoforidis	J. Colan	10	Chicago	Nov. 9	A. Davis	F. Moreles	1	Wash.,D.C.
May 22	T. Maurello	B. Pastor	10	New York	Nov.13	B. Jack	A. Stolz	7	New York
May 25	L. Savold	L. Nova	8	Washing'tn	Nov.16	L. Savold	J. Kapovich	2	Baltimore
May 25	F. Zivic	L. Jenkins	10	Pittsburgh	Nov.16	T. Larkin	F. Archer	10	Newark, N. J.
May 25	N. Mann	B. Weinberg	10	New Haven					
May 28	R. Robinson	M. Servo	10	New York	Nov.16	S. Rangel	F. Zivic	10	San Franc.

Amateur Boxing in 1942

National Amateur Boxing Championships, Boston, Mass., April 16-17.
112 lbs.—Leroy Jackson, Cleveland, O.
118 lbs.—Bernard Decussen, New Orleans, La.
126 lbs.—James Marlo, Fort Mitchell, N. Y.
135 lbs.—Robert McQuillan, Lackawanna, N. Y.
147 lbs.—Willard Buckless, Saugus, Mass.
160 lbs.—Samson Powell, Cleveland, O.
175 lbs.—Robert Foxworth, St. Louis, Mo.

Heavyweight—Paul Komar, Pittsburgh, Pa.

Eastern Intercollegiate Boxing Championships, University of Virginia, Charlottesville, Va., March 6-7.
120 lbs.—Gerald Auclair, Syracuse.
127 lbs.—Jess Fardella, Penn State.
135 lbs.—Robert Peden, Army.
145 lbs.—Robert Baird, Penn State.
155 lbs.—Mark McGarity, Coast Guard Academy.

165 lbs.—Carlo Ortenzi, Western Maryland.
175 lbs.—Norman Rathbun, Virginia.
Heavyweight—Salvatore Mirabito, Syracuse.
Team championship won by Maryland with 15 points.

National Intercollegiate Boxing Championships, Baton Rouge, La., March 27-28.
120 lbs.—Harper, Southwestern Louisiana Institute.
127 lbs.—Miyagawa, San Jose State.
135 lbs.—Rankin, Wisconsin.
145 lbs.—Jollymore, Wisconsin.
155 lbs.—Lutz, Wisconsin.
165 lbs.—Rathbun, Virginia.
175 lbs.—Markis, Wisconsin.

Heavyweight—Markis, Wisconsin.
Team title won by Wisconsin.

N. B. A. freezes titles of boxing champions

The National Boxing Association announced (Oct. 16, 1942) the freezing of boxing titles for champions in the armed services. "A man in the service is entitled to complete protection of his championship in all circumstances until he is able to defend; this is the N. B. A. policy" said Abe J. Green, head of the N. B. A.

Joe Louis and His Record in 57 Ring Contests

1934		
July 4—Jack Kracken, Chicago....... K.O.	1
July 11—Willie Davies, Chicago....... K.O.	3
July 29—Larry Udell, Chicago....... K.O.	2
Aug. 13—Jack Kranz, Chicago....... Won	8
Aug. 27—Buck Everett, Chicago....... K.O.	2
Sept. 11—Otto Bovchuk, Detroit....... K.O.	4
Sept. 25—Artolph Wiater, Chicago....... Won	10
Oct. 24—Art Sykes, Chicago....... K.O.	8
Oct. 30—Jack O'Dowd, Detroit....... K.O.	4
Nov. 14—Stanley Poreda, Chicago....... K.O.	1
Nov. 30—Charley Massera, Chicago....... K.O.	3
Dec. 14—Lee Ramage, Chicago....... K.O.	8

1935		
Jan. 4—Patsy Perroni, Detroit........ Won	10
Jan. 11—Hans Birkie, Pittsburgh....... K.O.	10
Feb. 21—Lee Ramage, Los Angeles...... K.O.	2
Mar. 8—Red Barry, San Francisco.... K.O.	3
Mar. 29—Natie Brown. Detroit........ Won	10
Apr. 12—Roy Lazaer, Chicago......... K.O.	3
Apr. 22—Biff Bennett, Dayton, O...... K.O.	3
Apr. 25—Roscoe Toles, Flint, Mich.... K.O.	6
May 3—Willie Davies, Peoria, Ill..... K.O.	2
May 7—Gene Stanton, K'l'm'zoo,Mich. K.O.	3
June 25—Primo Carnera, New York.... K.O.	6
Aug. 7—King Levinsky, Chicago....... K.O.	1
Sept. 24—Max Baer, New York........ K.O.	4
Dec. 13—Paulino Uzcudun, N. Y. C... K.O.	4

1936		
Jan. 17—Charley Retzlaff, Chicago..... K.O.	1
June   19—Max Schmeling, New York..... K.O. by 12
Aug. 17—Jack Sharkey, New York...... K.O.	3
Sept. 22—Al Ettore, Philadelphia....... K.O.	5
Oct. 9—Jorge Brescia, New York...... K.O.	3
Dec. 14—Eddie Simms, Cleveland....... K.O.	1

1937		
Jan. 11—Stanley Ketchell, Buffalo...... K.O.	2
Jan. 27—Bob Pastor, New York........ Won	10
Feb. 17—Natie Brown, Kansas City..... K.O.	4
*June 22—James J. Braddock, Chicago.... K.O.	8
Aug. 30—Tommy Farr, New York....... Won	15

1938		
Feb. 23—Nathan Mann, New York.... K.O.	3
Apr. 1—Harry Thomas, Chicago...... K.O.	5
June 22—Max Schmeling, New York.... K.O.	1

1939		
Jan. 25—John Henry Lewis, New York. K.O.	1
Apr. 17—Jack Roper, Los Angeles...... K.O.	1
June 27—Tony Galento, New York...... K.O.	4
Sept. 20—Bob Pastor, Detroit.......... K.O.	11

1940		
Feb. 9—Arturo Godoy, New York..... Won	15
Mar. 29—Johnny Paycheck, New York .. K.O.	2
June 20—Arturo Godoy, New York..... K.O.	8
Dec. 16—Al McCoy, Boston.......... K.O.	6

1941		
Jan. 31—Red Burman, New York...... K.O.	5
Feb. 17—Gus Dorazzio, Philadelphia.... K.O.	2
Mar. 21—Abe Simon, Detroit......... K.O.	13
Apr. 8—Tony Musto, St. Louis....... K.O.	9
May 23—Buddy Baer, Washington..... K.O.	8
June 18—Billy Conn, New York....... K.O.	13
Sept. 29—Lou Nova, New York........ K.O.	6

1942		
Jan. 9—Buddy Baer, New York...... K.O.	1
Mar. 27—Abe Simon, New York....... K.O.	6

Recapitulations—Bouts, 57; knockouts, 49; won, 7; knocked out by, 1.
Joe Louis—Joseph Louis Barrow—whose fists have won for him $2,263,784 in the boxing ring, joined the United States Army (Jan. 12, 1942) at Governors Island, New York. Louis was born (May 13, 1914) in Lexington, Ala.

HISTORY OF HEAVYWEIGHT CHAMPIONSHIP BOUTS

1889—July 8—John L. Sullivan beat Jake Kilrain, 75 rounds, Richbourg, Miss. (Last championship bare knuckle bout.)
*1892—Sept. 7—James J. Corbett defeated John L. Sullivan, 21 rounds, New Orleans. (Used big gloves.)
1894—Jan. 25—James J. Corbett beat Charley Mitchell, 3 rounds, Jacksonville, Fla.
*1897—March 17—Bob Fitzsimmons defeated James J. Corbett, 14 rounds, Carson City, Nev.
*1899—June 9—James J Jeffries beat Bob Fitzsimmons, 11 rounds, Coney Island, N. Y.
1899—Nov. 3—James J. Jeffries beat Tom Sharkey, 25 rounds, Coney Island, N. Y.
1900—James J. Jeffries knocked out James J. Corbett, 23 rounds, May 11, Coney Island, N. Y.
1902—July 25—James J. Jeffries knocked out Bob Fitzsimmons, 8 rounds, San Francisco, Cal.
1903—Aug. 14—James J. Jeffries knocked out James J. Corbett, 10 rounds, San Francisco, Cal.
1904—Aug. 26—James J. Jeffries knocked out Jack Munroe, 2 rounds, San Francisco, Cal.
1905—James J. Jeffries retired, July 3 Marvin Hart knocked out Jack Root, 12 rounds, Reno. Jeffries refereed and presented the title to the victor, Jack O'Brien also claimed the title.
1906—Feb. 23—Tommy Burns defeated Marvin Hart 20 rounds, Los Angeles, Cal.
1907—May 8—Tommy Burns defeated Jack O'Brien, 20 rounds, Los Angeles, Cal.
1907—July 4—Tommy Burns defeated Bill Squires, 1 round, Colma, Cal.
1907—Dec. 2—Tommy Burns defeated Gunner Moir, 10 rounds, London.
1908—Feb. 10—Tommy Burns defeated Jack Palmer, 4 rounds, London.
1908—March 17—Tommy Burns defeated Jem Roche, 1 round, Dublin.
1908—April 18—Tommy Burns defeated Jewey Smith, 5 rounds, Paris.
1908—June 13—Tommy Burns defeated Bill Squires, 8 rounds, Paris.
1908—Aug. 24—Tommy Burns defeated Bill Squires, 13 rounds, Sydney, New South Wales.
1908—Sept. 2—Tommy Burns defeated Bill Lang, 2 rounds, Melbourne, Australia.
*1908—Dec. 26—Jack Johnson stopped Tommy Burns, 14 rounds, Sydney, Australia. Police halted contest.
1909—May 19—Jack Johnson and Jack O'Brien, 6 rounds, draw, Philadelphia.
1909—June 30—Jack Johnson and Tony Ross, 6 rounds, draw, Pittsburgh, Pa.
1909—Oct. 16—Jack Johnson knocked out Stanley Ketchell, 12 rounds, Colma, Cal.
1909—Sept. 9—Jack Johnson and Al Kaufman, 10 rounds, no decision, San Francisco, Cal.
1910—July 4—Jack Johnson knocked out Jim

Jeffries, 15 rounds, Reno, Nev. (Jeffries came back from retirement.)
1912—July 4—Jack Johnson won on points from Jim Flynn, 9 rounds, Las Vegas, N. M., (contest stopped by police.)
1913—Nov. 28—Jack Johnson knocked out Andre Spaul, 2 rounds, Paris.
1913—Dec. 9—Jack Johnson and Jim Johnson, 10 rounds, draw, Paris.
1914—June 27—Jack Johnson won from Frank Moran, 20 rounds, Paris.
*1915—April 5—Jess Willard knocked out Jack Johnson, 26 rounds, Havana, Cuba.
1916—March 25—Jess Willard and Frank Moran, 10 rounds (no decision), New York City.
*1919—July 4—Jack Dempsey knocked out Jess Willard, Toledo, O. (Willard failed to answer bell for fourth round.)
1920—Sept. 6—Jack Dempsey knocked out Billy Miske, 3 rounds, Benton Harbor, Mich.
1920—Dec. 14—Jack Dempsey knocked out Bill Brennan, 12 rounds, New York City.
1921—July 2—Jack Dempsey knocked out Georges Carpentier, 4 rounds, Boyle's Thirty Acres, Jersey City, N. J.
1923—July 4—Jack Dempsey won on points from Tom Gibbons, 15 rounds, Shelby, Mont.
1923—Sept. 14—Jack Dempsey knocked out Luis Firpo, 2 rounds, New York City.
*1926—Sept. 23—Gene Tunney beat Jack Dempsey, 10 rounds, decision, Philadelphia.
1927—Sept. 22—Gene Tunney beat Jack Dempsey. 10 rounds, decision, Chicago.
1928—July 26—Gene Tunney knocked out Tom Heeney, 11 rounds, Yankee Stadium, New York; he announced, shortly after that, his retirement from the ring.
1930—June 12—Max Schmeling of Germany defeated Jack Sharkey, Boston, in fourth round when Sharkey fouled Schmeling in a bout which was generally considered to have resulted in the election of a successor to Gene Tunney.
*1932—June 21—Jack Sharkey defeated Max Schmeling, 15 rounds, decision, New York City.
*1933—June 29—Primo Carnera knocked out Jack Sharkey, six rounds, New York City.
*1934—June 14—Max Baer knocked out Primo Carnera, eleven rounds, New York City.
*1935—June 13—James J. Braddock defeated Max Bear, 15 rounds, New York City. (Judge's decision.)
*1937—June 22—Joe Louis knocked out James J Braddock, 8 rounds, Chicago.
1937—Aug. 30—Joe Louis defeated Tommy Farr, 15 rounds (Judge's decision), New York City.
1938—Feb. 23—Joe Louis knocked out Nathan Mann, 3 rounds, New York City.

1938—April 1—Joe Louis knocked out Harry Thomas, 5 rounds, New York City.
1938—June 22—Joe Louis knocked out Max Schmeling, one round, New York City.
1939—January 25—Joe Louis knocked out John H. Lewis, 1 round, New York City.
1939—April 17—Joe Louis knocked out Jack Roper, 1 round, Los Angeles.
1939—June 28—Joe Louis knocked out Tony Galento, 4 rounds, New York City.
1939—September 20—Joe Louis knocked out Bob Pastor, 11 rounds, Detroit, Mich.
1940—February 9—Joe Louis defeated Arturo Godoy in fifteen-round bout by decision, New York City.
1940—March 29—Joe Louis knocked out Johnny Paycheck, 2 rounds, New York City.
1940—June 20—Joe Louis knocked out Arturo Godoy, 8 rounds, New York City.

1940—Dec. 16—Joe Louis knocked out Al McCoy, 6 rounds, Boston.
1941—Jan. 31—Joe Louis knocked out Red Burman, 5 rounds, New York City.
1941—Feb. 17—Joe Louis knocked out Gus Dorazio, 2 rounds, Philadelphia.
1941—March 21—Joe Louis knocked out Abe Simon, 13 rounds. Detroit, Mich.
1941—April 8—Joe Louis knocked out Tony Musto, 9 rounds, St. Louis, Mo.
1941—May 23—Joe Louis beat Buddy Baer, 7 rounds, Washington, D. C.
1941—June 18—Joe Louis knocked out Billy Conn, 13 rounds, New York City.
1941—Sept. 29—Joe Louis knocked out Lou Nova, 6 rounds, New York City.
1942—Jan. 9—Joe Louis knocked out Buddy Baer, 1 round, New York City.
1942—March 27—Joe Louis knocked out Abe Simon, 6 rounds, New York City.

* Title changed hands.

Largest Championship Battle Gate Receipts

Date	Winner	Loser	Place	Gate Receipts
Sept. 22, 1927	Gene Tunney	J. Dempsey	Chicago	$2,650,000
Sept. 23, 1926	Gene Tunney	J. Dempsey	Philadelphia, Pa.	1,895,723
July 2, 1921	Dempsey	Carpentier	Jersey City, N. J.	1,626,580
July 21, 1927	Dempsey	Jack Sharkey	New York City	1,083,529
Sept. 14, 1923	Dempsey	Firpo	New York City	1,082,590
Sept. 24, 1935	Joe Louis	Max Baer	New York City	948,352
June 22, 1938	Joe Louis	Max Schmeling	New York City	940,096
July 26, 1928	Gene Tunney	Tom Heeney	New York City	691,014
June 22, 1937	Joe Louis	J. Braddock	Chicago, Ill	640,420
Sept. 29, 1941	Joe Louis	Louis Nova	New York City	583,821
June 21, 1936	Max Schmeling	Joe Louis	New York City	547,372
Sept. 11, 1924	Wills	Firpo	Jersey City, N. J.	462,850
July 23, 1923	Benny Leonard	Lew Tendler	New York City	452,648
July 4, 1919	Dempsey	Willard	Toledo, Ohio	452,522
June 18, 1941	Joe Louis	Billy Conn	New York City	451,743
July 12, 1923	Firpo	Willard	Jersey City, N. J.	434,269
June 21, 1932	Sharkey	Schmeling	New York City	429,000
June 14, 1934	Max Baer	Primo Carnera	New York City	417,630
July 2, 1925	Wills	Weinert	New York City	400,000
Feb. 27, 1929	Jack Sharkey	Young Stribling	Miami Beach, Fla	395,369
July 27, 1922	Benny Leonard	Lew Tendler	Jersey City, N. J.	367,862
May 12, 1923	Heavyweight charity bouts		New York City	350,000
Sept. 20, 1939	Joe Louis	Bob Pastor	Detroit, Mich.	347,870
June 25, 1935	Joe Louis	Carnera	New York City	328,655
Sept. 26, 1929	Jack Sharkey	Tom Loughran	New York City	320,355

Golden Gloves Championships, 1942

Inter-City Championships, New York vs. Chicago, New York City, March 30, won by New York, 9 bouts to 7, including alternate contests.

112-POUND CLASS
Championship—Ralph McNeil, New York, defeated Hank Ulrich.
Alternates—Melvyn Pullen, Chicago, defeated Lee Booker.

118-POUND CLASS
Championship—Jack Graves, Chicago, defeated Al Turner.
Alternate—Charles Riley, Chicago, knocked out Nick Picarello in 2:35 of second round.

126-POUND CLASS
Championship—Tommy Rotolo, New York, defeated Sammy Derrico.
Alternate—Victor Resto, New York, defeated Arloc Roye.

135-POUND CLASS
Championship—Morris Corona, Chicago, defeated Eugene Burton.
Alternate—Doc Henry, New York, defeated Julius Menendez.

147-POUND CLASS
Championship—Bob Burns, Chicago, defeated Benny Deans.
Alternate—Marvin Bryant, Chicago, defeated Joseph Bowman.

160-POUND CLASS
Championship—Joe Carter, New York, defeated Benny McCombs.

Alternate—Reginald Osborne, New York, defeated Forrest Gee.

175-POUND CLASS
Championship—Clent Conway, New York, defeated Tom Attra.
Alternate—Leroy Jeffries, Chicago, defeated Samuel Springer.

HEAVYWEIGHT CLASS
Championship—Jimmy Carollo, New York, defeated Hubert Hood.
Alternate—Robert Ramsey, New York, defeated James Phillips.

Tournament of Champions—New York City. March 18.
112-lb. Class—R. McNeil, Newark, N. J., defeated R. Dabney, Philadelphia, Pa.
118-lb. Class—A. Turner, Trenton, N. J., defeated C. Vinci, Rome, N. Y.
126-lb. Class—T. Rotolo, Syracuse, N. Y., defeated D. Matthews, Savannah, Ga.
135-lb. Class—E. Burton, New York, defeated R. McQuillan, Buffalo, N. Y.
147-lb. Class—B. Deans, Newark, N. J., defeated R. Vernon, Washington, D. C.
160-lb. Class—J. Carter, Syracuse, N. Y., defeated J. Rowsey, Huntington, W. Va.
175-lb. Class—C. Conway, New York, K.O. 1st round, J. Fowlks, Newark, N. J.
Heavyweight—J. Carollo, New York, defeated R. Ramsey, Huntington, W. Va.

James E. Sullivan Memorial Trophy Winners

Year	Name	Sport	Points	Year	Name	Sport	Points
1930	Bobby Jones, jr.	Golf	1625	1936	Glenn Morris	Track	1106
1931	Barney Berlinger	Track	425	1937	J. D. Budge	Tennis	1398
1932	J. A. Bausch	Track	687	1938	Don Lash	Track	459
1933	Glenn Cunningham	Track	611	1939	J. W. Burk	Rowing	1063
1934	W. R. Bonthron	Track	1072	1940	J. Gregory Rice	Track	1013
1935	W. L. Little. Jr	Golf	694	1941	Leslie MacMitchell	Track	848

The James E. Sullivan Memorial Trophy is awarded annually to the athlete who "by his performance, example and influence as an amateur and a man, has done the most during the year to advance the cause of sportsmanship." The A. A. U. polls sports leaders throughout the country in its search for the No. 1 sportsman of the year.

Intercollegiate Rowing at Poughkeepsie

The leading American rowing colleges (except Yale and Harvard) have sent eight-oared crews to compete over the four-mile course on the Hudson River at Poughkeepsie, N. Y., since 1895. Columbia won that year, defeating Cornell and Pennsylvania in that order. In 1896 Cornell defeated Harvard, Pennsylvania and Columbia.

In 1897 Cornell defeated Columbia and Pennsylvania on July 2, after defeating Yale and Harvard at New London on June 25. The following year, 1898, the three-mile course on Lake Saratoga was used, Pennsylvania defeating Cornell, Wisconsin and Columbia. In 1899 the crews returned to Poughkeepsie. Pennsylvania won that year, and subsequent winners were: 1900, Pennsylvania; 1901, Cornell; 1902, Cornell; 1903, Cornell; 1904, Syracuse; 1905, Cornell; 1906, Cornell; 1907, Cornell; 1908, Syracuse; 1909, Cornell; 1910, Cornell; 1911, Cornell; 1912, Cornell; 1913, Syracuse; 1914, Columbia; 1915, Cornell; 1916, Syracuse.

Racing was dropped during the war years and was resumed by four crews over a two-mile course on Lake Cayuga, Ithaca, N. Y., on June 19, 1920, when Syracuse won in 11 m. $2\frac{3}{5}$ sec. The colleges again returned to Poughkeepsie in 1921 and for four years rowed over a three-mile course, but resumed the four-mile course in 1925. The full results of the races from 1901 to 1935 inclusive will be found in The World Almanac for 1936 on page 818. The regatta was omitted in 1933.

California established a record for the course in 1939, 18 mins., $12\frac{3}{5}$ seconds for four miles.

Freshman races were rowed over a two-mile course at Poughkeepsie from 1896 to 1916, the winners being: 1896, Cornell; 1897, Cornell; 1898 (at Saratoga), Cornell; 1899, Cornell; 1900, Wisconsin; 1901, Pennsylvania; 1902, Cornell; 1903, Cornell; 1904, Syracuse; 1905, Cornell; 1906, Syracuse; 1907, Wisconsin; 1908, Cornell; 1909, Cornell; 1910, Cornell; 1911, Columbia; 1912, Cornell; 1913, Cornell; 1914, Cornell; 1915, Syracuse; 1916, Cornell. They rowed at Lake Cayuga in 1920 Cornell winning, and returned with the varsities to the Hudson in 1921 when Cornell won.

The Junior varsities first rowed at Poughkeepsie on the two-mile course in 1914, Cornell winning. In 1915 Cornell won and in 1916 Syracuse. The race was rowed on Lake Cayuga in 1920, Cornell winning. In 1926 the course was lengthened to three miles.

The results of the regattas at Poughkeepsie since 1923 (the regatta was omitted in 1933) are:

UNIVERSITY EIGHT-OAR CREWS; POUGHKEEPSIE, COURSE FOUR MILES

Year	Winner	Second	Third	Fourth	Fifth
1923, June 28	**Wash., 14.03 1-5**	Navy, 14.07 2-5	Col'bia, 14.15 4-5	Syracuse	Cornell
1924, June 17	**Wash., 15.02**	Wisc'n, 15.09 2-5	Cornell, 15.15 3-5	Pen'via, 15.23 3-5	S'acuse, 15.25
1925, June 22	**Navy, 19.24 4-5**	Wash., 19 28	Wisc'n, 19.58	Pen'via, 19.59	Cornell, 20.04
1926, June 28	**Wash., 19.28 3-5**	Navy, 19.29 3-5	S'acuse, 19.53 4-5	Pen'via 20.03 4-5	Col'bia 20.05 1-5
1927, June 29	**Col'bia., 20.57**	Wash., 20.59 3-5	Calif., 21.12 2-5	Navy, 21.21 1-5	Cornell, 21.23
1828, June 19	**Calif., 18.35 4-5**	Col'bia, 18.38	Wash., 18.46	Cornell, 19.01	Navy, 19.10
1929, June 24	**Col'bia, 22.58**	Wash., 23.08 4-5	Pen'via, 23.41 2-5	Navy, 23.58 4-5	Wisc'n, 24.09 2-5
1930, June 26	**Cornell, 21.42**	S'acuse, 21.54 4-5	M.I.T., 21.19	Calif., 22.24 4-5	Col'bia. 22.33 2-5
1931, June 16	**Navy, 18.54 1-5**	Cornell, 18.59	Wash., 19.00 3-5	Calif., 19.11 4-5	S'acuse, 19.19 4-5
1932, June 20	**Calif., 19.55**	Cornell, 20.05	Wash., 20.14 1-5	Navy, 20.19 4-5	Syrac., 20.24 2-5
1934, June 16	**Calif., 19.44**	Wash., 19.48 4-5	Navy, 19.50 2-5	Cornell, 19.58 2-5	Penn., 19.59
1935, June 18	**Calif., 18.52**	Cornell 18.52 3-5	Wash. 19.00 4-5	Navy, 19.02 4-5	S'acuse, 19.09 1-5
1936, June 22	**Wash., 19.09 3-5**	Calif ... 19.13 2-5	Navy .. 19.16 4-5	Col'bia. 19.27 1-5	Cornell. 19.34 3-5
1937, June 22	**Wash., 18:33 3-5**	Navy, 18.47 1-5	Cornell, 18.56 2-5	Syrac .. 18.57 1-5	Calif., 19.03 4-5
1938, June 27	**Navy, 18.19**	Calif. 18.20 1-5	Wash., 18.25 2-5	Col'bia. 18.27	Wisc., 18.34
1939, June 17	**Calif., 18.12 3-5**	Wash., 18.14	Navy, 18.22 4-5	Cornell 18.31 3-5	Syrac., 18.34 2-5
1940, June 18	**Wash., 22.42**	Cornell 22.45 3-5	S'acuse, 22.57	Navy, 23.02	Calif. 23.17
1941, June 25	**Wash., 18:53 3**	Calif., 19.02 3	Cornell, 19.14 6	S'acuse, 19.18 9	Princ'n, 19.23 4

1942—Not rowed—war.
In 1936, Pennsylvania (19.37) was sixth; Syracuse ($19.37\frac{1}{2}$) seventh.
In 1937, Columbia (19.20 2-5) was sixth; Wisconsin (19.24 3-5) seventh.
In 1938, Cornell (18:38 4-5) was sixth; Syracuse (18:40 1-5) seventh.
In 1939, Wisconsin (18:40 2-5) was sixth; Columbia (18.50) seventh.
In 1940, Columbia (24.02) was sixth; Wisconsin (24.06) seventh; Princeton (24.09) eighth.
In 1941, Wisconsin (19:29.4) was sixth; Rutgers (19:29.8) seventh; M. I. T. (19:32.8) eighth; Columbia (19:35.5) ninth.

Year	FRESHMEN EIGHTS: course two miles — Winner	Second	JUNIOR EIGHTS: course four miles — Winner	Second
1923, June 28	**Cornell ... 9.27 4-5**	Wash'ton.. 9.28	**Syracuse.. 9.50**	Cornell.... 9.53
1924, June 17	**Pennsylv'a 10.22 3-5**	Cornell........	**Pennsyl'a. 10.36 2-5**	Wash'ton.. 10.43
1925, June 22	**Syracuse.. 9.59**	Penn'via... 10.04	**Wash..... 10.26**	Cornell.... 10.31
1926, June 28	**Columbia. 11.28 3-5**	Calif...... 11.48 2-5	**Wash..... 15.40 1-5**	Penn'via.. 15.46 1-5
1927, June 29	**Navy...... 9.45**	S'acuse.... 9.50 1-5	**Wash..... 15.12 4-5**	Col'bia.... 15.23 4-5
1928, June 19	**Navy...... 9.42**	Cornell.... 9.49	**Navy..... 14.18 1-5**	Cornell.... 14.18 3-5
1929, June 24	**Syracuse.. 10.23 3-5**	Calif...... 10.33 3-5	**Cornell ... 15.21 1-5**	Col'bia.... 15.24
1930, June 26	**Syracuse.. 11.18 1-5**	Cornell.... 11.25 4-5	**Cornell ... 16.39**	Wash'ton.. 17.01
1931, June 16	**Wash..... 9.49 4-5**	Cornell.... 9.53 4-5	**Syracuse.. 14.29 3-5**	California.. 14.33 3-5
1932, June 20	**Syracuse.. 10.59**	Navy 11.05 4-5	**Syracuse.. 15.41**	California.. 15.45 1-5
1934, June 16	**Wash..... 10.50**	S'acuse.... 11.08 1-5	**Syracuse.. 15.40 3-5**	Navy..... 15.41 4-5
1935, June 18	**Wash..... 10.29**	Calif...... 10.41 2-5	**Wash..... 14.58 4-5**	Navy..... 15.04 4-5
1936, June 22	**Wash..... 10.19 3-5**	Calif...... 10.23 2-5	**Wash..... 14.42 1-5**	Navy..... 14.53 3-5
1937, June 23	**Wash..... 9.15 2-5**	Calif...... 9.20 2-5	**Wash..... 13.44**	Navy..... 13.55 3-5
1938, June 27	**California. 9.30 2-5**	Wash...... 9.31 2-5	**Wash..... 13.49 1-5**	California.. 13.50 2-5
1939, June 17	**Wash..... 9.31**	Colo....... 9.32 3-5	**Syracu ... 13.56 3-5**	Wash'ton.. 13.57 2-5
1940, June 18	**Cornell ... 10.55 1-5**	Princeton.. 11.02 3-5	**Wash..... 18.07 1-5**	Navy..... 18.23
1941, June 25	**Cornell ... 9.57 7**	Wiscon.... 10.03.4	**Calif...... 14.40.4**	Wash'ton.. 14.45.7

1942—Not rowed—war.
In the 1941 Freshman race Syracuse was third, Princeton fourth, M. I. T. fifth, Columbia sixth.
In the 1941 Junior Eights race Cornell was third, Columbia fourth.
*Course record. Freshman record, Cornell, 1909, $9.11\frac{3}{5}$.

Oxford-Cambridge Boat Race—$4\frac{1}{4}$ Miles

(**Recapitulation:** Victories, Cambridge 48, Oxford 42, dead heat 1. Best time since inauguration of races in 1841 is 18.03, made in 1934. For races back to 1841 see 1936 Almanac, page 819.)

Yr.	Date	Winner	Time	Yr.	Date	Winner	Time	Yr.	Date	Wnner	Time
1907	Mar. 23	**Cambridge**	**20.26**	1921	Mar. 30	**Cambridge**	**19.44**	1931	Mar. 21	**Cambridge**	**19.26**
1908	April 4	**Cambridge**	**19.20**	1922	April 1	**Cambridge**	**19.27**	1932	Mar. 19	**Cambridge**	**19.11**
1909	Mar. 27	**Oxford.....**	**19.50**	1923	Mar. 24	**Oxford.....**	**20.54**	1933	April 1	**Cambridge**	**20.57**
1910	Mar. 23	**Oxford.....**	**20.14**	1924	April. 5	**Cambridge**	**18.41**	1934	Mar. 17	**Cambridge**	**18.03**
1911	April 1	**Oxford.....**	**18.29**	1925	Mar. 28	**Cambridge**	**21.50**	1935	April 6	**Cambridge**	**19.48**
1912	April 1	**Oxford ....**	**22.05**	1926	Mar. 27	**Cambridge**	**19.29**	1936	April 4	**Cambridge**	**21.06**
1913	Mar. 13	**Oxford ....**	**20.53**	1927	April 2	**Cambridge**	**20.14**	1937	Mar. 24	**Oxford.....**	**22.39**
1914	Mar. 28	**Cambridge**	**20.23**	1928	Mar. 3	**Cambridge**	**20.25**	1938	April 2	**Oxford.....**	**20.30**
1915-19	No races account war			1929	Mar. 23	**Cambridge**	**19.24**	1939	April 1	**Cambridge**	**19.03**
1920	Mar. 27	**Cambridge**	**21.11**	1930	April 12	**Cambridge**	**19.09**	1940	Mar. 2	**Cambridge**	***9.28**

*Distance $1\frac{1}{2}$ miles on account of war and not counted in the record. 1941-1942—No races on account of war.

Polo Records

INTERNATIONAL POLO CUP SERIES

1921 (Hurlingham, England) — America, 2 matches; England, 0. America: 1, Louis E. Stoddard; 2, T. Hitchcock, jr.; 3, J. Watson Webb; Back, D. Milburn. England: 1, Lieut. Col. H. A. Tomkinson; 2, Major F. W. Barrett; 3, Lord Wodehouse; Back, Major Lockett.

1924 (**Meadow Brook, L. I.**)—United States, 2 matches; England, 0. United States: 1, J. Watson Webb; 2, Thomas Hitchcock, jr.; 3, Malcolm Stevenson; Back, Devereux Milburn. England: 1, Major T. W. Kirkwood; 2, Major F. B. Hurndall; 3, Major E. G. Atkinson; Back, Lewis L. Lacey.

1927 (**Meadow Brook, L. I.**)—America, 2 matches; England, 0. America: 1 Watson Webb; 2, Thomas Hitchcock, jr.; 3, Malcolm Stevenson; Back, Devereux Milburn. England: 1, Capt. R. George; 2, Capt. J. P. Denning; 3, C. T. I. Roark; Back, Major E. G. Atkinson.

1928 (**Meadow Brook, L. I.**)—America won 2 matches; Argentina, 1. America (1st and 2nd matches) 1, W. A. Harriman; 2, Thomas Hitchcock, jr.; 3, Malcolm Stevenson; Back, F. W. C. Guest. (3rd match) 1, Harriman; 2, E. A. S. Hopping; 3, Hitchcock; Back, Guest. Argentina (all matches) 1, Arturo Kenny; 2, Jack D. Nelson; 3, John B. Miles; Back, Lewis L. Lacey.

1930 (**Meadow Brook, L. I.**)—America won 2 matches; England, none. America: 1, Eric Pedley; 2, E. A. S. Hopping; 3, Thomas Hitchcock, Jr.; Back, Winston Guest. England: 1, Gerald Balding; 2, Lewis Lacey; 3, Capt. C. T. I. Roark; Back, Lieut. Humphrey Guinness.

1936 (Hurlingham, England)—United States won 2 matches to 0, by scores of 10-9 and 8-6. Line-ups: United States: 1, Eric Pedley; 2, Michael Phipps; 3, Stewart Iglehart; Back, Winston Guest. England: 1, H. Hesketh Hughes; 2, Gerald Balding; 3, Eric H. Tyrrell-Martin; Back, Capt. Humphrey P. Guinness.

1939 (Meadow Brook, L. I.)—America won 2 matches to 0, by scores of 11 to 7 and 9 to 4. Line-ups: United States: 1, Michael Phipps; 2, Thomas Hitchcock, Jr.; 3, S. B. Iglehart; back, W. F. C. Guest. England: 1, Robert Skene; 2, Aidan Roark; 3, Gerald Balding; back, Eric Tyrrell-Martin.

International Military Title Cup—Winner (cup presented by Meadow Brook Club): (1923) at West-bury, N. Y., U. S. Army team won over British Army team, 10-7, 12-10, 10-3. (1925) at Hurlingham Club, London, England, U. S. Army team won over British Army team, 8-4, 6-4.

U. S. POLO ASSOC. CHAMPIONSHIPS.

Open—(1927) Sands Point, 11; British India Army, 7. (1928) Meadow Brook, 8; U. S. Army, 5. (1929) Hurricanes, 11; Sands Point, 7. (1930) Hurricanes, 6; Templeton, 5. (1931) Santa Paula (Argentine), 11; Hurricanes, 8. (1932) Templeton, 16; Greentree, 3. (1933) Aurora, 14; Greentree, 11. (1934) Templeton, 10; Aurora 7. (1935) Greentree, 7; Aurora, 6. (1936) Greentree, 11; Templeton, 10. (1937) Old Westbury, 11; Greentree, 6. (1938) Old Westbury 16, Greentree 7. (1939) Bostwick Field 8; Greentree 7. (1940) Aknusti 5; Great Neck 4. (1941) Gulf Stream 10; Aknusti 6. (1942) Not held—war.

Junior—(1927) U. S. Army, 13; Rumson, 11. (1928) Old Oaks, 12; U. S. Army, 8. (1929) Old Aitken, 12; Mid West, 5. (1930) U. S. Army, 17; Whippany River, 7. (1931) Roslyn, 9; Aiken Knights, 6. (1932) U. S. Army, 11; Bahadur, 8. (1933) Aknust, 11; Aurora, 9. (1934) Burnt Mills, 5; United States Army, 4. (1935) Aiken Knights, 13; Burnt Mills, 3. (1936) Hurricanes, 6; Meadow Brook Ramblers, 4. (1937) Santa Barbara, 12; Narragansett, 7. (1938) Bostwick Field, 8; Aknusti 5. (1939) changed to National 20 Goal Championship-League of Nations 15; Hurricanes 9. (1940) Great Neck 12; Bostwick Field 7. 1941 (title changed to 20 championship) Bostwick Field 9; Hurricanes 4. (1942) Not held—war.

Intercollegiate Championship — (1928) Penn. Military College, 7½; Yale, 6½. (1929) Harvard, 6; Yale, 3. (1930) Yale, 11; Princeton, 0. (1931) Army, 6; Harvard 5. (1932) Yale, 13; Harvard, 9. (1933) Princeton, 10; Harvard, 9. (1934) Harvard, 12; Pennsylvania Military Academy, 2. (1935) Yale, 12; Harvard, 0. (1936) Harvard, 8; U. S. Military Academy, 7; (1937) U. S. Military Academy, 10; Cornell 6. (1938) Harvard, 7; Yale, 1. (1939) Yale, 12; Harvard 8. (1940) Yale 13; Princeton 1. (1942) Princeton 6; Yale 4.

OTHER POLO RESULTS

1942—Intercollegiate Indoor Championship Final —Yale 4, Princeton 3.

Amateur Wrestling in 1942

National A. A. U. Championships, New Orleans, La., April 10-11.

115 lbs.—W. Curtis, Crescent Club, Tulsa, Okla.
121 lbs.—R. Barber, University of Minnesota.
128 lbs.—S. Marks, Crescent Club, Tulsa, Okla.
135 lbs.—D. Lee, Y. M. C. A., Baltimore, Md.
145 lbs.—D. Arndt, Crescent Club, Tulsa, Okla.
155 lbs.—V. Logan, Crescent Club, Tulsa, Okla.
165 lbs.—J. Scarpello, Vental H. S., Vental, Okla.
175 lbs.—G. Inman, Bowman Field, Ky.
191 lbs.—S. Santo, Camp Polk, La.
Heavyweight—L. Levy, University of Minnesota.
Point Scores: Crescent Club, 28; New Orleans A. C., 11; University of Minnesota, 10; Baltimore Y. M. C. A., 9; Camp Polk, 8.

Eastern Intercollegiate Wrestling Association, State College, Pa., March 13-14, won by Penn State with 30 points.

121 lbs., *Charles Ridenour, Penn State. 128 lbs., Samuel Harry, Penn State. 136 lbs., *Warren Taylor, Princeton. 145 lbs., Glen Alexander, Penn State. 155 lbs., *Milton Bennett, Navy. 165 lbs., William Carmichael, Navy. 175 lbs., *Richard DiBattista, Pennsylvania. Heavyweight, Shuford Swift, Navy.
*Retained title.

National Collegiate A. A. Championships, East Lansing, Mich., March 27-28.

121 lbs.—M. Jennings, Michigan State.
128 lbs.—B. Jennings, Michigan State.
136 lbs.—Maxwell, Michigan State.
145 lbs.—Arndt, Oklahoma A. and M.
155 lbs.—Logan, Oklahoma A. and M.
165 lbs.—Smith, Oklahoma A. and M.
175 lbs.—Dibatista, Pennsylvania.

Heavyweight—Arms, Oklahoma A. and M.

Oklahoma A. and M. won the team title with a score of 31 points, with Michigan State second with 26.

Western Conference Championship, Chicago, Ill., March 14, won by Purdue University with 33 points.

121 lbs.—Malcolm MacDonald, Purdue.
128 lbs.—Casey Fredericks, Purdue.
136 lbs.—Mark Matovina, Purdue.
145 lbs.—Manly Johnson, Michigan.
155 lbs.—Red Seabrooke, Illinois.
165 lbs.—Norm Anthonisen, Illinois.
175 lbs.—John Roberts, Wisconsin.

Heavyweight—Frank Ruggieri, Purdue.

Water Log Rolling Championships
Gladstone, Mich., July 3-5, 1942

The 1942 World's Championship Roleo and Water Festival was held in Gladstone, Mich. (July 3-5). Jimmie Running, Beloit, Wis., won the title of "King of The White Waters" by defeating Walter Swanson, Kodiak, Alaska, in two straight falls, the first coming after 48 minutes 9 seconds and the second after 7 minutes 12 seconds. Running advanced to the finals by winning the second and third falls from Jim Johnson, Cloquet, Minn., after losing the first. Jimmie Herron, Kelso, Wash., was unable to defend the title won by him in 1938 and successfully defended in 1941 because of enlistment in the Coast Guard.

The first semi-final match saw Joe Connor, 1937 champion and runner-up in 1941, of Cloquet, battle Walter Swanson for 53 minutes and 14 seconds before Swanson won the first fall. Swanson pressed his initial advantage and took the second fall in 2 minutes 2 seconds. The consolation round was won by Ray Heideman, Eau Claire, Wis. Jay Swanson, Brinnon, Wash., won the Old Timers' Round for birlers over 50 years of age.

Mary Jean Malott, Anderson (Ind.) College coed, of Cornell, Wis., successfully defended her title by defeating Marietta Terrill, Stevens Point, Wis. The Junior title was won by Mark Olson, Marquette, Mich., who defeated Irving DeRoeck, Gladstone. Ted Springer, Minneapolis, 1941 Junior champion, was unable to defend his title because of illness.

44,189,669 Telephones in World, Jan. 1, 1941

Source: American Telephone and Telegraph Company

Countries	Total	Countries	Total	Countries	Total
North America:		**Europe:**		**Asia:**	
United States......	21,928,182	Belgium............	428,752	British India.......	83,378
Canada...........	1,461,038	Bulgaria...........	31,225	China.............	160,000
Central America....	35,609	Denmark...........	459,757	Japan.............	1,367,958
Mexico...........	178,726	Eire..............	46,726	Other Asia.........	328,000
West Indies:		Finland...........	186,573	Total...........	2,000,000
Cuba...........	68,483	France............	1,622,680	**Africa:**	
Puerto Rico......	17,987	Germany..........	4,226,504	Egypt............	67,983
Other West Indies.	32,632	Great Brit, No. Irel.	3,348,000	Union of So. Afr....	232,885
Other North America	20,552	Greece............	54,404	Other Africa.......	147,460
Total.........	23,743,209	Hungary...........	179,115	Total...........	451,460
South America:		Italy...............	685,815	**Oceania:**	
Argentina.........	460,857	Netherlands........	461,424	Australia...........	704,868
Bolivia...........	2,621	Norway...........	250,000	Hawaii............	41,568
Brazil............	290,910	Portugal..........	75,803	Netherlands Indies..	52,813
Chile.............	90,943	Roumania.........	92,107	New Zealand.......	228,346
Colombia.........	42,233	Russia............	1,272,500	Philippine Islands...	33,923
Ecuador..........	7,600	Spain.............	336,448	Other Oceania......	5,680
Paraguay.........	3,800	Sweden...........	908,653	Total...........	1,070,000
Peru.............	35,151	Switzerland........	474,033		
Uruguay..........	46,656	Yugoslavia.........	72,000	**Total world**.........	44,189,669
Venezuela.........	31,856	Other Europe......	680,000		
Other South America.	3,398	Total...........	15,900,000		
Total.........	1,025,000				

As of Jan. 1, 1942, there were 23,521,000 telephones in the United States.

TELEPHONES IN LARGE CITIES JAN. 1, 1940—NO LATER DATA AVAILABLE

Telephones in chief cities—New York, 1,669,904; Chicago, 997,174; Los Angeles, 456,564; Cleveland, 264,560; San Francisco, 290,990; Washington, 254,042; Minneapolis, 155,362; Seattle, 128,613; Denver, 108,244.

Buenos Aires, 268,956; Rio de Janeiro, 103,797; Mexico City, 95,673; Montevideo, 33,447. Brussels, 127,639; Copenhagen, 220,202; Dublin, 24,893; Paris, 437,139; Berlin, 599,911; Hamburg, 188,861; Vienna, 180,166; London, 717,468; Budapest, 107,906; Rome, 122,442; Amsterdam, 67,927; Oslo, 73,786; Stockholm, 184,722.

Sydney, 159,825; Melbourne, 135,518; Shanghai, 79,554; Tokio, 290,510; Manila, 25,715.

TELEPHONE CONVERSATIONS AND TELEGRAMS, 1939 OR 1938

Country	Talks	Tele-grams	Total	Country	Talks	Tele-grams	Total
	1,000	1,000	1,000		1,000	1,000	1,000
Australia........	637,000	17,998	654,998	Hungary.........	187,000	2,439	189,439
Belgium..........	320,000	5,900	325,900	Japan...........	5,339,000	68,475	5,407,475
Canada..........	2,774,000	11,629	2,785,629	Netherlands......	468,000	3,588	471,588
Denmark.........	726,000	1,748	727,748	Norway..........	281,000	3,489	284,489
Finland..........	309,000	811	309,811	Sweden.........	1,195,000	4,641	1,199,641
France..........	972,000	27,524	999,524	Switzerland......	335,000	2,039	337,039
Germany........	3,640,000	21,701	3,661,701	Union of S. Africa.	317,000	6,863	323,863
Gt. Brit., No. Ire..	2,255,000	59,484	2,314,484	United States.....	30,300,000	195,000	30,495,000

Annual Fire Losses in the United States

Source: 1879-1916, Journal of Commerce; since, National Board of Fire Underwriters

Year	Loss	Year	Loss	Year	Loss	Year	Loss
1880......	$74,643,400	1909......	$188,705,150	1920......	$447,886,677	1931......	$451,643,866
1885......	102,818,796	1910......	214,003,300	1921......	495,406,012	1932......	400,859,554
1890......	108,993,792	1911......	217,004,575	1922......	506,541,001	1933......	271,453,189
1895......	142,110,233	1912......	206,438,900	1923......	535,372,782	1934......	271,197,296
1900......	160,929,805	1913......	203,763,550	1924......	549,062,124	1935......	235,263,401
1902......	161,078,040	1914......	221,439,350	1925......	559,418,184	1936......	266,659,449
1903......	145,302,155	1915......	172,033,200	1926......	561,980,751	1937......	254,959,423
1904......	229,198,050	1916......	258,377,952	1927......	472,933,969	1938......	258,477,944
1905......	165,221,650	1917......	289,535,050	1928......	464,607,109	1939......	275,102,119
1906......	518,611,800	1918......	353,878,876	1929......	459,445,778	1940......	285,878,697
1907......	215,084,709	1919......	320,540,399	1930......	501,980,624	1941......	303,895,000
1908......	217,885,850						

Fires cost annually in the United States about 10,000 human lives.

A committee of the National Board of Fire Underwriters reported in May, 1942, that it had found no evidence of incendiary origin of fires in defense plants, adding: "The large increase in employment and the resulting comparatively high average earnings, together with the increasing value of commodities of all types, have tended to lessen fires for profit. It is only fair to say, however, that so far the number of incendiary fires is believed to have been somewhat below normal and that the effect of war conditions to date has been to lessen rather than to increase cases of arson."

Fire Prevention Awards to Cities

The grand award for the most notable work in fire protection and protection in the Inter-Chamber Fire Waste Contest (1941) was won by Cincinnati. The United States Chamber of Commerce and the National Fire Waste Council sponsor the contest. Winners in six population groups were announced (April 4, 1942) by the National Fire Waste Council was as follows

More than 500,000—Milwaukee.

250,000-500,000—Cincinnati.
100,000-250,000—Wichita, Kan.
50,000-100,000—Lakewood, Ohio.
20,000-50,000—Parkersburg, W. Va.
Less than 20,000—Valley City, N. D.

More than 500 communities participated in the contest which took into account the achievements for fire loss, intensive educational work in fire prevention, organization for fire defense and permanent improvements to eliminate fire hazards.

Construction and Housing in the United States

Source: United States Bureau of Labor Statistics

NUMBER AND PERCENTAGE OF FAMILIES PROVIDED FOR IN NEW DWELLINGS IN 257 IDENTICAL CITIES

Year	Number of families provided for in—				Percentage of families provided for in—		
	All types of dwellings	1-family dwellings	2-family dwellings (1)	Multi-family dwellings (2)	1-family dwellings	2-family dwellings (1)	Multi-family dwellings (2)
1925	491,032	225,222	86,133	179,677	45.9	17.5	36.6
1930	125,315	57,311	15,145	52,859	45.7	12.1	42.2
1931	98,158	48,310	11,310	38,538	49.2	11.5	39.3
1932	27,380	19,524	3,400	4,456	71.3	12.4	16.3
1933	25,885	14,443	2,128	9,314	55.8	8.2	36.0
1934	20,952	12,570	1,446	6,936	60.0	6.9	33.1
1935	55,490	31,021	3,008	21,461	55.9	5.4	38.7
1936	113,646	59,099	5,261	49,286	52.0	4.6	43.4
1937	117,307	66,238	7,316	43,753	56.5	6.2	37.3
1938	157,008	78,582	7,759	70,667	50.1	4.9	45.0
1939	203,392	117,693	16,302	69,397	57.8	8.1	34.1
1940	220,928	140,823	21,298	59,807	63.7	9.7	26.6
1941	232,073	162,894	19,396	49,783	70.2	8.4	21.4

1 Includes 1- and 2-family dwellings with stores. 2 Includes multifamily dwellings with stores.

PERMIT VALUATION OF VARIOUS CLASSES OF BUILDING CONSTRUCTION IN 257 IDENTICAL CITIES, 1921 TO 1941. Revised. Index numbers based on 5-year average, 1935-39=100

Year	Total building construction		New residential buildings		New nonresidential buildings		Additions, alterations, and repairs	
	Permit valuation	Index No.	Permit valuation	Index No.	Permit valuation	Index No.	Permit valuation	Index No.
1925	$4,028,066,479	363.8	$2,390,390,182	481.0	$1,300,494,326	345.8	$337,181,971	144.0
1926	3,826,927,204	345.7	2,222,874,645	447.3	1,262,738,028	335.8	341,314,531	145.8
1927	3,478,604,263	314.2	1,906,003,260	383.5	1,231,785,870	327.6	340,815,133	145.6
1928	3,304,699,712	298.5	1,859,423,751	374.1	1,135,569,986	302.0	309,705,975	132.3
1929	2,933,212,041	264.9	1,433,715,542	288.5	1,147,796,781	305.2	351,699,718	150.2
1930	1,697,724,944	153.3	601,269,847	121.0	849,386,873	225.9	247,068,224	105.5
1931	1,237,457,788	111.8	426,270,111	85.8	622,830,444	165.6	188,357,233	80.5
1932	481,219,448	43.5	103,445,244	20.8	275,509,435	73.3	102,264,769	43.7
1933	383,363,271	34.6	92,175,207	18.5	183,241,951	48.7	107,946,113	46.1
1934	413,335,750	37.3	78,322,545	15.8	197,407,829	52.5	137,605,376	58.8
1935	690,980,829	62.4	213,547,937	43.0	288,503,017	76.7	188,929,875	80.7
1936	1,074,041,134	97.0	460,957,356	92.7	376,062,438	100.0	237,021,340	101.2
1937	1,187,141,752	107.2	475,966,515	95.8	434,602,894	115.6	276,572,343	118.1
1938	1,185,561,486	107.1	580,028,372	116.7	382,633,246	101.8	222,899,868	95.2
1939	1,398,020,069	126.3	754,471,224	151.8	398,430,016	106.0	245,118,829	104.7
1940	1,760,881,878	159.0	797,284,564	160.4	720,323,251	191.6	243,274,063	103.9
1941	1,978,168,975	178.7	868,684,922	174.8	843,968,900	224.5	265,515,153	113.4

AVERAGE COST PER FAMILY OF NEW DWELLINGS IN 257 IDENTICAL CITIES

(Revised. This table does not show change in cost of erecting identical building, but does show change in cost of such buildings as were erected. Does not include land cost.)

Year	Average cost per new dwelling unit				Index numbers of cost per new dwelling unit (1935-1939=100)			
	All types of dwellings	1-family dwellings	2-family dwellings (1)	Multi-family dwellings (2)	All types dwellings	1-family dwellings	2-family dwellings (1)	Multi-family dwellings (2)
1925	4,445	4,593	4,422	4,271	112.6	115.6	117.5	106.3
1930	4,385	4,994	3,924	3,857	111.1	125.7	104.3	96.0
1931	4,226	4,836	3,607	3,644	107.1	121.8	95.9	90.7
1932	3,705	3,943	3,250	3,010	93.9	99.3	86.4	74.9
1933	3,495	3,845	3,112	3,040	88.5	96.8	82.7	75.6
1934	3,572	4,071	3,338	2,716	90.5	102.5	88.7	67.6
1935	3,779	4,228	2,953	3,245	95.7	106.4	78.5	80.7
1936	4,002	4,355	3,058	3,679	101.4	109.6	81.3	91.5
1937	4,009	4,352	3,110	3,641	101.6	109.6	82.7	90.6
1938	3,644	4,105	2,862	3,217	92.3	103.3	76.1	80.0
1939	3,673	3,970	2,868	3,359	93.1	99.9	76.2	83.6
1940	3,564	3,890	2,760	3,075	93.2	92.6	93.0	89.7
1941	3,691	3,980	2,774	3,105	96.6	94.7	93.4	90.6

1 Includes 1- and 2-family dwellings with stores. 2 Includes multifamily dwellings with stores.

The Average Father of 32,000,000 in the U. S.

Statisticians of the Census Bureau picture the average of 32,000,000 fathers in the United States as follows:

Age: 44.

The odds are 9 to 1 that he is a married man living with his wife and has one to two children living at home. The rest of the fathers are mostly widowers and a very small sprinkling of divorced males.

The chances are 3 to 2 that he will live in a city of 2,500 or more.

The odds are 8 to 1 that he has a job in private or non-emergency work.

If he works in an industrial establishment his yearly wage is about $1,100 or $1,200 a year.

It is 9 to 1 he is white and 3 to 2 he is a native American whose parents were born here.

He spends about $1,200 a year for family purchases in retail stores; he worries over a $480 annual tax bill.

About 2,250,000 fathers each year have the thrill of a childbirth in the home, about 25,000 of which involve twins, 274 triplets and 2 quadruplets.

One father in the United States has 27 children.

U. S. Government Crime Reports

Source: Federal Bureau of Investigation, Department of Justice

ESTIMATED NUMBER OF MAJOR CRIMES IN THE U. S., 1938-1940

Offense	No. of Offenses			Offense	No. of Offenses		
	1939	1940	1941		1939	1940	1941
Murder & non-negli.				Aggravated assault...	46,483	46,538	48,385
mans aughter......	7,514	7,540	7,562	Burglary............	311,104	316,369	302,475
Manslaught. by negli.	4,394	4,425	4,582	Larceny............	872,988	902,113	919,120
Rape...............	8,832	9,055	9,257	Auto theft.........	177.997	177,551	190,059
Robbery	55,242	53,435	49,832	Total...........	1,484,554	1,517,026	1,531,272

The total for 1930 was 1,333,526; (1937) 1,415,816; (1938) 1,433,812.

Penitentiaries: Alcatraz, Calif; Atlanta, Ga.; Fort Leavenworth, Kans.; Leavenworth, Kans.; Lewisburg, Pa.; McNeil Island, Wash.
Reformatories: Chillicothe, Ohio; El Reno, Okla.; Petersburg, Va.; Alderson, W. Va.
Medical center: Springfield, Mo.: Hospital; Maintenance unit.
Prison camps: Du Pont, Wash.; Kooskia, Idaho; Mill Point, W. Va.; Montgomery, Ala.; Tucson, Ariz.
Correctional institutions: El Paso, Tex.; Milan, Mich.; Male, Female, Sandstone, Minn.; San Pedro, Calif.; Male, Female, Tallahassee, Fla.
Detention headquarters: New Orleans, La.; New York, N. Y.
National Training School for Boys, Washington, D. C.

Lynchings in the United States Since 1900

Source: Monroe N. Work, Director, Department of Records and Research, Tuskegee Institute, Ala.

Yea..	W.	N.	Total	Year.	W.	N.	Total	Year.	W.	N.	Total	Year	W.	N.	Tota
1900..	9	106	115	1911..	7	60	67	1922..	6	51	57	1933..	4	24	28
1901..	25	105	130	1912..	2	61	63	1923..	4	29	33	1934..	0	15	15
1902..	7	85	92	1913..	1	51	52	1924..	0	16	16	1935..	2	18	20
1903..	15	84	99	1914..	3	49	52	1925..	0	17	17	1936..	0	9	9
1904..	7	76	83	1915..	13	54	67	1926..	7	23	30	1937..	0	8	8
1905..	5	57	62	1916..	4	50	54	1927..	0	16	16	1938..	0	6	6
1906..	3	62	65	1917..	3	35	38	1928..	1	10	11	1939..	1	2	3
1907..	2	58	60	1918..	4	60	64	1929..	3	7	10	1940..	1	4	5
1908..	8	89	97	1919..	7	76	83	1930..	1	20	21	1941..	0	4	4
1909..	13	69	82	1920..	8	53	61	1931..	1	12	13				
1910..	9	67	76	1921..	5	59	64	1932..	2	6	8	T.tal.	1,291	3,408	4,699

LYNCHINGS BY STATES

State	W.	N.	Tot.	State	W.	N.	Tot.	State.	W.	N.	Tot.	State	W.	N.	Tot.
Ala....	47	299	346	Iowa...	17	2	19	Nev...	6	0	6	S. D...	27	0	28
Ariz...	29	0	29	Kans...	35	19	54	N. J..	0	1	1	Tenn..	48	201	249
Ark...	59	226	285	Ky....	64	141	205	N. M..	33	3	36	Texas..	143	345	488
Calif..	41	2	43	La.....	56	334	390	N. Y...	1	1	2	Utah...	6	2	8
Colo...	66	2	68	Md....	2	27	29	N. C...	15	84	99	Va.....	16	83	99
Del....	1	0	1	Mich...	7	1	8	N. D...	13	3	16	Wash...	25	1	26
Fla....	28	251	279	Minn..	5	4	9	Ohio...	10	16	26	W. Va.	21	28	49
Ga....	37	483	520	Miss..	41	528	569	Okla...	82	41	123	Wis....	6	0	6
Idaho..	20	0	20	Mo....	51	70	121	Oreg...	20	1	21	Wyo...	30	5	35
Ill	14	17	31	Mont..	82	2	84	Penn...	2	6	8				
Ind ...	33	14	47	Nebr..	52	5	57	S. C...	4	155	159				

In the first half of 1942 one person was lynched, a Negro, in Missouri.

Prisoners in Federal and State Institutions in 1940

Source: The United States Bureau of the Census

Area	Institutions	Total prisoners received	Received from courts	Dec. 31	Area	Institutions	Total prisoners received	Received from courts	Dec. 31
	No.	No.	No.	No.		No.	No.	No.	No.
United States.	179	106,355	73,456	171,626	South Atlantic:				
					Delaware......	1	150	149	386
Fed. institutions	31	21,658	15,109	19,260	Maryland......	4	3,649	2,994	2,933
State institut'ns	148	84,697	58,347	146,325	Dist. of Columbia	2	841	668	1,597
					Virginia.......	1	1,713	1,665	4,144
New England:					West Virginia....	1	1,122	1,019	2,691
Maine......	3	401	337	608	North Carolina..	1	1,589	1,254	4,272
New Hampshire..	1	121	100	262	South Carolina..	1	727	611	1,276
Vermont.....	2	246	222	343	Florida........	1	1,434	1,359	3,648
Massachusetts...	4	2,000	915	2,993	Ea. So. Central:				
Rhode Island....	3	420	393	308	Kentucky......	3	2,212	1,895	4,537
Connecticut.....	3	811	541	1,146	Tennessee......	3	1,975	1,278	3,233
Middle Atlantic:					Alabama......	35	14,500	5,307	6,446
New York.....	13	6,984	3,633	15,353	W. So. Central:				
New Jersey.....	4	2,319	1,574	3,662	Arkansas........	2	932	833	1,904
Pennsylvania....	4	2,592	2,358	6,690	Louisiana.......	1	977	939	2,946
Ea. No. Central:					Oklahoma......	2	2,190	2,021	3,921
Ohio.......	4	4,680	2,532	8,758	Texas.........	1	3,136	2,663	6,070
Indiana.........	3	2,180	1,362	4,361	Mountain:				
Illinois.........	4	2,873	1,526	11,374	Montana.......	1	314	305	522
Michigan.......	4	4,058	2,395	7,656	Idaho.........	1	258	231	409
Wisconsin.......	5	5,117	4,906	2,671	Wyoming......	2	191	173	363
W. No. Central:					Colorado.......	2	749	691	1,556
Minnesota.....	3	1,136	887	2,589	New Mexico....	1	353	331	646
Iowa.........	3	917	753	2,574	Arizona........	1	368	335	796
Missouri.......	2	1,925	1,668	4,208	Utah..........	1	193	164	438
North Dakota...	1	283	263	353	Nevada........	1	177	165	255
South Dakota...	1	262	243	400	Pacific:				
Nebraska.......	3	548	483	1,064	Washington.....	2	946	742	2,312
Kansas........	3	1,041	780	2,431	Oregon........	1	571	530	1,038
					California.......	3	2,516	2,154	8,182

In 1940, 86 prisoners were executed. Prisoners, Dec. 31, 1941, numbered 165,827.

Leading Churches in the City of New York

Source: Official Denominational Records

MANHATTAN

Armenian Apostolic—Holy Cross Cathedral, 580 W. 180 St.

Baptist—Central, 92nd St. and Amsterdam Ave.; Riverside, 122nd St. and Riverside Drive; First, W. 79th St., corner Broadway; Judson Memorial, 65 Washington St. So.; Madison Ave. Church, cor. E. 31st St.; Metropolitan, W. 128th St. and 7th Ave.; Mount Morris, 5th Ave., near W. 127th St.

Christian Science (Church of Christ, Scientist)—First, Central Park West and 96th St.; Second, 10 W. 68th St.; Third, Park Ave. at 63rd St.; Fourth, Fort Washington Ave., at 185th St.; Fifth, 342 Madison Ave. near 43rd St.; Sixth, 1935 Anthony Ave., near Tremont Ave.; Seventh, Broadway at 111th St.; Eighth, 103 E. 77th St.; Ninth, 1457 Broadway at 42nd St.; Tenth, 171 McDougal St., near W. 8th St.; Eleventh, 39 W. 190th St.; Twelfth, 147 W. 123rd St.; Thirteenth, 311 W. 83rd St.; Fourteenth, 555 N. 141st St.; Society, 262 E. Tremont Ave.

Congregational—Tabernacle, Broadway and 56th St.

Disciples of Christ—Central Church, W. 81st St., near Columbus Ave.

Friends (Quaker)—Meeting Houses: (Hicksite), E. 15th St. and Rutherford Pl.; and (Orthodox), 144 E. 20th St.

Jewish—Temple Israel, W. 91st St., near B'way; Congregation B'nai Jeshurum, 88th St. and West End Ave.; Shearith Israel, Central Park West and 70th St.; Rodeph Sholom Temple, W. 83rd St., near Central Park West; Temple Emanu-El, 5th Ave. and 65th St.; Anshe Chesed, West End Ave. and 100th St.; Central, 55th St. and Lexington Ave.; West End, 160 W. 82nd; Free Synagogue, Carnegie Hall; Institutional Synagogue, 120 W. 76th St.

Lutheran—Advent, Broadway and 93d St.; Holy Trinity, Central Park West and 65th St.; Immanuel, Lexington Ave. and E. 88th St.; St. Peter's, Lexington Ave. and 54th St.; St. Luke's, 46th St. near Eighth Ave.

Methodist Episcopal—Calvary, 1885 University Ave.; Christ, 60th St., and Park Ave.! Church of All Nations, 9 2nd Ave.; Grace, 131 W. 104th St.; John St., 44 John St.; Metropolitan Duane, 58 7th Ave.; Park Ave., at 86th St.; St. Paul's, West End Ave. and 86th St.; Union, W. 48th St., near Broadway; Broadway Temple, 174th St.

Presbyterian—Brick, Park Ave. and E. 91st St., Broadway, at W. 114th St.; Central, Park Ave. and 64th St.; Fifth Ave., at 55th St.; First, 5th Ave. and 11th St.; Fourth, West End Ave. and 91st St.; Madison Ave., at 73rd St.; Rutgers, W. 73rd St., near Broadway; Scotch, Central Park West and 96th St.; West End, 165 W. 105th St.

Protestant Episcopal—Cathedral of St. John the Divine, W. 111th St., between Amsterdam and Morningside Avenues.; Ascension, 5th Ave. and 10th St.; Christ Church, 71th St. near Broadway; Eglise du Saint-Esprit (French), 223 E. 61st St.; Epiphany 74th St. and York Ave.); Grace, Broadway, Broadway and 10th St.; Heavenly Rest, 5th Ave. and 90th St.; Incarnation, 205 Madison Ave.; "Little Church Around the Corner" (Transfiguration), 5 E. 29th St.; St. Andrew's, 127th St. near 5th Ave.; St. Bartholomew's, 109 E. 50th St.; St. George's, Stuyvesant Sq.; St. James', Madison Ave. and 71st St.; St. Luke's, Convent Ave. and 141st St.; St. Mark's-in-the-Bouwerie, 2nd Ave. and 10th St.; St. Paul's Chapel, Broadway and Vesey St.; St. Thomas's, 5th Ave. and 53d St.; Trinity Church, Broadway at Wall St.

Reformed Church in America—Middle Collegiate, Second Ave., at 7th St.; Marble Collegiate, Fifth Ave., at 29th St.; Collegiate Church of St. Nicholas, Fifth Ave. at 48th St.; West End Collegiate, West End Ave. at 77th St.; Fort Washington Collegiate, Fort Washington Ave., at 181st St.

Roman Catholic—St. Patrick's Cathedral, Fifth Ave., at E. 50th St.; Ascension, 107th St., near Broadway; Holy Trinity, 205 W. 82d St.; Notre Dame, Morningside Drive and 114th St.; St. Agnes's, 143 E. 43d St.; St. Andrew's, Duane St. and Cardinal Place; St. Brigid's, 123 Ave. B; St. Cyril, St. Mark's Pl.; St. Francis Xavier, 42 W. 16th St.; St. Ignatius Loyola's, Park Ave. and E. 84th St.; St. Leo's, 11 E. 28th St.; St. Patrick's, Mott and Prince Sts.; St. Paul the Apostle's, Columbus Ave. and W. 6th St.; St. Peter's, 20 Barclay St.

Russian Orthodox—Cathedral of Holy Virgin Protection, 105 E. Houston St.

Salvation Army—Centennial Memorial Temple, 120 W. 14th St. There are other meeting places.

Seventh Day Adventist—City Temple, 564 W. 150th St.

Synodical Church of Russia—St. Nicholas Cathedral, 15 E. 97th St.

Among other places of worship in Manhattan **Unitarian**—All Souls, Lexington Ave. and 80th St.; Community, Park Ave. and 34th St.

Universalist—(Fourth), Church of the Divine Paternity, Central Park West and 76th St.

Greek Orthodox—Holy Trinity Cathedral, 319 E. 74th St.

Among other places of worship in Manhattan are: Church of the Strangers (Deems Memorial), 307 W. 57th St.; Divine Inspiration (Spiritualist), 20 W. 91st St.; Gospel Tabernacle, 44th St., and 8th Ave.; Labor Temple, 2nd Ave. and 14th St. New Jerusalem Church (Swedenborgian), 114 E. 35th St.; Pentecostal Glad Tidings, 325 W. 33rd St., Spiritualists', 123 W. 94th St.; Society of Ethical Culture, 2 W. 64th St.; Theosophical, 22 E. 8th St.

BROOKLYN

Baptist—Temple, 3d Ave. and Schermerhorn St.; Emmanuel, Lafayette Ave. and St. James Pl.; Hanson Place, at So. Portland Ave.; Sixth Ave., at Lincoln Pl.

Christian Science—First, New York Ave. and Dean St.

Congregational—Central (also St. Paul's), Hancock St., near Franklin Ave.; Clinton Ave., at Lafayette Ave.; Flatbush, Dorchester Rd. and E. 18th St.; Pilgrims, Henry and Remsen Sts.; Plymouth, Orange St., near Hicks St.; South, President and Court Sts.; (In 1934 the Church of the Pilgrims and Plymouth Church merged into the Plymouth Church of the Pilgrims.

Disciples of Christ—Flatbush, Dorchester and Marlborough Roads.

Friends—(Hickste). 110 Schermerhorn St.; (Orthodox), Lafayette and Washington Aves.

Jewish—Beth-El, 15th Ave. and 48th St.; Beth Judah, 904 Bedford Ave.; Beth Sholaum, 399 9th St.; Eighth Ave., at Garfield Pl.; Mt. Sinai, State and Hoyt Sts.

Lutheran—Emmanuel, 421 7th St.; Evangelical, Schermerhorn St., near Court St.; Good Shepherd, 4th Ave. and 75th St.; Redeemer, Ditmas Ave., at E. 21st St.; St. Luke's, Washington Ave., near DeKalb Ave.; St. Peter's Bedford Ave., near De-Kalb Ave.; Trinity, 4th Ave. and 46th St.; Zion, Henry St., near Clark St.

Methodist Episcopal—First, Henry and Clark Sts.; Grace, 7th Ave. and St. John's Pl.; Hanson Place Central, at St. Felix St.; New York Ave. at Dean St.; Simpson, Clermont and Willoughby Aves.

Moravian—Jay St., near Myrtle Ave.

Presbyterian—Bedford, Dean St. and Nostrand Ave.; Central, Marcy and Jefferson Aves.; First, Henry St., near Clark St.; Lafayette Ave., at So. Oxford St.; Memorial, 7th Ave. and St. John's Pl.; Spencer Memorial, Clinton and Remsen Sts.; Throop Ave., at Macon St.; Westminster, Clinton St. and 1st Pl.

Protestant Episcopal—Christ, Clinton and Harrison Sts.; Grace, Hicks St. and Grace Court; Holy Trinity, Clinton and Montague Sts.; Messiah, Greene and Clermont Aves.; Redeemer, Pacific St. and 4th Ave.; St. Ann's, Clinton and Livingston Sts.; St. John's, 7th Ave. and St. John's Pl.; St. Luke's, Clinton Ave., near Fulton St.

Reformed Church in America—Bethany, Clermont Ave., near Willoughby Ave.; First, of Williamsburgh, Bedford Ave. and Clymer St.; First, Flatbush and Church Aves.; Old First, 7th Ave. and Carroll St.

Roman Catholic—Holy Name of Jesus, Prospect Ave. and Prospect Park West; Our Lady of Lourdes, De Sales Pl., near Broadway; Our Lady of Mercy, Schermerhorn St., near Bond St.; Queen of All Saints, Lafayette and Vanderbilt Aves., St. Augustine's, 6th Ave. and Sterling Pl.; St. Charles Borromeo, Sidney Pl. and Livingston St.; St. Francis Xavier's, 6th Ave. and Carroll St.; St. James Pro-Cathedral Jay and Chapel Sts.

Seventh Day Adventist—Washington Ave., at Gates Ave.

Swedenborgian—Church of the New Jerusalem, Monroe Pl. and Clark St.

Unitarian—Saviour, Pierrepont St. and Monroe Pl.; Second, Clinton and Congress Sts.

Universalist—All Souls', Ditmas and Ocean Aves.

Miscellaneous—Brooklyn Spiritualist Soc., 58 Irving Pl.; Brooklyn Tabernacle, 17 Hicks St.; Christian and Missionary Alliance, 1560 Nostrand Ave.; Ethical Culture Soc., Academy of Music.

Museums and Points of Interest in Chicago

Source: Chicago Municipal Reference Library

Adler Planetarium—In Grant Park. Admission free, Wednesdays, Saturdays and Sundays. Other days 25 cents. Hours: Monday, Wednesday, Thursday and Saturday, 10 A. M. to 5 P. M.; demonstrations at 11 A. M. and 3 P. M. and 8 P. M. on Tuesdays and Fridays, when the planetarium is open from 10 A. M. to 9 P. M.; Sundays 2 P. M. to 5 P. M. with demonstrations at 2:30 and 3:30. Planets, stars, moon and entire celestial orbit reproduce all the mysteries of the universe.

Art Institute—Michigan Ave. foot of Adams St., covers 3 acres of floor space. Admission free: Wednesdays, Saturdays, Sundays and holidays; other days 25 cents. Hours: 9 A. M. to 5 P. M. weekdays; 12 noon to 5 P. M. Sundays. Collections of paintings (c. 1400), sculpture, prints and drawings, decorative arts (period rooms, etc.), oriental arts, Children's Museum. Ryerson and Burham Libraries (45,000 vols.); photos (70,000), etc. Goodman Memorial Theatre; Art School; Sunday free lectures.

Chicago Academy of Sciences and Museum of Natural History—In Lincoln Park at Clark St. and Ogden Ave.-Armitage Ave. Admission free every day. Hours 9 A. M. to 5 P. M. weekdays, 1 P. M. to 5 P. M. Sundays. Exhibits flora and fauna native to the region of Chicago; wild animals of the middle west. Free illustrated lectures on natural history subjects on Sundays at 3 P. M. during the winter.

Chicago Historical Museum—In Lincoln Park at Clark St. and North Ave. Admission free daily except Sunday, when fee is 25 cents. Free every day to children. Hours 9:30 A. M. to 5 P. M. weekdays, 1 P. M. to 6 P. M. on Sundays. Collection of American historical mementoes, including anchor dropped by Columbus when he discovered America, the death bed of Abraham Lincoln and relics of the explorers of the Northwest.

Field Museum of Natural History—see Index, Field Museum.

Museum of Science and Industry—Jackson Park, 57th St. and Lake Michigan. Open daily and Sundays 9:30 A. M. to 4 P. M. in winter; 6 P. M. in summer. Admission free every day. The Museum contains exhibits which show the important steps from primitive times to the present day, in the fields of physics, chemistry, agriculture, textiles and forestry, geology and mineral industries, power, transportation, civil engineering and architecture, the medical sciences, and printing and the graphic arts.

Shedd Aquarium—In Grant Park, Roosevelt road and Lake Michigan. Admission free Thursdays, Saturdays and Sundays; every day to children; other days entrance fee is 25 cents. Open 10 A. M. to 5 P. M. every day except Christmas and New Year's day. Contains 10,000 finny specimens ranging all the way from the walking fish of Africa to the weirdest exhibits of deep sea life.

Marquette Cross—At Damen avenue, on the bank of the south branch of the Chicago river. This huge cross marks the spot where Father Marquette camped during the winter of 1674-1675, after his exploration of the Mississippi.

Flagship of Columbus—In Jackson Park Yacht harbor. An exact replica of the Santa Maria, flagship of Christopher Columbus, presented by the Spanish government to the Chicago Columbian exposition in 1893.

Chicago Fire—At De Koven and Jefferson streets stands a marker on the spot formerly given over to the cowshed of the famed Mrs. O'Leary. Tradition recalls that it was a lamp upset by the flying heels of Mrs. O'Leary's cow that started the Chicago fire.

Oriental Institute—At the University of Chicago, Fifty-eighth street and University avenue. Admission free daily. A museum of ancient civilizations brought to Chicago by the explorations of Prof. Breasted. Babylon, Thebes, Persepolis, relics from the stables of Solomon, a model of the Tower of Babel, and a statue of Tutenkhamen, are displayed in the museum. Open, free, 10 A. M. to 5 P. M. Monday through Saturday, and 11 A. M. to 5 P. M. on Sunday from June to Nov. 30. From December to May 31, open from 1 to 5 P. M., Monday through Friday, while the Saturday and Sunday schedule is the same as that for the summer and fall months.

Union Stock Yards—Main entrance, Halsted Street and Exchange Avenue. Established 1865. Largest live stock market and meat packing center in the world. The gateway between the producing regions of the West and the consuming areas of the East. Tours through the stock yards have been discontinued for the duration of the war.

Hull House—Polk and Halsted streets. Founded by Miss Jane Addams as the first American settlement for the advancement of the unprivileged. Now under the direction of Miss Charlotte Carr.

University of Chicago Chapel—On the Midway at the University of Chicago campus. A structure of unusual grace and beauty, designed by the noted architect, Bertram Grosvenor Goodhue, and dedicated in 1929. Open daily to visitors from 9 A. M. to 6 P. M.; Sunday services at 11 A. M. and 4:30 P. M. are open to the public.

Chicago Zoological Gardens—Brookfield, a suburb southwest of the city, may be reached by street car, elevated or Burlington train. Open every day of the year. Admission free on Thursday, Saturday, Sunday and holidays; 25 cents on other days; children are always admitted free. A large and comprehensive collection of the world's mammals, birds and reptiles are shown in modern buildings and inclosures. Barless cages are used extensively, native habitations and backgrounds have been reproduced. Open during May to September from 9 A. M. to 7 P. M. week days and to 7 P. M. Sundays and holidays; during April to October hours 9 A. M. to 6 P. M. Sundays and holidays. From November to March, 9 A. M. to 4:30 P. M. week days, and to 5:30 P. M. Sundays and holidays.

Mayors of Chicago

Source: Historical Records

No.	Name	Elec.	No.	Name	Elec.	No.	Name	Elec.
1	William B. Ogden, D...	1837	21	John Wentworth, R.-Fus.	1857	42	Hempsted Washburne, R.	1891
2	Buckner S. Morris, Whig	1838	22	John Haines, R.......	1858	43	Carter H. Harriison, Sr., D	1893
3	Benj. W. Raymond, Whig	1839	23	John C. Haines, R......	1859	44	John P. Hopkns, D	1893
4	Alexander Lloyd, D ...	1840	24	John Wentworth, R....	1860	45	George B. Swift, R	1895
5	Francis C. Sherman, D	1841	25	Julian S. Rumsey, R...	1861	46	Carter H. Harrison, Jr., D.	1897
6	Benj. W. Raymond, D..	1842	26	Francis C. Sherman, D.	1862	47	Carter H. Harrison, Jr., D.	1899
7	Augustus Garrett, D....	1843	27	Francis C. Sherman, D.	1863	48	Carter H. Harrison, Jr., D.	1901
8	Alson S. Sherman, D...	1844	28	John B. Rice, R.......	1865	49	Carter H. Harrison, Jr., D.	1903
9	Augustus Garrett, D....	1845	29	John B. Rice, R.......	1867	50	Edward F. Dunne, D ...	1905
10	John B. Chapin, Whig.	1846	30	Roswell B. Mason, Peop.	1869	51	Fred A. Busse, R......	1907
11	James Curtiss, D......	1847	31	Joseph Medill, Cit.*....	1871	52	Carter H. Harrison, Jr., D.	1911
12	J. Woodworth, D.-Whig	1848	32	Harvey D. Colvin, Peop.	1873	53	William H. Thompson, R.	1915
13	J. Woodworth, D.-Whig	1849	33	Thomas Hoyne, R.†	1875	54	William H. Thompson, R.	1919
14	James Curtiss, D......	1850	34	Monroe Heath, R......	1876	55	William E. Dever, D....	1923
15	Walter Gurnee, D......	1851	35	Monroe Heath, R......	1877	56	William H. Thompson, R.	1927
16	Walter S. Gurnee, D...	1852	36	Carter H. Harrison, Sr., D.	1879	57	Anton J. Cermak, D....	1931
17	Charles M. Gray, D....	1853	37	Carter H. Harrison, Sr., D.	1881	58	Frank J. Corr, D.‡....	1933
18	Isaac L. Milliken, D....	1854	38	Carter H. Harrison, Sr., D.	1883	59	Edward J. Kelly, D.§...	1933
19	Levi D. Boone, Know-nothing..............	1855	39			60	Edward J. Kelly, D.....	1935
20	Thomas Dyer, D.......	1856	40	John A. Roche, R......	1887	61	Edward J. Kelly, D.....	1939
			41	DeWitt C. Cregier, D...	1889			

*"Fireproof" ticket.
†Elected but did not serve.
‡Elected by City Council, March 14, 1933, after death of Mayor Anton Cermak, and served as Acting Mayor until the election of a successor.
§Elected by City Council April 13, 1933, to serve unexpired term of Cermak.

added
BONUS
features for our
100th year!

THE
WORLD
ALMANAC ®

$1.75

and Book of Facts

1968

CENTENNIAL EDITION

Foreword by the President of the United States

Full color Maps and Flags of All Nations
A Million Facts at Your Fingertips
THE AUTHORITY--For 100 Years

Published by Newspaper Enterprise Association

A Foreword by

The President of the United States

During the past one hundred years, *The World Almanac* has become an American institution. In schools, libraries, and homes, it is an indispensable reference work.

A glance through the Almanac's index provides a panorama of American and world history — from John Adams to the Zip Code. And the Almanac acts as a mirror to the changing face of the world, reflecting growth and development of such proportions as would have staggered the reader of one hundred years ago.

In 1868, a large part of America was still a hostile wilderness in which men struggled for survival. Today, our nation extends from the Arctic Circle to the Caribbean, from the shores of the Atlantic to the reaches of the Pacific, and our struggle is toward a loftier ideal: toward a society that is both great and just, that feeds the hungry and shelters the homeless, that strives to make life a pleasure rather than a burden.

In 1868, the most rapid means of communication was the telegraph. Today, sounds and pictures leap across continents and through space, bringing us everything from foreign television productions to live pictures from the moon.

In 1868, Negroes were agonizing through the birth pangs of emancipation. Today, they are finally beginning to achieve their fair measure of justice and freedom.

No World Almanac reader of one hundred years ago could possibly have foreseen what would fill its pages in 1968. Who would have believed, for example, that within one hundred years the Almanac would contain a category on "Space Developments" with "Men in Space" as a subtitle?

The Almanac is more than a book of facts. It provides a concise history of man's thought, of his philosophical development from the Magna Carta to the United Nations. It clarifies the complexities of government, helps us to compute our income taxes, and presents a readable synopsis of the major events of the year.

I salute *The World Almanac* on its Centennial. May it continue, as a responsible friend and reliable teacher for hundreds of years to come.

Lyndon B. Johnson

The World Almanac

and Book of Facts for 1968

The 192nd anniversary of the signing of the Declaration of Independence, 1776, falls on July 4, 1968. The 181st anniversary of the signing of the Constitution of the United States, 1787, falls on September 17, 1968. The Government declared the Constitution in effect March 4, 1789.

☞   The Editor acknowledges with thanks the many letters, whether of helpful comment or criticism, that attest the usefulness of the WORLD ALMANAC, and invites suggestions for improvement of its services to readers. Address: 230 Park Avenue, New York, N.Y. 10017.

The WORLD ALMANAC does not decide wagers.

The Past 100 Years
The First Century of the World Almanac

Any history of the World Almanac would in fact be a capsule history of the past 100 years—a chronicle of the momentous events and often the trivia of human affairs.

But this is a personal history of the World Almanac—far from comprehensive, but perhaps of interest to our many readers who delight in facts in and of themselves, and to whom the World Almanac itself may be a subject of curiosity.

A full distillation of the events of the past 100 years can be found in other sections of this book. But only here will a reader learn that in 1870, the year the 15th Amendment was ratified, the World Almanac Index somehow wandered from the back to the front of the book, where it has remained ever since.

The World Almanac's first edition, a 120-page hand-set volume containing 12 pages of advertisments, was published by the New York World in 1868. That was the year in which President Andrew Johnson was acquitted in an impeachment trial in the U. S. Senate and in which Congress established the first 8-hour day for Government workers.

The first editor of the World Almanac was a newspaperman whose name was never recorded. The price of the first edition is not known, for it appeared nowhere in the volume. It probably sold for 20 cents or less, since the slightly larger edition of the next year listed its price on Page 70 as 20 cents a copy.

No credo was proclaimed in the World Almanac's first edition, but the idea was nevertheless established of a single volume encompassing generally useful information and a contemporary record of important persons and issues.

In the year 1868 America was in a period of transition. The Civil War had ended recently and the effort to "bind up the nation's wounds," which Abraham Lincoln had counseled, was proving to be a process almost as painful as the war itself.

Reconstruction was the issue of the day—and the World Almanac took due note of it, devoting 14 pages of the slim volume to a complete text of the Reconstruction Acts and a history of Reconstruction. This firsthand impression is still worthy of a reading by any student of American history.

In many ways the 1868 World Almanac was a remarkable first performance. For here was an almanac almost totally unlike its predecessors and contemporaries, which often contained jokes, fiction, weather prophecies, and doubtful "fact." Many features in the first edition are so vital that they have their counterparts in today's World Almanac.

Less vital perhaps, but not without interest to the modern reader, was a section called "Important Events of 1867"—an abbreviated form of today's Chronology. Among its items: Jan. 21—"Indians troublesome, and 8,000 U. S. troops ordered to the plains;" Mar. 23—"Winter Garden Theatre, New York, destroyed by fire;" Apr. 4—"Lindell House, St. Louis, burnt, loss $1,000,000;" and May 23 — "Queen's proclamation declaring the Dominion of Canada."

Pulitzer's Influence

In 1886 after Joseph Pulitzer had purchased the New York World and while he was making it the greatest newspaper of its day, the famed journalist turned his attention to the World Almanac and determined to make it a "compendium of universal knowledge." It was in that year that the Statue of Liberty was completed. Pulitzer had led the fund drive that made the Statue of Liberty a reality, and a picture of the statue appeared on the cover of the 1886 World Almanac.

By 1893, when the World Almanac printed a map of the grounds of the Columbian Exposition in Chicago, Pulitzer's "compendium of universal knowledge" was selling more than 100,000 copies each year. Today it is still the best-selling general information almanac, with annual sales of more than a million copies throughout the world.

The 1894 World Almanac published "Observations by Some of its Half Million Habitual Users," including Gov. William E. Russell of Massachusetts, who wrote: "A most useful and accurate compendium of information. I constantly refer to it."

Perhaps it was due to such observations that in 1894 the book's editor—a position that still was anonymous—changed its name to World Almanac and Encyclopedia. And this was the publication's full title until 1923, when it was changed to World Almanac and Book of Facts—a more accurate if less ambitious title. It was the 1923 edition that contained the first mention of the radio broadcasting industry. With many stations 'broadcasting music and other entertainment regularly," the World Almanac said, "fully 2,000,000 were 'listening in' nightly, and as the average cost of a radio set is $75, the amount invested is $150,000,000."

For a publication intensely concerned with recording the events of a world whose horizons were rapidly expanding the World Almanac showed a curious unconcern for recording its own history. The incandescent lamp, the telephone, the Spanish-American War, and even such an event as the creation of Sherlock Holmes by Dr. A. Conan Doyle in 1886—all of these things, and literally hundreds of thousands more, were faithfully recorded in the book. But not until 1923 did the name of the World Almanac's editor appear in its pages.

This distinction belongs to Robert Hunt Lyman, a newspaperman and scholar who guided the World Almanac until his retirement in 1937.

Successive editors—all newspapermen—have been E. Eastman Irvine, 1938-1948; Harry Hansen, 1947-1965; and Luman H. Long, the present editor.

The names of other members of the World Almanac editorial staff appear for the first time in the 1968 Centennial Edition. Notable among former editorial workers who served anonymously in recent years were Arthur Raymond, Robert T. Martin, and Robert W. Popp.

Through the years, the World Almanac continued to expand and to examine critically itself and its aim of being responsive to the needs of its readership. It was in the 1890s that the World Almanac first solicited the comment of its readers. Substantial revision in content continues to be made on the basis of reader criticism and suggestion.

Purchased by Newspaper Enterprise

Scripps-Howard acquired the New York World and the World Almanac in 1931, and the book was published thereafter by the New York World-Telegram and later by the World-Telegram & Sun. In 1966 the World Almanac was purchased by a Scripps-Howard feature service, Newspaper Enterprise Association, Inc., which is America's oldest and largest basic newspaper feature organization.

Boyd Lewis, president and editor of Newspaper Enterprise Association, said: "The reaction of NEA to the challenge of managing the World Almanac is a combination of pride and determination. We are extremely proud to have received the responsibility of carrying on the centuryold tradition of the World Almanac."

As part of an NEA program to spread the success of the World Almanac to even wider fields, the 1968 Centennial Edition is sponsored by a local newspaper in each of 33 great U. S. and Canadian cities.

Ranged beside the momentous matters of the past 100 years—such as the two World Wars and the awesome mushroom cloud produced by the first atomic bomb in 1945—the personal history of the World Almanac is, of course, of little consequence. It is the World Almanac's job to record and to clarify such events.

Proud Moments

The years have brought their moments of quiet pride to the World Almanac, in deeply satisfying, if unheralded ways.

During 3 years of World War II, at the request of the Government, the World Almanac made special printing runs of the book for distribution to the armed forces here and overseas. In 1944, 100,000 copies were made for the Government, the following year 150,000 and in 1946 a special 100,000 armed services edition.

A somewhat amusing tribute was indirectly paid the World Almanac in 1960 when the head of the Polish Communist Party, Wladyslaw Gomulka, rebuked American officials at an international fair in Poznan for distributing free copies of the book. Gomulka was believed to object to the book's factual history of Poland after World War II.

But the highest tribute that any reference work can receive is to know that it is being used as a source of information by people who cannot afford to be wrong. And in 1961 the World Almanac received such a compliment when a wire service photographer snapped a picture of President Kennedy's desk. There upon the desk was a copy of the World Almanac, ranged beside 5 other books. It was the only reference work.

In this centennial year, the World Almanac is aware of a new honor—the "Foreword" written by President Johnson.

It is certain that the anonymous editor of the 1868 World Almanac could not have imagined the truly cataclysmic changes in the world in the 100 years just past.

But the temptation remains to speculate on what the next 100 years may bring.

The article that follows was written by Dr. Isaac Asimov for this edition. Only time will tell how many of Dr. Asimov's speculations will one day be facts included in the World Almanac

The Next 100 Years

Science-Based Estimates of What the Century Ahead May Bring

By Isaac Asimov, Ph.D.

Associate Professor of Biochemistry at Boston University School of Medicine

[Author's note: Looking into the future is a little harder than looking into the past; and it gets harder each year. The manner in which the rate-of-change is increasing means that the next hundred years will probably see at least as many changes as did the last five hundred. If you imagine the man of 1468, a generation before Columbus' voyage, trying to portray the world of 1968, you will get an idea of the magnitude of the present task of trying to picture the world of 2068.

But we can try. We can suppose that great catastrophies like all-out nuclear war, world-girdling epidemics, or unbridled increase in population will not occur. Then, perhaps, we can dimly see something of what the world of a hundred years hence will be like. Here, at any rate, is one man's guess—]

The world's population is increasing quickly, and each year the World Almanac will be presenting its population statistics with a sharper sense of urgency. But population will level off. By 2000, when the world's population will have reached 6 billion, scientists expect that birth control will be well-established over most of the world. A plateau will have been reached and the main talk of the Twenty-first Century will be to keep it from being exceeded.

By 2068, a major effort will be in progress to increase the quality of the human population. Gene-analysis will be the technique used. Each child as born will have its gene content checked as routinely as its footprints are taken.

This gene-analysis will be an essential part of the medical records, since it will give information as to possible physical and mental weak points. The attempt will be to encourage only the birth of those children who may be expected to have a gene pattern that predisposes them toward excellence.

Increasingly, there will be a tendency to control not only the number of births but the right to parenthood. Perhaps the greatest social controversy of 2068 will be between those who favor an absolute right on the part of society to dictate who may or may not have children, and those who dispute man's understanding of what constitutes "excellence" and who advocate the "right-to-have-children."

Each side in the dispute may have to take into account the rapid development of "ectogenesis"; that is, the development of fetuses outside the human body.

This will have several advantages. Women will be freed of the biological task of actual child-bearing. Embryos can be nurtured under optimum conditions, something not always available in the natural womb. Genic analysis can be carried through before birth, thus allowing a more liberal policy on conception, since checks would be possible afterward.

The techniques involved in ectogenesis will be delicate and space-consuming, and even in 2068 the process will not be common. It will have become important enough, however, so that the World Almanac of the time may well list numbers of births in two columns: "natural" and "ectogenetic."

Computerization of the World

The goal of controlling quantity and quality of population would be quite impossible without some international agency making full use of computerized equipment.

In fact, the computer, as it develops steadily over the next century, will make the present division of the planet obsolete. The necessary controls that will keep 6 billion human beings alive and comfortable in 2068 can only be planet-wide in scope.

We will still be a world of nations in 2068, for tradition and self-esteem will keep us "national" in feeling. But the computers that alone will be able to guide the world economy and make the necessary decisions will transcend the nations, which will, in real importance, be at about the level of our county governments of today.

Since computers are designed to solve problems on a rational basis, the computerization of the world will be its rationalization as well. Decisions, for instance, will be directed that will alter conditions that give rise to social friction, thus minimizing the danger of national wars or internal rioting. This will be done not because wars or riots are immoral, but because they are irrational. And society will, by and large, obey the decisions of computers because to avoid doing so will bring disaster.

By 2068, the active desire to raise human intuition above the complex computer-driven calculations will be gone. There will still be "intuitionist" parties and societies in various parts of the globe that will refuse to use computers and will carry on anti-computer activities, but they will have no influence.

In fact, the computer will be an integral part of the domestic scene by 2068. The home computer that keeps tabs on bills, makes out checks, organizes shopping and menus, turns on appliances, keeps tabs on the family pet, and controls the cooking, will solve the servant problem.

There will even be a tendency to use self-contained mobile computers (or "robots") as a kind of literal servant-substitute. These, however, will still be a luxury in 2068. The tendency in that year will be in the other direction, instead; toward consolidation. More and more households will be tied in to a large community computer for the sake of greater efficiency.

And, of course, the Central Planetary Computer will keep track of all statistics, down to the minutest, for instant recall. The statistical contents of a reference book like the World Almanac will be largely computer-prepared and computer-checked, though it will still require the active and agile intelligence of the human personnel to decide *which* statistics and *how* the whole is to be organized.

Energy Problem to Be Solved

Energy will not be a problem in 2068. The key breakthrough into the practical use of fusion power will have been made at least a half-century before. The oceans will then offer a supply of deuterium as an energy fuel that will last in copious quantity for millions of years. By 2068,

417

man will have gone beyond that. There will be space stations circling Earth that will be capable of absorbing and transmitting solar energy to Earth, a source that will last for billions of years.

The world of 2068 will be one of infinite energy, and therefore one in which we can control the environment easily. For instance, the difficulty today in obtaining fresh water from the sea or metals from low-content slag, or in removing pollutants from air and water, is not any lack in understanding but is a matter of expense only. In 2068, with infinite energy at our disposal and very advanced techniques, expense will be no factor, and the world's resources can be mobilized with ease and efficiency to support 6 billion in far greater affluence than we can now support 3 billion, and without the accumulation of waste or pollution.

Food supply will be crucial, of course. The last decades of the 20th Century will see a greater and more intelligent use of the ocean as a food source. In the 21st Century, the great age of ocean-farming and ocean-herding will begin. Plants will be grown underwater and sea-life will be "domesticated"; that is, bred and cared for, so that the annual increase may be exploited without danger of overuse.

But the great trend in 2068 will be the use of microorganisms as food for mankind. Yeasts and algae can be grown far more rapidly and efficiently than the higher forms of life can. They can be flavored to suit and eventually can be prepared in varieties of forms, textures and tastes that will outshine more common classes of foods. They will also be carefully designed to supply optimal nutritional needs.

Food will become the product of gigantic laboratories and the percentage of space on land and sea which must be devoted to food will be decreasing in 2068. More and more of the Earth's surface can be turned into amusement resorts, parkland and wildlife refuges.

Underground Cities Predicted

Even Earth's surface load of cities will be declining in 2068. The 21st Century will see man burrowing underground.

The process will only be underway in 2068; the majority of mankind will still be living aboveground; but the future will be clear. Every city will already have its underground portion; many newer suburbs will be entirely underground.

The underground city will have as its chief advantage an utter freedom from weather viscissitudes or day-night change. Temperature will be equable the year round and there will be neither wind nor rain nor snow. Well-lit and well-ventilated, the underground cities will be computer-designed from the start for rationality and comfort. With the day-night cycle gone, the entire planet can eventually be put on a single "planet-time."

Nor will the underground dweller be deprived of the touch of nature. Quite the contrary. Where the modern city dweller may have to travel twenty miles to get out "in the country," the underground dweller will merely have to rise a few hundred feet in an elevator, for once a city is completely underground, the area above can be made into parkland.

With abundant energy and advanced computers lifting from the shoulders of mankind all forms of routinized and unrewarding labor, there will be room and scope for fun and creation.

In this endeavor, human beings will compete freely and with an increasing feeling of social equality. As the planet becomes a computer-guided community, the sense of "foreigner" will diminish.

Ghettos and slums will disappear as copious energy makes affluence possible for all and as computerized decisions modify conditions that would otherwise be brought about by irrational feelings of bigotry. Some people may still choose to be selective in their social and intimate associations, but there will be no great gaps in living standards or opportunity between one loose association and another; no economic barriers between them; and therefore no burning fears or hatreds.

With the declining birth-rate, the rise in ectogenesis, the disappearance of routine housework, and the conversion of all work into a low-muscle, high-brain endeavor that can be performed by either sex, it is clear that the woman of 2068 will be completely equal to man economically and socially. The family will no longer be an essential economic unit and sex will no longer be tied to child-birth. Sexual associations will be looser in 2068 and more casual. The sorrows of unrequited love and of jealousy will not disappear, but perhaps they can more easily be recovered from in the casual atmosphere of the time.

In 2068's world of leisure and comfort, the greatest industry will be that of supplying what may be called "amusement." Sports and shows of all sorts will still be popular, but there will be entirely new outlets. One-man reaction motors can place individuals in the air, so that the sensation of scuba-diving can become airborne. Trips to the Moon may be common and large space-stations may be established in orbit about the Earth for the chief purpose of supplying vacationers with no-gravity fun.

The casual life will allow greater individual tastes in style and manner of behavior. There probably will be chemicals to supply a world of inner illusion without adverse side-effects, and large sections of the population may choose to withdraw into themselves.

Matching the emphasis on amusement will be that on education. By 2068, a substantial percentage of the human race will be seriously devoting the major portion of their lives to a continuing program of education in a variety of fields.

Education will be quite comfortable and amusing in 2068. Closed-circuit television and microfilms will offer dramatic ways of transferring information. Computers will design courses in any subject to match the capacity and temperament of the individual. The central library of the planet will be open to everybody and anything in it available on demand through a computerized copying service.

Those who choose education as their goal will have a chance to develop what creativity they possess and to participate in the important work of the world of 2068, the further increase and refinement of knowledge.

Those groups who, in 2068, will be pushing hard for controlling the quality of births will undoubtedly have as their goal the increase in the percentage of those who would be so constituted, temperamentally, as to choose continuing education over passive amusement.

Colony on the Moon

Space will still offer an outstanding technological adventure in progress in 2068. A successful, self-supporting colony on the Moon will be celebrating more than half a century of existence. It will be a sizable community, increasing quickly in numbers and drawing a large immigration from Earth. Also the development of rational underground towns on the Moon and the discoveries by the Lunar colonists of techniques for the proper utilization of microorganisms for food will have stimulated similar changes on Earth.

Nor will the Moon serve merely as a human residential community. The greatest astronomical observatory will be established on its far side and huge research complexes will be working on chemical and physical techniques that utilize hard vacuums. A Lunar-based computer will analyze data from probes that circle the Sun at closer-than-Mercury distances and from satellites that circle the Earth, watching its atmospheric changes. Weather-forecasting on Earth will become a science and so will another kind of weather-forecasting; that of predicting changes in the Solar wind, necessary, if space travel is to be safe.

By 2068, there will also be a small colony on Mars and manned probes will have swept across the neighborhood of Venus and Mercury. Temporary landings will have been made on Ceres, the largest of the asteroids.

But the outer planets will still remain to be explored. In 2068, the news headlines will feature the preparation for manned flights to the moons of Jupiter. (These headlines, by the way, can be on television screens, called for at will, with any news item or feature reproduced on paper for your records, as desired, at the push of a button. Many, however, will wish to obtain printed newspapers, complete with comics and feature columns, for leisure reading and for absorption in depth—and that will be available, too.) Unmanned probes will have preceded

the flight, both to the neighborhood of Jupiter and to the planets beyond. It will be clear that by 2100 man will have explored to the limits of the Solar system.

Unsolved Problems to Remain

Are there any great unsolved problems that will face the world of 2068? In the fields of science and technology, two overriding ones will remain.

In the first place, the gap between the Solar system and other planets circling other stars will still be unbridgeable in 2068. Is the gap permanently unbridgeable, or can there exist techniques undreamed of, even in 2068, by which the distance can be crossed, without unbearable expenditure of energy and of time?

The importance of reaching the stars is that somewhere out there are other life forms and even, in all likelihood, other intelligences. To study other forms of life or to make contact with other intelligences would represent a chance at a monumental advance of knowledge.

Second, the thorough understanding of the human brain will still be an unattained goal in 2068. The biochemistry of other tissues will be solved in considerable detail by then and it will be possible to "create life" in the test-tube—that is, to synthesize nucleic acid molecules capable of reproducing themselves. But the big problem will remain; the intricate interrelationships of the human brain will still be out of sight.

A major push in this direction will be in progress in 2068. After all, a true understanding of what makes us tick will make it possible for mankind to guide itself all the better in a further rational advance that will, by 2168, make the world of 2068 seem, by comparison nothing more than a collection of cavemen huddled about a brushfire.

About the Author

Isaac Asimov was born in Russia in 1920, brought to Brooklyn, N. Y., 3 years later and reared there by his parents, who operated a candy store. He now lives in a suburb of Boston and is an associate professor of biochemistry at Boston University School of Medicine.

A prolific writer, in virtually every area of science fact and fiction, Dr. Asimov is the author of more than 80 books. Among them are Pebble in the Sky; End of Eternity; Kingdom of the Sun; The Human Body; Human Brain; and I, Robot. He has received the James T. Grady award for science writing from the American Chemical Society.

"I was a writer much before a teacher," Dr. Asimov says. "I began at 11. I would have started earlier if the thought had occurred to me."

He received his Ph.D. from Columbia University in 1948 and began teaching the next year. For 10 years he confined his writing efforts to weekends. Today, he teaches infrequently, but does help run a university magazine and is on a number of committees.

"Writing is a form of teaching anyway. All I did was abandon retail for wholesale teaching," Dr. Asimov explains.

U. S. Population Passes 200,000,000

The "Census Clock" in the Commerce Dept. in Washington, D. C., ticked past the 200,000,000 mark Nov. 20, 1967, in its theoretical counting of the U. S. population and proceeded toward the 250,000,000 figure which it may reach by 1980. Every 14½ seconds the "Clock" adds another person to the U. S. population by balancing births, deaths, immigration and emigration on the basis of current averages for these things.

The 200,000,000 Americans can be broken down roughly into the following categories:

• 102,000,000 are females, 98,000,000 males. The females have a life expectancy of 73.5 years. The males have a life expectancy of 66.5 years.

• 33,000,000 are white collar workers, 27,000,000 are blue collar workers.

• 12% of the population is non-white.

• 19,000,000 are over 65.

• 9,000,000 are foreign born.

• Two-thirds of the population live in metropolitan counties.

The U. S. population passed the 100,000,-000 milestone in 1915 and in 1950 hit the 150,000,000 mark. It is impossible to say for certain when the 250,000,000 figure will be reached since any alteration in the factors used to compute the population would change the rate of progression and a nuclear war or plague would throw all projections and assumptions out the window.

But barring catastrophe, some population theorists suggest that if you visit the Commerce Dept. building in the year 2015, or thereabout, you may be just in time to see the "Clock" register 500,000,000.

AGRICULTURE
Farms in United States by State—Number, Acreage, Value
Source: Bureau of the Census (Census of 1964)

| State | Farms | Land in Farms | Average value of land and buildings | | State | Farms | Land in Farms | Average value of land and buildings | |
			Per Farm	Per Acre				Per Farm	Per Acre
	No.	Acres	Dollars	Dollars		No.	Acres	Dollars	Dollars
U.S.	3,157,864	1,110,096,507	51,470	146.41	East So. Central	468,155	64,508,796	22,270	116.62
New England	41,972	7,745,828	36,222	196.28	Kentucky	133,038	16,265,180	22,422	182.59
Maine	12,875	2,590,022	21,050	102.07	Tennessee	133,446	15,266,212	21,088	183.99
N. Hamp.	4,648	903,197	25,339	131.78	Alabama	92,530	15,225,797	20,868	126.48
Vermont	9,247	2,524,371	30,341	111.46	Mississippi	109,141	17,751,607	24,801	153.30
Mass.	8,019	901,789	48,150	427.40	West So. Central	436,200	204,776,847	60,217	128.27
R. Island	1,115	105,135	47,255	512.31	Arkansas	79,898	16,574,299	37,549	181.35
Connecticut	6,068	721,314	69,407	577.11	Louisiana	62,467	10,411,045	40,859	246.31
Middle Atlantic	160,237	24,234,888	34,262	226.54	Oklahoma	88,726	36,077,472	50,995	125.09
New York	66,510	12,275,308	33,308	179.72	Texas	205,109	141,714,031	79,625	114.20
New Jersey	10,641	1,155,597	74,281	669.58					
Pa.	83,086	10,803,983	30,358	232.34	Mountain	134,114	267,894,536	104,075	52.10
E. No. Central	573,565	99,486,457	49,233	283.86	Montana	27,020	65,833,760	105,230	43.11
Ohio	120,381	17,619,167	44,638	304.04	Idaho	29,661	15,300,513	70,215	136.12
Indiana	108,082	17,933,226	52,490	314.87	Wyoming	9,038	36,818,632	117,848	28.92
Illinois	132,822	29,957,500	82,494	263.98	Colorado	29,797	38,257,577	92,393	71.96
Michigan	93,504	13,598,992	34,199	233.99	N. Mexico	14,206	47,646,966	121,680	36.31
Wisconsin	118,816	20,377,572	27,820	154.61	Arizona	6,477	40,559,493	330,241	52.72
West No. Central	763,782	283,683,320	52,216	129.58	Utah	15,759	12,994,823	60,445	73.23
Minnesota	131,163	30,804,980	39,536	167.78	Nevada	2,156	10,482,772	184,565	38.09
Iowa	154,162	33,758,321	59,901	273.36					
Missouri	147,315	32,691,618	34,050	153.07	Pacific	166,177	76,558,167	137,382	298.20
No. Dakota	48,836	42,717,360	59,342	67.80	Washington	45,574	19,052,538	65,609	157.35
So. Dakota	49,703	45,567,262	57,914	63.01	Oregon	39,757	20,509,302	60,307	117.09
Nebraska	80,163	47,792,663	66,232	111.01	California	80,846	36,996,327	216,071	471.14
Kansas	92,440	50,271,116	68,188	124.83	Alaska	382	19,594,440	47,150	9.17
South Atlantic	468,376	76,973,774	35,329	214.97	Hawaii	4,864	2,354,454	100,508	208.08
Delaware	4,401	717,013	60,237	362.64					
Maryland	20,760	3,180,696	66,975	435.02					
Dist. of Col.	N.A.	N.A.	N.A.	N.A.					
Virginia	80,354	12,001,860	28,634	189.68	Puerto Rico and Possessions				
W. Virginia	34,504	5,278,592	14,146	92.05					
N. Carolina	148,202	14,396,724	24,906	257.16	Puerto Rico	44,829	N.A.	N.A.	N.A.
S. Carolina	56,248	8,101,417	26,220	179.80	Guam	2,529	30,099	N.A.	N.A.
Georgia	83,366	17,886,931	30,498	141.63	Am. Samoa[2]	2,135	11,521	N.A.	N.A.
Florida	40,541	15,410,541	109,732	288.68	Virgin Isl.	466	39,539	166,441	1961.65

N.A.—not available. [1]Preliminary. [2]Not enumerated in 1964.

Farms in United States—Number, Acreage, Value
Source: Bureau of the Census

Year	Farms	Farms	Percent of Total Area in Farms	Cropland Harvested[1]	Value of Farm Land, Buildings
	Number	Acres	Per cent	Acres	Dollars
1850	1,449,073	293,561,000	15.6	....	3,272,000,000
1860	2,044,077	407,213,000	21.4	....	6,645,000,000
1870	2,659,985	407,735,000	21.4	....	7,444,000,000
1880	4,008,907	536,082,000	28.2	166,187,000	10,197,000,000
1890	4,564,641	623,219,000	32.7	219,706,000	13,279,000,000
1900	5,737,372	838,592,000	44.1	283,218,000	16,615,000,000
1910	6,361,502	878,798,000	46.2	311,293,000	34,801,000,000
1920	6,448,343	955,884,000	50.2	348,604,000	66,316,000,000
1930	6,288,648	986,771,000	51.8	359,242,000	47,880,000,000
1935	6,812,350	1,054,515,000	55.4	295,624,000	32,859,000,000
1940	6,096,799	1,060,852,000	55.7	321,242,000	33,642,000,000
1945	5,859,169	1,141,615,000	59.9	352,866,000	46,389,000,000
1950	5,382,162	1,158,566,000	60.9	344,399,000	$75,261,000,000
1959 (a)	3,703,894	1,120,157,789	58.9	311,285,249	138,987,659,000
1964	3,157,864	1,123,508,000	48.7	286,885,256	160,341,000,000

(a)Alaska and Hawaii not included

[1]For 1950 and earlier censuses figures for cropland harvested relate to the preceding year. Prior to 1924, this column shows the total acreage of crops for which figures are available, except for 1919, when 14,502,932 acres of corn cut for forage were included (most of this was probably duplicated in the acreage of corn harvested as grain). Beginning with 1924, the figures represent the actual land harvested. [2]Based on reports for only a sample of farms.

Farm Employment—Annual Averages
Source: Economic Research Service; Department of Agriculture
Index (1910-14 = 100 per cent)

Yr.	Total Aver. No.	Total Index	Family Aver. No.	Family Index	Hired Aver. No.	Hired Index	Yr.	Total Aver. No.	Total Index	Family Aver. No.	Family Index	Hired Aver. No.	Hired Index
	1,000 Persons	Per cent	1,000 Persons	Per cent	1,000 Persons	Per cent		1,000 Persons	Per cent	1,000 Persons	Per cent	1,000 Persons	Per cent
1915	13,592	100	10,140	100	3,452	102	1945	10,000	74	7,881	78	2,119	62
1920	13,432	99	10,041	99	3,391	100	1950	9,926	73	7,597	75	2,329	69
1925	13,036	96	9,715	96	3,321	98	1955	8,364	62	6,347	62	2,017	59
1930	12,497	92	9,307	92	3,190	94	1960	7,057	52	5,172	52	1,885	55
1935	12,733	94	9,855	97	2,878	85	1965	5,610	41	4,128	41	1,482	44
1940	10,979	81	8,300	82	2,679	79	1966	5,214	38	3,854	38	1,360	40

Farm Income and Government Payments, by States
Source: Economic Research Service; Department of Agriculture (Preliminary)

State	Cash receipts from farm marketings ($1,000) 1965	1966	Government payments by program 1966 (in $1,000) Conservation	Sugar Act	Wool Act	Soil Bank	Feed Grain Program	Wheat Program	Other[1]	Total
Alabama	646,454	647,252	5,784	.....	7	3,485	20,107	183	50,051	79,617
Alaska	4,523	4,543	66	.....	32	.....	.....	.....	.....	98
Arizona	505,709	500,104	1,582	.....	479	33	3,802	209	37,528	43,633
Arkansas	909,813	935,420	4,918	.....	13	2,781	3,129	50	74,818	85,709
California	3,696,107	3,948,048	6,015	11,720	2,670	599	10,983	552	71,339	103,881
Colorado	695,537	826,228	5,174	5,258	1,818	7,330	11,778	475	30,637	62,470
Connecticut	155,027	167,993	508	.....	5	17	194	.....	167	891
Delaware	125,619	128,188	231	.....	2	90	1,214	5	263	1,805
Florida	993,896	1,038,841	3,536	5,390	1	1,737	5,725	28	1,949	18,366
Georgia	964,407	1,015,809	7,729	.....	4	9,504	24,954	599	37,383	80,173
Hawaii	184,830	199,339	177	10,952	5	.....	.....	.....	.....	11,134
Idaho	505,429	541,964	2,804	6,676	1,554	1,418	.....	366	22,218	37,579
Illinois	2,338,323	2,763,091	8,591	36	.....	.....	93,313	609	17,109	121,063
Indiana	1,308,950	1,460,667	5,682	.....	382	1,276	72,059	818	11,874	92,091
Iowa	3,044,085	3,460,366	10,093	71	1,310	901	195,596	47	1,985	210,001
Kansas	1,205,774	1,532,998	8,067	861	506	9,275	63,474	1,367	142,091	225,641
Kentucky	675,257	711,255	6,408	.....	232	2,098	30,033	378	3,755	42,904
Louisiana	485,227	549,948	4,917	8,322	24	1,781	3,301	11	33,451	51,807
Maine	280,396	248,854	1,084	29	24	846	63	1	25	2,072
Maryland	329,408	332,529	859	.....	24	230	3,325	105	972	5,515
Massachusetts	164,930	170,875	521	.....	10	14	56	.....	33	634
Michigan	797,820	886,420	4,907	2,580	388	2,468	34,530	2,559	14,747	62,179
Minnesota	1,602,034	1,814,626	5,910	3,298	835	7,973	105,200	37	12,176	135,429
Mississippi	817,981	783,571	6,601	.....	16	1,573	13,631	35	102,671	124,527
Missouri	1,258,509	1,383,699	10,508	.....	504	4,039	83,864	2,042	37,544	138,501
Montana	418,310	503,329	5,077	1,842	1,946	3,263	4,062	448	47,816	64,454
Nebraska	1,331,321	1,680,427	6,717	2,629	483	3,678	118,148	600	43,150	175,405
Nevada	53,144	62,997	587	62	283	.....	43	26	540	1,541
New Hampshire	54,196	58,272	513	.....	9	119	9	.....	.....	647
New Jersey	256,570	274,079	689	.....	9	68	3,433	106	537	4,842
New Mexico	262,025	289,562	2,659	133	1,087	4,037	10,155	1,025	18,362	37,458
New York	938,377	1,002,248	4,487	375	150	2,975	9,261	1,250	3,671	22,169
North Carolina	1,174,071	1,295,187	6,527	.....	26	2,152	29,470	1,666	22,975	62,816
North Dakota	677,062	732,165	3,876	1,729	677	14,072	23,553	315	93,235	137,457
Ohio	1,110,195	1,301,819	6,102	1,623	1,054	1,669	52,302	1,386	17,066	81,202
Oklahoma	777,597	852,627	8,563	.....	132	7,512	10,768	1,415	78,890	107,280
Oregon	471,227	513,570	4,629	826	867	1,028	2,470	748	13,780	24,348
Pennsylvania	845,390	913,347	4,876	.....	212	1,763	11,084	937	3,550	22,422
Rhode Island	21,541	22,324	70	.....	1	.....	2	.....	.....	73
South Carolina	399,690	396,570	3,772	.....	2	6,359	11,880	890	30,094	52,997
South Dakota	754,286	880,133	3,615	.....	2,043	7,512	37,520	511	26,454	77,655
Tennessee	609,928	603,306	5,429	.....	93	3,527	21,894	466	35,592	67,001
Texas	2,468,571	2,698,583	19,252	1,366	7,792	16,901	109,867	4,017	292,539	451,734
Utah	161,421	187,500	1,660	891	1,435	1,248	1,252	122	3,106	9,717
Vermont	130,809	138,965	1,051	.....	8	296	116	.....	22	1,493
Virginia	503,080	506,552	4,675	.....	299	652	8,453	651	2,882	17,612
Washington	641,063	726,534	2,812	2,997	300	1,759	2,324	257	39,128	49,677
West Virginia	103,349	105,468	1,595	.....	253	619	1,196	39	153	3,855
Wisconsin	1,254,374	1,420,423	5,845	.....	219	2,619	40,369	89	4,568	53,709
Wyoming	170,461	204,102	2,321	1,689	2,945	533	879	147	3,121	11,635
Total U. S.	39,284,167	43,422,717	220,074	71,355	33,697	144,689	1,293,390	27,587	1,486,017	3,276,809

[1]Includes Milk Indemnity, $194,000; Great Plains Conservation, $9,152,000 Cotton Domestic Allotment, $69,551,000; Wheat Marketing Certificates $487,234,000; and Cropland Adjustment $51,016,000.

Index Numbers of Prices Received by Farmers
Source: Economic Research Service; Department of Agriculture
(1910-1914=100)

Year	All Farm Products	All Crops	Livestock[1]	Food Grains	Feed Grains and Hay	Feed Grains	Cotton	Tobacco	Oil-bearing Crops	Fruit	Commercial Vegetables[2]	Potatoes, Sweetpotatoes[3]	Meat Animals	Dairy Products	Poultry and Eggs	Wool
1910	104	105	102	109	96	97	118	84	120	100	....	83	101	100	100	117
1915	99	96	102	127	105	110	76	82	106	82	....	86	102	101	101	125
1920	211	235	190	249	202	209	262	233	208	188	....	294	171	202	222	214
1925	156	164	149	171	132	139	186	168	147	165	153	170	139	156	162	221
1930	125	115	134	93	106	109	104	140	111	149	128	162	133	142	128	119
1935	109	103	114	97	107	112	98	171	127	89	116	72	115	114	116	110
1940	100	90	109	84	85	86	83	134	103	81	122	89	108	129	98	160
1945	207	202	211	172	167	168	179	360	228	240	207	207	229	198		232
1950	258	233	280	224	193	198	282	402	276	194	211	166	240	249	186	341
1955	232	231	234	228	183	187	272	437	249	202	223	178	246	247	191	249
1960	238	222	253	203	152	151	254	500	214	242	228	203	296	259	160	235
1963	242	239	245	224	165	164	271	494	258	291	233	156	290	253	146	269
1964	237	239	236	190	167	166	262	490	256	36	247	229	270	256	142	291
1965	248	234	261	164	174	173	245	513	265	247	262	295	319	261	145	262
1966	266	235	292	185	181	181	215	553	293	243	288	200	356	293	161	275

[1]Livestock and livestock products. [2]For fresh market and processing beg. 1952. [3]Including dry edible beans.

Employees on Non-farm Payrolls Reach New High

Bureau of Labor Statistics reported on July 11, 1967, that the number of persons on non-farm payrolls reached a record high of 66,141,000 in June 1967. This topped the previous high of 65,904,000 set in Dec. 1966. The May-June employment increase was about 150,000 greater than seasonally expected. Over the year, non-farm payroll employment has risen by 1,500,000; nearly all of this increase took place in services, trade and government establishments.

BEST SELLING BOOKS IN 1967

(Listed according to frequency of citation in best-seller reports)

General

1. *Games People Play, Dr. Eric Berne
2. *Everything But Money, Sam Levenson
3. *How to Avoid Probate, Norman Dacey
4. *Human Sexual Response, Dr. William Masters & Virginia Johnson
5. *Rush to Judgment, Mark Lane
6. Edgar Cayce—The Sleeping Prophet, Jess Stearn
7. Madame Sarah, Cornelia Otis Skinner
8. Paper Lion, George Plimpton
9. The Jury Returns, Louis Nizer
10. The Death of a President, William Manchester
11. The Boston Strangler, Gerold Frank
12. The Autobiography of Bertrand Russell: 1872-1914
13. With Kennedy, Pierre Salinger
14. Division Street: America, Studs Terkel
15. Anyone Can Make a Million, Morton Shulman
16. Inside South America, John Gunther
17. *The Random House Dictionary of the English Language
18. The New Industrial State, John Kenneth Galbraith
19. A Modern Priest Looks at His Outdated Church, Father James Kavanaugh
20. Winston S. Churchill, Randolph S. Churchill
21. At Ease: Stories I Tell to Friends, Dwight D. Eisenhower
22. "Our Crowd," Great Jewish Families of New York, Stephen Birmingham
23. The Search for Amelia Earhart, Fred Goerner
24. The Passover Plot, Hugh J. Schonfield
25. Disraeli, Robert Blake
26. By-Line: Ernest Hemingway, William White
27. The Lawyers, Martin Mayer
28. That Quail, Robert, Margaret Stanger
29. Treblinka, Jean-Francois Steiner
30. Variety of Men, C. P. Snow
31. The Arrogance of Power, Sen. J. William Fulbright
32. Incredible Victory, Walter Lord
33. Harold Nicolson: The War Years, Nigel Nicolson
34. The Quotations of Mao
35. Due to Circumstances Beyond Our Control, Fred Friendly
36. A Man Called "Lucy," Pierre Accoce & Pierre Quet
37. The Bitter Heritage, Arthur Schlesinger, Jr.
38. Nicholas and Alexandra, Robert Massie

Fiction

1. *Valley of the Dolls, Jacqueline Susann
2. *The Secret of Santa Vittoria, Robert Crichton
3. *Tai-Pan, James Clavell
4. *Capable of Honor, Allen Drury
5. *The Adventurers, Harold Robbins
6. The Arrangement, Elia Kazan
7. *All in the Family, Edwin O'Connor
8. The Birds Fall Down, Rebecca West
9. *The Fixer, Bernard Malamud
10. The Eighth Day, Thornton Wilder
11. The Mask of Apollo, Mary Renault
12. Washington, D. C., Gore Vidal
13. Tales of Manhattan, Louis Auchincloss
14. The Captain, Jan de Hartog
15. The Chosen, Chaim Potok
16. The Plot, Irving Wallace
17. Rosemary's Baby, Ira Levin
18. Fathers, Herbert Gold
19. A Dream of Kings, Harry M. Petrakis
20. Go to the Widow-Maker, James Jones
21. Waiting for Winter, John O'Hara
22. A Night of Watching, Elliot Arnold
23. The King of the Castle, Victoria Holt
24. Under the Eye of the Storm, John Hersey
25. When She Was Good, Philip Roth
26. Night Falls on the City, Sarah Gainham
27. A Second-Hand Life, Charles Jackson
28. An Operational Necessity, Gwyn Griffin
29. All the Little Live Things, Wallace Stegner
30. The Time is Noon, Pearl S. Buck
31. The Candlesticks and the Cross, Ruth Freeman Solomon
32. Five Smooth Stones, Ann Fairbairn

*One of 10 best-sellers in 1966 according to Publishers' Weekly.

STATISTICS OF BOOK TRADE

The number of new books (titles) published in the U. S. rose from 28,595 in 1965 to a record 30,050 in 1966, according to Publishers' Weekly. The 1966 output was made up of 21,819 new titles and 8,231 new editions of previously published titles. The number of new books imported by the U. S. rose from 4,670 titles in 1965 to 6,347 (5,468 of them new titles) in 1966. Titles in print in paperback increased in 1966 by about 5,900, bringing the total to approximately 42,500.

British publishers issued in 1966 a record of 28,883 new books—22,964 new titles and 5,919 new editions of previously published titles.

For the U. S. in 1965, the last year for which complete statistics are available, trade books (publishers' name for general interest books such as novels and biographies) accounted for 7.3% of the $2.01 billion spent for books. Student text and reference books accounted for 51% of the total sales—and an estimated 90% of publishing profits. References for lawyers, doctors, engineers and businessmen accounted for another 10% of book sales. Book-club selections, which are mailed to readers, accounted for 9% of sales; juvenile books for 6.3%; Bibles and other religious books for 4.5%, and books published by university presses for 1.1%. Paperbacks accounted for almost 6% of the dollar volume.

During 1966, 310,000,000 paperback books were sold, highest in the industry's 28-year history.

was scheduled to end Nov. 26, 1967. Kurt Herbert Adler is general director and Howard K. Skinner is manager.

SANTA FE OPERA, Santa Fe, N. M., was destroyed by fire July 27, 1967. It was announced that work on the new open-air opera house has begun and was expected to be completed in time for the opening of the 1968 season on July 2, with a production of Madama Butterfly. In its short history the Santa Fe Opera has presented 41 operas, including 5 American and two world premieres. The repertory is usually divided between standard operatic favorites and unfamiliar recent works. Almost all the operas are sung in English.

ST. LOUIS MUNICIPAL OPERA, St. Louis, Mo., one of America's most famous summer theaters, presented a varied repertory for the 1967 season. The first evening opened with West Side Story. This was followed by Wish You Were Here, Do I Hear a Waltz?, Superman, The New Moon, The Unsinkable Molly Brown, Funny Girl, On a Clear Day, Gypsy, The King and I; in addition, the Royal Ballet performed Swan Lake, Giselle, and Romeo and Juliet. America's oldest summer musical theater, the St. Louis Municipal Opera presented its first performance June 15, 1919. Since that time, the theater has given over 230 different comic and light operas, operettas and musical comedies. The group that founded the theater believed that it should belong to all the people of St. Louis and thus they decided not to charge admission for a portion of the seats. Today, approximately 1,500 seats are free of charge. The total seating capacity of the outdoor amphitheater in Forest Park is 12,000.

ST. PAUL CIVIC OPERA ASSN., St. Paul, Minn., presented varied programs for its 1967-1968 season. After opening Oct. 9 with Sweet Charity, the Civic Opera went on to perform Faust with Jean Fenn and Don Giovanni with Giorgio Tozzi. The second half of the season had scheduled Pagliacci, Cavalleria Rusticana, Kiss Me Kate, On a Clear Day, to conclude with the Song of Norway Apr. 28, 1968.

TULSA OPERA, Tulsa, Okla., opened its 1967-1968 season Nov. 2, with Puccini's Madama Butterfly starring Renata Scotto as Butterfly and John Alexander as Lt. Pinkerton. The season was scheduled to close Mar. 23, 1968, with Donizetti's Don Pasquale featuring Gianna D'Angelo as Norina and Italo Tajo in the title role.

WASHINGTON, D. C. The New York Opera Festival, Felix Salmaggi general manager, was scheduled to present its tenth season of operas at the Carter Barron Amphitheatre, Washington, D. C., during the summer of 1968. The repertory included Aida, La Traviata, Il Trovatore, Rigoletto, La Boheme, Madama Butterfly, Tosca, Carmen, I Pagliacci, Cavalleria Rusticana and the Barber of Seville.

Movies of the Year (Oct. 1, 1966, to Oct. 1, 1967)
Selected and Rated by the New York Daily News Film Critics

After a steady advance in the previous two years, motion picture attendance hit a peak in 1967. Variety and quality accounted for the upsurge. Freed from the fear of the TV bogeyman and liberated by the elasticity of the moral code recently revised by the Motion Picture Assn. of America, American producers revitalized the industry by making films of distinction for intelligent fans. Some failed; most succeeded.

So many movies, attractive to the public, resulted in the biggest summer at the box-office in film history. The single month of August outgrossed any preceding month of any preceding year in money and attendance. A number of the films enjoying popularity around the country were made in 1966, notably Hawaii, Doctor Zhivago, The Sand Pebbles and A Man for All Seasons.

Of widely divergent nature were the big ones of 1967. Barefoot in the Park, a comedy of newlyweds, broke all records at Radio City Music Hall in New York Thoroughly Modern Millie, a musical of the 1920's starring the world's darling, Julie Andrews, is Universal Pictures' biggest grosser of all time. The Dirty Dozen, a tough, uncompromising war drama with Lee Marvin, is coining money for Metro-Goldwyn-Mayer. To Sir, With Love, starring Sidney Poitier as a Negro teacher in a London slum school, is doing the same for Columbia.

Listed below, alphabetically, are films rated by The New York Daily News star system. ★★★★ is for excellence; ★★★½★, very good; ★★★, good; ★★½★, mediocre; ★★, fair; ★½★, poor; ★, very poor. Documentaries, such as A King's Story, do not receive stars because they are photographic records of people and places, not fictional stories with actors playing the roles. Included are foreign films of merit.

Wanda Hale
N. Y. Daily News Movie Editor

Movie	Star rating	Cast	Director
Accident, The	★★★½★	Dirk Bogarde, Stanley Baker	Joseph Losey
Adventures of Bullwhip Griffin	★★★	Roddy McDowall, Suzanne Pleshette	James Neilson
After the Fox	★★½★	Peter Sellers, Victor Mature	Vittorio de Sica
Any Wednesday	★★★½★	Jane Fonda, Jason Robards	Robert Ellis Miller
Barefoot in the Park	★★★★	Robert Redford, Jane Fonda	Gene Saks
Battle of Algiers, The	★★★½★	Yacef Saadi, Jean Martin	Gillo Pontecorvo
Beach Red	★★★½★	Cornel Wilde, Rip Torn	Cornel Wilde
Big Mouth, The	★★★	Jerry Lewis, Harold J. Stone	Jerry Lewis
Blow-up	★★	Vanessa Redgrave, David Hemmings	Michaelangelo Antonioni
Bobo	★★★	Peter Sellers, Britt Ekland	Robert Parrish
Bonnie and Clyde	★★★½★	Warren Beatty, Faye Dunaway	Arthur Penn
Casino Royale	★★½★	Peter Sellers, Ursula Andress	John Huston, Ken Hughes, Val Guest, Robert Parrish, Joe McGrath
Covenant With Death, A	★	George Maharis, Laura Devon	Lamont Johnson
Countess From Hong Kong, A	★★½★	Marlon Brando, Sophia Loren	Charles Chaplain
Deadly Affair, The	★★★★	James Mason, Simone Signoret	Sidney Lumet
Defector, The	★★★	Montgomery Clift, Hardy Kruger	Raoul Levy
Dirty Dozen, The	★★★★	Lee Marvin, Ernest Borgnine	Robert Aldrich
Divorce American Style	★★★★	Dick Van Dyke, Debbie Reynolds	Bud Yorkin
El Dorado	★★★	John Wayne, Robert Mitchum	Howard Hawks
Enter Laughing	★★★½★	Jose Ferrer, Shelley Winters	Carl Reiner
Family Way, The	★★★★	Hayley Mills, John Mills	John and Roy Boulting
Fistful of Dollars, A	★★★	Clint Eastwood, Marianne Koch	Sergio Leone
Flim-Flam Man, The	★★★½★	George C. Scott, Sue Lyon	Irvin Kershner
For a Few Dollars More	★★½★	Clint Eastwood, Lee Van Cleef	Sergio Leone
Fortune Cookie, The	★★★	Jack Lemmon, Walter Matthau	Billy Wilder
Follow Me, Boys!	★★★	Fred MacMurray, Vera Miles	Norman Tokar
Funeral in Berlin	★★★½★	Michael Caine, Eva Renzi	Guy Hamilton
Funny Thing Happened on the Way to the Forum, A	★★★½★	Zero Mostel, Phil Silvers	Richard Lester
Games	★★★	Simone Signoret, James Caan	Curtis Harrington

Movie	Star rating	Cast	Director
Gambit	★★★½★	Shirley McLaine, Michael Caine..	Ronald Neame
Georgie Girl	★★★½★	James Mason, Lynn Redgrave...	Silvio Narizzano
Grand Prix	★★★½★	James Garner, Eva Marie Saint..	John Frankenheimer
Guide for the Married Man, A.	★★★½★	Walter Matthau, Robert Morse..	Gene Kelly
Hawaii	★★★	Julie Andrews, Max von Sydow..	George Roy Hill
Hombre	★★★★	Paul Newman, Fredric March....	Martin Ritt
Honey Pot, The	★★★★	Rex Harrison, Susan Hayward...	Joseph L. Mankiewicz
Hotel	★★★	Rod Taylor, Catherine Spaak...	Richard Quine
How to Succeed in Business Without Really Trying	★★★★	Robert Morse, Michele Lee.....	David Swift
Hurry Sundown	★★	Michael Caine, Jane Fonda.....	Otto Preminger
In Like Flint	★★½★	James Coburn, Lee J. Cobb.....	Gordon Douglas
In the Heat of the Night	★★★★	Sidney Poitier, Rod Steiger....	Norman Jewison
Is Paris Burning?	★★★★	Jean-Paul Belmondo, Charles Boyer	Rene Clement
King's Story, A	documentary	Orson Welles (narrator)	Harry Booth
La Guerre Est Finis	★★★	Yves Montand, Ingrid Thulin..	Alain Resnais
Luv	★★½★	Jack Lemmon, Peter Falk......	Clive Donner
Man For All Seasons, A	★★★★	Paul Scofield, Wendy Hiller...	Fred Zinnemann
Marat/Sade	★★★★	Ian Richardson, Patrick Magee..	Peter Brook
Naked Runner, The	★★★½★	Frank Sinatra, Peter Vaughan..	Sidney J. Furie
Night of the Generals, The	★★★½★	Peter O'Toole, Omar Sharif....	Anatole Litvak
Penelope	★★★	Natalie Wood, Ian Bannen.....	Arthur Hiller
Professionals, The	★★★★	Burt Lancaster, Lee Marvin....	Richard Brooks
Quiller Memorandum, The	★★★½★	George Segal, Alec Guinness...	Michael Anderson
St. Valentine's Day Massacre...	★	Jason Robards, George Segal...	Roger Corman
Sand Pebbles, The	★★★★	Steve McQueen, Richard Attenborough	Robert Wise
Taming of the Shrew, The	★★★★	Elizabeth Taylor, Richard Burton	Franco Zeffirelli
Texas Across the River	★★★	Dean Martin, Alain Delon.....	Michael Gordon
Thoroughly Modern Millie	★★★★	Julie Andrews, Mary Tyler Moore	George Roy Hill
Tiger Makes Out, The	★★½★	Eli Wallach, Anne Jackson....	Arthur Hiller
Tobruk	★★★	Rock Hudson, George Peppard..	Arthur Hiller
To Sir, With Love	★★★½★	Sidney Poitier, Christian Roberts.	James Clavell
Triple Cross	★★	Christopher Plummer, Romy Schneider	Terence Young
Two For The Road	★★★½★	Audrey Hepburn, Albert Finney..	Stanley Donen
Ulysses	★★★★	Milo O'Shea, Maurice Roeeves...	Joseph Strick
Up the Down Staircase	★★★	Sandy Dennis, Patrick Bedford.	Robert Mulligan
Venetian Affair, The	★★	Robert Vaughan, Elke Sommer..	Jerry Thorpe
War Wagon, The	★★★	John Wayne, Kirk Douglas.....	Burt Kennedy
Welcome to Hard Times	★★½★	Henry Fonda, Janice Rule.....	Burt Kennedy
Whisperers, The	★★★★	Dame Edith Evans, Eric Portman	Bryan Forbes
You're A Big Boy Now	★★★	Elizabeth Hartman, Geraldine Page	Francis Ford
You Only Live Twice	★★★½★	Sean Connery, Akiko Wakabayashi	Lewis Gilbert

RECORDINGS

Disc Sales Boom in 1967; Beatles Break Bing Crosby Mark

The U. S. record industry, riding a rapidly-growing boom, rang up close to a billion dollars in sales in 1967, an increase of 300% in a dozen years. Americans owned an estimated 40,000,000 phonographs and record players, triple the number only 20 years earlier.

The rising tempo of disc sales toppled previous, long-held marks. **The Beatles** claimed worldwide sales of over 210,000,000 records—a total achieved in only about four years—and these figures put them ahead of the all-time popularity king, **Bing Crosby**, during 1967.

Bing's total was reckoned at "over 200,000,000" but the exact number was uncertain, as was true of many figures in an industry where sales statistics are not readily available.

Both single records and albums are included in the Crosby and Beatles figures.

Bing still held the record for biggest sale of a single, 16,000,000 of Irving Berlin's "White Christmas." The Beatles top-selling single was "I Want to Hold Your Hand," 5,300,000 copies.

Another upset was in the top mark for sales of a long-play album. That spot was taken over by the movie soundtrack of "The Sound of Music" with 8,000,000 LP albums, passing the previous leader, the original cast recording of "My Fair Lady," which had 6,000,000 copies.

Crosby also benefited from the growing market. His "Merry Christmas" album, which had sold some 5,000,000 copies in various speeds and sizes, was selling at better than a quarter million annually. Bing had a total of 20 singles which sold over 1,000,000 each (mostly in the 1940s); his "Silent Night" sold over 10,000,000, and "Jingle Bells" over 7,000,000.

Elvis Presley is credited with 45 singles which sold more than 1,000,000 each, including "Hound Dog," 6,485,000 copies. His total sales were well over 100,000,000; those of his singles alone were put at 81,450,000.

By contrast, in the entire decade of the 1920s only a half-dozen records sold the magic number

of 1,000,000. There were many more in the '30s and still more in the '40s and '50s.

But by the '60s, the growing popularity of the LP albums cut chances of selling a million copies; the LPs were more expensive (although an LP may be just one disc, it is sold as an album, not a single).

Beginning in 1958, the Record Industry Assn. of America has awarded Gold Records for each single it certifies as selling 1,000,000 copies, and for each LP album with sales of $1,000,000 (in manufacturers sales reckoned at 50% of the list price).

Frank Sinatra has made 10 such LP albums with sales of over $1,000,000 each, one more than Presley and one less than The Beatles. Sinatra also has made 5 singles with over a million copies each, as well as many singles under that number.

Fats Domino made 22 records that sold over a million each, including "Blueberry Hill," with total sales (in the '50s and '60s) of 27,000,000 records. **Eddy Arnold**, though credited with only one record in the over-a-million class, "Bouquet of Roses" (1948), and one album with $1,000,000 in sales, reportedly has sold over 49,000,000 discs.

The only LP classical to sell a million copies was the Van Cliburn rendition of Tchaikovsky's "Piano Concerto No. 1," which sold nearly 2,000,000.

Leopold Stokowski hit a million copies with both "Tales from the Vienna Woods" and "Blue Danube Waltz." **Arthur Fiedler** did it with "Jalousie," **Jose Iturbi** hit the magic number with two singles, "Clair de Lune" and Chopin's "Polonaise in A-Flat," **Percy Faith** joined the club with "Song from Moulin Rouge" and "Theme from a Summer Place."

Among the top recording artists of all times were **Enrico Caruso** and **Arturo Toscanini**, but figures on their sales are not available.

Among others not named above who have sold several singles of more than a million each are: **Perry Como, Connie Francis,** 13; **Pat Boone,** 12; **Glenn Miller,** 9; **Artie Shaw, Frankie Laine,** 8;

Patti Page, Harry James, Kay Kyser, Little Richard, Ricky Nelson, 7; Guy Mitchell, Everly Brothers, 6; Nat King Cole, Al Jolson, Gene Autry, Chubby Checkers, Bobby Darin, The Platters, Bobby Rydel, Dean Martin, The Weavers, Doris Day, The Drifters, Hank Ballard & The Midnighters, 5.

Those who have sold at least 4 singles over a million each include: Guy Lombardo, Les Paul and Mary Ford, Ames Brothers, Paul Anka, Tony Bennett, Jimmy Dorsey, Tommy Dorsey, Eddie Fisher, Joni James, Vaughan Monroe, Jimmy Rodgers, Four Aces, The Coasters, Bill Black's Combo.

Among those who sold singles of a million each in the '30s and are not among those named above were: Rudy Vallee, "Stein Song," 1930; Jeanette MacDonald and Nelson Eddy, "Indian Love Call," 1935; Ella Fitzgerald, "A-Tisket, A-Tasket," 1938; Will Glahe, "Beer Barrel Polka," 1938; Cab Calloway, "Jumpin' Jive," 1939; Orrin Tucker, "Oh, Johnny," 1939.

The recorders who managed to sell a million copies in the '20s were Paul Whiteman, "Whispering," 1920, and "Three O'Clock in the Morning," 1922; Clyde McCoy, "Sugar Blues," 1923 (in 1946 McCoy again sold over a million copies of "Sugar Blues"); Vernon Dalhart, "Prisoner's Song," 1924; Gene Austin, "My Blue Heaven," 1927, and "Ramona," 1928.

Among artists who have had LP album sales of $1,000,000 each are:

..The Beatles, Mitch Miller, 11; Frank Sinatra, 10; Elvis Presley, Beach Boys, Kingston Trio, 9; Herb Alpert and the Tijuana Brass, Rolling Stones, Johnny Mathis, Andy Williams, 8; Barbra Streisand, 7; Harry Belafonte, 6; Mantovani, Ray Coniff, Bill Cosby, Roger Williams, Peter, Paul and Mary, 5.

Grammy Awards

On Mar. 2, 1967, the Grammy Awards for what were judged the best efforts of the recording industry in 1966 were announced by the National Academy of Recording Arts and Sciences. The Grammys are gold-plated statuettes in the form of early gramophones. The categories and winners were:

Record of the Year; STRANGERS IN THE NIGHT—Frank Sinatra—Producer: Jimmy Bowen.

Album of the Year; SINATRA: A MAN AND HIS MUSIC—Frank Sinatra—Producer: Sonny Burke.

Song of the Year; MICHELLE—Songwriters: John Lennon, Paul McCartney.

Best Instrumental Theme; BATMAN THEME—Composer: Neal Hefti.

Best Vocal Performance—Female; IF HE WALKED INTO MY LIFE (Single)—Eydie Gorme.

Best Vocal Performance—Male; STRANGERS IN THE NIGHT (Single)—Frank Sinatra.

Best Instrumental Performance (other than jazz); WHAT NOW MY LOVE—Herb Alpert & the Tijuana Brass.

Best Performance by a Vocal Group; A MAN AND A WOMAN—Anita Kerr Singers.

Best Performance by a Chorus; SOMEWHERE MY LOVE (Lara's Theme from "Dr. Zhivago")—Ray Coniff & Singers.

Best Original Score Written for a Motion Picture or TV Show; DR. ZHIVAGO—Composer: Maurice Jarre.

Best Score from an Original Cast Show Album; MAME (Original Cast)—Composer: Jerry Herman—Producer: Goddard Lieberson.

Best Comedy Performance; WONDERFULNESS—Bill Cosby.

Best Spoken Word, Documentary or Drama Recording; EDWARD R. MURROW—A REPORTER REMEMBERS—VOL. 1 THE WAR YEARS—Edward R. Murrow.

Best Recording for Children; DR. SEUSS PRESENTS: "IF I RAN THE ZOO" AND "SLEEP BOOK"—Marvin Miller.

Best Album Notes; SINATRA AT THE SANDS—Frank Sinatra—Annotator: Stan Cornyn.

Best Instrumental Jazz Performance—Group or Soloist with Group; GOIN' OUT OF MY HEAD—Wes Montgomery.

Best Original Jazz Composition; IN THE BEGINNING GOD—Composer: Duke Ellington.

Best Contemporary (R & R) Recording; WINCHESTER CATHEDRAL—New Vaudeville Band—Producer: Geoff Stephens.

Best Contemporary (R & R) Solo Vocal Performance—Male or Female; Single, ELEANOR RIGBY—Paul McCartney (The Beatles).

Best Contemporary (R & R) Group Performance—Vocal or Instrumental; Single, MONDAY, MONDAY—The Mamas & The Papas.

Best Rhythm & Blues Recording; CRYING TIME—Ray Charles—Producer: Tangerine Records.

Best Rhythm & Blues Solo Vocal Performance—Male or Female; Single, CRYING TIME—Ray Charles.

Best Rhythm & Blues Group—Vocal or Instrumental; Single, HOLD IT RIGHT THERE—Ramsey Lewis.

Best Folk Recording; BLUES IN THE STREET—Cortelia Clark—Producer: Felton Jarvis.

Best Sacred Recording (Non-Classical); GRAND OLD GOSPEL—Porter Wagoner & the Blackwood Bros.—Producer: Chet Atkins.

Best Country & Western Recording; ALMOST PERSUADED—David Houston—Producer: Billy Sherrill.

Best Country & Western Vocal Performance—Female; DON'T TOUCH ME, Single—Jeannie Seely.

Best Country & Western Vocal Performance—Male; ALMOST PERSUADED, Single — David Houston.

Best Country & Western Song; ALMOST PERSUADED—Songwriters: Billy Sherrill, Glenn Sutton.

Best Instrumental Arrangement; WHAT NOW MY LOVE (Herb Alpert & the Tijuana Brass)—Arranger: Herb Alpert.

Best Arrangement Accompanying a Vocalist or Instrumentalist; STRANGERS IN THE NIGHT (Frank Sinatra)—Arranger: Ernie Freeman.

Best Engineered Recording — Non-Classical; STRANGERS IN THE NIGHT (Frank Sinatra)—Engineer: Eddie Brackett.

Best Engineered Recording—Classical; WAGNER: LOHENGRIN—Leinsdorf cond. Boston Symphony, Pro Musica Chorus & Soloists—Engineer: Anthony Salvatore.

Best Album Cover, Photography; CONFESSIONS OF A BROKEN MAN—Porter Wagoner—Art Director: Robert Jones—Photographer: Les Leverette.

Best Album Cover, Graphic Arts; REVOLVER—The Beatles—Graphic Artist: Klaus Voormann.

Album of the Year; IVES: SYMPHONY NO. 1 IN D MINOR—Morton Gould cond. Chicago Symphony Orchestra—Producer: Howard Scott.

Best Performance—Orchestra; MAHLER: SYMPHONY NO. 6 IN A MINOR—Erich Leinsdorf cond. Boston Symphony Orchestra.

Best Chamber Music Performance—Instrumental or Vocal; BOSTON SYMPHONY CHAMBER PLAYERS (Selections by Mozart, Brahms, Beethoven, Fine, Copland, Carter, Piston) Boston Symphony Chamber Players.

Best Performance—Instrumental Soloist or Soloists; BAROQUE GUITAR (Bach, Sanz, Weiss, Etc.) Julian Bream.

Best Opera Recording; WAGNER: DIE WALKURE—Georg Solti cond. Vienna Philharmonic Orchestra—Principal Soloists: Nilsson, Crespin, Ludwig, King, Hotter—Producer: John Culshaw.

Best Choral Performance (Other Than Opera); A TIE: HANDEL: MESSIAH—Robert Shaw cond. Robert Shaw Chorale & Orchestra, and IVES: MUSIC FOR CHORUS (Gen. Wm. Booth Enters Into Heaven, etc.)—Gregg Smith cond. Columbia Chamber Orch., Gregg Smith Singers, Ithaca College Concert Choir, George Bragg cond. Texas Boys Choir.

Best Vocal Soloist Performance, PRIMA DONNA (Barber, Purcell, Etc.)—Leontyne Price, Soloist (Francesco Molinari—Pradelli cond. RCA Italiana Opera Orchestra).

ECONOMICS

United States Budget Receipts and Expenditures—1966-1967

Source: Treasury Department; each fiscal year ends June 30 (data preliminary)

Classification	Fiscal year 1966	Fiscal year 1967
RECEIPTS		
Internal Revenue:		
Individual income taxes:		
Withheld	$42,811,381,066	$50,476,959,074
Other	18,486,170,453	18,848,169,528
Total individual income taxes	61,297,551,519	69,325,128,603
Corporation income taxes	30,834,242,695	34,914,684,186
Excise taxes	13,398,112,011	14,130,143,102
Employment taxes:		
Federal Insurance Contributions Act and Self-Employment Contributions Act	19,005,488,017	25,562,637,832
Railroad Retirement Tax Act	683,630,962	790,447,686
Federal Unemployment Tax Act	567,014,254	602,744,198
Total employment taxes	20,256,133,234	26,955,829,717
Estate and gift taxes	3,093,921,881	3,000,869,434
Total internal revenue	128,879,961,342	148,326,655,044
Customs	1,811,170,211	1,971,799,790
Miscellaneous receipts:		
Interest	846,731,214	965,304,662
Dividends and other earnings	1,731,401,307	1,829,042,236
Realization upon loans and investments	359,473,577	601,869,862
Recoveries and refunds	131,782,639	173,657,040
Royalties	207,816,492	104,409,382
Sales of Government property and products	1,438,500,624	1,248,998,128
Seigniorage	648,804,126	836,734,039
Other	500,802,693	1,099,891,022
Total miscellaneous receipts	5,865,312,675	6,859,906,375
Subtotal gross receipts	**136,556,444,229**	**157,158,361,210**
Deduct: Refunds of receipts:		
Internal Revenue:		
Applicable to budget accounts:		
Individual income taxes	5,851,430,132	7,849,758,415
Corporation income taxes	761,215,081	937,365,678
Excise taxes	216,797,296	186,074,571
Estate and gift taxes	27,604,513	36,341,901
Applicable to trust accounts	353,620,351	499,774,094
Subtotal net internal revenue refunds	7,210,667,377	9,509,314,661
Custom	44,627,265	71,084,500
Other	285,306	107,400
Total refunds of receipts	7,255,579,949	9,581,006,563
Transfers to trust accounts	23,939,087,562	31,108,424,805
Interfund transactions	634,513,049	674,877,946
Total deductions	31,829,180,561	41,364,309,315
Net administrative budget receipts	**104,727,263,667**	**115,794,051,894**
EXPENDITURES		
Legislative Branch	231,505,145	249,679,120
The Judiciary	79,162,697	87,098,250
Executive Office of the President	26,282,285	27,775,919
Funds appropriated to the President:		
Alaska programs	5,433,400	2,601,212
Disaster relief	132,492,310	53,471,391
Emergency fund for the President	48,300	253,723
Expansion of defense production (net)	−151,995,216	−105,006,311
Expenses of management improvement	377,837	27,706
International Financial Institutions		−653,500,000
Office of Economic Opportunity	1,017,845,647	1,508,889,403
Peace Corps	94,378,056	110,972,438
Philippine education program		3,400,000
Public works acceleration	88,168,149	21,132,053
Southeast hurricane disaster	28,497,570	10,408,499
Other	218,636	226,293
Military assistance:		
Office of Secretary of Defense	73,586,963	59,154,080
Department of the Army	511,657,326	369,242,005
Department of the Navy	191,664,202	129,055,763
Department of the Air Force	280,128,581	331,012,449
All other Agencies	1,045,814	−5,630,223
Foreign military sales fund (net)	−89,947,987	−32,874,164
Total—Military	968,134,990	849,959,911
Economic:	2,140,610,112	2,295,059,004
Total—Funds appropriated to the President	4,324,209,797	4,097,896,226
Agriculture Department	5,948,579,581	5,817,132,995
Commerce Department	673,111,638	756,649,483
Defense Department:		
Military personnel	16,753,352,054	19,659,728,385
Operation and maintenance	14,709,815,173	18,892,534,289
Procurement	14,338,537,392	19,065,081,675
Research, development, test and evaluation	6,259,082,903	7,171,048,872
Military construction	1,333,564,021	1,500,368,537
Family housing	647,469,810	557,440,180
Civil Defense	86,051,014	100,084,925
Revolving and management funds	281,135,125	624,185,299
Total—Military functions	54,409,007,496	67,570,472,167
Civil Functions:		
Army: Corps of Engineers	1,250,447,986	1,278,327,965
The Panama Canal	32,254,062	25,015,964
Other	26,416,973	39,197,101
Navy—Wildlife conservation, etc.	−1,817	11,841
Air Force—Wildlife conservation, etc.	39,533	48,206
Total—Civil functions	1,309,158,738	1,342,601,079
Total—Defense Department	55,718,166,235	68,913,073,246

U. S. BUDGET RECEIPTS AND EXPENDITURES (continued)

Classification	Fiscal year 1966	Fiscal year 1967
Health, Education and Welfare Dept.	7,552,452,215	10,800,978,809
Housing and Urban Development Dept.	767,079,543	520,347,613
Interior Department.	1,437,365,817	1,509,923,854
Justice Department.	372,493,608	406,887,799
Labor Department.	503,381,803	506,424,647
Post Office Department.	888,195,731	1,182,581,033
State Department.	406,607,209	410,796,263
Transportation Department.	1,276,338,243	1,468,064,775
Treasury Department.	13,054,653,149	14,538,931,951
Interest on the public debt.	12,013,862,666	13,392,356,054
Atomic Energy Commission.	2,402,925,455	2,264,016,704
General Services Administration.	601,001,413	678,955,940
National Aeronautics and Space Administration.	5,932,988,770	5,425,596,586
Veterans Administration.	5,069,665,105	6,194,506,564
Other independent agencies:		
Alaska Development Committees.	137,870	185,379
American Battle Monuments Commission.	1,994,467	2,005,843
Central Intelligence Agency-construction.	359,732	1,431,915
Civil Aeronautics Board.	85,478,496	73,858,054
Civil Service Commission.	122,849,939	129,875,127
Commission of Fine Arts.	103,012	117,303
Commission on Civil Rights.	1,520,048	2,441,578
Equal Employment Opportunity Commission.	2,590,293	4,609,337
Export-Import Bank of Washington (net).	−385,023,380	−339,631,337
Farm Credit Administration.	−7,229,860	−13,175,266
Federal Coal Mine Safety Board of Review.	74,059	75,816
Federal Communications Commission.	17,217,322	17,965,489
Federal Home Loan Bank Board (net).	−255,457,882	−157,464,477
Federal Maritime Commission.	3,091,139	3,454,202
Federal Mediation and Conciliation Service.	6,550,185	7,078,811
Federal Power Commission.	13,402,065	14,080,581
Federal Radiation Council.	83,872	106,930
Federal Trade Commission.	13,647,651	14,108,765
Foreign Claims Settlement Commission.	1,852,725	1,654,625
Historical and memorial commissions.	120,084	120,398
Indian Claims Commission.	312,690	336,011
Intergovernmental Commissions.	1,414,708	1,347,479
Interstate Commerce Commission.	27,263,905	44,475,642
National Capital Housing Authority.	41,477	42,679
National Capital Planning Commission.	1,284,783	1,138,255
National Capital Transportation Agency.	1,978,387	2,976,380
National Foundation on Arts and Humanities.	1,227,982	9,003,355
National Labor Relations Board.	28,371,894	30,196,888
National Mediation Board.	1,906,625	1,981,263
National Science Foundation.	368,248,429	414,978,938
President's Adv. Co., on Labor-Management Policy.	44,284	1,218
Railroad Retirement Board.	16,558,000	17,201,000
Renegotiation Board.	2,450,399	2,518,634
Securities and Exchange Commission.	15,820,029	16,681,030
Selective Service System.	54,229,962	58,035,805
Small Business Administration.	−139,659,888	−238,972,565
Smithsonian Institution.	29,870,642	30,245,810
Subversive Activities Control Board.	363,112	330,446
Tariff Commission.	3,246,115	3,399,647
Tax Court of the United States.	2,125,892	2,171,885
Temporary Study Commissions.	5,417,304	7,800,501
Tennessee Valley Authority (net).	53,905,319	102,033,739
U. S. Arms Control and Disarmament Agency.	8,803,200	9,513,017
U. S. Information Agency.	166,597,584	183,640,629
Water Resources Council.	44,468	1,969,900
Total—Other independent agencies.	275,238,157	465,946,675
District of Columbia.	71,453,600	83,600,600
Interfund transactions (−).	−634,513,049	−674,877,946
Net administrative budget expenditures.	**106,978,344,155**	**125,731,987,115**
Administrative budget surplus (+) or deficit (−).	−2,251,080,487	−9,937,935,220

EFFECT OF OPERATIONS ON PUBLIC DEBT

Classification	Fiscal year 1966	Fiscal year 1967
Administrative budget surplus (−) or deficit (+).	+2,251,080,487	+9,937,935,220
Excess of trust receipts (−) or expenditures (+).	+11,723,308	−10,138,757,498
Excess of investments (+) or sales (−) in public debt and agency security (net).	+3,562,355,673	+10,850,927,796
Excess of sales (−) or redemptions (+) of government agency securities in market (net).	−4,077,314,625	−428,031,775
Increase (−) or decrease (+) in checks outstanding and deposits in transit (net) and other accounts.	+905,683,879	+800,789,447
Increase (−) or decrease (+) in public debt interest accrued.	+50,487,319	−12,393,110
Increase (+) or decrease (−) in cash held outside Treasurer's account.	+132,060,195	−73,023,619
Increase (+) or decrease (−) in balance of Treasurer's account.	−202,887,425	−4,648,382,684
Increase (+) or decrease (−) in public debt.	+2,633,188,811	+6,313,849,999
Gross debt at beginning of period.	317,273,898,983	319,907,087,795
Gross public debt at end of period.	**319,907,087,795**	**326,220,937,794**
Guaranteed debt of U. S. Government agencies.	461,547,275	512,196,075
Total public debt and guaranteed securities.	**320,368,635,070**	**326,733,133,869**
Deduct: Debt not subject to statutory limitation.	266,414,118	262,012,656
Total debt subject to statutory limitation.	**320,102,220,951**	**326,471,121,213**

United States Net Receipts and Expenditures

Source: Treasury Department; annual statements for year ending June 30

Yearly average	Receipts	Expenditures	Yearly average	Receipts	Expenditures	Yearly average	Receipts	Expenditures
	$1,000	$1,000		$1,000	$1,000		$1,000	$1,000
1789-1800[1]	5,717	5,776	1871-1875	336,830	287,460	1908	601,862	659,196
1801-1810[2]	13,056	9,086	1876-1880	288,124	255,598	1909	604,320	693,744
1811-1820[2]	21,032	23,943	1881-1885	366,961	257,691	1910	675,512	693,617
1821-1830[2]	21,923	16,162	1886-1890	375,448	279,134	1911	701,833	691,202
1831-1840[2]	30,461	24,495	1891-1895	352,891	363,599	1912	692,609	689,881
1841-1850[2]	28,545	34,097	1896-1900	434,877	457,451	1913	724,111	724,512
1851-1860	60,237	60,163	1901-1905	559,481	535,559	1914	734,673	735,081
1861-1865	160,907	683,735	1906	594,984	570,202	1915	697,910	760,586
1866-1870	447,301	377,642	1907	665,860	579,129	1916	782,534	734,056

Yearly Average	Receipts	Expenditures	Yearly Average	Receipts	Expenditures
1917	$1,124,324,795	$1,977,681,751	1943*	$21,986,700,787	$79,407,131,152
1918	3,664,582,865	[6]12,696,702,471	1944*	43,635,315,356	95,058,707,898
1919	5,152,257,136	18,514,879,955	1945*	44,475,303,665	98,416,219,788
1920	6,694,565,389	6,403,343,841	1946*	39,771,403,710	60,447,574,319
1921	5,624,932,961	5,115,927,690	1947*	39,786,181,036	39,032,393,376
1922	4,109,104,151	3,372,607,900	1948*	41,488,178,842	[7]33,068,708,998
1923	4,007,135,481	3,294,627,529	1949*	37,695,549,449	39,506,989,497
1924	4,012,044,702	3,048,677,965	1950*	36,494,900,837	[8]39,617,003,195
1925	3,780,148,685	3,063,105,332	1951*	47,567,613,484	44,057,830,859
1926	3,962,755,690	3,097,611,823	1952*	61,390,944,552	65,407,584,930
1927	4,129,394,441	2,974,029,674	1953	64,825,044,026	74,274,257,484
1928	4,042,348,156	3,103,264,655	1954	64,655,386,989	67,772,353,245
1929	4,033,250,225	3,298,859,486	1955	60,389,743,895	64,569,972,817
1930	4,177,941,702	3,440,268,884	1956	68,165,329,582	66,539,776,178
1931	3,115,556,923	[3]3,577,434,003	1957	71,028,649,978	69,433,078,427
1932	1,923,913,117	4,659,202,825	1958	69,116,717,311	71,936,171,353
1933	2,021,212,943	4,622,865,028	1959	67,915,348,624	80,342,335,375
1934	3,064,267,912	6,693,899,854	1960	77,763,460,220	76,539,412,798
1935	3,729,913,845	6,520,965,945	1961	77,659,424,905	81,515,167,453
1936	4,068,936,689	8,493,485,919	1962	81,409,092,072	87,786,766,580
1937	[4]4,978,600,695	7,756,021,409	1963	86,357,020,251	92,589,764,029
1938*	5,615,221,162	6,791,837,760	1964	89,458,664,071	97,684,374,794
1939*	4,996,299,530	18,858,457,570	1965	93,071,796,891	96,506,904,210
1940*	5,144,013,044	9,062,032,204	1966	106,978,344,155	104,727,263,667
1941*	7,102,931,383	13,262,203,742	1967 (prel.)	115,794,051,894	125,731,987,115
1942*	12,555,436,084	44,045,678,816			

*Revised to exclude from both net budget receipts and budget expenditures the appropriations of receipts to the Railroad Retirement Account.

(1) Average for period March 4, 1789, to Dec. 1, 1800.

(2) Years ended Dec. 31, 1801, to 1842; average for 1841-1850 is for the period Jan. 1, 1841, to June 30, 1850.

(3) Receipts from 1937 on have deducted appropriations to Federal old-age and survivors insurance trust fund.

(4) Expenditures for years 1932 through 1946 have been revised to include Government Corporations (wholly owned), etc. (net).

(5) Effective January 3, 1949, amounts refunded by the Government, principally for the overpayment of taxes, are being reported as deductions from total receipts rather than as expenditures. Also, effective July 1 1948, payments to the Treasury, principally by wholly owned Government corporations for retirement of capital stock and for disposition of earnings, are excluded in reporting both budget receipts and expenditures. Neither of these changes affects the size of the budget surplus or deficit. Beginning 1931 figures in each case have been adjusted accordingly for comparative purposes.

(6) Figures for 1918 through 1946 are revised to exclude statutory debt retirements (sinking fund, etc.)

(7) Excludes $3 billion transferred to Foreign Economics Corporation Trust Fund.

(8) Includes $3 billion representing expenditures made from the FEC Trust Fund.

Net Public and Private Debt

Sources: Office of Business Economics, U. S. Dept. of Commerce

(In billions of dollars)

	Public				Private								
							Individual and noncorporate						
							Farm		Nonfarm mortgage		Other nonfarm		
End of year	Public and private total	Total public	Federal[1]	State and Local[2]	Total private	Corporate	Production	Mortgage	1-4 family residential	Multifamily residential & commercial	Commercial	Financial	Consumer
1950	490.3	239.4	218.7	20.7	250.9	142.1	6.2	6.1	42.9	16.5	8.9	6.9	21.4
1955	672.3	269.8	231.5	38.4	402.5	212.1	9.7	9.1	83.8	24.9	12.4	11.6	38.9
1958	782.6	283.6	232.7	50.9	499.1	269.5	12.1	11.3	111.8	32.8	13.7	12.8	45.1
1959	846.2	298.8	243.2	55.6	547.4	283.3	11.7	11.3	124.3	36.5	15.3	13.4	51.5
1960	890.2	301.0	241.0	60.0	589.2	302.8	12.3	12.8	134.2	40.2	16.6	14.2	56.0
1962[3]	1,016.7	331.2	257.5	73.7	685.5	348.2	15.0	15.2	158.3	48.0	19.3	18.3	63.2
1963[3]	1,089.5	341.9	262.4	79.5	747.6	376.1	16.4	16.8	173.8	51.7	21.5	20.8	70.5
1964[3]	1,166.4	354.6	269.4	85.2	811.8	407.7	17.1	18.9	188.8	55.6	23.9	21.5	78.4
1965	1,257.6	367.6	272.5	95.1	890.0	451.2	18.1	21.2	204.5	58.7	25.7	22.6	87.9
1966	1,346.1	380.8	279.9	100.9	965.2	497.2	18.8	23.3	216.6	61.9	28.8	23.8	94.8

[1]Includes categories of debt not subject to the statutory debt limit. Net Federal Government debt is defined as the gross debt outstanding less Federal Government securities held by Federal agencies and trust funds, and Federal agency securities held by the U. S. Treasury and other Federal agencies. It thus equals Federal Government and agency debt held by the public.

[2]Data for State and local governments are for June 30 of each year.

[3]Figures for 1962 thru 1964 have been revised.

National Income by Type of Income
(Millions of dollars)

	1958	1959	1960	1962*	1963*[1]	1964[1]	1965[1]	1966
Compensation of employees..	257,816	279,093	294,226	323,632	341,004	365,720	393,932	435,719
Wage and salaries..........	239,926	258,187	270,844	296,091	311,095	333,683	359,052	394,620
Private..................	196,382	212,538	222,108	240,132	251,616	269,355	289,788	316,735
Military..................	9,767	9,873	9,804	10,756	10,849	11,692	12,143	14,669
Government civilian......	33,777	35,776	38,842	45,203	48,630	52,636	57,121	63,213
Supplements to wages, sal....	17,890	20,906	23,382	27,541	29,909	32,037	34,880	41,099
Empl. contrib. soc. ins.....	7,972	9,650	11,380	13,657	15,045	15,411	16,241	20,298
Other labor income........	9,918	11,256	12,002	13,884	14,864	16,626	18,639	20,801
Empl. contrib. priv. pen..	7,870	9,064	9,684	11,356	12,165	13,670	15,517	17,336
Other..................	2,048	2,192	2,318	2,528	2,699	2,956	3,122	3,465
Proprietors' income.......	46,607	46,550	46,209	50,111	51,013	52,315	56,682	59,277
Business and professional...	33,173	35,129	34,244	37,093	37,910	40,180	41,921	43,226
Income unic. enterprises...	33,229	35,269	34,263	37,076	37,944	40,259	42,291	43,596
Invent. valu. adjustment.	−56	−140	−19	17	−34	−79	−370	−370
Farm......................	13,434	11,421	11,965	13,018	13,103	12,135	14,761	16,051
Rental income of persons....	15,418	15,596	15,822	16,691	17,139	17,963	18,951	19,374
Corp. prof., inv. adjust..	41,117	51,676	49,904	55,660	58,933	66,276	74,898	82,196
Corp. profits before tax..	41,372	52,141	49,712	55,408	59,401	66,789	76,560	83,832
Corp. profits tax liability..	19,045	23,679	23,032	24,179	26,324	28,345	31,358	34,546
Corp. profits after tax...	22,327	28,462	26,680	31,229	33,077	38,444	45,202	49,286
Dividends...........	11,566	12,580	13,437	15,183	16,454	17,811	19,792	21,452
Undistributed profits....	10,761	15,882	13,243	16,046	16,623	20,633	25,410	27,834
Inventory valuation adj.....	−255	−465	192	252	−468	−513	−1,662	−1,636
Net interest................	6,804	7,110	8,361	11,593	13,838	15,794	17,917	20,163
Net interest................								
National income............	367,762	400,025	414,522	457,687	481,927	518,068	562,380	616,729

*The figures for 1962 and 1963 reflect the new depreciation guidelines issued by the Treasury Department July 11, 1962, and the investment tax credit provided in the Revenue act of 1962. [1]Revised.

Per Capita Personal Income, by States and Regions
Source: Department of Commerce. Office of Business Economics

State and region	Per capita income[1] (dollars)				State and region	Per capita income[1] (dollars)			
	1963	1964	1965	1966p		1963	1964	1965	1966p
United States........	2,455	2,579	2,746	2,940	Southeast............	1,837	1,950	2,089	2,256
					Virginia.........	2,095	2,264	2,419	2,581
New England......	2,698	2,843	2,995	3,223	West Virginia....	1,781	1,891	2,027	2,195
Maine...........	1,961	2,122	2,277	2,438	Kentucky........	1,837	1,887	2,045	2,205
New Hampshire..	2,347	2,428	2,547	2,761	Tennessee........	1,776	1,874	2,013	2,109
Vermont.........	2,013	2,130	2,312	2,590	North Carolina...	1,804	1,918	2,041	2,235
Massachusetts....	2,746	2,910	3,050	3,271	South Carolina...	1,580	1,696	1,846	2,027
Rhode Island....	2,507	2,652	2,823	2,980	Georgia.........	1,879	2,004	2,159	2,311
Connecticut......	3,118	3,234	3,401	3,678	Florida.........	2,145	2,285	2,423	2,576
					Alabama.......	1,676	1,777	1,910	2,039
Mideast..........	2,806	2,948	3,108	3,310	Mississippi......	1,436	1,485	1,608	1,751
New York........	2,978	3,127	3,278	3,480	Louisiana........	1,843	1,936	2,067	2,257
New Jersey......	2,965	3,069	3,237	3,414	Arkansas........	1,627	1,740	1,845	2,015
Pennsylvania.....	2,441	2,588	2,747	2,951					
Delaware........	3,013	3,121	3,392	3,563	Southwest........	2,095	2,191	2,324	2,492
Maryland........	2,675	2,828	3,001	3,220	Oklahoma.......	1,992	2,111	2,289	2,456
Dist. of Col......	3,370	3,527	3,708	3,969	Texas..........	2,105	2,208	2,338	2,511
					New Mexico.....	2,053	2,090	2,193	2,310
Great Lakes......	2,619	2,766	2,985	3,198	Arizona.........	2,220	2,272	2,370	2,528
Michigan.........	2,587	2,772	3,010	3,219					
Ohio............	2,509	2,641	2,829	3,027	Rocky Mountain....	2,324	2,379	2,536	2,678
Indiana..........	2,471	2,599	2,848	3,061	Montana........	2,265	2,255	2,438	2,615
Illinois..........	2,915	3,050	3,280	3,511	Idaho.........	2,048	2,131	2,395	2,441
Wisconsin........	2,374	2,534	2,724	2,935	Wyoming......	2,421	2,429	2,558	2,686
					Colorado.......	2,483	2,559	2,710	2,872
Plains...........	2,315	2,395	2,624	2,820	Utah.........	2,215	2,268	2,355	2,500
Minnesota.......	2,372	2,440	2,666	2,871					
Iowa............	2,303	2,392	2,676	2,931	Far West.........	2,910	3,038	3,174	3,385
Missouri.........	2,358	2,458	2,663	2,845	Washington......	2,622	2,714	2,906	3,280
North Dakota.....	2,003	1,991	2,279	2,400	Oregon........	2,472	2,600	2,761	2,938
South Dakota....	1,908	1,877	2,213	2,355	Nevada........	3,243	3,232	3,311	3,330
Nebraska........	2,277	2,383	2,629	2,819	California.......	2,997	3,133	3,258	3,449
Kansas..........	2,398	2,488	2,639	2,814	Alaska.........	2,862	3,082	3,187	3,272
					Hawaii.........	2,647	2,775	2,879	3,143

[1]Per capita personal income for each state is derived by the division of total personal income by total population. Personal income is a measure of the income received from all sources during the calendar year by the residents of each state. It comprises income received by individuals in the form of wages and salaries, net income of proprietors (including farmers), dividends, interest, net rents, and other items such as social insurance benefits, relief, veterans pensions and benefits, and allotment payments to dependents of military personnel. P—preliminary.

Gross National Product, National Income, and Personal Income
Source: Department of Commerce. Office of Business Economics
(In millions of dollars) Includes Alaska and Hawaii beginning in 1960

	1950	1955	1960	1963	1964	1965	1966
Gross national product...........	284,769	397,960	503,734	590,503	631,712	681,207	743,288
Less: Capital consumption allowances.........	18,342	31,474	43,408	52,601	56,048	59,589	63,506
Equals: Net national product.........	266,427	366,486	460,326	537,902	575,664	621,618	679,782
Less: Indirect business tax and nontax liability......	23,334	32,067	45,200	54,692	58,497	62,652	65,110
Business transfer payments........	778	1,245	1,878	2,329	2,522	2,565	2,686
Statistical discrepancy...........	1,488	2,093	−1,031	−294	−1,383	−1,609	−2,585
Plus: Subsidies minus current surplus of government enterprises..........	247	−63	243	752	1,253	1,010	2,158
Equals: National income.........	241,074	331,018	414,522	481,927	517,281	559,020	616,729
Less: Corporate profits and inventory valuation adjustment............	37,669	46,871	49,904	58,933	66,593	74,201	82,196
Contributions for social insurance......	6,870	11,135	20,672	26,868	27,969	29,214	38,166
Wage accruals less disbursement......	24	0	2	0	0	0	0
Plus: Government transfer payments to persons..	14,294	16,065	26,609	32,989	34,241	37,137	41,231
Net interest paid by gov't and consumers..	7,196	10,089	15,083	17,589	19,131	20,603	22,269
Dividends...............	8,838	10,478	13,437	16,454	17,340	19,173	21,452
Business transfer payments............	778	1,245	1,878	2,329	2,522	2,565	2,686
Equals: Personal income............	227,619	310,889	400,953	465,487	495,953	535,083	584,005

Cost of Living in Various Cities of the World

This comparison of the cost of living in various cities was drawn up in 1966 by the UN Statistical Bureau, based on prices for goods, services and housing for international officials stationed in these cities. Figures show relative costs, based on about 120 items. New York City was assigned the index figure 100. Thus, while expenditure for these items might be $1,000 in New York, it would be $880 for them in Copenhagen and $1,080 in Caracas. Figures with an asterisk (*) omit cost of housing (rent, utilities and domestic service) in cities where they were furnished at nominal cost by governments.

Index	City	Index	City
*115	Abdjan, Ivory Coast	86	Kuala Lumpur, Malaysia
*123	Accra, Ghana	*108	Lagos, Nigeria
95	Addis Ababa, Ethiopia	81	La Paz, Bolivia
83	Algiers, Algeria	94	Lima, Peru
83	Amman, Jordan	82	London, England
78	Ankara, Turkey	85	Lusaka, Zambia
90	Athens, Greece	*87	Manila, Philippines
85	Baghdad, Iraq	85	Mexico City, Mexico
92	Bangkok, Thailand	99	Mogadishu, Somalia
84	Beirut, Lebanon	*110	Monrovia, Liberia
68	Bogota, Colombia	66	Montevideo, Uruguay
82	Bonn, W. Germany	87	Montreal, Canada
*113	Brazzaville, Rep. of Congo	83	Nairobi, Kenya
80	Buenos Aires, Argentina	74	New Delhi, India
103	Bujumbura, Burundi	100	New York, U. S.
81	Cairo, United Arab Rep.	101	Paris, France
108	Caracas, Venezuela	89	Quito, Ecuador
82	Colombo, Ceylon	85	Rabat, Morocco
88	Copenhagen, Denmark	102	Rio de Janeiro, Brazil
111	Dakar, Senegal	93	Riyadh, Saudi Arabia
73	Damascus, Syria	92	Rome, Italy
87	Dar Es Salaam, Tanzania	83	San Jose, Costa Rica
86	Geneva, Switzerland	71	Santiago, Chile
91	Guatemala City, Guatemala	88	Seoul, South Korea
85	The Hague, Netherlands	96	Tananarive, Malagasy
94	Havana, Cuba	82	Tehran, Iran
73	Kabul, Afghanistan	97	Tripoli, Libya
85	Karachi, Pakistan	81	Tunis, Tunisia
94	Katmandu, Nepal	80	Vienna, Austria
*97	Khartoum, Sudan	92	Washington, D.C., U. S.
*132	Kinshasa, Dem. Rep. of Congo	*112	Yaounde, Cameroon

Average Consumer Price Indexes

Source: Bureau of Labor Statistics, United States Department of Labor

The Consumer Price Index measures the average change in prices of goods and services purchased by urban wage-earner and clerical-worker families and single workers living alone. Data for 56 large, medium size, and small cities are combined for the all-city average.

(1957-59=100)

Year and month	All items	Food	Housing					Apparel and Upkeep	Transportation	Medical care	Personal care	Reading and recreation	Other goods and services
			Total	Rent	Gas and electricity	Fuel and Utilities	Household furnishings & operation						
1964 Avg......	108.1	106.4	107.2	107.8	107.9	107.3	102.8	105.7	109.3	119.4	109.2	114.1	108.8
1965 Avg......	109.9	108.8	108.5	108.9	107.8	107.2	103.1	106.8	111.1	122.3	109.9	115.2	111.4
1966 Avg......	113.1	114.2	111.1	110.4	108.1	107.7	105.0	109.6	112.7	127.7	112.2	117.1	114.9
1967 Jan......	114.7	114.7	113.1	111.4	108.3	108.6	106.7	111.3	113.4	132.9	113.8	118.5	116.2
Feb......	114.8	114.2	113.3	111.7	108.3	108.7	107.0	111.9	113.6	133.6	114.1	118.6	116.3
Mar......	115.0	114.2	113.3	111.8	108.3	108.7	107.3	112.6	114.2	134.6	114.4	118.9	116.4
Apr......	115.3	113.7	113.6	111.9	108.4	108.8	107.7	113.0	115.1	135.1	114.9	119.4	116.5
May......	115.6	113.9	113.9	112.1	108.3	108.7	107.9	113.8	115.5	135.7	115.0	119.6	116.7
June.....	116.0	115.1	114.1	112.2	108.2	108.6	108.1	113.9	115.7	136.3	115.3	119.7	116.9
July.....	116.5	116.0	114.3	112.4	108.3	108.9	108.2	113.7	116.2	136.9	115.5	119.8	117.8
Aug......	116.9	116.6	114.7	112.6	108.5	109.1	108.3	113.8	116.4	137.5	116.1	120.0	118.8
Sept.....	117.1	115.9	115.0	112.8	108.9	109.4	108.8	115.1	116.8	138.5	116.4	120.5	119.7

INDEXES BY CITIES, ALL ITEMS AND FOOD (1957-59=100)

City	All Items (Annual Average)		Food (Annual Average)		City	All Items (Annual Average)		Food (Annual Average)	
	1965	1966	1965	1966		1965	1966	1965	1966
Average of 56 Cities...	109.9	113.1	108.8	114.2	Los Angeles, Calif.....	112.5	114.7	110.7	113.3
Atlanta, Ga...........	108.1	111.5	107.4	112.9	Milwaukee, Wis........	108.2	110.6	107.7	114.0
Baltimore, Md.........	109.6	113.4	109.3	115.9	Minneapolis, Minn.....	109.5	112.2	107.1	112.4
Boston, Mass..........	113.2	117.0	112.5	117.0	New York, N. Y........	112.2	116.0	109.8	115.1
Buffalo, N. Y.........	103.5	107.0	104.1	108.8	Philadelphia, Pa.......	110.6	113.7	107.2	113.1
Chicago, Ill..........	107.6	110.7	108.8	114.6	Pittsburgh, Pa........	110.2	113.0	107.5	111.8
Cincinnati, Ohio......	107.2	110.3	106.2	111.8	Portland, Ore.........	111.8	115.3	109.5	114.7
Cleveland, Ohio.......	106.9	109.7	104.8	110.9	St. Louis, Mo.........	109.9	113.5	111.5	117.8
Dallas, Texas.........	101.4	105.0	103.9	110.0	San Diego, Calif......	100.1	102.1	102.7	106.5
Detroit, Mich.........	106.4	111.1	105.0	112.2	San Francisco, Calif...	112.7	115.6	111.2	114.2
Honolulu, Hawaii......	102.1	105.1	103.5	107.0	Scranton, Pa..........	112.7	114.9	107.7	112.8
Houston, Tex..........	108.5	111.5	109.2	115.4	Seattle, Wash.........	111.0	114.1	110.3	114.1
Kansas City, Mo.......	113.3	116.3	111.3	117.2	Washington, D. C......	109.6	113.3	108.4	114.0

Occupational Earnings in Selected Cities

Source: Bureau of Labor Statistics, Dept. of Labor

(Average earnings[1] for selected occupations studied in 6 broad industry divisions, manufacturing, transportation, communication and other public utilities; wholesale trade, retail trade, insurance and real estate; and services. March—June 1967)

Occupation	N. Y.	Worcester, Mass.	Atlanta, Ga.	Houston, Texas	Chicago	Phoenix, Ariz.	Spokane, Wash.
Office Workers—Men			(Per week)				
Accounting clerks[2]	$122.00	$130.50	$126.50	$129.00	$127.00	$110.00	$127.50
Draftsmen[2]	168.50	147.50	151.50	167.00	162.50	158.00	....
Office boys	72.00	64.00	75.00	67.50	77.50	66.50	....
Tabulating operators[2]	122.50	......	128.00	132.50	130.50	......	....
Office Workers—Women							
Accounting clerks[2]	107.00	105.00	104.50	104.50	110.00	103.00	104.00
Billers (machine)	93.50	74.50	81.00	85.00	90.50	......	82.00
Bookkeeping (machine)[2]	103.50	92.50	92.50	97.00	103.00	105.00	......
Keypunch operators[2]	96.00	87.00	102.00	93.50	98.00	90.00	106.50
Nurses	126.50	111.50	120.50	126.00	121.50	121.50	......
office girls	70.00	68.00	67.50	66.00	72.00	......	75.50
Payroll clerks	101.00	87.50	91.00	96.00	100.00	91.50	102.50
Secretaries	118.00	102.50	108.00	113.00	113.00	103.00	100.00
Stenographers (general)	91.00	81.50	90.50	88.00	95.00	83.50	91.50
Switchboard operators[2]	102.00	89.50	100.00	92.50	100.00	92.50	......
Typists[2]	90.50	77.50	86.00	85.00	91.50	88.00	85.00
Maintenance, Custodial, and Material Handling							
Workers-Men			(Per hour)				
Carpenters	3.51	3.14	3.14	3.65	3.89	3.52	3.51
Electricians	3.58	3.51	3.68	3.76	3.79	3.74	3.77
Engineers (stationary)	3.79	3.24	3.27	3.21	3.89	3.15	3.41
Helpers, trades	2.97	2.58	2.41	2.61	2.83	2.51	2.93
Machinists	3.88	3.21	3.43	3.76	3.80	3.71	3.76
Mechanics, automotive	3.56	3.14	3.28	3.12	3.71	3.37	3.72
Painters	3.25	......	2.82	3.58	3.97	3.16	......
Plumbers	3.38	......	......	......	4.26	......	......
Guards and watchmen	2.22	2.16	1.87	1.69	2.24	2.10	2.90
Janitors, porters, cleaners	2.27	2.13	1.67	1.73	2.30	1.66	2.22
Laborers, material handling	2.77	2.48	2.04	2.02	2.70	2.40	2.99
Shipping packers	2.26	2.73	2.02	2.00	2.47	2.52	2.79
Shipping clerks	2.92	2.39	2.70	2.75	2.87	......	3.08
Truckdrivers (local)	3.40	3.02	2.71	2.53	3.41	2.98	3.45

[1]Weekly earnings relate to regular straight-time salaries that are paid for standard workweeks. Hourly earnings exclude premium pay for overtime, weekends, holidays, or late shifts. [2]More than one skill level surveyed. Earnings are for highest level surveyed.

Personal Consumption Expenditures for the U. S.

Source: Office of Business Economics, U. S. Department of Commerce.
(In millions of dollars) *Revised

	1940	1945	1950	1955	1960	1964*	1965	1966
Food and tobacco	22,032	43,520	58,120	72,236	87,510	100,671	106,791	115,446
Clothing, accessories and jewelry	8,852	19,645	23,709	27,982	33,032	40,564	43,427	48,406
Personal care	1,036	1,982	2,438	3,461	5,324	7,032	7,509	8,215
Housing	9,446	12,479	21,286	33,738	46,305	59,189	63,157	67,135
Household operation	10,479	15,530	29,461	37,322	46,306	58,255	61,577	66,658
Medical care	3,018	5,042	8,788	12,755	19,116	25,681	28,120	31,250
Personal business	3,326	4,656	6,858	10,049	14,974	20,066	22,055	23,992
Transportation	7,143	6,845	24,672	35,574	43,134	51,753	57,825	55,607
Recreation	3,761	6,139	11,147	14,078	18,295	24,573	26,304	28,673
Private education and research	632	936	1,618	2,339	3,718	5,217	5,585	6,667
Religious and welfare activities	1,012	1,735	2,282	3,257	4,748	5,527	5,609	6,475
Foreign travel and remittances—net	87	1,192	630	1,590	2,179	2,828	3,206	3,384
Total personal consumption expenditures	70,824	119,701	191,009	254,381	325,241	401,356	431,465	465,946

Employees in Non-Agricultural Establishments

ANNUAL AVERAGE BY INDUSTRY DIVISION
Source: Bureau of Labor Statistics, U. S. Dept. of Labor
(In thousands)

Year	Total	Mining	Contract construction	Manufacturing	Transportation and public utilities	Wholesale and retail trade	Finance, insurance, and real estate	Service, and miscellaneous	Government
1950	45,222	901	2,333	15,241	4,034	9,386	1,919	5,382	6,026
1955	50,675	792	2,802	16,882	4,141	10,535	2,335	6,274	6,914
1959	53,313	732	2,960	16,675	4,011	11,127	2,594	7,130	8,083
1960	54,234	712	2,885	16,796	4,004	11,391	2,669	7,423	8,353
1961	54,042	672	2,816	16,326	3,903	11,337	2,731	7,664	8,594
1962	55,596	650	2,902	16,853	3,906	11,566	2,800	8,028	8,890
1963	56,702	635	2,963	16,995	3,903	11,778	2,877	8,325	9,225
1964	58,332	634	3,050	17,274	3,951	12,160	2,957	8,709	9,596
1965	60,770	632	3,181	18,032	4,033	12,683	3,019	9,098	10,091
1966	63,864	628	3,281	19,081	4,137	13,220	3,086	9,582	10,850

Distilled Spirits and Beer Production

Source: Internal Revenue Service. (Figures show thousands of tax gallons or barrels)

Year fiscal	Distilled Spirits					Beer Tot.	Year fiscal	Distilled Spirits					Beer Tot.
	Whky.	Rm.	Bdy.	Alcoh.	Total*			Whky.	Rm.	Bdy.	Alcoh.	Total*	
	Gals.	Gals.	Gals.	Gals.	Gals.	Bbls.		Gals.	Gals.	Gals.	Gals.	Gals.	Bbls.
1940	98,993	2,478	18,427	261,022	387,183	54,892	1960	149,545	1,866	10,114	613,924	803,751	94,541
1945	41,562	2,888	26,596	1,101,286	1,174,391	86,608	1964	102,732	2,129	11,143	688,512	838,978	103,018
1950	118,760	1,781	5,364	391,126	521,770	88,807	1965	117,930	2,274	11,522	695,332	865,240	108,015
1955	103,927	2,005	4,008	465,069	593,982	89,791	1966	140,186	2,637	17,858	687,287	889,352	109,736

*Includes gin, Vodka and Okelehao.

Worktime Required to Buy Food and Other Articles

Source: Bureau of Labor Statistics, U. S. Dept. of Labor

Production workers in manufacturing in the United States in Sept. 1966, earned an average of $2.74 per hour, including overtime. At this rate, with average prices as they were at that time, he worked 12 minutes to earn enough to buy one pound of ground beef, 19 minutes for one pound of butter, and corresponding lengths of time for other articles, as shown below. A month's rent for a dwelling unit of average cost would be earned in about 3.1 working days. Prices of automobiles and equipment vary widely throughout the United States; roughly, however, a good used car could be bought for about 9 weeks' work, and a new car of one of the popular makes for about 26 weeks' work.

Article	Aver. retail price	Worktime Hrs.	Worktime Mins.	Article	Aver. retail price	Worktime Hrs.	Worktime Mins.
FOOD				Woman's skirt, wool......	$6.66	2	26
White flour..........1 pd	$ 0.121		3	Woman's slip, nylon, tricot,			
White wheat bread...1 pd	.230		5	plain...............	4.07	1	29
Rice, short grain....1 pd	.189		4	Nylon stockings, 1 pr.....	.97		21
Beef: Round steak				Man's work shoes, high....	12.01	4	23
(best grade)......1 pd	1.095		24	Man's street shoes, oxford...	18.92	6	54
Chuck roast				Boy's sneakers, oxford.....	5.45	1	59
(best grade)......1 pd	.618		14	Printed cotton percale cloth,			
Hamburger				36 inches wide, 1 yard...	.42		9
(ground beef)....1 pd	.547		12	**Medical**			
Pork: Chops, center				Penicillin prescription, 12			
cut...........1 pd	1.074		24	tablets.............	2.23		49
Bacon (sliced, best				Hospital, semiprivate room,			
grade)........1 pd	1.002		22	per day..........	30.52	11	8
Ham (whole,				Physician, house visit.....	9.89	3	37
smoked)........1 pd	.732		16	Dentist, extraction........	7.73	2	49
Fish: Frozen filet of				Dentist, filling..........	6.47	2	22
haddock........1 pd	.675		15	Eyeglasses, with examina-			
Canned tuna.....6½ oz.	.363		8	tion...............	32.49	11	51
Chicken (ready-to-				**MISCELLANEOUS**			
cook)..........1 pd	.418		9	Toothpaste, per oz.......	.17		4
Butter..........1 pd	.881		19	Man's haircut...........	2.10		46
Oleomargarine,				Permanent wave.........	13.40	4	53
colored........1 pd	.291		6	Washing machine electric,			
Shortening, hydrog-				automatic............	210.69	76	54
enated..........3 pds	.906		20	Vacuum cleaner, electric...	45.28	16	32
Cheese (American				Television set, 19-inch			
Cheddar).........1 pd	.882		19	portable............	144.89	52	53
Fresh milk, at grocery				Radio, 4 tubes, table model	16.60	6	4
store..........½ gal.	.514		11	Cigarettes, pack of 20.....	.32		7
Eggs (large, grade A).1 doz	.633		14	Cigarettes, carton (200			
Oranges, (size, ap-				cigarettes).........	2.80	1	1
proximately 5 pds				Beer, per 6 12-ounce cans			
per dozen)........1 doz	.872		19	or bottles..........	1.16		25
Potatoes..........1 pd	.073		2	Spirit blended whiskey, ⅕			
Cabbage..........1 pd	.117		3	gallon.............	4.70	1	43
Dried beans......1 pd	.197		4	Sheet, percale, 81 x 108			
Canned tomatoes....1 pd	.179		4	inches.............	3.14	1	9
Sugar..........1 pd	.121		3	Detergent, 20 ounces.....	.34		7
Coffee, can......1 pd	.825		18	Paper napkins, pkg of 80	.16		4
Teabags......pkg. of 48	.611		13	Laundry service: 10-pd			
CLOTHES				bundle finished........	2.48		54
Man's 2-piece suit, wool,				Dry cleaning: Man's 2-piece			
hard-finished worsted,				suit, cash and carry.....	1.41		31
medium grade......	62.09	22	40	Gas, 25 therms.........	4.12	1	30
Man's work pants, cotton..	3.91	1	26	Electricity, 250 kilowatt			
Man's business shirt,				hours.............	7.39	2	42
broadcloth...........	4.97	1	49	Automobile tires, (7.50 x 15)	26.14	9	32
Man's socks, argyle knit,				Gasoline, premium, gal.....	.37		8
cotton.............	.82		18	Bus fare, one..........	.25		5
Boy's undershirts........	.71		16				

Indexes of Retail Prices of Foods

Source: Bureau of Labor Statistics, United States Department of Labor (1957-59=100)

Year and month	Total food	Food at home	Cereals, bakery products	Meats, poultry, fish	Dairy products	Fruits, vegetables	Other foods
1962 Avg.......	103.6	102.2	107.6	101.7	104.1	105.0	96.1
1963 Avg.......	105.1	103.5	109.1	100.2	103.8	111.0	97.8
1964 Avg.......	106.4	104.7	109.6	98.6	104.7	115.3	101.6
1965 Avg.......	108.8	107.2	111.2	105.1	105.0	115.2	101.8
1966 Aug.......	114.2	112.6	115.8	114.1	111.8	117.6	103.9
1967 Jan........	114.7	112.3	118.8	110.3	116.4	115.3	104.9
Feb........	114.2	111.7	118.5	110.7	116.1	114.2	102.5
Apr........	113.7	110.8	118.5	109.0	115.7	114.2	101.4
June.......	115.1	112.3	118.3	111.6	116.3	119.9	100.0
Aug........	116.6	113.9	118.4	113.1	116.6	122.7	102.6
Sept.......	115.9	112.9	118.4	113.4	117.3	115.6	102.4

Average Percent Increase in Earnings

Source: Bureau of Labor Statistics, United States Department of Labor

Period and area Feb. 1966 to Feb. 1967	All industries				Manufacturing			
	Clerical men and women	Industrial nurses	Skilled maintenance trades	Unskilled plant workers	Clerical men and women	Industrial nurses	Skilled maintenance trades	Unskilled plant workers
United States........	4.3	5.3	4.1	4.3	3.6	5.0	4.2	4.0
Northeast..........	4.0	4.7	3.9	4.0	3.4	4.0	3.9	3.3
South............	4.4	4.6	3.7	5.0	3.6	4.4	3.8	4.1
North Central.....	4.6	5.8	4.4	4.5	3.5	5.9	4.5	4.5
West.............	4.5	5.9	4.4	3.7	4.6	5.6	4.4	4.0

Interest Laws and Consumer Finance Loan Rates

Source: Revised by Roger S. Barrett of Chicago, Editor Consumer Finance Law Bulletin

Most states have laws regulating interest rates. These laws fix a legal or conventional rate which applies when there is no contract for interest. They also fix a general maximum contract rate, but there are exceptions for particular purposes including consumer finance loan laws. In many states there are so many exceptions that the general contract maximum actually applies only to exceptional cases.

1. Legal rate of interest. The legal or conventional rate of interest applies to money obligations when no interest rate is contracted for and also to judgments. The rate is usually 6% a year, but in some states it is 5% or 7%.

2. General maximum contract rates. All states, except Colorado, Massachusetts, and New Hampshire have general laws fixing the maximum rate of interest which may be contracted for, unless another law authorizes a higher rate. The general maximum is fixed by the state constitution in Arkansas, California, Oklahoma, Tennessee, and Texas. The most common maximum rates are 6% and 8% a year, but some states permit 10% or 12%. Rhode Island permits 21%. Penalties for infraction range from forfeiture of interest to loss of the entire principal and even imprisonment. Loans to corporations are frequently exempted or subject to a higher maximum. Courts generally hold that installment sale charges are not interest, but installment sale charges are limited by laws in many states.

3. Specific enabling acts. In many states special statutes permit industrial loan companies and banks to charge interest and fees without regard to installment payments which yield 1½% a month or more. Credit unions may generally charge 1% a month. Pawnbrokers' rates vary widely. Building and loan associations, loans insured by the Federal Housing Administration, and frequently retail charge account credit are also specially regulated.

4. Consumer finance loan statutes. Consumer finance loan statutes are based on early models drafted by the Russell Sage Foundation (1916-42) to provide small loans to wage earners under license and other protective regulations. In general, licensed lenders may charge 2½% or 3% a month for $300 or less and reduced rates for additional amounts up to $1,000, $1,500 or more. A number of states permit add-on rates of 17% to 20% ($17 to $20 per $100) a year of the original principal for $300 and lower rates for additional amounts. An add-on of 17% ($17 per $100) per year yields about 2½% per month when the loan is paid in equal monthly installments. In the table below unless otherwise stated, monthly rates are based on reducing principal balances, annual add-on rates are based on the original principal for the full term, and two or more rates apply to different portions of balance or original principal.

The states with consumer finance loan laws and the rates of charge as of October 1, 1967, are as follows:

State	Maximum rate
	Monthly unless otherwise stated
Ala.	3% to $200, 2% to $300. Special rate up to $75
Alaska	4% to $300, 2½% to $600, 2% to $1,000; 5% for loans up to $50
Ariz.	3% to $300, 2% to $600, 1% to $1,000
Calif.	2½% to $200, 2% to $500, 5/6% to $5,000
Colo.	3% to $300, 1½% to $500, 1% to $1,500
Conn.	Annual Add-on: 17% to $300, 9% to $1,000
D. of C.	1% to $200
Fla.	3% to $300, 2% to $600
Hawaii	3½% to $100, 2½% to $300
Idaho	3% to $300, 2% to $500, 1% to $1,000
Ill.	3% to $150, 2% to $300, 1% to $800
Ind.	3% to $150, 2% to $300, 1½% to $1,000
Ia.	3% to $150, 2% to $300, 1½% to $700, 1% to $1,000
Kan.	3% to $300, 5/6% to $2,100
Ky.	3% to $150, 2% to $600, 1% to 800; or annual add-on of 20% to $150, 15% to $600, 11% to $800
La.	3½% to $150, 2½% to $300
Me.	2½% to $300, 1½% to $2,000; 25c minimum
Md.	3% to $300
Mass.	2½% to $200, 2% to $600; 1¾% to $1,000, ¾% to $3,000
Mich.	2½% to $300, 1¼% to $1,000
Minn.	2¾% to $300, 1½% to $600, 1¼% to $900
Miss.	Interest and service charges combined exceed 3% per month
Mo.	2.218% to $500, 8% per annum on any remainder
Mont.	Annual Add-on: 20% to $300, 16% to $500, 12% to $1,000. Special rate to $90
Nebr.	30% per annum to $300, 24% to $500, 18% to $1,000, 12% to $3,000
Nev.	Annual Add-on: 9% to $1,000, 8% to $2,500; monthly fee of 1% on first $200 and ½% on next $200
N. H.	2% to $600, 1½% to $1,500, 1½% on larger loans to $5,000
N. J.	24% per annum to $500, 22% to $1,000
N. M.	3% to $150, 2½% to $300, 1% to $1,000
N. Y.	2½% to $100, 2% to $300, ¾% to $800
N. C.	Annual Add-on: 20% to $100, 18% to $200, 15% to $300, 6% to $600. Special rate up to $75
N. D.	2½% to $250, 2% to $500, 1¾% to $750, 1½% to $1,000
Ohio	Annual Add-on: 16% to $500, 9% to $1,000, 7% to $2,000; or equivalent simple interest rate
Okla.	10% per annum plus various fees to $300
Ore.	3% to $300, 2% to $500, 1% to $1,500
Penna.	3% to $150, 2% to $300, 1% to $600
P. Rico	Annual Add-on: 20% to $300, 7% to $600
R. I.	3% to $300; 2½% for loans between $300 and $800; 2% for larger loans to $2,500
S. C.	Annual Add-on: 20% to $100, 18% to $300, 9% to $1,000; 7% for larger loans to $7,500, plus service fee. Special rate to $150
S. D.	3% to $300, ¾% to $2,500; $2 minimum
Tenn.	6% per annum plus fee of 1% per month to $300
Texas	Annual Add-on: 18% to $300, 8% to $2,500. Special rates to $100
Utah	3% to $300, 1% to $600
Vt.	2½% to $125, 2¼% to $300, 1% to $600
Va.	2½% to $300, 1½% to $600
Wash.	3% to $300, 1½% to $500, 1% to $1,000; $1 minimum
W. Va.	3% to $200, 2% to $600, 1½% to $800; or annual add-on of 19% to $200, 16% to $600, 12% to $800
Wisc.	2½% to $100, 2% to $200, 1% to $300
Wyo.	3½% to $150, 2½% to $300, 1% to $1,000; plus $1 for loans up to $50

Federal Deposit Insurance Corporation (FDIC)

The chief purpose of the Federal Deposit Insurance Corporation (FDIC) is to insure the deposits of all banks entitled to insurance benefits under the Federal Deposit Insurance Act. The major functions of the FDIC are to pay off depositors of insured banks closed without adequate provision having been made to pay depositors' claims, to act as receiver for all national banks placed in receivership and for state banks placed in receivership when appointed receiver by state authorities, and to prevent the continuance or development of unsafe and unsound banking practices. The FDIC's entire income consists of assessments on insured banks and income from investments; it receives no appropriations from Congress. It may borrow from the U. S. Treasury not to exceed $3 billion outstanding at any one time, but has made no such borrowings since it was organized in 1933. The FDIC surplus (Deposit Insurance Fund) as of Dec. 31, 1966, was $3,251,962,457.

Employment Security
SELECTED UNEMPLOYMENT INSURANCE DATA BY STATE
Fiscal year 1966-1967. State Program Only

State	Insured claim- ants[1]	Bene- ficiaries[2]	Exhaus- tions[3]	Initial claims[4]	Benefit payments		Funds available for bene- fits, June 30, 1967[6]	Employ- ers sub- ject to State law March 31, 1967
					Total amount[5]	Average weekly benefit for total unem- ployment		
	(1,000)	(1,000)	(1,000)	(1,000)	($1,000)	(dollars)	(millions)	(1,000)
Alabama.....	73	53	13	133	$18,796	$30.87	110	24
Alaska......	11	10	2	24	6,710	43.16	20	5
Arizona.....	38	30	6	82	11,547	37.68	76	18
Arkansas....	50	38	7	94	11,397	29.58	41	36
California....	910	725	154	1,878	462,349	50.46	841	349
Colorado....	28	29	4	60	9,897	47.71	71	18
Connecticut...	94	66	11	156	28,467	44.21	262	36
Delaware....	20	18	2	34	7,414	44.73	25	10
Dist. of Col...	17	12	2	29	7,165	43.72	71	21
Florida......	86	68	21	180	18,440	28.39	218	53
Georgia.....	104	70	16	141	17,915	33.59	239	33
Hawaii......	24	18	3	32	10,280	48.63	27	13
Idaho.......	21	18	4	38	7,436	42.64	36	15
Illinois......	266	194	30	448	78,464	43.47	565	93
Indiana.....	139	91	18	224	26,574	35.42	240	37
Iowa........	32	23	4	51	9,113	41.93	125	24
Kansas......	33	25	4	56	9,758	40.78	79	21
Kentucky....	72	53	8	117	17,387	35.95	142	25
Louisiana....	69	53	14	124	22,246	35.51	156	28
Maine.......	28	23	5	51	7,728	34.25	40	9
Maryland....	86	71	6	153	24,646	39.71	215	54
Massachusetts.	225	188	35	457	90,686	43.10	305	107
Michigan.....	396	264	32	663	111,368	47.38	624	125
Minnesota...	66	49	9	109	22,263	37.75	55	45
Mississippi...	39	28	4	72	6,811	26.13	76	14
Missouri.....	136	101	12	333	31,419	38.11	266	39
Montana....	19	15	4	32	5,598	31.64	20	16
Nebraska....	20	16	4	31	5,934	35.79	46	14
Nevada.....	27	23	6	53	12,526	43.05	27	10
N. Hampshire.	19	12	0	29	2,469	37.52	39	8
New Jersey...	316	241	50	544	111,538	40.92	385	69
New Mexico...	21	16	2	47	6,198	31.15	38	19
New York....	730	605	83	1,780	315,166	43.01	1,501	389
N. Carolina...	131	100	11	254	24,649	28.02	291	40
N. Dakota....	9	8	2	15	4,739	41.38	6	6
Ohio.........	203	168	14	433	61,603	40.45	552	102
Oklahoma....	35	27	7	77	10,196	27.35	58	20
Oregon......	80	64	8	189	27,514	37.15	114	40
Pennsylvania..	356	280	24	812	95,834	36.05	626	187
Puerto Rico...	71	66	35	194	15,985	17.59	71	11
Rhode Island..	47	34	6	97	12,504	39.84	68	22
S. Carolina....	70	45	10	114	13,350	31.43	119	17
S. Dakota....	5	4	1	9	1,581	32.70	16	7
Tennessee....	109	85	14	171	23,854	30.58	150	26
Texas........	129	85	26	216	27,638	30.81	309	83
Utah........	25	21	5	46	9,872	39.65	40	18
Vermont.....	11	9	1	21	3,610	38.20	17	6
Virginia.....	51	33	6	83	8,906	32.50	175	32
Washington...	104	85	14	230	34,085	33.23	272	62
West Virginia..	51	43	5	84	10,376	26.05	76	13
Wisconsin....	96	78	9	213	38,234	47.52	251	38
Wyoming....	5	5	1	11	2,264	40.48	13	9
Total 1966-67.	**5,805**	**4,490**	**779**	**11,524**	**$1,962,501**	**$41.05**	**$10,202**	**2,517**

[1]Claimants whose base-period earnings or whose employment—covered by the unemployment insurance program—was sufficient to make them eligible for unemployment insurance benefits as provided by State law. [2]Based on number of first payments.

[3]Based on final payments. Some claimants shown, therefore, actually experienced their final week of compensable unemployment toward the end of the previous fiscal year but received their final payments in the current fiscal year. Similarly, some claimants who served their last week of compensable unemployment toward the end of the current fiscal year did not receive their final payment in this fiscal year and hence are not shown. A final week of compensable unemployment in a benefit year results in the exhaustion of benefit rights for the benefit year. Claimants who exhaust their benefit rights in one benefit year may be entitled to further benefits in the following benefit year.

[4]Excludes intrastate transitional claims to reflect more nearly instances of new unemployment. Includes claims filed by interstate claimants in the Virgin Islands.

[5]Adjusted for voided benefit checks and transfers under interstate combined wage plan.

[6]Sum of balance in State clearing accounts, benefit-payment accounts, and unemployment trust fund accounts maintained in the U. S. Treasury.

How Unemployment Statistics Are Obtained
Source: Bureau of Labor Statistics, U. S. Department of Labor

The main source of unemployment statistics in the United States is the Current Population Survey, a sample survey of households, conducted monthly since 1940. The material is collected and tabulated by the Bureau of the Census under contract with the Bureau of Labor Statistics, which analyzes and publishes the data in *Employment and Earnings and Monthly Report on the Labor Force.*

In this survey trained interviewers obtain information from approximately 52,500 households each month; the households form a probability sample representative of the entire civilian noninstitutional population. Sufficient information is obtained to classify persons 16 years of age and over as (1) employed (2) unemployed or (3) not in the labor force. The labor force is simply the total of the employed and the unemployed, and is com-

monly referred to as the civilian labor force since it excludes the Armed Forces.

Under this system the unemployed consist of all civilians 16 years of age or older who did not work during the survey week (the week including the 12th of the month) but who looked for work in the previous 4 weeks, and were available for work during the survey week. Persons who never had a job are counted among the unemployed if they meet these criteria. Persons with jobs but on layoff and those planning to start new jobs within 30 days are also classified as unemployed. The data on the unemployed are analyzed by sex, age, previous occupation and industry, duration of unemployment, and other characteristics. The unemployment rate is the percent of the labor force who are unemployed.

State Sales Taxes; Types and Rates

Source: Analysis Staff, Tax Division, Treasury Dept. Data as of July 1, 1967

State	Type of tax[1]	Rates on retail sales: Tangible pers'l prop.	Selected service: Admissions	Selected service: Rest. meals	Selected service: Public utilities	Rates on other services and nonretail businesses
Alabama	Retail sales	[2]4%	4%	4%	....	Gross receipts of amusement operators 4%. Mining and manufacturing machinery, farm machines, 1.5%; transient lodging, 4%; closed circuit TV 10%.
Arizona[3]	Retail sales	3	3	3	1½	Meat packing ⅜%, wholesale sales of feed to poultry and livestock producers ½%; advertising printing, publishing, contracting, mining 1½%; amusement operators 3%.
Arkansas[4]	Retail sales	3	3	3	3	Printing and photography, transient lodging, coin-operated devices, 3%.
California[4]	Retail sales	5	....	4		Manufacturing, processing, printing, 4%.
Colorado[4]	Retail sales	3	....	3	3	Transient lodging, 3%.
Connecticut	Retail sales	3½	....	[5]3½	....	Transient lodging, 3½%.
Florida	Retail sales	[2]3	3	3	....	Rental income from vending and amusement machines 3%; fishing, hunting, camping, swimming and diving equipment 5% of wholesale price. Transient lodging 3%.
Georgia	Retail sales	3	3	3	3	Transient lodging 3%; receipts from amusement devices 3%.
Hawaii	Multiple-stage sales	4	4	4	....	Manufacturers, producers, wholesalers, sugar processors and pineapple canners and selected service businesses ½%; insurance solicitors 2%; contractors, sales representatives, professions, radio broadcasting stations, service businesses and other businesses not otherwise specified, transient lodging 4%.
Idaho	Retail sales	3	3	3	....	Producing, fabricating, processing, printing and transient lodging 3%
Illinois[4]	Retail sales	4¼	....	4¼	....	Remodeling, repairing and reconditioning tangible personal property 4¼%.
Indiana	Retail sales	2	....	2	2	Transient lodging 2%.
Iowa[4]	Retail sales	3	3	3	3	Commercial amusement devices and enterprises; transient lodging, repairs, barber and beauty parlor services, advertising, dry cleaning equipment rentals 3%.
Kansas	Retail sales	3	3	3	3	Transient lodging and coin-operated devices and commercial amusements 3%.
Kentucky	Retail sales	3	[6]3	3	3	Transient lodging, photographic services and sewer services, 3%.
Louisiana[4]	Retail sales	2	2	2	....	Laundry, dry cleaning, automobile and cold storage, printing, repair services to tangible personal property, transient lodging, 2%.
Maine	Retail sales	4½	....	4	4	Transient lodging 4%; proceeds from closed circuit TV, 2%.
Maryland	Retail sales	[2]3	....	[5]3	3	Farm equipment 2%; production, fabrication, or printing on special order, transient lodging 3%.
Massachusetts	Retail sales	3	....	4	....	Transient lodging 5%[7]. Farm equipment 2%, production, fabrication, or printing on special order, 3%.
Michigan	Retail sales	4	....	4	4	Transient lodging 4%.
Minnesota	Retail sales	3	3	3	3	Fabricating, printing, processing, transient lodging 3%.
Mississippi	Multiple-stage sales	[2]3½	....	3½	[8]3½	Wholesaling ⅛% (beer and motor fuel 3½%); farm tractors 1%; contracts exceeding $10,000 2%; extracting or mining, specified businesses including warehouses, laundry and dry cleaning, photo finishing, storage, termites or pest control services, specified repair services 3½%; cotton ginning 15c per bale. Transient lodging 3½%. Wholesale and retail sales of liquor, 3½%.
Missouri	Retail sales	3	3	3	3	Transient lodging, trailer camp rentals, 3%.
Nebraska	Retail sales	2½	2½	2½	2½	....
Nevada	Retail sales	2	....	2	....	Storage, 2%. A mandatory 1% county sales tax is imposed.
New Jersey	Retail sales	3	3	3	....	Producing, fabricating, storing, processing, installing maintenance and repair 3%. Transient lodging[7] 3%.
New Mexico[4]	Retail sales	[2]3	3	3	3	Liquor wholesalers ½%, extracting minerals (except coal, oil and gas) and timber ¾%; coal sold directly from mine ½%; smelting, refining or processing of minerals including oil and gas ¾%; contracting 1½%; professions and service businesses (including amusement) excluding wages and salaries 3%; farm implements & airplanes 1½%.

State	Type of tax[1]	Rates on retail sales — Tangible pers'l prop.	Selected service — Admissions	Selected service — Rest. meals	Selected service — Public utilities	Rates on other services and nonretail businesses
New York [4]	Retail sales...	2	2	42	2	Transient lodging[7] 2%. Producing, processing, printing, installation, repairing, storage and rental of safe deposit boxes 2%.
North Carolina	Retail sales...	3	....	3	....	Farm and industrial machinery, 1% ($80 maximum); boats ($120 maximum), air planes, 1½%; laundry and dry cleaning 3%; transient lodging 3%.
North Dakota		3	3	3	3	Transient lodging 3%.
Ohio	Retail sales...	4	3	3	....	Transient lodging, printing and reproducing, production and fabrication, 3%.
Oklahoma[3,4]	Retail sales...	22	2	2		Advertising (exclusive of newspapers, periodicals and billboards), printing, automobile storage, transient lodging, 2%
Pennsylvania	Retail sales...	5	....	55	5	Repairing, altering, laundering and cleaning of tangible personal property, cleaning, polishing, lubricating and inspection of motor vehicles, rental income of coin-operated amusement devices and transient lodging 5%.
Rhode Island	Retail sales...	5	....	5	5	Producing, processing, fabricating, printing, 5%.
South Carolina	Retail sales...	3	....	3	3	Transient lodging, laundry and dry cleaning, 3%.
South Dakota	Retail sales...	23	3	3	3	Amusement devices, transient lodging, 3%. Farm machinery, 2%. Professional fees (other than medical) 3%.
Tennessee [4]	Retail sales...	3	3	3	83	Transient lodging, parking lots and storage of motor vehicles, repair service, installations, laundry and dry cleaning, 3% industrial machinery, fuels to manufacturers, farm equipment and machinery, 1%; vending machines 1½% except tobacco products 2¼%.
Texas	Retail sales...	2	....	2	2	
Utah[3,4]	Retail sales...	3	3	3	3	Repairing, renovating, installing, transient lodging, laundry, dry cleaning, 3%.
Virginia[4,9]	Retail sales...	2	....	2		Transient lodging, storage, contracting, fabricating of tangible personal property, 2%.
Washington	Retail sales...	4.5	4.5	4.5	....	Transient lodging, auto parking and storage, other specified services, selected amusement and recreation activities 4.5%.
West Virginia	Retail sales...	23	3	3	....	All services except personal, professional and public utilities, transient lodging 3%.
Wisconsin	Retail services...	3	3	3	....	Laundry, dry cleaning, repair services, photography, transient lodging, 3%.
Wyoming	Retail sales...	3	3	3	3	Laundry, dry cleaning, garage services, photography repair, alteration of personal property, transient lodging 3%.
Dist. of Col.	Retail sales...	23	....	3	....	Transient lodging, 5%; food for off-premises consumption, 1%. Repair services 3%.

[1]All but a few states levy sales taxes of the single-stage retail type. Hawaii and Mississippi, levy multiple-stage sales taxes. The Arizona and New Mexico taxes, although applicable to some nonretail businesses are essentially a retail sales tax. Washington and West Virginia levy gross receipts taxes on all businesses, distinct from their sales taxes. Alaska also levies a gross receipts tax on businesses. The rates applicable to retailers (with exceptions) under these gross receipts taxes are as follows: Alaska, ½%, on gross receipts of $20,000–$100,000 and ¼% on gross receipts in excess of $100,000; Washington, 44/100%; and West Virginia, ½%. In Indiana, an additional tax of ½% is imposed on retailers under the gross income tax. New Jersey will impose a tax of 1/20 of 1% on retail stores with income in excess of $150,000.

[2]Motor vehicles are taxed at the general rates with certain exceptions. The following states apply different rates to motor vehicles under the sales and use tax laws: Alabama 1½%; Florida 2%; Mississippi 2% and North Carolina 1½% ($120 maximum). The following states exempt motor vehicles from their general sales and use taxes but impose special sales or gross receipts taxes on them under their motor vehicle tax laws: Maryland 3% titling tax; New Mexico 1½% excise tax; Oklahoma 2% excise tax; South Dakota 3% excise tax; West Virginia 3% titling tax; District of Columbia 3% titling tax.

[3]Arizona and Mississippi also tax the transportation of oil and gas by pipelines. Missouri, Oklahoma, and Utah do not tax transportation of property.

[4]In addition to the state tax, sales taxes are also levied by certain cities and/or counties.

[5]Restaurant meals below a specified price are exempt; Connecticut, Maryland and New York, less than $1; Pennsylvania 50 cents or less.

[6]Tax on the sale of tickets to prize fights and wrestling matches on closed circuit television is 5% of gross receipts. The 5% tax applies to payments received from broadcasting companies for the right to televise or broadcast such a match.

[7]Rooms which rent for $3 a day or less are exempt.

[8]Mississippi and Tennessee tax industrial sales of gas and electricity at 1%.

[9]The rate is scheduled to be increased to 3% July 1, 1968.

United States Foreign Trade with Leading Countries

Source: International Trade Analysis Division, Bureau
of International Commerce, Dept. of Commerce
(Value in millions of dollars)

Exports from the U. S. to the following areas and countries and imports into the U. S. from those areas and countries:	Exports, including re-exports		General imports	
	1965	1966	1965	1966
Total (including special category) see asterisk........	27,478	30,336	21,366	25,550
Western Hemisphere........................	9,917	11,434	9,202	10,829
Canada..	5,643	6,661	4,832	6,125
19 American Republics.....................	3,788	4,235	3,675	3,970
Central American Common Market......	341	361	279	303
Latin American Free Trade Association[1]	3,182	3,580	3,173	3,424
Bolivia....................................	42	47	31	28
Dominican Republic......................	76	88	111	128
Panama....................................	125	138	60	68
Bahamas......................................	107	134	24	24
Bermuda......................................	44	49	1	2
Jamaica......................................	87	115	125	133
Netherlands Antilles.........................	75	72	319	304
Surinam......................................	36	32	33	50
Trinidad and Tobago.........................	75	59	142	163
Europe.......................................	9,364	10,011	6,292	7,864
OECD countries , total [2]....................	8,978	9,536	6,007	7,509
Western Europe...............................	9,224	9,813	6,155	7,685
European Economic Community............	5,252	5,511	3,322	4,124
Belgium and Luxembourg..................	650	690	494	567
France....................................	971	1,007	615	698
Germany, Western.........................	1,650	1,674	1,341	1,797
Italy.....................................	893	914	620	743
Netherlands..............................	1,088	1,226	251	320
European Free Trade Association..........	2,789	2,956	2,348	2,960
Austria*..................................	57	55	66	80
Denmark..................................	208	184	147	202
Norway*..................................	130	144	124	129
Portugal*.................................	74	64	56	75
Sweden...................................	336	358	243	300
Switzerland...............................	369	415	306	388
United Kingdom..........................	1,615	1,737	1,405	1,786
Finland*....................................	76	64	84	97
Greece......................................	172	180	44	51
Ireland......................................	69	86	58	94
Spain..	472	518	133	163
Turkey......................................	205	265	83	96
Yugoslavia*..................................	149	173	61	74
Eastern Europe[2].............................	140	198	138	179
Asia and Oceania				
Asia[3]...	6,170	6,916	4,544	5,296
Iran...	195	230	88	115
Iraq...	49	46	20	21
Israel.......................................	224	210	62	77
Kuwait......................................	66	89	47	29
Lebanon.....................................	75	84	6	9
Saudi Arabia................................	137	152	106	96
Arabia Peninsula States[4]..................	29	27	41	32
United Arab Republic (Egypt).............	158	189	16	18
Japan..	2,080	2,365	2,414	2,964
Other Asia...................................	3,100	3,440	1,738	1,928
Ceylon*.....................................	10	16	33	33
Hong Kong..................................	191	229	343	416
India*.......................................	928	929	348	327
Indonesia...................................	42	60	165	179
Korea, Republic of..........................	274	339	54	85
Malaysia[5]....................................		46	212	177
Singapore...................................	91	51	....	15
Nansei and Nanpo Islands.................	41	44	9	8
Pakistan*...................................	336	239	45	68
Philippines..................................	348	348	369	398
Thailand*...................................	107	128	41	76
Taiwan......................................	234	237	93	117
South Viet-Nam[6]*...........................	191	311	3	2
Australia....................................	797	661	311	395
New Zealand and Western Samoa...........	133	127	130	180
Africa[7]......................................	1,071	1,160	861	960
North Africa, excluding Egypt.............	225	274	118	126
Algeria.....................................	20	67	8	3
Ethiopia....................................	22	24	64	45
Libya.......................................	65	59	30	57
Morocco....................................	56	63	6	10
Western and equatorial Africa..............	265	319	340	378
Angola......................................	13	17	48	53
Ghana......................................	36	53	59	46
Ivory Coast.................................	11	23	46	65
Liberia......................................	39	38	51	59
Nigeria......................................	74	103	60	52
Central and southern Africa................	581	568	402	456
Kenya......................................	24	28	13	22
Congo (Kinshasa)...........................	71	60	38	45
South Africa, Republic of[8].................	438	401	226	250
Zambia, Rhodesia, Malawi..................	23	47	14	11

*Recent changes in security regulations have permitted the inclusion of "special category shipments" to most countries and in all continental totals. Where the asterisk appears the "special category shipments" are excluded.

[1]Includes Paraguay. [2]Excludes Finland and Yugoslavia. [3]Includes United Arab Republic (Egypt). [4]Excludes Aden and Bahrain. [5]Includes former Federation of Malaya, Sarawak and Sabah (No. Borneo). [6]Prior to Jan. 1, 1966 includes North Vietnam. [7]Excludes UAR. [8]Includes SW Africa and British High Commission Territories of Bechuanaland, Basutoland and Swaziland.

U. S. Exports and Imports of Leading Commodities

Source: International Trade Analysis Division, Dept. of Commerce,
Office of International Regional Economics from basic data of the Bureau of the Census, March, 1967
(Value in millions of dollars)

Commodity	Exports		Imports	
	1965	1966	1965	1966
Total	$27,000	$29,899	$21,366	$25,550
Food and live animals[1]	4,003	4,567	3,460	3,948
Meat	136	130	426	600
Poultry	52	46	....	....
Dairy products and eggs[1]	192	125	....	....
Cheese	....	....	43	61
Grains and preparations[1]	2,638	3,196	95	128
Wheat and wheat flour[1][2]	1,185	1,537		
Rice[1]	244	230		
Coarse, grains[1]	1,115	1,340		
Corn[1]	833	881		
Grain sorghums	209	357		
Fruits and Nuts	339	340	339	368
Vegetables[1]	148	169	139	170
Sugar			442	501
Coffee, green or roasted			1,060	1,069
Beverages and Tobacco	517	624	553	642
Alcoholic beverages			426	497
Leaf Tobacco	378	472	121	137
Cigarettes	105	110		
Crude materials, inedible, except fuels	2,856	3,072	3,047	3,266
Hides and skins, except fur skins	109	155	80	89
Oil seeds, oil nuts, oil kernels	707	823	63	53
Synthetic rubber, including latex	161	175	182	177
Iron ore, and concentrates			444	462
Coal	477	468		
Petroleum and products	418	436	2,092	2,127
Animal and vegetable oils and fats	472	356	116	146
Soybean oil	124	124		
Chemicals	2,402	2,676	769	957
Medicinal and pharmaceutical products	256	269	58	75
Machinery and transport equipment	10,147	11,161	2,948	4,828
Power generating machinery	841	975	195	331
Automotive engines	67	101	32	114
Agricultural machinery	219	233	249	327
Tractors and parts	646	627	93	134
Metalworking machinery	332	338	63	135
Textile and leather machinery	207	227	157	221
Other machines	2,558	2,822	360	474
Electrical apparatus	1,660	1,901	640	1,016
Transport equipment[3]	3,214	3,484	1,148	2,135
Railway vehicles	140	116		
Automobiles, commercial, new	393	564	658	1,236
Aircraft, and parts	1,136	1,101	140	272
Other manufactured goods	4,839	5,279	7,521	8,636
Rubber manufactures	166	168	47	64
Paper and manufactures	389	444	870	986
Diamonds excluding industrial			308	375
Metals and manufactures	1,736	1,777	2,868	3,267
Iron and steel-mill products	607	537	1,140	1,182
Nonferrous base metals	539	582	1,198	1,468
Cotton	98	110	123	144
Furniture	41	47	60	81
Clothing	143	164	543	608
Other transactions	954	1,187	730	866

[1]Includes relief shipments. [2]Wheat equivalent. [3]Excludes parts for tractors.

U. S. Balance of Payments

Source: Office of Business Economics, Dept. of Commerce
(In millions of dollars. Excludes military transfers under grants. Revised)

	1955	1960	1961	1962	1963	1964	1965	1966
Recorded receipts	20,517	28,326	30,612	32,651	34,085	38,487	40,327	46,785
Exports of goods and services	19,804	27,325	28,631	30,350	32,426	37,099	39,147	43,039
Merchandise	14,280	19,489	19,954	20,604	22,071	25,297	26,244	29,168
Transportation	1,406	1,782	1,805	1,964	2,115	2,324	2,390	2,589
Foreign travel in U.S.	654	919	947	957	1,015	1,207	1,380	1,573
Miscellaneous services	820	1,450	1,582	1,750	1,919	2,135	2,401	2,617
Military transactions	200	335	402	656	657	747	844	847
Income on investments	2,444	3,350	3,941	4,419	4,649	5,389	5,888	6,245
Repayments on Government loans	414	636	1,274	1,280	970	703	902	1,234
Foreign capital other than liquid funds	297	365	707	1,021	689	685	278	2,512
Recorded payments	22,274	31,305	32,078	33,801	36,471	40,338	41,247	47,759
Imports of goods and services	17,795	23,324	23,122	25,305	26,573	28,637	32,203	37,937
Merchandise	11,527	14,732	14,510	16,187	16,992	18,621	21,472	25,510
Transportation	1,204	1,915	1,943	2,128	2,316	2,462	2,674	2,914
U. S. travel abroad	1,153	1,750	1,785	1,939	2,114	2,211	2,438	2,657
Miscellaneous services	521	795	896	858	891	1,027	969	1,088
Military expenditures	2,901	3,069	2,981	3,083	2,936	2,861	2,921	3,694
Income on investments	489	1,063	1,007	1,110	1,324	1,455	1,729	2,074
Private remittances	456	483	487	533	629	617	658	647
Private capital outflow	1,255	3,879	4,180	3,425	4,456	6,542	3,743	4,132
Government pensions and other transfers	141	214	235	245	262	279	366	383
Government grants and capital outflow	2,627	3,405	4,054	4,293	4,551	4,263	4,277	4,680
Unrecorded transactions, net[1]	515	−922	−904	−1,053	−285	−949	−415	−383
Balance of payments	−1,242	−3,901	−2,370	−2,203	−2,671	−2,800	−1,335	−1,357
Balanced by—								
Monetary reserve assets (increase [−])[2]		2,145	606	1,533	378	171	1,222	568
Foreign holdings of liquid dollar assets (decrease [−])	1,060	1,756	1,764	670	2,293	2,629	113	789

[1]Also called "errors and omissions." Believed to consist largely of unreported short-term capital flows.
[2]Includes gold, convertible currencies, and International Monetary Fund position.
[3]Includes U. S. Government nonmarketable medium-term convertible securities in the amount of $703 million in 1963, $376 million in 1964, $122 million in 1965, and $945 million in 1966.

EXPLORATION
Arctic Operations—1966-1967
Source: National Geographic Society and contemporary records

An 8-man American-Canadian team left Eureka, Ellesmere Island, Northwest Territories, Mar. 28, 1967, for the North Pole, each man driving a motorized sled. Not since Admiral Peary's conquest of the Pole 58 years earlier, in April, 1909, had there been an attempt made to reach the Pole by sled.

Each of the 250-pound snowmobiles towed an aluminum toboggan carrying more than 400 pounds of food (including food packs similar to those used by astronauts), supplies and equipment for the 1,600-mile round-trip.

Unexpectedly warm weather and rapidly melting ice turned them back before they had zig-zagged 300 miles. Among the problems they met were ice ridges nearly 50 feet high, being twice stranded on ice blocks and having to wait for the surrounding water to freeze over so they could get back on to solid ice, high winds and low temperatures.

They were about 80 miles north-northwest of their starting point when forced to turn back.

The expedition hoped to pinpoint for the first time the exact location of the geographic pole, and also to install a radar-signalling device to guide nuclear submarines.

The team plans to undertake this trip again next year.

American and Russian scientists continue to maintain a watch over the icy currents of the Arctic Ocean which flow clockwise around the North Pole. Personnel of the Navy's largest ice island station are constantly observing and recording conditions on and under the ice, under the water and in the atmosphere.

Other scientists, using icebreakers, small boats and planes, are gathering similar data about the more than 5,000,000 square miles of the Arctic Ocean.

Army scientists at Camp Century, Greenland, more than 100 miles inland from Thule Air Base, are analyzing nearly 10,000 years of Arctic history from a 5,000-foot core sample obtained when they drilled through the icecap. The underside of the icecap was penetrated at a depth of 4,500 feet. Frozen sand, pebbles and stone were found below that point.

In analyzing the core sample, special attention is being given to the composition of the ice, salt nuclei content, indications of volcanic eruptions and ascertaining whether or not the land beneath the ice ever laid beneath the sea. Already determined is that cosmic dust is settling on the earth 3 times faster than it did 700 years ago.

The Weather Bureau is seeking men to staff 5 Arctic weather stations. Needed are cooks, airstrip and machinery maintenance mechanics, electronic and meteorological technicians and supervisors. To obtain such personnel willing to be exposed to temperatures as low as 80° below zero, the pay ranges, roundly, from $7,100-$11,000 a year plus an Arctic bonus of $200 a month, an additional $100 per month for November through February duty, plus food, clothing, transportation and recreational facilities.

A 2,500-mile Asia-Europe passage along the north coast of Siberia has been opened to foreign shipping by the Soviet Union. Vessels may traverse that part of the route within Russia's territorial waters and make use of port facilities.

The nuclear-powered icebreaker Lenin is able to keep the route open for about 150 days a year. Prior to 1960 it was navigable for about 100 days a year.

From Archangel to Vladivostok is about 6,500 miles via this northern route. Ships using it pass through the Barents, Kara, Laptev, East Siberian, Chukchi, Bering and Okhotsk Seas. To sail the 15,000-mile southern route between these two points, ships would sail the Atlantic Ocean, the length of the Mediterranean, through the Suez Canal and traverse the Red, Arabian, South China and Japan Seas.

In 1958 the Soviet merchant fleet consisted of 735 ships capable of transporting 3,300,000 tons; in 1966 1,300 ships transported 9,400,000 tons, and it is expected that 13,100,000 tons will be transported by the Soviet fleet in 1970.

Two Russians sailed a reconditioned 24-foot fishing boat nearly 1,600 miles, from Archangel to former Mangazyea on a tributary of the Ob River, retracing a route used by fur traders until early in the 17th century. Using sails and outboard motors, they made their way along the Barents Sea Coast, through the Kara Strait, across the Kara Sea and probed the rivers of the Yamai Peninsula to reach the Gulf of Ob. Their venture took nearly 4 months.

This route was popular with traders wishing to avoid the Muscovy market. It was so popular that the Siberian merchants, who were losing money because they were being by-passed, brought so much pressure to bear on the government that Moscow finally closed the route.

EARLY EXPLORERS

1587—John Davis (England). Davis Strait to Sanderson's Hope, 72°12'N.

1596—Willem Barents and Jacob van Heemskerck (Holland). Discovered Bear Island, touched northwest tip of Spitsbergen, 79°49'N., rounded Novaya Zemlya, wintered at Ice Haven.

1607—Henry Hudson (England). North along Greenland's east coast to Cape Hold-with-Hope, 73°30', then north of Spitsbergen to 80°23'. Returning he discovered Hudson's Touches (Jan Mayen).

1616—William Baffin and Robert Bylot (England). Baffin Bay to Smith Sound.

1728—Vitus Bering (Russia). Proved Asia and America were separate by sailing through strait.

1733-40—Great Northern Expedition (Russia). Surveyed Siberian Arctic coast.

1741—Vitus Bering (Russia). Sighted Alaska from sea, named Mount St. Elias. His lieutenant, Chirikof, discovered coast.

1771—Samuel Hearne (Hudson's Bay Co.). Overland from Prince of Wales Fort (Churchill) on Hudson Bay to mouth of Coppermine River.

1778—James Cook (Britain). Through Bering Strait to Icy Cape, Alaska, and North Cape, Siberia.

1789—Alexander Mackenzie (North West Co., Britain). Montreal to mouth of Mackenzie River.

1806—William Scoresby (Britain). North of Spitsbergen to 81°30'.

1820-3—Ferdinand von Wrangel (Russia). Completed a survey of Siberian Arctic coast. His exploration joined that of James Cook at North Cape, confirming separation of the continents.

1845—Sir John Franklin (Britain) was one of many to seek the Northwest Passage—an ocean route connecting the Atlantic and Pacific via the Arctic. His two ships, (the Erebus and Terror), were last seen entering Lancaster Sound July 26. Dozens of relief expeditions sent out during next 14 years explored thousands of miles in the Arctic. In 1859 a record was found in a cairn at Point Victory, near Cape Victoria, telling of the death of Franklin in 1847 and the abandonment of the ships in 1848. Skeletons and other relics were found on King William's Island.

JEANNETTE DISASTER

Expeditions often came to grief when ships were caught in the ice and provisions ran out. Jas. Gordon Bennett, Jr., New York newspaper publisher, fitted out the steamer Jeannette to explore the Arctic 3 years under Lt. Commdr. Geo. Washington DeLong, 35, Annapolis graduate. DeLong left San Francisco July 8, 1879, for Siberian waters. Trapped in the ice by September, the ship was crushed in June, 1881, at 77° 15' N., 155° E. The crews split in two parties; DeLong and 11 others died of cold and starvation on the Lena River; 12 others survived at a village.

A. W. GREELY RESCUE

Lt. A. W. Greely, U. S. Signal Service, sent to the Arctic to establish a geographic station, left St. John's, NF., with 24 men July 7, 1882; reached Discovery Harbor Aug. 12, where he located station. Two men reached farthest north, 83° 24' 30" N. May 15, 1882. His ship, Proteus was crushed in ice, 1883. Commdr. Winfield S. Schley in the Thetis was put in charge of relief expedition May, 1884; Britain gave the schooner Alert. U. S. offered $25,000 reward. Schley met Greely and 5 other survivors at Cape Sabine, Smith Sound, June 22, 1884. Greely, later major general, was head of Signal Service and Weather Bureau and had charge of San Francisco relief, 1905. Died 1935, aged 91. In 1957 a Canadian Arctic expedition found a cairn on northern Ellesmere Island containing documents left there by Lt. Greely in 1882.

1888—Fridtjof Nansen (Norway) Crossed Greenland's icecap. 1893-96—Nansen in Fram drifted from New Siberian Isls. to Spitsbergen; tried

439

Polar dash in 1895, reached Franz Josef Land.

1896—Solomon A. Andrée (Sweden) and companion, in June, made first attempt to reach North Pole by balloon; failed and returned in August. On July 11, 1897, Andrée and 2 others started in balloon from Danes Isl., Spitsbergen, to drift across Pole to America, and disappeared. Over 33 years later, Aug. 6, 1930, Dr. Gunnar Horn (Norway) found their frozen bodies on White Isl., 82° 56' N, 29° 52' E.

1903-06—Roald Amundsen (Norway) first sailed Northwest Passage.

DISCOVERY OF NORTH POLE

Robert E. Peary began exploring in 1886 on Greenland, when he was 30. With his hq. at McCormick Bay he explored Greenland's coast 1891-92, tried for North Pole 1893, returned with large meteorites. In 1900 he reached northern limit of Greenland and 83° 50' N.; in 1902 he reached 84° 17' N; in 1906 he went from Ellesmere Isl. to 87° 06' N. He sailed in the Roosevelt, July, 1908, to winter off Cape Sheridan, Grant Land. The dash for the North Pole began Mar. 1 from Cape Columbia, Ellesmere Land. Peary reached the Pole, 90° N., April 6, 1909.

Peary had several supporting groups carrying supplies until the last group, under Capt. Robt. A. Bartlett, turned back at 87°47'N. Peary, Matthew Henson and 4 Eskimos proceeded with dog teams and sleds. They crossed Pole several times, finally built an igloo at 90°, remained 36 hours. Started south Apr. 7 at 4 p.m. for Cape Columbia. Eskimos were Coqueeh, Ootah, Eginwah and Seegloo. Adm. Peary died Feb. 20, 1920. Henson, a Negro, born Aug. 8, 1866, died in New York, N. Y., Mar. 9, 1955, aged 88. Ootah, last survivor, died near Thule, Greenland, May, 1955, aged 80.

1914—Donald MacMillan (U.S.). Northwest, 200 miles, from Axel Heiberg Island to seek Peary's Crocker Land.

1915-17—Vilhjalmur Stefansson (Canada) discovered Borden, Brock, Meighen and Lougheed Islands.

1918-20—Amundsen sailed Northeast Passage.

1925—Amundsen and Lincoln Ellsworth (U.S.) reached 87°44'N. in attempt to fly to North Pole from Spitsbergen.

1926—Richard E. Byrd and Floyd Bennett (U.S.). First over North Pole by air, May 9.

1926—Amundsen, Ellsworth, and Umberto Nobile (Italy) flew from Spitsbergen over North Pole May 12, to Teller, Alaska, in dirigible Norge.

1928—Nobile crossed North Pole in airship Italia May 24, crashed May 25. Amundsen lost while trying to effect rescue by plane.

1928—Sir Hubert Wilkins and Eielson. Flew from Point Barrow to Spitsbergen, 84°N.

SUBMARINE RECORDS

On Aug. 3, 1958, the Nautilus, under Comdr. William R. Anderson, became the first ship to cross the North Pole beneath the Arctic ice.

On Aug. 12, 1958, the nuclear submarine Skate, Comdr. James F. Calvert, became the second ship to make an underwater crossing of the North Pole.

In March, 1959, the Skate returned to the Arctic and, on its third attempt broke through at the North Pole, the first time any ship had been on the surface at 90° N.

The nuclear-powered U. S. submarine Seadragon, Comdr. George P. Steele II, made the first east-west underwater transit through the Northwest Passage during August, 1960. It sailed from Portsmouth, N. H., headed between Greenland and Labrador through Baffin Bay, then west through Lancaster Sound and McClure Strait to the Beaufort Sea. Traveling submerged for the most part, the submarine made 850 miles from Baffin Bay to the Beaufort Sea in six days. The vessel made a 300-foot dive to sail under an iceberg in Baffin Bay.

In February, 1960, the nuclear submarine Sargo traveled under the Arctic ice pack to and around the North Pole. The Sargo departed from and returned to Honolulu, and spent 31 days and 4 hours under the ice. The submarine successfully smashed its way through ice three feet thick.

Polar Expeditions—Antarctic, 1966-1967

Some 150 American scientists participated in nearly 50 scientific projects in Antarctica during the year—ranging from studies of the blood serum and muscle proteins of frigid water fishes to upper atmospheric physics.

Dr. Wernher Von Braun and other space experts visited McMurdo Sound to see if that area lends itself to testing vehicles, life-detection equipment and instruments being developed for lunar and planetary exploration. They inspected a number of stations and 5 dry valleys at the edge of the Transantarctic Mountains, about 50 miles from McMurdo Sound. Similarity of living conditions and effect on personnel, equipment operation under weather extremes, logistics and instruments being tested for the detection of living organisms were given special attention.

The dry valleys in "McMurdo Oasis" may be used as a natural training ground for astronauts. Little is known about these valleys, encompassing several thousand square miles, and there is diversity of thinking as to their origin. Some scientists think they were formed by volcanic activity; others believe that millions of years ago hard bedrock shifted and formed dams which kept glaciers from flowing; still others say the answer is the earth's temperature—that as one penetrates the earth at this spot in Antarctica the temperature increases more rapidly than anywhere else in the world.

Because of the winds and arid climate these valleys have no ice or snow cover—glaciers hang part way down the steep sides and sand dunes 100 feet high have been seen. Some lakes in these valleys are 200 feet deep, have a high salt content and warm bottom water (70°) during the summer. Microscopic life has been found near glacier streams and along lake shores.

A 2,700-mile stretch of "White Wilderness" along the Byrd Land Coast, from Edward VII Peninsula (near Little America) to Jones Mountains in Ellsworth Land, was charted by men from the U. S. Geological Survey. In some areas the land was so flat the surveyors mounted their theodolites and electronic equipment on 20-foot aluminum poles to make sightings as far as 10 miles away. As a part of the mapping program the Navy made aerial photographs of more than 400,000 square miles.

Geologists studied the structure and rock layers

of western Byrd Land, hoping to relate the mountains of this area to the Transantarctic and Ellsworth Mountains. Men working in eastern Byrd Land established gravity stations, gathered rock samples for laboratory analysis and drew geologic maps. Traces of magnetism in rocks were studied for evidence of different magnetic orientation of other geologic times.

Geodetic satellite observations were carried out at McMurdo Station for use in compiling a gravitational map of the earth. This information will be helpful in plotting satellite orbits, for navigation, and to other earth sciences. Geomagnetic measurements were recorded at Plateau Station.

Scientists are trying to obtain 30,000-year-old samples of Antarctic ice because of their importance in interpreting the major ice ages. Using knowledge gained from boring through the Greenland Icecap, they have set up and tested a deep-core drill for drilling an 8,679-foot hole at Byrd Station. From the samples obtained they hope to determine the rate of snow accumulation, temperature variations, rate of infall of extraterrestrial material and physical conditions of rock and ice at the bottom of the shaft.

More than a dozen scientists from the Environmental Science Services Administration spent the 1967 winter in Antarctica at Byrd, South Pole and Plateau Stations and on the USNS Eltanin. Personnel at Byrd and Pole Stations manned magnetic and seismological equipment, studied aurora displays and the abundance of alkaline metals in the atmosphere and meteorology. Geomagnetic observations were recorded at Plateau.

Research conducted aboard the USNS Eltanin embraced many areas of science, such as upper atmosphere physics, entomology, seismology, gravity, geomagnetism, meteorology, marine biology and physical and chemical oceanography.

A 3-story scientific research station (including living quarters) was erected at Palmer Peninsula early in 1967.

The United States' South Pole Station is sliding toward South America at a speed of about 150 feet per year and, at the same time, is sinking slowly into the ice. The sinking is indicated by increased gravitation—up about 1/10,000 of 1% in nine years.

Fifteen Antarctic areas have been set aside as Specially Protected Areas for the conservation of

Antarctic flora and fauna, upon the recommendation of a special committee established to set conservation criteria.

Dr. Robert C. Murphy of the American Museum of Natural History suggests Antarctica be made an international park for the preservation of flora and fauna, citing as disturbers of nature's balance the dogs that kill birds, ships that pump oily bilge water from their tanks while too close to shore, scientists who collect more specimens than needed (and who are often duplicating prior work), garbage, sewage and rubbish.

FOREIGN OPERATIONS

New Zealand's first decade of Antarctic research, which began Jan. 20, 1957, at Scott Station, came to an end at the close of the 1966-1967 season.

In 1957 it took 14 days aboard the wooden-hulled Endeavour to make the 2,500 mile ocean trip from Lyttelton, New Zealand, to McMurdo Sound; today a plane flies from Christchurch to the same area in 7 hours. Motorized toboggans have replaced dog teams and helicopters have replaced small single-engined planes.

Mapping the 180,000-square mile Ross Dependency was one of their major accomplishments. An extensive geological survey was completed; and much was learned from biological and upper atmosphere studies.

During the past season, New Zealand had a geological survey team make a two-month long study of the Mariner Glacier, some 300 miles north of Scott Station. During this same period New Zealanders placed two prefabricated huts in dry Wright Valley, near Lake Vanda, about 60 miles west of Scott. Six men, the first ever to winter in a dry valley, made meteorological, glaciological and upper atmosphere observations.

Early in the year men from an Argentinian Navy ship found a boat abandoned by French explorer Jean Baptiste Etienne August Charcot in 1903 at Port Charcot, Booth Island, where it had been buried in ice for 64 years.

The high point of the French research work was the firing of four two-stage Dragon rockets up to 250 miles into the upper atmosphere. Recording equipment in the rockets' nose cones measured upper atmosphere electrons and protons and magnetic phenomena. This type of research is particularly difficult because of the proximity of the Magnetic Pole and its effect upon guidance controls as well as recording equipment. Booster-equipped Arcas rockets, having a range of about a hundred miles, have been fired in this area.

The Chilean base, Presidente Aguirre Cerda, assumed the status of an Antarctic meteorological center, raising it to a technical level similar to that of Mirny and McMurdo. It is now the meteorological center for all British, Argentinian and Chilean stations in the Antarctic Peninsula region.

The 12th Soviet Expedition manned Mirny, Novolazarevskaya, Vostok and Molodezhnaya stations, where the Russians measured ice sheet thickness, obtained seismic and gravity readings and carried out research in numerous other fields.

One Russian expedition undertook a 1,900-mile three-month-long tractor and sled train trip from the Soviety Molodezhnaya Station via the Area of Inaccessibility to Novolazarevskaya. Another group made an 1,800-mile snow-train trip from Mirny to Vostok to Mirny.

An 80-foot high ice shelf at Halley Bay collapsed into the Weddell Sea, destroying the most ideal unloading site for Great Britain's largest base. Hundreds of tons of supplies and 1,500 barrels of fuel had already been put ashore before the ice collapsed. The next nearest suitable unloading site is about 50 miles away.

Australia's plans to build a model station near Wilkes this past summer were upset when its two supply ships were trapped by ice, one for nearly a month. The ships and personnel were saved.

EARLY HISTORY

Antarctica has been approached since 1773-75, when Capt. Jas. Cook (Britain) reached 71°10' S. Many sea and landmarks bear names of early explorers, Bellingshausen (Russia), discovered Peter I and Alexander I Islands, 1819-21. Nathaniel Palmer (U. S.) discovered Palmer Peninsula, 60°

W. 1820, without realizing that this was a continent. Jas. Weddell (Britain) found Weddell Sea, 74°15' S., 1823.

First to announce existence of the continent of Antarctica was Charles Wilkes (U.S.), who followed the coast for 1,500 mi., 1840. Adelie Coast, 140° E., was found by Dumont d'Urville (France), 1840. Ross Ice Shelf was found by Jas. Clark Ross (Britain), 1841-42.

1895—Leonard Kristensen, Norwegian whaling captain, landed a party on the coast of Victoria Land in Jan. 1895. They were the first ashore on the main continental mass, C. E. Borchgrevink, a member of that party, returned in 1899 with a British expedition, first to winter on Antarctica.

1902-04—Robert F. Scott (Britain) discovered Edward VII Peninsula. In 1902 he reached 82°17' S., 146°33' E. from McMurdo Sound.

1908-09—Ernest Shackleton in 1908 introduced the use of Manchurian ponies in Antarctic sledging. In 1909 he reached 88°23' S., discovering a route on to the plateau by way of the Beardmore Glacier and pioneering the way to the Pole.

DISCOVERY OF SOUTH POLE

1911—Roald Amundsen (Norway) with four men and dog teams reached the Pole Dec. 14, 1911.

1912—Capt. Scott reached the Pole from Ross Island Jan. 18, 1912, with four companions (Dr. E. A. Wilson, Lt. Bowers, Capt. Oates, and Petty Officer Edgar Evans), where they found Amundsen's tent. Of Scott's party, Oates and Evans died first; Scott, Wilson and Bowers died in a tent around March 29. They were found Nov. 12, 1912.

1928—First man to use an airplane over Antarctica was Hubert Wilkins (Britain).

1929—Richard E. Byrd (U. S.) established Little America on Bay of Whales. On 1600-mi. airplane flight begun Nov. 28 he crossed South Pole Nov. 29 with pilot Bernt Balchen, a radio operator and a photographer. Dropped U. S. flag over Pole, temp. 16° below zero.

1934-35—Richard E. Byrd (U.S.) led second expedition to Little America, which explored 450,000 sq. mi. Byrd wintered alone at an advance weather station in 80°08' S.

1934-37—John Rymill led British Graham Land expedition of 1934-37; discovered that Palmer Peninsula is part of Antarctic mainland.

1940—Richard E. Byrd (U. S.) charted most of coast between Ross Sea and Palmer Peninsula.

1946-47—U. S. Navy undertook Operation Highjump under Rear Admiral Byrd. Ships were commanded by Rear Admiral Richard H. Cruzen. Expedition included 13 ships and 4,000 men. 29 land-based flights from Little America and 35 by seaplanes from tenders, photomapped coastline and penetrated beyond Pole.

1946-48—Ronne Antarctic Research Expedition, Comdr. Finn Ronne, USNR, determined the Antarctic to be only one continent, with no strait between Weddell Sea and Ross Sea; discovered 250,000 sq. miles of land by flights to 79°S. Lat., and made 14,000 aerial photographs over 450,000 sq. miles of land. Mrs. Ronne and Mrs. H. Darlington, who accompanied their husbands, were the first women to winter on Antarctica.

1955-57—U. S. Navy's Operation Deep Freeze led by Adm. Richard E. Byrd. Supporting U. S. scientific efforts for the International Geophysical Year, the Operation was commanded by Rear Adm. George Dufek. It established five coastal stations fronting the Indian, Pacific, and Atlantic Oceans and also three interior stations; explored more than 1,000,000 sq. miles in Wilkes Land. Seven Navy men under Adm. Dufek landed by plane at the Pole Oct. 31, 1956, and landed radar reflectors.

1957-58—During the International Geophysical Year, July, 1957 through Dec., 1958, scientists from 12 countries conducted ambitious programs of Antarctic research. A network of some 60 stations on the continent and sub-Arctic islands studied oceanography, glaciology, meteorology, seismology, geomagnetism, the ionosphere, cosmic rays, aurora and airglow. A party from Ellsworth IGY station (US) south of Weddell Sea under the direction of Captain Finn Ronne explored beyond 1947 flight and delineated Berkner Island imbedded in the Filchner Ice Shelf. Pensacola Mountains, first sighted by Argentines in Oct., 1955 and seen by U. S. Navy in Jan., 1956, were accurately located. New mountain ranges about 11,000 ft. high were discovered in Edith Ronne Land.

Undersea Craft to Observe Marine Life in Gulf Stream

Construction has begun on the PX-15 mesoscaph, a new undersea craft designed by Dr. Jacques Piccard. In this 50-foot vessel he and four associates will drift for 6 weeks along the west edge of the Gulf Stream, from south Florida to Nova Scotia (about 1,500 miles) at depths ranging from 300 to 2,000 feet, observing marine life through 25 portholes.

UNITED STATES GOVERNMENT
AS OF NOVEMBER 1, 1967

Terms of office of the President and Vice President, from January 20, 1965 to January 20, 1969
No person may be elected President of the United States for more than two four-year terms.

PRESIDENT—Lyndon B. Johnson of Texas. Receives salary of $100,000 a year, taxable, and in addition an expense allowance, also taxable, of $50,000 to assist in defraying expenses resulting from his official duties. Also there may be expended not exceeding $40,000, nontaxable, a year for travel expenses and official entertainment. Congress in 1958 provided lifetime pensions of $25,000 a year, free mailing privileges, free office space, and up to $65,000 a year for office help for ex-Presidents and $10,000 annually for their widows.

VICE PRESIDENT—Hubert H. Humphrey of Minnesota. Salary $43,000 a year and $10,000 for expenses, all of which is taxable.

Order of succession to Presidency *See P. 207.*

The Cabinet
(Salaries $35,000 each)

Secretary of State—Dean Rusk, of New York.
Secretary of Treasury—Henry H. Fowler, Va.
Secretary of Defense—Robt. S. McNamara, Mich.
Attorney General—Ramsey Clark, Tex.
Postmaster General—Lawrence F. O'Brien, Mass.
Secretary of the Interior—Stewart L. Udall, of Arizona.
Secretary of Agriculture—Orville L. Freeman, of Minnesota.
Secretary of Commerce—Alexander B. Trowbridge, New York.
Secretary of Labor—William Willard Wirtz, Ill.
Secretary of Health, Education and Welfare—John W. Gardner, of New York.
Secretary of Housing and Urban Development—Robert C. Weaver, New York.
Secretary of Transportation—Alan S. Boyd, Fla.

The White House Staff

Special Assistants to the President—Joseph A. Califano, Jr., S. Douglass Cater, Jr., George E. Christian, E. Ernest Goldstein, Donald F. Hornig, Walt Whitman Rostow, W. Marvin Watson.
Special Assistant to the President for Consumer Affairs—Betty Furness.
Special Consultant to the President—Gen. Maxwell D. Taylor, USA, Retired.
Special Consultant to the President—J. P. Roche.
Special Counsel to the President—Harry C. McPherson, Jr.
Legislative Counsel to the President—Harold Barefoot Sanders, Jr.
Deputy Special Counsel to the President—Lawrence E. Levinson.
Associate Special Counsel to the President—W. DeVier Pierson.
Deputy Press Secretary to the President—Robert H. Fleming.
Administrative Assistant to the President—Mike N. Manatos.
Physician to the President—Vice Adm. George G. Burkley (MC), USN.
Armed Forces Aide to the President—Lt. Col. James U. Cross, USAF.
Personal Secretary to the President—Mrs. Juanita Duggan Roberts.
Press Secretary and Staff Director for the First Lady—Mrs. Elizabeth S. Carpenter.
Social Secretary—Mrs. Bess Abell.

EXECUTIVE AGENCIES

National Security Council—Members are the President, the Vice President, the Secretary of State, the Secretary of Defense, the Director of the Office of Emergency Planning, Walt Whitman Rostow, special assistant to the President, and Bromley Smith, exec. secy.
Bureau of the Budget—Charles L. Schultze, dir.
Council of Econ. Advisers—Dr. Gardner Ackley, chm.
Central Intelligence Agency—Richard Helms, Dir.
Natl. Aeronautics & Space Council—Edward C Welsh, exec. secy.
Of. of Economic Opportunity—Sargent Shriver, dir.
Office of Science & Tech.—Donald F. Hornig, dir.
Office of Emergency Planning—Price Daniel, dir.
Special Representative for Trade Negotiations—William M. Roth.

Department of State

Secretary of State—Dean Rusk.
Under Secretary—Nicholas deB. Katzenbach.
Under Sec. for Political Affairs—Eugene V. Rostow.
Deputy Under Secretaries—Foy D. Kohler (for political affairs), Idar Rimestad (for administration).
Ambassadors at Large—W. Averell Harriman, Henry Cabot Lodge.
Counselor—Robert R. Bowie.

Chmn. of Policy Planning Council—Henry D. Owen.
Assistant Secretaries for:
African Affairs—Joseph Palmer, II.
Congressional Relations—W. B. Macomber, Jr.
Economic Affairs—Anthony M. Solomon.
Educ. and Cultural Affairs—Charles Frankel.
European Affairs—John M. Leddy.
East Asian & Pacific Affairs—William P. Bundy.
Internatl. Organiz. Affairs—Joseph J. Sisco.
Inter-American Affairs—Covey T. Oliver.
Near-Eastern & So. Asian Affairs—L. D. Battle.
Public Affairs—Dixon Donnelley.
Bureau of Security & Consular Affairs—Barbara M. Watson (acting admin.).
Inspector Gen., For. Assisance—J. K. Mansfield.
Chief of Protocol—James W. Symington.
Dir. General, Foreign Service—John M. Steeves.
Director of Intelligence & Research—Thomas L. Hughes.
Director of Internatl. Scientific and Technological Affairs—Herman Pollack.
Insp. Gen. Foreign Service—Fraser Wilkins.
Foreign Service Inst.—George V. Allen.
Agency for Internatl. Development—William S. Gaud, administrator.
Advisory Committee on Foreign Aid—Charles P Taft, ch.
Peace Corps—Jack K. Vaughn, dir.
U. S. Rep. to the UN and Rep. in the Security Council—Arthur J. Goldberg, ambassador.

Treasury Department

Secretary of the Treasury—Henry H. Fowler.
Under Sec. of the Treasury—Joseph W. Barr.
Under Sec. for Monetary Affairs—Frederick L. Deming.
Assistant Secretaries—W. True Davis, Jr., Stanley S. Surrey, Robert A. Wallace, Winthrop Knowlton.
Deputy Under Sec. for Monetary Affairs—Peter D. Sternlight.
Fiscal Assistant Secretary—John K. Carlock.
Asst. Sec. for Adm.—Artemus E. Weatherbee.
Assistants to the Sec.—Joseph M. Bowman, Jr., Raymond J. Albright, R. Duane Saunders, James F. King.
Office of Budget and Finance—Ernest C. Betts, Jr., dir.
Bureaus of:
Accounts—Sidney S. Sokol, commissioner.
Customs—Lester D. Johnson, commissioner.
Engraving & Printing—James A. Conlon, dir.
Mint—Eva B. Adams, dir.
Narcotics—Henry L. Giordano, commissioner.
Public Debt—Donald M. Merritt, commissioner.
Internal Revenue Service—Sheldon S. Cohen, commissioner.
Comptroller of the Currency—William B. Camp
Treasurer of the U. S.—*Vacant.*
U. S. Savings Bonds—Glen R. Johnson, dir.
U. S. Secret Service—James J. Rowley, dir.

Department of Defense

Secretary of Defense—Robert S. McNamara.
Deputy Sec. of Defense—Paul H. Nitze.
Armed Forces Policy Council—Sec. of Defense Robert S. McNamara, chmn.
Dir. of Def. Research & Eng.—John S. Foster Jr.
Assistant Secretaries of Defense:
Administration—Solis Horwitz.
Comptroller—Robert N. Anthony.
Installations & Logistics—Thomas D. Morris.
Intl. Security Affairs—Paul C. Warneke.
Manpower—Alfred B. Fitt.
Public Affairs—Phil G. Goulding.
Systems Analysis—Alain C. Enthoven.
General Counsel—*Vacant.*
Joint Chiefs of Staff:
Chairman—Gen. Earle G. Wheeler, USA.
Chief of Staff, Army—Gen. Harold K. Johnson.
Chief of Naval Operations—Adm. Thomas H. Moorer, USN.
Chief of Staff, Air Force—Gen. John P. McConnell.
Commandant of the Marine Corps—Gen. Wallace M. Greene, Jr., USMC.
Joint Staff—Lt. Gen. B. E. Spivy, Jr., USA, dir.
Spec. Asst. to Joint Chiefs of Staff for Arms Control—Maj. Gen. B. F. Evans, USA.
Joint Command & Control Requirements Group—Maj. Gen. J. R. Russ, USA.
Defense Atomic Support Agency—Lt. Gen. Harold C. Donnelly, USAF, dir.
Defense Communications Agency—Lt. Gen. Alfred D. Starbird, USA, dir.
Defense Contract Audit Agency—William B. Petty, dir.
Defense Intelligence Agency—Lt. Gen. Joseph F. Carroll, USAF, dir.

Defense Supply Agency—Lt. Gen. Earl C. Hedlund, USAF, dir.

U. S. UNIFIED AND SPECIFIED COMMANDS

Alaskan Command—Lt. Gen. Robert A. Breitweiser, USAF.
Atlantic Command—Adm. Ephraim P. Holmes, USN.
Continental Air Defense Command—Lt. Gen. Raymond J. Reeves, USAF.
European Command—Gen. Lyman L. Lemnitzer, USA.
Pacific Command—Adm. U. S. Grant Sharp, Jr., USN.
Southern Command—Gen. Robert W. Porter, Jr., USA.
Strike Command—Gen. T. J. Conway, USA.
Strat. Air Command—Gen. Joseph J. Nazzaro, USAF.

INTERNATIONAL COMMANDS
Under North Atlantic Treaty Organization
Supr. Allied Commander, Europe (SACEUR)—Gen. Lyman L. Lemnitzer, USA.
Deputy SACEUR—Sir Thomas A. Pike (Britain).
Air Deputy to SACEUR—Gen. William S. Stone USAF.
C-in-C, Allied Forces, Northern Europe—Lt. Gen. Sir Robert Bray (Britain).
C-in-C, Allied Forces, Central Europe—Gen. J. A. Graf Von Kielmansegg (Germany).
C-in-C, Allied Forces, Southern Europe—Adm. Charles D. Griffin, USN.
C-in-C, Allied Forces, Mediterranean—Adm. Sir. John G. Hamilton (Britain).
Supr. Allied Comdr., Atlantic (SACLANT)—Adm. Thomas H. Moorer, USN.
Deputy SACLANT—V. Adm. D. G. Clutterbuck (Br.).
Comdr. Striking Fleet, Atlantic—V. Adm. Bernard A. Clarey, USN.
Allied Comdr. in Chief, Channel—Adm. Sir John Frewen (Britain).

DEPARTMENT OF THE ARMY
Secretary of the Army—Stanley R. Resor.
Under Secretary—David E. McGiffert.
Assistant Secretaries for:
Financial Management—Eugene M. Becker.
Installations & Logistics—Robert A. Brooks.
Research & Development—Russell D. O'Neal.
Civil Defense—Joseph Romm, act.
Chief of Public Information—Maj. Gen. Keith L. Ware.
Chief of Staff—Gen. Harold K. Johnson.
Surgeon General—Lt. Gen. Leonard D. Heaton.
Adjutant General—Maj. Gen. K. G. Wickham.
Chief of Engineers—Lt. Gen. William F. Cassidy.
U. S. Women's Army Corps—Col. Elizabeth P. Hoisington.
Natl. Guard Bureau—Maj. Gen. Winston P. Wilson.
Chief, Army Reserve—Maj. Gen. William J. Sutton.
U. S. Army Materiel Command—Lt. Gen. Frank S. Besson, Jr.
U. S. Army Combat Developments Command—Lt. Gen. Harry W. O. Kinnard.
U. S. Continental Army Command—Gen. James K. Woolnough.
Commanding Generals, U. S. Armies:
1st, Fort Meade, Md.—Lt. Gen. Jonathan O. Seaman.
3rd, Ft. McPherson, Ga.—Lt. Gen. John L. Throckmorton.
4th, Ft. Sam Houston, Tex.—Lt. Gen. Lawrence J. Lincoln.
5th, Chicago, Ill.—Lt. Gen. John H. Michaelis.
6th, Presidio of San Francisco, Calif.—Lt. Gen. Ben Harrell.
Military Dist. of Washington—Maj. Gen. Charles S. O'Malley, Jr.

DEPARTMENT OF THE NAVY
Secretary of the Navy—Paul R. Ignatius.
Under Secretary—Charles F. Baird.
Assistant Secretaries for:
Financial Management—Vacant.
Installations & Logistics—Graeme C. Bannerman.
Research & Development—Robert A. Frosch.
Judge Advocate Gen.—R. Adm. Wilfred Hearn.
Military Sea Transp. Service—V. Adm. Lawson P. Ramage, commander.
Chief of Naval Operations—Adm. Thomas H. Moorer.
Bureau Chiefs:
Medicine & Surgery—V. Adm. Robert B. Brown.
Naval Material—V. Adm. I. J. Galantin.
Naval Personnel—V. Adm. B. J. Semmes, Jr.
U. S. Marine Corps:
Commandant—Gen. Wallace M. Greene, Jr.
Asst. Commandant—Lt. Gen. L. F. Chapman, Jr.
Quartermaster Gen.—Maj. Gen. Paul R. Tyler.
Dir. of Women Marines—Col. B. J. Bishop.
Commandants, Naval Districts:
1st, Boston, Mass.—R. Adm. R. S. Benson.
3rd, New York, N. Y.—R.Adm. F. D. Foley.
4th, Philadelphia, Pa.—R. Adm. Robert H. Speck.
5th, Norfolk, Va.—R. Adm. Reynold D. Hogle.
6th, Charleston, S. C.—R. Adm. Jack S. Dorsey.
8th, New Orleans, La.—R. Adm. P. N. Charbonnet, Jr.
9th, Great Lakes, Ill.—R. Adm. H. A. Renken.
10th, New York, N. Y.—R. Adm. A. R. Matter.
11th, San Diego, Calif.—R. Adm. M E. Dornin.
12th, San Francisco, Calif.—R. Adm. W. H. Groverman, Jr.
13th, Seattle, Wash.—R. Adm. Wm. E. Ferrall.
14th, San Francisco, Calif.—R. Adm. R. B. Lynch.
15th, New York, N. Y.—R. Adm. E. P. Koch.
17th, Seattle, Wash.—R. Adm. D. M. White.
Naval District, Washington, D. C.—R. Adm. E. C. Loughlin.

DEPARTMENT OF THE AIR FORCE
Secretary of the Air Force—Dr. Harold Brown.
Under Secretary—Townsend W. Hoopes.
Assistant Secretaries for:
Financial Management—Thomas H. Nielsen.
Research & Development—Alexander H. Flax.
Installations & Logistics—Robert H. Charles.
Dir. of Info.—Maj. Gen. William C. Garland.
Dir. of Space Systems—Brig. Gen. Russell A. Berg.
Chief of Staff—Gen. John P. McConnell.
Vice Chief of Staff—Gen B. K. Holloway.
Secretary of the Air Staff—Col. James H. Watkins.
Scientific Advisory Board—Dr. H. G. Stever.
Surgeon General—Maj. Gen. Kenneth E. Fletcher.
Inspector General—Lt. Gen. Joseph H. Moore.
Judge Advocate—Maj. Gen. Robert W. Manss.
Major Air Commands:
U. S. Air Force Academy—Lt. Gen. Thomas S. Moorman.
Air Force Accounting and Finance—Brig. Gen. Thomas P. Corwin.
Office of Aerospace Research—Maj. Gen. Ernest A. Pinson.
Air National Guard—Maj. Gen. Winston P. Wilson.
Air Defense, Ent. AFB, Colo.—Lt. Gen. Arthur C. Agan.
Air Force Logistics, Wright-Patterson AFB, Ohio—Gen. Thomas P. Gerrity.
Air Force Systems, Andrews AFB, Md.—Gen. James Ferguson.
Air Training, Randolph AFB, Tex.—Lt. Gen. Sam Maddux, Jr.
Air University, Maxwell AFB, Ala.—Lt. Gen. John W. Carpenter III.
Continental Air Command, Robins AFB, Ga.—Lt. Gen. Henry Viccellio.
Headquarters Command, Bolling AFB, D. C.—Maj. Gen. Rollen H. Anthis.
Military Airlift, Scott AFB, Ill.—Gen. Howell M. Estes, Jr.
Strategic Air, Offutt AFB, Neb.—Gen. Joseph J. Nazzaro.
Tactical Air, Langley AFB, Va.—Gen. Gabriel P. Disosway.
Alaskan Air, Elmendorf AFB, Alaska—Lt. Gen. Robert A. Breitweiser.
U.S.A.F. Southern Command AT Albrook AFB. Balboa, Canal Zone—Maj. Gen. Robert J. Clizbe.
Pacific Air Forces, Hickam AFB, Hawaii—Gen. John D. Ryan.
U. S. Air Forces in Europe, Wiesbaden, Germany—Gen. Maurice A. Preston.
U. S. Air Force Security Service, San Antonio, Tex.—Maj. Gen. Louis E. Coira.
Air Force Communications Service, Scott AFB, Ill.—Maj. Gen. Robert W. Paulson.

Department of Justice
Attorney General—Ramsey Clark.
Solicitor General—Vacant.
Assistant Attorneys General:
Administrative—Ernest C. Friesen, Jr.
Antitrust Div.—Donald F. Turner.
Civil Div.—Carl Eardley, Acting.
Civil Rights Div.—John Doar.
Criminal Div.—Fred M. Vinson, Jr.
Internal Security Div.—J. Walter Yeagley.
Lands Div.—Edwin L. Weisl, Jr.
Legal Counsel—Frank Wozencraft.
Tax Div.—Mitchell Rogovin.
Fed. Bureau of Investigation—J. Edgar Hoover, dir.
Bureau of Prisons—Myrl Alexander.
Federal Prison Industries, Inc.—Myrl E. Alexander, assoc. commissioner.
Board of Parole—Walter Dunbar, chmn.
Immigration and Naturalization Service—Raymond F. Farrell, commissioner.
Board of Immigration Appeals—Thomas G. Finucane, chmn.
Pardon Attorney—Reed Cozart.

Post Office Department
Postmaster General—Lawrence F. O'Brien.
Deputy Postmaster General—Frederick C. Belen.
Exec. Asst. to Postmaster Gen.—Claude J. Desautels.

THE NINETIETH CONGRESS, SECOND SESSION

As of Nov. 20, 1967

The Congress must meet annually on Jan. 3, unless it has, by law, appointed a different day

The Senate

Terms are for 6 years and end January 3 of the year preceding name. Annual salary $30,000.

To be eligible for the U. S. Senate, a person must be at least 30 years of age, a citizen of the United States for at least 9 years, and a resident of the state from which he is chosen.

Democrats, 64; Republicans, 36. Total, 100. (*) Asterisk designates senior Senator.

President pro Tempore—Carl Hayden
Chaplain—Rev. Frederick Brown Harris, D.D.
Secretary of the Senate—Francis R. Valeo
Chief Clerk—Darrell St. Claire
Sergeant at Arms—Robert G. Dunphy

Majority Floor Leader—Mike Mansfield
Majority Whip—Russell B. Long
Majority Secretary—J. Stanley Kimmitt
Minority Floor Leader—Everett M. Dirksen
Minority Whip—Thomas H. Kuchel
Minority Secretary—J. Mark Trice

Terms Expire	SENATORS	P. O. Address
ALABAMA		
1973	John Sparkman......Dem	Huntsville
1969	Lister Hill*.........Dem	Montgomery
ALASKA		
1973	E. L. (Bob) Bartlett*..Dem	Juneau
1969	Ernest Gruening....Dem	Juneau
ARIZONA		
1971	Paul J. Fannin......Rep	Phoenix
1969	Carl Hayden*.......Dem	Phoenix
ARKANSAS		
1973	John L. McClellan*...Dem	Camden
1969	J. William Fulbright...Dem	Fayetteville
CALIFORNIA		
1971	George Murphy......Rep	Beverly Hills
1969	Thomas H. Kuchel*..Rep	Anaheim
COLORADO		
1973	Gordon Allott*......Rep	Lamar
1969	Peter H. Dominick...Rep	Englewood
CONNECTICUT		
1971	Thomas J. Dodd*....Dem	West Hartford
1969	Abraham Ribicoff.....Dem	Hartford
DELAWARE		
1973	J. Caleb Boggs......Rep	Wilmington
1971	John J. Williams*....Rep	Millsboro
FLORIDA		
1971	Spessard L. Holland*.Dem	Bartow
1969	George A. Smathers...Dem	Miami
GEORGIA		
1973	Richard B. Russell*...Dem	Winder
1969	Herman E. Talmadge.Dem	Lovejoy
HAWAII		
1971	Hiram L. Fong*......Rep	Honolulu
1969	Daniel K. Inouye.....Dem	Honolulu
IDAHO		
1973	Len B. Jordan......Rep	Boise
1969	Frank Church*......Dem	Boise
ILLINOIS		
1973	Charles H. Percy....Rep	Kenilworth
1969	Everett M. Dirksen*..Rep	Pekin
INDIANA		
1971	Vance Hartke*......Dem	Evansville
1969	Birch Bayh.........Dem	Terre Haute
IOWA		
1973	Jack Miller........Rep	Sioux City
1969	Bourke B. Hickenlooper*..Rep	Cedar Rapids
KANSAS		
1973	James B. Pearson...Rep	Prairie Village
1969	Frank Carlson*......Rep	Concordia
KENTUCKY		
1973	John Sherman Cooper*..........Rep	Somerset
1969	Thruston B. Morton.Rep	Glenview
LOUISIANA		
1973	Allen J. Ellender*....Dem	Houma
1969	Russell B. Long.....Dem	Baton Rouge
MAINE		
1973	Margaret Chase Smith*..........Rep	Skowhegan
1971	Edmund S. Muskie...Dem	Waterville
MARYLAND		
1971	Joseph D. Tydings...Dem	Havre De Grace
1969	Daniel B. Brewster*..Dem	Towson
MASSACHUSETTS		
1973	Edward W. Brooke...Rep	Newton Center
1971	Edward M. Kennedy*.Dem	Boston
MICHIGAN		
1973	Robert P. Griffin....Rep	Traverse City
1971	Philip A. Hart*.....Dem	Mackinac Is.
MINNESOTA		
1973	Walter F. Mondale...Dem	Minneapolis
1971	Eugene J. McCarthy*.Dem	St. Paul
MISSISSIPPI		
1973	James O. Eastland*...Dem	Doddsville
1971	John Stennis........Dem	DeKalb
MISSOURI		
1971	Stuart Symington*...Dem	St. Louis
1969	Edward V. Long.....Dem	Bowling Green

Terms Expire	SENATORS	P. O. Address
MONTANA		
1973	Lee Metcalf........Dem	Helena
1971	Mike Mansfield*.....Dem	Missoula
NEBRASKA		
1973	Carl T. Curtis......Rep	Minden
1971	Roman L. Hruska*...Rep	Omaha
NEVADA		
1971	Howard W. Cannon...Dem	Las Vegas
1969	Alan Bible*........Dem	Reno
NEW HAMPSHIRE		
1973	Thomas J. McIntyre..Dem	Laconia
1969	Norris Cotton*......Rep	Lebanon
NEW JERSEY		
1973	Clifford P. Case*....Rep	Rahway
1971	H. A. Williams, Jr...Dem	Westfield
NEW MEXICO		
1973	Clinton P. Anderson*.Dem	Albuquerque
1971	Joseph M. Montoya..Dem	Santa Fe
NEW YORK		
1971	Robert F. Kennedy..Dem	New York City
1969	Jacob K. Javits*....Rep	New York City
NORTH CAROLINA		
1973	B. Everett Jordan...Dem	Saxapahaw
1969	Sam J. Ervin, Jr.*...Dem	Morganton
NORTH DAKOTA		
1971	Quentin N. Burdick..Dem	Fargo
1969	Milton R. Young*....Rep	La Moure
OHIO		
1971	Stephen M. Young...Dem	Shaker Heights
1969	Frank J. Lausche*...Dem	Cleveland
OKLAHOMA		
1973	Fred R. Harris......Dem	Lawton
1969	A. S. Mike Monroney*Dem	Okla. City
OREGON		
1973	Mark O. Hatfield....Rep	Salem
1969	Wayne Morse*......Dem	Eugene
PENNSYLVANIA		
1971	Hugh Scott.........Rep	Philadelphia
1969	Joseph S. Clark*....Dem	Philadelphia
RHODE ISLAND		
1973	Claiborne Pell......Dem	Newport
1971	John O. Pastore*....Dem	Providence
SOUTH CAROLINA		
1973	Strom Thurmond*....Rep	Aiken
1969	Ernest F. Hollings...Dem	Charleston
SOUTH DAKOTA		
1973	Karl E. Mundt*.....Rep	Madison
1969	George McGovern....Dem	Mitchell
TENNESSEE		
1973	Howard H. Baker, Jr.Rep	Knoxville
1971	Albert Gore*........Dem	Carthage
TEXAS		
1973	John G. Tower......Rep	Wichita Falls
1971	Ralph Yarborough*...Dem	Austin
UTAH		
1971	Frank E. Moss......Dem	Salt Lake City
1969	Wallace F. Bennett*..Rep	Salt Lake City
VERMONT		
1971	Winston L. Prouty...Rep	Newport
1969	George D. Aiken*....Rep	Putney
VIRGINIA		
1973	William B. Spong, Jr..Dem	Portsmouth
1971	Harry F. Byrd, Jr.*...Dem	Winchester
WASHINGTON		
1971	Henry M. Jackson...Dem	Everett
1969	Warren G. Magnuson*Dem	Seattle
WEST VIRGINIA		
1973	Jennings Randolph*..Dem	Elkins
1971	Robert C. Byrd......Dem	Sophia
WISCONSIN		
1971	William Proxmire*...Dem	Madison
1969	Gaylord Nelson.....Dem	Madison
WYOMING		
1973	Clifford P. Hansen...Rep	Jackson
1971	Gale W. McGee*.....Dem	Laramie

ELECTION STATISTICS
Popular and Electoral Vote for President, 1964
Compiled by The World Almanac from official returns of the States.
Blank and void ballots are excluded from all totals.

States	Electoral vote		Popular vote							Total
	John-son Dem.	Gold-water Rep.	John-son Dem.	Gold-water Rep.	Hass Soc. Labor	De-Berry Soc. Worker	Munn Proh.	Kasper Nat'l States Rights	Other *	
Ala. (a)....		10	(a)	479,085					105	689,038
Alaska.....	3		44,329	22,930						67,259
Ariz.......		5	237,753	242,535	482					480,770
Ark.......	6		314,197	243,264				2,965		560,426
Calif.....	40		4,171,877	2,879,108	489	378	305		5,429	7,057,586
Colo......	6		476,024	296,767	302	2,537	1,356			776,986
Conn......	8		826,269	390,996					1,313	1,218,578
Del.......	3		122,704	78,078	113		425			201,320
D. of C...	3		169,796	28,801						198,597
Fla.......	14		948,540	905,941						1,854,481
Ga........		12	522,557	616,600						1,139,157
Hawaii....	4		163,249	44,022						207,271
Idaho.....	4		148,920	143,557						292,477
Ill.......	26		2,796,833	1,905,946					62	4,702,841
Ind.......	13		1,170,848	911,118	1,374		8,266			2,091,606
Iowa......	9		733,030	449,148	182	159	1,902		118	1,184,539
Kan.......	7		464,028	386,579	1,901		5,393			857,901
Ky........	9		669,659	372,977				3,469		1,046,105
La........		10	387,068	509,225						896,293
Me........	4		262,264	118,701					50	380,965
Md........	10		730,912	385,495					50	1,116,457
Mass......	14		1,786,422	549,727	4,755		3,735		159	2,344,798
Mich......	21		2,136,615	1,060,152	1,704	3,817	669		145	3,203,102
Minn. (b).	10		991,117	559,624	2,544	1,177				1,554,462
Miss......		7	52,618	356,528						409,146
Mo........	12		1,164,344	653,535					519	1,817,879
Mont......	4		164,246	113,032		332	499			278,628
Nebr......	5		307,307	276,847						584,154
Nev.......	3		79,339	56,094						135,433
N. H......	4		182,065	104,029						286,094
N. J......	17		1,867,671	963,843	7,075	8,181				2,846,770
N. M......	4		194,017	131,838	1,217		543			327,615
N. Y......	43		4,913,156	2,243,559	6,085	3,215			188	7,166,203
N. C......	13		800,139	624,844						1,424,983
N. D......	4		149,784	108,207		224	174			258,389
Ohio......	26		2,498,331	1,470,865						3,969,196
Okla......	8		519,834	412,665						932,499
Ore.......	6		501,017	282,779					2,509	786,305
Pa........	29		3,130,954	1,673,657	5,092	10,456			2,531	4,822,690
R. I......	4		315,463	74,615						390,078
S. C......		8	215,700	309,048					8	524,756
S. D......	4		163,010	130,108						293,118
Tenn......	11		635,047	508,965					34	1,144,046
Texas....	25		1,663,185	958,566					5,060	2,626,811
Utah.....	4		219,628	181,785						401,413
Vt........	3		107,674	54,868						162,542
Va........	12		558,038	481,334	2,895					1,042,267
Wash......	9		779,699	470,366	7,772	537				1,258,374
W. Va....	7		538,087	253,953						792,040
Wis.......	12		1,050,424	638,495	1,204	1,692				1,691,815
Wyo.......	3		80,718	61,998						142,716
Total U.S.	486	52	43,126,506	27,176,799	45,186	32,705	23,267	6,953	17,711	70,638,975

(a) Alabama did not list Johnson on ballot. There were 209,848 votes cast for the slate of unpledged Democratic electors. (b) Hass ran under the Industrial Government ticket.
*Scattering Vote: Ala. 105; Calif. 5,410; Conn. 1,313; Iowa 118; Mich. 145; N. Y. 188 and Pa. 2,531.
Write-in Vote: Ill. 62; Md. 50; Ore. 2,509; S. C. 8 and Tenn. 34.
Others: Mass. 159.
Constitution Party: Texas 5,060.
Universal Party: Calif. 19.

Major National Convention Cities since 1856
(Number in parentheses)

Atlantic City, N. J., (1)—Dem. 1964.
Baltimore, Md., (3)—Rep., 1864; Dem., 1872, 1912.
Charleston, S. C., (1)—Dem., 1860.
Chicago, Ill., (23)—Rep., 1860, 1868, 1880, 1884, 1888, 1904, 1908, 1912, 1916, 1920, 1932, 1944, 1952, 1960. Dem., 1864, 1884, 1892, 1896, 1932, 1940, 1944, 1952, 1956.
Cincinnati, O., (3)—Rep., 1876; Dem., 1856, 1880.
Cleveland, O., (2)—Rep., 1924, 1936.
Denver, Col.,(1)—Dem., 1908.
Houston, Tex., (1)—Dem., 1928.
Kansas City, Mo., (2)—Rep., 1928; Dem., 1900.
Los Angeles, Calif., (1)—Dem., 1960.
Minneapolis, Minn., (1)—Rep., 1892.
New York City, (2)—Dem., 1868, 1924.
Philadelphia, Pa., (7)—Rep., 1856, 1872, 1900, 1940, 1948; Dem., 1936, 1948.
St. Louis, Mo., (5)—Rep., 1896; Dem., 1876, 1888, 1904, 1916.
San Francisco, Calif., (3)—Rep., 1956, 1964; Dem., 1920.

Work of 90th Congress, First Session (1967)

The First Session of the 90th Congress convened Jan. 10, 1967. Although the two previous sessions of Congress had adjourned on Oct. 22 (1961 and 1966), this session was still at work on major legislation late in November.

Congress wrestled slowly with a host of problems new and old. Among them were President Johnson's proposed 10% income tax surcharge, expansion of Social Security, consumer protection, civil rights, crime, riots, aid to education, anti-poverty measures, the draft, foreign aid, air pollution control, new postal rates, higher military pay, etc.

The President several times urged Congress to take action on a number of his proposals; his tone, in these calls, was a moderate one.

Many of his programs were, however, effectively blocked or trimmed by Congress.

Important legislation passed by Congress and signed by the President included:

Extension of the Draft. This act extended the military draft for 4 years from June 30. It gave the President authority to end deferments for graduate school students except those in medical and some allied fields. It barred the President from ending undergraduate deferments unless he found it necessary to meet military manpower needs. It sanctioned the President's proposal to reverse the order of induction so as to call 19-year-olds before older men. Undergraduates and students in job training were to be deferred until graduation, leaving school or reaching their 24th birthday, whichever came first; they would then be put in the draft pool for 19-year-olds for a year; if not called in a year they would be given the same draft status as others in their age group. The President's proposal for a draft lottery was barred unless with approval of Congress. (See also Page 737.)

Foreign Aid. The foreign military and economic assistance authorization act set a ceiling of $2.67 billion to be spent in the current fiscal year, about a half billion less than the Administration sought. The House then slashed this figure, in its foreign aid appropriations bill, to $2.2 billion. It appeared unlikely that the Senate could or would raise this latter figure by much. It was the smallest appropriations bill in the 20 years of foreign aid programs, and about $1 billion less than the Administration request.

Air Pollution Control. The Air Quality Act authorized a 3-year, $428,000,000 program to combat air pollution. It empowered the Secretary of Health, Education and Welfare to seek a Federal Court injunction, in a pollution emergency, to shut down a specific factory or building or to immobilize all sources of pollution, including automobiles, in an entire city. The initiative in setting clean air standards was left to the states, but if they do not act promptly, the Secretary may step in and set standards.

New GI Benefits. This increased pensions and education and job-training benefits, extending them to veterans of 180 days or more service since Jan. 31, 1955 (the legal end of the Korean War). Cost was put at $285,603,000, more by $115,000,000 than the Administration requested. Eligibility for VA loan guarantees was extended to July 25, 1970; the maximum for a home loan was raised from $17,500 to $25,000.

Business Tax Credit. This act restored the 7% tax credit on business investments and the system of depreciation allowances.

End to Railroad Strike. This act ordered an end to a nationwide rail strike, involving 6 of the railroad unions in a wage dispute, and also ordered mediation between the railroads and the unions. The legislation was voted after the President sent Congress a message saying a 'national crisis" existed, threatening the nation's economy and security.

Debt Ceiling Raised. This action raised the permanent limit on the national debt from $285 billion to $358 billion for fiscal 1968. It also provided for a future "shifting" ceiling, allowing use of a temporary ceiling of $365 billion in succeeding years except that for each June 30 it would revert to $358 billion.

Product Safety. This act created a National Commission on Product Safety which would inform the public of dangerous products and of steps which should be taken to protect the public from hazards occurring in the home.

Teacher Corps Extended. This act extended for 3 years the Teacher Corps, with an authorization of $135,000,000, and changed its name, dropping the word National from the title. It also shifted much of the control of the organization from the Federal Government to local school agencies and provided that local districts should pay at least 10% of the salaries of corps members in their districts.

Educational TV. A corporation was established to help finance educational TV and radio programs.

First Veto. President Johnson vetoed a bill, passed by Congress, to raise life insurance for Federal employees. The cost would have been $61,000,000 in its first year, in contrast to Administration proposals that would have cost $13,000,000. It was President Johnson's first veto during the 90th Congress and his 23rd since becoming President.

Among issues on which Congress showed it did not want to go along with Presidential proposals were: anti-poverty measures, open housing, gun control, a wiretap ban, political campaign financing and some consumer protection steps.

Shirley Temple Black: "I Will Be Back."

With the old spunk and charm of Little Miss Marker, Mrs. Shirley Temple Black, defeated for a chance at a Congressional seat Nov. 14, 1967, by a fellow Republican in a special election in California's 11th District, smilingly told her supporters at a "victory" dinner: "Maybe I'll see you next year. I'm not going to give up. This is my first race and now I know how the game is played."

Mrs. Black, who as a child had added luster to the "silver screen" 30-odd years earlier in a series of motion pictures that captured America's heart, ran second to Paul N. McCloskey, Jr., who was to oppose Democrat Roy Archibald in a special mid-December run-off vote.

For a first try at elective office, Mrs. Black, 39, made a creditable showing, finishing ahead of 9 other male contenders.

Major Decisions of the U. S. Supreme Court, 1967

The court extended freedom of the press by ruling, 5-4, that "newsworthy" persons may not be awarded invasion-of-privacy damages for statements containing errors which give a false impression of a person, unless the falsehoods were deliberate or reckless. (Jan. 9.)

Refused to change a lower court decision giving newspapers broad immunity from libel suits for statements made by syndicated columnists. (Jan. 9.)

Unanimously held it is not a crime for a person to visit, with an up-to-date passport, countries to which travel is banned by the State Department. (Jan. 10.)

Ruled, 5-4, that admissions made by public employees under a threat of dismissal may not be used against them in criminal trials, holding that this violated the 5th Amendment protection against compulsory self-incrimination. (But the court did not hold that employees refusing to make statements could not be fired.) (Jan. 16.)

Loyalty Laws

Declared unconstitutional, 5-4, N. Y. State loyalty laws which required removal of school personnel for seditious words or acts, denied public employment to anyone advocating overthrow of the government by force, and required school and college teachers to sign certificates that they were not members of the Communist party; the court termed the laws "unconstitutionally vague." (Jan. 23.)

Rejected two appeals by James R. Hoffa, Teamsters president, to stay or throw out his conviction and 8-year sentence for jury tampering. (Feb. 27.)

Ruled, 5-3, that savings won by natural gas companies through the filing of consolidated U. S. income tax returns must be passed on to their consumers in the form of lower rates. (Mar. 13.)

Held, 5-4, the Constitution does not require police to disclose in court the identity of an informant who gave them a tip about a crime. (Mar. 20.)

Declined to hear the appeal of a man sentenced to 5 years for refusing to report for induction; the man asserted the U. S. was committing war crimes in Vietnam. (Mar. 20.)

Union Fines

Upheld, 5-4, the right of a union to prevent automation of its members' jobs by enforcing contract provisions against the use of prefabricated materials. (Apr. 17.)

Rejected an appeal by Muhammad Ali (Cassius Clay) for an injunction to block his induction; he charged discrimination because of a lack of Negroes on Kentucky draft boards. (Apr. 17.) Turned down two more appeals by the heavyweight boxing champion. (Apr. 24.)

Ruled, 6-3, that mail order houses cannot be forced to collect state or local use taxes (equivalents of sales taxes) on interstate sales by mail or common carrier. (May 8.)

Threw out 3 obscenity cases, holding, 7-2, that a group of "girlie" magazines and two paperback books were not obscene and noting that none of them involved the questions of sale of smut to minors, "obtrusive" presentation, or promotion of a "pandering" type. (May 8.)

Held, 8-1, that juvenile courts must grant children rights guaranteed adults, such as: timely notice of charges, a lawyer (appointed by the court if necessary), adequate warning of the privilege against self-incrimination, the right to remain silent, the right to confront and cross-examine complainants and witnesses. (May 16.)

Granted James R. Hoffa and 6 others a hearing in a Federal District Court on whether their conviction in a mail fraud case was tainted by Government eavesdropping. (May 22.)

Decided unanimously that its one-man, one-vote doctrine for legislative reapportionment did not apply to local school boards, terming them essentially administrative bodies. (May 22.)

Ruled, 6-3, that alien homosexuals may be excluded or deported from the U. S. under a 1952 Federal law barring persons afflicted with a "psychopathic personality." (May 22.)

Declared unconstitutional, 5-4, the voter-approved amendment to the California Constitution which gave property owners the right to discriminate in resale or rental of housing, terming it a violation of the U. S. Constitution's 14th Amendment. (May 29.)

Held, 5-4, that Congress lacks authority to pass laws stripping U. S. citizens of their citizenship for actions such as voting in a foreign election, and declared such a law unconstitutional. (May 29.)

Unanimously declared unconstitutional Virginia laws forbidding marriage between whites and nonwhites and indicating similar laws in 15 other states were also void. (June 12.)

Held, 5-4, it is legal for labor unions to fine members for working during a strike. (June 12.)

Eavesdropping Devices

Declared unconstitutional, 5-4, a N. Y. law permitting police to obtain judicial warrants to enter private property to plant concealed microphones, terming it a violation of the 4th Amendment limitations on police searches. (June 12.)

Held that the Constitution's protection of the press against libel suits brought for false statements (except where made with knowledge they were false or made with reckless disregard) extends not only to suits brought by public officials but also suits by other "public" figures. (June 12.)

Affirmed on a technicality, 5-4 ,the convictions of the Rev. Dr. Martin Luther King and 7 other Negro ministers for violating an Alabama court injunction against a 1963 Birmingham demonstration. (June 12.) Refused to re-examine the convictions. (Oct. 9.)

School Desegregation

Let stand a lower court decision ordering immediate desegregation of schools in 6 Southern states; also let stand a lower court decision that school officials in Cincinnati have no constitutional duty to reduce racial imbalance in schools unless it results from discriminatory actions by public officials. (Oct. 9.)

Reversed, 7-1, lower court rulings barring admission of foreign nudist magazines reportedly intended for the male homosexual market, but refused to upset the conviction of a Florida sculptor for displaying erotic statues for sale; the court intimated the criterion was "obtrusive" promotion. (Oct. 24.)

Refused to hear the appeal of 3 soldiers given court-martial sentences of 3 years for refusing to go to Vietnam; the soldiers claimed the war there was illegal and they could be adjudged war criminals if they participated in it. (Nov. 6.)

UNITED NATIONS
History, Membership, Organization and Purpose

The 22nd regular session of the United Nations General Assembly opened Sept. 19, 1967. *See Chronology for developments at UN sessions during 1967.*

The fifth emergency special session of the General Assembly adjourned Sept. 18, 1967, after adopting a resolution asking that the Middle East question be placed high on the agenda of the 22nd regular session. The emergency special session had been convened 3 months earlier at the request of the Soviet Union, with the concurrence of a majority of member states, to consider the situation in the Middle East.

In its fifth special session, Apr. 21-June 13, 1967, the General Assembly considered the question of South West Africa. The Assembly made a comprehensive review of the whole question of peace-keeping operations; it also decided to postpone the UN Conference on the Exploration and Peaceful Uses of Outer Space until 1968.

The membership of the UN rose to 122 states during the 21st regular session of the General Assembly, which ended Dec. 20, 1966. This resulted from the admission of 4 new nations—Barbados, Botswana, Guyana, and Lesotho—and the resumption of membership by Indonesia.

Foundations of the United Nations were laid at the Dumbarton Oaks Conference in Washington between the United States, the United Kingdom and the Soviet Union, Aug. 21-Sept. 28, 1944, and between

the United States, the United Kingdom and the Republic of China (Nationalist) Sept. 29-Oct. 7, 1944. Proposals to establish an organization of nations for maintenance of world peace led to the United Nations Conference on International Organization at San Francisco, Apr. 25-June 26, 1945, where the charter of the United Nations was drawn up. It was signed June 26 by 50 nations, and by Poland, one of the original 51, on Oct. 15, 1945. The charter came into effect Oct. 24, 1945, when the requisite ratification by the 5 permanent members of the Security Council, China, France, Soviet Union, United Kingdom and United States, and a majority of other signatories had been completed.

United Nations headquarters are located in New York, N. Y., between First Ave. and Roosevelt Drive and E. 42nd St. and E. 48th St. The General Assembly Bldg. (opened 1952), Secretariat, Conference and Library bldgs. are interconnected. The Dag Hammarskjold Library, built by a $6,200,000 grant from the Ford Foundation, was dedicated Nov. 16, 1961. It has room for 400,000 vols. To build the headquarters the U. S. Government advanced an interest-free loan of $65,000,000, payable in annual installments until 1982. John D. Rockefeller, Jr., contributed $8,000,000 for land and the City of New York contributed an est. $26,500,000 for adapting the site. United Nations has a post office originating its own stamps. *See Postal Information.*

Roster of the United Nations
(As of Sept. 19, 1967)

The 122 Members of the United Nations, with the dates on which they became Members.

Member	Date	Member	Date	Member	Date
Afghanistan	Nov. 19, 1946	Ghana	Mar. 8, 1957	Niger	Sept. 20, 1960
Albania	Dec. 14, 1955	Greece	Oct. 25, 1945	Nigeria	Oct. 7, 1960
Algeria	Oct. 8, 1962	Guatemala	Nov. 21, 1945	Norway	Nov. 27, 1945
Argentina	Oct. 24, 1945	Guinea	Dec. 12, 1958	Pakistan	Sept. 30, 1947
Australia	Nov. 1, 1945	Guyana	Sept. 20, 1966	Panama	Nov. 13, 1945
Austria	Dec. 14, 1955	Haiti	Oct. 24, 1945	Paraguay	Oct. 24, 1945
Barbados	Dec. 9, 1966	Honduras	Dec. 17, 1945	Peru	Oct. 31, 1945
Belgium	Dec. 27, 1945	Hungary	Dec. 14, 1955	Philippines	Oct. 24, 1945
Bolivia	Nov. 14, 1945	Iceland	Nov. 19, 1946	Poland	Oct. 24, 1945
Botswana	Oct. 17, 1966	India	Oct. 30, 1945	Portugal	Dec. 14, 1955
Brasil	Oct. 24, 1945	Indonesia	Sept. 28, 1950	Romania	Dec. 14, 1955
Bulgaria	Dec. 14, 1955	Iran	Oct. 24, 1945	Rwanda	Sept. 18, 1962
Burma	Apr. 19, 1948	Iraq	Dec. 21, 1945	Saudi Arabia	Oct. 24, 1945
Burundi	Sept. 18, 1962	Ireland	Dec. 14, 1955	Senegal	Sept. 28, 1960
Byelorussian Soviet		Israel	May 11, 1949	Sierra Leone	Sept. 27, 1961
Socialist Rep	Oct. 24, 1945	Italy	Dec. 14, 1955	Singapore	Sept. 21, 1965
Cambodia	Dec. 14, 1955	Ivory Coast	Sept. 20, 1960	Somalia	Sept. 20, 1960
Cameroon	Sept. 20, 1960	Jamaica	Sept. 18, 1962	South Africa	Nov. 7, 1945
Canada	Nov. 9, 1945	Japan	Dec. 18, 1956	Spain	Dec. 14, 1955
Central African		Jordan	Dec. 14, 1955	Sudan	Nov. 12, 1956
Republic	Sept. 20, 1960	Kenya	Dec. 16, 1963	Sweden	Nov. 19, 1946
Ceylon	Dec. 14, 1955	Kuwait	May 14, 1963	Syria²	Oct. 24, 1945
Chad	Sept. 20, 1960	Laos	Dec. 14, 1955	Tanzania³	Dec. 14, 1961
Chile	Oct. 24, 1945	Lebanon	Oct. 24, 1945	Thailand	Dec. 16, 1946
China	Oct. 24, 1945	Lesotho	Oct. 17, 1966	Togo	Sept. 20, 1960
Colombia	Nov. 5, 1945	Liberia	Nov. 2, 1945	Trinidad & Tobago	Sept. 18, 1962
Congo—Brassaville	Sept. 20, 1960	Libya	Dec. 14, 1955	Tunisia	Nov. 12, 1956
Congo, Dem. Rep.	Sept. 20, 1960	Luxembourg	Oct. 24, 1945	Turkey	Oct. 24, 1945
Costa Rica	Nov. 2, 1945	Madagascar	Sept. 20, 1960	Uganda	Oct. 25, 1962
Cuba	Oct. 24, 1945	Malawi	Dec. 1, 1964	Ukrainian Soviet	
Cyprus	Sept. 20, 1960	Malaysia¹	Sept. 17, 1957	Socialist Republic	Oct. 24, 1945
Czechoslovakia	Oct. 24, 1945	Maldive Islands	Sept. 21, 1965	Union of Soviet	
Dahomey	Sept. 20, 1960	Mali	Sept. 28, 1960	Socialist Repub's.	Oct. 24, 1945
Denmark	Oct. 24, 1945	Malta	Dec. 1, 1964	United Arab Rep.²	Oct. 24, 1945
Dominican Rep	Oct. 24, 1945	Mauritania	Oct. 27, 1961	United Kingdom	Oct. 24, 1945
Ecuador	Dec. 21, 1945	Mexico	Nov. 7, 1945	United States	Oct. 24, 1945
El Salvador	Oct. 24, 1945	Mongolia	Oct. 27, 1961	Upper Volta	Sept. 20, 1960
Ethiopia	Nov. 13, 1945	Morocco	Nov. 12, 1956	Uruguay	Dec. 18, 1945
Finland	Dec. 14, 1955	Nepal	Dec. 14, 1955	Venezuela	Nov. 15, 1945
France	Oct. 24, 1945	Netherlands	Dec. 10, 1945	Yemen	Sept. 30, 1947
Gabon	Sept. 20, 1960	New Zealand	Oct. 24, 1945	Yugoslavia	Oct. 24, 1945
Gambia	Sept. 21, 1965	Nicaragua	Oct. 24, 1945	Zambia	Dec. 1, 1964

[1] The Federation of Malaya joined the UN on Sept. 17, 1957. On Sept. 16, 1963, its name changed to Malaysia, following the admission to the new federation of Singapore, Sabah (North Borneo) and Sarawak. Singapore became an independent State Aug. 9, 1965 and a Member of the UN Sept. 21.

[2] Egypt and Syria were original Members of the United Nations from Oct. 24, 1945. Following a plebiscite held on Feb. 21, 1958, the United Arab Republic was established by a union of Egypt and Syria and continued as a single Member of the United Nations. On Oct. 13, 1961, Syria, having resumed its status as an independent State, resumed its separate membership in the Organization.

[3] Tanganyika was a Member of the United Nations from Dec. 14, 1961 and Zanzibar was a Member from Dec. 16, 1963. Following the ratification, on Apr. 26, 1964, of Articles of Union between Tanganyika and Zanzibar, the United Republic of Tanganyika and Zanzibar continued as a single Member of the United Nations, later changing its name to United Republic of Tanzania.

Population of Important Foreign Cities

Source: Latest census reports and latest official estimates; *(asterisk) denotes capital; Gr. denotes Greater, or metropolitan area

City	Population	City	Population	City	Population	City	Population
Afghanistan		Quebec	166,984	**Czecho-slovakia**		**Ghana**	
*Kabul	450,000	Quebec, Gr	413,397	Bratislava	262,380	*Accra	491,060
Kandahar	300,000	Regina	131,127	Brno	325,332	**Greece**	
Albania		St. Catharines	97,101	Ostrava	255,703	*Athens (incl.	
Tirane	156,950	St. John, Gr	101,192	Plzen (Pilsen)	138,421	Piraeus)	1,852,709
Algeria		St. John's, Gr	101,161	*Prague	1,017,156	Patras	95,364
*Algiers	883,879	Saskatoon	115,892	**Dahomey**		Thessaloniki	
Constantine	300,000	Sudbury	84,888	Cotonou	110,000	(Salonika)	309,205
Oran	430,000	Toronto	664,584	**Denmark**		**Guatemala**	
Andorra		Toronto, Gr	2,158,496	Aarhus	177,551	*Guatemala	
*Andorra La		Vancouver	410,375	*Copenhagen	1,342,878	City	690,000
Vella	5,501	Vancouver,Gr	892,286	Frederiksberg	112,211	Quezaltenango	56,921
Argentina		Windsor	192,544	Odense	109,681	**Guinea**	
Avellaneda	380,000	Windsor, Gr	211,697	**Dominican Republic**		*Conakry	112,490
*Buenos Aires	2,966,816	Winnipeg	257,005	*Santo		**Guyana**	
Cordoba	635,000	Winnipeg, Gr	508,759	Domingo	522,490	*Georgetown	165,000
General San		**Central Africa Rep.**		**Ecuador**		**Haiti**	
Martin	279,213	*Bangui	237,971	Guayaquil	651,542	Cap-Haitien	30,000
La Plata	410,000	**Ceylon**		*Quito	401,811	*Port-au-	
Lanus	244,473	*Colombo	510,947	**El Salvador**		Prince	250,000
Mar del Plata	270,000	Jaffna	94,248	*San Salvador	281,122	**Honduras**	
Rosario	761,300	Kandy	67,768	Santa Ana	72,839	*Tegucigalpa	170,535
Santa Fe	275,000	**Chad**		**Ethiopia**		San Pedro Sula	95,890
Tucuman	251,000	*Fort-Lamy	150,000	*Addis Ababa	600,000	**Hungary**	
Australia		**Chile**		Asmara	200,000	*Budapest	1,928,000
Adelaide	770,628	Concepcion	250,000	**Finland**		*Budapest, Gr.	1,951,000
Brisbane	777,935	*Santiago	2,550,000	*Helsinki(Hel-		Debrecen	148,000
*Canberra	93,311	Valparaiso	300,000	singfors)	518,000	Miskolc	171,000
Hobart	141,238	**China**		Tampere	147,000	Pecs	135,000
Melbourne	2,228,511	Amoy	240,000	Turku (Abo)	146,000	Szeged	116,000
Newcastle	143,061	Anshan	833,000	**France**		**Iceland**	
Perth	558,297	Canton	1,867,000	Bordeaux	254,122	*Reykjavik	78,982
Sydney	2,539,627	Changsha	709,000	Le Havre	184,133	**India**	
Austria		Changteh	300,000	Lille	199,033	Agra	517,699
Graz	248,620	Chengtu	1,135,000	Lyon	535,784	Ahmedabad	1,285,447
Innsbruck	107,914	Chenteh		Marseille	783,738	Allahabad	455,158
Linz	202,199	(Jehol)	510,000	Nantes	246,227	Amritsar	398,200
Salzburg	114,472	Chungking	2,165,000	Nice	294,976	Benares	573,558
*Vienna	1,638,584	Dairen	1,590,000	*Paris	2,811,171	Bangalore	959,803
Barbados		Fatshan	450,000	*Paris, Gr	8,569,238	Bombay	4,653,687
*Bridgetown	94,000	Foochow	400,000	St. Etienne	203,633	Calcutta	3,026,436
Belgium		Hangchow	784,000	Strasbourg	233,549	Calcutta	
Antwerp	657,485	HongKong,Br.	3,739,900	Toulouse	330,570	(Met.)	5,505,195
*Brussels	1,065,921	Hsinking		**Gabon**		*Delhi	2,369,464
Charleroi	283,426	(Changchun)	975,000	*Libreville	45,909	Howrah	1,611,373
Ghent	232,915	Kowloon	675,000	**Gambia**		Hyderabad	2,062,995
Liege	452,713	Lanchow	699,000	*Bathurst	28,896	Kanpur	987,227
Bolivia		Macao, Port.	187,772	**Germany, West**		Lucknow	662,196
Cochabamba	100,000	Nanking	1,419,000	Aachen	176,900	Madras	1,864,813
*La Paz	420,000	*Peking	4,010,000	Augsburg	210,800	Madurai	452,123
Santa Cruz	139,000	Pin-chiang		Berlin (West)	2,201,800	Nagpur	713,577
*Sucre	60,000	(Harbin)	1,552,000	Bielefeld	170,100	Patna	398,462
Botswana		Shanghai	6,900,000	Bochum	356,900	Poona	721,134
*Gaberones	6,000	Shenyang		*Bonn	141,700	**Indonesia**	
Brazil		(Mukden)	2,411,000	Bremen	592,400	Bandung	1,046,189
Belem	516,000	Sian	1,500,000	Brunswick	236,200	*Jakarta	
Belo Horizonte	1,015,000	Taiyuan	1,020,000	Cologne	854,500	(Batavia)	2,906,533
*Brasilia	300,000	Tientsin	3,220,000	Darmstadt	139,600	Jogjakarta	341,424
Curitiba	536,000	Tsinan	862,000	Dortmund	656,000	Makassar	603,767
Fortaleza	743,000	Tsingtao	1,121,000	Duesseldorf	700,100	Malang	374,554
Niteroi	285,000	Wenchow	631,276	Duisburg	490,300	Medan	532,129
Porto Alegre	840,000	Wuhan	2,146,000	Essen	726,800	Palembang	723,232
Recife	1,006,000	**China (Taiwan)**		Frankfurt	690,900	Semarang	520,565
Rio de Janeiro	3,977,000	Kaohsiung	693,680	Gelsenkirchen	373,600	Surabaya	1,310,631
Salvador	842,000	Keelung	268,817	Hamburg	1,857,000	Surakarta	445,305
Santos	271,000	Taichung	348,762	Hannover	559,000	**Iran**	
Sao Paulo	5,251,000	Tainan	386,980	Heidelberg	125,400	Abadan	302,189
Bulgaria		*Taipei	1,175,279	Karlsruhe	252,900	Hamedan	114,610
Plovdiv	220,000	**Colombia**		Kassel	214,700	Isfahan	339,909
*Sofia	800,953	Barranquilla	547,000	Kiel	269,900	Meshed	312,186
Varna	172,700	*Bogota	1,980,000	Krefeld	220,800	Shiraz	229,761
Burma		Bucaramanga	272,000	Luebeck	239,500	Tabriz	387,803
Mandalay	212,873	Cali	787,000	Ludwigshafen	176,800	*Tehran	2,317,116
Moulmein	116,165	Cartagena	285,000	Mannheim	326,900	**Iraq**	
*Rangoon	821,800	Medellin	925,000	Muelheim		*Baghdad	2,124,323
Burundi		**Congo—Brazzaville**		(Ruhr)	192,000	Basrah	673,623
*Bujumbura	75,000	*Brazzaville	136,200	Munich	1,210,500	Mosul	954,157
Cambodia		**Congo, Democratic Rep.**		Nuremberg	472,000	**Ireland**	
*Phnom-Penh.	450,000	Lubumbashi	200,000	Oberhausen	259,500	Cork	77,980
Cameroon		*Kinshasa	1,000,000	Stuttgart	632,700	*Dublin	537,448
Douala	187,000	**Costa Rica**		Wiesbaden	261,100	Drogheda	17,085
*Yaounde	93,269	*San Jose	173,725	Wuppertal	422,900	Galway	22,028
Canada		**Cuba**		**Germany, East**		Kilkenny	10,159
Calgary, Gr	330,575	Camaguey	204,254	*Berlin (East)	1,055,000	Limerick	50,786
Edmonton	376,925	*Havana, Gr.	1,517,700	Chemnitz		Waterford	28,216
Edmonton, Gr	401,299	Holguin	226,644	(Karl Marx		**Israel**	
Halifax	86,792	Marianao	229,576	Stadt)	287,000	Haifa	205,000
Hamilton	298,121	Santa Clara	144,630	Dresden	503,859	*Jerusalem	192,000
Hamilton, Gr.	449,116	Santiago de		Erfurt	189,770	Ramat Gan	102,600
Kitchener	93,255	Cuba	231,000	Halle	274,402	Tel Aviv-Jaffa.	394,400
Laval	196,088	**Cyprus**		Leipzig	595,203	**Italy**	
London	194,416	Famagusta	38,000	Magdeburg	265,141	Bari	340,000
London, Gr	207,396	Limassol	47,000	Rostock	179,352	Bologna	483,000
Montreal	1,222,255	*Nicosia	103,000			Catania	383,739
Montreal, Gr.	2,436,817					Florence	455,000
*Ottawa	290,741					Genoa	848,000
*Ottawa, Gr.	494,535					Messina	260,802
						Milan	1,672,000

City	Population	City	Population	City	Population	City	Population
Naples......	1,240,000	Tetuan......	101,352	**Somalia**		Lvov......	502,000
Palermo......	618,327	**Muscat and Oman**		*Mogadishu...	141,770	Magnitogorsk.	352,000
*Rome......	2,500,000	*Muscat......	6,208	**So. Africa**		Makeyevka....	410,000
Trieste......	281,000	Matrah......	14,000	Bloemfontein..	145,273	Minsk......	749,000
Turin......	1,114,300	**Nepal**		*Cape Town..	807,211	*Moscow......	6,412,000
Venice......	363,000	*Katmandu....	220,391	Durban......	681,492	*Moscow, Gr..	6,482,000
Verona......	236,700	**Netherlands**		Johannesburg.	1,152,525	Novokuznetsk.	484,000
Ivory Coast		*Amsterdam..	868,445	*Pretoria......	422,590	Odessa......	753,000
*Abidjan......	300,000	Arnhem......	129,628	**Spain**		Omsk......	746,000
Jamaica		Eindhoven....	177,002	Barcelona....	1,696,756	Perm......	785,000
*Kingston....	419,416	Enschede....	132,752	Bilbao......	350,884	Riga......	665,000
Japan		Groningen....	151,399	Cadiz......	128,460	Rostov......	737,000
Amagasaki...	488,000	The Hague....	602,448	Cordoba......	215,454	Saratov......	669,000
Fukuoka......	771,679	Haarlem......	172,087	Granada......	161,861	Sverdlovsk....	940,000
Hakodate....	250,457	Rotterdam....	732,232	*Madrid......	2,599,330	Tallin......	335,000
Hiroshima....	507,000	Tilburg......	143,962	Malaga......	324,949	Tashkent......	1,140,000
Kawasaki....	791,000	Utrecht......	265,432	Murcia......	264,505	Tbilisi......	830,000
Kita Kyushu.	1,070,367	**New Zealand**		Palma......	170,740	Tula......	371,000
Kobe......	1,216,579	Auckland....	548,300	Seville......	531,571	Ufa......	683,000
Kyoto......	1,364,977	Christchurch..	247,200	Valencia......	583,151	Vladivostok....	379,000
Nagasaki....	405,000	Dunedin....	108,700	Zaragoza....	377,412	Volgograd....	703,000
Nagoya......	1,935,430	*Wellington		**Sudan**		Voronezh....	592,000
Osaka......	3,214,330	(incl. Hutt).	282,500	*Khartoum....	135,000	Yaroslavl......	486,000
Sapporo......	735,000	**Nicaragua**		Omdurman....	167,000	Zaporozhie....	571,000
Sendai......	486,000	*Managua....	274,901	**Sweden**		Zhdanov......	373,000
Shizuoka....	363,000	**Niger**		Boras......	69,440		
*Tokyo, Gr...	11,021,579	*Niamey......	42,000	Goteborg......	442,799	**United Arab Republic**	
Yokohama....	1,788,796	**Nigeria**		Halsingborg..	79,547	**(Egypt)**	
Jordan		Ibadan......	750,000	Linkoping....	77,227	Alexandria....	1,587,700
*Amman......	311,134	Kano......	400,000	Malmo......	255,315	Assiut......	400,000
Kenya		*Lagos......	665,246	Norrkoping....	94,565	*Cairo......	3,518,200
*Nairobi......	300,000	Oghomosho..	343,279	Orebro......	85,646	Gizeh......	276,200
Korea		**Norway**		*Stockholm...	779,000	Port Said......	256,100
Inchon......	485,511	Bergen......	117,000	*Stockholm,		Suez......	219,000
Pusan......	1,419,808	*Oslo......	485,000	Gr......	1,354,000	Tanta......	209,500
Pyongyang...	1,225,000	Stavanger....	79,400	Uppsala......	94,608		
*Seoul......	3,470,880	Trondheim....	118,000	Vasteras......	107,082	**United Kingdom**	
Taegu......	811,406	**Pakistan**		**Switzerland**		ENGLAND	
Kuwait		Chittagong....	364,205	Basel......	216,000	Birmingham..	1,102,570
*Kuwait......	99,638	Dacca......	556,712	*Berne......	168,200	Bradford......	297,100
Laos		*Islamabad....	50,000	Geneva......	174,000	Bristol......	429,370
*Luang		Karachi......	1,912,598	Lausanne....	135,900	Coventry......	331,950
Prabang....	45,000	Lahore......	1,296,477	Zurich......	434,000	Kingston-upon	
*Vientiane....	138,000	Rawalpindi....	340,175	**Syria**		-Hull......	298,000
Lebanon		**Panama**		Aleppo......	547,030	Leeds......	508,000
*Beirut......	700,000	Colon......	79,893	*Damascus....	562,907	Leicester......	283,540
Sidon......	50,000	*Panama......	359,301	Hama......	173,000	Liverpool......	712,040
Tripoli......	80,000	**Paraguay**		Homs......	293,500	*London, Gr..	7,913,600
Lesotho		*Asuncion....	305,160	Lattakia......	109,216	Manchester..	625,250
*Maseru......	9,000	Concepcion...	33,886	**Tanzania**		Newcastle....	253,780
Liberia		Encarnacion...	35,186	*Dares Salaam	250,000	Nottingham..	310,280
*Monrovia....	80,992	Villarica......	30,000	Tanga......	55,000	Oxford......	109,510
Libya		**Peru**		**Thailand**		Plymouth....	213,980
*Bengazi......	137,295	Arequipa......	407,163	*Bangkok......	2,318,000	Portsmouth..	217,780
Misurata......	63,000	Callao......	219,420	Thonburi......	459,555	Sheffield......	486,490
*Tripoli......	213,506	Cuzco......	648,168	**Togo Rep.**		Stoke on-	
Liechtenstein		*Lima......	2,093,435	*Lome......	125,000	Trent......	276,300
*Vaduz......	3,957	**Philippines**		**Trinidad and**		WALES	
Luxembourg		Cebu......	299,700	**Tobago**		Barry......	42,430
*Luxembourg.	85,000	Davao......	269,300	*Port of Spain.	93,954	Cardiff......	250,705
Malagasy Rep.		Iloilo......	180,900	**Tunisia**		Merthyr	
*Tananarive..	380,000	Manila......	1,356,000	Bizerte......	46,681	Tydfil......	57,710
Malawi		Manila, Gr...	3,100,000	*Tunis......	680,000	Swansea....	170,600
Blantyre-		*Quezon City.	482,400	Sfax......	65,635	SCOTLAND	
Limbe......	130,000	Zamboanga...	158,000	Sousse......	48,172	Aberdeen....	183,463
Malaysia		**Poland**		**Turkey**		Dundee......	183,744
*Kuala		Bydgoszcz....	231,000	Adana......	422,123	Edinburgh....	468,765
Lumpur....	316,230	Gdansk		*Ankara......	1,067,048	Glasgow......	979,798
Penang......	234,930	(Danzig)....	313,500	Bursa......	212,518	NORTHERN	
Maldive Islands		Krakow......	509,000	Istanbul......	2,302,438	IRELAND	
*Male......	11,202	Lodz......	737,400	Izmir......	627,496	Belfast......	406,800
Mali		Poznan......	431,700	**Uganda**		Londonderry..	56,300
*Bamako......	120,000	Szczecin		*Kampala....	46,736	**Upper Volta**	
Malta		(Stettin)....	302,900	**USSR**		*Ouagadougou	100,000
*Valletta......	18,000	*Warsaw......	1,232,000	Alma-Ata....	653,000	**Uruguay**	
Sliema......	23,000	Wroclaw		Astrakhan....	361,000	*Montevideo..	1,173,114
Mauritania		(Breslau)....	465,600	Baku......	1,175,000	**Venezuela**	
*Nouakchott..	20,000	**Portugal**		Barnaul......	395,000	Barquisimeto..	245,476
Mexico		Funchal......	99,645	Cheliabinsk....	820,000	*Caracas......	1,638,860
Chihuahua....	206,000	*Lisbon......	817,326	Dniepro-		Maracaibo....	517,717
Guadalajara..	1,048,351	Porto......	305,445	petrovsk....	790,000	Valencia......	201,105
Juarez......	379,000	**Rhodesia**		Donetsk......	823,000	**Vietnam**	
Leon......	275,335	*Salisbury....	324,800	Erevan......	652,000	Haiphong....	369,248
Mexicali......	291,000	**Romania**		Frunse......	385,000	*Hanoi......	643,576
*Mexico......	3,118,059	Arad......	125,553	Gorky......	1,100,000	Hue......	104,500
*Mexico, D.F.	6,016,000	Braila......	125,263	Gorlovka......	340,000	*Saigon......	2,000,000
Monterey......	821,843	*Bucharest....	1,372,130	Irkutsk......	409,000	Tourane......	110,500
Puebla......	346,000	Cluj......	205,189	Ivanovo......	398,000	Vinh......	150,000
SanLuisPotosi	186,000	Ploesti......	173,831	Izhevsk......	360,000	**Western Samoa**	
Torreon......	217,000	Timisoara....	170,232	Karaganda....	489,000	*Apia......	25,000
Veracrus......	183,000	**Saudi Arabia**		Kazan......	804,000	**Yemen**	
Mongolian Rep.		Jedda......	147,859	Kemerovo....	358,000	Hodeida......	40,000
*Ulan Bator..	250,000	Mecca......	158,908	Khabarovsk....	420,000	*Sana......	75,000
Morocco		*Riyadh......	169,185	Kharkov......	1,092,000	*Taiz......	25,000
Casablanca..	965,277	**Senegal**		Kiev......	1,383,000	**Yugoslavia**	
Fes......	216,133	*Dakar......	400,000	Krasnoyarsk..	557,000	*Belgrade....	700,000
Marrakesh....	243,134	**Sierra Leone**		Krasnodar....	395,000	Ljubljana......	160,000
Meknes......	175,943	*Freetown....	128,000	Krivoy Rog....	498,000	Sarajevo......	206,000
*Rabat......	227,445	**Singapore**		Kuibyshev....	969,000	Skopje......	172,000
Tangier......	141,714	*Singapore....	1,820,000	Leningrad....	3,665,000	Zagreb......	471,000
				Lugansk......	339,000	**Zambia**	
						*Lusaka......	151,418

The War in Vietnam

Efforts Toward Settlement; Chronology of Conflict

As 1967 drew toward its close the Johnson Administration remained on the defensive at home over the continued escalation and drawn-out nature of the war in Vietnam and, as some saw it, the failure to move ahead against poverty and the country's domestic ills. In a speech in New York **Nov. 9** President Johnson castigated critics of his foreign and domestic policies. At one point he shouted: "Well that's just pure bunk" when "stand-patters" and "nay-sayers" argue that we cannot make social progress and fight the war in Vietnam. "And far off at the other end of the political spectrum," the President said, "are those who say, 'What America has built is rotten. Let's tear it apart.' I say they are both wrong. I say we can meet our commitments at home and abroad—and we will."

At a press conference **Nov. 1** the President had said the anti-war demonstrators' "private proposals and statements have not contributed to the solution we so eagerly seek" in Vietnam.

Repeated efforts to bring the war to the negotiation table and effect a cease-fire had been rejected by the North Vietnamese through the year and political observers speculated that Hanoi was going to stick out the shooting war at least until after the 1968 U. S. Presidential elections in the hope that President Johnson would be defeated if he sought reelection.

The present war is a sequel to an earlier war between the French and the forces of Ho Chi Minh (the present leader of North Vietnam). At the end of World War II, Vietnamese nationalist and Communist groups were determined to achieve independence, but the French attempted to re-establish colonial rule over the Indo-Chinese states (Cambodia, Laos and Vietnam). The strongest of the Vietnamese nationalist groups was Ho Chi Minh's Communist-led Vietminh (abbreviated name of the League for the Independence of Vietnam). On Sept. 2, 1945, Ho declared Vietnam independent and announced the creation of the Democratic Republic of Vietnam (DRVN). The French recognized 'the DRVN Mar. 6, 1946, "as a free state within the French union." However, a series of blunders and misunderstandings by both sides led to armed conflict and the beginning of the French-Vietminh war Dec. 19, 1946.

As the war progressed, the French sought to enlist non-Communist support by turning to ex-Emperor of Vietnam Bao Dai as a rallying-point for the Vietnamese. With French approval, he formed on July 1, 1949, the State of Vietnam with its capital in Saigon.

The U. S. recognized the new state Feb. 7, 1960, and to assist it, President Truman announced June 27 that the U.S. was sending a 35-man Military Assistance Advisory Group (MAAG) to Indo-China to advise the troops there in the use of American weapons. Other assistance measures soon followed. On Dec. 23 the U. S. signed a Mutual Defense Assistance Agreement with Vietnam and on Sept. 7, 1951, the U. S. agreed to provide direct economic assistance to the Saigon government.

The following is a chronological listing of major developments thereafter:

May 8 to July 21, 1954—Geneva Conference on Indo-China attended by France, Britain, Russia, U. S., Democratic Republic of Vietnam, State of Vietnam, Laos, Cambodia and Communist China. France and North Vietnam agreed: to partition of Vietnam along 17th parallel, ban on new troops or bases, scheduling of reunification elections in July 1956, creation of International Control Commission composed of India, Canada and Poland to supervise implementation of the agreement. U. S. and South Vietnam do not sign agreement.

May 8, 1954—French stronghold of Dien Bien Phu in North Vietnam falls to Communist forces.

Oct. 24, 1954—President Eisenhower offers South Vietnam economic aid.

Feb. 12, 1955—U. S. agrees to train South Vietnamese army.

Feb. 19, 1955—SEATO protocol extended to offer protective cover of organization to Vietnam.

Oct. 23, 1955—South Vietnamese national referendum deposes Bao Dai, creates republic with Ngo Dinh Diem as first president. Diem says reunification elections as specified by Geneva Conference impossible because of intimidation by North Vietnam. Reunification elections never held.

Oct. 22, 1957—First injuries of U. S. advisers in Vietnam reported.

July 8, 1959—First U. S. troops killed in combat.

May 5, 1960—Upon request of South Vietnam, U. S. increases number of military advisers from 327 to 685.

Oct. 26, 1960—President Eisenhower pledges continued assistance to South Vietnam.

Dec. 1960—North Vietnam announces formation of the National Liberation Front of South Vietnam. Acts of terrorism in the South increase.

Apr. 3, 1961—Kennedy Administration signs Treaty of Amity and Economic Relations with South Vietnam.

Dec. 14, 1961—President Kennedy declares U. S. prepared to help Republic of South Vietnam "preserve its independence."

June 2, 1962—Majority report of International Control Commission says evidence shows North Vietnam to be supporting, organizing and carrying out hostile acts in South Vietnam.

Dec. 1962—U. S. force in Vietnam stands at 4,000 men.

Nov. 1, 1963—President Diem assassinated. Series of coups follows.

Dec., 1963—U. S. force in Vietnam numbers 15,000.

Aug. 2-4, 1964—U. S. destroyers Maddox and C. Turner Joy attacked by North Vietnamese torpedo boats in Gulf of Tonkin. President Johnson orders immediate retaliatory attacks.

Aug. 7, 1964—Congress approves Gulf of Tonkin Resolution giving President power to "take all necessary measures to repel any armed attack against the forces of the United States and to prevent further aggression."

Dec. 1964—U. S. force in Vietnam numbers 23,000.

Feb. 1965—Continuous U. S. bombing raids over North Vietnam started in effort to force Communists to conference table. Hanoi says negotiations will not be considered until U. S. forces withdraw.

Apr. 17, 1965—President Johnson in speech at Johns Hopkins University offers billion dollar aid program to SE Asia as soon as peace is achieved.

May 13-19, 1965—U. S. halts air raids against North Vietnam. No response from Hanoi.

June 8, 1965—U. S. commanders authorized to send American troops into combat.

July, 1965—President Johnson authorizes increase of U. S. force from 75,000 men to 125,000.

Dec. 24, 1965-Jan. 31, 1966—U. S. again suspends bombing of North Vietnam in hope of bringing foe to conference table. Hanoi rejects all peace feelers.

Feb. 6-7, 1966—President Johnson and South Vietnamese Premier Nguyen Ky meet in Honolulu. "Declaration of Honolulu" issued at end of meeting, declaring the two countries will continue to resist aggression.

June 29, 1966—U. S. bombs major installations near Hanoi and Haiphong for first time.

July 30, 1966—U. S. bombs 6-mile-wide demilitarized zone between North and South Vietnam.

Nov. 1966—U. S. forces in Vietnam number 358,000 men, with 33,000 more stationed in Thailand.

Nov. 12, 1966—U. S. dead killed in action in Vietnam from Jan. 1, 1961 to date—4,904.

Dec. 2, 1966—UN Secy. Gen. U Thant pledges new effort to end war.

Dec. 30, 1966—Britain proposes peace conference. Hanoi rejects suggestion Jan. 4, 1967.

Dec. 31, 1966-Jan. 2, 1967—New Year's truce.

Jan. 5, 1967—Defense Dept. announces total U. S. casualties since Jan. 1, 1961 are 6,664 dead, 37,738 wounded.

Feb. 8-12—U. S. suspends air raids during Lunar New Year truce and two days beyond. No response from Hanoi.

Mar. 2, 1967—Sen. Robert F. Kennedy proposes Administration halt bombing as part of 3-point peace plan. Secy. Rusk says there is nothing new in the Kennedy proposals and that Hanoi has already rejected similar peace overtures.

Mar. 20-21, 1967—President Johnson confers with South Vietnamese leaders on Guam. War and election of civilian government in South Vietnam discussed.

Mar. 21, 1967—Ho Chi Minh rejects previously undisclosed proposal by President Johnson in February for peace talks.

(continued on page 44)

*U. S. Military Casualties in Vietnam

Source: Secretary of Defense. As of Nov. 11, 1967

Casualties from hostile forces action Since Jan. 1, 1961	Army	Navy[1]	Marine	Air force	Total
1. Killed....................	6,868	380	4,578	— 191	12,017
2. Wounded or injured:					
a. Died of wounds..........	827	40	561	17	1,445
b. Nonfatal wounds:					
Hospital care required...............	28,044	1,060	19,172	289	48,565
Hospital care not required...........	23,796	1,984	16,532	1,094	43,406
3. Missing:					
a. Died while missing..........	881	53	5	214	1,153
b. Returned to control..........	30	7	4	13	54
c. Current missing.............	66	88	60	392	606
4. Captured or interned:					
a. Died while captured or interned........	5	....	....	1	....
b. Returned to control..........	6				6
c. Current captured or interned.............	14	103	9	94	220
5. Deaths:					
a. From aircraft accidents/incidents					
Fixed Wing......................	45	97	28	356	526
Helicopter........................	430	25	128	11	594
b. From ground action.................	8,106	351	4,988	56	13,501
†Total deaths........................	8,581	473	5,144	423	14,621
Casualties Not the Result of Actions by Hostile Forces					
6. Current missing......................	27				27
7. Deaths:					
a. From aircraft accidents/incidents:					
Fixed Wing...........................	118	52	24	144	338
Helicopter...........................	473	12	77	....	562
b. From other causes..................	1,117	334	471	106	2,028
Total deaths..................	1,708	398	572	250	2,928

Combat Deaths for Other Forces (Since Jan. 1, 1961)	S. Vietnam[2]	Other Free World Forces	Enemy
Total deaths...........	51,184	1,563	237,156

†Sum of lines 1, 2a, 3a and 4a. [1]Navy figures include a number of Coast Guard casualties. [2]Republic of Vietnam Armed Forces.

*In an article copyrighted in October, 1967, by Newspaper Enterprise Association, it was stated that the total U.S. casualties in Vietnam would be actually 40% less than the figure reported by the Defense Department, if judged by the standards of World War II and the Korean War. The discrepancy, it was stated, resulted from a 1963 decision to count as wounded anyone receiving the Order of the Purple Heart. The military services award the Purple Heart for virtually any wound, no matter how superficial, the NEA article said.

The official figures above show that nearly half of the 91,971 nonfatally wounded did not require hospitalization. Of the 107,478 enemy-inflicted casualties reported through Nov. 11, 1967, according to Pentagon sources, 83% had returned to duty by that date or were expected to return to duty; 2.8% had been or were expected to be discharged for disability; 0.8% were missing or captured. The remaining 13.4% were killed in action, died of wounds or died while captured or missing.

Half of the nonfatal casualties who returned to duty had been outpatients (actually never off duty) or were off duty overnight or for only a day or two. One-fourth were hospitalized for 30 days and returned to duty. One-sixth were hospitalized for more than 30 days but less than 60 days and returned to duty. One-twelfth were hospitalized for more than 60 days and returned to duty.

Winners of Medal of Honor in Vietnam War

Source: Department of Defense. Data through Oct. 25, 1967

Capt. Roger H. C. Donlon, 30, U. S. Army, of Saugerties, N. Y. Award presented by President Johnson Dec. 5, 1964, for "conspicuous gallantry" in South Vietnamese battle July 6, 1964, during which Donlon received 4 wounds. (First Medal of Honor awarded since Korean War.)

*Sgt. Larry F. Pierce, 24, U. S. Army, of Wasco, Calif. Award presented posthumously by President Johnson Feb. 24, 1966. Pierce lost his life Sept. 20, 1965, when he threw himself on an exploding mine.

*Pfc. Milton L. Olive 3rd, 19, U. S. Army, of Chicago. Award presented posthumously by President Johnson Apr. 21, 1966. Olive was killed Oct. 22, 1965, when he threw himself upon a Vietcong grenade to save the lives of 4 members of his platoon. He was the first Negro to win the award in Vietnam, 8th Negro to be so honored.

Lt. Charles Q. Williams, U. S. Army, of Vance, S. C. Award presented by President Johnson June 23, 1966, for Williams' heroism in directing the defense of a Special Forces camp against an attack June 10, 1965, by Vietcong who outnumbered his men by 5 to 1. Though wounded, Williams managed to direct an evacuation by helicopter.

*Seabee Marvin Glen Shields, U. S. Navy, Port Townsend, Wash. Award presented posthumously by President Johnson Sept. 13, 1966. Shields was cited for heroism in a Vietnamese battle June 10, 1965, in which he saved the lives of many of his comrades; although twice wounded, he continued to supply his comrades with ammunition to return the fire. He was the first Seabee to win the award.

Sgt. Robert E. O'Malley, 23, U. S. Marine Corps, of Woodside, Queens (New York City). Award presented by President Johnson Dec. 6, 1966. O'Malley, the first Marine to win the Medal of Honor in Vietnam, was a corporal Aug. 18, 1965, when he leaped into an enemy trench and killed 8 Vietcong.

First Lt. Walter J. Marm, Jr., 25, U. S. Army, of Washington, Pa. Award presented by Secy. of the Army Stanley R. Resor Dec. 19, 1966. Marm was a second lieutenant Nov. 14, 1965, when he was credited with killing 18 North Vietnamese soldiers who were firing on his platoon.

Maj. Bernard F. Fisher, 40, U. S. Air Force, of Kuna, Idaho. Award presented by President Johnson Jan. 19, 1967, for Fisher's heroism in landing his plane under fire on a battle-torn airstrip in South Vietnam Mar. 10, 1966, and rescuing a fellow pilot who had crash-landed.

*Second Lt. Robert J. Hibbs, U. S. Army, of Cedar Falls, Iowa. Award presented posthumously by Secy. of the Army Stanley R. Resor Jan. 26, 1967. Hibbs was cited for his heroism on Mar. 5, 1966, when he rescued a wounded comrade at the cost of his own life.

*First Lt. Frank S. Reasoner, 27, U. S. Marine Corps, of Kellogg, Idaho. Award presented posthumously by Secy. of the Navy Jan. 31, 1967. Reasoner was killed July 12, 1965, while covering the evacuation of his radio operator while his unit was under attack by a much larger Vietcong force.

*Lance Corporal Joe C. Paul, 19, U. S. Marine Corps, of Vandalia, Ohio. Award presented posthumously Feb. 7, 1967, by Under Secy. of the Navy Robert H. Baldwin. Paul was fatally wounded Aug. 18, 1965, when he placed himself between the enemy and several wounded comrades to provide covering fire while they were evacuated.

Capt. Harvey C. Barnum, Jr., 26, U. S. Marine Corps, of Cheshire, Conn. Award presented Feb. 27, 1967, by Secy. of the Navy Paul H. Nitze. Barnum was a first lieutenant Dec. 18, 1965, when, after his company commander was killed, he took over and led a counterattack against heavy enemy fire.

Specialist 6 Lawrence Joel, 39, U. S. Army, of Winston-Salem, N. C. Award presented by President Johnson Mar. 9, 1967. The first medic to be so honored in the Vietnam War, Joel was cited for his heroism Nov. 8, 1965, in caring for the wounded although himself wounded and under fire.

*Specialist 4 Daniel Fernandez, 20, U. S. Army, of Los Lunas, N. M. Award presented posthumously by President Johnson Apr. 6, 1967. Fernandez was killed Feb. 18, 1966, when he threw himself on a Vietcong grenade to save the lives of 4 fellow soldiers.

*Staff Sgt. Peter S. Connor, 33, U. S. Marine Corps, a native of Orange, N. J. Award presented posthumously by President Johnson May 2, 1967. Connor was a platoon sergeant when he was fatally wounded Feb. 25, 1966, while hugging a grenade to his body to save his men from harm.

*Sgt. James W. Robinson, Jr., 26, U. S. Army, of Annandale, Va. Award presented posthumously by Secy. of the Army Stanley R. Resor July 12, 1967. In action against the Vietcong Apr. 11, 1966 Robinson dragged 3 wounded men to safety and was himself wounded. He seized two grenades and charged an enemy machine gun position, destroying it as he fell dead.

Gunnery Sgt. Jimmie E. Howard, 38, U. S. Marine Corps, of San Diego, Calif. Award presented by President Johnson Aug. 21, 1967. Howard was a staff sergeant June 16, 1966, when his 18-man platoon was attacked by a Vietcong battalion. His citation said his extraordinary courage and fighting spirit, despite his serious wounds, were largely responsible for preventing the loss of his entire platoon.

*Staff Sgt. Jimmy G. Stewart, 24, U. S. Army, of Columbus, Ga. Award presented posthumously Aug. 24, 1967, by Secy. of the Army Stanley R. Resor. Stewart was killed May 18, 1966, in a one-man stand to protect his wounded comrades, while he killed at least 8 Vietcong.

Sgt. David C. Dolby, 21, U. S. Army, of Oaks, Pa. Award presented by President Johnson Sept. 28, 1967. Dolby was a Specialist 4 May 21, 1966, when he took command from his dying platoon leader, rallied his men to stand fast under intense fire, and personally destroyed several enemy positions.

*First Lt. James A. Gardner, 23, U. S. Army, of Dyersburg, Tenn. Award presented posthumously Oct. 19, 1967, in Defense Dept. ceremony. Gardner died on his 23rd birthday in 1966 while waging a one-man rifle and grenade attack on enemy bunkers.

Maj. Howard V. Lee, 34, U. S. Marine Corps, of New York City. Award presented by President Johnson Oct. 25, 1967. Lee was a captain Aug. 8-9, 1966, when he went to the aid of a beleaguered platoon by helicopter, saved his men from capture and dealt the enemy a defeat.

*Awarded posthumously.

The Medal of Honor; Other Top U. S. Military Awards

The Medal of Honor is the highest military award for bravery that can be given to any individual in the United States of America. It is presented to its recipients, usually by the President, "in the name of the Congress of the United States," and for this reason it is often called the Congressional Medal of Honor.

The law, as amended in 1963, provides that the President may award the Medal of Honor to any person who, while a member of the armed forces, "distinguished himself conspicuously by gallantry and intrepidity at the risk of his life above and beyond the call of duty—(1) while engaged in an action against an enemy of the United States; (2) while engaged in military operations involving conflict with an opposing foreign force; or (3) while serving with friendly foreign forces engaged in an armed conflict against an opposing armed force in which the United States is not a belligerent party."

Criteria for awarding the medal to officers or enlisted men of the Army, Navy, Marine Corps, Air Force and Coast Guard are identical, although the actual medals vary slightly in design. On rare occasions, Congress has enacted special legislation to award the Medal of Honor for individual exploits in peacetime. The Navy Medal of Honor has been awarded for heroism by noncombatants on several occasions.

Distinguished Service Cross, Navy Cross, Air Force Cross. These decorations, all ranked on the same level, may be awarded to a person who, while serving in any capacity with the Army, Navy, Marine Corps or Air Force, "distinguishes himself by extraordinary heroism not justifying the award of a Medal of Honor."

Distinguished Service Medal. Awarded to any person who, while serving with the armed forces in any capacity, "distinguishes himself by exceptionally meritorious service to the United States in a duty of great responsibility."

Silver Star. Awarded to a person who, while serving in any capacity with the armed forces, "is cited for gallantry in action that does not warrant a Medal of Honor or Distinguished Service Cross."

Other Awards. Lesser awards for heroism or extraordinary achievement include the Bronze Star, Distinguished Flying Cross, Soldiers Medal, Navy and Marine Corps Medal, and Airman's Medal. The Purple Heart, originally for bravery, is now given to those wounded in action.

Debt Owed U. S. Arising from World War I as of June 30, 1967

Source: Treasury Department

Country	Original Indebtedness	Interest thru June 30, 1967	Cumulative Payments		Unmatured Principal*	Principal and interest due and unpaid*
			Principal	Interest		
Armenia........	$ 11,959,917	$ 28,587,070	$ 17	....	....	$ 40,546,970
Austria¹........	26,843,148	44,058	862,668	....	$ 882,626	25,141,913
Belgium........	419,837,630	318,884,720	19,157,630	$ 33,033,642	197,580,000	488,951,077
Cuba...........	10,000,000	2,286,751	10,000,000	2,286,751	....	....
Czechoslovakia	185,071,023	111,060,093	·¹,829,914	304,178	86,355,000	189,642,023
Estonia........	16,466,012	21,869,780	....	1,248,432	9,007,000	28,080,360
Finland........	8,999,999	11,476,565	²4,292,999	²11,476,565	4,707,000	....
France.........	4,089,689,588	3,246,978,853	226,039,588	260,036,302	1,772,868,667	5,077,723,883
Great Britain..	4,802,181,641	6,980,131,958	434,181,641	1,590,672,656	2,433,000,000	7,324,459,301
Greece.........	³34,319,843	3,230,509	983,922	3,143,133	21,205,921	12,217,378
Hungary⁴.......	1,982,555	2,775,445	73,995	482,924	1,095,545	3,105,536
Italy..........	2,042,364,319	339,839,470	37,464,319	63,365,560	1,168,900,000	1,112,473,909
Latvia.........	6,888,664	9,250,660	9,200	752,349	3,801,800	11,575,976
Liberia........	26,000	10,471	26,000	10,471	....	....
Lithuania......	6,432,465	8,612,114	234,783	1,003,173	3,487,367	10,319,255
Nicaragua⁵.....	141,950	26,625	141,950	26,625	....	....
Poland.........	207,344,297	279,443,464	⁶1,287,297	21,359,000	115,807,000	348,334,464
Rumania........	68,359,192	51,261,664	⁷4,498,632	⁷292,375	31,923,000	82,906,849
Russia.........	192,601,297	476,089,679	....	⁸8,750,311	....	659,940,665
Yugoslavia.....	63,577,712	25,825,277	1,952,712	636,059	35,389,000	51,425,218
Total......	$12,195,087,259	$11,917,685,236	$761,037,272	$1,998,830,514	$5,886,009,926	$15,466,844,782

*To arrive at the total outstanding figure add the figures in the two columns together.
¹The Federal Republic of Germany has recognized liability for securities falling due between March 12, 1938 and May 8, 1945.
²$6,360,250.26 has been made available for educational exchange programs with Finland pursuant to 20 U.S.C. 222-224.
³Includes $13,155,921.00 refunded by the agreement of May 28, 1964. The agreement was ratified by Congress Nov. 5, 1966.
⁴Interest payments from December 15, 1932 to June 15, 1937 were paid in pengo equivalent.
⁵The indebtedness of Nicaragua was canceled pursuant to the agreement of April 14, 1938.
⁶Excludes claim allowance of $1,813,428.69 dated December 15, 1929.
⁷Excludes payment of $100,000.00 on June 14, 1940 as a token of good faith.
⁸Principally proceeds from liquidation of Russian assets in the United States.

American Military Cemeteries and Memorials on Foreign Soil

Administered by the American Battle Monuments Commission, Washington, D. C.

(Numbers of graves, and numbers of commemorated missing in parentheses)

WORLD WAR I CEMETERIES

Aisne-Marne, near Belleau (Aisne) France (2288-1060)
Brookwood (Surrey) England (468-563)
Flanders Field, Waregem, Belgium (368-43)
Meuse-Argonne, Romagne (Meuse), France (14,-246-954)
Oise-Aisne, Seringes (Aisne), near Fere-en-Tardenois (Aisne), France (6012-241)
St. Mihiel, Thiaucourt (M. et M.), France (4,152-284)
Somme, Bony (Aisne), France (1837-333)
Suresnes (Seine), France (1541-974). In this cemetery rest also 24 of our unknown Dead of World War II. The World War I chapel was, by the addition of two loggias, converted into a shrine to commemorate our Dead of both Wars. Senior representatives of the American and French governments assemble here on ceremonial occasions to pay homage to our military Dead of these wars.

MONUMENTS

Andenarde, Belgium.
Bellicourt (Aisne), France.
Brest (Finistère), France.
Cantigny (Somme), France.
Château-Thierry (Aisne), France
Gibraltar.
Kemmel, near Ypres, Belgium.
Montfaucon (Meuse), France.
Montsec (Meuse), France.
Sommepy (Marne), France.
Tours (Indre et Loire), France.

WORLD WAR II CEMETERIES

Ardennes, near Neuville-en-Condroz, Belgium (5,-271-462)
Brittany, near St. James (Manche), France 4,410-498)
Cambridge, near Cambridge, England, (3,811-5125)
Epinal, near Epinal (Vosges), France (5,255-424)

Florence, near Florence (Tuscany), Italy (4,402-1409)
Henri-Chapelle, near Henri-Chapelle, Belgium (7,989-450)
Lorraine, St. Avold (Moselle), France (10,489-444)
Luxembourg, near Luxembourg (City), France (5,076-170)
Manila, near Manila, Republic of the Philippines (17,206-36.279)
Netherlands, Margraten, Holland (8,301-1722)
Normandy, near St. Laurent (Calvados), France (9,386-1557)
North Africa, Carthage, Tunisia (2,840-3724)
Rhône, Draguignan (Var), France (861-293)
Sicily-Rome, Nettuno, Italy (7,862-3094)

To commemorate those who met their deaths in the American coastal waters of the Atlantic and Pacific Oceans the Commission has erected a memorial in Battery Park, New York City, on which are inscribed 4,596 names, and at the Presidio of San Francisco, California, which carries 412 names.

World War II dead are also buried in Sitka National Cemetery, Sitka, Alaska, Puerto Rico National Cemetery, Bayamon, Puerto Rico, and the National Memorial Cemetery of the Pacific, Honolulu, Hawaii. These cemeteries, all on American soil, are under the jurisdiction of The Office of the Chief of Support Services, Department of the Army, Washington, D. C. 20315. At the Honolulu Cemetery the American Battle Monuments Commission has erected a memorial which records the names of 18,093 Missing of World War II and 8,187 Missing resulting from the Korean operations.

The Commission also maintains a cemetery in Mexico City where the remains of 750 Americans who gave their lives in the Mexican War (1846-1848) are buried.

The decoration of graves with natural cut flowers only, is permitted in the cemeteries under the control of The American Battle Monuments Commission. The Commission is glad to assist interested persons in arranging with local florists in foreign countries to furnish such decorations.

ADJUTANT GENERAL'S FIGURES OF CIVIL WAR DEATHS

Figures reported from the Adjutant General's Office previous to the above revision, and accepted for many years, are as follows:

Union Army, according to records in the office of the Adjutant General of the War Department in Washington—killed or died of wounds, 110,070 (6,365 officers, 103,705 men); died of disease, 224,586 (2,795 officers, 221,791 men); other deaths, 24,872 (424 officers, 24,448 men). Totals, 359,528 (9,584 officers, 349,944 men).

Confederate Army, estimated, no official records in the office of the Adjutant General of the War Department in Washington—killed in battle, 52,954 (2,086 officers, 50,868 men); died of wounds, 21,570 (1,246 officers, 20,324 men); died of disease, 59,297 (1,294 officers, 58,003 men). Total, 113,821 (4,626 officers, 129,195 men).

The Israeli-Arab War
Six Days That Shook The Middle East

The balance of power was shattered in the Middle East in 1967 as Israel in a spectacular six-day war smashed the armed forces of the United Arab Republic, Syria and Jordan in a display of military prowess that amazed the world.

In the initial hours of the war, June 5, Israeli planes, sweeping in low over the Mediterranean to avoid radar detection, destroyed some 450 Arab aircraft, most of them on the ground. With complete mastery in the air, Israeli ground forces swarmed over the Gaza Strip and chopped-up a 100,000-man Egyptian army in the Sinai Peninsula in a drive to the Suez Canal that broke the UAR blockade of the Gulf of Aqaba. In a simultaneous action, the Old City of Jerusalem was captured and all Jordanian territory west of the Jordan River bordering on Israel was occupied. On the third front, Israeli forces in a dogged ground battle secured

strategic heights 12 miles inside Syria from which Israeli border settlements in northern Galilee had been shelled for years.

By the time UN-arranged cease-fire agreements went into effect, Israel had conquered territory 4 times its own size, killed some 35,000 Arabs and captured thousands more, destroyed between 600 and 700 Soviet-built Egyptian tanks as well as capturing hundreds of tanks, armed personnel carriers and thousands of dollars worth of military equipment. Israeli losses of 679 dead and 2,563 wounded were reported June 11.

The prelude to the Israeli attack began with a series of what appeared to be routine border incidents with Syria—the kind of sporadic Arab terrorist raids and shelling that had broken out along Israel's borders ever since the 1956 Suez-Sinai campaigns. Clashes between the two

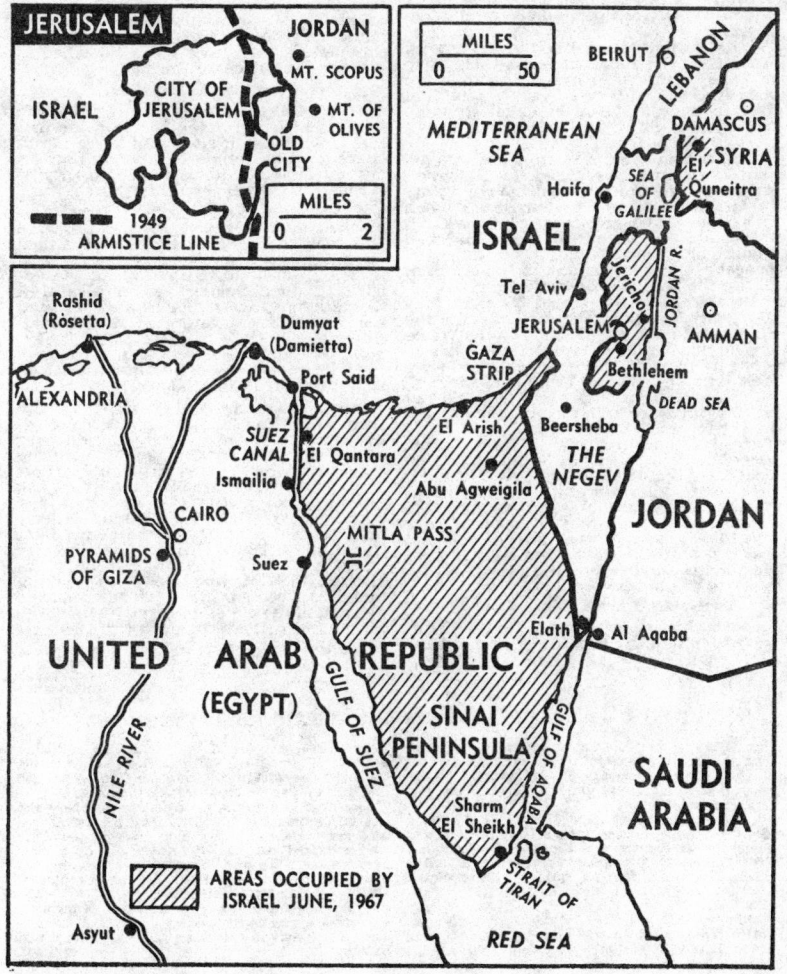

earlier in the year were followed by an Israeli "reprisal" raid Apr. 7 in which Syria lost 6 Russian-built jets. But finally, Arab terrorists incursions into the area of Galilee May 5 and May 8 provoked Israel to warn Syria in a note to the UN Security Council May 11 that Israel "regards itself as fully entitled to act in self-defense."

After this the crisis mounted rapidly as Egypt and Syria began to mass troops along the Israel border May 14-20—a move that Israel met by a partial mobilization of its reserves and corresponding build-up of its ground forces.

UN Force Withdrawn

Egyptian President Gamal Abdel Nasser, apparently stung by taunts from Jordan and Saudi Arabia that he had been hiding behind the skirts of the 3,400-man United Nations Emergency Force which for 10 years had patrolled the 117-mile long armistice line between Egypt and Israel, regained the world spotlight and Arab leadership May 18 by demanding the withdrawal of the UN force. UN Secy. Gen. U Thant yielded with "serious misgivings" to Nasser's demand and formally ended the UNEF's peace-keeping mission May 19.

With the withdrawal of the UN troops, Nasser rapidly reoccupied the Gaza Strip and the heights at Sharm el Sheikh at the mouth of the Gulf of Aqaba, leaving him free to impose a ban on Israel shipping through the Strait of Tiran to the Israeli port of Elath.

Nasser waited 3 days before announcing that the Strait was closed to all Israeli shipping. The move erased the gains won by Israel, France and Britain in 1956 when in a 5-day war Israel conquered the Sinai Peninsula and withdrew from Sharm el Sheikh only on the condition that the UN peacekeeping force maintain Israel's right to use the 3-mile-wide Strait of Tiran.

President Johnson urged the UAR May 23 to lift the blockade, saying that the U. S. considered the Gulf of Aqaba "to be an international waterway." Futile sessions of the UN Security Council were held but the Soviet Union rejected all peacekeeping proposals made in and out of the international forum, placing the blame for the crisis on Israel.

Nasser, apparently leading from strength, continued to taunt Israel in speeches, declaring at one point that "if war comes our main objective will be the destruction of Israel." For their part, the Israelis announced that they would take "political action" to end the blockade and Foreign Minister Abba Eban flew to London, Paris and Washington May 24-26 for a series of high-level talks.

Moshe Dayan Takes Over

But as the days passed, the UN floundered impotently, and the Western maritime powers vacillated on plans to run the blockade and open the Gulf, more militant political leaders in Israel came to the fore. On June 1 Maj. Gen. Moshe Dayan, hero of the 1956 Sinai campaign, was appointed Israel's Defense Minister. Convinced that Israel could count on no outside help in breaking the stranglehold on the port of Elath, Israel apparently decided to hit in force upon the next Arab provocation, and on June 5 shelling by the Jordanians and Syrians unleashed the Israeli attack.

Within 48 hours it was clear that the Arab forces had been routed, and the impasse at the UN broke as the 15-nation Security Council June 6 voted a cease-fire resolution after the Soviet Union dropped its demand that Israel withdraw its troops from the conquered territory. The same day Nasser broke off diplomatic relations with the U. S. and Britain, accusing them of having used their warplanes to aid the Israelis, a charge vehemently denied by both governments. June 9 Nasser announced he was resigning as president but the following day yielded to the "people's will" and said he would stay in office. The Soviet Union broke off diplomatic relations with Israel June 10, threatening "sanctions" if Israel failed to observe the UN cease-fire.

Cease-fire Is Accepted

All fighting was ended by June 10 as the Arabs and Israel accepted the cease-fire. But Israel made it clear that it would not be content to return to its old frontiers and on June 28 annexed the Old City of Jerusalem, formally reuniting the city.

A Soviet move to censure Israel was blocked in the Security Council June 14 and shortly afterward the Soviets called for an emergency session of the General Assembly in a bid to circumvent the Security Council. Soviet Premier Aleksei N. Kosygin flew to New York June 17 to head his country's delegation at the General Assembly. After a show of political coyness, President Johnson and the Soviet Premier met in a summit conference in Glassboro, N. J., June 23 and 25.

The UN ceasefire was observed by both sides with relatively minor violations until Oct. 21, when the Israeli destroyer Elath was sunk by the Egyptians, using Soviet-supplied guided missiles off Port Said. Forty-three Israelis were killed and 48 wounded in the attack. Israel and Egypt engaged Oct. 24 in a 3-hour artillery duel across the southern end of the Suez Canal, in which the Israelis left the city of Suez ablaze and claimed to have destroyed 80% of the UAR's oil refining facilities located there. The renewed fighting underscored the uneasiness of the peace and activated fears of a full-scale resumption of the war.

Expo 67 Breaks All Exposition Attendance Records

Canada's growing stature as a great nation drew international recognition in 1967 with celebrations of the 100th anniversary of the country's Confederation—most spectacularly with the huge success of Expo 67.

Total admissions to Expo 67 were 50,306,648, a record for a one-season world's fair; the previous holder of the record was the 1958 Brussels fair with 41,454,412. So popular was Expo 67 that the attendance came close to equalling the two-year total of the 1964-65 New York World's Fair, 51,607,037.

Most heavily attended of the pavilions was Soviet Russia's, which was also the costliest, with about 13,000,000 visitors. Canada's own exhibit drew 11,000,000. The U. S. pavilion, a sparkling geodesic sphere 250 ft. in diameter, was 3rd with 9,000,000 guests. Visitors from the U. S. accounted for 45% of Expo attendance, Canadians 53%.

The final attendance figures were far above the pre-fair estimate of 35,000,000, and the deficit was also considerably higher than expected, reaching an estimated $250,000,000, according to a Fair spokesman. This was to be shared 50% by the Canadian Government, 37.5% by the Province of Quebec and 12.5% by Montreal.

There were plans to keep much of Expo as a permanent municipal exhibit, including turning the U. S. pavilion into a gigantic arboretum and aviary.

Selective Service Act of 1967; Selective Service System

Source: Selective Service System, Washington, D. C.

Legislation providing for Selective Service has been in effect continuously since 1948. The induction provisions of the present Military Selective Service Act of 1967 were extended until July 1, 1971, by Act of Congress, June 20, 1967.

The Selective Service System registers, classifies, and selects men for induction into the Armed Forces. Most of the needs of the services are met by enlistments. But it is generally recognized that most men who enlist do so in order to choose a time to serve and a service of their choice, as an alternative to later induction. The military services rely on the prospect of induction to prompt enlistments. The Selective Service System, by induction, supplies the balance required to meet service needs.

The System also aids in maintaining the strength and the stability of the Reserve and National Guard. Deferments are provided for continued satisfactory participation in these reserve programs. Sufficient satisfactory participation in the Ready Reserve qualifies a man for Class IV-A as having completed service under the Military Selective Service Act of 1967.

The draft of married men into the Armed Forces was halted by Pres. Kennedy Sept. 10, 1963. The order changed the sequence of selection so that married men will be called only after all single men 19-26 have been called. Pres. Johnson on Aug. 26, 1965 changed the order of selection so that married men were no longer deferred. This was necessary because the pool of single men was no longer ample to fill draft quotas to meet the increased needs of the Armed Forces.

STANDBY RESERVE

In addition to helping maintain the active and reserve forces, the Selective Service System has statutory responsibility for the selective recall of the nation's Standby Reserve when their recall to duty is authorized. The System must make and keep current a determination of which individual members of the Standby Reserve are available for recall and which should remain in the civilian economy because of occupations vital to the nation or because recall would result in extreme hardship to dependents. The System is thus responsible for the proper utilization of this segment of the manpower resource. numbering at this time about 513,076 men and women as of June 30, 1967.

DEFERMENTS AND EXEMPTIONS

The law states that selection for service is to be accomplished in a manner "consistent with the maintenance of an effective national economy." The operation of the System has had the effect, through the prospect of deferment, of inducing men to prepare for, enter into, and remain in, civilian activities essential to national strength. The new Act of 1967 provides for the deferment of persons satisfactorily pursuing a full-time course of instruction at a college, university, or similar institution of learning who request such deferment. Such deferment shall continue until the registrant completes the requirements of his baccalaureate degree, fails to pursue satisfactorily a full-time course of instruction, or attains the age of 24, whichever occurs first.

A registrant who has received a student deferment after July 1, 1967, and has been awarded a baccalaureate degree may not subsequently be classified in I-S (C) or III-A on the role basis of fatherhood.

After Oct. 1, 1967, only graduate students pursuing medical studies or in other fields identified by the Director of Selective Service after receiving advice from the National Security Council may receive graduate student deferments. Students entering graduate school for the first time in October 1967 may be deferred for one year if entering the first class commencing after completing the requirements for admission. Students entering their second or subsequent year of graduate school without interruption in October 1967 may be deferred for one additional year to earn a master's degree or not to exceed a total of five years to earn a doctorate or professional degree or one additional year whichever is greater.

Deferments also are provided for fathers, extreme hardship to dependents, agricultural and industrial occupations, apprentices, some officials, sole surviving sons, some aliens, ministers and divinity students, and for those physically, mentally, or morally not qualified for military service.

INDUCTIONS

The number of men inducted since 1948 through June 1967 was 3,872,274, which included 103,467 for the Marine Corps and 30,080 for the Navy. Calls by month since January 1967 were: Jan. 15,600; Feb. 10,900; March 11,900; April 11,400; May 18,000; June 19,800; July 19,900; Aug. 29,000; Sept. 25,000; Oct. 17,000; Nov. 22,000; and Dec. 18,200.

Physicians, dentists and allied specialist categories are liable for service under the same conditions that apply to all registrants. The law gives the President authority to order these registrants to active duty involuntarily from the Reserve. It also provides that the Secretary of Defense may requisition registrants by specialty. The prospect of induction of these registrants on special calls influence them to apply for and accept reserve commissions. They are then ordered to two years of active duty as service needs dictate.

SEQUENCE OF SELECTION

Registrants are selected for induction in the following order: (1) Delinquents 19 and older in the order of dates of birth, oldest first; (2) Volunteers under 26 in order of volunteering; (3) Nonvolunteers 19 to 26 who do not have a wife with whom they maintain a home, oldest first; (4) Nonvolunteers 19 to 26 who have a wife with whom they maintain a home, oldest first; (5) Nonvolunteers over 26, youngest first; (6) Nonvolunteers 18½ to 19 years, oldest first.

CLASSIFICATION

The registrant is placed by the local board in one of the following classes.

Class I-A: Available for military service.

Class I-A-O—Conscientious objector available for non-combatant military service only.

Class I-C: Member of the Armed Forces of the United States, Environmental Science Services Administration, or the Public Health Service.

Class I-D: Member of reserve component or student taking military training.

Class I-O: Conscientious objector available for civilian work contributing to the maintenance of the national health, safety, or interest.

Class I-S: Student deferred by law until graduation from high school or attainment of age of 20, or until end of his academic year at a college or university.

Class I-W: Conscientious objector performing civilian work contributing to the maintenance of the national health, safety, or interest, or who has completed such work.

Class I-Y: Registrant qualified for military service only in time of war or national emergency.

Class II-A: Registrant deferred because of civilian occupation (except agriculture and activity in study).

Class II-C: Registrant deferred because of agricultural occupation.

Class II-S: Registrant deferred because of activity in study.

Class III-A: Registrant with a child or children; and registrant deferred by reason of extreme hardship to dependents.

Class IV-A: Registrant who has completed service; sole surviving son.

Class IV-B: Officials deferred by law.

Class IV-C: Aliens

Class IV-D: Ministers of religion or divinity students.

Class IV-F: Registrant not qualified for any military service.

Class V-A: Registrant over the age of liability for military service.

SELECTIVE SERVICE SYSTEM

The Selective Service System has a National Headquarters at 1724 F Street N. W., Washington 25, D. C.; a state hq. in each state and similar hq. for New York City, the District of Columbia, the Virgin Islands, Puerto Rico, Guam, and the Panama Canal Zone—a total of 56. Approximately 4,000 local draft boards of 3 or more unpaid civilians, function one in each county except in sparsely populated areas, or in heavily populated urban areas. An appeal board is situated in each Federal judicial district.

Deaths—Dec. 1, 1966 to Dec. 1, 1967

A

Abrams, Benjamin, 74; founder of Emerson Radio and Phonograph Corp.; White Plains, N. Y., June 23.

Alexander, A. L., 61; moderator of radio's "Good Will Court"; New York, Feb. 23.

Alger, Frederick Jr.; 59; former U. S. ambassador to Belgium; Grosse Pointe, Mich., Jan. 5.

al-Kuwatly, Shukri, 76; former president of Syria; Beirut, Lebanon, June 30.

Amberg, Richard, 55; publisher St. Louis Globe Democrat; New York, Sept. 3.

Andrews, Laverne, 51; singer; oldest of the Andrews Sisters trio; Hollywood, May 8.

Anfuso, Victor L., 61; N. Y. State Supreme Court Justice, ex-Congressman; New York, Dec. 28.

Angell, Sir Norman, 94; 1933 Nobel Peace Prize winner; Croydon, Surrey, England, Oct. 7.

Attlee, Clement, 84; former British Prime Minister; London, Oct. 7.

Auer, Mischa, 62; actor; Rome, Mar. 5.

B

Babson, Roger, 92; stock analyst; predicted '29 crash; Mountain Lake, Fla., Mar. 5.

Barden, Graham, 70; ex-Representative from N. C.; New Bren, N. C., Jan. 29.

Barnett, Claude A., 77; founder of the Associated Negro Press; Chicago, Aug. 2.

Barrows, Lewis O., 73; former gov. Maine; Pittsfield, Me., Jan. 30.

Barton, Bruce, 80, founder of Batten, Barton, Durstine & Osborn, ad agency; New York, July 5.

Bauhan, Rolf W., 74; architect; New Hope, Pa., Dec. 4.

Belaunde, Victor A., 83; Peruvian diplomat, UN Rep.; New York, Dec. 14.

Bickford, Charles, 78; actor; "Johnny Belinda"; Hollywood, Nov. 9.

Big Tree, Chief John, 92; posed for the Indian head nickel; Syracuse, New York, July 6.

Block, Martin, 64; pioneer radio disk jockey; Englewood, New Jersey Sept. 19.

Bracci, Francesco Cardinal, 87; canon law expert; Rome, Mar. 24.

Brain, Lord, 71; neurologist, medical leader; London, Dec. 29.

Branco, Humberto Castelo, 66; former president of Brazil; Rio De Janeiro, July 18.

Breen, Richard L., 47; screen writer, Sherman Oaks, Calif. Feb. 1.

Brereton, Gen. Lewis, 77; developed technique of dive bombing with Gen. Billy Mitchell; Washington, July 19.

Buckley, Charles, 76; politician; Bronx Cty. (N. Y.) Democrat; New York, Jan. 22.

Bullitt, William C., 76; first U. S. envoy to Soviet Union; Paris, Feb. 15.

Burnette, Smiley, 55; actor (Charlie Pratt in tv's "Petticoat Junction") Encino, Calif., Feb. 16.

C

Campbell, Donald, 45; holder world water speed record; Coniston, England, Jan. 4.

Campbell, Jimmy, 64; composer of "Show Me the Way to Go Home"; London, Aug. 18.

Campbell, Thomas, 62; publisher Iron Age magazine; New York, Oct. 11.

Cardijn, Joseph Cardinal, 85; founded Young Christian Workers movement; Louvain, Belgium, July 25.

Carnera, Primo, 60; former world heavyweight boxing champion; Sequals, Italy, June 29.

Cassado, Gaspar, 69; cellist; Madrid, Spain, Dec. 24.

Cassidy, Leslie M., 62; ex-pres. Johns-Manville Corp.; Short Hills, N.J. Feb. 7.

Chaffee, Lt. Cmdr. Roger B., 31; astronaut; Cape Kennedy, Fla. Jan. 27.

Chamberlain, Mrs. Neville, 84; widow of prime minister; London, Feb. 12.

Chaney, Maj. Gen. James E., 82; led invasion of Iwo Jima; New York, Aug. 22.

Choate, Mrs. Arthur, 80; active supporter of the Girl Scouts; Pleasantville, N. Y., May 17.

Christophoros II, 91; Patriarch of Alexandria and All Africa; Athens, July 24.

Ciriaci, Pietro Cardinal, 81; key figure in Roman Curia; Rome. Dec. 30.

Clark, Chase A., 83; former Idaho governor; Boise, Idaho, Dec. 30.

Clement, Dr. Rufus E., 67; president of Atlanta University; New York, Nov. 7.

Clyde, Andy, 75; actor; Hopalong Cassidy's early sidekick; Los Angeles, May 18.

Cockcroft, Sir John, 70; 1951 Nobel Prize winner in physics; London, Sept. 18.

Coltrane, John, 40; jazz saxophonist; Huntington, N. Y., July 18.

Compton, Dr. Wilson, 76; educator; Wooster, Ohio, Mar. 7.

Connor, Sir William, 57; British newspaper columnist Cassandra; London, Apr. 6.

Conway, Tom, 63; actor; Culver City, Calif., Apr. 22.

Copello, Santiago Luis Cardinal, 87; chancellor of the Roman Catholic Church; Rome, Feb. 9.

D

Da Costa, Albert, 43; tenor; sang 8 years with Metropolitan Opera; Kolding, Jutland, Nov. 8.

Dalla Torre, Count Guiseppe, 82; former director of Vatican newspaper; Rome, Oct. 17.

Danenhower, Sloan, 82; navigator on submarine Nautilus in 1931 Arctic expedition; Old Saybrook, Conn., Nov. 1.

Dante, Enrico Cardinal, 82; Vatican official; Rome, Apr. 24.

Darrow, Charles B., 78; inventor of the game Monopoly; Ottsville, Pa., Aug. 28.

Darwell, Jane, 87; Academy Award winner as Ma Joad in "The Grapes of Wrath." Hollywood, Aug. 13.

Day, James, 62; president of the Midwest Stock Exchange; Chicago, Nov. 8.

Dee, Sylvia, 52; lyricist; "Chickery Chick"; New York, June 12.

De Kallay, Nicholas, 79; former premier of Hungary; New York, Jan. 14.

de Seversky, Mrs. Alexander, 60; pilot and wife of aeronautical designer; Northport, N.Y., July 28.

Dibelius, Bishop Otto, 86; German Evangelical (Lutheran) Church leader; West Berlin, Jan. 31.

Dick, Dr. John, 86; co-developer of the Dick test for scarlet fever; Palo Alto, Calif., Oct. 10.

Disney, Walt, 65; movie producer, creator of Mickey Mouse and Donald Duck; Los Angeles, Dec. 15.

Donath, Ludwig, 67; actor; father in "The Jolson Story."; New York, Sept. 29.

Drewes, Alfred, 53; pres. of National Lead Co.; New York, June 6.

Dreyer, Dave, 72; songwriter; "Cecilia"; New York, Mar. 2.

Dunn, James, 61; actor; Academy Award winner for "A Tree Grows in Brooklyn"; Santa Monica, Calif., Sept. 3.

Duryea, J. Frank, 97; co-designer of first gas auto in U. S.; Saybrook, Conn., Feb. 15.

E

Eddy, Nelson, 65; singer; Miami Beach, Fla., Mar. 6.

Ehrenburg, Ilya, 76; Soviet writer; Moscow, Sept. 1.

Ekstrom, Edwin, 78; founder of the Greyhound Bus Co.; Corpus Christi, Texas, May 7.

Elman, Mischa, 76; violin virtuoso; New York, Apr. 5.

Epstein, Brian, 32; manager of the Beatles; London, Aug. 27.

Evelyn, Judith, 54; actress; "The Shrike"; New York, May 7.

F

Fabian, Dr. Bela, 77; anti-Communist Hungarian exile; San Juan, P. R., Dec. 25.

Farrar, Geraldine, 85; former Metropolitan Opera star; Ridgefield, Conn., Mar. 11.

Farrell, Dr. Eddie, 64; major league baseball player, dentist; Livingston, N. J., Dec. 20.

Fawcett, Robert, 64; magazine illustrator; Ridgefield, Conn., Apr. 13.

Fechteler, Adm. William, 71; ex-chief of Naval Operations; Washington, July 4.

Pelton, Verna, 76; actress; North Hollywood, Calif., Dec. 14.

Fogarty, John E., 53; Democratic Rep. from Rhode Island; Washington, Jan. 10.

Forbes, Esther, 76; winner Pulitzer Prize for history; Worcester, Mass., Aug. 12.

Foulois, Gen. Benjamin, 87; America's first combat pilot; Washington, Apr. 25.

Foxx, Jimmy, 59; Hall of Fame baseball great, hit 534 home runs; Miami, July 21.

G

Garden, Mary, 92; soprano; former star Chicago Civic Opera Co.; Aberdeen, Scot., Jan. 3.

Garner, John Nance, 98; Vice President of U. S. under FDR; Uvalde, Tex., Nov. 7.

Gassner, John W., 64; critic; Yale drama professor; New Haven, Conn., Apr. 2.

Genaro, Frankie, 65; ex-world flyweight boxing champ; New York, Dec. 27.

Gernsback, Hugo, 83; author, editor, publisher, "father of modern science fiction"; New York, Aug. 19.

Gibb, Margaret and Mary, 54; oldest Siamese twins in the U. S.; Holyoke, Mass., Jan. 7.

Gibbs, William, 81; designed ocean liner the United States; New York, Sept. 6.

Glasgow, Brig. Gen. William, 101; oldest graduate of West Point; El Paso, Texas, Aug. 4.

Gold, Michael, 74; author "Jews Without Money"; Terra Inda, Calif., May 14.

Goldfine, Bernard, 76; involved in 1958 Administration scandal with Sherman Adams; Boston, Sept. 21.

Gonzalez, Juan, 64; ex-president of Paraguay; Mexico City, Dec. 6.

Gorsch, Mrs. Marion, 85; first model for Phoebe Snow ad of the Delaware, Lackawanna & Western Railroad; New York, Aug. 3.

Graham, Robert C., 82; one of three brothers, makers of Graham-Paige autos; Washington, Ind., Oct. 3.

Greenfield, Albert M., 79; department store tycoon, exowner Tiffany's; Philadelphia, Jan. 5.

Grissom, Col. Virgil (Gus), 40; astronaut; Cape Kennedy, Fla., Jan. 27.

Guevara, Che, 39; Argentineborn Cuban revolutionary; Valle Grande, Bolivia, Oct. 8.

Guinness, Rupert, 93; Earl of Iveagh and former chief of Guinness brewery; London, Sept. 14.

Guthrie, Woody, 55; Folk singer and composer; New York, Oct. 3.

H

Hall, Edmond, 65; jazz clarinetist; Cambridge, Mass., Feb. 12.

Harlan, Kenneth, 71; silent film actor; Hollywood, Mar. 6.

Harriman, Mrs. J. Borden, 97; former minister to Norway; Washington, Aug. 31.

Hatvany, Lili, 76; playwright; (Tonight Or Never); New York, Nov. 12.

Heim, Jacques, 67; fashion house head; Paris, Jan. 7.

Herter, Christian A., 71; former U. S. Secretary of State, Republican Governor of Mass., 5-term Congressman; Washington, Dec. 30.

Heyrovsky, Prof. Jaroslav, 76; Nobel Prize chemistry winner; Prague, Mar. 27.

Himber, Richard, 59; band leader, magician; New York, Dec. 11.

Hinshelwood, Sir Cyril, 70; Nobel Prize winning chemist; London, Oct. 9.

Hobart, Alice Tisdale, 85; novelist; "Oil for the Lamps of China"; Oakland, Calif., Mar. 14.

Hoffman, Clare, 92; Michigan Congressman for 28 years; Allegan, Mich., Nov. 3.

Holland, Vyvyan, 80; writer; second son of Oscar Wilde; London, Oct. 10.

Holt, Rev. Dr. Ivan, 81; Methodist Bishop; Atlanta, Ga., Jan. 12.

Hopper, Edward, 84; artist; Painter of American loneliness; New York, May 15.

Hornbeck, Stanley K., 83; U. S. career diplomat; Washington, Dec. 10.

Howe, Prof. Mark, 60; constitutional law expert; Cambridge, Mass., Feb. 28.

Hughes, Langston, 65; poet; chronicler of Negro life; New York, May 22.

Hume, Benita, 60; actress; widow of Ronald Colman, wife of George Sanders; Egerton, England, Nov. 1.

Humphreys Jr., Harry, 66; exchairman and president of Uniroyal Inc.; White Plains, N. Y., Sept. 3.

Hurley, Margaret, 59; managing editor, Town and Country Magazine; New York, Nov. 11.

Hutheesing, Mrs. Krishna, 60; Author; sister of Nehru, London, Nov. 9.

J

Jacob, H. E., 78; biographer; Biography of Franz Joseph Haydn; Salzburg, Austria, Oct. 25.

Jergens, Andrew, 85; pres. Jergens toiletries; Cincinnati, Ohio, Feb. 22.

Juin, Marshal Alphonse-Pierre 78; last surviving French marshal; Paris, Jan. 27.

K

Kaiser, Henry J., 85; industrialist; Honolulu, Aug. 24.

Keane, Johnny, 55; mgr. baseball's St. Louis Cardinals; Houston, Tex., Jan. 6.

Kesselring, Joseph, 65; playwright; "Arsenic and Old Lace;" Kingston, N. Y., Nov. 5.

Kiplinger, Willard M., 76; founder of the Kiplinger Letters and Changing Times; Washington, Aug. 6.

Kiss, Max, 84; pharmacist; creator of Ex-Lax, Atlantic Beach, New York, June 22.

Kline, C. Mahlon, 86; honorary chairman Smith Kline & French Laboratories; Phila., Pa. Apr. 3.

Knollys, Viscount, 71; British industrialist; London, Dec. 3.

Koch, Ilse, 60; Nazi "beast of Buchenwald"; Aichach, Bavaria, Sept. 1.

Kodaly, Zoltan, 84; composer; Budapest, Hungary, Mar. 6.

Kosygin, Mrs. Aleksei N., late 50s; wife of the Soviet premier; Moscow, May 1.

Kroll, Hans, 69; former West German ambassador to Russia; Starnberg, West Germany, Aug. 8.

Krupp, Alfred, 59; last head of German steel empire; Essen, Germany, July 30.

Kuhn, Dr. Richard, 66; Nobel Prize winning biochemist, codiscoverer of vitamins; Heidelberg, Aug. 1.

L

Labarthe, Andre, 65; Information Minister French Provisional Govt., 1943; Paris, Nov. 12.

Lamont, Thomas, 68; banker; one-time partner of J. P. Morgan; New York, Apr. 10.

Landy, Alvin, 62; executive secretary American Contract Bridge League; Atlantic City, Sept. 23.

Lane, William Preston Jr., 74; ex-Gov. Maryland; Hagerstown, Feb. 6.

Lashly, Jacob, M., 85; former pres. American Bar Assn; St. Louis, Oct. 1.

Lee, Josh Bryan, 75; former Senator and Representative from Oklahoma; Norman, Oklahoma, Aug. 10.

Leigh, Vivien, 53; actress; Scarlett O'Hara in "Gone With the Wind"; London, July 8.

Lister, Walter B., 67; newspaperman; once city editor of 3 N.Y.C. newspapers; Philadelphia, May 3.

Lovejoy, Dr. Esther, 97; president emeritus of the American Women's Hospital Service; New York, Aug. 17.

Luce, Henry R., 68; founder Time-Life-Fortune magazine empire; Phoenix, Ariz., Feb. 28.

Luthuli, Albert, 69; former Zulu chief; Nobel Peace Prize winner; Goutville, South Africa, July 21.

Lyon, Alfred, 81; former pres. of Philip Morris, Inc.; Stamford, Conn., May 7.

M

Mack, Earle, T., 77; son of Connie Mack; Phila. Feb. 5.

MacNeal, Robert, 64; former president Curtis Publishing Co.; Somers Point, N. J. Oct. 31.

Magritte, Rene, 68; Belgian surrealist painter; Brussels, Aug. 15.

Mahoney, Will, 71, vaudeville dancer; Melbourne, Australia, Feb. 9.

Malinovsky, Marshal Rodion, 68; Soviet Defense Minister; Moscow, Mar. 31.

Mandell, Sammy, 63; former lightweight boxing champion; Oak Park, Ill., Nov. 7.

Mansfield, Jayne, 34; actress; "dumb blonde" of "Will Success Spoil Rock Hunter?"; New Orleans, June 29.

Manville, Tommy, 73; oft-wed asbestos millionaire; Chappaqua, N. Y., Oct. 8.

Marshall, Edison, 73; novelist; "Yankee Pasha"; Augusta, Ga., Oct. 29.

Martin, Edward, 87; ex-gov. Pennsylvania, Washington, Pa. Mar. 19.

Masefield, John, 88; Poet Laureate of England; London, May 12.

Mason, Dr. John, 82; Ethnologist; noted for his studies of the American Indian, Berwyn, Pa., Nov. 7.

Maurois, Andre, 82; biographer; Paris, Oct. 9.

May, Eugene, 62; noted test pilot; Mackay, Idaho, Dec. 5.

Maytag, L. B., 78; ex-pres. Maytag Co. washing machine manufacturer; Colorado Springs, Aug. 3.

McAdoo, Eleanor Wilson, 77; daughter of Pres. Wilson; Montecito, Calif., Apr. 5.

McCann, Richard, 57; director of the Pro Football Hall of Fame; Washington, Nov. 5.

McCullers, Carson, 50; writer; "The Member of the Wedding"; Nyack, N. Y., Sept. 29.

McGrath, Frank, 64; TV actor; cook in "Wagon Train"; Beverly Hills, May 13.

McLain, John, 63; drama critic; London, May 3.

McNaughton, Harry, 70; actor. Amityville, L. I., N. Y. Feb. 26.

Mikolajczyk, Stanislaw, 65; exhead polish Govt.-in-Exile in London; Chevy Chase, Md., Dec. 13.

Millsop, Thomas, 68; former board chairman National Steel Corp.; Weirton, W. Va., Sept. 12.

Monizer, Matvei G., 75; Soviet sculptor; Moscow, Dec. 20.

Montague, Theodore, 69; former pres. Borden Co.; Greenwich, Conn. Aug. 13.

Morehouse, Ward, 67; Broadway theater critic, playwright; New York, Dec. 7.

Moreno, Antonio, 78; silent film star; Beverly Hills, Feb. 15.

Morgan, Lt. Gen. Sir Frederick, 73; planned Allied invasion of Europe; London, Mar. 20.

Morgenthau, Henry Jr., 75; Secy. of the Treas. 1934-45; Poughkeepsie, N. Y. Feb. 6.

Morse, Sir Arthur, 75; influential Hong Kong banker; London, May 13.

Mossadegh, Dr. Mohammed, 86; ex-premier of Iran; Teheran, Mar. 5.

Muller, Hermann J., 76; discoverer of hereditary effects of x-rays; Indianapolis, Apr. 5.

Muni, Paul, 71; stage and screen actor; Santa Barbara, Calif., Aug. 25.

Muste, Rev. A. J., 82; pacifist leader; New York, Feb. 11.

N

Nesbit, Evelyn, 82; showgirl; figure Thaw-White murder case; Santa Monica, Calif., Jan. 17.

Nick the Greek (Dandalos), 80; noted gambler; Los Angeles, Dec. 25.

Nizam of Hyderabad, 80; ex-ruler of Indian state; Hyderabad, India, Feb. 24.

O

O'Hara, Geoffrey, 84; songwriter (K-K-K-Katy); St. Petersburg, Fla., Jan. 31.

Oppenheimer, Dr. J. Robert, 62; "father of the atom bomb"; Princeton, N. J. Feb. 18.

Orr, Carey, 77; Pulitzer Prize-winning cartoonist; Chicago, May 16.

Orsborn, Albert W. T., 80; head of Intl. Salvation Army 1946-54; London, Feb. 4.

Ouimet, Francis, 74; golfer; first amateur to win U. S. Open; Newton, Mass., Sept. 2.

P

Paddleford, Clementine, 67; food editor, N. Y. Herald Tribune; New York, Nov. 13.

Parker, Dan, 73; sportswriter; former sports editor New York Daily Mirror; Waterbury, Conn., May 20.

Parker, Dorothy, 73; humorist; "Men seldom make passes at girls who wear glasses"; New York, June 7.

Pell, Theodore Roosevelt, 89; former tennis champion; Sands Pt., N. Y. Aug. 18.

Pendleton, Nat, 60; movie actor; La Jolla, Calif., Oct. 11.

Persinger, Louis, 79; violin teacher of Menuhin, Ricci, Stern; New York, Dec. 31.

Peterson, Virgilia, 62; literary critic; Sharon, Conn., Dec. 24.

Pichon, Walter "Fats," 60; riverboat jazz pianist; Chicago, Feb. 26.

Pincus, Dr. Gregory, 64; one of three developers of the birth-control pill; Boston, Aug. 22.

Pinkerton, Robert A., 62; chairman Pinkerton's Inc. private detectives, Bay Shore, N. Y., Oct. 11.

Pott, Dr. William, 74; former president of Elmira College; Berkeley, Calif., Nov. 7.

Pu Yi, Henry, 61; last emperor of China; Tokyo, Oct. 17.

R

Rains, Claude, 77; actor; "The Invisible Man"; Sandwich, N. H., May 30.

Randall, Clarence B., 76; retired chairman of Inland Steel; Ishpeming, Mich., Aug. 4.

Rathbone, Basil, 75; actor; Sherlock Holmes of movies; New York, July 21.

Read, Adm. Albert C., 80; made first successful trans-Atlantic flight; Miami, Oct. 10.

Reinhardt, Ad, 53; painter; "black monk" of abstract expressionism; New York, Aug. 30.

Rice, Elmer, 74; dramatist; winner 1929 Pulitzer Prize for "Street Scene"; London, May 8.

Riis, Mrs. Jacob, 90; widow of the social reformer; New York, Aug. 4.

Ritter, Joseph Cardinal, 74; Archbishop of St. Louis; St. Louis, June 10.

Roberts, Roy, 79; newspaperman; ex-pres. Kansas City Star; Kansas City, Mo., Feb. 23.

Rockwell, George Lincoln, 49; founder and leader of the American Nazi Party; Arlington, Va., Aug. 25.

Rodriguez, Gen. Abelardo Luis, 77; ex-pres. Mexico; La Jolla, Calif., Feb. 13.

Rose, Dr. Morris, 56; Nuclear Physicist, Chief Physicist at Oak Ridge Natl. Lab., 1946-61; Charlottesville, Va., Nov. 10.

Ross, Barney, 57; boxing champion; Chicago, Jan. 18.

Roth, Dr. Ludwig, 58; pioneer rocket engineer; Redondo Beach, Calif., Oct. 31.

Ruby, Jack, 55; awaiting retrial for slaying of Lee Harvey Oswald; Dallas, Tex., Jan. 3.

Rudkin, Mrs. Margaret, 69; founder Pepperidge Farm Inc. bakery; New Haven, Conn., June 1.

Ruffini, Ernest Cardinal, 79; Archbishop of Palermo; Palermo, Italy, June 11.

Ruiz, Jose, 93; writer; Madrid, Spain, Mar. 2.

Ruman, Sig, 82; actor (Sgt. Schultz in "Stalag 17" film); San Diego, Calif., Feb. 14.

Runyon, John, 79; publisher Dallas Times Herald; Dallas, Tex., Jan. 20.

Ruotolo, Onorio, 78; Italian-born sculptor; New York, Dec. 18.

S

Saigh, Maximos IV Cardinal, 89; Patriarch of Antioch; Beirut, Lebanon, Nov. 5.

Sandburg, Carl, 89; poet, biographer of Lincoln; Flatrock, N. C. July 22.

Sargent, Sir Malcolm, 72; conductor; London, Oct. 3.

Sassoon, Siegfried, 80; poet; World War I anti-war poet; Warminster, England, Sept. 1.

Schaeffer, Fritz, 79; ex-West German Finance Minister; Munich, Mar. 29.

Scheiberling, Edward, 79; former national commander of the American Legion; Albany, N. Y., Sept. 10.

Schuyler, Philippa, 35; pianist; child prodigy; Danang, South Vietnam, May 9.

Shepard, Odell, 82; poet-politician; Pulitzer Prize biography winner 1937; New London, Conn., July 19.

Sheridan, Ann, 51; actress; "the oomph girl"; San Fernando Valley, Calif., Jan. 21.

Shumard, Robert, 46; crew member "Enola Gay" in Hiroshima atomic bombing; Dearborn, Mich., Apr. 24.

Smeterlin, Jan, 74; concert pianist; London, Jan. 18.

Smith, Gen. Holland McTeire (Howlin' Mad) 84; led Iwo Jima attack; San Diego, Calif., Jan. 12.

Smith, Raymond, 80; founder Harolds Club casino in Reno, Nev., Reno, May 24.

Smith, Willie, 58; saxophonist; Los Angeles, Mar. 7.

Spanier, "Muggsy," 64; jazz cornetist; Sausalito, Calif., Feb. 12.

Spence, Brent, 92; former Representative from Kentucky for 32 years; Fort Thomas, Ky., Sept. 18.

Squier, Carl B., 74; Sales Executive; Stunt Pilot, 13th Federally licensed pilot in U. S. Burbank, Calif., Nov. 5.

Stahlberg, Gideon, 59; international grand master of chess; Moscow, May 26.

Stewart, Rex, 60; jazz cornetist; sideman with Duke Ellington for 10 years; Los Angeles, Sept. 7.

Stone, George, 64; movie actor noted for gangster roles; Woodland Hills, Calif., May 26.

Storing, Dr. James A., 61; provost Colgate Univ.; Hamilton, N. Y., Feb. 9.

Strayhorn, Billy, 51; jazz composer; "Take the 'A' Train"; New York, May 31.

T

Tatum, Reese (Goose), 45; "clown prince of basketball"; El Paso, Tex., Jan. 18.

Tien, Thomas Cardinal, 76; only Chinese cardinal of the Roman Catholic Church; Chiayi, Taiwan, July 24.

Toklas, Alice, 89; author; companion of Gertrude Stein; Paris, Mar. 7.

Tolan, Eddie, 57; Olympic track star; Detroit, Jan. 31.

Trachtenberg, Alexander, 82; publisher of Marxist books in U. S.; New York, Dec. 16.

Tracy, Spencer, 67; actor; Hollywood, June 10.

Trahan, Al, 69; vaudeville comedian; New York, Dec. 14.

Tynan, Brandon, 91; actor; New York, Mar. 19.

U

Upjohn, Dr. Lawrence, 93; director of Upjohn Co. drug firm; Kalamazoo, Mich., June 2.

V

Van Doren, Irita, 75; literary critic; New York, Dec. 18.

Vanier, Maj. Gen. Georges, 78; governor general of Canada; Ottawa, Mar. 5.

W

Walker, Herbert, 71; ex-pres. Newspaper Enterprise Assn.; Leavenworth, Kan., Jan. 20.

Ward, Rev. Dr. Harry F., 93; ex-chairman American Civil Liberties Union; Palisades, N. J., Dec. 9.

Waxman, Franz, 60; Oscar-winning film composer; Los Angeles, Calif., Feb. 24.

Wells, Dr. C. Raymond, 71; ex-president American Dental Assn.; Chicago, Dec. 9.

White, Lt. Col. Edward H. 2nd, 36; astronaut; Cape Kennedy, Fla., Jan. 27.

Whorf, Richard, 60; stage, screen, TV actor-director; Santa Monica, Calif., Dec. 14.

Wickard, Claude, 74; former U. S. Secy. of Agriculture; Delphi, Ind., Apr. 29.

Wiley, Alexander, 83; former Republican senator from Wisconsin, Philadelphia, Oct. 26.

Wilson, Lyle C., 67; former vice-pres. of United Press International; Stuart, Fla., May 23.

Woodring, Harry, 77; Secy. of War in FDR cabinet; Topeka, Kan., Sept. 9.

Wortman, Mrs. Doris, 77; devised more than 3,000 Double-Crostic puzzles; Vineyard Haven, Mass., June 8.

X

Xceron, Jean, 77; non-objective painter; New York, Mar. 29.

Y

Yoshida, Shigeru, 89; former Premier of Japan; Oiso, Japan, Oct. 20.

Youssoupoff, Prince Felix, 81; killed Rasputin, mystic adviser to Czar Nicholas II; Paris, Sept. 27.

Z

Zbyszko, Stanislaus, 88; world wrestling champion; St. Joseph, Mo., Sept. 22.

UNITED STATES POPULATION
Growth Rate Slows; 30% of Population Enrolled in School or College
Source: U. S. Bureau of Census

The total population of the United States including members of the armed services overseas on April 1, 1967 reached 198,608,-000, according to Census Bureau estimates. This figure represented an increase of 18,-601,000 over the April 1, 1960 census count.

Elements of Change—The estimated rate of population growth in the United States in calendar year 1966 was 1.15%, a rate lower than in any year since the end of World War II. It compared with 1.23% in 1965 and the most recent previous low of 1.05% in 1945. The 1966 rate represents a continuing decline in the annual population growth rate that began in 1957—influenced primarily by the lowering of the *birth rate*. A total of 3,700,000 births occurred during 1966, a drop from 3,800,000 in 1965 and from 4,300,000 in 1957.

Deaths numbered about 1,876,000 in 1966, slightly more than in 1965. Since 1960, the death rate has remained virtually unchanged at about 9.5 deaths per thousand people. Since 1954, the death rate has fluctuated between 9.3 and 9.6 per thousand with no definite trend appearing in the 1954-1966 period.

Net civilian immigration, averaging about 390,000 annually since 1960, has contributed about 14.5% to population growth in that period. This represented an increase over the 300,000 annual average for the 1950's. The largest net gain from this source since 1950 was in 1966, when immigration added 456,000 persons to the population, and in 1965, when net immigration amounted to 397,000. These recent increases probably reflect the effect of the Immigration Act of 1965 and of the U. S.-Cuban agreement on the transfer of Cuban refugees to the United States, both of which took effect in 1965.

Educational Attainments and Projections—About 55,100,000 persons 5 to 34 years old were enrolled in school or college in the United States in the fall of 1966. This represents 30% of the total population.

Of these, about 32,900,000 were enrolled in grades 1 to 8, 13,400,000 in grades 9 to 12, and 6,100,000 in college. There were an additional 2,700,000 children in kindergarten excluding those below age 5.

The increase of enrollment in the last 6 years has been 8,800,000 or 19% over the 46,300,000 enrolled in Oct., 1960. The rate of increase varied considerably by level of school. During this 6-year period, there was a 70% gain in college enrollments, 30% in high schools (grades 9 to 12), and 8% in elementary schools (grades 1 to 8).

Increased enrollment in elementary and secondary schools was due primarily to increases in the population 5 to 17 years old rather than in changes in the percent of persons enrolled. College and professional enrollments, however, reflect both an increase in the percent enrolled among persons aged 18 and 34, and in increase in the total population at these ages.

In May, 1967, Census Bureau population specialists revised school enrollment projections for 1985 upward from those anticipated just a year earlier. College enrollment, according to the new projections, would rise to between 9,700,000 and 11,800,000 by 1985 from the October, 1966, total of 6,100,000 depending upon assump-

tions about the proportions of the population enrolled in colleges. A year earlier, specialists projected college enrollment to a 1985 range of between 9,000,000 and 11,-600,000 students. High school enrollment by 1985 would rise to a range of 13,800,000 to 17,300,000, the revised projections indicate. A year earlier, the projections for high school were in the range of 13,300,000 and 17,000,000. The 1966 total was 13,400,000. New projections for elementary and kindergarten call for a range of 35,400,000 to 47,700,000 pupils by 1985. A year earlier, the range was 34,300,000 to 46,600,000 pupils, and the total for October, 1966, was 35,600,000.

Farm Population Continues Down—An average of 11,595,000 persons lived on farms in rural areas of the United States in 1966. Of the total U. S. population, 5.9% or 1 in 17, lived on a farm. The 1966 estimate of farm residents is 768,000 lower than the 1965 estimate.

Since 1960, when there were 15,600,000 farm residents, the farm population has declined approximately 4,000,000 persons, an average annual decline of about 5%.

Family Income Up—Median income for all families in 1965 was $6,900, more than double the median figure of $3,000 in 1947. Despite rises in consumer prices, the gain in real income over 1947 is about 61%.

Over the past 18 years, median family income has increased at an average annual rate of 5% in current dollars and 3% in constant dollars. This increase in family income parallels the expansion of general economic activity in the U. S. for the same period during which time the Gross National Product increased at an annual rate of about 6% in current dollars and 4% in constant dollars.

Families receiving income under $3,000 have decreased from 50% in 1947 to 17% in 1965, and those receiving $10,000 or more have increased from 7% in 1947 to 25% in 1965.

Plans for the 1970 Decennial Census—In 1967, the Bureau of the Census reported to Congress on plans for the 1970 Census of Population and Housing in which every household will be included. In summary, the report said: 1) that the Census would be conducted principally by mail, although enumerators would be used to follow-up incomplete or non-response cases; enumerators would also be needed to canvass some rural and other areas which do not lend themselves to the mail-type census; 2) that local officials were cooperating in the revision of maps of their areas and in establishing address guides which make it possible for Census Bureau electronic computers to provide more effective application of statistics to local areas; 3) that preliminary results of a special census of Metropolitan New Haven in April, 1967, reaffirm results of previous test censuses concerning increased efficiency from the mail technique of census taking and from the application of computer technology speeding up results and refining statistical usages; and 4) that two or three "dress rehearsal" censuses would be conducted in 1968 in cities and areas of varying complexity prior to final firming of plans for the 1970 Census.

ESTIMATED POPULATION OF THE UNITED STATES

Date	Inc. armed forces overseas	Resident population	Date	Inc. armed forces overseas	Resident population
1960 Census	180,007,000	179,323,175	July 1, 1964..	192,120,000	191,372,000
July 1, 1961..	183,756,000	183,057,000	July 1, 1965..	194,592,000	193,815,000
July 1, 1962..	186,656,000	185,890,000	July 1, 1966..	196,920,000	195,936,000
July 1, 1963..	189,417,000	188,658,000	July 1, 1967..	198,979,113	197,836,000

POPULATION OF THE UNITED STATES, 1950-1960
By States, Regions, Geographic Divisions, Urban, Rural and Rank
Source: Bureau of the Census. *See States of the Union section for latest official estimates.*

Region, division and state	April 1, 1960 census	April 1, 1950 census	Pct. + or −	1960 census Urban	1960 census Rural	Per cent urban	Rank 1960	Rank 1950
UNITED STATES....	179,323,175	151,325,798	18.5	125,268,750	54,054,425	69.9	.....	.....
REGIONS								
Northeast.............	44,677,819	39,477,986	13.2	35,840,140	8,837,679	80.2	.....	.....
North Central......	51,619,139	44,460,762	16.1	35,481,254	16,137,885	68.7	.....	.....
South...............	54,973,113	47,197,088	16.5	32,160,250	22,812,863	58.5	.....	.....
West................	28,053,104	20,189,962	38.9	21,787,106	6,265,998	77.7	.....	.....
DIVISIONS:								
New England........	10,509,367	9,314,453	12.8	8,031,795	2,477,572	76.4		
Middle Atlantic.....	34,168,452	30,163,533	13.3	27,808,345	6,360,107	81.4		
E. No. Central......	36,225,024	30,399,368	19.2	26,434,937	9,790,087	73.0		
W. No. Central.....	15,394,115	14,061,394	9.5	9,046,317	6,347,798	58.8		
So. Atlantic........	25,971,732	21,182,335	22.6	14,851,516	11,120,216	57.2		
E. So. Central......	12,050,126	11,477,181	5.0	5,830,569	6,219,557	48.4		
W. So. Central.....	16,951,255	14,537,572	16.6	11,478,165	5,473,090	67.7		
Mountain...........	6,855,060	5,074,998	35.1	4,600,852	2,254,208	67.1		
Pacific.............	21,198,044	15,114,964	40.2	17,186,254	4,011,790	81.1		
NEW ENGLAND								
Maine...............	969,265	913,774	6.1	497,114	472,151	51.3	36	35
New Hampshire.....	606,921	533,242	13.8	353,766	253,155	58.3	45	44
Vermont............	389,881	377,747	3.2	149,921	239,960	38.5	47	46
Massachusetts......	5,148,578	4,690,514	9.8	4,302,530	846,048	83.6	9	9
Rhode Island.......	859,488	791,896	8.5	742,897	116,591	86.4	39	36
Connecticut.........	2,535,234	2,007,280	26.3	1,985,567	549,667	78.3	25	28
MID. ATLANTIC								
New York...........	16,782,304	14,830,192	13.2	14,331,925	2,450,379	85.4	1	1
New Jersey.........	6,066,782	4,835,329	25.5	5,374,369	692,413	88.6	8	8
Pennsylvania.......	11,319,366	10,498,012	7.8	8,102,051	3,217,315	71.6	3	3
E. NO. CENTRAL								
Ohio................	9,706,397	7,946,627	22.1	7,123,162	2,583,235	73.4	5	5
Indiana.............	4,662,498	3,934,224	18.5	2,910,149	1,752,349	62.4	11	12
Illinois.............	10,081,158	8,712,176	15.7	8,140,315	1,940,843	80.7	4	4
Michigan............	7,823,194	6,371,766	22.8	5,739,132	2,084,062	73.4	7	7
Wisconsin...........	3,951,777	3,434,575	15.1	2,522,179	1,429,598	63.8	15	14
W. NO. CENTRAL								
Minnesota..........	3,413,864	2,928,483	14.5	2,122,566	1,291,298	62.2	18	18
Iowa................	2,757,537	2,621,073	5.2	1,462,512	1,295,025	53.0	24	22
Missouri............	4,319,813	3,954,653	9.2	2,876,557	1,443,256	66.6	13	11
North Dakota.......	632,446	619,636	2.1	222,708	409,738	35.2	44	41
South Dakota.......	680,514	652,740	4.3	267,180	413,334	39.3	40	40
Nebraska...........	1,411,330	1,325,510	6.5	766,053	645,277	54.3	34	33
Kansas.............	2,178,611	1,905,299	14.3	1,328,741	849,870	61.0	28	31
SO. ATLANTIC								
Delaware...........	446,292	318,085	40.3	292,788	153,504	65.6	46	47
Maryland...........	3,100,689	2,343,001	32.3	2,253,832	846,857	72.7	21	24
Dist. of Col........	763,956	802,178	−4.8	763,956		100.0	.....	.....
Virginia............	3,966,949	3,318,680	19.5	2,204,913	1,762,036	55.6	14	15
West Virginia.......	1,860,421	2,005,552	−7.2	711,101	1,149,320	38.2	30	29
North Carolina.....	4,556,155	4,061,929	12.2	1,801,921	2,754,234	39.5	12	10
South Carolina.....	2,382,594	2,117,027	12.5	981,386	1,401,208	41.2	26	27
Georgia.............	3,943,116	3,444,578	14.5	2,180,236	1,762,880	55.3	16	13
Florida.............	4,951,560	2,771,305	78.7	3,661,383	1,290,177	73.9	10	20
E. SO. CENTRAL								
Kentucky...........	3,038,156	2,944,806	3.2	1,353,215	1,684,941	44.5	22	19
Tennessee..........	3,567,089	3,291,718	8.4	1,864,828	1,702,261	52.3	17	16
Alabama............	3,266,740	3,061,743	6.7	1,791,721	1,475,019	54.8	19	17
Mississippi.........	2,178,141	2,178,914	.....	820,805	1,357,336	37.7	29	26
W. SO. CENTRAL								
Arkansas...........	1,786,272	1,909,511	−6.5	765,303	1,020,969	42.8	31	30
Louisiana..........	3,257,022	2,683,516	21.4	2,060,606	1,196,416	63.3	20	21
Oklahoma..........	2,328,284	2,233,351	4.3	1,464,786	863,498	62.9	27	25
Texas..............	9,579,677	7,711,194	24.2	7,187,470	2,392,207	75.0	6	6
MOUNTAIN								
Montana............	674,767	591,024	14.2	338,457	336,310	50.2	41	42
Idaho...............	667,191	588,637	13.3	317,097	350,094	47.5	42	43
Wyoming...........	330,066	290,529	13.6	187,551	142,515	56.8	48	48
Colorado............	1,753,947	1,325,089	32.4	1,292,790	461,157	73.7	33	34
New Mexico........	951,023	681,187	39.6	626,479	324,544	65.9	37	39
Arizona.............	1,302,161	749,587	73.7	970,616	331,545	74.5	35	37
Utah...............	890,627	688,862	29.3	667,158	223,469	74.9	38	38
Nevada.............	285,278	160,083	78.2	200,704	84,574	70.4	49	49
PACIFIC								
Washington.........	2,853,214	2,378,963	19.9	1,943,249	909,965	68.1	23	23
Oregon.............	1,768,687	1,521,341	16.3	1,100,122	668,565	62.2	32	32
California..........	15,717,204	10,586,223	48.5	13,573,155	2,144,049	86.4	2	2
Alaska.............	226,167	128,643	75.8	85,767	140,400	37.9	50	50
Hawaii.............	632,772	499,794	26.6	483,961	148,811	76.5	43	45

U. S. Population Urban, Rural, White, Nonwhite
Source: Bureau of the Census (Census of 1960)

Area	All classes Total	All classes Male	All classes Female	White Male	White Female	Nonwhite Male	Nonwhite Female
Total.............	179,323,175	88,331,494	90,991,681	78,367,149	80,464,583	9,964,345	10,527,098
Urban............	125,268,750	60,733,005	64,535,745	53,631,145	56,797,187	7,101,860	7,738,558
Urbanized areas..	95,848,487	46,494,210	49,354,277	40,706,094	43,063,841	5,788,116	6,290,436
Central cities..	57,975,132	27,927,624	30,047,508	22,976,282	24,650,950	4,951,342	5,396,558
Urban fringe..	37,873,355	18,566,586	19,306,769	17,729,812	18,412,891	836,774	893,878
Other urban.	29,420,263	14,238,795	15,181,468	12,925,051	13,733,346	1,313,744	1,448,122
Places of 10,000 or more.	16,172,839	7,838,676	8,334,163	7,070,615	7,490,599	768,061	843,564
2,500 to 10,000.	13,274,424	6,400,119	6,847,305	5,854,436	6,242,747	545,683	604,558
Rural............	54,054,425	27,598,489	26,455,936	24,736,004	23,667,396	2,862,485	2,788,540
Places of 1,000 to 2,500.	6,496,788	3,149,869	3,346,919	2,909,209	3,086,545	240,660	260,374
Other rural.......	47,557,637	24,448,620	23,109,017	21,826,795	20,580,851	2,621,825	2,528,166

United States Population (Official Census), 1790-1880

Source: Bureau of the Census

1790—Connecticut 237,946; Delaware 59,096; Georgia 82,548; Kentucky 73,677; Maine 96,540; Maryland 319,728; Massachusetts 378,787; New Hampshire 141,885; New Jersey 184,139; New York 340,120; North Carolina 393,751; Pennsylvania 434,373; Rhode Island 68,825; South Carolina 249,073; Tennessee 35,691; Vermont 85,425; Virginia 747,610. Total 3,929,214.

1800—Connecticut 251,002; Delaware 64,273; Dist. of Col. 14,093; Georgia 162,686; Indiana 5,641; Kentucky 220,955; Maine 151,719; Maryland 341,548; Massachusetts 422,845; Mississippi 8,850; New Hampshire 183,858; New Jersey 211,149; New York 589,051; North Carolina 478,103; Ohio 45,365; Pennsylvania 602,365; Rhode Island 69,122; South Carolina 345,591; Tennessee 105,602; Vermont 154,465; Virginia 880,200. Total 5,308,483.

State	1810	1820	1830[1]	1840[1]	1850	1860	1870	1880
Alabama		9,046	127,901	309,527	590,756	771,623	964,201	996,992	1,262,505
Arizona							9,658	40,440
Arkansas	1,062	14,273	30,388	97,574	209,897	435,450	484,471	802,525
California					92,597	379,994	560,247	864,694
Colorado						34,277	39,864	194,327
Connecticut	261,942	275,248	297,675	309,978	370,792	460,147	537,454	622,700
Delaware	72,674	72,749	76,748	78,085	91,532	112,216	125,015	146,608
Dist. of Col.	24,023	33,039	39,834	43,712	51,687	75,080	131,700	177,624
Florida			34,730	54,477	87,445	140,424	187,748	269,493
Georgia	252,433	340,989	516,823	691,392	906,185	1,057,286	1,184,109	1,542,180
Idaho							14,999	32,610
Illinois	12,282	55,211	157,445	476,183	851,470	1,711,951	2,539,891	3,077,871
Indiana	24,520	147,178	343,031	685,866	988,416	1,350,428	1,680,637	1,978,301
Iowa				43,112	192,214	674,913	1,194,020	1,624,615
Kansas						107,206	364,399	996,096
Kentucky	406,511	564,317	687,917	779,828	982,405	1,155,684	1,321,011	1,648,690
Louisiana	76,556	153,407	215,739	352,411	517,762	708,002	726,915	939,946
Maine	228,705	298,335	399,455	501,793	583,169	628,279	626,915	648,936
Maryland	380,546	407,350	447,040	470,019	583,034	687,049	780,894	934,943
Massachusetts	472,040	523,287	610,408	737,699	994,514	1,231,066	1,457,351	1,783,085
Michigan	4,762	8,896	31,639	212,267	397,654	749,113	1,184,059	1,636,937
Minnesota					6,077	172,023	439,706	780,773
Mississippi	40,352	75,448	136,621	375,651	606,526	791,305	827,922	1,131,597
Missouri	19,783	66,586	140,455	383,702	682,044	1,182,012	1,721,295	2,168,380
Montana							20,595	39,159
Nebraska						28,841	122,993	452,402
Nevada						6,857	42,491	62,266
New Hampshire	214,460	244,161	269,328	284,574	317,976	326,073	318,300	346,991
New Jersey	245,562	277,575	320,823	373,306	489,555	672,035	906,096	1,131,116
New Mexico					61,547	93,516	91,874	119,565
New York	959,049	1,372,812	1,918,608	2,428,921	3,097,394	3,880,735	4,382,759	5,082,871
North Carolina	555,500	638,829	737,987	753,419	869,039	992,622	1,071,361	1,399,750
North Dakota							*2,405	36,909
Ohio	230,760	581,434	937,903	1,519,467	1,980,329	2,339,511	2,665,260	3,198,062
Oklahoma								
Oregon					13,294	52,465	90,923	174,768
Pennsylvania	810,091	1,049,458	1,348,233	1,724,033	2,311,786	2,906,215	3,521,951	4,282,891
Rhode Island	76,931	83,059	97,199	108,830	147,545	174,620	217,353	276,531
South Carolina	415,115	502,741	581,185	594,398	668,507	703,708	705,606	995,577
South Dakota						*4,837	*11,776	98,268
Tennessee	261,727	422,823	681,904	829,210	1,002,717	1,109,801	1,258,520	1,542,359
Texas					212,592	604,215	818,579	1,591,749
Utah					11,380	40,273	86,786	143,963
Vermont	217,895	235,981	280,652	291,948	314,120	315,098	330,551	332,286
Virginia	974,600	1,065,366	1,211,405	1,239,797	1,421,661	1,596,318	1,225,163	1,512,565
Washington						11,594	23,955	75,116
West Virginia							442,014	618,457
Wisconsin				30,945	305,391	775,881	1,054,670	1,315,497
Wyoming							9,118	20,789
Total U. S.	7,239,881	9,638,453	12,866,020	17,069,453	23,191,876	31,443,321	38,558,371	50,189,209

*1860 figure is for Dakota Territory; 1870 figures are for parts of Dakota Territory.
[1]U. S. total includes persons (5,318 in 1830 and 6,100 in 1840) on public ships in the service of the United States not credited to any region, division, or state.

United States Area and Population: 1790 to 1960

Source: Bureau of the Census

Area figures represent area on indicated date including in some cases considerable areas not then organized or settled, and not covered by the census. Area figures have been adjusted to bring them into agreement with remeasurements made in 1940.

Census date	Area (square miles)			Population			
	Gross	Land	Water	Number	Per sq. mile of land area	Increase over preceding census	
						No.	%
Conterminous U.S.[1]							
1790 (Aug. 2)	888,811	864,746	24,065	3,929,214	4.5	(X)	(X)
1800 (Aug. 4)	888,811	864,746	24,065	5,308,483	6.1	1,379,269	35.1
1810 (Aug. 6)	1,716,003	1,681,828	34,175	7,239,881	4.3	1,931,398	36.4
1820 (Aug. 7)	1,788,006	1,749,462	38,544	9,638,453	5.5	2,398,572	33.1
1830 (June 1)	1,788,006	1,749,462	38,544	12,866,020	7.4	3,227,567	33.5
1840 (June 1)	1,788,006	1,749,462	38,544	17,069,453	9.8	4,203,433	32.7
1850 (June 1)	2,992,747	2,940,042	52,705	23,191,876	7.9	6,122,423	35.9
1860 (June 1)	3,022,387	2,969,640	52,747	31,443,321	10.6	8,251,445	35.6
1870 (June 1)	3,022,387	2,969,640	52,747	[2]39,818,449	[2]13.4	8,375,128	26.6
1880 (June 1)	3,022,387	2,969,640	52,747	50,155,783	16.9	10,337,334	26.0
1890 (June 1)	3,022,387	2,969,640	52,747	62,947,714	21.2	12,791,931	25.5
1900 (June 1)	3,022,387	2,969,834	52,553	75,994,575	25.6	13,046,861	20.7
1910 (Apr. 15)	3,022,387	2,969,565	52,822	91,972,266	31.0	15,977,691	21.0
1920 (Jan. 1)	3,022,387	2,969,451	52,936	105,710,620	35.6	13,738,354	14.9
1930 (Apr. 1)	3,022,387	2,977,128	45,259	122,775,046	41.2	17,064,426	16.1
1940 (Apr. 1)	3,022,387	2,977,128	45,259	131,669,275	44.2	8,894,229	7.2
1950 (Apr. 1)	3,022,387	2,974,726	47,661	150,697,361	50.7	19,028,086	14.5
1960 (Apr. 1)	3,022,387	2,971,494	50,893	178,464,236	60.1	27,766,875	18.4
1950 (Apr. 1)[3]	3,615,211	3,552,206	63,005	151,325,798	42.6	19,161,229	14.5
1960 (Apr. 1)[3]	3,615,211	3,548,974	66,237	179,323,175	50.5	27,997,377	18.5

X Not applicable. [1]Excludes Alaska and Hawaii. [2]Revised to include adjustments for underenumeration in Southern States; unrevised number is 38,558,371. [3]Includes Alaska and Hawaii.

United States Population (Official Census), 1890-1960

Source: Bureau of the Census

State	1890	1900	1910	1920	1930	1940	1950	1960
Alabama....	1,513,401	1,828,697	2,138,093	2,348,174	2,646,248	2,832,961	3,061,743	3,266,740
Alaska....								226,167
Arizona....	88,243	122,931	204,354	334,162	435,573	499,261	749,587	1,302,161
Arkansas....	1,128,211	1,311,564	1,574,449	1,752,204	1,854,482	1,949,387	1,909,511	1,786,272
California...	1,213,398	1,485,053	2,377,549	3,426,861	5,677,251	6,907,387	10,586,223	15,717,204
Colorado....	413,249	539,700	799,024	939,629	1,035,791	1,123,296	1,325,089	1,753,947
Connecticut.	746,258	908,420	1,114,756	1,380,631	1,606,903	1,709,242	2,007,280	2,535,234
Delaware....	168,493	184,735	202,322	223,003	238,380	266,505	318,085	446,292
Dist. of Col..	230,392	278,718	331,069	437,571	486,869	663,091	802,178	763,956
Florida....	391,422	528,542	752,619	968,470	1,468,211	1,897,414	2,771,305	4,951,560
Georgia....	1,837,353	2,216,331	2,609,121	2,895,832	2,908,506	3,123,723	3,444,578	3,943,116
Hawaii....								632,772
Idaho....	88,548	161,772	325,594	431,866	445,032	524,873	588,637	667,191
Illinois....	3,826,352	4,821,550	5,638,591	6,485,280	7,630,654	7,897,241	8,712,176	10,081,158
Indiana....	2,192,404	2,516,462	2,700,876	2,930,390	3,238,503	3,427,796	3,934,224	4,662,498
Iowa....	1,912,297	2,231,853	2,224,771	2,404,021	2,470,939	2,538,268	2,621,073	2,757,537
Kansas....	1,428,108	1,470,495	1,690,949	1,769,257	1,880,999	1,801,028	1,905,299	2,178,611
Kentucky....	1,858,635	2,147,174	2,289,905	2,416,630	2,614,589	2,845,627	2,944,806	3,038,156
Louisiana...	1,118,588	1,381,625	1,656,388	1,798,509	2,101,593	2,363,880	2,683,516	3,257,022
Maine....	661,086	694,466	742,371	768,014	797,423	847,226	913,774	969,265
Maryland....	1,042,390	1,188,044	1,295,346	1,449,661	1,631,526	1,821,244	2,343,001	3,100,689
Massch'ts.	2,238,947	2,805,346	3,366,416	3,852,356	4,249,614	4,316,721	4,690,514	5,148,578
Michigan....	2,093,890	2,420,982	2,810,173	3,668,412	4,842,325	5,256,106	6,371,766	7,823,194
Minnesota..	1,310,283	1,751,394	2,075,708	2,387,125	2,563,953	2,792,300	2,982,483	3,413,864
Mississippi.	1,289,600	1,551,270	1,797,114	1,790,618	2,009,821	2,183,796	2,178,914	2,178,141
Missouri....	2,679,185	3,106,665	3,293,335	3,404,055	3,629,367	3,784,664	3,954,653	4,319,813
Montana....	142,924	243,329	376,053	548,889	537,606	559,456	591,024	674,767
Nebraska....	1,062,656	1,066,300	1,192,214	1,296,372	1,377,963	1,315,834	1,325,510	1,411,330
Nevada....	47,355	42,335	81,875	77,407	91,058	110,247	160,083	285,278
N. Hamp....	376,530	411,588	430,572	443,083	465,293	491,524	533,242	606,921
New Jersey..	1,444,933	1,883,669	2,537,167	3,155,900	4,041,334	4,160,165	4,835,329	6,066,782
New Mexico	160,282	195,310	327,301	360,350	423,317	531,818	681,187	951,023
New York...	6,003,174	7,268,894	9,113,614	10,385,227	12,588,066	13,479,142	14,830,192	16,782,304
No. Carolina	1,617,949	1,893,810	2,206,287	2,559,123	3,170,276	3,571,623	4,061,929	4,556,155
No. Dakota..	190,983	319,146	577,056	646,872	680,845	641,935	619,636	632,446
Ohio....	3,672,329	4,157,545	4,767,121	5,759,394	6,646,697	6,907,612	7,946,627	9,706,397
Oklahoma....	258,657	790,391	1,657,155	2,028,283	2,396,040	2,336,434	2,233,351	2,328,284
Oregon....	317,704	413,536	672,765	783,389	953,786	1,089,684	1,521,341	1,768,687
Penn....	5,258,113	6,302,115	7,665,111	8,720,017	9,631,350	9,900,180	10,498,012	11,319,366
Rhode Is....	345,506	428,556	542,610	604,397	687,497	713,346	791,896	859,488
So. Carolina	1,151,149	1,340,316	1,515,400	1,683,724	1,738,765	1,899,804	2,117,027	2,382,594
So. Dakota..	348,600	401,570	583,888	636,547	692,849	642,961	652,740	680,514
Tennessee...	1,767,518	2,020,616	2,184,789	2,337,885	2,616,556	2,915,841	3,291,718	3,567,089
Texas....	2,235,527	3,048,710	3,896,542	4,663,228	5,824,715	6,414,824	7,711,194	9,579,677
Utah....	210,779	276,749	373,351	449,396	507,847	550,310	688,862	890,627
Vermont....	332,422	343,641	355,956	352,428	359,611	359,231	377,747	389,881
Virginia....	1,655,980	1,854,184	2,061,612	2,309,187	2,421,851	2,677,773	3,318,680	3,966,949
Washington.	357,232	518,103	1,141,990	1,356,621	1,563,396	1,736,191	2,378,962	2,853,214
W. Virginia.	762,794	958,800	1,221,119	1,463,701	1,729,205	1,901,974	2,005,553	1,860,421
Wisconsin...	1,693,330	2,069,042	2,333,860	2,632,067	2,939,006	3,137,587	3,434,575	3,951,777
Wyoming....	62,555	92,531	145,965	194,402	225,565	250,742	290,529	330,066
Tot. U. S...	**62,947,714**	**75,994,575**	**91,972,266**	**105,710,620**	**122,775,046**	**131,669,275**	**150,697,361**	**179,323,175**

U. S. Center of Population, 1790 to 1960

Source: Bureau of the Census

Center of population is that point which may be considered as center of population gravity of the U. S. or that point upon which the U. S. would balance if it were a rigid plane without weight and the population distributed thereon with each individual being assumed to have equal weight and to exert an influence on a central point proportional to his distance from that point.

Year	North latitude	West longitude	Approximate location
CONTERMINOUS U.S.[1]			
1790..........	39 16 30	76 11 12	23 miles east of Baltimore, Md.
1800..........	39 16 6	76 56 30	18 miles west of Baltimore, Md.
1810..........	39 11 30	77 37 12	40 miles northwest by west of Washington D. C. (in Virginia).
1820..........	39 5 42	78 33 0	16 miles east of Moorefield, W. Va.[2]
1830..........	38 57 54	79 16 54	19 miles west-southwest of Moorefield, W. Va.[2]
1840..........	39 2 0	80 18 0	16 miles south of Clarksburg, W. Va.[2]
1850..........	38 59 0	81 19 0	23 miles southeast of Parkersburg, W. Va.[2]
1860..........	39 0 24	82 48 48	20 miles south by east of Chillicothe, Ohio.
1870..........	39 12 0	83 35 42	48 miles east by north of Cincinnati, Ohio.
1880..........	39 4 8	84 39 40	8 miles west by south of Cincinnati, Ohio (in Ky.)
1890..........	39 11 56	85 32 53	20 miles east of Columbus, Ind.
1900..........	39 9 36	85 48 54	6 miles southeast of Columbus, Ind.
1910..........	39 10 12	86 32 20	In the city of Bloomington, Ind.
1920..........	39 10 21	86 43 15	8 miles south-southeast of Spencer, Owen County, Ind.
1930..........	39 3 45	87 8 6	3 miles northeast of Linton, Greene County, Ind.
1940..........	38 56 54	87 22 35	2 miles southeast by east of Carlisle, Haddon township, Sullivan County, Ind.
1950..........	38 50 21	88 9 33	8 miles north-northwest of Olney, Richland County, Ill.
1960..........	38 37 57	88 52 23	4 miles east of Salem in Marion County, Ill.
UNITED STATES[3]			
1950..........	38 48 15	88 22 8	About 3 miles northeast of Louisville, in Clay County, Ill.
1960..........	38 35 58	89 12 35	6½ miles northwest of Centralia, Ill., and approximately 50 miles east of East St. Louis, Ill.

[1]Excludes Alaska and Hawaii.
[2]West Virginia was set off from Virginia Dec. 31, 1862, and admitted as a State June 20, 1863.
[3]Includes Alaska and Hawaii.

U. S. Population, White and Nonwhite, by States
Source: Bureau of the Census (Census of 1960)

State	All classes Male	All classes Female	White Male	White Female	Nonwhite Male	Nonwhite Female
Alabama	1,591,709	1,675,031	1,124,061	1,159,548	467,648	515,483
Alaska	128,811	97,356	101,194	73,352	27,617	24,004
Arizona	654,928	647,233	587,872	581,645	67,056	65,588
Arkansas	878,987	907,285	690,762	704,941	188,225	202,344
California	7,836,707	7,880,497	7,193,094	7,262,136	643,613	618,361
Colorado	870,467	883,480	843,575	857,125	26,892	26,355
Connecticut	1,244,229	1,291,005	1,189,653	1,234,163	54,576	56,842
Delaware	221,136	225,156	190,186	194,141	30,950	31,015
Dist. of Col	358,171	405,785	158,124	187,139	200,047	218,646
Florida	2,436,783	2,514,777	2,000,593	2,063,288	436,190	451,489
Georgia	1,925,913	2,017,203	1,391,735	1,425,488	534,178	591,715
Hawaii	338,173	294,599	112,915	89,315	225,258	205,284
Idaho	338,421	328,770	333,298	324,085	5,123	4,685
Illinois	4,952,866	5,128,292	4,435,687	4,574,565	517,179	553,727
Indiana	2,298,738	2,363,760	2,165,509	2,223,045	133,229	140,715
Iowa	1,359,047	1,398,490	1,344,933	1,383,776	14,114	14,714
Kansas	1,081,377	1,097,234	1,031,409	1,047,257	49,968	49,977
Kentucky	1,508,448	1,529,708	1,401,904	1,418,179	106,544	111,529
Louisiana	1,592,254	1,664,768	1,090,306	1,121,409	501,948	543,359
Maine	479,054	490,211	475,682	487,609	3,372	2,602
Maryland	1,533,200	1,567,489	1,273,444	1,300,475	259,756	267,014
Massachusetts	2,486,235	2,662,343	2,423,947	2,599,197	62,288	63,146
Michigan	3,882,868	3,940,326	3,520,422	3,565,443	362,446	374,883
Minnesota	1,692,962	1,720,902	1,671,493	1,700,110	21,469	20,792
Mississippi	1,067,933	1,110,208	625,011	632,535	442,922	477,673
Missouri	2,108,279	2,211,534	1,918,378	2,004,589	189,901	206,945
Montana	343,743	331,024	331,374	319,364	12,369	11,660
Nebraska	700,026	711,304	681,603	693,161	18,423	18,143
Nevada	147,521	137,757	136,298	127,145	11,223	10,612
New Hampshire	298,107	308,814	296,662	307,672	1,445	1,142
New Jersey	2,971,991	3,094,791	2,717,512	2,821,491	254,479	273,300
New Mexico	479,770	471,253	442,352	433,411	37,418	37,842
New York	8,123,239	8,659,065	7,421,364	7,865,707	701,875	793,358
North Carolina	2,247,069	2,309,086	1,684,797	1,714,488	562,272	594,598
North Dakota	323,208	309,238	316,637	302,901	6,571	6,337
Ohio	4,764,228	4,942,169	4,376,126	4,533,572	388,102	408,597
Oklahoma	1,147,851	1,180,433	1,041,202	1,066,698	106,649	113,735
Oregon	879,951	888,736	861,040	870,997	18,911	17,739
Pennsylvania	5,509,851	5,809,515	5,093,879	5,360,125	415,972	449,390
Rhode Island	421,845	437,643	411,265	427,447	10,580	10,196
South Carolina	1,175,818	1,206,776	775,754	775,268	400,064	431,508
South Dakota	344,271	336,243	330,434	322,864	13,837	13,379
Tennessee	1,740,690	1,826,399	1,459,508	1,518,245	281,182	308,151
Texas	4,744,981	4,834,696	4,159,510	4,215,321	585,471	619,375
Utah	444,924	445,703	436,198	437,630	8,726	8,073
Vermont	191,743	198,138	191,321	197,771	422	367
Virginia	1,979,372	1,987,577	1,571,139	1,571,304	408,233	416,273
Washington	1,435,037	1,418,177	1,381,261	1,370,414	53,776	47,763
West Virginia	915,035	945,386	871,178	898,955	43,857	46,431
Wisconsin	1,964,512	1,987,265	1,918,199	1,940,704	46,313	46,568
Wyoming	169,015	161,051	165,349	157,573	3,666	3,471
Total	88,331,494	90,991,681	78,367,149	80,464,583	9,964,345	10,527,098

Latest U. S. Population by Age, Color and Sex
Source: Bureau of Census
Estimates of the total population of the United States and Armed Forces Abroad, July, 1966

Age	All classes Total	All classes Male	All classes Female	White Male	White Female	Nonwhite Male	Nonwhite Female
All ages	196,842,000	96,900,000	99,942,000	85,432,000	87,820,000	11,468,000	12,121,000
Under 5 years	19,851,000	10,135,000	9,715,000	8,512,000	8,117,000	1,624,000	1,598,000
5 to 9 years	20,806,000	10,580,000	10,226,000	9,047,000	8,691,000	1,533,000	1,535,000
10 to 14 years	19,402,000	9,861,000	9,542,000	8,505,000	8,184,000	1,356,000	1,358,000
15 to 19 years	17,895,000	9,088,000	8,807,000	7,933,000	7,653,000	1,155,000	1,154,000
20 to 24 years	14,047,000	7,064,000	6,983,000	6,223,000	6,123,000	841,000	860,000
25 to 29 years	11,611,000	5,770,000	5,841,000	5,110,000	5,111,000	660,000	730,000
30 to 34 years	10,956,000	5,429,000	5,527,000	4,816,000	4,830,000	613,000	697,000
35 to 39 years	11,789,000	5,801,000	5,988,000	5,184,000	5,262,000	618,000	725,000
40 to 44 years	12,436,000	6,064,000	6,372,000	5,445,000	5,667,000	619,000	705,000
45 to 49 years	11,636,000	5,658,000	5,978,000	5,112,000	5,363,000	546,000	615,000
50 to 54 years	10,695,000	5,197,000	5,498,000	4,701,000	4,950,000	496,000	547,000
55 to 59 years	9,331,000	4,491,000	4,839,000	4,082,000	4,395,000	410,000	444,000
60 to 64 years	7,931,000	3,757,000	4,174,000	3,410,000	3,805,000	347,000	369,000
65 to 69 years	6,378,000	2,901,000	3,476,000	2,668,000	3,214,000	233,000	263,000
70 to 74 years	5,190,000	2,261,000	2,929,000	2,083,000	2,708,000	178,000	221,000
75 to 79 years	3,688,000	1,564,000	2,124,000	1,443,000	1,974,000	122,000	150,000
80 to 84 years	2,076,000	847,000	1,230,000	774,000	1,141,000	73,000	89,000
85 years and over	1,124,000	430,000	694,000	385,000	634,000	46,000	60,000
Under 1 year	3,666,000	1,872,000	1,793,000	1,564,000	1,490,000	309,000	303,000
1 to 4 years	16,185,000	8,263,000	7,922,000	6,948,000	6,627,000	1,315,000	1,295,000
5 to 13 years	36,525,000	18,567,000	17,958,000	15,926,000	15,314,000	2,640,000	2,644,000
14 to 17 years	14,300,000	7,268,000	7,032,000	6,298,000	6,062,000	970,000	969,000
18 to 21 years	12,878,000	6,518,000	6,360,000	5,736,000	5,571,000	782,000	789,000
14 years and over	140,466,000	68,198,000	72,268,000	60,994,000	64,389,000	7,204,000	7,880,000
18 years and over	126,167,000	60,930,000	65,237,000	54,696,000	58,326,000	6,234,000	6,911,000
21 years and over	116,100,000	55,829,000	60,271,000	50,202,000	53,971,000	5,627,000	6,300,000
62 years and over	23,052,000	10,172,000	12,880,000	9,318,000	11,884,000	854,000	997,000
65 years and over	18,457,000	8,004,000	10,453,000	7,352,000	9,670,000	652,000	783,000
Median age, years	27.8	26.5	29.0	27.4	30.0	20.4	22.4

U. S. Population, Nonwhite, by States and Races

Source: Bureau of the Census (Census of 1950-1960.)

State	Total		Negro		Indian		Japanese		Chinese	
	1960	1950	1960	1950	1960	1950	1960	1950	1960	1950
Alabama....	983,131	982,152	980,271	979,617	1,276	928	500	88	288	187
Alaska......	51,621	35,835	6,771	(1)	14,444	14,089	818	(1)	137	(1)
Ariz.......	132,644	95,076	43,403	25,974	83,387	65,761	1,501	780	2,936	1,951
Ark.......	390,569	428,004	388,787	426,639	580	533	237	113	676	592
Calif.......	1,261,974	671,050	883,861	462,172	39,014	19,947	157,317	84,956	95,600	58,324
Colo.......	53,247	28,436	39,992	20,177	4,288	1,567	6,846	5,412	724	458
Conn......	111,418	54,951	107,449	53,472	923	333	653	254	865	450
Dist. of Col..	418,693	284,313	411,737	280,803	587	330	900	353	2,632	1,825
Del.......	61,965	44,207	60,688	43,598	597	......	152	-14	191	85
Fls.......	887,679	605,254	880,186	603,101	2,504	1,011	1,315	238	1,023	429
Ga.......	1,125,893	1,064,001	1,122,596	1,062,762	749	333	885	128	686	511
Hawaii..	430,542	385,001	4,943	2,651	472	(1)	203,455	184,611	38,197	32,376
Idaho......	9,808	7,242	1,502	1,050	5,231	3,800	2,254	1,980	311	244
Ill........	1,070,906	666,118	1,037,470	645,980	4,704	1,443	14,074	11,646	7,047	4,207
Ind.......	273,944	175,712	269,275	174,168	948	438	1,093	318	952	496
Ia........	28,828	21,527	25,354	19,692	1,708	1,084	599	310	423	310
Kan.......	99,945	76,338	91,445	73,158	5,069	2,381	1,362	116	537	315
Kentucky...	218,073	202,716	215,949	201,921	391	234	774	74	288	335
La........	1,045,307	886,833	1,039,207	882,428	3,587	409	519	127	731	526
Me........	5,974	2,928	3,318	1,221	1,879	1,522	343	30	123	77
Md........	526,770	388,026	518,410	385,972	1,538	314	1,842	289	2,188	795
Mass.....	125,434	79,011	111,842	73,171	2,118	1,201	1,924	384	6,745	3,627
Mich.....	737,329	453,941	717,581	442,296	9,701	7,000	3,211	1,517	3,234	1,619
Minn.....	42,261	28,786	22,263	14,022	15,496	12,533	1,726	1,049	1,270	720
Miss......	920,595	990,282	915,743	986,494	3,119	2,502	178	62	1,244	1,011
Mo.......	396,846	299,060	390,853	297,088	1,723	547	1,473	527	954	519
Mont......	24,029	18,986	1,467	1,232	-21,181	16,606	589	524	240	209
Nebr......	36,566	24,182	29,262	19,234	5,545	3,954	905	619	290	202
Nev.......	21,835	10,175	13,484	4,302	6,681	5,025	544	382	572	281
N. H.......	2,587	967	1,903	731	135	74	207	25	152	93
N. J.......	527,779	323,744	514,875	318,565	1,699	621	3,514	1,784	3,813	1,818
N. M.....	75,260	50,976	17,063	8,408	56,255	41,901	930	251	362	166
N. Y.......	1,495,233	958,097	1,417,511	918,191	16,491	10,640	8,702	3,893	37,573	20,171
N. C......	1,156,870	1,078,808	1,116,021	1,047,353	38,129	3,742	1,265	98	404	345
N. D......	12,908	11,188	777	257	11,736	10,766	127	61	100	82
Ohio......	796,699	518,405	786,097	513,072	1,910	1,146	3,135	1,986	2,507	1,542
Okla......	220,384	200,825	153,084	145,503	64,689	53,769	749	137	398	397
Ore......	36,650	24,213	18,133	11,529	8,026	5,820	5,016	3,660	2,995	2,102
Pa.......	865,362	644,164	852,750	638,485	2,122	1,141	2,348	1,029	3,741	2,258
R. I.......	20,776	14,881	18,332	13,903	932	385	192	25	574	403
S. C.......	831,572	823,622	829,291	822,077	1,098	554	460	34	158	101
S. D......	27,416	24,236	1,114	727	25,794	23,344	188	56	89	44
Tenn......	589,336	531,461	586,876	530,603	638	339	507	104	487	230
Texas......	1,204,846	984,660	1,187,125	977,458	5,750	2,736	4,053	957	4,172	2,435
Utah......	16,799	11,953	4,148	2,729	6,961	4,201	4,371	4,452	629	335
Vt........	789	559	519	443	57	30	79	14	68	34
Va........	824,506	737,125	816,258	734,211	2,155	1,056	1,733	193	1,135	565
Wash......	101,539	62,467	48,738	30,691	21,076	13,816	16,652	9,694	5,491	3,408
W. Va......	90,288	115,270	89,378	114,867	181	160	176	46	138	99
Wis.......	92,874	41,885	74,546	28,182	14,297	12,196	1,425	529	1,010	590
Wyo......	7,144	6,520	2,183	2,557	4,020	3,237	514	450	192	106
Total....	**20,491,443**	**16,176,169**	**18,871,831**	**15,044,937**	**523,591**	**357,499**	**464,332**	**326,379**	**237,292**	**150,005**

State	Filipino *	All other **	State	Filipino *	All other **	State	Filipino *	All other **
	1960	1960		1960	1960		1960	1960
Ala..........	127	669	La.	754	509	Okla.........	267	1,197
Alaska.......	814	28,637	Me.	131	180	Ore.........	1,109	1,371
Ariz........	943	474	Md..........	1,670	1,122	Pa..........	1,640	2,761
Ark.........	83	206	Mass........	809	1,996	R. I........	424	322
Calif........	*65,459	20,723	Mich........	1,134	2,468	S. C........	328	237
Colo........	605	792	Minn........	646	860	S. D........	59	172
Conn........	726	802	Miss........	59	252	Tenn........	249	579
D. of C.....	1,158	1,679	Mo..........	719	1,124	Texas.......	1,623	2,123
Del.........	67	270	Mont........	253	299	Utah........	207	483
Fla.........	1,361	1,290	Nebr........	123	441	Vt..........	25	41
Ga..........	433	544	Nev.........	286	268	Va..........	1,857	1,368
Hawaii......	*69,070	114,405	N. H........	41	149	Wash........	*7,110	2,472
Idaho.......	193	317	N. J........	1,451	2,427	W. Va.......	105	310
Ill.........	3,587	4,024	N. M........	192	458	Wis.........	401	1,195
Ind.........	402	1,274	N. Y........	*5,403	9,553	Wyo.........	99	136
Ia..........	167	577	N. C........	343	708			
Kan.........	372	1,160	N. D........	47	121	**Total....**	**176,310**	**218,807**
Ky..........	236	435	Ohio........	943	2,107			

¹Not available.

*Filipino 1950—California 40,424; Hawaii 61,071; New York 3,719; Washington 4,274. All other states not available.

**All other total for 1950, 174,642.

Countries of Origin of Foreign Stock in the United States
BY NATIVITY, COLOR AND SEX

Country from which over 100,000 foreign born originate
Source: Bureau of the Census (Census of 1960)

Country of Origin	Total foreign stock			Foreign born[1]		Native of foreign or mixed parentage[2]	
	Total	White	Non-white	White	Non-white	White	Non-white
Austria	1,098,630	1,097,581	1,049	304,192	315	793,389	734
Belgium	140,266	140,028	238	50,210	84	89,818	154
Canada*	3,181,051	3,153,514	27,537	941,906	10,594	2,211,608	16,943
China	208,455	32,543	175,912	12,858	86,877	19,685	89,035
Cuba	124,416	116,354	8,062	74,921	4,229	41,433	3,833
Czechoslovakia	917,530	917,172	658	227,467	151	689,705	507
Denmark	399,350	398,806	544	84,989	71	313,817	473
Finland	240,827	240,525	302	67,540	84	172,985	218
France	351,681	349,360	2,321	110,864	718	238,496	1,603
Germany	4,320,664	4,312,638	8,026	986,564	3,251	3,326,074	4,775
Greece	378,586	377,973	613	158,894	273	219,079	340
Hungary	701,637	700,899	738	244,945	307	455,954	431
Ireland (Eire)	1,773,312	1,771,070	2,242	338,350	372	1,432,720	1,870
Italy	4,543,935	4,539,692	4,243	1,255,812	1,187	3,283,880	3,056
Japan	322,090	30,169	291,921	11,686	97,489	18,483	194,432
Lithuania	402,846	402,498	348	121,349	126	281,149	222
Mexico	1,735,992	1,724,838	11,154	572,564	3,333	1,152,274	7,816
Netherlands	398,658	398,151	507	118,160	255	279,991	252
Norway	774,756	774,081	673	152,644	54	621,437	619
Philippines	201,746	45,328	156,418	15,624	89,219	29,704	67,199
Poland	2,780,026	2,778,210	1,816	747,250	500	2,030,960	1,316
Rumania	233,805	233,540	265	84,471	104	149,069	161
Spain	126,163	125,167	996	44,815	184	80,352	812
Sweden	1,046,942	1,045,763	1,179	214,313	178	831,450	1,001
Switzerland	263,054	262,734	320	61,490	78	201,244	242
Turkey	106,225	105,790	435	51,887	341	53,903	94
United Kingdom							
England	1,826,825	1,820,740	6,085	526,157	2,048	1,294,583	4,037
Scotland	668,672	667,672	1,000	213,026	193	454,646	807
Wales	134,008	133,793	215	23,407	62	110,386	153
Northern Ireland	255,146	254,809	337	68,083	79	186,726	258
USSR	2,290,267	2,286,986	3,281	689,462	1,136	1,597,524	2,145
Yugoslavia	448,503	448,142	361	165,658	140	282,484	221
Total	32,396,362	31,686,566	709,796	8,741,558	304,037	22,945,008	405,759
Other Countries	1,653,992	1,391,773	262,219	552,434	140,062	839,339	122,157
Total all countries	34,050,354	33,078,339	972,015	9,293,992	444,099	23,784,347	527,916

*Includes Newfoundland.

[1]Foreign born—White, Male 4,507,502, Female 4,786,490. Nonwhite, Male 252,930, Female 191,169.

[2]Native of foreign or mixed parentage—White, Male 11,568,891, Female 12,215,456. Nonwhite, Male 266,746, Female 261,170.

Foreign Born in U.S. Standard Metropolitan Statistical Areas
See Pages 318-320 for total population
Source: Bureau of the Census (Census of 1960)

Country	Boston	Chicago	Cleveland	Detroit	Los Angeles-Long Beach	New York	Philadelphia	San Francisco Oakland
Austria	2,683	20,805	8,274	6,725	12,278	95,631	9,441	4,431
Belgium	777	3,451	298	6,840	2,855	6,413	760	979
Canada[1]	83,364	21,428	7,827	94,027	83,685	42,823	8,682	24,328
China	2,790	3,011	481	1,022	8,924	21,529	1,287	23,207
Cuba	385	1,736	212	400	2,194	30,018	788	416
Czechoslovakia	573	28,156	16,985	5,024	6,656	33,756	4,005	1,861
Denmark	949	6,093	456	1,628	6,275	7,205	811	4,680
Finland	1,622	2,036	1,030	1,966	2,152	8,200	468	2,382
France	2,118	3,872	986	2,339	7,860	23,875	3,166	6,460
Germany	8,744	74,120	16,496	25,942	43,056	199,685	32,643	25,052
Greece	7,787	14,995	2,212	5,873	4,849	32,250	2,962	4,740
Hungary	1,189	13,645	18,249	10,790	13,340	52,305	8,549	2,737
Ireland (Eire)	38,741	25,795	4,238	4,402	7,321	119,280	17,745	9,254
Italy	57,718	61,930	19,317	30,794	31,934	345,489	63,570	34,051
Japan	532	2,882	237	638	17,186	4,413	1,285	6,823
Lithuania	6,416	24,802	3,755	4,479	3,760	13,531	4,728	523
Mexico	248	23,450	447	3,565	117,004	3,909	557	18,977
Netherlands	1,082	6,462	800	2,777	12,814	7,433	1,004	3,786
Norway	2,106	9,854	523	1,164	6,483	24,783	1,213	4,635
Philippines	488	2,358	191	673	9,323	4,399	936	16,476
Poland	12,323	90,109	19,437	49,993	23,371	188,492	24,741	4,450
Rumania	760	6,893	3,540	5,219	5,433	27,085	4,258	1,063
Spain	325	485	178	782	2,630	12,193	591	4,005
Sweden	6,526	26,316	1,425	2,875	11,709	17,071	1,632	6,902
Switzerland	597	2,112	467	913	4,168	8,636	1,043	4,304
Turkey	3,701	1,902	492	3,500	4,425	13,213	1,623	1,282
United Kingdom								
England	14,728	18,530	7,613	23,479	47,250	58,259	18,441	16,966
Scotland	8,818	8,835	3,895	18,132	14,644	30,229	8,863	6,187
Wales	328	846	599	960	1,719	1,478	726	759
North'n Ireland	3,099	3,194	791	2,224	3,529	15,516	7,956	2,131
USSR	28,863	43,700	11,487	19,435	43,544	222,354	46,038	12,399
Yugoslavia	306	21,574	15,505	8,570	9,656	13,954	2,738	3,475
Other Countries	20,151	25,633	6,691	17,425	44,646	172,991	13,979	40,550
Total	320,328	601,010	175,134	364,575	616,673	1,858,898	297,229	300,241

[1]Includes Newfoundland.

Country of Birth of Foreign Born
Source: Bureau of the Census (1960 Census)

State	Total Foreign Born	Austria	Belgium	Canada¹	China	Czechoslov.	Denmark	England²	Finland	France	Germany
Alabama	14,955	357	78	1,171	124	223	114	2,350	39	465	3,196
Alaska	8,227	105	37	1,866	108	99	157	641	201	153	1,103
Arizona	70,318	1,061	268	6,234	1,053	643	430	4,101	219	624	4,273
Arkansas	7,457	250	69	687	251	175	63	1,128	21	143	1,457
California	1,343,686	21,269	5,012	149,351	40,796	10,847	17,503	121,442	6,809	20,585	95,279
Colorado	59,874	2,067	291	3,954	449	910	979	5,289	198	904	8,522
Connecticut	275,523	6,096	647	34,253	543	6,616	1,816	21,960	1,962	2,770	19,446
Delaware	14,650	330	87	912	60	201	64	1,982	41	150	1,726
Dist. of Col.	38,971	862	164	1,902	1,411	523	242	3,406	146	1,280	3,166
Florida	272,161	7,830	1,378	31,905	631	4,217	2,752	32,324	2,710	4,022	24,757
Georgia	25,300	649	173	2,048	344	316	179	3,616	94	776	6,906
Hawaii	68,897	141	92	1,312	3,541	75	78	1,229	28	202	1,287
Idaho	15,542	336	70	2,500	140	208	588	1,731	216	245	1,685
Illinois	686,093	23,288	6,495	25,268	3,520	30,345	7,087	37,179	2,297	5,684	87,707
Indiana	93,202	2,579	1,645	6,533	596	3,773	411	8,465	187	1,215	13,474
Iowa	56,278	845	565	2,725	246	2,307	4,864	3,917	88	662	14,368
Kansas	33,268	1,242	401	2,038	291	786	454	3,067	64	765	7,049
Kentucky	16,830	463	117	1,161	155	168	85	2,091	4	511	5,015
Louisiana	30,557	365	165	1,611	331	182	199	2,622	67	1,357	3,091
Maine	60,403	150	28	44,075	107	225	285	3,939	653	309	1,378
Maryland	94,174	2,468	435	5,847	974	2,187	639	9,453	481	1,618	15,239
Massachusetts	576,452	5,026	1,537	152,057	3,256	1,762	1,536	49,285	6,050	4,839	17,593
Michigan	529,624	10,649	9,034	126,095	1,628	10,005	3,009	57,217	9,111	3,526	43,655
Minnesota	143,874	3,753	881	13,722	760	3,592	4,717	5,936	8,717	635	18,129
Mississippi	8,058	63	32	567	546	56	83	1,150	34	211	1,083
Missouri	77,756	3,926	546	3,563	432	1,803	588	5,515	41	1,041	15,728
Montana	30,646	1,058	259	5,619	98	425	1,010	3,349	727	256	2,568
Nebraska	40,238	871	247	1,562	108	3,819	2,888	2,333	37	257	8,743
Nevada	13,133	343	76	1,798	322	57	330	1,381	57	621	1,120
N. Hampshire	44,772	423	298	26,301	81	109	118	3,630	542	333	1,639
New Jersey	615,474	22,397	2,723	17,674	2,028	16,341	3,704	55,203	2,163	7,290	81,505
New Mexico	21,408	320	108	1,123	211	149	84	1,810	23	395	1,949
New York	2,289,310	107,101	7,955	111,280	22,251	42,021	9,462	131,122	9,765	27,639	250,173
North Carolina	21,978	506	163	2,113	255	186	160	3,052	35	547	4,657
North Dakota	29,907	562	105	3,749	75	418	764	730	182	103	2,794
Ohio	396,610	17,340	1,380	20,643	1,473	29,304	1,139	34,760	2,216	3,312	46,988
Oklahoma	20,003	503	103	1,674	184	681	169	2,342	11	468	4,234
Oregon	71,314	1,520	409	15,853	1,161	950	1,813	7,366	2,227	782	6,907
Pennsylvania	603,490	36,750	2,018	14,432	1,738	34,846	1,303	52,030	947	5,361	54,878
Rhode Island	85,974	830	524	18,072	393	197	123	12,321	414	1,320	2,535
South Carolina	11,140	242	61	1,039	122	112	44	2,022	31	446	2,266
South Dakota	18,577	340	95	1,050	37	593	1,624	993	151	51	3,342
Tennessee	15,843	306	92	1,575	226	200	106	2,111	16	261	2,836
Texas	298,791	2,752	738	7,960	1,941	5,054	893	12,176	172	2,444	19,506
Utah	32,133	441	232	2,256	287	112	1,665	5,568	169	359	5,585
Vermont	23,336	133	27	15,092	59	107	98	1,997	269	179	746
Virginia	48,181	996	328	4,736	745	861	531	7,321	151	1,547	8,132
Washington	178,658	2,868	706	44,423	2,925	1,266	3,336	18,552	4,703	1,501	14,483
West Virginia	23,863	912	323	822	84	947	71	2,545	72	337	1,536
Wisconsin	171,519	8,411	1,020	7,505	547	6,679	4,400	7,519	1,946	899	43,554
Wyoming	9,663	412	57	774	91	140	303	1,535	120	182	827
Totals	9,738,091	304,507	50,294	952,500	99,735	227,618	85,060	764,893	67,624	111,582	989,815

¹Includes Newfoundland. ²Includes Scotland and Wales

State	Greece	Hungary	Ireland (Eire)	Italy	State	Greece	Hungary	Ireland (Eire)	Italy
Alabama	715	262	243	1,151	Nebraska	454	283	500	1,996
Alaska	63	110	82	101	Nevada	383	171	202	1,665
Arizona	599	798	610	2,450	N. Hampshire	2,006	121	1,221	1,138
Arkansas	229	130	108	525	New Jersey	7,396	27,389	22,386	137,356
California	14,491	19,799	21,340	102,366	New Mexico	321	99	188	809
Colorado	903	1,049	894	4,797	New York	36,579	60,382	131,764	440,063
Connecticut	3,459	7,954	12,262	65,233	North Carolina	1,549	253	268	567
Delaware	374	259	606	2,914	North Dakota	106	515	221	73
Dist. of Col.	1,774	639	1,005	3,086	Ohio	8,872	35,082	7,184	50,338
Florida	3,720	7,404	4,408	16,217	Oklahoma	387	256	203	710
Georgia	884	244	389	750	Oregon	897	866	1,378	3,024
Hawaii	48	117	115	249	Pennsylvania	8,816	23,823	22,534	131,149
Idaho	209	147	172	420	Rhode Island	858	220	4,426	18,438
Illinois	16,660	15,652	26,880	72,139	South Carolina	739	108	188	260
Indiana	3,517	5,816	1,073	4,756	South Dakota	183	79	161	174
Iowa	1,145	324	769	2,254	Tennessee	426	279	176	1,383
Kansas	431	274	496	1,024	Texas	2,034	1,238	2,228	4,568
Kentucky	400	299	437	911	Utah	1,537	79	139	1,437
Louisiana	356	303	563	5,470	Vermont	141	104	327	1,208
Maine	482	136	1,219	1,568	Virginia	1,709	811	945	2,468
Maryland	2,818	1,775	2,202	10,454	Washington	1,918	1,170	2,158	6,072
Massachusetts	13,519	1,871	51,428	86,921	West Virginia	1,292	1,380	235	5,882
Michigan	7,782	14,996	5,582	36,879	Wisconsin	1,891	5,787	945	8,479
Minnesota	1,176	1,297	1,398	3,541	Wyoming	498	95	254	555
Mississippi	247	46	159	923					
Missouri	1,833	2,636	2,513	9,033					
Montana	341	325	938	1,055	Totals	159,167	245,252	338,722	1,256,999

Country of Birth of Foreign Born

Source: Bureau of the Census (1960 Census)

States	Japan	Lithuania	Mexico	Netherlands	North Ireland	Norway	Philippines	Poland	Portugal	Romania	Spain
Alabama	329	136	141	144	68	128	113	415	12	56	44
Alaska	376	8	77	52	49	962	515	97	4	8	10
Arizona	538	339	35,834	529	202	434	554	1,489	59	278	291
Arkansas	137	74	209	44	29	58	63	198	4	82	38
California	38,332	5,068	248,542	23,513	7,258	15,723	44,635	31,877	13,921	7,718	10,897
Colorado	1,964	196	4,882	966	237	580	559	2,032	15	450	135
Connecticut	303	7,508	245	1,132	2,278	1,734	630	30,326	3,253	862	1,045
Delaware	133	79	51	250	242	110	34	1,599	35	61	32
Dist. of Col	642	385	330	308	122	227	877	1,943	117	187	390
Florida	945	2,126	1,312	3,132	1,690	2,744	1,307	11,770	443	2,519	3,475
Georgia	548	118	161	287	140	142	348	1,138	88	154	138
Hawaii	24,658	38	112	90	43	82	28,649	93	764	29	146
Idaho	497	20	1,010	383	96	725	64	134	4	48	961
Illinois	3,551	27,977	25,477	7,734	3,554	11,524	2,534	94,132	136	7,194	735
Indiana	601	1,410	5,058	1,729	499	440	283	9,600	25	1,587	382
Iowa	258	427	1,038	4,335	395	3,159	130	1,133	10	180	23
Kansas	1,154	81	3,495	323	134	239	408	836	9	89	93
Kentucky	603	137	116	152	107	49	118	511	11	119	40
Louisiana	396	45	3,714	367	111	362	594	742	46	144	374
Maine	304	574	63	69	176	366	112	773	73	35	25
Maryland	1,299	2,602	478	912	526	730	1,280	7,825	94	801	340
Massachusetts	1,397	13,387	403	1,902	4,848	3,401	703	36,536	21,453	1,042	579
Michigan	1,324	7,143	6,292	20,395	3,014	2,868	919	63,378	117	6,037	893
Minnesota	533	785	846	2,649	358	20,009	511	6,295	.....	902	32
Mississippi	160	50	232	88	30	87	96	134	8	31	51
Missouri	816	642	2,506	451	304	199	600	5,072	53	1,512	361
Montana	262	78	430	748	201	3,371	167	611	.....	141	38
Nebraska	307	763	1,521	258	119	367	103	1,836	4	160	43
Nevada	257	24	920	130	71	159	240	188	63	56	620
New Hampshire	165	607	28	115	191	303	104	1,907	91	33	52
New Jersey	1,832	6,667	769	10,928	6,672	6,432	1,115	63,689	4,027	4,030	3,626
New Mexico	467	57	10,725	226	56	103	181	182	4	33	110
New York	5,564	17,815	4,496	13,132	18,749	27,125	5,037	234,742	4,489	29,040	13,563
North Carolina	1,140	105	207	521	145	190	261	554	28	66	57
North Dakota	152	42	72	241	49	7,274	28	545	7	267	4
Ohio	1,256	5,473	2,639	2,233	1,835	1,079	652	34,597	226	9,134	1,075
Oklahoma	600	88	1,105	249	94	146	198	534	28	65	58
Oregon	1,297	261	1,000	1,178	376	3,908	728	1,110	98	335	221
Pennsylvania	1,307	13,301	1,437	1,781	9,388	1,669	1,204	63,386	836	6,565	1,443
Rhode Island	174	455	47	144	790	263	354	4,002	6,664	209	102
South Carolina	383	45	52	126	81	79	235	430	12	45	36
South Dakota	104	35	56	1,055	72	3,079	30	216	4	122	5
Tennessee	449	75	232	108	63	55	212	921	8	69	56
Texas	2,893	374	202,315	1,333	454	843	1,412	3,725	124	459	785
Utah	1,049	7	1,153	3,905	95	967	197	151	.....	21	134
Vermont	82	35	30	101	87	84	17	678	24	23	224
Virginia	1,273	480	270	716	476	571	1,386	1,398	101	190	260
Washington	5,625	485	3,407	3,495	1,039	18,522	3,999	2,458	46	442	228
West Virginia	115	364	194	49	86	25	82	1,896	27	154	564
Wisconsin	477	2,471	1,880	3,678	414	8,693	229	17,695	25	768	106
Wyoming	147	13	770	29	49	289	36	221	.....	23	59
Totals	109,175	121,475	575,902	118,415	66,162	152,698	104,843	747,750	57,690	84,575	44,999

State	Sweden	Switzerland	U.S.S.R.	Yugoslavia	State	Sweden	Switzerland	U.S.S.R.	Yugoslavia
Alabama	160	112	477	104	Nebraska	2,892	334	4,826	577
Alaska	442	74	155	139	Nevada	267	254	325	225
Arizona	894	346	1,800	731	New Hampshire	716	109	927	82
Arkansas	171	132	260	112	New Jersey	6,287	4,832	46,268	5,490
California	26,553	15,157	68,677	18,210	New Mexico	136	102	202	236
Colorado	2,468	460	7,583	1,628	New York	23,516	10,926	245,063	17,488
Connecticut	7,668	1,545	16,542	1,159	North Carolina	222	162	554	106
Delaware	146	92	944	90	North Dakota	1,838	102	7,851	71
Dist. of Col	447	357	3,884	223	Ohio	3,368	2,513	20,530	28,870
Florida	6,323	1,596	18,183	1,520	Oklahoma	191	149	1,281	138
Georgia	204	108	1,280	98	Oregon	4,538	1,685	4,349	998
Hawaii	78	58	183	20	Pennsylvania	4,603	2,331	59,894	18,450
Idaho	1,035	304	736	204	Rhode Island	2,019	152	3,960	55
Illinois	34,606	2,940	45,522	24,570	South Carolina	65	55	347	56
Indiana	1,710	436	3,113	5,531	South Dakota	1,430	161	2,480	69
Iowa	3,813	522	1,777	867	Tennessee	177	168	986	68
Kansas	1,243	337	2,735	1,252	Texas	1,625	743	3,472	627
Kentucky	128	253	699	148	Utah	1,316	870	229	305
Louisiana	179	84	760	358	Vermont	345	118	364	41
Maine	586	63	1,082	30	Virginia	387	332	1,859	251
Maryland	874	575	10,332	566	Washington	13,507	1,682	6,611	2,775
Massachusetts	13,607	956	38,604	625	West Virginia	56	132	774	1,017
Michigan	7,790	1,513	25,784	11,633	Wisconsin	5,519	3,633	9,145	9,364
Minnesota	25,323	673	6,676	4,328	Wyoming	451	126	822	428
Mississippi	84	16	233	145					
Missouri	947	88	6,837	2,578					
Montana	1,541	303	2,616	1,142	**Totals**	214,491	61,565	690,598	165,798

Population of Voting Age—Votes Cast for President 1964-1960

Source: Bureau of the Census
(Population includes armed forces stationed in each state. Percentages based on unrounded numbers.)

State	1964 Pop. of voting age	Votes cast Number (Rounded)	Per cent	1960 Pop. of voting age	Votes cast Number (Rounded)	Per cent
Alabama	1,915,000	690,000	36.0	1,834,000	570,000	31.1
Alaska	138,000	67,000	48.7	134,000	61,000	45.5
Arizona	879,000	481,000	54.7	732,000	398,000	54.5
Arkansas	1,124,000	560,000	49.8	1,043,000	429,000	41.1
California	10,916,000	7,058,000	64.7	9,660,000	6,507,000	67.4
Colorado	1,142,000	777,000	68.0	1,031,000	736,000	71.4
Connecticut	1,698,000	1,219,000	71.8	1,591,000	1,223,000	76.8
Delaware	283,000	201,000	71.0	267,000	197,000	73.6
District of Columbia	517,000	199,000	38.4	509,000	...	...
Florida	3,516,000	1,854,000	52.5	3,088,000	1,544,000	50.0
Georgia	2,636,000	1,139,000	43.2	2,410,000	733,000	30.4
Hawaii	395,000	207,000	52.5	360,000	185,000	51.3
Idaho	386,000	292,000	75.8	372,000	300,000	80.7
Illinois	6,358,000	4,703,000	74.0	6,281,000	4,757,000	75.7
Indiana	2,826,000	2,092,000	74.0	2,778,000	2,135,000	76.9
Iowa	1,638,000	1,185,000	72.3	1,664,000	1,274,000	76.5
Kansas	1,323,000	858,000	64.8	1,322,000	929,000	70.3
Kentucky	1,976,000	1,046,000	52.9	1,898,000	1,124,000	59.2
Louisiana	1,893,000	896,000	47.3	1,804,000	808,000	44.8
Maine	581,000	381,000	65.6	581,000	422,000	72.6
Maryland	1,995,000	1,116,000	56.0	1,845,000	1,055,000	57.2
Massachusetts	3,290,000	2,345,000	71.3	3,245,000	2,469,000	76.1
Michigan	4,647,000	3,203,000	68.9	4,580,000	3,318,000	72.4
Minnesota	2,024,000	1,554,000	76.8	2,001,000	1,542,000	77.0
Mississippi	1,243,000	409,000	32.9	1,171,000	298,000	25.5
Missouri	2,696,000	1,818,000	67.4	2,696,000	1,934,000	71.8
Montana	399,000	279,000	69.9	359,000	278,000	71.4
Nebraska	877,000	584,000	66.6	858,000	613,000	71.4
Nevada	244,000	135,000	55.5	175,000	107,000	61.2
New Hampshire	396,000	288,000	72.3	373,000	296,000	79.4
New Jersey	4,147,000	2,847,000	68.6	3,861,000	2,773,000	71.8
New Mexico	514,000	328,000	63.7	501,000	311,000	62.1
New York	11,330,000	7,166,000	63.2	10,881,000	7,291,000	67.0
North Carolina	2,753,000	1,425,000	51.8	2,557,000	1,369,000	53.5
North Dakota	358,000	258,000	72.2	355,000	278,000	78.5
Ohio	5,960,000	3,969,000	66.6	5,839,000	4,162,000	71.3
Oklahoma	1,493,000	932,000	62.5	1,416,000	903,000	63.8
Oregon	1,130,000	786,000	69.6	1,073,000	776,000	72.3
Pennsylvania	7,080,000	4,823,000	68.1	7,100,000	5,007,000	70.5
Rhode Island	568,000	390,000	68.6	540,000	406,000	75.1
South Carolina	1,380,000	525,000	38.0	1,266,000	387,000	30.5
South Dakota	404,000	293,000	72.6	392,000	306,000	78.3
Tennessee	2,239,000	1,144,000	51.1	2,093,000	1,052,000	50.3
Texas	5,922,000	2,627,000	44.4	5,534,000	2,312,000	41.8
Utah	522,000	401,000	76.9	468,000	375,000	80.1
Vermont	240,000	163,000	67.9	231,000	167,000	72.5
Virginia	2,541,000	1,042,000	41.0	2,313,000	771,000	33.4
Washington	1,759,000	1,258,000	71.5	1,718,000	1,242,000	72.3
West Virginia	1,053,000	792,000	75.2	1,083,000	838,000	77.3
Wisconsin	2,391,000	1,692,000	70.8	2,354,000	1,729,000	73.4
Wyoming	195,000	143,000	73.2	190,000	141,000	74.0
Total	**113,931,000**	**70,642,000**	**62.0**	**108,458,000**	**68,839,000**	**63.5**

Estimated Population of Voting Age for 1968

Source: Bureau of the Census

New England:
Maine 596,000
New Hampshire 418,000
Vermont 244,000
Massachusetts 3,379,000
Rhode Island 561,000
Connecticut 1,813,000

East South Central:
Kentucky 2,062,000
Tennessee 2,361,000
Alabama 2,037,000
Mississippi 1,308,000

Mountain:
Montana 412,000
Idaho 404,000
Wyoming 202,000
Colorado 1,211,000
New Mexico 562,000
Arizona 1,003,000
Utah 562,000

Nevada 285,000

Middle Atlantic:
New York 11,773,000
New Jersey 4,402,000
Pennsylvania 7,234,000

West North Central:
Minnesota 2,097,000
Iowa 1,653,000
Missouri 2,770,000
North Dakota 370,000
South Dakota 408,000
Nebraska 891,000
Kansas 1,339,000

East North Central:
Ohio 6,235,000
Indiana 2,946,000
Illinois 6,580,000
Michigan 4,853,000
Wisconsin 2,484,000

South Atlantic:
Delaware 306,000
Maryland 2,168,000
Dist. of Col. 515,000
Virginia 2,690,000
West Virginia 1,073,000
North Carolina 2,919,000
South Carolina 1,455,000
Georgia 2,834,000
Florida 3,924,000

West South Central:
Arkansas 1,188,000
Louisiana 2,032,000
Oklahoma 1,546,000
Texas 6,289,000

Pacific:
Washington 1,838,000
Oregon 1,193,000
California 12,052,000
Alaska 151,000
Hawaii 421,000

Do You Need A Birth Certificate?

Although a birth certificate is of great value in situations requiring documentation of date and place of birth, such as qualifying for Social Security or Medicare benefits, in obtaining a passport or in qualifying for certain jobs, many Americans do not possess such a certificate and may not be able to obtain one because the birth was not recorded or because records are not available.

In most instances a transcript from early census records is acceptable as a substitute for a birth certificate. The Bureau of the Census maintains a special office and a staff of trained researchers especially to provide this service, and charges a fee to cover the cost.

You may obtain an application form at your local Social Security Office or from the Personal Census Service Branch, Bureau of the Census, Pittsburg, Kan. 66762. Your application form should be accompanied by a check or money order in the amount of $4 for a regular search, or $5 for an expedited search.

Transcripts from a regular search of census records usually are available within 4 to 6 weeks; from an expedited search in about 2 weeks.

Applications should be made by the person himself or by a legally authorized representative.

Jewish Population by Countries and Cities

Source: Jewish Statistical Bureau, Dr. H. S. Linfield, Exec. Secy. Figures are 1967 estimates

North America	5,996,000	Australia and New Zealand	72,000
Central and South America	731,450	Africa	240,600
Europe	3,956,800		
Asia	2,785,650	World total	73,782,500

Country		Country		Country		Country	
Europe		Switzerland	20,000	Honduras	150	Pakistan	400
Albania	200	Turkey	43,000	Jamaica	1,000	Philippines	500
Austria	12,000	Yugoslavia	7,000	Mexico	30,000	Syria	2,000
Belgium	41,000			Nicaragua	200	Thailand	100
Bulgaria	7,000	**North America**		Panama	2,000	Yemen	2,000
Czechoslovakia	18,000	Canada	275,000	Paraguay	1,200		
Denmark	6,000	United States	5,721,000	Peru	4,000	**Africa**	
Finland	1,700			Trinidad	400	Abyssinia	12,000
France	520,000	**Central and**		Uruguay	50,000	Algeria	3,000
Germany	30,000	**South America**		Venezuela	9,000	Congo	300
Gibraltar	650	Argentina	450,000			Egypt	2,000
Great Britain	450,000	Barbados	100	**Asia**		Kenya	1,000
Greece	6,500	Bolivia	4,000	Aden	300	Libya	6,000
Hungary	80,000	Brasil	130,000	Afghanistan	800	Morocco	70,000
Irish Free State	4,000	Chile	30,000	Burma	200	Mozambique	150
Italy	35,000	Colombia	10,000	Cyprus	100	Rhodesia	6,000
Luxemburg	1,000	Costa Rica	1,500	China	250	Sudan	350
Malta	100	Cuba	2,500	Hong Kong	100	Tunisia	23,000
Netherlands	23,000	Curacao	700	India	16,000	Union of	
Norway	1,000	Dominican		Indonesia	100	South Africa	116,000
Poland	25,000	Republic	500	Iran	80,000	Zambia	800
Portugal	500	Dutch Guiana	500	Iraq	6,000		
Romania	120,000	Ecuador	2,000	Israel	2,669,000	**Australia and**	
Soviet Union	2,485,000	El Salvador	300	Japan	1,000	**New Zealand**	
Spain	3,000	Guatemala	1,200	Lebanon	6,000	Australia	67,000
Sweden	14,000	Haiti	200	Malaysia	800	New Zealand	5,000

ESTIMATED JEWISH POPULATION IN FOREIGN CITIES (Over 5,000)

Amsterdam	12,000	Glasgow	13,500	Melbourne	27,500	Strassbourg	14,000
Antwerp	13,000	Haifa	204,000	Milan	8,000	Sydney	23,000
Ascalon	35,000	Istanbul	30,000	Montreal	105,000	Teheran	30,000
Ashdod	23,000	Jerusalem	192,000	Moscow	285,000	Tel Aviv-Jaffa	393,000
Beersheba	65,000	Johannesburg	57,500	Nasareth	29,000	Tiberias	23,500
Berlin	6,000	Kharkov	80,000	Nice	20,000	Toronto	88,000
Bordeaux	6,500	Kiev	220,000	Ottawa	5,500	Toulouse	20,000
Brussels	25,000	Leeds	18,000	Paris	300,000	Tunis	10,000
Bucharest	65,000	Leningrad	165,000	Petach Tikvah	69,000	Vancouver	8,000
Budapest	65,000	Liverpool	7,500	Ramath Gan	162,000	Vienna	9,000
Buenos Aires	360,000	Lod (Lydda)	23,500	Rio de Janeiro	60,000	Warsaw	5,000
Burmingham	6,300	London (gr.)	280,000	Rome	12,000	Winnipeg	21,000
Casablanca	52,000	Lyons	25,000	Sao Paulo	55,000	Zurich	6,200
Copenhagen	6,000	Manchester	28,000	Santiago	25,000		
Elat	9,700	Marseilles	60,000	Stockholm	7,000		

ESTIMATED JEWISH POPULATION IN LARGE U. S. CITIES (Over 10,000)

Albany	11,000	Hollywood, Fla.	12,000	Queens	420,000	Pittsburgh	45,000
Atlanta	15,500	Houston	20,000	Richmond	11,000	Prince George	
Atlantic City*	10,000	Jersey City	13,000	N. Y. City environs:		County, Md	19,000
Baltimore	85,000	Kansas City	22,000	Nassau Co.	372,000	Providence	20,000
Bergen County	80,000	Long Beach Cal	12,000	Suffolk Co.	42,000	Rochester	21,500
Boston*	169,000	Los Angeles*	490,000	Westchester		St. Louis	57,000
Bridgeport*	14,500	Lynn	12,000	County	131,000	St. Paul	10,000
Buffalo	25,000	Miami	92,000	Newark:		San Diego	10,000
Camden	15,000	Milwaukee	27,000	Essex Co.	100,000	San Francisco*	71,000
Chicago*	270,000	Minneapolis	22,000	Oakland:		Seattle	11,000
Cincinnati	27,000	Montg'y Co.,		Alemeda		Springfield,	
Cleveland	85,000	Md.	47,000	and Contra		Mass.	12,000
Columbus	10,000	New Brunswick	10,000	Costa.	18,000	Stamford	10,000
Dallas	20,000	New Haven.	20,000	Orange Co.		Syracuse	11,000
Denver	22,000	New Orleans.	10,000	Calif.	30,000	Teaneck	12,000
Detroit	85,000	New York City	1,836,000	Passaic.	12,000	Waco*	12,000
Elizabeth*	16,500	Manhattan	250,000	Paterson	15,000	Washington*	90,000
Fairlawn	10,500	Bronx	395,000	Philadelphia*.	330,000	Worcester	10,000
Hartford	26,000	Brooklyn	760,000	Phoenix*	12,000		

*Indicates greater area.

Density of Population by States

BY SQUARE MILE, LAND AREA ONLY
Source: Bureau of the Census

State	1920	1950	1960**	State	1920	1950	1960**	State	1920	1950	1960**
Ala.	45.8	59.9	64.2	La.	39.6	59.4	72.1P	Okla.	29.2	32.4	33.8
Alaska*	0.1	0.2	.39P	Maine	25.7	29.4	31.3P	Oregon	8.2	15.8	18.4
Ariz.	2.9	6.6	11.5	Md.	145.8	237.1	313.5	Pa.	194.5	233.1	251.4
Ark.	33.4	36.3	34.2	Mass.	479.2	596.2	657.5	R. I.	566.4	748.5	819.3
Calif.	22.0	67.5	100.4	Mich.	63.8	111.7	136.3P	S. C.	55.2	69.9	78.7
Colo.	9.1	12.8	16.9	Minn.	29.5	37.3	43.1P	S. D.	8.3	8.5	9.0
Conn.	286.4	409.7	520.6	Miss.	38.6	46.1	46.0	Tenn.	56.1	78.8	86.2
Del.	113.5	160.8	225.2	Mo.	49.5	57.1	62.6P	Texas.	17.8	29.3	36.4
D. C.	7,292.9	13,150.5	12,442.3	Mont.	3.8	4.1	4.6	Utah	5.5	8.4	10.8
Fla.	17.7	51.1	91.5	Neb.	16.9	17.3	18.4P	Vt.	38.6	40.7	42.0
Ga.	49.3	58.9	67.8	Nev.	.9	1.5	2.6	Va.	57.4	83.2	99.3
Hawaii.	39.9	78.0	96.7P	N. H.	49.1	59.1	67.2	Wash.	20.3	35.6	42.8
Idaho.	5.2	7.1	8.1	N. J.	420.0	642.8	805.5	W. Va.	60.9	83.3	77.2
Illinois.	115.7	155.8	180.4P	N. M.	2.9	5.6	7.8	Wis.	47.6	62.8	72.6
Indiana.	81.3	108.7	128.8	N. Y.	217.9	309.3	350.8	Wyo.	2.0	3.0	3.4
Iowa.	43.2	46.8	49.2	N. C.	52.5	82.7	92.9P				
Kan.	21.6	23.2	26.6	N. D.	9.2	8.8	9.1	U.S.	*29.9	*42.6	50.5P
Ky.	60.1	73.9	76.2	Ohio.	141.4	193.8	236.7P				

* For purposes of comparison. Alaska and Hawaii included in above tabulation for 1920 and 1950 even though not states then. **Revised 1967. P-Preliminary.

Number of inhabitants per sq. mi. of Land Area in U. S. (1790) 4.5; (1800) 6.1; (1810) 4.3; (1820) 5.5; (1830) 7.4; (1840) 9.8; (1850) 7.9; (1860) 10.6; (1870) 13.0; (1880) 16.9; (1890) 21.2; (1900) 25.6; (1910) 31.0; (1920) 35.5; (1930) 41.2; (1940) 44.2; (1950) 50.7; (1960) 50.5 (Alaska and Hawaii included only in 1960).

Marital Status of United States Population by States
Source: Bureau of the Census (1960 Census)

States	Male 14 years old and over				Female 14 years old and over			
	Total	Single	Married	Widowed or divorced	Total	Single	Married	Widowed or divorced
Alabama.........	1,059,866	270,845	735,545	53,476	1,157,626	221,981	752,437	183,208
Alaska..........	89,132	30,756	52,958	5,418	59,626	9,236	45,821	4,569
Arizona........	435,986	108,368	301,183	26,435	435,196	76,873	298,782	59,541
Arkansas.......	606,401	145,217	423,049	38,135	643,007	108,663	428,607	105,737
California......	5,530,596	1,371,603	3,786,286	372,707	5,652,177	928,656	3,771,579	951,942
Colorado.......	594,842	144,886	414,228	35,728	616,527	109,310	415,785	91,432
Connecticut....	881,494	221,220	613,984	46,290	942,847	197,177	616,690	128,980
Delaware.......	151,235	36,305	106,852	8,078	157,955	29,546	107,250	21,159
Dist. of Col....	265,503	82,417	164,116	18,970	313,161	84,367	168,601	60,193
Florida........	1,730,220	374,544	1,241,993	113,683	1,827,398	272,521	1,249,347	305,530
Georgia........	1,290,444	335,377	891,632	63,435	1,397,751	261,801	909,846	226,404
Hawaii.........	232,805	84,965	134,421	13,419	193,684	44,376	128,528	20,780
Idaho.........	226,097	55,122	157,798	13,177	221,295	36,234	157,901	27,160
Illinois.......	3,498,909	862,301	2,421,448	215,160	3,719,766	705,238	2,439,625	574,905
Indiana........	1,580,100	357,882	1,127,277	94,941	1,670,751	288,626	1,132,436	249,689
Iowa........	941,937	225,414	663,565	52,958	999,250	186,617	665,925	146,708
Kansas........	754,886	174,588	537,048	43,250	783,472	129,835	537,325	116,312
Kentucky......	1,036,635	272,754	703,396	60,485	1,074,053	203,317	707,757	162,979
Louisiana......	1,037,798	267,633	716,265	53,900	1,126,618	220,706	734,376	171,536
Maine........	334,141	86,356	224,921	22,864	349,182	68,276	225,143	55,763
Maryland......	1,054,302	267,338	733,011	53,953	1,100,932	210,392	740,061	150,498
Massachusetts..	1,767,940	487,744	1,177,799	102,397	1,971,652	479,217	1,190,007	302,472
Michigan......	2,622,801	626,942	1,845,155	150,704	2,725,768	500,994	1,856,372	368,428
Minnesota.....	1,148,286	313,625	775,743	58,918	1,196,196	257,360	778,308	160,551
Mississippi....	693,456	190,286	465,811	37,359	746,017	147,842	478,764	119,429
Missouri.......	1,496,446	346,446	1,053,285	96,715	1,620,617	286,446	1,059,992	274,118
Montana.......	234,200	63,003	155,254	15,943	224,198	38,191	154,769	31,278
Nebraska......	488,723	120,473	341,033	27,217	507,502	92,119	341,875	73,534
Nevada.......	105,363	24,827	71,084	9,452	96,690	13,167	69,509	14,004
New Hampshire.	209,518	52,846	143,172	13,500	223,616	45,038	144,104	34,418
New Jersey.....	2,125,478	519,170	1,497,601	108,707	2,278,413	442,593	1,511,112	324,777
New Mexico....	305,452	79,090	210,812	15,550	301,432	56,403	209,892	35,101
New York......	5,888,946	1,537,321	4,035,908	315,717	6,498,895	1,407,437	4,109,697	981,738
North Carolina.	1,518,107	421,557	1,036,364	60,186	1,600,462	332,546	1,054,388	213,562
North Dakota...	217,868	69,007	139,140	9,721	208,074	44,814	139,138	24,128
Ohio..........	3,267,146	742,609	2,322,247	202,290	3,499,338	642,553	2,333,487	523,222
Oklahoma......	812,235	184,934	574,424	52,877	856,059	130,662	576,185	149,291
Oregon........	616,766	139,280	435,000	42,486	634,518	102,736	436,231	95,512
Pennsylvania...	3,915,461	987,646	2,701,373	226,442	4,270,170	904,654	2,740,734	624,757
Rhode Island...	303,887	84,312	202,075	17,500	323,812	72,513	203,042	48,286
South Carolina.	765,653	233,698	505,151	29,804	810,626	177,777	516,583	116,253
South Dakota...	233,532	66,168	155,237	12,127	229,543	44,426	155,464	29,667
Tennessee......	1,199,101	298,535	836,525	64,041	1,300,251	245,625	850,469	204,153
Texas.........	3,212,658	769,443	2,261,537	181,678	3,339,071	562,011	2,269,898	517,158
Utah..........	281,896	70,980	198,330	12,586	289,631	56,529	198,914	34,168
Vermont.......	132,187	36,571	87,567	8,049	141,327	30,724	88,365	22,280
Virginia.......	1,368,706	379,473	923,830	65,403	1,393,767	272,930	925,637	195,239
Washington....	1,003,704	247,500	687,435	68,769	1,001,924	162,947	687,228	151,705
West Virginia..	627,445	162,916	427,931	36,598	667,970	133,557	435,018	99,343
Wisconsin.....	1,347,890	352,665	919,328	75,897	1,395,184	285,762	921,919	187,592
Wyoming......	114,875	27,775	79,852	7,248	108,991	16,780	78,679	13,503
Total........	**61,362,055**	**15,412,733**	**42,416,979**	**3,532,343**	**64,913,989**	**12,380,049**	**42,749,302**	**9,784,638**

Males per 100 Females in U. S.
Source: Bureau of the Census

Ratio represents number of males per 100 females. Includes Alaska and Hawaii. Total resident population; only 1966 includes Armed Forces abroad

Age	1910	1920	1930	1940	1950	1960	1966[1]		
							Total	White	Non-white
All ages................	[2]106.2	[2]104.1	[2]102.6	100.8	98.7	97.1	97.0	97.3	94.6
Under 15 years.........	102.2	102.1	102.6	103.0	103.7	103.4	103.7	104.3	100.5
15 to 24 years.........	101.2	96.9	98.2	98.7	97.8	98.3	102.3	102.8	99.1
25 to 44 years.........	110.5	105.3	101.0	98.7	96.5	95.7	97.2	98.5	87.8
45 to 64 years.........	114.7	115.4	109.2	105.3	100.2	95.7	93.2	93.5	91.1
65 and over...........	101.2	101.5	100.6	95.7	89.7	82.8	76.6	76.0	83.2

[1] Estimated as of July 1. [2] Includes figures for "age not reported."

New Housing Units Started in U. S.
Source: Bureau of the Census (Preliminary)

1966	Inc. Farm	Non-Farm	1966	Inc. Farm	Non-Farm
Total, private and public...........	1,251,900	1,228,600	Regions:		
Private...........	1,220,200	1,196,900	Northeast.......	221,200	221,000
Public...........	31,700	31,700	North Central....	314,300	307,000
			South...........	505,200	489,500
Metropolitan.......	851,800	850,700	West...........	211,200	211,100
Private...........	830,700	829,600			
Public...........	21,100	21,100	**VALUATION of ALL PRIVATE CONSTRUCTION**		
			Authorized by building permits in 3,014 selected permit issuing places.		
Nonmetropolitan.....	401,000	377,900			
Private...........	389,500	367,200	**Total for 1966**		
Public...........	10,700	10,700	All private construction $21,913,400,000		
			Private residential construction .. $19,545,700,000		
Type of structure:			Estimated value of new construction put in place (including all types of construction, private and public), in the United States, including Alaska and Hawaii, for 1966 amounted to $74,369,000,000.		
1-family.........	794,700	771,400			
2-family.........	45,900	45,800			
3-or-more-family..	411,300	411,300			

Population of U.S. Cities of 100,000 or more
1960 CENSUS OF POPULATION
Source: Bureau of the Census

City	1960	1950	City	1960	1950
1—New York, N. Y.	7,781,984	7,891,957	66—Worcester, Mass.	186,587	203,486
2—Chicago, Ill.	3,550,404	3,620,962	67—Austin, Texas	186,545	132,459
3—Los Angeles, Calif.	2,479,015	1,970,358	68—Spokane, Wash.	181,608	161,721
4—Philadelphia, Pa.	2,002,512	2,071,605	69—St. Petersburg, Fla.	181,298	96,738
5—Detroit, Mich.	1,670,144	1,849,568	70—Gary, Ind.	178,320	133,911
6—Baltimore, Md.	939,024	949,708	71—Grand Rapids, Mich.	177,313	176,515
7—Houston, Texas	938,219	596,163	72—Springfield, Mass.	174,463	162,399
8—Cleveland, Ohio	876,050	914,808	73—Nashville, Tenn.	170,874	174,307
9—Washington, D. C.	763,956	802,178	74—Corpus Christi, Texas	167,670	108,287
10—St. Louis, Mo.	750,026	856,796	75—Youngstown, Ohio	166,689	168,330
11—Milwaukee, Wisc.	741,324	637,392	76—Shreveport, La.	164,372	127,206
12—San Francisco, Calif.	740,316	775,357	77—Hartford, Conn.	162,178	177,397
13—Boston, Mass.	697,197	801,444	78—Fort Wayne, Ind.	161,776	133,607
14—Dallas, Texas	679,684	434,462	79—Bridgeport, Conn.	156,748	158,709
15—New Orleans, La.	627,525	570,445	80—Baton Rouge, La.	152,419	125,629
16—Pittsburgh, Pa.	604,332	676,806	81—New Haven, Conn.	152,048	164,443
17—San Antonio, Texas	587,718	408,442	82—Savannah, Ga.	149,245	119,638
18—San Diego, Calif.	573,224	334,387	83—Tacoma, Wash.	147,979	143,673
19—Seattle, Wash.	557,087	467,591	84—Jackson, Miss.	144,422	98,271
20—Buffalo, N. Y.	532,759	580,132	85—Paterson, N. J.	143,663	139,336
21—Cincinnati, Ohio	502,550	503,998	86—Evansville, Ind.	141,543	128,636
22—Memphis, Tenn.	497,524	396,000	87—Erie, Pa.	138,440	130,803
23—Denver, Colo.	493,887	415,786	88—Amarillo, Texas	137,969	74,246
24—Atlanta, Ga.	487,455	331,314	89—Montgomery, Ala.	134,393	106,525
25—Minneapolis, Minn.	482,872	521,718	90—Fresno, Calif.	133,929	91,669
26—Indianapolis, Ind.	476,258	427,173	91—South Bend, Ind.	132,445	115,911
27—Kansas City, Mo.	475,539	456,622	92—Chattanooga, Tenn.	130,009	131,041
28—Columbus, Ohio	471,316	375,901	93—Albany, N. Y.	129,726	134,995
29—Phoenix, Ariz.	439,170	106,818	94—Lubbock, Texas	128,691	71,747
30—Newark, N. J.	405,220	438,776	95—Lincoln, Nebr.	128,521	98,884
31—Louisville, Ky.	390,639	369,129	96—Madison, Wisc.	126,706	96,056
32—Portland, Ore.	372,676	373,628	97—Rockford, Ill.	126,706	92,927
33—Oakland, Calif.	367,548	384,575	98—Kansas City, Kans.	121,901	129,553
34—Fort Worth, Texas	356,268	278,778	99—Greensboro, N. C.	119,574	74,389
35—Long Beach, Calif.	344,168	250,767	100—Topeka, Kans.	119,484	78,791
36—Birmingham, Ala.	340,887	326,037	101—Glendale, Calif.	119,442	95,702
37—Oklahoma City, Okla.	324,253	243,504	102—Beaumont, Texas	119,175	94,014
38—Rochester, N. Y.	318,611	332,488	103—Camden, N. J.	117,159	124,555
39—Toledo, Ohio	318,003	303,616	104—Columbus, Ga.	116,779	79,611
40—St. Paul, Minn.	313,411	311,349	105—Pasadena, Calif.	116,407	104,577
41—Norfolk, Va.	304,869	213,513	106—Portsmouth, Va.	114,773	80,039
42—Omaha, Nebr.	301,598	251,117	107—Trenton, N. J.	114,167	128,009
43—Honolulu, Hawaii	294,194	248,034	108—Newport News, Va.	113,662	42,358
44—Miami, Fla.	291,688	249,276	109—Canton, Ohio	113,631	116,912
45—Akron, Ohio	290,351	274,605	110—Dearborn, Mich.	112,007	94,994
46—El Paso, Texas	276,687	130,485	111—Knoxville, Tenn.	111,827	124,769
47—Jersey City, N. J.	276,101	299,017	112—Hammond, Ind.	111,698	87,594
48—Tampa, Fla.	274,970	124,681	113—Scranton, Pa.	111,443	125,536
49—Dayton, Ohio	262,332	243,872	114—Berkeley, Calif.	111,268	113,805
50—Tulsa, Okla.	261,685	182,740	115—Winston-Salem, N. C.	111,135	87,811
51—Wichita, Kans.	254,698	168,279	116—Allentown, Pa.	108,347	106,756
52—Richmond, Va.	219,958	230,310	117—Little Rock, Ark.	107,813	102,213
53—Syracuse, N. Y.	216,038	220,583	118—Lansing, Mich.	107,807	92,129
54—Tucson, Ariz.	212,892	45,454	119—Cambridge, Mass.	107,716	120,740
55—Des Moines, Iowa	208,982	177,965	120—Elizabeth, N. J.	107,698	112,817
56—Providence, R. I.	207,498	248,674	121—Waterbury, Conn.	107,130	104,477
57—San Jose, Calif.	204,196	95,280	122—Duluth, Minn.	106,884	104,511
58—Mobile, Ala.	202,779	129,009	123—Anaheim, Calif.	104,184	14,556
59—Charlotte, N. C.	201,564	134,042	124—Peoria, Ill.	103,162	111,856
60—Albuquerque, N. M.	201,189	96,815	125—New Bedford, Mass.	102,477	109,189
61—Jacksonville, Fla.	201,030	204,517	126—Niagara Falls, N. Y.	102,394	90,872
62—Flint, Mich.	196,940	163,143	127—Wichita Falls, Texas	101,724	68,042
63—Sacramento, Calif.	191,667	137,572	128—Torrance, Calif.	100,991	22,241
64—Yonkers, N. Y.	190,634	152,798	129—Utica, N. Y.	100,410	101,531
65—Salt Lake City, Utah	189,454	182,121	130—Santa Ana, Calif.	100,350	45,533
			San Juan, P. R.	432,377	224,767
			Ponce, P. R.	114,286	99,492

U. S. Population, Urban and Rural, by Color: 1950 and 1960
Source: Bureau of the Census

Includes Alaska and Hawaii. An urbanized area comprises at least 1 city of 50,000 inhabitants (central city) plus contiguous, closely settled areas (urban fringe).

Year and area	Total	White	Nonwhite	Percent distribution		
				Total	White	Non.
1950	151,326,000	135,150,000	16,176,000	100.0	100.0	100.0
Urban	96,847,000	86,864,000	9,983,000	64.0	64.3	61.7
Urbanized areas	69,249,000	61,925,000	7,324,000	45.8	45.8	45.3
Central cities	48,377,000	42,042,000	6,335,000	32.0	31.1	39.2
Urban fringe	20,872,000	19,883,000	989,000	13.8	14.7	6.1
Other urban	27,598,000	24,939,000	2,659,000	18.2	18.5	16.4
Rural	54,479,000	48,286,000	6,193,000	36.0	35.7	38.3
1960	179,323,000	158,832,000	20,491,000	100.0	100.0	100.0
Urban	125,269,000	110,428,000	14,840,000	69.9	69.5	72.4
Urbanized areas	95,848,000	83,770,000	12,079,000	53.5	52.7	58.9
Central cities	57,975,000	47,627,000	10,348,000	32.3	30.0	50.5
Urban fringe	37,873,000	36,143,000	1,731,000	21.1	22.8	8.4
Other urban	29,420,000	26,658,000	2,762,000	16.4	16.8	13.5
Rural	54,054,000	48,403,000	5,651,000	30.1	30.5	27.6

U. S. Cities with Standard Metropolitan Statistical Areas

POPULATION OF 220 SMSA'S AND THEIR CENTRAL CITIES
Areas over 1,000,000 population are numbered according to rank in 1965
Source: Bureau of the Census

Standard Metropolitan Statistical Area	1965 est.	1960 Metropol. area total	1960 In central cities	1950 Metropol. area total	1950 In central cities
United States (220 areas)	(1,000)	116,584,421	58,782,271	92,138,000	52,875,360
Abilene, Texas	126	120,377	90,368	85,517	45,570
Akron, Ohio	650	513,569	290,351	473,986	274,605
Albany, Ga.	89	75,680	55,890	43,617	31,155
Albany-Schenectady-Troy, N. Y.	697	657,503	278,900	589,359	299,091
Albuquerque, N. Mex.	288	262,199	201,189	145,673	96,815
Allentown-Bethlehem-Easton, Pa.-N. J.	515	492,168	215,710	437,824	208,728
Altoona, Pa.	137	137,270	69,407	139,154	77,177
Amarillo, Texas	168	149,493	137,969	87,140	74,246
Anaheim-Santa Ana-Garden Gr., Calif. (25)	1,107	703,925	288,772	216,224	60,089
Anderson, Ind.	130	125,819	49,061	103,911	46,820
Ann Arbor, Mich.	187	172,440	67,340	134,606	48,251
Asheville, N. C.	143	130,074	60,192	124,403	53,000
Atlanta, Ga. (21)	1,216	1,017,188	487,455	726,989	331,314
Atlantic City, N. J.	179	160,880	59,544	132,399	61,657
Augusta, Ga.-S. C.	237	216,639	70,626	162,013	71,508
Austin, Texas	247	212,136	186,455	160,980	132,459
Bakersfield, Calif.	319	291,984	56,848	228,309	34,784
Baltimore, Md. (12)	1,854	1,727,023	939,024	1,405,399	949,708
Baton Rouge, La.	255	230,058	152,419	158,436	125,629
Bay City, Mich.	109	107,042	53,604	88,461	52,523
Beaumont-Port Arthur, Texas	313	306,016	185,851	235,650	151,544
Billings, Mont.	84	79,016	52,851	55,875	31,834
Binghamton, N. Y.	297	283,600	75,941	246,834	80,674
Birmingham, Ala.	644	634,864	340,887	558,928	326,037
Bloomington-Normal, Ill.	90	84,000	....	....	....
Boise City, Idaho	99	93,460	34,481	70,649	34,393
Boston, Mass. (6)	3,205	2,589,301	697,197	2,410,572	801,444
Bridgeport, Conn.	746	337,983	156,748	275,888	158,709
Brockton, Mass.	296	149,458	72,813	119,728	62,860
Brownsville-Harlingen-San Benito, Texas	151	151,098	105,669	125,170	72,566
Buffalo, N. Y. (16)	1,320	1,306,957	532,759	1,089,230	580,132
Canton, Ohio	356	340,345	113,631	283,194	116,912
Cedar Rapids, Iowa	148	136,899	92,035	104,274	72,296
Champaign-Urbana, Ill.	133	132,436	76,877	106,100	62,397
Charleston, S. C.	296	254,578	65,925	195,107	70,174
Charleston, W. Va.	245	252,925	85,796	239,629	73,501
Charlotte, N. C.	360	316,781	201,564	239,086	134,042
Chattanooga, Tenn.-Ga.	292	283,169	130,009	246,453	131,041
Chicago, Ill. (see also consolidated areas) (3)	6,689	6,220,913	3,550,404	5,177,868	3,620,962
Cincinnati, Ohio-Ky. (17)	1,347	1,071,624	502,550	1,023,245	503,998
Cleveland, Ohio (11)	2,000	1,796,595	876,050	1,532,574	914,808
Colorado Springs, Colo.	176	143,742	70,194	74,523	45,472
Columbia, S. C.	289	260,828	97,433	186,844	86,914
Columbus, Ga.-Ala.	260	217,985	116,779	170,541	79,611
Columbus, Ohio	847	682,962	471,316	563,040	375,901
Corpus Christi, Texas	286	221,573	167,690	656,471	108,287
Dallas, Texas (19)	1,289	1,063,601	679,684	743,501	434,462
Davenport, Ia.-Rock Island-Moline, Ill.	339	319,375	183,549	280,748	160,656
Dayton, Ohio	791	694,623	262,332	545,723	243,872
Decatur, Ill.	122	118,257	78,004	98,853	66,269
Denver, Colo. (26)	1,073	929,383	493,887	612,128	415,786
Des Moines, Iowa	271	266,315	208,982	226,010	177,965
Detroit, Mich. (5)	3,987	3,762,360	1,670,144	3,016,197	1,849,568
Dubuque, Iowa	87	80,048	56,606	71,337	49,671
Duluth-Superior, Minn.-Wis.	267	276,596	140,447	252,777	139,836
Durham, N. C.	123	111,995	78,302	101,639	71,311
El Paso, Texas	344	314,070	276,687	194,968	130,485
Erie, Pa.	255	250,682	138,440	219,388	130,803
Eugene, Ore.	194	162,890	50,977	125,776	35,879
Evansville, Ind.-Ky.	223	222,890	141,543	212,664	128,636
Fargo-Moorhead, N. Dak.-Minn.	110	106,027	69,596	89,240	53,126
Fayetteville, N. C.	193	148,418	51,022	96,006	34,715
Flint, Mich.	459	416,239	196,940	306,757	163,143
Fort Lauderdale-Hollywood, Fla.	441	333,946	118,885	83,933	50,679
Fort Smith, Ark.	154	135,110	52,991	141,978	47,942
Fort Wayne, Ind.	259	232,196	161,776	183,722	133,607
Fort Worth, Texas	627	573,215	365,268	392,643	278,778
Fresno, Calif.	403	365,945	133,929	276,515	91,669
Gadsden, Ala.	94	96,980	58,088	93,892	55,725
Galveston-Texas City, Texas	157	140,364	99,240	113,066	83,188
Gary-Hammond-East Chicago, Ind.	596	573,548	347,687	408,228	275,768
Grand Rapids, Mich.	502	461,906	177,313	362,043	176,515
Great Falls, Mont.	82	73,418	55,357	53,027	39,214
Green Bay, Wis.	137	125,082	62,888	98,214	52,735
Greensboro-High Point, N. C.	267	246,520	181,637	191,057	114,362
Greenville, S. C.	267	255,806	66,188	208,210	58,161
Hamilton-Middletown, Ohio	208	199,076	114,469	147,203	91,646
Harrisburg, Pa.	391	371,653	79,697	317,023	89,544
Hartford, Conn.	765	549,249	162,178	420,009	177,397
Honolulu, Hawaii	571	500,409	294,194	353,020	248,034
Houston Texas (14)	1,696	1,243,158	938,219	806,701	596,163
Huntington-Ashland, W. Va.-Ky.-Ohio	260	254,780	114,910	245,795	117,484
Huntsville, Ala.	224	153,861	72,365	108,669	16,437
Indianapolis, Ind.	984	697,567	476,258	703,199	427,173
Jackson, Mich.	137	131,994	50,720	107,925	51,088
Jackson, Miss.	250	221,367	144,422	171,045	98,271
Jacksonville, Fla.	497	455,411	201,030	304,029	204,517
Jersey City, N. J.	619	610,734	276,101	647,437	299,017
Johnstown, Pa.	270	280,733	53,949	291,354	63,232
Kalamazoo, Mich.	181	169,712	82,089	126,707	57,704
Kansas City, Mo.-Kans. (22)	1,183	1,039,493	475,539	848,655	456,622
Kenosha, Wis.	114	100,615	67,899	75,238	54,368
Knoxville, Tenn.	390	368,080	111,827	337,105	124,769

Standard Metropolitan Statistical Area	1965 est. (1,000)	1960 Metropol. area total	1960 In central cities	1950 Metropol. area total	1950 In central cities
Lafayette, La.	98	84,656	40,400	57,743	33,541
Lafayette-West Lafayette, Ind.	96	89,000	.....	.....	.....
Lake Charles, La.	135	145,475	63,392	89,635	41,272
Lancaster, Pa.	289	278,359	61,055	234,717	63,774
Lansing, Mich.	336	298,949	107,807	244,159	92,129
Laredo, Texas	76	64,791	60,678	56,141	51,910
Las Vegas, Nev.	232	127,016	64,405	48,289	24,624
Lawton, Okla.	99	90,803	61,697	55,165	34,757
Lewiston-Auburn, Me.	91	70,295	65,258	68,426	64,108
Lexington, Ky.	159	131,906	62,810	100,746	55,534
Lima, Ohio	112	103,691	51,037	88,183	50,246
Lincoln, Nebr.	161	155,272	128,521	119,742	98,884
Little Rock-North Little Rock, Ark.	279	242,980	165,845	196,685	136,310
Lorain-Elyria, Ohio	240	217,500	112,714	148,162	81,509
Los Angeles-Long Beach, Calif. .....(2)	6,765	6,742,696	2,823,183	4,151,687	2,221,125
Louisville, Ky.-Ind.	771	725,139	390,639	576,900	369,129
Lubbock, Texas	185	156,271	128,691	101,048	71,747
Lynchburg, Va.	119	110,701	54,790	96,936	47,727
Macon, Ga.	201	180,403	69,764	135,043	70,252
Madison, Wis.	260	222,095	126,706	169,357	96,056
Manchester, N. H.	205	102,861	88,282	93,338	82,732
Mansfield, Ohio	126	118,000	.....	.....	.....
McAllen-Pharr-Edinburg, Tex.	202	181,000	.....	.....	.....
Memphis, Tenn.	740	627,019	497,524	529,577	396,000
Miami, Fla. .....(27)	1,061	935,047	291,688	495,084	249,276
Midland, Texas	67	67,617	62,625	25,785	21,713
Milwaukee, Wis. .....(20)	1,275	1,194,290	741,324	980,309	637,392
Minneapolis-St. Paul, Minn. .....(15)	1,612	1,482,030	796,283	1,151,053	833,067
Mobile, Ala.	391	363,389	194,856	272,102	129,009
Monroe, La.	112	101,663	52,219	74,713	38,572
Montgomery, Ala.	207	199,734	134,393	170,614	106,525
Muncie, Ind.	117	110,938	68,603	90,242	58,479
Muskegon-Muskegon Heights, Mich.	153	149,943	66,037	121,545	67,257
Nashville, Tenn.	512	463,628	170,874	381,609	174,307
New Bedford, Mass.	411	143,176	102,477	141,984	109,189
New Haven, Conn.	704	320,836	152,048	273,049	164,443
New London-Groton-Norwich, Conn.	216	170,981	72,688	134,612	68,184
New Orleans, La. .....(28)	1,027	868,480	627,525	712,393	570,445
New York, N. Y. (includes 5 boroughs of New York City plus Nassau, Rockland, Suffolk and Westchester Counties, N. Y.—see also consolidated areas below) .....(1)	11,366	10,694,633	7,781,984	9,555,943	7,891,957
New York, NE N.J. (SCA)	15,821	14,759,429	.....	.....	.....
Newark, N. J. .....(13)	1,851	1,689,420	405,220	1,468,458	438,776
Newport News-Hampton, Va.	272	224,503	202,920	154,977	143,227
Norfolk-Portsmouth, Va.	637	578,507	420,645	446,200	293,552
Odessa, Texas	93	90,995	80,338	42,102	29,495
Ogden, Utah	120	110,744	70,197	83,319	57,112
Oklahoma City, Okla.	585	511,833	324,253	392,439	243,504
Omaha, Nebr.-Iowa	516	457,873	301,598	366,395	251,117
Orlando, Fla.	372	318,487	88,135	141,833	52,367
Oxnard-Ventura, Calif.	318	199,138	69,379	114,647	38,101
Paterson-Clifton-Passaic, N. J. .....(18)	1,307	1,186,873	279,710	876,232	261,549
Pensacola, Fla.	224	203,376	56,752	131,260	43,479
Peoria, Ill.	320	313,412	103,162	271,847	111,856
Philadelphia, Pa.-N. J. .....(4)	4,664	4,342,987	2,002,512	3,671,048	2,071,605
Phoenix, Ariz.	818	663,510	499,170	331,770	106,818
Pine Bluff, Ark.	86	81,373	53,647	76,075	37,162
Pittsburgh, Pa. .....(9)	2,372	2,405,435	604,332	2,213,236	676,806
Pittsfield, Mass.	144	76,772	57,879	68,636	53,348
Portland, Maine	197	139,122	72,566	133,983	77,634
Portland, Ore.-Wash.	897	821,897	372,676	704,829	373,628
Providence-Pawtucket, R. I.-Mass.	739	816,148	288,499	763,902	330,110
Provo-Orem, Utah	118	106,991	54,441	81,912	37,288
Pueblo, Colo.	119	118,707	91,181	90,188	63,685
Racine, Wis.	160	141,781	89,144	109,585	71,193
Raleigh, N. C.	195	169,082	93,931	136,450	65,676
Reading, Pa.	283	275,414	98,177	255,740	109,320
Reno, Nev.	113	84,743	51,470	50,205	32,497
Richmond, Va.	484	436,044	219,958	350,035	230,310
Roanoke, Va.	173	158,803	97,110	133,407	91,921
Rochester, N. Y.	804	586,387	318,611	615,044	332,488
Rockford, Ill.	247	230,091	126,706	169,455	92,927
Sacramento, Calif.	737	502,778	191,667	259,429	137,572
Salem, Ore.	172	147,411	49,142	127,718	43,140
Saginaw, Mich.	208	190,752	98,265	153,515	92,918
St. Joseph, Mo.	95	90,581	79,673	96,826	78,588
St. Louis, Mo.-Ill. .....(10)	2,249	2,203,000	750,026	1,755,334	856,796
Salinas-Monterey, Calif.	222	198,000	.....	.....	.....
Salt Lake City, Utah	523	447,795	180,454	305,762	182,121
San Angelo, Texas	73	64,630	58,815	58,929	52,093
San Antonio, Texas	808	687,151	587,718	525,852	408,442
San Bernardino-Riverside-Ontario, Calif. .....(29)	1,026	1,033,000	222,871	451,688	132,604
San Diego, Calif. .....(24)	1,136	1,033,011	573,224	556,808	334,387
San Francisco-Oakland, Calif. .....(7)	2,918	2,783,359	1,107,864	2,135,934	1,159,932
San Jose, Calif.	885	642,315	204,196	290,547	95,280
Santa Barbara, Calif.	243	168,962	58,768	98,220	44,913
Savannah, Ga.	192	188,299	149,245	151,481	119,638
Scranton, Pa.	226	234,531	111,443	257,396	125,536
Seattle-Everett, Wash. .....(23)	1,179	1,107,213	557,087	844,572	467,591
Shreveport, La.	289	281,481	164,372	216,686	127,206
Sioux City, Iowa	114	120,017	89,159	114,318	83,991
Sioux Falls, S. Dak.	94	86,575	65,466	70,910	52,696
South Bend, Ind.	270	271,057	132,445	234,526	115,911
Spokane, Wash.	267	278,333	181,608	221,561	161,721
Springfield, Ill.	153	146,539	83,271	131,484	81,628
Springfield, Mo.	140	126,276	95,865	104,823	66,731
Springfield, Ohio	147	131,440	82,723	111,661	76,508
Springfield-Chicopee-Holyoke, Mass.	550	493,999	288,705	422,163	266,271
Steubenville-Weirton, Ohio-W. Va.	170	167,756	60,696	157,787	59,877
Stockton, Calif.	273	249,989	86,321	200,750	70,853
Syracuse, N. Y.	606	563,781	216,038	465,114	220,583

Standard Metropolitan Statistical Area	1965 est. (1,000)	1960 Metropol. area total	1960 In central cities	1950 Metropol. area total	1950 In central cities
Tacoma, Wash.	343	321,590	147,979	275,876	143,673
Tallahassee, Fla.	83	74,225	58,022	51,590	27,237
Tampa-St. Petersburg, Fla.	873	772,453	456,268	409,143	221,419
Terre Haute, Ind.	167	172,069	72,500	172,468	64,214
Texarkana, Texas-Ark.	100	91,657	50,000	94,580	40,628
Toledo, Ohio	657	630,647	318,003	530,822	303,616
Topeka, Kans.	149	141,286	119,484	105,418	78,791
Trenton, N. J.	296	266,392	114,167	229,781	128,009
Tucson, Ariz.	307	265,660	212,892	141,216	45,454
Tulsa, Okla.	433	418,974	261,685	327,900	182,740
Tuscaloosa, Ala.	118	109,047	63,370	94,092	46,396
Tyler, Texas.	93	86,350	51,230	74,701	38,968
Utica-Rome, N. Y.	346	330,771	152,056	284,262	143,213
Vallejo-Napa, Calif.	239	200,487	83,047	151,436	39,617
Waco, Texas.	156	150,091	97,808	130,194	84,706
Washington, D. C.-Md.-Va. ....(8)	2,408	2,001,897	763,956	1,464,089	802,178
Waterloo, Iowa.	124	122,482	71,755	100,448	65,198
West Palm Beach, Fla.	281	228,106	56,208	114,688	43,162
Wheeling, W. Va.-Ohio.	188	190,342	53,400	196,305	58,891
Wichita, Kans.	389	381,626	254,698	253,291	168,279
Wichita Falls, Texas.	130	129,638	101,724	105,309	68,042
Wilkes-Barre-Hazleton, Pa.	346	346,972	95,607	392,241	112,317
Wilmington, Del.-N. J.	468	414,565	95,827	301,743	110,356
Wilmington, N. C.	95	92,000			
Winston-Salem, N. C.	207	189,428	111,135	146,135	87,811
Worcester, Mass.	608	328,898	186,587	303,037	203,486
York, Pa.	290	290,242	54,504	246,934	59,953
Youngstown-Warren, Ohio.	523	509,006	226,337	416,544	218,186
Puerto Rico (3 areas)		818,241	596,810	679,858	515,641
Mayaguez.		83,850	50,147	87,307	58,944
Ponce.		145,586	114,286	126,810	99,492
San Juan.		647,979	432,377	465,741	357,205

STANDARD CONSOLIDATED AREAS OF NEW YORK AND CHICAGO

Standard Consolidated Areas combining metropolitan areas (SMSA)	1960	1950	Increase 1950 to 1960 Number	Increase 1950 to 1960 Percent
New York-Northeastern New Jersey	14,759,429	12,911,994	1,847,435	14.3
New York, N. Y., SMSA.	10,694,633	9,555,943	1,138,690	11.9
Newark, N. J., SMSA.	1,689,420	1,468,458	220,962	15.0
Jersey City, N. J., SMSA.	610,734	647,437	−36,703	−5.7
Paterson-Clifton-Passaic, N. J. SMSA.	1,186,873	876,232	310,641	35.5
Middlesex County, N. J.	433,856	264,872	168,984	63.8
Somerset County, N. J.	143,913	99,052	44,861	45.3
Chicago-Northwestern Indiana	6,794,461	5,586,096	1,208,365	21.6
Chicago, Ill., SMSA.	6,220,913	5,177,868	1,043,045	20.1
Gary-Hammond-East Chicago, Ind., SMSA.	573,548	408,228	165,320	40.5

Value of New Construction Put in Place in U. S.
Source: Bureau of the Census

Values in billions of dollars	Value put in place Annually 1965	Annually 1966	First 5 mos. 1966	First 5 mos. 1967[1]	Percentage change 1965 to 1966	1966 to 1967[2]
Total new construction	71,912	74,371	27,989	26,601	+3.4	−5.0
Private construction	49,840	50,446	19,404	17,235	+1.2	−11.2
Private residential bldgs. (non farm)	26,266	23,815	9,482	7,570	−9.3	−20.2
Public construction	22,072	23,925	8,585	9,366	+8.4	+9.1

[1]Preliminary. [2]First five months.

Households by Type, Color of Head and Residence
Source: Bureau of the Census (Numbers in thousands)

Type of household March 1966	Total No.	Total %	Color of head White No.	White %	Nonwhite No.	Nonwhite %	Residence Nonfarm No.	Nonfarm %	Farm No.	Farm %
All households...	58,092	100.0	52,135	100.0	5,954	100.0	54,875	100.0	3,214	100.0
Primary families...	48,169	82.9	43,426	83.3	4,742	79.6	45,221	82.4	2,947	91.7
Husband-wife....	42,060	72.4	38,600	74.0	3,460	58.1	39,376	71.8	2,684	83.5
Other male head.	1,165	2.0	993	1.9	172	2.9	1,069	1.9	96	3.0
Female head.	4,944	8.5	3,833	7.4	1,110	18.6	4,776	8.7	167	5.2
Primary individuals	9,923	17.1	8,709	16.7	1,212	20.4	9,654	17.6	267	8.3
Male.	3,292	5.7	2,759	5.3	532	8.9	3,161	5.8	130	4.0
Female.	6,631	11.4	5,950	11.4	680	11.4	6,493	11.8	137	4.3

Negro Population in 25 Largest Cities
Source: Bureau of the Census, Census of 1960.

City	Total	Negro	%	City	Total	Negro	%
New York	7,781,984	1,087,931	14.0	Dallas.	679,684	129,242	19.0
Chicago.	3,550,404	812,637	22.9	New Orleans.	627,525	233,514	37.2
Los Angeles.	2,479,015	334,916	13.5	Pittsburgh.	604,332	100,692	16.7
Philadelphia.	2,002,512	529,240	26.4	San Antonio.	587,718	41,605	7.1
Detroit.	1,670,144	482,223	28.9	San Diego.	573,224	34,435	6.0
Baltimore.	939,024	326,589	34.8	Seattle.	557,087	26,901	4.8
Houston.	938,219	215,037	22.9	Buffalo.	532,759	70,904	13.3
Cleveland.	876,050	250,818	28.6	Cincinnati.	502,550	108,754	21.6
Washington.	763,956	411,737	53.9	Memphis.	497,524	184,320	37.0
St. Louis.	750,026	214,377	28.6	Denver.	493,887	31,066	6.3
Milwaukee.	741,324	62,458	8.4	Atlanta.	487,455	186,464	38.3
San Francisco.	740,316	74,383	10.0	Minneapolis.	482,872	11,785	2.4
Boston.	697,197	63,165	9.1				

Educational Attainment by Age, Race and Sex

Source: Bureau of the Census

Age, race and sex March, 1966	Total population	None	Elementary school			High school		College			Median years complete
			1 to 4 years	5 to 7 years	8 years	1 to 3 years	4 years	1 to 3 years	4 years	5 yrs. or more	
White			(in thousands)								
Total, 14 years and over	122,849	1,553	3,548	10,895	18,170	27,292	38,488	12,181	6,995	3,727	12.0
14 to 17 years	12,268	66	60	1,601	3,267	7,152	112	9	....	....	9.5
18 and 19 years	5,870	28	8	118	141	1,862	2,948	765	....	....	12.3
20 to 24 years	11,295	57	61	227	404	1,741	5,067	2,732	789	216	12.6
25 years and over	93,416	1,403	3,420	8,948	14,357	16,535	30,362	8,675	6,206	3,511	12.1
25 to 29 years	9,853	60	77	326	453	1,663	4,534	1,288	989	464	12.5
30 to 34 years	9,536	51	125	410	570	1,686	4,163	1,159	894	479	12.5
35 to 44 years	21,478	124	440	1,203	1,985	4,101	8,769	2,097	1,732	1,027	12.3
45 to 54 years	20,001	165	476	1,807	2,969	4,041	6,889	1,833	1,162	660	12.1
55 to 64 years	15,599	220	673	2,122	3,615	2,852	3,473	1,285	800	558	10.2
65 years and over	16,949	783	1,629	3,080	4,765	2,192	2,534	1,013	629	323	8.6
Male, 14 years and over	58,835	737	1,949	5,601	9,000	12,896	16,149	6,039	3,838	2,626	11.8
14 to 17 years	6,227	32	40	920	1,671	3,524	40	....	....	....	9.4
18 and 19 years	2,833	21	2	73	66	994	1,274	403	....	....	12.2
20 to 24 years	5,238	39	36	119	207	745	2,011	1,550	368	163	12.7
25 years and over	44,537	646	1,872	4,488	7,055	7,632	12,824	4,086	3,470	2,464	12.0
25 to 29 years	4,791	33	36	184	231	798	1,987	664	513	344	12.6
30 to 34 years	4,698	34	64	218	291	717	1,819	615	566	374	12.6
35 to 44 years	10,514	48	253	655	1,096	1,959	3,623	1,009	1,065	807	12.3
45 to 54 years	9,741	87	290	922	1,493	1,997	3,009	875	645	424	12.0
55 to 64 years	7,453	109	388	1,086	1,823	1,346	1,424	555	394	328	9.7
65 years and over	7,340	335	841	1,423	2,121	815	962	368	287	187	8.5
Female, 14 yrs. and over	64,014	816	1,599	5,294	9,170	14,396	22,339	6,142	3,158	1,101	12.0
14 to 17 years	6,041	35	21	681	1,596	3,628	72	9	....	....	9.6
18 and 19 years	3,037	7	5	46	75	868	1,674	362	....	....	12.3
20 to 24 years	6,057	18	25	108	197	996	3,056	1,183	421	53	12.6
25 years and over	48,879	756	1,548	4,460	7,303	8,903	17,537	4,589	2,735	1,048	12.1
25 to 29 years	5,062	26	41	142	222	865	2,546	624	476	120	12.5
30 to 34 years	4,838	16	61	192	279	969	2,344	544	328	105	12.4
35 to 44 years	10,963	76	187	549	889	2,142	5,146	1,088	667	220	12.3
45 to 54 years	10,261	78	186	885	1,477	2,045	3,880	958	516	236	12.1
55 to 64 years	8,146	112	284	1,035	1,792	1,506	2,050	730	406	230	10.7
65 years and over	9,609	448	789	1,657	2,644	1,376	1,571	645	342	137	8.7
Nonwhite											
Total, 14 years and over	14,768	423	1,516	2,471	1,963	4,128	2,889	848	335	194	9.7
14 to 17 years	1,917	6	6	447	522	910	25	....	....	....	9.0
18 and 19 years	808	5	9	37	37	419	247	53	....	....	11.3
20 to 24 years	1,581	4	26	96	122	476	587	236	29	5	12.1
25 years and over	10,460	407	1,475	1,891	1,282	2,324	2,029	560	306	189	9.2
25 to 29 years	1,343	8	36	96	99	428	477	89	74	37	12.0
30 to 34 years	1,291	15	58	124	130	381	372	111	62	38	11.5
35 to 44 years	2,647	40	194	459	314	700	621	195	69	55	10.4
45 to 54 years	2,187	50	348	474	317	467	326	105	54	46	8.7
55 to 64 years	1,560	65	380	401	260	226	149	35	39	7	7.5
65 years and over	1,432	229	459	337	162	122	84	25	8	6	5.2
Male, 14 years and over	6,952	242	888	1,119	980	1,843	1,239	384	147	110	9.4
14 to 17 years	957	4	6	232	289	443	13	....	....	....	8.9
18 and 19 years	390	3	2	21	19	214	114	17	....	....	11.1
20 to 24 years	732	2	16	58	64	207	263	110	10	2	12.1
25 years and over	4,873	233	863	809	640	979	848	256	138	108	8.8
25 to 29 years	619	1	23	38	50	182	220	54	29	22	12.1
30 to 34 years	593	8	42	77	73	142	165	41	23	23	11.0
35 to 44 years	1,220	37	128	199	165	297	226	101	38	29	9.8
45 to 54 years	1,033	27	215	195	161	202	132	44	26	29	8.5
55 to 64 years	754	41	232	178	117	99	58	10	18	2	6.8
65 years and over	654	119	223	122	74	57	57	6	4	3	4.7
Female, 14 yrs. and over	7,816	180	628	1,352	983	2,286	1,650	464	188	85	10.0
14 to 17 years	960	2	....	216	264	467	12	....	....	....	9.0
18 and 19 years	419	2	7	16	19	205	133	36	....	....	11.4
20 to 24 years	849	2	10	38	58	269	324	126	19	3	12.1
25 years and over	5,588	175	611	1,083	642	1,343	1,182	303	169	80	9.6
25 to 29 years	724	6	13	59	49	246	257	35	45	15	11.9
30 to 34 years	698	7	16	47	57	239	208	70	40	15	11.8
35 to 44 years	1,427	3	66	260	149	402	395	93	31	26	10.8
45 to 54 years	1,155	24	132	279	156	264	194	61	28	17	8.9
55 to 64 years	807	24	148	223	143	127	91	25	21	5	8.1
65 years and over	777	111	236	215	88	65	37	19	4	2	5.6

Farm Population of the United States

Age and color	Both sexes		Male		Female	
	1966	1960	1966	1960	1966	1960
Total	11,595,000	15,669,000	6,002,000	8,184,000	5,593,000	7,485,000
White	10,143,000	13,092,000	5,249,000	6,871,000	4,894,000	6,221,000
Nonwhite	1,452,000	2,577,000	753,000	1,313,000	699,000	1,264,000
Under 14 years	3,338,000	4,995,000	1,742,000	2,586,000	1,596,000	2,409,000
White	2,742,000	3,851,000	1,430,000	1,995,000	1,312,000	1,856,000
Nonwhite	596,000	1,144,000	312,000	591,000	284,000	553,000
14 years and over	8,257,000	10,674,000	4,260,000	5,598,000	3,997,000	5,076,000
White	7,401,000	9,241,000	3,819,000	4,876,000	3,582,000	4,365,000
Nonwhite	856,000	1,433,000	441,000	722,000	415,000	711,000

American Territorial Expansion

When the War of the Revolution ended the 13 original states—Massachusetts, Rhode Island, Connecticut, New Hampshire, New York, New Jersey, Pennsylvania, Delaware, Maryland, Virginia, North Carolina, South Carolina and Georgia had a land and water area of 892,135 sq. mi., comprising New England, all land from Canada to Florida and from the Atlantic to the Mississippi. At the request of Congress (acting under the Articles of Confederation) the states gave their unorganized land to the Congress, which passed the Northwest Ordinance of 1787, and formed Northwest Terr., north of the Ohio river and another territory south of it.

France originally occupied and fortified a large area from Canada to the Gulf via the Great Lakes and the Mississippi, which it lost to Britain by the Treaty of 1763 after the French and Indian War, Britain yielded this territory to the U. S. by the Treaty of Paris, 1783. After fighting Indians and British in border campaigns, the U. S. took possession July 11, 1796.

LOUISIANA PURCHASE

The first accession to the United States was the Louisiana Purchase, 827,192 sq. mi. west of the Mississippi. This was held by Spain until ceded to France in 1800, with the proviso that it go back to Spain if France gave it up. In order to free navigation on the Mississippi President Jefferson sent James Monroe and Robert R. Livingston to Paris to buy the isle of Orleans (New Orleans) and West Florida, for which Congress voted $2,-000,000. Napoleon, defeated in San Domingo, offered the vast Louisiana area. The treaty was signed Apr. 30, 1803; Congress ratified it in October; the U. S. took possession at New Orleans Dec. 20, 1803. The U. S. paid $11,250,000 (60,000,000 francs), assumed claims of Americans against France, $3,750,000. Total cost $15,000,000.

Nobody knew the exact boundaries. After Mar. 10, 1804, the U. S. divided the Purchase into the Territory of Orleans, later the state of Louisiana, and the Territory of Louisiana. Included in the Purchase were the present state of Louisiana west to the Sabine River plus the port of New Orleans; the present areas of Arkansas, Missouri, Nebraska, Iowa and South Dakota; North Dakota except the northeast corner, held by Britain until the treaty of 1819; Minnesota west of the Mississippi; Kansas except a small part in the southwest; Oklahoma except the Panhandle no-man's-land; parts of Colorado and Montana. Sometimes Wyoming was claimed and the territory was thought to have run as far as the Pacific coast, but U. S., Britain, Spain and Russia had conflicting claims and settled them by treaty.

SPAIN GIVES UP FLORIDA

Spain, which still claimed East Florida and West Florida as far as Mobile, Ala., ceded all rights to the U. S. by treaty Feb. 22, 1819, ratified by Spain 1821. The U. S. gave up claims to an undetermined border in Texas and on the Rio Grande and assumed $5,000,000 worth of Spanish obligations to Americans; total cost, $6,674,057.

Spain, Britain, France and the Americans had fought in this territory. Spain's title was recognized in 1783. In 1810 the U. S. took possession of large areas along the Gulf, except Mobile, and West Florida declared itself independent and asked annexation. In 1814 Gen. Andrew Jackson took Pensacola from the British.

OREGON TERRITORY ORGANIZED

Organization of the Territory of Oregon in 1848 was not called an accession because the U. S. claimed title by (1) discovery and occupation; (2) a free interpretation of the Louisiana Purchase; (3) treaties with Spain, 1819, Great Britain, 1818, Russia, 1824. The northern boundary was settled by treaty with Britain in 1846.

The Territory extended from the crest of the Rockies to the Pacific coast, north of 42° N. Lat. and included the present states of Oregon, Washington, Idaho and parts of Montana and Wyoming.

ADMISSION OF TEXAS AS STATE

The third accession came when the Republic of Texas was admitted to the Union as a state, Dec. 29, 1845. This was part of a Mexican state settled by many U. S. citizens. Texas declared its independence in 1836, was recognized by the U. S. and applied for admission into the Union. It was bounded by the Rio Grande on the Southwest, and the Sabine, Red and Arkansas Rivers on the North and Northeast, and roughly comprised parts of present New Mexico, Colorado, Wyoming and a bit of Kansas as well as Texas of

today, 390,144 sq. mi. Today the state has 267,-339 sq. mi. Texas had declared for slavery and its admission was opposed by anti-slavery men. Since a two-thirds majority of the Senate could not be attained it was admitted, Mar. 1, 1845, by a joint resolution of Congress, requiring only a majority of both houses. Texas ratified the agreement July 4, 1845.

Texas formally became a state Dec. 29, 1845. Congress gave Texas the right to divide itself into as many as five states "of convenient size" and sufficient population, at its own discretion. The Lone Star flag of the republic has been retained as the state flag of Texas. It can be flown by the side of the Stars and Stripes, but not above it.

TERRITORY FROM MEXICO

At the end of the Mexican War the U. S. and Mexico signed the treaty of Guadelupe-Hidalgo, Feb. 2, 1848, which gave the fourth large accession of territory. This included the present states of Arizona, New Mexico, California, Nevada, Utah, and Colorado west of the Rockies. The Gila river was a boundary line. The U. S. paid $15,000,000 to Mexico and assumed claims of U. S. citizens against Mexico. The claim of Texas to part of New Mexico territory was settled in 1850 by paying Texas $10,000,000. Interest increased both totals.

Inexact boundaries and agitation by railroad men for the Gila river valley to build the Southern Pacific led President Franklin Pierce to send James Gadsden as ambassador to Mexico to negotiate concessions of land. Gadsden got the Mexican dictator, Santa Anna, to yield 29,640 sq. mi. for $10,-000,000 in 1853. This made the Rio Grande the boundary line on the South and the Colorado river on the West.

ALASKA FROM RUSSIA

Russia, which operated Alaska as a fur and fishing station at a loss, first offered to sell it during President Pierce's administration, about 1856. President Buchanan wanted to pay $5,000,-000 for it in 1860. Secy. Seward, an expansionist, signed a treaty with Baron Stoeckl, Russian minister, Mar. 30, 1867, to buy it for $7,200,000. Senate ratified it Apr. 9, 1867, and it was transferred to U. S. at Sitka Oct. 18, 1867, before it had been paid for. The House, by 113 to 43, appropriated the money July 14, 1868. The legend that the U. S. bought Alaska to repay Russia for checkmating Britain during the Civil War is without foundation.

ACQUISITION OF HAWAII

A British naval officer seized the kingdom of Hawaii, 1843, but was disavowed. Britain and France recognized its independent status 1843. France seized it, 1849, but restored it at once. In 1851 the King offered it to the U. S.; Danl. Webster, Secy. of State, refused it. Annexation was urged, 1854, but rejected. A reciprocity treaty with U. S., 1875, increased trade; it was renewed 1884 to include lease of Pearl Harbor as naval base. Jas. G. Blaine, Secy. of State, in 1881 had practically extended Monroe Doctrine to Hawaii. After revolution, 1893 (with American connivance) the republic, 1894, asked annexation. U.S. voted this July 7, 1898, effective Aug. 12, 1898, and assumed a national debt of $4,000,000.

ISLANDS FROM SPAIN

After the 1898 war with Spain, Spain by treaty of Dec. 10, 1898, ceded Puerto Rico, Guam and the Philippine islands for $20,000,000. An additional $100,000 was paid later for islands of the Philippines not in the original treaty. Puerto Rico is a free commonwealth electing its own executives. Guam is administered by the Dept. of the Interior. The Philippine Islands received their independence July 4, 1946, as the Republic of the Philippines.

PACIFIC AND CARIBBEAN

American Samoa in the Pacific. Port of Pago Pago was ceded 1872. Tutuila and other islands ceded to U.S. by convention with Great Britain and Germany, Dec. 2, 1899. Swain's Isl. annexed 1925. Dept. of the Interior.

Wake annexed Jan. 17, 1899, from Spain.

Midway Islands (Sand Isl., Eastern Isl.) occupied Sept. 30, 1867. Under Navy Dept.

Baker Island, discovered 1832, U. S. since 1857. Also Jarvis, and Howland. Under Interior Dept.

Virgin Islands in the Caribbean, the former Danish West Indies, comprising St. Croix, St. Thomas, St. John and islets, bought from Denmark Jan. 25, 1917, for $25,000,000.

Panama Canal Zone, acquired from the Republic of Panama.

United States Immigration Law, Latest Revision

Source: The Federal Statutes

Admission of immigrants into the United States is regulated by the Immigration and Nationality Act and its amendments.

Aliens wishing to enter the United States for permanent residence get immigrant visas from U. S. consuls located abroad. They must present documents of identity and nationality.

Aliens coming solely for a short stay, for business or study, and not as immigrants, also must get visas in U. S. consulates abroad and have documents of identity. If they live in contiguous foreign countries, such as Mexico and Canada, they must apply to consuls for identification cards for border crossing. All aliens on arrival must be inspected at U. S. ports by officers of the Immigration and Naturalization Service of the Dept. of Justice to determine admissibility.

Under the Immigration and Nationality Act (1952) aliens were divided into 3 classes; quota immigrants who came under the quota allotted to foreign nationals; nonquota immigrants who were outside quota limitations for special reasons and non-immigrants (visitors or seasonal workers).

Legislation signed by President Johnson, Oct. 3, 1965, effective Dec. 1, 1965, provided for the elimination of the national origins system effective June 30, 1968, with a phase-out during the interim period. A new selection system is established thereafter, based upon first-come, first-served without regard to place of birth, within new preference categories and subject to specified limitations and designed to prevent an unreasonable allocation of numbers to any one preference or to any foreign state.

CLASSES OF ALIENS

The Act of Sept. 11, 1957, to relieve hardship to immigrants, refugees, relatives, provided:

An illegitimate child may enter with its parents. The word *child* includes also an adopted child under 14 if latter has been two years with parent.

A law approved Sept. 26, 1961, gives authority to issue visas for permanent residence to individuals with tuberculosis who are spouses or children of a citizen or of an individual admitted for permanent residence.

A law approved July 14, 1960, gives the Attorney General authority to permit certain aliens living in the U. S. with temporary visas to acquire permanent visas without having to leave and reenter.

The following aliens are among those excludable:

Persons mentally retarded, insane, previously insane, psychopathic, mentally defective, sexual deviates, also those afflicted with any dangerous contagious disease or having a physical defect impairing the ability to earn a living.

Also chronic alcoholics, narcotic drug addicts, persons convicted of narcotic violations or suspected of illicit traffic in prohibited drugs.

Also paupers, beggars, stowaways; those convicted of or admitting moral turpitude, other than a political offense, with certain exceptions for those under 18. Also prostitutes and those engaged in commercialized vice.

The Act of Oct. 3, 1965 establishes new controls to protect the American labor market from the influx of skilled and unskilled foreign labor. Under the legislation the primary responsibility is placed upon the intending immigrant to obtain the Secretary of Labor's clearance prior to the issuance of a visa establishing that there are not sufficient workers in the United States at the alien's destination who are able, willing and qualified to perform the skilled or unskilled labor; and that the employment of the alien will not adversely affect wages and working conditions of the United States citizens similarly employed.

Also excluded are those who try to enter the U. S. by fraud and misrepresentation and those who abet such acts; those over 16 and physically capable of reading who cannot read and understand some language or dialect; those trying to enter the country from contiguous foreign territory or adjacent islands within two years after arrival there on a transport line that has not complied with the U. S. immigration laws.

Also those who left the U. S. to avoid military service in time of war or national emergency, unless they were nonimmigrants.

Provision is made by the Act of Oct. 3, 1965 for a waiver of the ground of exclusion based upon mental retardation if the alien is the spouse, unmarried son or daughter, parent, or the minor unmarried lawfully adopted child of a United States citizen or a permanent resident alien, or of an alien who has been granted an immigrant visa. A similar waiver is granted to aliens who have suffered a prior attack of insanity based upon the same relationships.

SUBVERSIVE ACTIVITIES

Excluded from the United States are persons who seek to enter to engage in activities against the public interest and likely to endanger the welfare, safety and security of the country. Any persons who probably would engage in espionage, sabotage, disorder or other activities inimical to the U. S. or who are members of organizations that must register under the Subversive Activities Control Act of 1950, are barred.

Also excluded are persons—except certain nonimmigrant officials and employees of foreign governments and international organizations—who are or have been anarchists, opposed to organized government, members of or affiliated with a communist or other totalitarian party; those who teach or advocate the overthrow of the U. S. Government by force or violence and advocate destruction of property and killing of government officials, or who are members of or affiliated with organizations with these aims.

Involuntary membership or affiliation with such organizations is not a reason for exclusion.

For more detailed information concerning the immigration law consult the nearest office of the U. S. Immigration & Naturalization Service, or any U. S. Consul abroad.

Normal Immigration Quotas

Source: Visa Office, U. S. Department of State

Quota area	Quota	Quota area	Quota	Quota area	Quota	Quota area	Quota
Afghanistan	100	France	3,069	Liechtenstein	100	San Marino	100
Albania	100	Gabon	100	Lithuania	[384	Saudi Arabia	100
Algeria	574	Germany	25,814	Luxemburg	100	Senegal	100
Andorra	100	Ghana	100	Malagasy Rep.	100	Sierra Leone	100
Arab Peninsula	100	Great Britain and		Malaysia	400	Somali Rep.	100
Australia	100	No. Ireland	65,361	Malawi	100	So. Africa Rep.	100
Austria	1,405	Greece	308	Mali	100	So.-W. Africa	100
Belgium	1,297	Guinea	100	Malta	100	Spain	250
Bhutan	100	Hungary	865	Mauritania	100	Sudan	100
Bulgaria	100	Iceland	100	Monaco	100	Sweden	3,295
Burma	100	India	100	Morocco	100	Switzerland	1,698
Burundi	100	Indonesia	200	Muscat & Oman	100	Syria	100
Cambodia	100	Iran (Persia)	100	Nauru	100	Tanganyika	100
Cameroon	151	Iraq	100	Nepal	100	Thailand (Siam)	100
Cen. African Rep.	100	Ireland (Eire)	17,756	Netherlands	3,136	Togo	100
Ceylon	100	Israel	100	New Guinea	100	Tonga	100
Chad	100	Italy	5,666	New Zealand	100	Tunisia	100
China	205	Ivory Coast	100	Niger	100	Turkey	225
Congo (former Fr.)	100	Japan	185	Nigeria	149	Uganda	100
Congo, Rep. of	100	Jordan	100	Norway	2,364	U.S.S.R.	2,697
Cyprus	100	Kenya	100	Pacific Isl. U. S.	100	United Arab Rep.	100
Czechoslovakia	2,859	Korea	100	Pakistan	100	Upper Volta	100
Dahomey	100	Kuwait	100	Palestine (Arab)	100	Viet-Nam	100
Dansig	100	Laos	100	Philippines	100	Western Samoa	100
Denmark	1,175	Latvia	235	Poland	6,488	Yemen	100
Estonia	115	Lebanon	100	Portugal	438	Yugoslavia	942
Ethiopia	100	Liberia	100	Rumania	289	Zambia	100
Finland	566	Libya	100	Rwanda	100	**Total**	**158,261**

Immigrants Admitted From All Countries

Source: Immigration and Naturalization Service, U. S. Dept. of Justice

Year	Number	Year	Number	Year	Number
1820.........	8,385	1891-1900....	3,687,564	1960.......	265,398
1821-1830....	143,439	1901-1910....	8,795,386	1961.......	271,344
1831-1840....	599,125	1911-1920....	5,735,811	1962.......	283,763
1841-1850....	1,713,251	1921-1930....	4,107,209	1963.......	306,260
1851-1860....	2,598,214	1931-1940....	528,431	1964.......	292,248
1861-1870....	2,314,824	1941-1950....	1,035,039	1965.......	296,697
1871-1880....	2,812,191	1958........	253,265	1966.......	323,040
1881-1890....	5,246,613	1959........	260,686	1820-1966..	43,614,313

Immigration from the close of the Revolutionary War to 1820 is estimated at 250,000.

Passports Issued and Renewed

Source: Passport Office, Dept. of State

[Passports are actual count; other data based on a sample. Data refer to number of passports issued, not travelers (except as noted). A single passport may cover more than one trip and more than one person]

Item	1950	1960	1962	1963	1964	1965	1966
New and renewed passports....	299,665	853,087	906,900	1,055,504	1,133,228	1,330,290	1,547,725
Object of travel:[1]							
Government.................	(N.A.)	115,910	106,690	145,034	180,328	191,140	215,585
Nongovernment.............	(N.A.)	737,177	800,210	910,470	952,900	1,139,150	1,332,140
Personal reasons[2].........	141,567	321,590	428,260	436,250	366,860	487,470	483,240
Pleasure[3]................	108,486	350,897	268,480	353,150	470,180	535,150	651,220
Business[4]................	27,364	24,540	73,890	86,000	78,300	76,210	135,250
Education.................	13,837	31,240	22,500	26,470	30,200	31,120	51,750
Religion..................	4,676	6,780	4,910	6,540	5,480	6,770	8,280
Health...................	1,069	1,460	1,490	1,350	1,140	500	710
Other....................	2,666	670	680	710	740	1,930	1,690
First area destination:							
Africa....................	4,827	8,440	12,810	12,350	16,120	19,580	22,680
Australia and Oceania......	2,059	35,220	28,610	32,650	36,880	50,750	58,450
Europe...................	243,771	669,662	687,280	794,964	864,598	992,800	1,115,855
Far East.................	5,558	55,960	85,000	102,010	95,640	111,310	165,660
North, Central and South America	33,003	58,935	63,970	70,890	72,880	99,620	120,590
Middle-East..............	10,447	24,670	28,940	42,390	46,710	56,080	64,070
Not stated[5].............	....	200	290	250	400	150	420
Mode of travel—departure:							
Ship.....................	200,800	226,245	161,963	165,141	114,621	39,340	49,765
Air......................	96,565	626,842	744,937	890,363	1,018,607	1,290,950	1,497,960
Not stated...............	2,300	....	....	....	....	....	....
Sex of traveler:							
Male.....................	155,595	419,615	458,415	534,490	579,520	700,080	810,850
Female...................	144,070	433,472	448,485	521,014	553,708	630,210	736,875
Citizenship of traveler:							
Native...................	174,723	710,172	777,000	918,364	1,011,597	1,236,797	1,374,075
Naturalized..............	124,942	142,915	129,900	137,140	121,631	93,493	173,650

[1] Data not entirely comparable because of changes in classifications in 1956, 1958, and 1961.
[2] Includes "Personal business," "Join husband," "Accompany husband," "Business and pleasure," and "Visit family." [3] Includes "Sightsee," "Vacation," "Visit," and "Tourist." [4] Includes applicants formerly listed under "Employment" and "Commercial business." [5] Beginning 1960, includes applicants who listed "World tour."

Status of American Woman Who Marries a Foreigner

Source: United Nations

She will automatically acquire the nationality of:

Afghanistan	Gabon*	Italy	Liechtenstein	Philippines	Spain
Austria	Greece*	Ivory Coast*	Monaco	Portugal*	Switzerland
Cambodia	Haiti	Jordan	Nepal	Rwanda (e)	Togo*
Ethiopia	Iran	Korea (Rep.)	Niger*	Saudi Arabia	Turkey
Finland	Iraq	Liberia	Peru	Somalia	

Automatically gains husband's nationality if she loses her own:

Belgium*	Cen. African Rep.*	Congo (a)	Rep.*	MalagasyRep.(b)	Tunisia
		Costa Rico (b)	France*	Mauritania*	
Cameroon*	China	Dominican	Laos*	Somaliland	

May acquire husband's nationality if she chooses:

Algeria (c)	Guyana	Libya	Nicaragua	Sudan	Upper Volta
Andorra	Indonesia	Luxemburg	Nigeria	Tanganyika	Venezuela
Bolivia	Ireland	Mali	Pakistan	Thailand	Vietnam, Rep.
Chad (d)	Jamaica	Mexico	Poland	United Arab	Zambia
Ecuador	Kenya	Morocco	San Marino	Rep.	
Gambia	Kuwait	Netherlands	Senegal		
Ghana	Lebanon	New Zealand	Sierra Leone	United Kingdom	

May acquire husband's nationality more easily than other aliens:

Australia	Colombia	Hungary	Malta	Syrian Arab	Rep. of S.
Brazil	Cuba	India	Norway	Rep.	Africa
Burma	Czechoslovakia	Israel	Panama	Trinidad-	Uruguay
Canada	Denmark	Japan	Singapore	Tobago	Western Samoa
Ceylon	El Salvador	Malawi	Sweden (b)	Uganda	Yugoslavia
Chile	Guatemala	Malaysia			

No effect on her nationality:

		Bulgaria	Honduras	Paraguay	USSR
Albania	Argentina	Germany (West)	Iceland	Romania	

*She may decline her husband's nationality. aShe may acquire her husband's nationality if she resides in the country 5 years following the marriage and unless she declines before the expiration of this date. bShe may acquire her husband's nationality by declaration. cShe must formally declare before the marriage that she repudiates her nationality of origin. dApplies only to marriages celebrated in Chad. eMarriage must be registered in civil office of Rwanda Government, which reserves right to oppose within one year the acquisition of nationality.

VITAL STATISTICS

Source: Division of Vital Statistics, National Center for Health Statistics, Public Health Service, U. S. Dept. of Health, Education & Welfare

First Half-Year, January-June, 1967

BIRTHS

The birth rate and the fertility rate continued to decline during the first half of 1967. Live births during the 6 months totalled 1,713,000, a decrease of 49,000 from the figure for the corresponding 6 months in 1966. The fertility rate for the first half of 1967 was 86.4, or 4 percent below the rate of 90.3 for the first half of 1966.

MARRIAGES

An estimated 873,000 marriages were performed in the first half of 1967 or 26,000 more than during the corresponding period in 1966. During June 1967, the marriage rate was 14.7 per 1,000 population, compared with 14.3 for June 1966.

DIVORCES

The January-June 1967 total for 40 reporting areas was 7 percent above the comparable figure for 1966 and 17 percent above that for 1965.

DEATHS

There were 25,000 fewer deaths in January-June 1967 than in January-June 1966. The rates for the first half of these 2 years were 9.5 and 9.9 per 1,000 population, respectively. For the same period, the infant mortality rate of 22.9 per 1,000 live births for 1967 was 5 percent lower than the rate of 24.0 for 1966. In June 1967 the infant mortality rate was 2.7 percent lower than in June 1966.

For the first half of 1967, the death rate for major cardiovascular-renal diseases was lower than for January-June 1966. Among diseases of the heart, the January-June 1967 rate for rheumatic fever and chronic rheumatic heart disease was lower by 10.0 percent than that for the corresponding period of 1966; that for nonrheumatic chronic endocarditis and other myocardial degeneration by 8.5 percent; and that for hypertensive heart disease by 14.3 percent. The rate for chronic and unspecified nephritis and other renal sclerosis was nearly 16% lower.

The cumulative rate for malignant neoplasms of 160.3 per 100,000 population was 5 percent higher for the first 6 months of 1967 than for the first half of 1966. The death rate for home accidents was 16 percent lower for January-June 1967 than for the comparable period of 1966.

PROVISIONAL STATISTICS

12 Months Ending with June 1967

	Number		Rate	
	1967	1966	1967	1966
Live births.........	3,582,000	3,697,000	18.2	19.0
Marriages.........	1,870,000	1,811,000	9.5	9.3
Deaths............	1,844,000	1,853,000	9.4	9.5
Infant deaths......	81,600	88,800	22.8	24.0
Population base (in millions)......			196.9	194.9

Annual Report for the Year 1966
Provisional Statistics

The general trends observed for the last few years continued in 1966. The birth rate decreased for the 9th consecutive year while the marriage rate showed its 4th consecutive annual increase. The death rate with a slight upward fluctuation, continued on its relatively level course. The divorce rate remained the same as in 1965.

BIRTHS

The birth and fertility rates continued to decline from their most recent peaks, which were reached in 1957. In 1966 the birth rate was 18.5 births per 1,000 population, and the fertility rate was 91.8 births per 1,000 women 15-44 years of age.

The current decline in fertility (which began in the late 1950's) has been brought about in part by changes in the age pattern of child-bearing. Women who are now 25 years of age are having relatively low birth rates because they had unusually high birth rates when they were younger. At the same time, women who are now under 25 years of age are having relatively low birth rates because they are apparently delaying some births until they are a little older. Also, these younger women may have fewer children altogether than did women who began their families in the late 1940's and the 1950's.

MARRIAGE AND DIVORCE

The marriage rate rose from 9.2 in 1965 to 9.4 in 1966. This was the 4th successive increase in the annual rate. Because of relatively low birth rates during the 1930's, the proportion of people in the peak marriage ages (about 18-29) was unusually low in 1958-62. By 1963 infants born in the early part of World War II began to enter the peak marriage ages; by 1966, those born in the high post-war birth rate years of 1947 and 1948 also reached these ages. This rise in the number of young people is a key factor in the recent increase in the marriage rate for the total population.

All of the nine geographic divisions registered rates in 1966 that were either about equal to or somewhat higher than those for 1965. Increases were greatest among the States of the Mountain and Pacific Divisions.

An estimated 494,000 decrees of divorce or annulment were granted in the United States in 1966 as compared with an estimated 481,000 for 1965. This represents an increase of 13,000, or 2.7 percent. The divorce rate was 2.5 per 1,000 population for both years. This was the highest national divorce rate since 1953.

DEATHS

An estimated 1,869,000 deaths occurred in the United States in 1966. This provisional rate is higher than the final rate of 943 deaths per 100,000 for 1965. In turn, the final rate for 1965 was higher than that for 1964 (940 deaths per 100,000).

A levelling off of the downward trend in total mortality began around 1954 and continued through the ensuing decade. This occurred despite the fact that infant deaths have constituted a diminishing segment of total deaths since the peak fertility year of 1957. In 1957 infant deaths made up 6.9 percent of all deaths in the United States as compared with 5.1 percent in 1965 and 4.5 percent in 1966. This reduction in the percent of infant deaths resulted both from the smaller number of infants in the population and from the decline in the infant mortality rate. The number of infant deaths per 1,000 live births dropped from 26.3 in 1957 to 24.7 in 1965, to 23.4 in 1966.

Disease of Heart—The death rate for diseases of heart increased from 367.4 per 100,000 population in 1965 to 375.1 in 1966. About 79 percent of all deaths assigned to this category were attributed to arteriosclerotic heart disease, including coronary disease.

Malignant Neoplasms—The increase for malignant neoplasms (the second leading cause of death), from 153.5 deaths per 100,000 in 1965 to 154.8 in 1966 resulted chiefly from the increase for malignant neoplasms of the respiratory system.

Accidents—Fatalities from accidents rose from 55.7 deaths per 100,000 population in 1965 to 57.3 deaths in 1966. This high level of accidental deaths continues because of the ongoing rise in motor vehicle fatalities—from 25.4 deaths per 100,000 population in 1965 to an estimated 27.2 deaths in 1966. This figure for 1966 is the highest death rate for this cause since 1941, when the motor vehicle fatality rate reached 30.0 deaths per 100,000. The death rate for other accidents declined somewhat during 1954-66: from 33.8 deaths per 100,000 in 1954 to 30.4 deaths in 1965 and 30.1 deaths in 1966.

Influenza and Pneumonia—Influenza and pneumonia had an estimated death rate for 1966 (32.8 deaths per 100,000) that was lower than that for the epidemic year 1966 (37.3 deaths per 100,000). Mortality from influenza and pneumonia reported by 122 cities in the U. S. showed some increases above the epidemic threshold from mid-February to mid-May 1966. However, there was no evidence of a widespread influenza epidemic in 1966.

POSTAL INFORMATION

United States Domestic Rates Going Up

Legislation increasing postal rates by $890,000,000 a year was enacted by the House of Representatives Oct. 11, 1967, and given favorable consideration by the Senate Committee on Post Office and Civil Service, with minor changes, Nov. 15, 1967.

FIRST CLASS

Under the new legislation, expected to become effective in January, 1968, it would cost 6 cents instead of 5 cents to mail an ordinary letter. It would cost 5 cents instead of 4 cents to mail a postal card.

GREETING CARDS

The new law would abolish the special low rate for greeting cards and other single-piece mailings entitled to third-class benefits. The rate for such mail would be 6 cents instead of 4 cents for the first 2 ounces and would be 2 cents for each additional ounce or fraction. In effect, this would make the cost of mailing an unsealed Christmas card the same as that of mailing an ordinary first-class letter.

First class includes written matter, namely letters, postal cards, post cards (private mailing cards) and all other matter wholly or partly in writing, whether sealed or unsealed, except manuscripts for books, periodical articles and music, manuscript copy accompanying proofsheets or corrected proofsheets of the same and the writing authorized by law on matter of other classes. Also matter sealed or closed against inspection.

AIR MAIL LETTERS

Air mail (up to 8 ounces): under the new legislation the rate would be 10 cents an ounce or fraction, instead of 8 cents, in the United States, its territories and possessions; also to Armed Forces outside the United States, when addressed APO or FPO, New York, N.Y., San Francisco, Calif., or Seattle, Wash. May be certified, registered, sent C.O.D. or special delivery. Government postal cards and private cards would be 8 cents instead of 6 cents. (Over 8 ounces consult Post Office).

SECOND CLASS

Single copy mailings by general public, under the new law would be 5 cents instead of 4 cents for first 2 ounces, and 1 cent for each additional ounce.

Bulk mailings by publishers, consult local postmasters for rates and permit.

THIRD CLASS

Third Class (limit up to but not including 16 ounces): Mailable matter not in 1st and 2nd classes.

Single mailing: Greeting cards (unsealed), small parcels, printed matter, booklets and catalogs, under the new law would be 6 cents instead of 4 cents for the first 2 ounces and 2 cents for each additional ounce or fraction.

Bulk material: Books, catalogs of 24 pages or more, seeds, cuttings, bulbs, roots, scions and plants: under the new law would be 16 cents instead of 12 cents for first pound and 16 cents for each additional pound or fraction.

Other matter: Newsletters, shoppers' guides, advertising circulars: under the new law, would be 22 cents instead of 18 cents a pound. Subject to a minimum rate for which Post Office should be consulted. Separate rates for some nonprofit organizations. Bulk mailing fee, $30 per calendar year. Apply to postmaster for permit.

PARCEL POST—FOURTH CLASS

Fourth Class or Parcel Post (16 ounces and over): Merchandise, printed matter, etc., may be sealed.

On parcels weighing less than 10 lbs. and measuring more than 84 inches, but not more than 100 inches in length and girth combined, the minimum postage charge shall be the zone charge applicable to a 10-pound parcel.

AIR PARCEL POST

Air Parcel Post (over 8 ounces to 70 lbs.): Packages not to exceed 100 inches in length and girth combined, including written and other matter of the first class, whether sealed or unsealed, fractions of a pound being charged as a full pound. Eight cents an ounce or fraction for all domestic air mail up to and including 8 ounces regardless of distance or zone.

Rates according to zone apply between the U. S. and Puerto Rico and the Virgin Islands.

SPECIAL HANDLING

Parcels weighing less than 10 pounds, measuring over 84 inches but not exceeding 100 inches in length and girth combined, are chargeable with a minimum rate equal to that for a 10 pound parcel for the zone to which addressed. Fourth class parcels will be handled and delivered as expeditiously as practicable (but not special delivery) upon payment, in addition to the regular postage: Up to 2 lbs., 25c; over 2 lbs. and up to 10 lbs., 35c; over 10 lbs., 50c. Such parcels must be endorsed, Special Handling.

AIR MAIL PARCEL POST

The projected scale shown below would become effective under the new law.

Air Mail Parcel Post (Effective January 1968)

Zones	Under 1 lb.	1-1½	1½-2	2-2½	2½-3	3-3½	3½-4	4-4½	4½-5	Each lb. or fract. over 5
1, 2, 3	$0.80	$0.98	$1.16	$1.40	$1.64	$1.88	$2.12	$2.36	$2.60	$0.48
4	.80	1.02	1.23	1.48	1.73	1.98	2.23	2.48	2.73	.50
5	.80	1.07	1.34	1.62	1.90	2.18	2.46	2.74	3.02	.56
6	.80	1.14	1.47	1.79	2.11	2.43	2.75	3.07	3.39	.64
7	.80	1.18	1.55	1.91	2.27	2.63	2.99	3.35	3.71	.72
8	.80	1.24	1.68	2.08	2.48	2.88	3.28	3.68	4.08	.80

Parcel Post Rate Schedule

(Effective Jan. 15, 1967)

1 lb., not exceeding	Zones							
	Local	1 & 2	3	4	5	6	7	8
2	$0.40	$0.50	$0.50	$0.55	$0.60	$0.70	$0.75	$0.80
3	.40	.55	.60	.65	.75	.85	.95	1.05
4	.45	.60	.65	.75	.85	1.00	1.10	1.25
5	.45	.65	.70	.80	.95	1.10	1.30	1.45
6	.45	.70	.80	.90	1.05	1.25	1.45	1.65
7	.50	.80	.85	1.00	1.15	1.40	1.60	1.85
8	.50	.85	.90	1.05	1.30	1.50	1.75	2.00
9	.55	.90	.95	1.15	1.40	1.65	1.90	2.20
10	.55	.95	1.05	1.20	1.50	1.75	2.10	2.40
11	.55	1.00	1.10	1.30	1.60	1.90	2.25	2.60
12	.60	1.05	1.15	1.35	1.70	2.00	2.40	2.75
13	.60	1.10	1.20	1.45	1.80	2.10	2.55	2.95
14	.65	1.15	1.30	1.50	1.90	2.25	2.70	3.10
15	.65	1.20	1.35	1.60	2.00	2.35	2.85	3.30
16	.65	1.25	1.40	1.65	2.10	2.45	3.00	3.45
17	.70	1.30	1.45	1.75	2.20	2.60	3.15	3.65
18	.70	1.35	1.50	1.80	2.30	2.70	3.30	3.80
19	.75	1.40	1.60	1.90	2.40	2.85	3.45	4.00
20	.75	1.40	1.65	1.95	2.50	2.95	3.60	4.15

(Consult the postmaster for parcels weighing over 20 pounds or measuring more than 72 inches, length and girth.)

SPECIAL DELIVERY

First class mail, up to 2 lbs., 30c; over 2 lbs. and up to 10 lbs., 45c; over 10 lbs., 60c. 2nd, 3rd and 4th class mail up to 2 lbs., 55c; over 2 lbs. and up to 10 lbs., 65c; over 10 lbs., 80c.

Registry. All mailable matter prepaid with postage at the first-class or airmail rate may be registered. The mailer is required to declare the value of mail presented for registration.

Insurance is applicable to 3rd and 4th class matter. Matter for sale addressed to prospective purchasers who have not ordered it or authorized its sending will not be insured.

C.O.D.: Unregistered—is applicable to 3rd and 4th class matter and sealed domestic mail of any class bearing postage at the 1st class rate. Such mail must be based on bona fide orders or be in conformity with agreements between senders and addressees. **Registered**—For details consult postmaster.

Certified mail service is available for any matter having no intrinsic value on which 1st class or air mail postage is paid. Receipt is furnished at time of mailing and evidence of delivery obtained. The fee is 30c in addition to postage. Return receipt, restricted delivery and special delivery are available upon payment of additional fees. No indemnity.

REGISTERED, INSURED, C. O. D. AND CERTIFIED MAIL

Indemnity and fees	Registration	Insurance	C.O.D.
Indemnity to $10.	.75	.20	.60
10.01 to 15......	.75	.20	.70
15.01 to 25......	.75	.30	.70
25.01 to 50......	.75	.30	.80
50.01 to 100.....	.75	.40	.90
100.01 to 150....	1.00	.50	1.00
150.01 to 200....	1.00	.60	1.00
200.01 to 400....	1.25		
400.01 to 600....	1.50	Limit $200.	
600.01 to 800....	1.75		
800.01 to 1,000..	2.00		

Consult postmaster for registry rates on articles valued above $1,000.

MONEY ORDERS

Money Orders: Must be purchased at the money order window of the post office or one of its stations. Maximum amount for which a single order may be issued, $100. When a larger sum is to be sent, additional orders must be obtained.

Domestic fees: From 1c to $10, 25c; $10.01 to $50, 35c; $50.01 to $100, 40c. Payable in the U. S., incl. Puerto Rico, Virgin Islands, Guam and Tutuila (Samoa).

Fees for sending money abroad: 1c to $10, 45c; $10.01 to $50, 65c; $50.01 to $100, 75c.

POST OFFICES IN UNITED STATES

As of Mar. 1, 1967 there was a total of 32,755 post offices throughout the United States and Possessions. Of this number 4,704 were First Class; 7,108 Second Class; 13,004 Third Class, and 7,939 Fourth Class.

Postal Savings System Ends

The Postal Savings System went out of business at midnight June 30, 1967, after more than 56 years of continuous operation. The "poor man's banking service" was ended by the Post Office because of increasing costs and a declining number of depositors. Some 600,000 savers still had unclaimed deposits of $60,000,000 with the Post Office when the system ended.

The Postal Savings System began operations Jan. 1, 1911, and had its most prosperous years during the Depression and World War II. In its peak year of 1947, it had 4,000,000 depositors with savings of more than $3 billion.

A maximum account of $2,500 and interest of 2% was maintained from the inception of the system.

But despite the low interest rate, the Postal Savings System was popular with the newly arrived immigrant, the conservative saver who did not trust banks, and the working man who could not conveniently get to an ordinary bank during normal business hours.

Postal savings always made a profit for the Post Office, which claimed to have earned $240,-000,000 from the service from 1911 to 1965.

Record Price Paid for U. S. Stamp

An 1869 U. S. stamp with an inverted center was bought for $35,000 at an auction in New York City Feb. 2, 1967—the highest price ever paid for an American stamp.

The 15-cent brown-and-blue stamp, which shows Columbus landing in America, was bought by Raymond H. Weill, a New Orleans stamp dealer.

At the same auction, $34,000 was paid for a Millbury, Mass., 5-cent postmaster provisional stamp which has a black portrait of George Washington on bluish paper.

Space 1967: Tragedy and Recovery
Source: Science Service, Washington, D. C. 20036

Tragedy marred the space efforts of both the United States and the Soviet Union in 1967, but the two countries vigorously set about picking up the pieces and getting back on course—although the courses are now somewhat different.

The U. S. was dealt the first blow on Jan. 27 when a violent fire, made even hotter by a pure oxygen atmosphere, swept through an Apollo spacecraft being tested on the launch pad. Astronauts Virgil Grissom, Edward White and Roger Chaffee died in the holocaust, and the resulting investigation shook the National Aeronautics and Space Administration.

Layer upon layer of officials was shuffled around by NASA and its main Apollo contractors as a result of the conditions that permitted the tragedy. Congress, alerted by the accident and pressured by the Vietnam war, decided that the space program's headlong pace had to slow down, and chopped half a billion dollars from NASA's requested budget.

Less than three months after the three astronauts became the first Americans to die in a spacecraft, Soviet Cosmonaut Vladimir Komarov, returning from the only manned space flight of the year, lost his life when his Soyuz spacecraft's reentry parachute lines became snarled. During the rest of the year, the Russians have flown more than a dozen objects believed to be unmanned versions of Soyuz, in an effort to overcome their manned flight difficulties.

While the manned part of the U. S. lunar program was having trouble, the unmanned spacecraft assigned to collecting advance information about the moon were going great guns. The Soviet Union sent nothing to the moon as late as November 1967, but three U. S. Lunar Orbiters and three Surveyors collected thousands of photographs of the moon and made chemical analyses of its surface.

The primary task of these probes—selecting a group of locations on the moon from which an Apollo landing site could be chosen—was completed a third of the way through the year.

The other big target of the year was Venus. The Soviet Venus 4 probe and the U. S. Mariner 5 raced toward the planet only two days apart, climaxing their journey when the Russian craft landed on the surface and the U. S. version flew by as planned about 2,400 miles out.

Together, the two probes painted a grim picture of earth's sister planet, with temperatures of more than 500 degrees and an atmosphere that is mainly unbreathable carbon dioxide. Strange optical effects caused by the dense atmosphere, scientists said, would include the impression of standing in a bowl, with the sides sloping up around the observer. In addition, a person on the surface—if he could see the wavelengths of light that could get through Venus' clouds—might even see the back of his own head, because light rays reflecting from it might be bounced around the entire planet.

Several countries besides the "big two" fared into space. France, Italy, Japan, England and the European Space Research Organization (ESRO) all launched satellites, though not all of them got into orbit.

In the future, space activity in the United States may well be less active, with Congress putting on the economic brakes. As a result, a number of foreign countries or groups of them, may achieve a bit more prominence. This could be counterbalanced, however, by a general slackening of far-out space projects if the U. S. slowdown reduces the competition.

It appears as though the big question facing space policy planners will be, "Will it pay for itself?" Satellites and programs specifically aimed at the commercial utilization of space are already starting to meet with more favor than their pure-research counterparts.

1967 SPACE CALENDAR
Source: Science Service, Washington, D. C. 20036

The following are the principal satellites, spacecraft and probes launched in 1967 up to Nov. 10. When available, initial orbital distances closest to (perigee) and farthest from (apogee) earth are shown in miles. The times represent the periods of the orbits. Unsuccessful launches are not listed.

PACIFIC 1 (U. S.) Jan. 11—Also known as Intelsat 2B, it hovers in synchronous orbit over the Pacific, and provides general communications between the U. S., Japan, Australia and the Philippines; Apollo tracking communications for NASA; and military communications for the Defense Communications Agency. 22,244-22,257 miles, 1,436.1 minutes.

IDCSP 8-15 (U. S.) Jan. 18—An eight-in-one launch brought to 15 the number of satellites in the Initial Defense Communication Satellite Program, which keeps the Pentagon in touch with Vietnam. Approx. 20,885-21,153 miles, 1,336 minutes.

COSMOS 138 (USSR) Jan. 19—The first of more than 50 launches this year in the Soviet Union's catch-all satellite series, an increase of more than 40 percent over last year's total. 120-182 miles, 89.2 minutes.

ESSA 4 (U. S.) Jan. 26—Lofted to replace ESSA 2, the Environmental Science Services Administration's fourth satellite got into orbit with only one of its two weather cameras working, but provides daily weather coverage to almost 200 worldwide Automatic Picture Transmission (APT) receivers. 822-894 miles, 113.4 minutes.

LUNAR ORBITER 3 (U. S.) Feb. 4—Took 182 pictures of potential Apollo landing sites on the moon, following its two successful predecessors of last year.

COSMOS 140 (USSR) Feb. 7—Though its mission was, as usual, unannounced this Russian probe was believed to have been a precursor of the Soyuz manned spacecraft series. 106-150 miles, 88.5 minutes.

D1C (France) Feb. 8—The first of two D1 geodetic satellites intended to provide more accurate triangulation data, particularly in the Mediterranean area, via lasers and doppler measurements. 360-833 miles, 104.3 minutes.

D1D (France) Feb. 15—Successful comrade to D1C. 368-1,172 miles, 110.2 minutes.

COSMOS 144 (USSR) Feb. 28—Equipped with two TV cameras for daytime cloud cover photos; infrared scanners for day and night observations and sensors to measure radiation emitted and reflected by the earth and its atmosphere, this satellite was the first in the USSR's proposed "Meteor" global weather-watching system. 388-388 miles, 96.9 minutes.

OSO 3 (U. S.) March 8—The third Orbiting Solar Observatory was successfully set to work with its nine experiments to replace OSO C, which failed to get into orbit in 1965. 336-354 miles, 95.9 minutes.

COSMOS 146 (USSR) March 10—Believed to be an unmanned test of manned spacecraft. 118-193 miles, 89.2 minutes.

ATLANTIC 2 (U. S.) March 22—Alias Intelsat 2C, this communications satellite is the Atlantic version of Pacific 1 (Intelsat 2B). 22,246-22,254 miles, 1,436.1 minutes.

ATS 2 (U. S.) April 5—The second in the multipurpose Applications Technology Satellite series, it got into the wrong orbit for its primary goal of trying out a gravity gradient stabilization system, but carried out communications and meteorological experiments. 115-6,947 miles, 218.9 minutes.

COSMOS 154 (USSR) April 8—Believed to be another manned flight precursor. 116-144 miles, 88.5 minutes.

SURVEYOR 3 (U. S.) April 17—It dug holes in the moon and photographed itself in action, as well as adding more than 6,300 photos to the Apollo landing-site search file.

ESSA 5 (U. S.) April 20—Replaced ESSA 3 in the Tiros Operational Satellite System (TOSS). 840-883 miles, 113.5 minutes.

SOYUZ 1 (USSR) April 23—In the only manned flight of the year by any country, Cosmonaut Vladimir Komarov orbited the earth 17 times, but was killed during reentry when the spacecraft's parachute lines fouled. 125-139 miles, 88.6 minutes.

SAN MARCO 2 (Italy) April 26—Launched from a floating platform off the coast of Kenya, the weather satellite was successfully placed in an equatorial orbit. 135-498 miles, 94.9 minutes.

COSMOS 156 (USSR) April 27—Joined Cosmos 144, but phased 95 degrees behind so that the two satellites would pass over the same areas six hours apart. 391-391 miles, 97 minutes.

VELA 7 and 8 (U. S.) April 28—These two nuclear-blast-detecting sky-spies were launched as part of a five-in-one shot which also included: ERS 18, to continue mapping the Van Allen radiation belts; OV5-1, to aid in solar flare prediction; and OV5-3, to investigate the effects of space on metals. Vela orbits approx. 67,521-70,332 miles, 6,696 minutes.

LUNAR ORBITER 4 (U. S.) May 4—The first Orbiter to be devoted more to scientific research than to Apollo site-picking, it sent 163 photos back to earth.

ARIEL 3 (U. K.) May 5—The third satellite in the U. S.-U. K. cooperative research program, first British-built one, orbit with all five of its experiments operating. 306-373 miles, 95.6 minutes.

EXPLORER 34 (U. S.) May 24—Also known as IMP-F, it was the fifth in the seven-satellite Interplanetary Monitoring Probe series, and carried 11 experiments to compare solar and galactic cosmic rays measured inside and outside earth's magnetosphere. 154-131,187 miles, 6,231 minutes.

MOLNIYA 1E (USSR) May 25—The fifth Soviet communications satellite, it could handle color and black-and-white TV, voice and telegraph transmissions. 286-24,737 miles, 319 minutes.

VENUS 4 (USSR) June 12—Part of it flew by the planet Venus, the other part landed on the planet's surface on Oct. 17, concluding that Venus was every bit as inhospitable as expected, with temperatures of more than 500 degrees F.

MARINER 5 (U. S.) June 14—Launched toward Venus two days after the Russian vehicle, the third U. S. Venus probe got there two days later also, found that Venus has an ionosphere and a glowing hydrogen corona as does earth, but that the mysterious planet lacks both a magnetic field and radiation belts.

AURORA 1 (U. S.) June 29—Launched as half of a double shot that included the Secor 9 geodetic satellite, the probe was designed to investigate the aurora borealis. 2370-2458 miles, 172.1 minutes.

DODGE (U. S.) July 1—This huge, spidery satellite was the Department of Defense's Gravity Experiment. 20,627-20,-868 miles, 1,319.1 minutes.

EXPLORER 35 (U. S.) July 22—Now in orbit around the moon, it measures the solar wind and other interplanetary data as influenced by the moon's presence.

OGO 4 (U. S.) July 28—The fourth Orbiting Geophysical Observatory collects a wide range of data as part of one of the most complicated satellite series ever flown by the United States. 257-551 miles, 97.7 minutes.

LUNAR ORBITER 5 (U. S.) Aug. 1—The final Orbiter in the series worked just as well as its predecessors, adding even more photos to the lunar art gallery.

BIOSATELLITE 2 (U. S.) Sept. 7—After its identical predecessor was lost over Australia with its cargo of wasps, wildflowers, frogs' eggs, pepper plants and other living things, the second satellite successfully ejected its cargo of flora and fauna out of orbit, providing geneticists with samples exposed to three days of radiation and weightlessness. 164-164 miles, 90.1 minutes.

SURVEYOR 5 (U. S.) Sept. 8—Besides the ever present cameras, the third success in the series (1 and 3 worked; 2 and 4 crashed) carried an automatic chemical laboratory that analyzed the moon directly beneath itself by observing the characteristic scattering of alpha particles bounced off the lunar elements. The spacecraft found that the lunar material was basaltic rock of which more than 75 percent was oxygen and silicon.

PACIFIC 2 (U. S.) Sept. 27—The latest addition to the U. S. communications satellite system, this one's other name is Intelsat 2D. 22,219-22,225 miles, 1,436.1 minutes.

OSO 4 (U. S.) Oct. 18—The 3,000th man-made object sent into space, the fourth Orbiting Solar Observatory carries nine experiments to monitor the sun for its effects on the communications blackout that plagues reentering spacecraft. 337-359 miles 95.8 minutes.

COSMOS 186 (USSR) Oct. 27—Another unmanned Soyuz spacecraft duplicate, it cruised along in orbit for three days until the launch of

COSMOS 188 (USSR) Oct. 30—When 188 got into orbit, it carried out automatic docking procedures with 186, remaining coupled for several orbits, after which 186 came back to a reported "soft landing in the preset area." Orbits for the two spacecraft while coupled: 124-171 miles, periods varying from 88 to 97 minutes.

ATS-3 (U. S.) Nov. 5—Packed with experimental meteorological and communications equipment, the third Applications Technology Satellite carried a new camera to take the first high-resolution color pictures of the earth's full disc. 22,229-22,255 miles, 1,440 minutes.

SURVEYOR 6 (U. S.) Nov. 7—Equipped with both a camera and a robot chemistry laboratory, this next-to-last Surveyor went to the moon to enable scientists to make broader generalizations about the moon's makeup.

APOLLO 4 (U. S.) Nov. 9—This unmanned flight marked the first launch of Apollo hardware since the Jan. 27 fire that killed three astronauts in their spacecraft; in addition, it was the first launch ever of the giant Saturn 5 booster that will send the Apollo crew to the moon.

ESSA 6 (U. S.) Nov. 10—The latest member of the Tiros Operational Satellite System, this weather-watcher is equipped with APT cameras to enable its use by low-cost, worldwide group stations. 874-922 miles, 114.8 minutes.

Meteor Showers Are Numerous Every Year

About a dozen meteor showers occur each year and the dates on which they take place may be found in the Calendar of Celestial Events. These showers are caused by the earth's passage through streams of meteoroids left in space by comets, of which they were a part. The meteoroids orbit the sun along the path originally followed by the comet and are encountered annually by the earth as it moves about the sun.

A shower of unusual intensity was visible over western North America during the early morning hours of Nov. 17, 1966. This was the Leonid Shower, produced by debris from Comet Tempel I which passed near the sun—and the earth—in April, 1966.

PREHISTORIC BOMBARDMENT

Canadian and American researchers have found evidence that the earth has been subjected to heavy bombardment from space on several occasions from 34,000,000 to 700,000 years ago.

The oldest of these catastrophes covered the eastern half of North America, the Atlantic Ocean and the northern half of Africa. Scars in the form of circular pits, sometimes a score of yards in diameter and often filled with water, have been located in northern Quebec, and fragments of metallic, stony and glassy objects define the area.

Central Europe received a fall of similar objects about 15,000,000 years ago and the most recent fall, about 700,000 years ago, struck the region including Australia and southeastern Asia.

The stony-metallic fragments are thought to originate in the asteroid belt, a region in space roughly between Mars and Jupiter in which travel thousands of minor planets ranging in size from 480 miles in diameter down to flying mountains a few miles across. Gravitational upheavals and collisions among asteroids are believed to provide fragments, some of which may reach the earth.

The glassy fragments, called tektites, are thought to be material resulting from collisions of large objects with the earth or the moon, scattered originally in liquid form and cooling after impact into drop-shaped, glassy particles.

METEORS

Meteoroids are celestial bodies, possibly associated with comets, that move through space with velocities up to 40 miles per second. Upon reaching the earth's atmosphere, they are vaporized by the heat of the friction of their passage into the atmosphere and are seen as meteors. An unusual number in a short period of time is called a meteor shower. Meteors are popularly known as falling stars or shooting stars. While most of them are consumed, a few fall to earth as fused metal or stone, and are called meteorites.

Many meteorites have been picked up in the United States, most of them small. A huge meteorite may lie embedded in the earth at Meteor Crater, on U. S. 6 near Canyon Diablo in Arizona. The crater is 1 mi. in diameter at the surface and over 500 feet deep, and is surrounded by a wall of earth filled with pyrites presumably originating with the meteor. A lake in the Ungava region of northern Quebec fills the Chubb Crater, discovered 1943, which is 7½ mi. around. Vast destruction of timber was caused by a meteorite that hit in the vicinity of Lake Baikal, in Siberia, June 30, 1908. A large meteor that split into fragments of 80 to 820 pounds fell Feb. 17, 1930, 14 mi. sw of Paragould, Ark.

On display in the American Museum-Hayden Planetarium, New York, N. Y. are three meteorites; a 34 ton 85 pound iron-nickel meteorite and another 3-ton one brought from Cape York, Greenland by Robert E. Peary in 1907 and a 14½ ton meteorite found in the Willamette region of Oregon in 1902.

COMETS

The origin of comets is not known. Dr. Jan Oort, a Dutch astronomer, presents the hypothesis that there is a wide, irregular cloud of comets around the outskirts of the solar system. From this cloud single comets may be drawn, from time to time, by the gravitational pull of one of the large outer planets and started on journeys through the solar system on long elliptical orbits about the sun.

Comets sufficiently bright to be seen without a telescope are rare. In October and November, 1965, a new comet, Ikeya-Seki, was visible in the morning skies before sunrise as the most spectacular comet since Halley's in 1910. Barring the unexpected appearance of an as yet unknown bright comet, possible at any time, the next certain bright comet due to appear is Halley's Comet, expected in 1986.

On page 659 are listed a few of the short-period comets that make fairly regular visits to the region of the earth.

U. S. Space Probes Enable Close Study of Lunar Surface

United States space probes, in both hard and soft landings on the moon, and other U. S. space vehicles orbiting the moon have made available to scientists valuable new material for detailed studies of the lunar surface.

During 1964 and 1965, three successful landings on the moon were made by moon probes of the Ranger series, designed to photograph the surface of the moon at close range. These three Ranger vehicles sent back nearly 18,000 pictures of the surface of the moon before crashing and destroying themselves. These pictures were taken at distances ranging from 300 miles to less than 2,000 feet from the moon.

On June 2, 1966, the first of the Surveyor vehicles made a soft landing on the moon near the crater Flamsteed in the Oceanus Procellarum, on the eastern side of the moon slightly north of the lunar equator. Its cameras took photographs from a height of about four feet.

Surveyor III duplicated this feat on April 19, 1967, by landing gently on the moon after some heart-stopping bounces which evidently did no damage to its instruments. It landed in the Oceanus Procellarum, not far from Surveyor I, apparently on the slope of a shallow crater so that its cameras saw the moon at a slight angle.

Meanwhile, three Lunar Orbiters are revolving about the moon, securing and transmitting photographs of much of the moon's surface in order to find the best landing place for the manned Apollo flight to take place in the future. Orbiter II is placed at a much greater distance from the moon than its two orbiting companions so that its cameras can secure pictures of large areas with the purpose of using them for making detailed lunar maps.

The Ranger vehicles revealed that there is hardly any of the moon's surface unmarked by craters, from the enormous depressions visible in telescopes from the earth to tiny holes inches across. There does not appear to be any overall cover of dust on the moon. The pictures sent back by Surveyor I show the surface strewn with small, loose rocks and rubble and the instruments on the vehicle registered a temperature of 280 degrees below zero, Fahrenheit, during the two-week lunar night through which it passed before its communication systems ceased to operate. One of the Orbiter pictures shows Surveyor I on the moon.

Surveyor III was equipped with a small metal claw with which it could dig into the surface material of the moon. The amount of current required to move this claw through the surface gave a measure of the density of this material and its composition. It appears to be dry and fine-grained, resembling silt or closely packed sand. Surveyor III took photographs during an eclipse of the moon which showed the reverse of that phenomenon from the lunar viewpoint—an eclipse of the sun by the earth. Its instruments registered a drop of about 400 degrees in temperature as the moon passed through the earth's shadow during the eclipse.

There are still several opinions as to the character of the lunar surface. Proponents of the "hot moon" hold that surface formations there are volcanic in origin but pulverized by meteorites. The "cold moon" advocates maintain that little or no volcanic activity has taken place and that the surface has been shaped entirely by meteorite impact. Still others see a combination of both factors responsible for the moon's surface with evidence of water, which has long since disappeared, in forming some of the landscape features. Water may be present under the insulating surface material. One of these opinions may be confirmed by subsequent Surveyor probes, or confirmation may not be possible until astronauts land on the moon to see for themselves.

Poles and Rotation of the Earth

POLES OF THE EARTH

Source: Coast and Geodetic Survey, ESSA

The geographic (rotation) poles, or points where the earth's axis of rotation cuts the surface, are not absolutely fixed in the body of the earth. The pole of rotation describes an irregular curve about its mean position.

Two periods have been detected in this motion: (1) an annual period due to seasonal changes in barometric pressure, load of ice and snow on the surface and to other phenomena of seasonal character; (2) a period of about 14 months due to the shape and constitution of the Earth.

In addition there are small but as yet unpredictable irregularities. The whole motion is so small that the actual pole at any time remains within a circle of 30 or 40 feet in radius centered at the mean position of the pole.

The pole of rotation for the time being is of course the pole having a latitude of 90° and an indeterminate longitude.

MAGNETIC POLES

The **north magnetic pole** of the earth is that region where the magnetic force is vertically downward and the **south magnetic pole** that region where the magnetic force is vertically upward. A compass placed at the magnetic poles experiences no directive force.

There are slow changes in the distribution of the earth's magnetic field. These changes were at one time attributed in part to a periodic movement of the magnetic poles around the geographical poles, but later evidence refutes this theory and points, rather, to a slow migration of "disturbance" foci over the earth.

There appear shifts in position of the magnetic poles due to the changes in the earth's magnetic field. The center of the area designated as the north magnetic pole was estimated to be in about latitude 70.5° N and longitude 96° W in 1905; from recent nearby measurements and studies of the secular changes, the position in 1965 is estimated as latitude 75.5° N and longitude 100.5° W. Improved data rather than actual motion account for at least part of the change.

The position of the south magnetic pole in 1912 was near 71° S and longitude 150° E; the position in 1965 is estimated as latitude 66.5° S. and longitude 139.9° E.

The direction of the horizontal components of the magnetic field at any point is known as magnetic north at that point, and the angle by which it deviates east or west of true north is known as the magnetic declination, or in the mariner's terminology the **variation of the compass.**

A compass without error points in the direction of magnetic north. (In general this is *not* the direction of the magnetic north pole.) If one follows the direction indicated by the north end of the compass, he will travel along a rather irregular curve which eventually reaches the north magnetic pole (though not usually by a great-circle route). However, the action of the compass should not be thought of as due to any influence of the distant pole, but simply as an indication of the distribution of the earth's magnetism at the place of observation.

ROTATION OF THE EARTH

Source: U. S. Naval Observatory

The speed of rotation of the earth about its axis has been found to be slightly variable. The variations may be classified as:

(a) **Secular.** Tidal friction acts as a brake on the rotation and causes a slow secular increase in the length of the day, about 1 millisecond per century.

(b) **Irregular.** The speed of rotation may increase for a number of years, about 5 to 10, and then start decreasing. The maximum difference from the mean in the length of the day during a century is about 5 milliseconds. The accumulated difference in time has amounted to 38 seconds. The cause is probably turbulent motion in the core of the earth.

(c) **Periodic.** Seasonal variations exist with periods of one year and six months. The cumulative effect is such that each year the earth is late about 30 milliseconds near June 1 and is ahead about 30 milliseconds near Oct. 1. The maximum seasonal variation in the length of the day is about 0.5 millisecond. It is believed that the principal cause of the annual variation is the seasonal change in the wind patterns of the Northern and Southern Hemispheres. The semi-annual variation is due chiefly to tidal action of the sun, which distorts the shape of the earth slightly.

The secular and irregular variations were discovered by comparing time based on the rotation of the earth with time based on the orbital motion of the moon about the earth and of the planets about the sun. The periodic variation was determined largely with the aid of quartz-crystal clocks. The introduction of the cesium-beam atomic clock in 1955 made it possible to determine in greater detail than before the nature of the irregular and periodic variations.

Four Eclipses in 1968

The time used in these tables is Eastern Standard Time. To obtain Central Standard Time, subtract 1 hour; Mountain Standard Time, subtract 2 hours; Pacific Standard Time, subtract 3 hours; Alaska-Hawaii Time, subtract 5 hours. A.M. light figures; P.M. black; O (zero) designates midnight, 12 designates noon.

FIRST ECLIPSE

A **Partial Eclipse of the Sun,** March 28, 1968. The eclipse is visible in the southern tip of South America, the South Pacific Ocean and Antarctica.

CIRCUMSTANCES OF THE ECLIPSE

	d	h	s
Eclipse begins	March 28	03	43.6
Greatest eclipse	March 28	06	59.9
Eclipse ends	March 28	08	16.7

SECOND ECLIPSE

A **Total Eclipse of the Moon,** April 12-13, 1968. The beginning of the penumbral phase of the eclipse is visible in Europe, most of Africa, the Atlantic Ocean, North America except the northwestern part of Alaska, South America, the southeast Pacific Ocean, New Zealand, Antarctica.

CIRCUMSTANCES OF THE ECLIPSE

	d	h	s
Moon enters penumbra	April 12	09	11.1
Moon enters umbra	April 12	10	10.0
Total Eclipse begins	April 12	11	22.5
Middle of the eclipse	April 12	11	47.4
Total eclipse ends	April 13	00	12.3
Moon leaves umbra	April 13	01	24.8
Moon leaves penumbra	April 13	02	23.6

Magnitude of the eclipse 1.117

THIRD ECLIPSE

A **Total Eclipse of the Sun,** September 22, 1968. The eclipse is visible over central Asia and Siberia. It is partial over Western Asia, Europe, northeastern Africa, the north Atlantic Ocean, Iceland and Greenland.

CIRCUMSTANCES OF THE ECLIPSE

	d	h	m
Eclipse begins	September 22	04	06.7
Central eclipse begins	September 22	05	43.9
Central eclipse ends	September 22	06	52.9
Eclipse ends	September 22	08	29.8

FOURTH ECLIPSE

A **Total Eclipse of the Moon,** October 6, 1968. The beginning of the penumbral phase is visible in North America, the western half of South America, the Pacific Ocean, most of Australia, New Zealand, the northeastern part of Asia, and the Arctic regions; the end visible in the northwestern part of North America, the Pacific Ocean except the southeastern part, Australia, New Zealand, most of the Indian Ocean, Asia, except the western part and the Arctic region.

CIRCUMSTANCES OF THE ECLIPSE

	d	h	m
Moon enters penumbra	October 6	03	44.3
Moon enters umbra	October 6	04	54.6
Total eclipse begins	October 6	06	09.9
Middle of the eclipse	October 6	06	42.0
Total eclipse ends	October 6	07	13.9
Moon leaves umbra	October 6	08	29.2
Moon leaves penumbra	October 6	09	39.7

Magnitude of the eclipse 1.174

Harvest Moon and Hunter's Moon

The Harvest Moon, the full moon nearest to the Autumnal equinox, ushers in a period of several successive days when the moon rises soon after sunset. This phenomenon gives farmers in north temperate latitudes extra hours of light in which to harvest their crops before frost and winter come—hence the name. The 1968 Harvest Moon falls on Oct. 6.

The next full moon after Harvest Moon is called the Hunter's Moon, accompanied by a similar phenomenon but less marked.

Developments in the Earth Sciences
United States Geological Survey

Water Resources: On the average in the U. S. about 30 inches of precipitation falls during the year, of which 21 inches is returned directly to the atmosphere by various natural processes. About 9 inches reaches the ocean as either streamflow or underground seepage. Man, in his efforts to supply his needs for water, works principally with the 9 inches that nature would ordinarily return to the oceans.

The U. S. Geological Survey is constantly searching for new ways to explore for and appraise water resources. Remote sensing of water conditions from aircraft and satellites, a recent development, shows promise of becoming a very effective tool in hydrologic investigations.

Many Federal agencies collect data on water resources, and in recent years a critical need for coordination of these activities became evident. To meet this need the Office of Water Data Coordination was established in the Geological Survey. This office was assigned the responsibility for: (1) the design and operation of a national network for acquiring data on the quantity and quality of surface water and ground water, including sediment in streams; (2) coordination of the national network and specialized water data acquisition; and (3) the establishment and maintenance of a central catalog of information on national network and specialized water data and on activities being planned or conducted to acquire such data. As of October 1967, sections of the catalog on the quality and quantity of surface water have been processed; and indexes to these sections have been published. Sections on ground water data and data collected in specialized hydrologic studies are being compiled.

Mineral Resources: During 1966 a heavy metals program was started to investigate possible new sources of metals such as gold and silver that are in short domestic supply. The program has pinpointed areas in Cortez, Nev., Ely, Nev., Cripple Creek, Colo. and northwest Wyo. as warranting further investigation.

One of the continuing programs of the Geological Survey is the systematic analysis of the regional geology throughout the U. S. to provide the broad framework needed for further detailed mineral resource appraisals as well as for the solution of land use and conservation problems.

The Survey in cooperation with the Bureau of Mines is evaluating the mineral potential of the lands considered for inclusion in the National Wilderness Preservation System. Mineral surveys have been completed or are in progress in 19 primitive areas being considered for Wilderness status. Reports on 12 of these areas have been published.

Natural Hazards: Supplementing regional studies are more comprehensive studies of areas that are prone to natural hazards. Chief among these are earthquake areas. The Survey is now engaged in a study of the active San Andreas fault and the related Hayward and Calaveras faults in Calif. These faults are being instrumented with seismographs, tiltmeters, strainmeters, magnetometer and gravity meters to detect and transmit by telephone lines to the Geological Survey's National Center for Earthquake Research in Menlo Park, Calif., any earth changes in the faults. These observations may one day provide a means to predict earthquakes.

Research under the Sea: Studies of the geologic environment of the Atlantic Continental Shelf are continuing and similar regional studies of the shelf areas of the Gulf of Mexico, and along the Pacific and Alaska Coasts were started in 1966.

On the Alaskan Shelf, studies identified many extensive submerged beaches and ancient drainage systems whose landward counterparts are known to contain rich placer deposits.

Through the use of color photography, multi-spectral photography, and infrared imagery, submarine fresh water springs were located 24 miles off the Fla. coast. These springs may prove to be important sources of supply for the heavily-populated coastal areas.

Lunar Geology: On the basis of photographs taken by Lunar Orbiters and Surveyor I and III, the Geological Survey recommended prime sites for the first Apollo landing. In addition, the Survey continued to develop instruments and techniques for effective geologic exploration of the lunar surface.

Ten of 44 geologic maps covering most of the moon's visible surface have been published. These maps show the distribution and relative age of the various lunar surface materials that can be identified and the many craters that are visible.

International Cooperation: During the past year the Survey provided 134 specialists to 30 countries and arranged academic or practical training in the United States for 94 earth scientists and engineers from abroad.

Conservation: Areas of Federal lands of great current public interest, because they hold great promise for making a substantial contribution to future demands for energy, and agricultural and industrial raw materials, are the Outer Continental Shelves and the vast deposits of undeveloped oil shale and associated minerals on Federal lands in Colo., Utah, and Wyo. The Survey is implementing programs to gather and analyze resource data which will permit an even more meaningful evaluation of the resources of both these areas.

Topographic mapping: The USGS publishes nearly 30,000 different maps in several standard scales and quadrangle sizes. These maps provide a wealth of information needed for planning and executing many kinds of work, such as geologic and mineral investigations, urban development and other land-use programs, forest and range management, hydrologic studies, soil conservation, recreation, and selection and preliminary surveying of construction sites for highways, dams, pipelines, transmission lines, and industrial plants. More than 7,500,000 copies were distributed in 1966.

Research: A continuing program of research and development in the Geological Survey provides new or improved instruments, materials, and procedures for topographic mapping and related activities. Although this program expends only a small percentage of the topographic mapping budget, over the past 15 years it has increased the efficiency of map production in terms of square miles mapped per man-year by more than 150%. Developments of the program have also had wide application in the worldwide mapping community.

Antarctic mapping: The Geological Survey has the primary responsibility for producing maps needed to support scientific investigations of the U. S. Antarctic Research Program. Current mapping is aimed at producing topographic maps for the mountainous areas of Antarctica.

National Atlas: The Geological Survey is preparing a 475-page National Atlas of the United States, which in a single volume will provide an accurate composite record of the physical environment of the country, its resources, economy, industry, population, history and social culture, and political sub-divisions. Approximately 325 pages are in some phase of preparation and 6 maps have been published and are available for purchase.

Mineral Production, Value and Royalty (Fiscal Year 1967[a])

Lands	Oil	Gas	Gas liquids	Other[b]	Value	Royalty
	Bls.	1,000 cu. ft.	Gallons	Tons		
Public	187,218,000	818,329,000	493,751,000	28,426,000	$850,916,000	$86,085,000
Acquired	10,477,000	25,481,000	460,000	193,000	40,051,000	4,572,000
Indian	32,347,000	128,408,000	71,379,000	11,580,000	130,390,000	16,396,000
Military	1,298,000	46,826,000	54,783,000		14,587,000	2,422,000
Outer continental shelf	199,000,000	1,100,000,000		1,930,000	855,000,000	145,000,000
Naval petroleum res. no. 2	3,100,000	5,000,000	13,000,000		12,000,000	1,500,000
Total	433,440,000	2,124,044,000	633,373,000	42,129,000	1,902,944,000	255,975,000

[a]Estimated in part. [b]All minerals except petroleum products; includes coal, potassium, sodium, etc.

Weather in 1967: Droughts, Floods, Billion-Dollar Hurricane

Droughts Come and Go. The blistering drought which beset the nation's Northeast for 5 years finally came to a rainy end in 1967 as that region was deluged with heavier downpours than it might have wished. But nature, balancing its bounty in a thoroughly unwelcome way, dealt the Pacific Northwest a prolonged summer dry spell which was to bring disaster to many of the nation's finest forests.

New Yorkers sloshed through their wettest summer in 25 years; during June, July and August 17.57 inches of rain fell on the metropolitan area, 6.12 inches above normal and 4 times the 4.31 inches that fell in the hot summer of 1966.

Wet Weekends in the East. If the damp urbanites and suburbanites complained that it seemed to rain every weekend, they were right; Labor Day provided the first weekend without precipitation since June 10-11. The Northeast also could complain, and rightfully, that there had been no spring; it was indeed unusually wet and chilly. But there was compensation when authorities largely lifted restrictions on the use of water.

Fires in the Northwest. By contrast, Portland, Ore., had its first rain in 72 days on Sept. 2, and even then it was only .4 of an inch. (Portland's old record was 61 days.) By late August, tinder-dry forests in northern Idaho and Montana, in Oregon, Washington and British Columbia, were hit by raging fires. Light showers eased the hazard early in September; heavy rains hit the area early in October.

California Brush Fires. A dry summer, topped off by hot desert winds in October, brought a series of dangerous brush fires to areas around Los Angeles. Fanned by gusts up to 70 m.p.h., the flames caused at least 3 deaths, destroyed scores of homes and caused damage in the millions.

Earlier in the year, drought damaged the winter wheat crops in Texas, Oklahoma, Kansas and Colorado. A severe 3-month drought caused death of some wildlife in Everglades National Park and damaged nearby Florida pastures but ended in June.

Blizzards and Big Snows. The Great Plains and Great Lakes areas were battered by powerful blizzards in mid-January; winds were near hurricane force in North Dakota and temperatures as low as −47° in Minnesota. On Jan. 26 a snowstorm dumped a record 23 inches on Chicago; in the next 10 days succeeding storms added another foot.

A major blizzard blasted the East Coast from Washington to southern New England Feb. 6-7, taking 18 lives. In New York City, it closed schools and paralyzed all forms of transport with 12.6 inches of snow and cold of 6°.

A "May Day Blizzard" struck the northern Great Plains with winds of 70 m.p.h. and 30 inches of snow in the Black Hills.

Tornadoes. Death-dealing twisters knew no season. On Jan. 24 a series of them struck the Midwest, killing 3 persons in Missouri, two in Illinois, one in Iowa, injuring over 200 and causing heavy property damage. A chain of tornadoes ripped the Midwest on Apr. 21, killing 55 and injuring more than 1,000 in northeastern Illinois; hundreds of homes were destroyed. In Oak Lawn, a Chicago suburb, at least 32 died; in Belvidere, 65 mi. from Chicago, some 17 were killed, many of them high school students.

Another string of killer twisters struck southern Minnesota and Iowa Apr. 30, taking 17 lives. Two tornadoes smashed ashore near Gulfport, Miss., Oct. 30, killing 3 persons.

Fairbanks Flooded. Five days of record rains swelled the Chena and Tanana Rivers in mid-August sending water 9 ft. deep through the streets of the central Alaska city; it was the worst flood in Fairbanks' history; damage was estimated at over $200,000,000.

Other floods caused widespread damage in Wisconsin in April; in Louisiana in April and again in May; in Tennessee and Nebraska in May, in Missouri in June and again in July.

3 Hurricanes at Once. The hurricane season started late but in early September Beulah, Chloe and Doria were all raging at the same time. Chloe finally dissipated in the mid-Atlantic and Doria appeared likely to do the same; but Chloe's last fling gave Doria a push which sent it slamming into the North Carolina coast, where it quickly lost its strength. But its spreading winds and high seas caused the death of a mother and two children aboard a small boat off New Jersey.

Beulah Spreads Havoc. The worst of the terrible trio, Beulah was spawned in the Atlantic, rampaged through the Caribbean, leaving 29 dead in Martinique, St. Vincent, the Dominican Republic and Haiti, roared across the Yucatan Peninsula and into the Gulf of Mexico with winds as high as 175 m.p.h.

On Sept. 20 it smashed its way ashore at the Texas-Mexico border near Brownsville and dealt Texas and Mexico damage reckoned at more than $1 billion. To the 29 dead in the Caribbean, it added 11 in Texas and at least 30 in Mexico. It dumped 20-30 inches of rain, flooding vast areas, and touched off at least 56 tornadoes to add to the terror and desolation.

More than 200,000 persons were left homeless in the vast flood disaster which followed in Beulah's wake. Thousands of Mexicans were flown to shelter in the U.S. The Mexican Government termed it the worst flood of the 20th Century. Only a tremendous effort by disaster relief agencies kept the death toll from soaring into the hundreds.

Snows Return Early. The first big autumn snowstorm hit the northern Great Plains and Great Lakes region Oct. 27, dropping 18 inches on Ironwood, Mich. The central Rockies had heavy snow; by Nov. 2 there was 26 inches at Berthoud Pass, near Denver. On Nov. 4-5, 20 inches fell on western New York.

Storms at Sea. Gale winds wrecked a trawler near Halifax, N.S., Feb. 21; all 18 aboard were reported drowned. Another storm sank the Soviet fishing boat Tukan off Denmark, Feb. 28, drowning 52 of the 79 aboard. A Lake Michigan squall sank numerous fishing boats Sept. 23; 7 persons were reported drowned.

The Meaning of "One Inch of Rain"

An acre of ground contains 43,560 square feet. Consequently, a rainfall of 1 inch over 1 acre of ground would mean a total of 6,272,640 cubic inches of water. This is equivalent of 3,630 cubic feet.

As a cubic foot of pure water weighs about 62.4 pounds, the exact amount varying with the density, it follows that the weight of a uniform coating of 1 inch of rain over 1 acre of surface would be 226,512 pounds, or 113¼ short tons.

The weight of 1 U. S. gallon of pure water is 8.345 pounds. Consequently a rainfall of 1 inch over 1 acre of ground would mean 27,143 gallons of water.

Medical Developments in 1967

Source: Science Service, Washington, D. C. 20036

Medical science in the year 1967, while mostly undramatic in terms of radical new cures, showed marked progress against the 3 top killers—heart disease, cancer and stroke.

Massive efforts to understand fully the work of drugs and their side effects are still in their infancy, with more promise than progress reported. Similar slow forward motion is being made toward increasing the chance that organ transplants can be routinely and successfully retained; classes of drugs that prevent the rejection of kidney and other organ transplants as foreign bodies to be attacked by the host body's defense mechanisms are promising, but still experimental. So, at year's end, are efforts to produce cheap and easy artificial kidneys that can be widely afforded and used at home.

In one breakthrough, a new vaccine against the baby-killing Rh disease was being stockpiled in expectation of approval for use by the National Institutes of Health. RhoGAM, as it is called, has been found effective in almost 100% of its test cases. The disease regularly killed 10,000 infants a year in the United States, 200,000 around the world.

Fight Against Major Killers

Meanwhile, medicine's persistent fight against the major killers is apparently beginning to pay off.

During 1967 statistics were compiled that show heart disease deaths cut down by 5% during the decade ended in 1965. Most startling drop: a cut of 46% in the incidence of high blood pressure deaths, partially due to new drugs such as guanethidine and mecamylamine.

Rheumatic heart disease deaths were cut 33% and stroke deaths dropped 20%. While coronary heart disease deaths climbed 11% in the decade, they have since fallen by 2%.

And, in the heart field, there are great advances in the offing.

Plastic Heart Valves

Although plastic heart valves have been installed in humans for a dozen years, they often caused dangerous blood clotting. During 1967, researchers reported that using frozen natural valves from cadavers or animals overcomes the clotting problem. On the heels of their announcement, doctors working with plastic valves overcame the problem in another way—the use of Dacron or polypropylene coated with silicone and dipped in heparin, an anticlotting agent.

The 15,000 people who are wearing implantable pacemakers to back up their unreliable hearts can look forward to new devices that will dispense with the batteries—which now have to be replaced at intervals of 3 years or less. One of the new pacers sponsored by the Atomic Energy Commission will derive power from the heat given off by the manmade radioisotope plutonium 238. Others take their power from the body itself, forming an electric cell in the bloodstream.

The artificial heart branch of the National Heart Institute awarded $8,700,000 during the year for research in assisting damaged or failing hearts, including pumping devices. The Heart Institute also awarded more than $5,000,000 to establish special units for the care of victims of acute heart attacks.

The Federal Heart, Cancer and Stroke regional program, authorized in February 1966, got underway in 1967. As of Nov. 1, 1967, medical programs in 49 regions covering 90% of the countrys' population had been approved and funded for planning activities, and 5 of these also had received money for operations.

Exercise was proven beneficial to victims of angina pectoris, the painful and disabling blockage of an artery. Researchers recommended walking as the best exercise for these patients because it does not require any quick spurts of energy such as when a cyclist suddenly has to climb a hill. Tests on a treadmill every day showed that symptoms improved so much that some of the patients were able to do almost any kind of exercise. Drugs such as nitroglycerine were continued during the exercise to minimize pain.

Leukemia Death Rates Drop

Death rates from leukemia, cancer of the blood-forming organs, went down for the first time in the United States. The National Cancer Institute is supporting a special program of virus-leukemia research for which the U. S. Congress appropriated more than $16,000,000 in 1967.

Pitting one type of virus against another, scientists developed new techniques permitting them to isolate leukemia-causing viruses from chickens and mice. Next, they're hoping these methods will uncover leukemia viruses in dogs and eventually in man. Dr. Robert J. Huebner of the National Cancer Institute predicts success may come during 1968.

A similar research effort is being launched to find out whether another group of viruses, called adenoviruses, cause human cancer. Certain types of these viruses which cause common respiratory diseases were shown to trigger cancer in rats. The initial study of what these viruses do to man will involve examination of blood serum and tissue extracts from 500 cancer patients.

Among the legislative changes during 1967 were liberalizing the abortion laws, especially in California, Colorado and North Carolina. The American Medical Association's House of Delegates accepted a Board of Trustees report on therapeutic abortion recommending similar changes. These follow the Model Penal Code of the American Law Institute. This code provides for the legal termination of pregnancy to preserve the life and health of the mother, or when there is a substantial risk of fetal abnormalities or when pregnancy is the result of rape or incest. Licensed physicians in accredited hospitals may perform therapeutic abortions after consultation with medical colleagues.

The war in Vietnam has shown a markedly lower figure for deaths following wounds than in Korea. Speedy transportation by helicopter to hospitals has further reduced the death toll. Research has produced new drug treatment against malaria. Daraprim with quinine has been found effective against Plasmodium falciparum malaria, which had become resistant to chloroquine.

Research in the United States and England linked several human diseases, including multiple sclerosis, with a tiny subvirus that causes the sheep disease, scrapie. This agent appears to be neither viral nor genetic, but may be a protein that reproduces in a different way from the nucleic acids, DNA and RNA. Other linked human diseases are amyotrophic lateral sclerosis, which killed the famous baseball player Lou Gehrig; a type of shaking palsy called Parkinsonism dementia and a disease of the Fore tribe of New Guinea called kuru.

In spite of apparent success of Medicare, hospital costs have continued to climb, with predictions of $100 a day for a room in some cases because of increased costs of labor and equipment. Studies showed that poor planning in some areas had permitted excessive beds and whole hospitals that should never have been built.

A preliminary report of successful rejoining of a damaged spinal cord was made by a group of surgeons. Although two more years of follow-up will be needed to assess the degree of function, one of seven patients—a quadriplegic—reportedly had regained use of his hands and upper trunk. Four of the other six persons who underwent similar operations had varying degrees of function, it was said. Considerable controversy over the report arose in medical circles.

Medical Signs and Abbreviations
Source: American Medical Association

℞ (Lat. Recipe)	....take	ad	....to, up to	gargarisma	....a gargle	q. 3 h...every three hours
℈	....drachm	adde	....add	gr	....grain	q.i.d....four times daily
f ℈	....fluid drachm	ad libitum...at pleasure		gtt	....drops	q.s.
℥	....ounce	agit	....shake	h.s.	....at bedtime	... as much as is sufficient
f ℥	....fluid ounce	aqua	....water	inject	....injection	sig	....sign, write
℥ ss	....half an ounce	b.i.d	....twice daily	lb	....pound	solutio	....a solution
℥ i	....one ounce	cap	....capsule	m	....mix	ss	....one-half
℥ iss one ounce and a half		cum, or c	....with	non. rep. or n.r.		stat	....at once
℥ ij	....two ounces	dilute	....dilute		do not repeat	sum	....to be taken
℈	....scruple	e.m.p	....as directed	p.c.	....after meals	tab	....tablet
♏	....minim, or drop	fac (mist)		pil	....pill	t.i.d....three times daily
O	....pint	....let a mixture be made		p.r.n....as circumstances		ung	....ointment
āā	....of each	fiant (ft)	....make		may require	ut dict......as directed
a.c.	....before meals	filtra	....filter	pulvis	....powder	

Drug Addiction Continues to Rise

The number of active drug addicts in the United States continued to increase in 1966 and the Bureau of Narcotics reported that as of Dec. 31, 1966 the number of known addicts stood at 59,720—an increase of 2,521 over the previous year.

More than 82% of all addicts in the country were reported from five states:

New York—31,191   Illinois—6,915   Michigan—1,667
California—7,212   New Jersey—2,107   All others—10,628

New York City accounted for 95% or 29,665 of all the addicts in the state in 1966. Almost 46% of the nation's addicts were between the ages of 21 and 30 at the end of 1966, the Bureau of Narcotics said. The number of active addicts under 21 years old was 2,118 or 3.5% of the addict population.

Suicide in Selected Countries
Source: World Health Organization
Average annual death rates per 100,000, 1962-1963*

Country	All ages	15-24	25-44	45-64	65 & over	Country	All ages	15-24	25-44	45-64	65 & over
Males						**Females**					
Hungary	35.5	29.7	41.7	56.3	87.8	Japan	14.3	19.7	14.0	16.7	46.9
Austria	29.5	20.5	33.6	56.8	61.1	Hungary	14.1	13.4	14.0	24.2	37.2
Sweden	24.0	12.9	28.2	49.4	48.3	Austria	11.1	6.3	13.7	20.3	24.5
Germany (west)	23.1	18.7	25.1	43.3	49.4	Germany (west)	10.4	6.6	10.9	21.7	22.0
Japan	21.3	23.9	22.3	28.0	66.9	Australia	9.9	3.8	13.0	21.5	14.0
France	20.8	6.8	19.8	46.1	63.9	Sweden	8.8	5.4	13.1	14.8	13.2
Australia	20.7	11.1	27.4	38.9	38.7	England, Wales..	7.9	2.8	8.7	17.3	19.2
United States						Belgium	6.4	2.8	5.9	14.2	18.5
White	18.0	9.3	19.7	35.1	45.0	France	6.2	3.7	5.8	12.8	17.7
Nonwhite	9.6	8.0	14.1	13.3	16.9	United States					
Poland	16.6	12.9	24.1	27.4	20.4	White	6.7	3.2	8.7	12.2	8.7
Belgium	16.2	7.1	13.2	33.5	62.2	Nonwhite	2.7	2.9	4.4	3.1	3.2
England, Wales..	12.7	7.0	13.6	24.4	36.4	Canada	3.9	2.4	5.2	7.6	5.2
Canada	12.6	8.5	14.8	25.3	22.1	Poland	3.5	3.6	4.0	6.6	4.9
Italy	7.1	3.8	6.0	14.8	22.7	Italy	2.9	2.8	2.9	5.3	7.1

*Age-adjusted on basis of U. S. total population, 1940.

HemisFair '68 Marks San Antonio's 250th Anniversary

HemisFair '68, a world's fair celebrating the 250th anniversary of the founding of San Antonio, offers numerous attractions to fair-goers from Apr. 6 to Oct. 6, 1968, on a 92.6-acre site close to the famed Alamo.

Theme of the Texas fair is "The Confluence of Civilizations in the Americas." More than a score of nations including the U. S. and Mexico planned pavilions, as did numerous Texas, national and international corporations.

The fair provided an amusements area, a 1.5-mile minirail and a mile of waterways, including an extension of the picturesque San Antonio River to provide transportation within the fair to boats, river taxis and dining barges. A Tower of the Americas, 622 ft. tall, featured observation decks and a revolving restaurant at the 550-ft. level.

Tickets at the gate were set at $2 for adults and $1 for children. Persons seeking to reserve lodging reservations or to purchase 20-ticket books at reduced advance prices were advised to write to Visitors Services, P. O. Drawer H, San Antonio, Tex. 78206.

COLLEGE BASKETBALL

Final Standings in 1966-1967 Season

BIG TEN

	Conference Games W	L	All Games W	L
Indiana	10	4	17	7
Michigan State	10	4	17	7
Iowa	9	5	16	8
Wisconsin	8	6	13	11
Purdue	7	7	15	9
Northwestern	7	7	11	11
Ohio State	6	8	13	11
Illinois	6	8	12	12
Minnesota	5	9	8	16
Michigan	2	12	8	16

PACIFIC EIGHT

	Conference Games W	L	All Games W	L
U.C.L.A.	14	0	26	0
Washington St.	8	6	15	11
Oregon State	8	6	14	14
Stanford	7	7	15	11
Southern Calif.	6	8	13	12
Washington	6	8	12	13
California	6	8	15	10
Oregon	1	13	9	17

SOUTHEASTERN

	Conference Games W	L	All Games W	L
Tennessee	15	3	21	5
Florida	14	4	21	4
Vanderbilt	14	4	21	5
Auburn	12	6	17	8
Mississippi State	8	10	14	11
Kentucky	8	10	13	13
Mississippi	7	11	13	13
Alabama	6	12	13	13
Georgia	5	13	9	17
Louisiana St. Un.	1	17	3	23

WEST COAST ATHLETIC

	Conference Games W	L	All Games W	L
Pacific	14	0	23	3
Loyola	10	4	16	10
Santa Clara	8	6	13	13
San Francisco	7	7	13	13
Santa Barbara	6	8	10	16
Pepperdine	5	9	9	17
San Jose State	4	10	9	15
St. Mary's	2	21	4	21

BIG EIGHT

	Conference Games W	L	All Games W	L
Kansas	13	1	22	3
Colorado	10	4	17	8
Nebraska	10	4	16	8
Kansas State	9	5	17	8
Iowa State	6	8	13	12
Oklahoma	5	9	8	17
Oklahoma State	2	12	7	18
Missouri	1	13	3	22

IVY LEAGUE

	Conference Games W	L	All Games W	L
Princeton	13	1	23	4
Cornell	11	3	19	7
Yale	11	3	14	5
Penn	7	7	11	14
Columbia	6	8	11	14
Harvard	4	10	11	14
Brown	3	11	10	16
Dartmouth	1	13	7	17

ATLANTIC COAST

	Conference Games W	L	All Games W	L
North Carolina	12	2	21	4
Duke	9	3	16	9
South Carolina	8	4	15	6
Clemson	5	7	17	9
Maryland	5	9	11	13
Wake Forest	5	9	8	17
Virginia	4	10	9	18
No. Carolina St.	2	12	7	18

METROPOLITAN

	Conference Games W	L	All Games W	L
St. Peter's	7	2	18	5
St. Francis	7	2	14	8
Manhattan	7	2	13	8
New York Univ.	6	3	10	16
Long Island Un.	5	4	19	6
Wagner	4	5	17	8
Iona	4	5	11	10
Seton Hall	3	6	7	17
Hofstra	2	7	12	13
Fairleigh Dickinson	0	9	4	19

SOUTHWEST

	Conference Games W	L	All Games W	L
S. Methodist Un.	12	2	19	5
Texas	8	6	14	10
Baylor	8	6	14	9
Tex. Christ. Un.	8	6	10	14
Texas Tech	7	7	9	14
Texas A.&M.	5	9	6	18
Rice	4	10	7	17
Arkansas	4	10	6	17

YANKEE

	Conference Games W	L	All Games W	L
Connecticut	9	1	17	6
Rhode Island	8	2	14	12
Massachusetts	7	3	14	11
New Hampshire	4	6	10	12
Maine	1	9	8	12
Vermont	1	9	10	15

TRI-STATE LEAGUE

	Conference Games W	L	All Games W	L
Long Island Un.	6	0	19	6
C.C.N.Y.	4	2	13	6
Bridgeport	3	3	16	9
Adelphi	2	4	14	10
Rider	2	4	11	12
Fairleigh Dickinson	2	4	4	19
C. W. Post	2	4	13	10

N.J. STATE

	Conference Games W	L	All Games W	L
Montclair	9	1	21	4
Trenton	9	1	16	8
Jersey City	5	5	10	12
Glassboro	3	7	6	18
Paterson	3	7	6	18
Newark	1	9	6	17

MISSOURI VALLEY

	Conference Games W	L	All Games W	L
Louisville	12	2	23	3
Tulsa	10	4	19	7
Wichita	9	5	14	12
Bradley	6	8	17	9
Cincinnati	6	8	17	9
St. Louis	5	9	12	13
North Texas	4	10	12	13
Drake	4	10	9	16

MID-AMERICAN

	Conference Games W	L	All Games W	L
Toledo	11	1	23	1
Marshall	10	2	18	6
Miami	7	5	14	10
Bowling Green	5	7	11	13
West'n Michigan	4	8	10	14
Ohio Univ.	4	8	8	15
Kent State	1	11	5	19

WESTERN ATHLETIC

	Conference Games W	L	All Games W	L
Brigham Young	8	2	14	9
Wyoming	8	2	13	13
New Mexico	5	5	18	7
Utah	5	5	15	11
Arizona	3	7	8	17
Arizona State	1	9	5	21

SOUTHERN CONFERENCE

	Conference Games W	L	All Games W	L
West Virginia	9	1	19	8
Davidson	8	4	15	12
William & Mary	8	5	14	11
Richmond	9	7	11	12
Citadel	6	7	8	17
George Washing.	5	7	6	18
Furman	4	6	9	15
East Carolina	4	8	7	18
Virginia Military	4	12	5	16

OHIO VALLEY

	Conference Games W	L	All Games W	L
W. Kentucky	13	1	23	2
Morehead State	8	6	16	8
E. Tennessee St.	8	6	17	9
Murray State	8	6	14	9
Austin Peay St.	7	7	14	9
Tennessee Tech.	6	8	12	11
Middle Tenn. St.	4	10	10	15
East. Ky.	2	12	5	18

BIG SKY

	Conference Games W	L	All Games W	L
Montana State	7	3	13	12
Gonzaga	7	3	19	6
Idaho State	5	5	10	15
Idaho	5	5	14	10
Weber State	5	5	18	7
Montana	1	9	6	17

INDIANA COLLEGE CONFERENCE

	Conference Games W	L	All Games W	L
Indiana State	11	1	21	5
Valparaiso	7	5	21	6
DePauw	6	6	10	12
Evansville	6	6	8	17
Butler	5	7	9	17
Ball State	4	8	7	14
St. Joseph's	3	9	10	15

MIDWEST CONFERENCE

	Conference Games W	L	All Games W	L
Beloit	14	4	18	4
Cornell	14	4	17	5
Ripon	12	6	14	8
Knox	11	7	14	8
St. Olaf	11	7	12	10
Carleton	9	9	11	11
Monmouth	8	10	9	13
Lawrence	7	11	—	—
Grinnell	2	16	2	20
Coe	2	16	2	20

FAR WESTERN

	Conference Games W	L	All Games W	L
UC Davis	12	2	21	7
Sacramento St.	10	4	15	11
San Francisco St.	10	4	14	12
Hayward St.	7	7	12	14
Chico St.	7	7	11	15
Humboldt St.	4	10	10	14
Nevada	4	10	5	20
Sonoma St.	2	12	6	14

OHIO CONFERENCE

	Conference Games W	L	All Games W	L
Wittenberg	12	1	17	7
Baldwin-Wallace	11	2	22	9
Kenyon	10	3	16	6
Otterbein	9	4	19	6
Denison	8	5	11	7
Marietta	7	5	13	8
Ohio Wesleyan	6	7	9	13
Capitol	5	8	7	14
Wooster	4	9	9	15
Oberlin	4	9	9	12
Hiram	4	9	8	13
Mt. Union	4	9	9	18
Heidelberg	3	10	3	18
Muskingum	3	10	—	—

Basketball Champions by Years

	National Invitation Tournament		National Collegiate A. A.	
	Winner	Runner-up	Winner	Runner-up
1954....	Holy Cross...........71	Duquesne...........62	La Salle...........92	Bradley...........76
1955....	Duquesne...........70	Dayton...........58	San Francisco...........77	La Salle...........63
1956....	Louisville...........93	Dayton...........80	San Francisco...........83	Iowa...........71
1957....	Bradley...........84	Memphis State...........83	North Carolina...........54	Kansas...........53
1958....	Xavier...........78	Dayton...........74	Kentucky...........84	Seattle...........72
1959....	St. John's...........76	Bradley...........71	California...........71	West Virginia...........70
1960....	Bradley...........88	Providence Coll...........72	Ohio State...........75	California...........55
1961....	Providence Coll...........62	St. Louis...........59	Cincinnati...........70	Ohio State...........65
1962....	Dayton...........73	St. John's...........67	Cincinnati...........71	Ohio State...........59
1963....	Providence Coll...........81	Canisius Coll...........66	Loyola (Chicago)...........60	Cincinnati...........58
1964....	Bradley...........86	New Mexico...........54	U. C. L. A...........98	Duke...........83
1965....	St. John's...........55	Villanova...........51	U. C. L. A...........91	Michigan...........80
1966....	Brigham Young...........97	N. Y. U...........84	Texas Western...........72	Kentucky...........65
1967....	Southern Illinois...........71	Marquette...........56	U. C. L. A...........79	Dayton...........64

U.C.L.A. 1966-67 National Basketball Champion

The United Press International board of coaches selected the U.C.L.A. Bruins as the top college basketball team for the 1966-67 season. The top twenty teams with points figured on a 10-9-8-7-6-5-4-3-2-1 basis for first through 10th place (first place votes in parentheses) follow:

1—U.C.L.A. (34) 349	8—Texas Western 84	14—Utah State 13
2—Louisville (1) 307	9—Tennessee 60	16—Pacific Univ. 12
3—North Carolina 232	10—Boston College 61	17—Providence 11
4—Kansas 204	11—Toledo 23	18—New Mexico 10
5—Princeton 167	12—St. John's 14	19—Duke 8
6—Houston 150	13—Tulsa 14	20—Florida 6
7—Western Kentucky 127	14—Vanderbilt 13	

NEA All-American Team, 1967

The following is the 1967 college All-American team selected for Newspaper Enterprise Assn. by the 10 NBA coaches and their talent scouts in the field.

First Team			Second Team		
Pos.	Name	Team	Pos.	Name	Team
F	Westley Unseld, Louisville		F	Clem Haskins, Western Kentucky	
F	Elvin Hayes, Houston		F	Sonny Dove, St. John's	
C	Lew Alcindor, UCLA		C	Mel Daniels, New Mexico	
G	Jim Walker, Providence		G	Bob Verga, Duke	
G	Bob Lloyd, Rutgers		G	Butch Beard, Louisville	

HONORABLE MENTION

Pat Riley, Kentucky; David Lattin, Texas Western; Cliff Anderson, St. Joseph's (Pa.); Lou Dampier, Kentucky; Walt Frazier, Southern Illinois; Earl Monroe, Winston-Salem; Tom Workman, Seattle; Harry Hollines, Denver; Jo Jo White, Kansas; Jim Burns, Northwestern; Larry Miller, North Carolina; Bob Lewis, North Carolina; Chris Thomforde, Princeton; Joe Allen, Bradley; Wes Bialosuknia, Connecticut.

Alcindor Named College Basketball Player of Year

Lew Alcindor, sophomore from U.C.L.A., was named by United Press International as the college basketball player of the year for 1966-67 in the annual balloting by newsmen and broadcasters from across the nation. The 7-foot-1⅜ inch star received 155 of 260 ballots cast. Jimmy Walker of Providence was second with 71 votes, Louisville's Westley Unseld received 10 and Bob Lloyd of Rutgers 7. Awards for previous years follow:

1955—Tom Gola, La Salle	1959—Oscar Robertson, Cincinnati	1963—Art Heyman, Duke
1956—Bill Russell, San Francisco	1960—Oscar Robertson, Cincinnati	1964—Gary Bradds, Ohio State
1957—Chet Forte, Columbia	1961—Jerry Lucas, Ohio State	1965—Bill Bradley, Princeton
1958—Oscar Robertson, Cincinnati	1962—Jerry Lucas, Ohio State	1966—Cazzie Russell, Michigan

Basketball Hall of Fame
Springfield, Mass.

The Naismith Memorial Basketball Hall of Fame was incorporated in 1959 to serve as a memorial to James Naismith, who invented the game of basketball for students of the School for Christian Workers (now Springfield College) in November, 1891, at Springfield, Mass. The following persons have been enshrined in the Basketball Hall of Fame for outstanding contributions to basketball:

College Players

Harold (Bud) Foster, Wisconsin; Victor Hanson, Syracuse; Charles (Chuck) Hyatt, Pittsburgh; Robert Kurland, Oklahoma State; Angelo (Hank) Luisetti, Stanford; Branch McCracken, Indiana; C. Edward Macauley, St. Louis; George Mikan, DePaul; Charles (Stretch) Murphy, Purdue; H. O. (Pat) Page, Chicago; Andy Phillip, Illinois; John Roosma, U. S. Military Academy; John Schommer, Chicago; Christian Steinmetz, Wisconsin; J. A. (Cat) Thompson, Montana State; John R. Wooden, Purdue.

Professional Players

Bennie Borgmann, Nat Holman, Joe Lapchick, John (Honey) Russell, Barney Sedran, Edward A. Wachter.

AAU Players

Forrest S. DeBernardi, Robert (Ace) Gruenig, Jack McCracken.

Coaches

Ernest A. Blood, Dr. H. Clifford Carlson, Everett S. Dean, Howard A. Hobson, Frank Keaney, George E. Keogan, Ward (Piggy) Lambert, Kenneth Loeffler, Dr. Walter E. Meanwell, Leonard D. Sachs.

Referees

George Hepbron, George Hoyt, Matthew P. Kennedy, Ernest Quigley, David Tobey, David Walsh.

Contributors

Dr. Forrest C. (Phog) Allen, Walter A. Brown, John W. Bunn, Dr. Luther Gulick, Edward J. Hickox, Paul D. (Tom) Hinkle, Edward S. (Ned) Irish, R. William Jones, William G. Mokray, Ralph Morgan, Frank (Pop) Morgenweck, Dr. James Naismith, John J. O'Brien, Sr., Harold Olsen, H. V. Porter, William Reid, Lynn St. John, A. A. Schabinger, Amos Alonzo Stagg, Oswald Tower, Arthur L. Trester.

Biddy Basketball Champions

Biddy basketball competition, with scaled down courts, equipment and shorter periods of play, is open to boys up to 12 and girls up to 13. Local, regional and national tournaments are held annually under jurisdiction of Biddy Basketball national headquarters, Scranton, Pa. National champions have been:

	Winner	Runner-up		Winner	Runner-up
1957.....	New Orleans, La...45	Atlantic City, N.J..42	1963.....	New Orleans, La...44	New York, N. Y...43
1958.....	Bridgeport, Conn.49	Puerto Rico...........46	1964.....	Chester, Pa..........61	Jersey City, N. J..55
1959.....	Bridgeport, Conn.50	New Orleans, La..36	1965.....	New York, N. Y.37	New Orleans, La..32
1960.....	Gary, Ind...........51	Jersey City, N.J...47	1966.....	New Orleans, La..53	Jersey City, N. J..38
1961.....	Jefferson, La......46	Wichita, Kan......42	1967.....	Wichita, Kans.....41	New Orleans, La..38
1962.....	Wichita, Kansas..41	Jefferson Parish, La...........40			

Professional Basketball

NATIONAL BASKETBALL ASSOCIATION

Eastern Division	W.	L.	Pct.	Pts.	Op.	Western Division	W.	L.	Pct.	Pts.	Op.
Philadelphia	68	13	.840	10143	9378	San Francisco	44	37	.543	9911	9679
Boston	60	21	.741	9684	9012	St. Louis	39	42	.481	9204	9334
Cincinnati	39	42	.481	9487	9507	Los Angeles	36	45	.444	9764	9736
New York	36	45	.444	9425	9672	Chicago	33	48	.407	9167	9407
Baltimore	20	61	.247	9353	9881	Detroit	30	51	.370	9015	9163

Eastern Divisional Championship—Philadelphia defeated Boston, 4 games to 1.
Western Divisional Championship—San Francisco defeated St. Louis, 4 games to 2.
Championship Series—Philadelphia defeated San Francisco, 4 games to 2.

Individual Scoring Leaders

	FG	FT	Pts.	Avg.*
R. Barry, San Fran.	1011	753	2775	35.6
O. Robertson, Cin.	838	736	2412	30.5
W. Chamberlain, Phil.	785	386	1956	24.1
J. West, L. A.	645	602	1892	28.7
E. Baylor, L. A.	711	440	1862	26.6
H. Greer, Phil.	699	367	1765	22.1
J. Havlicek, Bos.	684	365	1733	21.4
W. Reed, N. Y.	635	358	1628	20.9
B. Howell, Bos.	636	349	1621	20.0
D. Bing, Det.	664	273	1601	20.0

Field Goal Percentage Leaders (A)

	FG	FGA	Pct.
W. Chamberlain, Phil.	785	1150	.683
W. Bellamy, N. Y.	565	1084	.521
B. Howell, Bost.	636	1242	.512
O. Robertson, Cinc.	838	1699	.493
W. Reed, N. Y.	635	1298	.490
C. Walker, Phil.	561	1150	.488
B. Boozer, Chic.	538	1104	.487
T. Hawkins, L. A.	275	572	.481
H. Hairston, Cinc.	461	962	.479
D. Barnett, N. Y.	454	949	.478

Leaders in Rebounds

	No.	Avg.*
W. Chamberlain, Phil.	1957	24.2
B. Russell, Bost.	1700	21.0
J. Lucas, Cinc.	1547	19.1
N. Thurmond, S. F.	1382	21.3
B. Bridges, St. L.	1190	15.1
W. Reed, N. Y.	1136	14.6
D. Imhoff, L. A.	1080	13.3
W. Bellamy, N. Y.	1064	13.5
L. Ellis, Balt.	970	12.0
D. DeBusschere, Det.	924	11.8

Free Throw Percentage Leaders (A)

	FT	FTA	Pct.
A. Smith, Cinc.	343	380	.903
R. Barry, S. F.	753	852	.884
J. West, L. A.	602	686	.878
O. Robertson, Cinc.	736	843	.873
S. Jones, Bost.	318	371	.857
L. Siegfried, Bost.	294	347	.847
W. Jones, Phil.	223	266	.838
J. Havlicek, Bost.	365	441	.828
K. Loughery, Balt.	340	412	.825
E. Baylor, L. A.	440	541	.813

Leaders in Assists

	No.	Avg.*
G. Rodgers, Chic.	908	11.2
O. Robertson, Cinc.	845	10.7
W. Chamberlain, Phil.	630	7.8
J. West, L. A.	447	6.8
L. Wilkens, St. L.	442	5.7
H. Komives, N. Y.	401	6.2
K. C. Jones, Bost.	389	5.0
R. Guerin, St. L.	345	4.4
P. Neumann, S. F.	342	4.4

*Per game (A) minimum 220.

Podoloff Trophy Winners

Wilt Chamberlain of Philadelphia was selected as the winner of the Maurice Podoloff Trophy as the Most Valuable Player in the N. B. A. for the 1966-67 season. The award was determined in a poll of all players on the ten teams conducted by Newspaper Enterprise Association.

1956—Bob Pettit, St. Louis
1957—Bob Cousy, Boston
1958—Bill Russell, Boston
1959—Bob Pettit, St. Louis
1960—Wilt Chamberlain, Philadelphia
1961—Bill Russell, Boston
1962—Bill Russell, Boston
1963—Bill Russell, Boston
1964—Oscar Robertson, Cincinnati
1965—Bill Russell, Boston
1966—Wilt Chamberlain, Philadelphia
1967—Wilt Chamberlain, Philadelphia

N. B. A. SCORING LEADERS

Yr.	Scoring Champion	Pts.	Avg.	Yr.	Scoring Champion	Pts.	Avg.
1947	Joe Fulks, Philadelphia	1,389	23.2	1958	George Yardley, Detroit	2,001	27.8
1948	Max Zaslofsky, Chicago	1,007	21.0	1959	Bob Pettit, St. Louis	2,105	29.2
1949	George Mikan, Minneapolis	1,698	28.3	1960	Wilt Chamberlain, Philadelphia	2,707	37.9
1950	George Mikan, Minneapolis	1,865	27.4	1961	Wilt Chamberlain, Philadelphia	3,033	38.4
1951	George Mikan, Minneapolis	1,932	28.4	1962	Wilt Chamberlain, Philadelphia	4,029	50.4
1952	Paul Arizin, Philadelphia	1,674	25.4	1963	Wilt Chamberlain, San Francisco	3,586	44.8
1953	Neil Johnston, Philadelphia	1,564	22.3	1964	Wilt Chamberlain, San Francisco	2,948	36.5
1954	Neil Johnston, Philadelphia	1,759	24.4	1965	Wilt Chamberlain, San Fran., Phila.	2,534	34.7
1955	Neil Johnston, Philadelphia	1,631	22.7	1966	Wilt Chamberlain, Philadelphia	2,649	33.5
1956	Bob Pettit, St. Louis	1,849	25.7	1967	Rick Barry, San Francisco	2,775	35.6
1957	Paul Arizin, Philadelphia	1,817	25.6				

N. B. A. CHAMPIONS 1948-1967

Year	Regular Season		Playoffs	
	Eastern Division	Western Division	Winner	Loser
1948	Philadelphia	St. Louis	Baltimore	Philadelphia
1949	Washington	Rochester	Minneapolis	Washington
1950	Syracuse	Minneapolis	Minneapolis	Syracuse
1951	Philadelphia	Minneapolis	Rochester	New York
1952	Syracuse	Rochester	Minneapolis	New York
1953	New York	Minneapolis	Minneapolis	New York
1954	New York	Minneapolis	Minneapolis	Syracuse
1955	Syracuse	Ft. Wayne	Syracuse	Ft. Wayne
1956	Philadelphia	Ft. Wayne	Philadelphia	Ft. Wayne
1957	Boston	St. Louis	Boston	St. Louis
1958	Boston	St. Louis	St. Louis	Boston
1959	Boston	St. Louis	Boston	Minneapolis
1960	Boston	St. Louis	Boston	St. Louis
1961	Boston	St. Louis	Boston	St. Louis
1962	Boston	Los Angeles	Boston	Los Angeles
1963	Boston	Los Angeles	Boston	Los Angeles
1964	Boston	San Francisco	Boston	San Francisco
1965	Boston	Los Angeles	Boston	Los Angeles
1966	Philadelphia	Los Angeles	Boston	Los Angeles
1967	Philadelphia	San Francisco	Philadelphia	San Francisco

Hockey Champions in 1966-67

NATIONAL HOCKEY LEAGUE

Final Standings

	W	L	T	Pts.	GF	GA
Chicago Blackhawks....	41	17	12	94	264	170
Montreal Canadiens.....	32	25	13	77	202	188
Toronto Maple Leafs....	32	27	11	75	204	211
New York Rangers......	30	28	12	72	188	189
Detroit Red Wings......	27	39	4	58	212	241
Boston Bruins..........	17	43	10	44	182	253

LEADING SCORERS

	GP	G	A	Pts.	PIM
Stan Mikita, Chi........	70	35	62	97	12
Bobby Hull, Chi.........	66	52	28	80	52
Norm Ullman, Det.......	68	26	44	70	26
Ken Wharram, Chi.......	70	31	34	65	21
Gordie Howe, Det.......	69	25	40	65	53
Bobby Rousseau, Mtl....	68	19	44	63	58
Phil Esposito, Chi.......	69	21	40	61	40
Phil Goyette, N. Y......	70	12	49	61	6
Doug Mohns, Chi........	61	25	35	60	58
Henri Richard, Mtl......	65	21	34	55	28
Alex Delvecchio, Det.....	70	17	38	55	10
Dave Keon, Tor.........	66	19	33	52	2
Pierre Pilote, Chi.......	70	6	46	52	90
John Bucyk, Bos........	59	18	30	48	12
Ted Hampson, Det.......	65	13	35	48	4
Bruce MacGregor, Det...	70	28	19	47	14
Rod Gilbert, N. Y.......	64	28	18	46	12
Don Marshall, N. Y.....	70	24	22	46	4
Frank Mahovlich, Tor....	63	18	28	46	44
Dean Prentice, Det......	68	23	22	45	18
Ron Ellis, Tor..........	67	22	23	45	14
Bob Pulford, Tor........	67	17	28	45	28
Bob Nevin, N. Y........	67	20	24	44	6
Dennis Hull, Chi........	70	25	17	42	33
John Ferguson, Mtl......	67	20	22	42	177
Pit Martin, Bos.........	70	20	22	42	40
Bernie Geoffrion, N. Y..	58	17	25	42	42
Ralph Backstrom, Mtl....	69	14	27	41	39
Bobby Orr, Bos.........	61	13	28	41	102
Yvan Cournoyer, Mtl.....	69	25	15	40	14
Paul Henderson, Det.....	46	21	19	40	10
Harry Howell, N. Y.....	70	12	28	40	54
Red Kelly, Tor.........	61	14	24	38	4
Jean Beliveau, Mtl......	53	12	26	38	22
Chico Maki, Chi........	56	9	29	38	14
Eric Nesterenko, Chi.....	68	14	23	37	38
John McKenzie, Bos.....	69	17	19	36	98
Ed Westfall, Bos........	70	12	24	36	26
Orland Kurtenbach, N.Y..	60	11	25	36	58
Claude Larose, Mtl......	69	19	16	35	82
Pete Stemkowski, Tor....	68	13	22	35	75
Ken Hodge, Chi.........	68	10	25	35	59
Murray Oliver, Bos......	65	9	26	35	16
Gary Bergman, Det......	70	5	30	35	129
Earl Ingarfield, N. Y....	67	12	22	34	12
J. C. Tremblay, Mtl......	60	8	26	34	14
Pat Stapleton, Chi.......	70	3	31	34	54
Vic Hadfield, N. Y......	69	13	20	33	80
George Armstrong, Tor...	70	9	24	33	28
Jim Pappin, Chi.........	64	21	11	32	89
Gilles Tremblay, Mtl.....	62	13	19	32	16
Reg. Fleming, N. Y......	61	15	16	31	146
Andy Bathgate, Det......	60	8	23	31	24
Wayne Connelly, Bos.....	64	13	17	30	12
Ron Schock, Bos........	66	10	20	30	8
Larry Jeffrey, Tor.......	56	11	17	28	27
Brian Conacher, Tor.....	66	14	13	27	47
Ron Murphy, Bos.......	39	11	16	27	6
Doug Jarrett, Chi.......	70	5	21	26	76
Floyd Smith, Det.......	54	11	14	25	8
Eddie Shack, Tor.......	63	11	14	25	58
Tim Horton, Tor........	70	8	17	25	70
Ron Stewart, Bos.......	56	14	10	24	31
Claude Provost, Mtl......	64	11	13	24	16
Dick Duff, Mtl..........	51	12	11	23	23
Larry Hillman, Tor......	55	4	19	23	40
Tom Williams, Bos......	28	8	13	21	2
Leo Boivin, Det.........	69	4	17	21	78
Bill Hay, Chi...........	36	7	13	20	12
Jacques Laperriere, Mtl..	61	0	20	20	48
Dave Balon, Mtl.........	48	11	8	19	31
Ed Van Impe, Chi.......	61	8	11	19	111
Bob Dillabough, Bos......	60	6	12	18	14
Lou Angotti, Chi........	63	6	12	18	21
Ted Harris, Mtl.........	65	2	16	18	86
Mike Walton, Tor.......	31	7	10	17	13
Howie Young, Det.......	44	3	14	17	100
Leon Rochefort, Mtl......	27	9	7	16	6
Ray Cullen, Det.........	27	8	8	16	8
Ted Green, Bos.........	47	6	10	16	67
Terry Harper, Mtl.......	56	0	16	16	99
Gilles Marotte, Bos......	67	7	8	15	112
Jim Neilson, N. Y.......	61	4	11	15	65
Joe Watson, Bos........	69	2	13	15	38
Kent Douglas, Tor.......	39	2	12	14	48
Marcel Pronovost, Tor....	58	2	12	14	28
Wayne Hillman, N. Y....	67	2	12	14	43
Allan Stanley, Tor.......	53	1	12	13	20
Arnie Brown, N. Y......	69	2	10	12	61
Jean Ratelle, N. Y......	41	6	5	11	4
Wally Boyer, Chi........	42	5	6	11	15
John Brenneman, Tor....	41	6	4	10	4

STANLEY CUP PLAYOFF RESULTS

(BEST 4 OUT OF 7 GAMES)

Series "A"
Apr. 6 at Chicago—Toronto 2, Chicago 5
Apr. 9 at Chicago—Toronto 3, Chicago 1
Apr. 11 at Toronto—Toronto 3, Chicago 1
Apr. 13 at Toronto—Toronto 3, Chicago 4
Apr. 15 at Chicago—Toronto 4, Chicago 2
Apr. 18 at Toronto—Toronto 3, Chicago 1
Toronto won series "A" 4 games to 2.

Series "B"
Apr. 6 at Montreal—Montreal 6, New York 4
Apr. 8 at Montreal—Montreal 3, New York 1
Apr. 11 at New York—Montreal 3, New York 2
Apr. 13 at New York—Montreal 2, New York 1
Montreal won series "B" 4 games to 0.

Series "C"
Apr. 20 at Montreal—Toronto 2, Montreal 6
Apr. 22 at Montreal—Toronto 3, Montreal 0
Apr. 25 at Toronto—Toronto 3, Montreal 2
Apr. 27 at Toronto—Toronto 2, Montreal 6
Apr. 29 at Montreal—Toronto 4, Montreal 1
May 2 at Toronto—Toronto 3, Montreal 1
Toronto won Stanley Cup 4 games to 2.

1967 STANLEY CUP SCORING

	G	A	Pts.	PIM
Jim Pappin, Tor........	7	8	15	12
Pete Stemkowski, Tor.....	5	7	12	20
Jean Beliveau, Mtl........	6	5	11	26
Bob Pulford, Tor........	1	10	11	12
Henri Richard, Mtl.......	4	6	10	2
Frank Mahovlich, Tor.....	3	7	10	8
Dave Keon, Tor.........	3	5	8	0
Tim Horton, Tor........	3	5	8	25
Bobby Rousseau, Mtl.....	1	7	8	4
Ralph Backstrom, Mtl.....	5	2	7	6
Mike Walton, Tor........	4	3	7	2
Bobby Hull, Chi........	4	2	6	0

AMERICAN HOCKEY LEAGUE

Final Standings

EASTERN DIVISION

	W	L	T	Pts.	GF	GA
Hershey..........	38	24	10	86	273	216
Baltimore........	35	27	10	80	252	247
Quebec..........	35	30	7	77	275	249
Springfield.......	32	31	9	73	267	261
Providence.......	13	46	13	39	210	329

WESTERN DIVISION

	W	L	T	Pts.	GF	GA
Pittsburgh.......	41	21	10	92	282	209
Rochester........	38	25	9	85	300	223
Cleveland........	36	27	9	81	284	230
Buffalo..........	14	51	7	35	207	386

LEADING SCORERS

	GP	G	A	Pts.	PIM
Gordon Labossiere, Que...	72	40	55	95	71
Wayne Hicks, Que.......	72	31	60	91	34
Willie Marshall, Balt.....	68	33	56	89	22
Roger DeJordy, Hers.....	72	52	32	84	10
Mike Nykoluk, Hers.....	72	16	68	84	26
Dick Gamble, Roch......	72	46	37	83	22
Eddie Joyal, Roch.......	70	32	51	83	10
Jeannot Gilbert, Hers....	72	26	57	83	48
Gene Ubriaco, Hers......	69	38	43	81	50
Bill Sutherland, Que.....	67	40	38	78	27
Bronco Horvath, Roch....	72	29	49	78	54
Tom McCarthy, Clev.....	70	36	38	74	21
Guy Gendron, Que.......	68	28	45	73	72
Doug Robinson, Balt.....	63	39	33	72	89
Gary Jarrett, Pitt.......	68	29	42	71	28
Billy Harris, Pitt.......	70	34	36	70	29
Bruce Cline, Hers.......	70	28	42	70	29

WESTERN HOCKEY LEAGUE

Final Standings

	W	L	T	Pts.	GF	GA
Portland Buckaroos......	41	24	7	89	255	209
Seattle Totems........	39	26	7	85	228	195
Vancouver Canucks.....	38	32	2	78	228	215
California Seals........	32	30	10	74	228	242
Victoria Maple Leafs.....	30	34	8	68	224	232
Los Angeles Blades.....	29	38	5	63	260	286
San Diego Gulls.......	22	47	3	47	222	266

LEADING SCORERS

	GP	G	A	Pts.	PIM
Guyle Fielder, Sea.......	72	20	71	91	22
Art Jones, Port.........	65	38	51	89	26
Gordon Vejprava, Van....	71	36	46	82	27
Dick Meissner, L. A......	72	39	42	81	6
Warren Hynes, S. D......	69	25	53	78	18
Norm Johnson, L. A......	67	31	46	77	20
Milan Marcetta, Vic......	70	40	35	75	2
Larry Lund, Sea........	72	34	38	72	74
Howie Hughes, Sea......	70	26	45	71	27
Fred Hilts, S. D........	66	45	25	70	28

Central Hockey League

Final Standings

	W	L	T	Pts.	GF	GA
Oklahoma City Blazers	38	23	9	85	233	196
Omaha Knights......	36	24	10	82	262	203
Houston Apollos....	32	28	10	74	255	229
Memphis Wings......	30	32	8	68	230	259
St. Louis Braves.....	24	26	20	68	229	236
Tulsa Oilers.........	14	41	15	43	183	269

SCORING LEADERS

	GP	G	A	Pts.	PIM
Art Stratton, St. Louis....	67	34	56	90	46
Alex Faulkner, Memphis...	70	28	60	88	32
Paul Andrea, Omaha......	69	37	46	83	22
Norm Beaudin, Memphis...	65	39	37	76	32
Larry Mickey, Omaha......	63	33	41	74	86
George Konik, Omaha......	66	27	47	74	109
Terry Crisp, Okla. City....	69	31	42	73	37
Jim Johnson, Omaha......	64	26	46	72	20
Gerry Meinyk, St. Louis...	67	24	47	71	12
Ron Buchanan, Okla. City.	56	34	35	69	23
Bryan Campbell, Omaha...	65	26	42	68	46
Bill Inglis, Houston......	70	33	34	67	50
Andre Pronovost, Memphis	70	25	42	67	85
Andre Boudrias, Houston..	67	16	48	64	58
Real Lemieux, Memphis...	68	28	34	62	211

Ontario Junior League

Final Standings

	W	L	T	Pts.	GF	GA
Kitchener Rangers......	28	12	8	64	213	164
Niagara Falls Flyers....	23	15	10	56	238	195
Toronto Malboros......	23	15	10	56	208	184
Hamilton Red Wings....	22	21	5	49	172	161
St. Catharines Blk Hawks	19	20	9	47	175	155
London Nationals......	18	21	9	45	185	214
Montreal Canadiens....	16	23	9	41	176	204
Peterboro Petes........	15	23	10	40	183	219
Oshawa Generals.......	12	26	10	34	138	192

SCORING LEADERS

	GP	G	A	Pts.
Derek Sanderson, Niagara Falls...	47	41	60	101
Mickey Redmond, Peterboro......	48	51	44	95
Jim Lorentz, Niagara Falls.......	48	33	59	92
Gary Monahan, Peterboro........	47	30	54	84
Clem Tremblay, Niagara Falls.....	48	30	51	81
John Vanderburg, Peterboro......	48	23	51	74
Gary Unger, London...........	48	38	35	73
Walt Tkaczuk, Kitchener.......	48	23	47	78
Jude Drouin, Montreal.........	47	32	36	68
Gerry Meehan, Toronto........	48	26	42	60

Stanley Cup Champions

1936—Detroit Red Wings	1945—Toronto Maple Leafs	1953—Montreal Canadiens	1961—Chicago Black Hawks
1937—Detroit Red Wings	1946—Montreal Canadiens	1954—Detroit Red Wings	1962—Toronto Maple Leafs
1938—Chicago Black Hawks	1947—Toronto Maple Leafs	1955—Detroit Red Wings	1963—Toronto Maple Leafs
1939—Boston Bruins	1948—Toronto Maple Leafs	1956—Montreal Canadiens	1964—Toronto Maple Leafs
1940—New York Rangers	1949—Toronto Maple Leafs	1957—Montreal Canadiens	1965—Montreal Canadiens
1941—Boston Bruins	1950—Detroit Red Wings	1958—Montreal Canadiens	1966—Montreal Canadiens
1942—Toronto Maple Leafs	1951—Toronto Maple Leafs	1959—Montreal Canadiens	1967—Toronto Maple Leafs
1943—Detroit Red Wings	1952—Detroit Red Wings	1960—Montreal Canadiens	
1944—Montreal Canadiens			

All-Star Teams 1967

Position	First Team	Second Team
Goal	Ed Giacomin, New York	Glenn Hall, Chicago
Defense	Harry Howell, New York	Tim Horton, Toronto
Defense	Pierre Pilote, Chicago	Bobby Orr, Boston
Center	Stan Mikita, Chicago	Norm Ullman, Detroit
Right Wing	Ken Wharram, Chicago	Gordie Howe, Detroit
Left Wing	Bobby Hull, Chicago	Don Marshall, New York

HOCKEY TROPHY WINNERS

ROSS TROPHY Leading Scorer	NORRIS TROPHY Best Defenseman	CALDER TROPHY Best Rookie
1967—Stan Mikita, Chicago	Harry Howell, New York	Bobby Orr, Boston
1966—Bobby Hull, Chicago	Jacques Laperriere, Montreal	Brit Selby, Toronto
1965—Stan Mikita, Chicago	Pierre Pilote, Chicago	Roger Crozier, Detroit
1964—Stan Mikita, Chicago	Pierre Pilote, Chicago	Jacques Laperriere, Montreal
1963—Gordie Howe, Detroit	Pierre Pilote, Chicago	Kent Douglas, Toronto
1962—Bobby Hull, Chicago	Doug Harvey, New York	Bobby Rousseau, Montreal
1961—Bernie Geoffrion, Can.	Doug Harvey, Montreal	Dave Keon, Toronto
1960—Bobby Hull, Chicago	Doug Harvey, Montreal	Bill (Red) Hay, Chicago
1959—Dickie Moore, Canadiens	Tom Johnson, Montreal	Ralph Backstrom, Montreal
1958—Dickie Moore, Canadiens	Doug Harvey, Montreal	Frank Mahovlich, Toronto

HART TROPHY M. V. P.	VEZINA TROPHY Leading Goalie	LADY BYNG TROPHY Sportsmanship
1967—Stan Mikita, Chicago	Hall, De Jordy, Chicago	Stan Mikita, Chicago
1966—Bobby Hull, Chicago	Hodge, Worsley, Montreal	Alex Delvecchio, Detroit
1965—Bobby Hull, Chicago	Sawchuck, Bower, Toronto	Bobby Hull, Chicago
1964—Jean Beliveau, Montreal	Charlie Hodge, Montreal	Ken Wharram, Chicago
1963—Gordie Howe, Detroit	Glenn Hall, Chicago	Dave Keon, Toronto
1962—Jacques Plante, Montreal	Jacques Plante, Montreal	Dave Keon, Toronto
1961—Bernie Geoffrion, Mont.	Johnny Bower, Toronto	Red Kelly, Toronto
1960—Gordie Howe, Detroit	Jacques Plante, Montreal	Don McKenney, Boston
1959—Andy Bathgate, New York	Jacques Plante, Montreal	Alex Delvecchio, Detroit
1958—Gordie Howe, Detroit	Jacques Plante, Montreal	Camille Henry, New York

National Shuffleboard Championships in 1967

National Winter Singles Championships, West Palm Beach, Fla., Jan. 16-18—Men (open) William Folberth, Pinerest Trailer Park; (closed) Ernest Glenn, Ft. Lauderdale. Women (open) Mae Hall, St. Petersburg; (closed) Mary Hinkle, Bradenton.

National Winter Doubles Championships, Lakeland, Fla., Feb. 23-25—Men: Lew Tansky & Bob Litts, St. Petersburg. Women: Sara Chase & Lucy Magee, St. Petersburg.

National Summer Singles Championships, Toledo, Ohio, July 17-19—Men (open) Ernest Glenn, Ft. Lauderdale; (closed) Earl Baker, Trailer Estates. Women (open) Mary Shiley, Carey, Ohio; (closed) Joy Hauser, Palmetto, Fla.

National Summer Doubles Championships, Toledo, Ohio, July 20-22—Men: Jay Snoddy & Pete Cleveland, Lakeland, Fla. Women: Joy Hauser & Mable Glenn, Palmetto & Ft. Lauderdale, Fla.

World Track and Field Records

Source: International Amateur Athletic Federation; records approved to Oct. 16, 1967
*Asterisk indicates pending record. A number of new records await confirmation

Men

RUNNING

Event	Record	Holder	Country	Date	Where made
100 yds.	9.1 s.	Bob Hayes	U. S. A.	June 21, 1963	St. Louis, Mo.
		*Harry Jerome	Canada	July 15, 1966	Edmonton, Alb.
		*Charlie Greene	U. S. A.	June 15, 1967	Provo, Utah
220 yds.	19.5 s. (Straight course)	Tommie Smith	U. S. A.	May 7, 1966	San Jose, Calif.
220 yds.	20.2 s. (Turn)	Henry Carr	U. S. A.	Apr. 4, 1964	Tempe, Ariz.
440 yds.	44.9 s.	Adolph Plummer	U. S. A.	May 25, 1963	Tempe, Ariz.
	*44.8 s.	Tommie Smith	U. S. A.	May 20, 1967	San Jose, Calif.
880 yds.	1 m. 45.1 s.	Peter Snell	New Zealand	Feb. 3, 1962	Christchurch, N.Z.
	*1 m. 44.9 s.	Jim Ryun	U. S. A.	June 10, 1966	Terre Haute, Ind.
1 mile	3 m. 53.6 s.	Michel Jazy	France	June 9, 1965	Rennes, France
	*3 m., 51.1 s.	Jim Ryun	U. S. A.	June 23, 1967	Bakersfield, Calif.
2 miles	8 m. 22.6 s.	Michel Jazy	France	June 23, 1965	Melun, France
	*8 m., 19.8 s.	Ron Clarke	Australia	June 27, 1967	Vaesteraas, Sw.
3 miles	12 m., 52.4 s.	Ron Clarke	Australia	July 10, 1965	London, Eng.
6 miles	26 m. 47.0 s.	Ron Clarke	Australia	July 14, 1965	Oslo, Norway
10 miles	47 m., 12.8 s.	Ron Clarke	Australia	Mar. 3, 1965	Mentone, Aust.
15 miles	1 h., 12 m., 48.2 s.	Ron Hill	Gt. Britain	July 21, 1965	Bolton, Eng.
hour	12 mi., 1,006 yds.	Ron Clarke	Australia	Oct. 27, 1965	Geelong, Aust.

RUNNING—METRIC DISTANCES

Event	Record	Holder	Country	Date	Where made
100 meters	10.0 s.	Armin Hary	Germany	June 21, 1960	Zurich, Switzerland
		Harry Jerome	Canada	July 15, 1960	Saskatchewan, Canada
		Horacio Esteves	Venezuela	Aug. 15, 1964	Caracas, Venes.
		Bob Hayes	U. S. A.	Oct. 15, 1964	Tokyo, Japan
		*Jim Hines	U. S. A.	May 27, 1967	Modesto, Calif.
200 meters	19.5 s. (Straight course)	Tommie Smith	U. S. A.	May 7, 1966	San Jose, Calif.
200 meters	20.2 s. (Turn)	Henry Carr	U. S. A.	Apr. 4, 1964	Tempe, Ariz.
400 meters	44.9 s.	Adolph Plummer	U. S. A.	May 25, 1963	Tempe, Ariz.
		Otis Davis	U. S. A.	Sept. 6, 1960	Rome, Italy
		Carl Kaufman	Germany	Sept. 6, 1960	Rome, Italy
		Mike Larrabee	United States	Sept. 12, 1964	Los Angeles, Calif.
	*44.5 s.	Tommie Smith	U. S. A.	May 20, 1967	San Jose, Calif.
800 meters	1 m. 44.3 s.	Peter Snell	New Zealand	Feb. 3, 1962	Christchurch, N.Z.
1,000 meters	2 m. 16.2 s.	Juergen May	E. Germany	July 20, 1965	Erfurt, Germany
1,500 meters	3 m. 35.6 s.	Herb Elliott	Australia	Sept. 6, 1960	Rome, Italy
	*3 m., 33.1 s.	Jim Ryun	U. S. A.	July 8, 1967	Los Angeles, Cal.
2,000 meters	*4 m., 56.2 s.	Michel Jazy	France	Oct. 12, 1966	Paris, France
3,000 meters	7 m., 39.6 s.	Kipchoge Keino	Kenya	Aug. 27, 1965	Halsingborg
5,000 meters	13 m., 24.2 s.	Kipchoge Keino	Kenya	Nov. 30, 1965	Auckland, N. Z.
10,000 meters	27 m., 39.4 s.	Ron Clarke	Australia	July 14, 1965	Oslo, Norway
15,000 meters	44 m. 54.6 s.	Emil Zatopek	Czechoslovakia	Sept. 29, 1951	Stara Boleslav, Czecho.
20,000 meters	59 m., 22.8 s.	Ron Clarke	Australia	Oct. 27, 1965	Victoria, Aust.
25,000 meters	1 h., 15 m., 22.6 s.	Ron Hill	Gr. Britain	July 21, 1965	Bolton, Eng.
30,000 meters	1 h., 32 m., 34.6 s.	T. F. K. Johnston	Gr. Britain	Oct. 16, 1965	Walton, Eng.
3,000 meter stpl.	8 m., 26.4 s.	Gaston Roelants	Belgium	Aug. 7, 1965	Brussels, Belgium
1 hour	20, 232.56 m.	Ron Clarke	Australia	Oct. 27, 1965	Victoria, Aust.

HURDLES (10 hurdles)

Event	Record	Holder	Country	Date	Where made
120 yards	13.2 s.	Martin Lauer	Germany	July 7, 1959	Zurich, Switz.
		Lee Calhoun	U. S. A.	Aug. 21, 1960	Berne, Switz.
		*Willie Davenport	U. S. A.	Apr. 9, 1966	Baton Rouge, La.
		*Earl McCullouch	U. S. A.	July 16, 1967	Minneapolis, Minn.
220 yards	21.9 s.	Don Styron	U. S. A.	Apr. 2, 1960	Baton Rouge
440 yards	49.3 s.	G. C. Potgieter	South Africa	Apr. 16, 1960	Bloemfontein, S. A.
110 meters	13.2 s.	Martin Lauer	Germany	July 7, 1959	Zurich, Switz.
		Lee Calhoun	U. S. A.	Aug. 21, 1960	Berne, Switz.
200 meters	21.9 s.	Don Styron	U. S. A.	Apr. 2, 1960	Baton Rouge
200 meters	22.5 s.	Martin Lauer	Germany	July 7, 1959	Zurich, Switz.
	(Turn)	Glenn Davis	U. S. A.	Aug. 20, 1960	Berne, Switz.
400 Meters	49.1 s.	Rex Cawley	U. S. A.	Sept. 13, 1964	Los Angeles, Calif.

RELAY RACES

Event	Record	Holder	Country	Date	Where made
440 yds. (4x110) (2 turns)	39.6 s.	Southern Univ. (H. Nairn, G. Harris, W. Johnson, G. Anderson)	U. S. A.	May 28, 1966.	Modesto, Calif.
	*38.6 s.	Univ. of Southern Calif. (McCullough, Kuller, Simpson, Miller)	U. S. A.	June 17, 1967.	Provo, Utah
880 yds. (4x220)	1 m., 22.6 s.	Abilene Christian. (B. Woodhouse, J. Segrest, G. Petersen, B. Morrow)	U. S. A.	May 31, 1958.	Modesto, Calif.
	*1 m., 22.1 s.	San Jose State Coll. (Shackelford, Talmadge, Evans, Smith)	U. S. A.	May 13, 1967.	Fresno, Calif.

RELAY RACES

Event	Record	Holder	Country	Date	Where made
1 mile (4x440)	3 m., 04.5 s.	Arizona State Un. (M. Barrick, H. Carr, R. Freeman, U. Williams)	U. S. A.	Apr. 27, 1963	Walnut, Calif.
		Southern Univ. Track Club (R. Johnson, A. Gates, E. Mason, T. Lewis)	U. S. A.	May 29, 1965	Modesto, Calif.
2 miles (4x880)	7 m., 17.4 s.	U. of Southern Calif. (J. Link, D. Best, D. Buck, D. Carr)	U. S. A.	May 13, 1966	Los Angeles, Calif.
4 miles (4x1) (mile)	16 m. 09.0 s.	Univ. of Oregon (A San Romani, Jr., V. Reeve, K. Forman, D. Bur eson)	U. S. A.	May 12, 1962	Fresno, Calif.

RELAY RACES—METRIC DISTANCES

Event	Record	Holder	Country	Date	Where made
400 mtrs. (4x100)	39.0 s.	Nat'l team (P. Drayton, G. Ashworth, R. Stebbins, R. Hayes)	U. S. A.	Oct. 21, 1964	Tokyo, Japan
	*38.6 s.	Univ. of So. Calif. (McCullough, Kuller, Simpson, Miller)	U. S. A.	June 17, 1967	Provo, Utah
800 mtrs. (4x200)	1 m., 22 6 s.	Abilene Christian (B. Woodhouse, J. Segrest, G. Petersen. B. Morrow)	U. S. A.	May 31, 1958	Modesto, Calif.
	*1 m., 22.1 s.	San Jose State Coll. (Shackelford, Talmadge, Evans, Smith)	U. S. A.	May 5, 1967	Fresno, Calif.
1,600 mtrs. (4x400)	3 m., 00.7 s.	Nat'l team (O. Cassell, M. Larrabee, U. Williams, H. Carr)	U. S. A.	Oct. 21, 1964	Tokyo, Japan
	*2 m., 59.6 s.	Nat'l team (Frey, Evans, Smith, Lewis)	U. S. A.	July 24, 1966	Los Angeles
3,200 mtrs. (4x800)	7 m. 15.8 s.	Nat'l team (A. Baalllieux, A. Langenus, E. Leva, R. Moens)	Belgium	Aug. 8, 1956	Brussels, Belgium
6,000 mtrs. (4x1,500)	14 m., 49.0 s.	French Nat'l team (Vervoort, Nicolas, Jazy, Wadoux)	France	June 25, 1965	Paris, France

FIELD EVENTS

Event	Record	Holder	Country	Date	Where made
High jump	7 ft., 5¾ in.	Valery Brumel	USSR	July 21, 1963	Moscow, Russia
Long jump	27 ft., 4¾ in.	Ralph Boston	U. S. A.	May 29, 1965	Modesto, Calif.
Triple jump	55 ft., 10¼ in.	Josef Schmidt	Poland	Aug. 5, 1960	Olsztyn, Poland
Pole vault	17 ft., 5½ in.	Bob Seagren	U. S. A.	May 14, 1966	Glendale, Calif.
	*17 ft., 7¾ in.	Paul Wilson	U. S. A.	June 23, 1967	Bakersfield, Calif.
16 lb. shot put	70 ft., 7¼ in.	Randy Matson	U. S. A.	May 8, 1965	College Station, Tex.
	*71 ft., 5½ in.	Randy Matson	U. S. A.	Apr. 22, 1967	College Sta., Texas
Discus throw	213 ft., 11¾ in.	Ludvik Danek	Czecho.	Oct. 12, 1965	Czecho.
Javelin throw	300 ft. 11 in.	Terje Pedersen	Norway	Sept. 2, 1964	Oslo, Norway
16 lb. hammer throw	241 ft., 11 in.	G. Zsivotsky	Hungary	Sept. 4, 1965	Hungary
Decathlon	9,121 pts.	C. K. Yang	Taiwan	Apr. 27-28, 1963	Walnut, Calif.

WALKING

Event	Record		Holder	Country	Date	Where made
20 miles	2 h., 31 m., 33.0 s.		A Vedjakov	USSR	Aug. 23, 1958	Moscow, USSR
30 miles	4 h., 02 m., 33 s.		Christian Hohne	E. Germany	May 16, 1965	Potsdam

WALKING—METRIC DISTANCES

Event	Record	Holder	Country	Date	Where made
20,000 meters	1 h., 27 m., 05.0 s.	V. Golubnichiy	USSR	Sept. 23, 1958	Simferopol, USSR
30,000 meters	2 h., 17 m. 16.8 s.	A. Egorov	USSR	July 15, 1959	Leningrad, USSR
50,000 meters	4 h., 10 m., 51.8 s.	Christian Hohne	E. Germany	May 16, 1965	Potsdam
2 hours	26,429 meters	A. Egorov	USSR	July 15, 1959	Leningrad

Women
RUNNING

Event	Record	Holder	Country	Date	Where made
100 yards	10.3 s.	Marlene Mathews	Australia	Mar. 10, 1958	Sydney
		Wyomia Tyus	U. S. A.	July 17, 1965	Kingston, Jam.
220 yards	22.9 s.	Mary Burvill	Australia	Feb. 22, 1964	Perth, Australia
440 yards	52.4 s.	Judy Amoore	Australia	Feb. 2, 1965	Perth, Australia
880 yards	2 m., 02.0 s.	D. Willis	Australia	Mar. 3, 1962	Perth, Australia
60 meters	7.2 s.	Betty Cuthbert	Australia	Feb. 27, 1960	Sydney, Australia
		I. Bochkareva	USSR	Aug. 28, 1961	Moscow

(World Track and Field Records, continued)

RUNNING

Event	Record	Holder	Country	Date	Where made
100 meters...........	11.1 s..........	Irena Kirszenstein...	Poland......	July 9, 1965.	Prague
		Eva Klobukovska...	Poland......	July 9, 1965.	
		Wyomia Tyus....	U. S. A.....	July 31, 1965.	Kiev, USSR
200 meters.......	22.7 s........	Irena Kirszenstein...	Poland......	Aug. 8, 1965.	Warsaw, Poland
400 meters.......	51.9 s.......	Shin Guen Dan....	North Korea.	Oct. 23, 1962.	Pyongyang, No. Korea
800 meters........	2 m., 1.1 s...	Ann Packer........	Gr. Britain...	Oct. 20, 1964.	Tokyo, Japan

HURDLES

80 meters.......	10.3 s........	Irena Press........	USSR......	Oct. 24, 1965.	USSR

FIELD EVENTS

High jump........	6 ft., 3 in...	I. Balas........	Rumania...	July 15, 1961.	Sofia, Bulg.
Long jump........	22 ft., 2¼ in..	Mary Rand....	Gr. Britain..	Oct. 14, 1964.	Tokyo, Japan
Shot put........	61 ft........	Tamara Press....	USSR......	Sept. 19, 1965.	Kassel, Germany
Discus throw.....	195 ft., 10½ in.	Tamara Press....	USSR......	Aug. 11, 1965.	Moscow
Javelin..........	204 ft., 8½ in..	Elena Gorchakova...	USSR......	Oct. 16, 1964.	Tokyo, Japan
Pentathlon........	5,246 pts....	Irena Press........	USSR......	Oct. 16-17, 1964.	Japan

RELAY RACES

440 yards (4x110)....	45.2 s........	Nat'l team. (M. Cobb, M. Rand, D. Arden, D. Hyman)	Gr. Britain...	Aug. 5, 1963..	London, England
400 mtrs. (4x100)....	43.6 s........	Nat'l team... (T. Ciepla, I. Kirszenstein, H. Gorecka, E. Klobukowska)	Poland......	Oct. 21, 1964.	Tokyo, Japan
800 mtrs. (4x200).....	1 m., 35.1 s..	Nat'l team... (R. Lace, V. Laslovskaya, G. Popova, M. Itkina)	USSR........	July 14, 1963.	Moscow, USSR
880 yds. (4x220)......	1 m., 36.0 s..	Nat'l team... (H. Sadau, G. Birkemeyer, B. Mayer, C. Studnick)	E. Germany..	July 26, 1958.	Leipzig, Germany
1½ miles (3x880).....	6 m., 36.2 s..	Nat'l team... (A. Bacskai, A. Oros, A. Kazi)	Hungary.....	July 21, 1954.	Tata, Hungary
2,400 mtrs. (3x880)...	6 m., 27.4 s..	Nat'l team... (L. Yanvareva, D. Kozlova, L. Lysanko-Shevtsova)	Ukraine..... USSR	Sept. 3, 1958.	Kiev, USSR

Evolution of the World Record for the One Mile Run

The table below shows how the world record for the one-mile run has been lowered in the past 103 years.

Time	Individual	Year	Time	Individual	Year
4:56	Charles Lawes, Britain.............	1864	4:07.6	Jack Lovelock, New Zealand......	1933
4:36.5	Richard Webster, Britain.........	1865	4:06.8	Glenn Cunningham, U. S.........	1934
4:29	William Chinnery, Britain........	1868	4:06.4	Sydney Wooderson, Britain.......	1937
4:28.8	W. C. Gibbs, Britain.........	1868	4:06.2	Gunder Haegg, Sweden.........	1942
4:26	Walter Slade, Britain.........	1874	4:06.2	Arne Andersson, Sweden.........	1942
4:24.5	Walter Slade, Britain.........	1875	4:04.6	Gunder Haegg, Sweden.........	1942
4:23.2	Walter George, Britain.........	1880	4:02.6	Arne Andersson, Sweden.........	1943
4:21.4	Walter George, Britain.........	1882	4:01.6	Arne Andersson, Sweden.........	1944
4:19.4	Walter George, Britain.........	1882	4:01.4	Gunder Haegg, Sweden.........	1945
4:18.4	Walter George, Britain.........	1884	3:59.4	Roger Bannister, Britain.........	1954
4:18.2	Fred Bacon, Scotland.........	1894	3:58	John Landy, Australia.........	1954
4:17	Fred Bacon, Scotland.........	1895	3:57.2	Derek Ibbotson, Britain.........	1957
4:15.6	Thomas Conneff, U. S.........	1895	3:54.5	Herb Elliott, Australia.........	1958
4:15.4	John Paul Jones, U. S.........	1911	3:54.4	Peter Snell, New Zealand.........	1962
4:14.6	John Paul Jones, U. S.........	1913	3:54.1	Peter Snell, New Zealand.........	1964
4:12.6	Norman Taber, U. S.........	1915	3:53.6	Michel Jazy, France.........	1965
4:10.4	Paavo Nurmi, Finland.........	1923	3:51.3	Jim Ryun, U. S.........	1966
4:09.2	Jules Ladoumegue, France.........	1931	3:51.1	Jim Ryun, U. S.........	1967

71st Annual Boston Marathon

Boston, Mass., April 19, 1967

Dave McKenzie, a 24-year-old New Zealander, covered the traditional marathon distance of 26 miles 385 yards in the record-breaking time of 2 hours 15 minutes 45 seconds to win the 1967 Boston Marathon. The winning time was 48 seconds faster than the record for this event by Morio Shigematsu of Japan in 1965. The event drew 740 entries and 600 starters, 377 of whom finished within four hours. The leading finishers follow:

1—Dave McKenzie, New Zealand..........2:15:45
2—Tom Laris, New York A. C...........2:16:48
3—Yutaka Oaki, Japan...........2:17:17
4—Lou Castagnola, Wash. Sport Club...2:17:48
5—Antonio Ambu, Italy...........2:18:04
6—Andrew Boychuk, Toronto...........2:18:17
7—Takaski Inque, Japan...........2:20:41
8—Tooru Tarasawa, Japan...........2:21:17
9—Danny McFadzean, England.........2:22:06
10—Kalevi Ihaksi, Finland...........2:22:07
11—Eugene Comroe, So. Calif. Striders..2:25:16
12—John J. Kelley, Boston A. C........2:25:25
13—Efran Carmona, Mexico...........2:25:59

14—Mike Kimball, Santa Barbara A. C...2:26:26
15—Luis Buendia, Mexico...........2:27:23
16—Stephen Matthews, Denver T. C....2:27:52
17—Ambrose Burfoot, Wesleyan...........2:28:05
18—Ron Daws, Twin Cities...........2:28:42
19—Tom Osler, South Jersey T. C......2:29:04
20—William Harvey, New York...........2:28:22
21—Bill Clark, Camp Lejeune...........2:28:44
22—Jim McDonagh, Millrose A. A.......2:29:55
23—Orville Atkins, So. Calif. Striders...2:30:26
24—Jim Colpitts, Kessler A. F. B......2:31:04
25—Karl Wiser, Kegonsa T. C........2:31:05

American Track and Field Records

Source: Amateur Athletic Union. Records are those set by an American citizen anywhere in the world. Indoor records are for tracks not more than 220 yards per lap unless otherwise noted. A number of new records await confirmation. Italics indicate record pending.

OUTDOOR

Distance	Time	Holder	Where made	Date
100 yards	9.1 s.	Bob Hayes	St. Louis, Mo.	June 21, 1963
		Charlie Green	*Provo, Utah*	*June 17, 1967*
		Jim Hines	*Houston, Tex.*	*May 13, 1967*
220 yards	19.5 s.	Tommie Smith	San Jose, Calif.	May 7, 1966
220 yards (turn)	20.0 s.	Tommie Smith	Sacramento, Calif.	May 11, 1966
300 yards	30.2 s.	C. W. Paddock	Redlands, Calif.	Apr. 23, 1921
		Cliff Bourland	Los Angeles, Calif.	Apr. 17, 1943
440 yards	44.9 s.	Adolph Plummer	Tempe, Ariz.	May 25, 1963
	44.8 s.	*Tommie Smith*	*San Jose, Calif.*	*May 20, 1967*
600 yards	1 m., 08.5 s.	Willie Atterbury	Columbus, Ohio.	Apr. 20, 1957
880 yards	1 m., 44.9 s.	Jim Ryun	Terre Haute, Ind.	June 10, 1966
1,000 yards	2 m., 07.3 s.	Ernie Cunliffe	Palo Alto, Calif.	Jan. 7, 1961
1,320 yards	2 m., 54.8 s.	Jim Grelle	Woodland Hills, Calif.	Aug. 29, 1964
1 mile	3 m., 51.3 s.	Jim Ryun	Berkeley, Calif.	July 17, 1966
	3 m., 51.1 s.	*Jim Ryun*	*Bakersfield, Calif.*	*June 23, 1967*
2 miles	8 m., 25.2 s.	Jim Ryun	Los Angeles, Calif.	May 13, 1966
3 miles	12 m., 53.0 s.	Gerry Lindgren	Seattle, Wash.	May 14, 1966
4 miles	18 m., 27.4 s.	Peter McArdle	Yonkers, N. Y.	May 3, 1964
5 miles	23 m., 13.4 s.	Peter McArdle	Yonkers, N. Y.	May 3, 1964
6 miles	27 m., 11.6 s.	Billy Mills	San Diego, Calif.	June 27, 1965
		Gerry Lindgren	San Diego, Calif.	June 27, 1965
7 miles	33 m., 45.8 s.	George Brown	St. Paul, Minn.	Sept. 18, 1966
8 miles	38 m., 43.4 s.	George Brown	St. Paul, Minn.	Sept. 18, 1966
9 miles	43 m., 43.8 s.	George Brown	St. Paul, Minn.	Sept. 18, 1966
10 miles	48 m., 28.0 s.	Buddy Edelen	Hurlingham Park, Eng.	April 18, 1963
15 miles	1 h., 18 m., 10.8 s.	Ron Daws	St. Paul, Minn.	Sept. 18, 1965
20 miles	1 h., 50 m., 8.4 s.	Robert Scharf	Arlington, Va.	Jan. 16, 1966
	1 h., 46 m., 13.0 s.	*L. Castagnola*	*Arlington, Va.*	*Jan. 22, 1967*
1 hour	12 mi., 151 yd., 1 ft., 6 in.	Buddy Edelen	Dublin, Ireland	May 6, 1962
	11 mi., 1,719 yds.	*Michael Kimball*	*Culver City, Calif.*	*July 14, 1967*
2 hours	21 mi., 1,511 yds.	Robert Scharf	Arlington, Va.	Jan. 16, 1966

METRIC DISTANCES—OUTDOOR

Distance	Time	Holder	Where made	Date
100 meters	10.0 s.	Bob Hayes	Tokyo, Japan.	Oct. 15, 1964
	10.0 s.	*Jim Hines*	*Modesto, Calif.*	*May 27, 1967*
200 meters (straightaway)	19.5 s.	Tommie Smith	San Jose, Calif.	May 7, 1966
200 meters	20.0 s.	Tommie Smith	Sacramento, Calif.	May 11, 1966
300 meters	33.0 s.	Andrew Stanfield	Orebro, Sweden.	Aug. 18, 1949
400 meters (two turns)	44.9 s.	Otis Davis	Rome, Italy.	Sept. 6, 1960
		Adolph Plummer	Tempe, Ariz.	May 25, 1963
		Mike Larrabee	Los Angeles, Calif.	Sept. 12, 1964
	44.5 s.	*Tommie Smith*	*San Jose, Calif.*	*May 20, 1967*
500 meters	1 m., 01 s.	Mal Whitfield	Antwerp, Belgium.	July 25, 1949
600 meters	1 m., 17.0 s.	Jack Yerman	Buffalo, N. Y.	Aug. 23, 1959
800 meters	1 m., 44.9 s.	Jim Ryun	Terre Haute, Ind.	June 10, 1966
1,000 meters	2 m., 19.3 s.	Tom Courtney	Goteborg, Sweden.	July 4, 1954
1,500 meters	3 m., 36.1 s.	Jim Ryun	Berkeley, Calif.	July 17, 1966
	3 m., 33.1 s.	*Jim Ryun*	*Los Angeles, Calif.*	*July 8, 1967*
2,000 meters	5 m., 07.4 s.	Jim Grelle	Sidney, Aust.	Mar. 18, 1966
3,000 meters	7 m., 54.2 s.	Jim Beatty	Avranches, France.	Aug. 15, 1962
5,000 meters	13 m., 38.0 s.	Bob Schul	Compton, Calif.	June 5, 1964
		Gerry Lindgren	Los Angeles, Calif.	June 4, 1966
8,000 meters	23 m., 54.4 s.	George Brown	St. Paul, Minn.	Sept. 18, 1966
9,000 meters	27 m., 13.6 s.	Robert Scharf	Washington, D. C.	May 30, 1966
10,000 meters	28 m., 17.6 s.	Billy Mills	Augsburg, Germany.	Aug. 12, 1965
15,000 meters	45 m., 16.8 s.	L. G. Edelen	London, Eng.	Apr. 13, 1963
20,000 meters	1 hr., 2 m., 25.6 s.	Ken Moore	Eugene, Ore.	Mar. 11, 1966
25,000 meters	1 hr., 22 m., 14.2 s.	Ron Daws	St. Paul, Minn.	Sept. 18, 1965
30,000 meters	1 hr., 45 m., 28.4 s.	Richard Halmes	Arlington, Va.	Jan. 20, 1963

INDOOR

Distance	Time	Holder	Where made	Date
60 yards	5.9 s.	Bob Hayes	New York, N. Y.	Feb. 22, 1964
		Sam Perry	New York, N. Y.	Jan. 28, 1965
		Darrel Newman	San Francisco, Calif.	Feb. 26, 1965
		Charles Greene	Los Angeles, Calif.	Jan. 22, 1966
		Bill Gaines	Albuquerque, N. M.	Mar. 4, 1966
		Jim Hines	*Albuquerque, N. M.*	*Jan. 28, 1967*
100 yards	9.5 s.	David Sime	Washington, D. C.	Jan. 21, 1956
220 yards	22.2 s.	Theo. P. Ellison	Brooklyn, N. Y.	Mar. 1, 1935
300 yards	30.5 s.	James Lingel	Buffalo, N. Y.	Feb. 14, 1953
440 yards	47.6 s.	Ray Saddler	Louisville, Ky.	Feb. 27, 1965
	46.2 s.	*Tommie Smith*	*Louisville, Ky.*	*Feb. 18, 1967*
600 yards	1 m., 9.0 s.	Martin McGrady	Louisville, Ky.	Feb. 12, 1966
880 yards	1 m., 49.8 s.	Tom Farrell	New York, N. Y.	Feb. 11, 1965
	1 m., 48.9 s.	*Dave Patrick*	*Detroit, Mich.*	*Mar. 10, 1967*
1,000 yards	2 m., 7.9 s.	Ernie Cunliffe	Boston, Mass.	Jan. 28, 1961
	2 m., 06.8 s.	*Tom Von Ruden*	*San Diego, Calif.*	*Feb. 4, 1967*
1,320 yards	3 m., 01.2 s.	Joseph M. Deady	New York, N. Y.	Jan. 7, 1956
1 mile	3 m., 56.4 s.	Tom O'Hara	Chicago, Ill.	Mar. 6, 1964
2 miles	8 m., 30.8 s.	James F. Beatty	Chicago, Ill.	Mar. 9, 1963
3 miles	13 m., 25.4 s.	Billy Mills	New York, N. Y.	Feb. 19, 1965
	13 m., 16.2 s.	*Tracy Smith*	*Oakland, Calif.*	*Mar. 5, 1967*
4 miles	19 m., 39.8 s.	G. V. Bonhag	New York, N. Y.	Feb. 5, 1910
5 miles	24 m., 59.4 s.	G. V. Bonhag	New York, N. Y.	Mar. 16, 1909
6 miles	30 m., 42 s.	G. V. Bonhag	New York, N. Y.	Mar. 20, 1909
7 miles	35 m., 50.6 s.	G. V. Bonhag	New York, N. Y.	Mar. 20, 1909
10 miles	54 m., 21.2 s.	L. Tewanima	New York, N. Y.	Mar. 27, 1909
25 miles	2 h., 44 m., 50 s.	M. Maloney	New York, N. Y.	Jan. 8, 1909

METRIC DISTANCES—INDOOR

Distance	Time	Holder	Where made	Date
60 meters	6.6 s.	Jesse Owens	New York, N. Y.	Feb. 23, 1935
		Ben Johnson	New York, N. Y.	Feb. 26, 1938
		Ben Johnson	New York, N. Y.	Feb. 23, 1935
		Herbert Thompson	New York, N. Y.	Feb. 25, 1939

METRIC DISTANCES—INDOOR continued

Distance	Time	Holder	Where made	Date
100 meters.....	10.7 s..	Robt. Rodenkirchen...	Brooklyn, N. Y.......	Jan. 8, 1938
200 meters.....	22.2 s..	Theo. P. Ellison......	Brooklyn, N. Y.......	Mar. 1, 1935
400 meters.....	46.8 s..	Mike Larabee........	Berlin, Germany.....	Apr. 8, 1965
	46.2 s..	*Tommie Smith.......	*Louisville, Ky.......	*Feb. 18, 1967*
500 meters.....	1 m., 02.9 s	Mal Whitfield........	New York, N. Y.......	Feb. 23, 1953
600 meters.....	1 m., 20.3 s	James B. Herbert.....	New York, N. Y.......	Feb. 26, 1938
800 meters.....	1 m., 47.4 s.	Ted Nelson..........	Berlin, Germany.....	Apr. 9, 1965
1,000 meters....	2 m., 26.4 s.	Lloyd Hahn..........	New York, N. Y.......	Mar. 26, 1927
1,500 meters....	3 m., 43.6 s	Tom O'Hara..........	New York, N. Y.......	Feb. 27, 1964
2,000 meters....	5 m., 16.8 s	Jim Beatty..........	Chicago, Ill.........	Mar. 9, 1963
3,000 meters....	7 m., 56.6 s.	Billy Mills..........	Berlin, Germany.....	Apr. 7, 1965
4,000 meters....	11 m., 27.4 s.	Horace Ashenfelter...	New York, N. Y.......	Feb. 20, 1935
5,000 meters....	14 m., 30.9 s.	Donald Lash.........	New York, N. Y.......	Feb. 25, 1939

RACE WALKING—METRIC DISTANCES—INDOOR

1,500 meters...	6 m., 8.8 s..	Louis Welch........	Boston, Mass.......	Feb. 10, 1934
3,000 meters...	12 m., 49.0 s.	William Plant.......	Brooklyn, N. Y.......	Feb. 13, 1926
4,000 meters...	17 m., 51.2 s.	J. B. Pearman.......	New York, N. Y.......	Mar. 14, 1925
5,000 meters...	21 m., 50.6 s	William Plant.......	New York, N. Y.......	Feb. 3, 1925

RACE WALKING—METRIC DISTANCES—OUTDOOR

3,000 meters...	12 m., 52.4 s.	Ronald O. Laird.....	Poland.............	Aug. 4, 1965
5,000 meters...	22 m., 56.8 s.	Harry Hinkel........	Milwaukee, Wis.....	June 30, 1934
1,000 meters...	44 m., 59.6 s.	Ronald O. Laird.....	Walnut, Calif.......	May 16, 1964
15,000 meters...	1 h., 8 m., 14.4 s.	Ronald O. Laird.....	Walnut, Calif.......	May 16, 1964
20,000 meters...	1 h., 35 m., 25.8 s.	Ronald O. Laird.....	San Diego, Calif.....	Feb. 2, 1964

RACE WALKING—OUTDOOR

1 mile..........	6 m., 29.6 s.	F. P. Murray........	New York, N. Y......	Oct. 27, 1883
2 miles.........	13 m., 29.2 s.	Rudolp Halusa.......	Walnut, Calif.......	Apr. 16, 1966
3 miles.........	21 m., 7.8 s.	Ronald Zinn.........	Chicago, Ill.........	Oct. 31, 1964
4 miles.........	28 m., 34.0 s.	Ronald Zinn.........	Chicago, Ill.........	Oct. 31, 1964
5 miles.........	36 m., 4.2 s.	Ronald Zinn.........	Chicago, Ill.........	Oct. 31, 1964
6 miles.........	43 m., 28.0 s.	Ronald O. Laird.....	Walnut, Calif.......	May 16, 1964
7 miles.........	50 m., 50.6 s.	Ronald O. Laird.....	Walnut, Calif.......	May 16, 1964
8 miles.........	58 m., 15.8 s.	Ronald O. Laird.....	Walnut, Calif.......	May 16, 1964
9 miles.........	1 h., 5 m., 45.6 s.	Ronald O. Laird.....	Walnut, Calif.......	May 16, 1964
10 miles........	1 hr., 17.6 s.	Ronald O. Laird.....	Walnut, Calif.......	May 16, 1964
15 miles........	1 h., 57 m., 36.0 s.	Ronald O. Laird.....	San Diego, Calif.....	Feb. 20, 1966
20 miles........	2 h., 40 m., 12.0 s.	Ronald O. Laird.....	Chicago, Ill.........	Oct. 27, 1963
25 miles........	3 h., 39 m., 36.8 s.	Ronald O. Laird.....	San Diego, Calif.....	Feb. 25, 1966
1 hour.........	8 mil., 420 yds.	Ronald O. Laird.....	Walnut, Calif.......	May 16, 1964
2 hours........	15 mi., 125 ft., 6 in.	Ronald O. Laird.....	Chicago, Ill.........	Oct. 27, 1963

RACE WALKING—INDOOR

1 mile..........	6 m., 10.2 s.	Donald De Noon.....	Los Angeles, Calif...	Feb. 12, 1966
2 miles.........	13 m., 41.8 s.	William Plant.......	New York, N. Y......	Feb. 23, 1926
3 miles.........	21 m., 4.0 s.	William Plant.......	New York, N. Y......	Feb. 3, 1925
4 miles.........	28 m., 58.0 s.	William Plant.......	New York, N. Y......	Feb. 28, 1925

RELAY RACING

(Long track—More than 220 yards per lap. *Denotes indoor record.)

400 meters (4x100)—39.1s., United States National Team (Drayton, Ashworth, Stebbins, Hayes), Tokyo, Oct. 21, 1964.

440 yards (4x110)—(2 turns)—39.6s., Southern Univ. (Nair, Harris, Johnson, Anderson), Modesto, Calif., May 28, 1966. 39.6s., *Univ. of Southern Calif., Provo, Utah, June 17, 1967.*

800 meters (4x200)—1m. 22.6s., Abilene Christian (Woodhouse, Segrest, Peterson, Morrow), Modesto, Calif., May 13, 1958. 1m., 22.1s., *San Jose State, Fresno, Calif., May 13, 1967.*

880 yards (4x220)—1m. 22.6s., Abilene Christian (Woodhouse, Segrest, Peterson, Morrow), Modesto, Calif., May 31, 1958. 1m. 22.1s., *San Jose State Coll., Fresno, Calif., May 13, 1967.* *1m. 31.6s.* (7 turns), Henry Snyder H. S., Jersey City, N. J. (Harry Smith, Howard Smith, Branch, Cox), New York, N. Y., Feb. 1, 1958.

1000 meter medley relay (100, 200, 300, 400)—1m, 50s., United States Team (Whitfield, Dixon, Ault, Stanfield), Basle, Switzerland, Aug. 20, 1949.

1060 yards sprint medley (440, 100, 220, 300)—*1m. 51.3s., No. Carolina Coll. (McCray, Tate, Johnson, Roberts), New York, N. Y., Feb. 22, 1964.

1600 meters (4x400)—2m. 59.6 s., United States Team (Frey, Evans, Smith, Lewis), Los Angeles, Calif., July 24, 1966.

1 mile (4x440)—3m. 04.5s., Arizona State Univ. (Barrick, Carr, Freeman, Williams), Walnut, Calif., Apr. 27, 1963. Southern Track Club (Johnson, Gates, Mason, Lewis) Modesto, Calif., May 29, 1965. 3m., 3.5s., *San Jose State, Fresno, Calif., May 13, 1967.* *3m., 11.1s., Texas Southern Univ. (Saddler, Stevens, Duncan, Hines), Louisville, Ky., Feb. 27, 1965; Southern Univ. (Johnson, Gates, Mason, Lewis), Louisville, Ky., Feb. 12, 1966. *3 m., 10.2 s., Southern Univ., Louisville, Ky., Feb. 18, 1967.*

Two miles (4x880)—7m., 17.4s., Univ. of So. Calif. (Link, Bess, Buck, Carr), Los Angeles, Calif., May 13, 1966. *7m., 29.0s., Georgetown Univ. (McGovern, Schmitt, Duchini, Reilly), Louisville, Ky., Feb. 16, 1963. *7m., 25.6s., 49er Track Club, Albuquerque, N. M., Jan. 28, 1967.*

4 miles (4x1 mile)—*17m. 21.7s., Univ. of Pennsylvania (Venzke, Coan, McKniff, Dean), Buffalo, N. Y., Mar. 11, 1933.

6,000-meter relay—15m. 26.2s., United States team (Ryun, Dellinger, Young, Schul), Osaka, Japan, Oct. 25, 1964.

2,900 meters medley (400, 200, 800, 1,500)—6m. 58.9s., U. S. Army Team (H. Bright, G. Brown, H. Cryer, W. Druetzler), Buffalo, N. Y., June 28, 1953. *7m, 8.3s, New York A. C. (Stribling, O'Sullivan, Venzke, Graves), New York, N. Y., Feb. 25, 1939.

Medley (440, 220, 880, mile)—7m. 18.4 s., Univ. of Chicago T. C. (Caffey, Johnson, Wheeler, Coleman), Buffalo, N. Y., Aug. 18, 1957. *7m. 25 3s. New York University (Francis, Fangboner, Gares, MacMitchell), New York City, Feb. 22, 1941.

2½ miles distance medley (880, 440, 1320, 1 mile)—9m. 35s., Santa Clara Valley Youth Village (Gordon, Peake, Beatty, Tabori), Fresno, Calif. May 14, 1960. 9m., 33.8s., *Kansas Univ., Des Moines, Iowa, Apr. 29, 1967.*

HURDLE RACING

60 yards: High hurdles—*6.8s., Hayes Jones, Baltimore, Md., Feb. 29, 1964.

65 meters: High hurdles—*8.3s., Allan Tolmich, New York City, Feb. 22, 1941.

70 yards: High hurdles—*8.0s., Hayes Jones, Detroit, at Louisville, Ky., Feb. 17, 1962.

120 yards: High hurdles—13.2s., Lee Calhoun, Berne, Switzerland, Aug. 21, 1960. *Willie Davenport, Baton Rouge, La., Apr. 9, 1966; Earl McCullouch, Minneapolis, Minn., July 16, 1967.*

110 meters: High hurdles—13.2s., Lee Calhoun, Berne, Switzerland, Aug. 21, 1960. *15.8s., Sol Furth, Brooklyn, N. Y., Jan. 16, 1932.

200 meters: Low hurdles—21.9s., Donald A. Styron, Baton Rouge, La., Apr. 2, 1960. Around turn—22.5s., Glenn Davis, Berne, Switzerland, Aug. 20, 1960.

220 yards: Low hurdles—21.9s., Donald A. Styron, Baton Rouge, La., Apr. 2, 1960. Around turn—22.7s., Charles Tidwell, Berkeley, Calif., June 13, 1958.

400 meters: Intermediate hurdles—49.1s., Rex Cawley, Los Angeles, Calif., Sept. 13, 1964.

440 yards: Intermediate hurdles—49.6s., Rex Cawley, Albuquerque, N. M., June 15, 1963.

STEEPLECHASE

3,000 meters—8m., 34.2s., George Young, Tokyo, Oct. 15, 1964. 8m., 32.4s., *Pat Traynor, Dusseldorf, Ger., Aug. 17, 1967.*

2 miles—9m. 49.6s., Charles Jones, Dayton, Oh June 22, 1957. ***9m. 35.4s.**, Joseph P. McCluskey, New York, N. Y., Feb. 22, 1941.

JUMPING

Standing high jump—5 ft. 5¾ in., Leo Goehring, Travers Island, N. Y., June 14, 1913. ***5 ft. 6 in.**, Harold M. Osborn, St. Louis, Mo., April 4, 1936.

Running high jump—7 ft. 3¾ in., John Thomas, Stanford, Calif., July 1, 1960. ***7 ft. 3 in.**, John Thomas, Boston, Mass., Jan. 28, 1961; **John Rambo, San Francisco, Calif., Jan. 7, 1967.*

Standing broad jump—11 ft. 4⅞ in., Ray C. Ewry, St. Louis, Aug. 29, 1904.

Long jump—27 ft. 4¾ in., Ralph Boston, Modesto, Calif., May 29, 1965. ***26 ft. 6¼ in.**, Ralph Boston, New York, N. Y., Feb. 25, 1961. ***26 ft. 1½ in.**, *Robert Beamon, Oakland, Calif., Mar. 4, 1967.*

Triple Jump—54 ft. 11 in., Art Walker, Los Angeles, Calif., July 23, 1966. ***54 ft. 9½ in.**, Art Walker, Albuquerque, N. M., Mar. 5, 1966.

POLE VAULT

17 ft. 6¼ in., John Pennel, Los Angeles, Calif., July 24, 1966. **17 ft. 7¾ in.**, *Paul Wilson, Bakersfield, Calif., June 6, 1967.* ***17 ft. ¾ in.**, Bob Seagren, Cleveland, Ohio, Mar. 18, 1966. ***17 ft., 3 in.**, *Bob Seagren, Cleveland, Ohio, Feb. 18, 1967.*

THROWING 16-LB. HAMMER

Weight (including handle), 16 lbs., entire length 4 feet, thrown from 7-foot circle—**233 ft., 9 in.**, Harold Connolly, Walnut, Calif., May 29, 1965.

PUTTING 16-LB. SHOT

70 ft. 7¼ in., Randy Matson, College Station, Texas, May 8, 1965. **71 ft. 5½ in.**, *Randy Matson, College Station, Tex., Apr. 22, 1967.* ***64 ft. 11¾ in.**, Gary Gubner, New York, N. Y., Feb. 16, 1962. ***67 ft., 10 in.**, *Neal Steinhauer, Portland, Ore., Jan. 28, 1967.*

THROWING THE DISCUS

Weight, 4 lbs. 6½ oz. From 8 ft. 2½ in. circle—**210 ft. 6 in.**, Jay Sylvester, Long Beach, Calif., June 5, 1965.

THROWING THE JAVELIN

284 ft., John Tushaus, Los Angeles, Calif., May 13, 1966.

THROWING WEIGHTS

56-lb. weight for distance, thrown with both hands from a 7-ft. circle without follow—**45 ft. 6 in.**, Robert Backus, Salem, Mass., July 14, 1965. **48 ft., ¾ in.**, *George Frenn, Pasadena, Calif., June 4, 1967.*

56-lb. weight for height—**16 ft. 11¼ in.**, P. Donovan, San Francisco, Calif., Feb. 20, 1914.

35-lb. weight for distance—**65 ft. 6½ in.**, Al Hall, Travers Island, N. Y., June 8, 1963. **71 ft., 2 in.**, *Ed Burke, Sweden, Aug. 27, 1967.* ***71 ft., 2½ in.**, Harold Connolly, New York, N. Y., Feb. 20, 1960.

ALL-ROUND TRACK AND FIELD RECORD

8,265 points, Tom Pagani, Baltimore, Md., Aug. 5, 1962.

DECATHLON

8,230 pts., Russ Hodges, Los Angeles, Calif., July 23-24, 1966.

PENTATHLON

3,512 points, Jeff Bannister, Gorham, Maine, July 9, 1966.

78th Annual Boston Athletic Association Games

Boston, Mass. Jan. 28, 1967

50 Yds.—Mel Pender, U. S. Army. **Time—0:05.3.**

440 Yds.—Charley Mays, Grand Street Boys. **Time—0:49.1.**

600 Yds.—Martin McGrady, Central State. **Time—1:09.9.**

1,000 Yds.—Ergas Leps, Toronto T.C. **Time—2:08.1.**

One Mile—Sam Bair, Kent State. **Time—4:04.8.**

Two Miles—Kerry O'Brien, Australia. **Time—8:38.4.**

45 Yd. High Hurdles—Willie Davenport, Southern. **Time—0:05.4.**

One Mile Walk—Ron Daniel, N.Y.A.C. **Time—6:37.4.**

One Mile Relay—Baltimore Olympic Club (Skinner, Bernard, Roberts, Lee.) **Time—3:17.9.**

Two Mile Relay—Villanova (O'Leary, Nation, Hamilton, Patrick). **Time—7:30.4.**

Women's 50 Yds.—Jane Burnett, Sports International T.C. **Time—0:06.1.**

Women's 880 Yds.—Francine Kraker, Michigammes T.C. **Time—2:09.7.**

High Jump—John Thomas, Boston A.A., 7 ft.

Long Jump—Nate Slaughter, McGuire A.F.B., 22 ft. 9½ in.

Shot Put—Carl Wallin, Northeastern T.C., 56 ft. 1 in.

35 lb. Weight Throw—Bob Backus, N.Y.A.C., 64 ft. 6¼ in.

Pole Vault—Vince Bizzarro, Villanova, 16 ft. ¼ in.

60th Annual Millrose Games

Madison Square Garden, New York, N.Y., Jan. 26, 1967

60 Yds.—Charlie Greene, Nebraska. **Time—0:06.3.**

500 Yds.—Charley Mays, Grand Street Boys. **Time—0:57.**

Mel Sheppard 600 Yds.—Martin McGrady, Central State. **Time—1:10.9.**

880 Yds.—Bill Crothers, East York T.C. **Time—1:53.2.**

1,000 Yds.—Robert Zieminski, Georgetown. **Time—2:11.6.**

Wanamaker Mile—Dave Patrick, Villanova. **Time—4:03.7.**

Two Miles—Kerry O'Brien, Australia. **Time—8:39.6.**

60 Yd. High Hurdles—Willie Davenport, Southern. **Time—0:07.2.**

Women's 880 Yds.—Francine Kraker, Michigammes. **Time—2:11.8.**

Club Mile Relay—Baltimore Olympic Club (Skinner, Lee, Bernard, Roberts). **Time—3:18.4.**

College Mile Relay—Maryland State (Walker, Morris, Cayenne, Grimes). **Time—3:23.0.**

College Two Mile Relay—Fordham (May, Groark, Ohernon, Fath.) **Time—7:32.4.**

High Jump—John Thomas, Boston A.A., 7 ft. 1 in.

Pole Vault—Bob Seagren, Southern Calif., 16 ft. 7 in.

48th Annual Knights of Columbus Indoor Track Meet

Madison Square Garden, Feb. 3, 1967

60 Yds.—George Anderson, Houston Striders. **Time—0:06.3.**

500 Yds.—Jim Kemp, 49er T.C. **Time—0:56.2.**

600 Yads.—Ricardo Urbana, Georgetown. **Time—1:11.4.**

880 Yds.—Byron Dyce, N.Y.U. **Time—1:51.9.**

Invitation 880 Yds.—Noel Carroll, Ireland. **Time—1:51.1.**

1,000 Yds.—Franz-Josef Kemper, W. Germany. **Time—2:08.4.**

One Mile—Ergas Leps, Toronto. **Time—4:05.5.**

Two Miles—Dave Ellis, Toronto Olympic Club. **Time—8:49.0.**

Mile Relay—Maryland State (King, Walker, Morris, Cayenne). **Time—3:19.5.**

High Jump—John Thomas, Boston A.A., 7 ft. 2 in.

16 lb. Shot Put—George Allen, St. John's, 55 ft. 11 in.

35 lb. Weight Throw—Ed Doernberger, N.Y.A.C., 62 ft. 10½ in.

Pole Vault—Mel Hein, So. Calif. Striders, 15 ft. 6 in.

Los Angeles Times Indoor Track & Field Meet

Los Angeles, Calif., Feb. 11, 1967

60 Yds.—Larry Dunn, So. Calif. Striders. **Time—0:06.1.**

500 Yds.—Jim Kemp, 49ers T.C. **Time—0:56.7.**

600 Yds.—Dave Crook, 49ers T.C. **Time—1:11.4.**

1,000 Yds.—Franz-Josef Kemper, W. Germany. **Time—2:09.0.**

One Mile—Jim Grelle, Multnomah A. C. **Time—4:06.4.**

Two Miles—Ron Clarke, Australia. **Time—8:41.8.**

One Mile Relay—San Jose State (Shackelford, Talmadge, Evans, Smith). **Time—3:16.7.**

Two Mile Relay—Southern Calif. (Grant, Buck, Trentadue, Carr). **Time—7:51.6.**

High Jump—Otis Burrell, 49ers T.C., 7 ft. 1¼ in.

Long Jump—Bill Miller, Abilene, Texas, 25 ft. 10¾ in.

Triple Jump—Art Walker, So. Calif. Striders, 53 ft. 6½ in.

Shot Put—Dave Maggard, Santa Clara Youth Village, 62 ft.

Pole Vault—Bob Seagren, Southern Calif., 17 ft. ½ in.

World Swimming Records

Approved by International Swimming Federation to Oct. 16, 1967

Under a F.I.N.A. decision of May 1, 1957, only records made in 55-yards or 50-meter pools are accepted as world marks. A number of new records await confirmation.

MEN'S FREESTYLE

Distance	Time	Holder	Country	Where made	Date
100 meters.....	0:52.6......	Ken Walsh............	U.S.A.....		1967
110 yards.....	0:53.5......	R. B. McGregor........	Gt. Britain..	Blackpool, Eng......	Sept. 6, 1966
200 meters.....	1:55.7......	Don Schollander........	U.S.A.....	Chicago, Ill.........	Aug. 12, 1967
220 yards.....	1:57........	Don Schollander........	U.S.A.....	Vancouver, B.C.......	Aug. 27, 1966
400 meters.....	4:08.2......	Greg Charlton.........	U.S.A.....		1967
440 yards.....	4:12.2......	Greg Charlton.........	U.S.A.....	Vancouver, B.C.......	Aug. 26, 1966
800 meters.....	8:47.7......	Semen Belits-Gelman....	U.S.S.R....	Khartov, Russia.....	Aug. 3, 1966
	*8:44......	Mike Burton...........	U.S.A.....	Nagoya, Japan.......	Sept. 2, 1967
880 yards.....	8:55.5......	Murray Rose..........	Australia....	Vancouver, B.C.......	Sept. 5, 1964
1,500 meters....	16:34.1......	Mike Burton...........	U.S.A.....	Chicago, Ill.........	Aug. 13, 1967
1,650 yards....	17:11.0......	Jon Konrads...........	Australia....	Sydney, Aust........	Feb. 27, 1960

MEN'S BREASTSTROKE—SURFACE STROKE

Distance	Time	Holder	Country	Where made	Date
100 meters.....	1:06.9......	Georgi Prokopenko....	U.S.S.R.....	Moscow...........	Sept. 3, 1964
110 yards.....	1:08.2......	Ian O'Brien..........	Australia....	Kingston, Jamaica...	Aug. 12, 1966
200 meters.....	2:27.8......	Ian O'Brien..........	Australia....	Tokyo, Japan.......	Oct. 15, 1964
220 yards.....	2:28........	Ian O'Brien..........	Australia....	Kingston, Jamaica...	Aug. 6, 1966

MEN'S BUTTERFLY

Distance	Time	Holder	Country	Where made	Date
100 meters.....	0:56.3......	Mark Spitz...........	U.S.A.....	Santa Clara, Calif...	July 9, 1967
	*0:55.6......	Mark Spitz...........	U.S.A.....	Berlin, Germany.....	Oct. 7, 1967
110 yards.....	0:58.1......	Dan Sherry..........	Canada....	Blackpool, Eng......	Aug. 12, 1965
200 meters.....	2:06........	John Ferris..........	U.S.A.....	Tokyo, Japan.......	Aug. 30, 1967
	*2:05.7......	Mark Spitz...........	U.S.A.....	Berlin, Germany.....	Oct. 8, 1967
220 yards.....	2:08.4......	Kevin Berry.........	Australia....	Sydney, Aust........	Jan. 12, 1963

MEN'S BACKSTROKE

Distance	Time	Holder	Country	Where made	Date
100 meters.....	0:59.6......	Thompson Mann......	U.S.A.....	Tokyo, Japan.......	Oct. 16, 1964
	*0:58.4......	Roland Matthes......	E. Germany..	Berlin, Germany.....	Sept. 21, 1967
110 yards.....	1:01.5......	John Monckton.......	Australia....	Melbourne, Aust.....	Feb. 15, 1958
	*1:00.1......	Roland Matthes......	E. Germany..	Leipzig, E. Ger......	Sept. 26, 1967
200 meters.....	2:09.4......	Charles Hickcox......	U.S.A.....	Tokyo, Japan.......	Aug. 29, 1967
220 yards.....	2:12........	Peter Reynolds.......	Australia....	Kingston, Jamaica...	Aug. 9, 1966

MEN'S INDIVIDUAL MEDLEY

Distance	Time	Holder	Country	Where made	Date
200 meters.....	2:11.3......	Greg Buckingham.....	U.S.A.....	Chicago, Ill.........	Aug. 13, 1967
400 meters.....	4:45.4......	Richard Roth........	U.S.A.....	Tokyo, Japan.......	Oct. 14, 1964
440 yards.....	4:50.8......	Peter Reynolds.......	Australia....	Kingston, Jamaica...	Aug. 8, 1966

MEN'S FREESTYLE RELAYS

Distance	Time	Holder	Country	Where made	Date
400 m. (4x100).	3:32.6......	Nat'l team........... (Walsh, Havens, Charlton, Zorn)	U.S.A.....		1967
440 yds. (4x110)	3:35.6......	Nat'l team........... (Wenden, Dickson, Ryan, Windle)	Australia....	Kingston, Jamaica....	Aug. 11, 1966
800 m. (4x200)	7:52.1......	Nat'l team........... (Clark, Saari, Ilman, Schollander)	U.S.A.....	Tokyo, Japan.......	Oct. 18, 1964
880 yds. (4x220)	7:59.5......	Nat'l team........... (Wenden, Reynolds, Dickson, Windle)	Australia....	Kingston, Jamaica....	Aug. 5, 1966

MEN'S MEDLEY RELAYS

Distance	Time	Holder	Country	Where made	Date
400 m. (4x100).	3:57.2......	Nat'l team........... (Hickcox, Merten, Russell, Walsh)	U.S.A.....		1967
440 yds. (4x110)	4:03.2......	Nat'l team........... (Reynolds, O'Brien, Dunn, Wenden)	Australia....	Kingston, Jamaica....	Aug. 12, 1966

WOMEN'S FREESTYLE

Distance	Time	Holder	Country	Where made	Date
100 meters.....	0:58.9......	Dawn Fraser.........	Australia....	Sydney, Aust........	Feb. 29, 1964
110 yards.....	0:59.5......	Dawn Fraser.........	Australia....	Melbourne, Aust.....	Nov. 24, 1962
200 meters.....	2:09.7......	Pam Kruse..........	U.S.A.....	Philadelphia, Pa.....	Aug. 19, 1967
220 yards.....	2:11.6......	Dawn Fraser.........	Australia....	Sydney, Aust........	Feb. 27, 1960
400 meters.....	4:29........	Debbie Meyer........	U.S.A.....	Philadelphia, Pa.....	Aug. 18, 1967
440 yards.....	4:38.6......	Kathy Wainwright....	Australia....	Kingston, Jamaica...	Aug. 12, 1966
800 meters.....	9:22.9......	Debbie Meyer........	U.S.A.....		1967
880 yards.....	9:50.3......	Kathy Wainwright....	Australia....	Sydney, Aust........	Nov. 19, 1966
	*9:44.1......	Debbie Meyer........	U.S.A.....	London, Eng........	Sept. 30, 1967
1,500 meters....	17:50.2......	Debbie Meyer........	U.S.A.....	Philadelphia, Pa.....	Aug. 20, 1967
1,650 yards....	18:51.1......	Patty Caretto.......	U.S.A.....	Cardiff, Wales......	Aug. 20, 1965

WOMEN'S BREASTSTROKE—SURFACE STROKE

Distance	Time	Holder	Country	Where made	Date
100 meters.....	1:14.6......	Catie Ball...........	U.S.A.....	Philadelphia, Pa.....	Aug. 19, 1967
110 yards.....	1:18.3......	Sue Jones...........	U.S.A.....	Vancouver, B.C......	Aug. 25, 1966
	*1:17........	Catie Ball...........	U.S.A.....	London, Eng........	Sept. 30, 1967
200 meters.....	2:39.5......	Catie Ball...........	U.S.A.....	Philadelphia, Pa.....	Aug. 20, 1967
220 yards.....	2:47.7......	G. Prozumenschikova..	U.S.S.R....	Blackpool, Eng......	Apr. 11, 1964
	*2:46.9......	Catie Ball...........	U.S.A.....	London, Eng........	Sept. 30, 1967

*Denotes records awaiting official sanction.

World Swimming Records continued — WOMEN'S BUTTERFLY

Distance	Time	Holder	Country	Where made	Date
100 meters.....	1:04.5	Ada Kok.............	Netherlands..	Budapest............	Aug. 14, 1965
110 yards.....	1:05.1	Ada Kok.............	Netherlands..	Blackball, Eng......	May 30, 1964
200 meters.....	2:25.3	Ada Kok.............	Netherlands..	Groningen...........	Sept. 12, 1965
	*2:23	Toni Hewitt........	U. S. A......	Philadelphia, Pa....	Aug. 19, 1967
220 yards.....	2:29.9	Elaine Tanner.......	Canada......	Kingston, Jamaica...	Aug. 9, 1966

WOMEN'S BACKSTROKE

100 meters.....	1:07.4	Ann Fairlie........	So. Africa..	Beziers, France.....	July 23, 1965
110 yards.....	1:07.9	Ann Fairlie........	So. Africa..	Vancouver, B. C.....	Aug. 26, 1966
200 meters.....	2:26.4	Karen Muir.........	So. Africa..	Lincoln, Nebr.......	Aug. 18, 1966
220 yards.....	2:28.2	Karen Muir.........	So. Africa..	Vancouver, B. C.....	Aug. 25, 1966

WOMEN'S INDIVIDUAL MEDLEY

200 meters.....	2:25	Claudia Kolb.......	U. S. A......	Philadelphia, Pa....	Aug. 18, 1967
400 meters.....	5:08.2	Claudia Kolb.......	U. S. A......	Philadelphia, Pa....	Aug. 19, 1967
440 yards.....	5:25.1	Mary Ellen Olcese...	U. S. A......	Cardiff, Wales.....	Aug. 21, 1965

WOMEN'S FREESTYLE RELAYS

400 m. (4x100).	4:03.5	Santa Clara, S. C. (Gustavson, Ryan, Fritz, Watson)	U. S. A......	Philadelphia, Pa....	Aug. 18, 1967
440 yds. (4x110)	4:10.8	Nat'l team (Tanner, Hughes, Kennedy, Lay)	Gr. Britain	Kingston, Jamaica...	Aug. 5, 1966

WOMEN'S MEDLEY RELAYS

400 m. (4x100).	4:30	Nat'l team (Moore, Ball, Daniel, Fordyce)	U. S. A......		1967
440 yds. (4x110)	4:40.6	Nat'l team (Ludgrove, Harris, Gegan, Sillett)	Gr. Britain.	Kingston, Jamaica...	Aug. 8, 1966

English Channel Swimmers

The usual route of Channel swimmers, from Cape Griz Nez, France, to Dover, England, is about 20 miles. Those swimming in the opposite direction are so noted. Times are expressed in hours and minutes and are considered official by the Channel Swimming Association only if swimmers are accompanied by official observers. Capt. Matthew Webb of Great Britain, 1875, was the first person to span the Channel, swimming from Dover to Calais in 21 hrs. 45 min.

E. H. Temme, Britain, was first swimmer to swim the Channel both directions (1927, 1934). William Barnie, Scotland, was first to swim it both ways in one year (July and August, 1951). Gertrude Ederle was the first American woman to swim it (1926). Florence Chadwick, U. S. was first woman to swim the distance both ways (1950, 1951). In 1964, Leonore Modell, U. S., aged 14 years 5 months, became the youngest person ever to swim the Channel.

Antonio Abertondo of Argentina was the first man to swim the Channel round trip, Sept. 21-22, 1961 taking 18 hrs. 50 minutes from England to France, and 24 hrs. 25 min. for the return trip.

All-time Record, England to France—10 hrs. 21 min.—Nitindra Roy, India, 1967.

All-time Record, Either Direction—9:35—Barry Watson, Great Britain, 1964.

1960	*Helge Jensen, Canada	10:23	
	Michael Jennings, Great Britain	13:31	
	Alfredo Camarero, Argentina	12:23	
	A. Fakireddin, Lebanon	12:56	
	S. Hasselberg, Sweden	14:30	
	Brojen Das, Pakistan	14:43	
	Mary Kok, Netherlands	12:25	
1961	**Antonio Abertondo, Argentina	43:15	
	Brojen Das, Pakistan	10:35	
	Dogan Sahin, Turkey	14:21	
1962	(No official records set) (a)		
1963	Claudia McPherson, Canada	17:17	
	Derek Turner, England	15:39	
	P. Van Vooren, Belgium	15:09	
1964	Greta Andersen, United States	13:40	
	Leonore Modell, United States	15:27	
	Raymond Rousselle, Belgium	15:13	
	John Starrett, United States	12:45	
	Barry Watson, Great Britain	9:35	
	Robert Cossette, Canada	12:05	
	Joe Nagi, United States	12:03	
	*Gregory Schofield, Great Britain	15:35	
	*Ted Erikson, United States	12:35	

1965	*Pierre Van Vooren, Belgium	17:55
	*Greta Andersen, United States	13:49
	Derek Gill, Great Britain	17:07
	Linda McGill, Australia	11:12
	Keith Hancox, New Zealand	15:33
	Danilo Lopez, Guatemala	16:45
	Philip Gollop, Great Britain	14:31
	**Ted Erikson, United States	30:03
1966	Philip Kaye, Great Britain	16:16
	Graham McIntyre, Great Britain	16:42
	Deneze Le Pennec, Ch. Islands	20:50
	Abdul Malek, Pakistan	13:42
	Lt. Mustafa Etaati, Iran	15:04
	*Michael Jennings, Great Britain	13:02
1967	Thomas Hetzel, United States	18:54
	Elaine Gray, Great Britain	10:24
	*Nitindra Roy, India	10:21
	Geffrey Lake, Great Britain	15:21
	Norman Trusty, Great Britain	12:05
	*Phillip Gollop, Great Britain	13:45
	Mervyn Sharp, Great Britain	18:34
	Rosemary Franklin, Great Britain	17:50
	Linda McGill, Australia	13:02
	Linda McGill, Australia	9:55

*England to France   **Round trip.

(a) Fred Baldasare, American frogman from Cocoa Beach, Fla., became the first man to swim the Channel underwater July 11, 1962. He used aqualung equipment and was guided by a towed cage beneath the surface. Simon Patterson of England repeated the performance July 28.

Diving Championships in 1967
National A. A. U. Senior Diving Championships
Arlington, Texas, April 3-5

Men

One-Meter Diving—Luis Rivero, Indiana Univ. 516.70 pts.

Three-Meter Diving—Keith Russell, Dick Smith Swim Gym. 509.70 pts.

Platform Diving—Keith Russell, 548.90 pts.

Women

One-Meter Diving—Lesley Bush, Bloomington, Indiana. 443.10 pts.

Three-Meter Diving—Sue Gossick, Tarzana, Calif. 416.40 pts.

Platform Diving—Patty Simms, Arcadia, Calif. 266.25 pts.

Open and Invitation Golf Tournaments in 1967
MEN

Date	Event	Winner	Score	Prize
Jan. 15	San Diego Open	Bob Goalby	269	$13,000
Jan. 23	Bing Crosby Tournament, Pebble Beach, Calif.	Jack Nicklaus	283	16,000
Jan. 29	Los Angeles Open	Arnold Palmer	269	20,000
Feb. 5	Bob Hope Desert Classic, Palm Springs, Calif.	Tom Nieporte	349	17,600
Feb. 12	Phoenix Open	Julius Boros	272	14,000
Feb. 19	Tucson Open	Arnold Palmer	273	12,000
Mar. 5	Doral Open, Miami, Fla.	Doug Sanders	275	20,000
Mar. 12	Florida Citrus Open, Orlando, Fla.	Julius Boros	274	23,000
Mar. 19	Greater Jacksonville Open	Dan Sikes	279	20,000
Mar. 26	Pensacola Open	Gay Brewer, Jr.	262	15,000
Apr. 2	Greater Greensboro Open	George Archer	267	25,000
Apr. 9	Masters Golf Tournament, Augusta, Ga.	Gay Brewer, Jr.	280	20,000
Apr. 16	Tournament of Champions, Las Vegas	Frank Beard	278	20,000
Apr. 24	Greater Dallas Open	Bert Yancey	274	20,000
Apr. 30	Texas Open, San Antonio, Texas	Juan (Chi Chi) Rodrigues	277	20,000
May 7	Houston Champions Intl. Tournament	Frank Beard	274	23,000
May 14	Greater New Orleans Open	George Knudson	277	20,000
May 21	Colonial Country Club Tournament, Ft. Worth	Dave Stockton	278	23,000
May 28	Oklahoma City Open	Miller Barber	*278	13,000
June 4	Memphis Open	Dave Hill	272	20,000
June 11	Buick Open, Grand Blanc, Mich.	Julius Boros	283	20,000
June 19	U. S. Open	Jack Nicklaus	275	30,000
June 25	Cleveland Open	Gardner Dickinson	271	20,700
July 3	Canadian Open, Montreal	Billy Casper	*279	30,000
July 9	Speedway Open, Indianapolis, Ind.	Frank Beard	279	20,000
July 24	P. G. A. Championship, Denver	Don January	*281	25,000
July 30	Minnesota Golf Classic, Minneapolis	Lou Graham	286	20,000
Aug. 6	Western Open, Chicago	Jack Nicklaus	274	20,000
Aug. 13	American Golf Classic, Akron	Arnold Palmer	276	20,000
Aug. 20	Greater Hartford Open	Charlie Sifford	272	20,000
Aug. 30	Westchester Classic, Harrison, N. Y.	Jack Nicklaus	272	50,000
Sept. 4	Carling World Golf Tournament, Toronto	Billy Casper	*281	35,000
Sept. 10	World Series of Golf, Akron	Jack Nicklaus	144	50,000
Sept. 17	Philadelphia Golf Classic	Dan Sikes	276	22,000
Sept. 24	Thunderbird Golf Tournament, Clifton, N. J.	Arnold Palmer	283	30,000
Oct. 1	Atlanta Golf Classic	Bob Charles	282	22,000
Oct. 28	Sahara Tournament, Las Vegas	Jack Nicklaus	270	20,000
Nov. 5	Hawaiian Open, Honolulu	Dudley Wysong	*284	20,000

WOMEN

Date	Event	Winner	Score	Prize
Mar. 19	Orange Blossom Open, St. Petersburg, Fla.	Marilynn Smith	283	$1,875
Mar. 26	Venice Open Golf Tournament, Venice, Fla.	Kathy Whitworth	217	1,500
Apr. 2	Louise Suggs Open, Delray Beach, Fla.	Susie Maxwell	*224	1,500
Apr. 23	Raleigh (N. C.) Invitation Tournament	Kathy Whitworth	215	1,800
Apr. 30	Shreveport (La.) Kiwanis Tournament	Mickey Wright	219	1,500
May 7	Tall City Open, Midland, Tex.	Carol Mann	214	1,875
May 15	Dallas Civitan Open	Jo Ann Prentice	281	2,475
May 22	Babe Zaharias Open, Beaumont, Tex.	Marilynn Smith	210	1,500
June 11	Bluegrass Invitational, Louisville	Mickey Wright	208	1,500
June 18	Milwaukee Jaycee Open	Susie Maxwell	216	2,250
June 25	Buckeye Savings Tournament, Cincinnati	Carol Mann	207	2,100
July 2	Woman's National Open Golf Championship, Hot Springs, Va.	Catherine Lacoste	294	(a)
July 9	Lady Carling Open, Baltimore	Mickey Wright	207	2,250
July 16	Ladies P. G. A. Championship, Sutton, Mass.	Kathy Whitworth	284	2,625
Aug. 20	Women's Western Open, Pekin, Ill.	Kathy Whitworth	289	1,500
Aug. 27	Amarillo Texas Open	Sandra Haynie	212	1,950
Sept. 3	Ladies' World Series of Golf, Springfield, Ohio	Kathy Whitworth	*137	10,000
Sept. 10	Pacific Ladies' Golf Classic, Junction City, Ore.	Clifford Ann Creed	211	1,875
Oct. 29	Alamo Open, San Antonio, Tex.	Kathy Whitworth	213	1,875
Nov. 5	Corpus Christi Open	Clifford Ann Creed	214	1,725

*Won playoff of tie (a) Amateur

BRITISH AMATEUR GOLF CHAMPIONS

Year	Winner	Year	Winner	Year	Winner	Year	Winner
1907	John Ball	1925	R. Harris	1939	A. Kyle (U.S.)	1956	John Beharrell
1908	E. A. Lassen	1926	J. Sweetser (U. S.)	1940-45	(Not played)	1957	Reid Jack
1909	R. Maxwell	1927	Dr. W. Tweddell	1946	J. Bruen	1958	Joseph Carr
1910	John Ball	1928	T. P. Perkins	1947	W. Turnesa	1959	DeaneBeman(U.S.)
1911	H. H. Hilton	1929	C. Tolley	1948	F. Stranahan (U.S.)	1960	Joseph Carr
1912	John Ball	1930	R.T.Jones,Jr.(U.S.)	1949	Sam McCready	1961	Michael Bonallack
1913	H. H. Hilton	1931	E. Martin-Smith	1950	Frank Stranahan (U. S.)	1962	Richard Davies (U. S.)
1914	J. L. C. Jenkins	1932	J. De Forest	1951	Dick Chapman (U. S.)	1963	Michael Lunt
1915-1919	(Not played)	1933	M. Scott			1964	Gordon Clark
1920	Cyril J. Tolley	1934	W.L.Little,Jr.(U.S.)	1952	H. Ward (U. S.)	1965	Mike Bonallack
1921	W. I. Hunter	1935	W.L.Little,Jr.(U.S.)	1953	Joseph Carr	1966	Bobby Cole
1922	E. W. Holderness	1936	H. Thompson	1954	Doug Bachli (Aust.)	1967	Bob Dickson (U.S.)
1923	R. Wethered	1937	R.Sweeny.(U.S.bn)	1955	Lt. Joseph Conrad		
1924	E. W. Holderness	1938	C. Yates (U.S.)				

BRITISH OPEN GOLF CHAMPIONS

Year	Winner	Year	Winner	Year	Winner	Year	Winner
1904	Jack White	1924	W. Hagen (U. S.)	1937	T. H. Cotton	1955	Peter Thomson
1905	James Braid	1925	J. Barnes (U. S.)	1938	R. A. Whitecomb	1956	Peter Thomson
1906	James Braid	1926	R. T. Jones, Jr. (U. S.)	1939	D. Burton	1957	Bobby Locke
1907	Arnaud Massy			1940-45	(Not played)	1958	Peter Thomson
1908	James Braid	1927	R. T. Jones, Jr. (U. S.)	1946	S. Snead (U. S.)	1959	Gary Player
1909	J. H. Taylor			1947	F. Daly (Ireland)	1960	Kel Nagle (Aust.)
1910	James Braid	1928	W. Hagen (U. S.)	1948	T. H. Cotton	1961	Arnold Palmer (U. S.)
1911	H. Vardon	1929	W. Hagen (U. S.)	1949	Bobby Locke (So. Africa)	1962	Arnold Palmer (U. S.)
1912	Ed. Ray	1930	R. T. Jones, Jr. (U. S.)	1950	Bobby Locke (So. Africa)	1963	Bob Charles (N.Z.)
1913	J. H. Taylor	1931	T. Armour (U. S.)	1951	Max Faulkner	1964	Tony Lema (U. S.)
1914	H. Vardon	1932	G. Sarazen (U. S.)	1952	Bobby Locke (Africa)	1965	Peter Thomson
1915-1919	(Not played)	1933	D. Shute (U. S.)	1953	Ben Hogan (U. S.)	1966	JackNicklaus(U.S.)
1920	George Duncan	1934	T. H. Cotton	1954	P. Thomson (Aust.)	1967	Roberto de Vicenzo (Arg.)
1921	Jock Hutchison	1935	A. Perry				
1922	WalterHagen(U.S.)	1936	Alf. Padgham				
1923	A. H. Havers						

U. S. Tennis Championships

MEN'S SINGLES

Year	Champion	Final Opponent	Year	Champion	Final Opponent
1937	J. Donald Budge	Baron G. Von Cramm	1952	Frank Sedgman	Gardnar Mulloy
1938	J. Donald Budge	C. Gene Mako	1953	Tony Trabert	E. Victor Seixas, Jr.
1939	R. L. Riggs	W. Van Horn	1954	E. Victor Seixas, Jr.	Rex Hartwig
1940	D. McNeill	R. L. Riggs	1955	Tony Trabert	Ken Rosewall
1941	R. L. Riggs	F. L. Kovacs	1956	Kenneth Rosewall	Lewis Hoad
1942	F. R. Schroeder, Jr.	F. A. Parker	1957	Malcolm Anderson	Ashley Cooper
1943	Lieut. (J. G.)—J. R. Hunt	(C. G. Seaman)	1958	Ashley Cooper	Malcolm Anderson
		J. A. Kramer	1959	Neale A. Fraser	Alejandro Olmedo
1944	Sgt. Frank Parker	W. F. Talbert	1960	Neale A. Fraser	Rodney Laver
1945	Sgt. Frank Parker	W. F. Talbert	1961	Roy Emerson	Rodney Laver
1946	John Kramer	Thomas Brown, Jr.	1962	Rodney Laver	Roy Emerson
1947	John Kramer	Frank Parker	1963	Rafael Osuna	F. A. Froehling, 3d
1948	Richard Gonsales	Eric Sturgess	1964	Roy Emerson	Fred Stolle
1949	Richard Gonsales	F. R. Schroeder, Jr.	1965	Manuel Santana	Cliff Drysdale
1950	Arthur Larsen	Herbert Flam	1966	Fred Stolle	John Newcombe
1951	Frank Sedgman	E. Victor Seixas, Jr.	1967	John Newcombe	Clark Graebner

MEN'S DOUBLES

Year	Doubles Champions	Year	Doubles Champions
1936...	J. D. Budge and C. G. Mako	1952...	Mervyn Rose and E. Victor Seixas, Jr.
1937...	H. Henkle and Baron G. Von Cramm (Ger.)	1953...	Rex Hartwig and Mervyn Rose
1938...	J. D. Budge and C. G. Mako	1954...	E. Victor Seixas, Jr. and Tony Trabert
1939...	A. K. Quist & J. E. Bromwich (Aust.)	1955...	Kosei Kamo and Atsushi Miyagi
1940...	J. A. Kramer and F. R. Schroeder, Jr.	1956...	Lewis Hoad and Kenneth Rosewall
1941...	J. A. Kramer and F. R. Schroeder. Jr.	1957...	Ashley Cooper and Neale Fraser
1942...	Lt. Mulloy and W. F. Talbert	1958...	Hamilton Richardson and Alejandro Olmedo
1943...	J. Kramer and Frank Parker	1959...	Neale A. Fraser and Roy Emerson
1944...	Lt. W. D. McNeill and a/c R. Falkenburg	1960...	Neale A. Fraser and Roy Emerson
1945...	Lt. G. Mulloy and W. F. Talbert	1961...	Dennis Ralston and Chuck McKinley
1946...	G. Mulloy and W. F. Talbert	1962...	Rafael Osuna and Antonio Palafox
1947...	J. A. Kramer and F. R. Schroeder, Jr.	1963...	Dennis Ralston and Chuck McKinley
1948...	G. Mulloy and W. F. Talbert	1964...	Dennis Ralston and Chuck McKinley
1949...	John Bromwich and William Sidwell	1965...	Roy Emerson and Fred Stolle
1950...	John E. Bromwich and Frank Sedgman	1966...	Roy Emerson and Fred Stolle
1951...	Frank Sedgman & Kenneth McGregor (Aust.)	1967...	John Newcombe and Tony Roche

WOMEN'S SINGLES, DOUBLES, MIXED DOUBLES

Yr.	Singles Champions	Doubles Champions	Mixed Doubles Champions
1937	Miss A. Lizana (Chile)....	Miss A. Marble & Mrs. S. P. Fabyan.	Mrs. S. P. Fabyan & J. D. Budge
1938	Miss Alice Marble........	Miss A. Marble & Mrs. S. P. Fabyan	Miss A. Marble & J. D. Budge
1939	Miss Alice Marble........	Miss A. Marble & Mrs. S. P. Fabyan	Miss Alice Marble & H. C. Hopman
1940	Miss Alice Marble........	Miss A. Marble & Miss S. Palfrey..	Miss Alice Marble & R. L. Riggs
1941	Mrs. E. T. Cooke........	Mrs. E. T. Cooke & Miss M. Osborne	Mrs. E. T. Cooke & J. A. Kramer
1942	Miss Pauline Bets.......	Misses A. L. Brough & M. Osborne..	Miss A. L. Brough & F. R. Schroeder, Jr.
1943	Miss Pauline Bets.......	Misses A. L. Brough & M. Osborne..	Miss M. Osborne & W. F. Talbert
1944	Miss Pauline Bets.......	Misses A. L. Brough & M. Osborne..	Miss M. Osborne & W. F. Talbert
1945	Mrs. E. T. Cooke........	Misses A. L. Brough & M. Osborne..	Miss M. Osborne & W. F. Talbert
1946	Miss Pauline Bets.......	Misses A. L. Brough & M. Osborne.	Miss M. Osborne & W. F. Talbert
1947	Miss A. L. Brough.......	Misses A. L. Brough & M. Osborne..	Miss A. L. Brough & J. Bromwich
1948	Mrs. M. O. du Pont.....	Miss A. L. Brough & Mrs. M. O. du Pont.	Miss A. L. Brough & T. Brown, Jr.
1949	Mrs. M. O. du Pont.....	Miss A. L. Brough & Mrs. M. O. du Pont.	Miss A. L. Brough & E. Sturgess
1950	Mrs. M. O. du Pont.....	Miss A. L. Brough & Mrs. M. O. du Pont.	Mrs. M. O. du Pont & Kenneth MacGregor
1951	Maureen Connolly.......	Doris Hart and Shirley Fry.......	Doris Hart & Frank Sedgman
1952	Maureen Connolly.......	Doris Hart and Shirley Fry.......	Doris Hart & Frank Sedgman
1953	Maureen Connolly.......	Doris Hart and Shirley Fry.......	Doris Hart & E. Victor Seixas, Jr.
1954	Doris Hart.............	Doris Hart and Shirley Fry.......	Doris Hart & E. Victor Seixas, Jr.
1955	Doris Hart.............	A. Louise Brough and Mrs. Margaret du Pont	Doris Hart & E. Victor Seixas, Jr.
1956	Shirley J. Fry..........	A. Louise Brough and Mrs. Margaret du Pont	Mrs. Margaret du Pont and Kenneth Rosewall
1957	Althea Gibson..........	A. Louise Brough and Mrs. Margaret du Pont	Althea Gibson and Gardnar Mulloy
1958	Althea Gibson..........	Darlene Hard and Jeanne Arth.....	Mrs. M. O. du Pont and Neale Fraser
1959	Maria E. Bueno........	Darlene Hard and Jeanne Arth.....	Mrs. M. O. du Pont and Neale Fraser
1960	Darlene R. Hard........	Darlene R. Hard and Maria Bueno..	Mrs. M. O. du Pont and Neale Fraser
1961	Darlene R. Hard........	Darlene R. Hard and Lesley Turner.	Margaret Smith and Robert Mark
1962	Margaret Smith.........	Maria Bueno and Darlene Hard....	Margaret Smith and Fred Stolle
1963	Maria E. Bueno........	Margaret Smith and Robyn Ebbern.	Margaret Smith and Kenneth Fletcher
1964	Maria E. Bueno........	Billie Jean Moffitt & Karen Susman	Margaret Smith & John Newcombe
1965	Margaret Smith.........	Mrs. Carol Gardner & Nancy Richey	Margaret Smith & Fred Stolle
1966	Maria Bueno...........	Maria Bueno & Nancy Richey......	Donna Floyd Fales & Owen Davidson
1967	Billie Jean King........	Rosemary Casals & Billie Jean King	Billie Jean King & Owen Davidson

CLAY COURT CHAMPIONS

Yr.	Champion	Doubles Champions	Yr.	Champion	Doubles Champions
1947	Frank A. Parker	J. Schroeder-J. Tuero	1958	Bernard Bartsen	B. MacKay-S. Giammalva
1948	R. A. Gonsales	S. Match-T. Chambers	1959	B. Bartsen	B. Bartsen-G. Golden
1949	R. A. Gonsales	E. V. Seixas-S. Match	1960	Barry MacKay	Bob Hewitt-Marty Mulligan
1950	Herbert Flam	H. Flam-A. Larsen	1961	B. Bartsen	C. McKinley-R. D. Ralston
1951	Tony Trabert	T. Trabert-H. Richardson	1962	Chuck McKinley	R. Earnhart-M. Riessen
1952	Arthur Larsen	G. Golden-A. Larsen	1963	Chuck McKinley	M. Riessen-C. Graebner
1953	E. Vic Seixas, Jr.	B. Bartsen-G. Golden	1964	Dennis Ralston	C. McKinley-D. Ralston
1954	B. Bartsen	T. Trabert-E. V. Seixas, Jr.	1965	Dennis Ralston	C. Graebner-M. Riessen
1955	Tony Trabert	T. Trabert-H. Richardson	1966	Cliff Richey	D. Ralston-C. Graebner
1956	Herbert Flam	P. Contreras-A. Olmedo	1967	Arthur Ashe	M. Riessen-C. Graebner
1957	E. Victor Seixas, Jr.......	Ashley Cooper-Neale Fraser			

MEN'S INDOOR CHAMPIONS

Yr.	Singles	Doubles	Yr.	Singles	Doubles
1948	W. F. Talbert	J. Borotra and M. Bernard	1959	Alex Olmedo	Alex Olmedo-Barry MacKay
1949	R. A. Gonzales	Wm. Talbert and D. McNeill	1960	Barry MacKay	Andres Gimeno-Manuel Santana
1950	Don McNeill	Wm. Talbert and D. McNeill			
1951	William Talbert	Wm. Talbert and D. McNeill	1961	Richard Savitt	C. Crawford-R. Holmberg
1952	Richard Savitt	Wm. Talbert and Budge Patty	1962	Chas. McKinley	R. Laver-C. McKinley
1953	Arthur Larsen	A. Larsen and K. Nielsen	1963	Dennis Ralston	D. Ralston-C. McKinley
1954	Sven Davidson	W. F. Talbert and Tony Trabert	1964	Chas. McKinley	M. Santana-J. L. Arilla
1955	Tony Trabert	E. V. Seixas, Jr. and T. Trabert	1965	Jan Erik Lundqui	
1956	Ulf Schmidt	S. Giammalva & E. V. Seixas, Jr.			D. Ralston-C. McKinley
1957	Kurt Nielsen	Grant Golden-Barry MacKay	1966	C. Pasarel	B. Luts-S. Smith
1958	Richard Savitt	Grant Golden-Barry MacKay	1967	C. Pasarel	A. Ashe-C.Pasarell

WOMEN'S INDOOR CHAMPIONS

Yr.	Champion	Doubles Champions	Yr.	Champion	Doubles Champions
1947	Miss P. Bets	Miss D. Hart and Miss B. Scofield	1958	Nancy O'Connell	Carol Hanks and Nancy O'Connell
1948	Mrs. P. C. Todd	Miss D. Hart and Miss B. Scofield	1959	Lois Felix	Lois Felix and Katharine Hubbell
1949	Miss G. Moran	Miss G. Moran and Mrs. R. A. Buck	1960	Carole Wright	Mrs. Richard A. Buck and Ruth Jeffery
1950	Miss Nancy Chaffee	Miss Nancy Chaffee and Mrs. R. A. Buck	1961	Janet S. Hopps	Janet S. Hopps and Kay Hubbell
1951	Miss Nancy Chaffee	Miss Nancy Chaffee and Mrs. Richard Buck	1962	Carole Wright	Ruth Jeffery and Belmar Gunderson
1952	Mrs. Nancy Chaffee Kiner	Mrs. Nancy Chaffee Kiner and Mrs. Patricia Todd	1963	Carol Hanks	Carol Hanks and Mary Ann Eisel
1953	Mrs. Thelma Long	Mrs. Thelma Long and Mrs. Barbara Davidson	1964	Mary Ann Eisel	Mary Ann Eisel & Katharine Hubbell
1954	Mrs. Dorothy W. Levine	Mrs. Dorothy W. Levine and Mrs. Barbara Ward	1965	Nancy Richey	Carol Hanks Aucamp and Mary Ann Eisel
1955	Katharine Hubbell	K. Hubbell and R. Jeffery	1966	Billie Jean King	Billie Jean King & Rosemary Casals
1956	Lois Felix	L. Felix and K. Hubbell	1967	Billie Jean King	Carol Hanks Aucamp & Mary Ann Eisel
1957	Mrs. Dorothy Levine	Mrs. Dorothy Levine and Nancy O'Connell			

NATIONAL INTERCOLLEGIATE CHAMPIONS

Yr.	Singles	College	Doubles	College
1947	Gardner Larned	Wm. & Mary	R. Curtiss and S. Match	Rice Inst.
1948	Harry Likas	San Franc. U.	F. Kovaleski & B. Bartsen	Wm. & Mary
1949	Jack Tuero	Tulane	J. Brinks and Fred Fisher	Washington
1950	Herbert Flam	U. C. L. A.	H. Flam and W. E. Garrett	U. C. L. A.
1951	Tony Trabert	Cincinnati	Earl Cochell and Hugh Stewart	So. California
1952	Hugh Stewart	So. California	Hugh Ditzler and Cliff Mayne	California
1953	Hamilton Richardson	Tulane	Lawrence Huebner and Robert Perry	U. C. L. A.
1954	Hamilton Richardson	Tulane	Robert Perry and Ron Livingston	U. C. L. A.
1955	Jose Aguero	Tulane	Pancho Contreras and Joaquin Reyes	So. California
1956	Alejandro Olmedo	So. California	Alejandro Olmedo and Pancho Contreras	So. California
1957	Barry MacKay	Michigan	Crawford Henry and Ronald Holmberg	Tulane
1958	Alejandro Olmedo	So. California	Alejandro Olmedo and Edward Atkinson	So. California
1959	Whitney Reed	San Jose State	Ronald Holmberg and Crawford Henry	Tulane
1960	Larry Nagler	U. C. L. A.	Larry Nagler and Allen Fox	U. C. L. A.
1961	Allen Fox	U. C. L. A.	Rafael Osuna and Ramsey Earnhart	So. California
1962	Rafael Osuna	So. California	Rafael Osuna and Ramsey Earnhart	So. California
1963	Dennis Ralston	So. California	Dennis Ralston and Rafael Osuna	So. California
1964	Dennis Ralston	So. California	Dennis Ralston and Bill Bond	So. California
1965	Arthur Ashe	U. C. L. A.	Arthur Ashe and Ian Crookenden	U. C. L. A.
1966	Charles Pasarell	U. C. L. A.	Charles Pasarell and Ian Crookenden	U. C. L. A.
1967	Bob Luts	So. Calif.	Stan Smith & Bob Luts	So. Calif.

British (Wimbledon) Champions

Inaugurated 1877

Year	Men's singles	Women's singles	Year	Men's singles	Women's singles
1953	Victor Seixas	Maureen Connolly	1961	Rodney Laver	Angela Mortimer
1954	Jaroslav Drobny	Maureen Connolly	1962	Rodney Laver	Karen Hantse Susman
1955	Tony Trabert	Louise Brough	1963	Chuck McKinley	Margaret Smith
1956	Lewis Hoad	Shirley Fry	1964	Roy Emerson	Maria Bueno
1957	Lewis Hoad	Althea Gibson	1965	Roy Emerson	Margaret Smith
1958	Ashley Cooper	Althea Gibson	1966	Manuel Santana	Billie Jean King
1959	Alex Olmedo	Maria Bueno	1967	John Newcombe	Billie Jean King
1960	Neale Fraser	Maria Bueno			

Other Tennis Championships in 1967

Australian Championships, Adelaide, Australia—Men's Singles: Roy Emerson; Men's Doubles: John Newcombe-Tony Roche; Women's Singles: Nancy Richey; Women's Doubles: Lesley Turner-Judy Tegart.

Eastern Grass Court Championships, South Orange, N. J.—Men's Singles: Marty Riessen; Men's Doubles: William Bowrey-Owen Davidson; Women's Singles: Mrs. Billie Jean King; Women's Doubles: Rosemary Casals-Mrs. Billie Jean King.

French Championships, Paris, France—Men's Singles: Roy Emerson; Men's Doubles: Tony Roche-John Newcombe; Women's Singles: Francoise Durr; Women's Doubles: Francoise Durr-Carol Sherriff.

Italian Championships, Rome, Italy—Men's Singles: Marty Mulligan; Men's Doubles: Bob Hewitt-F. McMillan; Women's Singles: Lesley Turner;

Women's Doubles: Rosemary Casals-Lesley Turner.

Pennsylvania Grass Courts Championships—Men's Singles: Cliff Drysdale; Men's Doubles: Clark Graebner-Marty Riessen; Women's Singles: Mary Ann Eisel; Women's Doubles: Karen Krantzcke-Kerry Melville.

Women's Collegiate Championships, Stanford, Calif.—Singles: Nancy Rippy; Doubles: Jane Albert-Julie Anthony.

Wightman Cup Matches (Women's Team of U. S. and England)—U. S. 6, Great Britain 1. Series standing since 1932: U. S. 33, Great Britain 6.

Federation Cup (Women's Teams of all Nations), Berlin, Germany—Final Round: USA d. England 2-0.

Newport Invitation Tournament, Newport, R. I.—Men's Singles: Bill Bowrey; Men's Doubles: Bill Bowrey-Owen Davidson.

WORLD SERIES
Cardinals Defeat Red Sox in Seven Games
Composite Box Score

ST. LOUIS CARDINALS

	G	AB	R	H	2B	3B	HR	RBI	SO	BB	Bat. Avg.	PO	A	E	Fldg. Avg.
Lou Brock, lf	7	29	8	12	2	1	1	3	3	2	.414	13	0	0	1.000
Curt Flood, cf	7	28	2	5	1	0	0	3	3	3	.179	15	0	0	1.000
Roger Maris, rf	7	26	3	10	1	0	1	7	1	3	.385	15	0	1	.937
Orlando Cepeda, 1b	7	29	1	3	2	0	0	1	4	3	.103	53	0	0	1.000
Tim McCarver, c	7	24	3	3	1	0	0	2	2	4	.125	55	4	0	1.000
Mike Shannon, 3b	7	24	3	5	0	0	1	2	4	1	.208	5	13	2	.900
Julian Javier, 2b	7	25	3	9	3	0	1	4	6	0	.360	11	19	1	.968
Dal Maxvill, ss	7	19	1	3	0	1	0	1	1	4	.158	13	17	0	1.000
Bob Tolan	3	2	0	0	0	0	0	0	0	1	.000	0	0	0	.000
Ed Bressoud, ss	1	0	0	0	0	0	0	0	0	0	.000	0	0	0	.000
Bob Gibson, p	3	11	1	1	0	0	0	1	1	2	.091	2	3	0	1.000
Dick Hughes, p	2	3	0	0	0	0	0	0	3	0	.000	1	0	0	1.000
Ron Willis, p	3	0	0	0	0	0	0	0	0	0	.000	0	0	0	.000
Ed Spiezio	1	1	0	0	0	0	0	0	0	0	.000	0	0	0	.000
Larry Jaster, p	1	0	0	0	0	0	0	0	0	0	.000	0	0	0	.000
Joe Hoerner, p	2	0	0	0	0	0	0	0	0	0	.000	0	0	0	.000
Jack Lamabe, p	2	0	0	0	0	0	0	0	0	0	.000	0	1	0	1.000
Dick Ricketts, p	3	0	0	0	0	0	0	0	0	0	.000	0	0	0	.000
Nelson Briles, p	2	3	0	0	0	0	0	0	0	0	.000	0	4	0	1.000
Phil Gagliano	1	1	0	0	0	0	0	0	0	0	.000	0	0	0	.000
Ray Washburn, p	1	0	0	0	0	0	0	0	0	0	.000	0	1	0	1.000
Hal Woodeshick, p	1	0	0	0	0	0	0	0	0	0	.000	0	1	0	1.000
Steve Carlton, p	1	1	0	0	0	0	0	0	0	0	.000	0	1	0	.000
Total	7	229	25	51	11	2	5	24	30	17	.223	183	67	4	.984

BOSTON RED SOX

	G	AB	R	H	2B	3B	HR	RBI	SO	BB	Bat. Avg.	PO	A	E	Fldg. Avg.
Jerry Adair, 2b	5	16	0	2	0	0	0	1	3	0	.125	7	10	0	1.000
Dalton Jones, 3b	6	18	2	7	0	0	0	1	3	0	.389	4	8	0	1.000
Carl Yastrzemski, lf	7	25	4	10	2	0	3	5	1	4	.400	16	2	0	1.000
Ken Harrelson, rf	4	13	0	1	0	0	0	1	3	1	.077	5	0	0	1.000
John Wyatt, p	3	0	0	0	0	0	0	0	0	0	.000	0	0	0	.000
Joe Foy, 3b	6	15	2	2	0	0	0	1	5	1	.133	4	6	1	.923
George Scott, 1b	7	26	3	6	1	1	0	0	6	3	.231	70	4	0	1.000
Rico Petrocelli, ss	7	20	3	4	1	0	2	3	8	3	.200	11	21	2	.941
Dave Morehead, p	2	0	0	0	0	0	0	0	0	0	.000	0	0	0	.000
Ken Brett, p	2	0	0	0	0	0	0	0	0	0	.000	0	0	0	.000
Mike Andrews, 2b	5	13	0	4	0	0	0	1	1	0	.308	2	6	0	1.000
Reggie Smith, cf	7	24	3	6	1	0	2	3	3	2	.250	14	0	0	1.000
Russ Gibson, c	2	2	0	0	0	0	0	0	3	0	.000	9	0	0	1.000
Norm Siebern	3	3	0	1	0	0	0	0	1	0	.333	0	0	0	.000
Jose Tartabull, rf	7	13	1	2	0	0	0	1	0	2	.154	7	0	0	1.000
Jose Santiago, p	3	2	1	1	0	0	0	1	1	1	.500	0	3	0	1.000
Elston Howard, c	7	18	0	2	0	0	0	1	1	1	.111	23	1	0	1.000
Jim Lonborg, p	3	9	0	0	0	0	0	0	7	0	.000	1	2	0	1.000
Gary Bell, p	3	0	0	0	0	0	0	0	0	0	.000	1	2	0	1.000
George Thomas, rf	2	0	0	0	0	0	0	0	0	0	.000	0	0	0	.000
Gary Waslewski, p	2	0	0	0	0	0	0	0	1	0	.000	2	0	0	1.000
Lee Strange, p	1	0	0	0	0	0	0	0	0	0	.000	0	0	0	.000
Dan Osinski, p	2	0	0	0	0	0	0	0	0	0	.000	0	0	1	.000
Jerry Stephenson, p	1	0	0	0	0	0	0	0	0	0	.000	0	0	0	.000
Mike Ryan, c	1	2	0	0	0	0	0	0	1	0	.000	4	0	0	1.000
Total	7	222	21	48	6	1	8	19	48	17	.216	182	61	4	.984

Pitching Summary
ST. LOUIS CARDINALS

	G	CG	IP	H	R	BB	SO	HB	WP	W	L	Pct.	ER	ERA
Bob Gibson	3	3	27	14	3	5	26	0	1	3	0	1.000	3	1.00
Dick Hughes	2	0	9	9	6	3	7	0	0	0	1	.000	5	5.00
Ron Willis	2	0	1	2	4	1	1	0	0	0	0	.000	3	27.00
Joe Hoerner	2	0	⅔	0	0	0	0	0	0	0	0	.000	0	0.00
Jack Lamabe	3	0	2⅔	5	4	0	4	0	0	0	1	.000	2	27.00
Nelson Briles	2	1	11	7	2	1	3	0	0	1	0	1.000	2	1.64
Steve Carlton	1	0	6	3	2	5	0	0	1	0	1	.000	0	0.00
Ray Washburn	2	0	2⅓	2	0	2	0	0	0	0	0	.000	0	0.00
Larry Jaster	1	0	⅓	1	0	0	0	0	0	0	0	.000	0	0.00
Hal Woodeshick	1	0	1	1	0	0	0	0	0	0	0	.000	0	0.00
Total	7	4	61	48	21	17	48	0	2	4	3	.571	18	2.66

BOSTON RED SOX

	G	CG	IP	H	R	BB	SO	HB	WP	W	L	Pct.	ER	ERA
Jose Santiago	3	0	9⅔	16	6	3	6	0	0	0	2	.000	6	5.40
John Wyatt	2	0	3⅔	1	2	3	3	0	0	1	0	1.000	2	6.00
Jim Lonborg	3	2	24	14	3	2	11	0	0	2	1	.667	7	2.63
Gary Bell	3	0	5⅓	8	3	1	1	0	0	0	0	.000	3	5.40
Gary Waslewski	2	0	8⅓	4	2	2	7	0	0	0	0	.000	2	2.25
Lee Strange	1	0	2	3	1	0	0	0	0	0	0	.000	0	0.00
Dan Osinski	2	0	1⅔	2	1	1	2	0	0	0	1	.000	1	9.00
Jerry Stephenson	1	0	2	3	2	1	0	0	0	0	0	.000	2	9.00
Dave Morehead	2	0	3⅓	0	1	4	3	0	0	0	0	.000	0	0.00
Ken Brett	2	0	1⅓	0	0	0	2	0	0	0	0	.000	0	0.00
Total	7	2	61	51	25	17	39	0	2	3	4	.429	23	3.39

Composite Score by Innings

St. Louis	5	2	7	0	2	2	4	3	1	1—25
Boston	0	1	2	4	1	3	8	1	2—21

1967 World Series Box Scores
Gibson Notches Three Wins for Cardinals

The St. Louis Cardinals became world baseball champions by defeating the Boston Red Sox in the 1967 World Series, 4 games to 3. Led by Bob Gibson, the Cardinals improved their record to 8 world championships in 11 World Series, which represents the best of any National League club. Gibson, by starting, finishing and winning 3 games in one World Series, joined select company. Only Christy Mathewson of the Giants in 1905, Babe Adams of Pittsburgh in 1909, Jack Coombs of the Philadelphia Athletics in 1910, Stanley Covaleski of Cleveland in 1920 and Lew Burdette of Milwaukee in 1957 had done it before.

FIRST GAME
Fenway Park, Boston, Oct. 4
ST. LOUIS CARDINALS

	AB	R	H	RBI	PO	A
Brock, lf	4	2	4	0	2	0
Flood, cf	5	0	1	0	2	0
Maris, rf	4	0	0	0	0	0
Cepeda, 1b	4	0	0	0	6	0
McCarver, c	4	0	2	0	11	2
Shannon, 3b	4	0	0	0	0	2
Javier, 2b	4	0	2	0	1	1
Maxvill, ss	2	0	0	0	2	0
B. Gibson, p	4	0	0	0	0	0
Totals	34	2	10	2	27	6

BOSTON RED SOX

	AB	R	H	RBI	PO	A
Adair, 2b	4	0	0	0	2	2
Jones, 3b	4	0	1	0	2	0
Yastrzemski, lf	4	0	0	0	4	1
Harrelson, rf	3	0	0	0	0	0
Wyatt, p	0	0	0	0	0	0
cFoy	1	0	0	0	0	0
Scott, 1b	3	0	2	0	8	0
Petrocelli, ss	3	0	0	0	0	0
dAndrews	1	0	0	0	0	0
Smith, cf	3	0	1	0	1	0
R. Gibson, c	2	0	0	0	8	0
aSiebern, rf	1	0	0	0	0	1
bTartabull, rf	0	0	0	0	1	0
Santiago, p	2	1	1	1	0	1
Howard, c	0	0	0	0	1	0
Totals	31	1	6	1	27	5

a-Announced for R. Gibson in 7th.
b-Ran for Siebern in 9th.
c-Grounded out for Wyatt in 9th.
d-Filed out for Petrocelli in 9th.

St. Louis (N) .... 0 0 1 0 0 0 1 0 0—2
Boston (A) .... 0 0 1 0 0 0 0 0 1—1

	IP	H	R	ER	BB	SO
B. Gibson (W.)	9	6	1	1	1	10
Santiago (L.)	7	10	2	2	2	5
Wyatt	2	0	0	0	2	1

Errors—None. Double plays—Jones and Scott; Jones, Adair, and Scott. Left on bases—St. Louis 10, Boston 4. Two-base hits—Flood, Scott. Home run—Santiago. Stolen bases—Brock 2. Sacrifice —Howard.

Bases on balls—Off B. Gibson 1 (Scott), Santiago 2 (Maris, Maxvill), Wyatt 2 (Maxvill, Brock). Struck out—By B. Gibson 10 (Adair 2, Jones, Petrocelli 2, R. Smith, R. Gibson 2, Santiago), Santiago 5 (Flood, McCarver, B. Gibson, Javier, Cepeda), Wyatt 1 (Javier). Balk—Wyatt. Passed ball—R. Gibson.

How runs were scored—One in Cardinal third: Brock singled. Flood doubled Brock to third. Maris grounded out, Brock scoring.
One in Red Sox third: Santiago hit a home run into the left field stands.
One in Cardinal seventh: Brock singled and stole second. Flood grounded out, Brock taking third. Brock scored on a grounder by Maris.

Umpires—Stevens (A.) plate; Barlick (N.), first base; Umont (A.) second base; Donatelli (N.), third base; Runge (A.) left field; Pryor (N.), right field. Time of game—2:22. Attendance—34,796.

SECOND GAME
Fenway Park, Boston, Oct. 5
ST. LOUIS CARDINALS

	AB	R	H	RBI	PO	A
Brock, lf	4	0	0	0	4	0
Flood, cf	3	0	0	0	3	0
Maris, rf	3	0	0	0	0	0
Cepeda, 1b	3	0	0	0	9	1
McCarver, c	3	0	0	0	9	0
Shannon, 3b	3	0	0	0	1	1
Javier, 2b	3	0	1	0	1	4
Maxvill, ss	2	0	0	0	1	0
aTolan, ph	1	0	0	0	0	0
Bressoud, ss	0	0	0	0	0	0
Hughes, p	2	0	0	0	1	0
Willis, p	0	0	0	0	0	0
Hoerner, p	0	0	0	0	0	0
Lamabe, p	0	0	0	0	0	0
bRicketts, ph	1	0	0	0	0	0
Totals	28	0	1	0	24	3

BOSTON RED SOX

	AB	R	H	RBI	PO	A
Tartabull, rf	4	1	0	0	2	0
Jones, 3b	5	1	2	0	0	3
Yastrzemski, lf	4	2	3	4	3	0
Scott, 1b	4	1	1	0	12	1
R. Smith, cf	3	0	0	0	1	0
Adair, 2b	4	0	2	0	1	4
Petrocelli, ss	2	0	1	1	3	5
Howard, c	3	0	0	0	4	0
Lonborg, p	4	0	0	0	1	0
Totals	33	5	9	5	27	13

a-Grounded out for Maxvill in 8th.
b-Popped up for Lamabe in 9th.

St. Louis (N) .... 0 0 0 0 0 0 0 0 0—0
Boston (A) .... 0 0 1 0 1 0 3 0 x—5

	IP	H	R	ER	BB	SO
Hughes (L.)	5⅓	7	2	1	3	5
Willis	*⅔	1	2	2	2	1
Hoerner	⅔	1	1	1	0	2
Lamabe	1⅓	2	0	0	1	2
Lonborg (W.)	9	1	0	0	1	4

*-Faced two batters in 7th.

Error—Shannon. Runs batted in—Yastrzemski 4, Petrocelli. Left on bases—St. Louis 2, Boston 11. Two-base hit—Javier. Home runs—Yastrzemski 2. Stolen base—Adair. Sacrifice fly—Petrocelli.

Bases on balls—Hughes 3 (Yastrzemski, Scott, R. Smith), Willis 2 (Howard, Tartabull), Hoerner (Petrocelli), Lonborg (Flood). Struck out—By Hughes 5 (Jones, Scott, Lonborg, Tartabull, Petrocelli). By Willis (Lonborg). By Lamabe 2 (Howard, Lonborg). By Lonborg 4 (Shannon 2, Hughes 2).

How runs were scored—One in Red Sox fourth: Yastrzemski hit a home run into the right field stands.
One in Red Sox sixth: Scott and Smith walked. Shannon bobbled Adair's grounder, filling the bases. Petrocelli hit a sacrifice fly to center field, scoring Scott.
Three in Red Sox seventh: Tartabull walked. Jones beat out a hit down the third base line. Yastrzemski hit a home run into the right field bleachers.

Umpires—Barlick (N.) plate; Umont (A.) first base; Donatelli (N.) second base; Runge (A.) third base; Pryor (N.) left field foul line; Stevens (A.) right field foul line. Time of game—2:24. Attendance—35,188.

THIRD GAME
Busch Memorial Stadium, St. Louis, Oct. 7
BOSTON RED SOX

	AB	R	H	RBI	PO	A
Tartabull, rf	3	0	0	0	3	0
Jones, 3b	4	0	3	1	2	1
Yastrzemski, lf	3	0	0	0	0	1
Scott, 1b	4	0	0	0	8	0
Smith, cf	4	1	2	1	2	0
Adair, 2b	4	0	0	0	2	2
Petrocelli, ss	4	0	0	0	1	5
Howard, c	3	0	1	0	5	0
Bell, p	0	0	0	0	0	1
aThomas	1	0	0	0	0	0
Waslewski, p	1	0	1	0	0	0
bAndrews	1	0	1	0	0	0
Stange, p	0	0	0	0	0	0
cFoy	1	0	0	0	0	0
Osinski, p	0	0	0	0	0	0
Totals	31	2	7	2	24	11

ST. LOUIS CARDINALS

	AB	R	H	RBI	PO	A
Brock, lf	4	2	2	0	2	0
Flood, cf	4	0	1	3	0	0
Maris, rf	4	1	2	1	0	0
Cepeda, 1b	4	0	1	1	13	0
McCarver, c	4	1	1	0	5	1
Shannon, 3b	3	1	2	2	0	4
Javier, 2b	3	0	1	0	0	6
Maxvill, ss	3	0	0	0	2	4
Briles, p	3	0	0	0	2	2
Totals	**32**	**5**	**10**	**5**	**27**	**15**

a—Struck out for Bell in 3rd inning.
b—Singled for Waslewski in 6th inning.
c—Grounded out for Stange in 8th inning.

```
Boston (A)........... 0 0 0 0 0 1 1 0 0—2
St. Louis (N)........ 1 2 0 0 0 1 x—5
```

	IP	H	R	ER	BB	SO
Bell (L.)	2	5	3	3	0	1
Waslewski	3	0	0	0	3	0
Stange	2	3	1	0	0	0
Osinski	1	2	1	1	0	0
Briles (W.)	9	7	2	2	0	3

Error—Stange. Double plays—Bell, Petrocelli and Scott; Javier, Maxvill and Cepeda. Two-base hit—Cepeda. Three-base hit—Brock. Home runs—Shannon, Smith. Sacrifice—Tartabull. Left on bases—Boston 4, St. Louis 3.

Struck out—By Bell 1 (Maxvill), Waslewski 3 (Brock, Cepeda, Javier), Briles 3 (Jones, Thomas, Scott). Hit by pitch—By Briles (Yastrzemski).

How runs were scored—One in Cardinal first: Brock tripled to left center. Flood singled to center, scoring Brock.

Two in Cardinal second: McCarver singled. Shannon hit a home run over the left field fence.

One in Red Sox sixth: Andrews singled to center and moved to second on a grounder. Jones singled, scoring Andrews.

One in Cardinal sixth: Brock beat out a bunt. A pickoff attempt was thrown wild and Brock went to third. Maris singled, scoring Brock.

One in Red Sox seventh: Smith hit a home run to right field.

One in Cardinal eighth: Maris had an infield hit. Cepeda doubled, scoring Maris.

Umpires—Umont (A.) plate; Donatelli (N.) first base; Runge (A.) second base; Pryor (N.) third base; Stevens (A.) left field; Barlick (N.) right field. Time—2:15. Attendance—54,575.

FOURTH GAME
Busch Memorial Stadium, St. Louis, Oct. 8

BOSTON RED SOX

	AB	R	H	RBI	PO	A
Tartabull, rf	4	0	2	0	1	0
Jones, 3b	4	0	0	0	0	2
Yastrzemski, lf	4	0	2	0	3	0
Scott, 1b	4	0	1	0	9	0
Smith, cf	3	0	0	0	3	0
Adair, 2b	4	0	0	0	2	2
Petrocelli, ss	3	0	0	0	2	4
Howard, c	2	0	0	0	0	0
Morehead, p	0	0	0	0	0	0
bSiebern	1	0	0	0	0	0
Brett, p	0	0	0	0	0	0
Santiago, p	0	0	0	0	0	0
Bell, p	0	0	0	0	0	0
aFoy	1	0	0	0	0	0
Stephenson, p	0	0	0	0	0	0
Ryan, c	2	0	0	0	4	0
Totals	**32**	**0**	**9**	**0**	**24**	**8**

ST. LOUIS CARDINALS

	AB	R	H	RBI	PO	A
Brock, lf	4	1	2	0	2	0
Flood, cf	4	1	1	0	3	0
Maris, rf	4	1	1	2	2	0
Cepeda, 1b	4	1	1	0	11	0
McCarver, c	3	1	1	2	7	0
Shannon, 3b	3	0	0	0	0	2
Javier, 2b	4	0	2	1	0	2
Maxvill, ss	3	0	1	1	0	3
Gibson, p	3	0	0	0	0	2
Totals	**32**	**6**	**9**	**6**	**27**	**9**

a—Struck out for Bell in 3rd inning.
b—Flied out for Morehead in 6th inning.

```
Boston (A)........ 0 0 0 0 0 0 0 0 0—0
St. Louis (N)..... 4 0 2 0 0 0 0 x—6
```

	IP	H	R	ER	BB	SO
Santiago (L.)	⅔	6	4	4	0	0
Bell	1⅓	0	0	0	0	0
Stephenson	2	3	2	2	1	0
Morehead	3	0	0	0	1	2
Brett	1	0	0	0	1	1
Gibson (W.)	9	5	0	0	1	6

Two-base hits—Maris, Cepeda, Javier, Brock, Yastrzemski. Stolen base—Brock. Sacrifice fly—McCarver. Left on bases—Boston 6, St. Louis 6.

Bases on balls—By Stephenson 1 (Shannon), Morehead 1 (Gibson), Brett 1 (Maxvill), Gibson 1 (Smith). Struck out—By Morehead 2 (McCarver, Javier), Brett 1 (Javier), Gibson 6 (Scott, Adair, Petrocelli, Foy, Ryan, Smith). Wild pitch—Stephenson.

How runs were scored—Four runs in Cardinal first: Brock beat out an infield hit. Flood singled to left. Maris doubled to left, scoring Brock and Flood. Cepeda flied to right, Maris taking third after the catch. McCarver singled, scoring Maris. Javier singled to deep short. Maxvill singled, scoring McCarver.

Two in Cardinal third: Cepeda doubled to left and took third on a wild pitch. McCarver flied out, Cepeda scoring after the catch. Shannon walked. Javier doubled, scoring Shannon.

Umpires—Donatelli (N.) plate; Runge (A.) first base; Pryor (N.) second base; Stevens (A.) third base; Barlick (N.) left field; Umont (A.) right field. Time—2:05. Attendance—54,575.

FIFTH GAME
Busch Memorial Stadium, St. Louis, Oct. 9

BOSTON RED SOX

	AB	R	H	RBI	PO	A
Foy, 3b	5	1	1	0	2	4
Andrews, 2b	3	1	0	1	2	2
Yastrzemski, lf	3	0	1	0	2	0
Harrelson, rf	3	0	1	1	1	0
Tartabull, rf	0	0	0	0	0	0
Scott, 1b	3	1	0	0	14	0
R. Smith, cf	4	1	1	0	1	0
Petrocelli, ss	3	0	0	0	1	2
Howard, c	4	0	1	1	5	0
Lonborg, p	4	0	0	0	0	2
Totals	**32**	**3**	**6**	**2**	**27**	**10**

ST. LOUIS CARDINALS

	AB	R	H	RBI	PO	A
Brock, lf	4	0	0	0	2	0
Flood, cf	4	0	0	0	3	0
Maris, rf	4	1	2	1	3	0
Cepeda, 1b	4	0	0	0	5	0
McCarver, c	3	0	0	0	9	1
Shannon, 3b	3	0	0	0	1	3
Javier, 2b	3	0	0	0	4	3
Maxvill, ss	2	0	1	0	3	4
bRicketts, ph	1	0	0	0	0	0
Willis, p	0	0	0	0	0	0
Lamabe, p	0	0	0	0	0	1
Carleton, p	1	0	0	0	0	0
aTolan, ph	1	0	0	0	0	0
Washburn, p	0	0	0	0	0	0
cCagliano, ph	1	0	0	0	0	0
Bressoud, ss	0	0	0	0	0	0
Totals	**31**	**1**	**3**	**1**	**27**	**12**

a—Struck out for Carlton in 6th inning.
b—Grounded out for Maxvill in 8th inning.
c—Popped out for Washburn in 8th inning.

```
Boston (A)........ 0 0 1 0 0 0 0 0 2—3
St. Louis (N)..... 0 0 0 0 0 0 0 0 1—1
```

	IP	H	R	ER	BB	SO
Lonborg (W.)	9	3	1	1	0	4
Carlton (L.)	6	3	1	0	2	5
Washburn	2	1	0	0	0	2
Willis	0	1	2	1	2	0
Lamabe	1	0	0	0	1	0

Errors—Shannon, Petrocelli, Maris. Double plays—Javier, Maxvill and Cepeda; McCarver, Javier, McCarver, Javier, McCarver, Shannon, Lamabe, McCarver. Two-base hits—Yastrzemski, R. Smith. Home run—Maris. Sacrifice—Andrews. Left on base—Boston 7, St. Louis 3.

Bases on balls—By Carlton 2 (Yastrzemski, Harrelson). Struck out—By Lonborg 4 (Cepeda, Brock, Shannon, Tolan); Carlton 5 (Foy, Scott, Lonborg 2, Yastrzemski); Washburn 2 (Petrocelli, Foy); Lamabe 2 (Lonborg, Foy). Wild pitch—Carlton.

How runs were scored—One in Red Sox third: Foy singled. Shannon booted Andrews' slow grounder, Foy stopping at second. Harrelson singled, scoring Foy.

Two in Red Sox ninth: Scott walked and went to third on Smith's double. Petrocelli was intentionally passed, filling the bases. Howard singled to right, scoring Scott. Smith scored on a poor throw to the plate by Maris.

One in Cardinal ninth: Maris hit a home run.

Umpires—Runge (A.) plate; Pryor (N.) first base; Stevens (A.) second base; Barlick (N.) third base; Umont (A.) left field; Donatelli (N.) right field. Time—2:20. Attendance—54,575.

SIXTH GAME
Fenway Park, Boston, Oct. 11
ST. LOUIS CARDINALS

	AB	R	H	RBI	PO	A
Brock, lf.	5	2	3	2	0	0
Flood, cf.	5	0	1	1	2	0
Maris, rf.	4	0	2	0	2	0
Cepeda, 1b.	5	0	1	0	11	0
McCarver, c.	3	0	0	0	2	0
Shannon, 3b.	4	0	1	0	1	4
Javier, 2b.	4	1	1	0	2	3
Maxvill, ss.	3	0	0	0	2	2
Hughes, p.	1	0	0	0	0	0
aSpiezo	1	0	0	0	0	0
Willis, p.	0	0	0	0	0	0
Briles, p.	0	0	0	0	0	0
bTolan	0	1	0	0	0	0
Lamabe, p.	0	0	0	0	0	0
Hoerner, p.	0	0	0	0	0	0
Jaster, p.	0	0	0	0	0	0
Washburn, p.	0	0	0	0	0	0
Ricketts	1	0	0	0	0	1
Woodeschick, p.	0	0	0	0	0	0
Totals	36	4	8	4	24	12

BOSTON RED SOX

	AB	R	H	RBI	PO	A
Foy, 3b.	4	1	1	1	3	3
Andrews, 2b.	4	1	1	0	2	0
Yastrzemski, lf.	4	2	3	1	2	0
Harrelson, rf.	3	0	0	1	0	1
Bell, p.	0	0	0	0	0	1
Tartabull, rf.	0	0	0	0	0	0
dAdair	0	0	0	1	0	0
Scott, 1b.	3	0	0	0	10	0
Smith, cf.	4	1	2	2	4	0
Petrocelli, ss.	3	2	2	1	3	0
Howard, c.	4	0	0	0	4	0
Waslewski, p.	1	0	0	0	0	0
Wyatt, p.	0	0	0	0	0	0
cJones	1	1	1	0	0	0
Thomas, rf.	1	0	0	1	1	0
Totals	32	8	12	8	27	10

a-Grounded out for Willis in 5th.
b-Walked for Briles in 7th.
c-Singled for Wyatt in 7th.
d-Sacrificed for Tartabull in 7th.
e-Flied out for Washburn in 8th.

St. Louis (N) .... 0 0 2 0 0 0 2 0 0—4
Boston (A) .... 0 1 0 3 0 0 4 0 x—8

	IP	H	R	ER	BB	SO
Hughes	3⅔	5	4	4	0	2
Willis	⅓	0	0	0	0	0
Briles	2	0	0	0	0	1
Lamabe (L.)	⅓	2	2	2	0	0
*Hoerner	0	2	2	2	2	0
Jaster	⅓	2	0	0	0	0
Washburn	⅓	0	0	0	1	0
Woodeschick	1	1	0	0	0	0
Waslewski	5⅓	4	2	2	2	4
Wyatt (W.)	1⅔	1	2	2	1	0
Bell	2	3	0	0	1	0

*-Faced two men in seventh.

Error—Petrocelli. Two-base hits—Javier, Foy, Shannon. Home runs—Petrocelli 2, Yastrzemski, Smith, Brock. Stolen base—Brock. Sacrifice—Foy. Sacrifice fly—Adair. Left on base—St. Louis 9, Boston 7.

Bases on balls—Off Briles 1 (Yastrzemski), Washburn 1 (Petrocelli), Waslewski 2 (Maris, McCarver), Wyatt 1 (Tolan), Bell 1 (Maxvill). Struck out—By Hughes 2 (Harrelson, Waslewski), Waslewski 4 (Brock, Maris, Hughes, Flood). Hit by pitch—By Briles (Waslewski).

How runs were scored—One in Red Sox second: Petrocelli hit a home run.

Two in Cardinal third: Javier doubled to left. Brock singled, scoring Javier. Brock stole second and scored on Flood's single.

Three in Red Sox fourth: Yastrzemski hit a home run to left center. Smith hit a home run into the right field stands. Petrocelli homered onto the left field screen.

Two in Cardinals seventh: Tolan walked. Brock hit a home run to right center.

Four in Red Sox seventh: Jones singled. Foy doubled scoring Jones. Andrews singled scoring Foy. Yastrzemski singled sending Andrews to third. Adair hit a sacrifice fly to center, Andrews scoring after the catch. Scott singled to left. Smith singled to center scoring Yastrzemski.

Umpires—Pryor (N.) plate; Stevens (A.) first base; Barlick (N.) second base; Umont (A.) third base; Donatelli (N.) left field; Runge (A.) right field. Time—2:38. Attendance—35,188.

SEVENTH GAME
Fenway Park, Boston, Oct. 12
ST. LOUIS CARDINALS

	AB	R	H	RBI	PO	A
Brock, lf.	4	1	2	0	1	0
Flood, cf.	3	1	1	0	1	0
Maris, rf.	3	0	2	1	1	0
Cepeda, 1b.	5	0	0	0	6	2
McCarver, c.	5	1	1	0	12	0
Shannon, 3b.	4	1	0	0	0	0
Javier, 2b.	4	1	2	3	3	3
Maxvill, ss.	4	1	1	0	3	3
B. Gibson, p.	4	1	1	1	0	1
Totals	36	7	10	6	27	9

BOSTON RED SOX

	AB	R	H	RBI	PO	A
Foy, 3b.	3	0	0	0	2	3
Morehead, p.	0	0	0	0	0	0
Osinski, p.	0	0	0	0	0	0
Brett, p.	0	0	0	0	0	0
Andrews, 2b.	3	0	0	0	1	2
Yastrzemski, lf.	3	0	1	0	2	0
Harrelson, rf.	4	0	0	0	3	0
Scott, 1b.	4	1	1	0	9	0
R. Smith, cf.	3	0	0	0	2	0
Petrocelli, ss.	3	1	1	1	3	2
Howard, c.	2	0	0	0	4	1
bJones, 3b.	0	0	0	0	1	0
Lonborg, p.	2	0	0	0	0	0
aTartabull	1	0	0	0	0	0
Santiago, p.	0	0	0	0	0	0
cSiebern	0	0	0	1	0	1
R. Gibson	0	0	0	0	1	0
Totals	28	2	3	1	27	9

a-Struck out for Lonborg in 6th.
b-Walked for Howard in 8th.
c-Hit into force play for Santiago in 8th.

St. Louis (N.) .... 0 0 2 0 2 3 0 0—7
Boston (A.) .... 0 0 0 0 1 0 0 1 0—2

	IP	H	R	ER	BB	SO
B. Gibson (W.)	9	3	2	2	3	10
Lonborg (L.)	6	10	7	6	1	1
Santiago	2	0	0	0	0	0
Morehead	½	0	0	0	3	1
Osinski	½	0	0	0	0	0
Brett	½	0	0	0	0	0

Errors—Javier, Foy. Double play—Maxvill, Javier and Cepeda. Left on bases—St. Louis 7, Boston 3. Two-base hits—McCarver, Brock, Petrocelli. Three-base hits—Maxvill, Scott. Home runs—B. Gibson, Javier. Stolen bases—Brock 3. Sacrifice—Andrews. Sacrifice fly—Maris.

Bases on balls—Off B. Gibson 3 (Foy, Yastrzemski, Jones), Lonborg 1 (Flood), Morehead 3 (Brock, Flood, Maris). Struck out—By B. Gibson 10 (Harrelson 2, Scott 2, Petrocelli 2, Lonborg, Foy, Andrews, Tartabull), Lonborg 1 (Cepeda), Morehead 1 (Gibson). Wild pitches—Lonborg, Gibson.

How runs were scored—Two in Cardinal third: Maxvill tripled. Flood singled scoring Maxvill. Maris singled sending Flood to third. Flood scored on a wild pitch.

Two in Cardinal fifth: Gibson hit a home run. Brock singled. Brock stole second and third. Flood walked. Maris hit a sacrifice fly scoring Brock.

One in Red Sox fifth: Scott tripled and scored on a bad throw.

Three in Cardinal sixth: McCarver doubled. Foy booted Shannon's grounder. Javier hit a home run.

One in Red Sox eighth: Petrocelli doubled. Petrocelli went to third on a wild pitch. Jones walked. Siebern forced Jones at second, Petrocelli scoring on the play.

Umpires—Stevens (A.) plate; Barlick (N.) first base; Umont (A.) second base; Donatelli (N.) third base; Runge (A.) left field; Pryor (N.) right field. Time of game—2:23. Attendance—35,188.

5 Records Broken, 35 Tied in 1967 World Series

INDIVIDUAL RECORDS BROKEN

Most Stolen Bases in Series—7, Lou Brock, St. Louis.

Most Home Runs Allowed in one inning—3, Dick Hughes, St. Louis, Oct. 11, fourth inning.

INDIVIDUAL RECORDS TIED

Most Base Hits in one game—4, Lou Brock, St Louis, Oct. 4.

Most Base Hits, consecutive in one game—4, Lou Brock, St. Louis, Oct. 4.

Most One-Base Hits in one game—4, Lou Brock, St. Louis, Oct. 4.

Most One-Base Hits, consecutive in one game—4, Lou Brock, St. Louis, Oct. 4.

Most Runs Scored in Series—8, Lou Brock, St. Louis.

Hitting home run in first Series at bat—Jose Santiago, Boston, Oct. 4, third inning.

Most Home Runs, consecutive at bats—2, Rico Petrocelli, Boston, Oct. 11.

Most Stolen Bases in one game—3, Lou Brock, St. Louis, Oct. 12.

Most Stolen Bases in one inning—2, Lou Brock, St. Louis, Oct. 12, fifth inning.

Most Complete Games Won, Consecutive, total Series—5, Bob Gibson, St. Louis, two in 1964, three in 1967.

Most Games Won in one Series—3, Bob Gibson, St. Louis.

Most Games Won, Consecutive in One Series—3, Bob Gibson, St. Louis.

Most Games Won, Losing None in One Series—3, Bob Gibson, St. Louis.

Most Complete Games in One Series—3, Bob Gibson, St. Louis.

Most Games Lost in One Series—2, Jose Santiago, Boston.

Most Home Runs Allowed in One Series—5, Dick Hughes, St. Louis.

Most Home Runs Allowed in game—4, Dick Hughes, St. Louis, Oct. 11.

Most Putouts by outfielder in one inning—3, Reggie Smith, Boston, Oct. 11, seventh inning.

Most Double Plays by third baseman in one game—2, Dalton Jones, Boston, Oct. 4.

Most Double Plays Started by third baseman in one game—2, Dalton Jones, Boston, Oct. 4.

Fewest Chances by first baseman in one game—2, Orlando Cepeda, St. Louis, Oct. 5, one putout, one assist.

Fewest Chances by third baseman in one game—0, Mike Shannon, St. Louis, Oct. 12.

Fewest Chances by shortstop in one game—0, Rico Petrocelli, Boston, Oct. 4.

Fewest Chances by outfielder in one game—0, Roger Maris, St. Louis, Oct. 7; Lou Brock, St. Louis, Oct. 9; Curt Flood, St. Louis, Oct. 12.

CLUB RECORDS BROKEN

Most Home Runs by one club in one inning—3, Boston, Oct. 11, fourth inning.

Fewest One-Base hits, Both Clubs in Series—66, St. Louis, 33, vs. Boston 33.

Most Pitchers, Both Clubs in one game—11, St. Louis 8, vs. Boston 3, Oct. 11.

CLUB RECORDS TIED

Most Home Runs, consecutive by club in one inning—2, Boston, Oct. 11, fourth inning.

Most Home Runs by Pitchers, as Batsmen in One Series—2, Boston vs. St. Louis, 1.

Fewest Batsmen Hit by Pitcher, Club in one Series—0, St. Louis.

Fewest Pinch Runners Used by Club in One Series—0, St. Louis.

Most One-Hit Games by Club in One Series—1, Boston, Oct. 5.

Most Pitchers Used by Both Clubs in One Series—20, St. Louis 10, vs. Boston 10.

Most Pitchers Used by One Club in One Game—8, St. Louis, Oct. 11.

Most Pitchers Used by Club in One Inning—4, St. Louis, Oct. 11, Seventh Inning.

Most Double Plays, both clubs in one series—7, St. Louis 4, vs. Boston 3.

Fewest Passed Balls by Club in One Series—0, St. Louis.

Fewest Assists by Club in One Game—3, St. Louis, Oct. 5.

How Players Shared World Series Money

(Players share in first four games only)

Yr.	G.	Winning Players'	Share	Losing Players'	Share	Yr.	G.	Winning Players'	Share	Losing Players'	Share
1946	7	Cardinals	$3,757	Red Sox	$2,052	1957	7	Braves	$8,924	Yankees	$5,606
1947	7	Yankees	5,830	Dodgers	4,081	1958	7	Yankees	8,759	Braves	5,896
1948	6	Indians	6,772	Braves	4,570	1959	6	Dodgers	11,231	White Sox	7,275
1949	5	Yankees	5,665	Dodgers	4,227	1960	7	Pirates	8,417	Yankees	5,214
1950	4	Yankees	5,737	Phillies	4,801	1961	5	Yankees	7,389	Reds	5,356
1951	6	Yankees	6,446	Giants	4,951	1962	7	Yankees	9,882	Giants	7,291
1952	7	Yankees	6,026	Dodgers	4,200	1963	4	Dodgers	*12,794	Yankees	7,874
1953	6	Yankees	8,280	Dodgers	6,178	1964	7	Cardinals	8,622	Yankees	5,309
1954	4	Giants	11,147	Indians	6,712	1965	7	Dodgers	10,297	Twins	6,634
1955	7	Dodgers	9,768	Yankees	5,598	1966	4	Orioles	11,683	Dodgers	**8,189
1956	7	Yankees	8,714	Dodgers	6,934	1967	7	Cardinals	8,314	Red Sox	5,115

*Record winners' shares. **Record losers' shares.

In 1967 the winning St. Louis Cardinals (N) divided their share of the players' pool into 34 full shares and 3 fractional shares. The Boston Red Sox (A) voted 31 full shares and 10 fractional shares. Second place was worth $1,484 to each San Francisco Giant, $1,268 to each Detroit Tiger, and $1,171 to each Minnesota Twin; the Tigers and Twins finished tied for second in the American League. Third place meant $1,080 apiece to the Chicago Cubs, and fourth-place Cincinnati Reds got $465 and the fifth-place Philadelphia Phillies, $197. The Chicago White Sox fourth place money was $428 and the California Angels' fifth place share was $181.

World Series Attendance and Receipts Since 1946

Yr.	Clubs	G.	Atten.	Rcpts.	Yr.	Clubs	G.	Atten.	Rcpts.
1946	St. Louis (N)-Boston (A)	7	250,071	1,052,920	1957	Milw. (N)-N. Y. (A)	7	394,712	2,475,978
1947	N. Y. (A)-Brooklyn (N)	7	389,763	2,137,549	1958	N. Y. (A)-Milw. (N)	7	393,909	2,397,223
1948	Clevel'd (A)-Boston (N)	6	358,362	1,633,685	1959	L. A. (N)-Chicago (A) (*)	6	420,784	2,626,973
1949	N. Y. (A)-Brooklyn (N)	5	236,710	1,129,627	1960	Pitts (N)-N. Y. (A)	7	349,813	2,230,627
1950	New York (A)-Phila. (N)	4	196,009	953,469	1961	N. Y. (A)-Cincinnati(N).	5	223,247	1,480,095
1951	New York (A)-N. Y. (N).	6	341,977	1,633,457	1962	N. Y. (A)-San Fran. (N)	7	376,864	2,878,891
1952	N. Y. (A)-Brooklyn (N)	7	340,906	1,622,753	1963	L. A. (N)-N.Y. (A)	4	247,279	1,995,190
1953	N. Y. (A)-Brooklyn (N)	6	307,350	1,779,269	1964	St. Louis (N)-N. Y. (A)	7	321,807	2,243,187
1954	New York (N)-Clev. (A).	4	251,507	1,566,203	1965	L. A. (N)-Minn. (A)	7	364,326	2,975,041
1955	Brooklyn (N)-N.Y. (A).	7	362,310	2,337,515	1966	L. A. (N)-Balt. (A) (**)	4	220,791	2,047,142
1956	N. Y. (A)-Brooklyn (N).	7	345,903	2,173,254	1967	St. Louis (N)-Bos. (A).	7	304,085	2,350,607

Receipts since 1948 do not include fees for radio and television rights. This revenue customarily goes to players' pension fund. *Attendance record. **Receipts record for 4-game Series.

American Legion Junior Baseball World Champions

1951—Los Angeles, Calif.	1956—St. Louis, Mo.	1960—New Orleans, La.	1964—Upland, Calif.
1952—Cincinnati, Ohio	1957—Cincinnati, Ohio	1961—Phoenix, Ariz.	1965—Charlotte, N. C.
1953—Yakima, Wash.	1958—Cincinnati, Ohio	1962—St. Louis, Mo.	1966—Oakland, Calif.
1954—San Diego, Calif.	1959—Detroit, Mich.	1963—Long Beach, Calif.	1967—Tuscaloosa, Ala.
1955—Cincinnati, Ohio			

National League Records, 1967

FINAL STANDING OF CLUBS

	St. Louis	San Francisco	Chicago	Cincinnati	Philadelphia	Pittsburgh	Atlanta	Los Angeles	Houston	New York	Won	Lost	Percentage	Games Behind
St. Louis *Cardinals*	—	11	11	13	12	7	12	12	12	11	101	60	.627	—
San Francisco *Giants*	7	—	.8	10	10	10	8	13	12	13	91	71	.562	10½
Chicago *Cubs*	6	10	—	12	11	11	7	9	8	13	87	74	.540	14
Cincinnati *Reds*	5	8	6	—	10	10	13	8	15	12	87	75	.537	14½
Philadelphia *Phillies*	6	8	7	8	—	8	8	12	11	14	82	80	.506	19½
Pittsburgh *Pirates*	11	8	7	8	10	—	10	11	9	7	81	81	.500	20½
Atlanta *Braves*	6	10	11	5	10	8	—	8	11	7	77	85	.475	24½
Los Angeles *Dodgers*	6	5	9	10	6	7	10	—	8	12	73	89	.451	28½
Houston *Astros*	6	6	10	3	7	9	7	10	—	11	69	93	.426	32½
New York *Mets*	7	5	5	6	4	11	10	6	7	—	61	101	.377	40½

CLUB BATTING

	g.	ab.	r.	h.	hr.	sb.	pct.
Pittsburgh	163	5725	679	1585	91	79	.277
St. Louis	161	5566	695	1462	115	102	.263
Chicago	162	5464	702	1373	128	64	.251
Houston	162	5506	626	1372	93	89	.249
Cincinnati	162	5519	604	1366	109	90	.248
San Francisco	162	5524	652	1354	140	22	.245
Philadelphia	162	5401	612	1306	103	79	.242
Atlanta	162	5451	631	1307	158	55	.240
New York	162	5415	498	1288	83	57	.238
Los Angeles	162	5455	519	1285	82	57	.236

CLUB PITCHING

	g.	cg.	ip.	h.	r.	bb.	so.	era.
San Fran.	162	64	1475	1283	551	453	988	2.92
Cincinnati	162	34	1468	1328	563	497	1062	3.03
St. Louis	161	44	1465	1312	557	430	954	3.05
Phila.	162	46	1453	1372	581	404	964	3.10
Los Angeles	162	41	1473	1421	595	393	965	3.21
Atlanta	162	35	1464	1376	640	450	859	3.44
Chicago	162	47	1457	1352	624	464	885	3.47
New York	162	36	1434	1369	672	537	889	3.73
Pittsburgh	163	36	1458	1439	693	561	812	3.74
Houston	162	35	1446	1444	742	484	1053	4.02

INDIVIDUAL BATTING

Leaders—450 or More At Bats

Player—Club	G.	ab.	h.	hr.	rbi.	sb.	pct.
Clemente, Pitts.	147	585	209	23	110	9	.357
†Gonzalez, Phila.	149	508	172	9	59	10	.339
*Alou, Pitts.	139	550	186	2	28	16	.338
Flood, St. L.	134	514	172	5	50	2	.335
†Staub, Houston	149	546	182	10	74	0	.333
Cepeda, St. Louis	151	563	183	25	111	11	.325
Allen, Phila.	122	463	142	23	77	20	.307
Aaron, Atlanta	155	600	184	39	109	17	.307
Wills, Pitts.	149	616	186	3	45	29	.302
Davis, New York	154	577	174	16	73	9	.302

INDIVDUAL PITCHING

Leaders—162 or More Innings

Pitcher—Club	G.	ip.	h.	bb.	so.	w.	l.	era.
Niekro, Atl.	46	207	164	55	129	11	9	1.87
Bunning, Phila.	40	302	241	73	253	17	15	2.29
Short, Phila.	29	199	163	74	142	9	11	2.40
*Nolan, Cin.	33	227	193	62	206	14	8	2.58
Perry, S. Fran	39	293	231	84	230	15	17	2.61
*Singer, L. A.	32	204	185	61	169	12	8	2.65
*Hughes, St. L.	37	222	164	48	159	16	6	2.68
Drysdale, L. A.	38	282	268	60	195	13	16	2.74
Johnson, Atl.	29	210	191	38	85	13	9	2.74

Individual Batting (over 100 at-bats) Individual Pitching (over 50 innings)

ATLANTA BRAVES

Batting

	g.	ab.	r.	h.	hr.	rbi	sb.	pct.
Aaron	155	600	113	184	39	109	17	.307
Torre	135	477	67	132	20	68	2	.277
Alou	140	574	76	157	15	43	6	.274
Carty	134	444	41	113	15	64	4	.255
†Jones	140	455	72	115	17	50	10	.253
Boyer	154	572	63	140	26	96	6	.245
†Francona	109	327	35	78	6	31	0	.239
Millan	41	136	13	32	2	6	0	.235
Menke	129	418	37	95	7	39	5	.227
Woodward	136	429	39	97	0	25	0	.226
de la Hoz	74	143	10	29	3	14	1	.203
†Geiger	69	117	17	19	1	5	1	.162
Uecker	80	193	17	29	3	20	0	.150

Pitching

	g.	cg.	ip.	h.	bb.	so.	w.	l.	era.
Niekro	46	10	207	164	55	129	11	9	1.87
Johnson	29	6	210	191	38	85	13	9	2.74
Raymond	49	0	65	64	18	30	4	5	2.91
Ritchie	52	0	82	75	29	58	4	6	3.07
†Lemaster	31	8	216	184	73	148	9	9	3.33
Jarvis	32	7	194	195	62	118	15	10	3.66
†Kelley	39	1	98	88	42	75	2	9	3.77
†*Hernandez	46	0	52	60	14	27	0	2	4.15
Cloninger	16	1	77	85	31	55	4	7	5.14
Carroll	42	1	93	110	29	35	6	12	5.52

CHICAGO CUBS

Batting

	g.	ab.	r.	h.	hr.	rbi.	sb.	pct.
Santo	161	586	107	176	31	98	1	.300
Beckert	146	597	91	167	5	40	10	.280
†Williams	162	634	92	176	28	84	7	.278
Banks	151	573	68	158	23	95	2	.276
Phillips	144	448	66	120	17	70	24	.268
Hundley	152	539	68	144	14	60	2	.267
†Spangler	62	130	18	33	0	13	2	.254
*Jones	53	135	13	32	2	16	0	.252
†Kessinger	145	580	61	134	0	42	6	.231
†Thomas	77	191	16	42	2	23	1	.220
Savage	105	233	41	50	5	33	7	.215
*Popovich	49	159	18	34	0	2	0	.214

CINCINNATI REDS

Batting

	g.	ab.	r.	h.	hr.	rbi	sb.	pct.
‡Rose	148	585	86	176	12	76	11	.301
Perez	156	600	78	174	26	102	0	.290
†Pinson	158	650	90	187	18	66	26	.288
Helms	137	497	40	136	2	35	5	.274
*May	127	438	54	116	12	57	4	.265
Cardenas	108	378	30	96	2	21	3	.254
Pavletich	74	231	25	55	6	34	2	.238
†Robinson	55	130	19	31	1	10	3	.238
Harper	103	365	55	82	7	22	23	.225
Johnson	108	361	39	81	13	53	0	.224
‡Ruiz	105	250	32	55	0	13	9	.220
†Edwards	80	210	10	44	2	20	1	.210
†Shamsky	75	146	6	29	3	13	0	.199

Pitching]

	g.	cg.	ip.	h.	bb.	so.	w.	l.	era.
Abernathy	70	0	106	63	38	87	6	3	1.27
Nottebart	47	0	79	75	20	46	0	3	1.94
*Nolan	33	8	227	193	62	206	14	8	2.58
Queen	31	6	196	155	53	155	14	8	2.76
†Arrigo	32	1	74	61	35	57	6	3	3.04
Maloney	30	6	196	151	72	152	15	11	3.26
Pappas	34	5	218	218	38	129	16	13	3.34
†McCool	31	0	97	92	56	83	3	6	3.43
Ellis	32	8	176	197	67	79	8	11	3.84
Lee	31	0	57	57	28	36	3	3	4.42

*Rookie   †Left handed   ‡Switch hitter

HOUSTON ASTROS

Batting

	g.	ab.	r.	h.	hr.	rbi.	sb.	pct
†Staub	149	546	71	182	10	74	0	.333
*Rader	47	162	24	54	2	26	0	.333
Aspromonte	137	486	51	143	6	58	2	.294
Gotay	77	234	30	66	2	15	1	.282
†Morgan	133	494	73	136	6	42	29	.275
Davis	94	285	31	73	7	38	5	.256
Landis	50	143	19	36	1	14	2	.252
Wynn	158	594	102	148	37	107	16	.249
Harrison	70	177	13	43	2	26	0	.243
Brand	84	215	22	52	0	18	4	.242
†Mathews	101	328	39	78	10	38	3	.238
†Jackson	129	520	67	123	0	25	22	.237
Brandt	57	108	8	23	1	16	0	.213
*†Miller	64	190	16	39	1	14	2	.205
Bateman	76	252	16	48	2	17	0	.190

Pitching

	g.	cg.	ip.	h.	bb.	so.	w.	l.	era.
*Wilson	31	7	184	141	69	159	10	9	2.79
†Cuellar	36	16	246	233	63	202	16	11	3.04
Dierker	15	4	99	95	25	68	6	5	3.36
Eilers	35	0	59	68	17	27	6	4	3.81
Giusti	37	8	222	231	58	158	11	15	4.18
Latman	39	0	78	73	34	69	3	6	4.62
†Schneider	54	0	53	60	27	37	0	2	4.75
†Belinsky	27	0	115	112	54	80	3	9	4.77
†Sembera	45	0	60	66	19	48	2	6	4.80
*Von Hoff	10	0	50	52	28	22	0	3	4.86
†Blasingame	25	0	102	118	48	66	5	7	5.65

LOS ANGELES DODGERS

Batting

	g.	ab.	r.	h.	hr.	rbi.	sb.	pct
Ferrara	122	347	41	96	16	50	0	.277
†Roseboro	114	334	37	91	4	24	2	.272
Johnson	104	330	39	89	11	41	4	.270
Hunt	110	388	44	102	3	33	2	.263
†Lefebvre	136	494	51	129	8	50	2	.261
†Gabrielson	90	238	20	62	7	29	3	.261
†Davis	143	570	65	146	6	41	20	.256
†Parker	139	413	56	102	5	31	10	.247
Oliver	76	231	18	55	0	7	3	.238
Bailey	115	322	21	73	4	28	5	.227
†Fairly	153	486	45	107	10	55	1	.220
†Schofield	84	232	23	50	2	15	1	.216
Torborg	76	196	11	42	2	12	1	.214
†Michael	97	223	20	45	0	7	1	.202

Pitching

	g.	cg.	ip.	h.	bb.	so.	w.	l.	era.
†Perranoski	70	0	110	98	44	75	6	7	2.45
*Singer	32	7	204	185	61	169	12	8	2.65
†Brewer	30	0	101	78	31	74	5	4	2.67
Drysdale	38	9	282	268	60	195	13	16	2.74
Regan	55	0	96	108	32	52	6	9	3.00
†Osteen	39	14	289	298	52	151	17	17	3.21
Sutton	37	11	233	223	57	169	11	15	3.94
Miller	53	0	86	88	28	32	2	9	4.29

NEW YORK METS

Batting

	g.	ab.	r.	h.	hr.	rbi.	sb.	pct
Johnson	90	230	27	80	5	27	1	.348
Davis	154	577	72	174	16	73	9	.302
Swoboda	134	448	48	126	13	53	3	.281
*Kranepool	140	469	37	126	10	54	0	.269
†Harrelson	151	539	59	137	1	28	12	.254
Jones	129	411	46	101	5	30	12	.246
†Stahl	70	155	8	37	1	18	2	.239
Charles	101	323	32	77	3	31	4	.238
Buchek	124	411	35	97	14	41	3	.236
Boyer	56	166	17	39	3	13	2	.235
†Sullivan	65	147	4	32	0	6	0	.218
†Reynolds	101	136	16	28	2	9	1	.206
Grote	120	344	24	67	4	23	1	.195

Pitching

	g.	cg.	ip.	h.	bb.	so.	w.	l.	era.
R. Taylor	50	0	73	60	23	46	4	6	2.34
*Seaver	35	18	251	224	80	171	16	13	2.76
Selma	38	0	81	71	36	52	2	4	2.89
*†D. Shaw	40	0	51	40	23	44	4	5	3.00
Reniff	29	0	43	42	23	21	3	3	3.14
*Frisella	14	0	74	68	33	51	1	6	3.41
Cardwell	26	3	118	112	39	70	5	9	3.58
Koonce	45	2	96	97	28	52	5	5	3.75
†Hendley	22	2	83	82	31	46	5	3	3.90
Fisher	39	7	220	251	64	117	9	18	4.70
*Denehy	15	0	54	51	31	34	1	7	4.83

PHILADELPHIA PHILLIES

Batting

	g.	ab.	r.	h.	hr.	rbi.	sb.	pct
†Gonsalez	149	508	74	172	9	59	10	.339
Allen	122	463	89	142	23	77	20	.307
†Callison	149	556	62	145	14	64	6	.261
Rojas	147	528	60	137	4	45	8	.259
Lock	112	313	46	79	14	51	5	.252
†White	110	308	29	77	8	33	6	.250
*Sutherland	103	231	23	57	1	19	0	.247
Taylor	132	462	55	110	2	34	10	.238
†Briggs	105	332	47	77	9	30	3	.232
Oliver	102	314	37	69	10	40	2	.220

(Philadelphia cont.)

Batting

	g.	ab.	r.	h.	hr.	rbi.	sb.	pct.
Wine	135	363	27	69	2	28	3	.190
†Dalrymple	101	268	12	46	3	21	1	.172

Pitching

	g.	cg.	ip.	h.	bb.	so.	w.	l.	era.
Hall	48	1	86	83	12	48	10	8	2.20
Bunning	40	16	302	241	73	253	17	15	2.29
Farrell	57	0	104	87	23	77	10	6	2.34
*Short	29	8	199	163	74	142	9	11	2.40
L. Jackson	40	11	262	242	54	139	13	15	3.09
Wise	36	6	181	177	45	111	11	11	3.28
†*G. Jackson	43	0	84	87	43	83	2	3	3.86
Boozer	28	1	75	86	24	48	5	4	4.08
*Ellsworth	32	3	125	152	36	44	6	7	4.39

PITTSBURGH PIRATES

Batting

	g.	ab.	r.	h.	hr.	rbi.	sb.	pct.
Clemente	147	585	103	209	23	110	9	.357
†Alou	139	550	87	186	2	28	16	.338
Mota	120	349	53	112	4	57	3	.321
†Wills	149	616	92	186	3	45	29	.302
Pagan	81	211	17	61	1	19	1	.289
Alley	152	550	59	158	6	55	10	.287
†Stargell	134	462	54	125	20	73	1	.271
May	110	325	23	88	3	22	0	.271
Mazeroski	163	640	62	167	9	77	1	.261
Clendenon	131	478	46	119	13	56	4	.249
Pagliaroni	44	100	4	20	0	9	0	.200
†Luplow	96	215	24	42	4	17	1	.195

Pitching

	g.	cg.	ip.	h.	bb.	so.	w.	l.	era.
Face	61	0	74	62	22	40	7	5	2.43
McBean	51	5	131	118	43	54	7	4	2.47
Sisk	37	11	208	196	78	84	13	13	3.33
Blass	32	2	126	126	46	73	6	8	3.57
†Veale	33	6	203	184	119	176	16	8	3.64
†Pizarro	50	1	107	99	53	95	8	10	4.04
†Fryman	28	3	113	121	44	74	3	8	4.06
Ribant	38	2	172	186	40	75	9	8	4.08
Law	25	1	97	122	18	42	2	6	4.18
†O'Dell	27	1	87	88	41	33	5	6	5.79

ST. LOUIS CARDINALS

Batting

	g.	ab.	r.	h.	hr.	rbi.	sb.	pct.
Flood	134	514	68	172	5	50	2	.335
Cepeda	151	563	91	183	25	111	11	.325
†Brock	159	689	113	206	21	76	52	.299
†McCarver	138	471	68	139	14	69	8	.295
Javier	140	520	68	134	14	64	6	.281
*Maris	125	410	64	107	9	55	0	.261
†Tolan	110	265	35	67	6	32	12	.253
Shannon	130	482	53	118	12	77	7	.245
Maxvill	152	476	37	108	1	41	0	.227
Johnson	81	175	19	39	1	12	6	.223
Gagliano	74	217	20	48	2	21	0	.221
Spiezio	55	105	9	22	3	10	2	.210

Pitching

	g.	cg.	ip.	h.	bb.	so.	w.	l.	era.
Briles	49	4	155	139	40	94	14	5	2.44
†Hoerner	57	0	66	52	21	49	4	4	2.59
*Willis	65	0	81	76	43	44	6	5	2.67
*Hughes	37	12	222	164	48	159	16	6	2.68
†Carlton	30	11	193	173	59	168	14	9	2.98
Gibson	24	10	175	151	40	147	13	7	2.98
†Jaster	34	2	152	141	45	87	9	7	3.02
Lamabe	39	1	79	67	17	52	3	7	3.30
Washburn	27	3	186	190	42	98	10	7	3.53
†Jackson	38	1	107	116	30	43	9	4	3.95

SAN FRANCISCO GIANTS

Batting

	g.	ab.	r.	h.	hr.	rbi.	sb.	pct.
Alou	129	510	55	149	5	30	1	.292
Hart	158	558	98	167	29	99	1	.289
†McCovey	135	456	73	126	31	91	3	.276
Davenport	124	295	42	81	5	30	1	.275
Hiatt	73	153	24	42	6	26	0	.275
Brown	120	412	44	110	13	53	0	.262
Mays	141	486	83	128	22	70	6	.263
†Cline	74	130	13	33	0	2	4	.254
†Haller	141	445	54	114	14	49	0	.251
Schroder	62	135	20	31	0	7	1	.230
†Etheridge	40	115	13	26	1	15	0	.226
*Dietz	56	120	10	27	4	19	0	.225
Lanier	151	525	37	112	0	42	2	.213
Fuentes	131	344	27	72	5	29	4	.209
†Henderson	65	179	15	34	4	14	0	.190

Pitching

	g.	cg.	ip.	h.	bb.	so.	w.	l.	era.
Linzy	57	0	96	67	34	38	7	7	1.50
Perry	39	18	293	231	84	230	15	17	2.61
Marichal	26	18	202	195	42	.166	14	10	2.76
*Sadecki	35	10	188	165	58	144	12	6	2.78
†McCormick	40	14	262	220	81	150	22	10	2.85
Herbel	42	1	126	125	35	52	4	5	3.07
†Gibbon	28	3	82	65	33	62	6	2	3.07
McDaniel	41	0	73	69	24	61	2	8	3.70
Bolin	37	0	120	119	50	69	6	8	4.88

*Rookie   †Left handed   ‡Switch hitter

American League Records, 1967
FINAL STANDING OF CLUBS

	Boston	Minnesota	Detroit	Chicago	California	Baltimore	Washington	Cleveland	New York	Kansas City	Won	Lost	Percentage	Games Behind
Boston *Red Sox*...........	—	7	9	8	10	10	11	13	12	12	92	70	.568	—
Minnesota *Twins*........	11	—	10	9	11	10	10	8	12	10	91	71	.562	1
Detroit *Tigers*...........	7	8	—	10	10	15	9	10	10	12	91	71	.562	1
Chicago *White Sox*.....	10	9	8	—	11	11	8	12	12	8	89	73	.549	3
California *Angels*.......	8	7	8	7	—	11	6	14	9	14	84	77	.522	7½
Baltimore *Orioles*........	10	8	3	7	6	—	10	9	13	10	76	85	.472	15½
Washington *Senators*...	7	8	9	10	12	8	—	5	6	11	76	85	.472	15½
Cleveland *Indians*.......	5	10	8	6	4	9	13	—	9	11	75	87	.463	17
New York *Yankees*.......	6	6	8	6	9	5	12	9	—	11	72	90	.444	20
Kansas City *Athletics*..	6	8	6	10	4	8	6	7	7	—	62	90	.385	29½

CLUB BATTING

	g.	ab.	r.	h.	hr.	sb.	pct.
Boston........	162	5471	722	1394	158	70	.255
Detroit........	163	5410	683	1315	152	38	.243
Baltimore......	161	5456	654	1312	138	54	.240
Minnesota.....	164	5458	671	1309	131	55	.240
California.....	161	5307	567	1265	114	42	.238
Cleveland.....	162	5402	589	¹²82	131	52	.235
Kansas City...	161	5350	533	1244	69	133	.233
New York......	163	5444	522	1225	100	63	.225
Chicago.......	162	5383	531	1209	89	125	.225
Washington....	161	5439	550	1211	115	53	.223

CLUB PITCHING

	g.	cg.	ip.	h.	r.	bb.	so.	era.
Chicago.....	162	36	1490	1196	491	466	926	2.45
Minnesota	164	58	1461	1335	590	397	1094	3.15
California..	161	19	1430	1246	587	526	887	3.19
New York..	163	37	1481	1375	621	480	895	3.23
Cleveland..	162	49	1478	1258	613	559	1185	3.24
Detroit.....	163	46	1443	1229	587	473	1034	3.31
Baltimore..	161	29	1457	1219	592	567	1036	3.32
Boston......	162	41	1459	1307	614	476	1006	3.37
Washington	161	24	1473	1334	637	495	975	3.40
Kansas City	161	27	1428	1265	660	556	988	3.69

INDIVIDUAL BATTING
Leaders—450 or More At Bats

Player—Club	G.	ab.	h.	hr.	rbi.	sb.	pct.
†Yastrzemski, Bos.	161	579	189	44	121	10	.326
F. Robinson, Balt.	129	479	149	30	94	2	.311
Kaline, Detroit...	131	458	141	25	78	8	.308
Scott, Boston....	159	565	171	19	82	11	.303
Blair, Baltimore..	151	552	162	11	64	8	.293
†*Carew, Minn...	137	514	150	8	51	5	.292
Fregosi, California	151	590	171	9	56	9	.290
†Oliva, Minnesota.	146	557	161	17	83	11	.289
Freehan, Detroit..	155	517	146	20	74	1	.282
†Mincher, Calif...	147	487	133	25	76	0	.273

Individual Batting (over 100 at-bats)

INDIVIDUAL PITCHING
Leaders—162 or More Innings

Pitcher—Club	g.	ip.	h.	bb.	so.	w.	l.	era.
Horlen, Chicago...	35	258	188	58	103	19	7	2.06
†Peters, Chicago..	38	260	187	91	215	16	11	2.28
Siebert, Cleveland.	34	185	136	54	136	10	12	2.34
†John, Chicago....	31	178	143	49	110	10	13	2.48
†Merritt, Minn...	37	228	195	30	161	13	7	2.53
*Clark, California.	32	174	144	69	82	12	11	2.59
Hargan, Cleveland.	30	223	180	72	141	14	13	2.62
†Downing, N. Y..	31	202	158	61	171	14	10	2.63
Tiant, Cleveland..	33	214	177	67	219	12	9	2.73
Stange, Boston...	35	182	171	32	101	8	10	2.77

Individual Pitching (over 50 innings)

BALTIMORE ORIOLES

Batting	g.	ab.	r.	h.	hr.	rbi.	sb.	pct.
F. Robinson...	129	479	83	149	30	94	2	.311
Blair.........	151	552	72	162	11	64	8	.293
B. Robinson..	158	610	88	164	22	77	4	.269
*Haney.......	58	164	13	44	3	20	1	.268
D. Johnson...	148	510	62	126	10	64	4	.247
†Blefary......	155	554	68	134	22	81	4	.242
†Powell......	125	415	53	97	13	55	1	.234
*Snyder......	107	274	41	64	4	25	5	.234
Aparicio.....	134	546	55	127	4	31	17	.233
Etchebarren..	112	330	29	71	7	35	2	.215
Bowens.......	62	120	13	22	5	12	3	.183
*Belanger....	69	184	19	32	1	10	6	.174

Pitching	g.	cg.	ip.	h.	bb.	so.	w.	l.	era.
Drabowsky..	43	0	95	66	27	93	7	5	1.61
Watt........	49	0	104	68	37	93	3	5	2.25
*Hardin....	19	5	111	85	27	64	8	3	2.27
S. Miller...	42	0	81	63	36	62	3	10	2.56
*Phoebus...	33	7	208	177	114	179	14	9	3.33
Brabender..	14	3	94	77	23	71	6	4	3.35
†Richert....	37	6	187	156	56	132	9	16	4.37
E. Fisher...	46	0	90	82	26	55	4	3	3.60
Buzhardt...	35	0	100	114	42	40	3	10	3.96
Bunker......	29	1	88	83	30	51	3	7	4.09
*Dillman....	32	2	124	114	33	69	5	9	4.35
†McNally....	24	3	119	134	39	70	7	7	4.54

BOSTON RED SOX

Batting	g.	ab.	r.	h.	hr.	rbi.	sb.	pct.
†Yastrzemski..	161	579	112	189	44	121	10	.326
Scott.........	159	565	74	171	19	82	11	.303
†Jones........	89	159	18	46	3	25	0	.289
Conigliaro....	95	349	59	100	20	67	3	.287
Adair.........	117	414	47	112	3	35	2	.271
*Andrews.....	142	494	79	130	8	40	7	.263
Petrocelli....	142	491	53	127	17	66	2	.259
Harrelson.....	110	333	42	85	12	54	10	.255
Foy...........	130	446	70	112	16	49	8	.251
‡R. Smith.....	158	565	78	139	15	61	17	.246
†Tartabull....	113	247	36	55	0	10	6	.223
*Gibson......	50	138	8	28	1	15	0	.203
Ryan.........	79	226	21	45	2	27	2	.199
Howard.......	108	315	22	56	4	28	0	.178

CALIFORNIA ANGELS

Batting	g.	ab.	r.	h.	hr.	rbi.	sb.	pct.
Morton.......	79	201	23	63	0	32	0	.313
Fregosi......	151	590	75	171	9	56	9	.290
†Mincher.....	147	487	81	133	25	76	0	.273
Reichardt....	146	498	56	132	17	69	6	.265
†Hall........	129	401	54	100	16	54	4	.249
†Repoz.......	113	263	34	65	7	28	6	.247
Knoop........	159	511	51	125	9	37	2	.245
*Rodriguez...	29	130	14	31	1	8	1	.238
Cardinal.....	108	381	40	90	6	27	10	.236
†Satriano....	90	201	13	45	4	21	1	.224
‡Rodgers.....	138	429	29	94	4	41	1	.219
†Johnstone...	78	230	17	48	2	10	4	.209
Skowron......	70	131	8	27	1	11	0	.206
Held.........	84	182	19	37	5	23	0	.203
Schaal.......	99	272	32	51	6	20	2	.188

Pitching	g.	cg.	ip.	h.	bb.	so.	w.	l.	era.
Rojas........	72	0	122	106	39	83	12	9	2.43
*Clark.......	32	1	174	144	69	82	12	11	2.59
McGlothlin...	32	9	197	163	56	137	12	8	2.97
*Kelso.......	69	0	112	85	63	91	5	3	3.13
Cimino.......	46	0	88	73	31	78	3	3	3.17
Hamilton.....	26	0	119	104	63	74	9	6	3.25
†Wright......	20	1	77	76	24	35	5	5	3.27
†Brunet......	40	7	250	203	90	164	11	19	3.31
Coates.......	25	0	52	47	23	39	1	2	4.33

CHICAGO WHITE SOX

‡Batting	g.	ab.	r.	h.	hr.	rbi.	sb.	pct.
Boyer........	57	180	17	47	4	21	0	.261
‡Buford......	156	535	61	129	4	32	34	.241

BOSTON RED SOX (cont.)

Pitching	g.	cg.	ip.	h.	bb.	so.	w.	l.	era.
Osinski......	34	0	64	61	14	38	-3	1	2.53
Wyatt........	60	0	93	71	39	68	10	7	2.61
Stange.......	35	6	182	171	32	101	8	10	2.77
Lonborg......	39	15	273	228	83	245	22	9	3.16
Bell.........	38	9	226	193	71	154	13	13	3.31
Santiago.....	50	2	145	138	46	109	12	4	3.66
†Bennett.....	13	4	70	72	22	34	4	3	3.86
Brandon......	39	2	158	147	59	94	5	11	4.16

*Rookie   †Left handed   ‡Switch hitter

CHICAGO WHITE SOX (cont.)

Batting	g.	ab.	r.	h.	hr.	rbi.	sb.	pct.
Berry........	146	486	49	117	7	41	9	.241
*Williams....	104	275	35	66	3	15	3	.240
*Josephson...	63	189	11	45	1	9	0	.238
†McCraw.....	125	453	55	107	11	45	25	.236
†Martin.....	100	251	22	59	4	22	3	.235
Agee........	158	529	73	124	14	53	28	.234
†Ward.......	146	467	49	109	18	62	3	.233
Hansen......	157	499	35	116	8	51	0	.232
Colavito....	122	381	30	88	8	50	3	.231
McNertney...	56	123	8	28	3	13	0	.228
†Causey.....	124	292	21	66	1	28	2	.226

Pitching	g.	cg.	ip.	h.	bb.	so.	w.	l.	era.
Wilhelm.....	49	0	89	58	33	76	8	3	1.31
McMahon.....	63	0	109	68	40	83	6	2	1.98
Horlen......	35	13	258	188	58	103	19	7	2.06
Locker......	77	0	125	102	23	81	7	5	2.09
†Peters.....	38	11	260	187	91	215	16	11	2.28
†Wood.......	51	0	95	94	26	46	4	2	2.46
†John.......	31	9	178	143	49	110	10	13	2.48
†O'Toole....	15	1	54	53	18	37	4	3	2.83
Howard......	30	1	113	102	52	76	3	10	3.42

CLEVELAND INDIANS

Batting	g.	ab.	r.	h.	hr.	rbi.	sb.	pct.
†Davalillo..	139	359	47	103	2	22	6	.287
Horton......	127	401	37	114	10	53	3	.284
†Maye.......	115	298	43	77	9	27	3	.258
Alvis.......	161	637	66	163	21	70	3	.256
Azcue.......	86	295	33	74	11	34	0	.251
Hinton......	147	497	55	122	10	37	6	.245
†Wagner.....	135	433	56	105	15	54	3	.242
Salmon......	89	202	19	46	2	19	0	.228
Gonsales....	80	189	19	43	1	8	4	.228
Brown.......	152	485	39	110	7	37	4	.227
Demeter.....	71	164	22	37	6	16	0	.226
*Fuller.....	73	206	17	46	7	21	2	.223
†Whitfield..	100	258	24	56	9	31	3	.217
†Sims.......	88	272	25	55	12	37	2	.202
†King.......	88	170	14	30	1	14	1	.176

Pitching	g.	cg.	ip.	h.	bb.	so.	w.	l.	era.
Siebert.....	34	7	185	136	54	136	10	12	2.34
Hargan......	30	15	223	180	72	141	14	13	2.62
Williams....	16	2	79	64	24	75	6	4	2.62
Tiant.......	33	9	214	177	67	219	12	9	2.73
†Allen......	47	0	54	49	24	50	0	5	3.00
†O'Donoghue.	33	5	131	120	33	80	8	9	3.23
Pena........	50	0	91	73	22	73	4	4	3.56
†McDowell...	37	10	236	201	123	236	13	15	3.85
*Bailey.....	32	0	65	62	42	46	2	3	3.88
*Culver.....	53	0	75	71	32	40	7	3	3.96

DETROIT TIGERS

Batting	g.	ab.	r.	h.	hr.	rbi.	sb.	pct.
Kaline......	131	458	94	141	25	78	8	.308
Tracewski...	71	106	19	30	1	9	1	.283
Freehan.....	155	517	66	146	20	74	1	.282
†Green......	58	151	22	42	1	13	1	.278
Horton......	122	401	47	110	19	67	0	.274
†Northrup...	144	495	63	134	10	61	7	.271
Wert........	142	533	60	137	6	41	0	.257
†Cash.......	152	488	64	118	22	72	4	.242
†McAuliffe..	153	557	92	133	22	65	6	.239
†Lumpe......	79	177	19	41	4	17	0	.232
†Mathews....	36	108	14	25	6	19	0	.231
Stanley.....	145	334	38	70	7	25	9	.210
Oyler.......	148	368	33	76	1	24	2	.207

Pitching	g.	cg.	ip.	h.	bb.	so.	w.	l.	era.
*Marshall...	37	0	59	51	20	41	1	3	1.83
Gladding....	41	0	76	60	19	63	6	4	2.01
†*Hiller....	23	2	65	57	9	49	4	3	2.63
Wickersham..	36	0	85	72	34	43	4	5	2.75
†Lolich.....	31	11	204	165	56	174	14	13	3.04
Wilson......	39	12	264	216	92	184	22	11	3.27
Sparma......	37	11	218	186	85	152	16	9	3.76
McLain......	37	10	235	209	73	160	17	16	3.79
†Podres.....	21	0	63	58	11	34	3	1	3.86

KANSAS CITY ATHLETICS

Batting	g.	ab.	r.	h.	hr.	rbi.	sb.	pct.
†*Donaldson.	105	377	27	104	0	28	6	.276
Cater.......	142	529	54	143	4	46	4	.270
*Webster....	122	360	41	92	11	50	5	.256
Hershberger.	142	480	55	122	1	40	10	.254
†*Monday....	124	406	52	102	14	58	3	.251
Campaneris..	147	601	85	149	3	32	55	.248
†Gosger.....	133	356	31	86	5	36	5	.242
Roof........	114	327	23	67	6	24	4	.205
Nossek......	88	166	12	34	0	10	2	.205
Green.......	121	350	26	69	5	37	6	.197
*Bando......	47	130	11	25	0	6	1	.192
Duncan......	34	101	9	19	5	11	0	.188
†*Jackson...	35	118	13	21	1	6	2	.178
‡*Kubiak....	52	102	6	16	0	5	3	.157

*Rookie   †Left handed   ‡Switch hitter

KANSAS CITY ATHLETICS (cont.)

Pitching	g.	cg.	ip.	h.	bb.	so.	w.	l.	era.
Hunter......	35	13	260	209	84	196	13	17	2.80
Segui.......	36	0	70	62	31	52	3	4	2.94
†*Pierce....	49	0	98	79	30	51	3	4	3.03
†Lindblad...	46	1	116	106	35	83	5	8	3.57
Dobson......	32	4	198	172	75	111	10	10	3.68
Nash........	37	9	222	200	87	187	12	17	3.85
Krausse.....	48	0	160	140	65	95	7	17	4.28
Aker........	57	0	88	87	32	64	3	8	4.30
Odom........	29	0	104	94	68	65	3	8	5.02
Sanford.....	22	0	70	77	21	34	4	4	5.14

MINNESOTA TWINS

Batting	g.	ab.	r.	h.	hr.	rbi.	sb.	pct.
†*Carew.....	137	514	66	150	8	51	5	.292
†Oliva......	146	557	76	161	17	83	11	.289
Killebrew...	163	547	105	147	44	113	1	.269
Tovar.......	164	649	98	173	6	47	19	.267
Allison.....	153	496	74	128	24	76	6	.258
†Uhlaender..	133	415	41	107	6	49	4	.258
*Reese......	95	101	13	25	4	20	0	.248
Rollins.....	109	339	31	83	6	39	1	.245
†Nixon......	74	170	18	40	1	22	0	.235
Versalles...	160	581	63	116	6	50	5	.200
Zimmerman...	104	234	13	39	1	12	0	.167
Battey......	48	109	6	18	0	8	0	.165

Pitching	g.	cg.	ip.	h.	bb.	so.	w.	l.	era.
†Merritt....	37	11	228	195	30	161	13	7	2.53
Chance......	41	18	284	244	68	220	20	14	2.79
Worthington.	59	0	92	77	38	80	8	9	2.84
Perry.......	37	3	131	123	50	95	8	7	3.02
†Kaat.......	43	13	263	269	42	211	16	13	3.05
Boswell.....	37	11	223	162	107	205	14	12	3.27
Kline.......	54	0	72	71	15	36	7	1	3.63
Grant.......	27	2	95	121	18	50	5	6	4.74

NEW YORK YANKEES

Batting	g.	ab.	r.	h.	hr.	rbi.	sb.	pct.
‡Clarke.....	143	588	74	160	3	29	21	.272
Howser......	63	149	18	40	0	10	1	.268
†Pepitone...	133	502	45	126	13	64	1	.251
†Mantle.....	144	440	63	108	22	55	1	.245
†Whitaker...	122	441	37	107	11	50	2	.243
†Gibbs......	116	374	33	87	4	25	7	.233
‡White......	70	214	22	48	2	18	10	.224
Smith.......	135	426	38	95	9	38	0	.223
Amaro.......	131	417	31	93	1	17	3	.223
Tillman.....	52	127	9	28	3	13	0	.220
‡Tresh......	130	448	45	98	14	53	1	.219
*Robinson...	116	341	31	67	7	29	3	.196
Kennedy.....	79	179	22	35	1	17	2	.196
†*Hegan.....	68	118	12	16	1	3	7	.136

Pitching	g.	cg.	ip.	h.	bb.	so.	w.	l.	era.
Monbouquette.	35	2	135	123	17	54	6	5	2.33
Womack......	65	0	97	80	35	57	5	6	2.41
†Downing....	31	10	202	158	61	171	14	10	2.63
†Verbanic...	28	1	80	74	21	38	4	3	2.81
Stottlemyre.	36	10	255	235	88	151	15	15	2.96
†Peterson...	36	6	181	179	43	101	8	14	3.33
†Hamilton...	44	0	62	57	23	56	2	4	3.48
†Tillotson..	43	1	98	99	39	64	3	9	4.04
†Barber.....	32	4	172	150	115	116	10	18	4.08
Talbot......	29	2	139	132	54	60	6	8	4.21

WASHINGTON SENATORS

Batting	g.	ab.	r.	h.	hr.	rbi.	sb.	pct.
Howard......	149	519	71	133	36	89	0	.256
Casanova....	141	528	47	131	9	53	1	.248
McMullen....	146	563	73	138	16	67	5	.245
†Peterson...	122	405	35	97	8	46	0	.240
†Cullen.....	123	402	35	95	2	32	4	.236
‡Saverine...	89	233	32	55	0	9	8	.236
†Valentine..	151	456	52	107	11	44	17	.235
*H. Allen...	116	292	34	68	3	17	3	.233
†Epstein....	105	297	32	67	9	29	1	.226
†Nen........	109	238	21	52	6	29	0	.218
†*Stroud....	106	231	42	49	1	13	15	.212
‡B. Allen...	87	254	13	49	3	18	1	.193
Brinkman....	109	320	21	60	1	18	1	.188

Pitching	g.	cg.	ip.	h.	bb.	so.	w.	l.	era.
†Baldwin....	58	6	89	53	20	52	2	4	1.70
Bosman......	7	2	51	38	10	25	3	1	1.76
†Knowles....	61	0	113	91	52	86	6	8	2.71
Cox.........	54	0	73	67	21	32	7	4	2.71
Ortega......	34	5	220	189	57	121	10	10	3.03
†Bertaina...	23	4	117	107	51	87	7	5	3.08
Pascual.....	28	5	165	147	43	106	12	10	3.27
Priddy......	46	1	110	98	33	57	3	7	3.44
†Lines......	54	0	86	83	24	55	2	5	3.56
†*Moore.....	27	3	144	127	71	74	7	11	3.75
Humphreys...	39	0	93	93	41	55	6	2	4.26
*Coleman....	28	3	134	154	47	77	8	9	4.77

Major League No-Hit Games Since 1935
(Complete Nine-inning Games)

Date	Pitcher	Club	Score
1934—Sept. 18	Bobo Newsom (1)	St. Louis-Boston A	1-2
1934—Sept. 21	Paul Dean	St. Louis-Brooklyn N. (2nd game)	3-0
1935—Aug. 31	Vern Kennedy	Chicago-Cleveland A	5-0
1937—June 1	Bill Dietrich	Chicago-St. Louis A	8-0
1938—June 11	Johnny Vander Meer	Cincinnati-Boston N	3-0
1938—June 15	Johnny Vander Meer	Cincinnati-Brooklyn N. (night game)	6-0
1938—Aug. 27	Monte Pearson	New York-Cleveland A. (2nd game)	13-0
1940—April 16	Bob Feller (2)	Cleveland-Chicago A	1-0
1940—April 30	Tex Carleton	Brooklyn-Cincinnati N	3-0
1941—Aug. 30	Lon Warneke	St. Louis-Cincinnati N	2-0
1944—April 27	Jim Tobin	Boston-Brooklyn N	2-0
1944—May 15	Clyde Shoun	Cincinnati-Boston N	1-0
1945—Sept. 9	Dick Fowler	Philadelphia-St. Louis A	1-0
1946—April 23	Ed Head	Brooklyn-Boston N	5-0
1946—April 30	Bob Feller	Cleveland-New York A	1-0
1947—June 18	Ewell Blackwell	Cincinnati-Boston N. (night game)	6-0
1947—July 10	Don Black	Cleveland-Philadelphia A	3-0
1947—Sept. 3	Bill McCahan	Philadelphia-Washington A	3-0
1948—June 30	Bob Lemon	Cleveland-Detroit A	2-0
1948—Sept. 9	Rex Barney	Brooklyn-New York N. (night game)	2-0
1950—Aug. 11	Vern Bickford	Boston-Brooklyn N. (night game)	7-0
1951—May 6	Cliff Chambers	Pittsburgh-Boston N. (2nd game)	3-0
1951—July 1	Bob Feller	Cleveland-Detroit A. (1st game)	2-1
1951—July 12	Allie Reynolds	New York-Cleveland A. (night game)	1-0
1951—Sept. 28	Allie Reynolds	New York-Boston A. (first game)	8-0
1952—May 15	Virgil Trucks	Detroit-Washington A	1-0
1952—June 19	Carl Erskine	Brooklyn-Chicago N	5-0
1952—Aug. 25	Virgil Trucks	Detroit-New York A	1-0
1953—May 6	Bobo Holloman	St. Louis-Philadelphia A (night game)	6-0
1954—June 12	Jim Wilson	Milwaukee-Philadelphia N	2-0
1955—May 12	Sam Jones	Chicago-Pittsburgh N	4-0
1956—May 12	Carl Erskine	Brooklyn-New York N	3-0
1956—July 14	Mel Parnell	Boston-Chicago A	4-0
1956—Sept. 25	Sal Maglie	Brooklyn-Philadelphia N. (night game)	5-0
1956—Oct. 8	Don Larsen (3)	New York-Brooklyn N	2-0
1957—Aug. 20	Bob Keegan	Chicago-Washington A	6-0
1958—July 20	Jim Bunning	Detroit-Boston A	3-0
1958—Sept. 20	Hoyt Wilhelm	Baltimore-New York A	1-0
1959—May 26	Harvey Haddix (4)	Pittsburgh-Milwaukee N	0-2
1960—May 15	Don Cardwell	Chicago-St. Louis N. (2nd game)	4-0
1960—Aug. 18	Lew Burdette	Milwaukee-Philadelphia N	1-0
1960—Sept. 16	Warren Spahn	Milwaukee-Philadelphia N	4-0
1961—April 28	Warren Spahn	Milwaukee-San Francisco N. (night)	1-0
1962—May 5	Bo Belinsky	Los Angeles-Baltimore A (night game)	2-0
1962—June 26	Earl Wilson	Boston-Los Angeles A (night game)	2-0
1962—June 30	Sandy Koufax	Los Angeles-New York N (night game)	5-0
1962—Aug. 1	Bill Monbouquette	Boston-Chicago A (night game)	1-0
1962—Aug. 26	Jack Kralick	Minnesota-Kansas City A	1-0
1963—May 11	Sandy Koufax	Los Angeles-San Francisco N (night)	8-0
1963—May 17	Don Nottebart	Houston-Philadelphia N. (night)	4-1
1963—June 15	Juan Marichal	San Francisco-Houston N	1-0
1964—April 23	Ken Johnson (5)	Houston-Cincinnati N	0-1
1964—June 4	Sandy Koufax	Los Angeles-Philadelphia N	3-0
1964—June 21	Jim Bunning (6)	Philadelphia-New York N	6-0
1965—June 14	Jim Maloney (7)	Cincinnati-New York N (night)	0-1
1965—Aug. 19	Jim Maloney (8)	Cincinnati-Chicago N (1st game)	1-0
1965—Sept. 9	Sandy Koufax (6)	Los Angeles-Chicago N	1-0
1965—Sept. 16	Dave Morehead	Boston-Cleveland A	2-0
1966—June 10	Sonny Siebert	Cleveland-Washington A (night)	2-0
1967—Apr. 30	S. Barber, Stu Miller (9)	Baltimore-Detroit A	0-2
1967—June 18	Don Wilson	Houston-Atlanta N	2-0
1967—Aug. 25	Dean Chance	Minnesota-Cleveland A	2-1
1967—Sept. 10	Joe Horlen	Chicago-Detroit A	6-0

(1) Newsom pitched nine hitless innings, then allowed one hit in tenth. (2) Opening game of season. (3) Perfect game and first World Series no-hitter, no one reaching first base. (4) Haddix became the first modern major league pitcher to carry a perfect game beyond nine innings. He allowed one hit in the 13th and lost the game. (5) Lost game on two errors in ninth inning. (6) Perfect game. (7) Maloney pitched ten hitless innings, then allowed two hits in the eleventh. Struck out eighteen batters. (8) Ten innings. (9) Barber pitched 8⅔ innings, Miller ⅓ of an inning. Detroit scored two 9th-inning runs on a wild pitch and an error.

Professional Baseball Government

William D. Eckert, a retired lieutenant general of the United States Air Force, was elected commissioner of baseball Nov. 17, 1965, for a 7-year-term at an annual salary of $65,000. He succeeded Commissioner Ford C. Frick, who retired after serving in the post since 1952.

Commissioner—William D. Eckert.
Administrator—John J. McHale.
Secretary-Treasurer—Charles Segar.
Director of Public Relations—Joseph L. Reichler.
Office—680 Fifth Ave., New York, N. Y. 10019.

NATIONAL LEAGUE
President, secretary, treasurer—Warren C. Giles.
Director of Public Relations—David J. Grote.
Office—2601 Carew Tower, Cincinnati, Ohio.

AMERICAN LEAGUE
Pres. sec., treas.—Joseph Edward Cronin.
Director Public Relations—Bob Holbrook.
Office—520 Boylston Street, Boston 16, Mass.

NATIONAL ASSOCIATION
President—Philip Piton.
Director, Public Relations—Daniel F. O'Brien.
Office—720 East Broad Street, Columbus 15, Ohio.

1967 AMATEUR SOFTBALL ASSOCIATION

Division	Championship Site	Champion
Men's Fast Pitch	Springfield, Mo.	Sealmasters, Aurora, Ill.
Women's Fast Pitch	Stratford, Conn.	Brakettes, Stratford, Conn.
Men's Open Slow Pitch	Parma, Ohio	Jim's Sports, Pittsburgh, Penn.
Men's Industrial Slow	Jones Beach, N. Y.	Grumman Aircraft, Bethpage, N. Y.
Women's Slow Pitch	Sheboygan, Wisc.	Ridge Maintenance, Cleveland, O.
16" Slow Pitch	Chicago, Ill.	Sobies, Chicago, Ill.

Cy Young Award Winners

1956—Don Newcombe, Dodgers	1961—Whitey Ford, Yankees	1966—Sandy Koufax, Dodgers
1957—Warren Spahn, Braves	1962—Don Drysdale, Dodgers	1967—(NL) Mike McCormick, Giants
1958—Bob Turley, Yankees	1963—Sandy Koufax, Dodgers	(AL) Jim Lonborg, Red Sox
1959—Early Wynn, White Sox	1964—Dean Chance, Angels	
1960—Vernon Law, Pirates	1965—Sandy Koufax, Dodgers	

Home Run Distances in Baseball Parks

AMERICAN LEAGUE					NATIONAL LEAGUE				
Team	Name of park	Ft. from plate to fence			Team	Name of park	Ft. from plate to fence		
		RF	CF	LF			RF	CF	LF
New York.....	Yankee Stadium....	296	461	301	Atlanta.........	Atlanta Stadium....	330	402	330
Boston........	Fenway Park......	302	420	315	New York.....	Shea Stadium......	341	410	341
Cleveland.....	Municipal Stadium.	320	408	320	Houston......	Astrodome........	340	406	340
Detroit.......	Tiger Stadium.....	325	440	340	San Francisco..	Candlestick Park...	335	410	335
Chicago.......	White Sox Park....	352	415	352	Los Angeles....	Dodger Stadium....	330	410	330
Baltimore.....	Memorial Stadium..	309	410	309	Chicago.......	Wrigley Field......	353	400	355
Kansas City...	Municipal Stadium.	388	421	370	Pittsburgh.....	Forbes Field......	300	457	365
Minnesota....	Metropolitan Stad..	330	425	346	Cincinnati.....	Crosley Field......	366	387	328
California.....	Anaheim Stadium..	333	406	333	St. Louis......	Busch Mem. Stad...	330	414	330
Washington...	D. C. Stadium.....	335	410	335	Philadelphia....	Connie Mack Stad..	329	447	334

Baseball Parks Seating Capacity

Astrodome (Houston, Tex.)................	46,000	Forbes Field, Pittsburgh, Pa.............	35,000
Anaheim Stadium........................	44,500	Kansas City (Mo.) Municipal Stadium (a)..	32,561
Atlanta (Ga.), Stadium...................	50,893	Metropolitan Sta., Bloomington, Minn.....	45,182
Baltimore (Md.), Memorial Stadium........	52,184	Milwaukee County Stadium (a)...........	43,826
Busch Memorial Stadium, St. Louis, Mo....	49,450	Oakland-Alameda County Coliseum.......	53,000
Candlestick Park, San Francisco..........	42,500	Shea Sta., Queens, N. Y. C.............	55,300
Cleveland (Ohio) Municipal Stadium.......	74,056	Tiger Stadium, Detroit, Mich............	53,089
Connie Mack Stad., Philadelphia, Pa......	33,604	Washington (D. C.) Stadium.............	45,016
Crosley Field, Cincinnati, Ohio...........	29,468	White Sox Park, Chicago, Ill............	46,550
Dodger Stadium, (Chavez Ravine), L. A....	56,000	Wrigley Field, Chicago, Ill..............	36,644
Fenway Park, Boston, Mass..............	33,524	Yankee Stadium, New York, N. Y.........	67,000

(a) Currently without major league team.

Longest Games Played in the Major Leagues

NATIONAL LEAGUE—26 INNINGS, Boston, May 1, 1920

		R	H	E
Brooklyn	...........0 0 0 0 1 0 0 0 0 0 0 0 0 0 0 0 0 0 0 0 0 0 0 0 0 0—1	9	2
Boston	...........0 0 0 0 0 1 0 0 0 0 0 0 0 0 0 0 0 0 0 0 0 0 0 0 0 0—1	15	2

Game called on account of darkness after 3 hours and 50 minutes of play.
Batteries: Cadore and Krueger; Elliott; Oeschger and O'Neill, Gowdy.

AMERICAN LEAGUE—24 INNINGS, Boston, Sept. 1, 1906

		R	H	E
Philadelphia	..........0 0 1 0 0 0 0 0 0 0 0 0 0 0 0 0 0 0 0 0 0 0 3—4	16	2
Boston	..........0 0 0 0 0 1 0 0 0 0 0 0 0 0 0 0 0 0 0 0 0 0 0—1	15	1

Time of game 4 hours 47 minutes. Batteries—Coombs and Powers; Harris and Carrigan and Criger.

AMERICAN LEAGUE—24 INNINGS, Philadelphia, July 21, 1945

		R	H	E
Detroit	...........0 0 0 0 0 1 0 0 0 0 0 0 0 0 0 0 0 0 0 0 0 0 0—1	11	3
Philadelphia	...........0 0 1 0 0 0 0 0 0 0 0 0 0 0 0 0 0 0 0 0 0 0 0—1	16	1

Time of game, 4 hours 48 minutes; called on account of darkness. Batteries—Mueller (19⅔ innings),
Trout (4⅓) and Swift; Christopher (13), Berry (11) and Rosar.

LONGEST SCORELESS TIE—NATIONAL LEAGUE—19 INNINGS, Brooklyn, N. Y.
Sept. 11, 1946

		R	H	E
Cincinnati	.............0 0 0 0 0 0 0 0 0 0 0 0 0 0 0 0 0 0 0—0	10	2
Brooklyn	.............0 0 0 0 0 0 0 0 0 0 0 0 0 0 0 0 0 0 0—0	8	1

Game called on account of darkness after 4 hours and 40 minutes of play.
The Pittsburgh Pirates and the Boston Braves (National League) played 20 scoreless innings,
Aug. 1, 1918, before Pittsburgh won in the 21st inning, 2 to 0.

LONGEST SCORELESS TIE—AMERICAN LEAGUE—18 INNINGS—Detroit versus
Washington, July 16, 1909.

LONGEST 9-INNING GAME—4 Hrs. 52 Min.—Los Angeles, Calif., Oct. 2, 1962.

The longest nine-inning game in major league baseball history—4 hours 52 minutes—was played in
Chavez Ravine Stadium, Los Angeles, Calif., Oct. 2, 1962, between the San Francisco Giants and
the Los Angeles Dodgers in the second of three play-off games for the National League pennant. The
Dodgers won, 8-7.

**LONGEST DOUBLE-HEADER AND EXTRA-INNING GAME BY TIME—10 hrs. 23
Min.**—New York, N. Y., May 31, 1964.

The longest double-header in major league history—10 hours 23 minutes, including intermission time
—was played May 31, 1964, by the New York Mets and San Francisco Giants (N. L.). The Mets lost
to the Giants 8-6 in the 23rd inning of the second game which lasted 7 hours 23 minutes, longest game
by time in the major leagues. The Giants had scored a 5-3 victory in 2 hours 29 minutes in the first
game.

Rookie of the Year Award

Source: Baseball Writers' Assn.
1947—Combined Selection—Jackie Robinson, Brooklyn, 1b
1948—Combined Selection—Alvin Dark, Boston, N. L., ss

Year	National League	Year	American League
1949—Don Newcombe, Brooklyn, p		1949—Roy Sievers, St. Louis, of	
1950—Sam Jethroe, Boston, of		1950—Walt Dropo, Boston, 1b	
1951—Willie Mays, N. Y., of		1951—Gil McDougald, N. Y., 3b	
1952—Joe Black, Brooklyn, p		1952—Harry Byrd, Phil., p	
1953—Jim Gilliam, Brooklyn, 2b		1953—Harvey Kuenn, Detroit, ss	
1954—Wally Moon, St. Louis, of		1954—Bob Grim, N. Y., p	
1955—Bill Virdon, St. Louis, of		1955—Herb Score, Cleveland, p	
1956—Frank Robinson, Cinn., of		1956—Luis Aparicio, Chicago, ss	
1957—Jack Sanford, Phil., p		1957—Tony Kubek, N. Y., if-of	
1958—Orlando Cepeda, S. F., 1b		1958—Albie Pearson, Wash., of	
1959—Willie McCovey, S. F., 1b		1959—Bob Allison, Wash., of	
1960—Frank Howard, Los Angeles, of		1960—Ron Hansen, Balt., ss	
1961—Billy Williams, Chicago, of		1961—Don Schwall, Boston, p	
1962—Ken Hubbs, Chicago, 2b		1962—Tom Tresh, N. Y., if-of	
1963—Pete Rose, Cinn., 2b		1963—Gary Peters, Chicago, p	
1964—Richie Allen, Phil., 3b		1964—Tony Oliva, Minn., of	
1965—Jim Lefebvre, L. A., 2b		1965—Curt Blefary, Balt., of	
1966—Tommy Helms, Cinn., 3b		1966—Tommie Agee, Chicago, of	

Boxing Champions by Classes

Heavyweight .... *Vacant*
Light-Heavyweight (175 lbs.) .... Dick Tiger, Nigeria
Middleweight (160 lbs.) .... Emile Griffith, New York, N. Y.
Welterweight (147 lbs.) .... Curtis Cokes, Dallas, Tex.
Junior Welterweight (140 lbs.) .... Paul Fujii, Honolulu
Lightweight (135 lbs.) .... Carlos Ortiz, New York, N. Y.
Junior Lightweight (130 lbs.) .... Yoshiaki Numata, Japan
Featherweight (126 lbs.) .... Vincente Saldivar, Mexico
Bantamweight (118 lbs.) .... Fighting Harada, Japan
Flyweight (112 lbs.) .... Chartchai Chionoi, Thailand

Ring Champions by Years

HEAVYWEIGHTS

1882-1892	John L. Sullivan (A)
1892-1897	James J. Corbett (B)
1897-1899	Robert Fitzsimmons
1899-1905	James J. Jeffries (C)
1905-1906	Marvin Hart
1906-1908	Tommy Burns
1908-1915	Jack Johnson
1915-1919	Jess Willard
1919-1926	Jack Dempsey
1926-1928	Gene Tunney*
1928-1930	Vacant
1930-1932	Max Schmeling
1932	Jack Sharkey
1933	Primo Carnera
1934	Max Baer
1935-1936	James J. Braddock
1937-1949	Joe Louis*
1949-1951	Ezzard Charles
1951-1952	Joe Walcott
1952-1956	Rocky Marciano* (D)
1956-1959	Floyd Patterson
1959	Ingemar Johansson
1960-1962	Floyd Patterson
1962-1963	Sonny Liston
1964-1967	Cassius Clay* (E)

(A) London Prize Ring (bare knuckle champion).
(B) First Marquis of Queensberry Champion.
(C) Jeffries abandoned the title (1905) and designated Marvin Hart and Jack Root as logical contenders and agreed to referee a fight between them, the winner to be declared champion. Hart defeated Root in 12 rounds (1905) and in turn was defeated by Tommy Burns (1906) who immediately laid claim to the title. Jack Johnson defeated Burns (1908) and was recognized as champion. He clinched the title by defeating Jeffries in an attempted comeback (1910).
(D) After Marciano's retirement Apr. 27, 1956, Archie Moore claimed the heavyweight title. A series of eliminations began to determine Marciano's successor, ending when Floyd Patterson knocked out Archie Moore in the 5th round, Chicago, Ill., Nov. 30, 1956.
(E) Title declared vacant by the World Boxing Assn. and other groups in 1967 after Clay's refusal to fulfill his military obligation.

LIGHT HEAVYWEIGHTS

1903	Jack Root, George Gardner
1903-1905	Bob Fitzsimmons
1905-1912	Philadelphia Jack O'Brien*
1912-1916	Jack Dillon
1916-1920	Battling Levinsky
1920-1922	Georges Carpentier
1922	Gene Tunney (outpointed Levinsky and gained American title)
1922	Harry Greb (outpointed Tunney for American title)
1923	Battling Siki (knocked out Carpentier for world title)
1923	Gene Tunney* (outpointed Greb)
1923-1925	Mike McTigue (outpointed Siki for world title)
1925	Paul Berlenbach (outpointed McTigue)
1926-1927	Jack Delaney* (outpointed Berlenbach)
1927-1929	Tommy Loughran* (outpointed McTigue)
1930-1934	Maxey Rosenbloom (outpointed Jimmy Slattery, recognized as champion by the New York State Athletic Commission. National Boxing Association vacated Rosenbloom's title)
1934-1935	Bob Olin (outpointed Rosenbloom, recognized in New York as champion)
1935-1939	John Henry Lewis*
1939-1940	Melio Bettina (defeated Jack Fox in elimination tournament to gain title vacated by Lewis)
1939-1941	Billy Conn*
1941	Anton Christoforidis (won NBA elimination tourney for title)
1941-1949	Gus Lesnevich, Freddie Mills.
1949-1950	Freddie Mills
1950-1952	Joey Maxim
1953-1960	Archie Moore
1961	Harold Johnson (NBA); Archie Moore (New York, Mass.)

*Abandoned title.

1962-1963	Harold Johnson; Willie Pastrano; Archie Moore (Calif. only)*
1964-1965	Willie Pastrano
1965-1966	Jose Torres
1966	Dick Tiger

MIDDLEWEIGHTS

1884-1891	Jack "Nonpareil" Dempsey
1891-1897	Bob Fitzsimmons*
1897-1907	Tommy Ryan*
1907-1908	Stanley Ketchel, Billy Papke
1908-1910	Stanley Ketchel
1911-1913	Claimed by Billy Papke, Frank Klaus, Mike Gibbons, Ed McGoorty and George Chip
1914-1917	Al McCoy
1917-1920	Mike O'Dowd
1920-1923	Johnny Wilson
1923-1926	Harry Greb
1926	Tiger Flowers, Mickey Walker
1926-1931	Mickey Walker*
1931-1932	Gorilla Jones (NBA), Ben Jeby (New York)
1932-1937	Marcel Thil (NBA)
1933	Lou Brouillard (New York), Vince Dundee (New York)
1934	Teddy Yarosz (New York)
1935	Babe Risko (New York)
1936-1937	Freddie Steele (NBA and New York)
1938	Al Hostak (NBA), Solly Krieger (NBA), Fred Apostoli (New York)
1939-1940	Al Hostak (NBA)
1939	Fred Apostoli (New York), Ceferino Garcia (New York)
1940	Tony Zale (NBA), Ken Overlin (New York)
1941	Tony Zale (NBA), Billy Soose (New York)*
1942-1947	Tony Zale
1947-1948	Rocky Graziano
1948	Tony Zale, Marcel Cerdan
1949	Marcel Cerdan, Jake LaMotta
1950	Jake LaMotta, Ray Robinson (Penna. only)
1951	Ray Robinson (universal); Randy Turpin; Ray Robinson
1952	Ray Robinson*
1953-1955	Carl (Bobo) Olson
1955-1956	Ray Robinson
1957	Gene Fullmer, Ray Robinson, Carmen Basilio
1958	Carmen Basilio, Ray Robinson
1959	Gene Fullmer (NBA); Ray Robinson (New York)
1960	Gene Fullmer (NBA); Paul Pender (New York and Mass.)
1961	Gene Fullmer (NBA); Terry Downes (New York, Mass., Europe)
1962	Gene Fullmer, Dick Tiger (NBA); Paul Pender (New York and Mass.)*
1963	Dick Tiger (universal).
1964	Joey Giardello
1965-1966	Dick Tiger
1966-1967	Emile Griffith
1967	Nino Benvenuti
1967	Emile Griffith

WELTERWEIGHTS

1892	Danny Needham, Mysterious Billy Smith
1892-1894	Mysterious Billy Smith
1894-1896	Tommy Ryan
1896	Kid McCoy (outgrew class)
1900	Mysterious Billy Smith, Rube Ferns Matty Matthews
1901	Matty Matthews, Rube Ferns
1901-1904	Joe Walcott
1904-1906	Dixie Kid, Joe Walcott, Honey Mellody
1907-1911	Mike Sullivan
1911-1915	Vacant
1915-1919	Ted Lewis, Jack Britton
1919-1922	Jack Britton
1922-1926	Mickey Walker
1926	Pete Latzo
1927-1929	Joe Dundee
1929	Jackie Fields
1930	Jackie Fields, Jack Thompson, Tommy Freeman
1931	Freeman, Thompson, Lou Brouillard
1932	Jackie Fields
1933	Young Corbett, Jimmy McLarnin
1934	Barney Ross, Jimmy McLarnin

Major Professional Boxing Bouts in 1967

Oct. 21, 1966——Oct. 28, 1967

Date	Winner, weight	Loser, weight	Round	Site
	1966			
Oct. 21	Johnny Persol, 182	Amos Lincoln, 203	D-10	New York, N. Y.
*Oct. 21	Sandro Lopopolo, 139	Vincente Rivas, 140	KO-7	Rome, Italy
Oct. 21	Nino Benvenuti, 159	Pascal Di Benedetto, 160	KO-10	Rome, Italy
Oct. 22	Carlos Ortiz	Sugar Ramos	TKO-5	Mexico City
*Oct. 22	Flash Elorde	Vincente Derado	D-15	Philippines
*Nov. 14	Cassius Clay, 212	Cleveland Williams, 210	TKO-3	Houston, Tex.
Nov. 21	George Chuvalo, 210	Boston Jacobs, 184	TKO-3	Detroit, Mich.
Nov. 21	Joe Frazier, 205	Eddie Machen, 192	KO-10	Berkeley, Calif.
Nov. 28	George Chuvalo, 214	Dave Russell, 201	TKO-4	St. John, N. B.
*Nov. 28	Carlos Ortiz, 134	Flash Elorde, 134	KO-14	New York, N. Y.
*Nov. 28	Curtis Cokes, 145	Jean Josselin, 146	D-15	Dallas, Tex.
*Dec. 30	Chartchai Chionoi, 111	Walter McGowen, 110	TKO-9	Bangkok, Thailand
	1967			
*Jan. 3	Fighting Harada, 117	Jose Medel, 117	D-15	Nagoya, Japan
Jan. 12	Frank Joseph, 178	Stanford Bulla, 177	KO-6	New York, N. Y.
Jan. 12	Jerry Quarry, 194	Al Jones, 193	KO-5	San Francisco, Calif.
Jan. 17	Howard Winstone, 125	Richie Sue, 127	D-10	London
Jan. 18	Lloyd Marshall, 131	Maurice Cullen, 137	KO-9	London
Jan. 18	Jim Beattle, 244	Ed Hurley, 200	D-10	St. Paul, Minn.
Jan. 19	Nino Benvenuti, 162	Manfred Graus, 161	KO-2	Bologna, Italy
Jan. 20	Hubert Hilton, 193	Prentice Snipes, 189	KO-3	Baltimore, Md.
*Jan. 21	Emile Griffith, 152	Joey Archer, 160	D-15	New York, N. Y.
Jan. 25	Fernando Atzori, 111	Rene Libeer, 112	D-15	Florence, Italy
Jan. 26	Stan Harrington, 160	Fumio Kaigu, 160	KO-6	Tokyo, Japan
*Jan. 29	Vincente Saldiver	Mitsunori Seke	TKO-7	Mexico City
Jan. 31	Gomeo Brennan, 160	Carl Moore, 157	D-10	Phoenix, Ariz.
Feb. 3	Sandro Mazzinghi, 155	Jean Rolland, 156	KO-10	Milan, Italy
*Feb. 6	Cassius Clay, 212	Ernie Terrell, 212	D-15	Houston, Tex.
Feb. 10	Mario Lamagna, 161	Lai Phonso, 162	KO-5	Naples, Italy
Feb. 13	Floyd Patterson, 196	Willie Johnson, 187	KO-3	Miami Beach, Fla.
Feb. 13	Allen Thomas, 167	Eddie Jones, 172	KO-3	Las Vegas, Nev.
Feb. 21	Joe Frazier, 205	Doug Jones, 188	KO-6	Philadelphia, Pa.
Feb. 22	George Chuvalo, 216	Dick Wipperman, 195	KO-3	Akron, Ohio
Feb. 26	Bo Hoegberg, 159	Gil Diaz, 160	KO-2	Malmoe, Sweden
Feb. 27	Bob Foster, 173	Andres Selpa, 164	KO-2	Washington, D. C.
Mar. 6	Nino Benvenuti, 161	Milo Calhoun, 163	D-10	Rome, Italy
Mar. 9	Jerry Quarry, 194	Brian London, 203	D-10	Los Angeles, Calif.
Mar. 10	Ismael Laguna, 134	Frankie Narvaez, 135	D-12	New York, N. Y.
Mar. 21	George Chuvalo, 215	Buddy Moore, 205	KO-2	Walpole, Mass.
Mar. 21	Luis Rodriguez, 152	Benny Briscoe, 155	D-10	Philadelphia, Pa.
Mar. 21	Karl Mildenberger, 199	Billy Walker, 190	KO-8	London, England
*Mar. 22	Cassius Clay, 211	Zora Folley, 202	KO-7	New York, N. Y.
Mar. 22	Jimmy Ellis, 190	Johnny Persol, 179	KO-1	New York, N. Y.
Mar. 22	Eddie Cotton, 177	Bobby Stininato, 175	TKO-9	Auckland, Aust.
Mar. 30	Floyd Patterson, 197	Bill McMurray, 209	KO-1	Pittsburgh, Pa.
Mar. 30	Sonny Liston, 221	Dave Bailey, 213	KO-1	Goteborg, Sweden
Mar. 31	Joe Harris, 151	Curtis Cokes, 149	D-10	New York, N. Y.
Apr. 4	George Chuvalo, 217	Willie Besmanoff, 193	KO-3	Miami Beach, Fla.
Apr. 4	Fighting Harada, 124	Tiny Palacio, 125	D-12	Fukuoka, Japan
Apr. 6	Wayne Kindred, 195	Matt Blow, 203	D-10	Los Angeles, Calif.
Apr. 11	Joe Frazier, 207	Jeff Davis, 205	KO-5	Miami Beach, Fla.
Apr. 14	Joe De Nucci, 163	Rocky Halliday	D-10	Boston, Mass.
*Apr. 17	Nino Benvenuti, 159	Emile Griffith, 154	D-15	New York, N. Y.
Apr. 17	Henry Cooper, 194	Boston Jacobs, 192	D-10	Leicester, England
Apr. 28	Sonny Liston, 220	Elmer Rush, 214	KO-6	Stockholm, Sweden
Apr. 30	Paul Fuji, 140	Sandro Lopopolo, 139	KO-2	Tokyo, Japan
May 5	Carlos Cruz, 135	Frankie Narvaez, 135	D-10	San Juan, P. R.
May 15	Joe Harris, 160	Ted Wright, 159	D-10	Philadelphia, Pa.
May 16	Dick Tiger, 167	Jose Torres, 173	D-15	New York, N. Y.
*May 19	Curtis Cokes, 145	Francoise Povilla, 146	TKO-10	Dallas, Tex.
May 19	Carlos Duran, 165	Mario Lamagna, 160	D-12	Naples, Italy
June 4	Luis Rodriguez, 154	Rocky Rivero, 169	D-10	San Juan, P. R.
June 4	Ismael Laguna, 136	Alfredo Urbina, 135	D-10	Panama
June 10	d-Floyd Patterson, 194	d-Jerry Quarry, 192	D-10	Los Angeles, Calif.
June 13	Henry Cooper, 189	Jack Bodell, 200	KO-2	Wolverhampton, England
June 13	Mac Foster, 200	Lino Armesteris, 177	KO-3	Fresno, Calif.
*June 15	Yoshiaki Numata, 129	Flash Elorde, 130	D-15	Tokyo, Japan
*June 15	Vincente Saldiver, 125	Howard Winstone, 125	D-15	Cardiff, Wales
June 23	Renaldo Victoria, 130	Hector Rodrigues, 131	D-12	Pittsfield, Mass.
*July 4	Fighting Harada, 118	Bernardo Caraballo, 118	D-15	Tokyo, Japan
July 6	Holly Mims, 162	George Johnson, 162	D-10	Portland, Me.
July 11	Harry Scott, 160	Ruben Iricco, 158	D-10	Liverpool, England
July 19	Joe Frazier, 204	George Chuvalo, 217	KO-4	New York, N. Y.
*July 26	Chartchai Chionoi, 111	Punthip Keosoriya, 111	KO-3	Bangkok, Thailand
July 31	Mike Cruz, 140	Pablo Lopez, 141	KO-2	New York, N. Y.
Aug. 5	Jimmy Ellis	Leotis Martin	TKO-9	Houston, Tex.
Aug. 5	Thad Spencer	Ernie Terrell	D-12	Houston, Tex.
Aug. 15	Brian London, 198	James Woody, 201	D-10	Liverpool, England
Aug. 16	Frankie Narvaez, 135	Victor Baegra, 134	KO-4	New York, N. Y.
*Aug. 16	Carlos Ortiz, 135	Ismael Laguna, 135	D-15	New York, N. Y.
Aug. 31	Joe Harris, 152	Miguel Barreto, 146	D-10	Philadelphia, Pa.
Sept. 13	Akihisa Someya, 136	Isco Icyihari, 135	KO-8	Osaka, Japan
Sept. 15	Jerry Quarry, 194	Billy Daniels, 187	KO-1	Los Angeles, Calif.
Sept. 16	Oscar Bonavena	Karl Mildenberger	D-12	Frankfurt, West Germany
Sept. 19	Buster Mathis, 239	Ron Marsh, 186	KO-4	New York, N. Y.
*Sept. 19	Chartchai Chionoi, 110	Walter McGowan, 111	KO-7	London, Eng.
Sept. 22	John Famechon, 126	Don Johnson, 127	D-10	Melbourne, Aust.
Sept. 22	Don Fullmer	Ted Wright	D-10	Ogden, Utah
Sept. 25	Frankie Narvaez	Ray Adigun	D-10	Paris, France
Sept. 26	Joe De Nucci, 165	Bob Simmons, 168	KO-7	Bangor, Me.
*Sept. 29	Emile Griffith, 154	Nino Benvenuti, 159	D-15	New York, N. Y.
*Oct. 2	Curtis Cokes, 145	Charlie Shipes, 145	KO-8	Oakland, Calif.
Oct. 2	Joe Shaw, 150	Percy Manning, 153	KO-10	Philadelphia, Pa.
Oct. 3	Al Jones, 220	Jim Beattie, 247	KO-1	Miami Beach, Fla.
Oct. 3	Kim Ki-Soo, 154	Fred Little, 152	D-15	Seoul, Korea
Oct. 17	Joe Frazier, 204	Tony Doyle, 197	KO-2	Philadelphia, Pa.
Oct. 28	Jerry Quarry, 195	Floyd Patterson, 195	D-12	Los Angeles, Calif.

*Indicates championship bout. d-Draw.

Billiard Records
Source: Billiard Congress of America

THREE CUSHION RECORDS

High Runs

1919 Tiff Denton, 17 (world tournament)
1926 John Layton, 18 (Inter. League)
1927 Willie Hoppe, 20 (Amer. League)
1928 Willie Hoppe, 25 (exhibition)
1930 Gus Copulos, 17 (world tournament)
1936 Willie Hoppe, 15 (match)
1939 Joe Chamaco, 50 in 23 (Nat. League)
1940 Tiff Denton, 17 (world tournament) (safeties)
1945 Willie Hoppe, 20 (match) (optional cue ball)

High Averages in Innings

1925 Otto Reiselt, 50 in 16 (Inter League)
1925 Otto Reiselt, 100 in 57 (Inter. League)
1925 Otto Reiselt, 150 in 104 (Inter. League)
1930 John Layton, 50 in 23 (world tournament)
1939 Joe Chamaco, 50 in 23 (Nat. League) (no safeties)
1940 Jay N. Bozeman, 50 in 23 (world tournament) (safeties)
1944 Willie Hoppe, 50 in 20 (tournament; choice of cue balls)
1945 Welker Cochran, 60 in 20 (match; choice of cue balls)
1947 Willie Hoppe, 50 in 21 (match)

High Grand Averages

1941 Willie Hoppe, 1.16 per inning (tournament)
1942 Willie Hoppe, 1.25 (tournament; optional cue ball)
1945 Willie Hoppe, 1.36 (tournament; choice of balls)
1950 Willie Hoppe, 1.33 (tournament)

POCKET BILLIARDS WORLD CHAMPIONS

1937 Ralph Greenleaf
1938 James Caras
1939 James Caras
1940 Andrew Ponzi
1941 Willie Mosconi; Erwin Rudolph
1942 Irving Crane (challenge match)
1943 Andrew Ponzi (challenge match)
1944 Willie Mosconi (challenge match)
1945 Willie Mosconi
1946 Irving Crane (world's tournament)
1947 Mosconi (defeated Crane in challenge match)
     Mosconi defeated Caras (match)
1948 Mosconi defeated Ponzi (match)
1949 James Caras (tournament)
1950 Willie Mosconi (tournament)
1951 Willie Mosconi (tournament)
1952 Willie Mosconi (tournament)
1953 Willie Mosconi (tournament)
1954 (No tournaments)
1955 Irving Crane (challenge match)
1955 Willie Mosconi (tournament)
1956-1962 (No official tournaments)
1963 Luther Lassiter (tournament)
1964 Luther Lassiter (tournament);
     Arthur Cranfield (challenge match)
1965 Joe Balsis (tournament)
1966 Luther Lassiter (tournament)
1967 Luther Lassiter (tournament)

POCKET BILLIARDS RECORDS—14-1

High Runs

1929 Ralph Greenleaf, 126 (tournament)
1934 Andrew Ponzi, 153 (match; continuous billiards)
1935 Bennie Allen, 125 (tournament)
1935 George Kelly, 125 (tournament)
1939 Irving Crane, 309 (exhibition)
1939 Andrew Ponzi, 127 (league play)
1941 Willie Mosconi, 126 (league tournament)
1945 Willie Mosconi, 309 (exhibition)
1945 Willie Mosconi, 127 (match; single game)
1946 James Caras, 127 (match; single game)
1952 Willie Mosconi, 121 and low game of 2 innings (tournament)
1954 Willie Mosconi, 150 in two innings (1200-pt. match)
1954 Willie Mosconi, 526 (exhibition) (tournament)

Other Pocket Billiards Records

High single average—1929, Ralph Greenleaf, 63 (tournament). High individual grand average—1929, Ralph Greenleaf, 11.02 (tournament; 5x10 table); 1950, Willie Mosconi, 18.34 (tournament; 4½x9 table).
Best game—1956, Willie Mosconi (one inning).

18-1 BALKLINE

1926, Jake Schaefer, Jr.—high run in match play 212, high grand average in match play 60, high grand average in match play 36; 1927, Welker Cochran, Jr.—high run in exhibition 353, high grand average in exhibition 150; high grand average in exhibition 61.

18-2 BALKLINE

1910 Harry P. Cline
1910-1920 Willie Hoppe
1921-1922 Jacob Schaefer, Jr.
1923-1924 Willie Hoppe
1925 Edward Horemans (disputed match—Schaefer won in playoff). 1925; Jacob Schaefer, Jr.
1926 Erich Hagenlocher
1927 Welker Cochran
1928 Edward Horemans
1929 Jacob Schaefer, Jr.
1930-1933 no tournaments
1934 Welker Cochran.
     No tournaments since.

18-2 BALKLINE

High run match, 432—Jacob Schaefer, Jr., 1925; high average, 400—Jacob Schaefer, Jr., 1925; high grand average tournament, 57.14—Jacob Schaefer, Jr., 1925; high grand average in match, 93.75—Jacob Schaefer, Jr., 1925; high run exhibition match, 585—Jacob Schaefer, Jr., 1926; high grand average 2400 pts, 120—Jacob Schaefer, Jr., 1926; high run exhibition, 684—Welker Cochran, 1926.

14-1 BALKLINE

1914, Willie Hoppe—high run 303; high grand average 25.75; high single average 40.

Billiard Tournaments in 1967

World's Invitational—New York, N. Y., Luther Lassiter, Elizabeth City, N. C., def. Jack Breit, Houston, Tex.

Collegiate Champions—Three Cushion, William "Wiley" Williams of Louisiana State University. Pocket Billiards (Men), Richard Baumgarth of Purdue University. Pocket Billiards (Women), Shirley Glicen, University of Miami.

Long Beach International Pocket Billiard Tournament—Straight Pool, Luther Lassiter def. Joe Balsis. Nine-Ball, Joe Balsis def. Don Watson. One-Pocket, Ed Kelly def. Jack Breit.

Stardust Open—Eddie Taylor, Knoxville, Tenn. Runners-up, Danny Jones, Columbus, O., and Mike Eufemia, Long Island, N. Y.

U. S. Open Tournament—Men's Division, Jimmy Caras, Springfield, Pa., def. Luther Lassiter, Elizabeth City, N. C. Women's Division, Dorothy Wise, Redwood City, Calif., def. San Lynn Merrick, Kansas City, Mo.

Columbus Proprietor's Association Tournament—Larry Johnson, New York City.

National Open Three-Cushion Billiard Tournament—Bud Harris def. Bill Hynes.

Grand National Steeplechase

The Grand National (established 1837) is run over a course of 4 miles, 856 yards for 4-year-olds and up. The race was run (1837-1838) at Maghull and then without a break at Aintree, near Liverpool, except in the World War I years, 1916-1919, when it was moved to Gatwick.

Year	Winner	Owner	Year	Winner	Owner
1953	Early Mist	J. H. Griffin	1962	Kilmore	Nat Cohen and Ben Rosenfeld
1954	Royal Tan	J. H. Griffin	1963	Ayala	P. B. Raymond and Nat Cohen
1955	Quare Times	Mrs. W. Welman			
1956	E. S. B.	Mrs. L. Carver	1964	Team Spirit	J. Goodman-R. Woodward
1957	Sundew	Mrs. G. Kohn			
1958	Mr. What	D. J. Coughlan	1965	Jay Trump	Mrs. Mary Stephenson
1959	Oxo	John E. Bigg			
1960	Merryman II	Winifred Wallace	1966	Anglo	Stewart Levy
1961	Nicolaus Silver	Charles Vaughan	1967	Foinavon	Cyril Watkins

Course record—9.20¾—Golden Miller, 1934; Bogskar, 1940.

Indianapolis Speedway Winners
DISTANCE 500 MILES (Inaugurated 1911)

Year	Car and driver	Time	MPH	Year	Car and driver	Time	MPH
1949.	Blue Crown Spark Plug Special, William Holland	4:07:15.97	121.327	1959.	Leader Card Special, Rodger Ward	3:40:49.20	135.857
1950.	Wynn Friction Proofing oil Special, Johnny Parsons(1)	2:46:55.97	124.002	1960.	Ken-Paul Special, Jim Rathmann	3:36:11.36	138.775
1951.	Belanger Special, Lee Wallard	3:57:38.05	126.244	1961.	Bowes Seal Fast Spec., A. J. Foyt	3:35:37.49	139.130
1952.	Agajanian Special, Troy Ruttman	3:52:41.88	128.922	1962.	Leader Card Spec., Rodger Ward	3:33:50.33	140.292
1953.	Fuel Injection Special, Billy Vukovich	3:53:01.69	128.740	1963.	Agajanian-Willard Battery Special, Parnelli Jones	3:29:35.40	143.137
1954.	Fuel Injection Special, Billy Vukovich	3:49:17.27	130.840	1964.	Sheraton-Thompson, A. J. Foyt	3:23:35.83	147.350
1955.	John Zink Special, Bob Sweikert	3:53:59.53	128.209	1965.	Lotus Powered by Ford, Jimmy Clark	3:19:05.34	150.686
1956.	John Zink Special, Pat Flaherty	3:53:00.00	128.490	1966.	American Red Ball Spec., Graham Hill	3:27:52.53	144.317
1957.	Belond Exhaust Special, Sam Hanks	3:41:14.25	135.601	1967.	Sheraton-Thompson Spl., A. J. Foyt	3:18:24.42	151.207
1958.	Belond A P.Special, Jimmy Bryan	3:44:13.00	133.791				

(1) Race stopped at 345 miles, rain. Race Record—151.207 mph—A. J. Foyt, 1967.

National Automobile Champions

1949 Johnnie Parsons	1954 Jimmy Bryan	1958 Tony Bettenhausen	1962 Rodger Ward
1950 Henry Banks	1955 Bob Sweikert	1959 Rodger Ward	1963 A. J. Foyt
1951 Tony Bettenhausen	1956 Jimmy Bryan	1960 A. J. Foyt	1964 A. J. Foyt
1952 Chuck Stevenson	1957 Jimmy Bryan	1961 A. J. Foyt	1965 Mario Andretti
1953 Sam Hanks			1966 Mario Andretti

Other Sports Car Racing in 1967

Date	Event	Winner	Car
Jan. 7	New Zealand Grand Prix	Jackie Stewart	BRM
Jan. 21	Lady Wigram Trophy, New Zealand	Jim Clark	Lotus Climax V8
Feb. 5	Daytona 24 hour Continental	C. Amon-L. Bianchi	Ferrari P4
Apr. 1	Sebring Endurance Race	M. Andretti-B. McLaren	Ford Mark IV
Apr. 9	Barcelona Grand Prix, Formula 2	Jim Clark	Lotus
Apr. 17	Pau Formula 2 Grand Prix	Jack Brabham	Brabham-Honda
May 7	Grand Prix de Monaco	Denis Hulme	Repco Brabham
May 14	Targa Florio Road Race	P. Hawkins-R. Stommelen	Porsche 2195 prototype
May 21	U. S. Road Race	Mark Donohue	Sunoco Special
May 28	Nuerburgring Sports Car Race	U. Schuetz-J. Buzetta	Porsche
June 4	Dutch Grand Prix	Jim Clark	Lotus
June 11	24 hour Le Mans race	D. Gurney-A. J. Foyt	Ford Mark IV
June 18	Grand Prix of Belgium	Dan Gurney	All American Racers' Eagle
June 25	Reims Grand Prix for Formula 2	Jochen Rindt	Brabham-Cosworth-Ford
July 2	French Grand Prix	Jack Brabham	Formula 1 Repco-Brabham
July 15	British Grand Prix	Jim Clark	Lotus-Ford
Aug. 6	West Germany Grand Prix	Denis Hulme	Repco Brabham
Aug. 20	Grand Prix of Austria	Paul Hawkins	Ford G.T.-40
Aug. 27	Canadian Grand Prix	Jack Brabham	Brabham Repco
Sept. 10	Grand Prix of Italy	John Surtees	Japanese Honda
Sept. 24	U. S. Auto Club Championship	A. J. Foyt	Sheraton-Thompson Special
Oct. 1	Grand Prix of U. S.	Jim Clark	Lotus-Ford
Oct. 22	Grand Prix of Mexico	Jim Clark	Lotus-Ford

World Automobile Speed Records
Records approved to July 15, 1967
UNLIMITED CLASS

Start	Dist.	Date	Place	Driver	Car	Time	MPH
F	1 m	11-15-65	Bonneville, Utah	Craig Breedlove	Spirit of America	5.994	600.601
F	5 k.	10-6-59	Bonneville "	M. Thompson	Challenger I	32.38	345.3
F	5 m.	10-6-59	Bonneville "	M. Thompson	Challenger I	52.83	340.7
F	10 k.	10-6-59	Bonneville "	M. Thompson	Challenger I	1:08.28	327.6
F	10 m.	10-6-59	Bonneville "	M. Thompson	Challenger I	2:05.80	286.2
S	1 m.	10-5-65	Bonneville "	Bobby Summers	Plymouth Satellite	23.0255	156.35
S	100 m.	7-20-51	Bonneville, Utah	Ab Jenkins	Mormon Met. III	31:28.198	190.657
S	200 m.	9-4-50	Bonneville "	Ab Jenkins	Mormon Meteor	1:02:51.21	190.92
S	500 m.	7-22-40	Bonneville "	Ab Jenkins	Mormon Meteor	2:49:16.365	177.229
S	1000 m.	7-22-40	Bonneville "	Jenkins-Bergere	Mormon Meteor	5:47:12.849	172.804
S	1 hr.	9-4-50	Bonneville "	Ab Jenkins	Mormon Meteor	306.87Kms.	190.68
S	24 hr.	7-22-23-40	Bonneville "	Jenkins-Bergere	Mormon Meteor	3868.430M	161.184
S	48 hr.	9-21-23-36	Bonneville "	Jenkins-Stapp	Mormon Meteor	7134.08M	148.63

Nascar Racing in 1967
Source: Natl. Assn. for Stock Car Auto Racing, Inc.

Date	Site	Winner	Car	Winners purse
Jan. 29	Riverside International Raceway	Parnelli Jones	67 Ford	$18,720
Feb. 26	Daytona International Speedway	Mario Andretti	67 Ford	43,500
Mar. 19	Bristol International Speedway	David Pearson	67 Dodge	5,290
Apr. 2	Atlanta International Raceway	Cale Yarborough	67 Ford	21,035
Apr. 16	N. Wilkesboro Speedway	Darel Dieringer	67 Ford	5,340
Apr. 23	Martinsville Speedway	Richard Petty	67 Plym.	4,450
May 13	Darlington International Raceway	Richard Petty	67 Plym.	14,090
May 28	Charlotte Motor Speedway	Jim Paschal	67 Plym.	28,450
Jun. 18	N. Carolina Motor Speedway	Richard Petty	67 Plym.	16,175
July 4	Daytona International Speedway	Cale Yarborough	67 Ford	15,725
July 9	Trenton Speedway	Richard Petty	67 Plym.	4,350
July 23	Bristol International Speedway	Richard Petty	67 Plym.	6,050
Aug. 6	Atlanta International Raceway	Dick Hutcherson	67 Ford	16,500
Sep. 4	Darlington International Speedway	Richard Petty	67 Plym.	26,900
Sep. 24	Martinsville Speedway	Richard Petty	67 Plym.	4,400

Professional Bowlers Association Tournaments: 1967

Date	Event	Purse	Winner	Winner's share
Jan. 7	Tucson Open..............	$40,000	John Juni...........	$5,000
Jan. 14	Western Open, San Jose, Calif.	40,000	Jim St. John.......	5,000
Jan. 21	Las Vegas Open.........	50,000	Dave Davis.........	10,000
Jan. 28	Denver Open.............	35,000	Dave Davis.........	5,000
Feb. 4	St. Paul Open...........	50,000	Carmen Salvino...	10,000
Feb. 11	Brut Open, Kansas City, Mo.	50,000	Tim Harahan.......	10,000
Feb. 18	Buckeye Open, Toledo, Ohio.	40,000	Jim St. John.......	5,000
Feb. 25	Miller High Life Open, Milwaukee, Wis.	60,000	Dave Davis.........	10,000
Mar. 4	Ebonite Open, Edison, N. J.	50,000	Sam Baca...........	10,000
Mar. 11	Buffalo Open............	37,500	Nelson Burton, Jr....	5,000
Mar. 18	Tampa Bay Sertoma Open	40,000	Mike Durbin.......	5,000
Mar. 25	Mobile-Sertoma Open...	40,000	Carmen Salvino...	5,000
Apr. 2	Firestone Tournament of Champions, Akron, Ohio.	100,000	Jim Stefanich.....	25,000
June 10	Seattle Open............	27,500	Don Johnson.......	3,000
June 18	Portland Open..........	27,500	Les Schissler......	3,000
June 25	Fresno Open............	27,500	Dick Ritger........	3,000
July 2	El Paso Open...........	27,500	Bill Tucker........	3,000
July 9	Houston Open...........	27,500	Butch Gearhart....	3,000
July 16	Ft. Worth Open.........	27,500	Dave Soutar.......	3,000
July 23	Oklahoma City Open....	27,500	Butch Gearhart....	3,000
July 30	Ft. Smith (Ark.) Open..	27,500	Jim Stefanich.....	3,000
Aug. 6	Brockton (Mass.) Open..	30,500	Don Johnson.......	3,000
Aug. 13	Coast Guard Open, Grand Haven, Mich.	30,000	Jim Stefanich.....	3,000
Aug. 20	Waukegan Open.........	34,000	Jim Godman.......	3,000
Aug. 27	Green Bay Open........	27,500	Dave Davis.........	3,000
Sept. 4	Nebraska Centennial Open, Omaha, Nebr.	30,500	Dave Davis.........	3,000
Sept. 10	Lubbock (Texas) Open...	27,500	Fred Foremsky.....	3,000
Sept. 17	New Orleans Open.......	27,500	Bill Tucker........	3,000

PBA Leading Money Winners

Total winnings are from PBA, ABC Masters and BFAA All-Star tournaments only, and do not include numerous other tournaments nor earnings from special television shows and matches.

Year	Player	Total money	Year	Player	Total money
1959.........	Dick Weber..........	$ 7,672	1964.........	Bob Strampe........	$33,592
1960.........	Don Carter..........	22,525	1965.........	Dick Weber.........	47,675
1961.........	Dick Weber..........	26,280	1966.........	Wayne Zahn........	54,720
1962.........	Don Carter..........	49,972	1967.........	Dave Davis (a).....	41,715
1963.........	Dick Weber..........	46,333			

(a) As of Sept. 11, 1967.

The $100,000 Firestone Tournament of Champions

This is professional bowling's richest tournament and has been held each year since its inception in 1965, in Akron, Ohio, the home of the Professional Bowlers Association. First prize is $25,000. The tournament is limited to champions of PBA events and recognized major tournaments.

Year	Winner	Year	Winner	Year	Winner
1965..........	Billy Hardwick	1966..........	Wayne Zahn	1967..........	Jim Stefanich

Other Bowling Championships in 1967

26th Annual National All-Star Championships, St. Louis, Mo., May 19-28—Men: Les Schissler, Denver, Colo., average 215-44. Prize $15,000. Women: Gloria Bouvia, Portland, Ore., 195-19. Prize $5,000.

National Intercollegiate Championships, Miami Beach, Fla., Apr. 2. Doubles—Jack Connaughton, LaCrosse (Wis.) State U. and Charles Atwood, U. of Miami. Singles—Jack Connaughton, LaCrosse (Wis.) State U.; All-events—Jack Connaughton, LaCrosse (Wis.) State U. (No team competition held in 1967.)

Woman's International Bowling Congress Champions

Yr.	Individual	All Events	Two-Woman Teams	Five-Woman Teams
1964	Jean Havlish, St. Paul, Minn.......690	Jean Havlish, St. Paul, Minn.....1,980	Grace Werkmeister-Shirley Garms, Chicago, Ill.....1,248	Allgauer's Villa Moderne, Chicago, Ill.........2,920
1965	Doris Rudell, Whittier, Calif. ...659	Donna Zimmerman, Norwalk, Calif....1,833	Betty Kemnick-Mary Ann White, Denver, Colo....1,263	Belmont Bowl Pro Shop, Chicago, Ill.........2,929
1966	Gloria Bouvia, Portland, Ore......675	Kate Helbig, Mohnton, Pa.....1,835	Pat Spence-Martha Morgan, Hampton, Va.........1,231	Gossard Girls, Chicago, Ill..........2,755
1967	Gloria Paeth, Pt. Huron, Mich......652	Carol Miller, Milwaukee, Wisc.......1,862	Elaine Liburd-Joan Oieske, Union City & Lyndhurst, N. J.....1,252	The Orphans, Los Angeles.........2,970

RECORDS OF 300 GAMES IN WIBC SANCTIONED PLAY

Season

1966-67—Donna Crisler, Carbondale, Kan.; Doreen Daneri, Daly City, Calif.; Pat Dwyer, Medford, Ore.; Bonnie Flint, Placerville, Calif.; Nancy Forry, Ephrata, Pa.; Eva Frank, Norfolk, Neb.; Elois Gray, Harrisburg, Pa.; Mildred Ignizio, Rochester, N. Y.; Dorothy Kaleel, Houston, Tex.; Arlis Kuess, Big Bend, Wis.; Shirley Mansfield, San Antonio, Tex.; Shirley Miner, Covina, Calif.; Shirley Music, Gardena, Calif.; Connie Pick, Bellflower, Calif.; Jane Shira, Bothell, Wash.; Nancy Sillmann, Fullerton, Pa.; Arlene Van Hekken, Holland, Mich.; Barbara White, Lockport, N. Y.; Dolores Witte, Brownsville, Tex.

1965-66—Dione Agnone, LaCrescenta, Calif.; Virginia Celli, Jacksonville, Fla.; Betty Dart, Grand Forks AFB, N. Dak.; Joanne Doyle, Redwood City, Calif.; Mildred L. Gibson, Tulsa, Okla.;

Season

Winona Gums, N. Highlands, Calif.; Joan Holm, Chicago, Ill.; Janet Hoodenpyl, Orangevale, Calif.; Betty Knecht, Minneapolis, Minn.; Betty Mivelaz, Tujunga, Calif.; Marty Parish, Corpus Christi, Tex.; Nan Poquette, E. Lansing, Mich.; Ruth Retz, Benton Harbor, Mich.; Margarette Uncles, Silver Springs, Md.; Sylvia Wagstaff, Zanesville, Ohio; Margaret M. Wilson, Lemay, Mo.

1964-65 Marge Fincutter, Charlotte, N. C.; Gene E. Hagen, Alderwood Manor, Wash.; Evelyn Ham, Los Alamos, N. M.; Shirley Linn, Concord, Calif.; Syble Pointer, Madison, Tenn.; Donna M. Rusch, Janesville, Wis.; Marie Branning, Ft. Wayne, Ind.; Mildred Kielmann, Rotterdam Junction, N. Y.; Betty Jo Hember, Fairway, Kan.; Evelyn Marie Lanier, Austin, Tex.

World Duckpin Bowling Records

Source: National Duckpin Bowling Congress; to Aug., 1967

MEN—Teams

Single game—820, Strikemaster, Baltimore, Md., May 10, 1967.

Three game set—2,271, Holiday Lanes, Manchester, Conn., May 15, 1964.

Five game set—3,348 Kelly-Buick, Baltimore, Md.

Ten game set—6,460 Park Circle, Baltimore, Md., Jan 11-12, 1941.

Season average—658-6, Stalcup Furniture Co., Washington, D. C., 1966-67 season.

MEN—Doubles

Single game—367, Bob Cleary-Charles Earle, Baltimore, Md. April 8, 1965, John Ferrando-Frank Caruso, Stratford, Conn., April 30, 1965.

Three game set—929 Mike Avon and Paul Jarman, Washington, D. C., April 27, 1952.

Four game set—1,206, Roy DeVeau and Gerald Maloney, Manchester, Conn., 1965-66 season.

Five game set—1,428 Gene Sirbaugh and Andy Page, Atlanta, Ga., Feb. 14, 1953.

Ten game set—2,752 James Dietsch and John Weinkam, Baltimore, Md., March 26 and April 8, 1950.

Fifty game set—13,228, Art Anderson-Bob Covel, Mansfield-Middleboro, Mass., Apr.-May, 1965.

One hundred game set—26,889, Art Anderson-Bob Covel, Mansfield-Middleboro, Mass., Apr.-May, 1965.

High season average—262-113, Roy DeVeau and Gerald Maloney, 1965-66 season.

MEN—Individuals

Single game—246, Charles Guess, Mt. Jackson, Va., Oct. 18, 1964.

Three-game set—549, Robert Gallis, Laurel, Md., July 18, 1967.

Five game set—818, Frank Micalizzi, Washington, D. C., Jan. 10, 1965.

Ten game set—1,550, Frank Micalizzi, Washington, D. C., Jan. 10, 1965.

Fifty game set—6,994, Nick Tronsky, Kensington, Conn., March, 1966.

Seventy-five game set—10,301, Art Anderson, Mansfield, Mass., Apr.-May, 1965.

One hundred game set—13,674, Art Anderson, Mansfield, Mass., April-May, 1965.

One hundred game set (continuous bowling)—12,466 Gordon McIlwee, Winchester, Va., Dec. 18, 1940.

High season average—140-15, James Wolfensberger, Hagerstown, Md., 1966-67 season.

WOMEN—Teams

Single game—760, Sea King Seafood, Baltimore, Md., Jan. 30, 1964.

Three game set—2,064, Brunswick-Pikesville, Baltimore, Md., Apr. 23, 1964.

Five game set—3,004 Pine Grove Dairy, Portsmouth, Va., Apr. 29, 1955.

Ten game set—5,438, Evening Star Champions, Washington, D. C., Feb. 9-11, 1934.

High season average—600-74, Coppola Ford, Bridgeport, Conn., 1963-64 season.

WOMEN—Doubles

Single game—338 Hazel Wells and Ruby Hovanic, Bridgeport, Conn., May 9, 1949.

Three game set—887, Frances Kupec and Helen Sudol, Manchester, Conn., Feb. 4, 1966.

Five game set—1,298 Elizabeth Barger and Ethel Dize, Baltimore, Md., January, 1952.

Ten game set—2,572 Elizabeth Barger and Ethel Dize, Baltimore, Md., January, 1952.

Twenty game set—4,500 Dorothy O'Brien and Ida Simmons, Norfolk, Va., April, 1934.

High season average—252-68, Dorothy Bermani and Dorothy Czajka, Manchester, Conn., 1965-66 season.

WOMEN—Individuals

Single game—232, Vivian Walsh, Washington, D. C., Feb. 24, 1954.

Three game set—511, Terry Vaccaro, Manchester, Conn., Mar. 21, 1966.

Five game set—767, Mary Kuebler, Baltimore, Md., Dec. 26, 1963.

Ten game set—1,420, Mary Kuebler, Baltimore, Md., Dec. 26, 1963.

Fifty game set—6,433, Maxine Allen, Durham, N. C., December, 1951.

Seventy-five game set—9,537 Maxine Allen, Durham, N.C., January, 1952.

High season average—135-79, Elizabeth Barger, Baltimore, Md., 1964-65 season.

MIXED—Doubles

Single game—370, Maureen Gilberto & Howard Hampton, Hartford-Manchester, Conn., May 24, 1964.

Three game set—918, Sue Brown & George Stonesifer, Washington, D. C., Jan. 29, 1965.

Ten game set—2,736 Elizabeth Barger and William Brozey, Baltimore, Md., March 11, 1950.

Fifty game set—12,883 Maxine Allen, Durham, N.C., and Dave Volk, Baltimore, Md., January, 1952.

Seventy-five game set—19,381 Maxine Allen, Durham, N. C., and Dave Volk, Baltimore, Md., January, 1952.

National Duckpin Bowling Champions, 1967

Source: Natl. Duckpin Bowling Congress

Men's Singles—Charles Guess, Richmond, Va., 502.

Women's Singles—Shirley McAneney, Lowell, Mass., 429.

Men's Doubles—Joe Serapilia-Tony Fratini, Bristol-New Haven, Conn., 919.

Women's Doubles—Laura Morgan-Jean Stewart, Baltimore, Md., 803.

Men's Teams—LaPerle's Memorials, Plainfield, Conn., 2,064.

Women's Teams—Holiday Lanes, Manchester, Conn., 1911.

Men's All-Events—Albert Barnhart, Hagerstown, Md., 1335.

Women's All-Events—Jean Stewart, Baltimore, Md., 1260.

Mixed Doubles—Selina Conner-Wally Lookingland, Baltimore, Md., 884.

22nd Annual Rubberband Duckpin Bowling Championships

Pittsburgh, Pa., April 1-May 14

Men's Singles—Michael Planey, Monessen, Pa., 679.

Women's Singles—Jean Harris, Arlington, Va., 576.

Mens' Doubles—Alvin Macek-Richard Lew, Pittsburgh, Pa., 1,120.

Women's Doubles—Dottie Clark, Falls Church, Va., and Eunice Hicks, Kensington, Md., 1,020.

Men's All Events—Michael Planey, Monessen, Pa., 1,839.

Women's All Events—Lillian Parsons, Baltimore, Md., 1,519.

Men's Team Events—Rudel's Connellsville, Pa., 2,548.

Women's Team Events—Phil-Mar Inn, Major Girls, Baltimore, Md., 2,424.

Mixed Team Events (3 men & 3 women)—Monessen Leagues, Monessen, Pa., 2,957.

Mixed Double Event (one man & one woman)—Ann Brandenburg 513, Wayne Souder 578, Charlottesville, Va., 1,100.

Lawn Bowls Championships in 1967

NATIONAL OPEN TOURNAMENT, AMERICAN LAWN BOWLS ASS'N

Seattle, Wash., Aug. 31-Sept. 1

Rettie Memorial Trophy—Pomona, Calif., LBC. (L. G. Le Master, M. G. Robinson, L. E. Clark).

Chicago Cup—Vancouver South LBC, Vancouver, B. C. (F. Corcoran, F. Christianson, W. Long).

Wisconsin Cup—Lakeside LBC, Chicago, Ill. (Russell Kutz, John Cordes, Joe Ibe).

California Trophy (Doubles)—Seattle (C. I. Dickinson, C. E. Dickinson).

Lakeside Trophy (Doubles)—Lakeside LBC, Chicago, Ill. (Russell Kutz, John Cordes).

Western New York Trophy (Doubles)—James Candelet, No. Kingstown, R. I., and William Miller, Gary, Ind.

National Open Singles Trophy—Alex. "Bob" Veitch, Oakland, Calif.

Metropolitan Trophy (Singles)—Gordon Martin, Seattle, Wash.

Pacific Northwest Trophy (Singles)—William Veale, Kent, Wash.

United States Championships, A.L.B.A.—Buck Hill Falls, Pa., Sept. 5-9 (Singles)—Willis J. Tewksbury, Clearwater. (Doubles)—Harold L. Esch and Alfred G. Hughes, Orlando, Fla.

Thoroughbred Champions 1951-1966
Thoroughbred Racing Association

	American Champion	2-Year-Old Colt	2-Year-Old Filly	3-Year-Old Colt
1951	Counterpoint	Tom Fool	Rose Jet	Counterpoint
1952	Native Dancer	Native Dancer	Sweet Patootie	One Count
1953	Tom Fool	Porterhouse	Evening Out	Native Dancer
1954	Native Dancer	Nashua	High Voltage	High Gun
1955	Nashua	Nail	Nasrina	Nashua
1956	Swaps	Barbizon	Romanita	Needles
1957	Dedicate	Jewel's Reward	Idun	Bold Ruler
1958	Round Table	First Landing	Quill	Tim Tam
1959	Sword Dancer	Warfare	My Dear Girl	Sword Dancer
1960	Kelso	Hail to Reason	Bowl of Flowers	Kelso
1961	Kelso	Crimson Satan	Cicada	Carry Back
1962	Kelso	Never Bend	Smart Deb	Jaipur
1963	Kelso	Hurry to Market	Castle Forbes	Chateaugay
1964	Kelso	Bold Lad	Queen Empress	Northern Dancer
1965	Roman Brother	Buckpasser	Moccasin	Tom Rolfe
1966	Buckpasser	Successor	Regal Gleam	Buckpasser

	3-Year-Old Filly	Older Colt, Horse or Gelding	Older Filly or Mare	Steeplechase Horse
1951	Kiss Me Kate	Hill Prince	Bed O' Roses	Oedipus
1952	Real Delight	Crafty Admiral	Next Move	Oedipus
1953	Grecian Queen	Tom Fool	Sickle's Image	The Mast
1954	Parlo	Native Dancer	Lavender Hill	King Commander
1955	Misty Morn	High Gun	Parlo	Neji
1956	Doubledogdare	Swaps	Blue Sparkler	Shipboard
1957	Bayou	Dedicate	Pucker Up	Neji
1958	Idun	Round Table	Bornastar	Neji
1959	Silver Spoon	Round Table	Tempted	Ancestor
1960	Berlo	Bald Eagle	Royal Native	Benguala
1961	Bowl of Flowers	Kelso	Airmans Guide	Peal
1962	Cicada	Kelso	Primonetta	Barnaby's Bluff
1963	Lamb Chop	Kelso	Cicada	Amber Diver
1964	Tosmah	Kelso	Old Hat	Bon Nouvel
1965	What a Treat	Roman Brother	Old Hat	Bon Nouvel
1966	Lady Pitt	Bold Bidder	Summer Scandal	Tuscalee

1967 Candidates for Championship
The candidates for championship and their 1967 racing records through Oct. 11th follow:

Horse	Starts	1st	2nd	3rd	Earnings	Owner	Points
Two-Year-Old Colt							
Vitriolic........	11	4	4	2	$197,381	Ogden Phipps............	62
Captain's Gig....	4	3	1	0	101,343	H. F. Guggenheim........	57
What a Pleasure...	6	4	2	1	128,138	Wheatley Stable.........	28
Two-Year-Old Filly							
Queen of the Stage..	7	7	0	0	284,059	Ogden Phipps............	100
Shenow...........	13	7	4	1	170,534	Everett Lowrance........	47
Gay Matelda......	14	2	5	4	114,581	Christopher T. Chenery...	23
Three-Year-Old Colt							
Damascus.........	14	11	2	1	723,651	Mrs. E. W. Bancroft......	100
Dr. Fager........	7	5	0	1	374,524	Tartan Stable...........	50
In Reality.......	12	6	6	0	415,982	Frances A. Genter.......	20
Three-Year-Old Filly							
Gamely...........	13	4	3	2	102,997	William Haggin Perry.....	80
Furl Sail........	14	9	1	2	191,600	Mrs. E. K. Thomas.......	65
Quillo Queen.....	9	3	4	0	174,429	Martin Anderson.........	13
Older Colt, Horse or Gelding							
Buckpasser.......	6	3	2	1	224,840	Ogden Phipps............	100
Handsome Boy....	17	4	3	2	265,605	Hobeau Farm............	42
Native Diver.....	13	6	3	3	258,100	Mr. & Mrs. L. K. Shapiro.	11
Older Filly or Mare							
Straight Deal....	19	6	5	1	225,798	Mrs. E. D. Jacobs......	100
Mac's Sparkler...	11	3	5	1	146,009	Hobeau Farm............	32
Politely.........	9	6	0	2	112,004	Mrs. R. C. duPont.......	26

Largest Winnings By One Horse in a Year

Year	Horse	Dollars	Year	Horse	Dollars	Year	Horse	Dollars
1937..	Seabiscuit	168,580	1948..	Citation	709,470	1959..	Sword Dancer...	537,004
1938..	Stagehand......	189,710	1949..	Ponder..........	321,825	1960..	Bally Ache.....	455,045
1939..	Challedon......	174,535	1950..	Noor...........	346,940	1961..	Carry Back.....	565,349
1940..	Bimelich	111,005	1951..	Counterpoint....	250,525	1962..	Never Bend	402,969
1941..	Whirlaway	272,386	1952..	Crafty Admiral..	277,225	1963..	Candy Spots	604,481
1942..	Shut Out........	238,972	1953..	Native Dancer...	513,425	1964..	Gun Bow.....	580,100
1943..	Count Fleet	174,055	1954..	Determine.......	327,760	1965..	Buckpasser.....	568,096
1944..	Pavot..........	179,040	1955..	Nashua.........	752,550	1966..	Buckpasser.....	669,078
1945..	Busher..........	273,735	1956..	Needles........	440,850	1967*	Damascus......	723,651
1946..	Assault.........	424,195	1957..	Round Table.....	600,258			
1947..	Armed..........	376,325	1958..	Round Table.....	662,780			

*Through Oct. 1.

Record of Buckpasser

Year	Age	Sts.	1st	2nd	3rd	Unp.	Earnings
1965........	2	11	9	1	0	1	$568,096
1966........	3	14	13	1	0	0	669,078
1967........	4	6	3	2	1	0	224,840
Totals...		**31**	**25**	**4**	**1**	**1**	**$1,462,014**

Triple Crown Turf Winners, Owners and Jockeys
(Kentucky Derby, Preakness and Belmont Stakes)

Year	Horse	Owner	Jockey	Year	Horse	Owner	Jockey
1919	Sir Barton	J. K. L. Ross	J. Loftus	1941	Whirlaway	Warren Wright	E. Arcaro
1930	Gallant Fox	W. Woodward	E. Sande	1943	Count Fleet	Mrs. J. D. Hertz	J. Longden
1935	Omaha	W. Woodward	W. Sanders	1946	Assault	R. J. Kleberg	W. Mehrtens
1937	War Admiral	S. D. Riddle	C. Kurtsinger	1948	Citation	Warren Wright	E. Arcaro

Major Stakes Races 1967

Event	Track	Added Value	Winner	Dist. Furl.	Time	Jockey
3 YEAR OLDS AND UP						
American Hdcp.	Hollywood Pk.	50,000	Pretense	9	1:47	J. Sellers
Aqueduct Stakes	Aqueduct	100,000	Damascus	9	1:48.1	W. Shoemaker
Arlington Hdcp.	Arlington	50,000	Stupendous	8	1:35	L. Pincay
Bowling Green Hdep.	Aqueduct	50,000	Poker	13	2:41.2	W. Boland
Brooklyn Hdcp.	Aqueduct	100,000	Handsome Boy	10	2:00.1	E. Belmonte
Carter Hdcp.	Aqueduct	50,000	Tumiga	7	1:23.4	B. Feliciano
Dixie Hdcp.	Pimlico	50,000	War Censor	12	2:36.3	E. Fires
Donn Hdcp.	Gulfstream	50,000	Francis U.	9	1:50.2	Campbell
Grey Lag Hdcp.	Aqueduct	75,000	Moontrip	9	1:49.3	A. Cordero
Gulfstream Park Hdcp.	Gulfstream	100,000	Pretense	10	2:01.4	J. Sellers
Haskell Hdcp.	Monmouth	100,000	Handsome Boy	10	2:02	J. Vasquez
Hawthorne Gold Cup	Hawthorne	100,000	Dr. Fager	10	2:01.1	B. Baeza
Hialeah Turf Cup	Hialeah	75,000	War Censor	12	2:28.1	E. Fires
Hollywood Gold Cup	Hollywood Park	150,000	Native Diver	10	1:58.4	J. Lambert
Jockey Gold Cup	Aqueduct	100,000	Damascus	16	2:55.4	W. Shoemaker
John B. Campbell Hdcp	Bowie	100,000	Quinta	8½	1:43.3	S. Brooks
Manhattan Hdcp	Aqueduct	50,000	Munden Point	13	2:41.3	R. Ussery
Man O' War Stakes	Aqueduct	100,000	Ruffled Feathers	13	2:42.4	D. Hidalgo
Metropolitan Hdcp	Aqueduct	100,000	Buckpasser	8	1:34.3	B. Baeza
Michigan Mile	Detroit	100,000	Eastemo 2nd	9	1:48.2	C. Marques
*San Carlos Hdcp	Santa Anita	50,000	Native Diver	9	1:48.1	B. Baeza
San Fernando Stakes	Santa Anita	50,000	Buckpasser	7	1:22	J. Lambert
San Juan Capistrano Hdcp.	Santa Anita	125,000	Niarkos	14	2:50.1	A. Pineda
Seminole Hdcp	Hialeah	50,000	Advocator	9	1:49	J. Valesques
Stars and Stripes Hdcp.	Arlington	50,000	Climax II	9	1:49.3	L. Pincay
Surburban Hdcp	Aqueduct	100,000	Buckpasser	10	2:02.1	B. Baeza
Sunset Hdcp	Hollywood Pk	100,000	Hill Clown	12	2:27.4	W. Shoemaker
Tidal Hdcp	Aqueduct	50,000	Ft. Marcy	9	1:52.1	R. Turcotte
Tropical Park Hdcp	Tropical	50,000	El Benito	9	1:51	H. Gustines
U. N. Hdcp.	Atlantic City	100,000	Flit-To	9½	1:54	H. Woodhouse
Vosburgh Hdcp.	Aqueduct	50,000	Dr. Fager	7	1:21.3	B. Baeza
Washington Park Hdcp.	Arlington	100,000	Handsome Boy	10	1:37.3	E. Belmonte
Westchester Hdcp.	Aqueduct	50,000	Advocator	8	1:35.1	M. Ycasa
*Whitney Hdcp.	Saratoga	50,000	Stupendous	9	1:48.1	E. Belmonte
Widener Hdcp.	Hialeah	100,000	Ring Twice	10	2:00.3	W. Boland
Woodward Stakes	Aqueduct	100,000	Damascus	10	2:00.3	W. Shoemaker
✦4 year olds and up.						
3 YEAR OLDS AND UP, FILLIES AND MARES						
Barbara Fritchie Hdcp.	Bowie	50,000	Holly-O	7	1:21.4	F. Lovato
Beldame Stakes	Aqueduct	75,000	Mac's Sparkler	9	1:49.4	W. Boland
Black Helen Hdcp.	Hialeah	50,000	Mac's Sparkler	9	1:48.3	W. Boland
Delaware Hdcp.	Delaware	100,000	Straight Deal	10	2:02.1	R. Ussery
Ladies Hdcp.	Aqueduct	50,000	Sweet Folly	10	2:04.3	H. Gustines
Sheepshead Bay Hdcp.	Aqueduct	50,000	Indian Sunlight	9½	1:54.4	H. Gustines
Spinster Stakes	Keeneland	50,000	Straight Deal	9	1:49.1	H. Grant
Top Flight Hdcp.	Aqueduct	50,000	Straight Deal	9	1:49.3	A. Cordero
Vineland Hdcp.	Garden State	50,000	Straight Deal	9	1:51.1	H. Grant
3 YEAR OLDS						
American Derby	Arlington	100,000	Damascus	9	1:46.4	W. Shoemaker
Arlington Classic	Arlington	100,000	Dr. Fager	8	1:36	B. Baeza
Belmont Stakes	Aqueduct	125,000	Damascus	12	2:28.4	W. Shoemaker
Chicagoan Hdcp.	Arlington	75,000	Minnesota Mac	9	1:48.2	W. Shoemaker
Choice Stakes	Monmouth	50,000	In Reality	8½	1:43.4	E. Fires
Dwyer Hdcp.	Aqueduct	75,000	Damascus	10	2:03	W. Shoemaker
Flamingo	Hialeah	100,000	Reflected Glory	9	1:48.3	J. Valesques
Florida Derby	Gulfstream	100,000	In Reality	9	1:50.1	E. Fires
Gotham	Aqueduct	50,000	Dr. Fager	8	1:35.1	M. Ycasa
Illinois Derby	Sportsman Park	50,000	Royal Malabar	9	1:51.1	C. Stone
Jerome Hdcp.	Aqueduct	50,000	High Tribute	8	1:34.4	L. Pincay
Jersey Derby	Garden State	100,000	In Reality	9	1:48	E. Fires
Kentucky Derby	Churchill Downs	125,000	Proud Clarion	10	2:00.3	R. Ussery
Lawrence Realization	Aqueduct	50,000	Successor	13	2:44.3	B. Baeza
New Hampshire Sweepstakes	Rockingham	250,000	Dr. Fager	10	1:59.4	B. Baeza
Preakness	Pimlico	150,000	Damascus	9½	1:55.1	W. Shoemaker
Rockingham Special	Rockingham	75,000	Dr. Fager	9	1:48.1	B. Baeza
San Felipe Hdcp.	Santa Anita	50,000	Rising Market	8½	1:42.4	L. Pincay
Santa Anita Derby	Santa Anita	125,000	Ruken	9	1:49.5	F. Alveres
Saranac Hdcp.	Aqueduct	50,000	Bold Hour	8	1:36	J. L. Rotz
Travers Stakes	Saratoga	75,000	Damascus	10	2:01.3	W. Shoemaker
Withers Stakes	Aqueduct	50,000	Dr. Fager	8	1:33.4	B. Baeza
Wood Memorial	Aqueduct	100,000	Damascus	9	1:49.3	W. Shoemaker
3 YEAR OLDS, FILLIES						
Acorn Stakes	Aqueduct	50,000	Furl Sail	8	1:35.3	J. Vasques
Alabama Stakes	Saratoga	50,000	Gamely	10	2:03.1	W. Shoemaker
Coaching Club Amer. Oaks	Aqueduct	100,000	Quillo Queen	10	2:03.2	E. Cardone
Delaware Oaks	Delaware Park	50,000	Lewiston	9	1:51.2	G. Patterson
Gazelle Hdcp.	Aqueduct	50,000	Sweet Folly	9	1:50.2	H. Gustines
Kentucky Oaks	Churchill Downs	50,000	Nancy, Jr.	8½	1:44	J. Sellers
Monmouth Oaks	Monmouth	50,000	Quillo Queen	9	1:52.1	E. Cardone
Mother Goose Stakes	Aqueduct	50,000	Furl Sail	9	1:49.3	J. Vasques
2 YEAR OLDS						
Arlington-Wash. Futurity	Arlington	75,000	T. V. Commercial	7	1:23.4	P. Anderson
Champagne Stakes	Aqueduct	75,000	Vitriolic	7	1:24	W. Shoemaker
Cowdin Stakes	Aqueduct	125,000	Vitriolic	8	1:34.3	B. Baeza
Del Mar Futurity	Del Mar	50,000	Iron Ruler	7	1:21.3	L. Pincay
Futurity	Aqueduct	75,000	Baffle	6	1:09.3	W. Blum
			Captain's Gig	6½	1:15.4	W. Shoemaker
Hollywood Juvenile Champ.	Hollywood Pk.	100,000	Jim White	6	1:09.4	B. Hartack
Hopeful Stakes	Saratoga	75,000	What A Pleasure	6½	1:16.2	B. Baeza
Pimlico Futurity	Pimlico	75,000	Vitriolic	8½	1:45.1	B. Baeza
Sapling Hdcp.	Monmouth	100,000	Subpet	6	1:10.2	R. Broussard
2 YEAR OLDS, FILLIES						
Arlington-Wash. Lassie Stks.	Arlington	125,000	Shenow	6½	1:18.2	L. Pincay
Frisette Stakes	Aqueduct	75,000	Queen of the Stage	8	1:34.2	B. Baeza
Matron Stakes	Aqueduct	50,000	Q. of the Stage	6	1:10	B. Baeza
Selima Stakes	Laurel	50,000	Syrian Sea	8½	1:44.2	E. Belmonte
Sorority Stakes	Monmouth	100,000	Q. of the Stage	6	1:10	B. Baeza
Spinway Stakes	Saratoga	50,000	Q. of the Stage	6	1:01.1	B. Baeza

LEADING MONEY-WINNING HORSES OF THE WORLD

Horse	Sts.	1st	2nd	3rd	Amt. won	Horse	Sts.	1st	2nd	3rd	Amt. won
Kelso	62	39	12	2	$1,977,396	Hill Rise	39	13	6	8	$634,599
Round Table	66	43	8	5	1,749,869	Bardstown	31	15	7	1	628,752
Buckpasser	31	25	4	1	1,462,014	Jaipur	25	10	6	0	618,926
Nashua	30	22	4	1	1,288,565	Prove It	25	15	4	1	613,820
Carry Back	61	21	11	11	1,241,165	Tosmah	39	23	6	2	612,591
Citation	45	32	10	2	1,085,760	Olden Times	54	17	10	5	603,875
Swoon's Son	51	30	10	3	970,605	In Reality (a)	19	10	8	0	601,024
Roman Brother	42	16	10	5	943,473	Needles	21	11	3	3	600,355
Native Diver	81	37	7	12	926,500	Terrang	66	15	9	12	599,285
Stymie	131	35	33	28	918,485	Straight Deal (a)	61	17	15	7	581,991
T. V. Lark	72	19	13	6	902,194	Mark-Ye-Well	40	14	2	4	581,910
Swaps	25	19	2	2	848,900	Northern Dancer	18	14	2	2	580,806
Sword Dancer	39	15	7	4	829,610	Oil Capitol	80	19	10	9	580,756
Candy Spots	22	12	5	1	824,718	Determine	44	18	7	9	573,360
Mongo	46	22	10	4	820,766	Tom Fool	30	21	7	1	570,165
Armed	81	41	20	10	817,475	Whirlaway	60	32	15	9	561,161
Find	110	22	27	27	803,615	Quadrangle	26	10	5	6	559,386
Gun Bow	42	17	8	4	798,722	†Old Hat	80	35	18	9	556,401
Crimson Satan	58	18	9	9	796,077	On Trust	88	23	19	13	554,125
Native Dancer	22	21	1	0	785,240	Rejected	47	11	10	2	549,500
Cicada	42	23	8	6	783,674	Affectionately	52	18	8	6	546,660
First Landing	37	19	9	2	779,577	Tompion	39	11	11	6	545,173
Bold Ruler	33	23	4	2	764,204	Summer Tan	28	11	12	2	542,796
Bally Ache	31	16	9	4	758,522	Promised Land	77	21	10	16	541,707
Damascus (a)	18	14	3	1	749,516	Hasty Road	28	14	5	3	541,402
Bald Eagle	23	9	5	3	676,442	Ponder	41	14	7	4	541,275
Assault	42	18	6	7	675,470	Clem	47	12	8	13	535,681
Tom Rolfe	31	16	5	5	671,297	Dedicate	43	12	9	5	533,200
Social Outcast	58	18	9	6	668,300	Eddie Schmidt	101	20	10	18	526,292
Intentionally	34	18	7	2	652,258	Porterhouse	70	19	8	12	519,460
Hillsdale	41	23	6	4	646,935	Bold Lad	19	14	2	1	516,465
Crozier	34	10	12	3	641,733	Gallant Man	26	14	4	1	510,355
Never Bend	23	13	4	4	641,524	Talent Show	116	16	15	22	507,038
Ridan	23	13	6	2	635,074	Bobby Brocato	88	21	16	14	504,510

(a) Record to Oct. 1, 1967. †Not including 1967 record.

Shoemaker Passes $40,000,000 Mark as Money-Winner

Willie Shoemaker, the world's leading money-winning jockey, increased his mounts' earnings to $40,252,818 by Oct. 1, 1967. He had passed Eddie Arcaro in 1964. Arcaro had earned $30,039,543 lifetime. His complete record follows.

Year	Mounts	Wins	Seconds	Thirds	Unpl.	Percent	Amt. won
1949	1,089	219	195	147	528	.20	$458,010
1950	1,640	388	266	230	756	.24	844,040
1951	1,161	257	197	161	546	.22	1,329,890
1952	1,322	315	224	174	609	.24	1,049,304
1953	1,683	485	302	210	686	.29	1,784,187
1954	1,251	380	221	142	508	.30	1,876,760
1955	1,149	307	178	138	526	.27	1,846,884
1956	1,229	328	187	165	549	.27	2,113,335
1957	1,191	295	183	134	579	.25	2,544,782
1958	1,133	300	185	137	511	.26	2,961,693
1959	1,285	347	230	159	549	.27	2,843,133
1960	1,227	274	196	158	599	.22	2,123,961
1961	1,256	304	186	175	591	.24	2,690,819
1962	1,126	311	156	128	531	.28	2,916,844
1963	1,203	271	193	137	602	.23	2,526,925
1964	1,056	246	147	133	530	.23	2,649,553
1965	1,069	247	161	120	541	.23	2,228,977
1966	1,037	221	158	107	551	.21	2,671,198
1967 (Oct. 1)	930	224	132	95	479	.24	2,792,523
(19) years	23,037	5,719	3,697	2,850	10,771	.24	40,252,818

Leading Money Winning Owners *To Oct. 1, 1967

Yr.	Owner	Amt. won	Yr.	Owner	Amt. won
1941	Calumet Farm (Warren Wright)	$475,091	1955	Hasty House Farm (Mr. and Mrs. A. E. Reuben)	$832,879
1942	Greentree Stable (Mrs. Payne Whitney)	414,432	1956	Calumet Farm (Mrs. Gene Markey)	1,057,383
1943	Calumet Farm (Warren Wright)	267,915	1957	Calumet Farm (Mrs. Gene Markey)	1,150,910
1944	Calumet Farm (Warren Wright)	601,660	1958	Calumet Farm (Mrs. Gene Markey)	946,262
1945	Maine Chance Farm (Mrs. Elizabeth N. Graham)	589,170	1959	Cain Hoy Stable (H. F. Guggenheim)	742,081
1946	Calumet Farm (Warren Wright)	564,095	1960	C. V. Whitney	1,039,091
1947	Calumet Farm (Warren Wright)	1,402,436	1961	Calumet Farm (Mrs. Gene Markey)	759,856
1948	Calumet Farm (Warren Wright)	1,269,710	1962	Ellsworth Stable (Rex C. Ellsworth)	1,154,454
1949	Calumet Farm (Warren Wright)	1,128,942	1963	Ellsworth Stable (Rex C. Ellsworth)	1,096,863
1950	Brookmeade Stable (Mrs. Dodge Sloane)	651,399	1964	Wheatley Stable (Mrs. Henry C. Phipps)	1,073,572
1951	Greentree Stable (Mrs. C. S. Payson and J. H. Whitney)	637,242	1965	Marion H. Van Berg	895,246
1952	Calumet Farm (Mrs. Gene Markey)	1,283,197	1966	Wheatley Stable (Mrs. Henry C. Phipps)	1,225,861
1953	A. G. Vanderbilt	987,630	1967*	Hobeau Farm	897,891
1954	King Ranch (Robert J. Kleberg, Jr.)	837,615			

Record of Kelso

Year	Age	Sts.	1st	2nd	3rd	Unp.	Won
1959	2	3	1	0	2	0	$ 3,380
1960	3	9	8	0	0	1	293,310
1961	4	9	7	1	0	1	425,565
1962	5	12	6	4	0	2	289,685
1963	6	12	9	2	0	1	569,762
1964	7	11	5	3	0	3	311,660
1965	8	6	3	0	2	1	84,034
1966	9	1	0	0	0	1	500.
Totals	–	63	39	12	2	10	$1,977,896.

Winners of Famous Harness Stakes

THE HAMBLETONIAN (3-year-old trotters)

Yr. Winner	Best Time	Value	Yr. Winner	Best Time	Value
1938—McLin Hanover	2:02¼	$37,962	1953—Helicopter	2:01⅗	$117,118
1939—Peter Astra	2:04¼	40,502	1954—Newport Dream	2:02⅘	106,830
1940—Spencer Scott	2:02	43,658	1955—Scott Frost	2:00⅗	86,863
1941—Bill Gallon	2:05	38,729	1956—The Intruder	2:01⅗	98,591
1942—The Ambassador	2:04	38,954	1957—Hickory Smoke	2:00⅕	111,126
1943—Volo Song	2:02½	42,298	1958—Emily's Pride	1:59⅘	106,719
1944—Yankee Maid	2:04	33,577	1959—Diller Hanover	2:01⅕	125,284
1945—Titan Hanover	2:04	50,190	1960—Blaze Hanover	1:59⅗	144,590
1946—Chestertown	2:02½	50,905	1961—Harlan Dean	1:58⅖	131,573
1947—Hoot Mon	2:00	46,267	1962—A.C.'s Viking	1:59⅗	116,312
1948—Demon Hanover	2:02	59,941	1963—Speedy Scot	1:58	115,549
1949—Miss Tilly	2:01⅖	69,791	1964—Ayres	1:56⅘	115,281
1950—Lusty Song	2:02	75,209	1965—Egyptian Candor	2:04⅗	122,245
1951—Mainliner	2:02⅗	95,263	1966—Kerry Way	1:58⅘	122,540
1952—Sharp Note	2:02⅗	87,637	1967—Speedy Streak	2:00	122,650

Year	FOX STAKE 2-yr.-old pacers		LITTLE BROWN JUG 3-yr.-old pacers		HORSEMAN STAKE 2-yr.-old trotters		KENTUCKY FUTURITY 3-yr.-old trotters	
	Winner	Time	Winner	Time	Winner	Time	Winner	Time
1957	Thorpe Hanover	2:01⅘	Torpid	2:00⅘	Sharpshooter	2:05⅘	Cassin Hanover	2:02⅕
1958	Meadow Al	2:00⅗	Shadow Wave	2:01	Diller Hanover	2:03⅕	Emily's Pride	1:59⅗
1959	Bullet Hanover	1:57	Adios Butler	1:59⅗	Blaze Hanover	2:01⅗	Diller Hanover	2:01⅕
1960	Adios Cleo	1:59⅖	Bullet Hanover	1:58⅗	Harlan Dean	2:01⅖	Elaine Rodney	1:58⅗
1961	Coffee Break	1:58⅕	Henry T. Adios	1:58⅘	Safe Mission	2:03⅗	Duke Rodney	1:58⅘
1962	(rained out)		Lehigh Hanover	1:58⅘	(rained out)		Safe Mission	1:59⅕
1963	Race Time	1:58	Overtrick	1:57⅕	Smart Rodney	2:03⅘	Speedy Scot	1:57⅕
1964	Bret Hanover	1:58	Vicar Hanover	2:01	Noble Victory	2:00⅕	Ayres	1:58⅕
1965	Romeo Hanover	1:59	Bret Hanover	1:57	Kerry Way	2:02⅘	Armbro Flight	1:59
1966	Best of All	1:59⅗	Romeo Hanover	1:59⅗	Kimberly Dutchess	2:04⅗	Governor Armbro	2:00⅗
1967	Golden Money Maker	1:58⅘	Best of All	1:59	Nevele Pride	2:02⅕	Speed Model	1:59⅗

OTHER HARNESS RACING WINNERS IN 1967

Event	Winner	Best time	Value
The Dexter Cup (3-year-old) (trot)	Flamboyant	2:04 3-5	$183,463
The Messenger (3-year-old) (pace)	Romulus Hanover	1:59 1-5	178,064
Yonkers Futurity (3-year-old) (trot)	Pomp	2:04 4-5	150,000
Yonkers International Pace (1½ miles)	Romeo Hanover	3:05 3-5	100,000
United Nations Trot (1½ miles)	Perfect Freight	3:07 3-5	100,000
Roosevelt International Trot (1¼ miles)	Roquepine	2:43 4-5	100,000
Realization (4-year-old) (pace) (1 1/16 miles)	Romeo Hanover	2:08	91,664
American-National Maturity (4-year-old) (trot)	Carlisle	1:59 3-5	89,580
Realization (4-year-old) (trot) (1 1/16 miles)	Carlisle	2:14	88,664
The Adios (3-year-old) (pace)	Romulus Hanover	1:57 3-5	85,510
American-National Maturity (4-year-old) (pace)	Song Cycle	1:59 2-5	80,719
N. Y. Sires Stake (3-year-old) (trot)	Grig	2:09 2-5	68,875
N. Y. Sires Stake (3-year-old) (pace)	Bobby Ed	2:03	68,875
Fox Stake (2-year-old) (pace)	Golden Money Maker	1:58 4-5	67,037
N. Y. Exposition (3-year-old) (pace)	Feather Step	2:01	57,870
N. Y. Exposition (3-year-old) (trot)	Duchess Rose	2:06 4-5	56,000
Illinois Colt Stake (2-year-old) (pace)	John L. Purdue	2:03 1-5	55,275
Illinois Colt Stake (3-year-old) (pace)	Shore Will	2:00 1-5	51,700
Nassau Pace (1½ miles)	True Duane	3:06 2-5	50,000
Centennial Pace	Romulus Hanover	1:57 1-5	50,000
National Pacing Derby (1¼ miles)	True Duane	2:32 4-5	50,000
Gotham Trot (1¼ miles)	Roquepine	2:36 4-5	50,000
Good Time Pace (1¼ miles)	Adios Vic	2:29 4-5	50,000
National Championship Pace (1½ miles)	Adios Vic	3:08 3-5	50,000
American Trotting Championship (1¼ miles)	Perfect Freight	2:33	50,000
Midwest Pacing Derby	Star Carrier	2:00 4-5	50,000
Washington Pk. Inv. Pace	Cardigan Bay	1:59 4-5	50,000

LEADING DRIVERS

Yr.	Races Won		Grand Circuit		Money Won	
1952	Levi Harver	129	Frank Ervin	$174,991	Bill Haughton	$311,728
1953	Bill Haughton	116	Del Miller	234,490	Bill Haughton	374,527
1954	Bill Haughton	153	Joe O'Brien	218,837	Bill Haughton	415,577
1955	Bill Haughton	168	Joe O'Brien	219,957	Bill Haughton	599,445
1956	Bill Haughton	167	Joe O'Brien	242,787	Bill Haughton	572,945
1957	Bill Haughton	156	John Simpson	367,670	Bill Haughton	586,950
1958	Bill Haughton	176	Joe O'Brien	267,342	Bill Haughton	816,659
1959	William Gilmour	165	Joe O'Brien	263,636	Bill Haughton	711,435
1960	Del Insko	156	Del Miller	338,594	Del Miller	567,282
1961	Bob Farrington	201	Jimmy Arthur	248,211	Stanley Dancer	674,723
1962	Bob Farrington	203	Stanley Dancer	306,454	Stanley Dancer	760,343
1963	Donald Busse	201	Ralph Baldwin	299,899	Bill Haughton	790,086
1964	Bob Farrington	312	Stanley Dancer	269,080	Stanley Dancer	1,051,538
1965	Bob Farrington	310	Joe O'Brien	304,791	Bill Haughton	889,943
1966	Bob Farrington	283	George Sholty	293,531	Stanley Dancer	1,218,403

Record of Citation

Year	Age	Starts	1st	2nd	3rd	Unpl.	Won
1947.	2	9	8	1	0	0	$155,680
1948.	3	20	19	1	0	0	709,470
1949.	4 (Did not start due to injuries)						
1950.	5	9	2	7	0	0	$73,480
1951.	6	7	3	1	2	1	147,130
Tot..		45	32	10	2	1	$1,085,760

Citation was retired at age of 6, July 19, 1951. His last winning race, the Hollywood Gold Cup, Inglewood, Calif., July 14, 1951, brought his total winnings to $1,085,760. A bay colt by Bull Lea—Hydroplane II, he was bred and owned by the Calumet Farm.

Green Bay Wins First Super Bowl Game

The first professional football game between the champions of the National and American Leagues resulted in a 35-10 victory by the National League Champion Green Bay Packers over the Kansas City Chiefs on Jan. 15, 1967. The game was played at Memorial Coliseum in Los Angeles before 63,036 spectators plus an estimated 60,000,000 television viewers. For their victory the Packer players received $15,000 each, with $7,500 going to each losing Chief, in addition to the money the players received for winning their respective league championships.

SCORING

Green Bay Packers ....7 7 14 7—35
Kansas City Chiefs ....0 10 0 0—10

G.B.—McGee, 37, pass from Starr (Chandler, kick).
K.C.—McClinton, 7, pass from Dawson (Mercer, kick).
G.B.—Taylor, 14, run (Chandler, kick).
K.C.—FG, Mercer, 31.
G.B.—Pitts, 5, run (Chandler, kick).
G.B.—McGee, 13, pass from Starr (Chandler, kick).
G.B.—Pitts, 1, run (Chandler, kick).

GAME STATISTICS

	Packers	Chiefs
First downs	21	17
Rushing yardage	130	72
Passing yardage	228	167
Passes	16-24	17-32
Interceptions by	1	1
Punts	4-43	7-45
Fumbles lost	1	1
Yards penalized	40	26

INDIVIDUAL STATISTICS

Rushing—G. B.: Taylor, 16 attempts for 53 yards; Pitts, 11 for 45; Anderson, 4 for 30; Grabowski, 2 for 2. K. C.: Dawson 3 for 24; Garrett 6 for 17; McClinton 6 for 16; Coan 3 for 1.

Passing—G. B.: Starr, 16 completions in 23 attempts for 250 yards; Bratkowski, 0 in 1. K. C.: Dawson 16 in 27 for 211; Beathard 1 in 5 for 17.

Receiving—G. B.: McGee, 7 receptions for 138 yards; Dale, 4 for 59; Fleming, 2 for 22; Pitts, 2

for 32. K. C.: Burford, 4 for 67; Taylor, 4 for 57; Garrett, 3 for 28; McClinton, 2 for 34; Arbanas, 2 for 30; Carolan, 1 for 7; Coan, 1 for 5.

PLAYERS

GREEN BAY

Ends—Dale, Fleming, Davis, Aldridge, Long, Anderson, B. Brown.
Tackles—Skoronski, Gregg, Kostelnik, Jordan, Wright, Weatherwax.
Guards—Thurston, Kramer, Gillingham.
Centers—Curry, Bowman.
Linebackers—D. Robinson, Nitschke, Caffey, Crutcher.
Quarterbacks—Starr, Bratkowski.
Offensive Backs—E. Pitts, J. Taylor, Dowler, McGee, Anderson, Mack, Vandersea, Grabowski.
Defensive Backs—Jeter, Adderly, T. Brown, Wood, Hart, Hathcock.
Kicker—Chandler.

KANSAS CITY

Ends—Burford, Arbanas, Mays, Hurston, F. Pitts, Carolan, A. Brown.
Tackles—Tyrer, Hill, Rice, Buchanan, DiMidio.
Guards—Budde, Merz, Reynolds, Biodrowski.
Centers—Frazier, Gilliam.
Linebackers—Bell, Headrick, Holub, Corey, Abell, Stover.
Quarterbacks—Dawson, Beathard.
Offensive Backs—Garrett, McClinton, O. Taylor, Coan, Thomas.
Defensive Backs—Williamson, Mitchell, Hunt, J. Robinson, F. Smith, Ply.
Kickers—Mercer, Wilson.

Professional Football Player Draft

The first combined National Football League-American Football League player draft was held Mar. 14, 1967, in New York. The twenty-six clubs required 21 hours and 39 minutes of elapsed time to select 445 players. First round picks in order of selection follow:

Baltimore—(From New Orleans)—Smith, Charles (Bubba), T, 6-7, 283, Michigan State University.
Minnesota—(From New York Giants)—Jones, Clinton, HB, 6-0, 201, Michigan State University.
San Francisco—(From Atlanta)—Spurrier, Steve, QB, 6-2, 203, Florida.
Miami—Griese, Bob, QB, 6-0, 184, Purdue.
Houston—Webster, George, LB, 6-4, 212, Michigan State University.
Denver—Little, Floyd, HB, 5-11, 195, Syracuse.
Detroit—Farr, Mel, HB, 6-2, 198, UCLA.
Minnesota—Washington, Gene, FL, 6-3, 219, Michigan State University.
Green Bay—(From Pittsburgh)—Hyland, Bob, G, 6-5, 245, Boston College.
Chicago—Phillips, Loyd, DE, 6-3, 230, Arkansas.
San Francisco—Banaszek, Casimir, TE-LB, 6-3, 228, Northwestern.
New York Jets—Seiler, Paul, G, 6-4½, 255, Notre Dame.
Washington—McDonald, Ray, FB, 6-5, 248, Idaho.
San Diego—Billingsley, Ronald, DT, 6-8, 258, Wyoming University.

Minnesota—(From Los Angeles)—Page, Alan, DE, 6-5, 238, Notre Dame.
St. Louis—Williams, Dave, E, 6-2, 200, Washington.
Oakland—Upshaw, Gene, G-T, 6-5, 260, Texas A.&I.
Cleveland—Matheson, Bob, LB, 6-3, 230, Duke.
Philadelphia—Jones, Harry, B, 6-2, 195, Arkansas.
Baltimore—Detwiler, James, HB, 6-3, 215, Michigan.
Boston—Charles, John, DHB, 6-1, 196, Purdue.
Buffalo—Pitts, John, FL-DB, 6-5, 211, Arizona State University.
Houston—(From Dallas)—Regner, Thomas, G, 6-1, 245, Notre Dame.
Kansas City—Trosch, Eugene, DT, 6-6, 247, Miami (Fla.).
Green Bay—Horn, Donald, QB, 6-2, 193, San Diego State.
New Orleans—Kelley, Leslie, HB, 6-3, 214, Alabama.

Stadiums

For stadiums that house a major league baseball team see page 818. For college stadiums and arenas see page 846.

Name and location	Cap.*	Name and location	Cap.*
American Legion Memorial, Charlotte, N. C.	22,315	Los Angeles Memorial Coliseum	92,000
Balboa Stadium, San Diego, Calif.	34,500	Mississippi Memorial Stadium, Jackson	46,000
Bears Stadium, Denver, Colo.	34,549	Orange Bowl, Miami, Fla.	75,000
Buffalo War Memorial Stadium	44,500	Philadelphia Municipal Stadium	105,000
Columbus (Ga.) Memorial Stadium	35,000	Portland Civic Stadium	29,019
Cotton Bowl, Dallas, Tex.	75,504	Richmond (Va.) City Stadium	22,000
Gator Bowl, Jacksonville, Fla.	70,000	Roanoke (Va.) Victory Stadium	30,000
Kansas City Municipal Stadium	40,000	Rose Bowl, Pasadena, Calif.	100,577
Kentucky Exposition Stadium, Louisville	21,000	Rubber Bowl, Akron, Ohio	35,000
Kezar Stadium, San Francisco	60,000	San Diego Stadium	50,000
Ladd Memorial Stadium, Mobile, Ala.	40,605	Sicks Seattle Stadium	10,500
Lambeau Field, Green Bay, Wisc.	50,180	Soldier Field, Chicago	77,112
Legion Stadium, Birmingham, Ala.	68,821	Sugar Bowl, New Orleans, La.	80,985
Long Beach (Calif.) Veterans Memorial	15,000	Tampa Stadium, Tampa, Fla.	45,000

*Normal permanent seating capacity.

Continental Football League

The Continental League Championship game was played Dec. 4, 1966, at Philadelphia. The score was Philadelphia 20, Orlando 17, in sudden death overtime.

(College Football Hall of Fame, Coaches continued)

Ray Morrison (Southern Methodist, Vanderbilt, Temple, Austin) 1915-52
Clarence Munn (Albright, Syracuse, Michigan State) 1935-53
Earl (Greasy) Neale (Muskingum, W. Virginia Wesleyan, Marietta, Washington & Jefferson, Univ. of Virginia, W. Virginia Univ., Yale) 1915-40
Robert R. Neyland (Tennessee) 1926-52
Frank (Buck) O'Neil (Colgate, Syracuse, Columbia) 1902-22
Bennie Owen (Bethany of Kansas, Oklahoma) 1901-26
E. N. Robinson (Neb., Brown, Me.) 1896-1902
Knute K. Rockne (Notre Dame) 1918-30
E. L. (Dick) Romney (Utah State) 1919-48
William W. Roper (Princeton, Missouri, Princeton) 1906-30
Andrew L. Smith (Penn., Purdue, Calif.) 1909-25

Carl Snavely (No. Carolina, Bucknell, Cornell) 1926-52
Amos Alonzo Stagg (Chi., Col. of Pacific) 1892-1946
John R. (Jock) Sutherland (Lafayette, Pitts.) 1919-38
Frank W. Thomas (Chattanooga, Ala.) 1925-46
W. Wallace Wade (Alabama, Duke) 1923-50
Lynn (Pappy) Waldorf (Oklahoma St., Kansas St., Northwestern, U. of Calif.) 1925-51
Glenn S. (Pop) Warner (Georgia, Cornell, Carlisle, Pittsburgh, Stanford, Temple) 1895-1938
E. E. (Tad) Wieman (Secretary of Rules Committee Honors Court, Michigan, Princeton) 1927-42
John W. Wilce (Ohio State) 1913-28
Henry L. Williams (Army, Minnesota) 1891-1921
George W. Woodruff (Pennsylvania) 1894-1901
Fielding H. Yost (Ohio Wesleyan, Nebraska, Kansas, Stanford, Michigan) 1897-1926
Robert Zuppke (Illinois) 1913-41

Records of Post-Season Football Games

Figures in parentheses after games denote attendance.

ROSE BOWL
Pasadena, Calif.
Jan. 1
1947—Illinois 45, U.C.L.A. 14 (90,000)
1948—Michigan 49, Southern California 0 (93,000)
1949—Northwestern 20, California 14 (93,000)
1950—Ohio State 17, California 14 (100,963)
1951—Michigan 14, California 6 (98,939)
1952—Illinois 40, Stanford 7 (96,825)
1953—Southern California 7, Wisconsin 0 (100,000)
1954—Michigan State 28, U.C.L.A. 20 (100,000)
1955—Ohio State 20, So. California 7 (89,191)
1956—Michigan State 17, U.C.L.A. 14 (100,809)
1957—Iowa 35, Oregon State 19 (97,126)
1958—Ohio State 10, Oregon 7 (100,000)
1959—Iowa 38, California 12 (98,297)
1960—Washington 44, Wisconsin 8 (100,809)
1961—Washington 17, Minnesota 7 (97,314)
1962—Minnesota 21, U.C.L.A. 3 (98,214)
1963—So. California 42, Wisconsin 37 (98,698)
1964—Illinois 17, Washington 7 (96,957)
1965—Michigan 34, Oregon State 7 (100,423)
1966—U.C.L.A. 14, Michigan State 12 (100,087)
1967—Purdue 14, Southern Calif. 13 (101,455)

SUGAR BOWL
New Orleans, La.
Jan. 1
1953—Georgia Tech 24, Mississippi 7 (82,000)
1954—Georgia Tech 42, West Virginia 19 (75,000)
1955—Navy 21, Mississippi 0 (82,000)
1956—Georgia Tech 7, Pittsburgh 0 (80,175)
1957—Baylor 13, Tennessee 7 (81,000)
1958—Mississippi 39, Texas 7 (82,000)
1959—Louisiana State 7, Clemson 0 (82,000)
1960—Mississippi 21, Louisiana State 0 (83,000)
1961—Mississippi 14, Rice 6 (82,851)
1962—Alabama 10, Arkansas 3 (82,910)
1963—Mississippi 17, Arkansas 13 (82,900)
1964—Alabama 12, Mississippi 7 (80,785)
1965—Louisiana State 13, Syracuse 10 (65,000)
1966—Missouri 20, Florida 18 (67,421)
1967—Alabama 34, Nebraska 7 (82,000)

ORANGE BOWL
Miami, Fla.
Jan. 1
1953—Alabama 61, Syracuse 6 (68,280)
1954—Oklahoma 7, Maryland 0 (68,718)
1955—Duke 34, Nebraska 7 (68,750)
1956—Oklahoma 20, Maryland 6 (76,561)
1957—Colorado 27, Clemson 21 (72,552)
1958—Oklahoma 48, Duke 21 (76,318)
1959—Oklahoma 21, Syracuse 6 (75,281)
1960—Georgia 14, Missouri 0 (75,280)
1961—Missouri 21, Navy 14 (71,218)
1962—Louisiana State 25, Colorado 7 (62,381)
1963—Alabama 17, Oklahoma 0 (73,280)
1964—Nebraska 13, Auburn 7 (72,647)
1965—Texas 21, Alabama 17 (72,647)
1966—Alabama 39, Nebraska 28 (74,214)
1967—Florida 27, Georgia Tech 12 (72,426)

SUN BOWL
El Paso, Tex.
Jan. 1
1953—College of Pacific 26, Miss. So. 7 (11,000)
1954—Texas Western 37, Miss. Southern 14 (9,500)
1955—Texas Western 47, Florida State 20 (14,000)
1956—Wyoming 21, Texas Tech. 14 (14,500)
1957—George Washington 13, Texas Western 0 (13,500)
1958—Louisville 34, Drake 20 (12,000)
1959—Wyoming 14, Hardin-Simmons 6 (13,000)
1959, Dec. 31—N. M. St. 28, No. Texas St. 8
1960, Dec. 31—N. M. St. 20, Utah St. 14 (16,000)
1961—Dec. 30—Villanova 17, Wichita 9 (15,000)

1962, Dec. 31—W. Texas St. 15, Ohio U. 14 (16,000)
1963, Dec. 31—Oregon 21, So. Methodist 14 (26,500)
1964, Dec. 26—Georgia 7, Texas Tech 0 (28,000)
1965, Dec. 31—Texas Western 13, Texas Christian 12 (27,450)
1966, Dec. 24—Wyoming 28, Florida St. 20 (24,381)

COTTON BOWL
Dallas, Texas
Jan. 1
1953—Texas 16, Tennessee 0 (75,504)
1954—Rice 28, Alabama 6 (75,504)
1955—Georgia Tech 14, Arkansas 6 (75,504)
1956—Mississippi 14, Texas Christian 13 (76,504)
1957—Texas Christian 28, Syracuse 27 (68,000)
1958—Navy 20, Rice 7 (75,504)
1959—Air Force Acad. 0, Texas Christian 0 (75,504)
1960—Syracuse 23, Texas 14 (75,504)
1961—Duke 7, Arkansas 6 (74,000)
1962—Texas 12, Mississippi 7 (75,504)
1963—Louisiana State 13, Texas 0 (75,504)
1964—Texas 28, Navy 6 (75,504)
1965—Arkansas 10, Nebraska 7 (75,504)
1966—Louisiana St. 14, Arkansas 7 (76,200)
1966, Dec. 31—Georgia 24, S.M.U. 9 (75,440)

BLUE AND GRAY (NORTH-SOUTH)
Montgomery, Ala.
(Dec.)
1955—South 20, North 19 (19,000)
1956—North 14, South 0 (21,000)
1957—South 21, North 20
1958—North 16, South 0 (21,000)
1959—North 20, South 8 (20,000)
1960—North 35, South 7 (12,000)
1961—South 9, North 7 (18,000)
1962—North 10, South 6 (20,000)
1963—North 21, North 14 (20,000)
1964—North 10, South 6 (16,000)
1965—South 23, North 19 (18,000)
1966—North 14, South 9 (18,000)

SHRINE ALL-STAR GAME
(EAST-WEST)
San Francisco
1955, Dec. 31—East 29, West 6 (60,000)
1956, Dec. 31—West 7, East 6 (61,000)
1957, West 27, East 13
1958, Dec. 27—East 26, West 14 (60,000)
1960, Jan. 2—West 21, East 14 (60,000)
1960, Dec. 31—East 7, West 0 (59,000)
1961, Dec. 30—West 31, East 8 (59,000)
1962, Dec. 29—East 25, West 19 (59,000)
1963, Dec. 28—East 6, West 6 (60,128)
1965, Jan. 2—West 11, East 7 (60,000)
1965, Dec. 31—West 22, East 7 (56,121)
1966, Dec. 31—East 45, West 22 (52,741)

GATOR BOWL
Jacksonville, Fla.
1953, Jan. 1—Florida 14, Tulsa 13
1954, Jan. 1—Texas Tech 35, Auburn 13
1954, Dec. 31—Auburn 33, Baylor 13
1955, Dec. 31—Vanderbilt 25, Auburn 13
1956, Dec. 29—Georgia Tech 21, Pittsburgh 14
1957, Dec. 28—Tennessee 3, Texas A & M 0
1958, Dec. 27—Mississippi 7, Florida 3
1960, Jan. 2—Arkansas 14, Georgia Tech 7
1960, Dec. 31—Florida 13, Baylor 12
1961, Dec. 30—Penn State 30, Georgia Tech 15
1962, Dec. 29—Florida 17, Penn State 7
1963, Dec. 28—North Carolina 35, Air Force Academy 0 (50,018)
1965, Jan. 2—Fla. State 36, Okla. 19 (50,408)
1965, Dec. 31—Ga. Tech 31, Texas Tech 21 (60,127)
1966, Dec. 31—Tennessee 18, Syracuse 12 (60,312)

OTHER GAMES OF POST-1966 FOOTBALL SEASON

Camellia Bowl, Sacramento, Calif., Dec. 10—San Diego State 28, Montana State 7. **Tangerine Bowl,** Orlando, Fla., Dec. 10—Morgan State 14, West Chester 6. **Pecan Bowl,** Abilene, Tex., Dec. 10—North Dakota 42, Parsons 24. **Liberty Bowl,** Memphis, Tenn., Dec. 10—Miami 14, Virginia Tech 7. **Bluebonnet Bowl,** Houston, Tex., Dec. 17—Texas 19, Mississippi 0. **All Star Shrine Game,** Miami, Fla., Dec. 26—North 27, South 14. **Senior Bowl,** Mobile, Ala., Jan. 7—North 35, South 13. **Hula Bowl,** Honolulu, Hawaii, Jan. 7—North 28, South 27.

Contract Bridge Championships in 1966-1967
Winners of Major Events at 3 National Tournaments
Fall 1966—Spring and Summer 1967
Source: American Contract Bridge League

Board-a-Match Teams—Edgar Kaplan, New York, N. Y.; Norman Kay, Philadelphia, Pa.; Arthur Robinson, Strafford, Pa.; Robert Jordan, Bala Cynwyd, Pa.

Men's Teams—Lawrence Jolma, Portland, Ore.; Dr. Gary Stark, Oswego, Ore.; Tom Bussey, Vancouver, Wash.; J. R. Dunlap, J. R. Patterson, both Milwaukie, Ore.

Women's Teams—Agnes Gordon, Buffalo, N. Y.; Margaret Wagar, Atlanta, Ga.; Dorothy Hayden, Hastings-on-Hudson, N. Y.; Emma Jean Hawes, Ft. Worth, Tex.

Mixed Teams—Michael & Kathie Cappelletti, Alexandria, Va.; Michael Moss, Gail Shane, both New York, N. Y.

Spingold Knockout Teams—Edgar Kaplan, William Root, Alvin Roth, all New York, N. Y.; Norman Kay, Philadelphia, Pa.

Vanderbilt Knockout Teams—Lew Mathe, Los Angeles, Calif.; Ron Von Der Porten, San Francisco, Calif.; Lew Stansby, Oakland, Calif.; Mike Lawrence, Berkeley, Calif.; James Jacoby, Dallas, Tex.; G. Robert Nail, Houston, Tex.

Blue Ribbon Pairs—Charles Coon, New York,

N. Y., and Richard Zeckhauser, Great Neck, N. Y.

Life Master Men's Pairs—Carl Hudecek, Toledo, O., and Ray Zoller, Cincinnati, O.

Life Master Women's Pairs—Dorothy Hayden, Hastings-on-Hudson, N. Y., and Emma Jean Hawes, Ft. Worth, Tex.

Life Master Pairs—Lew Mathe, Los Angeles, Calif., and Phil Feldesman, New York, N. Y.

Men's Pairs—Art Price and Richard Lawrence, both Ann Arbor, Mich.

Women's Pairs—Terry Michaels, Washington, D. C., and Garner McDaniel, Houston, Tex.

Mixed Pairs—Mr. and Mrs. Robert Sharp, Miami Beach, Fla.

Open Pairs—Harvey Cohen and Maury Genud, both Los Angeles, Calif.

Senior and Advanced Senior Master Pairs—Harold Thaw and Alvin Levy, both Brooklyn, N. Y.

1967 World Championship, Miami Beach, Fla.—Italy (Walter Avarelli, Giorgio Belladonna, Massimo D'Alelio, Pietro Forquet, Benito Garozzo, Camillo Pabis Ticci; Guido Barbone, non-playing captain).

Oswald Jacoby Passes 10,000-Master-Point Mark in Bridge Play

Oswald Jacoby, America's No. 1 bridge champion and long the holder of the most Master Points in bridge play, accomplished the bridge equivalent of the four-minute mile by passing the 10,000-Master-Point mark Oct. 5, 1967. He is the first person ever to achieve this feat.

At a sectional tournament in Dallas, the nationally known bridge columnist of Newspaper Enterprise Association played himself right off the charts of the American Contract Bridge League, whose mechanized equipment for keeping track of accumulated Master Points can't handle figures this high.

"I guess I'll just have to start over," the bridge expert said, "or else they'll have to issue me a new card indicating I already have 10,000 points."

Sharing in the excitement over Jacoby's accomplishment were the members of his team: his son Jim (who co-authors with Oswald the daily "Win at Bridge" column which appears in more than 400 metropolitan newspapers across the country) and their wives: Mary Zita (Mrs. Oswald) and Judy (Mrs. Jim).

Playing Cards and Dice Chances

POKER HANDS (Four-Suit)

Hand	Number Possible	Odds Against
Royal Flush....	4	649,739 to 1
Other Straight Flush	36	72,192 to 1
Four of a kind	624	4,164 to 1
Full House....	3,744	693 to 1
Flush	5,108	508 to 1
Straight	10,200	254 to 1
Three of a kind	54,912	46 to 1
Two Pairs	123,552	20 to 1
One Pair 1,098,240		4 to 3 (1.37 to 1)
Nothing 1,302,540		1 to 1
Total 2,598,960		

BRIDGE

Perfect hand—In dealing a hand of 13 cards from 52, the probability of drawing a perfect hand —13 spades—is 1 in 635,013,559,600.

One suit—Chances of drawing 13 cards of one suit are 1 in 158,753,389,900.

PINOCHLE (AUCTION)

Odds Against Finding in "Widow" of Three Cards Open Places	Odds Against
1....................................5 to 1	
2....................................2 to 1	
3...................................Even	
4...................................3 to 2 for	
5...................................2 to 1 for	

DICE
Totals Probabilities on Two Dice

Total	Odds Against (Single toss)
2.......................................35 to 1	
3.......................................17 to 1	
4.......................................11 to 1	
5..8 to 1	
6.......................................31 to 5	
7..5 to 1	
8.......................................31 to 5	
9..8 to 1	
10......................................11 to 1	
11......................................17 to 1	
12......................................35 to 1	

Probabilities of Consecutive Winning Plays

No. Consecutive Wins	By 7, 11, or Point
1................................244 in 495	
2.................................24 in 100	
3..................................3 in 25	
4..................................1 in 17	
5..................................1 in 34	
6..................................1 in 70	
7..................................1 in 141	
8..................................1 in 287	
9..................................1 in 582	
10...............................1 in 1,181	

World and U. S. Checker Champions
U. S. CHECKER ASSOCIATION CHAMPIONS

World Three-Move Champion—Walter Hellman, Gary, Ind.

World Two-Move Champion—Dr. Marion Tinsley, Tallahassee, Fla.

World Free-Style Champion—Tom Wiswell, Brooklyn, N. Y.

World Blindfold Champion—Newell Banks, Detroit, Mich.

U. S. Junior Champion—Geoffrey Lewis, Southgate, Mich.

U. S. Team Champions—Chess & Checker Club of N. Y.

Canadian Match Champion—Prof. W. R. Fraser, Montreal.

U. S. CHECKER ASSOCIATION CHAMPIONS

U. S. Straight Champion—Walter Hellman, Gary, Ind.

Eastern U. S. Straight Champion—Harold Fryer, Brooklyn, N. Y.

Southern U. S. Straight Champion—Basil Case, Halleyville, Ala.

Central U. S. Straight Champion—Eugene Frazier, Parsons, Kan.

Western U. S. Straight Champion—Millard Hopper, Los Angeles, Cal.

World Freestyle (Spanish) Champion—Enrique Freeman (King Chico), New York, N. Y.

Golf House Library and Museum

Golf House, 40 East 38th Street, New York, N. Y., headquarters of the United States Golf Association, opened in January, 1951, houses the organization's library and unique golf museum and serves as a valuable information center for the public. Funds were raised by popular subscription for the center. It possesses a large collection of trophies, books, clubs of champions and other items.

State Automobile Speed Limits
(Except as otherwise posted)
Source: American Automobile Assn., Digest of Motor Laws 1967

Alabama: Interstate highways, 70 mph. daytime, 60 mph. nighttime; open highways, 60 mph. daytime, 50 mph. nighttime; residential districts, 25 mph.; business districts, school zones, etc., 15 mph.

Alaska: Open highways, 50 mph.; urban area, 35 mph.; residential and business districts, 30 mph.

Arizona: State highways, 65 mph. daytime, 60 mph. nighttime; other state highways, 50 mph. daytime, 45 mph. nighttime; residential areas, business districts, 25 mph.; school zones, 15 mph.

Arkansas: Interstate highways, 70 mph.; controlled access highways, 60 mph.; urban districts, 30 mph.; other locations, 60 mph.

California: Statewide limit, 65 mph. (except freeways posted for 70 mph.); residential and business districts, school zones, 25 mph.

Colorado: Open highways, 60 mph.; residential districts, 30 mph.; business districts, 25 mph.; open mountain highway, 40 mph.; winding mountain highway, 20 mph.

Connecticut: Super highways, 70 mph.; other highways, 60 mph.; residential and business, reasonable rate.

Delaware: Open highways, 4-lane, 60 mph., 2-lane, 50 mph.; residential and business districts, 25 mph.

District of Columbia: Expressways, 45 mph.; school and playground areas, 15 mph.; other roads, 25 mph.

Florida: Interstate highways, 70 mph. daytime, 65 mph. nighttime; open highway, 65 mph. daytime, 55 mph. nighttime.

Georgia: Interstate highways, 70 mph. daytime, 65 mph. nighttime; open highway, 60 mph. daytime, 50 mph. nighttime; residential, business and school areas, 25 mph.

Hawaii: Open highways, 45 mph.; residential and business districts, local ordinances govern.

Idaho: Interstate highways, 70 mph.; open highway, 60 mph. daytime, 55 mph. nighttime; urban and business districts, 35 mph.

Illinois: Expressways, 70 mph.; open highways, 65 mph.; urban areas, 30 mph.; school zones, 20 mph.

Indiana: Open highways, 65 mph.; residential district, 30 mph.; business district, 20 mph.

Iowa: Interstate limited access roads, 75 mph. daytime, 65 mph. nighttime; open highways, 70 mph. daytime, 60 mph. nighttime; suburban, 45 mph.; residential and school districts, 25 mph.; business districts, 20 mph.; secondary roads, 60 mph. daytime, 50 mph. nighttime.

Kansas: Interstate highways, 75 mph. daytime, 70 nighttime; open highways, 70 mph. daytime, 60 mph. nighttime; residential districts, 30 mph.; business districts, 20 mph.; Kansas turnpike, 80 mph.

Kentucky: Interstate highways, 70 mph.; open highways, 60 mph. daytime, 50 mph. nighttime; residential and business districts, 35 mph.

Louisiana: Open highways 4-lane, 70 mph.; other open highways, 60 mph.

Maine: Turnpikes, 70 mph. daytime, 65 mph. nighttime; open highways, 45 mph.; residential and business districts, 25 mph.; school zones at recess and when children going to and from school, 15 mph.

Maryland: Open country, expressways, 60 mph.; dual lane highways, 55 mph.; other highways, 50 mph.; residential and business districts, 30 mph.; thinly settled areas, 35 mph., other highways 30 mph.

Massachusetts: Turnpike, 65 mph.; divided highway, 50 mph.; other highways, 40 mph.; residential and business districts, 30 mph.; school zones, 20 mph.

Michigan: Freeways, 70 mph.; open highways, 65 mph. daytime, 55 mph. nighttime; residential and business districts, 25 mph.

Minnesota: Open highways, 65 mph. daytime, 55 mph. nighttime; all speeds in urban districts, 30 mph.

Mississippi: Open highways, 65 mph.; residential districts, 25 mph.; business districts, 20 mph.; school zones, 15 mph.

Missouri: Dual lane U. S. routes, 70 mph.; undivided U. S. routes, 70 mph. daytime, 65 mph. nighttime; other open highways, 65 mph. daytime, 60 mph. nighttime; municipalities, 45 mph.

Montana: Open highways, reasonable and prudent daytime, 55 mph. nighttime; residential and business districts, 25 mph.

Nebraska: Interstate highways, 75 mph.; open highways, 65 mph. daytime, 60 mph. nighttime; residential districts, 25 mph.; business districts, 20 mph.; on non-hard surfaced roads, 50 mph.

Nevada: Careful and prudent; residential and business, posted.

New Hampshire: Turnpike, 60 mph.; open highways, 50 mph.; rural residential districts, 35 mph.; urban and business districts, 25 mph.; school zones, 20 mph.

New Jersey: Turnpike, 60 mph.; open highways, 50 mph.; residential and business districts, 25 mph.

New Mexico: Open highways, 70 mph. daytime, 60 mph. nighttime; other highways, 60 mph. daytime, 50 mph. nighttime; residential and business districts, 25 mph.; school zones, 15 mph.

New York: New York State Thruway, 65 mph.; open highways, 50 mph.; school zones when children going to and from school, 15 mph.

North Carolina: Open highways, 55 mph.; residential districts, 35 mph.; business districts, 20 mph.

North Dakota: Interstate highways, 70 mph. daytime, 60 mph. nighttime; all other highways, 60 mph.; residential and business districts, 25 mph.; school zones, 20 mph.

Ohio: Ohio turnpike and expressways, 70 mph.; open highways, 60 mph. daytime, 50 mph. nighttime; within municipal corporations, 25 mph; school zones, 20 mph.

Oklahoma: Turnpikes and interstate highways, 70 mph.; open highways, 65 mph. daytime, 55 mph. nighttime; school zones, 25 mph.

Oregon: Open highways, 55 mph.; freeways up to 70 mph; residential districts, 25 mph.; business and school zones, 20 mph.

Pennsylvania: Turnpike, 65 mph.; open highways 55 mph.; residential and business districts, 25 to 35 mph.; school zones, 15 mph.

Rhode Island: Residential and business districts, 25 mph.; elsewhere, 50 mph. daytime, 45 mph. nighttime.

South Carolina: Interstate System 70 mph. daytime, 65 mph. night; State highways 60 mph. daytime, 55 mph. night; urban districts 30 mph.

South Dakota: Interstate highways, 75 mph. daytime, 70 mph. nighttime; open highways, 70 mph. daytime, 60 mph. nighttime; residential and business districts, 30 mph.; school zones, 15 mph.

Tennessee: Open highways, 65 mph. daytime, 55 mph. nighttime; school zones, 15 mph.

Texas: Federal or State roads, 70 mph. daytime, 65 mph. nighttime; other rural roads, 60 mph, daytime, 55 mph. nighttime; in urban districts, 30 mph.

Utah: Open highways, as posted; residential and business districts, 25 mph ; school zones, 20 mph.

Vermont: Interstate highways, 65 mph.; open highways, 50 mph.

Virginia: Open highways, 55 mph.; residential, business and school areas, 25 mph.

Washington: County roads, 50 mph.; cities and towns, 25 mph.; school zones, 20 mph.; in other locations, 60 mph.

West Virginia: Interstate highways, 70 mph.; turnpike, 60 mph.; open highways, 55 mph.; residential districts, 25 mph.; school zones, 15 mph.

Wisconsin: Interstate highways, 70 mph. daytime, 60 mph. nighttime; open highways, 65 mph. daytime, 55 mph. nighttime; residential and business districts, 25 mph.; school zone, 15 mph.

Wyoming: Open highways 4-lane divided, 70 mph.; open highways, 65 mph.; residential districts, 30 mph.; business and school districts, 20 mph.

Canal Zone: Outside town limits, 40 mph.; within town limits, 25 mph.

Guam: Roads, 45 mph.; school zones when children at recess or going to and from school, 10 mph.

Puerto Rico: Open highways, 45 mph.; urban districts and school zones, 25 mph.

American Automobile Traffic Volume Hits Another New High

Some 103,000,000 Americans took to the highways within their own country for at least one vacation or pleasure trip by automobile during 1967, establishing a new record. They spent $27 billion and traveled an estimated 174 billion miles. The total mileage traveled by the over 81,000,000 passenger cars registered in this country in 1967 amounted to 780 billion miles. In addition, nearly 200 billion miles were driven by the nearly 17,-000,000 trucks and buses. It is estimated that private passenger automobiles are used for 90% of all vacation and recreation trips in the U. S.

U. S. Auto Safety Rules Go Into Effect

The Department of Transportation's National Traffic Safety Bureau issued in 1967 a set of 20 motor vehicle construction standards and requirements designed to reduce the nation's tragic toll of accidents, injuries and deaths.

The auto safety rules were to apply to all vehicles manufactured after Jan. 1, 1968, for sale in the U. S.

The Department's National Highway Safety Bureau issued a set of 13 standards to be followed by all states in setting up highway safety programs. The states were to have the programs under way by Dec. 31, 1968.

Both sets of standards were issued under Federal laws passed in 1966.

Vehicle Construction Rules

Two-speed windshield wipers with washers and defrosters; new shatter-resistant windshields; outside rearview mirrors (2 in cases of small rear windows); limits on bright surfaces reflecting in driver's eyes; certain standards for lights, switches, turn signals, parking, tail and stop lights and reflectors.

Parking brakes capable of holding on a 30% grade, warning lights to indicate brake failure, an emergency substitute brake system in case of failure of main system, standards for hydraulic brake hoses.

Padding on instrument panels, sun visors, arm rests and backs of front seats; impact-absorbing steering columns; latches limiting likelihood of doors flying open in crashes; standards for seats, seat belts (front seat chest straps were under consideration).

All essential controls to be within driver's reach; shift lever sequence to be park position, reverse, neutral, forward drives; interlock to prevent starting engine in reverse or forward; engine-braking effect in lower gear.

Rupture-resistant fuel tanks and a ban on winged, spinner-type hub caps. Tire standards were being set late in 1967.

A company violating a standard may be fined $1,000 for each vehicle to a total of $400,000,000. Additional standards for future years were under study.

State Safety Standards

Annual inspection of all motor vehicles (but states may adopt experimental programs initially).

Only physically and mentally qualified persons to receive driver licenses; eyesight and knowledge-of-rules exams every 4 years; training courses for youthful drivers.

Uniform traffic laws and regulations within each state; steps to be taken for uniform national rules.

Establishment of procedures to determine the percentage of alcohol in a driver's blood, the maximum permissible level set at one-tenth of 1%.

Programs for ambulance and medical care facilities and trained emergency personnel.

Highways to be modernized; new highways to include traffic control devices, break-away signs, illumination of congested areas, rails on bridges.

Licenses, helmets and eye-protectors for motorcyclists; rearview mirrors; seats and footrests for passengers.

Organized systems of records on drivers, their vehicles and accidents in which they have been involved.

The Transportation Department may withhold 10% of Federal highway construction funds from states failing to comply.

Air Pollution Limits

Another set of standards affecting car construction were the air pollution limitations set for all 1968 cars by the Department of Health, Education and Welfare. These required pollution control modifications which would limit the amounts of carbon monoxide and hydrocarbons that may be emitted from the exhausts of new cars and light trucks.

Both domestic and foreign-made cars were affected by the construction standards set up by both the Transportation and Health-Education-Welfare Departments.

Rural Road Mileage in the United States

Source: Bureau of Public Roads; data are for year 1965

State	Total	Under state control	Under local control	Under federal control	State	Total	Under state control	Under local control	Under federal control
Alabama....	66,239	18,242	47,997	....	Nebraska...	97,003	9,292	87,424	287
Alaska.....	6,107	4,356	1,655	96	Nevada.....	45,069	6,209	38,859	1
Arizona....	33,702	4,987	16,357	12,358	N. Hamp....	12,844	3,924	8,834	86
Arkansas...	71,928	12,121	57,856	1,951	New Jersey..	21,094	1,776	19,318	....
California..	125,302	14,589	79,007	31,706	N. Mexico..	62,790	11,487	46,011	5,292
Colorado...	74,063	8,092	65,868	103	New York..	84,838	13,958	70,870	10
Connecticut.	5,205	1,499	3,706	....	N. Carolina.	71,300	69,717	....	1,583
Delaware...	3,444	3,444	....	....	N. Dakota..	104,120	6,308	97,269	543
Florida.....	60,824	15,471	45,353	....	Ohio.......	84,416	15,988	68,428	....
Georgia....	83,207	15,067	68,093	47	Oklahoma...	94,851	11,488	83,367	....
Hawaii.....	2,432	1,010	1,331	91	Oregon.....	75,026	5,841	34,455	34,930
Idaho......	50,647	4,667	26,769	19,211	Pa.........	88,918	42,630	45,980	308
Illinois.....	102,555	13,064	89,491	....	R. I........	819	333	486	....
Indiana.....	86,253	10,116	76,137	....	S. Carolina..	52,441	28,737	23,704	....
Iowa.......	99,743	9,133	90,610	....	S. Dakota..	82,398	8,104	72,619	1,675
Kansas.....	123,740	9,985	113,746	9	Tennessee...	67,495	8,092	58,462	941
Kentucky...	65,356	21,015	44,077	264	Texas......	197,078	57,827	139,251	....
Louisiana...	40,557	14,171	26,386	....	Utah.......	33,616	5,126	19,855	8,635
Maine......	18,633	10,830	7,658	145	Vermont....	12,874	2,190	10,660	24
Maryland...	21,355	4,930	16,310	115	Virginia....	51,350	48,862	740	1,748
Mass.......	7,409	1,078	6,331	....	Washington..	62,340	10,488	39,293	12,559
Michigan...	94,801	7,998	86,803	....	W. Virginia.	32,081	31,207	....	874
Minnesota..	110,228	11,274	97,175	1,779	Wisconsin...	87,258	10,600	76,592	66
Mississippi.	59,148	9,516	49,140	192	Wyoming...	75,084	5,443	65,707	3,934
Missouri....	99,596	29,899	69,099	598					
Montana...	70,639	11,422	51,304	7,913	Totals...	3,183,220	686,703	2,346,443	150,074

Municipal mileage—Under state control 64,635, under local control 441,811. Total rural and municipal mileage 3,689,666.

Motor-Vehicle Registrations in the U. S. Top 97,000,000 by 1968

Motor-vehicle registrations in the United States will reach 97,527,000 by Jan. 1, 1968, according to estimates by the Federal Highway Administration of the U. S. Dept. of Transportation. This represents an expected increase of more than 3,350,000 over the total registered a year earlier. Passenger car registrations will reach 81,051,000, a 3.4% increase over year-earlier figures, while trucks and buses will total 16,476,000, nearly 4% up, it was estimated.

California's estimated 10,700,000 registrations are followed by 6,400,000 in New York and nearly 6,000,000 in Texas. Ohio and Pennsylvania will have nearly 5,500,000 motor vehicles each by the beginning of 1968. Illinois and Michigan will have more than 4,000,000 each, Florida and New Jersey more than 3,000,000 each, and Minnesota will join Indiana, North Carolina, Massachusetts, Missouri and Georgia in the 2,000,000 registration class. There will be 15 additional states with registrations of more than 1,000,000 each.

Auto Registrations, Taxes, Gasoline, Drivers' Ages
Source: Bureau of Public Roads and American Automobile Association

State	Mini-mum age[*]	Registered automobiles, buses & trucks[1]	Gasoline State Tax per gallon	Gasoline Gross Tax collection	Motor fuel consumption[2] (1966) Highway	Motor fuel consumption[2] (1966) Non-highway	Motor fuel consumption[2] (1966) Total[3]
	(1967)	(1966) Number	(1967) Cents	1,000 Dollars	1,000 Gallons	1,000 Gallons	1,000 Gallons
Alabama.......	16	1,731,836	7	96,106	1,331,212	42,015	1,373,227
Alaska.......	18 (16)	108,128	8	6,386	69,592	16,901	86,493
Arizona.......	18 (16)	862,950	7	51,576	701,355	37,708	739,063
Arkansas.......	18 (14)	955,091	7.5	63,144	822,093	34,946	857,039
California.......	16	10,347,012	7	554,750	7,718,880	289,074	8,007,954
Colorado.......	16	1,200,777	[4]6	59,683	838,773	76,052	914,825
Connecticut....	21 (16)	1,459,148	6	64,454	1,043,021	23,881	1,066,902
Delaware.......	16	256,481	7	16,221	225,421	9,203	234,624
Florida.......	16 (14)	3,221,307	7	173,180	2,428,962	120,505	2,549,467
Georgia.......	16 (15)	2,099,247	6.5	122,829	1,847,087	56,630	1,903,717
Hawaii.......	20	324,521	[4]5	9,697	179,398	21,762	201,160
Idaho.......	16 (14)	445,823	6	21,177	314,011	45,365	359,376
Illinois.......	21 (16)	4,704,624	5	201,460	3,878,030	250,726	4,128,756
Indiana.......	18 (16)	2,550,539	6	134,651	2,159,021	138,487	2,297,508
Iowa.......	16 (14)	1,609,004	7	99,547	1,171,098	280,657	1,451,755
Kansas.......	16 (14)	1,405,256	5	58,716	1,001,915	157,522	1,159,437
Kentucky.......	18 (16)	1,574,632	[6]7	87,410	1,172,941	48,429	1,221,370
Louisiana.......	15	1,555,655	7	90,054	1,248,642	56,016	1,304,658
Maine.......	18 (15)	433,891	7	29,111	402,214	13,401	415,615
Maryland.......	21 (16)	1,533,643	7	88,929	1,264,247	33,234	1,297,481
Massachusetts..	18 (16½)	2,172,767	6.5	115,688	1,783,690	42,130	1,825,820
Michigan.......	18 (14)	3,024,120	6	202,287	3,422,775	225,274	3,648,049
Minnesota.......	18 (16)	1,942,781	6	96,497	1,458,924	194,691	1,653,615
Mississippi.......	15	956,842	7	65,588	862,514	38,229	900,743
Missouri.......	16	2,220,858	5	102,504	1,947,130	168,487	2,115,617
Montana.......	18 (15)	439,146	6	23,433	339,912	40,736	380,648
Nebraska.......	16	870,439	7.5	54,448	659,161	85,088	744,249
Nevada.......	16	279,000	[4]6	17,919	257,234	16,097	273,331
New Hampshire.	16	334,052	7	18,541	261,925	6,066	267,991
New Jersey.....	17 (16)	3,122,876	6	153,209	2,475,188	77,415	2,552,603
New Mexico....	18 (15)	549,206	6	31,091	513,062	17,849	530,911
New York.....	18 (16)	6,162,374	6	285,261	4,707,966	250,691	4,958,657
North Carolina.	18 (16)	2,307,008	7	141,341	1,961,087	79,539	2,040,626
North Dakota...	16 (13)	406,420	6	22,580	251,555	120,602	372,157
Ohio	21 (16)	5,238,498	7	279,449	3,937,077	184,017	4,121,094
Oklahoma.......	16	1,495,620	6.5	77,051	1,171,295	58,944	1,230,339
Oregon.......	16 (14)	1,167,112	6	52,526	902,917	50,775	953,692
Pennsylvania...	18 (16)	5,196,174	7	284,610	3,795,990	209,994	4,005,984
Rhode Island...	16	423,433	7	20,820	291,863	5,764	297,627
South Carolina.	16 (15)	1,147,120	7	70,948	970,608	41,146	1,011,754
South Dakota...	16 (14)	401,189	6	24,741	297,247	109,397	406,644
Tennessee.......	16 (14)	1,757,575	7	108,176	1,513,884	56,192	1,570,076
Texas.......	16 (14)	5,711,263	5	260,179	4,927,565	202,331	5,129,896
Utah.......	17 (16)	543,991	6	26,211	418,629	24,444	443,073
Vermont.......	18 (16)	179,457	6.5	10,830	167,802	6,823	174,625
Virginia.......	18 (16)	1,874,779	[6]7	122,258	1,658,385	67,113	1,725,498
Washington.....	18	1,756,294	7.5	94,606	1,242,698	57,321	1,300,019
West Virginia...	18 (16)	730,880	7	43,152	604,745	14,536	619,281
Wisconsin.......	16 (14)	1,890,218	[4]7	107,168	1,555,763	122,215	1,677,978
Wyoming.......	21 (16)	223,993	5	12,218	207,796	28,452	236,248
Dist. of Col.....	18 (16)	241,749	[4]7	14,081	243,874	3,548	247,422
Totals.....		94,176,799	[7]6.40	4,971,522	74,628,274	[8]4,358,420	78,986,694

[*]Source: American Automobile Association 1967 Digest of Motor Laws. Figures in parentheses are age limits for junior permits, school permits or in other special situations.
[1]Registrations include: Automobiles, private and commercial (inc. taxicabs) 77,959,287; publicly owned 372,201. Buses, private and commercial 157,725, publicly owned 165,472. Trucks private and commercial 14,726,526, publicly owned 795,588. Total private and commercial motor vehicles 92,843,538, publicly owned 1,333,261. (Total revised registration for 1965 90,360,721.) Motorcycles, private and commercial 1,735,411, publicly owned 17,390. [2]Total motor fuel consumed includes (in gallons) for private and commercial use, 77,215,180,000; for public use 1,771,514,000; [3]Losses allowed for evaporation handling, etc., not included in total are 614,267,000. [4]Tax rate changes in 1966 were as follows: California 7 to 6¢, Jan. 1; Colorado 7 to 6¢, Sept. 1; Mississippi, 8 to 10¢ (diesel), Sept. 1; Nevada, state tax rate is 6¢ but all counties may levy an additional one cent effective July 1; Wisconsin 6 to 7¢, July 1; District of Columbia, 6 to 7¢, Nov. 1. [5]Hawaii County tax rate is 8¢ and 5¢ in the other counties. [6]Trucks or combinations of more than two axles pay motor-fuel tax at rate of 9¢ per gallon in Kentucky and Virginia. [7]Weighted average tax rate. (For motor fuel was 6.42¢ per gallon.) [8]Does not include an estimated 4.4 billion gallons of aviation jet fuel.

Minimum Legal Age for Purchase of Alcoholic Beverages
Source: Distilled Spirits Institute, Inc., Washington, D. C. 20004

State	Years	State	Years	State	Years
Alabama.......	21	Kentucky.......	21	North Dakota.......	21
Alaska.......	21	Louisiana.......	18	Ohio (c).......	21
Arizona.......	21	Maine.......	21	Oklahoma (d).......	21
Arkansas.......	21	Maryland.......	21	Oregon.......	21
California.......	21	Massachusetts...	21	Pennsylvania.......	21
Colorado (c)....	21	Michigan.......	21	Rhode Island.......	21
Connecticut....	21	Minnesota.......	21	South Carolina (e)..	21
Delaware.......	21	Mississippi (h)..	21	South Dakota (g)...	21
Dist. of Col. (b)..	21	Missouri.......	21	Tennessee.......	21
Florida.......	21	Montana.......	21	Texas.......	21
Georgia.......	21	Nebraska.......	21	Utah.......	21
Hawaii.......	20	Nevada.......	21	Vermont.......	21
Idaho (a).......	21	New Hampshire..	21	Virginia (c).......	21
Illinois.......	21	New Jersey.....	21	Washington.......	21
Indiana.......	21	New Mexico.....	21	West Virginia (o)...	21
Iowa.......	21	New York.....	18	Wisconsin (f).......	21
Kansas (c).......	21	North Carolina (b)	21	Wyoming.......	21

(a) Beer 20. (b) Light wine, beer 18. (c) 3.2 beer 18. (d) 3.2 beer: male 21; female 18 off-sale, 21. (e) Beer and wine 18. (f) Beer 18. (g) 3.2 beer 19. (h) Beer less than 4% 18.

1967 Mobil Economy Run Achieved Better Gas Mileage

Despite some of the worst weather in the 31-year history of the Mobil Economy Run, which tests gasoline economy of American stock cars, the 1967 event saw an improvement in overall gasoline mileage from the previous year. The 41 late-model sedans drove 2,837.8 mi., leaving Los Angeles Apr. 4, 1967, and arriving in Detroit Apr. 9 after encountering snow, high winds, icy roads, a heavy rainstorm and a warehouse fire which spewed debris on the road. The overall average was 19.9884 mi. per gallon, compared to 19.5614 in 1966. Men drivers scored 19.8148 m.p.g., women 20.6058. Average speed, all cars, was 51.3612; men 51.3695; women 51.3316. The event is sanctioned by the U. S. Auto Club and the Federation International de l'Automobile.

Make and model (all automatic transmissions)	Miles per gallon	Driver	Make and model (all automatic transmissions)	Miles per gallon	Driver
CLASS A—COMPACT 6-CYLINDER			**CLASS D (Contd.)**		
Plymouth Valiant	24.57	Bob Checkley	Buick Special V8	19.71	John Rich
Dodge Dart 170	24.29	Bob Cahill	Dodge Coronet DeLuxe	18.98	Shirley Shahan
Ford Falcon 170	24.06	Byron Froelich	Ford Fairlane 500	18.89	Al Johnson
Ford Mustang	24.04	Per Nystrom	Chevrolet Malibu	18.60	George Decker
Rambler American 220	23.36	Les Viland	Oldsmobile Cutlass	17.06	Mandy Williams
Corvair Monza	22.83	Gordon Madison			
Chevy II 100	22.52	Betty Enoch	**CLASS E—STANDARD SIZE,**		
Camaro	22.36	Pat Sawyer	**LOW-PRICE 8-CYLINDER**		
CLASS B—COMPACT 8-CYLINDER			Chevrolet Impala SS	19.29	Don Royer
			Ford Custom 500	19.25	Kay Kimes
Plymouth Barracuda	22.31	Scott Harvey	Plymouth Fury II	19.15	Jim Latham
Dodge Dart	21.12	Jean Calvin	Chevrolet Bel Air	18.64	Tom Evans
Mercury Cougar	20.99	Ginny Sims			
Chevy II 100	20.57	Jack Kirkpatrick	**CLASS F—STANDARD SIZE,**		
Ford Mustang 2+2	20.72	Fran Foster	**MEDIUM PRICE 8-CYLINDER**		
Camaro	19.27	Carolyn Thomas	Buick LeSabre 400	18.74	Marta Retzlaff
CLASS C—INTERMEDIATE			Olds Delmont "88"	18.51	Stan Raymond
6-CYLINDER			Pontiac Catalina	18.19	Don Francisco
			Dodge Polara 318	17.94	Art Bertelsen
Mercury Capri	23.29	Bill Levy	Mercury Monterey	16.68	Billy Cox
Plymouth Belvedere I	22.30	Bob Binder			
Buick Spec. V6	21.92	Paula Murphy	**CLASS G—LUXURY CARS**		
Chevelle 300 DeLuxe	21.46	Mary Hauser	Chrysler 300	17.59	Hart Fullerton
Oldsmobile F-85	20.04	George Alsbury	Buick Electra 225	16.99	John Meyers
			Toronado	16.48	Mel Alsbury, Jr.
CLASS D—INTERMEDIATE			Oldsmobile "98"	15.93	Pete Novotny
8-CYLINDER CARS			Cadillac Calais	15.62	Tom Gillum, Jr.
Plymouth Belvedere II	20.01	Allan Brooks	Thunderbird	15.26	Stan Seeds
Mercury Caliente	19.81	Darrell Droke			

Passenger Car Production, U. S. Plants

Source: Automobile Manufacturers Association

	1965	1966	1967 6 mos.		1965	1966	1967 6 mos.
American Motors Corp.	346,367	279,225	108,004	**General Motors Corp.**			
				Chevrolet	1,821,266	1,431,022	616,407
Chrysler Corp.				Corvette	27,700	24,939	15,104
Plymouth	679,539	640,450	323,230	Chevelle	370,188	423,317	202,937
Dodge	547,531	532,026	210,078	Camaro	....	94,426	115,336
Chrysler	224,061	255,487	105,809	Chevy II	164,348	155,726	64,877
Imperial	16,422	17,653	5,472	Corvair	204,007	73,362	11,302
Total Chrysler	1,467,553	1,445,616	644,589	**Total Chevrolet**	2,587,509	2,202,792	1,025,963
				Pontiac	534,633	481,591	240,105
Ford Motor Co.				Tempest	326,019	384,794	156,800
Ford	1,048,388	948,462	461,952	Firebird	....	....	74,521
Fairlane	251,647	304,659	111,879	**Total Pontiac**	860,652	866,385	471,426
Falcon	208,970	131,793	25,772	Oldsmobile	400,664	318,667	136,782
Mustang	580,187	580,767	241,381	Toronado	16,983	37,420	8,350
Thunderbird	75,710	72,734	41,528	F-85	233,154	237,982	146,653
Total Ford	2,164,902	2,038,415	882,512	**Total Oldsmobile**	650,801	594,069	291,785
Mercury	193,069	153,680	56,849	Buick	368,973	315,639	181,494
Comet	162,335	133,165	32,022	Riviera	41,424	48,073	23,219
Cougar	....	48,013	82,241	Special	243,441	216,709	102,187
Total Mercury	355,404	334,858	171,112	**Total Buick**	653,838	580,421	306,900
Lincoln	45,470	52,169	20,753	Cadillac	196,595	205,001	119,536
				Total General Motors Corp.	4,949,395	4,448,668	2,215,610
Total Ford Motor Co.	2,565,776	2,425,442	1,074,377	Checker Motors	6,136	5,761	2,784
				Total passenger cars	9,335,227	8,604,712	4,045,364

Motor Bus Passenger Operations, Intercity Class I Carriers

Source: Interstate Commerce Commission

Year ended December 31	1963	1964	1965	1966
Number of carriers reporting	138	158	147	156
Miles of line, regular route	214,806	211,621	211 131	216,580
Regular route intercity service revenue........(dollars)	412,819,949	442,098,685	452,302,408	475,280,834
Local and suburban revenue........(dollars)	23,830,737	79,654,963	13,664,810	13,149,293
Charter or special service bus........(dollars)	46,124,051	63,829,994	61,172,462	69,743,934
Total operating revenue........(dollars)	545,509,468	656,485,751	604,677,139	640,990,577
Total expenses........(dollars)	465,538,489	570,882,528	511,470,607	545,753,076
Net operating revenue........(dollars)	79,970,979	85,603,223	93,206,532	95,237,501
Bus-miles in intercity line service	789,058,588	834,041,327	815,579,656	844,445,549
Bus-miles in local and suburban service	36,803,550	117,154,966	24,397,719	22,407,474
Bus-miles in charter or special service	79,630,929	103,643,274	98,821,490	112,256,094
Intercity revenue passengers carried (line service)	162,251,039	160,516,733	162,992,836	169,323,447
Local and suburban revenue passengers carried	48,934,167	296,511,245	29,475,279	26,956,727
Charter or special revenue passengers carried	15,061,244	29,861,540	20,714,320	26,969,666

AVIATION

U. S. Domestic Airline Passenger Traffic Continues Upward Zoom

Passenger traffic on U. S. scheduled domestic air carriers for the first 9 months of 1967 increased 27.4% over the corresponding period a year earlier, according to the Air Transport Assn. of America. In the first three-quarters of 1967 the 11 trunk lines, 13 local service lines and 3 helicopter lines flew 56.4 billion revenue passenger miles, compared to 44.3 billion flown in the first 9 months of 1966.

The size of the 9-month increase was partially due to the effect of the 43-day strike by the International Assn. of Machinists against 5 major airlines during most of July and August of 1966. Despite that strike, passenger traffic on the scheduled domestic air carriers for calendar 1966 increased 16.8% over the 1965 figure.

The pattern of traffic growth continued in the international operations of U. S. scheduled airlines. The 11 carriers involved flew 10.174 billion revenue passenger miles in the first 6 months of 1967, an increase of over 14% from the corresponding period in 1966.

New Safety Rules

The Federal Aviation Administration announced Sept. 19, 1967, sweeping new rules aimed at saving more lives in airplane crashes. An important new requirement is that new planes must have enough exits for a full load of passengers to get out in 90 seconds by using exits on only one side of the plane. The current requirement is 120 seconds.

The FAA rule changes include easier access to exits, better marking and lighting of exits, more protection for electric and fuel lines, less flammable material in walls and ceilings, and a rule that 75% of lights continue to burn even if the fuselage is broken open.

The FAA noted that most airline accidents occur on take-off, approach to an airport or landing, and that many passengers survive them. The FAA rules are designed to make these so-called survivable crashes more survivable. Fire, smoke and confusion are blamed for most passenger deaths in survivable accidents.

The FAA reported Oct. 4, 1967, that the number of civil aircraft landing facilities in the U.S. had topped the 10,000 mark for the first time. The 10,015 landing facilities included 9,209 airports, 419 heliports, and 307 seaplane bases as of Aug. 1, 1967.

Landing Facilities Increase

This represented an increase of 533 landing facilities since the end of 1966 despite the abandonment of 191 airports since that time. The count does not include fields devoted solely to military use, but does include those serving both civil and military air traffic in the 50 states. It also includes 17 landing facilities in Puerto Rico, 3 in the Virgin Islands, and 5 in the South Pacific.

As of Aug. 1, 1967, scheduled airlines handling interstate, international and territorial traffic served 542 airports in the 50 states. An additional 281 airports and seaplane bases in Alaska and 8 airports in Hawaii were served by intrastate carriers, making a total of 831 served by the certified route air carriers.

Landing facilities open to the general public total 6,846, while 3,169 are restricted to emergency or private use. One or more lighted runways are provided at 3,102 airports and paved runways at 3,003.

Texas continued to lead the nation with 881 landing facilities, followed by California with 669, Alaska 607, Illinois 446, Pennsylvania 443, and Ohio 384.

Busiest Airport

Although scheduled airliners do not land at Opa-Locka Airport, in Opa-Locka, Fla., it was the busiest airport in the nation as of June 30, 1967, according to the Federal Aviation Administration. During the year ended on that date, the FAA tower at Opa-Locka recorded 596,-949 traffic movements there, all by private planes. This was more than one landing or take-off for each of the 525,600 minutes in the year. Opa-Locka, with a population of 10,400 is some 10 miles northwest of Miami.

FAA figures on the 5 next busiest airports showed the following annual traffic movements: O'Hare International, Chicago, 588,527; Van Nuys, Calif., 543,324; Long Beach, Calif., 499,724; Fort Lauderdale, Fla., 451,910 and Kennedy International New York, 451,533. Of these, only O'Hare and Kennedy have heavy scheduled airline traffic.

Air traffic controllers at O'Hare handled a record 60,462 take-offs and landings—one every 44 seconds—during August, 1967. This was the highest monthly traffic count ever recorded by an FAA control tower.

The peak air traffic month occurred while extensive airport construction was in progress, including construction of a new 10,000 foot long east/west runway which intersects one of the existing prime use parallel runways.

The airport's record August traffic comprised 54,459 airline operations; 5,595 general aviation operations; 384 military operations; and 24 purely local flights. The tower's radar controllers handled 53,926 instrument operations during the month, of which 48,959 arrived or departed O'Hare. The remainder were instrument operations at other Chicago area airports which include: Midway Airport, Meigs Field, Glenview Naval Air Station, Palwaukee, Sky Harbor, Chicagoland, and Ft. Sheridan Army Air Base—all under O'Hare radar control.

On 17 of August's 31 days, O'Hare controllers recorded more than 2,000 daily operations. On two Fridays, traffic set new single day records of 2,225 operations on the 4th and 2,233 on the 11th. The daily average during the month was 1,975 operations.

Airline passengers during O'Hare's record month totaled 2,737,293.

Notable Ocean and Intercontinental Flights

Pilot, Plane	From	To	Mi.	Time	Date
DIRIGIBLE BALLOONS					
British R-34 (1)	East Fortune, Scot.	Mineola, N. Y.		108 hrs.	July 2-6, 1919
	Mineola, N. Y.	Pulham, Eng.		75 hr.	July 9-13, 1919
Amundsen-Ellsworth-Noble expedition	Spitsbergen	Teller, Alaska			May 1926
Graf Zeppelin	Friedrichshafen	Lakehurst, N. J.	6,630	4d 15h 46m	Oct. 11-15, 1928
	Germany	Lakehurst, N. J.		51h 17m	June 30-July 2, 1936
Hindenburg Zeppelin	Lakehurst, N. J.	Frankfort, Ger.		42h 53m	Aug. 9-11, 1936
USN ZPG-2 Blimp	S. Weymouth, Mass.	Africa }	7,000	275h	Mar. 4-16, 1957
	Africa	Key West, Fla. }			
AIRPLANES					
USN NC-4	Newfoundland	Lisbon, Port.			May 16-27, 1919
John Alcock-A. W. Brown (2)	St. John's, Nfld.	Clifden, Ireland	1,960	16h 12m	June 14-15, 1919
Richard E. Byrd (3)	Spitsbergen	North Pole	1,545	15h 30m	May 9, 1926
Chas. A. Lindbergh (4)	Mineola, N. Y.	Paris	3,610	33h 29m 30s	May 20-21, 1927
Chas. A. Levine-Clarence D. Chamberlin (5)	Roosevelt Field, Mineola, N. Y.	Eisleben, Ger.	3,911	42h 31m	June 4-6, 1927
Baron G. von Huenefeld, crew (6)	Dublin	Greenly Isl., Lab.		37 hrs.	Apr. 12-13, 1928
Sir Hubert Wilkins (8)	Point Barrow, Alaska	Spitsbergen			April 16, 1928
Sir Chas. Kingsford-Smith, crew (7)	Oakland, Calif.	Brisbane, Aust.			May 31-June 8 1928
Amelia Earhart Putnam, W. Stults, L. Gordon	Trepassy, Nfld.	Burry Port, Wales.		20h 40m	June 17-18, 1928
Richard E. Byrd (9)	Bay of Wales	South Pole			Nov. 28-29, 1929
Capt. D. Coste-M. Bellonte	Paris	Valley Stream, N. Y.	4,100	37h 18m 30s	Sept. 1-2, 1930
Lt. L. Challe-Lt. T. L. Borres	Seville, Spain	Natal, Brazil	3,600		Dec. 15-17, 1930
Wiley Post-Harold Gatty	Harbor Grace, Nfld.	England	2,200	16h 17m	June 23-24, 1931
Clyde Pangborn-Hugh Herndon, Jr. (10)	Tokyo	Wenatchee, Wash.	4,458	41h 34m	Oct. 3-5, 1931
Amelia Earhart Putnam (11)	Harbor Grace, Nfld.	Ireland	2,026½	14h 56m	May 20-21, 1932
James A. Mollison (12)	Portmarnock, Ire.	Pennfield, N. B.			Aug. 18, 1932
Amelia Earhart Putnam (11)	Honolulu, T. H.	Oakland, Calif.	2,408	18h 16m	Jan. 11-12, 1935
China Clipper (Pan Am. Airways) (13)	San Francisco	Manila, P. I.			Nov. 22-28, 1935
	Manila, P. I.	San Francisco			Dec. 1-6, 1935
Gromoff, Yumasheff, Danilin (USSR)	Moscow, USSR	San Jacinto, Calif.	6,262	62h 02m	July 12-14, 1937
Douglas C. Corrigan	Floyd Bennett Field	Dublin, Ire.		28h 13m	July 17-18, 1938
B-29 (Lt. Col. C. J. Miller)	Honolulu, T. H.	Washington, D. C.	4,640	17h 21m	Sept. 1, 1945
C-54 (Maj. G. E. Cain)	Tokyo	Washington, D. C.		31h 25m	Sept. 3, 1945
William P. Odom	Honolulu, T. H.	Teterboro, N. J.	5,300	36 hrs.	Mar. 8, 1949
USN Caroline Mars	Honolulu, T. H.	San Diego, Calif.		14h 17m	June 17-18, 1950
Col. David C. Schilling, USAF (14)	England	Limestone, Me.	3,300	10h 01m	Sept. 22, 1950
Chas. F. Blair, Jr.	New York	London	3,500	7h 48m	Jan. 31, 1951
Canberra Bomber	Aldergrove, Belfast, N. I.	Gander, Nfld.		4h 40m	Feb. 21, 1951
Chas. F. Blair, Jr. (15)	Bardufoss, Nor.	Fairbanks, Alaska.	3,300	10h 29m	May 29, 1951
Chas. F. Blair, Jr.	Fairbanks, Alaska	New York	3,450	9h 31m	May 30, 1951
Canberra Bomber	England	Australia		20h 20m	Mar. 16, 1952
British Comet	London	Johannesburg, S. Af.		23h 38m	May 2-3, 1952
Two U. S. S-55 Helicopters (16)	Westover AFB, Mass.	Prestwick, Scot.	3,410	42h 30m	July 15-31, 1952
RB-45 Tornado (17)	Anchorage, Alaska	Yokoto AFB, Japan.	3,460	9h 50m	July 29, 1952
Canberra Bomber (18)	Aldergrove, N. I.	Gander, Nfld.	2,073	4h 34m	Aug. 26, 1952
	Gander, Nfld.	Aldergrove, N. I.	2,073	3h 25m	Aug. 26, 1952
B-47B	California	Hawaii	2,463	4h 52m	Sept. 20, 1952
British Comet	London-Tokyo	Tokyo-London.	20,400	74h 52m	April 3-7, 1953
U.S. B-47	Limestone AFB, Me.	Fairford, Eng.	2,925	4h 45m	July 28, 1953
U.S. B-47	Fairford, Eng.	Tampa, Fla.	4,450	9h 53m	Aug. 4, 1953
British Comet	London	Rio de Janeiro	6,000	12h 30m	Sept. 13-14, 1953
Flt. Lieut. Roland Burton (Canberra PR-3 bomber in race)	England	New Zealand	12,270	23h 51m	Oct. 8-9, 1953
Comet II.	London	Khartoum, Egypt.	3,064	6h 22m	Jan. 22, 1954
Max Conrad (solo)	New York	Paris, France.		22h 23m	Nov. 7, 1954
10 U. S. F-84's	Stugate AFB, Eng.	Bergstrom AFB, Austin, Texas.	5,118	10h 48m	Aug. 17, 1955
Canberra Bomber	London (round trip)	New York	6,920	14h21m45.4s	Aug. 23, 1955
Capt. William F. Judd	New York	Paris.		24h 11m	Jan. 29-30, 1956
Pan American DC-7.	New York	Shannon, Ire.		7h 45m	Dec. 10, 1956
Bristol Britannia	New York	Rome.	4,700	12h 20m	Mar. 8, 1957
Three USAF F-100 Ca	London	Los Angeles, Calif.	6,710	14h 5m	May 13, 1957
Spirit of St. Louis II (USAF F-100F jet)	McGuire AFB, N. J.	Le Bourget, Paris.		6h 38m	May 21, 1957
Air France.	Los Angeles.	Paris.	6,102	16h 21m	Aug. 25, 1957
Soviet TU-104.	Vnukovo Airport, Moscow	McGuire AFB, N. J.	5,570	21h 54m	Sept. 3-4, 1957
	McGuire AFB, N. J.	Moscow.	5,570	11h 13m	Sept. 7, 1957
Soviet TU-104.	Moscow.	McGuire AFB, N. J.	5,570	18h 30m	Sept. 13-14, 1957
Lockheed Super Starliner (19)	New York	Athens, Greece.	5,000	14h 38m	Sept. 26, 1957
TWA Jetstream (20).	London.	San Francisco	5,900	23h 19m	Oct. 1-2, 1957
6 USAF B-52 bombers	U.S.-Argentina(no-stp)	Argentina-U. S.	10,425	21h 42m	Nov. 16-17, 1957
4 USAF RF-101s (21).	Tokyo	Honolulu.	3,850	6h 35m	Dec. 2, 1957
El Al Britannia	New York	London.		7h 44m	Jan. 9, 1958
USAF KC-135.	Tokyo.	Lajes AFB, Azores.	10,230	18h 48m	Apr. 7-8, 1958
Max Conrad (solo)	New York	Palermo, Sicily.	4,440	32h 55m	June 22-23, 1958
USAF KC-135.	New York.	London.	3,442	5h 27m 42.8s	June 27, 1958
USAF KC-135.	London.	New York.	3,460	5h 51m 24.8s	June 29, 1958

Pilot, Plane	From	To	Mi.	Time	Date
Capt. Mairon Boling	Manila, P. I.	Pendleton, Oreg.	6,979	45h 42m	Jy. 31-Au. 1/58
Comet IV jet airliner	New York	London	3,496	6h 27m	Aug. 12, 1958
Boeing 707 Clipper	New York	London		7h 28m	Sept. 8, 1958
USAF KC-135	Yokota AB, Japan	Washington, D. C.	7,100	12h 28m	Sept. 12, 1958
Comet IV jet airliner	New York	London	3,650	6h 12m	Oct. 4, 1958
Boeing 707 Clipper	New York	Paris		7h 1m	Nov. 4-5, 1958
Boeing 707	London	New York	3,700	7h 17m	Jan. 10, 1959
Max Conrad (solo)	Chicago	Rome	5,000	34h 3m	Mar. 5-6, 1959
Boeing 707-320	Seattle, Wash.	Rome	5,800	11h 6m	May 29, 1959
Max Conrad (solo)	Casablanca, Africa	Los Angeles	7,700	58h 36m	June 2-4, 1959
USSR TU-114 (22)	Moscow	New York	5,092	11h 6m	June 28, 1959
Boeing 707 airliner	San Francisco	Sydney, Australia	7,630	16h10m	July 2, 1959
Boeing 707-320	New York	Moscow	c.5,090	8h 54m	July 23, 1959
Pan Amer. Clipper	Honolulu, Hawaii	San Francisco	2,410	4h 25m	Aug. 25, 1959
USAF F-100 (group)	Darwin, Australia	Itazuke, Japan	c.3,000	6h 35m	Nov. 4, 1959
Boeing 707	New York	Paris		5h 44m	Nov. 10, 1959
Boeing 707	New York	Shannon, Ireland		5h 5m	Nov. 11, 1959
Max Conrad (solo)	Casablanca, Mor.	El Paso, Texas	6,911	56h 26m	Nov. 22-26, 1959
USAF B-58	New York	Paris		3h 10m 58s	May 26, 1961
Col. J. B. Swindal	Washington, D. C.	Moscow		8h 39m 02.2s	May 19, 1963
Mrs. Jerrie Mock (23)	Columbus, Ohio	Columbus, Ohio	23,206	29d 11h 59m	Mr. 19-Au. 18/64
Joan Merriam (24)	Oakland, Calif.	Oakland, Calif.	27,750	56d	Mr. 17-Ma. 12/64

Notable first flights: 1, Atlantic aerial round trip. 2, Non-stop transatlantic flight. 3, Polar flight. 4, Solo transatlantic flight in the Ryan monoplane the "Spirit of St. Louis." 5, Transatlantic passenger flight. 6, East-West transatlantic crossing. 7, U. S. to Australia flight. 8, Trans-Arctic flight. 9, South Pole flight. 10, Non-stop Pacific flight. 11, Woman's transoceanic solo flight. 12, Westbound transatlantic solo flight. 13, Pacific airmail and U. S. to Philippines crossing. 14, Non-stop jet transatlantic flight. 15, Solo across North Pole. 16, Transatlantic helicopter flight. 17, Non-stop jet Pacific flight. 18, Transatlantic round trip on same day. 19, Non-stop between New York and Athens; carried 59 passengers. 20, Non-stop London to San Francisco via polar route; carried 32 passengers. 21, Non-stop jet flight from Tokyo to Honolulu. 22, Non-stop between Moscow and New York. 23, First woman pilot to circle globe; first woman to fly both North Atlantic and Pacific. 24, Followed route Amelia Earhart partly completed in 1937.

Fastest Trips Around the World

Fast circuits of the earth have been a subject of wide interest since Jules Verne, French novelist, described an imaginary trip by Phileas Fogg in Around the World in 80 Days, assertedly occurring Oct. 2 to Dec. 20, 1872. Notable actual such events follow:

Craft, pilot	Terminal	(Mi.)	Time	Date
Nellie Bly	New York, N. Y.		72d 6h 11m	1889
George Francis Train	New York, N. Y.		67d 12h 03m	1890
Charles Fitzmorris	Chicago		60d 13h 29m	1901
J. W. Willis Sayre	Seattle		54d 09h 42m	1903
Henry Frederick			54d 07h 02m	1903
Col. Burnlay-Campbell			40d 19h 30m	1907
Andre Jaeger-Schmidt			39d 19h 42m 38s	1911
John Henry Mears			35d 21h 36m	1913
Two U.S. Army airplanes	Seattle (57 hops, 21 countries)	26,103	351h 11m	1924
Edward S. Evans and Linton Wells (New York World) (1)	New York	18,400	28d 14h 36m 05s	June 16-July 14, 1926
John H. Mears and Capt. C. B. D. Collyer	New York		23d 15h 21m 03s	June 29-July 22, 1928
Graf Zeppelin	Friedrichshafen, Ger. via Tokyo, Los Angeles, Lakehurst, N. J.	21,700	20d 04h	Aug. 14-Sept. 4, 1929
Wiley Post and Harold Gatty (Monoplane Winnie Mae)	Roosevelt Field, via Artic Circle	15,474	8d 15h 51m	June 23-July 1, 1931
Wiley Post (Monoplane Winnie Mae) (2)	Floyd Bennett Field, via Arctic Circle	15,596	115h 36m 30s	July 15-22, 1933
H. R. Ekins (Scripps-Howard Newspapers in race) (Zeppelin Hindenburg to Germany, airplanes from Frankfort)	Lakehurst, N. J., via Frankfort, Ger.	25,654	18d 11h 14m 33s	Sept. 30-Oct. 19, 1936
Howard Hughes and 4 assistants	New York, Paris, Moscow, Siberia, Fairbanks, Alaska	14,824	3d 19h 08m 10s	July 10-13, 1938
Mrs. Clara Adams (Pan American Clipper)	Port Washington, N. Y., ret. Newark, N. J.		16d 19h 04m	June 28-July 15, 1939
Globester, U. S. Air Transport Command	Washington, D. C.	23,279	149h 44m	Sept. 28-Oct. 4, 1945
Capt. William P. Odom (A-26 Reynolds Bombshell)	New York, via Paris, Cairo, Tokyo, Alaska	20,000	78h 55m 12s	Apr. 12-16, 1947
America, Pan American 4-engine Lockheed Constellation (3)	New York, eastward	22,219	101h 32m	June 17-30, 1947
Col. Edward P. F. Eagan	New York	20,559	147h 15m	Dec. 13, 1948
USAF B-50, Lucky Lady II (Capt. James Gallagher) (4)	Fort Worth, Texas	23,452	94h 01m	Feb. 26-Mar. 2, 1949
Thos. G. Lapphier, Jr.	New York	22,180	119h 47m	Dec. 2-7, 1949
Jean-Marie Audibert	Paris		4d 19h 38m	Dec. 11-15, 1952
Horace C. Boren	Idlewild Airport, New York		99h 16m	June 21-25, 1953
Pamela Martin	Midway Airport, Chicago		90h 59m	Dec. 5-8, 1953
Three USAF B-52 Stratofortresses (5)	Castle AFB, Merced, Calif., via Nfld., Morocco, Saudi Araba, India, Ceylon, P. I., Guam, Riverside, Calif.	24,325	45h 19m	Jan. 15-18, 1957
Joseph Cavoli	Cleveland, Ohio		89h 13m 37s	Jan. 31-Feb. 4, 1958
Miss K. Kanetake	Tokyo, via Bangkok, Karachi, Rome, Anchorage	18,580	73h 9m	July 28-31, 1958
Peter Gluckmann (solo)	San Francisco	22,800	29d	Aug. 22-Sept. 20 1959
Milton Reynolds	San Francisco		51h 45m 22s	Jan. 12-14, 1960
Sue Snyder	Chicago		62h 59m	June 22-24, 1960
Max Conrad (solo)	Miami, Fla.	21,219	8d 18h 35m 57s	Feb. 28-Mar. 8, 1961
Sam Miller & Louis Fodor	New York	25,946	46h 28m	Aug. 3-4, 1963
Henry G. Beaird	Wichita, Kans.	22,992	65h 38m 49s	May 23-26, 1966
Robert & Joan Wallick (6)	Manila, Philippines	23,557	5d 6h 17m 10s	June 1-7, 1966
Arthur Godfrey, Richard Merrill, Fred Austin, Karl Keller	New York	23,333	86h 9m 1s	June 4-7, 1966

1. Mileage by train and auto, 4,100; by plane, 6,300; by steamship, 8,000. 2. First to fly solo around northern circumference of the world, also first to fly twice around the world. 3. Inception of regular commercial global air service. 4. First non-stop round-the-world flight, refueled 4 times in flight. 5. First non-stop global flight by jet planes; refueled in flight by KC-97 aerial tankers; average speed, approx. 525 m.p.h. 6. Official world record for light planes.

English Channel Tunnel Construction to Start in 1969

The British and French Governments announced in 1967 that construction of the projected tunnel under the English Channel to link the two countries was expected to start in 1969. Construction is expected to take 5 or 6 years. The tunnel, whose cost is estimated at $434,000,000 to $476,000,000, may be bored through the chalk Channel bed between Dover and Calais or built in sections which would then be submerged. Two tubes enclosing railroad tracks are planned, with automobiles to be carried on special railroad cars. Distance from terminal to terminal would be some 40 miles, of which 20 miles would be underwater. The tunnel is to be built with private financing but operated by a joint public body.

Orange-Fish Rivers Tunnel, expected to be the world's longest, is under construction as part of a $602,000,000 project to irrigate and develop the arid heart of South Africa. Preliminary excavation for the 51½-mile tunnel began in 1967.

Canadian Bridge-Tunnel. The Canadian Government started construction early in 1966 of a $148,-000,000 tunnel-bridge-causeway project across Northumberland Strait linking New Brunswick and Prince Edward Island. The 9-mile crossing will carry both a railway and a highway. Completion is expected in 1971.

Chesapeake Bay Bridge-Tunnel, 17.6 mi. long, was opened for traffic April 15, 1964. It has 12½ mi. of concrete trestles 30 ft. above mean low water, 2 one-mile tunnels, 2 steel bridges, 4-man-made islands, 1½ mi. of earthfill causeway and approx. 5½ mi. of approach roadway, most of the latter 28 ft. wide. It connects Cape Charles, on the Eastern Shore of Virginia, with Chesapeake Beach between Norfolk and Virginia Beach on the mainland, thus providing a new route to Florida via the New Jersey Turnpike and U. S. 13. Cost of the project was over $200,000,000.

Great St. Bernard Tunnel between Italy and Switzerland was opened to vehicular traffic March 19, 1964. It is 3.4 mi. long and is entered at St. Rhemy, in the Aosta valley of Italy, and at Bourg St. Pierre in Switzerland. It has two lanes and is 24½ ft. wide and 14 ft. 9 in. high. It is more than 6,000 ft. above sea level, rising about 150 ft. toward the Swiss opening. The walls were lined with reinforced concrete.

Mont Blanc Tunnel a 7¼-mile two-lane vehicular roadway between France and Italy, was opened July 16, 1965, with Presidents Charles de Gaulle of France and Giuseppe Saragat of Italy joining in ceremonies. Running between Chamonix, France, and Courmayeur, Italy, it cuts the driving time between Rome and Paris by as much as 20 hours in winter, when alternate routes over the passes are closed. The tunnel, the second under the Alps, cost $70,000,000, shared by France and Italy with help from Switzerland.

Simplon Tunnel, running under the Alps between Brigue, Switzerland, and Iselle, Italy, is 12.3 miles long, the longest rail tunnel in the world. The first of its two tubes was completed in 1905; the second, 22 yards longer, in 1922.

Under-water Vehicular Tunnels in United States

Source: Bureau of Public Roads, Dept. of Transportation
Over 1,000 feet in length

Name	Location	Waterway	Length Feet
Brooklyn-Battery	New York, N. Y.	East River	9,117
Holland Tunnel	New York, N. Y.	Hudson River	8,557
Lincoln Tunnel	New York, N. Y.	Hudson River	8,216
Harbor Tunnel	Baltimore, Md.	Patapsco River	7,650
Hampton Roads	Norfolk, Va.	Hampton Roads	7,479
Queens Midtown	New York, N. Y.	East River	6,414
Sumner Tunnel	Boston, Mass.	Boston Harbor	5,650
Detroit-Windsor	Detroit, Mich.	Detroit River	5,135
Callahan Tunnel	Boston, Mass.	Boston Harbor	5,046
Elizabeth River	Norfolk, Va.	Elizabeth River	4,194
Posey Tube	Oakland, Calif.	Oakland Estuary	3,500
Bankhead Tunnel	Mobile, Ala.	Mobile River	3,109
Baytown Tunnel	Baytown, Tex.	Houston Ship Channel	3,009
Washburn Tunnel	Houston, Tex.	Ship Channel	2,936
Harvey Tunnel	Louisiana	Intracoastal Canal	1,080

Land Vehicular Tunnels in United States

over 1,500 feet long

Name	Location	Length Feet	Name	Location	Length Feet
Copperfield	Copperfield, Utah	6,989	Rays Hill	Penna. Turnpike	3,532
Sideling Hill	Penna. Turnpike	6,782	Low Level	Broadway, Calif.	2,944
Liberty Tubes	Pittsburgh, Pa.	6,336	Kalihi	Honolulu, Hawaii	2,780
Allegheny	Penna. Turnpike	6,070	West Virginia	W. Va. Turnpike	2,669
Zion Natl. Park	Rte. 1, Utah	5,766	Cross-Town	178 St. N.Y.C.	2,414
Tuscarora	Penna. Turnpike	5,326	F.D. Roosevelt Dr.	81-89 Sts. NYC	2,400
Kittatinny	Penna. Turnpike	4,727	Battery Park	New York City	2,300
Laurel Hill	Penna. Turnpike	4,541	Battery St.	Seattle, Wash.	2,140
Evans	Penna. Turnpike	4,379	Big Oak Flat	Yosemite Natl. Pk.	2,083
Blue Mountain	Penna. Turnpike	4,339	Internatl. Underpass	Los Angeles, Calif.	1,910
Wawona	Yosemite Natl. Pk.	4,233	Street-Car	Providence, R. I.	1,793
Squirrel Hill	Pittsburgh, Pa.	4,225	Broadway	San Francisco, Calif.	1,616
Fort Pitt	Penna. Turnpike	3,600	F.D. Roosevelt Dr.	42-48 Sts. NYC	1,600

Size and Dimensions of the Continents

Source: U. S. Naval Oceanographic Office

	Sq. mi.	Miles			Sq. mi.	Miles	
		N to S	E to W			N to S	E to W
No. America (inc. islands)	9,300,000	5,300	4,000	Africa	11,500,000	5,000	4,700
South America	6,800,000	4,750	3,100	Australia	2,950,000	1,970	2,440
Europe	3,750,000	2,400	3,800	Antarctica	5,300,000	.....	.....
Asia (inc. islands)	16,900,000	5,300	6,000				

Fertile regions occupy 33,000,000 sq. mi. Steppes 19,000,000 sq. mi. Deserts 5,000,000 sq. mi.

U. S. Geodetic Datum Point

The geodetic datum point of the United States is the Coast and Geodetic Survey's triangulation station *Meades Ranch* in Osborne County, Kansas, at latitude 39°13′26″.686 N and longitude 98°32′30″.506 W. (Frequently this is referred to as the geodetic center of the U. S., which has no meaning.) This geodetic datum point is a fundamental point from which all latitude and longitude computations originate for North America and Central America.

Deaths and Death Rates for Selected Causes

Source: National Center for Health Statistics, Public Health Service,
U. S. Dept. of Health, Education and Welfare

Rates per 100,000 population.

1966* Cause of death	Number	Rate	1966* Cause of death	Number	Rate
All Causes................	1,869,000	954.2	Nonrheumatic chronic endo-		
Tuberculosis, all forms.............	7,590	3.9	carditis and other myo-		
Tuberculosis of respiratory system	7,000	3.6	cardial degeneration.......	52,450	26.8
Tuberculosis, other forms.........	580	0.3	Other diseases of heart......	31,260	16.0
Syphilis and its sequelae..........	2,480	1.3	Hypertensive heart disease....	55,930	28.6
Dysentery, all forms..........	70	0.0	Other hypertensive disease....	11,470	5.9
Scarlet fever and streptococcal sore			General arteriosclerosis......	38,280	19.5
throat.........................	10	0.0	Other diseases of circulatory		
Diphtheria......................	40	0.0	system...................	28,280	14.4
Whooping cough.................	50	0.0	Chronic and unspecified nephritis		
Meningococcal infections..........	990	0.5	and other renal sclerosis......	10,690	5.5
Acute poliomyelitis..............	20	0.0	Influenza and pneumonia, except		
Measles........................	230	0.1	pneumonia of newborn........	64,230	32.8
Infectious hepatitus.............	620	0.3	Influenza.................	3,060	1.6
Other infective and parasitic diseases	6,060	3.1	Pneumonia, except pneumonia of		
Malignant neoplasms, incl. neoplasms			newborn..................	61,170	31.2
of lymphatic and hematopoietic			Bronchitis.................	6,750	3.4
tissues......................	303,300	154.8	Other bronchopulmonix diseases....	28,740	14.7
Malignant neoplasm of buccal cav-			Ulcer of stomach and duodenum....	10,190	5.2
ity and pharynx.............	6,120	3.1	Appendicitis................	1,850	0.9
Malignant neoplasm of digestive			Hernia and intestinal obstruction...	9,700	5.0
organs and peritoneum, not spec-			Gastritis, duodenitis, enteritis, and		
ified as secondary.............	94,770	48.4	colitis, except diarrhea of newborn.	6,560	3.3
Malignant neoplasm of respiratory			Cirrhosis of liver.............	26,410	13.5
system, not specified as secondary	55,450	28.3	Cholelithiasis, cholecystitis, and		
Malignant neoplasm of breast....	27,420	14.0	cholangitis................	4,530	2.3
Malignant neoplasm of genital			Acute nephritis, and nephritis with		
organs.......................	40,480	20.7	edema including nephrosis......	1,070	0.5
Malignant neoplasm of urinary			Infections of kidney............	9,850	5.0
organs.......................	14,110	7.2	Hyperplasia of prostate........	3,030	1.5
Malignant neoplasm of other and			Deliveries and complications of preg-		
unspecified sites.............	35,500	18.1	nancy, childbirth, and the puer-		
Leukemia and aleukemia..........	14,080	7.2	perium....................	980	0.5
Lymphosarcoma and other neo-			Abortion.................	100	0.1
plasms of lymphatic and hema-			Other complications........	880	0.4
topoietic tissues..............	15,370	7.8	Congenital malformations.......	18,130	9.3
Benign neoplasms and neoplasms of			Certain diseases of early infancy....	51,170	26.1
unspecified nature..............	4,680	2.4	Birth injuries, postnatal asphyxia,		
Asthma........................	4,390	2.2	and atelectasis.............	20,640	10.5
Diabetes Mellitus................	35,380	18.1	Infections of newborn.........	3,360	1.7
Anemias.......................	3,700	1.9	Other diseases peculiar to early		
Meningitis, except meningococcal and			infancy, and immaturity un-		
Turberculous.................	2,320	1.2	qualified..................	27,170	13.9
Major cardiovascular-renal diseases..	1,028,240	524.9	Symptoms, senility, and ill-defined		
Diseases of cardiovascular system..	1,017,550	519.5	conditions.................	25,110	12.8
Vascular lesions affecting central			All other diseases.............	57,230	29.2
nervous system.............	204,810	104.6	Accidents..................	112,300	57.3
Diseases of heart.............	734,710	375.1	Motor vehicle accidents......	53,280	27.2
Rheumatic fever and chronic			Nonmotor vehicle accidents....	59,020	30.1
rheumatic heart disease....	14,650	7.5	Accidents in the home........	24,760	12.6
Arteriosclerotic heart disease			Other nonmotor vehicle accidents.	34,260	17.5
including coronary disease..	580,420	296.3	Suicide....................	20,160	10.3
			Homicide...................	11,210	5.7

Due to rounding estimates of deaths, figures may not add to totals. *Provisional.

Principal Types of Accidental Deaths

Source: National Center for Health Statistics, Data for 1966 are National Safety Council estimates

Year	All types	Motor vehicle	Falls	Burns	Drown-ing	Fire-arms	Machin-ery	Poison gases	Other poisons
1960........	93,806	38,137	19,023	7,645	6,529	2,334	1,951	1,253	1,679
1962........	97,139	40,804	19,589	7,534	6,439	2,092	1,922	1,376	1,833
1963........	100,669	43,564	19,335	8,172	6,347	2,263	1,965	1,489	2,061
1964........	105,000	47,700	18,941	7,379	6,709	2,275	1,945	1,360	2,100
1965........	108,004	49,163	19,984	7,347	6,799	2,344	2,054	1,526	2,110
1966 (est.)..	113,000	53,000	20,000	7,900	7,000	2,600	2,100	1,500	2,100

DEATH RATES PER 100,000 POPULATION

1960........	52.1	21.2	10.6	4.2	3.6	1.3	1.1	0.7	0.9
1962........	52.3	22.0	10.5	4.1	3.5	1.1	1.0	0.7	1.0
1963........	53.4	23.1	10.2	4.3	3.4	1.2	1.0	0.8	1.1
1964........	54.9	24.9	9.9	3.9	3.5	1.2	1.0	0.8	1.1
1965........	55.7	25.4	10.3	3.8	3.5	1.2	1.1	0.8	0.1
1966 (est.)..	57.7	27.1	10.2	4.0	3.6	1.3	1.1	0.8	1.1

ACCIDENTAL INJURIES BY SEVERITY OF INJURY

1966 Severity of injury	Total*	Motor vehicle	Work	Home	Public Non-motor vehicle
All injuries..............	10,900,000	1,950,000	2,200,000	4,450,000	2,400,000
Deaths..................	113,000	53,000	14,500	29,500	19,500
Nonfatal injuries..........	10,800,000	1,900,000	2,200,000	4,400,000	2,400,000
Permanent impairments....	400,000	160,000	90,000	120,000	50,000
Temporary total disabilities	10,400,000	1,750,000	2,100,000	4,300,000	2,350,000

CERTAIN COSTS OF ACCIDENTAL INJURIES, 1966

Total....................	$12,200,000,000	$6,700,000,000	$3,000,000,000	$1,500,000,000	$1,200,000,000
Wage loss................	5,900,000,000	2,600,000,000	1,500,000,000	1,000,000,000	950,000,000
Medical expense..........	2,000,000,000	600,000,000	700,000,000	500,000,000	250,000,000
Overhead cost of insurance...	4,300,000,000	3,500,000,000	800,000,000	10,000,000	10,000,000

*Duplications between motor-vehicle, work and home are eliminated in total.

Health Insurance Coverage by Insurance Companies
Source: Health Insurance Institute, New York, N. Y.

At the beginning of 1967 there were more than 900 insurance companies actively issuing health insurance policies in the United States. Many of these companies were licensed to operate in all 50 states and the District of Columbia, some were licensed to operate in several states, and a few were licensed in only one state. These companies provided hospital expense protection to a net total of 97,404,000 persons. In 1940, they covered some 3,700,000 persons with hospital insurance.

There have been significant increases in four other types of health insurance provided by insurance companies—surgical expense insurance, regular medical expense insurance, major medical expense insurance, and loss of income insurance. As of Dec. 31, 1966, insurance companies provided protection against the cost of surgery to 90,294,000 persons, compared with 2,280,000 in 1940. Coverage under regular medical insurance, which pays for doctor's calls and other non-surgical care by doctors, was held by 60,840,000 persons at the end of 1966 compared with 200,000 in 1944, the first

year insurance companies offered regular medical expense protection. Major medical expense insurance, which provides benefits of $10,000 or more to pay for virtually all types of medical services, covered 56,742,000 persons at the end of 1966, compared with 108,000 in 1951, the first year major medical insurance was introduced nationally. Disability Income Insurance, which replaces income lost as a result of sickness or injury, protected through insurance company policies a total of 40,774,000 workers at the close of 1966 compared with 14,369,000 in 1946.

In 1966 insurance companies paid out $5,559,-000,000 in health insurance benefits. This total included $1,137,000,000 in loss of income benefit payments.

The Health Insurance Council in its 21st annual survey of the extent of voluntary health insurance coverage in the United States, reported that at the end of 1966 insurance companies, Blue Cross-Blue Shield and other health care plans, provided hospital insurance to 158,022,000 persons and paid out $10,159,000,000 in benefits.

Average Future Lifetime in United States
Source: U. S. Dept. of Health, Education and Welfare, National Center for Health Statistics, 1965 Data

Age interval	Number living[1]	Average remaining lifetime[2]				
		Total	White		Nonwhite	
			Male	Female	Male	Female
0-1	100,000	70.2	67.6	74.7	61.1	67.4
1-5	97,550	70.9	68.3	75.1	62.9	68.9
5-10	97,188	67.2	64.5	71.3	59.3	65.3
10-15	96,976	62.3	59.7	66.4	54.5	60.4
15-20	96,779	57.4	54.9	61.5	49.7	55.5
20-25	96,320	52.7	50.2	56.6	45.1	50.8
25-30	95,709	48.0	45.6	51.8	40.7	46.1
30-35	95,068	43.3	40.9	47.0	36.4	41.5
35-40	94,266	38.7	36.3	42.2	32.3	37.1
40-45	93,127	34.1	31.7	37.5	28.3	32.8
45-50	91,421	29.7	27.3	32.9	24.5	28.8
50-55	88,810	25.5	23.2	28.5	21.0	25.0
55-60	84,837	21.6	19.4	24.2	17.9	21.4
60-65	79,144	17.9	16.0	20.1	15.1	18.2
65-70	71,383	14.6	12.9	16.3	12.6	15.5
70-75	60,876	11.7	10.3	12.8	11.2	13.5
75-80	48,409	9.0	8.0	9.6	9.8	11.2
80-85	34,282	6.7	6.0	6.9	8.3	9.0
85 and over	19,887	4.7	4.3	4.7	6.5	6.8

[1]Of 100,000 born alive, number living at beginning of age interval.
[2]Average number of years of life remaining at beginning of age interval.

YEARS OF LIFE EXPECTED AT BIRTH*

Year	Total	Male	Female	Year	Total	Male	Female
1966[1]	70.1	66.7	73.8	1930	59.7	58.1	61.6
1965	70.2	66.8	73.7	1925	59.0	57.6	60.6
1960	69.7	66.6	73.1	1920	54.1	53.6	54.6
1955	69.5	66.6	72.7	1915	54.5	52.5	56.8
1950	68.2	65.6	71.1	1910	50.0	48.4	51.8
1945	65.9	63.6	67.9	1905	48.7	47.3	50.2
1940	62.9	60.8	65.2	1900	47.3	46.3	48.3
1935	61.7	59.9	63.9				

*Based on Death-Registration States 1900-1925, and United States 1930-1966. [1]Provisional.

Average Weight of Americans by Height and Age
Source: Society of Actuaries; from its 1959 report on a 4-year study of 5,000,000 persons
The figures represent weights in ordinary indoor clothing and shoes, and heights with shoes.

	MEN						WOMEN				
Height	20-24	25-29	30-39	40-49	50-59	Height	20-24	25-29	30-39	40-49	50-59
5'0"	122	128	131	134	136	4'10"	102	107	115	122	125
5'1"	125	131	134	137	139	4'11"	105	110	117	124	127
5'2"	128	134	137	140	142	5'0"	108	113	120	127	130
5'3"	132	138	141	144	145	5'1"	112	116	123	130	133
5'4"	136	141	145	148	149	5'2"	115	119	126	133	136
5'5"	139	144	149	152	153	5'3"	118	122	129	136	140
5'6"	142	148	153	156	157	5'4"	121	125	132	140	141
5'7"	145	151	157	161	162	5'5"	125	129	135	143	148
5'8"	149	155	161	165	166	5'6"	129	133	139	147	152
5'9"	153	159	165	169	170	5'7"	132	136	142	151	156
5'10"	157	163	170	174	175	5'8"	136	140	146	155	160
5'11"	161	167	174	178	180	5'9"	140	144	150	159	164
6'0"	166	172	179	183	185	5'10"	144	148	154	164	169
6'1"	170	177	183	187	189	5'11"	149	153	159	169	174
6'2"	174	182	188	192	194	6'0"	154	158	164	174	180
6'3"	178	186	193	197	199						
6'4"	181	190	199	203	205						

Flower of the Month
January—Carnation or Snowdrop. **February**—Violet or Primrose. **March**—Jonquil or Daffodil. **April**—Sweet Pea or Daisy. **May**—Lily of the Valley or Hawthorn. **June**—Rose or Honeysuckle. **July**—Larkspur or Water Lily. **August**—Poppy or Gladiolus. **September**—Aster or Morning Glory. **October**—Calendula or Cosmos. **November**—Chrysanthemum. **December**—Narcissus or Holly.
Baby Colors—Blue for boys. Pink for girls.

Social and Rehabilitation Service
Source: Dept. of Health, Education and Welfare

A new agency, the Social and Rehabilitation Service, was established in the Department of Health, Education, and Welfare, Aug. 15, 1967, to strengthen and realign the former functions of the Vocational Rehabilitation Administration, the Administration on Aging, the Welfare Administration, and the Mental Retardation Division of the Bureau of Health Service, Public Health Service. Miss Mary E. Switzer, former Commissioner of Vocational Rehabilitation, was appointed Administrator.

The reorganization, announced by HEW Secretary John W. Gardner, is designed to make possible a more unified attack on the problems of needy Americans, with special emphasis on the family and with a more concerted effort toward rehabilitation in the Department's social and welfare programs. A major goal is to give people who receive public assistance the help, the skills, and the incentives they need to become independent.

A Social and Rehabilitation Service Commissioner has been assigned to each of the 9 HEW regions and will supervise all programs and activities of the Service in his region and give approval to all state plans. This will enable states, communities, and voluntary private groups to establish closer working relationships with the Federal government on all SRS programs.

A large number of persons will benefit by the range of services now merged in SRS:

—About 7,600,000 persons (4% of the population) receive cash assistance at any given time under Federally-aided programs. These payments total $7.3 billion annually; 58% ($4.2 billion) comes from the Federal Government and the remainder from state and local governments.

—Almost 175,000 persons are rehabilitated for gainful employment each year through vocational rehabilitation programs.

—Over 6,000,000 needy persons receive medical services each year through Federally-assisted programs, including the new Title XIX Medicaid program.

—Over 600,000 children receive child welfare services related to adoption, foster care, or neglect.

—Over 450,000 crippled children receive medical services each year with Federal assistance.

—More than 250,000 women received family planning help last year through Childrens Bureau programs.

—More than 700 projects assisted by the Administration on Aging provide services for many of the 19,000,000 Americans over 65.

The combined 1967 appropriations of the HEW components joined in the Social and Rehabilitation Service totalled $4.8 billion in Federal funds. The new agency is staffed by about 1,900 employees in the following 5 major program units:

Rehabilitation Services Administration: responsible for programs aiding the handicapped, disabled Social Security applicants, crippled children, the mentally retarded, and for services for the blind and the permanently and totally disabled.

Children's Bureau: responsible for studies and investigations of the status of children, and for Federal-State child welfare, maternal and child health and juvenile delinquency programs, for health services to school children, and for family and child welfare services.

Administration on Aging: responsible for administration of the Older Americans Act, and for collecting and disseminating information on the status of Older Americans, for services for the aged (including insurance and assistance beneficiaries), for maintaining standards for services to OAA beneficiaries and for the Foster Grandparent program.

Medical Services Administration: responsible for medical assistance services by State and local agencies, including Title XIX programs (Medicaid).

Assistance Payments Administration: responsible for the money payment aspects of public assistance programs (Aid to Families with Dependent Children, Old Age Assistance, Aid to the Blind, and Aid to the Permanently and Totally Disabled) and for the administration of Work Experience and Community Work Training programs.

A significant aspect of the new SRS is the separation of cash payments and social service functions in public assistance. This was done to offer greater opportunities for recipients to obtain social and other rehabilitation services which could lead them to self support and terminate their need for public financial aid.

OLD-AGE AND SURVIVORS AND DISABILITY INSURANCE TRUST FUNDS
[In thousands]

Period and fiscal year	Receipts			Expenditures		Total assets at period end
	Net contribution income and transfers	Net interest received	Financial Transfers	Benefit payments	Administrative expenses	
1936-37	$265,000	$2,262		$27		$267,235
1940-41	688,141	55,958		64,342	$26,840	2,397,615
1945-46	1,238,218	147,766		320,510	37,427	7,641,428
1950-51	3,124,098	287,392		1,498,088	70,447	14,735,567
1955-56	6,442,370	487,450	$7,439	5,360,813	124,339	22,593,109
1958-59	8,460,081	576,713	− 124,441	9,388,377	227,504	23,208,045
1959-60	10,329,764	564,040	− 573,606	10,798,013	234,291	22,995,939
1960-61	12,314,678	591,713	− 336,882	11,888,527	272,188	23,404,734
1961-62	12,475,509	609,006	− 371,818	13,669,211	315,417	22,132,803
1962-63	14,404,383	582,043	− 442,132	15,015,262	329,040	21,332,795
1963-64	16,645,887	606,704	− 421,775	15,830,373	370,400	21,962,838
1964-65	17,032,456	648,372	− 459,253	16,618,084	379,145	22,187,184
1965-66	19,422,599	648,635	− 468,782	19,792,586	437,159	21,878,935
1966-67p	¹24,886,399	792,741	− 538,670	20,746,553	432,638	25,537,114
Cumulative *p to July 1967	$195,472,633	$10,647,944	− $3,701,976	$172,548,171	$4,317,112	$25,544,379

pPreliminary. ¹Beginning 1966 transfers from general funds for military wage credits.
*Cumulative totals are not totals of columns for several years are omitted.

Average Tuition Fee at Selected Colleges and Universities

Source: World Almanac Questionnaire

Fees for tuition charged per year by colleges and universities for courses, use of libraries, laboratories and other facilities, are a major part of student expenses. Tuition varies considerably, depending on the type of institution, its control and location. The lowest tuition fees are those of state-controlled or other public-controlled institutions for residents of their state, city, etc. Students from other states or areas have to pay more. In the following list, such state or other public institutions are shown with two figures. The lower one is the tuition fee for residents, the higher one the tuition fee for students from other states or areas.

It should be noted that the tuition fee does not cover room, board, and other personal expenses.

For location of College or University see pages 130-149.

School	Tuition	School	Tuition	School	Tuition
Akron, Univ. of...	456-1,000	Eastern Ill. U........	234-600	North Dakota State..	360-804
Alabama, Univ. of...	350-700	Emory & Henry.....	1,750	North Dakota Un. of	360-804
Albuquerque, Univ. of	900	Fairleigh Dickinson...	1,250	Notre Dame, Univ. of	1,600
Amherst............	1,700	Florida State........	300-550	Oberlin.............	1,750
Antioch............	1,800	Florida, Univ. of....	300-750	Ohio State..........	450-1,008
Arizona State Univ...	286-1,101	Fordham............	1,500	Ohio Univ...........	495-990
Arizona, Univ. of...	269-1,084	Franklin & Marshall..	1,900	Oklahoma State.....	270-690
Arkansas, Univ. of...	250-650	Furman Univ........	1,000	Oklahoma, Univ. of..	270-690
Auburn............	300-600	George Washington U.	1,625	Omaha, Univ. of (e)..	880
Baldwin-Wallace....	1,600	Georgetown U.......	1,400	Oregon State Univ...	330-900
Ball State Univ.....	300-501	Georgia............	333-753	Oregon, Univ. of....	369-999
Baylor.............	900	Gonzaga............	1,000	Otterbein...........	1,400
Berea..............	None	Grambling..........	127-727	Pennsylvania........	1,950
Bob Jones Univ.....	500	Grinnell............	1,925	Pennsylvania St.....	450-1,050
Boston Coll........	1,600	Hampton Inst.......	800	Pennsylvania, Univ. of	1,950
Boston Univ........	1,650	Hartford, Univ. of...	1,200	Pittsburgh, Univ. of..	450-1,400
Bowdoin...........	1,900	Harvard............	2,000	Portland, Univ. of...	1,100
Brandeis Univ......	1,900	Haverford..........	1,975	Princeton...........	1,950
Bridgeport, Univ. of..	1,200	Hofstra............	1,500	Purdue.............	330-950
Brigham Young (a)..	400	Houston, Univ. of....	202-502	Radcliffe...........	2,000
Brown.............	2,000	Howard Univ.......	500	Rice...............	1,500
Bryn Mawr.........	1,850	Idaho State Univ....	280-780	Rochester..........	2,000
Bucknell...........	1,750	Idaho, Univ. of.....	210-710	St. Bonaventure....	1,300
Butler Univ........	1,250	Illinois State Univ....	225-600	St. John's Univ.....	1,400
California..........	242-1,223	Illinois, Univ. of....	270-850	St. Lawrence Univ...	1,800
Carnegie Univ......	1,950	Indiana State Univ...	320-640	San Diego, Univ. of..	1,000
Case Inst. of Tech...	2,000	Indiana Univ........	330-960	Sarah Lawrence.....	2,350
Centenary Coll. of La.	800	Iowa State Univ.....	345-930	Seattle Univ........	1,200
Central Michigan Univ.	300-600	Jacksonville Univ. (c)	950	Seton Hall..........	1,080
Charleston, Coll. of...	1,200	John Brown Univ....	700	So. Carolina........	455-1,005
Chattanooga, Univ. of	900	John Carroll Univ...	2,090*	So. Dakota State Un..	323-850
Chicago, Univ. of....	1,980	Johns Hopkins......	2,000	So. Ill. Univ........	241-631
Cincinnati (b).......	915-960	Kansas, Univ. of....	338-798	So. Methodist.......	1,200
Clemson...........	150-400	Kansas State.......	325-788	Stanford...........	1,770
Colgate............	1,800	Kentucky, Univ. of...	280-820	Swarthmore.........	2,065
Colorado State.....	292-540	Lehigh.............	1,800	Syracuse Univ......	1,800
Colorado, Univ. of...	372-1,120	Little Rock Univ.....	600	Tampa, Univ. of....	1,100
Columbia...........	1,700	Louisville, Univ. of (d)	1,800	Tennessee..........	270-720
Connecticut........	190-590	Maine, Univ. of.....	400-1,000	Texas Christian Univ.	1,280
Cooper Union......	None	Marquette..........	1,100	Tufts Univ..........	1,900
Cornell............	2,050	Maryland, Univ. of..	366-766	Tulsa Univ..........	675
Corpus Christi, Un. of	660	Mass. Inst. of Tech...	1,900	Utah State Univ.....	327-801
Creighton Univ......	1,070	Mass., Univ. of.....	200-600	Utah, Univ. of......	390-888
Dallas, Univ. of.....	950	Miami.............	1,460	Vanderbilt Univ.....	1,460
Dartmouth.........	2,075	Mich. State.........	354-1,020	Vassar.............	1,800
David Lipscomb....	960	Michigan...........	348-1,000	Vermont, Univ. of...	600-1,800
Davidson..........	1,200	Midwestern.........	100-400	Villanova...........	1,400
Davis & Elkins......	1,400	Minnesota..........	378-840	Wake Forest Univ....	1,000
Dayton, Univ. of....	1,000	Mississippi.........	350-790	Washington State Un.	345-825
Defiance...........	1,350	Mississippi State....	342-792	Washington & Lee...	1,600
Delaware...........	350-820	Missouri, Univ. of...	330-500	Wayne State, Univ...	312-750
Denver............	1,500	Montana St. U......	375-983	Wesleyan Univ......	1,800
DePaul............	1,140	Montana...........	359-966	West Virginia Univ...	434-1,170
Depauw............	1,750	Nebraska...........	334-860	Western Reserve....	1,650
Detroit, Univ. of....	1,150	Nevada............	350-950	Wichita State Univ...	317-775
Dillard............	800	New Hampshire.....	480-1,375	Wisconsin, Univ. of...	325-1,050
Drake.............	1,200	New Mexico State...	396-906	Worcester Poly. Inst..	2,000
Dubuque...........	1,180	New Mexico, U. of...	408-918	Wyoming...........	345-961
Duke..............	1,637	New York State.....	425-625	Yale...............	1,950
Dunbarton.........	1,250	New York Univ......	1,900	Yeshiva Univ........	1,500
Duquesne..........	1,400	Niagara............	1,224		
Earlham...........	1,680	North Carolina......	175-600		

*Includes room and board. (a) Additional fee of $150 for non-members of the Church of Jesus Christ of Latter-Day Saints. (b) Residents of Cincinnati and Golf Manor—$525. (c) Residents of Duval County—$900. (d) Residents of Jefferson County—$1,200. (e) Residents of Omaha—$540.

Public School Attendance, Teachers, Expenditures

Source: U. S. Office of Education; Salaries cover supervisors, principals, and teachers

School year ended in	Pop. 5 to 17 yrs.	Pupils		Teachers[1]			Av. salary[2] per member	Total Expend.
		Enrolled	Av. daily attend.	Male	Female	Total		
1900....	21,404,322	15,503,110	10,632,772	126,588	296,474	423,062	$325	$214,964,618
1910....	24,239,948	17,813,852	12,827,307	110,481	412,729	523,210	485	426,250,434
1920....	27,728,788	21,578,316	16,150,035	95,654	583,648	679,302	871	1,036,151,209
1930....	31,571,322	25,678,015	21,264,886	141,771	712,492	854,263	1,420	2,316,790,384
1940....	29,805,259	25,433,542	22,042,151	194,725	680,752	875,477	1,441	2,344,048,927
1950....	30,788,000	25,111,427	22,283,845	194,968	718,703	913,671	3,010	5,837,643,000
1960....	43,881,000	36,086,771	32,477,440	392,700	962,300	1,355,000	5,174	15,613,255,000
1964....	48,005,000	41,025,000	37,405,005	487,967	1,080,007	1,567,974	6,240	21,444,434,000
1965(Fall)	50,209,000	42,144,000	38,435,000	534,000	1,182,000	1,716,000	6,700	25,801,995,000
1966(Fall)	51,005,000	43,055,000	39,366,000	556,400	1,231,600	1,788,000	7,110	27,945,843,000

[1]Prior to 1954 includes other nonsupervisory instructional staff (librarians and guidance and psychological personnel). [2]Average annual salary per member of instruction staff.

Vocational Education

Source: United States Office of Education

All Federal funds expended for vocational education are matched by state and local funds. This does not include expenditures for plant and equipment for vocational schools, for which Federal funds cannot be used.

ENROLLMENT IN FEDERALLY AIDED VOCATIONAL CLASSES

Year	Total*	Agri-culture	Trade and in-dustry	Home eco-nomics	Year	Total*	Agri-culture	Trade and in-dustry	Home eco-nomics
1925	676,687	93,125	429,071	154,491	1955	3,314,255	776,138	870,954	1,431,808
1930	981,882	188,311	618,604	174,967	1960	3,768,149	706,237	938,490	1,588,109
1935	1,178,896	325,685	503,865	349,346	1963	4,217,198	827,827	1,001,776	1,839,450
1940	2,290,741	584,133	758,409	818,766	1964	4,566,399	860,605	1,069,274	2,022,133
1945	2,012,931	446,953	522,733	890,464	1965	5,430,611	887,529	1,087,807	2,098,520
1950	3,364,613	764,975	804,602	1,430,366	1966 (prel.)	6,070,059	907,354	1,269,051	1,897,670

*Total figures since 1940 include enrollment in schools and classes for distributive occupations—(1945) 152,781; (1950) 364,670; (1955) 235,355; (1960) 303,784; (1954) 334,126; (1965) 333,342; (1966) 420,426. Total figures since 1957 include enrollment for practical nursing—(1966) 83,677. Total figures since 1959 include enrollment for Area Vocational Programs—(1966) 1,238,043.

ENROLLMENT IN FEDERALLY AIDED VOCATIONAL CLASSES BY STATES
Fiscal Year 1966 Provisional figures

State	Enroll-ment	State	Enroll-ment	State	Enroll-ment	State	Enroll-ment
Alabama	124,090	Indiana	78,515	Nevada	14,935	Tennessee	118,424
Alaska	6,442	Iowa	77,741	N. Hampshire	8,709	Texas	503,531
Arizona	45,116	Kansas	52,971	New Jersey	80,936	Utah	50,285
Arkansas	92,724	Kentucky	93,365	New Mexico	20,667	Vermont	15,177
California	748,009	Louisiana	110,117	New York	496,434	Virginia	157,324
Colorado	73,119	Maine	10,107	North Carolina	234,013	Washington	163,785
Connecticut	54,246	Maryland	134,023	North Dakota	21,389	West Virginia	49,309
Delaware	13,222	Massachusetts	143,147	Ohio	208,195	Wisconsin	177,687
Dist. of Col.	9,368	Michigan	265,332	Oklahoma	78,621	Wyoming	8,100
Florida	272,844	Minnesota	128,367	Oregon	50,098	Guam	1,239
Georgia	192,715	Mississippi	94,990	Pennsylvania	197,018	Puerto Rico	89,177
Hawaii	16,525	Missouri	94,261	Rhode Island	8,041	Virgin Islands	2,028
Idaho	21,761	Montana	14,390	South Carolina	127,004		
Illinois	153,392	Nebraska	50,358	South Dakota	16,696	Total	6,070,059

Circulation of Leading U. S. Magazines

General and farm magazines, exclusive of groups and comics, of the Audit Bureau of Circulations. Statistics based on average circulation per issue during the 6 months prior to Jan. 1, 1967. **Source:** Magazine Advertising Bureau of Magazine Publishers Assn., Inc.

Magazine	Circulation	Magazine	Circulation
Reader's Digest	17,222,440	House Beautiful	1,026,708
TV Guide	11,508,767	American Girl	1,003,932
McCall's	8,585,574	Co-Ed	970,702
Look	7,731,177	Ebony	946,115
Family Circle	7,512,516	Cosmopolitan	895,666
Life	7,408,123	National Enquirer	893,758
Woman's Day	7,158,582	TV-Radio Mirror	891,594
Better Homes & Gardens	7,055,967	Sunset	833,065
Ladies' Home Journal	6,824,478	Nation's Business	800,178
Saturday Evening Post	6,696,050	Modern Screen	795,718
Good Housekeeping	5,624,772	Sport	792,666
National Geographic	5,041,802	Ingenue	783,739
Redbook	4,334,342	Our Sunday Visitor	760,614
Playboy	3,923,266	Modern Romances	756,254
American Home	3,482,397	Teen	744,539
Time	3,466,326	Hot Rod Magazine	701,123
Farm Journal	3,022,929	Mademoiselle	676,692
American Legion	2,517,729	Together	616,325
True	2,462,750	Young Catholic Messenger	612,778
Boys' Life	2,422,033	Flower & Garden Magazine	608,244
True Story	2,290,729	True Confessions	604,378
Senior Scholastic Unit	2,034,246	Catholic Digest	600,231
Parents' Magazine	2,023,916	Simplicity Fashion Magazine	598,666
Newsweek	1,965,095	Lion	582,221
Junior Scholastic	1,736,590	Pageant	557,123
U. S. News & World Report	1,522,813	Lutheran, The	540,319
Popular Mechanics	1,486,185	Motor Trend	522,332
Workbasket	1,463,854	Business Week	519,497
Popular Science	1,404,104	McCall's Pattern Fashions	500,059
Elks	1,399,286	Motion Picture	497,737
Outdoor Life	1,397,897	National Observer	484,741
Argosy	1,389,765	New Yorker, The	471,865
Mechanix Illustrated	1,389,685	Capper's Weekly	464,819
Seventeen	1,384,357	Saturday Review	463,138
Field & Stream	1,380,766	Hairdo	458,464
Sports Afield	1,336,730	Fortune	454,312
Successful Farming	1,330,991	Forbes	445,137
Glamour	1,321,792	Vogue	437,373
V. F. W. Magazine	1,298,664	Farmer-Stockman	430,124
Scouting	1,286,482	Popular Photography	429,302
Progressive Farmer	1,267,354	Family Handyman	429,177
House & Garden	1,256,829	Harper's Bazaar	422,681
Sports Illustrated	1,211,802	Rotarian	419,560
NewsTime	1,191,787	Scientific American	415,004
Photoplay	1,148,290	Christian Herald	400,068
Columbia	1,142,059	Home Garden and Flower Grower	400,060
Grit	1,064,585	Westways	392,886
Presbyterian Life	1,060,724	Popular Electronics	385,246
Esquire	1,035,337	Car & Driver	384,869
Holiday	1,029,277	Coronet	382,422

Crime Continued To Increase In 1967

In the cities, suburbs and rural areas of the United States crime increased an average of 17% during the first 6 months of 1967 when compared to the corresponding period in 1966, the FBI's Uniform Crime Reports disclosed.

Crimes of violence increased 18% as a group, with individual increases of 30% in robbery, 20% in murder, 11% in aggravated assault and 7% in forcible rape, according to the crime reports voluntarily submitted to the FBI by law enforcement agencies throughout the country.

In crimes against property, auto theft was up 19%, burglary 18% and larceny 16% in the 6 months, the FBI said.

Large cities of 100,000 or more inhabitants reported an average increase in crime of 18%. The increase was also 18% in suburban areas and rural areas reported a jump of 15%. The upward trend was consistent for all geographic areas of the country, according to the reports.

Crime Index Trends by Geographic Region
(January-June, 1967 over 1966 in Percentage)

Region	Total	Murder	Forcible rape	Robbery	Aggravated assault	Burglary	Larceny $50 and over	Auto theft
Northeastern states........	+18	+25	+ 8	+28	+14	+18	+10	+26
North central states........	+20	+36	+ 4	+25	+15	+21	+19	+19
Southern states............	+16	+13	+11	+36	+ 9	+16	+13	+21
Western states.............	+16	+15	+ 6	+33	+ 8	+17	+18	+10

Locations of Federal Detention Areas
Source: U. S. Bureau of Prisons

Penitentiaries: Atlanta, Ga.; Leavenworth, Kans.; Lewisburg, Pa.; McNeil Island, Wash.; Marion, Ill.; Terre Haute, Ind. **Reformatories:** El Reno, Okla.; Petersburg, Va.; Women, Alderson, W. Va. **Medical center:** Springfield, Mo.; Hospital; Maintenance unit. **Prison camps:** Eglin Air Force Base, Florida; Montgomery, Ala.; Safford, Ariz. **Correctional institutions:** Danbury, Conn.; La Tuna, Tex.; Lompoc, Calif.; Texarkana, Tex.; Milan, Mich.; Tallahassee, Fla.; Seagoville, Tex.; Terminal Island, Calif.; Sandstone, Minn. **Detention headquarters center:** New York City; Florence, Arizona. **Institutions for juvenile and youth offenders:** Ashland, Ky.; Englewood, Colo.; National Training School for Boys, Washington, D. C. **Pre-release guidance centers:** Detroit, Mich.; Chicago, Ill.; Los Angeles, Calif.; Kansas City, Mo.; Atlanta, Ga.; Houston, Texas; Oakland, Calif.

Prisoners in State and Federal Prisons and Reformatories

1940.......	173,706	1955........	185,780	1958........	205,493	1962........	218,830
1945.......	133,649	1956........	189,421	1959........	207,446	1963........	217,283
1950.......	166,123	1957........	195,256	1960........	212,953	1964........	214,356
				1961........	220,149	1965........	213,736

Counterfeiting Growing U. S. Problem

The Secret Service reported that in fiscal 1967 it arrested 1,072 persons on counterfeiting charges and seized more than $10,000,000 in bogus currency—an all-time high for both categories. The Secret Service described counterfeiting as a growing enforcement problem because of the ease and speed with which large amounts of counterfeit bills can be produced with modern printing and photography methods and quickly dispersed across the country for widespread distribution.

The counterfeiting of coins decreased in fiscal 1967 to $15,000 from approximately $29,000 in the previous fiscal year.

The following table summarizes receipts of counterfeit money during fiscal years 1966 and 1967:

Counterfeit Money Received in U. S.
Fiscal Yrs. 1966 and 1967

Receipts of counterfeit notes and coins	1966	1967
Loss to the public.......	$962,060.99	$1,658,100.75
Seized before circulation.	8,098,417.35	8,587,845.49
Total...............	9,060,478.34	10,245,946.24

Maximum Penalties for First Degree Murder
INCLUDING CAPITAL PUNISHMENT

These penalties may apply to convictions for other crimes. Imprisonment for life may be imposed instead of death in all states.

State	Penalty	State	Penalty	State	Penalty
Alabama....	Electrocution	Maine......	Life Imprisonment	Pennsylvania	Electrocution
Alaska......	Life Imprisonment	Maryland...	Lethal Gas	Rhode Island	Life Imprisonment
Arizona.....	Lethal Gas	Mass........	Electrocution	So. Carolina.	Electrocution
Arkansas....	Electrocution	Michigan....	Life Imprisonment	So. Dakota..	Electrocution
California...	Lethal Gas	Minnesota...	Life Imprisonment	Tennessee ...	Electrocution
Colorado....	Lethal Gas	Mississippi...	Lethal Gas	Texas.......	Electrocution
Connecticut.	Electrocution	Missouri....	Lethal Gas	Utah.......	Hanging or Shooting
Delaware....	Hanging	Montana....	Hanging	Vermont(b)..	Life Imprisonment
Dist. of Col..	Electrocution	Nebraska....	Electrocution	Virginia.....	Electrocution
Florida......	Electrocution	Nevada.....	Lethal Gas	Washington..	Hanging
Georgia.....	Electrocution	New Hamp...	Hanging	W. Virginia..	Life Imprisonment
Hawaii......	Life Imprisonment	New Jersey..	Electrocution	Wisconsin ..	Life Imprisonment
Idaho.......	Hanging	New Mexico..	Lethal Gas	Wyoming....	Lethal Gas
Illinois......	Electrocution	New York (a)	Life Imprisonment	U. S. Govt...	Death or Life
Indiana.....	Electrocution	No. Carolina.	Lethal Gas	Am. Samoa..	Hanging
Iowa.......	Life Imprisonment	No. Dakota..	Life Imprisonment	Canal Zone..	Hanging
Kansas......	Hanging	Ohio........	Electrocution	Guam.......	Life Imprisonment
Kentucky...	Electrocution	Oklahoma...	Electrocution	Puerto Rico..	Life Imprisonment
Louisiana...	Electrocution	Oregon......	Life Imprisonment	Virgin Islands	Life Imprisonment

(a) the death penalty applicable to persons for killing a peace officer acting in the line of duty and to convicts under life sentence for killing a guard or inmate. (b) Electrocution for killing of prison personnel or unrelated second offense.

Number of Radios, TVs and Phonographs in Use

The growth of color television reached spectacular proportions in 1967 as the number of American households owning a color set jumped from 4,410,400 in 1965 to an estimated 11,502,800 by June of 1967, according to the U. S. Department of Commerce.

Only 7.4% of American homes had a color TV set two years earlier compared to 19.3% of the 59,600,000 households in the middle of 1967. Only 6 out of every 100 households had no television set of any kind and 24.9% had two or more sets in 1967, the Commerce Department reported.

Number of Radio and TV Sets In Use
(In Millions)
Source: Electronic Industries Assn.

Year	Auto radios	Home radios	Total radios	Television receivers B & W	Television receivers Color	Phono-graphs
1950......	18	81	99	10.6	....	16.8
1955......	29	91	120	37.4	....	24.0
1960......	40	116	156	55.5	.2	34.0
1961......	41	127	168	57.6	.4	35.7
1962......	43	140	183	60.8	.8	37.0
1963......	45	151	196	65.0	1.6	39.0
1964......	47	161	208	70.0	3.0	42.0
1965......	55	172	227	75.0	5.0	45.0
1966......	64	188	262	78.5	9.7	48.0

Commercial Broadcast Stations on the Air
(Includes Puerto Rico, Virgin Islands and Guam)
Source: Federal Communications Commission

Year	Total on air	AM radio	FM radio	Television
1965..............	5,814	4,040	1,270	572
1966..............	5,986	4,004	1,393	589
1967..............	6,253	4,085	1,560	608

Newspaper Reporters Honor TV-Radio Newsmen

For the first time, television and radio newsmen were honored by their colleagues of the Newspaper Reporters Assn. of N. Y. City when Gabe Pressman of WNBC-TV and Joe Famm and Paul Ehrlich of WABC-TV were named among the group's award winners for 1967.

Other awards went to Kitty Hanson, Daily News; Martin Tolchin, N. Y. Times; Fern Marja Eckman, N. Y. Post; Alex J. Michelini, United Press International, and Stanley Slom, Fairchild Publications.

Individual Income Tax Returns, 1965
Source: Internal Revenue Service, Treasury Department (Preliminary)

Adjusted gross income classes	Total number of returns	Adjusted gross income	Taxable income	Income tax after credits
Total.....................	67,596,300	[1]$429,201,239,000	$254,338,564,000	$49,529,695,000
No adjusted gross income..	397,372	[2]1,461,970,000	....	....
Under $600...............	4,180,301	1,354,449,000	....	....
$600 under $1,000.........	3,206,523	2,557,167,000	33,277,000	4,729,000
$1,000 under $2,000.......	7,298,124	10,737,934,000	2,299,719,000	328,528,000
$2,000 under $3,000.......	6,128,705	15,324,793,000	5,198,126,000	768,744,000
$3,000 under $4,000.......	6,038,731	21,125,457,000	8,842,641,000	1,356,103,000
$4,000 under $5,000.......	5,767,595	25,946,576,000	12,014,638,000	1,878,785,000
$5,000 under $6,000.......	5,460,768	30,007,117,000	15,202,262,000	2,409,293,000
$6,000 under $7,000.......	5,497,614	35,696,499,000	18,930,863,000	3,030,288,000
$7,000 under $8,000.......	4,979,631	37,264,838,000	20,692,469,000	3,357,284,000
$8,000 under $9,000.......	4,147,888	35,198,637,000	20,420,871,000	3,368,062,000
$9,000 under $10,000......	3,387,836	32,113,709,000	19,472,751,000	3,269,180,000
$10,000 under $15,000.....	7,714,561	91,767,810,000	60,825,711,000	10,711,983,000
$15,000 under $20,000.....	1,761,926	29,934,707,000	21,668,701,000	4,188,905,000
$20,000 under $50,000.....	1,393,902	39,645,180,000	30,859,710,000	7,439,877,000
$50,000 under $100,000....	188,910	12,440,366,000	10,204,314,000	3,654,120,000
$100,000 under $500,000...	43,963	7,164,497,000	5,773,052,000	2,752,102,000
$500,000 under $1,000,000.	1,404	946,146,000	759,857,000	408,405,000
$1,000,000 or more.........	646	1,434,327,000	1,109,602,000	603,307,000

[1]Adjusted gross income less deficit. [2]Deficit.

Public Days in Canada, 1968

New Year's Day, Jan. 1; Good Friday, April 12; Easter Monday, April 15; Victoria Day, May 20 (always first Monday preceding May 25); Queen's Birthday (usually celebrated on same date as Victoria Day); Dominion Day, July 1; Labour Day, Sept. 2; Thanksgiving Day, Oct. 14 (the second Monday of October); Remembrance Day, Nov. 11; Christmas, Dec. 25.

When the statutory holidays fall on Sunday, the following day is observed. Although the general observation of holidays on Mondays, in order to give people long weekends, has been a matter of discussion, no legislation has yet been passed on this regard, with the exception for Victoria Day.

Civic Holiday is not a statutory holiday, but any city, town or municipality may appoint any day as such by resolution of the Council or the statutory body. However, the first Monday in August is generally observed throughout Canada as Civic Holiday (August 5, in 1968).

Roman Catholic Statistics for the United States

Source: Official Catholic Directory copyright 1967 by P. J. Kenedy & Sons
All data in the tables, including population, are for the archdioceses and the dioceses named (1967).

ARCH-DIOCESES	Cler-gy	Par-ishes	Stu-dents	Catholic Pop.*	ARCH-DIOCESES	Cler-gy	Par-ishes	Stu-dents	Catholic Pop.*
Anchorage....	25	9	1,758	15,000	Kansas City-				
Atlanta.....	151	31	16,033	47,325	St. Joseph...	359	96	40,788	132,361
Baltimore....	749	133	111,199	478,370	La Crosse....	397	175	60,211	179,659
Boston.....	2,499	400	455,073	1,843,490	Lafayette, Ind..	173	61	20,220	77,062
Chicago.....	2,620	452	521,395	2,343,000	Lafayette, La..	308	145	88,843	387,709
Cincinnati...	934	260	157,476	530,295	Lansing.....	234	96	67,309	228,269
Denver.....	327	108	75,052	261,944	Lincoln.....	174	139	16,018	58,711
Detroit.....	1,448	329	356,861	1,536,476	Little Rock...	303	86	14,407	52,228
Dubuque....	553	201	71,416	216,170	Madison.....	290	137	51,747	180,640
Hartford....	749	203	178,478	784,455	Manchester...	449	122	64,449	137,996
Indianapolis..	475	164	55,755	207,889	Marquette...	180	92	29,980	107,672
Kan.City,Kan.	400	105	41,001	136,500	Miami.....	332	96	75,686	439,594
Los Angeles..	1,447	313	386,505	1,649,167	Mobile-Birm'ham	414	145	35,431	130,937
Louisville....	447	131	65,015	198,654	Monterey-Fresno	290	114	73,899	442,583
Milwaukee...	1,206	285	206,675	698,954	Nashville....	160	75	28,728	89,785
Newark.....	1,345	253	295,141	1,604,397	Natchez-Jackson	218	98	24,829	74,589
New Orleans..	570	158	142,916	621,000	New Ulm....	130	90	22,993	71,256
New York....	2,246	407	379,888	1,848,000	Norwich....	256	69	48,040	185,134
Omaha.....	410	143	59,847	181,793	Oakland....	460	82	75,206	348,732
Philadelphia..	1,760	312	356,729	1,352,553	Ogdensburg...	264	118	48,334	165,702
Portland, Ore.	436	114	51,722	201,568	Okla. City &				
St. Louis....	1,109	249	150,723	518,142	Tulsa...	286	127	29,034	110,793
St. Paul....	628	214	166,263	517,521	Owensboro...	88	71	14,452	41,813
San Antonio..	441	143	121,813	506,084	Paterson....	425	98	74,871	361,347
San Francisco.	801	142	157,085	828,779	Peoria.....	418	169	58,245	210,083
Santa Fe....	458	90	57,842	255,463	Pittsburgh...	884	316	230,396	930,157
Seattle.....	487	118	78,536	292,675	Portland, Me..	372	134	75,505	274,013
Washington...	1,194	122	118,364	376,102	Providence...	609	154	115,472	554,766
Byzan. Phila.	143	99	10,356	164,033	Pueblo.....	171	61	31,812	114,888
DIOCESES					Raleigh.....	168	109	21,505	56,010
Albany......	735	207	107,185	420,614	Rapid City...	122	60	13,767	41,072
Alexandria, La.	186	87	23,760	93,660	Reno......	79	36	12,632	80,000
Allentown....	386	151	53,786	245,679	Richmond....	405	117	76,452	256,000
Altoona-Johnstn	302	119	40,127	142,789	Rochester....	609	155	111,522	361,790
Amarillo....	100	55	16,776	81,500	Rockford....	344	97	52,860	187,070
Austin.....	155	77	23,629	135,285	Rockville, C'tr.	470	123	260,847	850,121
Baker, Ore...	52	30	7,301	25,078	Sacramento...	268	87	51,512	221,085
Baton Rouge..	149	64	38,389	172,810	Saginaw....	202	115	48,898	166,750
Beaumont....	77	32	18,734	83,605	St. Augustine..	272	121	58,668	199,946
Belleville....	240	133	33,779	118,833	St. Cloud....	363	146	43,590	139,241
Belmont Abbey.	49	1	784	574	Salina.....	147	102	19,034	61,291
Bismarck....	159	88	24,538	76,192	Salt Lake City.	102	35	14,629	52,668
Boise......	101	58	14,740	51,822	San Angelo...	73	35	18,105	60,488
Bridgeport...	375	84	80,678	302,884	San Diego....	475	163	87,899	330,999
Brooklyn....	1,388	225	310,878	1,575,366	Santa Rosa...	105	32	15,239	61,284
Brownsville...	85	43	34,321	250,000	Savannah....	89	34	13,226	33,373
Buffalo.....	1,220	271	204,508	916,887	Scranton....	628	233	90,771	360,279
Burlington...	276	102	41,211	137,966	Sioux City...	238	141	34,707	106,850
Camden.....	429	119	75,738	295,000	Sioux Falls...	217	123	34,589	103,939
Charleston...	151	65	15,682	43,794	Spokane....	223	57	21,527	67,831
Cheyenne....	64	39	7,458	49,000	Springfield, Ill..	374	143	48,934	179,848
Cleveland....	933	232	227,544	866,606	Springfield, Mass.	484	134	89,915	386,917
Columbus....	299	108	47,756	182,000	Springfield-Cape				
Corpus Christi.	162	63	41,737	190,058	Girardeau...	120	58	10,610	35,811
Covington....	238	84	31,165	92,817	Steubenville...	194	73	15,516	54,000
Crookston....	79	55	12,995	40,659	Stockton....	80	28	18,193	90,755
Dallas-Ft.Worth	303	97	45,704	157,166	Superior....	147	89	24,160	79,854
Davenport...	244	123	30,997	104,846	Syracuse....	501	165	119,917	396,166
Des Moines...	145	71	23,014	79,942	Toledo.....	411	161	83,663	297,767
Dodge City...	73	50	10,890	31,218	Trenton....	480	188	167,027	451,218
Duluth.....	155	90	26,034	104,503	Tucson.....	310	87	76,637	412,000
El Paso.....	131	67	48,584	170,470	Wheeling....	213	103	30,464	104,360
Erie......	357	125	66,579	215,635	Wichita.....	220	98	24,185	87,662
Evansville....	148	74	25,216	82,123	Wilmington...	203	51	31,513	121,573
Fairbanks....	40	18	3,414	12,029	Winona.....	230	130	35,671	114,049
Fall River....	399	108	67,997	284,598	Worcester....	531	128	92,181	349,327
Fargo......	192	128	27,565	100,238	Yakima.....	77	38	12,543	48,501
Ft.Wayne-S. Bend	471	86	50,899	153,297	Youngstown...	347	117	74,122	286,492
Gallup.....	105	51	19,065	78,375	Eastern Rite:				
Galveston-Houston	360	104	73,579	305,000	Byzan. Pitts..	147	121	20,061	223,923
Gary......	264	84	42,913	183,742	Passaic.....	102	75	10,438	96,273
Grand Island..	93	58	13,931	49,073	UkrainianGreek				
Grand Rapids..	280	130	61,523	193,286	Chicago.....	44	26	3,620	29,600
Great Falls...	125	69	19,664	75,565	Stamford....	103	57	5,197	87,630
Green Bay....	568	192	96,332	316,783	Military Ordin-				
Greensburg...	293	120	46,968	228,486	ariate**	...	...	...	2,000,000
Harrisburg...	250	90	46,918	184,646	Maronite....	52	43	12	150,980
Helena.....	164	57	19,216	79,500	Melkite.....	37	23	7	23,000
Honolulu....	29	62	40,268	225,000					
Jefferson City.	203	93	18,000	62,580	**Total 1967**	59,892	17,942	11,006,687	46,864,910
Joliet.....	412	103	79,914	280,265	**Total 1966**	59,193	17,765	10,918,213	46,246,175
Juneau.....	10	6	927	3,290					

*Archdiocese of New York includes the boroughs of Manhattan, Bronx and Richmond, and 7 counties of eastern New York. Cities and diocese of the same name do not have the same areas and in some cases the population of the diocese is greater than that of the city because of its greater area.
**Military Ordinariate under jurisdiction of His Eminence Cardinal Spellman as Military Vicar.
The first 29 dioceses are archdioceses; there are 124 other dioceses.
Cardinals 8 (Baltimore, Boston, Chicago, Los Angeles, New York, Philadelphia, St. Louis and Washington, D.C.). Archbishops 32, Bishops 229, Abbots 50, Priests 59,892, Brothers 12,539, Sisters 176,671 and 17,942 parishes with 17,375 pastors. There are 452 seminaries with 45,379 seminarians; 305 colleges with 431,070 students; 1,469 high schools with 697,634 students; 872 private high schools with 406,127 students; 10,528 elementary schools with 4,291,466 students; 399 private elementary schools with 78,379 students; 118 protective institutes with 11,806 students; full time teachers 205,687; 234 orphanages and infant asylums with 46,856 dependent children; 799 general hospitals, 136 special hospitals, 18,377,492 patients treated annually; 416 homes for the aged. Converts (1966) 117,478.

Racial Violence Sweeps American Cities

Racial violence blossomed across urban America in 1967 from Portland, Ore., to New York in what sociologists feared might become a permanent feature of the Negro civil rights revolution. The single bloodiest outbreak occurred July 23-30 in Detroit, where at least 40 people died, 2,000 were injured and 5,000 left homeless by rioting, looting and burning in the city's ghetto areas. The riot was finally quelled by 4,700 Federal paratroopers dispatched to the city by President Johnson July 24 to aid 8,000 National Guardsmen. The violence in Detroit followed 6 days of rioting in Newark, N. J. July 12-17 in which some 26 persons died, 1,500 were injured and more than 1,000 persons arrested.

Stung by the cost in lives and destruction of the Newark and Detroit riots, President Johnson July 27 appointed a Special Advisory Commission on Civil Disorders "to investigate the origin of the recent disorders in our cities" and in a nationwide television address proclaimed Sunday, July 30 a National Day of Prayer for Peace and Reconciliation. Congressional leaders of both parties July 25 called for an investigation of the riots, with some Congressmen professing to see Communist influence behind the violence. The Senate Permanent Subcommittee on Investigations set up a panel Aug. 1 to look into the cause of the riots and the Senate Judiciary Committee held hearings Aug. 2-3 on an anti-riot bill making it a Federal crime to cross state lines to incite a riot. The Bill had been passed by the House July 19.

In a joint statement July 26 four moderate Negro civil rights leaders appealed for an end to the riots but said that white Americans were "not blameless" because they generally supported restrictive practices against Negroes. The statement was issued by Dr. Martin Luther King, Jr., A. Philip Randolph, Roy Wilkins and Whitney Young.

Dr. King in a press conference in New York Apr. 16 had warned that at least 10 cities could "explode in racial violence" and named Cleveland, Chicago, Los Angeles, Washington, Newark, New York and Oakland, Calif., as potential riot cities. FBI Director J. Edgar Hoover May 3 accused King and other civil rights leaders of issuing an "open invitation" to violence in naming cities where trouble could be expected.

The same day as King's statement, Apr. 16, racial rioting erupted in Cleveland, followed by disturbances in Massillon, Ohio Apr. 17. The Cleveland outbreak had been preceded by rioting in Nashville, Tenn., Apr. 8-10 in which some 17 persons were injured and 80 arrested. The Nashville riot started near Negro Fisk University following a speech by Stokely Carmichael, militant leader of the Student Non-Violent Coordinating Committee. Carmichael's successor as chairman of SNCC, H. Rap Brown, was arrested in Washington July 26 on a fugitive warrant charging "inciting to riot" and "counseling to burn" in connection with rioting in Cambridge, Md., July 25 that followed a speech in which Brown exhorted 400 Negroes to "burn this town down."

The riots and disturbances failed to end with the "long hot summer." As the year progresesd more towns and cities were added to the list of racial unrest. Among them were: Alabama: Birmingham, Prattville. Arizona: Phoenix. California: San Francisco, Fresno, Long Beach, Marin City, San Bernardino. Connecticut: Hartford, New Britain, New Haven. Delaware: Wilmington. Florida: Tampa, West Palm Beach, Riviera Beach. Georgia: Atlanta. Illinois: Chicago, Cairo, East St. Louis, Rockford, Peoria, Elgin. Indiana: South Bend. Iowa: Des Moines, Waterloo. Michigan: Lansing, Kalamazoo, Flint, Grand Rapids, Saginaw, Pontiac. Missouri: Kansas City. Massachusetts: Boston. Minnesota: Minneapolis. New Jersey: Plainfield, Jersey City, New Brunswick, Paterson, Elizabeth, Englewood, Passaic, Palmyra. New York: New York City, Buffalo, Nyack, Rochester, Mt. Vernon, Peekskill, Newburgh, Wyandanch. North Carolina: Durham, Winston-Salem. Ohio: Dayton, Cincinnati, Toledo, Youngstown, Springfield, Hamilton. Oregon: Portland. Pennsylvania: Erie, Philadelphia, New Castle. Tennessee: Memphis. Wisconsin: Milwaukee. Washington, D.C.

British Pound Devalued

Britain devalued the pound Nov. 18, 1967, by 14.3%, from $2.80 to $2.40. The move climaxed a week of financial crisis as pressure built up against the pound following a report of a $300,000,000 British trade gap—the difference between exports and imports—for the month of October.

By Nov. 22, 18 other currencies, those of Israel, Hong Kong, Sierra Leone, Ceylon, Jamaica, Malta, Guyana, Malawi, Cyprus, Gambia, Mauritius, Barbados, Fiji, Bermuda, Ireland, Denmark, Spain and New Zealand, were similarly devalued and others were expected to follow suit. Most major powers said they would not devalue their currencies.

In announcing the devaluation and other stringent economic measures, it was revealed that Britain was due to get $3 billion in international credits to protect the pound from further pressure in the international money market.

In a move to protect the value of the dollar, the Federal Reserve System, the country's central bank, raised its official lending rate to member commercial banks from 4% to 4.5%. Major banks throughout the country, in turn, increased their prime or minimum interest rate from 5½% to 6%, an indication that the cost of borrowing might eventually cost the consumer more in the form of higher rates on home mortgages and other consumer borrowing.

For the man in the street in Britain, devaluation means he will have to pay more to buy any imported item. An imported American coat formerly costing £100 will now cost about £114.

For Americans buying imported British goods, devaluation means lower prices with a £100 item formerly selling for $280 in the U. S., now costing only $240.

Mar. 28, 1967—Peace plan proposal by U Thant calling for stand-still truce, preliminary talks and reconvening of Geneva Conference revealed. Accepted by U. S. and South Vietnam with reservations. Rejected by Hanoi.

Mar. .1967—Total U. S. force in Vietnam stands at 427,000.

Apr. 1, 1967—South Vietnamese constitution goes into effect.

May 2, 1967—U. S. commander in Vietnam, Gen. William C. Westmoreland, urges further buildup of American forces. Domestic debate over war intensifies.

May 11, 1967—U Thant expresses fear Vietnamese war is "initial phase of World War III."

June 23 and 25, 1967—President Johnson and Soviet Premier Kosygin meet in Glassboro, N. J. Discuss Vietnam as well as Mideast crisis. No agreement.

Aug. 3, 1967—President Johnson announces U. S. forces in Vietnam will be increased to 525,000 men by June 1968. Asks for 10% income tax surcharge to finance the war.

Aug. 11, 1967—U. S. extends air raids to within 10 miles of Chinese border.

Aug. 23, 1967—President Johnson appoints 20 Americans to observe South Vietnamese elections.

Sept. 3, 1967—Nguyen Van Thieu elected president, Nguyen Cao Ky, vice president.

Sept. 7, 1967—U. S. announces plans for fortified barrier south of demilitarized zone.

Nov. 2, 1967—Amb. Arthur Goldberg states unequivocally that the U. S. would be willing to have the Vietcong's political arm, the National Liberation Front, participate directly in a reconvened Geneva conference or be present in any discussion of the Vietnam question before the Security Council of the UN.

Nov. 11, 1967—Defense Dept. announces total U. S. casualties since Jan. 1, 1961 are 14,621 dead, 91,971 wounded.

Nov. 17, 1967—President Johnson warns Hanoi not to rely on the 1968 Presidential elections. "I think that whatever interpretation Hanoi might make that would lead them to believe that Uncle Sam, whoever may be President, is going to pull out and it will be easier for them to make an inside deal with another President than will be the present, they'll make a serious misjudgment."

Nov. 19, 1967—Gen. Westmoreland says: "We are winning a war of attrition" and within two years or less we may be able to "phase down the level of our military effort."

Basic Changes in Medical Care Seen Necessary

Declaring flatly that there is a "crisis" in American health care, the National Advisory Commission on Health Manpower submitted a report to President Johnson Nov. 20, 1967, recommending sweeping changes in current medical practice in the United States.

Among some 50 recommendations made by the 14-member panel were:

• Re-examination and re-licensing of doctors on a periodic basis to insure competence, as well as a routine review of a doctor's performance by other doctors in the same community.

• A pre-paid health care system.

• Economic incentives for high quality health care and economic penalties for inefficiency.

• A greater emphasis by health insurance plans on out-patient care to alleviate the pressure on hospital facilities.

The report made it clear that no amount of money or manpower alone would meet the crisis unless basic changes were made in the present system.

"Because the present system channels manpower into inefficient and inappropriate activities, added numbers by themselves cannot be expected to bring much improvement," the commission said.

The executive director of the commission, Dr. Peter S. Bing, said the number of doctors and hospital beds is growing at a faster rate than the population. He noted that the country was still faced by a medical crisis because of greater demand for care, increasing specialization by doctors which produce personnel shortages in some areas, and the growing complexity of hospital and medical practice.

In giving its recommendations, the commission stressed that it was not advocating a Federal health care plan and said that the problems involved were so large that the Government alone couldn't solve them.

On the question of economic incentives for doctors, the report suggested that a system wherein the physician would share in the profits of a hospital was an area worthy of exploration.

As for economic incentives for hospitals, the report said that equal payment should be made to any hospital in a given area based on the quality and quantity of service made available by the hospital.

The report warned that if the demand for medical care is not met through better utilization of available manpower and medical facilities, costs for health care in the U.S. will skyrocket.

President Johnson declared the report would be required reading for his Cabinet members and said he hoped it would be widely read outside of the Government.

Sen. McCarthy May Enter Primaries

Anti-Vietnam war sentiment crystallized about Minnesota Democrat Sen. Eugene J. McCarthy in early Nov., 1967, as it became apparent that the Senator was seriously considering entering Presidential primary elections in an attempt to take the Democratic nomination away from President Johnson in 1968.

The California Democratic Council's steering committee Nov. 12 urged Sen. McCarthy to make the race as it sought to form a "peace delegation" that would be pledged to support a peace slate to oppose the President in the June 1968 primary contest in that state. The resolution declared that Sen. McCarthy had "courageously announced his belief that the incumbent President must be challenged in state primaries and the 1968 Democratic convention."

The previous day Sen. McCarthy told a convention of college Democrats in Boston that party leaders who are in disagreement with the Administration's Vietnam policy "have an obligation to speak out and party unity is not a sufficient excuse for their silence."

Sen. Robert F. Kennedy, (D.-N.Y.) said Nov. 18 that if Sen McCarthy were to seek the Democratic presidential nomination "it would be a healthy influence on the Democratic party."

Sen. Kennedy seemed to qualify his previously stated intention of supporting and campaigning for President Johnson by saying: "I will support the nominee of the Democratic party. I would support the President and Mr. Humphrey if they are the nominees."

Sen. McCarthy said he would announce his decision shortly.

split with him over the President's controversial plan to enlarge the Supreme Court. Mr. Garner would have been 99 years old Nov. 22.

Saturn-5 A Success—America's hopes to land a man on the moon before 1970 received a boost **Nov. 9** when the 36-story high Saturn-5 rocket lifted off from Cape Kennedy in its first test and completed an 8 hour and 37 minute unmanned mission without a hitch. The 3-stage rocket, generating 160,000,000 horsepower, placed a 285,000 pound payload into earth orbit at a peak altitude of 119 miles. At command from the ground, the third rocket booster sent the orbiting payload speeding 11,286 miles into space, after which it plunged earthward developing speed of 25,000 mph, that which astronauts returning from the moon will encounter when they return to earth. The 12,060 pound capsule was recovered in the Pacific Ocean about 700 miles northwest of Hawaii —just 10 miles away from its target area.

The shot's official designation was Apollo 4.

DISASTERS

Strategic Air Command B-52-H jet bomber crashed near Rome, N. Y. **Nov. 2**, killing 6, injuring 2 . . . Brazil's Sadia Airlines plane **Nov.** 3 crashed near Curitiba, Brazil, killing 20, injuring 6 . . . 12 of 37 aboard killed when Iberia Airlines Caravelle jet crashed **Nov.** 4 as it approached London Airport . . . Express train jumped the tracks near London **Nov.** 5, 51 dead, 111 injured . . . Cathay Pacific Airways Convair 880 jet carrying 127 crashed into Hong Kong harbor on take-off **Nov.** 5, all but one survived . . . Father and 3 small sons killed **Nov.** 5 when their private plane crashed into Black Mt. near Whitehall, N. Y. . . . 15 workers killed by gas fumes **Nov.** 8 following dynamite explosion at construction project in central Peru . . . Milan-to-Palermo express ran into herd of buffalo, then hit another train **Nov. 9**, killing 14, injuring 70.

Highlights of the 1967 Elections

Voters in the off-year state and mayoralty elections had a chance, directly and indirectly, to express their opinions on a variety of questions ranging through such topics as racism, the Vietnam war and separation of church and state. The electorate's answer to these questions was open to varying interpretations, but seemed on the whole to be a reasoned response rather than an emotional one.

In mayoralty elections in Cleveland, Ohio; Gary, Ind.; and Boston, Mass., racism was repudiated by the voters. They elected Negro mayors in Cleveland and Gary and rejected a white woman candidate in Boston who campaigned on the slogan: "You know where I stand."

In Cleveland, the nation's 8th largest city in terms of population, Negro Democrat Carl B. Stokes needed the assistance of some 43,000 white voters in squeaking out an unofficial 2,501-vote win over his Republican opponent, Seth C. Taft. Taft is the nephew of the late Sen. Robert A. Taft.

The Gary contest was won by Democrat Richard G. Hatcher in a bitterly fought race with his white Republican opponent, Joseph B. Radigan. Hatcher got 39,330 votes to Radigan's 37,941. The vote was along racial lines and Radigan refused to concede defeat, but it appeared that Gary, with a Negro population of 55%, had elected its first Negro mayor.

White backlash failed to develop in Boston and Democrat Mrs. Louise Day Hicks, a member of the city's school board who is opposed to busing of Negro children into white schools, was defeated in the non-partisan election by white Democrat Kevin H. White, who got 100,828 votes to Mrs. Hicks' 89,755, in an unofficial tally. A Negro was elected to the 9-man city council.

Despite the fact that there seemed to be a growing number of Americans across the country desiring a quick end to the Vietnam war, voters in San Francisco turned down a proposal on the ballot, by 132,406 to 76,632, which would have made it the policy of their city and county "that there be an immediate cease-fire

and withdrawal of U.S. troops from Vietnam."

The question of separation of church and state arose in New York State, and is believed to have played a decisive role in the 2½ to 1 defeat of a new state constitution. One of the provisions of the proposed constitution would have repealed a ban against financial aid to church operated schools and led to a prolonged emotional controversy prior to the vote. But New Yorkers did approve a $2½ billion transportation bond issue, thus giving Republican Gov. Nelson Rockefeller another victory, since he had campaigned vigorously for its approval.

But it was in New Jersey, where Republicans captured both houses of the legislature by 3 to 1 margins, and Kentucky, where Louie B. Nunn was elected the first Republican governor since 1943, that the Republican national politicians professed to see an augury for the 1968 Presidential elections. The New Jersey Republicans had contended during the campaign that a big GOP win would be a repudiation of President Johnson and an indication of dissatisfaction with his conduct of the Vietnam war.

Nationally, the Democrats saw the election results as a party victory on the basis of winning performances in Cleveland, Gary and Philadelphia and the defeat of the San Francisco Vietnam proposal.

Other elections of general interest saw Mississippians elect Rep. John Bell Williams as governor. Williams, a Democrat and segregationist, defeated easily moderate Republican Rubel Phillips, who had told voters Mississippi had to change its racial attitudes. With most of the vote counted Williams had 293,188 to 126,753 for Phillips.

One Negro, Robert G. Clark, won a seat as a Representative in the Mississippi legislature. He is the first Negro to sit in that house since the end of Reconstruction.

In Hartford, Conn., voters chose attractive Republican Ann Uccello to be mayor by a slim 165-vote margin over the Democratic incumbent, George Kinsella.

Mother and Father of the Year

Mrs. Minnie Guenther of Arizona was chosen American Mother of 1967 by the American Mothers Committee, in connection with Mother's Day, May 14. Mrs. Guenther has 9 children.

Mayor John Lindsay of New York was selected Father of the Year 1967 by the National Father's Day Committee, in connection with Father's Day, June 18. Mayor Lindsay has 3 daughters and a son.

explosion **Dec. 28** near Lob Nor in Sinkiang Province. The energy yield of the explosion was described by the U. S. Atomic Energy Commission as "a few hundred kilotons." Initial examination of the radioactive debris indicated that thermonuclear material had been used and that China was a step closer toward developing a hydrogen bomb.

GENERAL

Car Safety Rules—Dr. William Haddon Jr., head of the Commerce Department's National Traffic Safety Agency, proposed 23 safety standards for 1968-model cars **Dec. 1.** The new standards differed in some respects from those proposed earlier by the Federal Government. Dr. Haddon stated that many of the proposed standards had been "already met by most vehicles to which they would apply." Henry Ford 2nd said **Dec. 14** that many of the new standards were "unreasonable, arbitrary and technically unfeasible." On **Dec. 31** General Motors Corp. told Dr. Haddon that "given certain conditions," it could comply with 16 of the agency's proposed 23 safety standards for 1968 cars.

Mutual Funds—In a special report to Congress **Dec. 2**, the Securities and Exchange Commission declared that mutual funds charged their customers "excessive" fees. The Commission asked Congress for legislation to remedy the situation. The report of the Commission, which took 4 years to prepare, urged a 5% ceiling on sales commissions and an enforceable requirement that management fees be "reasonable."

Farm Bureau—The American Farm Bureau held its 48th annual meeting in Las Vegas, Nevada, **Dec. 5-8.** The Federation members endorsed statements calling for the elimination of Federal controls on wheat and livestock feed grains. The statements were also critical of the Administration's Great Society anti-poverty program, the housewives' food store boycotts and church leaders' activities in civil rights and politics.

Republicans Meet — Twenty-seven GOP governors and governors-elect attended the Republican Governors Association **Dec. 9-10** in Colorado Springs, Colo. A statement issued **Dec. 10** declared that there was "a contagious spirit of confidence" in the party's future. The Association elected Gov. John A. Love of Colorado the new chairman to replace Gov. Robert E. Smylie of Idaho. The governors also approved a plan under which state governments would share in Federal tax revenue.

Democratic Governors vs. LBJ—Angry criticism of President Johnson and the Great Society program was voiced by Democratic governors in a meeting at White Sulphur Springs, W. Va., **Dec. 16.** Gov. Harold E. Hughes of Iowa, chairman of the group, said state leaders should have a greater part in developing party policy and that Washington should not try to impose programs on the states without taking into regard local problems. He also said President Johnson might have "a

Book on Kennedy Assassination Arouses Controversy

A controversy developed in **December** between the Kennedy family and William R. Manchester, author of a book on the assassination of President John F. Kennedy entitled *The Death of a President.* The Kennedys had chosen Manchester to write the book and he had signed an 11-point agreement with Sen. Robert F. Kennedy (D.-N. Y.) in March, 1964. According to press reports, the agreement was purported to have said in part: (1) the Kennedy family would cooperate with Manchester; (2) the final manuscript would be subject to the review of Mrs. Jacqueline Kennedy and Sen. Robert Kennedy; (3) the book would not be published before Nov. 22, 1968, unless Mrs. Kennedy designated an earlier date.

After Manchester finished his book in 1966, the President's widow charged that the author had broken faith with her. She declared that the book recorded some of her deepest, emotional thoughts and that she did not wish to have these exposed. Publication of the book, she stated, would cause her "great and irreparable injury" and "result in precisely the sensationalism and commercialism which we—Robert F. Kennedy and I—have sought so strenuously to avoid." To prevent publication, Mrs. Kennedy **Dec. 14** notified the firm of Harper & Row (which planned to publish the hard-bound volume of the book) and Look magazine (which planned to serialize the book) of her intention to pursue court action.

In answer to Mrs. Kennedy's charges, Manchester stated **Dec. 18:** "Mrs. Kennedy asked me to write this book; I did not seek the opportunity. Mrs. Kennedy gave me 10 hours of interviews; I did not, indeed could not, have conducted these interviews without her voluntary cooperation."

A source close to Sen. Robert Kennedy disclosed that the dispute involved more than just the questions of broken faith and the personal feelings of Mrs. Kennedy. The source said that Manchester's book depicted alleged tension between the Johnson and Kennedy aides at the time of the assassination.

Manchester said that Mrs. Kennedy did not object to the book until she learned of Look magazine's offer of $665,000 for the publication rights. A Kennedy family spokesman said that in addition to the Look offer, Manchester would receive the following sums for his book: $1,500,000 from paperback rights, $250,000 from the Book-of-the-Month Club, $150,000 from the hard-bound edition and $200,000 from foreign publication rights. Manchester, however, declared that after taxes and legal expenses "I may come out with something in the range of $500,000."

The Kennedy-Manchester controversy was partially resolved **Dec. 21** when Look magazine agreed to delete about 1,600 words from the serialized form of the book. The parts deleted dealt with the personal life of Mrs. Kennedy and her children. Later Harper & Row agreed to delete about 2,000 words. After the agreement, Manchester said: "Changes were made in about 250 places. A word here, a phrase there—some of Jackie's changes were baffling—but not a single incident is omitted." With Look and Harper & Row in agreement with the deletions, Stern magazine, which planned to serialize the book in Germany, also agreed to an abridged version **Jan. 25.**

In the dispute over broken faith, contractual obligations, publication royalties and political innuendos, one fact was clear. According to many leaders in the publishing industry—with all the publicity and a first printing by Harper & Row of 500,000 copies, *The Death of a President* was almost certain to become one of the leading best-sellers in book publishing history.

JFK Assassination Conspiracy Probe in New Orleans

In an exclusive story **Feb. 17, 1967,** the New Orleans States-Item revealed that New Orleans District Attorney James Garrison was investigating the assassination of John F. Kennedy in the belief that the President's death was the result of a conspiracy hatched in New Orleans by Lee Harvey Oswald, Cuban exiles and others.

The next day, the 46-year-old Garrison confirmed the probe, which he said had started in October, 1966, and claimed that his investigation had already shown the Warren Commission report was wrong in its finding of no conspiracy. "Arrests will be made. Charges will be filed and convictions obtained," Garrison declared.

In the days and weeks that followed, a bizarre conspiracy tale with an ill-assorted cast of characters unfolded and the investigation itself took many unexpected twists and turns. The following is a chronological summary of the major developments.

Feb. 22—David Ferrie, 49, homosexual, former airline pilot, found dead in his apartment. New Orleans coroner says death was from natural causes. Garrison says it is suicide and calls Ferrie "one of history's most important individuals."

Feb. 24—Garrison says his staff has "solved" the assassination. "It's my personal belief that Oswald did not kill anyone that day."

Mar. 1—Garrison orders arrest of Clay Shaw, 54, retired director of the International Trade Mart, on charge of "participation in a conspiracy to murder John F. Kennedy." Garrison claims that Shaw, alias Clay Bertrand, met with Oswald and Ferrie in Ferrie's apartment and planned to kill President Kennedy.

Mar. 14—Perry Russo, 25, an insurance agent, testifies before 3-judge panel that 3 times he saw Ferrie, "Leon Oswald" and "Clem" Bertrand together in Ferrie's apartment in September, 1963, and heard them plan to kill the President.

Mar. 16—Russo admits Garrison's investigators questioned him 3 times while he was under hypnosis.

Mar. 16—Dean Andrews, lawyer and part-time district attorney of Jefferson County, who helped in the Garrison investigation initially, is indicted for perjury for testifying that he could not say Clay Bertrand and Clay Shaw were the same person.

Apr. 1—Gordon Novel, 29, former New Orleans nightclub owner, arrested in Ohio on fugitive charge stemming from conspiracy to commit burglary. Garrison claims Novel is "a most important witness" in the case.

Apr. 4—Novel, freed on bail, calls investigation "complete fabrication."

Apr. 5—Clay Shaw pleads not guilty.

Apr. 5—Layton Martens indicted on perjury charges for denying he knew Novel.

May 8—Garrison says he will investigate CIA and FBI, charging them with withholding evidence.

May 12—Garrison claims he found Jack Ruby's phone number written in code in Oswald address book.

June 26—William Gurvich, chief investigator for Garrison, resigns, saying: "If there is any truth to Garrison's charges about there being a conspiracy, I can't find it."

July 18—Walter Sheridan, investigative reporter for NBC, surrenders to New Orleans authorities on Garrison charge that he and Richard Townley of WSDU-TV, New Orleans, had attempted to bribe or intimidate Perry Russo. Both men deny the charges.

Aug. 14—Dean Andrews found guilty of 3 counts of perjury by 5-man jury.

Sept. 4—Chief Justice Earl Warren tells newsmen in Tokyo that he hasn't seen a single fact to contradict the Warren Report conclusions, including Garrison's investigation.

Sept. 6—Garrison accuses Warren of attempting to "dynamite" the investigation.

Off-Beat News Stories of 1967

Micro-miniskirts, hippies, flower power, Twiggy and everything and anything psychedelic made big news in 1967. But the year also saw less publicized off-beat events such as the advent of the radage or cabbish, a dumpling-helicopter war and a court ruling that sauerkraut does not smell bad.

The development of the radage—a cross between a radish and a cabbage—was announced by Russian scientists in Moscow who claimed their new vegetable contained more Vitamin C than a lemon.

In Schleissheim, Germany, Hermann Winter fired 120 dumplings from a homemade catapult at low flying American helicopters and won a one-man war with the United States Army, which agreed not to fly the noisy choppers so low over Winter's home.

It was also in Germany that sauerkraut got the official blessing of the judiciary when a judge ruled that it did not smell bad and an Esslinger housewife could go on fermenting cabbage in the cellar of the six-family apartment house where she lived, even though her neighbors did not share the judge's opinion.

Barbecued spare-ribs enthusiasts also got something to chew on in the news when it was reported that a Hereford bull in McLean, Tex., was siring offspring with 14 pairs of ribs instead of the usual 14—a discovery which could lead to extra cuts of beef and maybe a plethora of ribs.

The cause of equal rights for men was dealt a blow in 1967 by a State Supreme Court justice in New York who dismissed a husband's suit to collect alimony from his wife. It is "unnatural," Justice Margaret M. J. Mangan ruled.

Alcoholic beverages found their place in the odd news items with the Soviet Defense Ministry appealing to parents to stop sending vodka-filled hot water bottles to their sons in the armed services; while Spaniards were urged to drink themselves out of a severe wine surplus. The last 10 years had seen wine production jump from 4.8 billion to 7.9 billion gallons—largely because of government subsidies to grape growers.

For a final alcoholic news story, British European Airways told its hostesses and stewards to quit drinking wine and liquor left over by disembarking passengers.

In New York's Greenwich Village—where fantasy and reality often get mixed up—a motion picture actor, playing the part of a man fleeing from two policemen, was beaten to the ground with a nightstick by a real police officer who happened upon the scene, sized up the situation and did his duty as he saw it.

One of the oddest news stories of the year originated in Picoaza, Chile. The town of 4,000 held a mayoral election and voted into office Pulvapies—a foot deodorant. The company's advertising slogan was: "Vote for any candidate, but if you want well-being and hygiene—vote for Pulvapies."